The Professional Chef®

The Professional Chef® *7th edition*

THE CULINARY INSTITUTE OF AMERICA

JOHN WILEY & SONS, INC.

THE CULINARY INSTITUTE OF AMERICA'S CONTENT LEADERS:

Tim Ryan
Executive Vice President

Victor Gielisse
Associate Vice President and Dean of Culinary, Baking and Pastry Studies

Library of Congress Cataloging-in-Publication Data:

The professional chef/by the Culinary Institute of America.—7th ed.

    p. cm.

   Rev. ed. of: The new professional chef, c1996.

   Includes bibliographical references and index.

   ISBN: 0-471-38257-4 (cloth: alk. paper)

    1. Quantity cookery. I. Culinary Institute of America. II. New professional chef.

TX820 .P738 2001

641.5'7—dc21   2001026112

Printed in the United States of America.

Cover inset and spine photographs by Ben Fink

Cover background photograph © 2002 Stone/Luc Hautecoeur

Back cover photography by Ben Fink (top, middle, bottom); The Culinary Institute of America (second, fourth)

Interior photography by The Culinary Institute of America and Ben Fink; for details, see credits on page 1036.

Cover and interior design by Vertigo Design, NYC

10   9   8   7   6   5   4

ACKNOWLEDGMENTS

The common wisdom says "Leave well enough alone." It is because the following people in The Culinary Institute of America's education division knew that "well enough" isn't the same thing as "as good as we can make it" that this revised edition of the book came into being: Tim Ryan, CMC; Victor Gielisse, CMC; and the Institute's associate deans Eve Felder; Ron DeSantis, CMC; Anthony Ligouri; Robert Briggs; John Storm; Timothy Rodgers; Uwe Hestnar; Dan Kish; and Thomas Gumpel. Working with this group to make the goal a reality were the following members of the Institute's editorial team: Mary Cowell, Director, Food and Beverage Institute; Mary Donovan, '83, Senior Editor; Jessica Bard, '95, Photo Editor; Jennifer Armentrout, '97, Editor and Writer; and Lisa Lahey, '00, Associate Editor and Writer.

The heart of this book is the detailed explanation of cooking methods in words and images, as well as an amazingly diverse collection of recipes, running the gamut from simple broths to multi-layered dishes composed of sauces, stuffings, garnishes, and side dishes. For their dedication to excellence in several areas (reading and critiquing the text, testing and reviewing the recipes, and being the hands you see in the photographs throughout the book), the following individuals are to be congratulated and thanked:

Wayne L. Almquist

Ken Arnone, '92, CCC

Ryan Doyle Baxter, '87

Elizabeth E. Briggs

Terrell Brunet, '88

Daniel M. Budd, '87

Shuiliang Cheng

Corky Clark, '71, CCE

Richard J. Coppedge, Jr., CMB

Gerard Coyac

Robert Danhi, '91

Philip Delaplane

Martin Frei, CEC

Peter P. Greweling, CMB

Nancy Griffin, '80

Thomas W. Griffiths, '80, CEC

Stephen Giunta, '83

George B. Higgins, Jr., '78, CMB

David Kamen, '88, CCE

Mo Kanner, '84

Thomas P. Kief, '78

Joseph Klug, '82

John Kowalski, '77, CEC, CCE

Xavier LeRoux

Alain Levy

Hubert J. Martini, CEC, CCA, AAC

Bruce S. Mattel, '80

Peter Michael, CMC, AAC

Patricia Mitchell, '84

Joe Mure

William Phillips

Paul Prosperi

Heinrick Rapp

Charles Rascoll

Dieter Schorner

Russell Scott

Katherine Polenz-Shepard, '73

Rudy Smith, '86, CEC

Daniel Turgeon, '85

Hinnerk von Bargen

Jonathan A. Zearfoss, CEC, CCE, CCP

There are many subjects a chef must master. To those who assisted in the development and review of chapters dedicated to management, food safety issues, nutrition, food identification and purchasing, recipes and culinary math, and the selection of equipment, a special thank you:

Linda A. Blocker, MS

Patrick Bottiglieri

W. W. John Canner, MS

Robert DelGrosso

Ezra Eichelberger

Craig Goldstein

Julia Hill

John J. Stein, '80, CFBE

Marianne Turow, '83

Rich Vergili

Mark Westfield

The staff of the CIA's storeroom (particularly Michael Murphy, Miles Curtis, Randy Baker, Edward Bakter, Lisa Paquin, and Richard Drino who appear in photographs throughout Part Two of this book).

The images in this book were created in the Institute's studios and kitchens. Many thanks to the photographers whose work complements the words throughout the book. Lorna Smith is the CIA staff photographer whose work graces the majority of the book including technique sequences, fruit and vegetable identification, and the conceptual and mise en place compositions. Many thanks also to contributing photographers Elizabeth Corbett Johnson and John Grubell for their significant additions to the book's art program. Ben Fink's evocative photography rounds out the book with dramatic images for the cover and end papers; part, chapter, and method openers; as well as the gallery shots that bring a selection of recipes to life. Thanks also to his talented assistants, especially prop stylist Philippa Brathwaite and food stylist Lilia Jordan.

Our thanks also to Villeroy & Boch for supplying some of the china used in the photographs. A project such as revising *The Professional Chef* calls upon the talents of the entire Institute. We express our gratitude for the help and support of the MIS department, especially Ron Mosimann, the calm voice at the other end of the help line, and the Stewarding Department for their generosity when we needed dishes, glassware, or other props. Our gratitude to the teams at John Wiley & Sons, Inc. and at Vertigo Design, Inc. for their tireless attention to detail.

It is in the crucibles of the classroom and the kitchen that this book came into being and comes to life. We thank all the students and alumni who have helped to make this book what it is. To all those students and recent graduates who helped with research, recipe testing, manuscript review, and photography, especially Lindsay Martin, '97; Andrew Vaughn, '00; Cheryl Hecht, '00; Deborah Hartman, '01; Kendra Glanbocky, '99; Heather Renz, '99; and Nicole Herd, '00; a hearty thank you. So many students assisted directly and indirectly with the development of text, research, and photography that we are unable to list all of them here. This book is for all of you. Take it with you on your culinary journey that it may serve you well throughout your career.

CONTENTS

INTRODUCTION

Becoming a chef is a career-long process. Cooking is a dynamic profession—one that provides some of the greatest challenges as well as some of the greatest rewards. There is always another level of perfection to achieve and another skill to master. It is our hope that this book will function both as a springboard into future growth and as a reference point to give ballast to the lessons still to be learned.

The Professional Chef, Seventh Edition, represents a total reworking of our classic text, *The New Professional Chef*, and, as such, it is more than simply an updating of material. The motivation for this new book was our desire to incorporate into one volume as many contemporary cooking concepts as possible, while remaining true to the principles that govern all good cooking. Increased awareness and interest in such areas as technology, agriculture, food safety, and nutrition, as well as an ever growing sophistication on the part of both experienced and novice culinarians and the guests they serve, have combined to change the way we view a culinary education.

By nature of its encyclopedic subject coverage, this text is suited to a variety of curricula, whether as part of an existing program or through independent study. An instructor may choose to use all or part of its contents; the student may use it to advance his or her learning by employing it as a broad, basic text or as a reference tool to answer specific questions about a particular technique. The techniques as explained in this book have all been tested in the Institute's kitchens. Each represents one of many possible variations. The fact that all variations are not included in this text does not imply that other methods are incorrect. Experience will teach the student many "tricks of the trade."

The title of this work should not put it into the rarified category of books to be used only by those working in restaurant or hotel kitchens. The basic lessons of cooking are the same whether one prepares food for paying guests or for one's family and friends. Therefore, we hope that those who look to cooking for a creative outlet will come to regard this book as a valuable tool.

This book is suited to a variety of teaching situations because the material is arranged in a logical, progressive sequence. Chapter One covers the history of cooking as a profession and examines the skills and attributes of a professional chef and other members of the foodservice profession. (For more information about table service and dining room operations, consult *Remarkable Service*.) Since foodservice is a business, some of the elementary aspects of food costing are discussed in Chapter Two, as is how to adapt recipes, from this book or any other, for use in a specific professional kitchen. Knowing how to adapt recipes is useful for scheduling, controlling costs, and improving quality. (For more details about culinary math, consult *Culinary Math*.) Nutrition and food science have become part of the everyday language of the professional kitchen, and Chapter Three reviews some basic concepts of nutrition and science, particularly as they relate to cooking. (For more information about nutritional cooking, consult *The Professional Chef's Techniques of Healthy Cooking*, Second Edition.) Food and kitchen safety are of increasing concern in all foodservice operations, and Chapter Four presents fundamental concepts and procedures for assuring that safe, wholesome food is prepared in a safe environment.

Counted among the basics in the kitchen is the ability to seek out and purchase the best possible ingredients. Part Two is a catalog of the ingredients and tools used in the professional kitchen and includes information regarding product specifications, purchasing, and such processing concerns as trim loss. Many of the photographs featured in this section were taken at the Institute's receiving dock and show the care and attention that must be given to the raw materials of the professional kitchen. There are separate chapters devoted to meats and poultry; fish; fruits, vegetables, and fresh herbs; dairy products and eggs; and nonperishable goods such as oils, flours, grains, and dried pastas. The information is presented in such a way that it can act as a quick reference to quality, seasonality, and appropriate cooking styles or techniques.

Cooking is not always a perfectly precise art, but a good grasp of the basics gives the chef or student the ability not only to apply the technique, but also to learn the standards of quality so that they begin to develop a sense of how cooking works. Part Three is devoted to stocks, sauces, and soups. The part opens with a chapter covering such basic mise en place techniques as preparing and using seasoning and aromatic combinations (bouquet garni and sachet d'épices), thickeners (roux and arrowroot), and mirepoix.

Part Four presents the techniques used to cook meats, poultry, and fish. The first chapter in this part is devoted to mise en place, and presents, in text and in photographs, such methods as coating products with breading or batter, seasonings, and marinades, and more. The next chapter covers basic fabricating methods for familiar cuts of meat, poultry, and fish. With these basic lessons in mind, the next group of chapters demonstrates how to grill, roast, sauté, pan fry, stir fry, steam, poach, stew, and braise. These important lessons are presented in clear step-by-step photographs, with explanatory text and a model recipe.

In Part Five, chapters concentrate on preparation techniques for vegetables, grains and legumes, pasta and dumplings, and potatoes. Part Six covers breakfast and garde manger, with chapters covering eggs, salad dressings and salads, sandwiches, and garde manger items such as pâtés and terrines. (For further information on these subjects, consult *Garde Manger: The Art and Craft of the Cold Kitchen*.) Baking and pastry is presented in Part Seven, with attention paid to the preparation of breads and rolls; cakes and cookies; pastry doughs and crusts; and a variety of fillings, icings, and glazes.

The recipes included in this book are an example of the wide range of possibilities open to the student once the basics are mastered. It should be noted that these recipes have both metric and American measurements. In the conversion from one system to another, quantities have usually been rounded to the nearest even measurement.

The recipe yields reflect real-life cooking situations: some items, such as stocks and soups, are prepared in large quantities, while others, such as sautés and grills, are prepared à la minute, for a few portions at a time. Larger roasts, braises, stews, and side dishes generally have yields of 10 or 20 servings; any marinades, sauces, or condiments included in the recipes that are prepared in advance are normally given in quantities to produce a yield of 10 servings. These yields may not always suit the student who is using the book outside of a professional kitchen. In most cases, they can be reduced or increased in order to prepare the correct number of servings. Baking recipe yields are based on specific weight ratios, however, and must be followed exactly.

The new look in this new edition reflects the way we think about teaching cooking. We learn best when we understand not only how to do something, but why we should do it that way. From this grounded approach, students at any level can confidently take new directions in their cooking careers.

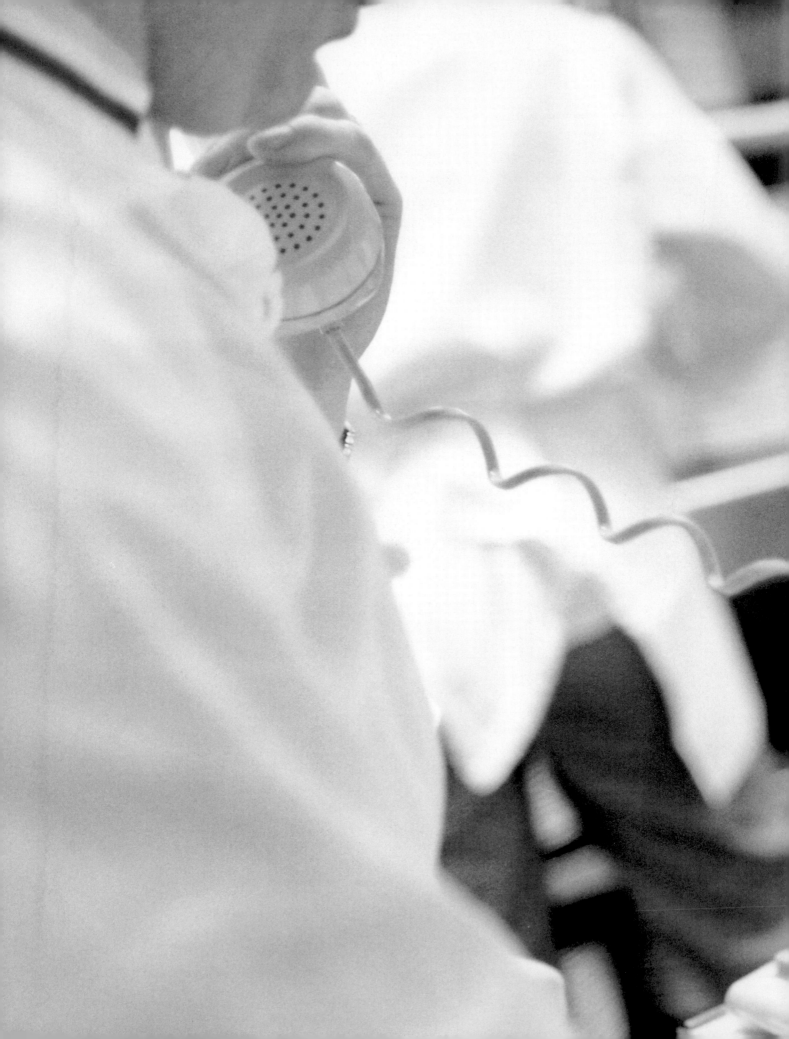

THE CULINARY PROFESSIONAL

PART ONE

A culinarian is a member of a
profession with a fascinating
history. Knowing where you have
come from may be the best way
to appreciate the choices, responsibilities, and opportunities that
await you as a professional chef.

INTRODUCTION TO
THE PROFESSION

The first restaurant (as we know restaurants today) opened in Paris in 1765, when M. Boulanger, a tavern keeper, served a dish of sheep's feet, or trotters, in a white sauce as a restorative. Although he was brought to court for infringing on a separate guild's monopoly, he won the case and was allowed to continue serving food. Once the precedent was established, other restaurants soon appeared.

The French Revolution (1789–99) had a particularly significant effect on restaurant proliferation, because many chefs who previously had worked for the monarchy or nobility fled France to escape the guillotine. Although some sought employment with the noble classes in other countries, others began to open their own establishments. Restaurants became increasingly refined operations, and although they were at first frequented only by men, this would change as customs in society and in the food service industry as a whole changed.

MAJOR CULINARY HISTORICAL FIGURES

THE FOLLOWING LIST of major historical figures in Western cuisine is by no means comprehensive. Further reading about influential people throughout the history of cooking is recommended. Refer to the Recommended Readings at the end of this book for other sources.

CATERINA DE MEDICI (1519–89), an Italian princess from the famous Florentine family, married the duc d'Orléans, later Henri II of France. She introduced a more refined style of dining, including the use of the fork and the napkin. Her Florentine chefs influenced French chefs as well, most particularly in the use of spinach.

ANNE OF AUSTRIA (1601–66), wife of Louis XIII, was a member of the Spanish Hapsburg family. Her retinue included Spanish chefs who introduced sauce espagnole and the use of roux as a thickener for sauces.

FRANÇOIS-PIERRE DE LA VARENNE (1615–78) was the author of the first cookbook to summarize the cooking practices of the French nobility. His *Le Vrai Cuisinier François* was published in 1651.

JEAN-ANTHELME BRILLAT-SAVARIN (1755–1826) was a French politician, gourmet, and renowned writer. His work *Physiologie de goût* (The Physiology of Taste) is highly regarded.

MARIE-ANTOINE CARÊME (1784–1833) become known as the founder of the *grande cuisine* and was responsible for systematizing culinary techniques. He had a profound influence on the later writing of Escoffier and was known as the "chef of kings, king of chefs."

CHARLES RANHOFER (1836–99) was the first internationally renowned chef of an American restaurant, Delmonico's, and the author of *The Epicurean*.

GEORGES-AUGUSTE ESCOFFIER (1847–1935) was a renowned chef and teacher and the author of *Le Guide culinaire*, a major work codifying classic cuisine that is still widely used. His other significant contributions include simplifying the classic menu in accordance with the principles advocated by Carême and initiating the brigade system. (See "The Kitchen Brigade System," later in this chapter.) Escoffier's influence on the food service industry cannot be overemphasized.

FERNAND POINT (1897–1955) was the chef-owner of La Pyramide restaurant in Vienne, France. He went even further than Escoffier in bringing about a change in cooking styles, and he laid the foundations for nouvelle cuisine.

PAUL BOCUSE and JEAN and PIERRE TROIGROS, who were disciples of Point, and ROGER VERGÉ and MICHEL GUÉRARD, known as the "Bande à Bocuse," were innovators and popularizers of nouvelle cuisine. Their considerable interaction and sharing of ideas have led to the growth and development of contemporary cuisine.

Most hotels and restaurants offered a simple table d'hôte, which provided little if any choice. The *grande cuisine*, a careful code established by Marie-Antoine Carême (1784–1833) that detailed numerous dishes and their sauces, was a cooking style well suited to royal and noble households but difficult to maintain in hotel kitchens, which usually had only rudimentary cooking equipment. When the Savoy Hotel opened in London in 1898 under the direction of César Ritz and Georges-Auguste Escoffier, the *grande cuisine* was replaced by a more refined and simplified approach referred to as *cuisine classique* (classic or classical cuisine).

The next major shift in French cuisine occurred gradually. Fernand Point (1897–1955) took Escoffier's message of simplification even further and laid the groundwork for the next upheaval in restaurant cooking styles. Several chefs, all influenced by Point, are credited with inventing nouvelle cuisine during the early 1970s, including such luminaries as Paul Bocuse, Alain Chapel, François Bise, and Jean and Pierre Troisgros. The end result was an entirely new approach to the selection of ingredients for a dish, cooking and saucing styles, and plate presentation. Smaller portions, more artful presentation, and the combination of new ingredients became the hallmarks of this cooking style.

Today, a growing global marketplace combined with an interest in multiculturalism and diversity has led to the popularization of many cuisines. Some chefs are blending cooking styles and ingredients from around the world to create new dishes (sometimes known as fusion cuisine). Other chefs are exploring the lesser-known traditions of regional and ethnic cooking styles. Still others have chosen a classical path, seeking to test their technical skills and culinary artistry against the standards of their mentors.

CAREER OPPORTUNITIES FOR CULINARY PROFESSIONALS

Culinary professionals are needed not just in hotel dining rooms and traditional restaurants but in a variety of settings — public and private, consumer-oriented and institutional. An increased emphasis on nutrition, sophistication, and financial and quality control means that all settings, from the white-tablecloth restaurant to the fast-food outlet, offer interesting challenges.

Hotels often have a number of different dining facilities, including fine-dining restaurants, room service, coffee shops, and banquet rooms. The kitchens are large, and there will often be separate butchering, catering, and pastry kitchens on the premises.

Preparing for service in a full-service restaurant.

Full-service restaurants, such as bistros, white-tablecloth establishments, and family-style restaurants, feature a full menu, and the patrons are served by trained wait staff.

Private clubs generally provide some sort of food service. It may be as simple as a small grill featuring sandwiches, or it may be a complete dining room. The difference is that the guests are paying members, and the food costs are generally figured differently than they would be for a public restaurant.

Many corporations operate *executive dining rooms.* The degree of simplicity or elegance demanded in a particular corporation determines what type of food is offered, how it is prepared, and what style of service is appropriate.

Institutional catering (used in schools, hospitals, colleges, airlines, and correctional institutions) often demands a single menu and a cafeteria where the guests serve themselves, choosing from the offered foods. Menu selections are based on the needs of the institution's guests, the operating budget, and the administration's expectations. Many institutional catering operations are run by large corporations, which frequently offer benefits and the opportunity for career advancement within the corporation.

Caterers provide a particular service, often tailored to meet the wishes of a special client for a particular event, whether it be a wedding, a cocktail reception, or a gallery opening. Caterers may provide on-site services (the client comes to the caterer's premises), off-site services (the caterer comes to the client's premises), or both.

Home meal replacement (carry-out) food service is growing in importance as more busy couples, single professionals, and families try to enjoy meals at home without having to spend time preparing them. These establishments prepare entrées, salads, side dishes, and desserts that are packaged to be taken home. Many supermarkets now offer this service to their customers.

THE KITCHEN BRIGADE SYSTEM

The brigade system was instituted by Escoffier to streamline and simplify work in hotel kitchens. It served to eliminate the chaos and duplication of effort that could result when workers did not have clear-cut responsibilities. Under this system, each position has a station and defined responsibilities, outlined below. In smaller operations, the classic system is generally abbreviated and responsibilities are organized so as to make the best use of work space and talents. A shortage of skilled personnel has also made modifications in the brigade system necessary. The introduction of new equipment has helped to alleviate some of the problems associated with smaller kitchen staffs.

The chef is responsible for all kitchen operations, including ordering, supervision of all stations, and development of menu items. He or she also may be known as the *chef de cuisine* or *executive chef*. The *sous chef* is second in command, answers to the chef, may be responsible for scheduling, fills in for the chef, and assists the station chefs (or line cooks) as necessary. Small operations may not have a sous chef. The range of positions in a classic brigade also include the following:

The SAUTÉ CHEF *(saucier)* is responsible for all sautéed items and their sauces. This position is often considered the most demanding, responsible, and glamorous on the line.

The FISH CHEF *(poissonier)* is responsible for fish items, often including fish butchering, and their sauces. This position is sometimes combined with the saucier position.

The ROAST CHEF *(rôtisseur)* is responsible for all roasted foods and related jus or other sauces.

The GRILL CHEF *(grillardin)* is responsible for all grilled foods. This position may be combined with that of rôtisseur.

The FRY CHEF *(friturier)* is responsible for all fried foods. This position may be combined with the rôtisseur position.

The VEGETABLE CHEF *(entremetier)* is responsible for hot appetizers and frequently has responsibility for soups, vegetables, and pastas and other starches. (In a full, traditional brigade system, soups are prepared by the soup station or *potager*, vegetables by the *légumier*.) This station may also be responsible for egg dishes.

Describing a new menu item to the wait staff is the chef's responsibility.

The ROUNDSMAN *(tournant)* or *swing cook* works as needed throughout the kitchen.

The COLD-FOODS CHEF *(garde-manger)*, also known as the *pantry chef*, is responsible for preparation of cold foods, including salads, cold appetizers, pâtés, and the like. This is considered a separate category of kitchen work.

The BUTCHER *(boucher)* is responsible for butchering meats, poultry, and, occasionally, fish. The boucher may also be responsible for breading meat and fish items.

The PASTRY CHEF *(pâtissier)* is responsible for baked items, pastries, and desserts. The pastry chef frequently supervises a separate kitchen area or a separate shop in larger operations. This position may be further broken down into the following areas of specialization: CONFISEUR (prepares candies, petits fours), BOULANGER (prepares unsweetened doughs, as for breads and rolls), GLACIER (prepares frozen and cold desserts), and DÉCORATEUR (prepares showpieces and special cakes).

The EXPEDITER or ANNOUNCER *(aboyeur)* accepts orders from the dining room and relays them to the various station chefs. This individual is the last person to see the plate before it leaves the kitchen. In some operations, this may be either the chef or sous chef.

The COMMUNARD prepares the meal served to staff at some point during the shift (also called the family meal).

The COMMIS, or apprentice, works under a station chef to learn the station and its responsibilities.

The dining room, or front-of-the-house, positions also have an established line of authority.

> The **MAÎTRE D'HÔTEL**, known in American service as the dining room manager, is the person who holds the most responsibility for the front-of-the-house operation. The maître d'hôtel trains all service personnel, oversees wine selection, works with the chef to determine the menu, and organizes seating throughout service.
>
> The **WINE STEWARD** (*chef de vin* or *sommelier*) is responsible for all aspects of restaurant wine service, including purchasing wines, preparing a wine list, assisting guests in wine selection, and serving wine properly. The wine steward may also be responsible for the service of liquors, beers, and other beverages. If there is no wine steward, these responsibilities are generally assumed by the maître d'hôtel.
>
> The **HEADWAITER** (*chef de salle*) is generally in charge of the service for an entire dining room. Very often this position is combined with the position of either captain or maître d'hôtel.
>
> The **CAPTAIN** (*chef d'étage*) deals most directly with the guests once they are seated. The captain explains the menu, answers any questions, and takes the order. The captain generally does any tableside food preparation. If there is no captain, these responsibilities fall to the front waiter.
>
> The **FRONT WAITER** (*chef de rang*) ensures that the table is properly set for each course, that the food is properly delivered to the table, and that the needs of the guests are promptly and courteously met.
>
> The **BACK WAITER** or **BUSBOY** (*demi-chef de rang* or *commis de rang*) is generally the first position assigned to new dining room workers. This person clears plates between courses, fills water glasses and breadbaskets, and assists the front waiter and/or captain as needed.

The maître d' keeps lines of communication open between the dining room and kitchen.

OTHER OPPORTUNITIES

In addition to the kitchen and dining room positions, a growing number of less traditional opportunities exist, many of which do not involve the actual production or service of foods.

> **FOOD AND BEVERAGE MANAGERS** oversee all food and beverage outlets in hotels and other large establishments.
>
> **CONSULTANTS** and **DESIGN SPECIALISTS** will work with restaurant owners, often before the restaurant is even open, to assist in developing a menu, designing the overall layout and ambience of the dining room, and establishing work patterns for the kitchen.
>
> **WELL-INFORMED SALESPEOPLE** help chefs determine how best to meet their needs for food and produce, introduce them to new products, and demonstrate the proper use of new equipment.
>
> **TEACHERS** are essential to the great number of cooking schools nationwide. Most of these teachers are chefs who are sharing the benefit of their experience with students.

FOOD WRITERS and CRITICS discuss food trends, restaurants, and chefs. It will always mean more, of course, if the writer is well versed in the culinary arts. Some prominent members of the food media, such as James Beard, Craig Claiborne, and Julia Child, have been influential teachers and have written landmark cookbooks in addition to contributing to newspapers and magazines and appearing on television.

FOOD STYLISTS and PHOTOGRAPHERS work with a variety of publications, including magazines, books, catalogs, and promotional and advertising pieces.

RESEARCH-AND-DEVELOPMENT KITCHENS employ a great many culinary professionals. These may be run by food manufacturers who are developing new products or food lines, or by advisory boards hoping to promote their products. Test kitchens are also run by a variety of both trade and consumer publications.

BECOMING A CULINARY PROFESSIONAL

Any profession has a great many sides; the culinary vocation is no different. A culinary professional is an artist, a businessperson, a scientist, and a cultural explorer, among other attributes. Acquiring the skills and knowledge necessary to succeed in this profession is a lifelong journey.

FORMAL EDUCATION AND TRAINING

A sound and thorough culinary education is a logical first step in the development of one's culinary career. In order to gain a grounding in basic and advanced culinary techniques and become fluent in the language of the trade, any aspiring professional will find formal training at an accredited school an excellent beginning.

Nothing substitutes for experience, however. It is only with hands-on practice that theory learned in class can be fully assimilated. The best culinary schools incorporate some measure of on-the-job training into their curriculum.

Some individuals receive their training entirely on the job, either in a special apprenticeship program or as a self-directed course of study, advancing from kitchen to kitchen, learning at the side of chefs who are involved in the day-to-day business of running a professional kitchen.

Cooking schools have been popular for over a century, and today there are more than eight hundred cooking schools in the United States. Of those schools, about fifty offer degree programs.

CONTINUING EDUCATION

Once initial training has been completed, continuing education is equally important, as the industry is constantly evolving. Attending classes, workshops, and seminars helps practicing culinary professionals hone skills in specialized areas while keeping up with new methods and new styles of cooking.

Evaluate your career, both as it is right now and as you would like it to be in the future, and then take the appropriate steps to keep on top of the latest information in the areas you are most concerned about. Magazines, newsletters, instructional videos, Web sites, government publications, and books are all excellent sources. To find out more in any given area, consider joining professional organizations in order to network with other professionals in the field.

NETWORKING

Creating a professional network is a task that should be taken seriously. Working with other professionals to share information and knowledge is an important avenue of growth, both professional and personal. Networks can be formal or informal. The way to begin is simply to introduce yourself to others in your field. Have business cards with you when you go out to other restaurants or to trade shows.

When you make a good contact, follow up with a phone call or a note. The communication that you develop with your peers will keep your own work fresh and contemporary, and an established network makes it much easier for you to find a new job or an employee.

Keeping current with basic skills and new trends is a lifelong task.

THE ATTRIBUTES OF A CULINARY PROFESSIONAL

Every member of a profession is responsible for the profession's image, whether he or she is a teacher, lawyer, doctor, or culinarian. Those who have made the greatest impression know that the cardinal virtues of the culinary profession are an open and inquiring mind, an appreciation of and dedication to quality wherever it is found, and a sense of responsibility. Success also depends on several character traits, some of which are inherent, some of which are diligently cultivated throughout a career. These include:

A COMMITMENT TO SERVICE. The food service industry is predicated on service; therefore, a culinary professional should never lose sight of what that word implies. Good service includes (but is not limited to) providing quality food that is properly and safely cooked, appropriately seasoned, and attractively presented in a pleasant environment — in short, making the customer happy. The degree to which an operation can offer satisfaction in these areas is the degree to which it will succeed in providing good (and, ideally, excellent) service. The customer must always come first.

A SENSE OF RESPONSIBILITY. A culinary professional's responsibility is fourfold: to him- or herself, to coworkers, to the restaurant, and to the guest. This should include respecting not just the customer and his or her needs but also staff, food, equipment, and the facility itself. Waste, recklessness, disregard for others, and misuse or abuse of any commodity are unacceptable. Abusive language, harassment, ethnic slurs, and profanity do not have a place in the professional kitchen. When employees feel that their needs are given due consideration, their self-esteem will increase and their attitude toward the establishment will improve; both will increase productivity and reduce absenteeism.

JUDGMENT. Although it is not easy to learn, good judgment is a prerequisite for becoming a professional. An ability to judge what is right and appropriate is acquired throughout a lifetime of experience. Good judgment is never completely mastered; rather, it is a goal toward which one should continually strive.

THE CHEF AS A BUSINESSPERSON

As you continue your career, you will move from positions where your technical prowess is your greatest contribution into those where your skills as an executive, an administrator, and a manager are more clearly in demand. This does not mean that your ability to grill, sauté, or roast foods to the exact point of doneness is less important than it was before. It does mean that you will be called on to learn and assume tasks and responsibilities that are more managerial, marking a shift in the evolution of your career.

Become a good executive. Executives are the individuals who develop a mission or a plan for a company or organization. They are also the ones responsible for developing a system to allow that plan to come to fruition. As an executive, you must shoulder a large portion of responsibility for the success or failure of your establishment. Executives don't operate in a vacuum, however. Nor do they emerge full-blown one day out of the blue. Even before you wear a jacket embroidered with "Executive Chef," you will have begun to exercise your abilities as an executive.

Become a good administrator. Once an overall goal or plan has been laid down, the next task is to implement and track that plan. Now your hat becomes that of an administrator. Some administrative duties may not sound at all glamorous — preparing schedules, tracking deliveries, computing costs, and so forth. If a restaurant is small, the executive and administrator will be the same person. That same person also might be the one who dons a uniform and works the line.

The best administrators are those who can create a feeling throughout the entire staff that each person has a stake in getting things done correctly. When you give people the opportunity to help make decisions and provide them with the tools they need to perform optimally, you will see that it is easier to achieve the goals you have established on an executive level.

Learn to use the important tools of your business; budgets, accounting systems, and inventory control systems all play a role. Many organizations, from the largest chains to the smallest one-person catering company, rely upon software systems that allow them to efficiently administer a number of areas: inventory, purchases, losses, sales, profits, food costs, customer complaints, reservations, payroll, schedules, and budgets. If you are not using a system capable of tracking all this information and more, you cannot be as effective as you need to be.

Become a good manager. Managing a restaurant, or any other business, is a job that requires the ability to handle four areas effectively: physical assets, information, people (human resources), and time. The greater your skills in managing any of these areas, the greater your potential for success. Many management systems today stress the use of quality as a yardstick. Every aspect of your operation needs to be seen as a way to improve the quality of service you provide your customers. As we look at what you might be expected to do in order to manage effectively, the fundamental question you need to ask, over and over, is this: How would a change (or lack of change) in a given area affect the quality of service or goods that you are offering your customer? Competition continues to increase, and unless your establishment is different, better, faster, or unique in some way, there is every chance that it may not survive, let alone prosper.

MANAGING PHYSICAL ASSETS

Physical assets are the equipment and supplies needed to do business. In the case of a restaurant, these might include food and beverage inventory, tables, chairs, linens, china, flatware, glassware, computers and point-of-sale systems, cash registers, kitchen equipment, cleaning supplies, and ware-washing machines. When we talk about managing physical assets, we are considering how anything that you must purchase or pay for affects your ability to do business well.

The first step in bringing the expenses associated with your physical assets under control is to know what your expenses actually are. Then you can begin the process of making the adjustments and instituting the control systems that will keep your organization operating at maximal efficiency.

One of the biggest expenses for any restaurant will always be food and beverage costs. You or your purchasing agent will have to work hard to develop and sustain a good purchasing system. The information found in Part Two of this book can help. Because each operation has different needs, there are no hard-and-fast rules, just principles that you will apply to your own situation.

MANAGING INFORMATION

You may often feel that you can never keep current in all the important areas of your work. Given the sheer volume of information being generated each day, you are probably right. The ability to tap into the information resources you need, using all types of media and technology, has never been more important.

Restaurants, menus, and trends in dining room design have all been dramatically impacted by such societal trends as busier, on-the-go lifestyles and increasing interest in world cuisines. Prevailing tastes in politics, art, fashion, movies, and music do have an effect on what people eat and where and how they want to eat it.

Information gathering can become a full-time task on its own. To make use of the information available, you must be able to analyze and evaluate carefully to sift out the important material from useless data.

Staying on top of the information explosion in the culinary field is especially important in today's market.

MANAGING HUMAN RESOURCES

Restaurant operations rely directly on the work and dedication of a number of people, from executives and administrators to line cooks, wait staff, and maintenance and cleaning staff. No matter how large or small your staff may be, the ability to engage all your workers in a team effort is one of the major factors in determining whether you will succeed or not.

Your goal should be to create an environment in which all staff feel they have a distinct and measurable contribution to make within the organization. The first task is establishing clear criteria, otherwise known as a job description. Training is another key component. If you want someone to do a job well, you first have to both explain and demonstrate the quality standards that you expect to see. You need to continually reinforce those standards with clear, objective evaluation of an employee's work through feedback, constructive criticism, and, when necessary, additional training or disciplinary measures.

The management of human resources includes several legal responsibilities. Everyone has the right to work in an environment that is free from physical hazards. This means that, as an employer, you must provide a work space that is well lit, properly ventilated, and free from obvious dangers, such as improperly maintained equipment. Employees must have access to potable water and bathroom facilities. Beyond this bare minimum, you may offer a locker room, a laundry facility that provides clean uniforms and aprons, or other such amenities.

Workers' compensation, unemployment insurance, and disability insurance are also your responsibility. You are required to make all legal deductions from an employee's paycheck and to report all earnings properly to state and federal agencies. Liability insurance (to cover any harm to your facility, employees, or guests) must be kept up-to-date and at adequate levels.

You may also choose to offer additional forms of assistance as part of an employee benefits package. Life insurance, medical and dental insurance, assistance with such things as dependent care, adult literacy training, and enrollment in and support for those enrolled in substance abuse programs are all items of which you should be aware. In an increasingly tight labor market, a generous benefits package can make the difference in the caliber of employee you are able to attract and retain.

You must keep a properly completed I-9 form on file for every employee, and you should be familiar with the regulations that could affect you or those you employ. The Immigration and Naturalization Service (INS) will provide the necessary information.

MANAGING TIME

It may seem that no matter how hard you work or how much planning you do, the days aren't long enough. Learning new skills, so that you can make the best possible use of the time you have, certainly ought to be an ongoing part of your career development. If you look over your operation, you will see where time is wasted. In most operations, the top five time wasters are: no clear priorities for tasks, poor staff training, poor communication, poor organization, and missing or inadequate tools to accomplish tasks. To combat these time wasters, use the following strategies.

Invest time in reviewing daily operations. Consider the way you, your coworkers, and your staff spend the day. Does everyone have a basic understanding of which tasks are most important? Do they know when to begin a particular task in order to bring it to completion on time? It can be an eye-opening experience to take a hard look at where the workday goes. Once you see that you and your staff need to walk too far to gather basic items or that the person who washes the dishes is sitting idle for the first two hours of the shift, you can take steps to rectify the problem. You can try to reorganize storage space. You may decide to train the dishwasher to do some prep work, or you can rewrite the schedule so that the shift begins two hours later. Until you are objective about what needs to be done and in what order, you can't begin the process of saving time.

Invest time in training others. If you expect someone to do a job properly, take enough time to explain the task carefully. Walk yourself and your staff through the jobs that must be done, and be sure that everyone understands how to do the work, where to find necessary items, how far each person's responsibility extends, and what to do in case a question or emergency comes up. Give your staff the yardsticks they need to evaluate the job and determine if they have done what was requested, in the appropriate fashion, and on time. If you don't invest this time up front, you may find yourself squandering precious time following your workers around, picking up the slack, and handling work that shouldn't be taking up your day.

Learn to communicate clearly. Whether you are training a new employee, introducing a new menu item, or ordering a piece of equipment, clear communication is important. Be specific, use the most concise language you can, and be as brief as possible without leaving out necessary information. If tasks are handled by a number of people, be sure to write each task out, from the first step to the last. Encourage people to ask questions if they don't understand you. If you need help learning communication skills, consider taking a workshop or seminar to strengthen any weak areas.

Take steps to create an orderly work environment. If you have to dig through five shelves to find the lid to the storage container you just put the stock in, you haven't been using your time wisely. Planning work areas carefully, thinking about all the tools, ingredients, and equipment you need for preparation and throughout service, and grouping like activities together are all techniques that can help you organize your work better. Poor placement of large and small tools is a great time waster. Use adequate, easy-to-access storage space for common items such as whips, spoons, ladles, and tongs. Electrical outlets for small equipment ought to be within reach of everyone. While you may be forced to work within the limits of your existing floor plan, be on the lookout for products or storage strategies that can turn a bad arrangement into one that works smoothly and evenly.

Purchase, replace, and maintain all necessary tools. A well-equipped kitchen will have enough of all the tools necessary to prepare every item on the menu. If you are missing something as basic as a sieve, your cream soups won't have the right consistency. If you have a menu with several sautéed appetizers, entrées, and side dishes, are you and your line cooks waiting around while the pot washer scrambles to get you restocked with sauté pans? If you can't purchase new equipment, then think about restructuring the menu to even out the workload. If you can't remove a menu item, then invest in the tools you need to prevent a slowdown during service.

THE CHALLENGES OF THE RESTAURANT INDUSTRY

Professionals in the restaurant industry face numerous opportunities and challenges, more than enough to keep a career vibrant and growing throughout their entire professional lives. The raw material of the profession—food—has taken on enormous political, economic, and ethical importance to those within the profession. Finding sources of high-quality and wholesome foods that meet the specifications of an individual operation, as well as controlling food costs through intelligent purchasing and kitchen practices, are vital to a healthy business operation.

The staffing of a professional kitchen is a constant challenge. The pool of qualified and trained personnel has not caught up with the industry's demand. It falls to the chef, then, to train new staff properly and to be certain that, as new ingredients, methods, or equipment come into the kitchen, the staff is given additional training and practice. Professional workers in the kitchen have started to require higher wages, benefits, and improved working conditions. These demands must be addressed and then folded into the operating budget of any foodservice establishment.

Cooking in a professional kitchen is a business. This fundamental aspect of the culinarian's work finds its expression in such key areas as facility management, marketing, and customer service. Facility management, such as keeping equipment in working order, upgrading equipment and technology, cleaning, and decorating, has a strong impact on the guest. Marketing is no longer limited to placing an ad in the paper, but also includes such activities as community outreach, Web sites, direct mail, appearances on radio or television, and live demonstrations. Customer service is, of course, at the heart of every challenge facing today's professional chef. The best way to deliver customer service that encourages repeat visits is to know the customer so well that you can anticipate and fulfill a need before the customer has voiced it.

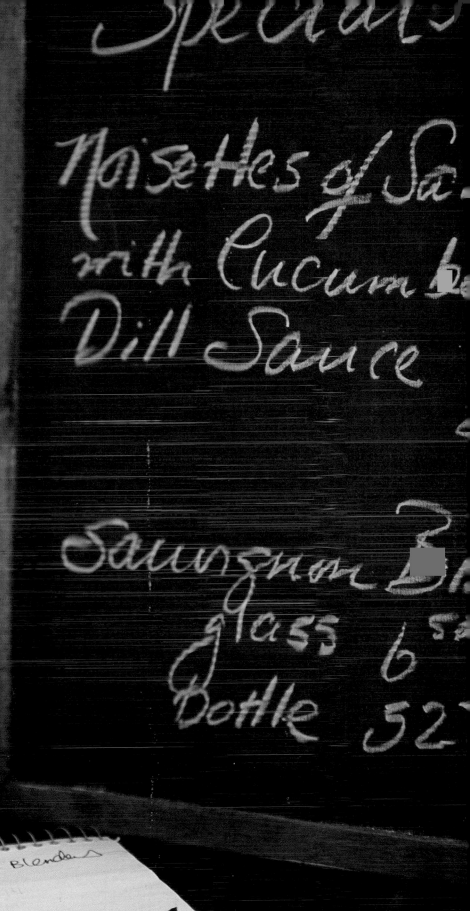

CHAPTER TWO

Menus are used in the dining room to give both waitstaff and guests important information about what the establishment offers. Recipes give detailed instructions to aid kitchen staff in producing menu items. But, more than that, carefully designed menus and comprehensive recipes can help the professional chef streamline kitchen operations and control costs.

MENUS AND RECIPES

MENUS

A menu is a powerful tool. It is a marketing and merchandising vehicle. It establishes and reinforces the total restaurant concept, from the style of china and flatware selected to staff training needs. It can assist the chef in organizing the day's work, ordering food, reducing waste, and increasing profits.

The way a menu is developed or adapted, as well as the way menu prices are established, is a reflection of how well the operation's concept or business plan has been defined. Sometimes the menu evolves as the business plan is refined. In other scenarios, the concept comes first and the menu comes later. In still others, the menu may be the guiding principle that gives a particular stamp to the way the restaurant concept evolves. (Menu development and menu pricing strategies are discussed in greater detail in other books and publications; consult the list of resources in Recommended Readings.)

Menus tell guests what items are available and how much they cost. They tell the kitchen staff additional vital things, such as whose responsibility it is to prepare the dish's components or to plate and garnish it. Menu items are typically assigned to a specific station. As the menu changes — daily, weekly, or seasonally — the tasks for that station also change. The preparation of certain garnishes, side dishes, sauces, or marinades may be organized so that the work is done by each individual chef or cook, or it may be the specific duty of a single prep cook. À la carte menus call for certain types of advance work and mise en place to help the chef adjust to the unpredictable work flow. Banquet menus call for different advance work strategies.

Even if a written menu is not provided to the guest, some form of recorded list is essential to the smooth operation of a professional kitchen.

Consult the menu, determine which items you or your staff are responsible for, and then read the recipes for those items carefully so that you understand all the tasks that must be performed in advance of service as well as at the time of plating and serving the food.

RECIPES

A recipe is a written record of the ingredients and preparation steps needed to make a particular dish. The form a recipe takes depends on who will ultimately be using the recipe and the medium in which the recipe will be presented. (For more information about writing recipes for publication, see Recommended Readings.)

Before starting to cook from any recipe, the first step is always to read through the recipe in its entirety to gain an understanding of exactly what is required. This step will alert you to any surprises that the recipe might contain, such as requiring an unusual piece of equipment or an overnight cooling period. This is also the point at which you must decide if any modifications to the recipe are in order. Perhaps the recipe makes only ten portions and you want to make fifty, or vice versa. You will have to convert the recipe (see page 21). In increasing or decreasing the yield, you may discover that you need to make equipment modifications as well to accommodate the new volume of food. Or you might decide that you want to omit, add, or substitute an ingredient. All of these decisions should be made before any ingredient preparation or cooking begins.

Once you have read through and evaluated or modified the recipe, it is time to get your mise en place (the ingredients and equipment) together. In many recipes, the ingredient list will indicate how the ingredient should be prepared (for example, being parboiled or cut into pieces of a certain size) before the actual cooking or assembling begins.

MEASURING INGREDIENTS ACCURATELY

Accurate measurements are crucial to recipes. In order to keep costs in line and ensure consistency of quality and quantity, ingredients and portion sizes must be measured correctly each time a recipe is made.

Ingredients are purchased and used according to one of three measuring conventions: count, volume, or weight. They may be purchased according to one system and measured for use in a recipe according to another.

Count is a measurement of whole items as one would purchase them. The terms *each*, *bunch*, and *dozen* all indicate units of count measure. If the individual item has been processed, graded, or packaged according to established standards, count can be a useful, accurate way to measure ingredients. It is less accurate for ingredients requiring some advance preparation or without any established standards for purchasing. Garlic cloves illustrate the point well. If a recipe calls for 2 garlic cloves, the intensity of garlic in the dish will change depending upon whether the cloves you use are large or small.

Volume is a measurement of the space occupied by a solid, liquid, or gas. The terms *teaspoon (tsp)*, *tablespoon (tbsp)*, *fluid ounce (fl oz)*, *cup*, *pint (pt)*, *quart (qt)*, *gallon (gal)*, *milliliter (mL)*, and *liter (L)* all indicate units of volume measure. Graduated containers (measuring cups) and utensils for which the volume is known (such as a 2-ounce ladle or a teaspoon) are used to measure volume.

Cutting meat into portions ensures that customers get consistent value and that portions are neither too large nor too small. Consult standardized recipes for established portioning guidelines.

Volume measurements are best suited to liquids, though they are also used for solids, especially spices, in small amounts. Tools used for measuring volume are not always as precise as necessary, especially if you must often increase or decrease a recipe. Volume measuring tools need not conform to any regulated standards. Therefore, the amount of an ingredient measured with one set of spoons, cups, or pitchers could be quite different from the amount measured with another set.

Weight is a measurement of the mass or heaviness of a solid, liquid, or gas. The terms *ounce (oz)*, *pound (lb)*, *gram (g)*, and *kilogram (kg)* all indicate units of weight measure. Scales are used to measure weight, and they must meet specific standards for accuracy. In professional kitchens, weight is usually the preferred type of measurement because it is easier to attain accuracy with weight than it is with volume.

STANDARDIZED RECIPES

The recipes used in a professional kitchen are known as standardized recipes. Unlike published recipes, standardized recipes are tailored to suit the needs of an individual kitchen. Preparing well-written and accurate standardized recipes are a big part of the professional chef's work in all foodservice settings, as they include much more than just ingredient names and preparation steps. Standardized recipes establish total yields, portion sizes, holding and serving practices, and plating information, and they set standards for cooking temperatures and times. These standards help to ensure consistent quality and quantity, and permit chefs to monitor the efficiency of their work and reduce costs by eliminating waste.

They also allow the wait staff to become familiar with a dish, so they can answer guests' questions accurately and honestly. For example, the type of oil used in a dish may matter very much to a guest, especially if it is an oil to which he or she has an allergy.

Standardized recipes can be recorded by hand or electronically, using a recipe management program or other computerized database. They should be recorded in a consistent, clear, easy-to-follow form and should be readily accessible to all staff members. Instruct kitchen staff to follow standardized recipes to the letter unless instructed otherwise, and encourage service staff to refer to standardized recipes when a question arises about ingredients or preparation methods.

As you prepare a standardized recipe, be as precise and consistent as you can. Include as many of the following elements as necessary:

Name/title of the food item or dish

Yield information for the recipe, expressed as one or more of the following: total weight, total volume, total number of portions

Portion information for each serving, expressed as one or more of the following: a specific number of items (count), volume, weight

Ingredient names, expressed in appropriate detail, specifying variety or brand as necessary

Ingredient measures, expressed as one of more of the following: count, volume, weight

Ingredient preparation instructions, sometimes included in the ingredient name, sometimes expressed in the method itself as a step

Equipment information for preparation, cooking, storing, holding, and serving an item

Preparation steps detailing mise en place, cooking methods, and temperatures for safe food handling (see "Hazard Analysis Critical Control Points (HACCP)," page 66)

Service information, describing how to finish and plate a dish, add side dishes, sauces, and garnishes, if any, and listing proper service temperatures

Holding and reheating procedures, describing procedures, equipment, times and temperatures for safe storage

Critical control points (CCPs) at appropriate stages in the recipe to indicate temperatures and times for safe food-handling procedures during storage, preparation, holding, and reheating

RECIPE CALCULATIONS

Often you will need to modify a recipe. Sometimes a recipe must be increased or decreased. You may be adapting a recipe from another source into a standardized format, or you may be adjusting a standardized recipe for a special event, such as a banquet or a reception. You may need to convert from volume measures to weight, or from metric measurements to the U.S. system. You will also need to be able to translate between purchase units and recipe measurements. In some circumstances you may be called upon to increase or decrease the suggested portion size for a recipe. Or you may want to determine how much the food in a particular recipe costs.

USING A RECIPE CONVERSION FACTOR (RCF) TO CONVERT RECIPE YIELDS

To adjust the yield of a recipe to make either more or less, you need to determine the recipe conversion factor. Once you know that factor, you first multiply all the ingredient amounts by it. Then you convert the new measurements into appropriate recipe units for your kitchen. This may require converting items listed originally as a count into a weight or a volume, or rounding measurement into reasonable quantities. In some cases you will have to make a judgment call about those ingredients that do not scale up or down exactly, such as spices, salt, and thickeners.

$$\frac{\text{Desired yield}}{\text{Original yield}} = \text{Recipe conversion factor (RCF)}$$

NOTE: The desired yield and the original yield must be expressed the same way before you can use the formula. If your original recipe says that it makes five portions, for example, and does not list the amount of each portion, you may need to test the recipe to determine what size portion it actually makes. Similarly, if your recipe lists the yield in ounces and you want to make 3 quarts of the soup, you need to convert quarts into fluid ounces before you can determine the recipe conversion factor.

The new ingredient amounts usually need some additional fine tuning. You may need to round the result or convert it to the most logical unit of measure. For some ingredients, a straightforward increase or decrease is all that is needed. For example, to increase a recipe for chicken breast from five servings to fifty, you would simply multiply 5 chicken breasts by 10; no further adjustments are necessary. Other ingredients, such as thickeners, aromatics, seasonings, and leavenings, may not multiply as simply, however. If a soup to serve four requires 2 tablespoons of flour to make a roux, it is not necessarily true that you will need 20 tablespoons (or 1¼ cups) of flour to thicken the same soup when you prepare it for forty. The only way to be sure is to test the new recipe and adjust it until you are satisfied with the result.

Other considerations when converting recipe yields include the equipment you have to work with, the production issues you face, and the skill level of your staff. Rewrite the steps to suit your establishment at this point. It is important to do this now, so you can uncover any further changes to the ingredients or methods that the new yield might force. For instance, a soup to serve four would be made in a small pot, but a soup for forty requires a larger cooking vessel. However, using a larger vessel might result in a higher rate of evaporation, so you may find that you need to cover the soup as it cooks or increase the liquid to offset the evaporation.

CONVERTING PORTION SIZES

Sometimes it will happen that you also need to modify the portion size of a recipe. For instance, say you have a soup recipe that makes four 8-ounce portions, but you need to make enough to have forty 6-ounce portions. To make the conversion:

1. Determine the total original yield and the total desired yield of the recipe.

Number of portions x Portion size = Total yield

Example: 4 x 8 fl oz = 32 fl oz (total original yield)

40 x 6 fl oz = 240 fl oz (total desired yield)

2. Determine the recipe conversion factor and modify the recipe as described above.

Example: $\dfrac{240 \text{ fl oz}}{32 \text{ fl oz}} = 7.5$ (recipe conversion factor)

Confusion often arises between weight and volume measures when ounces are the unit of measure. It is important to remember that weight is measured in ounces, but volume is measured in fluid ounces. A standard volume measuring cup is equal to 8 fluid ounces, but the contents of the cup may not always weigh 8 ounces. One cup (8 fluid ounces) of cornflakes weighs only 1 ounce, but one cup (8 fluid ounces) of peanut butter weighs 9 ounces. Water is the only substance for which it can be safely assumed that 1 fluid ounce equals 1 ounce. For all other ingredients, when the amount is expressed in ounces, weigh it; when the amount is expressed in fluid ounces, measure it with an accurate liquid (or volume) measuring tool.

Measuring spoons measure an ingredient using volume, a quick and easy way to scale ingredients used in very small amounts, such as this gumbo filé powder.

CONVERTING VOLUME MEASURES TO WEIGHT

You can convert a volume measure into a weight if you know how much a cup of an ingredient (prepared as required by the recipe) weighs. This information is available in a number of charts or ingredient databases. (See "Weights and Measures Equivalencies" Appendix Three).

You can also calculate and record the information yourself as follows:

Prepare the ingredient as directed by the recipe — sift flour, chop nuts, mince garlic, grate cheeses, and so forth.

Set the measuring device on the scale and reset the scale to zero (known as tare).

Fill the measuring device correctly. For liquids, use graduated measuring cups or pitchers and fill to the desired level. To be sure that you have measured accurately, bend down until the level mark on the measure is at your eye level. The measuring utensil must be sitting on a level surface for an accurate measurement. Use nested measuring tools for dry ingredients measured by volume. Overfill the measure, then scrape away the excess as you level off the measure.

Return the filled measuring tool to the scale and record the weight in either grams or ounces on your standardized recipe.

CONVERTING BETWEEN U.S. AND METRIC MEASUREMENT SYSTEMS

The metric system, used throughout most of the world, is a decimal system, meaning that it is based on multiples of 10. The gram is the basic unit of weight, the liter is the basic unit of volume, and the meter is the basic unit of length. Prefixes added to the basic units indicate larger or smaller units. For instance, a kilogram is 1,000 grams, a milliliter is 1/1,000 of a liter, and a centimeter is 1/100 of a meter.

The U.S. system, familiar to most Americans, uses ounces and pounds to measure weight, and teaspoons, tablespoons, fluid ounces, cups, pints, quarts, and gallons to measure volume. Unlike the metric system, the U.S. system is not based on multiples of a particular number, so it is not as simple to increase or decrease quantities. Instead, either the equivalencies of the different units of measure must be memorized or a chart must be kept handy (see page 996).

Most modern measuring equipment is capable of measuring in both U.S. and metric units. If, however, a recipe is written in a system of measurement for which you do not have the proper measuring equipment, you will need to convert to the other system.

TO CONVERT OUNCES AND POUNDS TO GRAMS: Multiply ounces by 28.35 to determine grams; divide pounds by 2.2 to determine kilograms

TO CONVERT GRAMS TO OUNCES OR POUNDS: Divide grams by 28.35 to determine ounces; divide grams by 453.59 to determine pounds

TO CONVERT FLUID OUNCES TO MILLILITERS: Multiply fluid ounces by 29.58 to determine milliliters

TO CONVERT MILLILITERS TO FLUID OUNCES: Divide milliliters by 29.58 to determine fluid ounces

METRIC PREFIXES

kilo = 1,000

hecto = 100

deka = 10

deci = 1/10

centi = 1/100

milli = 1/1000

CONVERTING TO A COMMON UNIT OF MEASURE

To convert measurements to a common unit (by weight or volume), use the following chart. This information is used both to convert scaled measurements into practical and easy-to-use recipe measures and to determine costs.

RECIPE MEASURE	COMMON CONVERSION TO VOLUME	COMMON UNIT (U.S.)
1 pound	N/A	16 ounces
1 gallon	4 quarts	128 fluid ounces
1 quart	2 pints	32 fluid ounces
1 pint	2 cups	16 fluid ounces
1 cup	16 tablespoons	8 fluid ounces
1 tablespoon	3 teaspoons	1 fluid ounce

CALCULATING AS PURCHASED COST (APC)

Most food items purchased from suppliers are packed and priced by wholesale bulk sizes, such as by the crate, case, bag, carton, and so on. Yet in kitchen production, the packed amount is not always used for the same purpose and may often be broken down and used for several items. Therefore, in order to allocate

TOP *These carrots were purchased by the bunch and still have tops attached, increasing the amount of trim loss.*

MIDDLE *Some cuts produce a minimum of trim. The oblique cut takes advantage of the natural shape of the carrot and increases the carrot you have left after trimming and cutting to serve to the guest.*

BOTTOM *Certain preparation techniques, such as tournéing, can increase the amount of trim. Not all trim counts as loss. Here, the chef peeled the carrot before tournéing in order to make use of the wholesome trim for mirepoix.*

the proper prices to the recipe being prepared, it is necessary to convert purchase pack prices to unit prices, which are expressed as price per pound, each, by the dozen, by the quart, and the like.

If you know the cost of a pack with many units, calculate the cost per unit by dividing the as-purchased cost of the pack by the number of units in the pack.

$$\frac{\text{APC Total}}{\text{Number of units}} = \text{APC per unit}$$

If you know the unit price of an item, you can determine the total cost by multiplying the as-purchased cost per unit (APC) by the number of units.

$$\text{APC per unit} \times \text{Number of units} = \text{Total APC}$$

CALCULATING THE YIELD OF FRESH FRUITS AND VEGETABLES AND DETERMINING YIELD PERCENTAGE

For many food items, trimming is required before the items are actually used. In order to determine an accurate cost for these items, the trim loss must be taken into account. From this information, the yield percentage will be important in determining the quantity to order.

First, record the as-purchased quantity (APQ) from the invoice, or weigh the item before trimming or cutting.

Example: APQ = 5 lb (or 80 oz) carrots

Trim the item and cut as desired, saving trim and edible portion quantity in separate containers. Weigh each separately and record their weights in a costing form.

As-purchased quantity (APQ) − trim loss = Edible portion quantity (EPQ)

Example: 80 oz carrots (APQ) − 8.8 oz carrot trim = 71.2 oz sliced carrot

Next, divide the EPQ by the APQ.

$$\frac{\text{Edible portion quantity}}{\text{As-purchased quantity}} = \text{Yield percentage}$$

$$\text{Example:} \frac{71.2 \text{ oz sliced carrot (EPQ)}}{80 \text{ oz carrots (APQ)}} = .89$$

To convert the decimal to a percentage, multiply by 100:

Yield percentage = 89%

CALCULATING THE AS-PURCHASED QUANTITY (APQ) USING YIELD PERCENTAGE

Because many recipes assume the ingredients listed are ready to cook, it is necessary to consider the trim loss when purchasing items. In this case, the edible portion quantity must be converted to the as-purchased quantity, which, when trimmed, will give the desired edible portion quantity. The yield percentage is used as a tool when ordering.

$$\frac{EPQ}{Yield\ Percentage} = APQ$$

Example: A recipe requires 20 pounds of cleaned shredded cabbage. The yield percentage for cabbage is 79 percent. When the 20 pounds is divided by 79 percent (0.79), the result, 25.3 pounds, will be the minimum amount to purchase.

Generally, the as-purchased quantity obtained by this method is rounded up, since the yield percentage is an estimate. Some chefs increase the figure by an additional 10 percent to account for human error as well.

It should be kept in mind that not all foods have a loss. Many processed or refined foods have 100 percent yield, such as sugar, flour, or dried spices. Other foods have a yield percentage that depends on how they are served. If, for example, the ingredient is to be served by the piece (half a cantaloupe), or if a recipe calls for it by count (15 strawberries), the yield percentage is not considered; the correct number of items must be purchased in order to create the correct number of servings. However, if you are making a fruit salad and you know you need 2 ounces of cubed melon and 1 ounce of sliced strawberries per serving, you must consider the yield percentage when ordering.

CALCULATING EDIBLE PORTION QUANTITY (EPQ) USING YIELD PERCENTAGE

Sometimes it is necessary for you to determine how many portions can be obtained from raw product. For example, if you have a case of fresh green beans that weighs 20 pounds and you need to know how many 4-ounce servings are in the case, what you need to do first is determine the yield percentage for green beans, either by referring to a list of yield percentages (see Appendix) or by performing a yield test. Once you know the yield percentage, you can compute the weight of the green beans after trimming.

The edible portion represents the part of any ingredient that can be served to the guest, such as the glazed carrots shown here.

APQ x Yield percentage = EPQ

Example: 20 lb green beans (APQ) x .88 (yield %) = 17.6 lb green beans (EPQ)

The edible portion quantity (EPQ) would be 17.6 pounds. The second step would be to compute how many 4-ounce servings would be in 17.6 pounds. If necessary, convert the portion size (here, 4 ounces) of the same unit of measure as the edible portion quantity (here, 1 pound). There are 16 ounces in 1 pound; 1 portion is equal to ¼ (or .25) pound.

$$\frac{EPQ}{\text{Portion Size}} = \text{Number of servings}$$

$$\text{Example: } \frac{17.6 \text{ lb green beans (EPQ)}}{.25 \text{ lb serving size}} = 70.4 \text{ servings}$$

You would be able to obtain seventy full servings from the case of green beans. You should round down the number of portions since it would not be plausible to serve a partial portion to a guest.

CALCULATING EDIBLE PORTION COST

As discussed earlier, recipes often assume ingredients are ready to cook, so when it comes to costing a recipe, the edible portion cost (EPC) per unit can be calculated from the as-purchased cost (APC) per unit, as long as the edible portion is expressed in the same unit of measure as the cost unit.

$$\frac{APC}{\text{Yield Percentage}} = EPC$$

$$\text{Example: } \frac{\$.106/\text{oz carrots (APC)}}{.75 \text{ (yield \% for tournéed carrots)}} = \$.141/\text{oz tournéed carrots (EPC)}$$

$$EPQ \times EPC = \text{Total cost}$$

Example: 4 oz tournéed carrot (EPQ) x $.141/oz tournéed carrot (EPC) = $.564 per serving (total cost)

CALCULATING THE VALUE OF USABLE TRIM

Often, some of the trimmings from a food may be used to prepare other foods. For example, if you have tournéed a carrot, rather than cutting it into dice or rounds, you can maximize your profit from the carrot by using the trim to prepare a soup, purée, or other dish. Using the information from your yield test, you can calculate the value of the trim. First, determine the use for the trim, then find the cost per unit and yield percentage for that ingredient, as if you had to buy it to prepare the dish. For instance, if you use the trim from carrot tournés to prepare

TOP *This strip loin is trimmed of excess fat before cutting steaks.*

MIDDLE *This steak is trimmed and ready to portion. Inedible trim (gristle and fat) is held separately. Usable trim for grinding or other uses is also kept separately.*

BOTTOM *Consult the standardized recipe for portioning information and cut the steak into the desired portion. Be sure to use a scale to keep sizes consistent.*

THE BUTCHER'S YIELD TEST

The purpose of a butcher's yield test is to find the accurate costs of fabricated meats, fish, and poultry. This is done by determining the amount of usable meat and trim from a particular fabrication, and to calculate the value of all edible cuts, including not only the portion of meat served to the guest, but also the value of bones used for stock and of trim used for ground meat, pâtés, soups, or other dishes.

GENERAL PROCEDURES

Select the item to be tested and record the as-purchased weight. (Make sure you use the same scale for the entire test.) Fabricate the item to desired specifications. Keep all parts (bones, fat, usable cuts, usable trim) in separate tubs or trays, and record all weights.

Use current prices for the meat item as purchased. Use market values for fat, bones, and usable trim. For instance, if you save the lean meat to make ground meat, the value of that part of the trim is the price you would have to pay to purchase ground meat.

1. DETERMINE THE AS-PURCHASED COST (APC)

   As-purchased weight x as-purchased price per lb = APC

   Example: 28 lb x $1.30 = $36.40 (APC)

2. FABRICATE THE MEAT.

   Example: #103 beef rib trimmed to #109 beef rib (roast ready)

3. DETERMINE THE TOTAL TRIM WEIGHT AND VALUE.

   Trim weight fat   x Market price per lb = Trim value (fat)
   +
   Trim weight bones x Market price per lb = Trim value (bones)
   +
   Trim weight trim   x Market price per lb = Trim value (trim)

   _____

   Total Trim Weight   Total Trim Value

   Example: 3 lb fat x $0.10/lb = $0.30

        4 lb bones x $0.30/lb = $1.20

        5 lb usable trim x $1.30/lb = $6.50

        12 lb total trim weight = $8.00 total trim value

4. DETERMINE THE NEW FABRICATED WEIGHT (NFW).

   As-purchased weight - total trim weight = NFW

   Example: 28 lb as-purchased weight –

        12 lb total trim weight = 16 lb (NFW)

5. DETERMINE THE NEW FABRICATED COST (NFC).

   APC – total trim value = NFC

   Example: $36.40 - $8.00 = $28.40 (NFC)

6. DETERMINE THE NEW FABRICATED PRICE PER POUND (NFPP)

   $$\frac{NFC}{NFW} = NFPP$$

   Example: = $1.77 (NFPP)

7. DETERMINE THE COST FACTOR (CF).

   $$\frac{NFPP}{\text{As-purchased price per pound}} = CF$$

   Example: = 1.36 (CF)

8. DETERMINE THE YIELD PERCENTAGE.

   $$\frac{NFW}{\text{As-purchased weight}} = \text{Yield percentage}$$

   Example: $\dfrac{16 \text{ lb}}{28 \text{ lb}}$ = 57% (yield percentage)

9. DETERMINE THE NUMBER OF PORTIONS OF FINAL PRODUCT FROM THE FABRICATION.

   NFW x 16 oz = total number of ounces

   $$\frac{\text{Total number of ounces}}{\text{Portion size}} = \text{number of portions}$$

   Example: How many 12-oz portions can be obtained from 16 lb of trimmed meat?

   16 lb x 16 oz = 256 oz

   $$\frac{256 \text{ oz}}{12 \text{ oz}} = 21.33, \text{ or 21 portions}$$

10. DETERMINE THE COST PER PORTION.

   $$\frac{NFPP}{16} = \text{Cost of 1 oz}$$

   Cost of 1 oz x Portion size = Cost per portion

   Example: What is the cost of one 12-oz portion?

   $$\frac{\$1.77}{16} = .1106, \text{ or 11.06 cents (cost of 1 oz)}$$

   .1106 x 12 oz = $1.277 (cost per portion)

a soup, the food cost for the carrot trim is the same as for a carrot that has been trimmed and chopped.

$$\text{Example: } \frac{\text{As-purchased cost of carrots per ounce (\$.106)}}{.89 \text{ (yield percentage for chopped carrots)}} = \$.119 \text{ (value of usable carrot trim for soup per ounce)}$$

Some products produce trim that can be used in a variety of ways. The strip loin shown on page 28 produces trimmings that can be used in a variety of ways. For example, the chef may use some of the trim to prepare a clarification that might otherwise require ground meat, and more of the trim to make a filling for fajitas that might otherwise require the purchase of a cut of sirloin. Also, some restaurants sell trimmed fat to rendering companies. Finding additional uses for trim brings the cost of edible portions down, reduces costs overall, and helps to eliminate waste.

For more information on any of the above culinary math topics, refer to *Culinary Math*.

USING RECIPES EFFECTIVELY

Recipes are meant to provide instructions. However, in the professional kitchen, a recipe can be much more than that. It can be used as a powerful tool to improve efficiency and organization, and to increase profits. When you know the approximate yield percentage for onions and carrots, you can get the right amount for a recipe in a single visit to the walk-in, instead of having to make several trips. If you understand the difference between the price you paid per pound for the whole beef tenderloin and how much you are actually paying per pound for the trimmed meat you serve to the guest, you can be more effective at reducing loss and decreasing the operation's overall food cost.

Learning to read recipes carefully and to use them to be more productive is an important step in developing your professional skills.

The American people have become increasingly aware of the fact that good nutrition plays an important part in maintaining physical health and overall well-being. Consequently, culinary professionals must be aware of the nutritional content of their dishes. They must also understand the chemical and physical changes that occur when food is cooked.

THE BASICS OF NUTRITION AND FOOD SCIENCE

NUTRITION

People choose to eat certain foods for a number of different reasons. One of the most important reasons is, of course, taste. But in addition to flavor, every food contains calories as well as a variety of substances known as nutrients, which are essential to our bodies for energy, growth, repair, and maintenance.

CALORIES

Foods provide human beings with the energy needed to perform vital functions. This energy is measured in kilocalories, defined as the amount of energy or heat required to raise the temperature of 1 kilogram of water by 1 degree Celsius. In general use, the term *calorie* is normally substituted for *kilocalorie*.

There is a direct correlation between calories consumed and actual body weight. Calorie intake needs to equal calorie expenditure in order for a person to maintain weight. Consuming more calories than expended will result in weight gain, while consuming fewer calories than expended will cause weight loss.

Although foods consist of many components, calories come from only four sources: carbohydrates, proteins, fats, and alcohol. Carbohydrates and proteins contain 4 calories per gram, fats have 9 calories per gram, and alcohol carries 7 calories per gram. Therefore, a food containing 10 grams of fat will contain 90 calories from fat.

TOP *Fruits and vegetables are part of a healthy lifestyle.*

BOTTOM *Foods high in carbohydrates.*

Any food source that has a good supply of nutrients in relation to the number of calories it contains is considered nutrient-dense. Whole grains, fresh fruits and vegetables, lean meats, poultry, and low-fat dairy products are all nutrient-dense foods. Foods and beverages that contribute little or nothing besides calories include beer, wine, and other forms of alcohol, doughnuts, jams and jellies, and candy.

In order to maintain good health, the United States Department of Agriculture (USDA) recommends that 55 to 60 percent of a person's daily calorie intake should come from carbohydrates, and protein should contribute 12 to 15 percent. Fat calories should be limited to a maximum of 30 percent.

CARBOHYDRATES

Carbohydrates are the preferred energy source of the brain and nervous system. They provide energy for muscle movement and red blood cells, and they play a role in the regulation of fat metabolism. Fifty-five to 60 percent of a person's daily calories should come from carbohydrates — in a 2,000-calorie diet, that is approximately 1,100 to 1,200 calories (275 to 300 grams of carbohydrate).

Carbohydrates are composed of smaller units containing carbon, hydrogen, and oxygen, otherwise known as sugars, and are classified as simple or complex. Simple carbohydrates, such as sucrose (table sugar), fructose (fruit sugar), and lactose (the sugar found in milk), are more quickly broken down into glucose and absorbed by the body than complex carbohydrates, found in plant-based foods such as grains, legumes, and vegetables.

FIBER

Fiber, a form of carbohydrate that is not digestible, is a non-nutritive but essential component of a healthy diet. Fiber is not a single compound, but a mixture of several components found in complex carbohydrates: cellulose, hemicelluloses, and lignin. These substances make up the structural building materials in the plant cell wall. The other components of fiber, pectin and gums, are involved with plant cell structure and metabolism. The proportion of these fiber components varies from food to food.

Fiber is divided into two basic types: soluble and insoluble. Soluble fiber dissolves in water. Good sources include beans, fruits, vegetables, oats, and barley. Soluble fiber plays a role in lowering high serum cholesterol levels and reducing the risk of heart attack by binding with cholesterol-rich bile acids in the intestinal tract. When the fiber and bile acids are excreted, cholesterol molecules are eliminated as well. Soluble fiber also helps to regulate the body's use of sugars, slowing their digestion and release into the bloodstream, thereby delaying the onset of hunger.

Insoluble fiber does not dissolve in water. Instead, it absorbs water and provides bulk in the diet, causing a feeling of fullness and aiding in bodily waste removal. Insoluble fiber also may play a role in reducing the risk of certain types of cancer, as well as possibly reducing the risk of type 2 diabetes. Sources of insoluble fiber include most fruits and vegetables, wheat bran, popcorn, nuts, and whole-grain flours and meals.

FAT

In recent years fat has become the focus of countless articles, books, diet plans, and advertising claims, many of which give the false impression that fat is the ultimate dietary villain, to be avoided at all costs. While it is true that excess fat in the diet is unhealthy because it raises the risk of coronary artery disease, obesity, and certain cancers, it is still an essential nutrient that provides energy and fulfills vital bodily functions. Fat is essential in making the fat-soluble vitamins A, D, E, and K available to our bodies. Fat is digested slowly, providing a lasting sensation of fullness (known as satiety), and slows the digestion of carbohydrates and protein ingested along with it, thus giving the body time to absorb the nutrients contained in foods. Lastly, fat has a crucial role in the development of flavor in cooking.

Fats are grouped into three main categories according to their degree of saturation, a term that refers to the molecular structure of the fat. A single fat is actually a number of chains, known as fatty acids, composed of carbon, hydrogen, and oxygen linked together. The individual fatty acids can be saturated, monounsaturated, or polyunsaturated, depending on how many open sites there are for hydrogen atoms to bond with a carbon atom. Saturated fatty acids cannot accept any more hydrogen, monounsaturated fatty acids have one open site on the chain, and polyunsaturated fatty acids have more than one site open.

Current dietary recommendations are that fat should account for 30 percent of calories at most, and most of the fat should be mono- and polyunsaturated. Saturated fats should not exceed 10 percent of total daily calories because they have been shown to have an adverse effect on serum cholesterol levels. In a 2,000-calorie diet, these limits translate to approximately 600 calories from all fats (about 67 grams), with no more than 200 of these calories (22 grams) coming from saturated fats.

Although consuming more than the recommended amount of fat is often associated with obesity, what many people fail to recognize is that fat is not in and of itself the cause of obesity. Fat doesn't necessarily make people fat; excess calories do. But fat is calorie-dense. One gram of fat contains 9 calories, whereas 1 gram of carbohydrate or protein contains only 4 calories. It is therefore quite easy to consume a great many calories in just a few bites when eating foods that are high in fat.

Recently two particular types of fats have received a great deal of media coverage. The first of these is known as trans fat. When liquid oils are made into margarines or shortenings during a process known as hydrogenation, additional hydrogen atoms are forced to bond with the liquid unsaturated fats, effectively increasing their saturation levels and causing them to become more solid at room temperature. This process results in the formation of trans fats (trace amounts of trans fats also occur naturally in some foods).

Until recently, trans fats were thought to be the lesser of two evils when compared to saturated fats in terms of their effect on serum cholesterol levels. The most current research, however, seems to indicate that trans fat is more detrimental than originally thought. It raises blood cholesterol levels and may be carcinogenic. However, Americans generally tend to consume much less trans fat than saturated fat, so current dietary advice places more of an emphasis on reducing saturated fat in the diet.

Commercially baked goods, margarines, and foods fried in or containing shortening that is solid at room temperature are the main sources of trans fats in the American diet. On nutrition labels, trans fats are not listed, but the Food and Drug Administration (FDA) is currently considering a petition to include them in a separate category on nutrition labels. For now, the best way to tell if a product contains trans fats is to look at the ingredients. If the label lists a hydrogenated fat, chances are trans fats are present also. If hydrogenated fat is one of the first few ingredients, the product should be used sparingly.

Omega-3 fatty acids have also been in the nutrition spotlight. These polyunsaturated fatty acids occur in fatty fish, dark green leafy vegetables such as spinach and broccoli, and certain nuts and oils such as walnuts and canola oil. They have been shown to be quite effective in reducing the risk of heart disease by lowering the amount of cholesterol manufactured in the liver and reducing the likelihood of blood clot formation around deposits of arterial plaque. Omega-3 fatty acids may also slow or prevent tumor growth, stimulate the immune system, and lower blood pressure.

CHOLESTEROL

Cholesterol is not the same thing as cooking fats or fats found in the body, but it is a fat-related compound. Cholesterol is a *sterol*, a subcategory of *lipids* (the scientific name for all substances commonly known as fat). There are two types of cholesterol: dietary and serum. Dietary cholesterol does not exist in any plant foods; it is found only in animal foods. Serum, or blood, cholesterol is found in the bloodstream and is essential to life.

The liver manufactures about 1,000 milligrams of serum cholesterol daily, which is used to provide a fatty protective jacket around nerve fibers. In the skin, a derivative of cholesterol is made into vitamin D with the aid of sunlight. Cholesterol also functions in the outer membranes of the cells and as a building block for certain hormones. It is not essential to consume cholesterol, because humans are capable of producing it from other dietary components. Furthermore, foods high in cholesterol also tend to have higher amounts of fat. For these reasons, it is recommended that daily dietary cholesterol should not exceed 300 milligrams, regardless of how many calories are consumed.

TOP *Foods high in visible and hidden fats.*

BOTTOM *Dishes high in cholesterol include fried calamari (squid), liver and onions, and beef tenderloin with hollandaise sauce.*

Cholesterol is transported by two main types of proteins in the blood, high-density lipoproteins (HDL) and low-density lipoproteins (LDL). LDL takes cholesterol into the circulatory system, and HDL clears cholesterol out of the circulatory system. A high level of HDL is desirable because it usually indicates a reduced risk of heart disease. LDL is a sticky substance that tends to deposit cholesterol in areas of high blood flow, such as arterial walls. These deposits may build up and eventually block the arteries so that blood cannot flow easily, causing a condition called atherosclerosis. Such a condition can lead to aneurysms, coronary and cerebral thrombosis, embolism, heart attack, and stroke.

The consumption of saturated fat has been shown to raise the level of LDL in the blood more than the consumption of dietary cholesterol. It is for this reason that health experts recommend limiting saturated fat to less than 10 percent of daily caloric intake.

Studies show that people who eat more monounsaturated fat have lower serum cholesterol levels and a lower incidence of heart disease. When total fat consumption is limited to 30 percent of daily calories and most of the fats are monounsaturated fats, there appears to be a positive effect on levels of HDL. Polyunsaturated fats have also been shown to lower serum cholesterol levels. However, large amounts of these fatty acids may also lower HDL.

Recent years have seen a move toward greater use of monounsaturated fats, such as olive oil, in cooking. However, it should be emphasized that the idea is not to simply add more unsaturated fats to the diet, but to substitute unsaturated fats for saturated fats.

PROTEIN

Like fats and carbohydrates, protein is an essential dietary component, providing calories that can be used by the body as a source of energy. It is also essential for the growth and maintenance of body tissues; for the production of hormones, enzymes, and antibodies; and for the regulation of bodily fluids. Protein should account for about 12 to 15 percent of calories; in a 2,000-calorie diet, that translates to approximately 240 to 300 calories (60 to 75 grams). Children, pregnant women, and nursing mothers will require more protein to support growth. Illness, infections, attacks on the immune system, and malnutrition can also affect how much protein the body needs and how well it can use the protein it receives.

The average American eats 100 to 120 grams of protein daily, nearly twice the recommended level. Too much protein can be as detrimental to the body as too little because excess protein is linked to osteoporosis, dehydration, and gout. An excess of protein can also damage the liver and kidneys.

The basic building blocks of protein are known as amino acids. The multitude of proteins found in a human cell are composed of about twenty amino acids, most of which are produced by the body. The eight essential amino acids that cannot be produced in the body must be supplied by the diet. All protein-rich foods contain some or all of these eight. Certain other amino acids are considered to be conditionally essential — normally the body can produce these from the eight essential ones, but when intake of the latter is insufficient, a dietary source of conditionally essential amino acids becomes important.

Foods are categorized as containing either complete protein or incomplete protein. Those providing complete protein contain all eight essential amino acids. Meats, poultry, fish, and other animal products are good sources of complete protein, but they are not necessarily the healthiest sources, as many of these foods also contain high amounts of saturated fat and cholesterol.

Vegetables, grains, legumes, and nuts do not contain all the essential amino acids. However, each of these food groups contains different types and ratios of the essential amino acids, and when combined, they can provide complete proteins. This process of combining complementary proteins has been referred to as *mutual supplementation*. The traditional dishes from cuisines that rely on plant foods as their major source of protein are excellent examples of this practice: lentils and rice, pasta and beans, tortillas and beans, tofu and rice, or hummus and pita bread.

Recent studies have shown that the body does not require that all eight essential amino acids be consumed in the same meal. A diet balanced over the course of the day with various complementary protein sources normally supplies all the amino acids required by a healthy individual.

WATER

Water contains no calories, but humans need it to live. It is in our tissues, blood, bones, teeth, hair, and skin. In fact, we are nearly 60 percent water.

Water is critical to the body's chemical reactions. It dissolves minerals and other compounds, transports nutrients to each cell, removes impurities from the bloodstream and the body, and forms an integral part of the cells themselves. Because water cannot be easily compressed, it can cushion joints, organs, and sensitive tissues such as the spinal cord. Water maintains pressure on the eyes'

THE AMINO ACIDS

ESSENTIAL	CONDITIONALLY ESSENTIAL	OTHERS
Isoleucine	Arginine	Alanine
Leucine	Cysteine	Aspartic acid
Lysine	Histidine*	Cystine
Methionine	Tyrosine	Glutamic acid
Phenylalanine		Glutamine
Threonine		Glycine
Tryptophan		Proline
Valine		Serine

*Essential for infants and small children

Water is a noncaloric, but essential, nutrient.

Including a variety of foods rich in vitamins and minerals is the best way to meet dietary requirements for these nutrients, as well as to produce visually exciting and flavorful plates.

optic nerves for proper vision, stabilizes blood pressure, and helps regulate body temperature. Excess heat, from exertion or climate, transforms water into a vapor through sweating. This energy exchange cools the body by carrying heat out and away from the body. The human body generally loses about a quart of water daily through the cleansing and cooling processes. Water must be replenished daily, by drinking fluids and eating foods that contain water.

VITAMINS AND MINERALS

Vitamins and minerals, like water, are noncaloric nutrients. Although they are important to overall health, they are generally needed in smaller quantities than the energy-providing nutrients. Daily Values (DVs), formerly known as U.S. RDAs, have been established for many, though not all, of the vitamins and minerals known to be important to good health.

VITAMINS Vitamins are classified as either water-soluble or fat-soluble. Water-soluble vitamins dissolve in water and are easily transported throughout the body in the bloodstream. Toxic levels of these vitamins in the body are possible but unlikely because when consumed in large amounts, the excess is released from the body along with waste water. A small amount of the water-soluble vitamins can be stored briefly in lean tissue, such as muscles and organs, but the body's supplies must be replenished daily.

The B-complex vitamins (thiamin, riboflavin, niacin, folate, biotin, pantothenic acid, B_6, and B_{12}) and vitamin C are water-soluble. B-complex vitamins are found in grains, legumes, vegetables, and meats. They are critical for the proper release of energy in the body. B-complex vitamin deficiencies may result in beriberi, anemia, or pellagra. Because B_{12} is found only in animal foods, strict vegetarians need to supplement their diets by taking vitamin B_{12} supplements or eating foods fortified with this vitamin.

Vitamin C, found in fruits and vegetables, increases the body's absorption of iron and is imperative to the growth and maintenance of body tissues because it promotes the production of collagen, the protein substance that helps hold tissue together. It also boosts the immune system and possibly reduces serum cholesterol levels. Vitamin C has antioxidant properties, which means that it protects cells from damage by oxygen and may protect against heart disease and cancer.

Unlike the water-soluble vitamins, fat-soluble vitamins are stored in fat tissue and cannot be easily flushed from the body once ingested. The fat-soluble vitamins are A, D, E, and K. They are found in a variety of food sources and often will occur together in plant foods and fish oils. In the proper amounts, these fat-soluble vitamins are basic to health, but greatly exceeding the DVs for these vitamins causes the body to store them in virtually limitless amounts, making it easy for toxic levels to accumulate. Once toxic levels are reached, a variety of dangerous conditions may develop, some of which can be fatal.

The form of vitamin A found in animal foods is known as retinol. Vitamin A itself is not found in plant foods, but a pigment known as beta-carotene, which the body uses to produce vitamin A, is contained in orange, deep yellow, and dark green leafy vegetables. Beta-carotene cannot normally be converted to vitamin A quickly enough to reach a toxic level. Excess beta-carotene may, however, cause a person to appear yellowish, because it is stored in fat layers just beneath the skin.

Vitamin D is responsible in part for the proper formation of bones. A lack of vitamin D results in the disease called rickets, a condition in which bones grow abnormally. People with limited exposure to sunlight, which is necessary to produce vitamin D in the body, may need to eat foods fortified with vitamin D, such as milk and cereal, to get the amounts needed for proper health.

Vitamin E is an antioxidant, like vitamin C, that protects the body from damage by free radicals (reactive forms of oxygen produced by the body's metabolic processes) and may have cancer-fighting potential. It is found in a variety of foods and is not difficult to obtain from dietary sources unless a person is following a low-fat diet.

Vitamin K is associated with proper clotting. Although it is produced by bacteria found in the intestines, a person who eats a varied and healthy diet obtains about half the DV from food, particularly dark green leafy vegetables.

MINERALS The body needs certain minerals in varying amounts. Some, such as calcium, phosphorus, sodium, potassium, and magnesium, are called macrominerals because they are required in relatively large amounts. Others, including fluoride, iodine, and iron, are known as trace minerals or microminerals because the body needs only minute amounts. Regardless of the relative amounts required by the body, they are all essential to maintaining good health.

Calcium is the body's most abundant mineral. Ninety-nine percent of the calcium needed by the body is used in the development of bones and teeth. The remaining 1 percent is used to regulate blood pressure and to aid in muscle contraction, transmission of nerve impulses, and clotting of the blood. A deficiency in calcium can cause stunted growth and loss of bone density. Good sources of calcium include dairy products such as milk and yogurt, broccoli, and leafy greens.

In addition to playing a key role in all energy-releasing reactions, phosphorus is also used by the body in conjunction with calcium for maintaining bone and tooth structure. A phosphorous deficiency, while rare, may result in weakness, impaired heart function, and neurological problems. Phosphorus is present in animal protein, nuts, cereals, and legumes.

Salt brings out the flavors in foods when it is used at the correct point in cooking and is added only in amounts at which its own flavor is just barely perceptible.

Sodium and potassium, otherwise known as electrolytes, are essential to the regulation of body functions, as they help maintain the body's normal fluid balance. They are also involved in nerve and muscle functions. Because sodium is plentiful in many foods, deficiencies are uncommon, but when one occurs, loss of appetite, muscle cramps, confusion, and forgetfulness may result. Diets high in sodium may aggravate hypertension in people who already suffer from this condition. Virtually all fruits and vegetables are good sources of potassium. Potassium deficiency symptoms are similar to those of a sodium deficiency and include weakness, falling blood pressure, and confusion.

Magnesium is used in the body to promote healthy bone and tooth structure, muscle contraction, nerve transmission, and bowel function. The American diet tends to be deficient in this mineral. A lack of magnesium can cause possible growth failure, behavioral disturbances, tremors, weakness, and seizures. Good food sources of magnesium include green vegetables, nuts, legumes, and whole grains.

Fluoride is incorporated in teeth and bones, helps to prevent tooth decay, and may play a role in preventing osteoporosis. Many community water supplies contain fluoride. It is also present in saltwater fish and shellfish, and in tea.

Iodine is essential for the normal functioning of the thyroid gland and also helps to regulate energy metabolism, cellular oxidation, and growth. A deficiency in iodine will result in goiter, or enlargement of the thyroid gland. Since the early 1900s, when goiter was common in the midwestern United States, iodine has been added to table salt (iodized salt) in this country; this has resolved this deficiency problem.

About 75 percent of the body's iron is found in the blood, where it is an important component of hemoglobin, a pigment in red blood cells that carries oxygen from the lungs to the cells. The remaining iron functions as a component of myoglobin, the oxygen-supplying molecule found in muscles, and as part of certain enzymes involved in cellular energy metabolism. Iron deficiency is a worldwide health problem, particularly for women of childbearing age, that causes a form of anemia in which the blood cells lack sufficient hemoglobin. Individuals suffering from an iron deficiency may appear pale and suffer from weakness and an impaired immune system. The best sources of iron are liver and red meat, but it is also found in whole grains, legumes, green leafy vegetables, and dried fruit.

PHYTOCHEMICALS AND ANTIOXIDANTS

Research about phytochemicals and antioxidants has provided good news for people concerned with healthy eating, because after years of hearing about foods that are bad for us and should be avoided, the focus can be shifted to identifying foods that have some promising potential and should be eaten more freely.

Phytochemicals, like vitamins, are compounds that occur naturally in fruits, vegetables, legumes, and grains. The difference between phytochemicals and vitamins is that vitamins have been recognized as being essential to life and have set deficiency levels, whereas the benefits of phytochemicals are a recent and still emerging discovery. As more is learned about phytochemicals, deficiency levels may eventually be established for some of these compounds. Although phyto-chemicals are a relatively new subject for scientific study, research results so far indicate that they are quite effective in reducing the risk of cancer, heart disease, and other chronic ailments.

In general, phytochemicals seem to function in a combination of three different ways. Some have antioxidant properties, some affect hormone levels, and some work with enzymes that may eliminate carcinogens. Certain phytochemicals, such as digitalis and quinine, have been used for medical purposes for centuries. The anticancer effects of plant-based substances are only beginning to be explored.

Antioxidants are a subcategory of the phytochemical family. They are essential for combating the cellular damage caused by free radicals. Free radicals are present in particularly great quantities during times of stress, illness, and exposure to toxins.

Antioxidants include vitamins A, C, and E, and the mineral selenium. The family of pigments called carotenoids, which are found in leafy green vegetables and yellow, orange, and red vegetables, are also antioxidants. There are over six hundred different carotenoids found in nature, and about fifty of these may be used by the body. Lycopene, for example, which is found most abundantly in tomatoes, seems to interfere with the growth of cancer cells and may reduce the risk of prostate cancer and perhaps other cancers.

Every plant food seems to have a different mix of phytochemicals, which work together to provide health benefits. Tomatoes, for instance, have been estimated to contain over a hundred different phytochemicals. Therefore, the best way to capitalize on the benefits of phytochemicals is to eat a wide variety of fruits, vegetables, grains, and legumes.

Choose brightly colored vegetables from a variety of groups to be sure your dishes introduce phytochemicals and antioxidants to your menu options.

DIETARY GUIDELINES AND RECOMMENDATIONS

The food guide pyramids are the most current and widely recognized graphic representation of recommended daily food allowances in America. The four food groups, taught to schoolchildren since the 1950s, advocated eating a variety of foods, but did not include the information that a diet emphasizing foods from certain categories was preferable. The introduction of the first food guide pyramid by the USDA in 1992 marked a whole new way of understanding the importance of various foods within the diet.

Since then, other pyramids have followed suit to show the health benefits of certain cultural foodways, such as those of traditional Mediterranean, Latin American, and Asian societies. Still other pyramids illustrate the specific dietary requirements for special groups, such as vegetarians, children, and senior citizens. Although each pyramid has a different focus, all aim to help people eat well and live better.

THE USDA FOOD GUIDE PYRAMID

In an effort to help people make better food choices to prevent or reduce incidence of these diseases, the USDA replaced the four food groups with the USDA Food Guide Pyramid. The pyramid presents a plan for a healthy diet by suggesting daily serving ranges for each of six categories of food. The base of the

The average American diet overemphasizes foods high in saturated fats, particularly animal products such as meat and cheese, and processed and refined foods full of sweeteners, hydrogenated shortenings, sodium, and empty calories. (Pyramid adapted from the U.S. Department of Agriculture and U.S. Department of Health and Human Services.)

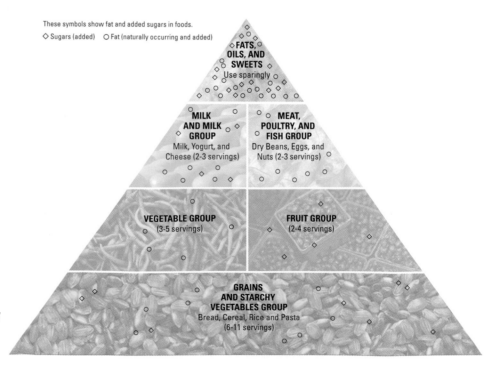

These symbols show fat and added sugars in foods.
◇ Sugars (added)   ○ Fat (naturally occurring and added)

FATS, OILS, AND SWEETS
Use sparingly

MILK AND MILK GROUP
Milk, Yogurt, and Cheese (2-3 servings)

MEAT, POULTRY, AND FISH GROUP
Dry Beans, Eggs, and Nuts (2-3 servings)

VEGETABLE GROUP
(3-5 servings)

FRUIT GROUP
(2-4 servings)

GRAINS AND STARCHY VEGETABLES GROUP
Bread, Cereal, Rice and Pasta
(6-11 servings)

pyramid represents the food groups that should comprise the largest part of the diet. The number of recommended servings will vary depending on individual caloric requirements, so some people find it easier to think of daily food allowances as a percentage of daily calories rather than a number of servings permitted each day. To translate the USDA Food Guide Pyramid suggestions, approximately 55 to 60 percent of daily calories should come from carbohydrates, no more than 30 percent from fat, and 12 to 15 percent from protein.

The broad base of the USDA pyramid shows representations of a variety of grain-based foods — pasta, rice, cereals, breads, and other grains. Whole or minimally processed grains are preferable because they contain nutrients that are lost during milling, refining, and other processing. In addition to stripping out nutrients, processing may also add refined sugars or fats not normally found in the whole grain. Six to eleven servings of these foods is optimal.

Fruits and vegetables make up the second largest component of the diet. Again, the closer these items remain to their natural state, the more nutrients are retained and the less fat and refined sugar are added. Three to five servings of vegetables and two to four servings of fruits are recommended by the USDA.

Two to three servings of dairy products should be included in the daily diet. Many dairy foods, such as cream and cheese, are loaded with fat and calories, but low fat alternatives to whole-milk products have improved immensely in recent years. Substituting a lower-fat milk, cheese, or yogurt can reduce the fat in a dish without sacrificing calcium or protein, and in most cases the taste is not affected.

Meats, poultry, fish, and eggs — the traditional centerpieces of many American meals — are still included, but the recommended serving size has been reduced to a 3-ounce portion, which is about the size of a deck of cards. Although not traditionally thought of as focal points of a meal, beans and nuts are also included in this food group because they are good sources of protein. Two to three servings totaling no more than 6 to 9 ounces are recommended each day.

Fats, oils, and sweets, which are represented at the peak of the pyramid, are suggested in very limited quantities, although no specific number of servings is recommended. In fact, the suggestion is to "use sparingly." For many individuals, keeping track of fats, oils, and sweets is difficult, since they are hidden in other foods. In order to limit consumption of these kinds of foods, the USDA suggests that people choose lower-fat foods from the other food groups most often and choose fewer foods that are high in sugars, such as candy, sweet desserts, and soft drinks. Additionally, fats and sugars added to foods in cooking or at the table, such as butter, gravy, salad dressing, sugar, and jelly, should be used in small quantities.

USDA FOOD GUIDE PYRAMID SERVING SIZES

FOOD GROUP	SUGGESTED DAILY SERVINGS	WHAT COUNTS AS A SERVING
Bread, cereal, rice, pasta	6 to 11 servings from entire group (include several servings of whole-grain products daily)	1 slice of bread ½ hamburger bun or English muffin (whole-grain or enriched) 1 small roll, biscuit, or muffin 5 to 6 small or 3 to 4 large crackers ½ cup cooked cereal, rice, or pasta 1 ounce ready-to-eat cereal
Fruits	2 to 4 servings from entire group	1 whole fruit such as a medium apple, banana, or orange ½ grapefruit 1 melon wedge ¾ cup fruit juice ½ cup berries ½ cup chopped, cooked, or canned fruit ¼ cup dried fruit
Vegetables	3 to 5 servings (include all types regularly; use dark green leafy vegetables and dry beans and peas several times a week)	½ cup cooked vegetables ½ cup chopped raw vegetables 1 cup raw leafy green vegetables, such as lettuce or spinach ¾ cup vegetable juice
Meats, poultry, fish, dry beans and peas, eggs, nuts	2 to 3 servings from entire group	Amounts should total 6 to 9 ounces of cooked lean meat, poultry without skin, or fish a day (count 1 egg, ½ cup cooked beans, or 2 tablespoons peanut butter as equivalent to 1 ounce of meat)
Milk, yogurt, cheese	2 servings (3 servings for women who are pregnant or breast-feeding, teenagers, and young adults to age 24)	1 cup milk 8 ounces yogurt 2 ounces processed cheese
Fats, sweets, and alcoholic beverages	Use fats and sweets sparingly; if you drink alcoholic beverages, do so in moderation	

Every five years the USDA revises its dietary guidelines for Americans based on the latest medical and scientific findings. Although these guidelines speak to people on a personal level and cover lifestyle choices as well as dietary ones, it is helpful for chefs and other culinary professionals to be aware of them. The 2000 dietary guidelines for Americans are as follows:

Aim for a healthy weight.

Be physically active each day.

Let the Food Guide Pyramid guide your food choices.

Choose a variety of grains daily, especially whole grains.

Choose a variety of fruits and vegetables daily.

Keep food safe to eat.

Choose a diet that is low in saturated fat and cholesterol and moderate in total fat.

Choose beverages and foods to moderate your intake of sugars.

Choose and prepare foods with less salt.

If you drink alcoholic beverages, do so in moderation.

THE MEDITERRANEAN PYRAMID

The Mediterranean Pyramid was generated from a conference series, "Public Health Implications of Traditional Diets," undertaken by the Harvard School of Public Health, Oldways Preservation & Exchange Trust, and the World Health Organization (WHO). It represents a diet based on the traditional diets of Greece and southern Italy, areas where people once had the world's lowest rates

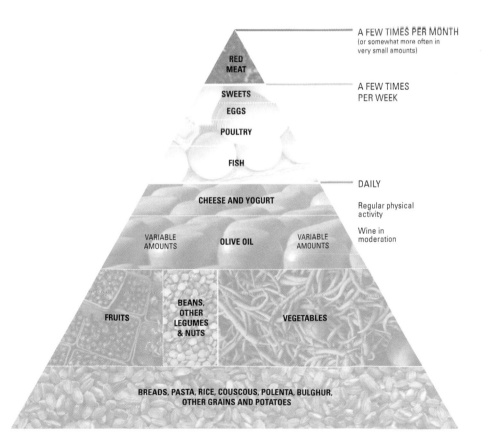

A FEW TIMES PER MONTH
(or somewhat more often in very small amounts)

A FEW TIMES PER WEEK

DAILY

Regular physical activity

Wine in moderation

Adapted and reprinted with permission from Oldways Preservation & Exchange Trust. © 1994 Oldways Preservation & Exchange Trust.

of heart disease, obesity, diabetes, hypertension, and many forms of cancer. Researchers believe that diet plays a significant role in this statistic. In fact, as Western dietary and lifestyle habits have made greater inroads on these traditional cultures, once-rare diseases are now cropping up in increasing numbers.

Rather than considering the diet strictly in terms of how many calories a particular food contains, this pyramid prioritizes food choices to maximize the health benefits of certain foods. The food choices are representative of a typical Mediterranean diet prior to the 1960s, before Western influence on food choices was widespread.

Some foods are recommended for daily consumption, while others should only be consumed a few times per week or month. Each day, foods rich in carbohydrates, such as polenta, rice, couscous, potatoes, breads, pasta, and other grains, make up the bulk of the meals. Fruits, vegetables, beans, and nuts round out the daily diet. Olive oil, high in monounsaturated fat, is specified as the Mediterranean Diet's principal source of fat. Cheeses and yogurt are also typically consumed daily. Olive oil, cheese, and yogurt may contain significant amounts of fat, but their rich nutrient content, including vitamins, antioxidants, and minerals, justifies using them in small amounts daily.

Fish, poultry, eggs, and sweets can be consumed a few times each week in the Mediterranean model. Red meats are limited to a few times per month, or more often if eaten in small quantities. These protein-rich foods, featured so prominently in the typical American diet, are used more as condiments to add flavor to the grains, legumes, and vegetables that make up the bulk of food in the Mediterranean diet.

Continuing research into the significant health advantages of the Mediterranean culture has revealed that diet is just one of several contributing factors. Genetics and certain lifestyle behaviors — a less stressful pace of life, regular daily physical activity, and communion with family and friends — are also likely factors. This feature, along with the option to include wine in moderation, further distinguishes this pyramid from the USDA pyramid.

THE VEGETARIAN PYRAMID

The growing number of people following vegetarian diets has focused special attention on how to structure a healthy diet or create a meal plan or menu options when animal foods are eliminated or greatly reduced. The results of this research have led several organizations to develop vegetarian pyramids. The one featured here was designed by the American Dietetic Association specifically for vegetarians.

Vegans, the strictest of vegetarians, do not eat any foods of animal origin, preferring instead to base their diets exclusively on vegetables, fruits, grains, nuts, and legumes. People who adhere to vegan diets have to be especially careful to consume foods that will supply all of their nutritional needs. The Vegan Vegetarian Food Guide (page 48), which incorporates many of the same elements as the USDA Food Guide Pyramid, addresses these special needs.

As in the Vegetarian Pyramid, foods are grouped into categories, and appropriate numbers of servings are suggested from within each category. The differences between the USDA Pyramid and the Vegetarian Pyramid begin in the first tier: The number of recommended servings from the bread/grain/cereal group is greater in the vegetarian pyramid (8 to 12 versus 6 to 11). This is simply to help a person who follows such a restricted diet obtain enough total calories for the day. In fact, the range of servings for several of the groups is greater than those in the USDA pyramid.

In the second tier, in addition to calling for a larger range of daily servings for fruit, the vegetarian pyramid makes a distinction between dark green leafy vegetables (kale, mustard and collard greens, spinach, and similar foods) and other types of vegetables. This is to help ensure that vegans, who abstain from dairy products, get all the calcium they need. Dark green leafy vegetables are also a good source of iron, which can be difficult to obtain in a meat-free diet.

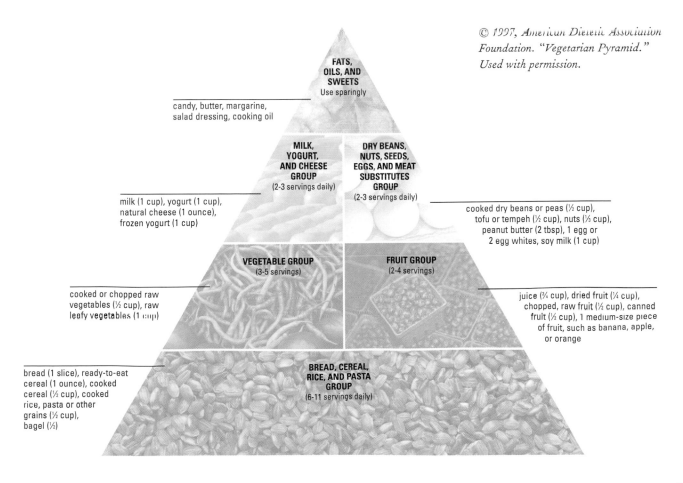

© 1997, American Dietetic Association Foundation. "Vegetarian Pyramid." Used with permission.

VEGAN VEGETARIAN FOOD GUIDE PYRAMID SERVING SIZES

FOOD GROUP	SUGGESTED DAILY SERVINGS	WHAT COUNTS AS A SERVING
Breads, grains, cereals	8 to 12	1 slice of bread ½ hamburger bun or English muffin (whole-grain or enriched) 1 small roll, biscuit, or muffin 5 to 6 small or 3 to 4 large crackers ½ cup cooked cereal, rice, or pasta 1 ounce ready-to-eat cereal
Fruit	2 to 6	1 whole fruit such as a medium apple, banana, or orange ½ grapefruit 1 melon wedge ½ cup juice ½ cup berries ½ cup chopped, cooked, or canned fruit ¼ cup dried fruit
Vegetables	4 to 6 servings dark green leafy vegetables	½ cup cooked vegetables ½ cup raw vegetables 1 cup raw leafy vegetables, such as lettuce or spinach ½ cup vegetable juice
Fortified soy drinks and tofu*	2 to 3	1 cup soy milk 6 ounces (1 cup) tofu
Nuts and seeds	1	2 ounces (⅓ cup) nuts or seeds 2 tablespoons nut or seed butter
Legumes and other plant proteins	1 to 3	½ cup cooked beans, peas, or lentils ½ cup tofu, soy product, or meat analog
Fats and sugars	Use sparingly	1 teaspoon oil or margarine 2 to 3 teaspoons salad dressing ⅛ avocado 5 olives 1 teaspoon sugar, jam, jelly, syrup

*Soy drinks should be fortified with calcium, vitamin D, and vitamin B_{12}. Tofu should be made with calcium sulfate, not magnesium sulfate. Check the Nutrition Facts label on soy products.

The third tier (which in the USDA pyramid represents the dairy and meat/poultry/fish groups) contains soy, nuts and seeds, legumes, and other plant proteins. In order to ensure that they are providing their bodies with enough usable protein, vegetarians should consume a combination of these foods over the course of a day.

The one nutrient that is virtually impossible to obtain in sufficient quantities on a vegan diet is vitamin B_{12}. Vegans must eat foods fortified with this vitamin, such as fortified soy milk or cereal, or they must take a B_{12} supplement daily.

In addition to the three food guide pyramids featured here, several organizations have developed pyramid models of other traditional cuisines or of diets suited for special population groups. Oldways Preservation & Exchange Trust, in conjunction with the Harvard School of Public Health, has also developed Asian, Latin American, and vegetarian pyramids. The American Dietetic Association has pyramids for older Americans and children, as well as pyramids modeled on the cuisines of India, China, southeastern America, Italy, Mexico, and Native America. For more information on these pyramids, contact these organizations directly (see Recommended Readings for addresses).

FOOD SCIENCE BASICS

There are dozens of scientific principles at work in cooking. As an introduction to the topic of food science, this section provides a cursory overview of the most basic of these principles. For more information on any of the following subjects, refer to the Recommended Readings for a list of food science references.

HEAT TRANSFER

Cooking is the act of applying heat to foods to prepare them for eating. When foods are cooked, changes in flavor, texture, aroma, color, and nutritional content occur.

There are three ways that heat is transferred to foods. *Conduction* is the direct transfer of heat between adjacent molecules. An example of conduction is cooking on a flattop range. Heat is transferred from the molecules of the hot range surface to the molecules of the adjacent pan bottom, then from the pan bottom to the pan sides and the food contained within the pan. The pan must be in direct contact with the range for conduction to occur.

Some materials are better conductors of heat than others. Generally, most metals are good conductors, while gases (air), liquids, and nonmetallic solids

Water boils in a pot over a conduction top.

INDUCTION COOKING

INDUCTION COOKING is a relatively new cooking method that transfers heat through a specially designed cooktop made of a smooth ceramic material over an induction coil. The induction coil creates a magnetic current that causes a metal pan on the cooktop to heat up quickly, yet the cooktop itself remains cool. Heat is then transferred to the food in the pan through conduction. Cookware used for induction cooking must be flat on the bottom for good contact with the cooktop, and it must be made of ferrous (iron-containing) metals, such as cast iron, magnetic stainless steel, or enamel over steel. Cookware made of other materials will not heat up. Induction cooking offers the advantages of rapid heating and easy cleanup because there are no nooks on the smooth surface of the cooktop for spilled foods to get stuck in, nor do spilled foods cook on the cool surface.

(glass, ceramic) are not. Because it relies on direct contact, conduction is a relatively slow method of heat transfer, but the slow, direct transfer of heat between adjacent molecules is what allows a food to be cooked from the outside in, resulting in a completely cooked exterior with a moist and juicy interior.

Convection is the transfer of heat through gases or liquids. When either of these substances is heated, the portions of the gas or liquid closest to the heat source warm first and become less dense, causing them to rise and be replaced by cooler, denser portions of the gas or liquid. Convection, therefore, is a combination of conduction and mixing.

Convection occurs both naturally and through mechanical means. Natural convection is at work in a pot of water placed on the stove to boil. Conduction transfers heat from the stove to the pot to the water molecules in contact with the interior of the pot. As these water molecules heat up, convection causes them to move away and be replaced by cooler molecules. This continual movement results in convection currents within the water. If a potato is added to the water, the convection currents transfer heat to the surface of the potato, at which point conduction takes over to transfer heat to the interior of the potato.

Mechanical convection occurs when stirring or a fan is used to speed and equalize heat distribution. When you stir a thick sauce to heat it faster and keep it from scorching on the bottom of the pan, you are creating mechanical convection. Convection ovens use fans to rapidly circulate hot air, allowing them to cook foods more quickly and evenly than conventional ovens do. (Natural convection occurs in conventional ovens as air in contact with the heating element circulates, but the majority of heat transfer in a conventional oven is the result of infrared radiation.)

Radiation is the transfer of energy through waves of electromagnetic energy that travel rapidly through space. Radiation does not require direct contact between the energy source and the food being cooked. When the waves traveling through space strike matter and are absorbed, they cause molecules in the matter to vibrate more rapidly, increasing the temperature. Two types of radiation are important in the kitchen: infrared and microwave.

Examples of sources of infrared radiation are the glowing coals of a charcoal grill or the glowing coils of an electric toaster, broiler, or oven. Waves of radiant energy travel in all directions from these heat sources. Foods or cookware that absorb the energy waves are heated. Dark, dull, or rough surfaces absorb radiant energy better than light-colored, smooth, or polished surfaces. Transparent glass permits the transfer of radiant energy, so conventional oven temperatures should be lowered by approximately 25°F to offset the additional energy transfer that occurs when glass baking dishes are used.

Microwave radiation, produced by microwave ovens, transfers energy through short, high-frequency waves. When these microwaves are absorbed by foods, they cause the food molecules to begin vibrating faster, creating heat. Microwave radiation cooks foods much faster than infrared radiation because it penetrates foods several inches deep, whereas infrared is mainly absorbed at the surface. Depending on their composition, foods react differently to microwaves. Foods with high moisture, sugar, or fat content absorb microwaves best and heat up more readily.

Microwave cooking has a few drawbacks, however. It is best suited to cooking small batches of foods. Meats cooked in a microwave oven lose greater amounts of moisture and easily become dry. Microwave ovens also cannot brown foods, and metal cannot be used in them because it reflects the microwaves, which can cause fires and damage the oven.

EFFECTS OF HEAT ON STARCHES AND SUGARS: CARAMELIZATION, MAILLARD REACTION, AND GELATINIZATION

As discussed previously in this chapter, carbohydrate comes in various forms, and each form reacts differently when exposed to heat. The two forms of carbohydrate that are of interest from a basic food science perspective are sugar and starch.

When exposed to heat, sugar will at first melt into a thick syrup. As the temperature continues to rise, the sugar syrup changes color, from clear to light yellow to a progressively deepening brown. This browning process is called caramelization. It is a complicated chemical reaction, and in addition to color change, it also causes the flavor of the sugar to evolve and take on the rich complexity that we know to be characteristic of caramel. Different types of sugar caramelize at different temperatures. Granulated white sugar melts at 320°F (160°C) and begins to caramelize at 338°F (170°C).

In foods that are not primarily sugar or starch, a different reaction, known as the Maillard reaction, is responsible for browning. This reaction involves sugars and amino acids (the building blocks of protein). When heat is applied, these components react and produce numerous chemical by-products, resulting in a brown color and intense flavor and aroma. It is this reaction that gives coffee, chocolate, baked goods, dark beer, and roasted meats and nuts much of their rich flavor and color.

Though the Maillard reaction can happen at room temperature, both caramelization and the Maillard reaction typically require relatively high heat (above 300°F) to occur rapidly enough to make an appreciable difference in foods. Because water cannot be heated above 212°F (100°C) unless it is under pressure, foods cooked with moist heat (boiling, steaming, poaching, stewing)

TOP *Sugar cooked until caramelization.*

BOTTOM *The browning of meats through the Maillard reaction.*

ABOVE *When starch is combined with water or another liquid and heated, individual starch granules absorb the liquid and swell.*

TOP *Lemon juice is added to milk to denature its proteins as a first step in making cheese.*

BOTTOM *The acid causes the milk's proteins to clump together, or coagulate, giving the milk a curdled appearance. To make cheese, the liquid (known as whey) is allowed to drain from the cheese curds.*

will not brown. Foods cooked using dry-heat methods (sautéing, grilling, or roasting) will brown. It is for this reason that many stewed and braised dishes begin with an initial browning of ingredients before liquid is added.

Starch, a complex form of carbohydrate, has powerful thickening properties. When starch is combined with water or another liquid and heated, individual starch granules absorb the liquid and swell. This process, known as gelatinization, is what causes the liquid to thicken. Gelatinization occurs at different temperatures for different types of starch. As a general rule of thumb, root-based starches (potato and arrowroot, for instance) thicken at lower temperatures but break down more quickly, whereas cereal-based starches (corn and wheat, for example) thicken at higher temperatures but break down more slowly. High levels of sugar or acid can inhibit gelatinization, while the presence of salt can help it.

DENATURING PROTEINS

At the molecular level, natural proteins are shaped like coils or springs. When natural proteins are exposed to heat, salt, or acid, they denature — that is, their coils unwind. When proteins denature, they tend to bond together, or coagulate, and form solid clumps. An example of this is a cooked egg white, which changes from a transparent fluid to an opaque solid. As proteins coagulate, they lose some of their capacity to hold water, which is why protein-rich foods give off moisture as they cook, even if they are steamed or poached. Fortunately, some heat-induced denaturation is reversible through cooling. This is why roasted foods should be allowed to rest before carving; as the temperature falls, some of the water that was forced into spaces between the proteins is reabsorbed and the food becomes moister. Denatured proteins are easier to digest than natural proteins.

FUNCTION OF COOKING FATS

Depending on their molecular structure, some fats are solid at room temperature, while others are liquid at the same temperature. Liquid fats are known as oils. Solid fats soften and eventually melt into a liquid state when exposed to heat.

In addition to being a vital nutrient, fat performs a number of culinary functions. It provides a rich flavor and silky mouth feel or texture that most people find very enjoyable and satisfying. Fat also carries and blends the flavors of other foods, and makes available to us flavor compounds and nutrients that are soluble only in fat. An appealing visual element is provided by fat when a food appears to be moist, creamy, fluffy, or shiny, among other things. During the baking process, fat performs a multitude of chemical functions, such as tenderizing, leavening, aiding in moisture retention, and creating a flaky or crumbly texture. In cooking, fat transfers heat to foods and prevents them from sticking. It also holds the heat in food, emulsifies or thickens sauces, and creates a crisp texture when used for frying.

One important aspect of fat is its ability to be heated to relatively high temperatures without boiling or otherwise breaking down. This is what allows fried foods to brown and cook quickly. If heated to high enough temperatures, however, fat will begin to break down and an acrid flavor develops, effectively ruining anything cooked in it. The temperature at which this occurs, known as the smoke point, is different for each type of fat. Generally, vegetable oils begin to smoke around 450°F (232°C), while animal fats begin to smoke around 375°F (191°C). Any additional materials in the fat (emulsifiers, preservatives, proteins, carbohydrates) lower the smoke point. Because some breakdown occurs at moderate temperatures and food particles tend to get left in the fat, repeated use in cooking also lowers the smoke point.

STATES OF AND FUNCTION OF WATER IN COOKING

Water is the primary substance in most foods. Fruits and vegetables contain up to 95 percent water; raw meat is about 75 percent water. At sea level, pure water freezes (becomes solid) at 32°F (0°C) and boils (turns to water vapor, or steam) at 212°F (100°C). Boiling leads to evaporation, which makes reduction possible.

Water is a powerful solvent. Many vitamins, minerals, and flavor compounds are soluble in water. When salt or sugar is dissolved in water, the freezing point is lowered and the boiling point is raised. An important aspect of solutions is their pH, which is a measure of their acidity or alkalinity. Pure water, which is neutral, has a pH of 7. Anything above 7 indicates an alkaline (basic) solution; a pH below 7 indicates an acidic solution. Practically all foods are at least slightly acidic. The pH of a solution is important in cooking for a number of reasons, including the effects it has on the flavor, color, texture, and nutritional quality of foods.

Allowing green vegetables to cook too long in boiling water leaches out their color (as evidenced by the green tint of the cooking water) as well as robbing them of flavor, texture, and vitamins and minerals.

FORMING EMULSIONS

An emulsion occurs when two substances that do not normally mix are forced into a mixture in which one of the substances is evenly dispersed in the form of small droplets throughout the other substance. Under normal conditions, fat (either liquid oil or solid fat) and water do not mix, but these two substances are the most common ingredients in culinary emulsions.

An emulsion consists of two phases, the dispersed phase and the continuous phase. An emulsified vinaigrette is an example of an oil-in-water emulsion, meaning that the oil (the dispersed phase) has been broken up into very small droplets

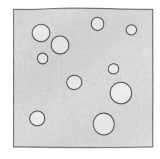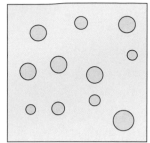

An oil-and-water emulsion (left) consists of oil droplets suspended in water. A water-in-oil emulsion (right) is water droplets suspended in oil.

suspended throughout the vinegar (the continuous phase). Butter is an example of a water-in-oil emulsion, in which the water occurs as very small droplets suspended in the fat.

Temporary emulsions, such as vinaigrettes, form quickly and require only the mechanical action of whipping, shaking, or stirring, but they do not remain emulsified for long. To make an emulsion stable enough to keep the oil in suspension, additional ingredients, known as emulsifiers, are necessary to attract and hold together both the oil and liquid. Commonly used emulsifiers include egg yolks (which contain the emulsifier lecithin), mustard, and glace de viande. Natural starches, such as those in garlic, or modified starches, such as cornstarch or arrowroot, are also used.

THE IMPORTANCE OF NUTRITION AND FOOD SCIENCE TO THE PROFESSIONAL CHEF

Nutrition and food science are exacting studies, both dedicated to discovering and clarifying the complexities of food when it is cooked (or otherwise changed through chemical and physical actions) and consumed.

The chef can prepare and serve wonderful food without being able to identify the food's role in a healthy diet or the scientific principle at play. However, a general knowledge of how heat affects food and how bodies assimilate foods gives the chef the freedom to develop new dishes that meet a client's needs. It also aids the chef during such problem-solving moments as changing the cooking method, finding a suitable short cut for a long or complex recipe, or substituting an ingredient. These challenges may be inspired by a need to liven up a menu, cut costs, streamline production, or introduce a new technique or ingredient. Or, you may want or need to know something about nutrition or science in order to train your staff in the dining room or the kitchen.

This chapter only begins the discussion of nutrition and food science. Books and articles written on these topics should be part of every chef's professional reading, even if the goal is not specifically to cut calories or prepare a lecture on the nature of emulsions. As chefs, scientists, food manufacturers, and dietitians continue to explore how our diets affect our bodies and how the act of cooking affects our food, there will be more discoveries. There may be new products, new equipment, and new styles of service, all arising from a deeper and more thorough understanding of the chef's basic raw material — food.

The importance of food and kitchen safety cannot be overemphasized. Few things are as detrimental to a food service establishment as an officially noted outbreak of a food-borne illness caused by poor sanitary practices. In addition to providing a sanitary atmosphere and adhering to procedures for safe food handling, it is also important to ensure a safe working environment. This chapter covers the causes of food-borne illnesses and prevention procedures and also includes checklists to help the staff achieve sanitary and safe kitchen conditions.

FOOD AND
KITCHEN SAFETY

FOOD-BORNE ILLNESS

Foods can serve as carriers for many different illnesses. The most common symptoms of food-borne illnesses include abdominal cramps, nausea, vomiting, and diarrhea, possibly accompanied by fever. These symptoms may appear within a matter of hours after consumption of the affected food, although in some cases several days may elapse before onset. In order for a food-borne illness to be declared an official outbreak, it must involve two or more people who have eaten the same food, and it must be confirmed by health officials. The table on page 58–60 gives a detailed list of food-borne illnesses and symptoms.

Food-borne illnesses are caused by *adulterated foods* (foods unfit for human consumption). The severity of the illness depends on the amount of adulterated food ingested and, to a great extent, on the individual's susceptibility. Children, the elderly, and anyone whose immune system is already under siege generally will have much more difficulty than a healthy adult in combating a food-borne illness.

The source of the contamination affecting the food supply can be chemical, physical, or biological. Insecticides and cleaning compounds are examples of *chemical contaminants* that may accidentally find their way into foods. *Physical contaminants* include such things as bits of glass, rodent hairs, and paint chips. Careless food handling can mean that even an earring or a plastic bandage could fall into the food and result in illness or injury.

Biological contaminants account for the majority of food-borne illnesses. These include naturally occurring poisons, known as toxins, found in certain wild mushrooms, rhubarb leaves, green potatoes, and other plants. The predominant biological agents, however, are disease-causing microorganisms known as *pathogens*, which are responsible for up to 95 percent of all food-borne illnesses. Microorganisms of many kinds are present virtually everywhere, and most are helpful or harmless, if not essential; only about 1 percent of microorganisms are actually pathogenic (responsible for causing illness).

Food-borne illnesses caused by biological contaminants fall into two subcategories: intoxication and infection. *Intoxication* occurs when a person consumes food containing toxins from bacteria, molds, or certain plants and animals. Once in the body, these toxins act as poison. Botulism is an example of an intoxication.

In the case of an *infection*, the food eaten by an individual contains large numbers of living pathogens. These pathogens multiply in the body and generally attack the gastrointestinal lining. Salmonellosis is an example of an infection.

Some food-borne illnesses have characteristics of both an intoxication and an infection. *E. coli* 0157:H7 is an agent that causes such an illness.

The specific types of pathogens responsible for food-borne illnesses are fungi, viruses, parasites, and bacteria. *Fungi*, which include molds and yeast, are more adaptable than other microorganisms and have a high tolerance for acidic conditions. They are more often responsible for food spoilage than for food-borne illness. Fungi are important to the food industry in the production of cheese, bread, and wine and beer.

Viruses do not actually multiply in food, but if through poor sanitation practice a virus contaminates food, consumption of that food may result in illness. Infectious hepatitis, caused by eating shellfish harvested from polluted waters (an illegal practice) or poor hand-washing practices after using the rest room, are examples. Once in the body, viruses invade a cell (called the host cell) and essentially reprogram it to produce more copies of the virus. The copies leave the dead host cells behind and invade still more cells. The best defenses against food-borne viruses are good personal hygiene and obtaining shellfish from certified waters.

Parasites are pathogens that feed on and take shelter in another organism, called a host. The host receives no benefit from the parasite and, in fact, suffers harm or even death as a result. Amebas and various worms, such as *Trichinella spiralis,* which is associated with pork, are among the parasites that contaminate foods. Different parasites reproduce in different ways. An example is the parasitic worm that exists in the larva stage in muscle meats. Once consumed, the life cycle and reproductive cycle continue. When the larvae reach adult stage, the fertilized female releases more eggs, which hatch and travel to the muscle tissue of the host, and the cycle continues.

Bacteria are responsible for a significant percentage of biologically caused food-borne illnesses. In order to better protect food during storage, preparation, and service, it is important to understand the classifications and patterns of bacterial growth.

Bacteria are classified by their requirement for oxygen, the temperatures at which they grow best, and their spore-forming abilities. *Aerobic bacteria* require the presence of oxygen to grow. *Anaerobic bacteria* do not require oxygen and may even die when exposed to it. *Facultative bacteria* are able to function with or without oxygen.

In terms of sensitivity to temperature, bacteria fall into the following categories:

1. Mesophilic bacteria grow best between 60° and 100°F (16° and 38°C). Because the temperatures of human bodies as well as commercial kitchens fall within that range, mesophilic bacteria tend to be the most abundant and the most dangerous.

2. Thermophilic bacteria grow most rapidly between 110° and 171°F (43° and 77°C).

3. Psychrophilic bacteria prefer cooler temperatures, between 32° and 60°F (0° and 15°C).

FOOD-BORNE ILLNESSES

DISEASE AND IN-CUBATION PERIOD*	SYMPTOMS	CAUSE	FOOD INVOLVED	PREVENTIVE MEASURES
Botulism (12 to 36 hours)	Sore throat, vomiting, blurred vision, cramps, diarrhea, difficulty breathing, central nervous system damage (possible paralysis). Fatality rate up to 70%.	*Clostridium botulinum:* anaerobic bacterium that forms spores with high resistance to heat. Found in animal intestines, water, and soil.	Refrigerated or improperly canned foods; low-acid foods, such as spinach, tuna, green beans, beets, fermented foods, and smoked products. Rare in commercially canned foods.	Toxin is sensitive to heat, so maintain a high temperature while canning food and boil 20 minutes before serving. Do not use food in swollen cans; do not use home-canned food for commercial use.
Staphylococcus (2 to 4 hours)	Vomiting, nausea, diarrhea, cramps.	*Staphylococcus aureus:* facultative bacterium found in the nose, in the throat, and in skin infections of humans.	Foods that are high in protein, moist, handled much, and left at temperatures that are too warm. Milk, egg custards, turkey stuffing, chicken/tuna/ potato salads, gravies, reheated foods.	Store foods below 40°F (4°C) and reheat thoroughly to 165°F (74°C). People with infected cuts, burns, or respiratory illnesses should not handle food.
Ergotism (varies)	Hallucinations, convulsions, gangrene of extremities.	Ergot is a mold that grows on wheat and rye.	Wheat and rye.	Do not use moldy wheat or rye.
Chemical poisoning (minutes to hours)	Varies.	Pesticides on fruits and vegetables, cyanide in silver polish, zinc inside tin cans, copper pans.		Wash fruits and vegetables before using. Discard polish with cyanide. Wash utensils after polishing. Store pesticides away from food. Avoid cooking and storing foods in opened cans. Don't allow food to touch unlined copper.
Plant and animal toxins (varies — often rapid)	Varies.	Alkaloids; organic acids.		Avoid poisons. Identify wild mushrooms. Don't ingest too much nutmeg, green-skinned potatoes, fava beans, raw soybeans, blowfish, moray eel, or shark liver.
Shigellosis (12 to 48 hours)	Diarrhea, fever, cramps, dehydration.	*Shigella spp:* found in feces of infected humans, food, and water.	Beans, contaminated milk, tuna/turkey/macaroni salads, apple cider, and mixed, moist foods.	Safe water sources, strict control of insects and rodents, good personal hygiene.
Infectious hepatitis (10 to 50 days)	Jaundice, fever, cramps, nausea, lethargy.	*Hepatitis A:* virus grows in feces of infected humans and human carriers. Transmitted by water and from person to person. Infects the liver.	Shellfish from polluted water, milk, whipped cream, cold cuts, potato salad.	Cook clams, shellfish, and so on thoroughly, to a temperature exceeding 150°F (65°C). Heat-treat or otherwise disinfect suspected water and milk. Enforce strict personal hygiene.

*Incubation period is the time between infection and onset of symptoms.

DISEASE AND IN-CUBATION PERIOD*	SYMPTOMS	CAUSE	FOOD INVOLVED	PREVENTIVE MEASURES
Salmonellosis (6 to 48 hours)	Headache, diarrhea, cramps, fever. Can be fatal or lead to arthritis, meningitis, and typhoid.	*Salmonella spp.*: aerobic bacilli that live and grow in the intestines of humans, animals, birds, and insects.	Eggs, poultry, shellfish, meat, soup, sauces, gravies, milk products, warmed-over food.	Since *Salmonella* can be killed by high temperatures, cook to proper temperatures and reheat leftovers to an internal temperature of 165°F (74°C). Eliminate rodents and flies, wash hands after using the bathroom, avoid cross contamination.
Bacillus cereus (8 to 16 hours)	Cramps, diarrhea, nausea, vomiting.	*Bacillus cereus*: anaerobic bacterium that produces spores and is found in soil and many foods.	Cereal products, cornstarch, rice, custards, sauces, meat loaf.	Spores are able to survive heating, so reheat to 165°F (74°C) and keep foods properly cold.
Streptococcus (1 to 4 days)	Nausea, vomiting, and diarrhea	Various species of *Streptococcus* bacteria, which are facultative. Some are transmitted by animals and workers contaminated with feces, others from the nose and throat of infected humans.	Milk, pudding, ice cream, eggs, meat pie, egg/potato salads, poultry.	Cook foods thoroughly and chill rapidly. Ensure strict personal hygiene. Use pasteurized dairy products.
Trichinosis (4 to 28 days)	Fever, diarrhea, sweating, muscle pain, vomiting, skin lesions.	*Trichinella spiralis*: a spiral worm that lives in the intestines, where it matures and lays eggs and later invades muscle tissue. Transmitted by infected swine and rats.	Improperly cooked pork allows larvae to live.	Cook pork to 150°F (65°C). Avoid cross contamination of raw meats. If frying, cook to 170°F (75°C).
Perfrigens (9 to 15 hours)	Diarrhea, nausea, cramps, possible fever, vomiting (rare).	*Clostridium perfrigens*: spore-forming anaerobic bacterium that can withstand most cooking temperatures and is found in soil, dust, and the intestinal tract of animals.	Reheated meats, raw meat, raw vegetables, soups, gravies, and stews.	Quickly cool meat that is to be eaten later and reheat to 165°F (74°C). Avoid cross contamination of raw meat and cooked meat. The only way to kill spores is to pressure-cook at 15 lb steam pressure to reach 250°F (120°C).
Listeriosis (1 day to 3 weeks)	Nausea, vomiting, headache, fever, chills, backache, meningitis, miscarriage.	*Listeria monocytogenes*: aerobic bacteria found in soil, water, mud, humans, domestic and wild animals and fowl.	Unpasteurized milk and cheese, vegetables, poultry, meats, seafood, and prepared, chilled ready-to-eat foods.	Use only pasteurized dairy products. Cook foods thoroughly. ** Avoid cross contamination, clean and disinfect surfaces, and avoid pooling of water.

**When serving at-risk populations (e.g., children or the elderly), reheat prepackaged cold cuts; serve only pasteurized apple cider.

FOOD-BORNE ILLNESSES (CON'T)

DISEASE AND IN-CUBATION PERIOD*	SYMPTOMS	CAUSE	FOOD INVOLVED	PREVENTIVE MEASURES
Campylobacetiriosis (3 to 5 days)	Diarrhea, fever, nausea, abdominal pain, headache.	*Campylobacter jejuni:* microaerophile bacteria (requiring low oxygen levels) found in intestinal tract of domestic and wild animals.	Unpasteurized milk and dairy products, poultry, beef, pork, and lamb.	Thoroughly cook food. Avoid cross contamination.
Norwalk virus gastroenteritis (24 to 48 hours)	Nausea, vomiting, diarrhea, abdominal pain, headache, low-grade fever.	*Norwalk and Norwalk-like viruses:* found in the intestinal tracts of humans.	Raw shellfish, raw vegetable salads, prepared salads, water with fecal contamination.	Obtain shellfish from approved certified sources. Avoid fecal contamination by scrupulous personal hygiene. Thoroughly cook foods. Use chlorinated water.
E. coli 0157:H7 enteritis (12 to 72 hours)	Nausea, vomiting, diarrhea, or bloody diarrhea. ***	*Escherichia coli:* aerobic bacteria found in the intestinal tracts of animals, particularly cattle, and humans.	Raw and undercooked ground beef and other meats, imported cheeses, unpasteurized milk.	Thoroughly cook ground beef.** Avoid cross contamination. Avoid fecal contamination. Practice scrupulous hygiene.

*Incubation period is the time between infection and onset of symptoms.
**When serving at-risk populations (e.g., children or the elderly), reheat prepackaged cold cuts; serve only pasteurized apple cider.
***Other strains of *E. coli* cause diarrheal illness.

These foods all meet the requirements for potentially hazardous foods: moisture, moderate pH, and a protein source.

Bacteria reproduce by means of fission — one bacterium grows and then splits into two bacteria of equal size. These bacteria divide to form four, the four form eight, and so on. Under ideal circumstances, bacteria will reproduce every twenty minutes or so. In about twelve hours, one bacterium can multiply into sixty-eight billion bacteria, more than enough to cause illness.

Certain bacteria are able to form endospores, which serve as a means of protection against adverse circumstances such as high temperature or dehydration. Endospores allow an individual bacterium to resume its life cycle if favorable conditions should recur.

Bacteria require three basic conditions for growth and reproduction: a protein source, readily available moisture, and a moderate pH. The higher the amount of protein in a food, the greater its potential as a carrier of a food-borne illness. The amount of moisture available in a food is measured on the water activity (Aw) scale. This scale runs from 0 to 1, with 1 representing the Aw of water. Foods with a water activity above 0.85 support bacterial growth.

A food's relative acidity or alkalinity is measured on a scale known as pH. A moderate pH — a value between 4.6 and 10 on a scale that ranges from 1 to 14 — is best for bacterial growth, and most foods fall within that range. Adding highly acidic ingredients, such as vinegar or citrus juice, to a food can lower its pH and extend its shelf life.

Many foods provide the three conditions necessary for bacterial growth and are therefore considered to be potentially hazardous. Meats, poultry, seafood, tofu, and dairy products (with the exception of some hard cheeses) are all categorized as potentially hazardous foods. Foods do not necessarily have to be animal-based to contain protein, however; vegetables and grains also contain protein. Cooked rice, beans, pasta, and potatoes are therefore also potentially hazardous, as are sliced melons, sprouts, and garlic-and-oil mixtures.

Food that contains pathogens in great enough numbers to cause illness may still look and smell normal. Disease-causing microorganisms are too small to be seen with the naked eye, so it is usually impossible to ascertain visually that food is adulterated. Because the microorganisms, particularly the bacteria, that cause food to spoil are different from the ones that cause food-borne illness, food may be adulterated and still have no "off" odor.

TOP *Some kitchens use color-coded cutting boards to avoid cross contamination between meat, poultry, fish, and vegetables.*

BOTTOM *Wooden cutting boards will remain sanitary if properly cleaned.*

Although cooking food will destroy many of the microorganisms present, careless food handling after cooking can reintroduce pathogens that grow even more quickly without competition for food and space from microorganisms that cause spoilage. Although shortcuts and carelessness do not always result in food-borne illness, inattention to detail increases the risk of creating an outbreak that may cause serious illness or even death. The various kinds of expenses that a restaurant can incur as the result of an outbreak of food-borne illness can be staggering. In addition, negative publicity and loss of prestige are blows from which many restaurants can simply never recover.

AVOIDING CROSS CONTAMINATION

Many food-borne illnesses are a result of unsanitary handling procedures in the kitchen. Cross contamination occurs when disease-causing elements or harmful substances are transferred from one contaminated surface to another.

Excellent personal hygiene is one of the best defenses against cross contamination. The employee who reports for work even though he or she has a contagious illness or an infected cut on the hand puts every customer at risk. Anytime the hands come into contact with a possible source of contamination, especially the face, hair, eyes, and mouth, they must be thoroughly washed before continuing any work.

TO CUT DOWN on cross contamination and avoid spreading illness, wash your hands as often as you need to, and wash them correctly. The 1999 FDA Food Code states that hands and forearms should be washed using soap and 110°F (43°C) water for twenty seconds. You should wash your hands at the beginning of each shift and each new task, after handling raw foods, after going to the bathroom, after handling money or other nonfood items, and upon returning to the kitchen, to name a few points in the workday.

First, wet your hands, then apply soap. Use enough soap to work up a good lather. Use a nail brush to clean under your nails and around the cuticles if necessary, and scrub well. Lathering should take at least twenty seconds. The "Happy Birthday" song takes about ten seconds to sing. In order to be sure you have lathered for twenty seconds, try singing this song to yourself twice while washing your hands. Rinse your hands thoroughly in warm water, and dry them completely using paper towels.

Food is at greatest risk of cross contamination during the preparation stage. Ideally, separate work areas and cutting boards should be used for raw and cooked foods. Equipment and cutting boards should always be cleaned and thoroughly sanitized between uses. For example, before cutting a piece of pork on a surface that was used to cut chicken, it is important to clean and sanitize not only the cutting surface, but also your hands, the knife, and the sharpening steel. Wiping cloths for this purpose should be held in a double-strength sanitizing solution and placed near each workstation to encourage use.

All food must be stored carefully to prevent contact between raw and cooked items. Place drip pans beneath raw foods to catch drips and prevent any splashing. Do not handle ready-to-eat foods with bare hands. Instead, use a suitable utensil (deli tissue, spatula, tongs, or the like) or single-use food-handling gloves (to be used only for a single task and replaced before beginning a new task).

KEEPING FOODS OUT OF THE DANGER ZONE

An important weapon against pathogens is the observance of strict time and temperature controls. Generally, the disease-causing microorganisms found in foods need to be present in significant quantities in order to make someone ill. (There are exceptions, with *E. coli* 0157:H7 being one.) Once pathogens have established themselves in a food source, they will either thrive or be destroyed, depending upon how long foods are in the so-called danger zone.

There are pathogens that can live at all temperature ranges. For most of those capable of causing food-borne illness, however, the friendliest environment is one that provides temperatures within a range of 41° to 140°F (5° to 60°C) — the danger zone. Most pathogens are either destroyed or will not reproduce at temperatures above 140°F (60°C). Storing food at temperatures below 41°F (5°C) will slow or interrupt the cycle of reproduction. (It should also be noted that intoxicating pathogens may be destroyed during cooking, but any toxins they have produced are still there.)

When conditions are favorable, pathogens can reproduce at an astonishing rate. Therefore, controlling the time during which foods remain in the danger zone is critical to the prevention of food-borne illness. Foods left in the danger zone for a period longer than four hours are considered adulterated. Additionally, one should be fully aware that the four-hour period does not have to be continuous, but is cumulative, which means that the meter starts running again every time the food enters the danger zone. Therefore, once the four-hour period has been exceeded, foods cannot be recovered by heating, cooling, or any other method.

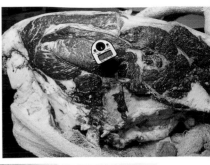

RECEIVE AND STORE FOODS SAFELY It is not unheard of for foods to be delivered to a food service operation already contaminated. To prevent this from happening to you, inspect all goods to be sure they arrive in sanitary conditions. Make a habit of checking delivery trucks for signs of unsanitary conditions, such as dirt or pests. If the truck is a refrigerated or freezer unit, check the ambient temperature inside to see that it is adequate. Use a thermometer to check the temperature of the product as well. Check expiration dates. Verify that foods have the required government inspection and certification stamps or tags. Randomly sample bulk items, as well as individual packages within cases. Reject any goods that do not meet your standards. Once you have accepted a delivery, move the items immediately into proper storage conditions. Break down and discard cardboard boxes as soon as possible because they provide nesting areas for insects, especially cockroaches.

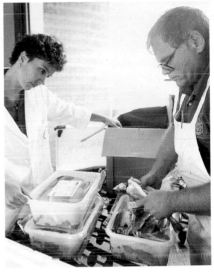

TOP *Meat must be received at the proper temperature.*

BOTTOM *Make sure your fish is from known waters.*

Refrigeration and freezing units should be regularly maintained and equipped with thermometers to make sure that the temperature remains within a safe range. Although in most cases chilling will not actually kill pathogens, it does drastically slow down reproduction. In general, refrigerators should be kept between 36° and 40°F (2° to 4°C), but quality is better served if certain foods can be stored at these specific temperatures:

Meat and poultry: 32° to 36°F (0° to 2°C)

Fish and shellfish: 30° to 34°F (-1° to 1°C)

Eggs: 38° to 40°F (3° to 4°C)

Dairy products: 36° to 40°F (2° to 4°C)

Produce: 40° to 45°F (4° to 7°C)

Separate refrigerators for each of the above categories is ideal, but if necessary, a single unit can be divided into sections. The front of the unit will be the warmest area, the back the coldest.

Reach-in and walk-in refrigerators should be put in order at the end of every shift. Before being put in the refrigerator, food should be properly cooled, stored in clean containers, wrapped, and labeled clearly with the contents and date. Store raw products below and away from cooked foods to prevent cross contamination by dripping. Because air circulation is essential for effective cooling, avoid overcrowding the box, and make sure the fan is not blocked.

Do not stack trays directly on top of food; this will reduce the amount of air that can circulate and may also result in cross contamination. Use the principle of "first in, first out" (FIFO) when arranging food, so that older items are in the front.

Dry storage is used for foods such as canned goods, spices, condiments, cereals, and staples such as flour and sugar, as well as for some fruits and vegetables that do not require refrigeration and have low perishability. As with all storage, the area must be clean, with proper ventilation and air circulation. Foods should not be stored on the floor or near the walls, and there must be adequate shelving to prevent overcrowding. The FIFO system should be practiced, and all containers should be labeled with a date. Cleaning supplies should be stored in a separate place.

HOLD COOKED OR READY-TO-SERVE FOODS SAFELY

Keep hot foods hot and cold foods cold. Use hot-holding equipment (steam tables, double boilers, bain-maries, heated cabinets or drawers, chafing dishes, and so on) to keep hot foods at or above 140°F (60°C). Do not use hot-holding equipment for cooking or reheating; it cannot be counted on to raise the temperature of the food through the danger zone quickly enough.

Use cold-holding equipment (ice or refrigeration) to keep cold foods at or below 41°F (5°C). If using ice, the foods should be in a container of some sort, not directly on the ice. Be sure to use a perforated insert and drip pan to allow melting ice to drain away from foods. Sanitize the pans after each use.

COOLING FOODS SAFELY

One of the leading causes of food-borne illness is improperly cooled foods. Cooked foods that are to be stored need to be cooled down to below 41°F (5°C) as quickly as possible. Cooling to below 41°F (5°C) should be completed within four hours, unless you use the two-stage cooling method endorsed by the Food and Drug Administration in its 1999 Model Food Code. In the first stage of this method, foods must be cooled down to 70°F (21°C) within two hours. In the second stage, foods must reach 41°F (5°C) or below within an additional four hours, for a total cooling time of six hours.

Soup being cooled in an ice-water bath.

The proper way to cool hot liquids is to place them in a metal container (plastic containers insulate rather than conduct heat and are not a good choice), then place the container in an ice-water bath that reaches the same level as the liquid inside the container. Bricks or a rack set under the container will allow the cold water to circulate better. Stir the liquid in the container frequently so that the warmer liquid at the center mixes with the cooler liquid at the outside edges of the container, bringing overall temperature down more rapidly. Stirring also discourages potentially dangerous anaerobic bacteria from multiplying at the center of the mixture.

Semisolid and solid foods should be refrigerated in single layers in shallow containers to allow greater surface exposure to the cold air and thus quicker chilling. For the same reason, large cuts of meat or other foods should be cut into smaller portions, cooled to room temperature, and wrapped before refrigerating.

REHEATING FOODS SAFELY

Improperly reheated foods are another frequent culprit in food-borne illness. When foods are prepared ahead and then reheated, they should move through the danger zone as rapidly as possible and be reheated to at least 165°F (74°C) for at least fifteen seconds. As long as all proper cooling and reheating procedures are followed each time, foods may be cooled and reheated more than once.

An instant-read thermometer gives you an accurate reading.

Food handlers must use the proper methods and equipment for reheating potentially hazardous foods, which should be brought to the proper temperature over direct heat (burner, flattop, grill, or conventional oven) or in a microwave oven. A steam table will adequately hold reheated foods above 140°F (60°C), but it will not bring foods out of the danger zone quickly enough. Instant-read thermometers should always be used to check temperatures. The thermometer should be carefully cleaned and sanitized after each use.

THAWING FROZEN FOODS SAFELY

Frozen foods may be safely thawed in several ways. Once thawed, they should be used as soon as possible and for optimal quality and flavor should not be refrozen. The best — though slowest — method is to allow the food to thaw under refrigeration. The food should still be wrapped and should be placed in a shallow container on a bottom shelf to prevent any drips from contaminating other items stored nearby or below.

If there is not time to thaw foods in the refrigerator, covered or wrapped food may be placed in a container under running water of approximately 70°F (21°C) or below. Be sure to clean and sanitize the sink both before and after thawing. Use a stream of water strong enough to wash loose particles off the food, but do not allow the water to splash on other food or surfaces.

Individual portions that are to be cooked immediately may be thawed in a microwave oven. Liquids, small items, or individual portions may also be cooked

HAZARD ANALYSIS CRITICAL CONTROL POINTS (HACCP)

HACCP IS AN ACRONYM that is fast becoming a commonly used term in food service and food safety. It stands for Hazard Analysis Critical Control Points, which is a scientific state-of-the-art food safety program originally developed for astronauts. HACCP takes a systematic and preventive approach to the conditions that are responsible for most foodborne illnesses. It is preventive in nature; it attempts to anticipate how food safety problems are most likely to occur, and then it takes steps to prevent them from occurring.

The HACCP system has been adopted by both food processors and restaurants, as well as by the FDA and USDA.

At this time, there are no particular mandates that HACCP must be used by all food service establishments. However, instituting such a plan may prove advantageous on a variety of levels.

If you decide to begin instituting HACCP procedures in your restaurant, you should know that an initial investment of time and human resources is required. It is becoming obvious, however, that this system can ultimately save money and time, as well as improve the quality of food you are able to provide your customers.

The heart of HACCP is contained in the following seven principles:

1. ASSESS THE HAZARDS.

The first step in an HACCP program begins with a hazard analysis of the menu item or recipe. It requires a close look at the process of putting that menu item together, beginning with the delivery of the starting ingredients. Every step in the process must be looked at by first designing a flow chart that covers the period from "dock to dish." In addition, it is best to have all persons involved in the flow of the food present when setting up an HACCP program, for the person receiving the food on the loading dock may have an important bit of information that can help set up the program and identify the true flow of food.

The types of hazards that you would be concerned with are biological, chemical, or physical conditions that could cause a food to be unsafe for consumption. The biological hazards are typically microbiological, though toxicity (such as from poisonous mushrooms) should not be ignored. The microbiological hazards include bacteria, viruses, and parasites.

2. IDENTIFY THE CRITICAL CONTROL POINTS.

The next decision to make, after you have established a flow diagram and identified the potential hazards, is to identify the critical control points (CCPs). From the moment food is received at a food service establishment, you have the ability to control what happens to that food item, including not accepting it from your vendor if it does not meet your specifications. You must decide which of the different control points (steps) are critical ones. One of the most difficult aspects of putting an HACCP program together is to not overidentify these critical control points, because it could lead to a cumbersome amount of paperwork. In addition, a profusion of CCPs could obscure the real control issues. A critical control point is the place in the utilization of the food in a restaurant where you have the ability to prevent, eliminate, or reduce an existing hazard or to prevent or minimize the likelihood that a hazard will occur. To quote the 1999 FDA Food Code, a critical control point is "a point

or procedure in a specific food system where loss of control may result in an unacceptable health risk."

As a tip for getting started, the cooking step, as a rule, is a critical control point. Other critical control points are usually associated with time/temperature relationships (thawing, hot-holding, cold-holding, cooling, and reheating). Some other considerations that need to be addressed in identifying a critical control point are: At this step, can food be contaminated? Can the contaminants increase or survive? Can this hazard be prevented through some kind of intervention (commonly referred to as corrective action)? Can hazards be prevented, eliminated, or reduced by steps taken earlier or later in the flow? Can you monitor, measure, and document the CCP?

3. ESTABLISH CRITICAL LIMITS AND CONTROL MEASURES.

Critical limits are generally standards for control measures for each critical control point. Many have already been established by local health departments, but you may

without thawing, but larger pieces of solid or semisolid foods that are cooked while still frozen become overcooked on the outside before they are thoroughly done throughout. Do not thaw food at room temperature; it is an invitation to pathogens.

want to establish new critical limits for your food operation that exceed the regulatory standard, or a new standard that meets with health department approval. The 1999 FDA Food Code refers to these possibilities as "variances."

By way of example, an established critical limit for the cooking step in preparing a chicken dish is a 165°F (74°C) final internal temperature. This critical limit prevents the possibility of a patron coming down with salmonellosis. If you were to hold this chicken on the line before actual service, it would have to be kept at 140°F (60°C) to prevent any proliferation of pathogenic microbes. Holding would be a step in this process that would be considered critical.

Control measures are what you can do ahead of time to facilitate the achievement of your critical limit. For example, in cooking chicken to 165°F (74°C), you should make sure your equipment is working well. Before you roast chicken, you should turn the oven on prior to putting the chicken in it. If you are going to monitor the temperature of the chicken with a thermometer, you must make sure it is accurately calibrated. You also have to know how to cook and take internal temperatures. Therefore, training is often a control measure, too.

4. ESTABLISH PROCEDURES FOR MONITORING CCPS.
Critical limits for each critical control point have to identify what is to be monitored. You must also establish how the CCP will be monitored and who will do it. For example, one employee may be designated to monitor the temperature of roasting chicken with a properly cali-

brated thermometer. For each batch, the employee is instructed to check the internal temperature of the largest chicken and the one in the middle of the pan.

Monitoring helps improve the system by allowing for the identification of problems or faults at particular points in the process. This allows for more control or improvement in the system because it provides an opportunity to take corrective action if the critical limit was not met.. Monitoring lets you know if the desired results were achieved. In the example of the chicken, did you cook it to an acceptable temperature (the critical limit for chicken is 165°F [74°C])?

5. ESTABLISH CORRECTIVE ACTION PLANS.
If a deviation or substandard level occurs for a step in the process, a plan of action must be identified. For example, if a roasted chicken was held at an incorrect temperature (120°F [60°C]) for too long in a steam table, the corrective action would be to discard it. If frozen fish arrives from the purveyor with a buildup of ice, indicating that it had been defrosted and refrozen again, the fish should be rejected. Specific corrective actions must be developed for each CCP, because each food item and its preparation can vary greatly from one kitchen to the next.

6. SET UP A RECORD-KEEPING SYSTEM.
Keep documentation on hand to demonstrate whether the system is working or not. Recording events at CCPs ensures that critical limits are met and preventive monitoring is occurring. Documentation typically consists of time/temperature logs, checklists, and forms.

An important point to remember is to keep the forms readily accessible and easy

to fill out. Having a temperature log at a grill station on a clipboard for the cook to record internal temperatures of one out of every ten orders that goes out to customers is a typical and realistic responsibility for a line cook. Having a reliable and accurately calibrated thermometer on hand is also necessary; these are readily available. Do not make the logs or forms too complicated or cumbersome for recording. This could encourage "dry lab," which is the falsifying of records.

7. DEVELOP A VERIFICATION SYSTEM.
This step is essentially to establish procedures to ensure that the HACCP plan is working correctly. Have a supervisor, executive chef, or outside party verify that the plan is working. If procedures are not being followed, try to find out what modifications you can make so it does work better. The most difficult part of putting an HACCP plan together is just going through it the first time. After the initial paperwork, it essentially involves monitoring and recording. As your employees become accustomed to filling out the forms correctly, they will be establishing positive behaviors that promote food safety. These new behaviors will naturally spill over into the preparation of other recipes, making the development of an HACCP plan for other dishes easier.

THE WAY IN WHICH an individual operation may apply these principles will vary. Not only is it permissible to make the system fit your establishment's style, it is imperative. Chain restaurants, for example, receive and process foods differently from à la carte restaurants.

SERVING FOODS SAFELY

The potential to transmit food-borne illness does not end when the food leaves the kitchen. Restaurant servers should also be instructed in good hygiene and safe food-handling practices. Hands should be properly washed after using the rest room, eating, smoking, touching one's face or hair, and handling money, dirty dishes, or soiled table linens (particularly napkins). Ideally, there should be servers who are designated to serve foods and other servers who are responsible for clearing used dishes and linens.

Servers should touch only the edges and bottoms of plates as they transport them from kitchen to dining room. When setting tables, they should never touch the parts of flatware that will ultimately come in contact with food, and they should handle glassware by the stems or bases only. Clean side stands, trays, and tray stands before the start of each shift and as necessary during service. Handle napkins as little as possible; always fold them on a clean surface. Table linens should be used only once. Carry plates, glasses, and flatware in such a way that food contact surfaces are not touched. Serve all foods using the proper utensils; handle ice and rolls with tongs, never with fingers.

CLEANING AND SANITIZING

Cleaning refers to the removal of soil or food particles, whereas *sanitizing* involves using moist heat or chemical agents to kill pathogenic microorganisms. For equipment that cannot be immersed in a sink, or for equipment such as knives and cutting boards, during food preparation use a wiping cloth, soaked in a double-strength sanitizing solution and then wrung out, to clean and sanitize it between uses. Iodine, chlorine, or quaternary ammonium compounds are all common sanitizing agents. Check the manufacturer's instructions for procedures for use.

Small equipment, tools, pots, and tableware should be run through a ware-washing machine or washed manually in a three-compartment sink. The many kinds of ware-washing machines all use some sanitation method, such as very hot water (usually 180° to 195°F [82° to 91°C]) or chemical agents.

Hard water, which contains high levels of iron, calcium, or magnesium, may interfere with the effectiveness of detergents and sanitizing agents and may also cause deposits that can clog machinery. Water-softening additives can prevent these problems. After sanitizing, equipment and tableware should be allowed to air-dry completely, because using paper or cloth toweling could result in cross contamination.

TOP *Servers should touch only the edges and bottoms of plates as they transport them from kitchen to dining room.*

MIDDLE *Servers should handle glassware by the stems or bases only.*

BOTTOM *In a three-compartment sink, the first basin is used for washing, the second for rinsing, and the third for sanitizing by means of a thirty-second immersion in hot water or an immersion in a chemical sanitizer.*

KEEPING PESTS OUT

Careful sanitation procedures, proper handling of foods, and a well-maintained facility all work together to prevent a pest infestation. Besides being destructive and unpleasant, rats, mice, roaches, and flies may also harbor various pathogens. Take the following steps to prevent infestation:

Clean all areas and surfaces thoroughly.

Wipe up spills immediately and sweep up crumbs.

Cover garbage and remove every four hours.

Elevate garbage containers on concrete blocks.

Keep food covered or refrigerated.

Check all incoming boxes for pests and remove boxes as soon as items are unpacked.

Store food away from walls and floors, and maintain cool temperatures and good ventilation.

Prevent pests from entering the facility by installing screened windows and screened, self-closing doors.

Fill in all crevices and cracks, repair weak masonry, and screen off any openings to buildings, including vents, basement windows, and drains.

If necessary, consult a professional exterminator.

KITCHEN SAFETY

These basic safety items — a poster showing first aid for choking, a phone with the number of the fire department and other emergency numbers posted, a first-aid kid, and a fire extinguisher — should be within easy reach. Everyone in the kitchen should know how to use them properly.

In addition to the precautions necessary to guard against food-borne illness, care must also be taken to avoid accidents to staff and guests. The following safety measures should be practiced.

HEALTH AND HYGIENE

Maintain good general health; have regular physical and dental checkups. Do not handle food when ill. Attend to cuts or burns immediately. Keep any burn or break in the skin covered with a clean, waterproof bandage and change it as necessary. Cover the face with a tissue when coughing or sneezing, and wash hands afterward.

Observe the fundamentals of good personal hygiene. Keep hair clean and neat, and contain it if necessary. Keep fingernails short and well maintained, with no polish. Keep hands away from hair and face when working with food. Do not smoke or chew gum when working with food. Begin each shift in a clean, neat uniform. Do not wear the uniform to or from work or school. Store the uniform and all clothing in a clean locker. Do not wear jewelry other than a watch and/or a plain ring, to reduce risk of personal injury and/or cross contamination.

WORKING SAFELY

Knives and other tools can do serious damage. To walk with a knife in a crowded kitchen, hold the knife with the blade pointing down and the blade facing backward.

Clean up grease and other spills as they occur. Use salt or cornmeal to absorb grease, then clean the area.

Warn coworkers when you are coming up behind them with something hot or sharp.

Alert the pot washer when pots, pans, and handles are especially hot.

Beware of grill fires. Do not attempt to put them out with water. Removing excess fat and letting any marinades drain completely away from foods helps prevent flare-ups.

Keep fire extinguishers in proper working order and place them in areas of the kitchen where they are most likely to be needed.

Remove lids from pots in such a manner that the steam vents away from the face, to avoid steam burns.

Bend at the knees, not the waist, to lift heavy objects.

Pick up anything on the floor that might trip the unwary.

Learn about first aid, CPR, and mouth-to-mouth resuscitation. Have a well-stocked first-aid kits on hand (see page 75).

Make sure that all dining room and kitchen staff know how to perform the Heimlich maneuver on a choking person. Post instructions in readily visible areas of the kitchen and dining room.

Handle equipment carefully, especially knives, mandolines, slicers, grinders, band saws, and other pieces of equipment with sharp edges.

Use separate cutting boards for cooked and raw foods, and sanitize after using.

Wash hands thoroughly after working with raw foods.

Use tasting spoons, and use them only once — do not "double-dip." Do not taste foods with fingers or with kitchen utensils.

Store any toxic chemicals (cleaning compounds and pesticides, for example) away from food, to avoid cross contamination.

Use only dry side towels for handling hot items.

Use instant-read thermometers (and sanitize them after using) to ensure that adequate temperatures are reached.

Post emergency phone numbers for the ambulance, hospital, and fire department near every phone.

It takes only a few seconds for a simple flare-up on the grill or in a pan to turn into a full-scale fire. Grease fires, electrical fires, even a waste container full of paper going up when a match is carelessly tossed into it are easy to imagine happening in any busy kitchen. A comprehensive fire safety plan should be in place and a standard part of all employee training.

The first step to take in avoiding fires is to make sure that the entire staff, for both the kitchen and the dining room, is fully aware of the potential dangers of fire everywhere in a restaurant. If you see someone handling a situation improperly, get the situation under control, and then take the time to explain what your concern is and how to avoid the situation in the future.

Be sure that all equipment is up to code. Frayed or exposed wires and faulty plugs can all too easily be the cause of a fire. Overburdened outlets are another common culprit. Any equipment that has a heating element or coil must also be maintained carefully, to be sure that workers are not likely to be burned as well as to prevent fires.

Another key element in any good fire safety program is thorough training. Everyone should know what to do in case of a fire. Having frequent fire drills is a good idea. Instruct your kitchen staff in the correct way to handle a grill fire and grease fire.

There should also be fire extinguishers in easily accessible areas. Check each extinguisher to see what type of fire it is meant to control, and make sure you understand when and how to operate each type.

Proper maintenance of extinguishers and timely inspections by your local fire department are vital. Fire control systems, such as an Ansul system, need to be serviced and monitored so that they will perform correctly if you need them. Above all, make sure you never try to put out a grease, chemical, or electrical fire by throwing water on the flames.

Everyone should know where the fire department number is posted and who is responsible for calling the department in case of need. The exits from all areas of the building should be easy to find, clear of any obstructions, and fully operational. Your guests will have to rely on you and other staff to get them safely through any crisis that requires them to exit the building quickly. Identify one spot outside the building at a safe distance where everyone should assemble when they've exited safely. Then you will know immediately who may still be inside the building and need to be rescued by firefighters.

The main rule for fire is to be prepared for all possibilities. You cannot assume it won't happen to you.

More than simply completing the look of the chef, the parts of the typical chef's uniform play important roles in keeping workers safe as they operate in a potentially dangerous environment. The chef's jacket, for instance, is double-breasted, which creates a two-layer cloth barrier between the chest area and steam burns, splashes, and spills. The double-breasted design also means that the jacket can easily be rebuttoned on the opposite side to cover any spills. The sleeves of the jacket are long and should be worn long, not rolled up, to cover as much of the arm as possible in order to protect against burns and scalding splashes.

The same is true of pants. Shorts, while they may seem like a good idea for such a hot environment, are inappropriate because they offer no protection. Pants should be worn without cuffs, which can trap hot liquids and debris. Ideally, pants should have a snap fly and be worn without a belt; in case hot grease is spilled on the legs, this allows for extremely fast removal of the pants, which could lessen the severity of the burn.

Be it a tall white toque or a favorite baseball cap, chefs wear hats to contain their hair, preventing it from falling into the food. Hats also help absorb sweat from overheated brows. Neckerchiefs serve a similar sweat-absorbing role.

The apron is worn to protect the jacket and pants from excessive staining. Most chefs use side towels to protect their hands when working with hot pans, dishes, or other equipment. They are not meant to be used as wiping cloths. Side towels used to lift hot items must be dry in order to provide protection. Once they become even slightly wet, they can no longer insulate properly.

While athletic shoes are very comfortable, they are not ideal for working in a kitchen. If a knife should fall from a work surface, most athletic shoes would offer very little protection. Hard leather shoes with slip-resistant soles are recommended, both because of the protection they offer and the support they can give your feet. A job that involves standing for several hours at a time puts a premium on good-quality, supportive, protective footgear.

Jackets, pants, side towels, aprons, and shoes can harbor bacteria, molds, parasites, and even viruses. Because these pathogens can be transmitted with ease from your uniform to foods, a sanitary uniform is important. If possible, wear your uniform at work only, not when traveling to and from the job, when you can pick up pathogens along the way.

Proper laundering can sanitize your uniform to make it safe and clean. Use hot water, a good detergent, and a sanitizer, such as borax or chlorine bleach, to remove bacteria and grime. Automatic dish-washing soap (used in household machines) contains an enzyme to help break up stuck-on food. These same enzymes can help to release food stains on uniforms. Add a half cup of coarse dishwasher detergent to the wash water.

REGULATIONS, INSPECTION, AND CERTIFICATION

Federal, state, and local government regulations work to ensure the wholesomeness of the food that reaches the public. Any new food service business should contact the local health department well in advance of opening, to ascertain the necessary legal requirements. A professional chef moving to a new area to work should contact local authorities for ordinances specific to that area. Some states and local jurisdictions offer sanitation certification programs. Regulations and testing vary from area to area; in some cases, each kitchen is required to have at least one worker who has been certified. Certification is often available through certain academic institutions.

THE OCCUPATIONAL SAFETY AND HEALTH ADMINISTRATION (OSHA)

OSHA is a federal organization that was instituted in 1970 and falls under the purview of the Health and Human Services Administration. Its goal is helping employers and workers to establish and maintain a safe, healthy work environment.

Among OSHA's regulations is the mandate that all places of employment must have an adequate and easily accessible first-aid kit on the premises. In addition, if any organization has more than ten employees, records must be kept of all accidents and injuries to employees that require medical treatment. Any requests for improvements to the safety of the workplace, including repair or maintenance of the physical plant and equipment necessary to perform one's job, must be attended to by the organization.

As money for many health and human services organizations has dwindled, OSHA's ability to make on-site inspections has also been reduced. It now concentrates its efforts on providing services where the risk to worker safety is greatest. This does not mean that small businesses can operate with impunity, for employees can call OSHA's offices and report violations.

This act is intended to make public places accessible and safe for those with a variety of disabilities. Any new construction or remodeling done to a restaurant must meet ADA standards. This includes being sure that telephones are located so that they can be reached by a person in a wheelchair, and providing toilets with handrails. Most contractors will have the necessary information, but if you are unsure, contact a local agency.

A SPECIAL NOTE ABOUT SMOKERS

Many restaurants have banned smoking completely, either voluntarily, as a result of public pressure, or because of legislative mandates. While this may improve the air quality within the restaurant itself and provide a more pleasant dining experience for nonsmoking guests, there is one thing that should be kept in mind: Simply banning smoking in the dining room and the bar may not ban smoking from the entire premises. Common sense will tell you that smokers will very likely smoke cigarettes up to the moment they walk in the door, and light up as soon as they step back outside. One carelessly flung match or a single smoldering cigarette butt can spell ruin.

Place sand-filled buckets or urns near the areas where you expect or prefer to have smokers take their cigarette breaks. If you do allow smoking in your restaurant, make sure that bartenders, bus people, and wait staff have a safe way to dispose of the contents of ashtrays.

Of course, smoking should never be allowed in the kitchen area.

DRUGS AND ALCOHOL IN THE WORKPLACE

One final topic that is of great importance in the workplace is the right of all workers to be free from the hazards imposed by a coworker who comes to work under the influence of drugs or alcohol. The abuse of any substance that can either alter or impair one's ability to perform his or her job is a serious concern. Reaction times are slowed. The ability to concentrate and to comprehend instructions is reduced. Inhibitions are often lowered, and judgment is generally impaired.

People's lives may be at stake: A poorly judged effort when emptying the hot oil from the deep fryer could result in permanent disability. A playful attempt at passing a knife could literally put out an eye. Forgetting to take the time to properly store and reheat foods could lead to an outbreak of food-borne illness that could kill someone. The responsibilities of a professional working in any kitchen are too great to allow someone suffering from a substance abuse problem to diminish the respect and trust you have built with your customers and staff.

FIRST-AID SUPPLIES

Adhesive strips in assorted sizes

Rolled stretch-fabric bandages

Sterile gauze dressings, individually wrapped

Rolled gauze bandage

First-aid adhesive tape

Cotton swabs (For applying antiseptic or removing particles from eye)

Tourniquet

Tongue depressors (for small splints)

Scissors

Tweezers

Needle (for removing splinters)

Rubbing alcohol (for sterilizing instruments)

Mild antiseptic (for wounds)

Antibiotic cream

Syrup of ipecac (to induce vomiting)

Petroleum jelly

Aspirin or acetaminophen

PART TWO

TOOLS AND INGREDIENTS IN THE PROFESSIONAL KITCHEN

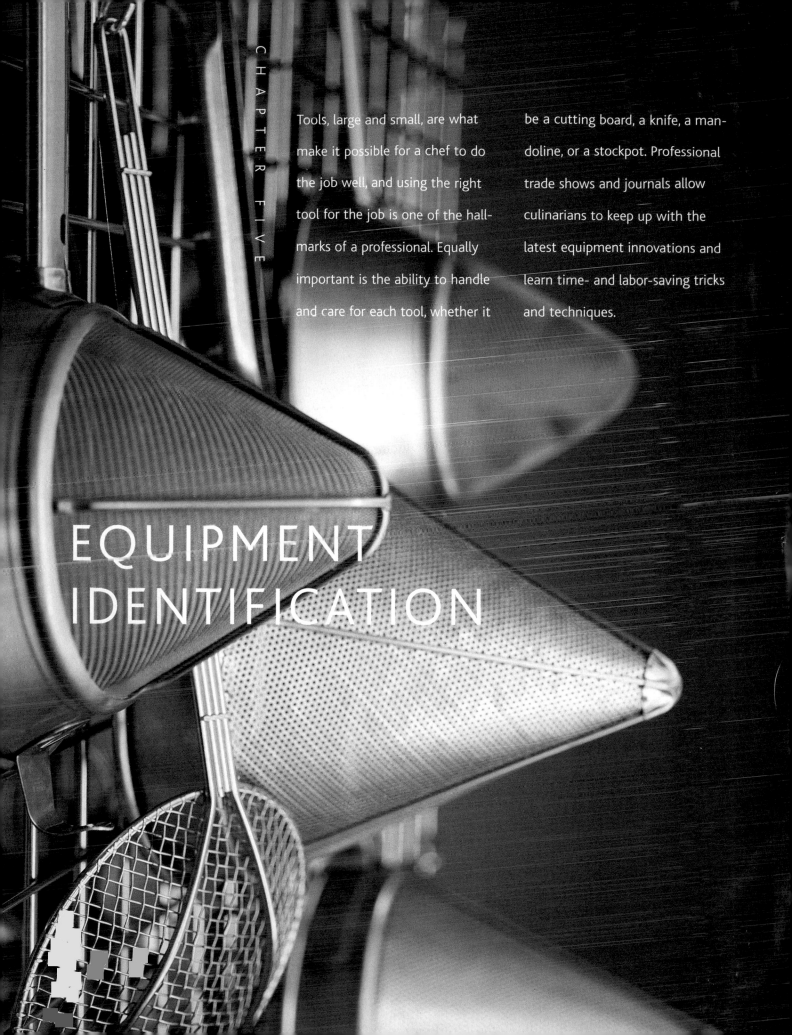

Tools, large and small, are what make it possible for a chef to do the job well, and using the right tool for the job is one of the hallmarks of a professional. Equally important is the ability to handle and care for each tool, whether it be a cutting board, a knife, a mandoline, or a stockpot. Professional trade shows and journals allow culinarians to keep up with the latest equipment innovations and learn time- and labor-saving tricks and techniques.

EQUIPMENT IDENTIFICATION

KNIVES

Assembling a personal collection of knives is one of the first steps in becoming a professional. Just as an artist or craftsperson gathers together the tools necessary for painting, sculpting, or drawing, you will need to select knives that allow you to do your work in the safest and most efficient way. The knives you choose will become as important to you as your own fingers — quite literally an extension of your own hands.

The following rules concerning knife care, use, and storage are automatic behavior for all true professionals.

1. HANDLE KNIVES WITH RESPECT. Knives can be damaged if they are handled carelessly. And they can damage people. Good-quality knives are expensive tools, manufactured to last a lifetime. Each professional has his or her own set of knives, and you should never use someone else's personal knife without first obtaining permission. Handle it with the same care that you would your own, and be sure to return it promptly.

Many people will have their name professionally engraved on the blade of the knife, so that they can identify which knives belong to them. If you work in a large kitchen, this is generally a good idea.

2. KEEP KNIVES SHARP. Learn the proper techniques for both sharpening and honing knives. A sharp knife not only performs better but is safer to use, because less pressure is required to cut through the food. When too much pressure is exerted, there is a good possibility of the knife slipping and causing injury to the user.

Various tools are used to sharpen knives. A steel should be within reach at all times. Use a stone periodically to sharpen knives, or use a sharpening machine. Severely dulled or damaged blades may need to be reground in order to restore the edge. Regrinding is usually done on sharpening wheels by professionals who specialize in the maintenance of knives.

3. KEEP KNIVES CLEAN. Clean knives thoroughly immediately after using them. Don't leave them lying on or near the sink. Work carefully, and pay attention to what you are doing, so that you don't cut yourself as you wipe down the blade. Sanitize the entire knife, including the handle, bolster, and blade, as necessary, so that the tool will not cross-contaminate food. Also, keeping knives clean helps to extend their lives. Always dry knives carefully before storing.

Never drop a knife into a pot sink. It could be dented or nicked by heavy pots, and someone who reaches into the sink could be seriously injured by the blade. Do not clean knives in a dishwasher. Wooden handles are likely to warp and split. The jostling that might occur could nick or break the blade beyond repair.

4. USE SAFE HANDLING PROCEDURES FOR KNIVES. In addition to the etiquette involved in borrowing a knife, there are other standards of behavior that should be remembered. When you are passing a knife, lay it down on a work surface so that the handle is extended toward the person who will pick it up. Whenever you must carry a knife from one area of the kitchen to another, hold the knife straight down at your side with the sharp edge facing behind you, and let people know you are passing by with something sharp. Ideally, you should sheathe or wrap the knife before walking anywhere with it, or transport it in a carrier.

When you lay a knife down on a work surface, be sure that no part of it extends over the edge of the cutting board or worktable. That will prevent people walking by from brushing against it or knocking it onto the floor. Be sure the blade is facing away from the edge of the work surface.

Knives are intended for specific cutting tasks. They are not built for opening bottles and cans, prying loose lids, and the like. Using them inappropriately can, at best, nick or mar the blade. At worst, the blade can break, and pieces may fly off into the surrounding area.

5. USE AN APPROPRIATE CUTTING SURFACE. Cutting directly on metal, glass, or marble surfaces will dull and eventually damage the blade of a knife. To prevent dulling, always use wooden or composition cutting boards.

6. KEEP KNIVES PROPERLY STORED. There are a number of safe, practical ways to store knives, including in knife kits or rolls for one's personal collection, and in slots, racks, and magnetized holders. Storage systems should be kept just as clean as knives. Cloth or vinyl rolls should be washed and sanitized periodically.

THE PARTS OF A KNIFE

To select a knife of good quality that fits your hand well and is suitable for the intended task, you need a basic knowledge of the various parts of a knife.

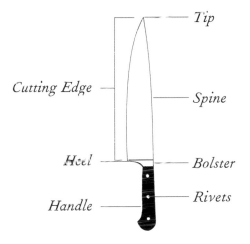

BLADES Currently, the most frequently used material for blades is high-carbon stainless steel. Other materials, such as stainless steel and carbon steel, are also available.

For many years, *carbon steel* was used to make most knife blades. Although carbon steel blades take a better edge than either regular or high-carbon stainless steel, they tend to lose their sharpness quickly. Also, carbon steel blades will discolor when they come into contact with high-acid foods such as tomatoes or onions. Carbon steel blades must be treated carefully to avoid discoloration, rusting, and pitting. They should be washed and thoroughly dried between uses and before storage. The metal is brittle and can break easily under stress.

Stainless steel is much stronger than carbon steel and will not discolor or rust. It is difficult to get a good edge on a stainless-steel blade, although once an edge is established, it tends to last longer than the edge on a carbon steel blade.

High-carbon stainless steel is a relatively recent development that combines the advantages of carbon steel and stainless steel. The higher percentage of carbon allows the blade to take and keep a keener edge; the fact that it is stainless steel means that it will not discolor or rust readily.

The most desirable type of blade for general use is *taper-ground*, meaning that the blade has been forged out of a single sheet of metal and has been ground so that it tapers smoothly from the spine to the cutting edge, with no apparent beveling. Frequently used knives should have taper-ground blades.

Hollow-ground blades are made by combining two sheets of metal. The edges are then beveled or fluted. Although hollow-ground blades often have very sharp edges, the blade itself lacks the balance and longevity of a taper-ground blade. This type is often found on knives, such as slicers, that are used less frequently.

TANGS The tang is a continuation of the blade that extends into the knife's handle. Knives used for heavy work, such as chef's knives or cleavers, should have a full tang; that is, the tang is as long as the entire handle. A partial tang does not run the full length of the handle. Although blades with partial tangs are not as durable as those with full tangs, they are acceptable on knives that will be used less frequently. Rat-tail tangs are much narrower than the spine of the blade and are encased in the handle (not visible at the top or bottom edges); these tangs tend not to hold up under extended use.

HANDLES A preferred material for knife handles is rosewood, because it is extremely hard and has a very tight or fine grain, which helps to prevent splitting and cracking. Impregnating wood with plastic protects the handle from damage caused by continued exposure to water and detergents. Some state codes require that plastic handles be used in butcher shops, because they are considered more sanitary than wood. Care must be taken to clean plastic handles thoroughly, however, because grease is more difficult to remove from plastic than from wood.

The handle should fit your hand comfortably. Manufacturers typically produce handles made from various materials and in varying shapes, intended to achieve a more custom fit to suit a variety of hand sizes. Spend some time holding the knife. A comfortable fit will improve the ease and speed with which you can work. A poor fit can result in fatigue or cramping. People with very small or very large hands should be sure that they are not straining to hold the handle. Some knives are especially constructed to meet the needs of left-handed chefs.

RIVETS Metal rivets are usually used to secure the tang to the handle. The rivets should be completely smooth and lie flush with the surface of the handle, to prevent irritation to the hand and so that there is no place for debris and microorganisms to collect.

BOLSTERS In some knives there is a collar or shank, known as a bolster, at the point where the blade meets the handle. This is a sign of a well-made knife, one that will hold up for a long time. Some knives may have a collar that looks like a bolster but is actually a separate piece attached to the handle. These knives tend to come apart easily and should be avoided.

TYPES OF KNIVES

A wide array of knives is available to suit specific functions. As you continue to work in professional kitchens, your knife kit will grow to encompass not only the basics — chef's or French knife, boning knife, paring knife, and slicer — but also a number of special knives, such as a tourné knife, serrated knife, utility knife, and flexible-bladed knife.

Chef's knives

Slicing knives

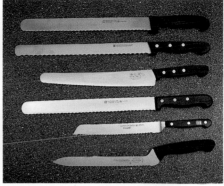

The knives a chef will accumulate over the course of his or her career will almost undoubtedly include a number of special knives that are not discussed below. There are, for example, several special knives and cutting tools found exclusively in the bakeshop; still others are

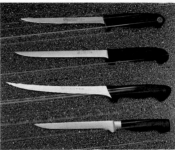

Filleting knives

required for butchering meats and fabricating fish. This list is intended as a guide to the knives that may be found in nearly any well-outfitted knife kit.

CHEF'S KNIFE or FRENCH KNIFE. This all-purpose knife is used for a variety of chopping, slicing, and mincing chores. The blade is normally 8 to 14 inches long.

UTILITY KNIFE. This smaller, lighter chef's knife is used for light cutting chores. The blade is generally 5 to 7 inches long.

Paring knives

PARING KNIFE. This short knife, used for paring and trimming vegetables and fruits, has a 2- to 4-inch blade.

BONING KNIFE. A boning knife is used to separate raw meat from the bone. The blade, which is thinner and shorter than the blade of a chef's knife, is about 6 inches long and is usually rigid.

FILLETING KNIFE. Used for filleting fish, this knife is similar in shape and size to a boning knife but has a flexible blade.

SLICER. This knife is used for slicing cooked meat. It has a long blade with a round or pointed tip. The blade may be flexible or rigid and may be taper-ground or have a fluted edge that consists of a series of ovals ground along the edge.

Boning knives

CLEAVER. Used for chopping, the cleaver is often heavy enough to cut through bones. It has a rectangular blade and varies in size according to its use.

TOURNÉ KNIFE. This small knife, similar to a paring knife, has a curved blade to make cutting the curved surfaces of tournéed vegetables easier.

The key to the proper and efficient use of any knife is making sure that it is sharp. A knife with a sharp blade always works better and more safely because it cuts easily, without requiring the chef to exert pressure, which may cause the knife to slip and cause injury. Knife blades are given an edge on a sharpening stone and maintained between sharpenings by honing with a steel.

SHARPENING STONES Sharpening stones are essential to the proper maintenance of knives. The blade is sharpened by passing its edge over the stone at a 20-degree angle. The grit — the degree of coarseness or fineness of the stone's surface — abrades the blade's edge, creating a sharp cutting edge. When sharpening a knife, always begin by using the coarsest surface of the stone, and then move on to the finer surfaces.

A stone with a fine grit should be used for boning knives and other tools on which an especially sharp edge is required. Most stones may be used either dry or moistened with water or mineral oil. Once oil has been used on a stone's surface, that practice should be continued. The standard size for sharpening stones is 8 by 2 inches. Three basic types of stones are commonly available:

CARBORUNDUM STONES have a fine side and a medium side.

ARKANSAS STONES are available in several grades of fineness. Some consist of three stones of varying degrees of fineness mounted on a wheel.

DIAMOND-IMPREGNATED STONES are also available. Although they are expensive, some chefs prefer them because they feel these stones give a sharper edge.

Grinding wheels, electric sharpeners, leather strops (such as those used to sharpen barber's blades), and other grinding tools may be necessary to replace or restore the edge of a badly dulled knife.

Opinion is split about whether a knife blade should be run over a stone from heel to tip or tip to heel. Similarly, some chefs prefer to use a lubricant such as mineral oil on their stones, while others swear by water. Like many other aspects of cooking, which method to use is a matter of preference and training. Most chefs do agree, however, that consistency in the direction of the stroke used to pass the blade over the stone is important. Once you find the method that suits you best, be sure to use the same technique every time.

Before using a stone, be sure that it is properly stabilized. No matter which method you use, keep the following guidelines in mind:

1. Allow yourself enough room to work.

2. Anchor the stone to keep it from slipping as you work. Place carborundum or diamond stones on a damp cloth or rubber mat. A triple-faced stone is mounted on a rotating framework that can be locked into position so that it cannot move.

Sharpening Method One

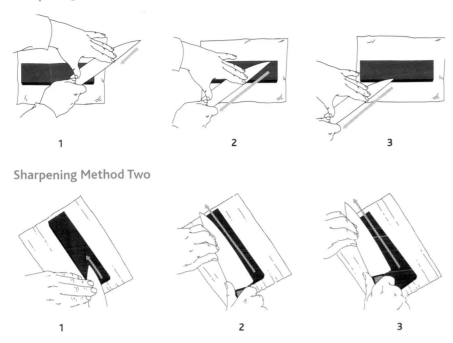

1   2   3

Sharpening Method Two

1   2   3

METHOD ONE *1. Use four fingers of the guiding hand to maintain constant pressure.*

2. Draw the knife across the stone gently.

3. Draw the knife off the stone smoothly. Turn the knife over and repeat the process on the other side.

METHOD TWO *1. Push the blade over the stone's surface, using the guiding hand to keep pressure even.*

2. Continue to push the entire length of the blade over the stone.

3. Push the knife off the stone smoothly. Turn the knife over and repeat the process on the other side.

3. Lubricate the stone with mineral oil or water. Be consistent about the type of lubricant you use on your stone. Water or mineral oil helps reduce friction as you sharpen your knife. The heat caused by friction may not seem significant, but it can eventually harm the blade.

4. Begin sharpening the edge on the coarsest grit you require. The duller the blade, the coarser the grit should be.

5. Run the entire edge over the surface of the stone, keeping the pressure on the knife even. Hold the knife at the correct angle as you work. A 20-degree angle is suitable for chef's knives and knives with similar blades. You may need to adjust the angle by a few degrees to properly sharpen thinner blades, such as slicers, or thicker blades, such as cleavers.

6. Always sharpen the blade in the same direction. This ensures that the edge remains even and in proper alignment.

7. Make strokes of equal number and equal pressure on each side of the blade. Do not oversharpen the edge on coarse stones. After about ten strokes on each side of the blade, move on to the next finer grit.

8. Finish sharpening on the finest stone, and wash and dry the knife thoroughly before use or storage.

STEELS A steel should be used both immediately after sharpening the blade with a stone and also between sharpenings to keep the edges in alignment. It should also be within reach anytime you are using your knives. The length of the steel's working surface can range from 3 inches for a pocket version to over 14 inches. Hard steel is the traditional material for steels. Other materials, such as glass, ceramic, and diamond-impregnated surfaces, are also available.

METHOD ONE *1. Start with the knife nearly vertical, with the blade resting on the steel's inner side.*

2. Rotate the wrist as the blade moves along the steel in a downward motion.

3. Keep the blade in contact with the steel until the tip is drawn off the steel. Repeat the process with blade resting on the steel's outer side.

METHOD TWO *1. Hold the steel in a near-vertical position with the tip resting on a nonslippery surface. Start with the heel of the knife against one side of the steel.*

2. Maintain light pressure and use an arm action, not a wrist action, to draw the knife down the shaft of the steel in a smooth motion.

3. Finish the first pass by drawing the blade all the way along the shaft up to and including the tip. Repeat the entire action, this time with the blade against the steel's other side.

Steeling Method One

1   2   3

Steeling Method Two

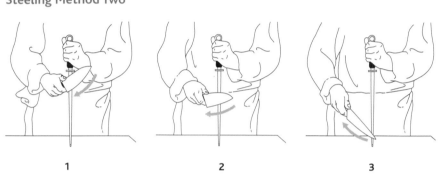

1   2   3

Steels come with coarse, medium, and fine grains, and some are magnetic, which helps the blade maintain proper alignment and also collects metal shavings. A guard or hilt between the steel and the handle protects the user, and a ring on the bottom of the handle can be used to hang the steel.

When using a steel, the knife is held almost vertically, with the blade at a 20-degree angle, resting on the inner side of the steel. The blade should be drawn along the entire length of the steel.

Shown here are two methods for steeling knives. There are more techniques you may have an opportunity to learn. Whichever method you choose, these guidelines will help you make effective use of your steel:

1. Allow yourself plenty of room as you work, and stand with your weight evenly distributed. Hold the steel with your thumb and fingers safely behind the guard.

2. Draw the blade along the steel so that the entire edge touches the steel. Work in the same direction on each side of the blade to keep the edge straight.

3. Be sure to keep the pressure even to avoid wearing away the metal in the center of the edge. Over time, this could produce a curve in the edge. Keep the knife blade at a 20-degree angle to the steel.

4. Use a light touch, stroking evenly and consistently. Lay the blade against the steel; don't slap it. Listen for a light ringing sound; a heavy grinding sound indicates that too much pressure is being applied.

5. Repeat the stroke on the opposite side of the edge to properly straighten the edge. If a blade requires more than five strokes per side on a steel, it probably should be sharpened on a stone.

HAND TOOLS

A number of small hand tools other than knives belong in a knife kit. Following are just some of the many that are available.

ROTARY OR SWIVEL-BLADED PEELER. This is used to peel the skin from various vegetables and fruits. The swivel action accommodates the contours of various products. Because the blade is sharpened on both sides, it will peel in both an upward and a downward motion. Using it correctly will greatly increase the speed with which you can prep vegetables.

PARISIENNE SCOOP (MELON BALLER). This is specifically designed for scooping out balls or ovals (depending upon the shape of the scoop) from vegetables and fruits.

KITCHEN FORK. The fork is used to test the doneness of braised meats and vegetables, for lifting finished items to the carving board or plate, and to steady the item being carved. A kitchen fork should not be used to turn foods being sautéed, grilled, or broiled, because the tines will pierce the food and let the juices run out.

PALETTE KNIFE (METAL SPATULA). This is a flexible, round-tipped tool used in the kitchen and bakeshop for turning pancakes or grilled foods, spreading fillings and glazes, and a variety of other functions. A palette knife with a serrated edge is useful for preparing and slicing sandwiches.

WHIPS/WHISKS. These tools are used to beat, blend, and whip foods. Balloon whips are sphere-shaped and have thin wires to incorporate air for making foams. Sauce whips are narrower and frequently have thicker wires. The chef should have a number of whips in various sizes.

OFFSET SPATULA. This spatula is used to turn or lift foods on grills, broilers, and griddles. It has a wide, chisel-edged blade set in a short handle.

PASTRY BAG. This plastic, canvas, or nylon bag is used to pipe out puréed foods, whipped cream, and various toppings. Pastry bags have uses in both the kitchen and the bakeshop. Disposable pastry bags are becoming more common. They are more sanitary than reusable bags.

PROPER CARE AND CLEANING OF ROLLING PINS

ROLLING PINS are made from hard, tight-grained woods, which prevent fats and flavorings used in rolled doughs from penetrating the pin. Rolling pins should never be washed with water. Doing this could ruin the integrity of the pin by warping or distorting the grain of the wood. Always use a dry cloth to wipe the pin clean directly after use. Store rolling pins securely so they do not roll and become dented. Damage to the surface of the pin will relay imperfections to the dough being rolled.

ROLLING PIN. There are two basic types of rolling pins. The French-style pin is a long cylinder of wood, which is rolled over dough with the palms of the hands. The second type, a rod-and-bearing pin, is heavier and wider than the French-style pin. A rod-and-bearing pin has a lengthwise shaft at the center of the wooden cylinder through which runs a metal rod with two wooden handles at either end. Bearings facilitate ease of rolling. Other specialized types of rolling pins are manufactured for specific tasks.

In addition to the hand tools listed here, many others, such as cherry pitters, strawberry hullers, and tomato knives (also known as tomato witches), are used in the professional kitchen for various specific functions. Tools designed to scale fish, open clams and oysters, or even cut eggs can also be found in some knife kits.

Among the many other kinds of small kitchen tools are rubber scrapers, ladles of various sizes, skimmers to be used on the surface of stocks or soups, "spiders" for lifting foods out of liquids or fats, spoons of various shapes and materials, scoops, and plastic or wooden cutting boards.

SMALL EQUIPMENT

The tools outlined in this section are available in any well-equipped kitchen. For the sake of clarity, they have been categorized here according to their general function: measuring, straining and sifting, mixing, and storage.

MEASURING EQUIPMENT

Measurements are determined in many different ways in a professional kitchen, depending upon the ingredient to be measured and the system employed by a specific recipe. This makes it important to have equipment for liquid and dry volume measures calibrated for both the U.S. and metric systems, as well as a variety of scales for accurate measurement by weight. Thermometers should display both Fahrenheit and centigrade temperatures.

Following is a selection of the most essential measuring equipment.

GRADUATED MEASURING PITCHERS. These are used for measuring liquids and are generally available in pint, quart, and gallon sizes.

SCALES. These are used to weigh ingredients for preparation and portion control. Ounce/gram and pound/kilo scales both should be available. Scales may be spring-type, balance beam, or electronic.

THERMOMETERS. An instant-read thermometer is used to measure foods' internal temperature. The stem, inserted in the food, gives an instant reading. Candy and deep-fat thermometers are also helpful.

MEASURING SPOONS. Measuring spoons come in tablespoon, teaspoon, half-teaspoon, and quarter-teaspoon sizes. Some sets also have half-tablespoon and eighth-teaspoon measures.

SIEVES AND STRAINERS

Sieves and strainers are used to sift, aerate, and help remove any large impurities from dry ingredients. They are also used to drain or purée cooked or raw foods. Sieves and strainers should be cleaned immediately after use and stored properly. The delicate mesh of some strainers is highly vulnerable to damage; never drop these into a pot sink, where they could be crushed or torn.

Below is a list of some of the most common and useful types of sieves and strainers.

FOOD MILL. This is a type of strainer used to purée soft foods. A flat, curving blade is rotated over a disk by a hand-operated crank. Most professional models have interchangeable disks with holes of varying fineness. An exception is the Foley food mill, which has a mesh disk that is fixed in place. Note: Many mixing machines may be used as food mills through the addition of attachments that allow them to strain and purée foods.

DRUM SIEVE (TAMIS). This sieve consists of a tinned-steel, nylon, or stainless-steel screen stretched in an aluminum or wood frame. A drum sieve is used for sifting or puréeing. A champignon (mushroom-shaped pusher) or a rigid plastic scraper is used to push the food through the screen.

CONICAL SIEVE (CHINOIS). This sieve is used for straining and/or puréeing food. The openings in the cone can be of varying sizes, from very large to very small. A fine-mesh conical sieve is also known as a bouillon strainer.

COLANDER. This stainless-steel or aluminum sieve, with or without a base, is used for straining or draining foods. Colanders are available in a variety of sizes.

Colander

RICER. This is a device in which cooked food, often potatoes, is placed in a pierced hopper. A plate on the end of a lever pushes the food through the openings in the hopper. Garlic presses and french-fry cutters operate on the same principle.

CHEESECLOTH. This light, fine mesh gauze is frequently used along with or in place of a fine conical sieve and is essential for straining some sauces. It is also used for making sachets. Before use, cheesecloth should be rinsed thoroughly in hot water and then cold water to remove any loose fibers. Cheesecloth also clings better to the sides of bowls, sieves, and so forth when it is wet.

BOWLS FOR MIXING

Most kitchens are equipped with a variety of bowls, usually made of a nonreactive material, such as stainless steel. Copper bowls are often included in the kitchen's stock of mixing bowls, because they are considered best for whipping egg whites. Bowls should be reserved for mixing, if at all possible, rather than being used for storage.

Mixing bowls

STORAGE CONTAINERS

Foods in the kitchen may be stored raw, partially prepared, or cooked. It is crucial to have an adequate stock of containers to hold foods safely in the refrigerator or freezer. In addition to plastic or stainless-steel containers (which may or may not have fitted lids), you will also require butcher's paper, plastic wrap, foil, and freezer wrap. Tools for securing and marking stored foods include freezer or masking tape and waterproof markers.

POTS, PANS, AND MOLDS

Various materials and combinations of materials are used in the construction of pots, pans, and molds. Because form and function are closely related, it is important to choose the proper equipment for the task at hand.

Pots made of copper transfer heat rapidly and evenly; because direct contact with copper will affect the color and consistency of many foods, copper pots are generally lined. (An exception is the copper pan used to cook jams, jellies, chocolates, and other high-sugar items, often known as a preserving pan.) Great care must be taken not to scratch linings made from a soft metal, such as tin. If the lining becomes scratched or wears away, it may be repaired by re-tinning. Copper also tends to discolor quickly, so its proper upkeep requires significant time and labor.

Cast iron has the capacity to hold heat well and transmit it very evenly. The metal is somewhat brittle, however, and must be treated carefully to prevent pitting, scarring, and rusting. Cast iron is sometimes coated with enamel to simplify care and increase its useful life.

Stainless steel is a relatively poor conductor of heat, but it is often used because it has other advantages, including easy maintenance. Other metals, such as aluminum or copper, are often sandwiched with stainless steel to improve heat conduction. Stainless steel will not react with foods; this means, for example, that white sauces will remain a pure white or ivory color.

Blue-steel, black-steel, pressed-steel, or rolled-steel pans are all prone to discoloration but transmit heat very rapidly. These pans are generally thin and are often preferred for sautéing foods because of their quick response to changes in temperature.

Aluminum is also an excellent conductor of heat; however, it is a soft metal that wears down quickly. When a metal spoon or whip is used to stir a white or light-colored sauce, soup, or stock in an aluminum pot, the food may take on a gray color. Anodized or treated aluminum tends not to react with foods and is one of the most popular metals for pots used in contemporary kitchens. The surfaces of treated aluminum pans tend to be easier to clean and care for than most other metals, with the exception of stainless steel.

Nonstick coatings on pans have some use in professional kitchens, especially for restaurants that offer foods cooked with less fat and oil. These surfaces are not as sturdy as metal or enamel linings, so care must be taken to avoid scratching them during cooking and cleaning, or allowing empty pans to preheat over extremely high heat. New methods of adding nonstick coatings as well as new mate-

PROPER CARE AND CLEANING OF COPPER PANS

THIS TECHNIQUE for cleaning and shining copper cookware has been used by chefs for many years and is still favored because it is fast, inexpensive, and efficient.

Mix equal parts of flour and salt, then add enough distilled white vinegar to form a paste. The vinegar will react with the copper to erase any discoloration caused by oxidation and heat. Any other acid, such as lemon juice, would work equally well, but white vinegar is typically the most economical choice. The salt acts as a scouring agent, and the flour provides the binder.

Coat copper surfaces completely with this paste, then vigorously massage clean with a cloth. Clean the lined cooking surfaces as you would other pots and pans, with a gentle scouring pad and cleanser.

NOTE: Delicate copper serving dishes and utensils should be cleaned with a commercial cream or polish without abrasives, to avoid scratching.

CHEFS WHO USE PANS made of cast iron or rolled steel, which are porous metals, often season their pans to seal the pores. Seasoning preserves the cooking surface and creates an essentially nonstick coating.

To season a pan, pour enough cooking oil into the pan to evenly coat the bottom by about ⅛ inch. Place the pan in a 300°F (150°C) oven for one hour. Remove the pan from the oven and let cool. Wipe away any excess oil with paper towels. This procedure should be repeated every so often to renew the seal.

To clean a seasoned pan, use a bundle of paper towels to scour salt over the surface of the pan until the food particles have been removed. This procedure effectively cleans the pan without stripping away the seal, as soap, water, and a scouring pad would.

rials used to create these coatings have produced more durable nonstick pans, suitable for many cooking situations.

The following guidelines should be observed for the choice of a pan or mold.

1. CHOOSE A SIZE APPROPRIATE TO THE FOOD BEING COOKED. Be familiar with the capacity of various pots, pans, and molds. If too many pieces of meat are crowded into a sauteuse, for instance, the food will not brown properly. If the sauteuse is too large, however, the fond (caramelized drippings from the meat) could scorch. If a small fish is poached in a large pot, the cuisson (cooking liquid) will not have the proper intensity of flavor. It is also easier to overcook the fish in a too-large pot. If the pot is too small, there may not be enough cuisson available for the sauce.

2. CHOOSE MATERIAL APPROPRIATE TO THE COOKING TECHNIQUE. Experience has shown, and science has verified, that certain cooking techniques are more successful when used with certain materials. For instance, sautéed foods require pans that transmit heat quickly and are sensitive to temperature changes. Braises, on the other hand, require long, fairly gentle cooking, and it is more important that the particular pot transmit heat evenly and hold heat well than that it respond rapidly to changes in heat.

3. USE PROPER HANDLING, CLEANING, AND STORING TECHNIQUES. Avoid subjecting pots to heat extremes and rapid changes in temperature (for example, placing a smoking-hot pot into a sinkful of water) because some materials are prone to warping. Other materials may chip or even crack if allowed to sit over heat when they are empty or if they are handled roughly. Casseroles or molds made of enameled cast iron or steel are especially vulnerable. In order to protect the seasoning of cast-iron or rolled-steel pans, do not clean the surface with detergents or abrasives such as steel wool or cleansing powders.

Be sure to dry pans before storing — air drying is best — to prevent the pitting and rusting of some surfaces, as well as to keep them clean and sanitary. Proper and organized storage prevents dents, chips, and breakage, and it also expedites the work, because staff can more readily find what they need.

POTS AND PANS FOR STOVETOP COOKING

Pots and pans used on the stovetop may be made from a variety of materials, but they must be able to withstand direct heat from a flame. A poorly produced pot will have weak spots and will eventually warp. Different manufacturers, however, may use different styles of handles, loops, or lids.

Following is a list of the most common stovetop pots and pans.

STOCKPOT (MARMITE). This large pot is taller than it is wide, and has straight sides. Some stockpots have a spigot at the base so that the liquid can be drained off without lifting the heavy pot. Anodized aluminum and stainless steel are the preferred materials.

Sauce pan

SAUCE PAN. This pan has straight or slightly flared sides (a pan with flared sides may be known as a fait-tout) and has a single long handle.

SAUCE POT. This pot is similar in shape to a stockpot, although not as large, with straight sides and two loop handles for lifting.

RONDEAU. This is a wide, fairly shallow pot with two loop handles. When made from cast iron, these pots are frequently known as griswolds, and they may have a single short handle rather than two loop handles. A brasier is similar to a rondeau and may be square instead of round.

Sauce pot

SAUTEUSE. This shallow skillet with sloping sides and a single long handle is often referred to as a sauté pan.

SAUTOIR. This shallow skillet has straight sides and a single long handle. It is often referred to as a sauté pan.

OMELET PAN/CRÊPE PAN. This shallow skillet has very short, slightly sloping sides and is most often made of rolled or blue steel.

Sauté pans

BAIN-MARIE (DOUBLE BOILER). These are nesting pots with single long handles. The bottom pot is filled with water that is heated to gently cook or warm the food in the upper pot. The term bain-marie also refers to the stainless-steel containers used to hold food in a steam table.

GRIDDLE. This is a heavy round or rectangular surface for griddling. A griddle is flat with no sides and may be built directly into the stove. There may be a groove or indentation around the edge to allow grease to drain away.

FISH POACHER. This is a long, narrow pot with straight sides and includes a perforated rack for holding the fish.

Omelet pan

STEAMER. This consists of a set of stacked pots or bamboo baskets with a tight-fitting lid. The upper pot has a perforated bottom and is placed over the second pot, which is filled with boiling or simmering water. The perforations allow the steam to rise from the pot below to cook the food above. Tiered steamers are also available.

SPECIALTY POTS AND PANS. Woks, couscousières, paella pans, and grill pans (the latter is essentially a skillet with ridges that can simulate grilling) are among the stovetop pots and pans used to prepare special, usually ethnic, dishes.

PANS FOR OVEN COOKING

Pans used in ovens are produced from the same basic materials used to make stovetop pots and pans; in addition, glazed and unglazed earthenware, glass, and ceramic are also used. The heat of the oven is less intense than that of a burner, making it possible to use these more-delicate materials without risk of cracking and shattering. It is important to remember not to submerge these materials in water immediately after removing them from the oven.

Pans are available in several gauges (*gauge* refers to the thickness of the metal). Heavy-gauge pans are usually preferred; some very delicate items, such as wafer-type cookies, may even be baked on doubled pans.

Pans also come with different surfaces. Shiny pans are used for baking items containing large amounts of sugar and fat, which could burn or scorch easily during cooking. The shiny surface tends to reflect some of the heat away from the pan, slightly slowing down the cooking process. Darker surfaces hold heat better and are used for items in which a well-developed crust and a deeper color are desirable.

Below are listed some of the most commonly used types of bakeware.

ROASTING PAN. This rectangular pan with medium-high sides is used for roasting or baking and comes in various sizes.

SHEET PAN. This shallow, rectangular pan is used for baking and may be full or half size.

HOTEL PANS. These are rectangular pans, used occasionally for preparing foods but more often as containers to hold cooked foods in steam tables, hot boxes, or electric or gas steamers. They are also frequently used to marinate meats or for food storage under refrigeration. They may be shallow, divided, half size, or deep. Chafing dishes usually are of standard sizes, so most hotel pans will fit them properly.

PÂTÉ MOLD. A deep rectangular metal mold, the pâté mold used for pâté en croûte usually has hinged sides to facilitate removal of the pâté. Special shapes (oval, triangular, and others) may be available.

Sheet pans

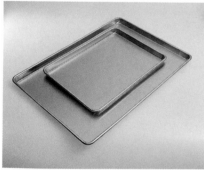

Hotel pans

TERRINE MOLD. The terrine mold may be rectangular or oval, with a lid. Traditionally an earthenware mold, it may also be made of enameled cast iron.

GRATIN DISH. A shallow oval baking dish, this may be ceramic, enameled cast iron, or enameled steel.

SOUFFLÉ DISH. These round, straight-edged ceramic dishes come in various sizes.

TIMBALE MOLD. This small metal or ceramic mold is used for individual portions of various molded, cooked vegetables, usually made with a custard base.

SPECIALTY MOLDS. These include dariole, savarin, ring, and other molds that are used to achieve varying shapes.

CAKE PANS. These pans have straight sides and are available in various sizes (diameters and heights) and shapes (round, square, or rectangular).

SPRINGFORM PANS. These are similar to cake pans, but their sides have springs that can be released in order to remove the cake from the pan more easily. Springform pans are often used for delicate cakes and to mold Bavarian cream-filled cakes as they chill.

LOOSE-BOTTOMED TART PANS. These shallow, round pans have a removable bottom. The sides may be scalloped or straight and are generally shorter than those of pie pans. Small versions are called tartlet pans.

PIE PANS. Pie pans are round pans with flared sides. They are deeper than tart pans.

LOAF PANS. These deep pans are usually rectangular. The sides may be straight or slightly flared. Loaf pans are used for preparing a variety of breads. Pullman loaf pans have lids and produce square loaves.

MUFFIN TINS. These are pans with small, round sections for producing muffins of various sizes.

TUBE PANS. These deep, round pans have a tube in the center and are used to create a specific effect. Some styles are similar to springform pans, having removable sides. Tube pans are most often used for chiffon and angel food cakes.

KUGELHOPF FORMS. These special tube pans with a fluted design are traditionally used to prepare a sweet, yeast-raised cake flavored with dried fruits and nuts.

Whip/Whisks

Wooden Spoons

Tongs

Kitchen Spoons

Large Palette Knife

Rolling Pin

Zester

Measuring Spoons

Parisienne Scoop

Skimmer

Swivel Peeler

Cork Screw

Plastic Graduated
Measuring Cups

Scale

Aluminum Graduated
Measuring Cups

Scoops

Instant-Read
Thermometer

Spider

Ladles

LARGE EQUIPMENT

When working with large equipment, safety precautions must be observed and proper maintenance and cleaning consistently done in order to keep this equipment functioning properly and to prevent injury or accident.

1. Obtain proper instruction in the machine's safe operation. Do not be afraid to ask for extra help.

2. First turn off and then unplug electrical equipment before assembling it or breaking it down.

3. Use all safety features: Be sure that lids are secure, hand guards are used, and the machine is stable.

4. Clean and sanitize the equipment thoroughly after each use.

5. Be sure that all pieces of equipment are properly reassembled and left unplugged after each use.

6. Report any problems or malfunctions promptly, and alert coworkers to the problem.

GRINDING, SLICING, MIXING, AND PURÉEING EQUIPMENT

Grinders, slicers, and puréeing equipment all have the potential to be extremely dangerous. The importance of observing all the necessary safety precautions cannot be overemphasized. As these tools are essential for a number of different operations, all chefs should be able to use them with confidence.

MEAT GRINDER. This is a freestanding machine or an attachment for a standing mixer. A meat grinder should have dies of varying sizes and in general will have a feed tray and a pusher. All food contact areas should be kept scrupulously clean. To make sure all the food has been pushed through the worm, feed a twisted coil of plastic wrap or parchment paper through the feed tube until it hits the plate.

BLENDER. A blender consists of a base, which houses the motor, and a removable lidded jar with a propellerlike blade in its bottom. Speed settings for the motor, of which there may be as many as eighteen or as few as two, are in the base. Jars are made of stainless steel, plastic, or glass, and are available in several capacities. Blenders are excellent for puréeing, liquefying, and emulsifying foods because the tall, narrow shape of the jar keeps food circulating and in close contact with the blade.

FOOD PROCESSOR. This is a processing machine that houses the motor separately from the bowl, blades, and lid. Food processors can grind, purée, blend, emulsify, crush, knead, and, with special disks, slice, julienne, and shred foods.

Food processor, blender

IMMERSION BLENDER. This long and slender one-piece machine (also known as a hand blender, stick blender, or burr mixer) is like an inverted regular blender. The top part of the machine houses the motor, which generally runs at just one speed. A plastic hand-hold with an on/off button extends from the top of the motor. A stainless-steel driveshaft, which varies in length depending on the model, extends from the motor and ends with the blade, which is immersed in the food being puréed. An immersion blender serves the same functions as a regular blender. The advantage of using an immersion blender over a regular blender is that large batches of food can be puréed directly in the cooking vessel, while a regular blender requires the user to work in small batches and transfer the food to the jar from the cooking vessel. Some immersion blenders have magnetic bottoms, which allow them to stand up and run unattended.

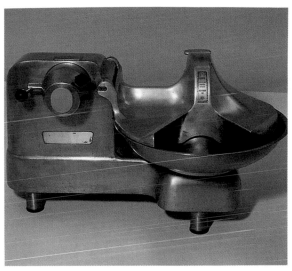

Buffalo chopper

VERTICAL CHOPPING MACHINE (VCM). This machine operates on the same principle as a blender. A motor at the base is permanently attached to a bowl with integral blades. As a safety precaution, the hinged lid must be locked in place before the unit will operate. The VCM is used to grind, whip, emulsify, blend, or crush foods.

FOOD CHOPPER (BUFFALO CHOPPER). The food is placed in a rotating bowl that passes under a hood, where blades chop the food. Some units have hoppers or feed tubes and interchangeable disks for slicing and grating. Food choppers are available in floor and tabletop models and are generally made of aluminum with a stainless-steel bowl.

FOOD/MEAT SLICER. This machine is used to slice foods in even thicknesses. A carrier moves the food back and forth against a circular blade, which is generally carbon steel. There may be separate motors to operate the carrier and the blade. To avoid injury, all the safety features incorporated in a food slicer, especially the hand guard, should be used.

Mandoline

MANDOLINE. This slicing device has blades of high-carbon steel. Levers adjust the blades to achieve the cut and thickness desired. As with food slicers, be sure

Standing mixer

to use the guard — the carrier that holds the food — to prevent injury. The mandoline can be used to make such cuts as slices, juliennes, gaufrettes, and batonnets.

STANDING MIXER. This electric mixing machine has large bowls of varying capacities, and may be referred to as a 20-quart mixer, a 40-quart mixer, and so forth. The bowl is locked in place and the beater, whip, paddle, or dough hook rotates through the batter or dough. These machines have varying speeds. These large mixers are usually set directly on the floor, or on a low table. Smaller, table-top models with a 5-quart capacity are often used for smaller batches.

KETTLES AND STEAMERS

Kettles and steamers enable a chef to prepare large amounts of food efficiently, since the heat is applied over a much larger area than is possible when a single burner is used. Cooking times for dishes prepared in steamers and large kettles are often shorter than for those prepared on a range top.

STEAM-JACKETED KETTLE. This freestanding or tabletop kettle circulates steam through the walls, providing even heat. Units vary; they may tilt, may be insulated, and may have spigots or lids. Available in a range of sizes, these kettles are excellent for producing stocks, soups, and sauces. They are generally made of stainless steel and sometimes have a specially treated non-stick surface. Gas or electric models are available.

Steam-jacketed kettle

TILTING KETTLE. This large, relatively shallow freestanding unit (also known as a Swiss brasier, tilting skillet, and tilting fry pan) is used for braising, stewing, and sautéing large quantities of meats or vegetables at one time. Most tilting kettles have lids, allowing for steaming as well. They are usually made of stainless steel and are available in gas or electric models.

PRESSURE STEAMER. Water is heated under pressure in a sealed compartment, allowing it to reach temperatures above the boiling point, 212°F/100°C. The cooking time is controlled by automatic timers, which open the exhaust valves at the end. The doors cannot be opened until the pressure has been released.

CONVECTION STEAMER. The steam is generated in a boiler and then piped to the cooking chamber, where it is vented over the food. Pressure does not build up in the unit; it is continuously exhausted, which means the door may be opened at any time without danger of scalding or burning.

DEEP-FAT FRYER. This piece of equipment consists of a gas or electric heating element and a large stainless-steel reservoir that holds the fat. A thermostat allows the user to control the temperature of the fat. Stainless-steel wire mesh baskets (most models accommodate one or two baskets) are used to lower and lift foods from the fat. Some models are self-straining; others require the user to manually drain and strain the fat to remove food particles.

RANGES AND OVENS

It is difficult to imagine a kitchen without a stove. The stovetop is known as the range; the oven is usually below the range. There are a number of different variations on this standard arrangement, however.

Gas or electric ranges are available in many sizes and with various combinations of open burners, flattops (not to be confused with griddle units), and ring-tops. Open burners and ring-tops supply direct heat, which is easy to change and control. Flattops provide indirect heat, which is more even and less intense than direct heat. Foods that require long, slow cooking, such as stocks, are more effectively cooked on a flattop. Small units known as candy stoves or stockpot ranges have rings of gas jets or removable rings in a flattop, allowing for excellent heat control.

Ovens cook foods by surrounding them with hot air, a gentler and more even source of heat than the direct heat of a burner. Although many types of food are prepared in ovens, they are most commonly used for roasting and baking. Different ovens are available to suit a variety of needs, and both the establishment's menu and its available space should be evaluated before determining what type and size oven to install.

OPEN-BURNER RANGE. This is an individual grate-style burner that allows for easy adjustment of heat.

FLATTOP RANGE. This consists of a thick plate of cast iron or steel set over the heat source. Flattops give relatively even and consistent heat but do not allow for quick adjustments of temperature.

RING-TOP RANGE. This is a flattop with plates that can be removed to widen the opening, supplying more or less heat.

INDUCTION COOKTOP. This type of burner relies on the magnetic attraction between the cooktop and steel or cast iron in the pan to generate heat. The cooktop itself remains cool. Reaction time is significantly faster than with traditional burners. Pans may not contain copper or aluminum.

CONVECTION OVEN. In a convection oven, fans force hot air to circulate around the food, cooking it evenly and quickly. Some convection ovens have the capacity to introduce moisture. They are available in gas or electric models, in a range of sizes, with stainless-steel interiors and exteriors and glass doors. Special features may include infrared and a convection-microwave combination.

CONVENTIONAL/DECK OVENS. The heat source is located on the bottom, underneath the deck, or floor, of the oven. Heat is conducted through the deck to the cavity. Conventional ovens can be located below a range top or as individual shelves arranged one above another. The latter are known as deck ovens, and the food is placed directly on the deck, instead of on a wire rack. Deck ovens normally consist of two to four decks, though single-deck models are available. Some deck ovens have a ceramic or firebrick base. Deck ovens usually are gas or electric, although charcoal- and wood-burning units are also available. The basic deck oven is most often used only for roasting, but several variations are available for other purposes.

COMBI OVEN. This piece of equipment, powered by either gas or electricity, is a combination steamer and convection oven. It can be used in steam mode, hot-air convection mode, or heat/steam (combi) mode. Combi ovens are available in a number of different configurations.

MICROWAVE OVEN. This type of oven uses electricity to generate microwave radiation, which cooks or reheats foods very quickly. Microwave ovens are available in a variety of sizes and power ratings. Some models double as convection ovens.

OTHER STYLES. Additional styles of ovens include pizza ovens, rotary ovens for spit roasting, conveyor ovens, and rotating deck ovens.

GRIDDLES AND GRILLS

Two other oven/range features, the griddle and the grill, are part of the traditional commercial food service setup.

GRIDDLE. Similar to a flattop range top, a griddle has a heat source located beneath a thick plate of metal, generally cast iron or steel. The food is cooked directly on this surface. A griddle may be gas or electric.

GRILL/BROILER/SALAMANDER. In a grill, the heat source is located below the rack; in a broiler or salamander, the heat source is above. Some units have adjustable racks, which allow the food to be raised or lowered to control cooking speed. Some grills burn wood or charcoal or both, but units in restaurants are often either gas or electric with ceramic "rocks" that create a bed of coals, producing the effect of a charcoal grill. Salamanders are small broilers, used primarily to finish or glaze foods.

SMOKERS

A true smoker will treat foods with smoke (after they have been properly brined and cured, if necessary) and can be operated at either cool or hot temperatures. Smokers generally have racks or hooks, allowing foods to smoke evenly.

Small home-style smokers can be used in some operations if you will be preparing a small volume of specialty items such as smoked trout or cheese, as long as there is proper ventilation.

REFRIGERATION EQUIPMENT

Maintaining adequate refrigeration storage is crucial to any foodservice operation; therefore, the menu and the available refrigeration storage must be evaluated and coordinated. All units should be maintained properly, which means regular and thorough cleaning, including the door gaskets. Such precautions will help reduce spoilage and thus reduce food costs. Placing the units so that unnecessary steps are eliminated will save time and labor. Both of these factors will save money for the operation.

Several types of refrigeration devices are available, including:

WALK-IN. This is the largest style of refrigeration unit and usually has shelves that are arranged around the walls. It is possible to zone a walk-in to maintain appropriate temperature and humidity levels for storing various foods. Some walk-ins are large enough to accommodate rolling carts for additional storage. Some units have pass-through or reach-in doors to facilitate access to frequently required items. Walk-ins may be situated in the kitchen or outside the facility. If space allows, walk-ins located outside the kitchen can prove advantageous, because deliveries may be made at any time without disrupting service.

REACH-IN. A reach-in may be a single unit or part of a bank of units, available in many sizes. Units with pass-through doors are especially helpful for the pantry area, where salads, desserts, and other cold items can be retrieved by the wait staff as needed.

ON-SITE REFRIGERATION. These are refrigerated drawers or undercounter reach-ins, which allow foods on the line to be held at the proper temperature. This eliminates unnecessary walking, which can create a hazard during peak periods.

PORTABLE REFRIGERATION. This is basically a refrigerated cart that can be placed as needed in the kitchen.

DISPLAY REFRIGERATION. These are display cases that are generally used in the dining room for desserts, salads, or salad bars.

PROFESSIONAL CHEFS AND THEIR TOOLS

Some tools and equipment used in the professional kitchen are the same today as they were centuries ago. Others are brand-new innovations, using advanced technology, such as computer chips or infrared. The ability to select, use, and safely maintain all equipment is fundamental to the smooth and efficient operation of a kitchen. As new pieces of equipment are developed and introduced, it is the chef's responsibility to learn how they might benefit the operation and his or her development as a culinarian.

CHAPTER SIX

For most restaurants, the purchase, preparation, and service of meats is one of the most expensive areas of the business —but also one of the most potentially profitable. In order to get the most value out of the meats purchased, it is important to understand how to select the right cut for a particular cooking method.

MEAT, POULTRY, AND GAME IDENTIFICATION

MEAT BASICS

The meat, poultry, and game cuts that a restaurant should buy will depend upon the nature of the particular operation. A restaurant featuring predominantly à la minute preparations — especially those with a preponderance of grilled or sautéed items — will need to purchase extremely tender (and more expensive) cuts. A restaurant that uses a variety of techniques may be able to use some less tender cuts, for example, the veal shank in a braise such as osso buco.

Meats can be purchased in a number of forms and at varying degrees of readiness to cook. The chef should consider several factors when deciding what type of meat to buy. Storage capacity, the equipment required to prepare a menu item, the kitchen staff's ability to fabricate cuts, and the volume of meat required must all be taken into consideration. Once this information is evaluated, you can determine whether it is more economical to purchase large pieces, such as whole legs of veal, or prefabricated meats, such as veal already cut into a top round or perhaps even precut scaloppine.

Meats should be checked for wholesomeness and freshness. Cut surfaces should appear moist, but not shiny. The meat should have a good color, which varies by type as well as by cut. The meat should also smell appealing. Packaged meats should arrive with the packaging intact with no punctures or tears.

The tables accompanying the sections that follow contain key pieces of information about beef, veal, pork, and lamb adapted from *The Meat Buyer's Guide* by The National Association of Meat Purveyors (NAMP), including item numbers as assigned by the NAMP and an average range in size for a cut. Appropriate cooking methods for various cuts have also been included.

STORAGE

Meats, poultry, and game should be loosely wrapped and stored under refrigeration. When possible, they should be held in a separate unit, or at least in a separate part of the cooler. They should always be placed on trays to prevent them from dripping onto other foods or the floor.

The chef should separate different kinds of meats; for example, poultry should not come into contact with beef, or pork products into contact with any other meats. This will prevent cross contamination.

Meats packed in Cryovac (a special type of plastic wrapping) can be stored directly in the Cryovac, as long as it has not been punctured or ripped. Once unwrapped, meats should be rewrapped in air-permeable paper, such as butcher's paper, because airtight containers promote bacterial growth that could result in spoilage or contamination. Variety meats, poultry, and uncured pork products, which have short shelf lives, should be cooked as soon as possible after they are received. Meat stored at the proper temperature and under optimal conditions can be held for several days without noticeable loss of quality.

INSPECTION AND GRADING

Government inspection of all meats is mandatory. Inspections are required at various times — on the farm or ranch, at the slaughterhouse (antemortem), and again after butchering (postmortem). This is done to ensure that the animal is free from disease and that the meat is wholesome and fit for human consumption. Inspection is a service paid for by tax dollars.

Most states have relinquished the responsibility for inspecting meats to federal inspectors. Those states that still administer their own inspections of meat must at least meet, if not exceed, federal standards.

Quality grading, however, is not mandatory. The U.S. Department of Agriculture (USDA) has developed specific standards used to assign grades to meats, and also trains graders. The packer may, however, choose not to hire a USDA grader and may assign its own grade instead. The costs involved in grading meats are absorbed by the individual meat packer, not the taxpayer, since it is voluntary.

Depending upon the particular animal, the grader will consider overall carcass shape, ratio of fat to lean, ratio of meat to bone, color, and marbling of lean flesh. The grade placed on a particular carcass is then applied to all the cuts from that animal. Only a small percentage of meats produced will be graded prime. Choice and select are more often available. Grades lower than select are generally used for processed meat and are of no practical importance to the restaurant (or retail) industry.

Some meats may also receive yield grades. This grade is of the greatest significance to wholesalers. It indicates the amount of salable meat in relation to the total weight of the carcass. Butchers refer to this as "cutability." In other words, it is a measure of the yield of edible meat from each pound of the carcass.

KOSHER MEATS

Kosher meats are specially slaughtered, bled, and fabricated in order to comply with religious dietary laws. In this country, only beef and veal forequarters, poultry, and some game are customarily used for kosher preparations. Kosher meats are butchered from animals that have been slaughtered by a *shohet*, or spe-

TOP *Inspection stamp*

MIDDLE *USDA grade shields*

BOTTOM *Yield grade*

Kosher stamp

cially trained rabbi. The animal must be killed with a single stroke of a knife and then fully bled. All the veins and arteries must be removed from the meat. This process would essentially mutilate the flesh of loins and legs of beef and veal; therefore, these are generally not sold as kosher.

MARKET FORMS OF MEAT

After slaughtering, inspection, and grading, the animal carcass is cut into manageable pieces. *Sides* are prepared by making a cut down the length of the backbone. *Quarters* are made by cutting sides into two pieces, dividing them between specific vertebrae. *Saddles* are made by cutting the animal across the belly, again at a specified point. The exact standards for individual animal types govern where the carcass is to be divided.

The next step is to cut the animal into what are referred to as *primal cuts*. There are uniform standards for beef, veal, pork, and lamb primals. These large cuts are then further broken down into *subprimals*. These cuts are generally

trimmed and packed. There may be even more fabrication or butchering done in order to prepare steaks, chops, roasts, stew, or ground meat. These cuts are referred to as *retail cuts*.

The amount of butchering done in packing plants has increased over the past several years. While it is still possible to purchase *hanging meat*, most operations will buy what is referred to as *boxed meat*. This indicates that the meat has been fabricated to a specific point (primal, subprimal, or retail cut), then packed in Cryovac, boxed, and shipped for sale to purveyors, butchers, chain retail outlets, and so forth.

BEEF

Many special types of beef are available throughout the world, including Kobe beef from Japan, Limousin beef from France, and, in this country, Brae, Certified Angus, natural, organic, and aged beef.

Organic and *natural* have not yet been clearly defined by the USDA in regard to beef. The terms are currently used in accordance with standards set by individual groups, and those standards can vary widely from one state to another, and from one group to another. Some groups may indicate how long the land must be free from specific chemical herbicides and pesticides, others may not. If organic meats are used in a restaurant, it is important to learn more about the standards used in raising and butchering the meat.

Aged beef was formerly more readily available and had greater consumer acceptance than it enjoys today. Aging is traditionally done for a number of meats, including beef, venison, and game birds. The meat is allowed to hang, uncovered, in a temperature- and humidity-controlled environment such as a meat locker. Enzymes naturally present in the meat begin to break down the meat fibers. This gives the meat a more pronounced or "higher" flavor and increases tenderness, but at the same time it reduces the overall yield. Some butchers still age meats and will work with individual restaurants to custom-age meats to exact specifications.

If you opt to purchase any of these meats for use on your menu, be sure that you identify them as such.

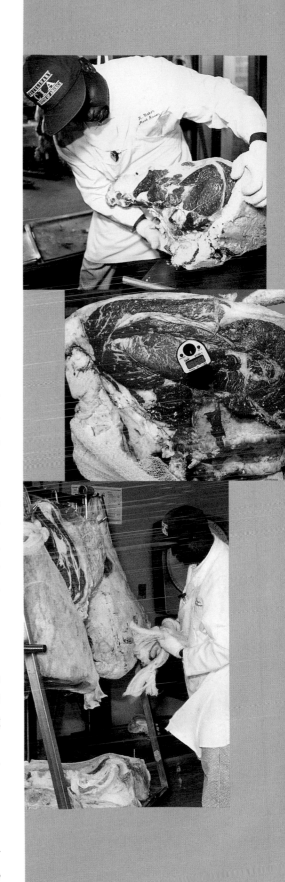

The beef industry is of great importance to the United States. We devote nearly 600 million acres of land to pasture in order to raise livestock. We produce more beef than any other nation in the world. We also consume more on a per capita basis than any other country in the world with the exception of Argentina.

Restaurants that feature beef, such as steak or chop houses, are an institution. Even if your restaurant features only one or two entrées based on beef, you cannot take shortcuts with this all-American commodity. Take the time to do your homework and learn which cooking methods work best with specific cuts. Get a good working knowledge of average yields from the cuts you feature on your menu. Consider ways to maximize yield and profit without cutting into the customer's perception of dollar value.

CHUCK

This large primal cut contains some of the animal's most exercised muscles. This means that, as a general rule, cuts from the shoulder will be best when prepared by one of the moist-heat or combination cooking methods. Long, slow cooking brings out the flavor of these cuts and ameliorates any toughness.

In addition to cuts for braising, stew meat and ground beef are often prepared from the chuck.

RIB

The rib contains many of the most prized roasts and steaks. These cuts are tender and well suited to dry-heat cooking methods such as sautéing, roasting, grilling, and broiling.

Beef rib

Rib roast, trimmed and tied

Boneless rib eye roast

The term *prime rib* really has no specific meaning and should be avoided in menu copy. It is often a confusing term, as it may lead the customer to assume that the beef is graded prime. Rib roasts may be bone-in or boneless. There are many specific menu terms used throughout the country as descriptors for the size of the cut, including *king cut, queen's cut, English cut,* and *double cut*. Doneness is generally of great concern.

Steaks cut from the rib may be bone-in or boneless.

LOIN

The loin yields a variety of cuts prized by those who value tenderness in beef. The tenderloin is one very important subprimal fabricated from the loin. Some terms often used in conjunction with cuts from the tenderloin include *chateaubriand, tournedos, medallions, fillet mignon,* and *tenderloin tips*.

Roasts from the loin may be referred to as *strip loins* or *New York strips*. A variety of steaks are also available, either fabricated on site or purchased from your purveyor, allowing you to indicate weight and fat trim.

ROUND

Some of the cuts from this primal are best when braised, stewed, or simmered, while others, if handled properly, can be roasted with great success. These cuts

Strip loin, top view

Tenderloin, top view

Top round

Bottom round

are generally less tender than those from the rib and the loin, but there are instances when a top round or even a carefully roasted bottom round may make more sense than a more expensive cut from the rib or loin. Roast beef sandwiches can be prepared from any well-cooked cut of meat, and since economics dictate that the lower your food cost, the greater your margin of profit, you may want to make some tests before deciding that bottom round is only for pot roast.

Good-quality, lean ground meat is made from the round as well.

Beef shank

SHANK

The foreshank and hindshank are available and may be used for braising or stews. One additional use made of this meat in many kitchens is as an ingredient in the clarification of consommés.

FLANK AND SKIRT STEAK

These cuts have become increasingly popular in recent times. Both steaks are found along the very edge of the rib and loin portion of the animal. The fibers, though long and relatively coarse, are even. There is enough intramuscular fat to ensure that the meat stays tender, as long as it is carefully sliced and not overcooked.

Beef flank steak

BRISKET

Brisket may be found fresh or corned. Fresh brisket is often favored for pot roasts and other braises. It responds well to slow cooking in a sauce. Corned beef has been brined and cured with spices. It is traditionally prepared by simmering, with or without root vegetable accompaniments. Sliced corned beef is a favorite sandwich meat.

Skirt steak, trimmed

MISCELLANEOUS CUTS OF BEEF

Oxtail is an intensely flavored cut, excellent in stews, soups, and braises. It may be purchased whole or as cross cuts.

Fresh *heart* can be prepared in the same way that any cut of well-exercised muscle is handled — by braising or stewing. The meat has a rich flavor and a deep color.

Beef *liver* is darker and more deeply flavored than other livers. It, like heart, is not commonly found in restaurants or homes. However, aficionados of liver

Beef brisket

and onions, liver pies and puddings, and other dishes including liver can be found in this country and in others where variety meats are accorded a more welcome place on the table.

Tongue is available fresh, smoked, or cured. Japan and other Asian countries esteem tongue highly, making it more difficult to obtain in this country than it used to be. This cut is best prepared by simmering in a flavored court bouillon or broth, and it is often served pickled or with a sharply flavored sauce. Sliced tongue sandwiches are a deli specialty, where its leanness and unique texture shine.

Tripe is the edible lining of the first and second stomachs of a cow. The type of tripe most often found is referred to as *honeycomb tripe*. One of the most famous recipes for this meat is tripes à la mode de Caen, a long-cooked braise finished with Calvados.

BEEF

ITEM	PRODUCT NAME	WEIGHT RANGE (IN POUNDS)	SUGGESTED COOKING METHODS
103	Rib	28–38	Roast, sauté, pan-fry, broil, grill
104	Rib, oven-prepared, regular	22–30	Roast, sauté, pan-fry, broil
107	Rib, oven-prepared	19–26	Roast, sauté, pan-fry, broil
107A	Rib, oven-prepared, blade bone in	19–26	Roast, sauté, pan-fry, broil
109	Rib, roast-ready	16–22	Roast
109A	Rib, roast-ready, special, tied	16–22	Roast
109B	Rib, blade meat	3 and up	Stew, braise
109C	Rib, roast-ready, cover off	15–21	Roast
109D	Rib, roast-ready, cover off, short-cut	14–20	Roast
110	Rib, roast-ready, boneless, tied	13–19	Roast
112	Rib, rib eye roll	6–10	Roast, sauté, pan-fry, broil
112A	Rib, rib eye roll, lip on	7–11	Roast, sauté, pan-fry, broil
113	Chuck, square-cut	79–106	Roast, braise, simmer
114	Chuck, shoulder clod	15–21	Roast, braise, simmer
144A	Chuck, shoulder clod, roast	15–21	Roast
144A	Chuck, shoulder clod, roast, tied	15–21	Roast, braise
115	Chuck, square-cut, boneless	65–88	Roast, braise
116B	Chuck, chuck roll, tied	15–21	Roast, braise
117	Foreshank	8–12	Braise, simmer
118	Brisket	14–20	Braise
120	Brisket, boneless, deckle off	8–12	Braise
121	Plate, short plate	27–35	Braise, cook in liquid
121C	Plate, skirt steak (diaphragm), outer	2 and up	Sauté, braise, grill, broil
121D	Plate, skirt steak, inner	3 and up	Sauté, braise, grill, broil
121E	Plate, skirt steak, skinned, outer	2 and up	Sauté, braise, grill, broil
123	Short ribs	3–5	Braise
123A	Short plate, short ribs, trimmed	Amount as specified	Braise, broil, grill
123B	Rib, short ribs, trimmed	Amount as specified	Braise, broil, grill
123C	Rib, short ribs	Amount as specified	Braise, broil, grill

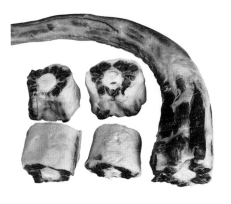

Oxtail

Smoked tongue

Tripe

ITEM	PRODUCT NAME	WEIGHT RANGE (IN POUNDS)	SUGGESTED COOKING METHODS
124	Rib, back ribs	Amount as specified	Braise, broil, grill
125	Chuck, armbone	88–118	Braise, roast
126	Chuck, armbone, boneless (3-way)	70–90	Braise, roast
126A	Chuck, armbone, boneless, clod out	57–77	Braise, roast
158	Round	71–95	Roast, braise, simmer, broil, sauté, grill
158A	Round, diamond-cut	76–102	Roast, braise, simmer, broil, pan-fry, sauté
159	Round, boneless	53–71	Roast, braise, simmer, broil, pan-fry, sauté
160	Round, shank off, partially boneless	57–76	Roast, braise, simmer, broil, pan-fry, sauté
161	Round, shank off, boneless	51–71	Roast, braise, simmer, broil, pan-fry, sauté
163	Round, shank off, 3-way, boneless	50–66	Roast, braise, simmer, broil, pan-fry, sauté
164	Round, rump and shank off	48–64	Roast, braise, simmer, broil, pan-fry, sauté
165	Round, rump and shank off, boneless	43–57	Roast, braise, simmer, broil, pan-fry, sauté
165A	Round, rump and shank off, boneless, special	46–60	Roast, braise, simmer, broil, pan-fry, sauté
165B	Round, rump and shank off, boneless, special, tied	46–60	Roast, braise
166	Round, rump and shank off, boneless, tied	46–57	Roast, braise
166A	Round, rump partially removed, shank off, boneless, tied	52–70	Roast, braise
166B	Round, rump and shank partially removed, handle on	52–70	Roast, braise, simmer, broil, pan-broil, pan-fry, sauté
167	Round, knuckle	9–13	Braise
167A	Round, knuckle, peeled	8–12	Braise
167B	Round, knuckle, full	12–16	Braise
169	Round, top (inside)	17–23	Braise, roast
170	Round, bottom (gooseneck)	23–31	Stew, braise, roast
170A	Round, bottom (gooseneck), heel out	20–28	Roast, braise, simmer, broil, pan-broil, pan-fry, sauté
171	Round, bottom (gooseneck), untrimmed	21–29	Roast, braise, simmer, broil, pan-broil, pan-fry, sauté

BEEF (CONT')

ITEM	PRODUCT NAME	WEIGHT RANGE (IN POUNDS)	SUGGESTED COOKING METHODS
171A	Round bottom (gooseneck) untrimmed, heel out	20–28	Roast, braise, simmer, broil, pan-broil, pan-fry, sauté
171B	Round, outside round	10–16	Roast, braise, simmer, broil, pan-broil, pan-fry, sauté
171C	Round, eye of round	3 and up	Roast, braise, simmer, broil, pan-broil, pan-fry, sauté
172	Loin, full loin, trimmed	37–52	Sauté, pan-fry, broil, grill
172A	Loin, full loin, diamond-cut	42–57	Sauté, pan-fry, broil, pan-broil, grill
173	Loin, short loin	24–35	Sauté, pan-fry, broil, pan-broil, grill
174	Loin, short loin, short-cut	20–30	Sauté, pan-fry, broil, pan-broil, grill
175	Loin, strip loin	14–22	Sauté, pan-fry, broil, pan-broil, grill
176	Loin, strip loin, boneless	10–14	Sauté, pan-fry, broil, pan-broil, grill
179	Loin, strip loin, short-cut	10–14	Sauté, pan-fry, broil, pan-broil, grill
180	Loin, strip loin, short-cut, boneless	7–11	Sauté, pan-fry, broil, pan-broil, grill
181	Loin, sirloin	19–28	Sauté, pan-fry, broil, pan-broil, grill
182	Loin, sirloin butt, boneless	14–19	Sauté, pan-fry, broil, pan-broil, grill
183	Loin, sirloin butt, boneless, trimmed	10–15	Sauté, pan-fry, broil, pan-broil, grill
184	Loin, top sirloin butt	10–14	Sauté, pan-fry, broil, pan-broil, grill
185	Loin, bottom sirloin butt	6–8	Sauté, pan-fry, broil, pan-broil, grill
185A	Loin, bottom sirloin butt, flap	3 and up	Sauté, pan-fry, broil, pan-broil, grill
185B	Loin, bottom sirloin butt, ball tip	3 and up	Sauté, pan-fry, broil, pan-broil, grill
185C	Loin, bottom sirloin butt, tri-tip	3 and up	Sauté, pan-fry, broil, pan-broil, grill
185D	Loin, bottom sirloin butt, tri-tip, defatted	3 and up	Sauté, pan-fry, broil, pan-broil, grill
186	Loin, bottom sirloin butt, trimmed	3–5	Sauté, pan-fry, broil, pan-broil, grill
189	Loin, full tenderloin	5–7	Sauté, pan-fry, broil, pan-broil, grill
189A	Loin, full tenderloin, side muscle on, defatted	4–6	Sauté, pan-fry, broil, pan-broil, grill
189B	Loin, full tenderloin, side muscle on, partially defatted	4–6	Sauté, pan-fry, broil, pan-broil, grill
190	Loin, full tenderloin, side muscle off, defatted	3 and up	Sauté, pan-fry, broil, pan-broil, grill
190A	Loin, full tenderloin, side muscle off, skinned	3 and up	Sauté, pan-fry, broil, pan-broil, grill
191	Loin, butt tenderloin	2–4	Sauté, pan-fry, broil, pan-broil, grill
192	Loin, short tenderloin	3 and up	Sauté, pan-fry, broil, pan-broil, grill
193	Flank steak	1 and up	Braise, sauté, pan-fry, grill
134	Beef bones	Amount as specified	Simmer
135	Diced beef	Amount as specified	Braise, stew, simmer, sauté
135A	Beef for stewing	Amount as specified	Braise, stew, simmer, sauté
136	Ground beef	Amount as specified	Bake, broil, pan-broil, pan-fry, braise, sauté
136A	Ground beef and vegetable protein product	Amount as specified	Roast, pan-fry, sauté
136B	Beef patty mix	Amount as specified	Roast, pan-fry, sauté

VEAL

Considered by some to be the finest meat available, veal nowadays is essentially an off-shoot of the dairy industry. Dairy cows must be bred in order to produce milk. Once the calves are born, they are generally separated from their mothers and raised to a specific age. The practices used in raising veal for slaughter have been cause for concern among many individuals, though a full consideration of this issue is outside the scope of this book.

Veal shoulder roast

Fine veal is known as *milk-fed* or *nature-fed*. Calves that never receive grain, grass, or adult feed have finely textured meat with a pale pink color. Because the overall ratio of meat to bone is necessarily less than it would be in a full-grown heifer or steer, there are proportionately fewer cuts of veal.

Veal, like beef, may be split in two halves, known as the fore and hind quarters. Alternatively, it may be cut into a foresaddle and a hindsaddle, which is accomplished by splitting the carcass at a point between the eleventh and twelfth ribs.

The primal cuts for veal are the shoulder (chuck), shank, rack (rib), loin, and leg. Organ meats (offal) from veal are highly prized, especially the sweetbreads, liver, head, and brains.

SHOULDER (CHUCK)

Cuts from this part of the animal may be handled in the same way that beef chuck cuts are used. Stew meat and ground meat are commonly fabricated from less desirable cuts or the trim from roasts used for braises.

Veal shank

SHANK

The veal foreshank is most commonly available, though it may be possible to procure the hind shank as well. The foreshank is generally meatier and typically is braised. Osso bucco is one of the most famous dishes made from the shank. There are many regional variations on this dish.

Veal rib

RACK (RIB)

The rib may be roasted whole (bone-in or as a boneless rolled roast). Portion-sized cuts from the rib are referred to as *chops*. The rib bones may be left attached and are generally frenched, meaning that the bone has been scraped free of all meat, cartilage, and sinew.

LOIN

The veal loin, like the beef loin, is prized for its tender meat. The flesh of the loin has an even texture and delicate color. The cuts from the loin include chops, roasts, and medallions or similar boneless portion-sized cuts.

Veal loin

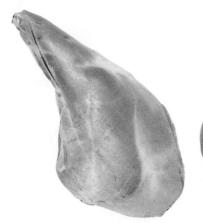

Veal leg

Top round

LEG

The leg yields numerous cuts, perhaps the most familiar of which is the cutlet. Veal cutlets fabricated from the top round have the best texture and cook the most evenly. It is possible to make cutlets from other areas of the leg, including the bottom round. Some butchers may even fabricate them from the chuck.

Veal legs may be purchased whole and broken down into their various components. This offers the chef a good bit of flexibility but requires some knowledge of meat-cutting techniques. The general instruction given is to follow the natural seams in the meat, which separate one large muscle group from another. If an operation is capable of butchering a leg of veal, the initial cost per pound is less than if subprimals or portion-sized cuts are purchased. There is also a greater opportunity to control costs through the use of lean trim and bones in other preparations.

There are many names for cutlets, and they vary from one cuisine to another; *scallops*, *scaloppine*, and *escalopes* are some of the more familiar. A cutlet that has been pounded and grilled is often referred to on the menu as a *paillard*.

BREAST

Veal breast is a richly flavored cut that responds well to slow, gentle cooking. It is relatively easy to remove the bones from the breast and a pocket can be cut to fill the breast with a stuffing or forcemeat, and the breast rolled and tied.

ORGAN MEATS/VARIETY MEATS AND BY-PRODUCTS

Veal breast

Veal organ meats (also called variety meats) such as calf's liver, tongue, and bones are among those most familiar and popular in American kitchens. Sweetbreads (the thymus gland), brains, and heart can also be found. A relatively small proportion of the U.S. public is interested in these specialty items, but cuisines around the world prize them.

Calf's liver, top view

Calf's brains

Calf's kidney

Cooking methods for these cuts vary. Sweetbreads are generally poached and then prepared in a sauce or used as a garnish in forcemeats. Brains may be cooked à la meunière or prepared, as in a classic French dish, with scrambled eggs. Tongue is generally simmered until tender, then sliced; it may also be pickled or smoked. Heart is braised. The bones and veal feet are excellent for preparing stocks and foundation sauces.

Calf's heart

Calf's tongue

VEAL

ITEM	PRODUCT NAME	WEIGHT RANGE (IN POUNDS)	SUGGESTED COOKING METHODS
304	Foresaddle, 11 ribs	44–86	Roast, pan-fry
306	Hotel rack, 7 ribs	9–14	Roast, pan-fry
307	Rack, rib eye	3–5	Roast, pan-fry
308	Chuck, 4 ribs	40–70	Braise, roast
309	Chuck, square-cut	20–36	Braise, roast
309B	Chuck, square-cut, boneless	19–33	Braise, roast
309D	Chuck, square-cut, neck off, boneless, tied	18–32	Braise, roast, pan-fry
310	Chuck, shoulder clod	4–7	Braise, roast, pan-fry
310A	Chuck, shoulder clod, special	4–7	Braise, roast
310B	Chuck, shoulder clod, roast	4–7	Braise, roast, pan-fry
310C	Chuck, scotch tender	½–1	Braise
311	Chuck, square-cut, clod out, boneless, tied	18–32	Braise, roast
312	Foreshank	2–4	Braise, simmer
313	Breast	6–10	Braise, roast
314	Breast with pocket	6–10	Braise, roast
330	Hindsaddle, 2 ribs	50–88	Braise, roast, pan-fry, broil, grill
331	Loin	10–18	Braise, roast
332	Loin, trimmed	8–14	Braise, roast, pan-fry, broil, grill
344	Loin, strip loin, boneless	3–6	Braise, roast, pan-fry, broil, grill
344A	Loin, strip loin, boneless, special	2–5	Braise, roast, pan-fry, broil, grill
346	Loin, butt tenderloin	1–1½	Roast, pan-fry, broil, grill
346A	Loin, butt tenderloin, skinned	½–1	Roast, pan-fry, broil, grill
347	Loin, short tenderloin	½–1	Roast, pan-fry, broil, grill
334	Leg	40–70	Roast, braise, pan-fry, broil
335	Leg, boneless, roast-ready, tied	15–26	Roast, braise
336	Leg, shank off, boneless, roast-ready, tied	11–19	Roast, braise
337	Hindshank	2–4	Braise, simmer
338	Shank, osso buco	1–3	Braise, simmer
341	Back, 9 ribs, trimmed	15–25	Braise, roast, pan-fry
348	Legs, TBS, 4 parts	24–32	Pan-fry, sauté, broil, grill
348A	Leg, TBS, 3 parts	16–24	Pan-fry, sauté, broil, grill
349	Leg, top round, cap on	8–12	Roast, braise, pan-fry, sauté, broil
349A	Leg, top round, cap off	6–8	Roast, braise, pan-fry, sauté, broil
395	Veal for stewing	Amount as specified	Stew, simmer
396	Ground veal	Amount as specified	Roast, pan-fry, sauté

PORK

Today, pork is among the most popular meats sold in the United States, despite growing concerns over fat and cholesterol in the diet. Pigs have been specifically bred over many generations in order to produce leaner cuts of meat. They are slaughtered and butchered in facilities that handle no other type of meat, to prevent the spread of diseases such as trichinosis. Chefs and consumers alike are more conscious than ever of how to handle pork to avoid food-borne illnesses.

While beef remains the number-one favorite in restaurants across the country, pork continues to grow in popularity as dishes that showcase its special qualities take their place on menus. Barbecued spareribs, tender chops and cutlets, and a range of smoked and cured meats are all to be found.

Purchasing agents, chefs, and consumers alike will seldom see on pork the inspection stamps or grading shields often found on beef, veal, or lamb. This is due to several factors. The inspection stamp is applied to the carcass before it is cut into wholesale and retail cuts, and trimming and cutting will generally remove the stamp. Also, quality grades are less frequently assigned to pork than they are to other meats. Packers will often use their own grading system, instead of paying for federal graders to be on hand. This does not necessarily mean that you cannot be certain that various cuts of pork will be of good quality, as the grading systems used by major packers are clearly defined and generally are reliable guides.

The pork carcass, once split into two halves along the backbone, is divided in a slightly different manner than most other meats. Instead of a primal rib, the loin is cut long. This is done to maximize the number of cuts possible from the prized loin. However, chops cut from the rib end are generally called *rib chops*. Those from the leg end may be referred to as *sirloin chops*.

SHOULDER OR BUTT

Roasts, stew meat, and ground pork are often made from this primal and the sub-primals it produces. The ratio of fat to lean is somewhat higher than in other portions of the animal. This makes it highly desirable for use in sausages and other items prepared by the charcutière. For more information, refer to *Garde Manger: The Art and Craft of the Cold Kitchen*.

There are many regional names given to cuts from the shoulder, including *daisy ham*, *Boston butt*, and *picnic ham* (or butt). Because of the greater abundance of fat in these cuts, it is possible to roast them with some success. However, they are generally best for stewing and braising.

Boston butt

LOIN

This is the largest single primal cut from the pig. It is intentionally cut longer than the loins for beef, veal, or lamb. The loin is often roasted, bone-in or boneless. One rather impressive cut produced from the rib portion of the loin is the crown roast. This is occasionally prepared for banquet service. The roast may be stuffed before it is roasted.

Cuts from the loin include chops of various thickness. The composition of the chop varies greatly from one end of the loin to the other. Boneless cutlets are also prepared from the loin. They are generally sautéed, grilled, or broiled. Thick chops are often stuffed and baked. Chops from the shoulder end of the loin may be braised.

The tenderloin, a prized subprimal of the loin, is often available. Noisettes and medallions are often fashioned from the tenderloin. These cuts are sautéed, grilled, or broiled.

A boneless smoked loin (sometimes referred to in the United States as Canadian bacon) is also popular. One of its classic uses is as a component of eggs Benedict. (See below for more information about bacon, salt pork, and other cured pork products.)

Trimmed pork loin

Pork chops from the arm, center, and leg sections

HAM (LEG)

This primal cut is often referred to as the ham, whether or not it has been cured. Fresh pork roasts or hams are quite different in flavor and texture from cured hams.

Ham steaks (available fresh, cured, or smoked) are also common. They are popular breakfast items and also have a place on lunch and dinner menus.

Cured or smoked hams are occasionally fully cooked and ready to eat, though these items may often benefit from simmering or roasting to enhance tenderness and flavor. Others, including such hams as prosciutto and Smithfield, are often simply sliced thinly and eaten as is, or they may be used as a special flavoring ingredient in pasta dishes, appetizers, or other preparations.

Stew meat and ground pork are also produced from the lean trim that results when smaller cuts are fabricated from this primal.

Pork tenderloin

SPARERIBS

Spareribs are similar to beef short ribs, breast of veal, and breast of lamb. This cut has more bone than meat, but it is immensely popular throughout the country.

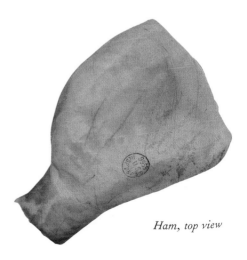

Ham, top view

Other cuisines have also developed trademark preparations that feature this succulent cut. Spareribs are sold whole or cut into portions. Baby back ribs and country-style ribs are also available.

CURED PORK AND PORK BY-PRODUCTS

It has often been said that you can use everything on the pig except the oink. Even in our society, where we tend to prefer recognizable cuts such as roasts, chops, and steaks, we enjoy a number of specialty items produced from the pig.

Bacon is made by curing and/or smoking the belly. This classic breakfast item may be sold as slab bacon, with or without the rind, or sliced. Special types of bacon, such as pancetta, are produced by different cuisines.

Fatback, used for larding, barding, and lining pâté and terrine molds, comes from the clear fat along the animal's back. It is referred to as *clear fat* to distinguish it from the belly, sometimes known as *streak of lean,* an apt description of bacon's composition. Jowl bacon is not as well suited for cooking as strips, but it is excellent for use as a cooking or flavoring ingredient.

Ham hocks, pig's feet and knuckles, and even snouts are used to produce a variety of regional and ethnic dishes. These items are available fresh, cured, and smoked. They are often simmered and traditionally are paired with peasant foods (including beans and greens); they are also used in soups.

Pork liver, heart, and kidneys are sometimes available, but in the United States their use is limited both by availability and by consumer acceptance.

Spareribs

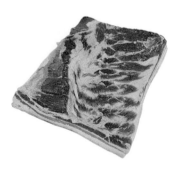

Slab bacon

Smoked slab bacon and Canadian bacon

PORK

ITEM	PRODUCT NAME	WEIGHT RANGE (IN POUNDS)	SUGGESTED COOKING METHODS
401	Fresh ham	17–26	Roast, braise, simmer, broil, pan-fry
401A	Fresh ham, short shank	17–26	Roast, braise, simmer, broil, pan-fry
402	Fresh ham, skinned	17–26	Roast, braise, simmer, broil, pan-fry
402A	Fresh ham, skinned, short shank	17–26	Roast, braise, simmer, broil, pan-fry
402B	Fresh ham, boneless, tied	8–12	Roast, braise
402C	Fresh ham, boneless, trimmed, tied	8–12	Roast, braise
402D	Fresh ham, outside, trimmed, tied	6 and up	Roast, braise
402E	Fresh ham, outside, trimmed, tied	6 and up	Roast, braise
403	Shoulder	12–20	Roast, braise, simmer, broil, pan-broil, pan-fry
404	Shoulder, skinned	12–20	Roast, braise, simmer, broil, pan-broil, pan-fry
405A	Shoulder, picnic, boneless	4–8	Roast, braise, simmer
405B	Shoulder, picnic, cushion, boneless	Amount as specified	Roast, braise, simmer
406	Shoulder, Boston butt	4 and up	Roast, braise, simmer, broil, pan-fry
406A	Shoulder, Boston butt, boneless	4 and up	Roast, braise, simmer, broil, pan-fry
407	Shoulder butt, cellar-trimmed, boneless	3–7	Roast, braise, simmer, broil, pan-fry
408	Belly	12–18	Sauté, pan-fry, simmer
409	Belly, skinless	9–13	Sauté, pan-fry, simmer
410	Loin	14–22	Roast, braise, pan-fry
411	Loin, bladeless	14–22	Sauté, pan-fry, simmer
412	Loin, center-cut, 8 ribs	6–10	Roast, braise, pan-fry
412A	Loin, center-cut, 8 ribs, chine bone off	5–9	Roast, braise, pan-fry, sauté, braise, grill
412B	Loin, center-cut, 8 ribs, boneless	4–6	Roast, braise, pan-fry, sauté, braise, grill
412C	Loin, center-cut, 11 ribs	7–11	Roast, braise, pan-fry, sauté, braise, grill
412D	Loin, center-cut, 11 ribs, chine bone off	6–10	Roast, braise, pan-fry, sauté, braise, grill
412E	Loin, center-cut, 11 ribs, boneless	5–7	Roast, braise, pan-fry, sauté, braise, grill
413	Loin, boneless	8–12	Roast, braise, pan-fry, sauté, braise, grill
413A	Loin, boneless, tied	8–12	Roast, braise
413B	Loin, boneless, tied, special	8–12	Roast, braise
414	Loin, Canadian back	4–6	Roast, braise, pan-fry
415	Tenderloin	1 and up	Roast, braise, grill, pan-fry, sauté
415A	Tenderloin, side muscle off	1 and up	Roast, braise, grill, pan-fry, sauté
416	Spareribs	2 1/2–5 1/2	Braise, smoke, broil, grill
416A	Spareribs, St. Louis-style	2–3	Braise, smoke, broil, grill
416B	Spareribs, breast bones	1/2–3/4	Braise, smoke, broil, grill
417	Shoulder hocks	3/4 and up	Braise, simmer
418	Trimmings	Amount as specified	Braise, simmer
420	Pig's feet, front	1/2–3/4	Simmer
421	Neck bones	Amount as specified	Simmer
422	Loin, back ribs	1 1/2–2 1/4	Braise, broil, grill
423	Loin, country style ribs	3 and up	Braise, broil, grill
435	Diced pork	Amount as specified	Braise, simmer, sauté
496	Ground pork	Amount as specified	Roast, sauté, pan-fry

LAMB AND MUTTON

Lamb has grown in popularity over the last several years, and the impression that it will have a "sheepy" flavor is fading fast because of better methods for breeding, raising, and feeding sheep. Improved breeding techniques also mean that lamb is no longer available only in the spring (the traditional time for lambing).

Because lamb is slaughtered when still quite young, it is tender, and most cuts can be cooked by any method. Spring lamb and hothouse lamb are not fed grass or grain because once the lamb begins to eat grass, the flesh loses some of its delicacy. As the animal ages, the flesh will darken in color, take on a slightly coarser texture, and have a much more pronounced flavor. Sheep slaughtered under the age of 1 year may still be labeled lamb; if slaughtered after that, however, they must be labeled mutton.

Like veal, lamb is cut into a foresaddle and hindsaddle and may also be cut into sides. The major lamb cuts are the rib (known also as the rack), shoulder, breast, shank, loin, and leg.

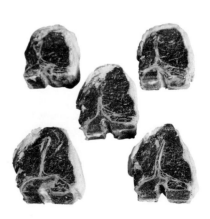

Full rack of lamb

Frenched rack with a single rib chop

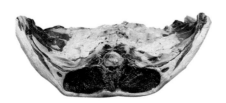

Lamb loin chops

Lamb loin saddle

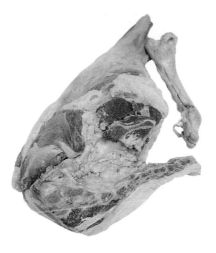

Square-cut shoulder of lamb

Leg of lamb with shank

Boneless leg of lamb, tied

LAMB

ITEM	PRODUCT NAME	WEIGHT RANGE (IN POUNDS)	SUGGESTED COOKING METHODS
204	Rack	5–9	Roast, grill, broil, pan-fry
204A	Rack, roast-ready, single	2–4	Roast, grill, broil, pan-fry
204B	Rack, roast-ready, single, frenched	2–4	Roast, grill, broil, pan-fry
204C	Rack, roast-ready, single, frenched, special	1½–3½	Roast, grill, broil, pan-fry
206	Shoulder	19–27	Roast, grill, broil, pan-fry
207	Shoulder, square-cut	13–19	Roast, grill, broil, braise, pan-fry, roast, braise
208	Shoulder, square-cut, boneless, tied	6–8	Roast, braise
209	Breast	7–11	Braise, simmer, broil, grill
209A	Ribs, Denver-style	5–9	Braise, simmer, broil, grill
210	Foreshank	2–3	Braise, simmer
230	Hindsaddle	27–38	Roast, braise, grill, sauté
231	Loin	8–12	Roast, grill, broil, pan-fry, sauté
232	Loin, trimmed	5–9	Roast, grill, broil, pan-fry, sauté
232A	Loin, short-cut, trimmed	3–7	Roast, grill, broil, pan-fry, sauté
232B	Loin, double, boneless, tied	2–5	Roast
233	Leg	19–27	Roast, braise, grill, broil, pan-broil, pan-fry, sauté
233A	Leg, lower shank off, single	9–14	Roast, grill, broil, pan-fry
233B	Leg, boneless, tied	8–13	Roast
233C	Leg, shank off, single	4–7	Roast
233E	Leg, hind shank	1 and up	Roast, braise
233F	Leg, hind shank, heel on	1 and up	Roast, braise
234	Leg, lower shank off, partially boneless	6–9	Roast, braise
234A	Leg, shank off, single, partially boneless	8–11	Roast, braise
234B	Leg, shank off, boneless, tied	8–11	Roast, braise
236	Back, trimmed	11–15	Braise, pan-fry
238	Hindsaddle, long-cut, trimmed	29–41	Roast, grill, broil, pan-fry, sauté
240	Leg, three-quarters single	7–11	Roast
241	Leg, steamship	6–10	Roast
245	Sirloin, boneless	2–4	Pan-fry, sauté
295	Lamb for stewing	Amount as specified	Stew, braise, simmer
295A	Lamb for kebobs	Amount as specified	Roast, broil, grill
296	Ground lamb	Amount as specified	Roast, pan-fry

VENISON AND OTHER FURRED GAME

Depending upon the area of the country, several types of furred game — including venison, wild boar, elk, and bear — may be available. Game meats of all sorts have become increasingly popular. This is due in part to increased customer sophistication and the fact that game meats are typically lower in fat and cholesterol than their domesticated counterparts.

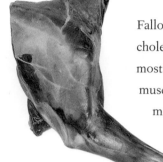

Venison shoulder, outside

Fallow deer (a farm-raised deer) produces a lean, tasty meat with less fat and cholesterol than beef. The loin and the rib are quite tender and are suitable for most cooking techniques, especially roasting, grilling, and sautéing. The leg muscles receive more exercise and are best when prepared by moist-heat methods or combination techniques.

The same general rules that determine how to cook a cut of beef or venison will work for other large game meats, such as wild boar, elk, and bear:

1. Cuts from less-exercised portions of the animal may be prepared by any technique and are commonly cooked with dry-heat methods such as grilling or roasting.
2. Well-exercised areas of the animal, such as the leg (or haunch), shank, and shoulder, are best when cooked by moist-heat or combination methods. These cuts are also used for preparing pâtés and other charcuterie items.

Rabbit, raised domestically, is available throughout the year. The loin meat is delicate in flavor and color, and it has a tendency to dry out if not handled carefully. Traditional preparation methods include roasting, braising, and "jugging," which preserves the meat by cooking and storing it in fat. The loin and legs are often prepared by two separate techniques — the loin is roasted or sautéed and the legs, which are more exercised, are cooked by stewing or braising.

Venison saddle (outside)

Venison top round

Venison haunch, outside

Rabbit (side view)

DOMESTIC POULTRY

As better rearing methods have been developed, chicken and other poultry, once reserved for special occasions, have become commonplace in restaurants and homes.

Poultry production is now a big business, with breeding, care, and feeding all scientifically controlled.

Poultry entrées are among the most popular on most menus. Chicken has a subtle and familiar flavor that lends itself well to a number of different cooking techniques: roasting, grilling, stewing, poaching, and frying.

Like other meats, all poultry must undergo a mandatory inspection for wholesomeness. It may be graded as USDA A, B, or C, depending on the shape of the carcass; the ratio of meat to bone; freedom from pinfeathers, hair, and down; and number (if any) of tears, cuts, or broken bones.

After postmortem inspection, the birds are plucked, cleaned, chilled, and packaged. They can be purchased whole or in parts. The younger the bird, the more tender its flesh will be. As birds age, their flesh toughens, and the cartilage in the breast hardens. The windpipe and bill of ducks and geese will also harden.

Poultry is classified by size and age (maturity), as shown in the table on page 128. Other terms you may see are *natural*, *free-range*, and *organic*. Just as these terms may not have a clear meaning when applied to beef, they are equally unclear in relation to the methods used to raise poultry. Some chefs are inclined to prefer birds raised in a free-range environment, for these are likely to have been allowed at least some exercise in a lot, rather than spending their entire lives in a cage. They may be allowed to forage for some of their feed, but a commercial operation of any size usually needs to carefully regulate the care and feeding of birds intended for sale to the public. This means that feed formulas will be prepared, and certain health precautions, including immunizations and treatment with antibiotics, may be necessary. Organically raised birds may be free of chemically produced growth enhancers or steroids, but it is important to ask questions about any product that is sold to you under any of these labels.

CHICKEN

Chickens are usually sold as broilers, fryers, or roasters, according to their size. Very small chickens, or baby chickens, are sometimes available, and may be referred to as *poussins*. Chickens are sold whole or as parts. They may be roasted, grilled or broiled, baked in pieces, sautéed, pan-fried, or deep-fried.

Stewing hens or fowls are more mature and are best simmered, stewed, or braised. They are excellent for soups.

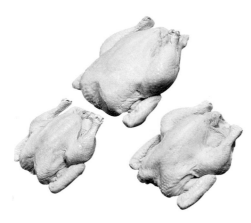

Clockwise from top: roaster, fryer, broiler

Chicken feet and cock's combs, though difficult to obtain, are traditional elements in stocks and soups, providing excellent flavor and body.

Chicken livers, gizzards, hearts, backs, and necks are also sold and have various applications in the kitchen. Schmaltz, or rendered chicken fat, is also available, and is an important component in kosher cooking.

CORNISH GAME HEN

Cornish game hens, also called Rock Cornish hens, are the result of crossbreeding. They are small, relatively plump birds. The ratio of light meat to dark meat is greater than in other birds.

TURKEY

Benjamin Franklin made a strong case for naming the turkey as the national bird of the United States. This large bird has gained in popularity over the years, and turkey products are finding their way onto the menu year-round, instead of only at Thanksgiving.

Stewing hen

Turkeys are classified as either young hens/toms or mature hens/toms. In general, the meat-to-bone ratio is best at weights over 12 pounds.

Turkey is increasingly available as parts: breast with neck and back attached, boneless breast meat, legs or thighs only, even portion-cut scallops or cutlets. Turkey has a more distinct flavor than chicken and as such may be preferred by some consumers. The traditional turkey club sandwich remains popular on all menus.

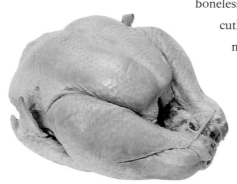

Wild turkey is infrequently available through special purveyors. It must meet certain health and safety standards in order to be sold legally in restaurants. If you are unsure, contact your local health department for more information.

Turkey

GEESE AND DUCKS

Ducklings (ducks under 1 year of age) are generally roasted. Full-grown ducks may be roasted but also are braised, stewed, or made into confit. Pekin duck, Long Island duck, moulard duck, and Muscovy duck are the breeds commonly found in this country.

It is possible to purchase duck parts, including the breasts, legs, and liver. The breast is often sautéed, grilled, or pan-seared. Legs are typically slow-roasted or braised. The fattened liver of the moulard duck, known as foie gras, is produced commercially in this country, making it more easily available as a fresh product.

Foie gras shrinks when cooked, so great care should be taken to sauté it correctly. It is also used in a variety of sausages, gratins, and other charcuterie preparations.

Geese are referred to as goslings when young. These birds are generally suited to roasting. Geese over 1 year old may be better stewed or braised.

GAME BIRDS

Traditionally, chefs could obtain most game birds only during the hunting season, usually late fall and early winter. Today, many game birds are raised on farms year-round. However, many game birds, especially those allowed to range freely, will still be at their best from October through December or January, when they are sufficiently fattened for the winter. While game birds may be raised on farms, they are not usually subjected to controlled breeding.

Young fowl should have soft, smooth, pliable skin. The breastbone cartilage should be flexible, as it is for domestic fowl. The flesh should be tender, with a slightly gamy taste. The types of game birds most often used today in cooking are the following:

QUAIL. The smallest of the game birds, these are traditionally spit-roasted, poêléed, or poached.

SQUAB. Squab is a small pigeon not yet able to fly.

SNIPE. Snipe is available in three sizes, large, common, and small, and has traditionally been considered by gourmets to be one of the finest of all game birds.

WILD DUCK. Teal, a small duck, is considered a delicacy. As wild duck ages, the flesh may take on a fishy or oily taste.

PHEASANT. One of the meatiest of all game birds, pheasant may be roasted or braised. Domestically raised pheasant will not have a pronounced gamy flavor.

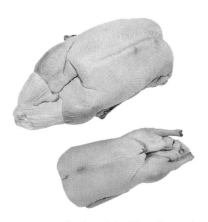

Goose (top) and duckling (bottom)

Moulard duck

Pheasant, squab, quail

POULTRY

NAME	WEIGHT RANGE (IN POUNDS)	SUITABLE COOKING METHODS
Cornish game hen, Rock Cornish hen	¾–2	Very tender, suitable for all cooking techniques
Chicken, broiler	1½–2	Very tender, suitable for all cooking techniques
Chicken, fryer	2½–3½	Very tender, suitable for all cooking techniques
Chicken, roaster	3½–5	Very tender, suitable for all cooking techniques
Chicken, stewing hen*	3½–6	Mature bird, requires slow, moist cooking
Capon (castrated male chicken)	5–8	Very tender, usually roasted or poêléed
Young hen or tom turkey	8–22	Very tender, suitable for all cooking techniques
Yearling turkey	10–30	Fully mature but still tender, usually roasted
Duckling, broiler or fryer	2–4	Very tender, usually roasted, but suitable for most techniques
Duckling, roaster	4–6	Tender, usually roasted
Young goose or gosling	6–10	Tender, usually roasted
Guinea hen or fowl	¾–1½	Related to pheasant; tender, suitable for most techniques
Squab (domestic pigeon that has not begun to fly)	Under 1	Light, tender meat, suitable for sautéing, roasting, grilling; as bird ages, the meat darkens and toughens

*Note: Very mature turkeys, ducks, and geese are also available, though not listed here; they are tough, with hardened cartilage and windpipes.

Fish were once plentiful and inexpensive, but because of various factors, including increased popularity, pollution of fishing beds, and the search for variety, demand has begun to outstrip supply. Also, many countries have passed regulations limiting commercial fishing in specific waters.

What this means to most chefs and consumers is that many longtime menu favorites, including bluefish, true striped bass, and red snapper, are increasingly unavailable. However, aquaculture, or farm-raising of fish, is growing, and it is becoming one of the few reliable sources of fresh fish.

FISH AND SHELLFISH IDENTIFICATION

FISH BASICS

The health benefits of fish are becoming increasingly widely known, and although many Americans traditionally have favored red meats both at home and when they eat out, a large number are ordering fish entrées more often. The chef should be familiar with a wide variety of fish and be able to select absolutely fresh fish of the best quality. The first step in this process is assessing the purveyor or market. The fishmonger should properly handle, ice, and display the fish and should be able to answer any questions regarding the fish's origin and its qualities: lean or oily, firm-textured or delicate, appropriate for moist-heat methods or able to withstand a grill's heat.

MARKET FORMS

Fish can be purchased fresh in one of the market forms described below. Fish may also be purchased frozen, smoked, pickled, or salted.

WHOLE FISH. This is the fish as it was caught, completely intact.

DRAWN FISH. The viscera (guts) are removed, but head, tail, and fins are still intact.

DRESSED FISH. Viscera, scales, and fins are removed. The head and tail may also be removed, depending upon the fish. Also known as pan-dressed, these fish are usually appropriate for a single serving.

STEAKS. These are cross-section cuts, with a portion of the backbone in each cut. The skin is generally not removed. Steaks are usually available only from large round fish (for example, salmon, tuna, or swordfish), although one flat fish, the halibut, may also be cut into steaks.

FILLETS. This is a boneless piece of fish, removed from either side of the backbone. The skin may or may not be removed before cooking, but, when purchased, the fish's skin should be attached to be sure that the fish received is the one that was ordered.

SHUCKED. Shucking is the removal of a mollusc or fish from the shell; this term also refers to the item's market form sold as meat only, along with natural juices known as liquor. Molluscs such as oysters, clams, and mussels may be available shucked; scallops are nearly always sold shucked.

To ensure that fish are of the best quality, the chef should carefully inspect the fish, checking for as many as possible of the following signs of freshness and quality.

When the fish arrives, smell it, checking for an odor. Fish should have a fresh, clean briny aroma. Very strong odors are a clear indication that the fish is aging

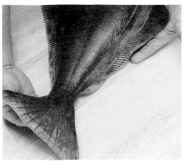

Looking at the fins and tail.

Feeling the skin.

Checking the gills.

Checking the belly.

or was improperly handled or stored. Aroma is the primary indicator of freshness used for whole, drawn, pan-dressed, or filleted fish.

The skin, if any, should feel slick and moist. The scales, if any, should be firmly attached. The fins and tail should be moist, flexible, and full, and should not appear ragged or dry. Press the flesh. It should feel firm and elastic. There should be no visible indentation when you lift your finger.

Eyes should be clear and full. As the fish ages, the eyes will begin to lose moisture and sink back into the head. (*Note:* The walleyed pike's eyes normally appear milky.)

Check the gills for a good red to maroon color, with no traces of gray or brown, and they should be moist and fresh-looking. The exact shade of red will depend on the fish type.

If you are receiving drawn or pan-dressed fish, open the belly flap. There should be no sign of "belly burn," which occurs when the guts are not removed promptly and the stomach enzymes begin to dissolve the flesh, causing it to come away from the bones. There should also be no breaks or tears in the flesh.

If a fish smells fresh and looks fresh but has a slight browning of the gills, it may still be acceptable. If a fish smells bad, no matter how clear the eyes or firm the flesh, reject it.

Ideally, the chef should purchase only the amount of fish needed for a day or two and should store it properly, as described below. When the purveyor is able to make deliveries only once or twice a week, proper storage becomes critical.

Under correct storage conditions, fish and shellfish can be held for several days without losing any appreciable quality. When the fish arrives, the following things should be done.

TOP *Pans for storing fish.*

BOTTOM *Icing fish. They should be positioned in the ice as if they were swimming.*

1. CHECK THE FISH CAREFULLY FOR FRESHNESS AND QUALITY. The fish may be rinsed at this point; scaling and fabricating should be delayed until close to service time.

2. PLACE THE FISH ON A BED OF SHAVED OR FLAKED ICE IN A PERFORATED CONTAINER; STAINLESS STEEL OR PLASTIC IS PREFERRED. The fish should be belly down, and the belly cavity should be filled with shaved ice as well.

3. COVER WITH ADDITIONAL ICE; THE FISH MAY BE LAYERED, IF NECESSARY, WITH SHAVED OR FLAKED ICE. Cubed ice can bruise the fish's flesh. It also will not conform as closely to the fish. Shaved or flaked ice makes a tighter seal around the entire fish. This prevents undue contact with the air, slowing loss of quality and helping to extend safe storage life.

4. SET THE PERFORATED CONTAINER INSIDE A SECOND CONTAINER. In this way, as the ice melts, the water will drain away. If fish is allowed to sit in a pool of water, some flavor and texture loss will occur. The longer it sits, the greater the loss of quality.

5. RE-ICE FISH DAILY. Even when properly iced, the fish will gradually lose some quality. To slow this loss, remove the fish from its storage container, place the fish in a clean container, and add fresh ice.

Fish purchased as fillets should be stored in metal or plastic containers set on or in the ice. They should not be in direct contact with the ice, however, because as it melts much of the flavor and texture of the scallops or fish would be lost.

Frozen fish, including ice-glazed whole fish (fish repeatedly coated with water and frozen so that the ice builds up in layers, coating the entire fish) and frozen fillets should be stored at 0° to -20°F/-1° to -29°C until it is ready to be thawed and cooked. (Storage at -10°F/-23°C is ideal and will greatly extend shelf life.)

Do not accept any frozen fish with white frost on its edges. This indicates freezer burn, the result of improper packaging or thawing and refreezing of the product.

COMMONLY AVAILABLE FISH

There are numerous different fish species commonly used for food and an even greater number of names for these fish. The name a fish will go by depends upon the region in which it is sold. However, basic groupings can be used to sort fish.

The skeletal structure of finfish can be used as the initial way to separate this large category into smaller groupings. There are three basic skeletal types:

1. Round fish, such as trout, bass, perch, and salmon, have a backbone along the upper edge. There are two fillets on either side. A round fish has one eye on each side of its head.

2. Flatfish, such as the various flounders and Dover sole, have a backbone that runs through the center of the fish. There are four fillets, two upper and two lower. Both eyes are on the same side of the head.

3. Nonbony fish, such as ray, skate, shark, and monkfish, have cartilage rather than bones.

Fish come in a wide range of flavors and textures. Some fish are naturally lean, while others are more oily; some have an extremely delicate and subtle flavor, while others are robust and meaty.

The best way to pair a fish with a cooking technique is to consider the flesh. Oily fish — bluefish and mackerel, for example — are often prepared by dry-heat techniques such as grilling or broiling. Fish with moderate amounts of fat (salmon and trout) work well with any technique, with the possible exception of deep-frying. Very lean fish, such as sole or flounder, are most successfully prepared by poaching ,sautéing, pan-frying, or deep-frying. There are some classic preparations, however, that combine certain fish with specific techniques.

ANCHOVY

Anchovies are round fish with relatively fatty flesh and firm texture when fresh. The most common form for the anchovy is the canned fillet packed in oil, with or without capers. In addition, they are sold as anchovy paste and smoked fillets and may also be available fresh. The salted and oil-packed fillet is a classic component of Caesar salad.

Herring, smelt, anchovies

BASS

Bass are round fish, considered to be moderately fatty with a fairly firm, smooth texture. Saltwater species are harvested in both the Atlantic and Pacific. Black sea bass feed primarily on shrimp, crabs, and mollusks. They have firm, well-flavored flesh that can be prepared by all cooking techniques. Considered to hold a close resemblance to a Mediterranean fish called the sea bream, black sea bass generally weigh from 1 to 3 pounds but may be larger in the fall. Other bass — striped bass, sea bass, pike, and red snapper, for example — are not necessarily taxonomically related but share culinary similarities.

Black sea bass

True striped bass

Hybrid striped bass

Some freshwater species are found in the United States, but those fished from clean salt waters tend to have the best texture and flavor. Unfortunately, because striped bass can tolerate polluted waters, its sale has been severely restricted. A hybrid striped bass is a farm-raised freshwater species and has a darker and oilier flesh than saltwater striped bass.

BLUEFISH

A round fish with a relatively strong flavor and oily flesh, bluefish is taken from both the Atlantic and Gulf of Mexico waters. The fish should be drawn as soon as possible after it is caught and should be purchased only when very fresh. Young bluefish generally have an excellent flavor, as they feed on mollusks and shrimp. The flesh has a loose, flaky texture and is excellent broiled or grilled. The strip of dark-colored flesh in the fillet has a more pronounced flavor and may be removed before cooking.

CATFISH

Catfish are round fish, farmed and marketed under carefully controlled conditions. Catfish should be skinned before cooking and are commonly sold as skinless fillets. The

Catfish

flesh is delicately flavored, lean, and very firm, almost rubbery in texture. This fish can be prepared by any cooking technique; a traditional preparation is dipped in cornmeal and pan-fried.

COD

Cod is a round fish that has lean, firm white flesh with a mild flavor. The cod family has a number of distinct species, including Atlantic cod, haddock, cusk, whiting, hake, and pollock, each with different identifying marks. Cod may be

Cod

poached, used in chowder, or steamed, and it is also available salted (in which case it is known as salt cod or *baccala*). *Finnan haddie* is split, smoked haddock.

DOVER SOLE

One of the only true soles is the Dover sole, a flat fish with a compact, oval shape and firmly textured, delicately flavored flesh. Dover sole is so highly esteemed that hundreds of different dishes have been devised to feature it. Dover sole is available fresh or frozen. Note that although many species of flounder have been dubbed "sole," they should not be confused with Dover sole.

Dover sole, top and bottom

DOLPHIN FISH (MAHI MAHI)

This round fish, harvested from the Pacific and Atlantic Oceans, has firm flesh with a sweet, delicate flavor. It is a round fish and not the mammal that we also call a dolphin. It can be prepared by all cooking techniques and is excellent in ceviche. The skin should be removed before cooking.

EEL

Eels are round fish with rich, oily flesh. Eels spawn in the Sargasso Sea, which is part of the North Atlantic, and then begin the journey back to the coasts of either Europe or America. They are available live, whole, skinned, in fillets, smoked, and jellied. One of the most famous eel dishes is matelote, a French stew.

Eel

FLOUNDER

Flounder is often sold in the United States under the market name of *sole*. Lemon sole, gray sole, and white sole are all forms of flounder, a flat, disk-shaped fish with both eyes on the same side of its head. *Plaice*, another flounder species, is often sold as *dab (sand dab* or *roughback)*. Flounder is generally quite delicate, with a tendency to flake readily. It is particularly suited to shallow poaching and steaming and is also commonly cut into "fingers" and deep-fried. Readily available whole, flounder is also sold skinned and cut into fillets.

Flounder, top view

Flounder, bottom view

Grouper

GROUPER

There are several kinds of grouper, all members of the sea bass family. One of the most commonly available is red grouper. Grouper is a round fish and, similar to other bass, has lean, firm, white flesh that is best when sautéed, pan-fried, steamed, or shallow-poached. The skin should be removed before cooking.

HALIBUT

Halibut is a flat fish with firm, white meat and a delicate flavor. The halibut can grow to be quite large and may be cut into steaks or fillets. A halibut of 10 to 40 pounds is considered small; they can grow to be over 200 pounds. Halibut is available as a farm-raised fish.

Halibut (head removed)

MACKEREL

King mackerel

Spanish mackerel

Mackerel is an oily, soft-textured round fish, once regularly sold salted. Spanish and king mackerel both are considered fish of eating quality, but the Spanish mackerel is conceded to be the best. The flesh flakes easily when cooked. Mackerel is best when prepared by dry-heat cooking techniques and is commonly broiled.

MONKFISH

Monkfish is a nonbony fish, prized for the fillet from the tail. Monkfish has a firm, dense texture and sweet taste. This fish has been known by a number of names, including *angler fish*, *goosefish*, *lawyer fish*, and *belly fish*. The French name is *lotte*. Suitable for any cooking technique, it is commonly used in fish stews such as cioppino and bouillabaisse.

Monkfish

PERCH

Perch is a round freshwater fish with a lean and delicate flesh. The best perch are harvested from the fresh waters of lakes and reservoirs. Small perch may be deep-fried and served whole; large fish are cut into fillets and then either pan-fried, steamed, or shallow-poached.

PIKE

Pike

Most famous for its use in *quenelles de brochet*, walleyed pike is a round fresh water fish that has sweet, white, firm-textured flesh that is relatively lean but stands up well to dry-heat techniques. It is also commonly poached or used to prepare mousses or terrines. It should not be confused with pickerel, a fish of virtually no culinary importance.

POMPANO

Considered by some to be one of the finest saltwater fish for eating, pompano is becoming increasingly expensive. Pompano is a round fish with moderately fatty, firm, well-flavored flesh and is often broiled or prepared en papillote. Most pompano comes from the Gulf of Mexico.

Pompano

SALMON

This firm, moderately oily round fish has a distinctively colored flesh, ranging from light pink to a deep orange-pink. A number of different species, including Coho, king, and Atlantic, are available. The Atlantic species is commonly farm-raised.

Coho salmon

Salmon may be prepared using any technique; among the more popular presentations are poached, baked in pastry (coulibiac), and grilled. Salmon is available fresh, smoked, or cured as *gravad lox*. Salmon shares flavors, textures, and culinary treatments with trout.

Atlantic salmon

SHAD

Shad, a round fish, usually enter the rivers of the Atlantic coast from the Gulf of St. Lawrence to northern Florida from December to May. The flesh of both sexes, which is sweet and white but extremely bony, and the roe of the female are highly regarded. A traditional preparation method for shad and shad roe is to sauté or pan-fry them with bacon. The American Indians used to smoke-roast the fish, a technique referred to as "planking."

SHARK

Shark are nonbony fish. Mako and blue shark are commonly available, and other types of shark, including yellowtip and blacktip, are also important in the marketplace. Shark may sometimes be sold to the unwary as swordfish, so be sure to check the pattern of the strip of dark-colored flesh (see illustration) and only pay for what was ordered, as shark is generally less expensive than swordfish. The flesh of shark is sweet and relatively firm and moist, but the skin is extremely tough. Shark is commonly made into steaks and grilled, broiled, or sautéed.

Shark, cut into steak

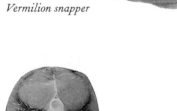

Red snapper

SKATE, RAY

The flesh of the skate, or ray, is sweet and firm and has been compared to scallops. Like shark and monkfish, skate is a nonbony fish. It is sold as wings, which should be skinned prior to sautéing, although they may be poached with the skin on. Skate wings are easier to skin after poaching. One famous presentation method is to sauté the skate and serve it with beurre noir.

SNAPPER

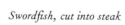

Vermilion snapper

There are a number of different snappers. These round fish have flesh that is firm, moist, and finely textured. One of the most popular is red snapper, the supply of which has become greatly reduced. True red snapper comes from the Gulf of Mexico and adjacent Atlantic waters. Among other desirable snapper species are vermilion, silk, mutton, mangrove, gray, beeliner, pink, and yellowtail. Almost any preparation technique can be used; snapper is often prepared en papillote or baked.

SWORDFISH

Swordfish has an extremely firm texture with a unique flavor. Commonly cut into steaks and grilled, swordfish is similar to shark, a nonbony fish that is usually less expensive. Swordfish's darker strip of flesh has an umbrella-shaped pattern, which is one way to distinguish it from shark, which has a round pattern.

Swordfish, cut into steak

TROUT

The trout is a moderately fatty round fish with delicately textured flesh. With the exception of some special trout species, such as the steelhead, all trout sold in restaurants comes from commercial hatcheries. Rainbow trout and brown trout are among the most commonly available types. They are excellent when pan-fried in a manner similar

Trout

to catfish, roasted, or poached. Truite au bleu is a famous preparation in which freshly killed trout is poached in a vinegar court bouillon until the blue color is barely set. Smoked trout is also available.

TUNA

A member of the mackerel family, tuna is a round fish with firm, moderately oily flesh and a distinctive strip of darker-colored flesh along its back. Tuna's flesh is similar to that of swordfish in texture, but it flakes more readily after cooking. Its flavor is unique, and the flesh's color ranges from a deep pinkish beige to a dark maroon. Tuna is often roasted or cut into steaks and grilled. Also popular is canned tuna — labeled as albacore, white, or light meat, packed in either oil or water. Canned tuna is essential for tonnato sauce and salade niçoise.

Tuna fillet

TURBOT

A disk-shaped flat fish esteemed for its snowy white, moist, finely textured flesh, turbot may grow large enough to be cut into steaks or fillets. It is generally steamed or poached to highlight its delicacy and whiteness.

WEAKFISH

Weakfish is harvested in the United States from Massachusetts to Florida. It is also marketed as squeteaque, drum, croaker, and sea trout. Its lean and flaky flesh makes it a popular fish for grilling and pan frying. The spotted squeteaque, most abundant in North Carolina and the other southern states, is commonly called salmon trout.

Weakfish

SHELLFISH

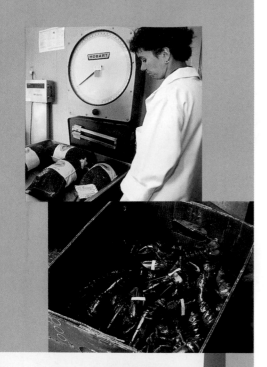

Shellfish can be broken into four distinct categories based on their skeletal structure:

1. Univalves (single-shelled mollusks), such as abalones and sea urchins
2. Bivalves (with two shells joined by a hinge), such as clams, mussels, oysters, and scallops
3. Crustaceans (with jointed exterior skeletons or shells), such as lobster, shrimp, and crayfish
4. Cephalopods, such as squid and octopus, with tentacles attached directly to the head

Check live shellfish for signs of movement — lobsters and crabs should move about. Clams, mussels, and oysters should be tightly closed. As they age, they will start to open. Any shells that do not snap shut when tapped should be discarded; the shellfish are dead. If a bag contains many open shells, the delivery should be rejected.

Crabs, lobsters, and other live shellfish should be packed in seaweed or damp paper upon delivery. If a lobster tank is not available, they can be stored directly in their shipping containers until they are to be prepared. Do not allow fresh water to come into direct contact with lobsters or crabs, as it will kill them.

Clams, mussels, and oysters purchased in the shell should be stored in the bag in which they were delivered, but should not be iced as they last better at temperatures between 35° and 40°F/1° and 4°C. The bag should be closed tightly and lightly weighted to keep the shellfish from opening.

ABALONE

The abalone has one shell and a suction cup that attaches firmly to rocks; it must be pried loose. Most abalone comes from California, and state law there prohibits the exportation of live abalone, so most of the country must rely on frozen or canned abalone. The meat, which is cut into steaks and pounded before sautéing or grilling, becomes extremely tough if overcooked.

CONCH

True conch comes from the Caribbean and is more accurately classified as a gastropod, a class of large mollusk. Conch is sold out of the shell and may also be found ground. It is used in salads, ceviche, chowders, and fritters. Further north, the whelk, which is much smaller and grayish in color, is sold as conch.

SNAILS

Fresh snails, also called *escargots*, are imported from France. There are, on average, thirty-two snails per pound. They are traditionally served in their shells with a compound butter as an appetizer. Fresh snails are far superior to canned snails.

Land snails

| Clams | Mussels | Oysters |

CLAMS

Clams are available in the shell, shucked (and possibly frozen), and canned. Clams sold as live should be checked to ensure that the shells are tightly closed and that they have a sweet smell.

Clams, like oysters, may be marketed by the name of the bed from which they were taken, and local preferences for species will vary. The following terms are commonly applied to clams.

HARD-SHELL CLAM OR QUAHOG. There are two kinds of hard-shell clams. Littlenecks are small hard-shell clams often eaten raw on the half shell. Cherrystones are the next largest size and are also commonly eaten raw. If hard-shell clams are more than 3 inches in diameter, they are generally referred to as quahogs and are used for chowder or fritters.

SOFT-SHELL CLAMS. These are generally steamed and used in fritters.

MUSSELS

Most commercially available mussels are farm-raised and are sold live in the shell. Mussels are commonly prepared à la marinière (steamed with wine, garlic, and lemon) or as the major component of billi-bi (a velouté soup garnished with mussels), although there are a great many other presentations.

Mussels steamed and served in the shell should be debearded first.

OYSTERS

Oysters are sold live in the shell or shucked. As with clams, they are generally marketed by the name of the beds from which they were harvested, and local preference will vary greatly. Some of the most famous presentations include raw on the half shell, oyster stew, oyster omelets, and oysters Rockefeller, a dish that includes spinach and Pernod.

SCALLOPS

Three species of scallop are of commercial importance: bay scallops, sea scallops, and calico scallops. Sea scallops can become quite large (2 to 3 inches in diameter); bay and calico scallops are smaller. Bay scallops (northern and southern) are generally considered superior in quality to calicos.

Scallops

Most scallops are sold shucked. Occasionally shucked scallops with the roe attached may be found. Even less frequently they are sold still in the shells, though farm-raised scallops in the shell are sometimes available.

Coquilles St. Jacques is customarily thought of as a cream-based scallop gratin; it is also the name for scallop in French, and refers to the fact that St. James wore the shell of the scallop as his personal emblem.

CRAB

Common kinds of crab include blue, Dungeness, king, and spider. Blue crab, which is found on the Atlantic coast, especially around Chesapeake Bay, is sold live or as pasteurized or canned meat.

In the spring through late summer, when the crab molts, blue crabs are sold as *soft-shell crabs,* which are commonly pan-fried or sautéed. Hard-shell crabs may be boiled or steamed. The meat may be removed and used in a variety of preparations, including one of the most famous, crab cakes.

Dungeness crab is common on the Pacific coast. King crab and spider crab are valued mainly for their legs, although the whole crab can be used. To harvest crab legs, fishermen simply twist off the legs (which grow back) and return the crab to the sea. Legs are cooked and frozen on the ship in most cases, and the claw may be cracked (especially in the case of stone crab).

Jonah crab is a larger relative of the stone crab. It is found from Nova Scotia to Florida. The meat of the crab is excellent for crab cakes and can be fried or baked.

Spider crab

CRAYFISH

Freshwater crayfish (also known as *crawfish*) is widely available year-round because it can be farmed. Crayfish may be purchased live or precooked and frozen (either whole or tail meat only). Crayfish are used extensively in Creole and Cajun cooking and are also a classic garnish. Crayfish étouffé and jambalaya are two of the most popular crayfish dishes.

LOBSTER

American lobster, harvested from the cool waters around New England, is generally the most prized; it is available live or cooked and canned. The meat is firm and succulent, and virtually all parts of the lobster inside the shell are edible. The female may contains the egg sac, known as the roe. It is considered a delicacy; however, lobsters with visible egg sacs cannot be legally harvested. Both sexes possess the green tomalley, or liver, another prized part.

To determine the sex of the lobster, feel the appendages where the tail meets the body. In the female they will be soft and feathery, whereas in the male they are rigid. The female's tail is generally broader.

Other types of lobster include the rock lobster (often sold as frozen tails; rock lobster is the market name for *spiny lobster*), Dublin Bay prawn, and lobsterette.

Clockwise from top left: Dungeness crab, Maine lobster, crayfish, shrimp (head on), shrimp (head off), blue crab

SHRIMP

Shrimp is one of the most popular crustaceans. Shrimp are most commonly available frozen, as fishermen generally remove the heads and flash-freeze the shrimp on the boat in order to preserve flavor and quality. Fresh shrimp are highly perishable, but they may be available in some regions of the United States, notably the Gulf of Mexico and Chesapeake Bay regions, and there are both saltwater and freshwater species. The flesh has a sweet flavor and a firm, almost crisp texture. Some common presentations include cold (as shrimp cocktail), deep-fried, baked, sautéed, and grilled.

Shrimp are sold according to the number in a pound, known as the *count*. The table on the following page shows the counts for various sizes of shrimp.

SHRIMP COUNT PER POUND

COMMERCIAL NAME	COUNT (NUMBER OF SHRIMP PER POUND), SOLD IN THE SHELL	COUNT (NUMBER OF SHRIMP PER POUND), SOLD PEELED AND DEVEINED
Colossal	15 or fewer	20 or fewer
Extra-jumbo	16–20	20–25
Jumbo	21–25	26–31
Extra-large	26–30	32–38
Large	31–35	39–44
Medium-large	36–42	45–53
Medium	43–50	54–63
Small	51–60	64–75
Extra-small	61 and over	76 and over

Octopus

OCTOPUS

Octopus has a firm texture and a sweet marine flavor. It is generally sold fresh and cleaned of its ink and beak, but it may also come frozen. Octopus may be presented in a variety of ways, including ceviche, chowders, and salads.

SQUID

Squid is one of the most widely available forms of seafood. It has always been an established part of Mediterranean and Asian cuisines and is continuing to gain popularity in the United States. Squid are available in a range of sizes; small squid are frequently stuffed and cooked whole in a sauce, whereas large squid are cut into rings, fried, and served with a spicy sauce. There are many different presentations, however, because squid are suited to most cooking techniques.

Fruits, vegetables, and herbs have always been an important part of the human diet, but today consumers are more aware than ever of the important role these foods play in maintaining overall health and fitness. This chapter provides professional chefs with the information they need to take full advantage of the abundance of fresh produce now available, including tips on availability, determination of quality, and proper storage.

FRUIT, VEGETABLE, AND FRESH HERB IDENTIFICATION

GENERAL GUIDELINES

SELECTION

Fruits, vegetables, and herbs should look fresh, but what constitutes a fresh appearance varies from one item to another. In general, fruits and vegetables should be free of bruises, mold, brown or soft spots, and pest damage; they should have colors and textures appropriate to their type; and any attached leaves should be unwilted. Fruits should be plump, not shriveled. Specific information on particular types of produce is given in the sections below.

GRADING

Since it is usually not possible to examine produce until it has been delivered to the restaurant, one way to help ensure quality is to buy according to grade. The grading information in the tables is based on U.S. Department of Agriculture standards. Lower-grade items, particularly fruits, may be used successfully in preparations such as baked pies and puddings, where appearance is not a factor.

Some items are graded according to state standards, so the chef should try to obtain local grading information from state agricultural departments. When the quality of fresh produce cannot be guaranteed, one possible solution is to buy frozen fruits and vegetables. Most vegetables and some fruits are available frozen, and these are preferable to poor-quality fresh produce. Peas, corn, spinach, and most berries, for example, freeze well.

AVAILABILITY

Traditionally, chefs have selected fruits and vegetables when they are in season, because they are at their best then. For some produce, this is still true. Locally-grown sweet corn, apricots, peaches, and strawberries that have not been shipped are often superior. However, some items ship particularly well. Examples are asparagus, head lettuces, broccoli, some melons, apples, and citrus fruits.

Another advantage of using local growers is that so-called boutique farmers may have specialty produce (wild lettuces, golden beets, and yellow tomatoes, for example) that is not available through large commercial purveyors.

More and more vegetables can be grown hydroponically, that is, in nutrient-enriched water rather than soil. Hydroponic growing takes place indoors under regulated temperature and light, so any growing season may be duplicated. Hydroponically grown lettuces, spinach, herbs, and tomatoes are all readily available. Although they have the advantage of being easy to clean, these products may have a less pronounced flavor than conventionally grown fruits and vegetables.

Once the produce has been obtained, following certain storage guidelines can ensure that its quality remains high. Most foodservice establishments store produce for no more than three or four days, although length of storage depends on the business's volume, the kind of available storage facilities, and delivery frequency. The ideal is to let the purveyor handle the produce as long as possible.

With a few exceptions (bananas, potatoes, dry onions), ripe fruits and vegetables should be refrigerated. Unless otherwise specified, produce should be kept at a temperature of 40° to 45°F/4° to 7°C, with a relative humidity of 80 to 90 percent. The ideal situation is to have a separate walk-in or reach-in refrigerator for fruits and vegetables.

Most fruits and vegetables should be kept dry, because excess moisture can promote spoilage. Most produce should therefore not be peeled, washed, or trimmed until just before use. The outer leaves of lettuce, for example, should be left intact; carrots should remain unpeeled. The exceptions to this rule are the leafy tops on vegetables such as beets, turnips, carrots, and radishes. They should be removed and either discarded or used immediately because even after harvesting, the leaves absorb nutrients from the root and increase moisture loss.

Fruits and vegetables that need further ripening, notably peaches and avocados, should be stored at room temperature, 65° to 70°F/18° to 21°C. Once the produce is ripe, it should be refrigerated so that it does not become overripe.

Certain fruits (including apples, bananas, and melons) emit ethylene gas as they sit in storage. Ethylene gas can accelerate ripening in some unripe fruits but can also promote spoilage in fruits and vegetables that are already ripe. For this reason, unless they are being used deliberately as a ripening agent, ethylene-producing fruits should be stored separately. When separate storage space is unavailable, place ethylene-producing fruits in sealed containers.

Some fruits and vegetables, including onions, garlic, lemons, and melons, give off odors that can permeate other foods. Dairy products are particularly susceptible to odor absorption and should always be stored away from fruits and vegetables. Certain fruits, such as apples and cherries, also absorb odors. They too should be well wrapped or stored separately.

Many vegetables begin to lose quality after three or four days. Although citrus fruits, most root vegetables, and hard squashes have a longer storage life, most restaurants do not hold even these items for more than two to three weeks.

FRUITS

Fruits are customarily used in sweet dishes, such as pies, puddings, ice creams, and dessert sauces. They are a classic finale for meals, with or without a plate of cheese. And of course, a plate of fresh seasonal fruits, fruit salad, or fruit soup can be refreshing and delicious. But fruits are used in savory dishes as well. Fruit is an excellent foil for richly flavored or oily meat, poultry, and fish, and dried fruits find their way into compotes, stuffings, and sauces. For example, the bright flavors of citrus fruits and grapes are frequently used in combination with poultry, veal, or fish, and rhubarb traditionally is served with mackerel. And applesauce is a favorite accompaniment to crisp, buttery potato latkes.

APPLES

Apples are perhaps America's favorite fruit. According to surveys from the International Apple Institute, apples account for nearly 14 percent of all tree fruits sold in this country. The most commonly available varieties are Golden and Red Delicious, McIntosh, Granny Smith, Rome Beauty, Fuji, and Gala. There are, however, thousands of other varieties grown in orchards throughout the country. A little searching results in a find that makes your apple tart uniquely flavorful.

Different varieties of apple have particular characteristics. Some are best for eating out of hand or in other preparations where they are left fresh and uncooked. Other types are considered best for pies and baking. These fruits tend to retain a recognizable shape and some texture even when baked. Still others are selected for their ability to cook down into a rich, smooth purée for applesauce. For cider, a blend of apples is usually chosen, to give the finished drink a full, well-balanced flavor.

Fresh apples can be held in climate-controlled cold storage for many months without significant loss of quality. This makes it possible to get good fresh apples throughout the year. Dried apples, prepared applesauce, apple juice (bottled or frozen concentrate), cider, spiced or plain pie fillings, and a host of other prepared items made from apples can also be purchased.

The flesh of many apples will begin to turn brown once they are cut open and come in contact with air. Dousing them in water that has had a little lemon juice added will help prevent browning but may not be desirable if a truly pure apple taste is important.

The following list discusses the characteristics of a selection of apple varieties.

CRABAPPLES are very small, tart, and red with a blush of yellow or white. Their peak season is the fall. They are typically used in sauces, pickles, and relishes.

GOLDEN DELICIOUS APPLES are sweet, juicy, and crisp with a golden, freckled skin. Their peak season is September to May. They are all-purpose apples that stay white after cutting longer than other varieties.

GRANNY SMITH APPLES are all-purpose apples with green skin and white to light green flesh. They are tart, extremely crisp, and fine-textured. Their peak season is April to July.

GREENING APPLES have green skin and firm flesh with a mild, sweet-tart flavor. Their peak season is October to March. They are used for pies and sauces as well as baking and freezing.

JONATHAN APPLES have bright red skin flecked with yellow-green and tender, semitart flesh. Their peak season is September to January. They are eaten out of hand and used for pies and sauces. They can also be frozen.

MCINTOSH APPLES are primarily red, streaked with yellow or green. Their flesh is very white. The peak season for McIntoshes is September to June. They are eaten out of hand and used for sauces and cider. They can also be frozen.

NORTHERN SPY APPLES are crisp, firm-textured, and juicy with a sweet-tart taste. Their peak season is October to November. They are excellent in pies.

RED DELICIOUS APPLES have bright red skin speckled with yellow and flesh that is yellow-white with a firm texture and sweet taste. Their peak season is September to June. They are all-purpose apples.

ROME BEAUTY APPLES have bright red skin and flesh that is firm with a mild tart-sweet flavor. Their peak season is October to June. They are all-purpose apples.

Cameo   *Ida Red*

WINESAP APPLES have bright red skin with some yellow-green and flesh that is firm, tart-sweet, and aromatic. Their peak season is October to June. They are eaten out of hand and used for pies, sauces, baking, or freezing.

There are many other varieties of apples available only in certain areas of the country. If you have any questions, ask your purveyor or other reputable source for the best use for a particular variety.

Red Delicious   *Lady*

Strawberries, raspberries, blueberries, and blackberries are so seasonal that for most people, seeing a particular berry in the market means that spring has arrived or summer is at its height. Some varieties can be found at virtually any time of the year, giving chefs the options they need to purchase berries of the best quality for both seasonal and year-round menu offerings.

Strawberries

Berries tend to be highly perishable (with the exception of cranberries) and are susceptible to bruising, mold, and overripening in fairly short order. Inspect all berries and their packaging carefully before you accept them. Juice-stained cartons or juice leaking through the carton is a clear indication that the fruit has been mishandled or is old. Once berries begin to turn moldy, the entire batch goes quickly.

Cranberries are almost always cooked. Other berries can be featured as fresh fruit or used as a flavoring, purée, or sauce in a number of dishes. They may also be used to flavor vinegars, marinades, or dressings. When fresh berries are out of season, IQF (individually quick-frozen) berries are often a perfectly fine substitute. Dried berries can be used to great advantage in winter fruit compotes, stuffings, breads, or other sweet and savory dishes. Some classic preparations that use berries include strawberry shortcake, fresh berry cobblers, pies, jams, jellies, and ice creams. The following list covers a selection of berry varieties.

BLUEBERRIES are blue/purple with a dusty silver-blue bloom. Their peak season is late summer. They are eaten fresh and used in baked goods, in jams, and as flavoring for vinegar. They are also dried.

BOYSENBERRIES are a hybrid of raspberry, blackberry, and loganberry. They are eaten fresh and made into preserves, wine, or syrup.

CLOUDBERRIES are orange-red, similar to raspberries.

CRANBERRIES are shiny red (some have a white blush), dry, and sour. Their peak season is the fall. They are generally cooked to make relishes, sauces, and jellies, although there are some raw chopped relishes. They may also be frozen or dried.

CURRANTS may be red, black, or white. Red is generally sweetest. Their peak season is midsummer. They are generally cooked for use in relishes, jams, jellies, wines, cordials, or syrups.

ELDERBERRIES are small and purple-black. They are made into jams, jellies, wines, or cordials.

GOOSEBERRIES have a smooth skin (some with a papery husk still attached). They may be green, golden, red, purple, or white. Some have fuzzy skins. They are crushed in fools or used in compotes, relishes, jams, and jellies.

MULBERRIES resemble but are unrelated to raspberries. They are juicy with a slightly musty aroma. Their peak season is midsummer. They are used in wines, syrups, and cordials.

RASPBERRIES are actually clusters of tiny fruits (drupes), each containing a seed. Sweet and juicy, raspberries may be red, black, or white. The dewberry is a type of raspberry. Raspberries have two peak seasons: early summer and late summer. They are eaten fresh and used in baked items, syrups, purées and sauces, cordials, and syrups. They are also used to flavor vinegar.

STRAWBERRIES are red shiny, heart-shaped berries with seeds on the exterior. Their peak season is late spring into early summer. They are eaten fresh and used in shortcakes, baked goods, purées, and preserves.

CITRUS FRUITS

Citrus fruits are characterized by extremely juicy, segmented flesh and skins that contain aromatic oils. Grapefruits, lemons, limes, oranges, and tangerines are the most common citrus fruits. They range in flavor from the sweetness of oranges to the tartness of lemons.

Oranges come in four basic types: juice, eating, Mandarin, and bitter. Juice types have smooth skin that is somewhat difficult to peel. They are usually plump and sweet, which makes them ideal for juicing. Varieties include the small Valencia and the blood orange (with orange skin and red pulp). Eating types include the navel, which is large, seedless, and easy to peel. Mandarin types, such as the tangerine and clementine, have thin skins that peel very easily. They may or may not have seeds. Bitter oranges such as Seville and bigarade are used almost exclusively for making marmalade. In fact, a hollandaise sauce variation flavored with the juice and rind of a bitter orange is called bigarade sauce.

Grapefruits have yellow skin with an occasional rosy blush where the sun hits them. They are juicy, tart-sweet, and available with either white (actually yellow), pink, or red flesh.

The following list covers a selection of citrus fruits.

BLOOD ORANGES have orange skin with a blush of red. They are aromatic and have pockets of dark red or maroon flesh. They are juiced, eaten fresh, or used in sauces or as a flavoring ingredient.

Oranges   *Lemons*   *Limes*

JUICE ORANGES have orange skin mottled with green. They are extremely juicy with a smooth, sweet flavor and are used for juice.

MANDARINS have deep orange, smooth skin with a "nipple" on one end. The skin is loosely attached to the flesh. Mandarins are seedless and usually eaten fresh or canned.

NAVEL ORANGES have relatively smooth orange skin. They are seedless and may be juiced or eaten fresh. The zest may be used as is or candied.

SEVILLE ORANGES have a sour flavor. They are typically made into marmalade.

TANGERINES are orange with a lightly pebbled to smooth skin that is loosely attached to the fruit. They are juicy with a sweet-tart flavor and usually have many seeds. They are juiced or eaten fresh.

TEMPLE ORANGES have orange skin with a slightly pebbled texture. They have a juicy, slightly tart flavor and are eaten fresh.

UGLI FRUITS are hybrid citrus, with wrinkled yellow-green skin and pink-yellow seedless flesh also known as uniq fruit. They are eaten fresh.

MEYER LEMONS are thought to be a lemon-orange cross. They look like a large orange with a small "nipple." The flesh is a light orange-yellow color, and the juice is sweeter than regular lemon juice. Meyer lemons are juiced, zested (the zest may be candied), or used as flavoring and in baked items.

LEMONS have yellow-green to deep yellow skin, seeds, and extremely tart flesh. They are juiced, zested (the zest may be candied), or used as flavoring.

PERSIAN LIMES have dark green, smooth skin and flesh that is tart and seedless. They are juiced, zested (the zest may be candied), or used as flavoring.

KEY LIMES are light green. They are juiced or used as flavoring. Their most famous use is in key lime pie.

PINK GRAPEFRUITS have yellow skin with a pink blush. The flesh is pink. They are juiced or eaten fresh.

RED GRAPEFRUITS have yellow skin with a red blush. The flesh is deep red with a mellow sweet-tart flavor. They are juiced or eaten fresh.

WHITE GRAPEFRUITS have yellow skin, sometimes with a green blush. The flesh is pale yellow; seedless varieties are available. They are eaten fresh, juiced, zested (zest may be candied), or used as flavoring.

GRAPES

Grapes, either with seeds or without, are juicy fruits that grow in clusters on vines. Technically, they are berries, but because they include so many varieties and have so many different uses, they are usually grouped separately from other berries.

Of the many kinds available for both eating and wine making, two of the most popular are Thompson Seedless, which is appropriate for both cooking and eating out of hand, and Napoleon Red, a good table variety. Grapes also are dried to form raisins. Harvested at different times in different locales, they can usually be found throughout the year.

There are some classic dishes that make use of grapes as an ingredient. The most famous is sole Véronique, poached fillet of sole in a cream sauce garnished with peeled seedless grapes. For the most part, though, grapes are used in fruit platters, as an accompaniment to cheese plates, or in salads. The following list covers a selection of grape varieties.

THOMPSON SEEDLESS GRAPES are green with thin skins. Available year-round, they are used as a table grape and are also dried as raisins.

CONCORD GRAPES have thick skins that may be deep purple, red, or white. The skins slip easily from the flesh. Their peak season is late summer into fall. They are used for juices, jams, jellies, syrups, and preserves.

BLACK GRAPES have deep purple skins. These table grapes are usually seedless. Their peak season is summer, but they may be available sporadically at other times, especially winter.

RED EMPEROR GRAPES have a light to deep red, tightly adhering thin skin, occasionally with green streaking. They have seeds. The peak season for these table grapes is summer, though they are available year-round as an imported item.

BLACK CORINTH GRAPES are small, red to light purple, seedless table grapes. Their peak season is late summer.

Green table grapes

Pineapples

Mango

Pomegranates

Kiwi

Blueberries
Raspberries

Lemons

Papaya

Strawberries

Persimmons

Figs

Star fruit
(carambóla)

Honeydew   *Cantaloupe*

MELONS

Melons are fragrant, succulent fruits, most of which are related to squashes and cucumbers. They also come in many varieties and range from the size of an orange to that of a watermelon. The four major types are cantaloupes, watermelons, winter melons (honeydew, casaba, crenshaw), and muskmelons.

The ability to determine when a melon is ripe is one that eludes some people. Depending upon the type, you will look for a variety of different signs. Cantaloupe melons should have a "full slip." This means that the melon ripened on the vine and grew away from the stem, leaving no rough edge. Unripe cantaloupes usually have a scarred or rough end. Other melons may become slightly soft at the stem end when properly ripened, though for certain varieties this indicates that they are over the hill. Aroma and heaviness for size are the best keys to determining ripeness, regardless of variety. The following list covers a selection of melon varieties.

CANTALOUPES have netting or veining over the surface of their skins. Their flesh is smooth, orange, juicy, and fragrant. Their peak season is summer. Signs of ripeness include a full slip, coarse netting, yellow to buff ground color, and pleasant melon aroma.

CASABA MELONS have skin that is light to yellow green. Their peak season is early fall. Signs of ripeness include a smooth, velvety feel to the skin and a melon aroma.

CRENSHAW MELONS are salmon-colored with very fragrant flesh. Their peak season is early fall. Signs of ripeness include a rich melon aroma and slight softening near the stem.

GALLIA MELONS have green flesh that tastes and smells like cantaloupe. Their peak season is early summer.

HONEYDEW MELONS are juicy and have green flesh. Their peak season is summer. Signs of ripeness include a velvety to slightly sticky feel to the skin. The skin should be yellow with no greenish cast.

MUSKMELONS are deeply ridged and have bright orange, aromatic flesh. Their peak season is mid- to late summer. Signs of ripeness include a yellow to buff base color (not green) and a full slip.

PERSIAN MELONS have dark green skin with yellow markings and yellow-orange flesh. Their peak season is summer. Signs of ripeness include heaviness for their size and some yielding when pressed.

WATERMELONS are large, oblong-shaped green melons with red or yellow flesh. There are some seedless varieties. Their peak season is mid- to late summer. In a ripe melon, the underside of the fruit, where it rested on the ground, has some color and is not dead white.

PEARS

Pears are to the French what apples are to the Americans. They also come in many varieties, with the most commonly available being Bartlett, Bosc, Comice, d'Anjou, and Seckel. It is difficult to find perfectly ripe pears in the market; because the flesh of pears is extremely fragile, they are picked for shipping before they have fully ripened. The fruit will soften at room temperature.

In addition to being eaten out of hand, pears are often poached whole or used in sorbet. The best uses for several varieties are listed below.

Bartlett pears

BARTLETT PEARS usually have green skin, which turns yellow as the fruit ripens. Some Bartlett varieties are red. Their peak season is in the fall. They are eaten fresh and poached.

BOSC PEARS have a long neck and dark russeted skin. They turn brown when ripe. Their peak season is in the late fall. They are eaten fresh, poached, and baked.

COMICE PEARS are round with a short neck and stem. They are greenish-yellow in color and may have a reddish blush. They are very sweet and juicy and are eaten fresh in salads and desserts. Comice pears are available from August through April.

Bartlett and Bosc

Red Bartlett (top) and Seckel (bottom)

D'Anjou

D'ANJOU PEARS have green skin that becomes yellow as they ripen, and may have brown scarring. Their peak season is in the fall. They are eaten fresh, poached, and baked.

SECKEL PEARS have green skin with a red blush. They are small and crisp. Their peak season is in the fall. They are eaten fresh.

WILLIAM PEARS have a long neck, yellow skin, and strong perfume. Their peak season is in the fall. They are used in preserves and to flavor the cordial Poire William.

RHUBARB

Although technically a vegetable, rhubarb has been classified here as a fruit because of the way it is used. Often known as *pie plant,* it grows in long stalks with broad, somewhat curly leaves. Only the reddish green stalks are eaten; the leaves should not be used because they contain large quantities of oxalic acid, a toxic compound. Rhubarb is crisp and very sour, so it is usually cooked and sweetened. In addition to being served as a dessert, it is classically combined with rich, oily fish such as mackerel or bluefish.

STONE FRUITS

Peaches, nectarines, apricots, plums, and cherries are often referred to as stone fruits because they have one large central pit, or stone. In North America, they typically come into peak season throughout the late spring and summer. Stone fruits need to be handled delicately because their flesh has a tendency to bruise easily. Stone fruits are used in preserves, shortcakes, pies, and cobblers, as well as in savory dishes. In addition to their fresh form, these fruits are also commonly available canned, frozen, and dried. Fruit brandies, wines, and cordials flavored with peaches, cherries, and plums are produced in many countries.

PEACHES are sweet and juicy, have a distinctively fuzzy skin, and come in many varieties. All peaches fall into one of two categories, clingstone or freestone. Clingstone peaches have flesh that clings to the pit, whereas the flesh of freestone peaches separates easily. Peach flesh comes in a range of color, from white to creamy yellow to yellow-orange to red, with a whole host of combinations possible.

APRICOTS resemble peaches in some ways. They have slightly fuzzy skin but are smaller, with somewhat drier flesh. The skin ranges in color from yellow to golden orange, and some have rosy patches.

NECTARINES are similar in shape, color, and flavor to peaches, and they are classified similarly, as either clingstone or freestone. They have smooth skin, and some varieties may have flesh whose texture closely resembles that of plums.

Nectarines

Figs

CHERRIES are grown in numerous varieties and come in many shades of red, from the light crimson of Queen Anne to the almost black Bing. They vary in texture from hard and crisp to soft and juicy, and flavors run the gamut from sweet to sour. Cherries are available in a number of different forms. They may be found fresh throughout their growing season, and are also sold canned or dried. Fillings for danish, pies, and other pastries can also be found, as well as cherry syrups and cherry-flavored cordials. Kirschwasser, a clear cordial, is often used in bakeshops and kitchens.

Bananas

PLUMS can be as small as an apricot or as large as a peach. The possible colors include green, red, purple, and various shades in between. When ripe, they are sweet and juicy, and some have sour skins that contrast nicely with their succulent flesh. Plums fall into two categories, dessert and cooking. Cooking plums are generally drier and more acidic than dessert plums, but both types can be eaten raw. Greengage plums, with green skin and flesh, are sweet and a popular dessert variety. Damson plums have purple skin with a silver-blue bloom; they are the best known cooking plums, used in preserves, conserves, and pies, and are also eaten fresh. Santa Rosa plums are red with light yellow flesh and are eaten fresh. Black Friar plums also are eaten fresh; they have dark purple skins with a silvery bloom and deep red to purple flesh. Prune plums, or Italian plums, are small, with purple skin and green flesh that is relatively dry and separates cleanly from the pit; they are eaten fresh and dried as prunes.

TROPICAL FRUITS

A wide variety of fruits fall into this category, which is named for the general climatic conditions under which the fruits are grown. Bananas are the most familiar. Unlike most fruits, bananas are almost always picked green and allowed to ripen in a controlled environment. In this category are dates, figs, guava, kiwis, mangos, papayas, pineapples, plantains, pomegranates, passion fruit, and star fruit. An ever-increasing number of tropical fruits are available through regular and specialty resources.

GENERAL FRUIT INFORMATION

FRUIT TYPE	GRADES AVAILABLE	PACK, COUNT, AND/OR WEIGHT	YIELD PERCENTAGE	AVAILABLE FORMS
Apples	U.S. Extra Fancy, U.S. No. 1, No. 2	Carton/box (variable count, cell-packed or loose, 34–43 lb/15.4—19.5 kg)	76%	Fresh, sliced, frozen, dried, canned
Apricots	U.S. No. 1, No. 2	Lug (22 lb/10 kg)	80%	Fresh, dried (sulfured, unsulfured)
Bananas	U.S. No. 1, No. 2	Box (40 lb/18 kg; average count for No. 1 grade is 115)	75%	Fresh, dried
Berries	U.S. No. 1	Basket (half pint, pint, or quart); flat (12 baskets, 10 lb/4.5 kg)	90–100%	Fresh, dried, IQF,* frozen in syrup
Cherries	U.S. No. 1	Lugs, 20 lb/9 kg; California lugs, 18 lb; flats, 12 lb/5.4 kg	80%	Fresh, dried, frozen, canned
Citrus	U.S. Fancy, No.1, Combination, or No. 2	Case (count varies by variety from 32 to 100)	65% (varies by use)	Fresh, frozen juice concentrate
Figs	U.S. No. 1	Case (35 count.)	80%	Fresh, dried, IQF
Grapes	U.S. Fancy, Extra No. 1, No. 1.	Lug/carton (12, 17, or 23 lb/ 5.4, 7.7, or 10.4 kg)	93%	Fresh, dried (raisins)
Kiwis	U.S. Fancy, No. 1, No. 2	Case (39 count)	89%	Fresh
Mangos	No Federal Grades	Case (12 count)	62%	Fresh, purée
Melon	U.S. No. 1, Commercial, No. 2	Case (5 count)	65–70%	Fresh
Nectarines	U.S. Extra No. 1, No. 1	Case (25 lb/11.3 kg)	87%	Fresh, IQF frozen
Papayas	U.S. No. 1, No. 2	Carton/flat (8 to 14 count)	84%	Fresh, purée
Peaches	U.S. Extra Fancy No. 1, Fancy No. 2	Lug/case (35 lb/15.9 kg)	75%	Fresh, IQF slices, frozen in syrup, canned halves, canned slices
Pears	U.S. Extra Fancy No. 1, Fancy No. 2	Case (40 to 90 count, by variety)	87%	Fresh, dried, canned, sliced, IQF slices
Persimmons	No Federal Grades	Flat (11–13 lb/5–6 kg, 25 count)	85%	Fresh
Pineapples	U.S. Fancy No. 1, No. 2	Case (5 count)	62%	Fresh, canned (sliced, crushed, chunks), juice
Plums	U.S. No. 1	Lug/case (28 lb/12.7 kg)	78%	Fresh
Pomegranates	No Federal Grades	Case (24 count)	58%	Fresh
Rhubarb	U.S. No. 1	Case (20 lb/9 kg); box (5 lb/2.25 kg); bulk (varies)	90%	Fresh, IQF pieces

*IQF = individually quick-frozen

VEGETABLES

Vegetables include a number of foods that botanically are classified as fruits. Tomatoes, for example, are really fruits. Their culinary application is the guiding principle for placing them in this section, rather than the previous one.

As we continue to explore other cuisines and to reexamine the more familiar dishes of the regions of our own country, we are becoming more adventurous in our selection of vegetables and the ways they are served — with meats or on their own as appetizers, salads, and entrées.

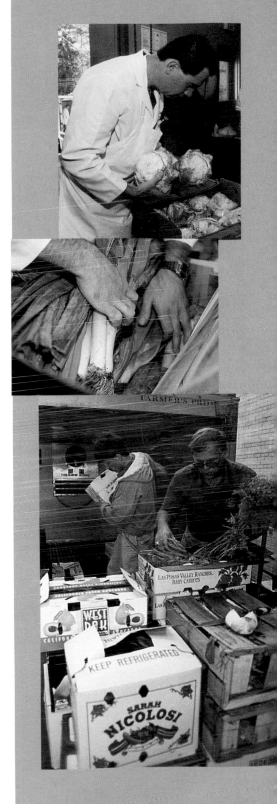

AVOCADOS

These egg- or pear-shaped vegetables have green to black leathery skin, which can be smooth or bumpy. Avocado flesh is buttery smooth and delicately flavored, green near the skin and yellow toward the center. Cut surfaces must be treated with lemon or lime juice to prevent browning.

Haas avocados have dark, pebbly skin and a more pronounced pear shape than other varieties. Florida varieties are smoother and brighter green in color. If avocados are not ripe when you purchase them, hold them at room temperature, around 70°F/21°C, until they soften. Use ripe avocados as soon as possible. If they must be stored in the refrigerator, allow them enough time to warm slightly before serving them, so that their full flavor is allowed to develop.

Avocado

CABBAGE FAMILY

The cabbage (brassica) family includes broccoli, Brussels sprouts, cauliflower, kale, kohlrabi, collard greens, and many kinds of cabbage. All have a similar flavor. Some members of this family, such as cauliflower and green cabbage, are referred to as heading cabbages. Others, such as bok choy, form loose heads. Still others do not form a head, but are prized for their roots; turnips and rutabagas are also members of the brassica family, but they are more commonly thought of as root vegetables. The following list covers a selection of brassica varieties.

BROCCOLI is usually dark green, sometimes with a purple cast. The peak season is summer, though imported broccoli is available year-round. Quality indicators include tight flowers, stem ends that are not split, and firm leaves.

Broccoli

Napa cabbage

BROCCOLI RABE (also *broccoli raab, rapini*) is leafy and green with small florets and stems. The peak season is summer to fall. Quality indicators include no yellowing of flowers, firm leaves, and bright white to light green stems.

BRUSSELS SPROUTS are small, round, cabbage-shaped, and light green. The peak season is late fall to winter, though they can be found year-round from storage or imports. Quality indicators include firmly attached leaves and bright stem ends.

BOK CHOY is a loose-head cabbage with deep green glossy leaves and green to white stems. The peak season is summer into fall, though it is available year-round. Quality indicators include fresh, firm stems and leaves that are not withered. Baby bok choy (shown on page 165) may be served uncooked.

NAPA CABBAGE is a long, heading cabbage with a light yellow-green color. The peak season is summer into fall, but it is available year-round. Quality indicators include no browning or withering of leaves and relative heaviness for size.

GREEN CABBAGE is a tight, round heading cabbage. The color may range from light to medium green. The peak season is late summer to fall, but it is available year-round. Quality indicators include loose wrapper leaves that should be firm, no withering, no browning or bore holes, and relative heaviness for size. Early varieties are less tight. Winter or storage cabbages are more firmly packed.

RED CABBAGE is a tight, round heading cabbage ranging in color from deep purple to maroon. The stems on individual leaves are white, giving a marbled appearance when cut. The peak season is late summer to fall, though it is available year-round. Quality indicators include loose wrapper leaves with a greenish cast. The head should be very glossy, with creamy white veining.

SAVOY CABBAGE is a moderately tight, round heading cabbage. The leaves are textured, giving a waffled appearance. The peak season is summer to fall. Quality indicators include a fresh appearance, color that ranges from moderate to light green, and loose wrapper leaves that should be firm.

CAULIFLOWER is a snowy to creamy white flowering head with green leaves. The peak season is late summer to fall, though it is available throughout the year in most areas. Quality indicators include firmly attached wrapper leaves, no wilting, and no evidence of yellowing, browning, or opened flowers.

KOHLRABI (also known as *cabbage turnip*) is a round, turnip-shaped bulb with stems and leaves attached. The peak season is early summer, though it is periodically available throughout the year. Quality indicators include firm bulbs with no evidence of cracking, firm green leaves, and no evidence of yellowing.

Cucumbers, eggplant, and the many squash varieties are all members of the gourd family. They have fairly tough rinds, thick flesh, and flat, oval seeds. Summer squashes (zucchini, yellow, crookneck, pattypan) are picked when they are immature to ensure a delicate flesh, tender seeds, and thin skins. Winter squashes (acorn, butternut, Hubbard, pumpkin, spaghetti) are characterized by their hard rind and seeds.

Cucumbers are a common ingredient in salad bowls and crudité platters and are frequently a part of uncooked sauces or soups such as salsa or gazpacho. They can also be served cooked or as a part of a creamed soup.

SLICING CUCUMBERS are long, narrow, and green, occasionally with a pale green or yellow underside. They are used in salads, relishes, and uncooked sauces, and for pickling.

KIRBY CUCUMBERS are short, chubby cylinders with green skin, deep ridges, and warts. They are eaten fresh and pickled.

ENGLISH, BURPLESS, or SEEDLESS CUCUMBERS are long, even cylinders with some ridging and no seeds. They are used for salads and crudités.

Summer squashes have relatively subtle flavors, which make them popular for use in vegetable stews or soups as a vehicle for other flavors.

PATTYPAN SQUASH is yellow (it may also be mottled or streaked with green) and has a flattened ball shape. It is generally steamed, sautéed, or pan-fried.

CHAYOTE (also known as mirliton) is pear-shaped and light green with deep ridging between its halves. Its large seed is edible. It is generally steamed, sautéed, stir-fried, stuffed, or pan-fried.

CROOKNECK SQUASH has yellow skin and a bent, narrow neck. It is generally steamed, sautéed, or pan-fried.

YELLOW SQUASH is yellow with an elongated pear shape. It is generally steamed, sautéed, or pan-fried.

ZUCCHINI is probably the most familiar of the summer squashes. It has a cylindrical shape and is green with

English cucumbers   *Yellow squash*   *Zucchini*

flecks of yellow (a golden variety is deep yellow with green at the stem end). It is generally steamed, sautéed, or pan-fried. It is also used in fritters and quick breads.

Winter squash finds its way into all categories of food as well, from soups to cakes, pies, quick breads, and side dishes. These squash have a more pronounced flavor than summer squash. Frozen and canned squash is often available, as well as fresh squash.

ACORN SQUASH is dark green (some varieties may have an orange blush or be virtually all orange) with deep ridges and an acorn shape. It is generally baked, puréed, simmered, glazed with honey or maple syrup, or used to make soups.

BUTTERNUT SQUASH has tan, orange, or light brown skin and an elongated pear shape. It is generally baked, puréed, simmered, glazed with honey or maple syrup, or used to make soups.

HUBBARD SQUASH is dusty green and very warty. It is generally baked, puréed, simmered, glazed with honey or maple syrup, or used to make soups.

PUMPKINS are dark orange with deep ridges. They are generally baked, puréed, simmered, glazed with honey or maple syrup, or used to make soups, pies, or breads.

SPAGHETTI SQUASH is yellow and has a zeppelin shape. When cooked, its flesh separates into spaghettilike strands. It is generally steamed or roasted, and it may be served with herbs or sauces.

Eggplant comes in a range of shapes and sizes, from the slender Japanese varieties to very large specimens. Although many swear by their own technique for removing the bitterness from eggplant, the best advice is to choose eggplant that is not overly large for its type. Roasted eggplant is used in numerous dishes, ranging from Middle Eastern dips to luscious soups. It is wonderful grilled, pan-fried, braised, or stewed. Ratatouille, a famous French vegetable stew, makes liberal use of eggplant.

PURPLE (STANDARD) EGGPLANT may have a rounded or elongated pear shape with glossy purple-black skin and green leaves at the stem end. It is generally stewed, braised, roasted, or grilled.

JAPANESE EGGPLANT has a long, narrow, cylinder shape with glossy purple-black skin. It is generally stewed, braised, roasted, or grilled.

WHITE EGGPLANT may be long or round (egg-shaped). Some are streaked with purple. It is generally stewed, braised, roasted, or grilled.

Eggplant

LEAFY VEGETABLES

This category includes both salad greens and cooking greens. Salad greens include lettuces of all types, as well as other leafy vegetables, such as Belgian endive and watercress, that are typically eaten raw as part of a salad. Today's chef has more options than ever before regarding the type and quality of greens featured in the salad bowl. Special mixes, such as mesclun or baby lettuces, can be purchased. Some mixes include herbs and edible flowers, such as nasturtiums, chrysanthemums, or pansies. Salad greens are highly perishable and require delicate handling. You will find through experience that some lettuces keep better than others.

ARUGULA has tender leaves ending in rounded teeth. It has a pungent, peppery flavor, becoming very biting as it ages.

BELGIAN ENDIVE has a tight, oblong head with white leaves and some yellow or green at the tips. It is slightly bitter and is often prepared as a braised vegetable as well as being used as a salad item.

BOSTON (BUTTERHEAD) LETTUCE is a heading lettuce with soft, tender leaves. It has a mild, delicate flavor and may also be braised as a vegetable in addition to being used as a salad item.

CURLY ENDIVE (also known as *frisée*) is a heading lettuce with sharp teeth on curly leaves. Its interior leaves are light yellow. It is slightly to very bitter.

ESCAROLE is a heading lettuce with scalloped edges on its leaves. It is slightly to very bitter and is often used in soups and stews and as a cooking green.

ICEBERG LETTUCE is a tight heading lettuce with pale green leaves. It has a very mild flavor.

LEAF LETTUCE is a loose-head lettuce with tender leaves that may be all green or tipped with red. It is usually mild, becoming bitter with age.

OAK LEAF lettuce is tender with deep scalloping on its leaves. It has a nutty flavor.

MÂCHE (also known as lamb's lettuce or corn salad) has very tender, rounded leaves and an extremely delicate flavor.

RADICCHIO is a heading form of endive with deep red to purple leaves and white veining. It is bitter.

Green leaf lettuce

Mâche

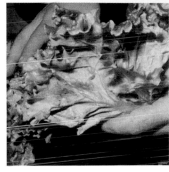
Red leaf lettuce

Baby bok choy

ROMAINE LETTUCE grows as a long, cylindrical head. The outer leaves are heavily ribbed. The inner leaves, sometimes known as the heart, have a milder, sweeter flavor than the outer leaves.

WATERCRESS has rounded scallops on its leaves and a peppery flavor.

Chefs across the country are beginning to make use of the wide variety of cooking greens. A resurgence of interest in authentic regional dishes from this country and other cuisines around the world is partly responsible. Another important factor is the public's awareness of the potent vitamin and mineral "cocktails" they deliver. Cooking greens can be eaten raw, as long as they have been harvested while still quite young. In fact, many mesclun mixes include one or two of these greens. Still, the most common way to serve these greens is as a cooked dish.

Cooking greens have a rather limited shelf life and should be used as soon after purchase as possible. Some types are perfect for quick stir-fries. Others are best when treated to a long, slow simmer, with or without the addition of ham hocks, bacon, or other smoked pork items. The following list covers a selection of cooking greens.

BEET GREENS have flat leaves with red ribbing. They are available year-round, especially during the summer into fall. They are generally steamed, sautéed (especially with garlic), or braised.

Swiss chard

COLLARD GREENS have large, flat, rounded leaves. Their peak season is fall. They are generally steamed, sautéed (especially with garlic), or braised.

DANDELION GREENS have narrow leaves with deep teeth on the edges. Their peak season is spring. They are generally steamed, sautéed (especially with garlic), or braised.

KALE has ruffled leaves. The peak season is late fall. It is generally steamed, sautéed (especially with garlic), or braised.

MUSTARD GREENS have deeply scalloped, narrow leaves. Their peak season is summer. They are generally steamed, sautéed (especially with garlic), or braised.

SPINACH LEAVES are deep green and may be deeply lobed or flat, depending upon variety. They are available year-round. They are generally steamed, sautéed (especially with garlic), or braised.

Frisée

SWISS CHARD has deeply lobed, glossy dark green leaves. The stems and ribs may be white, deep ruby, or variegated. The peak season is fall. It is generally steamed, sautéed (especially with garlic), or braised.

TURNIP GREENS have broad, flat green leaves with a coarse texture. Their peak season is summer into fall. They are generally steamed, sautéed (especially with garlic), or braised.

MUSHROOMS

Mushrooms are varieties of fungus. Some varieties are edible and delicious; some are edible but of little culinary consequence; still others are toxic, producing a host of unpleasant effects ranging from cramps and headaches to death. Knowing your purveyor is of great importance when you have wild mushrooms on the menu.

Cultivated mushrooms include familiar common white mushrooms as well as exotic varieties such as shiitakes and oyster mushrooms. There are still some varieties of mushroom that cannot be successfully farm-raised yet and are offered to either the purveyor or the chef by professional or amateur foragers.

Of the mushrooms that are edible, most are completely edible, but if the stem is tough or has a sticky skin, it should be trimmed away. Many mushrooms are available dried as well as fresh. Dried versions of morels, shiitake, and wood ears are sometimes preferred for certain dishes, as they deliver an even more intense flavor than fresh. The following list covers a selection of mushroom varieties.

BOLETUS MUSHROOMS have rounded, golden brown caps that are usually fused to bulbous white stems. Their tender, smooth, cream-colored flesh stays pale when cooked, and has an earthy to meaty flavor. They are highly perishable. Their sticky caps may be peeled. Also known as *boletes*, *cèpes* or *ceps*, and *porcini*, these are available fresh or dried.

CHANTERELLES are trumpet-shaped with yellowish stems and frilly brown caps with a delicate, almost fruity aroma. Their convoluted shape holds dirt, so they should be washed and dried well. They require longer cooking than other mushroom types. They are also known as *gallinaccio*, *cantarello*, and *finferlo*.

CREMINI MUSHROOMS are a firm, dark brown variation of the standard white mushroom. They are used in many of the same applications as white mushrooms, but they have a somewhat fuller flavor. Other names for this variety are common *brown mushroom* and *Roman mushroom*.

MORELS have delicate, spongy flesh with an earthy, nutty, or spicy flavor. They have blunt, deeply pitted, cone-shaped hollow caps and stems. Their color is pale tan to dark brown or gray. They tend to hold dirt and may be washed using a small brush to remove dirt and worms. They are also known as *morille* and *spugnole*.

Button mushrooms

Portobello mushrooms

Trumpet Royal mushrooms

Shiitake mushrooms

Chanterelle mushrooms

Oyster mushrooms

OYSTER MUSHROOMS are fan-shaped, like an oyster shell. They have smooth cream- to gray-colored caps and a short creamy white stem and gills. They grow on tree trunks and range from dime size to several inches across. They may require longer cooking than other types of mushrooms. Another name for these is *oak mushroom*.

PORTOBELLO MUSHROOMS are fully matured cremini mushrooms. They have very large (4 to 6 inches on average) flat caps with fully exposed gills. When cooked, they have a dense texture and meaty flavor. Portobello stems are very woody and are usually used only to flavor stocks, soups, and sauces.

SHIITAKE MUSHROOMS have dark brown umbrella-shaped caps with cream-colored stems and gills (the caps may show cream-colored cracks as well). Their flavor is earthy, woodsy, and slightly meaty. Their tough stems are usually removed before use.

TRUFFLES are a rounded, knobby, rough-skinned variety of mushroom. They grow underground and are found with the help of specially trained dogs or pigs, which are used to sniff them out. Truffles have a heady, earthy aroma and flavor. Black truffles, the finest of which come from France, are always cooked, and there are many classic recipes that call for them. White truffles, the finest of which come from Italy, are often served raw, thinly shaved over risotto and other rice and pasta dishes. Canned truffles and truffle essence are available.

Onions and their relations belong to the lily family. All varieties share a pungent flavor and aroma. It is hard to imagine a kitchen without a good supply of this basic item. Garlic, shallots, and dry and green onions are used in so many dishes and in so many guises that they are quite rightly considered indispensable.

Onions are part of that most fundamental aromatic combination, mirepoix. Garlic is called for in so many preparations that it is nearly taken for granted; roasted, chopped or slivered, it can be found as a topping for flatbreads, a flavoring for sauces, or the main ingredient in soups or sauces. Over the past several years, sweet onions have become widely available at certain times of the year. These varieties are often featured either raw or as grilled or broiled dishes.

Onions fall into two main categories, reflecting the state in which they are used: cured (dried) and fresh (green). Dry onions should be stored in a relatively cool, dry area of the kitchen in the bags or boxes in which they are received. Fresh onions should be stored under refrigeration. One additional member of this family not included here is chives; their main culinary application is similar to that of fresh herbs.

BOILING ONIONS are small round onions with white skins. They are used in stews, soups, and compotes.

CIPPOLINI ONIONS are round, flattened small onions with yellow papery skins. They are baked, grilled, and cooked en casserole.

GARLIC (standard and elephant) grows in a bulb covered with white or red-streaked papery skin; the individual cloves also are encased in skin. It is used as a flavoring ingredient and may be roasted or puréed.

Red onions

Leeks

Spanish onions

White onions

Scallions

LEEKS are long fresh onions with white root ends and dark green tops. They are grilled, steamed, or braised, and often are served cold. They are used extensively in soups, stews, and sauces as a main ingredient or secondary flavoring.

PEARL ONIONS are small, oval onions. They may be white, yellow, or red. They are boiled, pickled, or brined and often served in stews and braises.

RAMPS are wild leeks with small white stem ends and flat green tops. They are stewed or sautéed.

RED ONIONS have a round, flattened shape with red papery skin. Their flesh is red and white. They are grilled, eaten raw in salads, and used in compotes and marmalades.

SCALLIONS (green onions) are fresh onions with white root ends becoming green at tops. The entire plant is used, except for the roots. They are eaten raw as crudités and in salads and as an ingredient in uncooked sauces. They are also cooked in many Asian dishes.

Ramps

SHALLOTS may be cloves bunched together or single shallots, with light brown papery skin. Their flesh is white/purple. They are used primarily as a flavoring ingredient.

SPANISH ONIONS are large onions with yellow to yellow-brown skin. Their flesh is milder than that of yellow onions. They are used as an aromatic ingredient in soups, stews, sauces, and braises.

SWEET ONIONS (Walla Walla, Vidalia, Maui) generally have a flattened shape. The skin varies by type from white to tan. The flesh is very sweet. They are eaten raw in salads, or grilled or sautéed.

YELLOW ONIONS are moderately sized with yellow-brown, papery skin and pungent flesh. They are used as an aromatic ingredient in soups, stews, sauces, and braises.

WHITE ONIONS are moderately sized with white, papery skin. They are used as an aromatic ingredient in soups, stews, sauces, and braises.

PEPPERS

There are two basic types of peppers: *sweet peppers,* which are sometimes called *bell peppers* because of their shape, and *chiles,* which are related to sweet peppers but usually are smaller and contain spicy, volatile oils.

Sweet peppers come in many colors — green, red, yellow, even creamy white and purple. All peppers start out green, but special varieties will ripen into rich, vibrant colors. Sweet peppers have similar flavors, though red and yellow varieties tend to be sweeter than green peppers. Still, it is acceptable to substitute one color for another. The only big difference in most dishes will be their appearance.

Red peppers   *Green peppers*   *Jalapeños*

Sweet peppers are hollow, except for whitish ribs and a core with a cluster of small seeds. Generally, both ribs and core are removed before use. One of the most popular ways to prepare sweet peppers is to roast them and toss them with a good-quality oil, fresh herbs, and cracked black pepper. They are featured in sauces such as coulis, in antipasto, as the topping for grilled breads or pizzas, and in salads.

Look for firm peppers when examining a delivery or the offerings in the local farmer's market. The skin should be tight and glossy, with no puckering or wrinkling. The flesh should be thick and crisp. Depending upon the variety, the color may be mottled or streaked and the pepper may be more or less deeply ridged. Peppers will keep well for several days, but if some peppers in a box begin to soften or develop brown spots, check the entire box immediately and use all acceptable peppers as soon as possible. Once they start to lose quality, it goes quickly.

A whole host of fresh and dried chiles are available. The hotter the chile, the more important it is to handle it carefully. Use sensible precautions when working with such powerhouses as habaneros or banana chiles. Wear gloves, wash your cutting surface and knife, and avoid contact with sensitive tissue such as the eyes.

Chiles are available fresh, canned, dried (whole, flaked, and ground), and smoked. Frequently, dried and/or smoked chiles are given a name different from that of the fresh version.

ANAHEIMS are tapered, deep green, and glossy. A red variety is known as the Colorado chile. They are available fresh and dried.

BANANA CHILES (also called *Hungarian wax peppers*) are small, tapered, and pale yellow to yellow-green. They are considered one of the hottest chiles. They are used in sauces and stews, and may be pickled.

HABANEROS are small (about the size of a cherry tomato), lantern-shaped, and wrinkled. They are extremely hot.

Anaheims

Scotch bonnets

Poblanos

SCOTCH BONNETS are similar to habaneros. Both are used in sauces and bottled condiments. The Scotch bonnet is a standard ingredient in Jamaican jerk seasoning.

JALAPEÑOS are medium to very hot. They are compact and tapered, and may be deep green or red. They are available fresh, pickled, and canned whole or sliced. Chipotles are dried, smoked jalapeños and are available dried or canned in adobo sauce.

POBLANOS are mild, very deep green to black, and tapered, with a flattened shape. Poblanos are often stuffed, battered, and fried to make the dish chiles rellenos. Dried ripe poblanos are called anchos.

SERRANOS are tiny, skinny, dark green, and very hot. They may be used in place of jalapeños, or use jalapeños in their place.

POD AND SEED VEGETABLES

Pod and seed vegetables include fresh legumes, such as peas, beans, and bean sprouts, as well as corn and okra. All are best eaten young and fresh, when they are at their sweetest and most tender. Once picked, their natural sugars begin to be converted into starch. Garden peas and sweet corn are especially prone to flavor loss. They can lose their sweetness as soon as a day after being harvested, and after a few days they become mealy.

If possible, purchase pod and seed vegetables from local growers to minimize the amount of time between picking and serving. This is especially important with peas and corn, which are highly perishable. Peas, beans, and corn are also available in dried form, as discussed in Chapter Ten, "Dry Goods Purchasing and Identification." Some fresh peas and beans are eaten whole, when the pods are still fleshy and tender — for example, sugar snap peas, snow peas, green beans, and wax beans. In other cases, the peas or beans (such as limas, scarlet runners, and black-eyed peas) are removed from their inedible pods.

Below is a list of beans with edible pods.

GREEN BEANS are long, slender beans with an even, matte green color. Their peak season is mid- to late summer. They are available fresh or frozen and are generally served as a side dish or pickled. Wax beans, or yellow beans, are similar in texture and flavor.

HARICOTS VERTS have velvety skin and are smaller and more slender than regular green beans. Their peak season is mid- to late summer. They are typically served as a side dish.

ROMANO BEANS are similar in color to regular green beans, but they are wider and flatter, with a more developed flavor. Their peak season is mid- to late summer. They are often braised with ham or bacon.

BURGUNDY BEANS or purple beans are similar in shape to regular green beans, but with deep purple to maroon skin that turns green as they are cooked. Their peak season is mid- to late summer. They are typically served as a side dish.

There are also a variety of beans with inedible pods. All the beans in the following list are available both fresh and dried.

FAVA BEANS grow in pods that are long, large, and light green. The beans are a delicate green color and are almost kidney-shaped. Their peak season is spring to early summer. They are frequently cooked and puréed. They may be cooked and eaten cold. Large beans must be peeled before eating.

Snow peas *Green beans*

CRANBERRY BEANS grow in pods that are white streaked with red. The beans are a creamy white mottled with red. Their peak season is midsummer. They are cooked and served whole as a side dish or in soups. They may also be braised or puréed.

BORLOTTI BEANS grow in pods that are green to buff. The beans are creamy white. Their peak season is early to midsummer. They are cooked and served whole as a side dish or in soups. They may also be braised or puréed.

FLAGEOLETS grow in pods that are green. The beans are a light green. Their peak season is midsummer. They are cooked and served whole as a side dish or in soups. They may also be braised or puréed.

BLACK-EYED PEAS grow in pods that are green, often mottled with brown. The peas are round and tan with a black "eye." Their peak season is throughout summer and into fall. They are cooked and served whole as a side dish or in soups. They may also be braised or puréed. Hoppin' John is a well-known dish using black-eyed peas.

Wax beans

Fava beans

Sugar snap peas

Several varieties of peas are commonly found in the market.

GARDEN PEAS, also called *petit pois*, grow in pods that are tapered and rounded, and they should "squeak" when rubbed together. The peas are round and light drab green when raw. Their peak season is early spring to summer. They can be steamed, stewed, puréed, and used in soups.

SNOW PEAS have flat pods and are drab green when raw. The pod is edible. Their peak season is early spring to summer. They are usually steamed or stir-fried.

SUGAR SNAP PEAS have pods that are a deeper green than garden or snow peas. The pod is edible. Their peak season is early spring to summer. They are usually steamed or stir-fried.

POTATOES

Potatoes, once America's favorite side dish, later maligned by those watching their weight as too fattening and by sophisticated diners as pedestrian, are now back in the limelight as a terrific source of various nutrients. Today, you can choose from a wide variety of special potatoes, as well as the more familiar favorites, to establish a repertoire of potato dishes that belong in virtually any category of the menu.

Sweet potatoes and yams share culinary characteristics with potatoes. Like potatoes, they are starchy, tuberous vegetables that can be baked, steamed, or boiled. Botanically, sweet potatoes (members of the genus *Impomoea*) and yams (members of the genus *Dioscorea*) are unrelated to each other. Neither is botanically related to the white potato (member of the nightshade family, genus *Solanum*). In general, sweet potatoes tend to be a little moister and more deeply colored than yams. Yams are said to have a more understated flavor than sweet potatoes, but both are noticeably sweeter than white potatoes.

To retain quality potatoes should be kept dry, away from excess heat and light, and in a well ventilated area.

CHEF'S POTATOES are firm, smooth, and relatively round, with white to light tan skin and shallow eyes. They are available year-round (fresh in late summer into fall) in a range of sizes. The younger the potato, the moister it is. Chef's potatoes are used for salads, purées, soups, and other dishes. They tend to be too moist for baking.

RED POTATOES are firm, smooth, and relatively round, with light pink to dark red skin and shallow eyes. They are available year-round (fresh in late summer into fall) in a range of sizes. The younger the potato, the moister it is. Red potatoes are used for salads, purées, soups, and other dishes. They are excellent for oven-roasting.

RUSSET or IDAHO POTATOES are oblong with brown russeted skin. They are available year-round (fresh in late summer into fall). These potatoes are best for baking and for frying.

HEIRLOOM POTATOES include a number of special potatoes, shown at right, that have become increasingly available. The varieties include purple potatoes, such as caribe potatoes, with deep purple skin and blue or white flesh, and elongated potatoes, known as fingerling or banana potatoes, which typically have tan or brown skin and flesh that ranges from white to a creamy yellow. Different varieties have different starch contents. Experiment with unfamiliar varieties to determine their culinary characteristics.

Peruvian blue   *Russian banana*

Ruby crescent

YUKON GOLD POTATOES, also called *Yellow Finn potatoes*, have brown, tan, or red skin with buttery golden flesh. They are available year-round (fresh in late summer into fall). They can be baked, puréed, or used in casseroles and salads.

IRISH POTATOES are relatively round but generally misshapen, with deep eyes. They are available in the late summer and are best for boiling.

SALT POTATOES are small, no more than 1 inch in diameter. They are available year-round (fresh in late summer into fall) and are best for boiling and steaming.

NEW POTATOES are the same as chef's potatoes, but no more than 1–1½ inches in diameter. They are available in the early summer and are best for steaming and oven-roasting with herbs.

BLISS POTATOES are the same as red potatoes, but no more than 1–1½ inches in diameter. They are available in the early summer and are best for steaming and oven-roasting with herbs.

SWEET POTATOES have light to deep orange skin with deep orange, moist flesh, dense texture, and sweet flavor. They may be rounded or tapered. They are available year-round (fresh in late summer into fall) and can be roasted, boiled, puréed, or used in casseroles and soups.

YAMS have tan to light brown russeted skin with pale to deep yellow flesh. They are available year-round (fresh in late summer into fall) and can be roasted, boiled, puréed, or used in casseroles and soups.

Russet potatoes   *Red potatoes*

Sweet potatoes   *Chef's potatoes*

Sugar Pumpkin

Cheese Pumpkin

Acorn Squash

Sweet Corn

Onions

Delicata Squash

Garlic

Ginger

Cauliflower

Horseradish

Red Cabbage

Butternut Squash

Garlic

Shallots

Brussels Sprouts

Carrots with tops

ROOTS AND TUBERS

Roots and tubers serve as nutrient reservoirs for the upper part of the plant. Consequently, they are rich in sugars, starches, vitamins, and minerals. Popular root vegetables include beets, carrots, celeriac, parsnips, radishes, rutabagas, and turnips. Salsify, a relatively unfamiliar root to most Americans, is also part of this group; it may be white or black, and has a flavor that some consider similar to oysters, others say is like that of asparagus, and still others compare to artichoke hearts.

Tubers are enlarged, bulbous roots capable of generating a new plant. In addition to potatoes, described above, this category includes Jerusalem artichokes, a vegetable that is not native to Jerusalem and which is not technically an artichoke.

Roots and tubers should be stored dry and unpeeled. If they come with greens attached, these should be fresh at the time of purchase and cut off as soon as possible thereafter. When they are properly stored, most roots and tubers will retain good quality for several weeks.

BEETS

BABY BEETS are small, red, and ball-shaped. They are available throughout summer and into fall (greens are available from midspring). They can be roasted or boiled and are frequently glazed or used in salads.

RED BEETS are deep red or maroon and may be medium-sized or large. They may be sold with or without tops. They are available throughout summer and into fall (greens are available from midspring). They can be roasted or boiled and are frequently glazed or used in salads and soups (borscht). They are also pickled.

Horse carrots

GOLDEN BEETS are small, yellow to golden-orange, and ball-shaped. They are available throughout summer and into fall. They can be roasted or boiled and are frequently glazed or used in salads.

CARROTS are one of the most popular vegetables, and are available year-round. They are sold in bags or crates, and may be known as horse carrots. Some carrot varieties are short, others long, still others slender, and others relatively thick. As carrots age, the core becomes tough, woody, and fibrous. Carrots may be harvested when immature, as baby carrots. Carrots are also available with the green tops still attached. The tops should be cut away before storage to prevent wilting.

Beets

CELERIAC is closely related to celery. It develops a large knobby root with a crisp texture and intense celery flavor. Only the root portion of the vegetable is eaten. Although it is available year-round, it is best in the fall and winter. It is served raw in salads or crudité, or it may be cooked in the same manner as potatoes.

Good-quality celeriac is heavy and firm, free of deep dents, cuts, or soft spots. If the stems and leaves are attached, they should be fresh and green.

JERUSALEM ARTICHOKES, or sunchokes, are tubers that resemble a small nubby potato. They have a sweet, almost nutty, taste and a crisp texture. They can be eaten raw or cooked, and can be found in markets year-round. Jerusalem artichokes are at their most plentiful from late fall through early spring.

Look for clean, firm tubers with unblemished, glossy tan or matte brown skin with no greenish tinge or signs of sprouting or mold.

JÍCAMA is a white-fleshed tuber that can weigh from half a pound to five pounds or more. It has a thin brown skin and crisp, juicy, relatively bland-tasting flesh. Look for hard, unblemished jícama roots that are heavy for their size. Typically served raw in slices or sticks in salads, it may also be stir-fried or boiled and baked, as for a potato.

PARSNIPS are shaped similarly to carrots, with pale yellow to off-white skin and flesh and a mild celery-like fragrance. Parsnips are available year-round, although the supply is lowest during the summer months. Very large parsnips are likely to have tough, woody cores. They should taper smoothly to a slender tip. The roots should be firm and fairly smooth with a few hairlike rootlets. Most parsnips are sold without the leafy tops, but if they are still attached, they should look fresh and green.

TURNIPS

PURPLE-TOPPED TURNIPS, also called *white turnips*, are white and similar in shape to beets, with a purple blush on the stem end. They are available fresh from late fall into the early winter months, and throughout winter from storage. They are used in soups and as a side dish.

RUTABAGAS, or swedes, are large, ball-shaped, and usually coated with wax. They are also known as *yellow turnips*. They are available fresh from late fall into the early winter months, and throughout winter from storage. They are used in soups and as a side dish, often puréed.

RADISHES

RED RADISHES are small and ball-shaped or slightly elongated. They may be cherry red, striped, white, or specialty colors (purple, orange, etc.). They are available fresh from early spring and fall crops and throughout the year from storage or imports. They may be sold in cello packs or in bunches with green tops. They are generally used raw in salads and crudité platters.

Turnips

Daikon radishes

Red radishes

DAIKON RADISHES are carrot-shaped with white flesh that has a mild radish flavor. They are available year-round. They are either cooked or served raw, often grated or julienned as a garnish.

SALSIFY (OYSTER PLANT)

WHITE SALSIFY is similar in appearance to a parsnip. It is available from fall into winter. It is usually served as a side vegetable, often creamed.

BLACK SALSIFY is a long, stick-shaped vegetable with black matte skin. It is available from fall into winter. It is usually served as a side vegetable, often creamed.

SHOOTS AND STALKS

This family consists of plants that produce shoots and stalks used as vegetables. Globe artichokes (thistlelike plants that are members of the aster family), asparagus (another member of the lily family), celery, fennel, and fiddleheads (which are part of the growth cycle of a fern) are examples. The stalks should be firm, fleshy, and full, and should show no evidence of browning or wilting.

TOMATOES

These succulent vegetables are actually berries. They are grown in hundreds of varieties, in colors from green to yellow to bright red. Basic types include small, round cherry tomatoes, oblong plum tomatoes, and large beefsteak tomatoes. All have smooth, shiny skin, juicy flesh, and small, edible seeds. Most tomatoes grown commercially are picked unripe and allowed to ripen in transit. Most chefs prefer to find locally grown varieties whenever possible, since vine-ripened tomatoes may have especially rich flavors and are typically very juicy.

Fiddlehead ferns

Fennel

Celery

Asparagus

Artichokes

Recently growers have been able to produce several special varieties of tomatoes for the market, including special low-acid golden varieties of both slicing and cherry tomatoes. Heirloom species can also be found occasionally.

There are no hard-and-fast rules about which tomatoes work best under which circumstances, but there is a certain etiquette. Slicing tomatoes, including deeply ridged beefsteaks and other varieties, are favored for use in salads and other uncooked preparations. Plum, or Roma, tomatoes, with their relatively drier flesh, are preferred for sauces and purées. The following list covers several varieties of tomatoes.

Slicing tomatoes

BEEFSTEAK TOMATOES are large, deep red, deeply ridged, and juicy. Their peak season is late summer. They are usually served fresh in salads and sandwiches.

CHERRY TOMATOES are small red or yellow tomatoes that grow in clusters. The yellow version is low in acid. Their peak season is mid- to late summer. They are usually served fresh in salads and crudité platters.

Plum tomatoes

CURRANT (CRANBERRY) TOMATOES are very small red or yellow tomatoes that grow in clusters. The yellow version is low in acid. Their peak season is mid- to late summer. They are usually served fresh in specialty items.

PEAR TOMATOES are small, pear-shaped red or yellow tomatoes. Their peak season is mid- to late summer. They are usually served fresh in salads or crudité platters.

PLUM (ROMA) TOMATOES are egg-shaped and red with a relatively greater proportion of flesh to seeds than other tomatoes. Their peak season is late summer. They are typically used in sauces, purées, soups, and other cooked dishes.

Heirloom tomatoes

YELLOW SLICING TOMATOES are large, round, smooth-skinned, low-acid tomatoes. Their peak season is mid- to late summer. They are served fresh in salads and other uncooked preparations.

TOMATILLOS are small, round green berries with a light green to brown papery husk that must be removed before use. They taste like green tomatoes. Their peak season is mid- to late summer. They are usually cooked before use in sauces.

Tomatillos

GENERAL VEGETABLE INFORMATION

VEGETABLE BY TYPE	GRADES AVAILABLE	PACK/WEIGHT AND/OR COUNT	YIELD PERCENTAGE	AVAILABLE FORMS
Artichokes, globe	U.S. No. 1, No. 2	Half carton (20 lb/9 kg; 18, 24, 48 or 60 count)	40%	Fresh, frozen, marinated, canned in brine
Asparagus	U.S. No. 1, No. 2	Case/pyramid (30 lb/13.6 kg)	Varies	Fresh (green, white), canned (pieces), frozen (pieces)
Avocados	U.S. No. 1, Combination, No. 2	Case (36 count)	50%	Fresh, purée, canned
Beans	U.S. No. 1, Combination, No. 2	Case (varies by type)	Varies	Fresh, frozen, canned
Beets	U.S. No. 1, No. 2	Case (25 lb/11.3 kg, 24-bunch count)	75%	Fresh, frozen, canned
Broccoli	U.S. Fancy, No. 1, No. 2	Case (14-bunch count)	65%	Fresh, frozen (pieces, spears, chopped)
Brussels sprouts	U.S. No. 1, No. 2	Flat (12 pints)	75%	Fresh
Cabbage	U.S. No. 1, Commercial	Case (varies by type)	75%	Fresh
Carrots	U.S. Extra No. 1, No. 1, No. 1 Jumbo, No. 2	Case (varies by type)	85%	Fresh
Cauliflower	U.S. No. 1	Case (12 heads)	58%	Fresh, frozen (florets)
Celeriac	U.S. No. 1	Case (12 lb/5.4 kg)	75%	Fresh
Celery	U.S. Extra, No. 1, No. 2	Carton (weight and count vary)	75%	Fresh
Chiles	No Federal Grades	Case, bulk (by lb/kg)	85%	Fresh
Corn, sweet	U.S. Fancy, No. 1, No. 2	Case, crate, or bag (weight and count vary)	48%	Fresh, frozen (kernels), canned (kernels)
Cucumbers	U.S. Fancy, Choice, Extra No. 1, No. 1 Small, No. 1 Large	Carton, bushel, California lug (weight and count vary)	93% (peeled) or 68% (peeled and seeded)	Fresh
Eggplant	U.S. Fancy, No. 1, No. 2	Case (weight and count vary)	81%	Fresh
Fennel	U.S. No. 1	Case (24 each)	45%	Fresh
Greens, cooking	Varies By Type	Case (weight varies)	Average of 65%	Fresh
Kohlrabi	No Federal Grades	Case (24 lb/11 kg)	58%	Fresh
Lettuces	Varies By Type	Case, flat (weight varies)	Average of 70%	Fresh
Mushrooms	(Grading For Domestic Only) No. 1, No. 2	Basket (3 lb/1.3 kg); case or flat (weight varies), bulk (by lb/kg)	Average of 95%	Fresh, dried, canned
Onions, cured (dry)	U.S. No. 1, Export No. 1, Commercial, No. 1, Boilers, No. 1 Picklers, No. 2	Bag (25–50 lb/11.3–22.7 kg)	85%	Fresh
Onions, green (fresh)	U.S. No. 1, No. 2	Case (48-bunch count)	90%	Fresh
Parsnip	U.S. No. 1, No. 2	Case (12 lb/5.4 kg)	80%	Fresh, frozen
Peas	U.S. No. 1, Fancy	Case or bunch (weight and count vary)	Varies by type	Fresh, frozen, canned
Peppers, sweet	U.S. Fancy, No. 1, No. 2	Case (weight varies)	Average of 80%	Fresh
Potatoes	Varies By Type	Case, bag (weight varies)	Varies by use	Fresh
Squashes, summer	U.S. No. 1, No. 2	Case (weight and count vary)	80%	Fresh
Squashes, winter	U.S. No. 1, No. 2	Case (weight and count vary)	75%	Fresh, frozen (pieces), canned (pieces)
Tomatoes	U.S. No. 1, Combination, No. 2, No. 3	Case (weight and count vary)	Varies by use	Fresh, canned, dried
Turnips	U.S. No. 1, No. 2	Case (25 lb/11.3 kg)	80%	Fresh
Rutabagas	U.S. No. 1, No. 2	Case (50 lb/22.7 kg)	80%	Fresh

HERBS

Herbs are the leaves of aromatic plants and are used primarily to add flavor to foods. Most herbs are available both fresh and dried, although some (thyme, bay leaf, rosemary) dry more successfully than others. Aroma is a good indicator of quality in both fresh and dried herbs. An herb's scent can be tested best by using the fingers to crumble a few leaves and then smelling those leaves. A weak or stale aroma indicates old and less potent herbs. Fresh herbs also may be judged by appearance. They should have good color (usually green), fresh-looking leaves and stems, and no wilt, brown spots, sunburn, or pest damage.

Herbs can be used to flavor numerous preparations. They should enhance and balance, not overpower, a dish's flavors. Only occasionally, and with a purpose, should the herb's flavor be dominant. When used with discretion, herbs can transform the taste of plain foods into something special. Overuse or inappropriate use can cause, at best, a dish that tastes of nothing but herbs or, at worst, a culinary disaster.

Certain herbs have a special affinity for certain foods. Guidelines stating which herbs are most effectively paired with which foods are not cast in stone, but following them can familiarize the chef with the way herb-food combinations work and can serve as a springboard for future experimentation.

Fresh herbs should be minced or cut in chiffonade as close to serving time as possible. They are usually added to a dish toward the end of the cooking time, to prevent the flavor from cooking out. Dried herbs are usually added early in the process. For uncooked preparations, fresh herbs should be added well in advance of serving, to give them a chance to blend with the other elements.

In general, herbs should be stored loosely wrapped in damp paper or cloth. If desired, the wrapped herbs may then be placed in plastic bags to help retain freshness and reduce wilting of leaves. They should be kept at 35° to 45°F/ 2° to 7°C). Some leafy herbs, especially watercress and parsley, may be held by trimming the stems and placing the bunch in a jar of water. Wrap damp toweling around the leaves or cover with a plastic bag to prevent wilting.

Foodservice operations that grow herbs may have an excess at certain times of the season. These may be used for making compound butters, pestos, or flavored vinegars or oils. The following list covers a selection of herb varieties.

BASIL has leaves that are pointed and green. Purple varieties and large- or small-leafed varieties are available. There are also specialty types with cinnamon, clove, and other flavors. The peak season is summer, but it is usually available year-round. Uses for basil include flavoring for sauces, dressings, and chicken, fish, and pasta dishes; pesto sauce; and infusing oils and vinegars.

BAY LEAVES are smooth and rigid. Their peak season is summer, but they are usually available dried year-round. Bay leaves are used to flavor soups, stews, stocks, sauces, and grain dishes.

Mint

Basil

Chives

Tarragon

Chervil

Dill

Oregano

Cilantro

Sage

Thyme

Marjoram

Flat-leaf Parsley

Rosemary

CHERVIL is similar in shape to parsley but with finer leaves and a mild licorice flavor. The peak season is summer. It is a component of fines herbes. The whole small leaves, or pluches, are often used to garnish egg, chicken, and shellfish dishes.

CILANTRO is similar in shape to flat-leaf parsley, with a pronounced, unique flavor. It peaks in mid- to late summer. It is a component of many Asian, South American, and Central American dishes.

DILL has a feathery shape with a strong aroma. It peaks in late summer. It is used to flavor sauces, stews, and braises (especially central and east European dishes). Dill seeds are used to make pickles.

MARJORAM has small, rounded leaves with a flavor similar to oregano. It peaks in the summer. It is used in Greek, Italian, and Mexican dishes. It is especially suitable for vegetable dishes.

MINT has pointed, textured leaves. The size varies by type, as does the particular flavor. Mint peaks throughout summer. It is used to flavor sweet dishes and beverages, as a tisane, and in some sauces. Mint jelly is traditional with lamb.

OREGANO has small oval leaves. It peaks throughout summer. It is used with a variety of sauces and with poultry, beef, veal, lamb, and vegetables.

PARSLEY has feathered leaves. It may be curly or flat (Italian parsley). It is available year-round. Parsley is a component of fines herbes and of bouquet garni. It is used as a garnish and a flavoring for sauces, soups, dressings, and other dishes.

ROSEMARY LEAVES are shaped like pine needles and have a resiny aroma and flavor. It is available year-round. Large branches of rosemary can be used as skewers. Rosemary is popular in Middle Eastern dishes, grilled foods, and marinades. Dried rosemary is nearly as intense in flavor as fresh.

SAGE has large green leaves that may be furry or velvety. It peaks in summer. It is popular as a flavoring in stuffings, sausages, and some stews.

SUMMER SAVORY has a flavor similar to thyme. Winter savory is more like rosemary. It peaks in the summer and fall. It is used in salads, stuffings, and sauces.

TARRAGON has narrow leaves with a pronounced licorice flavor. It peaks in summer. Tarragon is a component of fines herbes and is the main flavoring of béarnaise sauce. It is also used with chicken, fish, veal, and egg dishes.

THYME has very small leaves. Different varieties are available with special flavors (including nutmeg, mint, lemon). It peaks in the summer. Thyme is used to flavor soups, stocks, stews, and braises.

A concentrated source of many nutrients, dairy products and eggs hold a prominent place on menus, on their own and as key ingredients in many preparations. Béchamel sauce, for example, is based on milk. Cream, crème fraîche, sour cream, and yogurt are used to finish sauces, to prepare salad dressings, and in many baked goods. Cheeses may be served as is, perhaps as a separate course with fruit, or as part of another dish. Fondue, raclette, and Welsh rarebit are classic dishes from around the world that feature cheese. And eggs appear not just on their own, in breakfast dishes to dessert soufflés, but in numerous sauces, especially emulsified ones such as hollandaise and mayonnaise.

DAIRY AND EGG PURCHASING AND IDENTIFICATION

PURCHASING AND STORAGE

Although dairy products and eggs are two different products, freshness and wholesomeness are important for both. Both are also highly perishable. For these reasons, careful purchasing and storage procedures are extremely important.

The table below provides holding temperatures and average shelf life of eggs and various dairy products. Milk and cream containers customarily are dated to indicate how long the contents will remain fresh enough to use. Because the freshness period will vary, the chef should not combine milk and cream from different containers, to avoid contamination.

When used in hot dishes, milk or cream should be brought to a boil before being added to other ingredients. If milk curdles, it should not be used. Unfortunately, detecting spoilage by simply smelling or tasting unheated milk is often impossible.

When considering storage arrangements for dairy products, flavor transfer is a particular concern. Storing all milk, cream, and butter away from foods with strong odors is preferable. Cheeses should be carefully wrapped, both to maintain moistness and to prevent the odor from permeating other foods and vice versa.

Eggs should be refrigerated and the stock rotated to ensure that only fresh, wholesome eggs are served. The chef should inspect eggs carefully upon delivery, making sure that shells are clean and free of cracks. Eggs with broken shells should be discarded because of the high risk of contamination.

PROPER STORAGE TIMES AND TEMPERATURES FOR DAIRY PRODUCTS AND EGGS

PRODUCT	STORAGE TIME	TEMPERATURE
Milk, fluid, pasteurized (whole, low-fat, nonfat)	1 week	35°–40°F/2°–4°C
Milk, evaporated		
Unopened	6 months	60°–70°F/16°–21°C
Opened	3–5 days	35°–40°F/2°–4°C
Milk, sweetened, condensed		
Unopened	2–3 months	60°–70°F/16°–21°C
Opened	3–5 days	3°–40°F/°–4°C
Milk, nonfat dry		
Unopened	3 months	60°–70°F/16°–21°C
Reconstituted	1 week	35°–40°F/2°–4°C
Buttermilk	2–3 weeks	35°–40°F/2°–4°C
Yogurt	3–6 weeks	35°–40°F/2°–4°C
Cream		
Table or whipping	1 week	35°–40°F/2°–4°C
Ultrapasteurized	6 weeks	35°–40°F/2°–4°C
Whipped, pressurized	3 weeks	35°–40°F/2°–4°C
Ice cream	4 weeks	-10° to 0°F/-23° to -18°C
Butter	3–5 days	35°F/2°C
Margarine	5–7 days	35°F/2°C
Cheese, unripened, soft	5–7 days	35°–40°F/2°–4°C
Cheese, ripened, soft, semisoft	5–7 days	35°–40°F/2°–4°C
Cheese, ripened, hard	2–3 months	35°–40°F/2°–4°C
Cheese, very hard	2–3 months	35°–40°F/2°–4°C
Cheese foods	2–3 weeks	35°–40°F/2°–4°C
Cheese, processed		
Unopened	3–4 months	60°–70°F/16°–21°C
Opened	1–2 weeks	35°–40°F/2°–4°C
Eggs, whole, in shell	5–7 days	33°–38°F/1°–3°C
Eggs, whole, fluid	2–3 days	29° to 32°F/-1° to 0°C
Eggs, frozen	1–2 months	-10° to 0°F/-23° to -18°C
Eggs, dried	1–2 months	40°F/4°C

DAIRY PRODUCTS

Milk is invaluable in the kitchen, whether it is served as a beverage or used as a component in dishes. Fermented or cultured milk products, such as sour cream, yogurt, and buttermilk, are prized for their rich yet tangy flavor. Butter is used as a spread, as an ingredient in numerous dishes, as a final enrichment for sauces, and as a cooking fat for sautéing. Cheeses of all sorts have become increasingly popular as specialty or farmhouse-style cheeses are coming into the market. The ability to select, store, and serve cheeses can greatly enhance any restaurant that features cheese as a menu offering. Dairy products, such as dry milk powder, evaporated or condensed milk, and ice cream, are also part of the well-stocked kitchen's mise en place.

MILK

U.S. federal regulations govern how milk is produced and sold, to ensure that it is clean and safe to use.

Most milk sold in the United States has been pasteurized. In pasteurization, the milk is heated to 145°F (63°C) for 30 minutes or to 161°F (72°C) for 15 seconds in order to kill bacteria or other organisms that could cause infection or contamination. Milk products with a higher percentage of milkfat than whole milk are heated to either 150°F (65°C) for 30 minutes or to 166°F (74°C) for 30 seconds for ultrapasteurization.

The date stamped on milk and cream cartons can be seven, ten, or sixteen days from the point of pasteurization. It is an indicator of how long the unopened product will remain fresh and wholesome, assuming that it has been properly stored and handled.

Milk is also generally homogenized, which means that it has been forced through an ultrafine mesh at high pressure in order to break up the fat globules it contains. This fat is then dispersed evenly throughout the milk, preventing it from rising to the surface. Milk may also be fortified with vitamins A and D. Low-fat and skim milk are almost always fortified, because removing the fat also removes fat-soluble vitamins.

State and local government standards for milk are fairly consistent. Milk products are carefully inspected before and after processing. Farms and animals (cows, sheep, and goats) are also inspected, to ensure that sanitary conditions are upheld. Milk that has been properly produced and processed is labeled grade A.

Milk comes in various forms and is classified according to its percentage of fat and milk solids. The table on page 190 describes the kinds of available milks and creams.

CREAM

Milk, as it comes from the cow, goat, or sheep, contains a certain percentage of fat, known as *milkfat* or *butterfat*. Originally, milk was allowed to settle long enough for the cream, which is lighter than the milk, to rise to the surface. Today, a centrifuge is used to spin the milk. The cream is driven to the center, where it can be easily drawn off, leaving the milk behind.

Cream, like milk, is homogenized and pasteurized, and may also be stabilized to help extend shelf life. Some chefs prefer cream that has not been stabilized or ultrapasteurized, because they believe it will whip to a greater volume. Two forms of cream are used in most kitchens: heavy (whipping) cream and light cream. Half-and-half, a combination of whole milk and cream, does not contain enough milkfat to be considered a true cream; its milkfat content is approximately 10.5 percent.

ICE CREAM

In order to meet government standards, any product labeled as ice cream must contain a certain amount of milkfat. For vanilla, it is no less than 10 percent milkfat. For any other flavor, the requirement is 8 percent. Stabilizers can make up no

FORMS OF MILK AND CREAM

FORM	DESCRIPTION	TYPE OF CONTAINER
MILK		
Whole	Contains no less than 3.25% milkfat.	Bulk, gallon, half gallon, quart, pint, half pint
Low-fat	Usually contains 0.5 to 2% milkfat and is generally labeled accordingly.	Same as whole milk
Nonfat	Contains less than 0.5% milkfat.	Same as whole milk
Powdered or dry	Milk from which water is completely removed. Made from either whole or skim milk and labeled accordingly.	Bulk (50 lb, 24 oz)
Evaporated	Milk that has been heated in a vacuum to remove 60% of its water. May be made from whole or skim milk and is labeled accordingly.	Cans (14.5 oz, 10 oz, 6 oz)
Sweetened condensed	Evaporated milk that has been sweetened with 40% sugar by weight.	Same as evaporated
CREAM		
Heavy or whipping	Must contain at least 36% milkfat. Light whipping cream is occasionally available, containing 30 to 35% fat.	Quarts, pints, half pints
Light	Contains between 18 and 30% fat.	Same as heavy cream
Half-and-half	Contains between 10.5 and 18% fat. Used as a lightener for coffee.	Same as heavy cream; also in portion sizes

more than 2 percent of ice cream. Frozen dairy foods that contain less fat must be labeled as ice milk. Premium ice cream may contain several times more fat than is required by these standards. The richest ice creams have a custard base (a mixture of cream and/or milk and eggs), which gives them a dense, smooth texture.

Ice cream should readily melt in the mouth, and when it melts at room temperature, there should be no separation. The appearance of "weeping" in melting ice cream indicates an excessive amount of stabilizers.

Other frozen desserts similar to ice cream are sherbet, sorbet, frozen yogurt, and frozen tofu. Sherbet does not contain cream, so it is far lower in butterfat than ice cream; however, it does contain a relatively high percentage of sugar in order to achieve the correct texture and consistency when frozen. Some sherbets will contain a percentage of either eggs or milk, or both. Although the word *sherbet* is the closest English translation of the French word *sorbet*, sorbets are commonly understood to contain no milk.

Frozen yogurt and tofu often contain stabilizers. They may be lower in total fat than ice cream, or even fat-free, but some brands are still high in calories due to a high sugar content.

Test a variety of these products to determine which brands offer the best quality for the best price. Refer to Chapter Thirty-Five for information about preparing frozen desserts in your own kitchen.

BUTTER

Anyone who has accidentally overwhipped cream has been well on the way to producing butter. Historically, butter was churned by hand. Today it is made mechanically by high-speed mixing of cream that contains between 30 and 45 percent milkfat. Eventually the milkfat clumps together, separating out into a solid mass, which is butter; the fluid that remains is referred to as buttermilk (most buttermilk sold today, however, is nonfat milk that has been cultured).

The best-quality butter has a sweet flavor, similar to very fresh heavy cream. If salt has been added, it should be barely detectable. The color of butter will vary depending upon the breed of cow and time of year, but is usually a pale yellow.

The designation *sweet butter* indicates only that the butter is made from sweet cream (as opposed to sour). If unsalted butter is desired, be sure that the word *unsalted* appears on the package.

Salted butter may contain no more than a maximum of 2 percent salt. The salt can aid in extending butter's shelf life but can also mask a slightly "old" flavor or aroma. Old butter will take on a very faintly cheesy flavor and aroma, especially when heated. As it continues to deteriorate, the flavor and aroma can become quite pronounced and extremely unpleasant, much like sour or curdled milk.

The best-quality butter, labeled grade AA, is made from sweet cream and has the best flavor, color, aroma, and texture. Grade A butter also is of excellent quality. Both grades AA and A contain a minimum of 80 percent fat. Grade B may have a slightly acidic taste, as it is made from sour cream.

FERMENTED AND CULTURED MILK PRODUCTS

Yogurt, sour cream, crème fraîche, and buttermilk are all produced by inoculating milk or cream with a bacterial strain that causes fermentation to begin. The fermentation process thickens the milk and gives it a pleasantly sour flavor.

Yogurt is made by introducing the proper culture into milk (whole, low-fat, or nonfat may be used). Available in a variety of container sizes, yogurt can be purchased plain or flavored with different fruits, honey, coffee, or other ingredients.

Sour cream is a cultured sweet cream that contains about 16 to 22 percent fat. It comes in containers of various sizes, beginning with a half pint. Low-fat and nonfat versions of sour cream are available.

Crème fraîche is similar to sour cream but has a slightly more rounded flavor, with less bite. It is often preferred in cooking because it tends to curdle less readily than sour cream when used in hot dishes. This product is made from heavy cream with a butterfat content of approximately 30 percent. The high butterfat content helps account for its higher cost. Although crème fraîche is available commercially, many operations make their own by heating heavy cream, adding a small amount of buttermilk, and allowing the mixture to ferment at room temperature until thickened and lightly soured.

Buttermilk, strictly speaking, is the by-product of churned butter. Despite its name, it contains only a very small amount of butterfat. Most buttermilk sold today is actually nonfat milk to which a bacterial strain has been added. Usually sold in pints or quarts, buttermilk is also available as a dried powder for baking uses.

CHEESE

The variety of cheeses produced throughout the world is extensive, ranging from mild, fresh cheeses (pot cheese or cottage cheese) to strongly flavored, blue-veined cheeses (Roquefort or Gorgonzola) and hard grating cheeses (Parmesan or Romano). Cheeses are used in many dishes and require careful handling and selection. Some cheeses are excellent for cooking, while others become a hopelessly stringy mass when subjected to heat. Selecting the right cheese for the intended effect is important, because cheese can be quite expensive.

Most cheeses are made through the following procedure: Milk is combined with the appropriate starter (either rennet, which contains an enzyme, or an acid such as tartaric acid or lemon juice), causing the milk solids to coagulate into curds. The remaining liquid is known as the whey. The curds are then processed in various ways, depending on the type of cheese desired. They may be drained and used immediately, as fresh cheese, or they may be pressed, shaped, inoculated with a special mold, and aged. Whey is also used to make some cheeses.

Cheese is made from a variety of different milks — cow's milk, goat's milk, sheep's milk, even buffalo's milk. The type of milk used will help to determine the cheese's ultimate flavor and texture.

Natural cheeses are considered "living" in much the same way that wine is considered living. The cheese will continue to grow, developing or aging to maturity (ripening), and finally spoiling (overripening). Processed or pasteurized cheeses and cheese foods, on the other hand, do not ripen and their character will not change.

Cheeses may be grouped according to the type of milk from which they are made, texture, age, or ripening process. The terms used are:

Fresh cheese

Soft or rind-ripened cheese

Semisoft cheese

Hard cheese

Grating cheese

Blue-veined cheese

Fresh cheeses include cottage cheese, fresh goat cheese, mozzarella, fromage blanc, ricotta, and quark. These cheeses are moist and very soft. They have a flavor that is generally termed mild, but fresh cheese made from goat's or sheep's milk may seem strong to some tastes. The table on page 196 lists and describes several fresh cheeses.

Soft cheeses, such as Brie or Camembert (see page 195), usually have a surface mold. This soft, velvety skin is often edible, though some people find it too strong to enjoy. The cheese ripens from the outside to the center. When fully ripe, a soft cheese should be nearly runny, with a full flavor. The table on page 197 lists and describes several soft cheeses.

Semisoft cheeses are more solid than soft cheeses but do not grate easily. They can be sliced, however. An inedible wax rind may be used to coat the cheese, in order to preserve moisture and extend shelf life. Edam, Muenster, and Port Salut are among the best-known semisoft cheeses. These cheeses are

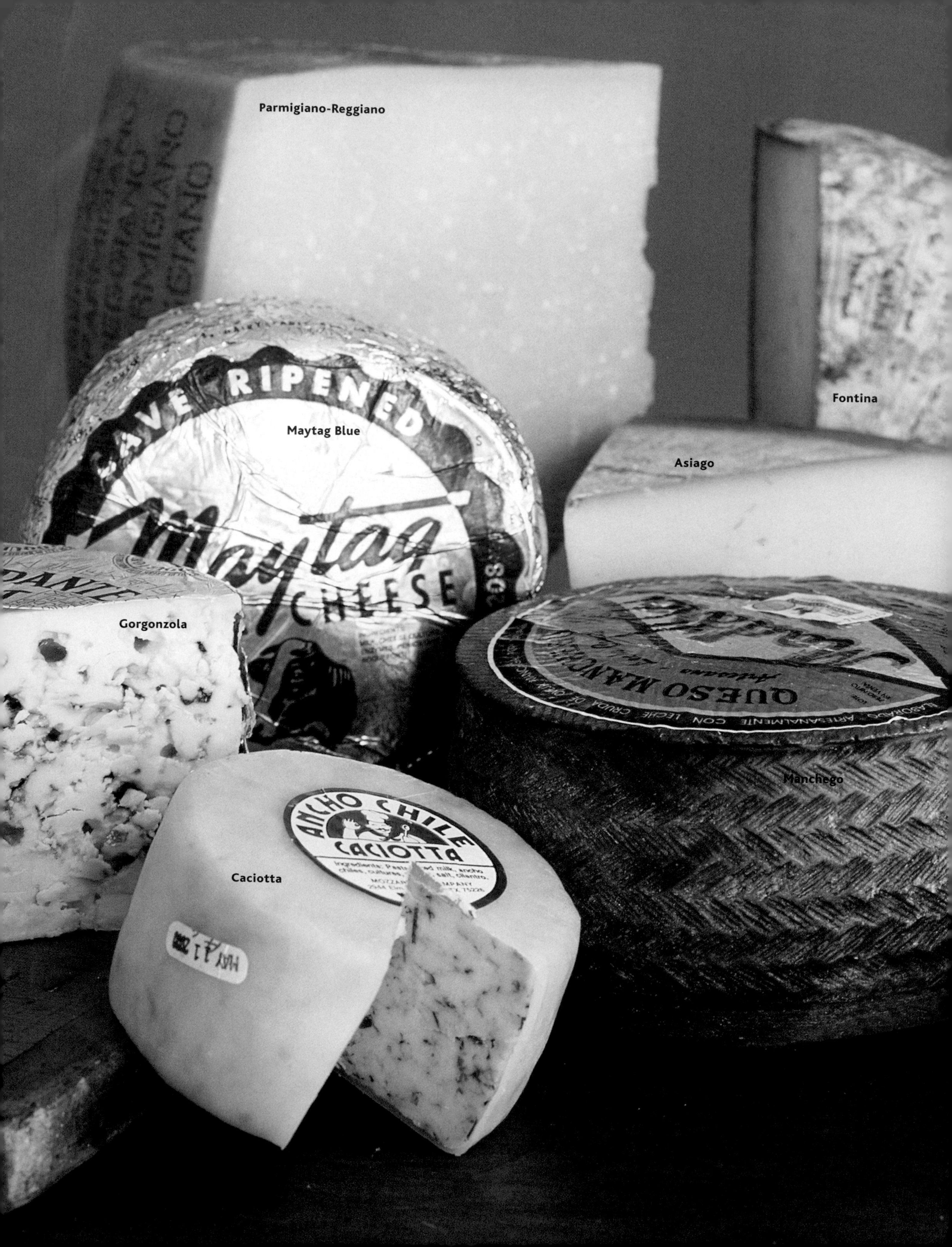

Parmigiano-Reggiano

Fontina

Maytag Blue

Asiago

Gorgonzola

QUESO MANCHEGO

Manchego

ANCHO CHILE
CACIOTTA

Caciotta

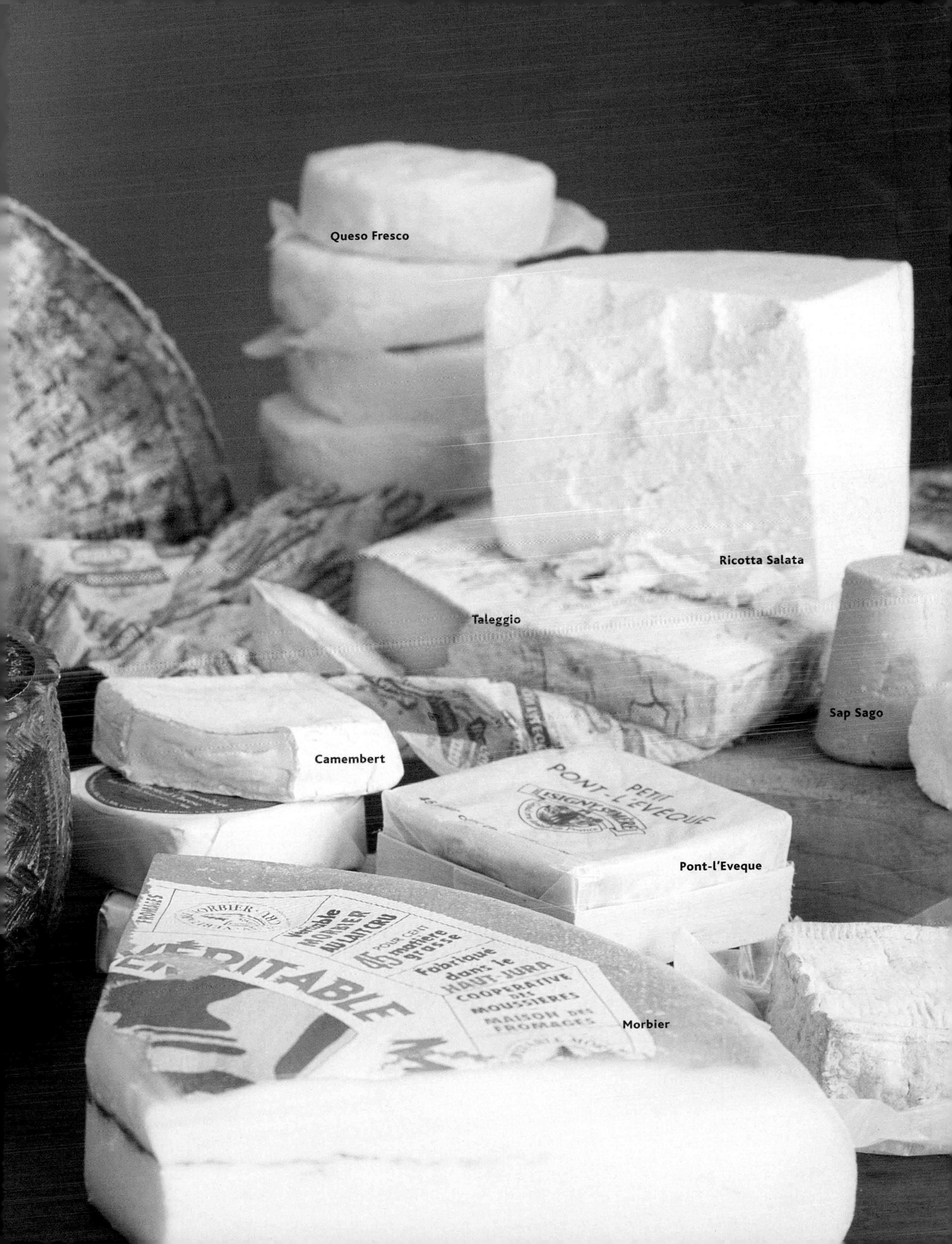

Queso Fresco
Ricotta Salata
Taleggio
Sap Sago
Camembert
PETIT PONT-L'EVEQUE
Pont-l'Eveque
Fabriqué dans le HAUT-JURA
COOPERATIVE DES MOUSSIERES
MAISON DES FROMAGES
Morbier

allowed to age for specific periods of time, though not quite as long as hard or grating cheeses. The table on the facing page lists and describes several semisoft cheeses.

Hard cheeses, such as Gruyère, Cheshire, and Cheddar, have a drier texture than semisoft cheeses and a firm consistency. They slice and grate easily. Cheddar cheese, though it originated as a farmhouse cheese in England, is extremely popular in the United States. In fact, its popularity is so widespread that some people refer to it as American cheese. Be aware, however, that the sliced processed cheese also known as American cheese is not the same product. The table on page 198 lists and describes several hard cheeses.

Grating cheeses, such as Sap Sago (see page 195), Parmesan, and Romano, are typically grated or shaved rather than cut into slices because of their crumbly texture. The best-quality Parmesan, Parmigiano-Reggiano (see page 195), is imported from the Reggiano region of Italy. It is used as a table or eating cheese.

FRESH CHEESE

TYPE/MILK USED	SHAPE AND COLOR	FLAVOR	TEXTURE
Bucheron (raw goat's)	Log, white	Slightly tangy	Soft, creamy
Chèvre (goat's)	Block, pyramid, button, wheel, log	Mild to tangy (depending on age), may be flavored with herbs or peppercorns	Soft to crumbly (depending on age)
Cottage (whole or skim cow's*)	Curds, white	Mild	Soft, moist
Cream (whole cow's plus cream)	Block, white	Mild, slightly tangy	Soft, creamy
Feta (sheep's, goat's, or cow's)	Block, white	Tangy, salty	Soft, crumbly
Fromage blanc (whole or skim cow's)	Soft, white	Mild, tangy	Soft, slightly crumbly
Mascarpone (whole cow's milk and/or cream)	Soft, pale yellow	Buttery, slightly tangy	Soft, smooth
Montrachet (raw goat's)	Log, white	Slightly tangy	Soft, creamy
Mozzarella (whole or skim cow's or buffalo's)	Irregular sphere, white	Mild, sometimes smoked (depending on age)	Tender to slightly elastic
Neufchâtel (whole or skim cow's†)	Block, white	Mild, slightly tangy	Soft, creamy
Ricotta (whole, skim, or low-fat cow's‡)	Soft curds, white	Mild	Soft, moist to slightly dry, grainy

*Cream may be added to finished curds.
†May have added cream.
‡May have added whey.

Domestically produced versions of these cheeses are available, as are blends of Parmesan and Romano. These cheeses are almost inescapably linked in the public mind with pasta dishes and may actually be referred to as "pasta cheese." The table on page 198 lists and describes several grating cheeses.

Blue-veined cheeses, such as Roquefort and Gorgonzola (see page 194), have consistencies that range from smooth and creamy to dry and crumbly. Their blue veining is the result of injecting a special mold into the cheese before ripening. The table on page 198 lists and describes several blue-veined cheeses.

SOFT AND RIND-RIPENED CHEESE

TYPE/MILK USED	SHAPE AND COLOR	FLAVOR	TEXTURE
Brie (pasteurized, whole or skim cow's or goat's, sometimes cream)	Disk, light yellow	Buttery to pungent	Soft, smooth, with edible rind
Camembert (raw or pasteurized whole cow's or goat's)	Disk, light yellow	Slightly tangy	Soft, creamy, with edible rind
Explorateur (whole cow's and cream)	Wheel, pale yellow	Rich, mild	Soft and creamy
Limburger (whole or low-fat cow's)	Block, light yellow, brown exterior	Very strong flavor and aroma	Soft, smooth, waxy
Pont-l'Évêque (whole cow's)	Square, light yellow	Piquant, strong aroma	Soft, supple, with small holes and edible golden yellow crust

SEMISOFT CHEESE

TYPE/MILK USED	SHAPE AND COLOR	FLAVOR	TEXTURE
Bel Paese (whole cow's)	Wheel, light yellow	Mild, buttery	Semisoft, creamy, waxy
Brick (whole cow's)	Block, light yellow	Mild to pungent (depending on age)	Semisoft, elastic, with many tiny holes
Edam (whole or part-skim cow's)	Loaf or sphere (may be coated with wax)	Mild to tangy (depending on age)	Elastic, may be slightly crumbly with tiny holes
Fontina (whole cow's or sheep's)	Wheel, medium yellow	Nutty flavor, strong aroma	Elastic, firm, smooth
Havarti (cream-enriched cow's)	Loaf or wheel, medium yellow	Buttery (may be flavored with dill or caraway)	Semisoft, creamy, with small holes
Morbier (whole cow's)	Wheel, light yellow with edible ash layer	Mild	Semisoft, smooth
Monterey jack (whole cow's)	Wheel or block, light yellow	Mild to pungent (may be flavored with jalapeño peppers)	Semisoft to very hard (depending on age)
Muenster (whole cow's)	Wheel or block, light yellow (rind may be orange)	Mild to pungent (depending on age)	Semisoft, smooth, waxy with small holes
Port Salut (whole or low-fat cow's)	Wheel or cylinder, white with russet exterior	Buttery, mellow to sharp	Semisoft, smooth
Taleggio (raw cow's)	Square, light yellow	Creamy	Semisoft with holes

HARD CHEESE

TYPE/MILK USED	SHAPE AND COLOR	FLAVOR	TEXTURE
Cantal (whole cow's)	Cylinder, light yellow	Mild to sharp, slightly nutty	Hard
Cheddar (whole cow's)	Wheel, light or medium yellow	Mild to sharp (depending on age)	Hard
Cheshire (whole cow's)	Cylinder, light or medium yellow (may have blue marbling)	Mellow to piquant	Hard
Derby (whole cow's)	Cylinder, honey-colored	Mild (may be flavored with sage)	Firm
Double Gloucester (whole cow's)	Large wheel, bright yellow-orange, colored with annatto	Full-flavored	Firm, smooth, creamy
Emmenthaler or Swiss (raw or pasteurized part-skim cow's)	Wheel, light yellow	Mild, nutty	Hard, smooth, shiny with large holes
Gjetost (whole cow's and goat's)	Small block, light brown	Butter, caramel, slightly tangy	Hard
Gouda (whole cow's)	Wheel (may be coated with wax)	Mild, creamy, slightly nutty	Hard, smooth, may have tiny holes
Jarlsberg (whole cow's)	Wheel, light yellow	Sharp, nutty	Hard with large holes
Manchego (whole sheep's)	Cylinder, light yellow	Full and mellow	Elastic to hard (depending on age) with holes
Provolone (whole cow's)	Pear, sausage, round, other, light yellow to golden brown	Mild to sharp (depending on age), may be smoked	Hard, elastic

GRATING CHEESE

TYPE/MILK USED	SHAPE AND COLOR	FLAVOR	TEXTURE
Asiago (whole or part-skim cow's)	Cylinder or flat block, light yellow	Mild to sharp	Semisoft to hard (depending on age)
Parmigiano Reggiano, Parmesan (part-skim cow's)	Cylinder, light yellow	Sharp, nutty	Very hard, dry, crumbly
Ricotta salata (whole sheep's)	Cylinder, off-white	Pungent	Hard
Romano, pecorino (whole sheep's, goat's, or cow's)	Cylinder	Very sharp	Very hard, dry, crumbly
Sap Sago (buttermilk, whey, and skim cow's)	Flattened cone, light green	Piquant, flavored with clover leaves	Very hard, granular

BLUE CHEESE

TYPE/MILK USED	SHAPE AND COLOR	FLAVOR	TEXTURE
Bleu, blue (whole cow's or goat's)	Cylinder, white with blue-green veins	Piquant, tangy	Semisoft, possibly crumbly
Bleu de Bresse (whole cow's or goat's)	Wheel, light yellow with blue veins	Piquant but mild for blue	Soft, creamy, slightly crumbly
Danish blue (whole cow's)	Blocks, drums, white	Strong, sharp, salty	Firm, crumbly
Fourme d'Ambert (whole cow's)	Cylinder, medium yellow with blue-green marbling and reddish yellow rind	Sharp, pungent	Semisoft, crumbly
Gorgonzola (whole cow's and/or goat's)	Wheel, medium yellow with blue marbling	Tangy, piquant	Semisoft, dry for blue
Maytag Blue (whole cow's)	Cylinder, medium yellow with blue marbling	Strong, salty	Hard, crumbly
Roquefort (raw sheep's)	Cylinder, white with blue-green marbling	Sharp, pungent	Semisoft, crumbly
Stilton (whole cow's)	Cylinder, medium yellow with blue-green marbling	Piquant, but mild for blue	Hard, crumbly

EGGS

Eggs are one of the kitchen's most important items. From mayonnaise to meringues, soups to sauces, appetizers to desserts, they are prominent on any menu. The ability to select the right egg for a particular dish (shell egg, yolks only, whites only, or pasteurized eggs) is critical to the success of any dish that includes eggs as an ingredient. To learn more about cooking eggs, see Chapter Twenty-Six.

Today's consumer is well aware of the potential for food-borne illness through eggs. Therefore, we will look first at basic rules for safe handling of eggs and foods containing eggs.

- All eggs in the shell should be free from cracks, leaking, and obvious holes.

- Raw egg yolks are a potentially hazardous food, due to the possible presence of *Salmonella enteritidis* bacteria. Salmonella bacteria are killed when the eggs are held at a temperature of at least 140°F (60°C) for a minimum of 3½ minutes. The bacteria is also killed instantly at 160°F (71°C). Fried eggs or poached eggs with runny yolks should be prepared only at customer request.

- Any foods containing eggs must be kept at safe temperatures throughout handling, cooking, and storage. Cooling and reheating must be done quickly.

EGG STRUCTURE AND USES

The egg is composed of two main parts, the white and the yolk. Various membranes help keep the yolk suspended at the center of the white and help prevent contamination or weight loss through evaporation.

Whole eggs, as well as whites and yolks separately, play a number of important culinary roles. Whole eggs are used as the main component of many breakfast dishes and can be prepared by scrambling, frying, poaching, or baking, or in custards. In baked goods, whole eggs are used as a glaze and to add nourishment, flavor, and color.

The egg white consists almost exclusively of water and a protein called albumen. Its ability to form a relatively stable foam is crucial to the development of proper structure in many items: angel food cakes, soufflés, meringues. Egg whites are a key ingredient in clarifying stocks and broths to produce consommés. They may also replace some or all of other binders used in some forcemeats, especially mousselines made from fish, poultry, or vegetables.

The yolk contains protein, a significant amount of fat, and a natural emulsifier called lecithin. The yolk has the ability to foam also. This function, plus its ability to form emulsions, makes egg yolks crucial to the preparation of such items as mayonnaise, hollandaise sauce, and génoise (sponge cake). Yolks are also responsible for providing additional richness to foods, as when they are included as a liaison in sauces or soups.

Eggs are graded by the U.S. Department of Agriculture on the basis of external appearance and freshness. The top grade, AA, indicates that the egg is fresh, with a white that will not spread unduly once the egg is broken, and a yolk that rides high on the white's surface. The yolk is anchored in place by membranes known as the chalazae.

Eggs come in a number of sizes: jumbo, extra large, large, medium, small, and pee wee. Younger hens produce smaller eggs, which are often regarded as of better quality than larger eggs. Medium eggs are best for breakfast cookery, where the cooked egg's appearance is important. Large and extra-large eggs are generally used for cooking and baking, where the whole egg's appearance is less critical.

Eggs are also sold in several processed forms: bulk, or fluid, whole eggs (which sometimes includes a percentage of extra yolks to obtain a specific blend); egg whites; and egg yolks. Pasteurized eggs are used in preparations such as salad dressings, eggnog, or desserts where the traditional recipe may have indicated that the eggs should be raw. These products generally are available in liquid or frozen form.

Dried, powdered eggs are also sold and may be useful for some baked goods or in certain specific circumstances. For instance, on board a ship, it may not be possible to properly store fresh eggs for the duration of a voyage.

Egg substitutes may be entirely egg-free or may be produced from egg whites, with dairy or vegetable products substituted for the yolks. These substitutes are important for people who require a reduced-cholesterol diet.

CHAPTER TEN

A broad spectrum of dry goods forms part of any foodservice operation's basic needs. Whole grains, meals, and flours; dried legumes; dried pasta and noodles; nuts and seeds; sugars, syrups, and other sweeteners; oils and shortenings; vinegars and condiments; coffee, tea, and other beverages; dry goods for baking; dried herbs and spices; and cooking wines, liqueurs, and cordials must be chosen, purchased, and stored with the same degree of care as required by fresh meats or produce.

DRY GOODS IDENTIFICATION

Dry goods are also occasionally referred to as nonperishable goods. However, these ingredients, like perishable goods, lose quality over time. Keeping an adequate stock on hand is essential to a smooth-running operation, but having too much ties up necessary space and money. Rotating dry goods and observing a rule of "first in, first out" is just as important for dry goods as for more perishable foods.

PURCHASING AND STORAGE

Well-organized kitchens maintain a par stock of dry goods. This means that enough of an item is stored to ensure that all menu offerings, as well as any items for special events, can be prepared from what is on hand. There should also be a slight overstock, in case of an unusually busy weekend or other contingencies. Excessive overstock, however, can monopolize valuable storage space.

Dry goods may be purchased in bulk, sold by the case, or bought in single units. Inspect all dry goods as they arrive, just as carefully as produce, meats, and fish are inspected, to ensure that the delivery matches the order. Check bags, boxes, cans, or other containers to make sure they are intact and clean and that they are not dented, broken, or in any way below standard.

Although dry goods do have long shelf lives, most of them are of the best quality when they are relatively fresh. Store dry goods in an area that is properly dry, ventilated, and accessible. All goods should be placed above floor level, on shelving or pallets. Some dry items, such as whole grains, nuts and seeds, and coffee (if it is not vacuum-packed), are best stored in the refrigerator or even the freezer.

GRAINS, MEALS, AND FLOURS

This broad category extends from whole grains such as rice and barley to cornmeal and pastry flour. Grains are versatile and universal foods enjoyed worldwide, in every cuisine and culture. While they are important sources of nutrition, it is also their subtle but satisfying flavors and textures that give them such culinary importance.

Traditional dishes based on grains have been brought up to date, and what might once have been considered stodgy dishes have been turned into exciting new menu items. Grains that were once seldom prepared in professional kitchens, such as wheat berries and barley, have come to be appreciated for their special flavors and textures.

Grains are the fruit and seed of cereal grasses. For the most part, they are inexpensive and readily available, and provide a valuable and concentrated source of nutrients and fiber. Although grains differ in appearance from other fruits (apples and pears, for example), their structure is quite similar.

Wheat and corn are of primary importance in Western countries, such as the United States and Canada. Rice is fundamental to many Asian cuisines. In fact, in many Asian languages, the word for rice is the same as that for food. Other cultures rely upon grains such as oats, rye, and buckwheat.

Whole grains are grains that have not been milled. They tend to have a shorter life span than milled grains and therefore should be purchased in amounts that can be used in a relatively short period of time: two to three weeks. Milled grains have been polished, that is, they have had the germ, bran, and/or hull removed. Although milled grains tend to last longer, some of their nutritive value is lost during processing.

Milled grains that are broken into coarse particles may be referred to as *cracked*. If the milling process continues, meals and cereals (cornmeal, farina, cream of rice) are formed. Finally, the grain may be ground into a fine powder, known as *flour*.

Various methods are used for milling: crushing between metal rollers, grinding between stones, or cutting with steel blades in an action similar to that of a food processor. Stone-ground grains may be preferred in some cases, because they remain at a lower temperature during this process as compared to other types of milling and so retain more of their nutritive value. The following lists describe some of the available forms for several different grains.

Types of processed wheat (clockwise from top left): whole wheat flour, wheat bran, cracked wheat, wheat berries, wheat germ, bleached all-purpose flour.

WHEAT

WHOLE: Unrefined or minimally processed whole kernels.

CRACKED: Coarsely crushed, minimally processed kernels.

BULGUR: Hulled, cracked hard or soft wheat, parboiled and dried.

SEMOLINA: Polished wheat kernel (bran and germ removed), whole or ground.

COUSCOUS: Semolina pellets, often parcooked.

FARINA: Polished, medium-grind wheat cereals.

BRAN: Separated outer covering of wheat kernel; flakes.

GERM: Separated embryo of wheat kernel; flakes.

WHEAT FLOUR

WHOLE OR GRAHAM: Finely ground whole kernels (graham flour is slightly coarser than whole wheat flour).

ALL-PURPOSE: Finely ground polished kernels; usually enriched; may be bleached.

BREAD: Finely ground polished hard wheat kernels; usually enriched; may be bleached.

CAKE: Very finely ground polished soft wheat kernels; usually enriched and bleached.

PASTRY: Very finely ground polished soft wheat kernels; usually enriched and bleached.

SELF-RISING: Very finely ground polished soft wheat kernels to which baking powder and salt have been added; usually enriched and bleached.

RICE

BROWN: Hulled grains, bran intact; short, medium, or long grain; may be enriched.

WHITE: Polished grains, usually enriched, long or short grain.

CONVERTED: Parcooked polished grains, may be enriched.

BASMATI: Delicate, extra-long grain, polished.

ITALIAN: Short grain, polished; types include arborio, Piedmontese, and Carnaroli.

WILD: Long, dark brown grain not related to regular rice.

GLUTINOUS: Round, short grain, very starchy; black (unhulled) or white (polished).

RICE FLOUR: Very finely ground polished rice.

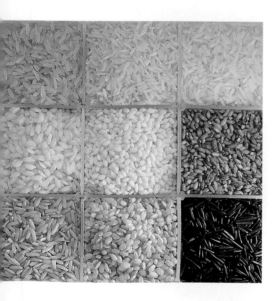

*Rices (from left to right, top to bottom):
long grain, converted, jasmine, arborio,
sushi, Japanese red, long grain brown,
short grain brown, wild.*

CORN

HOMINY: Hulled and degerminated kernels; dry or canned.

GRITS: Ground hominy.

MEAL: Medium-fine ground hulled kernels; white or yellow.

MASA: Corn processed with lime to remove hull, then ground.

MASA HARINA: Ground dried masa.

CORNSTARCH: Very finely ground hulled and degerminated kernels.

BARLEY

POT OR SCOTCH: Unpolished kernels.

BARLEY MEAL: Ground unpolished kernels.

PEARL: Polished kernels.

BARLEY FLOUR: Ground polished kernels.

OATS

OATS: Whole groats.

OATMEAL: Steel-cut; rolled; flakes; quick-cooking; instant.

OAT BRAN: Separated outer covering of grain; flakes.

OTHERS

BUCKWHEAT: Whole groats; coarsely cracked groats (kasha); flour.

MILLET: Whole; flour.

RYE: Whole berries; cracked; flour.

SORGHUM: Whole; flour; syrup.

Grains (from left to right, top to bottom): rolled oats, steel-cut oats, oat groats, cracked wheat, barley, Job's tears, kasha, wheat berries, quinoa, teff, amaranth, spelt.

DRIED LEGUMES

Legumes, or beans, are seeds that grow in pods. These seeds can be used in the kitchen fresh or dried. When fresh, they are considered vegetables. Dried, they are known collectively as legumes. Lima beans, for example, are treated as a vegetable when fresh and a legume when dried. Legumes are a potent source of nutrients, and they have a higher protein content than most grains.

Dishes that combine legumes and grains, such as the southern favorite hoppin' John (black-eyed peas and rice) or Cuban black beans and rice, contain a particularly effective balance of essential nutrients, including complete proteins as well as an impressive amount of complex carbohydrates, dietary fiber, vitamins, and minerals.

Although in theory they have a lengthy shelf life, as do most dry goods, legumes are best when used within six months of purchase. Store dried legumes in a cool, dry, well-ventilated area. Before using, discard any beans or peas that appear moldy, damp, or wrinkled. It should be noted that as beans age they will take longer to cook. The table on the facing page includes a description and standard purchase forms for the most common dried legumes.

ABOVE *Left to right, from the top: baby beans, rice beans, brown lentils, canary beans, large red kidney beans, pinto beans, green lentils, whole peas/mashy peas, navy beans, fava beans, beluga beans (black lentils), hominy.*

RIGHT *Left to right, from the top: navy beans, red lentils, brown lentils, adzuki beans, calypso beans, chickpeas, black beans, black-eyed peas, baby lima beans, yellow split peas, red kidney beans, Great Northern beans, pink beans, lima beans, green split peas.*

BEANS, LENTILS, AND PEAS

NAME	DESCRIPTION	PURCHASE FORM
BEANS		
Adzuki beans	Small, reddish brown with white ridge on one side, slightly sweet flavor	Dried
Black beans, turtle beans	Shiny, brownish black, medium-sized, rounded or kidney-shaped	Dried, canned
Black-eyed peas	Cream-colored with black patch around hilum, medium-sized, kidney-shaped	Dried, canned, fresh
Cannelini	Medium-sized, white, smooth, long, kidney-shaped	Dried, canned
Chickpeas	Medium-sized, acorn-shaped, light tan to brown	Dried, canned
Fava beans, broad beans	Large, flat, green (fresh) to brown (dried)	Fresh, dried; larger, baby
Flageolet	Medium-sized, smooth, flat, oval, green or white; a type of haricot	Dried
Kidney beans	Long, curved kidney shape, pink to maroon	Dried, canned
Lentils	Small, green, brown, yellow, orange, or dark green (French)	Dried
Lima beans	Medium-sized, flat, white to light green	Canned, frozen
Mung beans	Small, round, green or yellow	Fresh or dried; whole, skinless, split, sprouted
Navy beans	Small, smooth, rounded, white; a type of haricot	Dried, canned
Pigeon peas	Small, nearly round, off-white with orange-brown mottling	Dried, canned
Pinto beans	Medium-sized, kidney-shaped, mottled pink	Dried, canned
Soissons	Medium-size, oval, white; a type of haricot	Dried
Soybeans	Medium-size, rounded, black or yellow	Fresh or dried; salted, fermented, soy sauce, other (see "Bean Products," below)
BEAN PRODUCTS		
Bean paste, soy	Thick sauce of fermented soybeans, flour, and salt	Bottled or canned, whole or ground beans
Bean paste, hot	Soybean paste with crushed chile peppers	Bottled or canned
Bean paste, sweet/red	Puréed red beans and sugar	Bottled or canned
Miso	Japanese soybean paste	Foil pouches, jars
Tofu (soybean curd)	Off-white, soft, curdled bean protein	Cakes, packed in water or pressed
PEAS		
Fresh	See Chapter Eight	Fresh, frozen, canned
Dried	Green or yellow, smooth or wrinkled	Split or whole

DRIED PASTA AND NOODLES

Linguine

Dried pasta is a valuable convenience food. It stores well, cooks quickly, and comes in an extensive array of shapes, sizes, and flavors, as described in the table below. This range of shapes and flavors provides a base for a number of preparations, from a simple spaghetti dish to Asian and Middle Eastern specialties.

Pasta and noodles are made from a number of different flours and grains. Good-quality dried pastas from wheat flour are customarily made from durum semolina. Many pastas are flavored or colored with vegetables, such as spinach, peppers, or tomatoes.

Lasagne

Spaghetti

Pappardelle

Fettuccine nests

Orecchiette

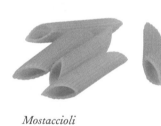
Mostaccioli

Ditalini

Spinach fusilli

Manicotti

Conchiglie

Orzo

Farfalle

Regular couscous

Israeli couscous

Soba

Rice sticks

DRIED PASTA AND NOODLES

NAME (ITALIAN/ENGLISH)	DESCRIPTION (SHAPE, BASE FLOUR)
Acini di pepe/peppercorns	Tiny, pellet-shaped. Made with wheat flour.
Anelli/rings	Medium-small, ridged, tubular pasta cut in thin rings. Made with wheat flour.
Arrowroot vermicelli	Very thin Chinese noodles. Made with arrowroot dough enriched with egg yolks.
Bucatini	Hollow, spaghetti-shaped pasta. Made with wheat flour.
Cannelloni/large pipes	Large cylinders. Made with wheat flour.
Capellini/hair	Very fine, solid, cylindrical; the finest is capelli d'angelo (angel hair). Made with wheat flour.
Cavatelli	Medium-thin, hollow, ridged pasta twisted into a spiral and cut into short lengths. Made with wheat flour.
Cellophane noodles	Very thin, transparent noodles; in bunches or compressed bundles. Made with mung bean starch.
Conchiglie/shells	Large or medium ridged shell shape; conchigliette are small shells. Made with wheat flour.
Couscous	Small, grain-shaped pasta. Made with semolina.
Ditali/thimbles	Narrow tubes cut in short lengths. Ditalini are tiny thimbles. Made with wheat flour.
Egg flakes	Tiny, flat squares. Made with wheat flour enriched with egg.
Egg noodles	Usually ribbons, in varying widths; may be cut long or short, packaged loose or in compressed bundles; may have spinach or other flavorings. Made with wheat flour enriched with egg yolks.
Elbow macaroni	Narrow, curved tubes cut in short lengths (about 1 inch). Made with wheat flour.
Farfalle/butterflies	Flat, rectangular noodles pinched in center to resemble butterfly or bow; may have crimped edges. Farfallini are tiny butterflies. Made with wheat flour.
Fedelini	Very fine ribbon pasta, similar to capellini. Made with wheat flour.
Fettuccine	Long, flat, ribbon-shaped, about $1/4$ inch wide. Made with wheat flour.
Fiochetti/bowties	Rectangles of flat pasta curled up and pinched slightly in the center to form bow shapes. Made with wheat flour.
Fusilli/twists	Long, spring- or corkscrew-shaped strands; thicker than spaghetti. Made with wheat flour.
Lasagne	Large, flat noodles about 3 inches wide; usually with curly edges. Made with wheat flour.
Linguine	Thin, slightly flattened, solid strands, about $1/8$ inch wide. Made with wheat flour.
Mafalda	Flat, curly-edged, about $3/4$ inch wide; sometimes called lasagnette or mafaldine. Made with wheat flour.
Manicotti/small muffs	Thick, ridged tubes; may be cut straight or on an angle. Made with wheat flour.
Mostaccioli/small mustaches	Medium-size tubes with angle-cut ends; may be ridged (rigati). Made with wheat flour.
Orecchiette/ears	Smooth, curved rounds of flat pasta, about $1/2$ inch in diameter. Made with wheat flour.
Orzo/barley	Tiny, grain-shaped. Made with wheat flour.
Pappardelle	Wide flat pasta, cut into varying lengths. Made with wheat flour.
Pastina/tiny pasta	Miniature pasta in any of various shapes, including stars, rings, alphabets, seeds/teardrops. Made with wheat flour.
Penne/quills or pens	Same as mostaccioli.
Rice noodles	Noodles in various widths (up to about $1/8$ inch); rice sticks are long, straight ribbons; rice vermicelli is very thin. Made with rice flour.
Rigatoni	Thick, ridged tubes cut in lengths of about $1 1/2$ inches. Made with wheat flour.
Rotelle/wheels	Wheel-shaped. Made with wheat flour.
Rotini/cartwheels	Small six-spoked wheels. Made with wheat flour.
Soba (Japanese)	Noodles the approximate shape and thickness of fedelini or tagliarini; buckwheat flour
Somen (Japanese)	Long, thin noodles resembling vermicelli. Made with wheat flour. Tomago somen is enriched with egg yolks.
Spaghetti/little strings	Solid, round strands ranging from very thin to thin; very thin spaghetti may be labeled spaghettini. Made with wheat flour.
Tagliatelle	Same as fettuccine; may be mixed plain and spinach noodles, called paglia e fieno (straw and hay). Made with wheat flour.
Tubetti/tubes	Medium-small (usually about as thick as elbow macaroni), tubular, may be long or cut in lengths of about an inch; tubettini are tiny tubes. Made with wheat flour.
Udon (Japanese)	Thick noodles, similar to somen. Made with wheat flour.
Vermicelli	Very fine cylindrical pasta, similar to capellini. Made with wheat flour.
Ziti/bridegrooms	Medium-size tubes; may be ridged (rigati); may be long or cut in approximately 2-inch lengths (ziti tagliate). Made with wheat flour.

*Where base flour is listed as wheat, usually durum semolina is used. Wheat pastas may be made from other flours, including whole wheat and buckwheat, and they may be flavored with vegetables and/or herb purées.

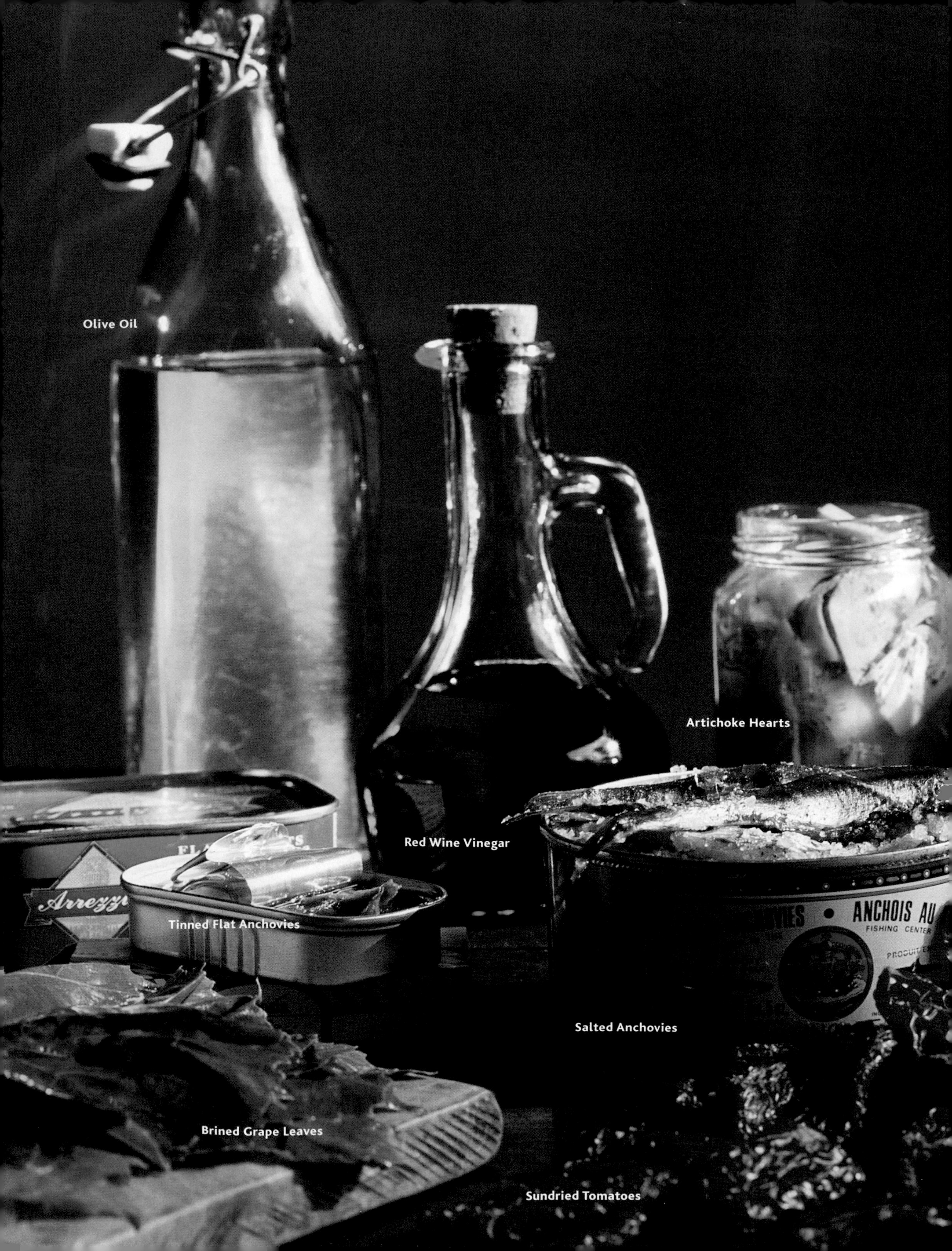

Olive Oil
Artichoke Hearts
Red Wine Vinegar
Tinned Flat Anchovies
ANCHOIS AU
FISHING CENTER
Salted Anchovies
Brined Grape Leaves
Sundried Tomatoes

Pepperoncini

Caper Berries

Capers

Kalamata Olives

Oil-Cured Olives

Dried Porcini Mushrooms

OILS AND SHORTENINGS

Oils are produced by pressing a high-oil-content food such as olives, nuts, corn, avocados, or soybeans. The oil then may be filtered, clarified, or hydrogenated in order to produce an oil or shortening that has the appropriate characteristics for its intended use.

The hydrogenation process causes the oil to remain solid at room temperature; in this state it is known as shortening. A product labeled "vegetable shortening" is made from vegetable oil, whereas one labeled just "shortening" may contain animal products.

Several different oils and shortenings are required in every kitchen. Oils for salads and other cold dishes should be of the best possible quality, with a perfectly fresh flavor. First pressings of olive oil or nut oils are often chosen for these purposes because of their special flavors.

Cooking oils may have a neutral flavor; those used for frying should have a high smoking point as well (the table on page 214 lists the smoking point of several fats and oils). Shortenings used for baking should also be neutral in flavor. Oils and shortenings should be stored in a dry place away from extremes of heat and light. The following list describes several oils and fats.

BUTTER-FLAVORED OILS/SHORTENINGS: Vegetable oils (usually blended) flavored with real or artificial butter flavor.

CANOLA OIL (RAPESEED OIL): A light, golden-colored oil, similar to safflower oil; low in saturated fat; extracted from the seeds of a variety of turnips (the same plant as the vegetable broccoli rabe).

COCONUT OIL: A heavy, nearly colorless oil extracted from fresh coconuts. Used primarily in blended oils and shortenings and prepared, processed, and packaged foods.

CORN OIL: A mild-flavored refined oil. It is medium yellow in color, inexpensive, and versatile.

COTTONSEED OIL: A pale yellow oil extracted from the seed of the cotton plant.

FRYING FATS: Blended oils or shortenings (usually based on processed corn or peanut oils) designed to have a high smoking point and long fry life. May be liquid or plastic at room temperature.

GRAPESEED OIL: This light, aromatic medium yellow oil is a by-product of wine making.

LARD: Solid pork fat. May be treated to neutralize flavor.

OLIVE OIL: Oil varies in weight and may be pale yellow to deep green depending on fruit used and processing. Cold-pressed olive oil is superior in flavor to thermally refined oil. The finest olive oil available is extra-virgin olive oil. Virgin olive oil is the next best grade. Both types of virgin olive oils must be produced without the use of heat, which can lead to alterations in the oil's character. They are therefore generally used for cold preparations. The most widely marketed grade of olive oil is known simply as "olive oil," the term for what was previously called "pure olive oil" or "100 percent pure olive oil." Suitable for cooking, it is a blend of refined olive oil (from flawed virgin oil that has been thermally treated to remove its undesirable characteristics) and virgin olive oil. Last, there is olive-pomace oil, which is extracted from pomace (the pulpy residue from which the virgin oil has been extracted) with the aid of solvents and then blended with virgin olive oil.

OIL SPRAYS: Vegetable oils (usually blended) packaged in pump or aerosol sprays. Used for lightly coating pans and griddles.

PEANUT OIL: A pale yellow refined oil, with a very subtle scent and flavor. Some less-refined types are darker with a more pronounced peanut flavor.

SAFFLOWER OIL: A golden-colored oil with a light texture. Made from a plant that resembles a thistle. Usually refined.

A selection of oils (from left to right): corn, sesame, extra virgin olive, white truffle, peanut, sweet almond, walnut.

SALAD OIL: Mild-flavored vegetable oils blended for use in salad dressings, mayonnaise, and the like.

SESAME OIL: Two types: a light, very mild, Middle Eastern type and a darker Asian type pressed from toasted sesame seeds. Asian sesame oil may be light or dark brown. The darker oil has a more pronounced sesame flavor and aroma. Asian sesame oil has a low smoking point, so it is used primarily as a flavoring rather than in cooking.

SHORTENING, BAKING FAT: Blended oil solidified using various processes, including whipping in air and hydrogenation. Designed for plasticity and mild flavor. May have real or artificial butter flavor added. Usually emulsified to enable absorption of more sugar in baked goods. May contain animal fats unless labeled as vegetable shortening.

SOYBEAN OIL: A fairly heavy oil with a pronounced flavor and aroma. More soybean oil is produced than any other type. Used in most blended vegetable oils and margarines.

SUNFLOWER OIL: A light, odorless, and nearly flavorless oil pressed from sunflower seeds. Pale yellow and versatile.

VEGETABLE OIL: Made by blending several different refined oils. Designed to have a mild flavor and a high smoking point.

WALNUT OIL: A medium yellow oil with a nutty flavor and aroma. It is cold-pressed and more perishable than most other oils, so it should be used soon after purchase. Used primarily in salads. (Other nut oils include almond and hazelnut.)

SMOKING POINTS OF SELECTED FATS

NAME	USES	APPROXIMATE MELTING POINT	APPROXIMATE SMOKING POINT*
Butter, whole	Baking, cooking	95°F/36°C	300°F/150°C
Butter, clarified	Cooking	95°F/36°C	300°F/150°C
Canola oil	Cooking, salad dressings	60°F/15°C	420°F/215°C
Coconut oil	Coatings, confectionery, shortening	75°F/24°C	350°F/175°C
Corn oil	Frying, salad dressings, shortening	12°F/-11°C	450°F/230°C
Cottonseed oil	Margarine, salad dressings, shortening	55°F/13°C	420°F/215°C
Frying fat	Frying	105°F/40°C	465°F/240°C
Lard	Baking, cooking, specialty items	92°F/33°C	375°F/190°C
Olive oil	Cooking, salad dressings	32°F/0°C	375°F/190°C
Peanut oil	Frying, margarine, salad dressings, shortening	28°F/-2°C	440°F/225°C
Safflower oil	Margarine, mayonnaise, salad dressings	2°F/-17°C	510°F/265°C
Shortening, emulsified vegetable	Baking, frying, shortening	115°F/46°C	325°F/165°C
Soybean oil	Margarine, salad dressings, shortening	-5°F/-20°C	495°F/257°C
Sunflower oil	Cooking, margarine, salad dressings, shortening	2°F/-17°C	440°F/225°C

*The smoking point of any oil will be reduced after it is used for cooking.

NUTS AND SEEDS

With the exception of the peanut, which grows underground in the root system of a leguminous plant, nuts are the fruits of various trees. They are available in various forms: in the shell, roasted, shelled, blanched, sliced, slivered, chopped, and as butters.

Nuts have a number of culinary uses, adding a special flavor and texture to dishes.

They are relatively expensive and should be stored carefully to keep them from becoming rancid. Nuts that have not been roasted or shelled will keep longer. Shelled nuts may be stored in the freezer or refrigerator if space allows. In any case, they should be stored in a cool, dry, well-ventilated area and checked periodically to be sure they are still fresh.

Macadamias

Sunflower seeds (in shell, shelled)   *Cashews (roasted, raw)*   *Walnuts (in shell, shelled)*   *Pistachios (in shell, shelled)*

Almonds (slivered, sliced)   *Coconut, sweetened shredded, unsweetened desiccated*   *Peanuts (in shell, shelled, some with skins attached)*   *Pumpkin seeds*

Some of the seeds used in the kitchen are considered spices (celery or fennel seed, for example), and others, including sunflower and pumpkin seeds, are treated more like nuts. Seeds are usually available whole or as a paste and should be stored in the same manner as nuts. The table on page 216 lists commonly available nuts and seeds.

Pine nuts

Hulled sesame seeds

Poppy seeds

Black sesame seeds

NUTS AND SEEDS

NAME	DESCRIPTION	PURCHASE FORM
Almond	Teardrop-shape seed of a fruit that resembles the apricot. Pale tan woody shell. Bitter and sweet types available. Bitter requires cooking; sweet may be used raw or cooked.	Whole in shell. Shelled: whole, blanched, slivered, ground. Almond paste, other products.
Brazil	Large, oval nut; grows in clusters of segments. Each segment is a hard, wrinkled, three-sided brown seed containing the rich nut.	Whole in shell. Shelled
Cashew	Kidney-shape nut that grows as the appendage of an applelike fruit, which is not usually eaten. It is always sold hulled, as its skin contains irritating oils similar to those in poison ivy.	Shelled: raw or toasted.
Chestnut	Fairly large, round to teardrop-shaped nut; hard, glossy dark brown shell.	Raw (whole in shell). Canned: whole in water or syrup, puréed.
Coconut	Melon-sized fruit that grows on a type of palm. The "nut," its woody brown seed, is covered with hairy fibers and surrounds a layer of rich white nutmeat. The inside of the nut is hollow and contains thin white juice (coconut water).	Whole in shell. Flaked (may be sweetened). Coconut cream. Other products.
Hazelnut	Small, nearly round nut; shiny, hard shell with matte spot where cap was attached. Nutmeat is rich and delicately flavored.	Whole in shell. Shelled: whole, chopped.
Macadamia	Nearly round, rich, sweet nut native to Australia.	Shelled and roasted in coconut oil.
Peanut	Seed grows inside a fibrous pod among the roots of a leguminous plant.	Whole in shell, raw or roasted. Shelled: whole, skinned, raw or roasted. Peanut butter.
Pecan	Medium-brown, smooth and glossy oval-shaped shell. Two-lobed nutmeat has a rich flavor.	Whole in shell. Shelled: halved or chopped.
Pine nut	Tiny, cream-colored, elongated kernel is the seed of a Mediterranean pine. Fairly perishable.	Shelled: raw or roasted.
Pistachio	Cream-colored shell; green nutmeat with distinctive, sweet flavor.	Whole in shell: roasted, usually salted, natural or dyed red. Occasionally shelled, chopped.
Poppy seeds	Tiny, round, blue-black seeds with a rich, slightly musty flavor.	Whole.
Pumpkin seeds	Flat, oval cream-colored seeds with semihard hull and soft, oily interior.	Whole in shell: raw or roasted. Shelled: raw or roasted.
Sesame seeds	Tiny, flat, oval seeds; may be black or tan; oily, with rich, nutty flavor.	Whole: hulled or unhulled. Paste (tahini).
Sunflower seeds	Small, somewhat flat, teardrop-shaped light tan oily seed with woody black-and-white shell; grown primarily for oil.	Whole in shell. Shelled.
Walnut	Mild, tender, oily nutmeat; grows in convoluted segments inside hard light brown shell. White walnuts, or butternuts, and black walnuts are North American varieties. Butternuts are richer, and black walnuts are stronger in flavor.	Whole in shell. Shelled: halved, chopped. Pickled (whole).

DRIED HERBS AND SPICES

Many of the herbs discussed in Chapter Eight, "Fruit, Vegetable, and Fresh Herb Identification," are also available in dried form. Some herbs, such as rosemary, sage, and bay leaves, dry successfully, whereas others will retain very little flavor.

Spices are aromatics produced primarily from the bark and seeds of plants. Most spices' flavors are quite intense and powerful. Spices are nearly always sold in dried form and may be available whole or ground. In addition, the chef may use spice blends, such as curry powder, quatre épices, chili powder, Chinese five-spice powder, pâté spice, and pickling spice. Recipes for several spice blends may be found in Chapter 15.

Dried herbs are often stored incorrectly, which compounds the problem of flavor loss. They are often stored too close to the top of the range and are kept for too long. A chef should buy only the amount of dried herbs that can be used within two or three months and should store them away from heat. Herbs that have a musty or "flat" aroma should be discarded. If at all possible, the chef should try to find fresh herbs.

Whole spices will keep longer than ground spices, although most spices will retain their potency for about six months if they are properly stored. They should be kept in sealed containers in a cool, dry spot, away from extreme heat and direct light. Check spices from time to time to be sure they are still potent, discarding any that have lost their flavor or have become stale or musty-smelling. For optimal flavor, purchase whole spices and grind them as close as possible to the time they are to be used.

Basil *Bay leaves* *Dill weed*

Epazote *Marjoram* *Oregano*

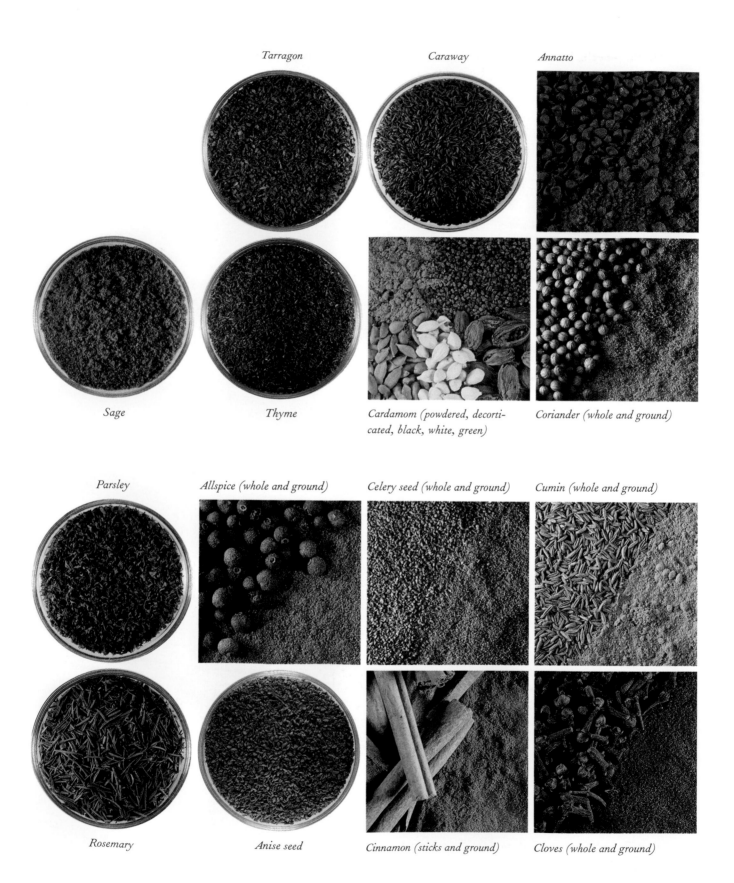

Tarragon

Caraway

Annatto

Sage

Thyme

Cardamom (powdered, decorticated, black, white, green)

Coriander (whole and ground)

Parsley

Allspice (whole and ground)

Celery seed (whole and ground)

Cumin (whole and ground)

Rosemary

Anise seed

Cinnamon (sticks and ground)

Cloves (whole and ground)

Old Bay seasoning

Garlic powder

Poultry seasoning

Fennel seed

Ground ginger

Saffron

Fenugreek

Juniper berries (whole and ground)

Star anise

Onion powder

Filé powder

Mustard (whole and ground)

Nutmeg (whole and ground)

Tumeric

Quatre épices   *Chili powder*   *Garam masala*

Curry powder   *Barbecue spice mix*   *Chinese five-spice powder*

SPICE BLENDS

Ready-made spice blends for virtually all ethnic or regional cuisines are widely available. Whenever possible, do an evaluation of three or more brands to find the best quality and value. Store spice blends as you would any spice: away from heat, direct light, or moisture. You may prefer to prepare your own blends using the recipes on pages 352–354.

DRIED FRUITS AND VEGETABLES

The United States processes over 1 billion pounds of dried fruit per year. Federal and state standards have been established for some (but not all) types of dried or low-moisture fruits and vegetables. Because the fruit is allowed to mature fully before being harvested and dried, there is greater potential for damage and defects. Low-moisture fruits and vegetables (raisins, sun-dried tomatoes, etc.) are somewhat perishable and should be carefully stored. Purchase no more than a one-month supply. Vacuum- or chemically-dried vegetables are not as perishable but should be stored in a cool, dry area. There is a great variety in the price and quality of dried fruits and vegetables. You will need to experiment to determine what is the best quality available in your area.

SALT AND PEPPER

Salt was once one of the most prized of all seasonings, as revealed in the expression "below the salt" — nobles, who sat at the head of the table (above the salt), were allowed to use salt, while lesser folk, sitting below the salt, had to rely on herbs to flavor their food. Another spice common today, pepper, was at one time the single most expensive seasoning in the world.

Salt and pepper should be stored in a dry place. In very humid weather, salt may cake together; mixing a few grains of rice in with the salt will help to prevent this. Whole peppercorns will retain their flavor almost indefinitely, releasing it only when crushed or ground. Check ground or cracked pepper for pungency if its age is in question.

SALT

Salt is readily available in numerous forms.

TABLE SALT: Most commonly used in cooking and as a table condiment. Consists of small, dense, granular cubes that adhere poorly to food, dissolve slowly in solution, and are difficult to blend.

IODIZED SALT: Table salt to which iodine has been added as a preventive against goiter, an enlargement of the thyroid gland caused by iodine deficiency.

KOSHER SALT: Granular salt that has been compressed so that each grain has a greater surface area. It is flaky, and compared to table salt, it is lighter in weight, dissolves more readily, and adheres better to food. Diamond Crystal kosher salt is formed through an evaporation process similar to sea salt and is a lighter version of regular kosher salt.

Salt (from left to right, top): kosher, curing salt, popcorn salt; (bottom) fine sea salt, coarse sea salt, table salt

SEA SALT AND BAY SALT: Collected through the evaporation of natural salt water. Consists of thin, flaky layers. Adheres well to food and dissolves quickly. These salts also contain various other trace minerals that occur naturally in the waters from which they are collected. As such, sea and bay salts from different areas of the world taste different. All are generally more complex in flavor than table and kosher salts. Sea and bay salts can be purchased in fine-grain and larger crystal forms.

CANNING AND PICKLING SALTS: Contain no additives and are very pure. Processed specifically to prevent clouding of the brine and discoloration of food undergoing salt curing.

POPCORN SALT: A superfine salt.

ROCK SALT: A very coarse salt used in crank ice-cream makers and as a bed for shellfish. Has a gray tint from the usually harmless impurities it contains. Some rock salts may contain arsenic; those that are safe to consume are marked as edible.

SALT SUBSTITUTES: Contain either no sodium or a reduced amount (light salt).

CURING SALT: A blend of 94 percent salt and 6 percent sodium nitrite. Used in a variety of charcuterie items, especially those to be cold-smoked. Usually dyed pink to differentiate it from other salts. Saltpeter, which is potassium nitrate, is occasionally used in place of curing salt.

PEPPER

Today, most kitchens require a number of different peppers for different uses. Not all of the peppers listed below are related botanically; however, they all share a pungent, fiery flavor and aroma. Freshly ground pepper is preferable, because it is more pungent and has a fresher flavor.

BLACK PEPPERCORNS: Available as whole berries, cracked, or ground. The Telicherry peppercorn is one of the most prized. Mignonette, or shot pepper, is a combination of coarsely ground or crushed black and white peppercorns.

WHITE PEPPERCORNS: Black peppercorns are allowed to ripen and then the husks are removed. May be preferred for pale or lightly colored sauces. Available in the same forms as black peppercorns.

GREEN PEPPERCORNS: Unripe peppercorns that are packed in vinegar or brine; also available freeze-dried (they must be reconstituted in water before use).

PINK PEPPERCORNS: Dried berries from the baics rose plant. Generally freeze-dried. Not a true peppercorn.

SZECHWAN PEPPERCORNS: Berries from the prickly ash tree, grown in the Szechwan province of China. Each berry contains a small seed. Typically sold dried.

CAYENNE: A special type of chile, originally grown in Cayenne in French Guyana. The chile is dried and ground into a fine powder. The same chile is used to make hot pepper sauces.

CHILE (RED PEPPER) FLAKES: Dried whole red chile peppers that are crushed or coarsely ground.

PAPRIKA: A powder made from dried pimientos. Available as mild, sweet, or hot. Hungarian paprikas are considered superior in flavor.

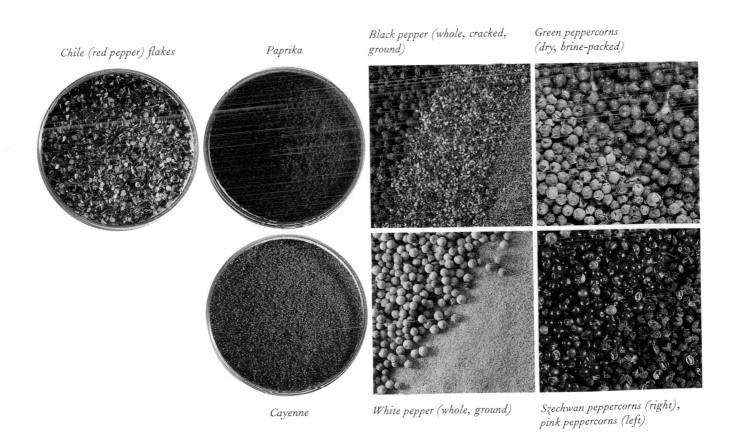

Chile (red pepper) flakes   *Paprika*   *Black pepper (whole, cracked, ground)*   *Green peppercorns (dry, brine-packed)*

Cayenne   *White pepper (whole, ground)*   *Szechwan peppercorns (right), pink peppercorns (left)*

SUGARS, SYRUPS, AND OTHER SWEETENERS

Once a symbol of wealth and prosperity, sugar is now so commonplace and inexpensive that it takes a good deal of effort to avoid using it. Sugar is extracted from plant sources (sugar beets or sugar cane) and then refined into the desired form. Most syrups (maple syrup, corn syrup, molasses, and honey) are also derived from plants.

Table sugar has a number of important roles in the kitchen and bakeshop, in addition to being required on the table to sweeten beverages. Syrups and other sweeteners, such as honey and sugar substitutes, may also be necessary, depending on a particular kitchen's menu and the guests' needs. The following are several types of sweeteners and their descriptions.

SUGARS

BROWN: Granular; refined sugar with some impurities left in or some molasses added; light to medium brown; moister than white sugar; slight molasses flavor.

MUSCOVADO: Granular brown sugar that has undergone little processing; soft and moist; dark brown with pronounced molasses flavor.

DEMERARA: Partially refined sugar in large crystals, golden brown, dissolves slowly.

TURBINADO: Coarse granular sugar that is slightly more refined than Demerara sugar; golden brown.

WHITE, COARSE: Pure, refined sugar in large crystals; dissolves slowly; also known as preserving sugar.

WHITE, GRANULATED: Pure, refined sugar in small, evenly sized crystals.

WHITE, SUPERFINE: Pure, refined sugar in very small crystals; dissolves quickly; also known as bar sugar.

CONFECTIONERS': Very finely powdered, pure refined sugar; usually mixed with a small amount of cornstarch to prevent clumping; also known as 10X.

WHITE, LUMP: Pure, refined, granulated sugar pressed into small cubes or tablets; also known as cube sugar.

SYRUPS

CORN: Liquefied sugar extracted from corn; less sweet than sugar; comes in light (pale yellow) and dark (deep amber).

MAPLE: Liquefied sugar made from the concentrated sap of the sugar maple; golden brown.

TREACLE: A liquid by-product of sugar refining, not widely used in the United States; light or dark; flavor resembles molasses.

FLAVORED: Sugar or other syrup with added flavoring; common types are cassis (black currant), grenadine (pomegranate), maple.

MOLASSES: Thick, dark brown liquid by-product of sugar refining; rich flavor but less sweet than sugar; comes in sulfured, unsulfured, and blackstrap.

HONEY: Thick, pale straw yellow to deep brown liquid; creamed honeys are moist and granular; may be packaged with honeycomb, whole or in pieces; sweeter than sugar.

CHOCOLATE

Chocolate is produced from beans, known as cocoa beans, which grow in a pod on the cacao tree. For the ancient Aztecs, cocoa beans served not only to produce drinks and as a component of various sauces, but also as currency. Today chocolate is usually found in a variety of sweets, including cakes, candies, and other desserts, although it is also used in a variety of savory entrées, such as mole poblano, a turkey dish of Mexican origin.

The chocolate extraction process is lengthy and has undergone a great deal of refinement since the days of the Aztecs. The first stage involves crushing the kernel into a paste; at this point it is completely unsweetened and is called chocolate liquor. The liquor is then further ground to give it a smoother, finer texture, and sweeteners and other ingredients may be added. The liquor may be pressed, causing cocoa butter to be forced out. The cocoa solids that are left are ground into cocoa powder. The cocoa butter may be combined with chocolate liquor to make eating chocolate, or it may be flavored and sweetened to make white chocolate. Cocoa butter also has numerous pharmaceutical and cosmetic uses.

Chocolate should be stored, well wrapped, in a cool, dry, ventilated area. Under most conditions it should not be refrigerated, since this could cause moisture to condense on the surface of the chocolate; if the weather is hot and humid, however, it may be preferable to refrigerate or freeze the chocolate to prevent loss of flavor. Sometimes stored chocolate develops a white "bloom"; the bloom merely indicates that some of the cocoa butter has melted and then recrystallized on the surface. Chocolate with a bloom can still be used safely. If properly stored, chocolate will last for several months. Cocoa powder should be stored in tightly sealed containers in a dry place. It will keep almost indefinitely. The table below lists descriptions and purchase forms of various chocolate products.

CHOCOLATE AND RELATED PRODUCTS

TYPE	DESCRIPTION	PURCHASE FORM
Chocolate liquor	The chocolate-flavored portion of chocolate; obtained by grinding and liquefying chocolate nibs.	(See unsweetened chocolate)
Cocoa butter	The vegetable fat portion of chocolate; removed for cocoa; added for chocolate.	Tubs (plastic at room temperature)
Cocoa	Chocolate from which all but 10–25% of the cocoa butter has been removed.	Powder
Cocoa, Dutch-process	Chocolate from which all but 22–24% of the cocoa butter has been removed; treated with alkali to reduce its acidity.	Powder
Cocoa, breakfast	Cocoa with at least 22% cocoa butter.	Unsweetened powder
Cocoa, low-fat	Cocoa with less than 10% cocoa butter.	Powder
Cocoa, instant	Cocoa that has been precooked, sweetened (it usually contains about 80% sugar), and emulsified to make it dissolve more easily in liquid; may have powdered milk added.	Powder
Chocolate, unsweetened (bitter/baking)	Solid chocolate made with about 95% chocolate liquor and 5% cocoa butter.	Blocks or bars
Chocolate, bittersweet	Solid chocolate made with 35–50% chocolate liquor, 15% cocoa butter, and 35–50% sugar; interchangeable with semisweet chocolate; may have added ingredients.	Blocks, bars, chunks, chips
Chocolate, semisweet	Solid chocolate made with about 45% chocolate liquor, 15% cocoa butter, and 40% sugar; interchangeable with bittersweet chocolate; may have added ingredients.	Blocks, bars, chunks, chips
Chocolate, sweet	Solid chocolate made with 15% chocolate liquor, 15% cocoa butter, and 70% sugar; may have added ingredients.	Blocks, bars, chunks, chips
Chocolate, milk	Solid chocolate made with 10% chocolate liquor, 20% cocoa butter, 50% sugar, and 15% milk solids; may have added ingredients.	Blocks, bars, chunks, chips
Chocolate, coating (couverture)	Solid chocolate made with 15% chocolate liquor, 35% cocoa butter, and 50% sugar; high fat content makes it ideal for coating candy, pastries, and cakes.	Blocks, bars, chunks, chips
Confectionery coating	Solid, artificial chocolate made with vegetable fat other than cocoa butter; usually contains real chocolate flavoring in chocolate-flavored types; other flavors available.	Blocks, bars, chunks, chips
Chocolate, white	Solid chocolate made with cocoa butter or other vegetable fats, sugar, milk solids, and vanilla flavoring; contains no chocolate liquor; may contain artificial yellow color and/or other added ingredients.	Blocks, bars, chunks, chips
Chocolate syrup	Chocolate or cocoa, sugar and/or other sweeteners, water, salt, flavorings.	Bulk, jar, can
Chocolate sauce	Same as chocolate syrup but thicker; may have added milk, cream, butter, and/or other thickeners.	Bulk, jar, can
Carob	A dark brown, somewhat chocolatelike flavoring produced from the carob bean; unsweetened carob is somewhat sweet, so it requires less added sugar than chocolate (about three-quarters the usual amount).	Blocks, bars, chunks, powder

MISCELLANEOUS DRY GOODS

VINEGARS AND CONDIMENTS

Vinegars and most condiments are used to introduce sharp, piquant, sweet, or hot flavors into foods. They may be used as an ingredient or served on the side, to be added according to a guest's taste. A well-stocked kitchen should include a full range of vinegars, mustards, relishes, pickles, olives, jams, and other condiments. In general, vinegars and condiments should be stored in the same manner as oils and shortenings.

EXTRACTS

The chef uses a variety of flavoring extracts for cooking and baking. Herbs, spices, nuts, and fruits are used to prepare extracts, which are alcohol-based. Common flavors include vanilla, lemon, mint, and almond.

Extracts can lose their potency if they are allowed to come in contact with air, heat, or light. To preserve flavor, store in tightly capped dark jars or bottles away from heat or direct light.

LEAVENERS

Leaveners are used to give foods a light, airy texture. Chemical leaveners, such as baking soda (sodium bicarbonate) and baking powder (a combination of baking soda, cream of tartar, and talc), work rapidly. Baking powder is usually double-acting, which means that one reaction happens in the presence of moisture, when liquids are added to dry ingredients, and a second occurs in the presence of heat, as the item bakes in the oven.

Yeast leavens foods by the process of fermentation, which produces alcohol and carbon dioxide. The gas is trapped by the dough, creating a number of small pockets, and the alcohol burns off during baking.

Chemical leaveners should be kept perfectly dry. Dried yeast can be held for extended periods, but fresh yeast has a short shelf life, only a few weeks under refrigeration.

THICKENERS

Thickeners are used to give liquid a certain amount of viscosity. The process of forming an emulsion is one way to thicken a liquid, as is the process of reduction. In addition, various thickening ingredients can be used. These include the following:

ARROWROOT: A starchy root that is ground and highly refined. In comparison to cornstarch, usually less arrowroot is needed to achieve the same degree of thickening.

FROM TOP RIGHT *cornstarch, potato starch, rice flour, tapioca, and arrowroot.*

CORNSTARCH: The refined, finely ground endosperm of the corn kernel.

FILÉ GUMBO POWDER: Powdered sassafras root; used in Cajun and Creole cookery.

GELATIN: A protein that, when properly combined with a liquid, will cause the liquid to gel as it cools. Available in powdered form and in sheets.

Thickeners should be stored in tightly sealed containers in dry storage. They will keep almost indefinitely.

COFFEE, TEA, AND OTHER BEVERAGES

A good cup of coffee or tea is often the key to a restaurant's reputation. The chef should identify brands and blends that best serve the establishment's specific needs. Whereas some operations prefer to select whole coffee beans, others may be better served by buying preground, portioned, vacuum-packed coffee. Many restaurants serve brewed decaffeinated coffee, and some offer espresso and cappuccino, both regular and decaffeinated.

Teas come in many varieties, including decaffeinated black teas and herbal teas. Most are blends and are available in single-serving bags or in loose form.

Although coffee and tea generally keep well, they will lose a lot of flavor if stored too long or under improper conditions. Whole beans or opened containers of ground coffee should be kept cool (ideally, refrigerated); teas should be stored in cool, dry areas, away from light and moisture.

Prepared mixes (powdered fruit drinks or cocoa mixes, for example) also should be kept moisture-free. Frozen juices and other beverages should remain solidly frozen until needed. Canned juices should be kept in dry storage. Remember to rotate stock, and check all cans, boxes, and other containers for leaks, bulges, or mold.

WINES, CORDIALS, AND LIQUEURS

A general rule of thumb for selecting wines, cordials, and liqueurs for use in cooking and baking is this: If it is not suitable for drinking, it is not suitable for cooking.

Among the common ones used in the kitchen are brandies and cognacs, Champagne, dry red and white wines,

Spiced   *Black*

Green   *Herbal (tisane)*

Port, Sauternes, Sherry, stouts, ales, beers, and sweet and dry vermouth. For baking purposes, the chef should keep on hand bourbon, crème de cassis, fruit brandies, gin, Kahlúa, rum, and scotch. Items listed for the kitchen can, of course, be used in the bakeshop, and vice versa.

Purchase wines and cordials that are affordably priced and of good quality. Table wines (Burgundies, Chablis, and Chardonnays, for example) lose their flavor and become acidic once opened, especially when subjected to heat, light, and air. To preserve flavor, keep them in closed bottles or bottles fitted with pouring spouts, and refrigerate when not needed. Fortified wines (Madeiras, Sherries, and Ports, for example) are more stable than table wines and can be held in dry storage if there is not enough room to refrigerate them. The same also applies to cordials, cognacs, and liqueurs.

PREPARED, CANNED, AND FROZEN FOODS

Only you, as the chef, can determine how and when to use convenience foods, depending upon the requirements and capabilities of the kitchen and the quality of the convenience foods available. It may make sense, for example, to purchase prepared and frozen doughs (puff pastry, brioche, phyllo dough), instead of producing them on the premises. Other commonly used convenience foods include frozen vegetables such as corn, peas, and spinach.

Canned products also have valid uses in the contemporary kitchen. Depending upon the season, some canned items may be of better quality than below-standard fresh produce. An obvious example is canned tomatoes, which are often superior to out-of-season fresh tomatoes. Quality, determined by good taste, yield, price, and color, will vary from product to product.

Other convenience foods that may have a place in the kitchen include mayonnaise and prepared bases. In all cases, remember to choose products that are of good quality.

For storage purposes, frozen goods should be kept solidly frozen until they are needed. Canned goods should be rotated on the shelves to ensure that the first in is the first out (FIFO rule).

PART THREE

STOCKS, SAUCES, AND SOUPS

Good cooking is the result of carefully developing the best possible flavor and most perfect texture in any dish. Basic flavoring and aromatic combinations constitute the flavor base in many stocks, sauces, and soups; thickeners contribute to a rich, smooth mouth feel in sauces, soups, and stews; and liaisons lend body.

MISE EN PLACE FOR STOCKS, SAUCES, AND SOUPS

BOUQUET GARNI AND SACHET D'EPICES

A bouquet garni or sachet d'épices adds flavors to stocks, sauces, and soups by gently infusing the liquid with their aroma.

Bouquet garni and sachet d'épices are two basic aromatic preparations called for over and over again. These combinations of aromatic vegetables, herbs, and spices are meant to enhance and support the flavors of a dish. Certain basic techniques and ingredient proportions should be observed, as outlined in the following methods for both bouquets garnis and sachets d'épices.

A bouquet garni is made up of fresh herbs and vegetables, tied into a bundle. If a leek is used to wrap the other bouquet garni ingredients, it must be thoroughly rinsed first to remove the dirt. Enclose the herbs in the leek leaves or celery. Cut a piece of string long enough to leave a tail to tie the bouquet to the pot handle. This makes it easy to pull out the bouquet when it is time to remove it.

A sachet contains such ingredients as peppercorns, other spices, or herbs tied up in a cheesecloth bag. A standard bouquet or sachet can be modified a little (add some carrot or a garlic clove) or a lot (use cardamom, ginger, ground turmeric, and cinnamon) to produce different effects. A sachet infuses a liquid with flavor, in the same way that a teabag is used to make a cup of tea.

For a small batch (less than a gallon), add the sachet or bouquet in the last 15 to 20 minutes. For batches of several gallons or more, add about 1 hour before the end of the cooking time. Consult specific recipes and formulas for guidance.

Whenever you add a bouquet or sachet to a stock or soup, taste the dish before and after adding it to learn more about how it affects the dish's flavor profile. If the aromatics have been combined following a basic formula and simmered long enough to infuse the dish with their aroma, the dish should be flavored but not overwhelmed by them.

A STANDARD BOUQUET GARNI, ADEQUATE TO FLAVOR 1 GALLON/3.75 LITERS OF LIQUID, INCLUDES:	*1 sprig of thyme* *3 or 4 parsley stems*	*1 bay leaf* *2 or 3 leek leaves and/or 1 celery stalk, cut crosswise in half*
A STANDARD SACHET D'EPICES, ADEQUATE TO FLAVOR 1 GALLON/3.75 LITERS OF LIQUID, INCLUDES:	*3 or 4 parsley stems* *1 sprig of thyme or 1 teaspoon/5 milliliters dried thyme*	*1 bay leaf* *1 teaspoon/5 milliliters cracked peppercorns.*

STANDARD BOUQUET GARNI

Rinse leeks to use as a wrapper.

Leave a long tail on the string.

Tie the bouquet securely.

STANDARD SACHET D'ÉPICES

Ingredients for a standard sachet.

Tie ingredients in cheesecloth.

MIREPOIX

Vegetables, herbs, and smoked meats with very intense flavors are often added for flavor and aroma.

White mirepoix (left) cut very fine. Standard mirepoix cut small (middle) and large (right).

Matignon.

Mirepoix and similar combinations are intended to provide a subtle but pleasing background flavor, supporting and improving the flavor of the finished dish. Mirepoix is the French name for a combination of onions, carrots, and celery, but it is not the only such combination, even in the French culinary repertoire. Other common combinations include onions, carrots, celery (both Pascal and celeriac), leeks, parsnips, garlic, diced ham, tomatoes, shallots, mushrooms, peppers and chiles, and ginger are among the ingredients commonly referred to as aromatics. They may be used in various combinations, as dictated by the cuisine and the dish itself.

Even when used in relatively small amounts, aromatic ingredients make a significant contribution to a dish. One pound/ 450 grams of mirepoix is enough to flavor 1 gallon/3.75 liters of stock, soup, sauce, stew, braise, or marinade and, according to the ratio above, would include 8 ounces/ 225 grams onion, 4 ounces/115 grams carrot, and 4 ounces/155 grams celery.

To get the best flavor from mirepoix and similar preparations, thoroughly rinse and trim all the vegetables first. Onion skin will give a simmering liquid an orange or yellow tint, which may not be desirable. Scrubbing but not peeling carrots and

parsnips can cut down prep time. Nevertheless, some chefs peel all vegetables on the premise that flavor is extracted into the dish more easily; others peel them only when they are not strained out of the finished dish.

Regardless of whether or not the vegetables are peeled, cut them into pieces of a relatively uniform size, with the dimensions matching the cooking time of the dish. The shorter the simmering time, the smaller and thinner the cut; the longer the time, the large and thicker the cut. Make larger cuts for long simmering dishes, like pot roasts or brown veal stock. Cut mirepoix small or slice it for use in uncooked marinades, pan gravies, and dishes that simmer up to 3 hours. Slice mirepoix very fine or chop fine for fumets and stocks that simmer less than 1 hour.

Mirepoix will add a distinct aroma to a dish, even if the cut-up vegetables are simply added to the pot as it simmers. But sweating, smothering, or browning them in fat significantly changes the flavor. Start by cooking onions and leeks in the fat first, then the carrots, and finally the celery.

White stocks or cream soups generally call for cooking the mirepoix over low heat in fat until it starts to give off some juices, known as sweating. If the pot is covered as

Celery is added once onions and carrots are browned.

Stir in tomato paste.

the aromatics sweat, they are considered smothered. Mirepoix can cook until it turns a deep rich brown (sometimes referred to as caramelized), either on the stovetop or in the oven.

Tomato paste or purée is often added to the mirepoix for added flavor and color. Add it, if required, once the mirepoix ingredients are partly cooked. Cook the tomato paste until it turns rusty brown and has a sweet aroma. This technique is called pinçage, from the French pincer, to stiffen or pinch, which is a fairly good description of what happens to the tomatoes as they cook in hot fat.

Cook until celery softens and its color deepens.

Cook carefully until deeply browned to complete pinçage.

MIREPOIX VARIATIONS

STANDARD MIREPOIX is used for a variety of stocks and soups and typically includes the following ingredients (by weight): 2 parts onion, 1 part carrot, 1 part celery.

Tomato paste or purée is often included for brown stock, gravy, stew, or soup. In addition to standard mirepoix, the following aromatic vegetable combinations are also used:

WHITE MIREPOIX:
Used to flavor white stocks and soups that should have a pale ivory or white color. Leeks and parsnips replace some of the onions and the carrots.

CAJUN TRINITY:
Used in many Louisiana Creole and Cajun dishes, such as gumbo. Made up of a combination of onions, celery, and green pepper.

MATIGNON (SOMETIMES CALLED EDIBLE MIREPOIX):
Typically includes onions, carrots, celery, and ham cut into very neat dice. Mushrooms and assorted herbs and spices may be added as desired. Used to garnish a dish as well as to flavor it.

BATTUTO:
Extensively used in Italian soups, sauces, stews, and meat dishes. Includes olive oil or chopped lard, pancetta, or fatback, with garlic, onions, parsley, carrots, celery, and/or green peppers. Once sautéed, a battuto becomes known as a soffritto.

ROUX

Roux thickens sauces, soups, and stews, as well as lending those dishes a special flavor.

Cooking flour in fat inactivates an enzyme that, if not destroyed by high heat, interferes with flour's thickening ability. Cooking flour also changes the flour's raw cereal taste to a toasty or nutty flavor. Both the flavor and the color become deeper the longer the roux cooks. In addition to improving raw flour's flavor and color, cooking flour in fat helps to keep the starch in the flour from forming long strands or clumps when the roux is combined with a liquid. (See page 51 for more on thickening with starches and gelatinization.)

Although roux is being supplanted by other thickeners in the American kitchen, it is still used extensively, perhaps because of the European culinary heritage. Dark roux is particularly important in Creole and Cajun cuisine, where it gives gumbos and stews a unique character.

Roux can be prepared with any type of white wheat flour. Flours vary in their starch to protein ratio. Cake flour, for instance, has a higher proportion of starch to protein than bread flour. A cake flour roux will therefore have more thickening power than a bread flour roux. All-purpose flour has a thickening

power between the two. Rouxs called for in this book were tested using all-purpose flour.

Clarified butter is the most common fat used for making roux, but whole butter, vegetable oils, rendered chicken fat, or fats rendered from roasts may also be used. Each fat will have a different influence on a finished dish's flavor.

Heat the fat over medium heat and add the flour, stirring to combine. The basic ratio (by weight) for a roux is 6 parts flour to 4 parts fat. The roux should be very smooth and moist, with a glossy sheen, not dry or greasy. It should look "like sand at low tide." Adjust the roux's texture by adding more flour or fat.

Stir the roux as it cooks to keep it from scorching and continue to cook it to the desired color. To reduce the chances of scorching, large quantities of roux may be placed in a moderate (350 to 375°F/175 to 190°C) oven to complete cooking.

The three basic colors of roux are white (barely colored or chalky), blond (golden straw color, with a slightly nutty aroma), and brown or dark (deep brown, with a strong nutty aroma). Once the roux is properly cooked, it is ready to use now, or it may be cooled and stored for later (see page 64).

Break up cold roux.

Roux can be combined with liquid in two ways. Cool roux may be added to hot liquid, or cool liquid may be added to hot roux. For either approach, though, follow these general guidelines:

- Avoid temperature extremes to prevent lumping.

- Cool or room-temperature roux can be incorporated into hot liquid more easily than ice-cold roux can because the fat is not as solid.

- Very cold liquid should not be used, as it will initially cause the roux to harden.

- Extremely hot roux should be avoided, because it may spatter when combined with a liquid and cause serious burns.

The full thickening action of the roux becomes evident when the liquid has reached approximately 200°F/93°C. Long cooking sauces and soups are further thickened though reduction.

The same weight of white roux has more thickening power than a darker roux, because the browning process causes some of the starch in the flour to break down, making it unavailable for thickening. The darker the roux, the less thickening power it has.

Melt the fat.

Stir in flour until smooth.

Adjust for proper consistency.

CLARIFIED BUTTER

Clarified butter is made by heating whole butter until the butterfat and milk solids separate.

The purpose of clarifying butter is to remove the milk solids and water from whole butter. This makes it possible to cook with butter at a higher temperature than would be possible with whole butter. Clarified butter is commonly used to make roux. Some chefs also prefer it for warm butter sauces, such as hollandaise and béarnaise.

Using salted butter is not recommended because the concentration of salt in the resulting clarified butter is unpredictable. Unsalted clarified butter can always be salted as it is used.

Heat the butter over low heat until foam rises to the surface and the milk solids

drop to the bottom of the pot. The remaining butterfat becomes very clear. Skim the surface foam as the butter clarifies.

Pour or ladle off the butterfat into another container, being careful to leave all of the water and milk solids in the pan bottom. After whole butter is clarified, some of its volume is lost due to skimming, decanting, and discarding the water and milk solids. One pound (450 grams) of whole butter yields approximately 12 ounces (340 grams) of clarified butter.

Ghee, which is used in some Asian cuisines, is a type of clarified butter. It has a nutty flavor because the milk solids brown before they are separated from the butterfat.

Melt butter.

Skim foam.

Decant clarified butter.

PURE STARCH SLURRIES

To use a pure starch in a dish, dilute it in cold water to produce a slurry.

Arrowroot, cornstarch, and other pure starches have greater thickening power, ounce for ounce, than flour and do not require an extended simmering time like roux.

Arrowroot, cornstarch, tapioca, potato starch, and rice flour are all pure starches. They are made into slurries by dissolving them in cold liquid. Thoroughly blend the starch and liquid to about the consistency of heavy cream. Slurries can be blended in advance and held to use during à la minute preparations. If not used immediately, the starch will settle out of the liquid and move to the bottom of the container. Stir the slurry just before use to recombine the starch evenly throughout the liquid.

Pour or ladle it into simmering liquid. When added to a simmering dish, slurries quickly thicken it, making it easy for the chef to control the final consistency of the dish. Whisk constantly to prevent lumping and scorching. Bring the liquid back to a boil and cook just until the sauce reaches the desired thickness and clarity.

Dishes thickened with slurries have limited holding periods. Be sure to check periodically for quality if they must be held in a steam table. They have somewhat different qualities but may be substituted one for the other, following the formula below.

ARROWROOT. Thickening power roughly equivalent to cornstarch but more translucent. Does not gel and weep when cooled. Freezes well. Fairly expensive.

CORNSTARCH. Translucent. Thickens when heated, but gels and weeps upon cooling. Thickening power diminishes with excessive heating. Does not freeze well. Inexpensive.

TAPIOCA/CASSAVA FLOUR. Translucent. Thickening power slightly greater than cornstarch. Available from Asian-food purveyors. Moderately priced.

POTATO STARCH. Translucent. More thickening power than cornstarch. Moderately priced.

RICE FLOUR. Translucent. Relatively weak thickening power. Freezes well. Fairly expensive.

FROM TOP RIGHT *cornstarch, potato starch, rice flour, tapioca, and arrowroot.*

Blend starch with cold liquid and stir to recombine.

TO SUBSTITUTE A PURE STARCH FOR ROUX, USE THE FOLLOWING FORMULA:

Weight of flour in roux (multiply weight of roux by 0.6 to determine weight of flour) × Thickening power of replacement starch (see below)
= Weight of replacement starch required (estimated)

EXAMPLE: TO SUBSTITUTE ARROWROOT IN A RECIPE THAT CALLS FOR 10 OUNCES OF ROUX:

10 ounces roux × 0.6 = 6 ounces flour
6 ounces flour × 0.5 (arrowroot thickening power) = 3 ounces arrowroot

THICKENING POWERS

Rice flour: 0.6   Cornstarch: 0.5   Arrowroot: 0.5   Tapioca: 0.4   Potato starch: 0.2

LIAISON

The mixture of egg yolks and cream that is used to enrich and slightly thicken sauces and soups is called a liaison.

Liaisons add body and sheen to a dish. They are not thickeners in the same way that roux and pure starch slurries are, but the combination of cream and eggs, when properly simmered in a dish, gives more body as well as a light golden-ivory color. A liaison also adds flavor to a sauce or soup and gives it a smooth texture.

Egg yolks normally begin to coagulate at 149°F/65°C. The addition of cream raises the coagulation point to 180° to 185°F/82°

to 85°C. Blend the cream and egg yolks together until evenly blended.

Adding a portion of the hot liquid to the liaison avoids a drastic heat change, which could cause the yolks to curdle. This process, known as tempering, reduces temperature extremes so the finished soup or sauce remains smooth. Gradually add about one-third of the hot liquid to the liaison, a ladleful at a time, whipping constantly.

When enough hot liquid has been added, return the tempered liaison to the soup or sauce. Return the pot to low heat and gently warm the mixture, stirring frequently, until it thickens slightly. Do not allow the mixture to go beyond 185°F/85°C or the egg yolks might curdle.

For reasons of quality, add the liaison as close to service time as possible. Hold soups and sauces thickened with a liaison above 140°F/60°C for food safety reasons but below 185°F/85°C to maintain quality.

Blend the liaison.

Add hot liquid to the liaison.

Return tempered liaison to the dish.

FOR ENOUGH LIAISON TO THICKEN 24 FLUID OUNCES/720 MILLILITERS LIQUID, THE BASIC RATIO (BY WEIGHT) IN A LIAISON IS:

3 parts cream (8 fluid ounces/240 milliliters)

1 part egg yolk (about 3 large yolks or 2½ fluid ounces/75 milliliters)

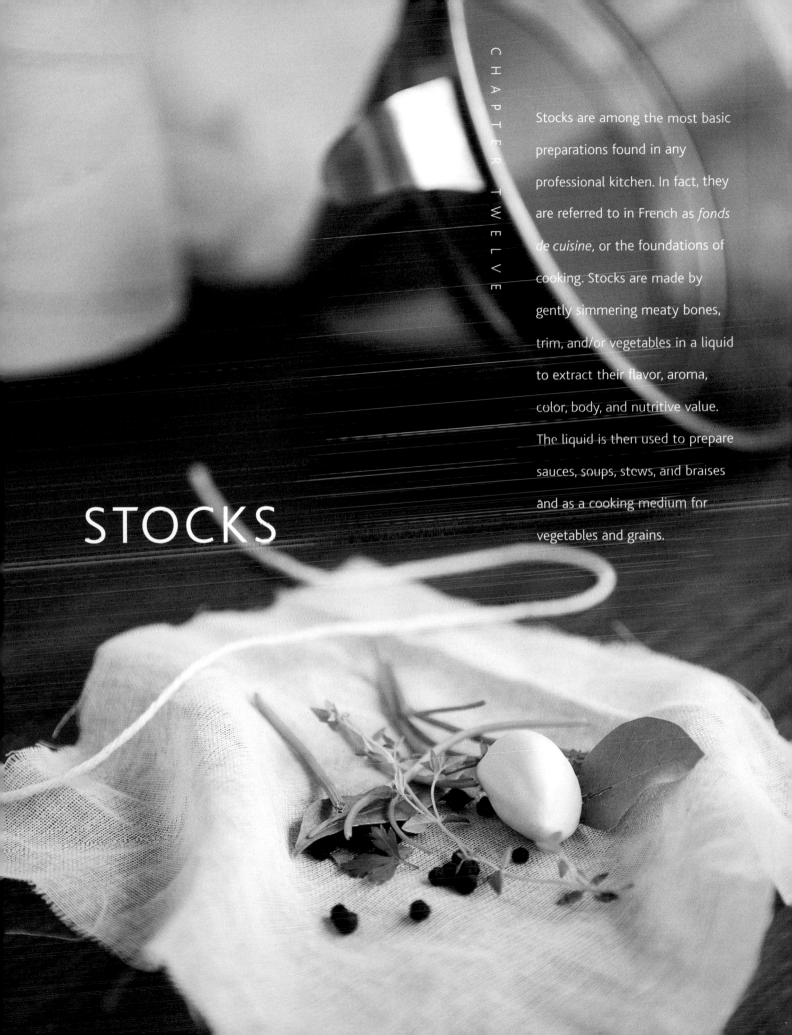

CHAPTER TWELVE

STOCKS

Stocks are among the most basic preparations found in any professional kitchen. In fact, they are referred to in French as *fonds de cuisine,* or the foundations of cooking. Stocks are made by gently simmering meaty bones, trim, and/or vegetables in a liquid to extract their flavor, aroma, color, body, and nutritive value. The liquid is then used to prepare sauces, soups, stews, and braises and as a cooking medium for vegetables and grains.

STOCK

White and brown stocks and fumets are the three basic types of stock.

White stocks are made by combining all of the ingredients with a cool liquid and gently simmering them over gentle heat.

Brown stocks indicate roasting or sautéing the bones and mirepoix in enough fat to produce a rich mahogany color before simmering. Fumets (sometimes known as essences) call for sweating or smothering the main ingredients before simmering, often with the addition of a dry white wine.

FOR A STOCK THAT HAS GOOD FLAVOR, AROMA, COLOR, AND BODY, OBSERVE THE FOLLOWING FORMULAS.

INGREDIENTS FOR 1 GALLON/ 3.75 LITERS OF MEAT OR POULTRY STOCK, INCLUDE:

8 pounds/3.6 kilograms bones and trimmings to 6 quarts/5.75 liters cool liquid

1 pound/450 grams mirepoix

1 standard sachet d'épices or bouquet garni

INGREDIENTS FOR 1 GALLON/ 3.75 LITERS OF FISH OR SHELLFISH STOCK, INCLUDE:

10 pounds/4.5 kilograms bones and trimmings to 5 quarts/4.75 liters cool liquid (sometimes including 1 to 2 quarts/1 to 2 liters dry white wine)

1 pound/450 grams white mirepoix (sometimes including mushroom trimmings)

1 standard sachet d'épices or bouquet garni

FOR GOOD FLAVOR and body use meat and fish bones, whether acquired as a by-product of meat and fish fabrication or purchased for stock. Bones from younger animals contain a high percentage of cartilage and other connective tissues that break down into gelatin during simmering and give the stock body. Knuckle, back, and neck bones are good for stock making. Include any wholesome trim from fabrication, if available, to further bolster flavor. Cut bones into 3-inch lengths for quicker and more thorough extraction of flavor, gelatin, and nutritive value. If bones are purchased frozen, thaw them before using to make stock.

Rinse all bones, fresh or frozen, well before putting them into the stockpot, to remove blood and other impurities that can compromise the quality of the stock. For brown stocks, prepare the bones and trim by roasting them first; for more information, see page 252. For additional information on selecting and preparing ingredients for fish and vegetable stocks, see pages 253 and 254.

Trim and cut mirepoix to a size that will allow for good flavor extraction. A 1/2-inch/12-mm dice or slice is good for simmering time of 1 hour. Cut vegetables larger or smaller for longer or shorter simmering times. The mirepoix and tomato paste called for in brown stocks are roasted or sautéed until browned before being added to the stock.

Stocks also include a sachet d'épices or bouquet garni containing aromatics suited to the type of stock being made. Because the stock will eventually be strained, some chefs do not tie up sachet or bouquet ingredients. However, tying makes it easy to remove the aromatics if their flavor becomes too strong.

Pots used for stocks are usually taller than they are wide. This type of pot creates a smaller surface area so the evaporation rate is minimized during simmering. Some stockpots have spigots at the bottom that can be used to remove the finished stock without disturbing the bones. Steam-jacketed kettles are often used to produce large quantities of stock. Court bouillons, fumets, and essences that do not have long simmering times can be prepared in rondeaus or other wide shallow pots. Tilting kettles are used when available for large-scale production.

Ladles or skimmers should be on hand to remove scum from the stock as it simmers. Cheesecloth, sieves, and colanders are used to separate the bones and vegetables from the stock. A thermometer and metal containers for cooling, as well as plastic containers for storing the stock, should be on hand. Tasting spoons will also be needed.

1. Combine the bones with a cool liquid and bring slowly to a simmer. Skim as necessary.

For the best flavor and clearest stock, start with a cool liquid (water or remouillage) to gently extract flavor and body. Maintain a bare simmer throughout the cooking process. Bubbles should break the surface of the stock infrequently. The French use the verb *frémir*, to tremble, to describe the action of the bubbles as the stock cooks.

Conscientious skimming, along with proper temperature regulation, produces the clearest stocks. Apart from the aesthetics of a clear, limpid stock, as opposed to a cloudy one, the impurities that leave a stock cloudy are the same elements that will quickly spoil and sour a stock. The clearer the stock, the longer its shelf life.

2. Add the aromatic ingredients at the appropriate point for the best flavor development.

The right time to add mirepoix to all stocks except fish stocks and court bouillons is about 1 hour before the end of cooking time. Adding the aromatics at this point will allow enough time for the best flavor to be extracted but not so much time that the flavor is broken down and destroyed. Taste the stock to determine whether or not it is necessary to adjust the standard formula.

Since fish stocks, fumets, essences, and court bouillons do not have extended cooking times, the mirepoix ingredients are normally cut smaller and added near the beginning of the simmering time, and they remain in the stock throughout cooking.

TOP *Cool water allows a slow rise in cooking temperature. This will let any blood or other impurities that might cloud the finished stock be released into the water, where they will coagulate and rise to the surface.*

BOTTOM *The liquid should cover the bones by no more than 2 inches.*

ABOVE *Once the impurities have risen to the surface, they can readily be skimmed away. The French verb* dépouiller, *literally to skin, is used to describe the skimming process. The careful and consistent skimming of stocks determines how clear the finished stock will be.*

ABOVE *To make mirepoix or a similar aromatic vegetable combination, rinse, trim, and cut the vegetables into roughly even-sized pieces.*

3. Simmer until the desired flavor, body, and color are achieved.

Smell and taste the stock as it develops so that you can begin to learn the stages it goes through, and notice when it has reached its peak. Once the stock reaches that point, further cooking will cause flavors to deaden and become flat. Even the color of the stock may be slightly off if it simmers too long. The following cooking times are approximate; they will vary according to numerous factors, such as ingredient quality, total volume, and cooking temperature.

WHITE BEEF STOCK: 8 to 10 hours

WHITE AND BROWN VEAL AND GAME STOCKS:
   6 to 8 hours

WHITE POULTRY AND GAME BIRD STOCKS:
   4 to 6 hours

FISH STOCK AND FUMET:
   30 minutes to 1 hour

VEGETABLE STOCKS: 30–40 minutes,
   depending on the specific
   ingredients and the size of
   the vegetable cut

4. Strain and use immediately or cool properly.

Ladle the stock out of the pot and through a fine wire mesh sieve or a colander lined with rinsed cheesecloth. Disturb the solid ingredients as little as possible for a clear stock.

Once you have removed as much stock as possible by ladling, drain the remaining stock through a colander into a bowl. Then strain the stock through cheesecloth or a fine sieve to remove any remaining impurities, if desired. Reserve the bones and mirepoix to prepare a remouillage if desired (see page 250).

If not using immediately, cool the stock (see pages 64–65), checking with a thermometer to determine when it has cooled to 40°F/4°C. Skim any fat that rises to the surface or wait until it has hardened under refrigeration and simply lift it away before reheating the stock for later use.

5. Evaluate the quality of the finished stock.

Evaluate the stock on the basis of four criteria: flavor, color, aroma, and clarity. If the correct ratio of bones, mirepoix, and aromatics to liquid has been used and the correct procedure has been followed, the flavor will be well balanced, rich, and full-bodied with the major flavoring ingredient dominating and the flavors of the aromatics unobtrusive.

Quality white stocks are clear and light to golden in color when hot. Brown stocks are a deep amber or brown because of the preliminary roasting of the bones and mirepoix. Vegetable stocks vary in color according to type.

ABOVE *As the stock simmers, fat rises to the surface and solid ingredients start to fall to the bottom. Continued simmering reduces the stock slightly, intensifying the flavor. The stock shown here has a rich color, and looks ready to strain.*

ABOVE *Rinse cheesecloth thoroughly before draping it in a sieve. Rinsing removes fibers and makes the cloth adhere to the strainer better.*

ABOVE *Steam-jacketed kettles are often used to produce large quantities of stock. Some stockpots have spigots near the bottom to draw off the finished stock without disturbing the bones.*

8 lb / 3.6 chicken bones (meaty) cut into 3-inch/75mm lengths

6 qt / 5.75 L cold water or remouillage, or as needed (see page 251)

salt (optional), as needed

MIREPOIX

8 oz / 225 g medium-dice onions

4 oz / 115 g medium-dice carrots

4 oz / 115 g medium-dice celery

sachet d'épices, containing 2 to 3 parsley stems, $1/2$ tsp/2 mL fresh or dried thyme, $1/2$ tsp/2 mL cracked black peppercorns, 1 bay leaf, and 1 garlic clove

CHICKEN STOCK

1 Rinse the bones under cool running water and place in a stockpot.

2 Add cold water or remouillage to cover the bones by about 2 inches. Add salt to taste if desired.

3 Slowly bring the stock to a simmer. Skim the surface as necessary.

4 Simmer for 3 to 4 hours. Add the mirepoix and sachet and continue to simmer the stock 1 more hour, skimming as necessary and tasting from time to time.

5 Strain the stock through a sieve or a colander lined with rinsed cheesecloth. The stock may be used at this point, or it may be properly cooled, labeled, and stored.

MAKES 1 GALLON/3.75 LITERS

NOTES

Replace 2 pounds of the chicken bones with turkey necks for an extra rich, gelatinous stock.

Add or replace aromatic ingredients to achieve a particular flavor. For example:

Ginger, lemongrass, and fresh or dried chiles

Juniper berries for game stocks

Strongly flavored herbs, such as tarragon or rosemary

Wild mushroom stems

White Veal Stock, made from veal bones that are gently simmered with mirepoix and a sachet, was originally called **Ordinary Stock**. Simmer for 6 to 8 hours.

White Beef Stock is made by replacing chicken bones with an equal amount of beef bones. Often, chefs like to include a piece of veal shank to add body to the stock. Simmer for 8 to 10 hours.

Stocks for Jus Lié-style Pan Sauces Brown the bones in a pot. (Chicken is shown here, but other birds and meats can be substituted.) Combine them with just enough stock or water to barely cover and simmer over low heat for 4 to 6 hours (a lesser quantity of liquid is used in relation to the bones than for a regular stock). Brown the mirepoix and tomato paste; add to the stock. Deglaze the pan used to brown the mirepoix with water or wine and add to the stock. Add a bouquet garni or sachet and simmer for 1 hour more.

When making smaller batches of a stock, it is more efficient to brown the bones directly in the pot on top of the stove.

Adding stock to the browned bones produces a very rich stock that is suitable as a sauce base.

The finished stock is strained into a bain-marie. A thickener such as arrowroot can be added as needed when preparing pan sauces.

Making stocks takes both time and money. If your kitchen prepares stocks, you should be sure you follow the correct procedures for cooling and storing them. Select a stock to use in a dish based upon either recipe requirements or the effect you hope to achieve, but make sure that any stock you use is still flavorful and wholesome.

REMOUILLAGE

Some chefs like to reserve the simmered bones and mirepoix to prepare a remouillage by simmering them a second time. The word translates from French as a "rewetting"—a good way to explain how remouillage is made. Remouillage may also be made from the clarification raft used to prepare consommé (see page 300). This secondary stock can be used as the liquid for stocks, broths, as a cooking medium, or reduced to a glace.

GLACE

Glace is a highly reduced stock or remouillage. As a result of continued reduction, the stock acquires a jellylike or syrupy consistency and its flavor becomes highly concentrated. When chilled, a glace takes on a rubbery consistency. Glaces are used to bolster the flavor of other foods, particularly sauces. When they are reconstituted with water, they may also serve as a sauce base in much the same way as a commercially prepared base. Glaces are made from different kinds of stock; the most common is *glace de viande,* made from brown veal or beef stock or remouillage.

STORING STOCK

Cool and store stocks the right way (see pages 64–65). Always check a stock before using it to make sure it is still flavorful and wholesome. Boil a small amount and taste it. The aroma should be appealing, not overly pungent or sour.

COMMERCIAL BASES

A stock of excellent quality, even though it may require up to eight hours of cooking time, can represent significant savings in a kitchen that regularly produces wholesome trim from meat and fish fabrication and vegetable preparation. Not all kitchens prepare stocks today, either because meaty bones and trim are not readily available on a consistent basis or because they do not have the space or manpower to successfully prepare and hold stocks. Commercially prepared bases are then used in place of stocks. Even in kitchens that do prepare stocks, bases are helpful to have on hand to deepen and improve the stock's flavor.

Bases are available in highly reduced forms, similar to the classic *glace de viande*, or dehydrated (powdered or cubed). Not all bases are created equal, however. Read the labels carefully. Avoid bases that rely on high-sodium ingredients for flavor. Quality bases are made from meats, bones, vegetables, spices, and aromatics. If possible, taste-test three or more brands. Prepare them according to the package instructions and taste each one. Judge the base on its flavor, saltiness, balance, and depth.

Having decided that a base meets your standards for quality and cost, learn how to make any adjustments you find necessary. For example, you might sweat or roast more vegetables and simmer them in a diluted base, perhaps along with browned trim, to make a rich brown sauce.

Good-quality stocks and prepared bases are an important way to streamline operations, reduce costs, improve quality, and ensure consistency. However, they are only as good as their basic ingredients and the chef's understanding of what makes a stock as flavorful as it can possibly be.

RECIPES

BROWN VEAL STOCK

BROWN STOCKS ARE OFTEN USED AS THE FOUNDATION OF BROWN SAUCES SUCH
AS DEMIGLACE OR *JUS LIÉ*. IF THE STOCK IS RICH AND FULLY FLAVORED, IT MAY NOT
BE NECESSARY TO ADD MORE AROMATICS AND FLAVORINGS TO THE SAUCE,
BEYOND THOSE REQUIRED TO MAKE A SPECIFIC SMALL OR DERIVATIVE SAUCE.
VARIATIONS ON THIS BASIC RECIPE FOLLOW. THEY TELL IN DETAIL HOW TO PRE-
PARE BROWN STOCKS FROM POULTRY AND MEATS OTHER THAN VEAL.

makes 1 gallon/3.75 liters

4 fl oz/120 mL oil, or as needed

8 lb/3.6 kg veal bones, including knuckles and trim if available,
rinsed and dried

6 qt/5.75 L cold water

MIREPOIX

8 oz/225 g large-dice onions

4 oz/115 g large-dice carrots

4 oz/115 g large-dice celery

6 oz/170 g tomato paste

sachet d'épices containing 2 to 3 parsley stems, ½ tsp/2 mL fresh
or dried thyme, ½ tsp/2 mL cracked peppercorns, 1 bay leaf,
and 1 garlic clove

salt (optional), as needed

1 To condition the roasting pan, heat the pan and enough oil
   to lightly film the pan in a 425° to 450°F/220° to 230°C
   oven. Add the bones to the pan and return to the oven.
   Roast the bones, stirring and turning from time to time,
   until the bones are a deep brown, about 30 to 45 minutes.

2 Transfer the bones to a stockpot, and add cool water.
   Deglaze the roasting pan with a little additional cool
   water, and add the released drippings to the stockpot.
   Bring the stock to a simmer slowly over low heat. Adjust
   the heat if necessary to establish an even, gentle simmer
   and continue to cook, skimming the surface as necessary.

3 While the stock is simmering, heat a *rondeau* over
   medium-high heat. Add enough oil to film the pan. Add
   the mirepoix and cook, stirring occasionally, until the
   onions are a deep golden brown, about15 to 20 minutes.
   Add the tomato paste and continue to cook, stirring frequently, until it takes on a rusty brown color and gives off
   a sweet aroma, about 1 to 2 minutes. Add a few ladles of
   the stock to the *rondeau* and stir well to release the drippings; add this mixture to the stock after it has simmered
   for about 5 hours. Add the sachet at the same time.

4 Continue to simmer the stock, skimming as necessary and
   tasting from time to time, until it has developed a rich flavor and a noticeable body, about 1 more hour.

5 Strain the stock. It may be used now (degrease by skimming if necessary), or it may be rapidly cooled and stored
   for later use.

Brown Game Stock (Jus de Gibier) Replace veal bones with an
equal amount of game bones. Include fennel seeds and/or
juniper berries in a standard sachet d'épices.

Estouffade Estouffade, a traditional component of
Espagnole or brown sauce, is a particularly rich brown
stock. Combine veal and beef bones totaling 8 to 9
pounds, with an unsmoked ham knuckle.

Brown Lamb Stock Lamb stock can be flavored with one or
more of the following herbs and spices in a standard
sachet d'épices: mint stems, juniper berries, cumin seeds,
caraway seeds, rosemary.

Brown Pork Stock Stock made from fresh or smoked pork
bones is often used as an ingredient in bean or potato
dishes or pork- or ham-based soups (see page 331). Add
one or more of the following herbs and spices to a standard sachet d'épices: oregano stems, crushed red pepper,
caraway seeds, mustard seeds.

Brown Chicken Stock Replace the veal bones with an equal
weight of chicken bones and lean trim.

Brown Duck Stock Replace the veal bones with an equal
weight of duck bones and lean trim (or bones of other
game birds, such as pheasant). Include fennel seeds and/
or juniper berries in a standard sachet d'épices, if desired.

FISH FUMET

FUMETS (SOMETIMES CALLED ESSENCES) ARE CONCENTRATED, HIGHLY AROMATIC STOCKS. FISH FUMET IS PREPARED BY SWEATING FISH BONES ALONG WITH VEGETABLES SUCH AS LEEKS, MUSHROOMS, AND CELERY, THEN SIMMERING THESE INGREDIENTS IN WATER, OFTEN WITH SOME DRY WHITE WINE.

FOR FISH STOCKS, USE ONLY BONES FROM LEAN FLATFISH LIKE SOLE AND TURBOT. BONES FROM OILY FISH LIKE SALMON AND TUNA ARE TOO STRONGLY FLAVORED AND HAVE TOO HIGH A FAT CONTENT. THE ENTIRE FISH CARCASS, INCLUDING THE HEAD IF IT IS VERY FRESH, CAN BE USED. IF INCLUDING THE HEAD, CUT AWAY THE GILLS FIRST. THEY WILL DISCOLOR THE STOCK AND GIVE IT AN OFF TASTE. ICE FISH BONES OVERNIGHT TO EXTRACT BLOOD, WHICH CAN CLOUD THE STOCK.

makes 1 gallon/3.75 liters

4 fl oz/120 mL oil

11 lb/5 kg fish bones

WHITE MIREPOIX

4 oz/115 g thinly sliced onions

4 oz/115 g thinly sliced leeks

4 oz/115 g thinly sliced parsnips

4 oz/115 g thinly sliced celery

10 oz/285 g mushroom trimmings (optional)

1 gal/3.75 L cold water

1 qt/1 L dry white wine

sachet d'épices containing 2 to 3 parsley stems, ½ tsp/2 mL fresh or thyme, ½ tsp/2 mL cracked black peppercorns, 1 bay leaf and 1 garlic clove

salt (optional)

1 Heat the oil in a *rondeau*, or wide shallow pot, and add the bones and mirepoix.

2 Cover and sweat the bones and mirepoix.

3 Add the water, wine, sachet, and salt, if using, and bring to simmer.

4 Simmer for 35 to 40 minutes, skimming the surface as necessary.

5 Strain the stock. It may be used now or it may be rapidly cooled and stored for later use.

Shellfish Stock Replace the fish bones with an equal amount of crustacean shells (shrimp, lobster, crab). Sauté the shells in hot oil until the color deepens. Add a standard mirepoix (see page 246), and sauté until golden. Add up to 3 oz/85 g tomato paste and cook briefly to deepen the color and aroma. Add enough water to cover the shells and simmer for 35 to 40 minutes. Cool and store as for Fish Fumet.

Fish Stock Sometimes used to make very clear broth or consommé. Combine the bones with cool liquid(s) and aromatics and simmer gently for 30 to 45 minutes. This method is sometimes called the swimming method, to distinguish it from fumet made by the so-called sweating method.

A fumet, as well as a vegetable stock or court bouillon, is best prepared in a rondeau or other wide shallow pot to encourage the best flavor development. Tilting kettles are used when available for large-scale production.

VEGETABLE STOCK

This stock can be used in any recipe calling for stock, particularly when preparing meatless soups, entrees, and side dishes.

makes 1 quart/1 liter

2 fl oz/60 mL vegetable oil

4 oz/115 g sliced onions

4 oz/115 g chopped leeks

2 oz/60 g chopped celery

2 oz/60 g chopped green cabbage

2 oz/60 g chopped carrots

2 oz/60 g chopped tomato

3 garlic cloves, crushed

1½ qt/1.5 L cold water

sachet d'épices containing 2 to 3 parsley stems, ½ tsp/2 mL thyme, ½ tsp/2 mL cracked black peppercorns, 1 bay leaf, 1 garlic clove, 1 tsp/4 mL fennel seeds, and 3 cloves

1. Heat the oil in a *rondeau*, or wide shallow pot, and add the vegetables.

2. Cover and sweat the vegetables for 3 to 5 minutes.

3. Add the water and sachet; simmer for 30 to 40 minutes.

4. Strain the stock. It may be used now, or it may be cooled and stored for later use (see pages 64–65).

Roasted Vegetable Stock Roast the vegetables first in a large pan, turning to make sure all sides are evenly roasted. Combine them with the water and simmer for 30 to 40 minutes. If desired, fresh or dried chiles may be roasted with the other vegetables for a specific flavor.

COURT BOUILLON

A court bouillon, or short broth, is often prepared as the cooking liquid for fish by simmering aromatic vegetables in water with an acid such as wine or vinegar. When fish bones or shells are simmered in the court bouillon, it is called a nage.

makes 1 gallon/3.75 liters

5 qt/4.75 L cold water

8 fl oz/240 mL white wine vinegar

salt (optional), as needed

12 oz/340 g sliced carrots

1 lb/450 g sliced onions

pinch of dried thyme

3 bay leaves

10 to 12 parsley stems

½ tsp/3 mL peppercorns

1. Combine all the ingredients, except the peppercorns, and simmer for 50 minutes.

2. Add the peppercorns and simmer for 10 minutes more.

3. The court bouillon may be used now as a cooking medium, or it may be rapidly cooled and stored for later use (see pages 64–65).

A court bouillon may be prepared as a part of the cooking process, or it may be prepared in large batches and used as required.

CHAPTER THIRTEEN

Sauces are often considered one of the greatest tests of a chef's skill. The successful pairing of a sauce with a food demonstrates technical expertise, an understanding of the food, and the ability to judge and evaluate a dish's flavors, textures, and colors.

SAUCES

BROWN SAUCE

At one time the term "brown sauce" was equated exclusively with the classic sauces Espagnole and demiglace. Today it may also indicate jus de veau lié, pan sauces, or reduction-style sauces based on a brown stock.

Espagnole sauce is prepared by bolstering a brown stock with additional aromatics and thickening it with roux. Demiglace is made by combining equal parts of espagnole and brown stock and reducing by half. Jus liés are made by reducing brown stocks (with added flavorings if desired) and thickening them with a pure starch slurry. Pan sauces and reduction sauces are produced as part of the roasting or sautéing cooking process; thickeners can be either roux, reduction, or pure starch slurries. Regardless of the approach taken, though, the end goal is the same — to make a basic brown sauce that is good enough to be served as is but can also be used as the foundation for several other specific sauces.

INGREDIENTS FOR 1 GALLON/
3.75 LITERS BROWN SAUCE
INCLUDE:

4½ quarts/4.25 liters Brown Stock (see page 252)

4 pounds/1.8 kilograms additional bones and trim

1 pound/450 grams large-cut mirepoix, well-browned

oil, for browning bones and trim and mirepoix

3 to 4 ounces/85 to 115 grams tomato paste or purée

12 ounces/340 grams roux (see page 238) or 1 ounce/30 grams arrowroot or other pure starch

1 sachet d'épices or bouquet garni

THE ULTIMATE SUCCESS of this sauce depends directly on the base stock, usually Brown Veal Stock (page 252). The stock must be of excellent quality with a rich appealing flavor and aroma and well-balanced flavor without any strong notes of mirepoix, herbs, or spices that might overwhelm the finished sauce.

Bones and trim are added to the sauce to improve the flavor of the base stock. If the stock is extremely flavorful, additional bones and trim may not be necessary. If used, cut them into small pieces for better and faster flavor development.

Mirepoix, cut into large dice, may be added to the sauce base; if there is sufficient flavor in the stock, then it may be unnecessary. Mushroom trimmings, herbs, garlic, or shallots may also be added to the sauce as it develops.

Roux (see page 238) may be prepared ahead of time, or it may be prepared as part of the sauce-making process. The thickener of choice for *jus lié* is arrowroot, though another pure starch, such as potato starch or cornstarch, may be used. Arrowroot is preferred because it results in a translucent, glossy sauce.

Jus lié is generally prepared in a saucepan or pot that is wider than it is tall. This is the most effective means of extracting flavors fully and quickly into the finished sauce. You will also need a kitchen spoon, ladle, or skimmer to skim the developing sauce, and tasting spoons, fine strainers, and containers to hold the finished sauce. Additional containers are necessary for both cooling and storing the sauce.

MAKE THE BROWN SAUCE

1. Brown the trim and/or bones and mirepoix.
The flavor of the base stock is usually fortified with well-browned meaty bones and lean trim meat and mirepoix, or a commercial base. Browning these ingredients will enrich the finished sauce and help darken its color. Brown them by roasting in a little oil in a hot oven (425° to 450° F/220° to 230° C) or over medium to high heat on the stovetop in the same pot that will be used to simmer the sauce. Let the bones, trim, and mirepoix reach a deep golden-brown color.

ABOVE *Tomato paste gives depth of flavor and color.*

2. Add the tomato paste and cook out until rust-colored.
Allowing the tomato paste to "cook out" *(pincé)* reduces excessive sweetness, acidity, or bitterness, which might affect the finished sauce. It also encourages the development of the sauce's overall flavor and aroma. When browning the mirepoix in the oven, add the tomato paste to the roasting pan with the vegetables. If browning the mirepoix on the stovetop, add the paste when the vegetables are nearly browned. (Tomato paste cooks out very quickly on the stovetop. Do not let it burn.) Deglaze the pan and add the deglazing liquid to the sauce.

3. Add the brown stock to the bones and/or trim and mirepoix and simmer for 2 to 4 hours, skimming as necessary throughout the cooking time. Let the sauce base simmer long enough for the richest possible flavor to develop. Simmering develops flavor in two ways: It extracts flavor from the bones, trim, and mirepoix; and it reduces the volume of liquid, concentrating flavor. (Optional: Add a prepared roux now, if desired, to prepare a sauce Espagnole.)

Skim the surface often throughout simmering time. Pulling the pot off center on the burner encourages impurities to collect on one side of the pot, where they are easier to collect.

Taste the sauce base frequently as it develops and adjust the seasoning as necessary by adding aromatics or seasonings. Remove from the heat once the desired flavor is achieved.

4. Strain the sauce.
Optional: For jus lié, add a pure starch slurry now, if desired, and simmer until thickened either before or after straining. Use a fine-mesh sieve or a double thickness of cheesecloth. It is now ready to finish for service, or it may be rapidly cooled and stored (see page 64).

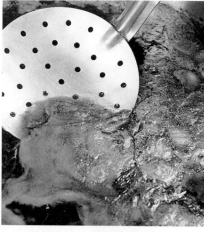

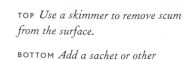

ABOVE *Brown stock, already brought to a simmer to shorten overall cooking time, is added to the bones, trim, and mirepoix. If desired, the chef could add seasonings and aromatics as the stock heats to infuse it with additional flavor.*

TOP *Use a skimmer to remove scum from the surface.*

BOTTOM *Add a sachet or other aromatics as flavor develops.*

TOP *This sauce base will thicken as needed in smaller amounts for service.*

BOTTOM *Unless the sauce is to be served immediately, all or part of it should be cooled quickly in an ice bath and stored.*

5. Finish as desired and hold at 165°F/73°C for service.

Return the sauce to a simmer and make any necessary adjustment to its flavor or consistency. (If the sauce requires thickening, either reduce it by simmering over high heat or add a starch slurry now.)

If the sauce has already been thickened, either with a roux or arrowroot or by reduction, no additional thickener is necessary.

Brown sauces can be finished for service by adding reductions, fortified wines, garnishes, and/or whole butter (see Finishing a Brown Sauce, page 261).

Brown sauces sometimes develop a skin when they are held uncovered. To avoid this, the sauce can be topped with melted whole or clarified butter to make an airtight seal. Alternately, a fitted cover for the bain-marie can be put on top, or a piece of parchment paper or plastic wrap cut to fit the pan can be placed directly on the surface of the sauce.

6. Evaluate the quality of the finished brown sauce.

A brown sauce of excellent quality has a full, rich flavor. The initial roasting of bones, trimmings, and/or mirepoix gives the finished sauce a pleasant roasted or caramel aroma, readily discernible when the sauce is heated, and a predominant flavor of roasted meat or vegetables. The aromatics, mirepoix, and tomatoes should not overpower the main flavor. There should be no bitter or burnt flavors, which can be caused by over-reduction or burning the bones, mirepoix, or tomato paste.

Good brown sauces have a deep brown color without any dark specks or debris. The color is affected by the color of the base stock, the amount of tomato paste or purée (too much will give a red cast to the sauce), the amount of caramelization on the trim and mirepoix, proper skimming, the length of simmering time (reduction factor), as well as any finishing or garnishing ingredients.

The texture and, to some extent, the color of a brown sauce depend on the type of thickener used. A roux-thickened brown sauce (Espagnole) is opaque with a thick body. A sauce thickened with puréed mirepoix is also thick and opaque but with a slightly rougher, more rustic texture. A sauce thickened with both roux and reduction (demiglace) is translucent and highly glossy with a noticeable body, although it should never feel tacky in the mouth. A pure starch-thickened sauce (*jus lié*) has a greater degree of clarity than other brown sauces as well as a lighter texture and color.

ABOVE *Brown sauce will gel and become less translucent once cold. Returning the sauce to a simmer re-establishes its clarity.*

ABOVE *Add pure starch slurries gradually to avoid over-thickening the sauce. It should be thickened to a light syrup consistency.*

2 fl oz / 60 mL vegetable oil

4 lb / 1.8 kg lean veal trim

MIREPOIX

8 oz / 225 g medium-dice onions

4 oz / 115 g medium-dice carrot

4 oz / 115 g medium-dice celery

4 oz / 115 g tomato purée

4$\frac{1}{2}$ / qt 4.5 L BROWN VEAL STOCK (page 252)

sachet d'épices, containing 2 to 3 parsley stems, $\frac{1}{2}$ tsp/2 mL thyme, $\frac{1}{2}$ tsp/2 mL cracked black peppercorns, 1 bay leaf, and 1 garlic clove

1 oz / 30 g arrowroot or cornstarch, diluted with cold water or stock to make a slurry

salt, as needed

pepper, as needed

JUS DE VEAU LIÉ

1 Heat the oil in a *rondeau* over medium heat. Add the trim and mirepoix and sauté, stirring from time to time, until the veal, onions, and carrots have taken on a rich brown color, about 25 to 30 minutes.

2 Add the tomato purée and continue to cook over medium heat until it turns a rusty brown color and has a rich sweet aroma, about 1 minute.

3 Add the stock and bring to a simmer. Continue to simmer, skimming as necessary, until a good flavor develops, 2 to 4 hours, depending on the size cut used for the trim and mirepoix. Add the sachet, if desired, during the last hour of cooking time.

4 Strain this sauce base. It can now be finished, or it may be rapidly cooled and stored for later use (see page 64).

5 Return the sauce base to a simmer. Stir the slurry to recombine if necessary and gradually add to the sauce base, adding just enough to achieve a good coating consistency. (nappé). The amount of slurry needed depends on the batch itself and its intended use.

6 Taste the sauce and adjust the seasoning. Hold at 165°F/67°C for service.

MAKES 1 GALLON/3.75 LITERS

Jus de Volaille Lié Replace the Brown Veal Stock with a Brown Chicken Stock (page 252) and replace the veal bones and trim with an equal weight of chicken bones and trim.

Jus de Canard Lié Replace the Brown Veal Stock with a Brown Duck Stock (page 252) and replace the veal bones and trim with an equal weight of duck bones and trim.

Jus d'Agneau Lié Replace the Brown Veal Stock with Brown Lamb Stock (page 252) and replace the veal bones and trim with an equal weight of lamb bones and trim.

Jus de Gibier Lié Replace the Brown Veal Stock with Brown Game Stock (page 252) and replace the veal bones and trim with an equal weight of venison bones and trim.

FINISHING A BROWN SAUCE

A brown sauce can be served as is or used to prepare derivative brown sauces. The main ways of finishing a brown sauce to create special sauces are through reductions, garnishes, fortified wines, or finishing with butter

REDUCTIONS
For small amounts of sauce, wine (with or without aromatics) may be used to deglaze the sauté pan or roasting pan or the wine and aromatics may be simmered separately and then added to a large batch of finished sauce, as you might do for banquet service.

GARNISH ITEMS
High-moisture items like mushrooms, shallots, or tomatoes are usually cooked before being added to a sauce. The sauce is then simmered again to return it to the correct consistency and to develop flavors fully. Then, the final seasoning adjustments are made.

FORTIFIED WINES
Port, Madeira, Marsala, or sherry are often blended into the simmering sauce just before serving.

FINISHING WITH BUTTER *(MONTER AU BEURRE)*
This step can be employed to enrich any brown sauce. Cold or room temperature butter is swirled or whisked into the sauce just before serving.

WHITE SAUCE

The white sauce family includes the classic sauces velouté and béchamel, both produced by thickening a liquid with roux.

A classic velouté, which translates from French as "velvety, soft, and smooth to the palate," is prepared by thickening a white stock (veal, chicken, or fish) with blond roux. In Escoffier's time, a béchamel sauce was made by adding cream to a relatively thick velouté sauce. Today, it is made by thickening milk (sometimes infused with aromatics for flavor) with a white roux.

TO PREPARE 1 GALLON/3.75 LITERS OF A WHITE SAUCE, YOU WILL NEED:

1 gallon/3.75 liters flavorful liquid (white stock for velouté, milk for béchamel)

1 sachet d'épices or bouquet garni or other aromatics (white roux, minced onions, or mushroom trimmings, for instance) and seasonings as appropriate

an appropriate amount of roux

FOR A LIGHT CONSISTENCY FOR SOUPS:

add 10 to 12 ounces/285 to 340 grams blond or white roux

FOR MEDIUM CONSISTENCY (FOR MOST SAUCES):

increase the amount of roux to 12 to 14 ounces/340 to 400 grams

FOR HEAVY CONSISTENCY (FOR A BINDER FOR CROQUETTES, FILLINGS, STUFFINGS, OR BAKED PASTA DISHES):

increase the amount of roux to 16 to 18 ounces/450 to 510 grams

LIQUIDS USED TO MAKE white sauces include white stocks (veal, chicken, fish, or vegetable) and milk. They may be brought to a simmer separately, and, if desired, infused with aromatics and flavorings to produce a special flavor and/or color in the finished sauce.

Blond roux is the traditional thickener for veloutés; blond or white roux may be used for a bechamel (the darker the roux, the more golden the sauce will be). Roux may be prepared in advance, or produced by cooking fat and flour together with the aromatics. The amount of roux (see page 238) determines the thickness of a white sauce.

Additional mirepoix, mushroom trimmings, or members of the onion family are sometimes added, either to bolster the flavor of the sauce or to create a specific flavor profile. Cut them into small dice or slice them thin to encourage rapid flavor release into the sauce.

White sauces scorch easily if they are not tended, and can take on a grayish cast if prepared in an aluminum pan. Choose a heavy-gauge nonaluminum pot with a perfectly flat bottom for the best results. Simmer white sauces on a flattop for gentle, even heat, or use a heat diffuser if available.

MAKE THE WHITE SAUCE

1. Sweat the appropriate aromatics in fat.
Vegetables are occasionally allowed to sweat to make a flavor base for a white sauce. Any meat trimmings included should be gently cooked with them.

2. (Optional) Add flour and cook, stirring frequently.
A roux may be cooked in the pot, as part of the sauce-making process, by adding flour to the oil and aromatics in the pot. Add more oil or butter as needed to produce a roux. Let the roux cook for about 4 to 5 minutes or to a light blond color. Some recipes call for a prepared roux to be added to the aromatics to soften. In other recipes, the liquid is added to the aromatics and brought to a simmer; then a prepared roux is whisked into the simmering liquid.

ABOVE *Cook aromatic ingredients, such as mushrooms, onions, and shallots, gently in clarified butter or oil until they soften and become translucent. Since the finished sauce should have a pale color, there should be no browning.*

ABOVE *Add a measured amount of flour to the vegetables and oil in the pot.*

ABOVE *Stir the flour into the fat and vegetables until it is evenly blended. Let the roux cook over low heat for several minutes to remove the raw flavor from the flour and reach the desired color. For velouté, a blond roux is desirable.*

3. Add the liquid to the roux gradually. Add a sachet d'épices or bouquet garni, if desired.

Many chefs add cool or room-temperature stock or milk to the roux. Others prefer to bring the liquid to a simmer separately, which allows them to adjust the liquid's seasoning with salt, pepper, or other aromatic ingredients. If the liquid is preheated, it should be removed from the heat so that its temperature drops slightly, making it cooler than the hot roux.

Add the liquid in stages, whisking until very smooth between additions.

4. Add other seasoning or aromatics and simmer for 30 minutes to 1 hour, stirring frequently and tasting throughout cooking time.

Very rich stocks may not require additional aromatics. If desired, either infuse the liquid with them when preheating or add a sachet or bouquet garni once the sauce returns to a simmer.

A simmering time of at least 30 minutes is long enough to cook away any raw flavor from the roux, but many chefs recommend simmering for 1 hour for the best flavor development.

Using a wooden spoon, stir the sauce occasionally while simmering. Make sure that the spoon scrapes the bottom and corners of the pot to prevent scorching. Scorching is of more concern with béchamel than with velouté because the milk solids tend to settle. Use a flattop or heat diffuser, if available.

Taste the sauce frequently as it develops, adjusting the seasoning as necessary. To test the texture, hold a small amount of the sauce on your tongue and press it against the roof of your mouth. If the sauce is properly cooked, there will be no tacky, gluey, or gritty sensation.

TOP *Add a small amount of stock.*

BOTTOM *Whisk until there are no more lumps of roux before adding more stock.*

TOP *Continue adding stock, whisking constantly, until fully incorporated.*

BOTTOM *Add a sachet during the final 15 to 20 minutes of simmering to add the aroma of herbs and spices to the sauce.*

5. Strain the sauce.

As the sauce simmers, it almost inevitably develops a thick skin on its surface as well as a heavy, gluey layer on the bottom and sides of the pot. Straining the sauce removes any lumps and develops a very smooth texture. The sauce is ready to use now, or it may be cooled and stored for later use.

6. Finish as desired and hold at 165°F (73°C) for service.

Return the sauce to a simmer over low heat, stirring frequently. Make any necessary adjustments to the consistency (thicken by simmering a little more or by adding a bit more roux or slurry; thin by adding more of the appropriate base liquid); and add any finishing ingredients.

For white sauce derivative sauces, the base sauce may be flavored with a reduction or essence and garnished. White sauces are also often finished with cream.

White sauces may develop a skin if held uncovered. To avoid this, some chefs like to top the sauce with melted whole or clarified butter to make an airtight seal; others prefer to use a fitted cover on the bain-marie or place a piece of parchment paper or plastic wrap cut to fit directly on the surface of the sauce.

7. Evaluate the quality of the finished white sauce.

An excellent white sauce meets several criteria. The flavor reflects the liquid used in its preparation: white veal, chicken, or fish stock or milk. It has a pale color, with absolutely no hint of gray. Although a white sauce will never be transparent, it should be translucent, lustrous, and have a definite sheen. A good white sauce is perfectly smooth, with noticeable body and no hint of graininess. It is thick enough to coat the back of a spoon yet still easy to pour from a ladle.

ABOVE *For a truly velvety texture, use the wringing method to strain the sauce through a double thickness of rinsed cheesecloth.*

ABOVE *Add a small amount of stock or water to film the pan before reheating velouté. This helps the sauce soften readily and avoids scorching.*

4½ qt / 4.25 L CHICKEN STOCK (page 248)

6 fl oz / 180 mL clarified butter or vegetable oil

WHITE MIREPOIX

2 oz / 60 g small-dice onions

2 oz / 60 g small-dice leek

2 oz / 60 g small-dice celery

2 oz / 60 g small-dice parsnips

8 oz / 225 g all-purpose flour

sachet d'épices, containing 2 to 3 parsley stems, ½ tsp/2 mL thyme, ½ tsp/2 mL
   cracked black peppercorns, 1 bay leaf, and 1 garlic clove

salt, as needed

ground white pepper, as needed

CHICKEN VELOUTÉ

1 Heat the butter in a saucepan over medium heat. Add the white mirepoix and cook,
   stirring from time to time, until the onions are limp and have begun to release their
   juices into the pan, about 15 minutes. They may take on a light golden color but should
   not be allowed to brown.

2 Add the flour and stir well to combine. Cook over low to medium heat, stirring frequently, until a pale or blond roux forms, about 12 minutes.

3 Add the stock to the pan gradually, stirring or whisking to work out any lumps. Bring
   to a full boil, then lower the heat to establish a simmer. (Use a heat diffuser, if desired,
   to avoid scorching.) Add the sachet, if desired, and continue to simmer, skimming as
   necessary, until a good flavor and consistency develop and the starchy feel and taste of
   the flour have cooked away, 45 minutes to 1 hour.

4 Strain the sauce through a fine sieve. Strain a second time through a double thickness
   of rinsed cheesecloth, if desired, for the finest texture. The sauce can now be finished,
   or it may be cooled and stored for later use (see page 64).

5 Return the sauce to a simmer. Taste and adjust with salt and pepper. Finish the sauce
   as desired.

MAKES 3½ QUARTS/3.3.LITERS

NOTES

To make a very rich sauce, simmer the stock with addition trim to fortify the flavor. Use 4 lb/1.8 kg chicken
trim, wing tips, or backs in a 1-gallon/3.85 liter batch.

Ordinary Velouté Replace the Chicken Stock with White Veal Stock (page 249) and replace the chicken trim, if desired, with an equal weight of veal trim.

Fish Velouté Replace the Chicken Stock with Fish Stock or Fumet (page 253) and replace the chicken trim, if desired, with an equal weight of lean fish trim.

Shrimp Velouté Replace the Chicken Stock with Shellfish Stock (page 253) and replace the chicken trim, if desired, with an equal weight of shrimp shells.

Vegetable Velouté Replace the Chicken Stock with Vegetable Stock (page 254). Use 2 lb/900 g mirepoix or white mirepoix rather than 8 oz/225 g, and add up to 1 lb/450 g additional vegetables (celery, mushrooms, leeks, etc.) to produce a specific flavor. For a completely meatless version, use oil rather than butter.

TOMATO SAUCE

Tomato sauces of all sorts, from simply seasoned fresh tomato sauces to complex and highly seasoned versions, are featured in cuisines around the world.

Tomato sauce is a generic term used to describe any sauce that is based mainly on tomatoes. Tomato sauces can be made several ways. They may be raw, or they may be cooked, anywhere from ten minutes to several hours. In some versions, olive oil is used as the only cooking fat. For others, rendered salt pork or bacon is required. Some recipes call for roasted veal or pork bones; others are made strictly from tomatoes and the desired vegetables. Some tomato sauces are puréed until smooth; others are left chunky. Escoffier's tomato sauce relied on roux as a thickener.

GOOD TOMATO SAUCE can be made from fresh or canned tomatoes. When fresh tomatoes are at their peak, it may be a good idea to use them exclusively. At other times of the year, good-quality canned tomatoes are a better choice. Plum tomatoes, sometimes referred to as Romas, are generally preferred for tomato sauces because they have a high ratio of flesh to skin and seeds. Fresh tomatoes may be skinned and seeded for sauce, or they may be simply rinsed, cored, and quartered or chopped. Canned tomatoes come peeled and whole, puréed, or a combination of the two. Tomato paste is sometimes added to the sauce as well.

There are dozens of choices for additional flavoring ingredients. Some recipes call for a standard mirepoix as the aromatic vegetable component. Others rely more simply on garlic and onions. Still others call for the inclusion of a ham bone or other smoked pork bones. Let your recipe or your palate be your guide.

Choose a heavy-gauge pot that is made of nonreactive materials such as stainless steel or anodized aluminum because tomatoes have a high acid content. The gauge of the pot is also important. Because of the high sugar content of some tomatoes, you will need to establish an even heat without hot spots so the sauce will not scorch.

If the sauce is to be puréed, a food mill is typically used. For a very smooth texture, you may wish to use a blender, food processor, or immersion blender.

TO MAKE 1 GALLON/3.75 LITERS OF TOMATO SAUCE, YOU WILL NEED:

10 to 12 pounds/4.5 to 5.5 kilograms fresh tomatoes or 9 pounds/4 kilograms canned tomatoes or 2 No. 10 cans

4 to 6 ounces/120 to 180 milliliters oil or other cooking fat

12 ounces/340 grams minced onions and/or 1 ounce/30 grams garlic

salt and pepper to taste

YOU MAY ALSO NEED, DEPENDING UPON YOUR FORMULA OR INTENDED USE, ONE OR MORE OF THE FOLLOWING INGREDIENTS OR PREPARATIONS:

tomato purée and/or paste

carrots or mirepoix

fresh and/or dried herbs

smoked meats

stock

thickeners (roux or pure starch slurries)

1. Sweat or sauté the aromatic vegetables.

The gentle release of flavor from the aromatic vegetables into the fat helps the flavor to permeate the sauce better. The way the vegetables are cooked influences the flavor of the finished sauce: The vegetables are usually sweated in a fat until they become tender, but for a more complex roasted flavor, they may be sautéed until lightly browned.

2. Add the tomatoes and any remaining ingredients and simmer until the flavor is fully developed, stirring frequently, skimming, and tasting throughout cooking time.

Cooking time varies, depending on the ingredients, but in general, the less cooking time, the better for any sauce based on fruits or vegetables. Extended cooking diminishes their fresh flavors. Most tomato sauces should be cooked just long enough for the flavors to meld together. If a tomato sauce that is not going to be puréed is too watery, strain and reduce the excess liquid separately to avoid overcooking.

Stir tomato sauce frequently throughout preparation, and check the flavor occasionally. If it becomes necessary to correct a harsh or bitter flavor, sweat a small amount of chopped onions and carrot and add them to the sauce. If the flavor is weak, add a small amount of reduced tomato paste or purée. Too sweet a sauce may be corrected by adding stock or water or more tomatoes.

ABOVE *Cook the onions until tender and properly done (here, the chef has chosen to allow them to brown slightly) before adding the tomatoes.*

ABOVE *For this recipe, tomato purée is added for additional body.*

ABOVE *As the rings on the pot's side show, tomato sauces reduce as they cook, concentrating the flavor and improving the texture.*

3. Purée the sauce, if desired.
Use a food mill, food processor, blender, or immersion blender to purée the sauce. If using a food processor or blender, a small amount of oil added during puréeing will emulsify the sauce, creating a lighter yet thicker consistency.

4. Finish as desired.
Check the balance and seasoning of the sauce and make any necessary adjustments to its flavor and consistency by adding salt, pepper, fresh herbs, or other ingredients as indicated by the recipe. At this point, the sauce is ready to be served, or it may be finished for service as desired (see recipes), or it may be cooled and stored (see page 64).

5. Evaluate the quality of the finished tomato sauce.
Tomato sauces are opaque and slightly coarse, with a concentrated flavor of tomatoes and without any trace of bitterness, excess acidity, or sweetness. Ingredients selected to flavor the sauce should provide only subtle underpinnings. Tomato sauces should pour easily.

ABOVE *Puréeing the sauce through a food mill removes any skin or seeds that were not removed from the tomatoes before cooking the sauce.*

ABOVE *If desired, add fresh herbs, according to recipe or intended use. Here, a chiffonade of fresh basil is added. Taste the sauce and adjust the salt level as it simmers.*

TOP *This sauce was puréed using the coarse openings on a food mill for a pleasing, rustic texture.*

BOTTOM *This unpuréed sauce has good body but can be ladled easily over pasta.*

4 to 6 fl oz / 120 to 180 mL olive oil

8 oz / 225 g diced onions

4 garlic cloves, minced or sliced very thin

7 lb / 3.15 kg fresh plum tomatoes, rinsed, cored, and chopped

20 fl oz / 600 mL tomato purée

$^1/_2$ cup torn or chopped basil leaves

salt, as needed

pepper, as needed

TOMATO SAUCE

1 Heat the olive oil in a *rondeau*, or wide shallow pot, over medium heat. Add the onions and cook, stirring occasionally, until they take on a light golden color, about 12 to 15 minutes.

2 Add the garlic and continue to sauté, stirring frequently, until there is a pleasing garlic aroma, about 1 minute.

3 Add the tomatoes and tomato purée. Bring the sauce to a simmer and cook over low heat, stirring from time to time, for about 45 minutes (exact cooking time depends on the quality of the tomatoes and their natural moisture content) until a good saucelike consistency develops.

4 Add the basil and simmer for 2 to 3 minutes more, to infuse the sauce with the aroma of basil. Taste the sauce and adjust with salt and pepper if necessary.

5 The sauce is ready to finish now. It may be puréed through a food mill fitted with a coarse disk, or broken up with a whisk to make a rough purée, or left chunky.

6 The sauce is ready to serve now, or it may be finished as desired (see Notes) or cooled and stored (see page 64).

MAKES 1 GALLON/3.75 LITERS

NOTES

This recipe calls for a combination of plum tomatoes and tomato purée. However, good-quality fresh tomatoes may be used exclusively. Opinions differ about peeling and seeding the tomatoes, but they must be rinsed and cored. If the tomatoes are not peeled and seeded, purée the sauce through a food mill fitted with a coarse disk.

With canned tomatoes, it may be necessary to drain off some of the liquid, if there is too much. Some chefs purée whole canned tomatoes in a food mill before preparing the sauce.

Adding carrots with the onions can help compensate for tomatoes with an acidic flavor. If the sauce does not seem to be developing the desired sweetness, sauté some carrots separately and add them to the sauce as it simmers.

Vegetables, such as mushrooms, leeks, or celery, may be added along with the onions to create a ragù.

Fresh herbs, including oregano, basil, marjoram, or thyme, may be added both early in the cooking process and at the end of cooking time. Some chefs prefer to add some of the herbs along with the garlic and the rest at the end of the cooking time, which layers the flavor of the herbs.

Add dried herbs, such as oregano, basil, thyme, or marjoram, as well as spices and seeds (crushed red pepper, fennel seed, etc.) along with the garlic to allow them to open their flavors and infuse the sauce.

Add ground or diced raw meat, poultry, fish, or shellfish, as well as cured meats such as bacon or ham, along with the onions to produce a specific flavor in the finished sauce.

Add cooked shellfish, cooked vegetables or meats, additional herbs, wines, vinegars, grated cheese, or extra-virgin olive oil to the sauce as finishing ingredients.

Tighten the sauce so that it will not separate as it sits (sometimes called weeping) by adding a little arrowroot or cornstarch slurry. This is a helpful technique for banquet or volume service situations.

HOLLANDAISE SAUCE

Since the largest part of a hollandaise is butter, the success or failure of the sauce depends not only on skillfully combining egg yolks, water, acid, and butter into a rich, smooth sauce, but also on the quality of the butter itself.

Hollandaise sauce is prepared by emulsifying melted or clarified butter and water (in the form of an acidic reduction and/or lemon juice) with partially cooked egg yolks. A number of similar warm egg emulsion sauces, as this group of sauces is sometimes known, can be prepared by varying the ingredients in the reduction or by adding different finishing and garnishing ingredients such as tarragon (as pictured above). The group includes béarnaise, Choron, and mousseline sauces. Hollandaise can also be combined with whipped cream and/or velouté to prepare a glaçage, which is used to coat a dish that is then lightly browned just before service under a salamander or broiler.

MELTED WHOLE BUTTER or clarified butter may be used in a hollandaise. Some chefs like melted whole butter for the rich, creamy butter flavor it imparts to the sauce, which is best for most meat, fish, vegetable, and egg dishes. Others prefer clarified butter, for a stiffer, more stable sauce, which is of particular advantage if the sauce is to be used in a glaçage. Whatever the approach, the butter must be quite warm (about 145°F/63°C) but not too hot for the sauce to come together successfully.

In general, the ratio of egg to butter is 1 egg yolk to every 2 to 3 ounces of butter. As the volume of sauce increases, the amount of butter that can be emulsified with 1 egg yolk also increases. A hollandaise made with 20 yolks, for instance, can usually tolerate more than 3 ounces of butter per yolk.

Pasteurized egg yolks may be used for hollandaise, if desired. However, the method outlined here cooks the yolks enough that any salmonella bacteria present, which is the major concern with eggs, are destroyed.

An acidic ingredient is included in hollandaise both for flavor and for the effect it has on the protein in the egg yolks (see page 52). The acidic ingredient, which can be either a vinegar reduction or lemon juice, also provides the water necessary to form an emulsion. Whether to use a reduction or lemon juice is determined by the desired flavor of the finished sauce. A reduction will impart a more complex flavor, particularly if lemon juice is also used as a final seasoning.

TO MAKE A 10-PORTION (2 FLUID OUNCES/60 MILLILITERS PER PORTION) BATCH OF HOLLANDAISE SAUCE YOU WILL NEED:

4 egg yolks or an equivalent quantity of pasteurized egg yolks (3½ ounces/100 grams)

12 fluid ounces/340 milliliters melted whole butter or clarified butter

a reduction made from white wine or cider vinegar, minced shallots, and peppercorns

a small amount of water to refresh and cool the reduction

lemon juice, salt, and pepper to taste

1. Make the reduction.

A standard reduction for hollandaise consists of dry white wine, white wine vinegar, minced shallots, and cracked peppercorns, cooked over direct heat until nearly dry. Cool and moisten the reduction with a small amount of water, then strain the reduction into a stainless-steel bowl.

2. Add the egg yolks to the reduction and whisk over barely simmering water until thickened and warm (145°F/63°C).

Be sure that the water is just barely simmering with no visible signs of surface action, just plenty of steam rising from the surface.

If the yolks seem to be getting too hot and coagulating slightly around the sides and bottom of the

bowl, remove from the heat. Set the bowl on a cool surface and whisk until the mixture has cooled very slightly. Continue cooking over simmering water.

When the yolks have tripled in volume and fall in ribbons into the bowl, remove them from the simmering water. Do not overcook the yolks or they will lose their ability to emulsify the sauce.

ABOVE *Cook the ingredients for the reduction over moderate heat until the liquid is almost completely cooked away (à sec).*

TOP *Add the egg yolks to the strained reduction. The bowl is set over a pan of simmering, not boiling, water.*

BOTTOM *Whisk the eggs into the reduction over simmering water. As they become warm, they cook into a* sabayon.

ABOVE *The yolks increase in volume as they cook. When they are properly cooked you can see "trails" left as the whisk drags through the yolks.*

3. Gradually whisk in the warm butter.
Stabilize the bowl by setting it on a towel or in a pot that has been draped with a towel to keep the bowl from slipping.

Add the butter slowly in a thin stream, whisking constantly as it is incorporated. The sauce will begin to thicken as more butter is blended in. If the sauce becomes too thick, add a bit of water or lemon juice. This makes it possible to finish adding the correct amount of butter without breaking the sauce.

If the sauce does start to break, try adding a small amount of water and whisking until the sauce is smooth before adding more butter. If that doesn't work, cook another egg yolk over simmering water until thickened, as directed in step 2, and then gradually whisk in the broken hollandaise. Note, however, that a sauce restored in this manner will not have the same volume as a sauce that did not have to be rescued, and it will not hold as well.

If the sauce becomes too hot, the egg yolks will begin to scramble. To correct this problem, remove the sauce from the heat and add a small amount of cool water. Whisk the sauce until it is smooth and, if necessary, strain it to remove any bits of overcooked yolk.

4. Season to taste.
Add seasonings such as lemon juice, salt, pepper, and cayenne, as desired, when the sauce is nearly finished. Lemon juice will lighten the sauce's flavor and texture, but do not let it become a dominant taste. Add just enough to lift the flavor. If the sauce is too thick, add a little warm water to regain the desired light texture.

Certain ingredients may be added to produce a specific sauce at this point. Add meat glaze (glace de viande), tomato purée, essences or juices, or other semi-liquid or liquid ingredients to the sauce gradually to avoid thinning it too much. Including flavoring ingredients may mean that other seasonings and flavorings need to be adjusted once more.

Some hollandaise-style sauces are finished with minced herbs. Herbs should be properly rinsed and dried, then cut into uniform mince or chiffonade with a very sharp knife to retain the most color and flavor. Fine-dice tomato or citrus suprêmes may also be added to certain hollandaise-style sauces; these garnishes should be properly cut and allowed to drain, so that excess moisture does not thin the sauce.

ABOVE *Twist a clean side towel into a circle to hold the bowl steady, or drape the towel over an empty pot and set the bowl into the pot. It is helpful to have a second person ladle the butter into the bowl.*

ABOVE *Continue adding butter and whisking until the sauce is thickened and all the butter is incorporated. If the sauce becomes too thick and the butter does not blend in easily, add a little warm water to loosen the sauce enough to absorb the remaining butter.*

5. **Evaluate the quality of the finished hollandaise.**

The predominant flavor and aroma of a good hollandaise sauce is that of butter. The egg yolks contribute a great deal of flavor as well. The reduction ingredients give the sauce a balanced taste, as do the lemon juice and any additional seasonings. Hollandaise should be a lemon-yellow color with a satiny smooth texture. (A grainy texture indicates that the egg yolks have overcooked and begun to scramble.) The sauce should have a luster and not appear oily. The consistency should be light and pourable.

6. **Serve immediately or hold at or near 145°F/63°C for no more than 2 hours.**

Most kitchens have one or two spots that are the perfect temperature for holding hollandaise, usually above the stove or ovens or near (but not directly under) heat lamps. Holding hollandaise presents an unusual challenge, however. The sauce must be held below 150°F/65°C to keep the yolks from curdling, but at this temperature the sauce hovers just above the danger zone for bacterial growth. The acid from the reduction and/or lemon juice helps keep some bacteria at bay, but the sauce should still never be held longer than 2 hours.

Some kitchens prepare batches of hollandaise to be finished to order with the appropriate flavorings and garnishes. Be sure that the containers used are perfectly clean. Stainless-steel bain-maries, ceramic containers, or vacuum bottles with wide necks are good choices. Keep all spoons and ladles used to serve the sauce meticulously clean, and never reintroduce a tasting spoon, bare fingers, or other sources of cross contamination into the sauce.

ABOVE *Some chefs like to use a spoon, rather than a ladle, to apply hollandaise to a dish, because it is easier to control where the sauce goes.*

TOP *Mousseline Sauce (page 279).*

MIDDLE *Choron Sauce (page 290).*

BOTTOM *Béarnaise Sauce (page 289).*

1 tbsp / 15 mL chopped shallots

½ tsp / 3 mL cracked peppercorns

2 fl oz / 60 mL white wine or cider vinegar

2 fl oz / 60 mL water, or as needed

3½ oz / 100 g egg yolks, fresh or pasteurized (about 4)

12 fl oz / 360 mL melted or clarified butter, kept warm (145°F/63°C)

2 tsp / 10 mL strained lemon juice

salt

ground white pepper

pinch of cayenne (optional)

HOLLANDAISE SAUCE

1 Combine the shallots, peppercorns, and vinegar in a small pan and reduce over medium heat until nearly dry *(à sec)*.

2 Add the water to the reduction and strain into a stainless-steel bowl.

3 Add the egg yolks and set over simmering water. Cook, whisking constantly, until the yolks triple in volume and fall in ribbons from the whisk.

4 Remove the cooked egg yolks from the simmering water and set on a clean side towel to keep the bowl from slipping. Gradually ladle in the hot melted butter in a thin stream, whisking constantly. As the butter is blended into the egg yolks, the sauce will thicken. If it becomes too tight and the butter is not blending in easily, you may need to add a little water or lemon juice to loosen the yolks enough to absorb the remaining butter.

5 Taste the sauce and add lemon juice, salt, pepper, and cayenne, if desired, as needed. The sauce is ready to serve at this point, or it may be finished as desired. The sauce can be held for no longer than 2 hours at 145°F/63°C. This can be accomplished by holding the sauce in hot (not simmering or boiling) water or in an insulated bottle.

MAKES 20 FLUID OUNCES/600 MILLILITERS

Mousseline Sauce Prepare a hollandaise sauce as directed above. Whip 5 fl oz/150 mL heavy cream to medium peaks and fold into the batch of hollandaise, or fold whipped cream into individual portions at the time of service.

Maltaise Sauce Prepare a hollandaise sauce as directed above, with the following change: Add 2 fl oz/60 mL blood orange juice to the reduction. Finish the hollandaise with 2 tsp/10 mL of grated or julienned blood orange zest and 1½ fl oz/45 mL blood orange juice.

BEURRE BLANC

Beurre blanc, a warm butter sauce, is said to have been first created by Mme. Clémence, a renowned French chef, as an accompaniment to the salmon and other freshwater fish that abounded in the Loire River.

Traditionally, beurre blanc is prepared as an integral part of the shallow-poaching process with the cooking liquid *(cuisson)* used for the reduction. Another common practice is to prepare a reduction separately and make the beurre blanc in a larger batch so it can be used as a grand sauce is used, to prepare derivative sauces. As with hollandaise, beurre blanc derivatives are prepared by either varying the ingredients in the reduction or altering the garnish ingredients. Beurre rouge, for instance, is made by using red wine in the reduction.

TO MAKE 1 QUART/1 LITER OF BEURRE BLANC YOU WILL NEED:	*1½ lb/680 grams butter*	*heavy cream (optional)*	*ground white pepper*
	a reduction made from 8 fluid ounces/240 milliliters dry white wine, 3 fluid ounces/90 milliliters vinegar, shallots, and peppercorns	*salt*	*lemon juice*

SELECT AND PREPARE THE INGREDIENTS AND EQUIPMENT

THE QUALITY OF THE BUTTER is critical to the success of a beurre blanc. Unsalted butter is best because salt can always be added to taste later on. Check the butter carefully for a rich, sweet, creamy texture and aroma. Cube the butter and keep it cool or at room temperature.

A standard reduction for a beurre blanc is made from dry white wine and shallots. (When prepared as part of a shallow-poached dish, the cooking liquid is cooked down to become the reduction, see page 500.) Other ingredients often used in the reduction include vinegar or citrus juice; chopped herbs including tarragon, basil, chives, or chervil; cracked peppercorns; and sometimes garlic or ginger, lemongrass, saffron, and other flavoring ingredients.

A small amount of reduced heavy cream is occasionally added to stabilize the emulsion. If cream is used, reduce it by half separately. Carefully simmer the cream until it thickens and has a rich, ivory-yellow color. The more the cream is reduced, the greater its stabilizing effect. The more stable the sauce, the longer it will last during service. However, the flavor of cream will dominate the fresh taste of the butter.

Be sure that the pan is of a nonreactive metal. Bi-metal pans, such as copper or anodized aluminum lined with stainless steel, are excellent choices for this sauce.

A whisk may be used to incorporate the butter into the sauce, but many chefs prefer to allow the motion of the pan swirling over the burner or flattop to incorporate the butter. Straining is optional for this sauce, but if you choose to strain either the reduction or the finished sauce, you will need a sieve. Once the sauce is prepared, it may be kept warm in the container used to prepare it, or it may be transferred to a clean bain-marie, ceramic vessel, or wide-necked vacuum bottle.

1. Prepare the reduction.

This initial reduction of acid, shallots, and peppercorns (or other aromatics as required by recipe) gives the sauce much of its flavor. Combine the reduction ingredients and reduce over fairly brisk heat to a syrupy consistency *(à sec)*. If preparing the sauce as an integral part of a shallow-poached dish, simply reduce the *cuisson* (see page 500).

2. Gradually incorporate the chilled butter into the reduction.

Reduce the heat to low. Add the butter a little at a time and blend it in with a fork or a whisk or by keeping the pan in constant motion. The action is similar to that used in finishing a sauce with butter *(monter au beurre)*.

If the sauce looks oily rather than creamy or if it appears to be separating, it has gotten too hot. Immediately pull the pan off the heat and set it on a cool surface. Continue to add the chilled butter a little at a time, whisking until the mixture regains the proper creamy appearance. Then continue to incorporate the remainder of the butter over low heat.

If the butter takes a very long time to become incorporated into the sauce, increase the heat under the pan very slightly.

ABOVE *A nonreactive pan (stainless steel or anodized aluminum, for example) wider than it is tall, gives the chef control over the sauce as it develops. The chef has opted to add a little reduced cream to stabilize the finished sauce.*

ABOVE *Keep the butter a little cooler than room temperature. Some chefs prefer to have the butter slightly softened, but this requires extra vigilance to be sure that the sauce won't break as it is prepared. Melted or runny butter rarely produces a good sauce.*

TOP *Temperature control is the key to preparing this sauce. The chef has the pan half on and half off the flat-top to help control the cooking speed and avoid breaking the sauce.*

BOTTOM *The butter is fully incorporated at this point, and the chef has removed it from the heat.*

3. Make the necessary final adjustments to flavor.

Adjust the seasoning. If you did not strain the reduction earlier, you now have the option of straining the sauce. If you do choose to strain, work quickly to keep the sauce warm.

4. Serve immediately or keep warm.

To prepare a large batch of beurre blanc and hold it through a service period, use the same holding techniques described for hollandaise (see page 278). The sauce may deteriorate over time, however, and must be monitored for quality.

5. Evaluate the quality of the finished beurre blanc.

The flavor of beurre blanc is that of whole butter, with piquant accents from the reduction. The finishing and/or garnishing ingredients also influence the flavor. If cream is included, it should not have a dominant flavor. A good beurre blanc is creamy in color, although garnishes of herbs, purées, and other ingredients may change the color. The sauce should have a distinct sheen. The body should be light. If the sauce is too thin, it probably does not contain enough butter. Conversely, a beurre blanc that is too thick includes too much butter or cream. The texture should be frothy, and the sauce should not leave an oily or greasy feeling in the mouth.

ABOVE *The beurre blanc may be strained at this point, or the reduction ingredients can also be left in the sauce for texture and garnish.*

ABOVE *Emulsion sauces are difficult to hold. Be sure that the beurre blanc is kept warm, not hot. Here, the finished sauce is held in a doubled bain-marie in a hot-water bath to keep the temperature as consistent as possible.*

2 tbsp / 30 mL minced shallots

6 to 8 black peppercorns

8 fl oz / 240 mL dry white wine

2 fl oz / 60 mL lemon juice

3 fl oz / 90 mL cider vinegar or white wine

8 fl oz / 240 mL reduced heavy cream (optional; see Notes)

1½ lb / 680 g cubed butter, cool or at room temperature

salt, as needed

ground white pepper, as needed

1 tbsp lemon zest, grated or minced (optional)

BEURRE BLANC

1 Combine the shallots, peppercorns, wine, lemon juice, and vinegar in a saucepan. Reduce over medium-high heat until nearly dry *(à sec)*.

2 Add the reduced heavy cream, if using, and simmer the sauce for 2 to 3 minutes to reduce slightly.

3 Add the butter a few pieces at a time, whisking constantly to blend the butter into the reduction. The heat should be quite low as you work. Continue adding butter until the full amount has been incorporated.

4 Taste the beurre blanc and adjust with salt and pepper. Finish the sauce by adding the lemon zest. Hold this sauce as you would a hollandaise (see page 278).

MAKES 1 QUART/1 LITER

NOTE
Reduce cream by half before measuring.

THE PURPOSE OF SAUCES

Most sauces have more than one function in a dish. A sauce that adds a counterpoint flavor, for example, may also introduce textural and visual appeal. Sauces generally serve one or more of the following purposes.

INTRODUCE COMPLEMENTARY OR COUNTERPOINT FLAVORS

Sauces that are classically paired with particular foods illustrate this function. Suprême sauce is made by reducing a chicken velouté with chicken stock and finishing it with cream. This ivory-colored sauce has a deep chicken flavor and a velvety texture. When served with chicken, the color and flavor of the sauce complement the delicate meat and help intensify its flavor. The cream in the sauce rounds out the flavors.

Charcutière sauce is made with mustard and cornichons. This sauce is pungent and flavorful. When served with pork, the sharpness of the sauce introduces a counterpoint flavor, cutting the meat's richness and providing a contrast that is pleasing but not startling to the palate. The sauce brings out the pork's flavor but might overwhelm a more delicate meat like veal.

ADD MOISTURE OR SUCCULENCE

A sauce can add moisture to naturally lean foods (e.g., poultry, fish), or when using cooking techniques that tend to have a drying effect, such as grilling or sautéing. Grilled foods are frequently served with a warm butter emulsion sauce like béarnaise or with compound butter or with salsa or chutney. Beurre blanc is often served with shallow-poached lean white fish to add a bit of succulence to the dish.

ADD VISUAL INTEREST

A sauce can enhance a dish's appearance by adding luster and sheen. Lightly coating a sautéed medallion of lamb with a jus lié creates a glossy finish on the lamb, giving the entire plate more eye appeal. Pooling a red pepper coulis beneath a grilled swordfish steak gives the dish a degree of visual excitement by adding an element of color.

ENHANCE FLAVORS

A sauce that includes a flavor complementary to a food brings out the flavor of that food. The mild sweetness of poultry is heightened by a sauce flavored with tarragon. The rich flavor of beef is highlighted by a pungent sauce made with green peppercorns, which deepen and enrich the overall taste.

ADJUST TEXTURE

Many sauces include a garnish that adds texture to the finished dish. Chicken Chasseur is enhanced by a sauce finished with tomatoes and mushrooms. A dish that has a distinct texture, such as pan-fried soft-shelled crab, is enhanced by a smooth sauce.

SAUCE PAIRING

Certain classic sauce combinations endure because the composition is well balanced in all areas: taste, texture, and eye appeal. When choosing an appropriate sauce, it should be:

- SUITABLE FOR THE STYLE OF SERVICE. In a banquet setting or in any situation where large quantities of food must be served rapidly and at the peak of flavor, choose a sauce that may be prepared in advance and held in large quantities at the correct temperature without affecting quality.

  In an à la carte kitchen, sauces prepared à la minute are more appropriate.

- MATCHED TO THE MAIN INGREDIENT'S COOKING TECHNIQUE. Pair a cooking technique that produces flavorful drippings (fond), such as roasting or sautéing, with a sauce that makes use of those drippings.

  Similarly, beurre blanc is suitable for foods that have been shallow-poached because the cooking liquid (cuisson) can become a part of the sauce.

- APPROPRIATE FOR THE FLAVOR OF THE FOOD WITH WHICH IT IS PAIRED. Dover sole is perfectly complemented by a delicate cream sauce. The same sauce would be overwhelmed by the flavor of grilled tuna.

  Lamb has its own strong flavor that can stand up to a sauce flavored by rosemary. The same sauce would completely overpower a delicate fish.

GUIDELINES FOR PLATING SAUCES

- **MAINTAIN THE TEMPERATURE OF THE SAUCE.** Check the temperature of the sauce, of the food being sauced, and of the plate. Be sure that hot sauces are extremely hot, warm emulsions sauces are as warm as possible without danger of breaking, and cold sauces remain cold until they come in contact with hot foods.

- **CONSIDER THE TEXTURE OF THE FOOD BEING SERVED.** Pool the sauce beneath the food, spreading it in a layer directly on the plate if the food has a crisp or otherwise interesting texture.

  Spoon or ladle the sauce evenly over the top of the food if it could benefit from a little cover or if the sauce has visual appeal.

- **SERVE AN APPROPRIATE PORTION OF SAUCE.** There should be enough sauce for every bite of the sauced food but not so much that the dish looks swamped. Not only does this disturb the balance between the items on the plate, it makes it diffi-cult for the waiter to carry the food from the kitchen to the guest's table without at least some of the sauce running onto the rim, or worse, over the edge of the plate.

RECIPES

SAUCE ESPAGNOLE

makes 1 gallon/3.75 liters

3 fl oz/90 mL vegetable oil

MIREPOIX
8 oz/225 g medium-dice onions
4 oz/115 g medium-dice carrots
4 oz/115 g medium-dice celery

2 fl oz/60 mL tomato paste
1½ gal/5.75 L BROWN VEAL STOCK (page 252), hot
12 oz/340 g brown roux (see page 238)
sachet d'épices, containing 2 to 3 parsley stems, ½ tsp/2 mL dried thyme, ½ tsp/2 mL cracked black peppercorns, 1 bay leaf, and 1 garlic clove

1 Heat the oil and brown the onions. Add the remainder of the mirepoix and continue to brown.

2 Add the tomato paste and cook for several minutes until it turns a rusty brown.

3 Add the stock and bring to a simmer.

4 Whip the roux into the stock. Return to a simmer and add the sachet.

5 Simmer for about 1 hour, skimming the surface as necessary.

6 Strain through a double thickness of rinsed cheesecloth. The sauce is ready to use now, or it may be cooled and stored for later use.

DEMIGLACE

makes 2 quarts/2 liters

2 qt/2 L BROWN VEAL STOCK (page 252)
2 qt/2 L SAUCE ESPAGNOLE (above)

1 Combine the stock and the espagnole in a heavy-gauge pot and simmer over low to moderate heat until reduced by half. Skim the sauce frequently as it simmers.

2 Strain the sauce. The sauce is ready to serve now, or it may be cooled and stored for later service (see page 64).

BROWN SAUCE DERIVATIVES
(Classically Based on Demi-Glace)

SAUCE	FLAVORINGS
BERCY	Shallots, pepper, white wine, butter, dice of poached marrow, parsley
BORDELAISE	Red wine reduction, glaçe de viande, poached marrow
CHARCUTIÈRE	Robert sauce (below) with julienne of cornichons
CHASSEUR	Mushrooms, shallots, white wine, tomato concassé
CHÂTEAUBRIAND	Shallots, thyme, bay leaves, mushroom trimmings, white wine, butter, tarragon, parsley
DIABLE	White wine reduction, pepper mignonette, shallots, cayenne
DIANE	Poivrade sauce (below) with cream
ESTRAGON	Tarragon
FINANCIÈRE	Madère sauce (below) with truffle essence
FINES-HERBES	White wine, fines herbes, lemon juice
LYONNAISE	Onions filed in butter, white wine, and vinegar
MADÈRE	Madeira wine
MOSCOVITE	Poivrade sauce (below) with an infusion of juniper berries, toasted sliced almonds, plumped currants, marsala wine
PÉRIGUEUX	Truffle essence, chopped truffles, madeira wine
PÉRIGOURDINE	Foie gras puree, sliced truffles
PIQUANTE	Reduction of white wine, vinegar, shallots; garnished with cornichons, chervil, tarragon, pepper
POIVRADE	Reduction of white wine, peppercorns, butter
PORTO	Port with shallots, thyme, lemon and orange juice and zest, cayenne
ROBERT	White wine, onions, mustard, butter
ROMAINE	Pale caramel dissolved with vinegar (gastrique), garnished with grilled pine nuts, plumped raisins and currants
SOLFÉRINO	Shallots, maître d'hôtel butter, tomato essence, cayenne, lemon
ZINGARA	Tomatoes, mushroom julienne, truffles, ham, tongue, cayenne, madeira wine

BÉCHAMEL SAUCE

makes 3 ½ quarts/3.5 liters

2 fl oz/60 mL oil or clarified butter
2 oz/60 g minced onions
1 lb/450 g white roux (see page 238)
4 ½ qt/4.25 L milk
salt, as needed
ground white pepper, as needed
grated nutmeg (optional), as needed

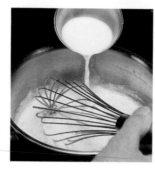 

1 Heat the oil or butter and add the onions. Sauté over low to moderate heat, stirring frequently, until the onions are tender and translucent, with no color, 6 to 8 minutes.

2 Add the roux to the onions and cook until the roux is very hot, about 2 minutes.

3 Add the milk to the pan gradually, whisking or stirring to work out any lumps. Bring the sauce to a full boil, then reduce the heat and simmer until the sauce is smooth and thickened, about 30 minutes. Stir frequently and skim as necessary throughout cooking time.

4 Adjust the seasoning to taste with salt, pepper, and nutmeg.

5 Strain through a double thickness of rinsed cheesecloth.

6 The sauce is ready to use now, or it may be cooled and stored for later use (see page 64).

Mornay Sauce Combine the finished béchamel with 8 oz/ 115 g *each* of grated gruyère and Parmesan. Finish with up to 2 oz/60 g whole butter, if desired.

Cream Sauce Add 1 pt/480 mL heated heavy cream to the finished béchamel. Simmer to a good flavor and consistency.

Cheddar Sauce Combine the finished béchamel with 1 lb/ 450 g of grated sharp cheddar.

TOP LEFT Oignon piqué, *an onion studded with cloves and a piece of bay leaf, can be added to give extra depth of flavor to a béchamel. Or use sweated minced onions, a clove or two, a piece of bay leaf, and a sprig of fresh thyme instead.*

BOTTOM LEFT *Béchamel calls for milk and/or cream, rather than the stocks used for velouté.*

TOP RIGHT *This béchamel is ready to use as a binder for croquettes, to finish creamed vegetable dishes, or as an ingredient in dishes like vegetable lasagne or croquettes.*

BOTTOM RIGHT *Béchamel can be finished with a variety of cheeses. Here, grated Gruyère is added to prepare a Mornay sauce.*

TOMATO COULIS

makes 2 quarts/2 liters

2 fl oz/60 mL olive oil

8 oz/225 g minced onions

1/2 oz/15 g minced garlic

8 fl oz/240 mL tomato purée

12 fl oz/360 mL red wine

2¹/₂ lb/1.15 kg plum tomato concassé

1 qt/1 L CHICKEN STOCK (page 248)

2 basil sprigs

1 thyme sprig

1 bay leaf

salt, as needed

pepper, as needed

1 Heat the olive oil and sauté the onions until they are translucent, about 6 to 8 minutes. Add the garlic and sauté it briefly. Add the tomato purée and cook for several minutes, until it turns a rusty brown.

2 Add the red wine, tomatoes, stock, basil, thyme, and bay leaf. Simmer for about 45 minutes. Remove and discard the herbs.

3 Pass through a food mill fitted with the coarse disk. Adjust the consistency if necessary.

4 Taste and season the sauce with salt and pepper. The sauce is ready to use now or it may be cooled and stored for later use (see page 64). Cool the sauce and hold it under refrigeration.

SUPRÊME SAUCE

makes ¹/₄ quarts/1.75 liters

2 qt/2 L CHICKEN VELOUTÉ (page 266)

1 pt/480 mL heavy cream, heated

1 lb/450 g sliced mushrooms (optional)

salt, as needed

ground white pepper, as needed

3 oz/85 g butter (optional)

1 Combine the velouté and heavy cream. (Add the mushrooms at this point, if desired.) Simmer, stirring and skimming the surface frequently, until the sauce coats the back of a spoon.

2 Strain the sauce and adjust the seasoning to taste with salt and pepper.

3 Finish the sauce with butter, if desired.

BÉARNAISE SAUCE

makes 20 fluid ounces/600 milliliters

1 tbsp/15 mL chopped shallots

¹/₂ tsp/3 mL cracked black peppercorns

1 tbsp dried tarragon

2 tarragon stems, chopped

2 fl oz/60 mL tarragon vinegar

1 fl oz/30 mL dry white wine

2 fl oz/60 mL water

6 egg yolks

1 pint/480 mL melted or clarified butter, warmed to 145°F/63°C

2 tbsp/30 mL chopped tarragon

1 tbsp/15 mL chopped chervil

salt, as needed

1 Combine the shallots, peppercorns, dried tarragon, tarragon stems, and vinegar. Reduce until nearly dry.

2 Add the wine and water to the reduction and strain into a stainless-steel bowl.

3 Whip the egg yolks together with the reduction and place over simmering water. Cook, whisking constantly, until the eggs are thickened and form ribbons when they fall from the whisk (165°F/73°C).

4 Add the butter in a thin stream, whipping constantly, until all of the butter is added and the sauce is thickened.

5 Add the chopped tarragon and chervil and adjust the seasoning to taste with salt. The sauce is ready to serve now. It may be held warm (145°F/63°C) for up to 2 hours.

Paloise Sauce (Mint Sauce) Replace the tarragon stems in the reduction with mint stems; replace the tarragon vinegar with cider vinegar; and replace the chopped tarragon and chervil with 3 tbsp/15 mL of chopped mint leaves.

BÉARNAISE REDUCTION

If a kitchen prepares béarnaise or similar warm butter sauces often, larger batches of reduction may be prepared in advance to make it easier to prepare smaller batches of the sauce during service.

makes about 4 fluid ounces/120 milliliters

1 tbsp/15 mL chopped shallots

12 cracked black peppercorns

³/₄ oz/20 g tarragon, chopped

6 fl oz/180 mL tarragon vinegar

4 fl oz/120 mL dry white wine

2 fl oz/60 mL water

1 Combine the shallots, peppercorns, tarragon, vinegar, and wine in a saucepan. Bring to a simmer, then reduce until nearly dry.

2 Add the water to the reduction. The reduction may be used to prepare a sauce or it may be cooled and stored for later use.

CHORON SAUCE

makes 1 quart/1 liter

2 tbsp/30 mL chopped shallots

12 black peppercorns

3 tbsp/45 mL dried tarragon

2 fresh tarragon stems, chopped

6 fl oz/180 mL cider vinegar, or as needed

1 fl oz/30 mL dry white wine

2 fl oz/60 mL water, or as needed

8 oz/225 g egg yolks (about 9)

27 oz/800 g clarified butter, warm (about 165°F/73°C)

lemon juice, as needed

1¹/₂ oz/45 g tomato purée

salt, as needed

pepper, as needed

cayenne pepper, as needed (optional)

1 Combine the shallots, peppercorns, dried tarragon, fresh tarragon, and vinegar in a small pan and reduce over medium heat until nearly dry.

2 Add the wine and water to the reduction and strain into a stainless-steel bowl.

3 Whip the egg yolks with the reduction and place over simmering water. Cook, whisking constantly, until the yolks triple in volume and form ribbons when they fall from the whisk (165°F/73°C).

4 Add the butter by the ladleful, whisking constantly, until all of the butter is added and the sauce is thickened. Adjust the sauce if necessary with lemon juice, vinegar, or water.

5 Stir in the tomato puree and taste the sauce. Add lemon juice, salt, pepper, and cayenne, if desired, as needed.

6 The sauce is ready to serve, or it may be held warm (165°F/73°C) for up to 2 hours.

BARBECUE SAUCE

makes 24 fluid ounces/720 milliliters

2 oz/60 mL oil or clarified butter

6 oz/180 g minced red onion

2 cloves garlic, minced to a paste

10 oz/300 mL orange juice concentrate

8 oz/240 mL WHITE BEEF STOCK (page 249)

6 oz/180 mL ketchup

4 oz/120 mL Heinz "57" sauce

4 oz/120 mL Worcestershire sauce

¹/₂ tsp/1 g celery seeds

¹/₂ tsp/1 g chopped chervil

salt, as needed

pepper, as needed

1 Heat the oil or butter in a 5-quart saucepot. Add onions and sauté over low to moderate heat, stirring frequently, until the onions are tender and translucent, with no color, about 6 to 8 minutes.

2 Add the garlic and sauté until an aroma is apparent, about 1 minute.

3 Add the remaining ingredients and simmer over low heat for 15 minutes, stirring occasionally and skimming as needed.

4 Taste the sauce and adjust the seasoning with salt and pepper if necessary. The sauce is ready to use now, or it may be properly cooled and stored for later use.

CHAPTER FOURTEEN

A well-prepared soup always
makes a memorable impression.
Soups offer a full array of flavoring ingredients and garnishing
opportunities. Soups also allow
the chef to use trimmings and
leftovers creatively, an important
profit-making consideration for
any foodservice establishment.

SOUPS

BROTH

Stocks and broths are very similar. In fact, the techniques for both are identical.

Meat, poultry, fish bones, and trimmings, or vegetables, possibly roasted or seared, are slowly simmered along with aromatic vegetables, spices, and herbs to produce a clear and flavorful liquid with some body.

The major distinction between broths and stocks is that broths are intended to be served as is, whereas stocks are used in the production of other dishes. Meat and poultry broths have a more pronounced flavor than their stock counterparts because they are based on meat rather than bones. By the same token, broths lack the body of stocks because of the absence of gelatin from bones. Fish and vegetable broths are made from the same basic ingredients as fish and vegetable stocks, so the difference between them is really one of intended end use and word choice.

If a broth's cooking speed is carefully regulated so that it is never more than an even, gentle simmer and if the surface is skimmed as necessary, a broth can be as clear, full-bodied, and rich as any consommé, without clarification.

Frequently, the meat or poultry used to prepare broths can work for other preparations, if they are cooked until fully tender and no longer. The meat can be julienned or diced to use as a garnish, or it can be served as a second course to follow the soup.

THE BEST BROTHS are made from the most flavorful meat, poultry, fish, shellfish, crustaceans, vegetables, and aromatics. Choose meat cuts from more exercised parts of the animal because the more fully developed the muscle, the more pronounced the flavor. The same is true of poultry broths, where stewing hens or more mature game birds are the best choice for deep flavor.

Fish freshness is of primary concern, as is the relative leanness or oiliness of the fish. It is best to use lean, white-fleshed fish, such as sole, flounder, halibut, or cod. Richer, oilier types of fish, such as bluefish or mackerel, tend to lose their savor when their delicate oils are subjected to high temperatures for even short periods. Shellfish and crustaceans cooked in the shell in a small amount of liquid produce excellent broth. It must then be strained very carefully to remove all traces of grit or sand.

For vegetable broths, wholesome trim from several vegetables can be combined to make a broth, or a specific recipe can be followed. Consider the strength of the vegetable's flavor and how that might affect the broth's balance.

Cabbage family members such as cauliflower or cabbage can become overwhelmingly strong.

Many broths are started with the simplest of all liquids: cool, fresh water. Using a stock, remouillage, or broth as the base liquid will produce what is sometimes referred to as a "double broth."

Additional ingredients can be selected to add flavor, aroma, and color to a broth. Aromatic herb and vegetable combinations such as mirepoix, sachet d'épices, or bouquet garni are traditional. Contemporary broths may call for such ingredients as dried tomatoes, lemon grass, wild mushrooms, or ginger to give the broth a unique character.

Garnishing broths adds visual and textural interest. Simple garnishes, such as a fine brunoise of vegetables or chervil pluches, are traditional. Other choices include diced or julienned meats; pieces of fish or shellfish; croutons; dumplings, quenelles, and wontons; noodles; and rice. The recipes found in this book and in many other books illustrate the breadth of possibilities.

When assembling the equipment, select a pot large enough to accommodate the broth as it cooks. There should be sufficient room at the top of the pot to allow some expansion during cooking, as well as to make it easy to skim away any impurities on the surface. The pot should be tall and narrow rather than short and wide. If available, select a pot with a spigot to make it easier to strain the broth.

You will also need skimmers and ladles, storage or holding containers, strainers, tasting spoons and cups, and a kitchen fork to remove any large pieces of meat.

FOR A BROTH THAT HAS GOOD FLAVOR, AROMA, COLOR, AND BODY, OBSERVE THE FOLLOWING FORMULAS.

INGREDIENTS FOR 1 GALLON/ 3.75 LITERS OF MEAT OR POULTRY BROTH, INCLUDE:

10 to 12 pounds/4.5 to 5.5 kilograms meat or poultry (including bones) to 6 quarts/5.75 liters cool liquid

1 pound/450 grams mirepoix

1 standard sachet d'épices or bouquet garni

INGREDIENTS FOR 1 GALLON/ 3.75 LITERS OF FISH OR SHELLFISH BROTH, INCLUDE:

10 to 12 pounds/4.5 to 5.5 kilograms fish or shellfish (including bones or shells) to 4 quarts/3.75 liters cool liquid

1 pound/450 grams white mirepoix (sometimes including mushroom trimmings)

1 standard sachet d'épices or bouquet garni

INGREDIENTS FOR 1 GALLON/ 3.75 LITERS OF VEGETABLE BROTH, INCLUDE:

6 to 8 pounds/2.75 to 3.6 kilograms vegetables to 4 quarts/3.75 liters cool liquid

1 pound/450 grams mirepoix

1 standard sachet d'épices or bouquet garni

1. Combine major flavoring ingredients, appropriate seasonings, and cool liquid and bring gently to a simmer, skimming as necessary. Begin with cool liquid to gently extract as much flavor as possible as the liquid slowly heats up. Gentle simmering establishes a natural clarification process and encourages impurities (fat and scum) to collect on the surface, where they can be skimmed away.

   Avoid a hard boil, which could cook the flavor out of the ingredients. Vigorous boiling action also causes fat and impurities to be mixed back into the broth, clouding the mixture.

2. Add remaining ingredients and aromatics at appropriate intervals. Sachet d'épices or bouquet garni ingredients release their flavors quickly. They are added near the end of cooking time. Rather than intensifying the flavor, continued cooking could actually cook away the delicate, volatile oils that hold their flavor essence.

3. Simmer until flavor, color, and body are fully developed. Since the cooking times for broths vary widely, consult specific recipes for guidance. Taste the broth from time to time as it simmers to be sure that it is developing properly, and make corrections if necessary. If a clove in the sachet d'épices threatens to overwhelm the broth, remove it. If there is a lack of rich, roasted flavors, add an oignon brûlé. Final seasoning and flavor adjustments, however, are generally done after the major flavoring ingredients have given up the maximum flavor. Meat and poultry should be cooked until fork tender. Fish, shellfish, and crustaceans should be simmered briefly until just cooked through. Vegetables should be extremely soft but not cooked into shreds.

ABOVE *Add enough cold liquid to cover the main ingredient completely.*

TOP *Vegetables are added at staggered intervals.*

BOTTOM *Parsley stems, fresh thyme, a bay leaf, and cracked peppercorns are included in the sachet for this broth.*

ABOVE *The broth cooks down as it simmers, concentrating its flavor.*

4. Strain and degrease the broth.
To keep the soup clear, first lift the meat or chicken and vegetables from the broth before straining. Line a sieve or colander with rinsed, doubled cheesecloth. A fine wire-mesh sieve or a paper filter can also be used. Skim as much fat from the surface as possible before garnishing and serving, or proper cooling and storage (see pages 64–65).

5. Bring the broth to service temperature and garnish as desired.
If the broth has been cooled, lift away any congealed fat and return the broth to a simmer. Prepare and heat the garnish.

6. Evaluate the quality of the finished broth.
A good broth is clear, rich-tasting, and aromatic, with good flavor and noticeable body.

The selection of fresh, high-quality ingredients, the right proportion of flavoring ingredients to liquid, careful regulation of heat as the broth simmers, thorough skimming, adequate cooking time, and adjustments to the broth's seasoning throughout cooking time result in the highest quality broth possible. Proper handling of the soup during storage and reheating assures that the broth maintains its quality.

TOP *Reserve the poultry and let it cool enough to handle easily.*

BOTTOM *To maintain clarity, ladle, don't pour, the broth out of the pot.*

ABOVE *Cut some of the meat into neat dice or julienne for a garnish. Use the remainder in another preparation (salads, fillings, etc.).*

ABOVE *This broth has a golden color and is quite clear. Broths typically have a few droplets of fat on the surface, a sign of a rich, full-flavored soup.*

2 stewing hens (about 5 lb/2.25 kg)

1½ gal / 5.75 L cold water

salt, as needed

MIREPOIX

6 oz / 170 g chopped onions

3 oz / 85 g chopped carrots

3 oz / 85 g chopped celery

8 oz / 225 g chopped tomatoes (optional)

sachet d'épices, containing 3 chopped parsley stems, 1 bay leaf, ½ tsp / 2 mL
  cracked peppercorns, ½ tsp / 2 mL fresh or dried thyme leaves, and 1 garlic clove

pepper, as needed

GARNISH (as shown on page 292)

10 oz / 285 g diced cooked chicken breast meat

10 oz / 285 g HERBED PASTA (page 706), cut into 1 in/5 cm squares, cooked

6 oz / 170 g carrot paysanne, cooked until tender

6 oz / 170 g celery paysanne, cooked until tender

CHICKEN BROTH

1 Rinse and disjoint the hens.

2 Bring the hens, water, and salt to taste to a simmer, skim the surface, and simmer gently for 2 hours.

3 Add the mirepoix and continue to simmer for 30 minutes. Continue skimming and adjust seasoning as necessary throughout cooking.

4 Add the sachet and simmer for 30 minutes more.

5 Lift the hens, mirepoix, and sachet from the broth. Strain the broth and degrease it. The broth is ready to finish now, or it may be cooled rapidly and stored for later service.

6 Return the broth to a simmer. Adjust seasoning with salt and pepper and add the garnish to individual portions or the batch. Serve in heated bowls or cups.

MAKES 1 GALLON/3.75 LITERS; 20 PORTIONS (6 FLUID OUNCES/180 MILLILITERS EACH)

BEEF BROTH Replace stewing hen with an equal amount of beef shank, chuck, bottom round, oxtail, or short ribs. A portion of veal shank/shin may also be added.

VEAL BROTH Replace stewing hen with an equal amount of veal shank/shin, chuck, bottom round, or calf's head.

HAM OR SMOKED PORK BROTH Replace stewing hen with an equal amount of hocks (fresh or smoked), meaty ham bones, or Boston butt.

LAMB BROTH Replace stewing hen with an equal amount of lamb shank, leg, shoulder, or neck.

TURKEY OR GAME BIRD BROTH Replace stewing hen with an equal amount of necks, backs, or legs of chicken, turkey, guinea hen, duck, pheasant, goose, or other poultry or game bird.

FISH BROTH Replace stewing hen with an equal amount of lean white fish, such as cod, halibut, hake, flounder, or pike. Use white mirepoix to keep a light color.

SHELLFISH BROTH Replace the stewing hen with an equal amount of shrimp, lobster, crayfish, and/or crab.

VEGETABLE BROTH Replace stewing hen with 7 lb/3.15 kg of combined onions, garlic, leeks, shallots, celery, celeriac, carrots, parsnips, mushrooms, tomatoes, fennel, broccoli stems, or others as deemed appropriate by recipe or intended use.

GARNISHES

MEAT Garnish each portion with diced or julienned meat, chicken, or fish.

GARDEN VEGETABLES Garnish each portion with fine-dice, fully cooked, well-seasoned vegetables (carrots, celery, leeks, turnips, peas) and diced cooked meat.

BARLEY Garnish each portion with diced, fully cooked, well-seasoned vegetables and 1 tablespoon cooked seasoned barley per portion.

SPÄTZLE Garnish each portion with hot, well-seasoned plain, herbed, or spinach spätzle.

CONSOMMÉ

A consommé is a perfectly clear broth.

Consommés are exceptionally rich in flavor and are crystal clear, an effect achieved by combining a high-quality stock or broth with a clarification mixture. To assure a high-quality consommé, the chef must choose ingredients carefully, keep the clarification mixture very cold until it is time to cook the consommé, and monitor the temperature of the consommé as it cooks at a slow simmer. Once the consommé has developed a rich flavor and color, it must be carefully strained and degreased to produce a crystal-clear soup, with no traces of fat, and an intense and satisfying flavor.

CLASSIC CONSOMMÉS

HUNDREDS OF CLASSICALLY CODIFIED garnishes for consommés exist, ranging from such humble items as neatly diced root vegetables to the esoteric edible gold leaf featured in a recipe found in Escoffier's *Le Guide Culinaire*. They draw on influences as diverse as Asian cuisines, Caribbean dishes, and Italian provincial cooking styles. No matter what the garnish selected may be, it is important that it be as well prepared as the consommé. Vegetable cuts should be neat and precise. Royales should be delicately set, soft, and supple in the mouth. The seasoning selected for the garnish should enhance the flavor of the consommé, not distract from it.

CONSOMMÉ BRUNOISE
Consommé garnished with small cubes of carrot, turnip, celery, leeks, peas, and chervil

CONSOMMÉ CÉLÈSTINE
Consommé lightly thickened with tapioca and garnished with julienne of crêpes mixed with chopped truffles or herbs

CONSOMMÉ JULIENNE
Consommé garnished with julienne of carrot, leek, turnip, celery, and cabbage plus green peas and chiffonade of sorrel and chervil

CONSOMMÉ PRINTANIER
Consommé garnished with balls of carrot and turnip, peas, and chervil

CONSOMMÉ ROYALE
Chicken consommé garnished with cubes or lozenges of royale (custard)

CONSOMMÉ CHASSEUR
Game consommé garnished with julienne of mushrooms and game quenelles or profiteroles stuffed with game purée

CONSOMMÉ DIPLOMATE
Chicken consommé lightly thickened with tapioca and garnished with julienne of truffles and rondels of chicken forcemeat blended with crayfish butter

CONSOMMÉ GRIMALDI
Consommé clarified with fresh tomato purée; garnished with dice of royale (custard) and julienne of celery

CONSOMMÉ MIKADO
Chicken consommé with tomato flavor, garnished with dice of tomato and chicken

STOCK FOR CONSOMMÉ should be of high quality and very fresh. To check for quality, bring a small amount to a boil, then smell and taste it. If there is any doubt about the quality of the stock, use a fresher batch or prepare new stock.

The clarification is a combination of lean ground meat, egg whites, mirepoix, herbs and spices, and tomato or other acidic ingredients. All of these ingredients serve multiple functions in preparing a well-balanced consommé. This mixture of ingredients produces a crystal-clear flavorful soup by removing impurities from the stock and bolstering its flavor. Whenever possible, grind the meat along with the mirepoix vegetables for the best flavor and quality in the finished consommé. Whether or not you grind the meat in house, be sure to keep it, as well as the egg whites, refrigerated so that it remains wholesome and flavorful.

Mirepoix vegetables should be cut small or ground so that they become part of the raft and release their flavors quickly. A variety of aromatic vegetables such as onions, carrots, celery, garlic, leeks, parsnips, and mushrooms are typical. Mix the clarification ingredients (except for the acid) thoroughly and chill, if time permits, for several hours or overnight. An acid, such as tomatoes, is added just before the stock is blended into the clarification to help the raft form properly, as well as for its flavor. An oignon brûlé may also be included to give additional flavor and color. Other flavoring items are used as necessary or appropriate to achieve a special flavor.

Herbs and spices are also included in the clarification mixture. Sprigs or stems of tarragon, parsley, chervil, dill, thyme, or other fresh herbs; cloves, bay leaf, peppercorns, juniper berries, or star anise; ginger and lemon grass are often featured in contemporary renditions of consommé.

The equipment needs for consommés are the same as those described earlier for broths, with the following special considerations: the pot should have a heavy bottom to help prevent the clarification ingredients from sticking and scorching, and it should be taller than it is wide. The even heat of steam kettles and flat-top ranges, if available, are ideal for making consommé.

FOR A CONSOMMÉ THAT HAS GOOD FLAVOR, AROMA, COLOR, AND BODY, OBSERVE THE FOLLOWING FORMULAS TO PRODUCE 1 GALLON/3.75 LITERS.

THE CLARIFICATION INCLUDES:

1 pound/450 grams mirepoix

3 pounds/1.3 kilograms lean ground meat, poultry, or fish

10 egg whites

an acid, such as tomatoes or lemon juice

THE BASE LIQUID IS:

5 quarts/4.75 liters stock or broth

SEASONING AND FLAVORING OPTIONS INCLUDE:

salt and pepper

a sachet d'épices or bouquet garni

oignon brûlé

others as desired

1. Blend clarification ingredients well and add cold stock.

Have the clarification ingredients very cold (below 40° F/4° C) at the start of cooking time. Some chefs prefer to grind the clarification mixture the day before making the consommé to allow it plenty of time to chill. The acid (tomatoes or lemon juice, for instance) is added just before cooking the consommé.

Add enough cold stock to loosen the clarification. The rest of the stock can be brought to a simmer separately to shorten the overall cooking time of the consommé.

2. Bring to a simmer, stirring frequently, until the raft begins to form. Continue to stir the consommé as it heats up so that the clarification ingredients do not stick to the pot and scorch.

Adjust the heat until only a few small bubbles break the surface. If there is a strong simmering or boiling action, the large soft mass known as the raft might break apart before it has sufficiently cleared and flavored the consommé. On the other hand, if the cooking speed is too slow, impurities may not rise from the bottom of the pot to the top, where they can be trapped by the raft.

Add an oignon brûlé, if desired. The skin can be left on the onion for even more color in the finished consommé.

ABOVE *Blend the tomatoes, and any additional aromatics into the clarification mixture.*

ABOVE *The stock added to the clarification is very cold.*

ABOVE *Add salt for the best flavor in the finished dish.*

3. Simmer without stirring once the clarification ingredients cook together into a raft.

As the consommé continues to simmer, the natural meat and eggs will coagulate, forming the raft. The simmering action of the soup carries impurities from the bottom of the pot to the raft, where they are trapped. This action clarifies the soup. The simmering action may also cause a small hole to form in the raft. If a small opening does not form on its own, use a spoon or ladle to gently poke through the raft so that you can taste the consommé as it develops and make any necessary seasoning adjustment. The hole should be just large enough to accommodate a small ladle.

4. Simmer gently until flavor, color, and body are fully developed.

Recipes usually provide a cooking guideline (generally from 1 to 1½ hours), long enough to bolster the soup's flavor and clarify it properly. Baste the raft occasionally as the consommé simmers. When the raft begins to sink slightly, assuming that this happens after a reasonable cooking time rather than because the heat wasn't adjusted properly, the consommé is properly simmered.

Pour a small amount into a soup bowl or plate to assess its clarity visually.

HOW THE RAFT FORMS

The clarification will rise to the surface of the stock as the raft continues to cook.

TOP *Clarification mixture and stock are stirred together until homogenous.*

MIDDLE *As the temperature rises, the clarification ingredients begin to turn gray and coalesce into a large, soft mass that is known as a raft. This occurs in the temperature range of approximately 120° to 125°F/49° to 52° C.*

BOTTOM *Once the raft forms, stop stirring the consommé to allow the raft to come together.*

ABOVE *The raft traps heat, in the same way that a lid on a pot does. Here the cooking action of the soup has broken a small hole in the raft.*

ABOVE *Basting the raft prevents it from breaking apart or sinking too quickly. This assures the fullest possible flavor and clarity.*

5. Strain and finish or cool the consommé.
Use a fine-wire mesh sieve, a conical sieve lined with a coffee filter, or carefully rinsed cheesecloth to strain the finished consommé.

Avoid breaking up the raft as you strain the consommé and don't pour the consommé and raft into a strainer, because this will release impurities. Adjust seasoning and make any necessary adjustments.

6. Degrease.
A consommé should be completely fat-free. The consommé is now ready for garnishing and service or to be cooled and stored (see pages 64–65).

7. Evaluate the quality of the finished consommé.
A consommé of excellent quality has a well-balanced, rich, full, deep flavor, reflecting the flavor of the major ingredient, and a discernible body. It is perfectly clear, completely fat-free, and aromatic.

The selection of fresh, high-quality ingredients, having the clarification ingredients as cold as possible when they are combined with the stock, the proper relationship of flavoring ingredients and aromatics to liquid, adequate cooking time, careful regulation of heat as the broth simmers, careful skimming, and seasoning adjustments throughout cooking time result in the highest quality consommé possible. Careful handling of the consommé during storage and reheating assures that it maintains its quality.

TOP *Carefully enlarge the opening in the raft. (This step is unnecessary if using a pot with a spigot. In that case, arrange strainer under the spigot and let the consommé drain slowly out of the pot.)*

BOTTOM *Strain the consommé (a paper filter is shown here) into a clean bain-marie to hold for service or for storage.*

ABOVE *Blot the consommé with absorbent paper, as shown here, or refrigerate it. Any fat will congeal and be easy to lift away before reheating the soup.*

ABOVE *Note the clarity and color of the finished consommé.*

8 oz / 225 g minced or ground onions

4 oz / 115 g minced or ground carrots

4 oz / 115 g minced or ground celery

3 lb / 1.35 kg lean ground beef

10 egg whites, beaten

12 oz / 340 g chopped tomatoes

5 qt / 4.75 L WHITE BEEF STOCK (page 249), cold

2 tbsp / 30 mL kosher salt, or as needed

sachet d'épices, containing 3 parsley stems, $\frac{1}{2}$ tsp / 2 mL fresh or dried thyme, 1 bay leaf, $\frac{1}{2}$ tsp / 2 mL cracked black peppercorns, 1 clove, and 2 allspice berries

2 oignons brûlés (optional)

BEEF CONSOMMÉ

1 Blend the ingredients for the clarification and add the stock.

2 Bring the mixture to a slow simmer, stirring frequently, until the raft forms. Add some of the salt. Add the sachet and oignons brûlés (if using). Stop stirring when raft begins to form (120° to 125°F/50° to 52°C).

3 Simmer slowly for 1 to 1½ hours, or until the desired flavor and clarity are achieved. Baste the raft occasionally.

4 Strain the consommé through a paper filter or doubled cheesecloth. The consommé is ready to finish now, or it may be rapidly cooled and stored for later service.

5 Degrease hot consommé by skimming or blotting with parchment paper, or degrease cold consommé by lifting the hardened fat from the surface.

6 Taste the consommé and adjust seasoning. Return to a simmer and garnish as desired.

MAKES 1 GALLON / 3.75 LITERS; 20 PORTIONS (6 FLUID OUNCES/180 MILLILITERS EACH)

NOTES

If the first clarification was less than successful, clarify a second time by combining 1 gallon/3.75 liters of cold consommé with no more than 4 beaten egg whites, a small amount of mirepoix, and 1 tablespoon/ 15 milliliters of the tomato purée or lemon juice that was used in the first clarification. Bring the consommé slowly to a boil. As the egg whites coagulate, the impurities will be trapped. This emergency measure, however, tends to remove not only the impurities but some flavor as well. This is why no more than 4 egg whites should be used.

HEARTY BROTHS

Hearty broths are full in flavor and have more texture and body than clear broths do.

Hearty broths are based on clear broths or stock. The vegetables are cut into uniform size and the soup is simmered until all the ingredients are tender. Meats, grains, and pasta are frequently included to add body.

When additional ingredients are cooked directly in the broth, these soups lack the clarity of broth or consommé. Hearty broths may also be made from a single vegetable; for example, onion soup.

HEARTY BROTHS INCLUDE vegetables chosen both for their own flavors and for their aromatic qualities. Each recipe indicates quantities of each type. Prepare each vegetable by trimming, peeling, and cutting it into neat and even-size pieces so that they cook uniformly and have an attractive appearance.

Some hearty broths also include meat, poultry, or fish. Trim and cut meat, poultry, or fish to suit the style of soup you are preparing. After cooking in the soup, these ingredients are often diced or julienned and returned to the soup just before it is finished for service. Other ingredients might include beans, whole grains, pasta, or similar ingredients. For a relatively clear soup, cook these starchy ingredients separately and add them to the soup as a garnish. A more rustic approach calls for these ingredients to be cooked in the broth as part of the soup making process. Such soups tend to have more body and are sometimes referred to as hearty vegetable soups.

Clear broths, good-quality stocks, and other liquids, including water, vegetable essences, or juices, are used as the liquid base for vegetable soups. Be sure to taste the liquid and add seasonings as necessary from the start of cooking time up to and including just before service. Refer to specific recipes for ingredient suggestions. Bring the broth to a simmer over low heat while preparing the other ingredients, along with seasonings and aromatics as needed. This will improve the flavor of the finished broth and help reduce overall cooking time, since the soup will come to the correct cooking speed more quickly.

Garnishes are as varied as the soups themselves. Croutons are common, and they may be an integral part of the preparation, as in French onion soup gratinée. Other garnishes, such as pesto, grated cheese, or even beaten eggs, can be added to vegetable soups just before they are served. Purées of red peppers, chiles, tomato, or sorrel may also be added at the last moment for a dash of color and flavor.

Most vegetable soups are prepared from start to finish in a single pot. The pot should be taller than it is wide to allow the soup to cook gently and evenly at a constant simmer.

Skimmers, ladles, and spoons are all used throughout cooking time. Tasting spoons and cups should be on hand, so that you can monitor the soup's flavor development. Storage or holding containers will also be needed.

Fortified wines such as sherry, vinegar, or citrus juices may be used for last-minute flavor adjustments.

FOR A HEARTY BROTH THAT HAS GOOD FLAVOR, AROMA, COLOR, AND BODY, OBSERVE THE FOLLOWING FORMULAS TO PRODUCE 1 GALLON/3.75 LITERS.

ONE OR MORE OF THE FOLLOWING MAIN FLAVORING INGREDIENTS, TO EQUAL 4 POUNDS/1.8 KILOGRAMS:

vegetables

meat, poultry, or fish

legumes

pasta

THE BASE LIQUID IS:

3 quarts/2.8 liters stock or broth

SEASONING AND FLAVORING OPTIONS INCLUDE:

salt and pepper

1 sachet d'épices or bouquet garni

oignon brûlé, or others as desired

FINISHING AND GARNISHING OPTIONS INCLUDE:

fresh herbs or herb pastes, such as pesto

plain or flavored oils

croutons

grated cheese

fortified wines, or others as desired

1. Cook the aromatic vegetables in fat to the desired stage, adding them at intervals to develop the best flavor, texture, and color.

Onions, garlic, leeks, celery, carrots, and parsnips are basic aromatic ingredients of many vegetable soups. Sweating them in a small amount of fat begins the process of releasing their flavors into the soup.

Some tender vegetables, such as broccoli florets, asparagus tips, and other delicate types, are generally not allowed to sweat. They are added at staggered intervals, according to individual cooking times. Consult recipes for specific instructions on cooking the vegetables.

2. Add liquid and bring to a simmer, stirring, skimming, and adjusting seasoning throughout cooking time. Add main flavoring ingredients at appropriate intervals (see sidebar at right).

Depending upon the flavor of the broth, appropriate seasoning is also added at this point. As you season the soup now, bear in mind that the soup will be simmering for about 1 hour longer.

A slow simmer is the best cooking speed for most soups. The vegetables and meats will release the best flavor, and the appearance of vegetables will be more attractive when cooked at a simmer. A hard boil tends to cook food to shreds. Continue to add ingredients at the appropriate point so that they cook properly and develop a good flavor.

TOP *Cutting vegetables neatly and in about the same size promotes even cooking and visual appeal. The onions here have been cut into julienne so that, once cooked, they will fit in the bowl of a soup spoon.*

BOTTOM *Sweating onions.*

TOP *As the sugars in the onions brown, the flavor becomes deeper and more complex.*

BOTTOM *These onions are ready to use as the basis of a rich onion soup.*

ABOVE *Add broth or good-quality stock.*

Additional aromatic ingredients, such as a sachet d'épices or bouquet garni, are also added at the end so that they will cook just long enough to release flavor into the soup.

Skim the surface as needed throughout preparation. The scum that is thrown by the soup needs to be removed for the best finished quality and appearance of the soup.

Taste the soup frequently as it cooks and make adjustments as necessary.

Once the soup has reached its peak flavor, it is ready for final seasoning, garnishing and service. Or it may be cooled and stored (see pages 64–65).

3. Evaluate the quality of the finished soup.

Clear vegetable soups are not as clear as broth or consommé. Unlike in strained soups, the vegetables are part of the soup itself and serve to give it texture and body. When properly cooked, vegetables should have appealing colors with no graying. Meats, poultry, fish, and starchy ingredients, such as potatoes and beans, hold their shape but have a very soft texture.

MEATS, POULTRY, AND FISH

Cuts of meat that are more mature and less tender should be added to the soup early in the cooking process so that they will flavor the broth properly and finish cooking at the same time as the other ingredients. Add fish or shellfish to hearty broths close to the end of cooking time to prevent them from becoming overcooked.

GRAINS AND PASTA

Allow grains and pasta a little more time than would be necessary to cook in boiling salted water.

LEGUMES

Lentils and black-eyed peas are added to the soup along with the stock so that they will cook fully. Other beans may need to be cooked separately (see pages 672–673).

DENSE OR STARCHY VEGETABLES

Turnips, carrots, potatoes, winter squash, rutabagas, beets, parsnips, and potatoes cut to small dice typically require 30 to 45 minutes to fully cook.

GREEN VEGETABLES

Peas, green beans, and leafy vegetables such as spinach or kale are added during the final 15 to 20 minutes of simmering time for the soup. Some chefs prefer to blanch these vegetables to help set the colors before adding them to a soup.

TOMATOES

In some cases, tomatoes may be added at the beginning of cooking time, along with the aromatic ingredients, to act as a broth flavoring. A tomato garnish may be added during the final 5 or 10 minutes of simmering time.

HERBS AND SPICES

Dried herbs and most spices are added to the soup along with the aromatics to flavor the broth throughout cooking time. Fresh and dried herbs and spices may also be added in the form of a sachet or bouquet during the final 15 to 20 minutes of simmering time or before service for the freshest flavor.

ABOVE *Cook the soup at a bare simmer to coax the flavor out of the vegetable and into the broth. Skim frequently for the best flavor, texture, and sheen.*

ABOVE *The interplay of flavors, the melting texture, and the rich color in this onion soup are the result of proper selection and handling of ingredients, judicious seasoning, and good technique.*

3 lb / 1.35 kg onions, sliced thin

2 oz / 60 g clarified butter

3½ qt / 3.3 L WHITE BEEF STOCK (page 249) or CHICKEN STOCK (page 248)

4 oz / 120 mL Calvados (optional)

sachet d'épices, containing 3 parsley stems, 1 bay leaf, ½ tsp / 2 mL cracked black
   peppercorns, and ½ tsp / 2 mL fresh or dried thyme

salt, as needed

pepper, as needed

ONION SOUP

1 Sauté the onions in clarified butter over moderate heat, stirring occasionally, until deep
golden brown, about 40 to 45 minutes. Add a little stock, if necessary, to prevent burning.

2 Add the Calvados and stir to deglaze the pot. Cook down until the liquid is syrupy.
Add the remaining stock and the sachet.

3 Simmer until the soup is properly flavored, about 20 to 25 minutes. The soup is ready
to serve now or it may be rapidly cooled and stored.

4 Adjust seasoning with salt and pepper to taste. Serve in heated bowls or cups.

MAKES 1 GALLON/3.75 LITERS; 20 PORTIONS (6 FLUID OUNCES/180 MILLILITERS EACH)

NOTES

Other stocks, including white veal stock, chicken stock, or combinations of stocks can be used to prepare a
good onion soup.

Sherry may be used to finish the soup just before it is served, if desired.

White Onion Soup Gently cook the onions in butter or oil over low heat until they are limp
but not colored. If desired, add up to 6 ounces of flour as a thickener. In some classic
recipes, the onions are puréed, then either returned to the soup or spread on a crouton.

Onion Soup Gratinée Garnish each portion with a crouton. Top generously with grated
Gruyère and brown under a salamander or broiler, or bake in a moderate oven until
lightly browned.

CREAM SOUPS

According to classic definitions, a cream soup is based on a béchamel sauce — milk thickened with roux — and is finished with heavy cream.

A velouté soup is based on a light velouté sauce — stock thickened with roux — and is finished with a liaison of heavy cream and egg yolks. Contemporary chefs no longer draw a distinction between the two; they frequently substitute a velouté base for the béchamel in cream soups or even use the term *cream* to refer to a purée soup that has been finished with cream.

THE MAIN FLAVORING INGRE-DIENT for some soups is often a single vegetable, such as broccoli or asparagus, or chicken or fish. If poultry or fish is simmered in the soup to give flavor and body, be sure to trim, truss, or cut those ingredients as appropriate.

Vegetables, whether used as main flavoring ingredients or as aromatics, should be well rinsed, then peeled, trimmed, and cut into small and uniform pieces so they cook evenly.

A well-seasoned, full-bodied broth, stock, or light velouté should be on hand. Milk or a light béchamel is sometimes appropriate. Bring the liquid up to a simmer, along with seasonings, aromatics, or other ingredients meant to provide flavor. Refer to specific recipes for guidance.

Thickeners, including prepared roux, flour, potatoes, or the natural thickening of the puréed main ingredient, give cream soups their texture. However, added thickeners are unnecessary if the base liquid is a prepared velouté. Assemble finishing ingredients, final flavoring and seasonings, and garnishes ahead of time, to be ready to add at the right time. Bring cream to a simmer before adding to simmering soup. Blend liaisons and temper them just before the soup is served.

Pots with heavy-gauge flat bottoms, made of nonreactive materials, such as stainless steel, anodized aluminum, or enameled cast iron, are a good choice for cream soups. Simmer cream soups on flat tops or a heat diffuser to prevent hot spots from developing and scorching the soup.

Wooden spoons, ladles, and skimmers are generally required throughout the cooking process. Blenders (countertop and immersion style), food processors, and food mills are used singly or in combination to purée the soup. For a velvety texture in the finished soup, you may also need fine mesh strainers or cheesecloth to strain the soup a final time.

FOR A CREAM SOUP THAT HAS GOOD FLAVOR, AROMA, COLOR, AND BODY, OBSERVE THE FOLLOWING FORMULAS TO PRODUCE 1 GALLON/3.75 LITERS.

ONE OR MORE MAIN FLAVORING INGREDIENTS, TO EQUAL 3 POUNDS/1.3 KILOGRAMS:

vegetables

meat, poultry, or fish

THE BASE LIQUID IS:

2 ½ to 3 quarts/2.5 to 2.8 liters stock or broth

2 ½ to 3 quarts/2.5 to 2.8 liters prepared velouté

THICKENING OPTIONS INCLUDE:

prepared blond roux

flour

potatoes

SEASONING AND FLAVORING OPTIONS INCLUDE:

salt and pepper

a sachet d'épices or bouquet garni

FINISHING AND GARNISHING OPTIONS INCLUDE:

1 pint/480 milliliters heavy cream or liaison

dice or julienne of main flavoring ingredient

mince or chiffonade of herbs

1. Cook the aromatic vegetables to develop a good flavor base.

White mirepoix is a common aromatic combination for cream soups. For some soups, the main flavoring ingredient(s) may also be added in the first stages of cooking. Cook gently over low heat in oil or whole or clarified butter until the vegetables are tender and translucent and begin to release their juices.

The amount of fat you use to sweat the vegetables will be determined by how you intend to introduce the roux into the soup. If the roux is to be made as part of the overall process (as shown here), sweat the aromatics in enough fat to also make the roux. If you intend to use a premade velouté or béchamel or a prepared roux, use only enough fat to smother the aromatics and keep them from burning.

2. Stir the flour, if using, into the fat and cook out the roux.

Cook the roux just long enough for it to take on a pale golden color. If using a premade velouté or béchamel (both of which already contain a roux) or a prepared roux, omit this step. Instead, add these once the soup is at a simmer. Alternately, a potato may be included to thicken the soup.

ABOVE *White mirepoix is used for the aromatic base in this soup, to preserve it's light green color.*

ABOVE *Add the chopped broccoli to release some of its flavor into the cooking fat. Stir well to coat the broccoli evenly and start the cooking process.*

TOP *Flour is added here to create the roux for the soup.*

BOTTOM *Stir the flour into the mixture well to combine it evenly with the cooking fat and allow it to cook until the flour is barely blond.*

3. Add the liquid base for the soup and bring it to a simmer. Add other ingredients, if using, at staggered intervals.

Slowly whisk in the hot broth, stock, velouté, or béchamel. Bring the soup just up to a simmer, stirring frequently. Check the soup's seasoning and make any necessary adjustments.

Certain ingredients are added to the soup at intervals, depending upon how dense they are and the effect extended cooking might have on them. Tender new peas will become gray and pasty if allowed to cook for too long. A sachet d'épices left in the soup too long may lose its fresh flavor. Consult individual recipes for specific instructions on when to add ingredients.

4. Simmer until the main ingredient is fully cooked and tender and the soup has a good flavor, stirring, skimming, and adjusting seasoning throughout cooking time.

Cream soups usually need 1 hour of simmering time to develop flavor and thicken properly. Stir frequently to prevent scorching.

Skimming the soup removes excess fat and impurities to create good flavor, color, and texture in the finished soup. Pull the pot slightly to the side of the burner; the fat and impurities collect on one side of the pot, where it is easy to skim them away.

Taste the soup often as it develops and add additional seasonings and aromatics as needed.

5. Purée the soup (if necessary) and strain it.

Use a food mill, blender, or food processor to purée vegetable cream soups. Cream soups based upon meat, fish, or poultry are not necessarily puréed. Puréed cream soups need to be strained using either a fine wire-mesh sieve or rinsed doubled cheesecloth. If using a fine mesh sieve, push the solids against the sides to extract the purée. Straining produces the velvet-smooth texture of a good cream soup by removing all fibers.

The soup should have the desired flavor and consistency at this point. Make any necessary adjustments to consistency now. The soup is ready to rapidly cool and store to finish and serve later (or to serve as a chilled soup), or it may be finished now.

ABOVE *Add simmering broth to the vegetable mixture. The broth should be very hot.*

ABOVE *Stir frequently to avoid scorching.*

ABOVE *Puréeing using a food mill.*

6. Finish and garnish the soup.

Cream soups can be finished and garnished by individual portion or by batches, according to the kitchen's needs. For a hot cream soup, return the soup to a simmer over moderate heat and add enough hot cream to enrich the soup, without overwhelming the main ingredient's flavor. Return the soup to a simmer and adjust the seasoning if necessary.

Cook the garnish fully and season it well. This must be done as a separate operation since garnish ingredients don't actually simmer in the soup as it cooks.

Add the heated and seasoned garnish, if desired, and serve at once in heated bowls or cups.

To finish a cold cream soup, add chilled cream to the soup. Adjust the seasoning if necessary (cold foods often need more seasoning than the same dish served hot), and add the chilled and seasoned garnish. Serve at once in chilled bowls or cups.

7. Evaluate the quality of the finished cream soup.

Good cream soups have a rich flavor, balancing the main flavoring ingredient(s) and supporting aromatic and finishing flavors, velvety texture, and a lightly thickened consistency, similar to heavy cream. Very thick cream soups often have a pasty feel and taste due either to too much thickener or to overcooking.

Disappointing flavor and color indicate that not enough of the main flavoring ingredient(s) was used or too much liquid was added. Too much cream can detract from the major flavor of the soup, masking the original taste.

TOP *Simmer the soup, checking for flavor, consistency, and seasoning, before adding hot cream.*

BOTTOM *Cut the garnish to a suitable size. For example, broccoli florets should be small enough to fit in the bowl of a spoon easily.*

ABOVE *Garnishes must be very hot when added to hot soup. Reheat them in a flavorful liquid to further enhance the soup's flavor.*

ABOVE *This cream soup shows the proper thickness, a velvety texture, and a perfectly smooth consistency. The garnish is bright, vibrant, and fully cooked.*

4 lb / 1.8 kg broccoli

6 fl oz / 180 mL clarified butter or vegetable oil

8 oz / 225 g chopped onions

4 oz / 115 g chopped celery

4 oz / 115 g chopped leeks

5 oz / 140 g flour

2 qt / 2 L CHICKEN STOCK (page 248), hot

1 pint / 480 mL heavy cream, hot

salt, as needed

pepper, as needed

CREAM OF BROCCOLI SOUP

1 Remove stems from broccoli; peel and cut into dice. Reserve separately. Reserve 12 oz/ 340 g of florets for garnish. Chop the remaining broccoli and reserve separately.

2 Heat the butter or oil and add the onions, celery, leeks, and broccoli stems. Sweat, stirring frequently, until the onions are tender and translucent with no color, about 6 to 8 minutes.

3 Add the flour and stir well to combine. Continue to cook, stirring frequently, until a blond roux forms, about 12 minutes.

4 Add the stock to the pot gradually, whisking or stirring to work out any lumps. Bring the soup to a full boil, then reduce the heat and simmer until the soup is smooth and thickened, about 45 to 60 minutes. Stir frequently and skim as needed.

5 Purée the soup. (Strain the soup through a sieve, if desired, for a smooth consistency.) The soup is ready to finish now, or it may be rapidly cooled and stored.

6 Return the soup to a simmer. Add the cream as necessary for correct flavor and adjust seasoning with salt and pepper. Add broccoli florets to individual portions or to larger batches.

MAKES 1 GALLON/3.75 LITERS; 20 PORTIONS (6 FLUID OUNCES/180 MILLILITERS EACH)

Cream of Asparagus (Crème Argenteuil) Replace the broccoli with an equal weight of asparagus stems. Garnish with blanched asparagus tips.

Cream of Lettuce (Crème Choisy) Replace the broccoli with an equal weight of shredded lettuce (romaine, Boston, etc.). Garnish with a chiffonade of fines herbes.

Cream of Celery (Crème Céleri) Replace the broccoli with an equal weight of celery or celeriac. Garnish with diced blanched celery.

PURÉE SOUPS

Purée soups are slightly thicker than cream soups and have a somewhat coarser texture.

Often based on dried peas, lentils, or beans or on such starchy vegetables as potatoes, carrots, and squash, purée soups are usually entirely puréed, though occasionally some of the solids are left whole for textural interest, as in Senate Bean Soup (page 339) or Caribbean-Style Purée of Black Bean (page 333). Although not necessary, finishing ingredients like milk or cream are sometimes used. Purée soups are frequently garnished with croutons or small dice of a complementary meat or vegetable.

MANY PURÉE SOUPS are based on dried beans: Great Northern, navy beans, black beans, lentils, and split peas, for example. Beans (other than lentils) may be soaked for several hours before cooking. The beans absorb some liquid, the overall cooking time is shortened, and the beans cook more evenly.

Other purée soups are made from relatively starchy vegetables such as potatoes, squash, carrots, or turnips. These have to be peeled and diced or sliced. Since they are puréed, neatness is not critical, but relative uniformity of size is necessary for the ingredients to cook evenly.

Onions, garlic, carrots, celery, mushrooms, and tomatoes are often found in purée soups. Other vegetables are suggested by specific recipes, peppers for example. Vegetables may be roasted or grilled beforehand for extra flavor. Consult specific recipes for preparation and cutting instructions.

Water, broth, or stock are the most frequently used base liquids. Check the freshness of broths or stocks that have been stored before using them in a soup.

Many purée soups call for a bit of rendered salt pork, smoked ham, bacon, or other cured pork products. In some instances, these ingredients should be blanched first to remove any excess salt: Cover them with cool water, bring the water to a simmer, and then drain and rinse. Consult specific recipes for guidance. An alternative is to use a ham-based broth.

Besides cured pork, ingredients used to season purée soups are as diverse as chiles, dried mushrooms, hot sauce, citrus zest or juice, and vinegar. Garnishes include chopped herbs, croutons, diced meats, toasted or fried tortillas, salsas, dollops of sour cream, and so forth.

Equipment requirements for purée soups are quite similar to those for cream soups. Look for pots that have heavy bottoms to help avoid scorching or the development of hot spots. If available, a heat diffuser or other similar device should be used keep the heat even. Tasting spoons and cups must be on had so that you can check the flavor of the soup throughout cooking time.

Wooden spoons, ladles and skimmers are generally required throughout the cooking process. Puréeing equipment such as a food mill (at left), blender, or food processor is necessary to finish the soup. You will also need containers for cooling or holding the soup.

FOR A PURÉE SOUP THAT HAS GOOD FLAVOR, AROMA, COLOR, AND BODY, OBSERVE THE FOLLOWING FORMULAS TO PRODUCE 1 GALLON/3.75 LITERS.	MAIN FLAVORING INGREDIENT OPTIONS INCLUDE:	THE BASE LIQUID IS:	*mirepoix*
	3 to 4 pounds/1.3 to 1.8 kilograms vegetables such as potatoes or squash	*2 ½ to 3 quarts/2.5 to 2.8 liters stock or broth*	*tomatoes*
		SEASONING AND FLAVORING OPTIONS INCLUDE:	*lemon juice or vinegar*
	1 pound/450 grams dried legumes, such as lentils	*salt and pepper*	**FINISHING AND GARNISHING OPTIONS INCLUDE:**
		1 sachet d'épices or bouquet garni	*croutons*
		smoked ham or pork	*diced meat from ham*

1. Lightly brown the aromatic vegetables.

If the recipe calls for minced salt pork or bacon, render it over low heat to release the fat. Or heat the butter or oil. Add the onions, garlic, shallots, leeks, or other aromatic vegetables. Cook over low to medium heat until a rich aroma develops or until they take on a rich golden hue, anywhere from 20 to 30 minutes.

TOP *Rendering the salt pork starts the process of building a flavor base. It also provides the fat necessary to sweat or brown the aromatic vegetables.*

BOTTOM *Stir in the aromatic vegetables in stages. The onions are added first and allowed to brown over medium heat. Cook the aromatic vegetables, stirring from time to time, to allow them to release their flavors.*

2. Add the liquid. Add the remaining ingredients at the appropriate intervals and simmer until the soup is well flavored and all ingredients are very tender.

Dry, dense, tough, fibrous, or starchy ingredients (dry beans, root vegetables, winter squash, for instance) are added at the beginning of cooking time, usually as soon as the stock or broth has returned to a simmer. Since the soup is puréed before service, it is less critical that these ingredients not overcook than in a hearty broth, where the ingredients are intended to retain their shape during cooking and service. Sachets or bouquets garni are added during the final 30 minutes of cooking time.

Many purée soups are based on legumes. These soups may call for a ham hock or similar smoked pork cut to be added to the soup as soon as the stock or broth returns to a simmer to properly flavor the broth and the main ingredients. Remove them from the soup once they have added the desired flavor. Cut the lean meat into neat dice and reserve it to add as a garnish.

Stir the soup frequently as it cooks to prevent starchy ingredients from sticking to the bottom of the pan. Add more stock or other liquid as necessary during cooking time. The starchy or dry ingredients used in many purée soups will absorb different amounts of liquid as they cook, depending upon their maturity. Skim the soup as it cooks to remove any impurities or scum, and adjust the seasoning as necessary.

ABOVE *Add simmering stock to shorten overall cooking time. Add seasonings and aromatics to the stock as it heats, or add them to the soup as it simmers. Add the sachet d'épices or bouquet garni near the end of cooking time. Other aromatics may be selected to create a specific flavor.*

ABOVE *The soup can be puréed in the pot without an initial straining. Be sure to remove and discard the sachet or bouquet first.*

3. Purée and adjust the seasoning and consistency.

Different types of puréeing equipment will produce different textures in the finished soup. Rustic or home-style purées may be relatively coarse and may even rely simply upon the starch in the main ingredient to give the soup its thickened texture. A food mill fitted with a coarse disk can also be used for a textured purée. Food processors and blenders produce very smooth soups.

At this point, the soup is ready to be finished for service or cooled and stored (see pages 64–65).

4. Evaluate the quality of the finished purée soup.

Purée soups are somewhat thicker and have a slightly coarser texture than other thick soups, but they should still be liquid enough to pour easily from a ladle into a bowl. The flavor should be well developed.

One of the major criticisms of purée soups is that they are too thick. Purée soups should pour easily from a ladle and have a consistency similar to heavy cream. A proper balance between solid ingredients and liquid results in a soup with a pleasing, robust flavor.

ABOVE *An immersion blender (sometimes called a "burr" mixer or a stick mixer) is used here to purée the soup to a very fine consistency. Other equipment choices will produce other textures in the finished soup.*

ABOVE *Once the soup has been heated for service and checked for flavor, consistency, and seasoning, it is ready to serve. Croutons and chopped herbs have been selected to garnish this purée. For a bit of extra richness, a bit of softened butter can be swirled on top of the soup just before it leaves the kitchen for the dining room.*

6 oz / 170 g small-dice bacon

8 oz / 225 g medium-dice onions

4 oz / 115 g medium-dice carrots

1 lb / 450 g lentils

1 gal / 3.75 L WHITE BEEF STOCK (page 249), VEGETABLE STOCK (page 254),
   CHICKEN STOCK (page 248), or water

salt, as needed

pepper, as needed

sachet d'épices, containing 3 parsley stems, 1 bay leaf, ½ tsp / 2 mL cracked black
   peppercorns, ½ tsp / 2 mL fresh or dried thyme

1 fl oz / 30 mL lemon juice

GARNISH

3 oz / 85 g whole butter

8 oz / 225 g croutons (see page 771), or as needed

1 oz / 30 g chopped chervil

PURÉE OF LENTILS

1 Render the bacon over low heat. Add the onions and carrots and cook until tender and
   lightly browned, about 15 minutes.

2 Add the lentils, stock, salt, and pepper. Bring to a simmer and skim.

3 Add the sachet d'épices and simmer for 30 minutes or until lentils are tender enough
   to purée easily.

4 Strain the mixture, reserving the soup broth. Remove and discard the sachet.

5 Purée the solids and add enough reserved soup broth to achieve the proper consistency. Add lemon juice to taste. The soup is ready to finish now, or it may be rapidly
   cooled and stored for later service.

6 Return the soup to a simmer. Adjust seasoning with salt and pepper. Garnish individual portions with whole butter, croutons, and chervil and serve in heated bowls or
   cups.

MAKES 1 GALLON/3.75 LITERS; 20 PORTIONS (6 FLUID OUNCES/180 MILLILITERS EACH)

BISQUES

Traditionally bisques are based on crustaceans, such as shrimp, lobster, or crayfish, and thickened with rice, rice flour, or bread.

In fact, the term bisque is derived from the use of dry bread, called *biscuit* in French, as the thickener. The crustacean shells are usually puréed along with the other ingredients. The end result is a soup with a consistency like that of a cream soup.

Contemporary bisques may be based on ingredients other than crustaceans and rely on a vegetable purée or roux as the thickener. A vegetable-based bisque is prepared in the same manner as a purée soup. If the main vegetable does not contain enough starch to act as a thickener, rice, roux, or a starchy vegetable such as potato may be used to provide additional thickness. After the vegetables are tender, the soup is puréed until smooth. Consequently the distinction between a purée and a bisque is not always clear.

CRUSTACEAN MEAT AND SHELLS are rinsed well, then coarsely chopped. Shellfish is scrubbed clean. Consult specific recipes for guidance.

Check fumets, stocks, or broths used to prepare a bisque before use if they have been stored. Bring a small amount to a boil and taste it for any sour or off odors.

Peel, trim, and chop any vegetables to be used in the bisque. Chopped onion and garlic or mirepoix is generally a part of the soup. Other ingredients frequently used to add flavor and color include tomato paste, paprika, brandy, and wine.

Thicken the soup with roux or flour, rice, or rice flour. However, added thickeners are unnecessary if using a prepared velouté. Cream is a finishing ingredient for most bisques. Diced cooked pieces of the main flavoring ingredient are traditionally used to garnish a bisque.

The equipment requirements for bisque are identical to those of cream soup (page 310) and include a heavy-gauge pot, puréeing equipment, and a strainer or cheesecloth, as well as equipment for holding, serving, or storing bisques.

FOR A SHELLFISH BISQUE THAT HAS GOOD FLAVOR, AROMA, COLOR, AND BODY, OBSERVE THE FOLLOWING FORMULAS TO PRODUCE 1 GALLON/3.75 LITERS.

MAIN FLAVORING INGREDIENT OPTIONS INCLUDE:

2 pounds/900 grams crustacean shells (shrimp, crab, lobster, or a combination)

THE BASE LIQUID OPTIONS ARE:

3 quarts/2.8 liters shellfish stock, fumet, or broth, or 3 quarts/2.8 liters shellfish velouté

THICKENING OPTIONS INCLUDE:*

prepared blond roux

flour

rice (whole grains or rice flour)

**added thickeners are unneccessary if using a prepared velouté*

SEASONING AND FLAVORING OPTIONS INCLUDE:

salt and pepper

1 sachet d'épices or bouquet garni

1 pound/450 grams mirepoix

tomato paste or purée

FINISHING AND GARNISHING OPTIONS INCLUDE:

1 pint/480 milliliters heavy cream

dice or other cuts of cooked shrimp, lobster, crab

sherry

1. Rinse the shells well and chop larger shells, such as crab or lobster. Drain and dry them well before searing.

Bisques get their color and flavor from shrimp, lobster, crab, or crayfish shells. Use one type of crustacean or a combination.

Sear the shells in the cooking fat, stirring frequently, until they turn a bright pink or red.

2. Add the aromatic vegetables and other aromatic ingredients at this point.

Add the mirepoix to the pan and cook it over medium heat for 20 to 30 minutes, or until the vegetables are tender and the onions are a light brown. Tomato paste is often added at this point and allowed to cook until it has a sweet aroma and a deep color. Spices such as paprika are added to the shells and other aromatics to cook in the fat.

3. If necessary, add the flour or roux to the shells. Add the liquid and bring the soup to a simmer.

Some bisque recipes indicate the addition of flour to prepare a roux as part of the soup-making process. If necessary, add a bit more oil or butter to the shells, then stir in the roux and cook, stirring constantly, for 4 to 5 minutes. Or, add a prepared roux to the shells and cook long enough to soften the roux.

A good-quality stock or broth is as important to the flavor of a bisque as the shells are. If available, a prepared light velouté (see page 262) made from a shellfish or fish stock thickened with a blond roux may be used. In that case, there is no need to add either flour or a prepared roux.

At this point, add wine and additional herbs or aromatics, such as a sachet d'épices or bouquet garni.

TOP *Remove shells and reserve the meat for garnish.*

BOTTOM *Cook the shells until they change color and become opaque, stirring frequently. Add onions and cook until they are light golden. Add minced garlic to the onions after they have cooked.*

ABOVE *For the best finished flavor, be sure to add seasonings at the appropriate points as you cook the bisque. Paprika has the best flavor and appearance in a dish when it is allowed to sauté briefly in a little fat.*

ABOVE *Add the flour and cook until it is thick, pasty, and tacky.*

Taste the soup and make modifications to the seasoning or consistency during cooking. Add more liquid, if necessary, to maintain a good balance between the liquid and solids as the soup cooks.

4. Simmer until the flavor is fully developed.

A bisque takes about 45 minutes to 1 hour to cook properly. At that point, all ingredients (except, obviously, the shells) should be relatively tender, so they will purée easily.

Skim the bisques throughout the cooking process.

5. Purée the soup.

Remove and discard the sachet or bouquet before puréeing the bisque. Use a blender (immersion or countertop) to purée the bisque to a fairly smooth and even consistency. Pulverizing the shells and puréeing the aromatic vegetables helps to release even more flavor into the soup. If time allows, return the puréed bisque to a simmer for several minutes and make any appropriate adjustments to the soup's seasoning or consistency before straining.

TOP *Add simmering fumet to the pot. Bringing the fumet to a simmer while preparing the aromatic flavor base makes cooking more efficient in the professional kitchen.*

BOTTOM *Use a whisk to work out any lumps that might form.*

ABOVE *Stir frequently and monitor the heat. A bisque, like any other soup with starchy ingredients, can scorch quickly if left untended for even a few minutes.*

ABOVE *Use an immersion blender to purée the soup before straining it through cheesecloth.*

6. Strain the bisque.
Use rinsed cheesecloth to strain a shellfish bisque. Cheesecloth removes all traces of the shell and gives the bisque a very fine, delicate texture. This is a two-person task. First, set a sieve or colander in a clean pot. Drape the rinsed cheesecloth in the sieve or colander and pour the bisque through it. Most of the bisque will pass through the cheesecloth. Each person holds two corners of the cheesecloth and lifts the corners up in an alternating sequence (known as the milking method). When only solids remain in the cheesecloth, each person gathers his or her corners together and twists in opposite directions to finish straining the bisque (known as the wringing method). The bisque is ready to finish now or it may be rapidly cooled and stored for later service.

7. Finish the bisque and add any garnish ingredients.
Return the bisque to medium heat and bring it to a simmer. Taste the soup and make any seasoning adjustments. Separately, bring the cream to a simmer and add it gradually to the bisque. There should be enough cream to enrich the soup and add a smooth flavor and mouthfeel, but not so much that the cream masks the main ingredient.

8. Evaluate the quality of the finished bisque.
A good bisque reflects the flavor of the main ingredient. If cream is added to round out and mellow the soup, it does not mask the main flavor. All bisques are slightly coarse or grainy, with a consistency similar to heavy cream. A crustacean bisque is pale pink or red in color, a shellfish bisque ivory, and a vegetable bisque a paler shade of the main vegetable.

ABOVE *When only the solids remain, each person gathers the ends of the cheesecloth and twists (working in opposite directions) to extract as much flavor as possible from the shells and into the soup.*

ABOVE *Reheat the soup before service, checking for flavor, consistency, and texture. Make necessary adjustments before finishing with heated cream.*

ABOVE *Serve shrimp bisque garnished with shrimp.*

2 lb / 900 g shrimp shells

6 oz / 170 g clarified butter

8 oz / 240 g minced onions

1 garlic clove, minced to a paste

1 oz / 30 g tomato paste

1 tbsp / 15 mL Hungarian paprika

2 oz / 60 mL brandy

6 oz / 180 g all-purpose flour

3 qt / 3 L SHELLFISH STOCK (page 253) or FISH STOCK (page 253), hot

1 lb 8 oz / 720 g diced cooked shrimp

26 fl oz / 780 mL heavy cream

salt, as needed

pepper, as needed

½ tsp Worcestershire sauce (optional)

½ tsp cayenne pepper or Tabasco sauce, as needed

3 oz / 90 mL dry sherry

SHRIMP BISQUE

1 Rinse the shells thoroughly and drain them.

2 Heat the butter in a soup pot over medium-high heat. Add the shells and cook, stirring occasionally, until they are bright red, about 10 to 12 minutes. Add the onions and cook over medium heat, stirring occasionally, until they are a light brown, 5 to 6 minutes. Add the garlic and continue to cook until the aroma is apparent, about 1 minute.

3 Add the tomato paste and paprika and cook over medium heat, stirring occasionally, for 3 to 4 minutes. Add the brandy and stir well to deglaze the pan. Continue to cook until the brandy is almost completely cooked away.

4 Add the flour to make a roux and continue to cook over medium heat, stirring frequently, for 6 to 8 minutes.

5 Gradually add the stock, whisking constantly to work out any lumps. Bring to a boil, then reduce the heat to establish an even, gentle simmer. Simmer for 45 minutes, skimming the surface occasionally.

6 Purée the solids until smooth. Strain the puréed soup through a fine wire-mesh sieve or rinsed cheesecloth. The soup is ready to finish for service, or it may be rapidly cooled and stored.

7 To finish the soup for service, return the desired number of portions to a simmer and add diced shrimp and cream. Simmer until the shrimp is cooked through, 3 to 4 minutes. Taste the soup and adjust seasoning with salt, pepper, Worcestershire sauce, and cayenne or Tabasco sauce. Finish with the sherry and serve in heated bowls.

MAKES 1 GALLON/3.75 LITERS; 20 PORTIONS (6 OUNCES/180 MILLILITERS)

GENERAL GUIDELINES FOR SOUP

TOP *Cook soup at a gentle simmer, just long enough to develop good flavor and body. Taste soup frequently and skim as necessary.*

MIDDLE *Adjust soup seasonings throughout cooking time, adding a little at a time and carefully checking the flavor after each addition as well as just prior to service, when the soup is at the correct temperature.*

BOTTOM *Soup seasonings can range from fresh minced herbs to hot sauce.*

COOKING

Add vegetables at staggered intervals, according to cooking times. Stir the soup from time to time throughout the cooking process, to prevent starchy ingredients from sticking to the bottom of the pot and for the best flavor, texture, and appearance. When the flavor is fully developed and all of the ingredients are tender, the soup may be finished or garnished and served right away, or it may be cooled and stored (see pages 64–65). Although some soups develop a more rounded, mellow flavor if served the day after they are prepared, no soup benefits from hours on the stove. Not only will the flavor become dull and flat, but the nutritive value will be greatly decreased.

ADJUSTING CONSISTENCY

Thick soups, especially those made with starchy vegetables or dried beans, may continue to thicken during cooking, storage, and reheating or holding. As a rule, creams and bisques are about as thick as cold heavy cream and liquid enough to pour from a ladle into a bowl. Purées are somewhat thicker.

For a soup that is too thin, a small amount of starch slurry may be added. Have the soup at a simmer or slow boil when the slurry is added, then stir constantly and continue to simmer for 2 or 3 minutes.

ADJUSTING FLAVOR AND SEASONING

Season soup throughout the cooking process. Meat or poultry glaze may be added to bolster a weak broth or consommé, but this will affect the clarity. Chopped fresh herbs, a few drops of lemon juice, Tabasco sauce, Worcestershire sauce, or grated citrus zest may be added to brighten a soup's flavor.

DEGREASING

Some soups, especially broth-based ones, may be prepared in advance, then cooled and refrigerated. It is then easy to remove the fat, which congeals on the surface, before reheating the soup. If the soup is to be served just after it is prepared, skim as much fat as possible from the surface. Clear soups may be blotted with strips of paper towel or unwaxed brown butcher paper to remove any traces of fat before serving. Float the strips on the surface, then carefully lift them off. Consommés should be completely fat-free, but broths and clear vegetable soups characteristically have some droplets of fat on the surface.

FINISHING

Some soups may be prepared to a specific point and then cooled and stored (see pages 64–65). Garnish clear soups just before service to prevent them from becoming cloudy and to keep the garnish fresh. Some garnishes are added, portion by portion, to heated cups or bowls just prior to service. In other cases, such as for buffet service, the garnish may be added to the entire quantity of soup.

Finish cream and liaison soups just prior to service. Do this for two reasons: The soup will have a fresher flavor, and its shelf life will be greater. Bring cream to a boil before adding it to soup to check freshness and to prevent it from lowering the soup's temperature. Temper a liaison to prevent curdling (see pages 64–65).

Make final seasoning adjustments after the soup is finished. Always check the seasoning immediately before service.

REHEATING

If a soup has been prepared in advance, reheat only the amount needed for a particular service period. Maintaining food at high temperatures for extended periods often has undesirable effects on flavor. One good way to maintain optimum quality and minimize waste is to reheat individual portions to order. Sometimes, however, this approach is not practical. Learn the best way to make use of the equipment available for service to determine how to get foods to service temperature. Getting foods through the danger zone quickly (see pages 64–65) is important.

Bring clear soup just up to a boil. Check seasoning and consistency and add the appropriate garnishes before serving.

Reheat thick soups gently. Pour a thin layer of water or stock into a preheated heavy-gauge pot before adding the soup. Reheat the soup over low heat at first, stirring frequently until it softens slightly. The heat can then be increased slightly and the soup brought to a simmer. If a soup has already been finished with cream, or with sour cream or a liaison in particular, do not let it come all the way up to a boil, or it may curdle. A temperature of 180°F/82°C is adequate for both quality and food safety concerns. Check seasoning and consistency and add any garnishes just before serving.

In order to reheat individual portions of soup in the microwave oven, pour the soup into a microwave-safe bowl and cover with plastic wrap. Heat it for about one minute at high power, then stir to distribute the heat evenly. Return the soup to the microwave and heat until the soup is very hot.

Check the temperature regularly of soups held in a steam table. If they consistently fall short of a desirable temperature (at least 165°F/73°C for most soups and sauces), then adjust the thermostat on the steam table, have it repaired, or learn to compensate by quickly bringing individual servings to the correct temperature over direct heat or in a microwave.

Broth garnished with julienne of the right length for the spoon.

GARNISHING

Garnishes may provide contrasts of flavor and texture or they may introduce a complementary flavor. They may also provide additional or contrasting color. In all cases, they should be thoughtfully selected, well prepared, and well seasoned.

Shape large garnishes, such as dumplings, wontons, or quenelles, to a size that does not allow them to overwhelm the soup cup or plate selected for service. It is equally important that they not be too difficult for the guest to eat. They should be soft enough to cut through with the edge of a soup spoon.

Since service temperature is extremely important for all soups, remember to bring the garnish to service temperature before adding it to the soup. There are several ways to do this:

- Heat the garnish in a steamer or in a small quantity of broth or consommé and hold in a steam table.

- Cut delicate items into shapes that will allow the heat of the soup to warm them thoroughly. (If they are small and relatively thin, they will not cause the soup's temperature to drop too severely.)

- Keep large items like dumplings, wontons, or quenelles warm and lightly moistened in a steam table or on the shelf over the range.

SERVING

Hot soups should be served very hot. The thinner the soup, the more important this is. Since consommés and broths lose their heat rapidly, they should be nearly at a boil before they are ladled into heated cups. The more surface area exposed to the air, the quicker the soup will cool. This is one reason that consommés and other broth-style soups are traditionally served in cups rather than in the flatter, wider soup plates or bowls often used for cream soups and purées. Serving thin soups in cups also makes it easier for servers to transport the soup without spilling. Cold soups should be thoroughly chilled and served in chilled cups, bowls, or glasses.

Try to plate all soups, but especially consommé, only when the server is in the kitchen, ready to pick up the order. That way, soups will not lose heat as they sit on the line waiting for the server. Use soup cup covers, if available.

Take the time to explain to anyone involved in serving soups the importance of keeping hot soups very hot and taking them quickly from the kitchen to the guest. Show all servers or line cooks the way that a soup should look when it is served to the guest with garnishes and additional elements, such as grated cheese or fine oils, to pass or serve at tableside.

Add garnishes as close to service as possible. If garnishes are prepared in advance, they should be cooled and stored separately, then reheated at service time.

RECIPES

CHICKEN CONSOMMÉ ROYALE

makes 1 gallon/3.75 liters; 20 portions

CLARIFICATION

8 oz/225 g small-dice or minced onions

4 oz/115 g small-dice or minced carrots

4 oz/115 g small-dice or minced celery

3 lb/1.3 kg lean ground chicken

10 egg whites, beaten to a froth

12 oz/340 g chopped tomatoes

5 qt/4.75 mL CHICKEN STOCK (page 248)

salt, as needed

sachet d'épices, containing 3 parsley stems, ½ tsp/2 mL thyme leaves, ½ tsp/2 mL cracked black peppercorns, and 1 bay leaf

2 oignons brûlés (optional)

ROYALE CUSTARD (recipe follows)

1 Blend the ingredients for the clarification and add the stock. Stir to combine thoroughly.

2 Bring the mixture to a slow simmer, stirring frequently, until the raft forms. Add some of the salt. Add the sachet and oignons brûlés (if using). Stop stirring when the raft begins to form (120°F/50°C). Simmer slowly for 1 to 1½ hours, or until the desired flavor and clarity are achieved. Baste the raft occasionally. Adjust the seasoning as needed.

3 Strain the consommé through a paper filter or rinsed doubled cheesecloth. The consommé is ready to finish now, or it may be properly cooled and stored for later service. Degrease hot consommé by skimming or degrease cold consommé by lifting the hardened fat from the surface.

4 To finish the consommé for service, return it to a simmer, place a portion of royale in a heated consommé cup, and ladle the hot consommé over the royale. Serve at once.

ROYALE CUSTARD

makes 10 garnish portions

12 fl oz/360 mL heavy cream or milk

3 eggs

salt, as needed

ground white pepper, as needed

1 Whisk together the heavy cream or milk and eggs to make a custard. Season to taste with salt and pepper. Pour the custard into a liberally greased 9-inch/225-mm baking pan.

2 Set the pan in a hot-water bath and bake it in a 350°F/175°C oven until a knife blade inserted in the custard's center comes out clean, about 40 to 45 minutes. Cut the custard into the desired shapes to use as a garnish.

CHICKEN NOODLE SOUP

makes 1 gallon/3.75 liters; 20 portions (6 fluid ounces/180 milliliters each)

1 stewing hen, quartered

sachet d'épices, containing 2 to 3 parsley stems, ½ tsp/2 mL fresh or dried thyme, ½ tsp/2 mL cracked black peppercorns, 1 bay leaf, and 1 garlic clove

5 qt/4.75 L CHICKEN STOCK (page 248)

salt, as needed

pepper, as needed

MIREPOIX

6 oz/170 g medium-dice onions

3 oz/85 g medium-dice carrots

3 oz/85 g medium-dice celery

GARNISH

5 oz/140 g diced chicken meat

8 oz/225 g cooked corn kernels (optional)

4 oz/115 g cooked diced celery

2 oz/60 g chopped parsley

10 oz/285 g cooked egg noodles

1 Combine the hen, sachet, stock, salt, and pepper. Simmer for 1½ hours, skimming as necessary.

2 Add the mirepoix and simmer for 1½ hours more.

3 Remove the hen and let stand until cool enough to handle. Remove and dice the meat and set aside.

4 Strain the broth. The broth is ready to be finished now, or it may be rapidly cooled and stored for later service.

5 Return the broth to a simmer. Adjust seasoning with salt and pepper. Add the garnish to individual portions or to batches of the appropriate size for service.

PURÉE OF SPLIT PEA

makes 20 portions

2 oz/60 g minced bacon

2 fl oz/60 mL vegetable oil

12 oz/340 g chopped onions

4 oz/115 g chopped celery

1 tsp/5 mL chopped garlic

1 gal/3.75 L CHICKEN STOCK (page 248)

1 lb/450 g large dice potatoes

1½ lb/680 kg green split peas

2 smoked ham hocks

2 bay leaves

salt, as needed

pepper, as needed

8 oz/225 g croutons (see page 771)

1 Cook the bacon in the oil until the bacon has rendered. Add the onions and celery and sauté until the onions become transparent, about 10 to 12 minutes. Add the garlic and sauté until an aroma develops, about 1 minute; do not brown.

2 Add the stock, potatoes, split peas, ham hocks, and bay leaves and bring to a simmer. Allow the soup to simmer for 1½ hours or until the peas are very tender. Remove the ham hocks and reserve. Dice lean meat for garnish if desired.

3 Purée the soup through a food mill or sieve and/or with a blender or processor until smooth. The soup is ready to finish for service now, or it may be properly cooled and stored for later service.

4 To finish the soup, return it to a simmer over medium heat. Add the reserved diced ham if desired. Adjust consistency with additional stock if necessary. Adjust the seasoning with salt and pepper to taste and garnish with the croutons.

NOTES

To make a smoked pork stock for this soup, combine the stock with the ham hocks and a sachet made from peppercorns and bay leaves. Simmer while preparing the rest of the soup's mise en place, or for about 1½ hours. Strain, reserving the ham hocks separately.

For a heartier version, purée half of the soup and return the purée with the meat in step 4.

A blond roux may be incorporated into the stock in step 4. This will give the soup greater stability if it must be held on a steam table.

Yellow Split Pea Soup Replace the green split peas with yellow split peas.

CREAM OF TOMATO SOUP

makes 1 gallon/3.75 liters; 20 portions (6 fluid ounces/180 milliliters each)

2 oz/60 g small-dice bacon (optional)

3 fl oz/90 mL butter or oil

8 oz/225 g small-dice carrots

4 oz/115 g small-dice celery

4 oz/115 g small-dice onions

2 garlic cloves, minced

4 oz/115 g flour

2 qt/2 L CHICKEN STOCK (page 248)

2 lb/900 g chopped fresh or canned tomatoes

24 fl oz/720 mL tomato purée

salt, as needed

ground white pepper, as needed

4 parsley stems

2 bay leaves

2 cloves

1 pint/480 mL heavy cream, hot

GARNISH

8 oz/225 g croutons (see page 771)

1 Render the bacon and/or add some oil or butter to heat. Add the carrots, celery, onions, and garlic and sweat until vegetables are tender, about 8 to 10 minutes. Add oil or butter if needed, to prepare the roux, then add the flour and blend well. Cook out to make a blond roux, about 12 minutes.

2 Add the stock and blend well. Add the chopped tomatoes, tomato purée, salt, and pepper and simmer about 30 minutes.

3 Add the parsley, bay leaves, and cloves and simmer for 30 minutes. Strain this soup base well. The base may be finished now or it may be rapidly cooled and stored for later service.

4 Return the soup base to a simmer. Add the cream as necessary for correct flavor and adjust seasoning with salt and pepper. Garnish individual portions with croutons.

Cream of Tomato with Rice Add 1 lb/450 g of cooked long-grain white rice to the tomato soup immediately prior to serving, or garnish individual portions of soup with 3 tablespoons/45 mL of cooked rice each.

CHEDDAR CHEESE SOUP

makes 1 gallon/3.75 liters; 20 portions (6 fluid ounces/180 milliliters each)

WHITE MIREPOIX

6 oz/170 g medium-dice onions

3 oz/85 g medium-dice mushrooms

3 oz/85 g medium-dice celery

1 oz/30 g minced garlic

4 fl oz/120 mL clarified butter

4 oz/115 g flour

3 qt/3 L CHICKEN STOCK (page 248) or VEGETABLE STOCK (page 254), or as needed

8 fl oz/240 mL dry white wine or lager beer

2 lb/900 g grated Cheddar cheese

½ oz/15 g dry mustard

1 pint/480 mL heavy cream, hot

Tabasco sauce

Worcestershire sauce

salt, as needed

ground white pepper, as needed

GARNISH

4 oz/115 g green pepper julienne (peeled and cooked)

4 oz/115 g red pepper julienne (peeled and cooked)

1 Sweat the mirepoix and garlic in the butter until limp.

2 Add the flour to make a blond roux and cook out for 12 minutes.

3 Add the stock gradually, whisking constantly to work out any lumps. Simmer for 45 minutes, or until the soup has a good flavor and a velvety texture. Strain through a fine mesh sieve or doubled cheesecloth. The soup is ready to finish now, or it may be rapidly cooled and stored for later service.

4 Return the soup to a simmer. Set aside 1 ounce of the wine (or lager) to dilute the mustard. Add the remaining wine and the cheese and continue to heat the soup gently until the cheese melts. Do not boil.

5 Blend the dry mustard and reserved wine or lager. Add the mustard mixture and the cream to the soup and bring the soup back to a simmer. Adjust the consistency with stock, if necessary. Season Tabasco and Worcestershire sauces, salt, and pepper to taste.

6 Add the peppers to the soup or use them to garnish individual portions.

CHILLED FRESH SPRING PEA PURÉE WITH MINT

makes 1 gallon/3.75 liters; 20 portions (6 fluid ounces/180 milliliters each)

8 oz/225 g minced leeks

8 oz/225 g minced onions

2 tbsp vegetable oil

14 oz/400 g shredded green leaf lettuce

2 lb 12 oz/1.25 kg fresh peas

5 pints/2.4 L VEGETABLE BROTH (page 254)

sachet d'épices, containing 6 chervil stems, 6 parsley stems, and 6 white peppercorns

salt, as needed

ground white pepper, as needed

10 to 12 fl oz/300 to 360 mL light cream or half-and-half

GARNISH

2 tbsp mint and/or chervil chiffonade

1 Sweat the leeks and onions in oil until tender and translucent.

2 Add the lettuce and peas, cover, and smother briefly.

3 Add the broth, sachet, salt, and pepper and bring to a boil. Simmer until all the ingredients are tender. Skim and stir the soup periodically.

4 Remove and discard the sachet. Purée the soup until smooth. Refrigerate. The soup is ready to finish now, or it may be rapidly stored for later service.

5 Add cream to the cold soup. Adjust seasoning with salt and pepper. Add the garnish to individual portions or to batches of the appropriate size.

CARIBBEAN-STYLE PURÉE OF BLACK BEAN

makes 1 gallon/3.75 liters; 20 portions (6 fluid ounces/180 milliliters each)

3 lb/1.35 kg dried black beans (4 lb 4 oz/1.9 kg cooked beans)

4 oz/115 g bacon fat

1 lb 8 oz/340 g medium-dice Spanish onions

1 gal/3.75L CHICKEN STOCK (page 248)

2 smoked ham hocks

sachet d'épices, containing 3 parsley stems, 1 bay leaf, $1/2$ tsp/2 mL cracked black peppercorns, and $1/2$ tsp/2 mL fresh or dried thyme

salt, as needed

6 fl oz/180 mL dry sherry wine

$1/2$ tsp ground allspice (optional)

pepper, as needed

GARNISH

8 fl oz/240 mL sour cream

12 oz/340 g tomato concassé

5 oz /140 g minced green onions

1 Soak the beans overnight in enough cold water to cover. Drain and rinse.

2 Heat the bacon fat, add the onions, and sweat until translucent.

3 Add the beans, stock, ham hocks, sachet d'épices, and salt. Simmer until the beans are tender. Remove and discard the sachet.

4 Remove the ham hocks. Dice the meat to add as a garnish, if desired.

5 Remove half of the beans and purée until smooth. Return the purée to the soup. The soup is ready to finish now, or it may be rapidly cooled and stored for later service.

6 Return the soup to a simmer. Add the sherry, allspice, if using, and diced ham, if desired. Adjust the seasoning with salt and pepper. Garnish individual portions with sour cream, tomato concassé, and green onions.

NOTES

Smoked pork broth may be used in place of ham hocks.

For a meatless version, replace the chicken stock with vegetable stock and omit the ham hocks. Replace the bacon fat with vegetable oil.

Other seasonings to consider for this soup include garlic, cilantro, chipotle peppers, and lemon or lime juice in place of the sherry.

Other possible garnishes for this soup include chopped cilantro, diced jícama, minced onions, chopped hard-cooked eggs, grated Monterey Jack cheese, and/or toasted tortilla strips.

VICHYSSOISE

makes 1 gallon/3.75 liters; 20 portions (6 fluid ounces/180 milliliters each)

20 oz/570 g finely chopped leeks

6 oz/170 g minced onions

$1^1/2$ fl oz/45 mL vegetable oil

2 lb 8 oz/1.15 kg diced peeled potatoes

5 pints/2.4 L CHICKEN STOCK (page 248)

sachet d'épices, containing 1 clove, 4 parsley stems, $1/2$ tsp/2 mL cracked black peppercorns, and 1 bay leaf

salt, as needed

ground white pepper, as needed

24 fl oz/720 mL half-and-half

2 oz/60 g snipped chives

1 Sweat the leeks and onions in the oil until tender and translucent.

2 Add the potatoes, stock, sachet, salt, and pepper. Bring to a full boil, then simmer until the potatoes start to fall apart, about 25 to 30 minutes. Remove and discard the sachet.

3 Purée the soup. Cool rapidly and refrigerate. The soup is ready to finish now, or it may be stored for later service.

4 Add the half-and-half to the soup, fold in the chives, and season with salt and pepper.

Corn Chowder

Seafood Gumbo

Gazpacho

POTAGE GARBURE

Larousse Gastronomique defines *garbure* as a broth of the Béarnais district, with the name being derived from *garbe* (meaning a "sheaf" or "bunch" in that dialect), referring to the vegetables used to prepare the broth.

makes 1 gallon/3.75 liters; 20 portions

4 oz/115 g ground salt pork

2 oz/60 g olive oil

8 oz/225 g thinly sliced carrots

8 oz/225 g thinly sliced onions

12 oz/240 g thinly sliced leeks

3 qt/2.8 L CHICKEN STOCK (page 248)

12 oz/240 g thinly sliced potatoes

12 oz/240 g thinly sliced green cabbage

12 oz/240 g chopped tomato (flesh only)

salt, as needed

pepper, as needed

croutons (see page 771)

1 Heat the salt pork and olive oil in a soup pot over moderate heat until the fat renders from the salt pork.

2 Add the onions, carrots, and leeks and stir until the vegetables are coated with fat. Cover the pan and smother over low heat until the vegetables are tender and translucent, about 10 to 12 minutes, stirring from time to time.

3 Add the stock, potatoes, cabbage, and tomato and simmer over low to medium heat until the potatoes are just starting to fall apart, about 20 to 25 minutes. Skim the surface of the soup as needed during cooking time. Taste the soup periodically to monitor cooking time and adjust seasoning as the soup simmers.

4 Purée the soup to a coarse texture. The soup is ready to finish now, or it may be properly cooled and stored at this point.

5 To finish the soup for service, return the soup to a boil. (Hold the soup at 180°F/82°C for service.) Taste the soup and adjust as necessary with salt and pepper. Serve each portion garnished with a crouton.

PAN-SMOKED TOMATO BISQUE

makes 2 quarts/2 liters; 10 portions (6 fluid ounces/180 milliliters each)

5 oz/140 g peeled, seeded, and quartered tomatoes

2 oz/60 g diced onions

2 oz/60 g diced celery

2 oz/60 g diced leeks

1 oz/30 g diced parsnips

24 fl oz/720 mL VEGETABLE STOCK (page 254)

1 lb 12 oz/800 g canned plum tomatoes with juice

8 fl oz/240 mL tomato purée

1 oz/30 g sun-dried tomatoes

2 tbsp chopped thyme

4 oz/115 g cooked white rice

salt, as needed

pepper, as needed

2 fl oz/60 mL balsamic vinegar

GARNISH

5 fl oz/150 mL AÏOLI (page 784)

10 slices French bread, toasted

⅓ oz/45 g TAPENADE (page 824)

1 Place the quartered tomatoes on a rack in a roasting pan containing a thin layer of hardwood chips. Cover with a tight-fitting lid or aluminum foil and place over direct heat. Smoke for 6 to 8 minutes. Remove the tomatoes and cut into small dice; reserve.

2 Sweat the onions, celery, leeks, and parsnips in a small amount of stock until tender. Stir in the remaining stock, tomatoes with juice, tomato purée, sun-dried tomatoes, and thyme. Simmer for 30 minutes.

3 Add the rice and simmer for 15 minutes. Purée until smooth. The soup is ready to finish now, or it may be rapidly cooled and stored for later service.

4 Return the soup to a simmer. Adjust seasoning with salt and pepper. Garnish individual portions with smoked tomato concassé and aïoli. Accompany each portion with a slice of French bread spread thinly with tapenade.

PUMPKIN BISQUE

makes 1 gallon/3.75 liters; 20 portions (6 fluid ounces/180 milliliters each)

6 oz/170 g medium-dice onions

5 oz/140 g medium-dice celery

3 oz/85 g medium-dice leeks

1 tbsp/15 mL chopped garlic

1 oz/30 g unsalted butter

5 oz/140 g pumpkin flesh

1 gal/3.75 L CHICKEN STOCK (page 248)

salt, as needed

2 fl oz/60 mL white wine

1 tsp/5 mL grated ginger

1 tsp/5 mL ground nutmeg (optional)

GARNISH

pumpernickel croutons (see page 771)

1 Sauté the onions, celery, leeks, and garlic in butter.

2 Add the pumpkin, stock, and salt and simmer until all the vegetables are tender, about 35 to 40 minutes.

3 Bring the wine to a simmer. Add the ginger, remove from the heat, and steep until cooled to room temperature. Strain.

4 Purée the solids with enough liquid to achieve the desired consistency. The soup is ready to finish now or it may be rapidly cooled and stored for later service.

5 Return the soup to a simmer. Add the wine to the soup and season with nutmeg and salt. Garnish individual portions with croutons.

GAZPACHO

makes 1 gallon/3.75 liters; 20 portions (6 fluid ounces/180 milliliters each)

1³/₄ oz/50 g minced jalapeños

1 lb 12 oz/800 g tomato concassé

10 oz/285 g small-diced green peppers

5 oz/140 g diced green onions

10 oz/285 g peeled, seeded, and diced cucumbers

10 oz/285 g small-dice celery

³/₄ oz/20 g chopped basil

2 tsp/10 mL chopped tarragon leaves

2 qt/2 L CHICKEN STOCK (page 248)

2 fl oz/60 mL olive oil

3 fl oz/90 mL balsamic vinegar

4 tsp/20 mL Worcestershire sauce

salt, as needed

ground white pepper, as needed

Tabasco sauce, as needed

GARNISH

8 oz/225 g croutons (see page 771), or as needed

1 Combine all ingredients except the croutons and refrigerate until well chilled. Purée the soup to a coarse, but even, texture.

2 Garnish individual portions with croutons.

NOTES

Other vegetables and herbs that might be included are red peppers, Italian peppers, mild green chiles, jícama, parsley, and cilantro.

Gazpacho is a seasonal soup that should be prepared only when tomatoes are at the height of their season. To strengthen the tomato flavor, if necessary, add tomato or other vegetable juices.

Use a vegetable broth to make a vegetarian version of this soup.

Gazpacho has a short refrigerator shelf life. The tomatoes will sour quickly. It is best when prepared on a daily basis.

see photograph on page 335

SEAFOOD GUMBO

GUMBO IS A TERM DERIVED FROM THE AFRICAN WORD FOR OKRA. GUMBOS ARE GENERALLY THICKENED WITH ONE OR A COMBINATION OF THE FOLLOWING: ROUX, FILE POWDER, OR OKRA.

makes 1 gallon/3.75 liters; 20 portions (6 fluid ounces/180 milliliters each)

2 lb/900 g shrimp (31/35 count)
10 crabs, cut in half

MIREPOIX

12 oz/340 g medium-dice onions
6 oz/170 g medium-dice carrots
6 oz/170 g medium-dice celery

4 oz/115 g butter
1 gal/3.75 L FISH STOCK (page 253)
1/2 oz/15 g seafood seasoning
salt, as needed
cayenne pepper, as needed
6 slices bacon, chopped
4 oz/115 g fine-dice onions
2 oz/60 g fine-dice celery
2 oz/60 g fine-dice green peppers
2 tbsp/30 mL minced garlic
2 tsp/10 mL dried thyme
2 tsp/10 mL dried basil
2 tsp/10 mL oregano
2 tsp/10 mL marjoram
1 bay leaf
8 oz/225 g brown roux (see pages 238–239)
8 oz/225 g tomato concassé
1 lb/450 g okra, sliced 1/2 inch/15 mm thick
2 tbsp vegetable oil, or as needed
8 oz/225 g cooked long-grain rice
Worcestershire sauce, as needed
Tabasco sauce, as needed

1 Peel, devein, and dice the shrimp. Reserve the shells and meat separately.

2 Sauté the shrimp shells, crab, and mirepoix in the butter until the shells turn bright red.

3 Add the stock, seafood seasoning, and salt and pepper to taste. Simmer for 45 minutes, until the broth is flavorful. Strain and reserve the broth.

4 Pick the crab meat from the shells and reserve.

5 Render the bacon until limp but not browned. Add the onions, celery, green peppers, garlic, and dried herbs. Sauté until the onions are lightly browned.

6 Add the broth and bring to a simmer. Thicken the soup with the roux, then add the tomato concassé.

7 Sauté the okra in the oil until softened and add to the soup. Simmer the soup until the okra is tender, about 12 to 15 minutes. Add the rice.

8 Sauté the diced shrimp and add to the soup. Adjust the seasoning with the Worcestershire, Tabasco, salt, and pepper.

NOTES

Instead of preparing a separate broth, use a previously prepared shellfish broth. Reserve the shells from this recipe for use in other broths, soups, or fumets.

Instead of adding the rice directly to the soup, it can be added to individual portions. Use about 2 tablespoons cooked rice per portion.

see photograph on page 335

SENATE BEAN SOUP

makes 1 gallon/3.75 liters

1½ lb/680 g dried navy beans

1 gallon/3.75 L CHICKEN STOCK (page 248)

2 smoked ham hocks

2 fl oz/60 ml vegetable oil

6 oz/170 g small-dice onions

6 oz/170 g small-dice carrots

6 oz/170 g small-dice celery

1 oz/30 g minced garlic

1 oignon piqué (optional)

sachet d'épices, containing 3 chopped parsley stems, 1 bay leaf,
   ½ tsp/3 mL cracked black peppercorns, ½ tsp/3mL fresh or dried
   thyme, and 1 garlic clove

1 lb/450 g large-dice chef's potatoes

1 tsp/5 mL Tabasco sauce (optional)

1 tbsp/15 mL salt

1 tsp/5 mL ground white pepper

GARNISH

1½ cups/360 mL croutons (see page 771)

1 Soak the beans overnight in enough cold water to cover.

2 Drain and rinse the beans.

3 Combine the beans, stock, and ham hocks. Simmer, skimming and stirring from time to time, for 2 hours. Strain the broth. Remove the ham hocks, dice the meat, and reserve.

4 Heat the oil. Add the onions, carrots, and celery and sweat until the onions are translucent, 4 to 5 minutes. Add the garlic and sauté it until an aroma is apparent. Add the beans, broth, oignon piqué, sachet, and potatoes and simmer until the beans and potatoes are tender, about 1 to 1½ hours. Remove and discard the oignon piqué and sachet.

5 Purée half of the soup. Recombine the purée and reserved ham with the remaining soup. Adjust the consistency with additional broth if necessary. Return the soup to a simmer and adjust the seasoning with Tabasco, salt, and pepper to taste. Garnish individual portions at service time with croutons.

NOTES

The soup can also be prepared as follows: Soak, drain, and rinse the beans. Simmer the beans with the stock and ham hocks, skimming and stirring from time to time, for 1 hour. Add the potatoes, oignon piqué, and sachet and continue to simmer until the beans are very tender, about 45 minutes to 1 hour. Remove and discard the oignon piqué and sachet. Remove the ham hocks, dice the meat, and reserve.

Purée half of the soup and recombine. Sweat the vegetables in bacon fat, lard, or oil. Add them and the diced ham to the soup at service time.

MINESTRONE

makes 1 gallon/3.75 liters; 20 portions (6 fluid ounces/180 milliliters each)

2 oz/60 g salt pork

2 fl oz/60 mL olive oil

1 lb/450 g paysanne-cut onions

8 oz/225 g paysanne-cut celery

8 oz/225 g paysanne-cut carrots

8 oz/225 g paysanne-cut green peppers

8 oz/225 g paysanne-cut green cabbage

½ oz/15 g minced garlic

1 lb/450 g tomato concassé

1 lb/450 g CHICKEN STOCK (page 248)

salt, as needed

pepper, as needed

4 oz/115 g cooked chickpeas

6 oz/170 g cooked black-eyed peas

6 oz/170 g cooked ditalini

GARNISH

5 oz/140 g grated Parmesan

1 Render the salt pork in the oil. Do not brown.

2 Add the onions, celery, carrots, peppers, cabbage, and garlic and sweat until the onions are translucent.

3 Add the tomato concassé, stock, and salt and pepper to taste. Simmer until the vegetables are tender, about 25 to 30 minutes. Do not overcook.

4 Add the chickpeas, black-eyed peas, and ditalini. Simmer the soup until all the ingredients are tender, 10 to 12 minutes more. The soup is ready to finish now, or it may be rapidly cooled and stored for later service.

5 Return the soup to a simmer. Adjust seasoning with salt and pepper.

6 Garnish individual portions with the Parmesan.

MANHATTAN–STYLE CLAM CHOWDER

makes 1 gallon/3.75 liters; 20 portions

30 chowder clams, washed

1 pint/1.5 L water

24 fl oz/720 mL clam juice

3 oz/85 g salt pork, minced to a paste

1 fl oz/30 mL vegetable oil

8 oz/225 g medium-dice onions

8 oz/225 g medium-dice celery

4 oz/115 g medium-dice carrots

4 oz/115 g medium-dice leeks

4 oz/115 g medium-dice green peppers

1 tsp/5 mL minced garlic

1 lb/450 g tomato concassé

1 bay leaf

1 thyme sprig

1 oregano sprig

12 oz/340 g medium-dice potatoes

salt, as needed

ground white pepper, or as needed

1 tsp Tabasco sauce, as needed

1/2 tsp Worcestershire sauce, or as needed

1/2 tsp Old Bay Seasoning, or as needed

1 Steam the clams in the water and clam juice in a covered pot until they open.

2 Strain the clam broth through a filter or cheesecloth and reserve. Pick the clams and chop and reserve the meat.

3 Render the salt pork in the oil. Add the onions, celery, carrots, leeks, and green peppers and sweat until soft.

4 Add the garlic and sauté until an aroma is apparent.

5 Add the reserved clam broth, tomato concassé, bay leaf, thyme, and oregano. Simmer for 30 minutes.

6 Add the potatoes and simmer until tender, about 20 minutes. Remove and discard the herbs. The soup is ready to finish now, or it may be rapidly cooled and stored for later service.

7 Degrease the soup by skimming hot soup or by lifting the hardened fat from cold soup.

8 Return the soup to a simmer. Add the clams and adjust seasoning with salt, pepper, Tabasco, Worcestershire, and Old Bay.

NOTE

Clams must be alive at the time they are to be cooked. For more information on selecting clams, see page 141.

NEW ENGLAND–STYLE CLAM CHOWDER

makes 1 gallon/3.75 liters; 20 portions (6 fluid ounces/180 milliliters each)

30 chowder clams

2 qt/2 L FISH STOCK (page 253) or water, as needed

4 oz/115 g salt pork, minced to a paste

4 oz/115 g minced onions

4 oz/115 g fine-dice celery

3 1/2 oz/100 g flour

12 oz/340 g small-dice potatoes

1 qt/1 L heavy cream, scalded

salt, as needed

ground white pepper, as needed

1/2 tsp Tabasco sauce, or as needed

1/2 tsp Worcestershire sauce, or as needed

1 Steam the clams in the stock or water in a covered pot until they open.

2 Strain the broth through a filter or cheesecloth and reserve. Pick the clams and chop and reserve the meat.

3 Render the salt pork. Add the onions and celery and sweat until they are translucent, about 6 to 7 minutes.

4 Add the flour and cook 5 to 6 minutes to make a blond roux.

5 Combine the reserved clam broth and enough additional stock to make 2 qt/2 L. Gradually add to the roux and incorporate completely, working out any lumps. Simmer for 30 minutes, skimming the surface as necessary.

6 Add the potatoes and simmer until tender. The soup is ready to finish now, or it may be rapidly cooled and stored for later service.

7 Return the soup to a simmer. Add the reserved clams and cream. Adjust the seasoning with salt, pepper, Tabasco, and Worcestershire.

CORN CHOWDER

makes 1 gallon/3.75 liters; 20 portions (6 fluid ounces/180 milliliters each)

4 oz/115 g ground salt pork

6 oz/170 g small-dice onions

6 oz/170 g small-dice celery

4 oz/115 g small-dice green peppers

4 oz/115 g small-dice red peppers

4 oz/115 g flour

2 qt/2 L CHICKEN STOCK (page 248)

salt, as needed

ground white pepper, as needed

2 lb/900 g corn kernels

2 lb/900 g small-dice potatoes

1 bay leaf

1 pint/480 mL heavy cream

1 pint/480 mL milk

Tabasco sauce, as needed

Worcestershire sauce, as needed

1 Render the salt pork. Add the onions, celery, and peppers and sweat until the onions are tender and translucent, about 6 to 7 minutes.

2 Add the flour and cook 5 to 6 minutes to make a blond roux.

3 Gradually add the stock, whisking to work out any lumps. Add the salt and pepper. Simmer for 30 to 40 minutes.

4 Purée half of the corn and add it to the soup with the remaining whole corn kernels, potatoes, and bay leaf. Simmer until the corn and potatoes are tender, about 25 to 30 minutes. Remove and discard the bay leaf. The soup is ready to be finished now, or it can be rapidly cooled and stored for later service.

5 Return the soup to a simmer. Combine the cream and milk and add to the soup. Adjust seasoning with salt, pepper, Tabasco, and Worcestershire sauce.

see photograph on page 334

WONTON SOUP

makes 20 portions

2 oz/60 g minced green onion

1/4 oz/7 g minced ginger

vegetable or peanut oil as needed

3 1/2 qt/3.3 L CHICKEN STOCK (page 248)

1 fl oz/30 mL black soy sauce

salt, as needed

ground white pepper, as needed

GARNISH

4 oz/115 g ham julienne

3 eggs, beaten and cooked into thin omelet, cut into julienne (see pages 738–739)

6 oz/170 g blanched and chopped spinach leaves or watercress

20 WONTONS (recipe follows)

1 Sauté the green onions and ginger in the oil over moderate heat until aromatic, about 1 minute. Add the chicken stock, bring to a simmer, and add the soy sauce, salt, and pepper to taste. Simmer until the soup has a good flavor, about 10 minutes.

2 Just before serving the soup, add the garnish ingredients and recheck the seasoning. To serve, place a hot wonton in a heated soup cup and ladle the soup over the wonton. Serve at once.

WONTONS

makes 20 wontons

STUFFING MIXTURE

8 oz/225 g ground pork

4 oz/115 g chopped Chinese cabbage

4 fl oz/120 mL CHICKEN STOCK (page 248)

1 tbsp/15 mL soy sauce

1 tbsp/15 mL sesame oil

salt, as needed

ground white pepper, as needed

20 wonton skins

1 egg, lightly beaten

1 Combine all the ingredients for the wonton stuffing. Fry or poach a small sample to check the seasoning and consistency and adjust as needed.

2 Lay a wonton skin on a work surface, place 1/2 tsp/2 mL of the stuffing mixture on the wonton wrapper, brush edges with a little of the beaten egg. Fold in half to form a triangle, and press the edges to seal them. Overlap two of the points, and press to seal. Simmer the wontons in seasoned broth or water until the wonton filling reaches 170°F/75°C. Drain and keep warm, or cool and store for later service.

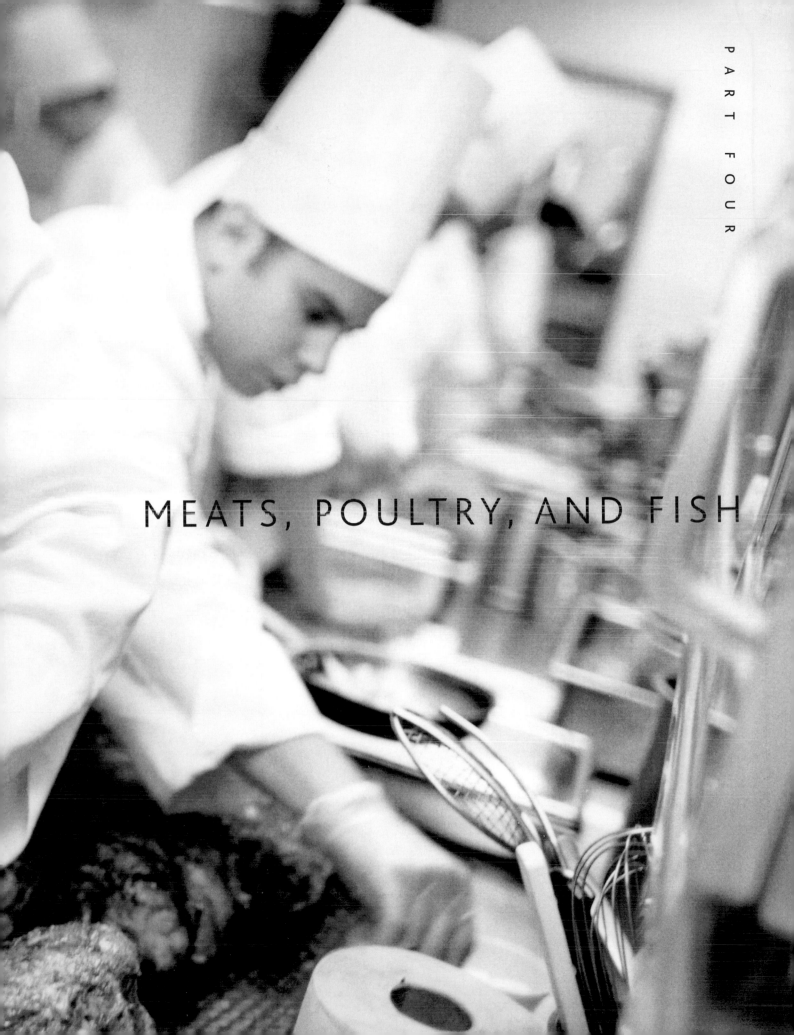

PART FOUR

MEATS, POULTRY, AND FISH

Bringing out the best flavor in meats, poultry, and fish is a skill that seems to come naturally to a professional chef. Another hallmark of the professional is an ability to cook meats, poultry, and fish to the perfect degree of doneness. This skill develops through concentration and practice as well as an understanding of how to reach that point.

MISE EN PLACE FOR MEATS, POULTRY, AND FISH

SEASONINGS

Adding seasonings at the proper point in the cooking process is key to giving a finished dish the fullest possible flavor.

The array of seasonings runs from simple (salt, pepper) to complex blends of herbs and spices and marinades with oils, acids, and aromatics, which may include onions, garlic, fresh or dried herbs, or spices. In every case, though, seasonings are meant to enhance flavor, not detract from or over-whelm the dish. Liquid marinades may change the texture of foods in addition to flavoring them.

Salt and pepper are taken so much for granted that some beginning cooks fail to apply these two seasonings early enough during cooking or in enough quantity to bring out the best flavor in cooked foods. Salt and pepper added before cooking bring out the inherent flavors in foods. If these seasonings are added only after the cooking is complete, the salt and pepper may take on too much significance in the finished dish's flavor.

It is generally better to apply salt and pepper separately. Using the fingertips to apply salt is a good way to control the amount of salt added, and to apply a more even coat.

Salt and pepper are fundamental, but spice and herb blends, which combine vari-ous spices, herbs, and other aromatics, can create a particular flavor profile. Like salt and pepper, they may be applied directly to the raw meat, poultry, or fish. To intensify the flavor of seeds and spices, toast them either on the stovetop or in a moderate oven just before grinding. Be sure to pay close attention. They can go from perfectly toasted to scorched very quickly.

To toast seeds or spices in the oven, spread them out on a dry sheet pan and place in a moderate oven just until a pleas-ant aroma is apparent. Stir often to ensure even browning. Remove immediately and transfer to a fresh pan or plate to cool.

To toast spices and seeds on the stovetop, spread them in a shallow layer in a preheated, dry sauté pan and toss, shake, or swirl the pan until a rich, penetrating aroma arises. Transfer them to a cool pan to avoid scorching.

Fresh herbs and other ingredients such as garlic, fresh or dry bread crumbs, or grated cheeses can be blended into a paste or coating. They are sometimes moistened with some oil, prepared mustard, or similar ingredients to create a texture than can easily adhere to a food, or make it easier to blend it into a dish as a final seasoning. Fresh herbs can trap dirt in their leaves. Rinse them well to remove sand or grit. Thorough drying improves the flavor and texture of the blend by preventing water clinging to the leaves from diluting the herbs' flavor.

When a spice blend is used as a dry rub (also called a dry marinade) to coat food, the food is left to stand after application, under refrigeration, to absorb the flavors. Very often, these rubs contain some salt to help intensify all the flavors in the dish. Dry rubs may be left on the food during cooking or they may be scraped away first. Spice blends may also be added to aromatic vegetables as they cook during the initial stages of preparing a braise or stew. The fat used to cook the vegetables releases the flavor of the spices and infuses the dish more effectively than if the spice blend were simply added to a simmering dish. Barbecued beef and Jamaican jerked pork are examples of dishes that may be prepared using a dry rub.

Marinades generally contain one or more of the following: oil, acid, and aromatics (spices, herbs, and vegetables). Oils protect food from intense heat during cooking and help hold other flavorful ingredients in contact with the food. Acids, such as vinegar, wine, yogurt, and citrus juices, flavor the food and change its texture. In some cases, acids firm or stiffen foods (e.g., the lime juice marinade that "cooks" the raw fish in ceviche); in others, it breaks down connective fibers to make tough cuts of meat more tender (for example, the effect of the red wine marinade used over several days to prepare beef bourgignonne). Aromatics provide specific flavors

Marinating times vary according to the food's texture. Tender or delicate foods such as fish or poultry breast require less time. A tougher cut of meat may be marinated for days. The ratio of acid to other ingredients may also affect timing. High-acid marinades such as those used to prepare ceviche have the desired effect within 15 or 20 minutes of applying them to a food. Others are best left in contact with foods for several hours; still others require several days to work.

Some marinades are cooked before use; others are not. Sometimes the marinade is used to flavor an accompanying sauce or may itself become a dipping sauce. Marinades that have been in contact with raw foods can be used in these ways, provided that they are boiled for several minutes first to kill any lingering pathogens.

To use a liquid marinade, add it to the ingredient and turn the ingredient to coat evenly. Cover and marinate, under refrigeration, for the length of time indicated by the recipe, the type of meat, poultry, or fish, and the desired result. Brush or scrape off excess marinade before cooking and pat dry, particularly if the marinade contains herbs or other aromatics that burn easily.

STUFFINGS

Stuffings can add flavor, moisture, and texture to a dish.

Keep forcemeats over an ice bath for quality as well as food safety.

The easiest stuffings are simply herbs and vegetables and fruits. These simple stuffings are easy to insert into the cavity of a bird or fish or under their skins, and options include quartered or halved onions, garlic cloves, lemons or oranges, sprigs or bunches of fresh herbs. Simple though they may be, they can still have dramatic impact on flavor.

Bread and particularly forcemeat stuffings offer more complex results. Bread stuffings are prepared by cubing or breaking. breads (peasant style, corn, French, or Italian style). They are generally flavored with aromatic vegetables (typically cooked in some fat to develop their flavor), herbs, and spices. Some bread stuffings are moistened with stocks or broths. Eggs may be included to bind the stuffing, though they are optional. Additional ingredients, such as cooked sausages, seafood, or mushrooms, may also be included.

Grain-based stuffings are based upon rice, barley, kasha, or other grains that have been cooked until just tender (use the pilaf or boiling methods; see pages 674 and 682). Once cooked, the grains should be allowed to cool completely before the stuffing is added to meat, poultry, or fish. These stuffings can be seasoned, moistened, and bound as for bread-based stuffings.

Forcemeat stuffings can be prepared using any of the forcemeat methods or recipes included in Chapter Thirty. These mixtures must be handled carefully to keep them well chilled and wholesome. They are often used to fill delicate cuts of meat and fish (for instance, to fill fish fillets before they are rolled into paupiettes and shallow-poached).

Another important consideration with stuffings, along with flavor and quality, is proper handling for food safety. Any stuffing ingredients that require precooking should be cooled to below 40°F/4°C before being combined with other stuffing elements. The finished mixture should also be chilled well before stuffing. During final cooking, stuffings must reach the minimum safe temperature for the food they were stuffed into. Stuffing in a chicken breast or leg, for instance, must reach 165°F/73° C. For this reason, whole chickens and turkeys are rarely stuffed in professional kitchens. By the time the stuffing would reach the necessary temperature, the meat would be overcooked. Instead, stuffings for whole roasted birds are more often baked separately, in which case they are known as dressings.

STANDARD BREADING

The standard breading procedure is the most efficient way to coat a number of items, using a consistent sequence.

Standard breading is done to create a crisp crust on fried foods. It is prepared by coating foods with flour, egg wash, and/or bread crumbs.

Be sure to season the food before applying any coating, and always handle food properly for the best flavor and in such a way as to prevent cross-contamination, which can lead to foodborne illnesses.

Flour and similar meals or powders, such as cornstarch, are used to lightly dredge or dust foods before they are dipped in an egg wash.

Egg wash is made by blending eggs (whole, yolks, or whites) and water or milk. A general guideline calls for about 2 ounces of milk for every 2 whole eggs. Some items are dipped into milk or buttermilk before applying breading, rather than using egg wash. And for some dishes, this step is not necessary; the natural moisture of the food holds the bread-crumb coating in place without requiring egg wash.

Bread crumbs may be dry or fresh. Fresh white bread crumbs (called *mie de pain* in French) are prepared by grating or processing a finely textured bread, such as white Pullman bread with the crust removed.

Dry bread crumbs (called *chapelure* in French) are prepared from slightly stale bread that may be further dried or toasted in a warm oven.

Other ingredients may be used in place of or in addition to bread crumbs. Options include nuts, seeds, shredded coconut, corn flakes, potato flakes, shredded potatoes, grated cheese, ground spices, garlic paste, or chopped herbs.

Blot the food dry with absorbent toweling and season as desired. Hold it in one hand and dip it in flour. Shake off any excess flour and transfer the food to the container of egg wash. Switch hands, pick up the food, and turn it if necessary to coat it on all sides. Transfer it to the container of bread crumbs. Use your dry hand to pack bread crumbs evenly around the food. Shake off any excess, then transfer the food to a rack set over a holding tray. Store breaded food in single layers, but if you must stack the pieces, use parchment or wax paper to separate the layers.

Discard any unused flour, egg wash or bread crumbs. The presence of juices, drippings, or particles of the food you just coated will contaminate these products, making them unsafe for use with other foods. Even sifting the flour or crumbs or straining the egg wash will not be sufficient to prevent cross-contamination and eliminate the potential for food poisoning.

TOP *The standard breading procedure.*

MIDDLE *Sift bread crumbs to remove any lumps as you work.*

BOTTOM *An herbed bread-crumb coating is applied to a beef steak.*

GENERAL GUIDELINES FOR DETERMINING DONENESS IN MEATS, POULTRY, AND FISH

As the noted chef André Soltner once observed, "One must cook a piece of meat a thousand times before he even begins to understand how it cooks."

A chef must rely not only upon a thermometer, but also on his or her senses when cooking. Those senses are put to a greater test in determining doneness in à la minute cooking because one can't actually taste what one is serving, the way one can a soup or a sauce.

THE WAY IT SMELLS. As foods near doneness, their smells change. Aromas intensify and become easier to identify. Each cooking method produces a particular aroma. Grilled and broiled foods should have a pleasing smoky, burnt aroma, indicating rich, deep flavor. Poached and steamed foods have a subtler smell.

THE WAY IT FEELS. Foods should be easy to cut and chew. Touch foods (with a gloved finger) to gauge resistance. The less well done a piece of meat is, the softer and more yielding it will feel. Practice is needed to become adept at judging doneness by touch. Also keep in mind that texture varies in different cuts of meat.

THE WAY IT LOOKS. As meat cooks, the exterior will change color. The interior colors also change, an important factor when determining doneness in meats cooked to customer preference (rare, medium, or well done). If the meat appears pale or even gray, it has not been properly cooked. The juices that run from the meat, although minimal, should be the correct color; the rarer the meat, the bloodier the juices should appear. Appearance is also an important factor in knowing when to turn a piece of meat. When the meat's upper surface begins to appear very moist (there may even be moisture beads), the meat should be turned. Thin pieces may start to change color at the edges when they are ready for turning.

For quick reference, consult the following temperatures and descriptions for the degree of doneness of various meats, poultry, and seafood. Temperatures are based on the USDA's safe cooking temperatures. Specific health codes, which vary from area to area, may differ.

These temperatures are final resting temperatures. Most meats, poultry, and fish need to be removed from the pan, grill, or oven before they reach their final temperature to avoid overcooking and drying out. Heat is retained by foods even after they are removed from the heat source. That residual heat causes the food to keep cooking, a phenomenon referred to as carryover cooking. Internal temperatures taken just as the food is removed from the oven, for example, and again after resting will show a temperature difference of anywhere from a few degrees to ten, fifteen, or more. Factors that play a role in changes in internal temperature during resting include the size of the food being prepared and the presence or absence of stuffing and bones.

TEMPERATURES AND DESCRIPTIONS
OF DEGREES OF DONENESS

	FINAL RESTING TEMPERATURE	DESCRIPTION
FRESH BEEF, VEAL, AND LAMB		
Rare	135°F/58°C	Interior appearance shiny
Medium rare	145°F/63°C	
Medium	160°F/70°C	
Well done	170°F/75°C	
FRESH PORK		
Medium	160°F/70°C	Meat opaque throughout, slight give, juices with faint blush
Well done	170°F/75°C	Slight give, juices clear
HAM		
Fresh ham	160°F/70°C	Slight give, juices with faint blush
Precooked (to reheat)	140°F/60°C	Meat already fully cooked
POULTRY		
Whole birds (chicken, turkey, duck, goose)	180°F/82°C	Leg easy to move in socket, juices with only blush
Poultry breasts	170°F/75°C	Meat opaque, firm throughout
Poultry thighs, legs, wings	180°F/82°C	Meat releases from bone
Stuffing (cooked alone or in bird)	165°F/73°C	
GROUND MEAT AND MEAT MIXTURES		
Turkey, chicken	165°F/73°C	Opaque throughout, juices clear
Beef, veal, lamb, pork	160°F/70°C	Opaque, may have blush of red, juices opaque, no red
SEAFOOD		
Fish	145°F/63°C or until opaque	Still moist, separates easily into segments
Shrimp, lobster, crab		Shells turn red, flesh becomes pearly opaque
Scallops		Turn milky white or opaque and firm
Clams, mussels, oysters		Shells open

RECIPES

GARAM MASALA, VERSION 1

makes 1¾ ounces/50 grams

¼ cup/60 mL coriander seeds

2 tbsp/30 mL cumin seeds

1 tbsp/15 mL black peppercorns

2 tsp/10 mL green cardamom seeds

2 cinnamon sticks

1 cloves

1 nutmeg

1 Toast all the spices except the nutmeg in a small pan.

2 Grind the spices in a spice mill or with a mortar and pestle. Grate the nutmeg into the mixture.

3 Store in a sealed container in a cool dark place.

GARAM MASALA, VERSION 2

makes about 1¾ ounces/50 grams

10 cardamom pods, green or black

1 tbsp/15 mL whole coriander seeds

1 tbsp/15 mL cumin seeds

1 cinnamon stick, broken into small pieces

1 tsp/5 mL cloves

2 tsp/10 mL black peppercorns

¼ tsp/1 mL ground nutmeg

2 bay leaves

1 Break open the cardamom pods and remove the seeds. Combine all the ingredients except the nutmeg and bay leaves. Roast in a 350°F/175°C oven for 5 minutes. Remove and cool slightly.

2 Grind the spices with the nutmeg and bay leaves in a spice mill or with a mortar and pestle.

3 Store in a sealed container in a cool dark place.

CHINESE FIVE SPICE

makes about 2½ ounces/75 grams

½ oz/15 g star anise

½ oz/15 g cloves

½ oz/15 g Szechwan peppers

½ oz/15 g fennel seeds

½ oz/15 g ground cinnamon or cassia

1 Grind the spices in a spice mill or with a mortar and pestle.

2 Store in a sealed container in a cool dark place.

BARBECUE SPICE MIX

makes about 2 ounces/60 grams

½ oz/15 g paprika

½ oz/15 g CHILI POWDER, either made as on page 353 or purchased

½ oz/15 g salt

2 tsp/10 mL ground cumin

2 tsp/10 mL sugar

1 tsp/5 mL dry mustard

1 tsp/5 mL ground pepper

1 tsp/5 mL dried thyme

1 tsp/5 mL dried oregano

1 tsp/5 mL CURRY POWDER, either made as on page 353 or purchased

½ tsp/5 mL cayenne

1 Combine all spices and mix well.

2 Store in a sealed container in a cool dark place.

CHILI POWDER

makes about 2 ounces/60 grams

1¹⁄₂ oz/45 g dried chiles, ground
¹⁄₂ oz/15 g ground cumin
1 tsp/5 mL dried oregano
¹⁄₂ tsp/5 mL garlic powder
¹⁄₄ tsp/1 mL ground coriander
¹⁄₄ tsp/1 mL ground cloves (optional)

1 Combine all the spices, including the cloves, if desired.

2 Store in a sealed container in a cool dark place.

NOTES

Some commercially prepared chili powder is actually a blend similar to this one. This Chili Powder should not be confused with the powdered chiles called for in some recipes. Be sure to use pure ground chiles in recipes that call for them.

CURRY POWDER

makes about 1 ounce/30 grams

³⁄₄ oz/20 g cumin seeds
¹⁄₄ oz/10 g coriander seeds
1 tsp/5 mL whole mustard seeds
4 dried red chiles, or to taste
1 tbsp/15 mL ground cinnamon
¹⁄₄ oz/10 g ground turmeric
1 tbsp/15 mL ground ginger

1 Combine all the seeds and chiles. Roast in a 350°F/175°C oven for 5 minutes. Remove and cool slightly. Split the chiles and remove the seeds.

2 Grind the whole spices, ground spices, and chiles in a spice mill or with a mortar and pestle until evenly blended.

NOTE

Add paprika, cloves, or fresh curry leaves to the blend if desired.

FINES HERBES

makes 4 ounces/115 grams

1 oz/30 g chervil leaves, chopped
1 oz/30 g chives, chopped
1 oz/30 g parsley leaves, chopped
1 oz/30 g tarragon leaves, chopped

1 Combine all the herbs and mix well.

NOTE

Add burnet, marjoram, savory, lavender, or watercress to the herb mixture to adjust the flavor, if desired. These herbs should be added near the end of cooking time because they do not hold their flavor long. Some typical uses include a flavoring for omelets or crepes, or as the final addition to soups and consommés.

QUATRES EPICES

makes about 2 ounces/60 grams

1¹⁄₄ oz/35 g peppercorns
¹⁄₂ oz/15 g ground nutmeg
¹⁄₄ oz/7 g ground cinnamon
¹⁄₈ oz/4 g cloves

1 Grind the peppercorns, nutmeg, cinnamon, and cloves in a spice mill or with a mortar and pestle.

2 Store in a sealed container in a cool dark place.

RED CURRY PASTE

makes 5 ounces/140 grams

2 tsp/10 mL coriander seeds

1 tsp/5 mL fennel seeds

1 tsp/5 mL cumin seeds

1 tsp/5 mL black peppercorns

30 oz/850 g red peppers, roasted, seeded, and peeled

3 oz/85 g jalapeños, roasted, seeded, and peeled

2 chipotles packed in adobo

2 fl oz/60 mL olive oil

1/2 oz/15 g chopped shallots

3/4 oz/20 g minced garlic

1 stalk lemongrass, bottom 4 inches, minced

3/4 oz/20 g minced ginger

1/4 tsp/1 mL ground nutmeg

zest of 1 lime

1 tsp/5 mL salt

1 Roast the coriander, fennel, cumin, and black peppercorns in a 350°F/175°C oven for 5 minutes. Remove and cool slightly.

2 Grind in a spice mill or with a mortar and pestle.

3 Combine with the remaining ingredients in a food processor or blender and pureé until very fine.

4 Store in a sealed container under refrigeration.

SEASONING MIX FOR SPIT-ROASTED MEATS AND POULTRY

makes about 2 1/2 ounces/75 grams

1 1/2 oz/45 g kosher salt

1/2 oz/15 g dry mustard

1 tbsp/15 mL ground black pepper

2 tsp/10 mL dried thyme

2 tsp/10 mL dried oregano

2 tsp/10 mL ground coriander

2 tsp/10 mL celery seeds

1 Combine all the ingredients and mix well.

2 Store in a sealed container in a cool dark place.

ASIAN-STYLE MARINADE

makes 1 pint/480 milliliters

6 fl oz/180 mL hoisin sauce

6 fl oz/180 mL sherry

2 fl oz/60 mL rice wine vinegar

2 fl oz/60 mL soy sauce

1/2 oz/15 g garlic minced

1 Combine all the ingredients.

2 Add the food to be marinated or pour the marinade over it. Let marinate, under refrigeration, as required.

BARBECUE MARINADE

makes 1 pint/480 milliliters

10 fl oz/300 mL vegetable oil

5 fl oz/150 mL cider vinegar

1 fl oz/30 mL Worcestershire sauce

1 tbsp/15 mL brown sugar

2 tsp/10 mL dry mustard

1 tsp/5 mL Tabasco sauce

1 tsp/5 mL garlic powder

1 tsp/5 mL onion powder

1/4 oz/8 g minced garlic

1 Combine all the ingredients.

2 Add the food to be marinated or pour the marinade over it. Let marinate, under refrigeration, as required.

FISH MARINADE

makes 8 fluid ounces/240 milliliters

6 fl oz/180 mL olive oil

2 fl oz/60 mL lemon juice or dry white wine or white vermouth

1/4 oz/7 g minced garlic

1 tsp/5 mL salt

1 tsp/5 mL pepper

1 Combine the ingredients.

2 Add the food to be marinated or pour the marinade over it. Let marinate, under refrigeration, as required.

RED WINE GAME MARINADE

makes 1 quart/1 liter

12 fl oz/360 mL dry red wine

2 fl oz/60 mL olive oil

2 fl oz/60 mL red wine vinegar

2 tsp/10 mL dried thyme

1 tsp/5 mL juniper berries

1 tsp/5 mL dried savory

1 tsp/5 mL pepper

3 parsley sprigs

1/4 oz/8 g minced garlic

1 carrot, diced

1 onion, diced

1 celery stalk, diced

1 bay leaf

1 Combine all the ingredients.

2 Add the food to be marinated or pour the marinade over it. Let marinate, under refrigeration, as required.

LAMB MARINADE

makes 1 pint/480 milliliters

4 fl oz/120 mL dry red wine

4 fl oz/120 mL red wine vinegar

2 fl oz/60 mL olive oil

1 tbsp/15 mL sugar

1 tbsp/15 mL dried mint

1 tsp/5 mL salt

1 tsp/5 mL juniper berries

2 bay leaves

2 slices onion

1 parsley sprig

1 thyme sprig

1 garlic clove, minced

pinch ground nutmeg

1 Combine all the ingredients.

2 Add the food to be marinated or pour the marinade over it. Let marinate, under refrigeration, as required.

LATIN CITRUS MARINADE (MOJO)

makes 10 fluid ounces/300 milliliters

6 fl oz/180 mL orange juice

3 fl oz/90 mL lemon juice

1 fl oz/30 mL lime juice

1 tbsp/15 mL ground annato seeds

1 garlic clove, chopped

1 tsp/5 mL salt

1/2 tsp/3 mL dried oregano

1/2 tsp/3 mL ground cumin

1/4 tsp/1 mL ground cloves

1/4 tsp/1 mL ground cinnamon

1/4 tsp/1 mL ground pepper

1 Combine all the ingredients.

2 Add the food to be marinated or pour the marinade over it. Let marinate, under refrigeration, as required.

RED WINE MARINADE FOR GRILLED MEATS

makes 1 pint/480 milliliters

8 fl oz/240 mL red wine

6 fl oz/180 mL olive oil

2 fl oz/60 mL lemon juice

1/4 oz/8 g minced garlic

1 tsp/5 mL salt

1 tsp/5 mL pepper

1 Combine all the ingredients.

2 Add the food to be marinated or pour the marinade over it. Let marinate, under refrigeration, as required.

ROSEMARY AND GIN MARINADE FOR GAME MEATS

makes 1 pint/480 milliliters

8 fl oz/240 mL gin

8 fl oz/240 mL dry vermouth

1 bay leaf

8 peppercorns

3 oz/85 g minced onion

1 oz/30 g minced carrot

1 oz/30 g minced celery

1 tsp/5 mL minced garlic

1 tbsp/15 mL chopped rosemary leaves

1 Combine all the ingredients.

2 Add the food to be marinated or pour the marinade over it. Let marinate, under refrigeration, as required.

TERIYAKI MARINADE

makes 1 pint/480 milliliters

6 fl oz/180 mL soy sauce

6 fl oz/180 mL peanut oil

3 fl oz/90 mL dry sherry

1 oz/30 g honey

$\frac{1}{4}$ oz/8 g garlic cloves, minced

$\frac{1}{4}$ oz/10 g grated ginger

2 tbsp/30 mL grated orange zest (optional)

1 Combine all the ingredients, including the orange zest, if desired.

2 Add the food to be marinated or pour the marinade over it. Let marinate, under refrigeration, as required.

Meat, poultry, and fish are the most costly part of the food budget of a foodservice operation, whatever the scale. For the most part the size and scope of the operation determine the form in which it purchases meats, poultry, and fish. For operations with limited labor and storage resources, quality prefabricated boxed meats, poultry, and fish are a perfectly acceptable purchasing form.

FABRICATING MEATS, POULTRY, AND FISH

Chefs with the means to do so often prefer to perform many fabrication tasks in-house to control portion size and to be sure that the quality of each portion is the same each time—important considerations when it comes to the establishment's reputation. Depending on the prevailing local market rates for food and labor, in-house fabrication may be less expensive than buying prefabricated menu cuts. As a further economic benefit, trim and bones can be used to prepare other dishes (e.g., stocks, soups, sauces, and forcemeats).

MEAT FABRICATION

General similarities exist between cuts of beef, veal, lamb, venison, or pork, if they come from the same part of the butchered animal. The rib and the loin contain the most tender cuts. They tend to cost more than cuts from the shoulder; cuts from the shoulder are often more exercised and tough. The leg may contain tender cuts as well as cuts that are quite tough. Proper handling during fabrication prepares meats for subsequent cooking. Most of the techniques described here do not require any special knowledge of the bones in a cut of meat or of the animal's overall anatomy, although reference to sections of Chapter Six, Meats, Poultry, and Game Purchasing and Identification (pages 105–127), will be helpful.

Since the tenderloin is one of the most expensive cuts of meat, extra care should be taken to leave the meat as intact as possible. Use a very sharp knife and pay close attention to be sure that only silverskin, fat, and gristle are removed, not edible meat.

Lift and pull away the fat covering of an untrimmed tenderloin. This fat pulls away easily, and the blade of the boning knife is used to steady the tenderloin as the fat cover is pulled away.

Completely remove the silverskin. This tough membrane, which gets its name from its somewhat silvery color, tends to shrink when exposed to heat and cause uneven cooking. A tenderloin of beef is shown here, but the same techniques can be applied to pork, veal, and lamb tenderloin as well as to other cuts of meat with silverskin, including top round of beef and of veal and loin cuts of venison and other large game.

1 (ABOVE) *Pull and cut away the strip of fat and meat known as the chain.*

2 (ABOVE) *The chain is completly removed. It can be further cleaned of excess fat and used in a variety of preparations, including stocks, broths, sauces, and soups or as ground meat. Position the tenderloin so that the tail is on the same side as your guiding hand.*

3 (ABOVE) *Work the tip of a boning knife under the silverskin and hold it tight against the meat. Glide the knife blade just underneath, angling the blade upward slightly. Work so that your cuts move toward the head (the larger end of the tenderloin) as much as possible.*

Boneless cuts from the tenderloin of beef and the loin or tenderloin of veal, lamb, or pork may be called medallions, noisettes (so named because they are like little nuts of meat), or grenadins (large cuts from the loin). The terms noisette and medallion are often used interchangeably to refer to a small, boneless, tender cut of meat weighing from 2 to 6 oz/60 to 170 g. Tournedos and châteaubriand are special terms generally used only for beef tenderloin cuts. Tournedos are typically cut from the thinner end of the tenderloin to weigh 5 oz/140 g. Châteaubriand serves two and is cut from the center of the tenderloin; it typically weighs 10 oz/285 g.

After the medallions or similar boneless cuts are portioned, they may then be wrapped in cheesecloth and molded to give them a compact, uniform shape. Not only does this give the meat a more pleasing appearance, it also helps the medallion to cook evenly.

1 (ABOVE) *Cut cheesecloth into a square large enough to wrap the meat portion easily.*

2 (ABOVE) *Gather the cheesecloth together and twist to tighten it around the meat. As you twist the cloth with one hand, press down on the meat firmly, with even, moderate pressure, using the broad side of a knife blade or similar flat tool.*

3 (ABOVE) *Once shaped, the medallions look uniform, even though they were cut from different sections of the tenderloin.*

FABRICATING BONELESS MEATS

Meats to be sautéed or pan fried, grilled, or stewed are often fabricated from larger boneless cuts, such as rounds, loins, and/or tenderloins. These cuts are typically composed of more than one muscle. Each muscle has its own grain, or direction in which the meat fibers are arranged. Breaking a larger cut into individual sections allows the chef to cut each piece of meat properly for the recipe or menu item.

1 (TOP LEFT) *Follow the natural seams in the meat (here a veal bottom round) to divide a large cut into smaller ones. This makes it possible to cut each muscle against the grain for the best texture in the finished dish as well as to easily trim out any internal gristle or fat.*

2 (BOTTOM LEFT) *Using the same technique as described for a beef tenderloin, trim away fat and silverskin. Pay attention to the angle of your knife blade. The blade should be angled upward slightly to prevent removing edible meat.*

3 (TOP RIGHT) *Have two or more holding containers available. You will need to keep trimmed and cut meat in one container. Have another available for wholesome trim to use in stocks, sauces, or forcemeats.*

4 (BOTTOM RIGHT) *This veal is ready to use in a stew. Other possible fabrication techniques include tying to roast whole, butterflying to grill, or cutting into scallops or émincé.*

CUTTING AND POUNDING CUTLETS

A meat cutlet or scallop is a thin boneless cut of meat prepared from the loin, the tenderloin, or any other sufficiently tender cut of meat, such as the top round. Cutlet, *scaloppine* in Italian, *escalope* in French are different words for the same cut and are used as fitting in a menu's particular style.

Cutlets are often pounded to ensure an even thickness over their entire surface so that they can be rapidly sautéed or pan fried. A paillard is a

pounded cutlet that is grilled rather than sautéed or pan fried. Adjust the weight of the mallet and strength of the blow to match the meat. Turkey cutlets (slices of turkey breast), for example, require a more delicate touch than pork cutlets. Be careful not to tear or overstretch the meat while pounding it.

SHREDDING AND MINCING MEATS

The French word for this cut is *émincé*, or cut into slivers. Meat is cut against the grain into thin strips of a length and width appropriate for the dish. Since the meat is generally sautéed, the cut should be one of the most tender. A loin of veal is shown here, but this same technique can be used for beef, lamb, or even pork. Be sure to trim the meat completely before cutting it into émincé.

1 (TOP) *Cut pieces of the same thickness, weight (generally ranging from 1 to 4 ounces/30 to 115 grams), and circumference.*

2 (BOTTOM) *Place the meat between two layers of plastic wrap. Use a pounding and pulling motion to evenly thin the cutlet. Increased surface area and decreased thickness promote rapid cooking.*

3 (ABOVE) *Arrange the pounded cutlets in a single layer on a parchment-lined sheet pan and keep well chilled until ready to bread or prepare in some other manner.*

ABOVE *Cut the meat with the grain into long, evenly shaped pieces. The length and width of the finished émincé are determined by this cut. The thickness is determined by cross cuts made against the grain. Once cut, the émincé may be pounded, if appropriate, using the same technique as for pounding cutlets. Blot the pounded émincé dry before cooking.*

CUTTING BONE-IN CHOPS

Chops and steaks are made from bone-in cuts from the rib or loin. Large bones can be difficult to saw through, but the bones of cuts from the rib and loin of pork, lamb, venison, and beef are more manageable.

Cut away the backbone, often referred to as the chine bone, completely away from the rib bones without cutting into the meat muscle. The feather bones, which are located near the chine bone, are also cut away from the meat before slicing it into chops.

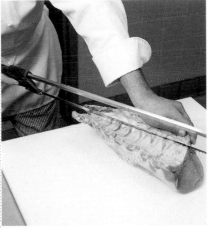

1 (TOP LEFT) *First, cut through the chine bone using a handsaw. Completely sever the bone, but do not cut into the meat.*

2 (BOTTOM LEFT) *Using your guiding hand to hold the chine bone away from the meat, work with the tip of a boning knife to make smooth strokes along the feather bones, cutting the meat cleanly away from the bones.*

3 (TOP RIGHT) *Continue cutting until the chine bone and the feather bones are completely released from the meat.*

4 (BOTTOM RIGHT) *Cut between each rib bone with a scimitar as shown or with a chef's knife to make individual chops. The cut should be very smooth to create a smooth surface on the chops. Once cut, the meat can be shaped using the technique demonstrated with a beef tenderloin medallion on page 360.*

TRIMMING A STRIP LOIN AND CUTTING BONELESS STEAKS

Steaks can be purchased already portioned and trimmed, but cutting attractive, consistently sized steaks in-house can keep the kitchen's food cost down.

The strip loin has a tail, sometimes referred to as a lip, running along one edge of the muscle. This heavy layer of fat is cut away first, taking care not to cut the interior loin muscle as you work. Once the fat cover is trimmed to the desired thickness, the chain is removed.

Steaks cut from the sirloin end of the steak will contain a V-shaped streak of collagen. While steaks cut from this end are as tender as those cut from the rib end, the collagen itself is tough, and can give the impression that the steak is tough. These steaks are sometimes referred to as vein steaks.

1 (ABOVE) *Start to remove the tail on the strip loin by making a cut down the length of the boneless loin.*

2 (TOP) *Hold the fat cover taut as you run the knife blade down the length of the loin, angling the blade up slightly.*

3 (BOTTOM) *A strip loin may have a section known as the chain. Remove the chain from the strip loin and reserve it for another use.*

4 (TOP) *Turn the loin over and trim away any gristle, sinew, or excess fat.*

5 (BOTTOM) *The trimmed loin is ready to cut into portions. Save edible trim (the pan on the right) for other uses. Discard inedible trim (the pan on the left).*

Adjust the thickness of the cut to produce equal-sized steaks of the desired weight. Hold cut steaks under refrigeration, until ready to cook.

A whole pork loin often costs less per pound than a trimmed boneless loin. Removing the fat and bones is relatively easy, and the bones and any lean trim can then be roasted and used to prepare a rich brown jus or stock. It may take some time at first to learn how to properly trim and bone a loin for a roast or cutlets.

The novice should cut slowly and stop to examine the loin between cuts. The first step when working with a pork loin is to remove the tenderloin, if it is still intact. Next, cut away the fat cover to the desired thickness. Pass the knife close to the bones, scraping them clean so that as little meat as possible is left on the bones. Use the tip of the knife to cut around joints and between bones and the flat part of the blade for longer, sweeping strokes.

Once the loin has been trimmed and boned, it can be used to prepare a wide variety of menu cuts, including medallions, cutlets, and émincé.

6 (TOP) *Use a scimitar, a knife with a long curved blade, to make it easier to cut neat slices.*

7 (BOTTOM) *Weigh each steak as it is cut. Make each portion the same size.*

1 (ABOVE) *Remove the excess fat covering the edge of the loin to expose the tips of the bones using smooth, even strokes.*

2 (ABOVE) *Make smooth strokes along the rib bones to free the meat. Pull the meat away to make it easy to see. When all the meat is freed from one side of the bones, turn the loin over and free the meat from the other side.*

Although this procedure may look difficult, it is possible to do it successfully by following the steps shown in the accompanying photographs. A leg of lamb has the same basic structure as a veal or venison leg. They all require the same general fabrication method.

A leg of lamb can be boned out to use in a number of different ways. It can be butterflied and grilled, or rolled, tied, and roasted. The meat can be divided along the natural seams to make small roasts, or sliced into cutlets or cubes.

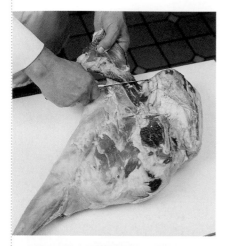

1 (TOP) *First, using a boning knife, remove the flank, a portion of muscle that is loosely attached to the underside of the leg.*

2 (BOTTOM) *Cut into the fat at the point closest to the lean muscle tissue. Pull and cut the fat cover and the fell, rolling the leg as you work.*

3 (TOP) *Cut the butt tenderloin (a small piece near the hip bone) away from the leg, but do not sever it completely from the rest of the meat.*

4 (BOTTOM) *Remove the tail bone from the pelvic bone. The cut is made at the joint between the two bones.*

5 (TOP) *Work the tip of the knife around the pelvic bone.*

6 (BOTTOM) *When the meat has been freed from the pelvic bone, lift the bone up and away from the leg.*

The leg is covered with layer of fat and a membrane, known as the fell. The fat and membrane should be removed carefully, leaving as much edible meat intact as possible. The leg contains the hind shank bone, the pelvic bones (consisting of the hip bone and the aitch bone), a portion of the back bone and tail, and the leg bone (also known as the femur).

As you cut into the meat to remove the bones, use an overhand grip to hold your boning knife and cut with the top of the blade as you work around bones and joints. Work the knife tip along the bone to remove as much meat as possible.

 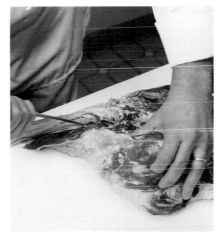 

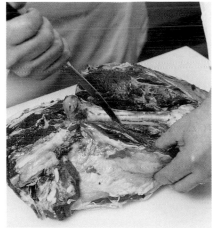 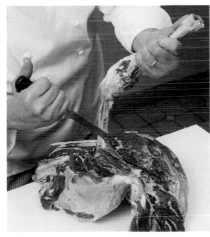 

7 (TOP) *Turn the leg and look for a seam of fat that runs parallel and close to the top of the femur. Make a cut into the meat, following the seam, until you reach the femur bone.*

8 (BOTTOM) *Cut the meat cleanly away from the femur bone. Note how little meat is left clinging to the bone.*

9 (TOP) *As you continue to expose the femur bone, the hind shank bone will also become visible.*

10 (BOTTOM) *Cut the meat away from the hind shank bone. Lift the femur and the hind shank bone away from the meat and continue to cut it completely free from the meat.*

11 (TOP) *Remove the kneecap, or patella.*

12 (BOTTOM) *Use your fingers to check for a large fat deposit in the leg of meat. Remove and discard it.*

FRENCHING A RACK OF LAMB

This technique is one of the more complicated fabrication techniques, but it is not especially difficult to master. Trimmed and frenched racks or chops can be ordered from a meat purveyor, of course, but the chef can exercise greater control over trim loss if the work is done in the kitchen. The same technique can be used to french individual rib chops of lamb, veal, or pork. Any lean trim can be used to prepare jus or a stock.

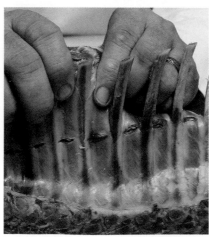

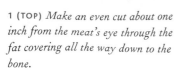

1 (TOP) *Make an even cut about one inch from the meat's eye through the fat covering all the way down to the bone.*

2 (BOTTOM) *Set the rack on one end and make a stabbing cut between each bone, using the initial cut as a guide.*

3 (TOP) *Use the tip of a boning knife to score the thin membrane covering the bones. This will allow them to break through the membrane easily.*

4 (BOTTOM) *Push the bones through the membrane. Place your thumbs against the fleshy side of the bone and your forefingers between the bones.*

5 (ABOVE) *Lay the rack so that the bones are facing down. Make an even cut to sever the meat surrounding the bone ends. It should pull away easily.*

In recent years, as Americans have become less squeamish about organ meats, the demand for properly prepared liver, kidneys, tongue, sweetbreads, and other kinds of variety meats has grown. Because these cuts are difficult for the consumer to find in a grocery store, or even a butcher's shop, many people are uncomfortable with or unsure of proper preparation techniques.

Liver

Liver is prepared before cooking by removing any silverskin, tough membranes, veins, or gristle before sautéing. When subjected to intense heat, silverskin shrinks more rapidly than meat; thus the liver would pucker and cook unevenly.

Kidneys

The unique flavor of kidneys will come through as long as they are perfectly fresh and properly handled. Soak kidneys in salted water for 12 hours, then rinse well and soak in milk for another 12 to 24 hours.

Rinse the kidneys, then cut them in half and remove all the fat and veins. In some cases, recipes may indicate that the kidneys be blanched first. Peel the kidneys by pulling away the membrane covering them.

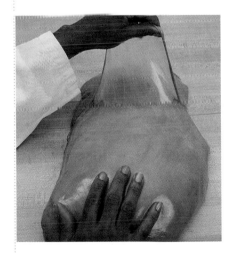

ABOVE *Clean the liver by pulling away the membrane.*

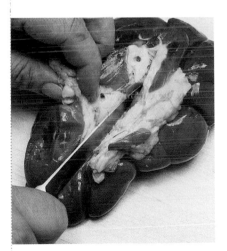

1 (ABOVE) *Make a cut through the center of the kidneys, dividing them into two equal pieces.*

2 (ABOVE) *Lift up the kidney fat and use the tip of a sharp knife to cut it away from the kidneys.*

Sweetbreads

Sweetbreads need to be thoroughly rinsed in cold water to remove all traces of blood. They are then blanched in a court bouillon, peeled, and pressed to give them a firmer, more appealing texture. The sweetbreads can then be prepared à la meunière (floured and sautéed), used to prepare terrines, or utilized in other preparations.

Tongue

Tongue is a muscle that is quite tough. This cut of meat may be sold with the skin. It is easier to remove the skin from the cooked tongue.

Gently simmer the tongue in a flavorful broth or bouillon, though, and it will become very tender. Let the tongue cool in the cooking liquid to bolster its flavor.

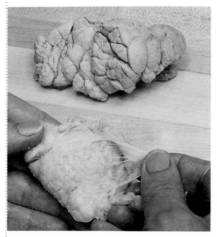

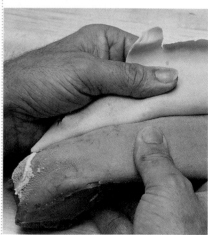

1 (TOP) *After blanching the sweetbreads, let them cool enough to handle easily. Pull away the membrane covering the meat.*

2 (BOTTOM) *To give the sweetbreads a uniform texture, roll the peeled lobes in cheesecloth and tighten the cloth to give them a compact, uniform shape.*

3 (TOP) *Place the rolled sweetbreads in a mold and top with a cover plate, such as a piece of wood cut to fit the mold's opening.*

4 (BOTTOM) *Top the cover plate with a weight to further compact the sweetbreads. Press them under refrigeration for several hours before using.*

1 (TOP) *Use the tip of a knife to trim the skin from the underside of a cooked tongue. Lift away from the tongue as the cuts are made to prevent removing too much meat.*

2 (BOTTOM) *The skin will peel away easily from the top of the tongue.*

Once the tongue is cooled, carefully peel it to remove the skin. The skin will cling more tightly near the base of the tongue and must be cut away with a sharp knife. It will peel away easily near the tip of the tongue using just your fingers.

Once peeled, tongue can be used in a variety of ways: It can be cut into julienne or dice and used as a garnish for sauces, soups, or pâtés. It may be sliced thin and served hot or cold, or used as a liner for terrine molds. It is a classic part of the Alsatian dish choucroute.

Marrow

Marrow—the soft inner substance of bones—is often used as a garnish for soups, sauces, and other dishes. Certain bones, known as marrow bones, have a significant amount of marrow that is relatively easy to remove using the technique below.

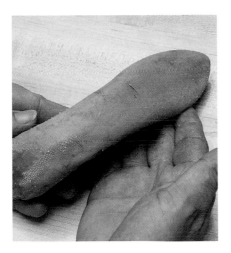

3 (ABOVE) *The completely peeled tongue is ready to slice.*

1 (TOP) *Place the marrow bones in a container and cover with cold water. Add salt to help draw away any excess blood and other impurities.*

2 (BOTTOM) *After the marrow bones have soaked for a few hours, push the marrow out using your thumb.*

3 (ABOVE) *The marrow is completely freed.*

TYING A ROAST

Tying a roast with secure knots that have the right tension is one of the simplest and most frequently required types of meat fabrication. It ensures that the roast will be evenly cooked and that it will retain its shape after roasting. Although simple, the technique is often one of the most frustrating to learn. For one thing, knot tying is not always easy. As long as the string is taut enough to give the roast a compact shape without being too tight, however, the result will be fine. There is one trick to keep in mind that will make initial attempts easier. Leave the string very long, so that it will wrap easily around the entire diameter of the meat. Or leave the string attached to the spool, and cut it only when the entire roast is tied. There are other methods used for tying roasts than the two shown here. If you have the chance to learn other methods, you will be better able to adapt to different cuts of meat with ease.

Both techniques illustrated here work for either boneless or bone-in roasts. The choice of technique is a matter of personal preference.

Technique One

For this tying technique, cut several lengths of string. Each piece should be long enough to wrap completely around the meat with sufficient additional length to tie the knots.

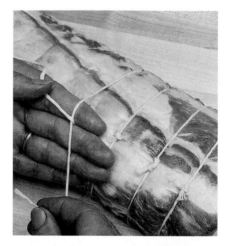

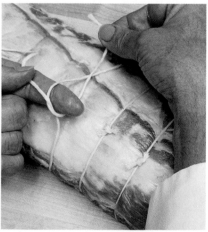

1 (TOP) *Pass one length of string around the meat and cross one end of the string over the other end.*

2 (BOTTOM) *Make a loop by passing one end around the index finger of your left hand.*

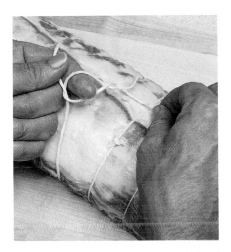

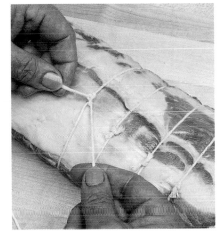

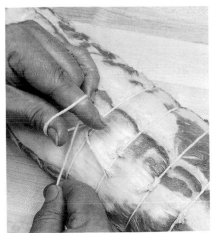

3 (TOP) *Loop the string back underneath itself.*

4 (BOTTOM) *Still working with the same end of the string, pass the tail of the string back through the opening where your fingertip was.*

5 (TOP) *Pull both ends of the string to tighten well until the string is pressing firmly against the meat.*

6 (BOTTOM) *Loop one end of the string completely around your thumb and forefinger and pull the other end of the string through the loop.*

7 (TOP) *Pull both ends of the string to tighten securely. Trim any long string tails so that the knots are neat.*

8 (BOTTOM) *Repeat tying lengths of string at even intervals until the entire piece of meat is securely tied.*

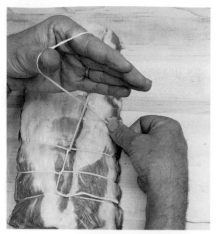

Technique Two

For this technique, the string is left attached to the spool, rather than being cut into lengths. Tie the end of the string around the thicker end of the meat (any knot that holds securely may be used). Then, loop the string around the meat in a series of half-hitch knots. Finally, work the string back through the loops to keep them in place during handling and cooking.

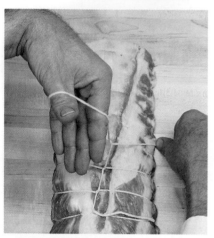
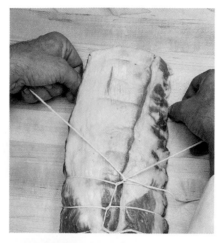
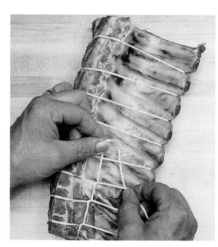

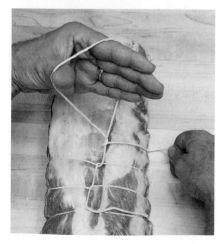
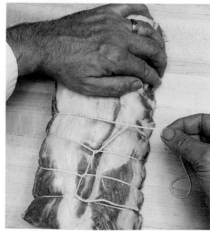
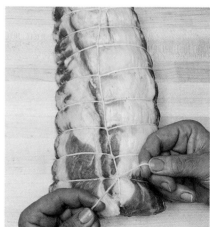

1 (TOP) *Pass the string around your outspread fingers and thumb with the string coming from behind the fingers, around the thumb, and then back behind itself.*

2 (MIDDLE) *Twist the loop around so that the base of the loop twists back on itself.*

3 (BOTTOM) *Spread the hand open to enlarge the loop.*

4 (TOP) *Continue to enlarge the loop until it is wide enough to pass easily around the meat, completely encircling it.*

5 (BOTTOM) *Pull the loose end of the string until the loop is securely tightened around the meat. Continue until the entire piece of meat has been secured with loops.*

6 (TOP) *Turn the piece of meat over. Pass the loose end of the string through the loop, then pass it back underneath the loop. Pull the string tight and continue down the length of the meat.*

7 (BOTTOM) *Once the string has been wrapped around each loop from one end to the other, turn the meat back over. Cut the loose end and tie the string securely to the first loop.*

GRINDING MEATS

Grinding meat calls for scrupulous attention to safe food handling practices (see pages 56–69). This fabrication technique applies to meats, as well as poultry and fish. Observe the following procedures for best results:

- Unplug the grinder before assembling or disassembling.

- Cut the meat into dice or strips that will fit easily through the grinder's feed tube.

- Chill meats thoroughly before grinding. Chill all grinder parts that will come in contact with the food by either refrigerating them or submerging them in ice water.

- Do not force the meat through the feed tube with a tamper. If they are the correct size, the pieces will be drawn easily by the worm.

- Be sure that the blade is sharp. Meat should be cut cleanly, never mangled or mashed, as it passes through the grinder.

1 (ABOVE) *Clean the grinder well and put it together correctly. Make sure that the blade is sitting flush against the die. In this position, the blade cuts the food neatly, rather than tearing or shredding it.*

2 (ABOVE) *For all but very delicate meats (salmon or other fish, for example), begin with a die that has large openings. The meat will appear quite coarse.*

3 (TOP) *Grind through progressively smaller dies until the desired consistency is achieved.*

4 (BOTTOM) *A final pass through a fine die gives the ground meat a more refined texture, and further blends the lean meat and fat.*

POULTRY FABRICATION

Poultry, always popular and readily available, is, for the most part, among the least costly of meats used for entrées and other menu items. Fabrication techniques are demonstrated here on a chicken, the bird most commonly used in restaurants. These techniques can be applied to virtually all poultry types, not only chicken but squab, ducks, pheasant, turkey, and quail, with some modification to adapt to size (smaller birds require more delicate, precise cuts; larger or older birds, a heavier blade and greater pressure to break through tough joints and sinew).

PREPARING A SUPRÊME

A suprême is a semi-boneless poultry breast half, usually from a chicken, pheasant, partridge, or duck, so named because the suprême of the chicken is the best (suprême) chicken portion. One wing joint, often frenched, is left attached to the breast meat (see Technique Two, page 378). If the skin is removed from the suprême, it may be referred to as a côtelette. Suprêmes may be sautéed, poached, or grilled.

Technique One

To prepare a chicken suprême from a whole chicken by this technique, you must first cut away the first wing joint and then remove the legs. The breast meat and the first joint of the wing are cut away from the bird's carcass. Reserve the carcass for stock or broth.

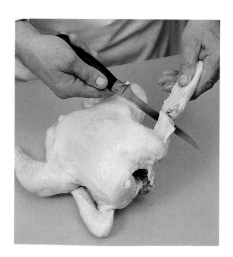

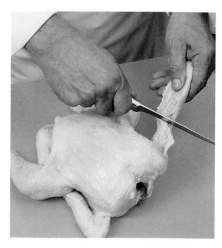

1 (ABOVE) *Use the tip of a boning knife to make a cut that circles around the second joint of the wing bone. Make sure to cut through the web skin as well.*

2 (ABOVE) *Bend the wing bone at the second joint, to snap it. Continue to cut through the joint until the first two joints are removed.*

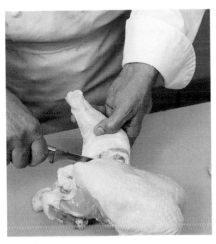

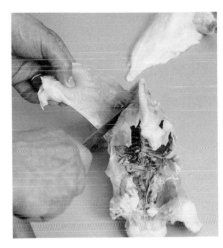

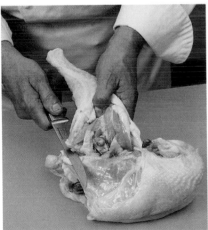

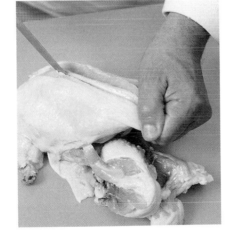

3 (TOP) *Cut through the skin between the thigh and the breast.*

4 (BOTTOM) *Bend the leg backward, away from the body, to expose the ball socket. Then make a cut that runs along the backbone up to the ball and socket.*

5 (TOP) *Hold the chicken stable with the heel of your knife, and pull the leg away from the body firmly and evenly. This will remove the leg and the oyster cleanly from the backbone structure. Repeat on the other side.*

6 (BOTTOM) *With the breast bone facing up, cut along either side of the keel bone with the knife. Use your guiding hand to steady the bird.*

7 (ABOVE) *Remove the breast meat from the rib cage with delicate cuts. Use the tip of the knife to free the meat from the bones, running the tip along the bones for the best yield.*

Technique Two

In contrast to Technique One, suprêmes are prepared by cutting the bones away from the breast, rather than cutting the breast away from the bones. The wing tips and legs should be cut away, as shown in Technique One. Then, the backbone is cut out, the breast is opened out like a book, and the breast bone and rib bones are cut away.

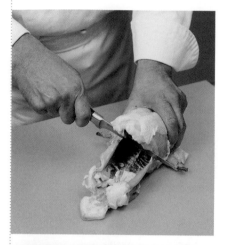

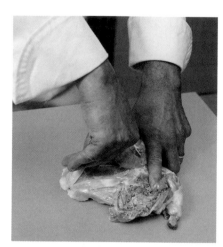

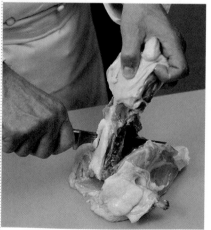

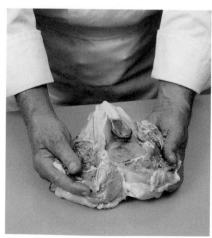

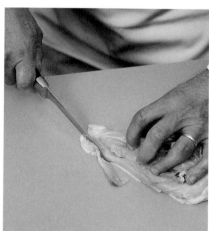

1 (TOP) *Cut through the connective tissue holding the breast and keel bone to the backbone without severing the backbone.*

2 (BOTTOM) *Cut from the tail to the neck opening down either side of the backbone. Pull upward slightly while cutting down, exerting enough pressure to cut through the rib bones.*

3 (TOP) *Lay out the whole breast, with the bones facing up. Use the tip of a boning knife to cut through the white cartilage at the very top of the keel bone.*

4 (BOTTOM) *Open out the breast like a book. This bending action will expose the keel bone.*

5 (TOP) *Grab the keel bone firmly and pull it and the attached cartilage away from the breast meat. The cartilage may break away from the keel bone. Be sure to remove the entire structure.*

6 (BOTTOM) *After the breast is cut into two portions, trim away any remaining cartilage or connective tissue.*

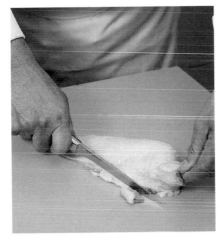

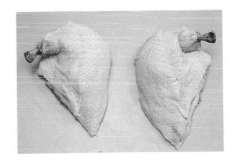

7 (TOP) *Hold the breast as shown and carefully cut the bones away from the meat. Cut down to the wing joint, but be careful not to cut the wing bone away from the suprême.*

8 (BOTTOM) *Carefully cut away the bones at the wing joint.*

9 (TOP) *Trim away excess skin from the breast.*

10 (BOTTOM) *Use the blade to scrape the meat on the wing bone to expose the bone completely. This is known as frenching the bone.*

11 (ABOVE) *The finished suprêmes.*

The object of trussing or tying a bird, any bird, is to give it a smooth, compact shape so that it will cook evenly and retain moisture. Several different methods for trussing poultry exist, some involving trussing needles, some requiring only string. One simple way of tying with string is shown here.

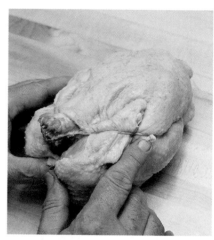

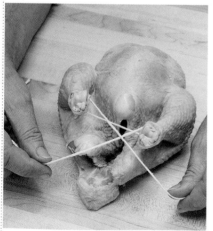
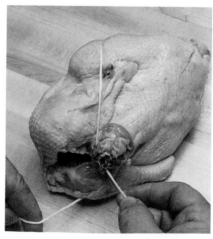

1 (TOP) *Cut away the first two wing joints. Pass the middle of a long piece of string underneath the joints at the end of the drumstick, and cross the ends of the string to make an X.*

2 (BOTTOM) *Pull the ends of the string down toward the tail and begin to pull the string back along the body.*

3 (TOP) *Pull both ends of the string tightly across the joint that connects the drumstick and the thigh and continue to pull the string along the body toward the bird's back, catching the wing underneath the string.*

4 (BOTTOM) *Pull one end of the string securely underneath the backbone at the neck opening.*

5 (TOP) *Tie the two ends of the string with a secure knot.*

6 (BOTTOM) *A properly trussed bird.*

Chicken and other birds may be halved or quartered before or after cooking. Cutting into halves is an especially important technique for use on smaller birds, such as Cornish game hens and broiler chickens, that are to be grilled. These birds are small enough to cook through completely before the skin becomes scorched or charred. One half of the bird is usually sufficient for a single portion. If the bones are left intact during grilling, they provide some protection against shrinkage.

This technique is also used to cut ducks in half after they have been roasted. In many restaurants, the ducks needed for an evening's service will be roasted in advance, then halved and partially deboned; at service, then, it is necessary only to reheat the duck and crisp the skin in a hot oven. The wing tips and backbone should be saved for use in the preparation of stock.

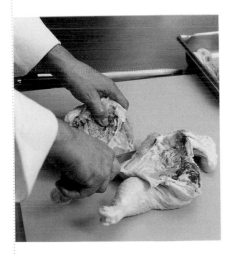  

1 (ABOVE) *Remove the backbone and keel bone as shown in Technique Two for preparing suprêmes on page 378. Cut the chicken into halves by making a cut down the center of the breast to divide the bird in half.*

2 (ABOVE) *Separate the leg and thigh from the breast and wing by cutting through the skin just above where the breast and thigh meet.*

3 (ABOVE) *The chicken is now quartered. The pieces may be grilled, baked, or stewed, as desired.*

DISJOINTING A RABBIT

The technique for disjointing a rabbit is similar to that for a chicken. Rabbit is a relatively lean, mildly flavored meat. The loin and rib sections are leaner than the legs, in much the same way that chicken breast is leaner than the legs. By removing the legs and shoulder, you can apply two different cooking methods to one rabbit — moist heat for the legs, dry heat for the loin — to achieve the most satisfactory results.

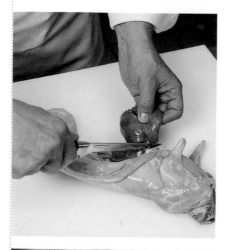

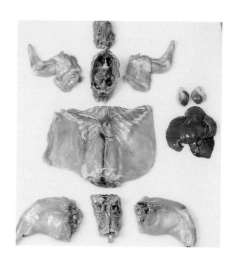

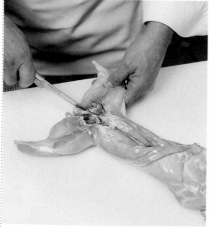

1 (TOP) *Spread open the belly cavity of the rabbit and pull out the kidneys and liver. Sever any membrane attaching the liver to the cavity. Reserve the liver for another use.*

2 (BOTTOM) *Remove the hind legs by cutting through the joint and cut through the meat to separate the hind leg from the loin.*

3 (TOP) *To separate the front legs and shoulder from the rest of the body, pull the leg away from the body and cut through the joint.*

4 (BOTTOM) *Trim the loin by cutting away the hind and front portions to produce the saddle.*

5 (ABOVE) *A fully disjointed rabbit is shown here, including the saddle, forelegs and shoulder sections, hind legs, liver, kidneys, and usable trim.*

FISH FABRICATION

Most fish fall into one of two categories: round or flat. Time, practice, and experience will help determine which of a number of techniques to use to fabricate a particular fish. Different methods can achieve virtually the same results, and the methods shown here are not always the only way to proceed.

The basic procedure for scaling—the first step in preparing the fish before any further fabrication is done—applies to all types of fish. Methods differ slightly, however, for gutting round fish and flat fish.

Similarly, the technique for filleting a round fish is different from that used for a flatfish. In determining how to fabricate a fish, knowledge of that particular fish's specific properties is important (see Chapter Seven, Fish and Shellfish Identification).

Other seafood, including lobster, shrimp, crayfish, and crab; shellfish such as clams, oysters, and mussels; and cephalopods like squid and octopus, also must be carefully handled to maintain quality and wholesomeness.

SCALING AND TRIMMING FISH

Most fish, though not all, have scales, which must be removed as a first step in fabricating fish. The best way to remove scales is with a fish scaler; but other tools (e.g., the dull side of a knife, a table crumber, a spoon handle) can be used if a scaler is not available. The fins and tails can be cut away at this point or later when the fish is gutted.

ABOVE *To scale fish, work from the head toward the tail, gripping the fish behind the eyes, and have water flowing over the fish to help keep the scales from flying around. Do not pinch the fish too tightly, as this could bruise the flesh.*

ABOVE *Cut away the fins and tail with either a sharp knife or a pair of scissors to pan dress the fish. A pan-dressed fish may have the head cut away as well, but if the fish is to be filleted or cut into steaks, this step may not be necessary.*

GUTTING A FISH

Frequently, fish viscera (guts) are removed soon after the fish is taken from the water, right on the fishing boat. The enzymes in the viscera can begin to break down the flesh rapidly, leading to spoilage. If a fish has not been gutted, this step should be performed right after it has been scaled. A salmon is used to illustrate the technique for round fish and a flounder for flat fish.

Round Fish

Flat Fish

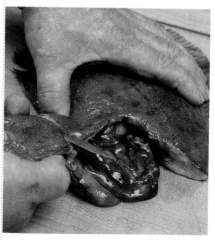

1 (TOP) *To gut a round fish, make a slit in the fish's belly.*

2 (BOTTOM) *Pull the guts away.*

3 (ABOVE) *Rinse the belly cavity thoroughly under cold running water to remove all traces of viscera and blood.*

1 (TOP) *To gut a flat fish, cut around the head, making a V-shaped notch.*

2 (BOTTOM) *Pull the head away from the body, twisting it. The guts will come away with the head.*

CUTTING FISH INTO STEAKS

Fish steaks are simply cross-cuts of the fish and are relatively easy to cut. The fish is scaled, gutted, and trimmed of its fins. Steaks can be of virtually any thickness. Darnes, a French term, are thick steaks. There are few flat fish large enough to cut into steaks; halibut is one that can be fabricated in this fashion.

Round Fish	Flat Fish

3 (ABOVE) *Rinse the belly cavity thoroughly under cold running water to remove all traces of viscera and blood.*

ABOVE *Scale, gut, and trim the round fish (in this case salmon). Using a chef's knife, make crosswise cuts through the fish to make steaks of the desired size.*

1 (TOP) *Scale, gut, and trim the flat fish (in this case halibut). Cut the fish in half along the backbone with a chef's knife.*

2 (BOTTOM) *Make crosswise cuts through the halved flat fish to the size desired.*

Fillets are one of the most common fabrications for fish. These boneless and (usually) skinless fish pieces can be sautéed, grilled, baked, or formed into paupiettes or cut into tranches or goujonettes.

Round Fish

Round fish are fabricated into two fillets, one from each side of the fish. Lay the fish on a cutting board with the backbone parallel to the work surface and the head on the same side as your dominant hand.

1 (ABOVE) *Using a filleting knife, cut behind the head and gill plates. Angle the knife so that the cutting motion is down and away from the body. This cut does not cut the head of the fish away from the body.*

2 (ABOVE) *Without removing the knife, turn it so that the cutting edge is pointing toward the tail of the fish. Position the knife so that the handle is lower than the tip of the blade. This will improve the yield by keeping the knife's edge aimed at the bones, rather than the flesh. Run the blade down the length of the fish, cutting against the backbone. Avoid sawing the knife back and forth.*

3 (TOP) *By cutting evenly and smoothly, you will split the tail, as shown. Lay the fillet skin side down on the work surface or in a hotel pan.*

4 (BOTTOM) *Without turning the fish over, insert the blade just underneath the backbone. Lay your guiding hand flat on top of the bone structure to keep the fish stable. Keep the knife parallel to the cutting surface.*

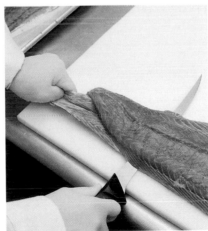

5 (TOP) *Run the blade the entire length of the fillet. The cutting edge should be angled upward very slightly to cut against the bone.*

6 (BOTTOM) *Remove the belly bones by making smooth strokes against the bones to cut them cleanly away.*

7 (TOP) *Cut away the remnants of the backbone by running the blade just underneath the line of backbone, lifting it up and away from the fillet as you cut.*

8 (BOTTOM) *To remove the skin, lay the fillet parallel to the edge of the cutting surface. Hold the knife so that the cutting edge is against the skin; pull skin taut with your guiding hand as you cut the fillet free.*

9 (ABOVE) *Locate the pin bones by running a fingertip over the fillet. Use needle-nose pliers or tweezers to pull out the bones. Pull them out in the direction of the head of the fillet (with the grain) to avoid ripping the flesh.*

Flat Fish

Flat fish can be fabricated into two fillets, one from the top and one from the bottom of the fish. They can also be fabricated into four fillets by remov- ing the fillet from each side of the backbone on the top and again on the bottom of the fish. These fillets are sometimes known as quarter fillets.

Making Two Fillets

Making Four (or Quarter) Fillets

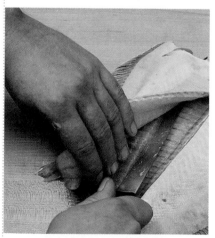

1 (ABOVE) *To make two fillets from a flat fish, use a filleting knife to cut the flesh away from the bones, start-ing on an outer edge and working from the tail toward the head.*

2 (TOP) *Adjust the direction and length of your strokes to go over the ridge of bones in the center of the fillet. Hold the fillet up and away from the bones as you work to see the bone structure.*

3 (BOTTOM) *Continue cutting to the other edge and remove the top fillet in a single piece. Repeat on the other side.*

1 (TOP) *Position the fish with the head pointing away from you and cut to one side of the center ridge.*

2 (BOTTOM) *Make cuts along the bones, working from the center to the edge.*

Dover Sole

Dover sole is handled in a special way. Many chefs like to skin the fish before filleting. The skin is freed from the tail using a filleting knife, and then it is simply pulled away.

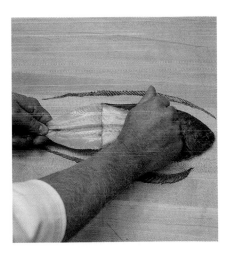

3 (ABOVE) *After the fillet is removed, you can see the roe sack and the belly portion. These should be trimmed away from the fillet as part of its preparation for cooking.*

1 (TOP) *Cut away the fins with kitchen scissors.*

2 (BOTTOM) *Make an initial cut to free the skin from the flesh at the tail.*

3 (ABOVE) *Hold the tail firmly and pull the skin away before filleting.*

TRANCHE

A tranche is simply a slice of the fillet. It is cut by holding the knife at an angle while cutting to expose more surface area and give the piece of fish a larger appearance. A tranche can be cut from any relatively large fillet of fish—for example, salmon, halibut, or tuna. Though this cut is normally associated with sautéed or pan-fried dishes, a tranche is often grilled or broiled.

GOUJONETTE

The name for this cut is derived from the French name for a small fish, the *goujon*. Goujonettes are small strips cut from a fillet; they are often breaded or dipped in batter and then deep-fried. This cut has about the same dimensions as an adult's index finger. Goujonettes are normally cut from lean white fish, such as sole or flounder.

PAUPIETTE

A paupiette is a rolled thin fillet, often—but not necessarily—filled with a forcemeat or other stuffing. Properly prepared, it resembles a large cork. Paupiettes are generally made from lean fish, such as flounder or sole, although they may also be made from some moderately fatty fish, such as trout or salmon. The most common preparation technique for paupiettes is shallow-poaching.

ABOVE *Using a very sharp slicer, slice across the fillet at approximately a 45-degree angle. The greater the angle of the knife, the more surface area will be exposed.*

ABOVE *Make even, finger-size cuts from the prepared fillet by cutting at an angle across the grain of the flesh.*

ABOVE *Prepare a fillet and trim as necessary. Then roll the fillet, working from the head to the tail. Stand the rolled fish on one of its edges.*

SHELLFISH FABRICATION

The main shellfish categories are crustaceans, with jointed skeletons on the exterior of their bodies; molluscs, with a single (univalve) or a hinged (bivalve) shell; or cephalopods, with tentacles. Lobster, shrimp, crayfish, and crab, all crustaceans; molluscs, including clams, oysters, and mussels; and cephalopods, like squid and octopus, are prepared before cooking using a variety of fabrication techniques.

WORKING WITH LIVE LOBSTER

Lobster is best when purchased alive. The first step in preparing a lobster to boil or steam is to kill it. Lobsters can also be split before they are broiled or baked.

The edible meat can be removed from a lobster, as shown, to produce a large tail portion and intact claw sections as well as smaller pieces from the knuckles and legs. The lobster's tomalley and coral (if any) should be removed and used as an ingredient in stuffing, sauce, or butter.

1 (ABOVE) *Leave the bands on the lobster's claws and lay it, stomach-side down, on a work surface. Insert the tip of a chef's knife into the base of the head.*

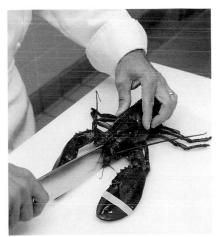

2 (ABOVE) *Pull the knife all the way down through the shell, splitting the head in half.*

3 (ABOVE) *Split the tail by reversing the direction of the lobster and positioning the tip of the knife at the point where you made your initial cut. Then, cut through the shell of the tail section.*

COOKED LOBSTER

The flesh of a lobster or other crustacean adheres tightly to the shell until it has been cooked. Lobster that will be served out of the shell or used in salads, stuffings, or as a garnish can be cooked whole by steaming, grilling, or deep poaching. Once the lobster is cool enough to handle, the meat can be removed from the shell easily.

1 (TOP) *Hold the tail section securely in one hand, hold the body of the lobster with the other. Twist your hands in opposite directions, pulling the tail away from the body.*

2 (BOTTOM) *Pull the tail meat out of the shell. It should come away in one piece.*

3 (TOP) *Use the heel of a chef's knife to crack the claws.*

4 (BOTTOM) *Use your fingers to pry the shell away from the meat. The claw meat should also come out in a single piece, retaining the shape of the claw.*

5 (TOP) *Use the knife to cut through the knuckles.*

6 (BOTTOM) *Pull out the knuckle meat.*

Shrimp are cleaned by removing the shell and then the vein that runs along the back of the shrimp, either before or after cooking. Shrimp that have been boiled or steamed in the shell are moister and plumper than shrimp that were peeled and deveined before cooking. Shrimp that will be served cold — in appetizers or salads, for example — can be cooked in the shell. Shrimp dishes that are sautéed or grilled usually call for the shrimp to be peeled and deveined before cooking. The shells can be reserved for other uses, such as making shrimp stock, bisque, or shellfish butters.

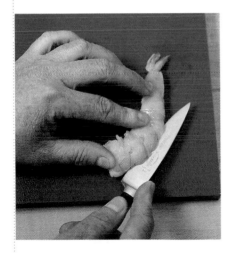 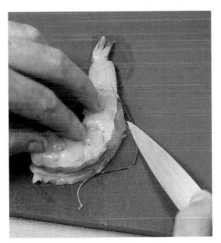 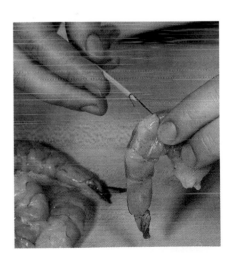

1 (ABOVE) *To devein shrimp, lay the shelled shrimp on a work surface, with the curved outer edge of the shrimp on the same side as your cutting hand. Slice into the shrimp with a paring or utility knife; make a shallow cut for deveining, a deeper cut for butterflying the shrimp.*

2 (ABOVE) *Use the tip of the knife to scrape out the vein, or intestinal tract.*

ABOVE *As an alternative, to remove the vein without cutting the shrimp, hook it with a toothpick or skewer and pull it out completely.*

CLEANING AND PICKING CRAYFISH

Crayfish share many similarities with lobster, but they are much smaller. (They can also be purchased frozen, whole or as just tails.) It is relatively simple to remove the vein from the crayfish before cooking, though this may be done afterward, if preferred. If live, pick them through and discard any dead ones. Remove the vein before or after cooking. Crayfish may be boiled or steamed in the shell. They can be served as is, whole, or they can be peeled after cooking to pick out the tail meat. Techniques for removing the vein and peeling the tail meat are shown here.

CLEANING SOFT-SHELLED CRAB

A seasonal favorite, soft-shelled crabs are considered a great delicacy. They are not especially difficult to clean once their various parts are identified.

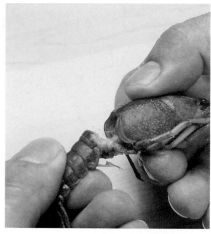

1 (ABOVE) *To remove the intestine from live uncooked crayfish, gently twist the middle fan of the tail to the left and right, then pull it away from the tail. The intestine will come away, as shown.*

2 (TOP) *Poach or steam the crayfish, and allow to cool until they can be handled. Pull the tail section away from the body. The vein can be pulled away from the cooked meat at this point, if not already removed.*

3 (BOTTOM) *Crack open the shell and pull the tail meat away.*

1 (TOP) *Peel back the pointed shell and scrape away the gill filament on each side.*

2 (BOTTOM) *Cut the eyes and mouth away from head just behind the eyes, and squeeze gently to force out the green bubble, which has an unpleasant flavor.*

Soft-shelled crabs are commonly prepared by sautéing or pan-frying, and the shell may be eaten along with the meat.

Oysters and clams are sold live in the shell and already shucked, but since they are often served on the half shell, it is important to be able to open them with ease. In addition, freshly shucked oysters and clams are often used for cooked dishes.

Scrub all mollusks well with a brush under cold running water before opening them. Any that remain open when tapped are dead and should be discarded. If a shell feels unusually heavy or light, check it. Occasionally, empty shells or shells that have filled with clay or sand will be found.

Oysters

Oysters are opened by prying open the hinge holding the two shells together. When opening oysters (and clams), be sure to reserve any juices, which are sometimes referred to as liquor. The liquor adds great flavor to soups, stews, and stocks.

3 (TOP) *Bend back the tail flap (or apron) and pull with a slight twisting motion. The intestinal vein is drawn out of the body at the same time.*

4 (BOTTOM) *The cleaned crab with the gill filaments, head, and tail flap removed.*

1 (ABOVE) *Wear a wire mesh glove to hold the oyster, positioned so that the hinged side is facing outward. Work the tip of an oyster knife into the hinge holding the upper and lower shells together and twist it to break open the hinge.*

2 (ABOVE) *Once open, slide the knife over the inside of the top shell to release the oyster from the shell. Make a similar stroke to release the oyster from the bottom shell.*

Clams

Wear a wire mesh glove to protect the hand holding the clam. Work the side of a clam knife into the seam between the upper and lower shells.

Mussels

Mussels are rarely served raw, but the method for cleaning them before steaming and poaching is similar to that used for clams. Unlike clams and oysters, mussels often have a dark, shaggy beard. It is normally removed before cooking.

1 (ABOVE) *Place the clam in your hand so that the hinged side is toward the palm of your hand. The fingers of your gloved hand can be used to both help guide the knife and give it extra force.*

2 (TOP) *Twist the blade slightly, like a key in a lock, to pry open the shell.*

3 (BOTTOM) *Once the shell is open, slide the knife over the inside of the top shell to release the clam from the shell. Make a similar stroke to release the clam from the bottom shell.*

1 (TOP) *Hold the mussel under cold running water. Use a brush with stiff bristles to thoroughly scrub the mussel and remove all sand, grit, and mud from the outer shell.*

2 (BOTTOM) *Pull the beard away from the shell. Removing the beard kills the mussel, so perform this step as close to service as possible.*

Octopus and squid belong to a category of shellfish known as cephalopods. They must be properly cleaned and cut to make the most of their flavor and texture in any cooked dish. Small squid and octopi are tender and moist when properly handled, even when cooked quickly and at high temperatures. Larger ones are better prepared by braising or stewing.

Octopus

Octopus is typically sold already cleaned. However, you may need to occasionally remove the viscera and beak (sometimes known as the eye). If the octopus you purchase has already been cleaned, simply cut the head away from the legs, and cut into the appropriate size. Baby octopi are typically cooked whole.

1 (ABOVE) *Use the tip of a filleting knife to cut around the eye and lift it from the octopus.*

2 (ABOVE) *Peel the skin away from the body by pulling firmly.*

3 (ABOVE) *Pull the suction cups away from the tentacles if desired. The octopus is ready to use.*

Squid

The squid mantle can be cut into rings to sauté, pan fry, or deep fry; or the squid may be left whole to grill or braise, with or without a stuffing. If desired, the ink sac can be saved and used to prepare various dishes, which will turn a dramatic black color.

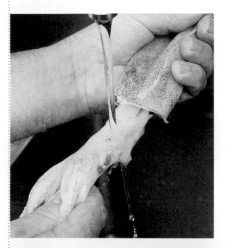 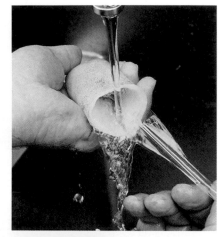 

1 (TOP) *Pull the mantle and the tentacles apart under running water. The eye, ink sac, and intestines will come away with the tentacles.*

2 (BOTTOM) *Pull away as much of the skin as possible from the mantle. Discard the skin.*

3 (TOP) *Pull the transparent quill from the mantle and discard.*

4 (BOTTOM) *Cut the tentacles away from the head by making a cut just above the eye. If desired, the ink sac may be reserved. Discard the rest of the head.*

5 (ABOVE) *Open the tentacles to expose the beak. Pull it away and discard. The tentacles may be left whole if they are small or cut into pieces if large.*

CHAPTER SEVENTEEN

Some cooking methods rely on dry heat without fats or oils. The food is cooked either by a direct application of radiant heat (grilling and broiling) or by indirect heat in an oven (roasting and baking). The result of these cooking methods is a highly flavored exterior and a moist interior.

GRILLING AND BROILING, ROASTING AND BAKING

GRILLING AND BROILING

Grilling and broiling are quick techniques that are used for naturally tender, portion-size or smaller pieces of meat, poultry, or fish. By contrast, roasting and baking require a longer cooking time and are frequently used with larger cuts of meat, whole birds, and dressed fish.

Grilling cooks food with radiant heat from a source located below it. Some of the juices are actually reduced directly on the food while the rest drip away. Grilled foods have a smoky, slightly charred flavor resulting from the flaring of the juices and fats that are rendered as the food cooks, as well as from direct contact with the rods of the grill rack.

Broiling is similar to grilling but uses a heat source located above the food rather than below. Frequently, delicate foods like lean white fish are brushed with butter or oil, put on a heated, oiled sizzler platter, and then placed on the rack below the heat source instead of directly on the rods. Items prepared in this manner may still be referred to as "broiled" on a menu, even though this is not broiling in the strictest sense of the word and is actually closer to baking.

TENDER PORTION-SIZE CUTS of poultry, cuts of meat from the loin, rib, or top round areas, and fillets of such fatty fish as tuna and salmon are suited to grilling and broiling. Lean fish may also be grilled or broiled if they are coated with oil or an oil-based marinade.

If necessary, pound meats and fish lightly to even their thickness. Meat should be trimmed of any fat, silverskin, and gristle. Some foods are cut into strips, chunks, or cubes and then threaded on skewers. The food itself should be seasoned and in some cases lightly oiled.

Different parts of the grill are hotter than others. Divide the grill into zones of varying heat intensity, including a very hot section for quickly searing foods and an area of moderate to low heat for slow cooking and for holding foods. (If the grill is wood or charcoal fired, set aside an area for the igniting fuel, which is too hot and smoky to cook foods over.) Zones may also be allocated for different types of foods, in order to prevent an undesirable transfer of flavors. Developing a system for placing foods on the grill or broiler, whether by food type or by range of doneness, helps speed work on the line.

Special woods such as mesquite, hickory, or apple are frequently used to impart a special flavor. Like hardwood chips, herb stems, grapevine trimmings, and other aromatics can be soaked in cold water; they are then thrown on the grill fire to create aromatic smoke. The sauce that accompanies a grilled item is prepared separately.

Pan-grilling involves cooking foods on top of the stove in a heavy cast-iron or other warp-resistant metal pan over intense heat. Special pans with thick ridges, which create marks similar to a grill and which

FOR A SINGLE ENTRÉE-SIZE PORTION, YOU WILL NEED:

a portion-size cut of meat, poultry, or fish; 6 to 8 ounces / 170 to 225 grams is a common standard (although some operations have their own standards)

seasonings, including salt and pepper or marinades, rubs, glazes, or barbecue sauce, if desired

sauces and other accompaniments, including compound butters, brown sauces, vegetable coulis, or salsas.

hold the food up and away from any juices or fat that might collect, may be used.

Grills and broilers must be well maintained and kept clean to produce a good-quality grilled or broiled entrée. Take the time to prepare the grill before service, during service, and at the end of service.

It is necessary to re-lubricate the rods throughout a service period, so keep a small container of oil and a cloth as part of the grill station mise en place.

Metal skewers need to be cleaned and oiled before use; wooden skewers should be soaked in water to prevent them from charring too much or catching on fire. Sizzler plates, tongs, offset spatulas, flexible spatulas, and brushes to apply glazes, marinades, or barbecue sauces should be part of the grill station's equipment mise en place, as well as all items necessary for service (heated plates, spoons, or ladles).

Hand racks for delicate foods or those that might be awkward to turn easily should also be cleaned and oiled between uses to prevent the skin from sticking and tearing.

TOP *Scour the rods well with a wire grill brush between service periods to remove any build-up of charred food particles.*

BOTTOM *Rub the rods with a cloth dipped in vegetable oil to lubricate and clean them before preheating the grill.*

ABOVE *Be sure that the collar on the handle is well secured once the food has been properly positioned.*

1. Place the seasoned food on the preheated grill or broiler rods to start cooking and to mark it.

It does make a difference which side of the food goes onto the grill first. The best-looking, or presentation, side always goes face down on the rods first. When the food comes into contact with the heated rods, marks are charred onto the surface of the food. To mark foods with a crosshatch on a grill or broiler, gently work the spatula or tongs under the food and give it a quarter turn (90°).

Because many barbecue sauces contain sugar and burn easily, it is usually a good idea to partially cook the food before applying the sauce. That way, as the food finishes cooking, the sauce glazes and caramelizes lightly without burning. A single coat of sauce may be applied to each side of the food, or, to build up a thicker, slightly crusty coat of sauce, the food may be brushed repeatedly with light coats of sauce.

2. Turn the food over and continue cooking to the desired doneness.

Since most foods cooked by grilling or broiling are relatively thin and tender, they do not require much more cooking time once they have been turned over. Thicker cuts or those that must be cooked to a higher internal doneness may need to be moved to the cooler portion of the grill or broiler, so that they don't develop a charred exterior. Or they may be removed from the grill or broiler altogether and finished in the oven.

For banquets, foods can be quickly marked on the rods of a grill or broiler, just barely cooking the outer layers of the food. Then they can be laid out on racks over sheet pans and finished in the oven. This approach allows you to expand the potential output of the grill or broiler. For food safety reasons, exercise extreme care in chilling the food quickly if it is to be held for any length of time.

3. Evaluate the quality of the finished grilled or broiled food.

Properly prepared grilled and broiled foods have a distinctly smoky flavor, which is enhanced by a certain amount of charring and by the addition to the grill of hardwood or sprigs or stalks of some herbs. This smoky flavor and aroma should not overpower the food's natural flavor and the charring should not be so extensive that it gives the food a bitter or carbonized taste. Any marinades or glazes should support and not mask the food's natural flavor.

ABOVE *Let the food cook undisturbed on the first side before turning it completely over. This develops better flavor and also lets the food's natural fats (if any) to release the food from the grill without tearing.*

ABOVE *Even thin pieces of meat or fish will retain some heat, allowing them to continue to cook after they have been removed from the heat. Remove the meat or fish when it is still slightly underdone, so it does not end up overcooked by the time it is served.*

ABOVE *Compound butter is a common accompaniment to grilled and broiled foods. Be sure to warm dishes including compound butters under a broiler or salamander or in a hot oven very briefly so that the butter sauces the entrée.*

salt, as needed

pepper, as needed

10 sirloin steaks (8 oz / 225 g each)

vegetable oil, as needed

10 oz / 300 g MAÎTRE D'HÔTEL BUTTER (recipe follows)

GRILLED (OR BROILED) SIRLOIN STEAK

1 Season the steaks with salt and pepper and dip in oil. Allow any excess to drain away before placing on rods.

2 Place the steak presentation side down on the grill or broiler rods. Grill or broil undisturbed for about 2 minutes. (Optional: Give each steak a quarter turn — 90° — during broiling to achieve grill marks.)

3 Turn the steaks over and complete cooking to the desired doneness, about 2 to 4 minutes more (135°F/57°C for rare, 145°F/63°C for medium rare, 160°F/71°C for medium, 170°F/77°C for well done).

4 Top each steak with a slice of the maître d'hôtel butter and heat under a broiler or salamander until the butter begins to melt. Serve at once.

MAKES 10 PORTIONS

MAÎTRE D'HÔTEL BUTTER

makes 10 ounces/285 grams, or ten portions

8 oz / 225 g unsalted butter, room temperature

2 oz / 60 g minced parsley

2 tsp / 10 mL lemon juice

salt, as needed

pepper, as needed

1 Work the butter by hand or with a paddle attachment until it is soft. Add the remaining ingredients and blend well. Adjust the seasoning with salt and pepper.

2 The compound butter is ready to use now, or it may be rolled into a log or piped into shapes and chilled for later service.

Pimiento Butter Prepare the compound butter as directed above, replacing the parsley with an equal amount of very fine dice roasted pimientos or red peppers.

Basil Butter Prepare the compound butter as directed above, replacing the parsley with an equal amount of finely minced basil.

Sun-Dried Tomato and Oregano Butter Prepare the compound butter as directed above, including 1 tbsp/15 mL minced oregano and 1 oz/30 g very fine dice sun-dried tomatoes.

ROASTING

Roasting, whether by pan roasting, baking, smoke roasting, or poêléing, is a way of cooking by indirect heat in an oven. Spit roasting is more like grilling or broiling. Either way, the result is a crusty exterior and tender interior.

Spit roasting, one of the earliest cooking methods, involves placing the food on a rod, which is turned either manually or with a motor. The radiant heat given off by a fire or gas jets cooks the food while constant turning creates a basting effect and ensures that the food cooks evenly. The tradition of serving roasted and grilled foods on toasted bread or a crouton began when pieces of bread were placed below the spit-roasting food to trap escaping juices. In contemporary kitchens, drip pans are placed under the spit.

Roasting, as it is most often practiced today, however, is more similar to baking than it is to spit roasting. Roasted foods are cooked through contact with dry, heated air held in a closed environment, an oven. As the outer layers become heated, the food's natural juices turn to steam and penetrate the food more deeply. The rendered juices, also called pan-drippings or fond, are the foundation for sauces prepared while the roast rests. Roasting commonly refers to large, multiportion meat cuts, whole birds, and dressed fish.

Baking, on the other hand, is the term used for portion-size foods that are cooked in the oven. Another difference between the two is that roasted foods are frequently seared first in hot fat on the stovetop or in the oven, while baked foods are not. Still, there are no ironclad distinctions in modern kitchens: Which foods are roasted and which are baked is largely a matter of usage.

SMOKE ROASTING IS AN ADAPTATION of roasting that allows foods to take on a rich, smoky flavor. The food cooks in a smokebath, in a tightly closed roasting pan, or in a smoking set-up. This can be done over an open flame or in the oven. Unlike smoked foods made in traditional charcuterie operations, the food does not have to be brined and cured before smoking. Smoke roasting does not preserve foods, and any food left too long in the smokebath can develop an acrid, unappetizing aroma and taste.

Poêléing, a technique most often associated with white meats and game birds, is sometimes called butter roasting. Meats are cooked in butter and their own juices in a covered vessel on a bed of aromatic vegetables known as a *matignon*. The matignon becomes a garnish served as part of the sauce.

Tender meats from the rib and loin give the best results. Tender cuts from the leg, such as top round, are also excellent when roasted. Young, tender birds may be roasted whole, as may dressed fish. Chicken and fish are roasted whole or cut into pieces and baked.

Trim away any excess fat and silverskin. Keeping a layer of fat or poultry skin helps to baste foods naturally as they roast. Season meats, poultry, and fish before roasting to fully develop their flavor. For additional flavor during roasting, herbs or aromatic vegetables may be used to stuff the cavity or to insert under the skin.

Foods such as whole birds, chicken breasts, and chops are frequently stuffed before roasting. Season the stuffing and chill it to below 40°F/4°C before combining it with raw meat, fish, or poultry. Allow enough time for the seasonings to interact

FOR AN ENTRÉE-SIZE PORTION OF MEAT, POULTRY, OR FISH, YOU WILL NEED:

meat, fish, poultry, trimmed as desired, trussed, or tied (may be portioned before roasting or baking, or carved into portions after roasting)

seasonings

2 fluid ounces/60 milliliters prepared pan sauce or pan gravy or other sauce as appropriate

TO PREPARE PAN GRAVY, YOU WILL NEED:

stock (fortified or regular)

mirepoix or other aromatic vegetables/ingredients

a thickener such as roux or pure starch slurry. In some cases, the puréed mirepoix may be used to thicken. Reduction is used to thicken some pan sauces.

with the food before starting to roast. Adding a hot stuffing to a cold food could result in food poisoning. Keep all foods at the correct temperature at each stage of preparation.

Place fresh herbs in the cavity of a bird before trussing for a simple stuffing. Or, rub seasonings on the skin or slip them under the skin.

A good roasting pan is flat-bottomed with relatively low sides to encourage hot air to circulate freely around the roasting food. Select a pan that holds the food comfortably but is not so large that the pan juices scorch. Food to be roasted may be set on a roasting rack, which permits the hot air to be in contact with all of the food's surface, but good results are also possible when foods are set directly in very shallow roasting or baking pans. The pan should remain uncovered.

Butcher's twine or skewers may also be needed, as well as an instant-read thermometer and a kitchen fork. An additional pan to hold the roasted food while a sauce is being made from the pan-drippings will also be needed. Strainers and skimmers or ladles are needed to prepare the sauce. Have a carving board and an extremely sharp carving knife nearby for final service.

Best results are achieved when the oven is at the correct roasting temperature before the roasting pan is put into the oven. If searing foods in a very hot oven, heat the oven to 425° to 450°F/220° to 230°C. Roast large cuts such as prime rib or turkey at a low to moderate temperature throughout roasting; a deeply browned exterior is the result of the extended roasting time. Start smaller or more delicate foods at a low to moderate temperature and then brown them at the very end of roasting by increasing the temperature of the oven from 300° to 325°F/150° to 175°C to 350° to 375°F/175° to 190°C.

BARDING AND LARDING

TWO TRADITIONAL preparation techniques for roasted foods that are naturally lean are barding (tying thin sheets of fatback, bacon, or caul fat around a food) and larding (inserting small strips of fatback into a food). The extra fat helps keep the meat tender and juicy. Venison, wild boar, game birds, and certain cuts of beef or lamb may be candidates for barding or larding. Variations using different products are also employed to add flavor to roasted foods. For example, a roast, rather than being larded with fatback, may be studded with slivers of garlic. The garlic will not have the same tenderizing effect as the fatback, but it will add plenty of flavor.

Today, with increased concern over the amount of fat in diets, every trace of visible fat or skin is often removed in an effort to reduce fat, even though the amount of fat released from skin or fat layers as foods roast does not penetrate far into the meat. Fat and skin provide some protection from the drying effects of an oven without dramatically changing the amount of fat, and foods stripped of their natural protection of fat or skin can become dry and lose flavor. If roasts are drastically trimmed, an alternative "skin" should be added in the form of a coating or crust made from such ingredients as seasoned dried potato flakes, rice flakes, corn flakes, cornmeal, or finely ground dried mushrooms. Or the fat or skin may be left in place during roasting and removed just before serving.

1. Sear the food (optional). Arrange in a roasting pan, and place in a pre-heated oven.

Once the foods have been seasoned and tied or trussed, if necessary, they may be seared in hot fat on the stovetop, under a broiler, or in a very hot oven. Some foods are not seared, especially large cuts, since an extended roasting time will produce a deeply colored exterior even without an initial searing.

2. Arrange in a roasting pan, and place in a preheated oven.

Arrange the food on in the roasting pan so that hot air can come into contact with all sides of the meat, poultry, or fish. A rack will help improve air circulation. There should be enough room in the pan so that foods fit comfortably.

3. Roast, adjusting oven temperature as necessary. Baste as necessary throughout cooking time.

There are several different theories regarding oven temperatures for roasting. Some items are traditionally roasted very quickly at high temperatures. Others are begun at low temperatures, then finished at a higher temperature. Still others are started at a high temperature, then finished at lower temperatures. In all cases, it is necessary to monitor the cooking speed to avoid over- or under-cooking foods.

Basting returns some moisture to the food, preventing it from drying out. The basting liquid also imparts additional flavor. Alternative basting liquids such as melted butter, oil, or marinades are particularly useful if the food is lean and does not release enough fat of its own for basting.

ABOVE *The birds are comfortably arranged on a rack, with enough room for hot air to circulate around them. Wing tips, which will be part of the pan sauce, are added directly to the pan to brown.*

ABOVE *The fat and juices released by the food itself are the traditional basting liquid, but a separately prepared basting liquid, such as a marinade, glaze, or flavored or plain butter, may also be used.*

4. Add mirepoix or other aromatic ingredients for a pan sauce or gravy to the roasting pan (optional).

Onions, carrots, celery, garlic, or other aromatic vegetables or herbs may be added to the roasting pan to brown and roast in the pan drippings. They take on a deep color and absorb some of the flavor from the drippings, so that they can properly flavor and color the finished pan sauce.

5. Roast foods to the correct doneness and let them rest before serving.

Meats, fish, poultry, and game are generally cooked to a specified internal temperature (see page 351). The most reliable way to determine doneness in roasted foods is to use a thermometer. When the meat is nearly done, remove it from the pan and allow it to rest. Cover the food loosely with foil to keep it moist and place it in a warm spot to rest.

Allow a resting period of about 5 minutes for small items, 15 to 20 minutes for medium items, and up to 45 minutes for very large roasts. This is done because as foods roast their juices become concentrated in

the center. A resting period before cutting into the food gives the juices time to redistribute evenly throughout. Resting also lets the temperature of the food equalize, which benefits texture, aroma, and flavor. Resting also plays a key role in carryover cooking, which should be thought of as the last stage of cooking.

Though less accurate than a thermometer, some chefs rely on a doneness test that involves using a metal skewer inserted into the food (at an angle, away from bones, and in the item's thickest portion). Hold the skewer just below your lower lip. The hotter the skewer feels to the lip, the more well done the item is.

ABOVE *If preparing a pan sauce or gravy, add the mirepoix to the roasting pan during the last 30 to 45 minutes of cooking time, so that it can develop a good rich flavor and color.*

ABOVE *To get the most accurate read, the thermometer must be inserted at least as far as the small dimple on the stem. Notice that the stem is inserted into the item's thickest part, away from any bones.*

ABOVE *Another way to test a whole roasted bird for doneness is to pierce the bird at the point where the thigh meets the breast. When done, juices run nearly clear. Or check the juices that have accumulated in the cavity. When done, they no longer have a red or pink hue.*

6. Brown the food and clarify the fat.
Roasted foods are usually served with a pan sauce based on the accumulated drippings from the food. Jus and pan gravy are the most frequently prepared pan sauces. Before preparing any pan sauce, be sure that the drippings are not scorched. Scorched drippings result in a bitter, unpalatable sauce.

Cook the drippings over medium heat until the mirepoix is browned and the fat is transparent and clear. The juices will have separated from the fat and cooked down to a fond on the bottom of the pan.

7. Degrease the pan and prepare the roux.
For a pan gravy, pour off the fat, but leave enough to prepare a roux by cooking the fat and some flour together.

8. (Optional) prepare a jus lié.
To prepare a jus-style sauce, pour off all of the remaining fat and deglaze the pan, if desired, with wine or another liquid. Add a stock that suits the meat. Simmer until the flavor is well developed, about 15 to 20 minutes. Skim the jus as it simmers to remove fat and particles from the surface. Adjust the seasoning and strain to finish the jus. To prepare a jus lié, thicken the jus with an arrowroot or cornstarch slurry just before straining.

ABOVE *To make a pan gravy, place the roasting pan on the stovetop and cook over direct heat to reduce the drippings in the pan and clarify the fat.*

TOP *Pour off the excess fat, leaving only enough to prepare an adequate amount of roux.*

BOTTOM *Sprinkle in the measured flour and stir frequently for a few minutes to brown the roux before adding the liquid.*

9. Add the stock and simmer the pan gravy or jus until thickened and well flavored. Strain.

Hold finished pan gravy or jus in a steam table or water bath like any other sauce. To keep a skin from forming on the pan gravy, top with a layer of clarified butter, a piece of parchment, or a tight-fitting cover.

10. Carve, if necessary, and serve with sauce and garnish, if desired. Large roasted foods must be carved or cut into portions correctly to make the most of the item. The three items carved in the sidebar on the following pages — a whole duck, a rib roast of beef, and a ham — should be considered prototypes. For example, because they are similar in structure, a ham would be carved in the same manner as a leg of lamb.

11. Evaluate the quality of roasted foods.

The flavor and aroma of a food that has been well roasted contribute to an overall sensation of fullness, richness, and depth. This is due in part to the nature of the food and in part to the browning process. The color varies according to the type of food, but roasted foods in general are nicely browned. The color has a direct bearing on the flavor as well as appearance. Foods that are too pale lack eye appeal and depth of flavor. Well roasted foods are tender and moist. The skin, if left on the food, should be crisp, creating a contrast with the texture of the meat.

TOP *Gradually add the stock to the pan and stir constantly to work out any lumps. Be sure the liquid is not too hot or it may spatter.*

BOTTOM *Use a fine wire-mesh sieve to strain the pan gravy into a clean holding container.*

ABOVE *A 2½-lb/1-kg chicken typically produces two entrée-sized portions. Cut the chicken in half through the breastbone. Be sure to wear gloves when working with foods that will not be cooked after handling and before service to the guest.*

CARVING A ROAST DUCK

When a guest orders duck, this presentation is the most user-friendly. Most of the bones are removed so that the leg portion has only the drumstick bone and the breast portion has a single wing bone. The two are nestled together so that the boneless breast and thigh meat overlap. The guest can simply cut into the meat, without having to work around bones.

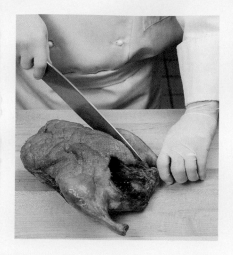

Cut the legs away from body at the point where leg meets the breast. Pulling away the leg will reveal the ball joint.

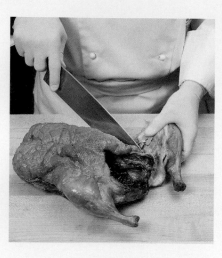

Pull the leg away from the body and cut through the ball-and-socket joint to sever it completely.

Use the tip of the knife to cut along either side of the keel bone.

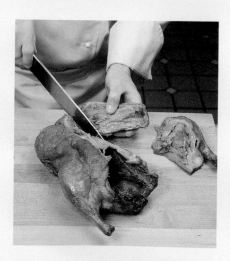

Carve the breast away from the rib cage with as little trim loss as possible by making the edge of the blade run as close to the bones as you can.

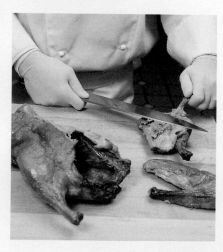

Pull the thigh bone up and away from the thigh meat. Use the knife as shown to separate the bone at the leg joint.

To nest the leg and breast portions for presentation, position the leg portion on the bottom and the breast portion overlapping the leg, with the drumstick bone and the wing bone on opposite sides.

CARVING A RIB ROAST

A beef rib roast is a large cut, and is easiest to handle when turned on its side. This carving method can also be used for a rack of veal or venison. These smaller roasts need not be turned on their sides, and cuts are made from top to bottom, between the bones. The meat can be cut away from the bones, as shown here, to make slices, or the bones may be left in place to produce chops.

Lay the rib roast on its side. Using a meat slicer, make parallel cuts from the outer edge toward the bones.

Use the knife tip to cut the slices of meat away from the bone. Store cut side up if need be to prevent juice loss.

CARVING A LEG OF HAM IN THE DINING ROOM

This carving method may also be used for legs of lamb and steamship rounds.

To steady the leg, hold the shank bone firmly in one hand with a clean side towel or cloth napkin. Cut away the end piece. This is usually served only by special request.

Make parallel cuts from the shank end down to the bone. Continue cutting slices of meat from the leg, cutting away from the bone to make even slices. The initial cuts are made vertically, until the bone is reached.

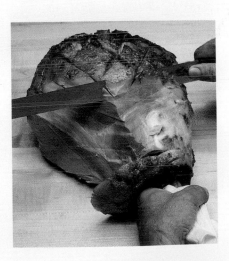

When the slices become very large, begin to cut the meat at a slight angle, first from the left side, then from the right side, alternating until the leg is entirely sliced.

Holding the ham steady, trim away the excess fat cover using a chef's knife. The amount you trim away is a matter of preference, but most diners today favor a cleaner trim, such as is shown here.

Stand the ham on end, with the sirloin end resting on the board. Hold the shank end with your guiding hand to keep the ham stable. Make a cut into the lean meat just below the stifle joint on the shank end and follow the natural curve of the femur bone. Cut close to the bone for the best yield.

At the ball and socket joint, cut around the joint. This first cut will not cut the meat completely away from the bone.

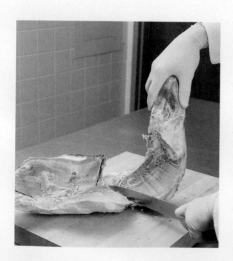

Repeat the same sequence of cuts on the second side of the bone to completely free the meat. The meat appears to have a V-shaped notch where it was cut away from the bone.

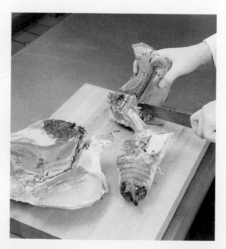

Cut away the meat from the back side of the femur bone. Try to keep the pieces of meat as intact as possible.

Carve the ham into slices with a ham or meat slicer as shown. The ham could also be sliced on an electric meat slicer, if you are preparing a large quantity for a banquet or other volume feeding situation.

5 chickens, wing tips removed (2½ lb / 1 kg each)

salt, as needed

ground white pepper, as needed

5 thyme sprigs

5 rosemary sprigs

vegetable oil or butter, as needed

4 oz / 115 g diced onion

2 oz / 60 g diced carrot

8 oz / 225 g diced celery

2 oz / 60 g flour

½ oz / 15 g tomato paste (optional)

1 pint / 480 mL CHICKEN STOCK (page 248), hot

ROAST CHICKEN WITH PAN GRAVY

1 Season the chickens with salt and pepper and place one sprig of thyme and rosemary in each cavity.

2 Rub the skin with oil and truss each chicken with twine.

3 Place the chickens, breast side up, on a rack in a roasting pan. Scatter the wing tips in the pan.

4 Roast at 400°F/205°C for 40 minutes, basting from time to time. Scatter the onions, carrots, and celery around the chicken and continue to roast another 30 to 40 minutes or until the thigh meat registers 180°F/82°C.

5 Remove the chickens from the roasting pan and allow them to rest.

6 Place the roasting pan on the stovetop and cook until the mirepoix is browned and the fat is clear. Pour off all but 1 oz/30 g of the fat.

7 Add the flour and cook out the roux for 4 to 5 minutes. (Optional: Add the tomato paste to the roux and cook out 2 minutes more.) Whisk in the stock until completely smooth.

8 Simmer the gravy for 20 to 30 minutes, or until it reaches the proper consistency and flavor. Degrease and adjust seasoning. Strain through a fine mesh sieve. Cut the chickens in half and serve with pan gravy.

MAKES 10 PORTIONS

RECIPES

BROILED SIRLOIN STEAK WITH MUSHROOM SAUCE

makes 10 portions

10 sirloin steaks (10 oz/285 g each)
salt, as needed
pepper, as needed
vegetable oil, as needed
MUSHROOM SAUCE (recipe follows)

1 Season the steaks with salt and pepper and dip in oil. Allow any excess to drain away before placing on rods.

2 Place the steaks presentation side down on the grill or broiler rods. Grill or broil undisturbed for about 2 minutes. (Optional: Give each steak a quarter turn [90°] during broiling to achieve grill marks.)

3 Turn the steaks over and complete cooking to the desired doneness, about 2 to 4 minutes more (135°F/57°C for rare, 145°F/63°C for medium rare, 160°F/70°C for medium, or 170°F/75°C for well done).

4 Top each steak with mushroom sauce. Serve at once.

MUSHROOM SAUCE

makes 10 servings

1 oz/30 g minced shallots
1¹⁄₂ oz/45 g unsalted butter
1¹⁄₂ lb/680 g sliced white mushrooms
5 fl oz/150 mL dry white wine
20 fl oz/600 mL DEMIGLACE (page 287) or JUS DE VEAU LIÉ (page 260)
salt, as needed
pepper, as needed

1 Sweat the shallots in the butter over medium heat.

2 Add the mushrooms, and continue to sauté until their juices have cooked away.

3 Add the wine to deglaze the pan. Cook until the wine is reduced. Add the demiglace or jus de veau and simmer 5 minutes more, or until the sauce has a good consistency and flavor.

4 Season with salt and pepper. Keep warm until needed.

BARBECUED STEAK WITH HERBED CRUST

makes 10 portions

BREAD CRUMB TOPPING

2 tsp/10 mL minced garlic
¹⁄₂ oz/15 g chopped parsley
6 oz/170 g bread crumbs
6 oz/170 g butter, melted
salt, as needed
pepper, as needed

10 sirloin steaks (6 oz/170 g each)
salt, as needed
pepper, as needed
1 tbsp/15 mL minced garlic
vegetable oil, as needed
12 fl oz/360 mL BARBECUE SAUCE (page 290), or as needed

1 Combine all of the ingredients for the bread crumb topping and blend well.

2 Season the steaks with salt and pepper, rub with garlic, and dip in oil. Allow any excess to drain away before placing on rods.

3 Place the steaks on the grill or broiler rods. Grill or broil undisturbed for about 2 minutes. Brush lightly with barbecue sauce. Turn the steaks over, brush with sauce, and cook about 2 minutes more, until rare (internal temperature of 135°F/57°C).

4 Top the steaks with the bread crumb mixture and finish in a hot oven to brown and crisp the topping. Serve the steaks at once, with additional barbecue sauce if desired.

BLACKENED BEEF WITH CORN AND PEPPER SAUCE

makes 10 portions

3³/₄ lb/1.75 kg trimmed beef tenderloin

BLACKENING MIXTURE

2 tbsp/30 mL CURRY POWDER (page 353)

1 tbsp/15 mL ground fennel seeds

2 tsp/10 mL salt

1 tsp cracked black pepper

pinch ground cayenne, or as needed

CORN AND PEPPER SAUCE (recipe follows)

1 Cut the beef tenderloin into 10 equal medallions, 5 to 6 oz/ 140 to 170 g each.

2 Mix together all the ingredients for the blackening mixture.

3 Season the medallions with the blackening mixture.

4 Place the medallions presentation side down on the grill rods. Grill or broil undisturbed for about 2 minutes.

5 Turn the medallions over and complete cooking to the desired doneness, about 2 to 4 minutes more (135°F/57°C for rare, 145°F/63°C for medium rare, 160°F/70°C for medium, or 170°F/75°C for well done).

6 Pool the sauce on heated plates and top each one with a medallion.

CORN AND PEPPER SAUCE

makes 10 portions

5 ears corn, husks on

6 oz/170 g large-dice onions

2 tsp/10 mL olive oil

2 oz/60 g tomato paste

10 fl oz/300 mL dry red wine

1¹/₂ pt/720 mL WHITE BEEF STOCK (page 249), or as needed

1 bay leaf

1 thyme sprig

1 tbsp/15 mL butter

6 oz/170 g red pepper brunoise

6 oz/170 g green pepper brunoise

1 tsp/5 mL minced jalapeños

¹/₂ oz/15 g garlic, minced to a paste

¹/₂ tsp/3 mL ground turmeric

1 tsp/5 mL CURRY POWDER (page 353), or as needed

1 Dampen the corn husks and roast the corn in a 375°F/190°C oven for 15 minutes. Remove the corn from the oven. Husk the ears, slice the kernels from the cob with a knife, and reserve the kernels and cobs separately.

2 Grill the cobs over hot coals until they are evenly browned. Reserve the cobs.

3 Sauté the onions in the olive oil until browned. Add the tomato paste and sauté. Add the wine and reduce until nearly dry.

4 Add the stock, bay leaf, thyme, and grilled cobs. Simmer until the sauce is reduced by one quarter. Strain the sauce and adjust seasoning. Reserve the sauce.

5 Return the pan to medium heat and melt the butter. Add the red and green peppers, reserved corn kernels, jalapeños, garlic, turmeric, and curry. Sauté the mixture until the peppers are tender.

6 Return the strained sauce to the pan and simmer until all the vegetables are tender.

BROILED STRIP STEAK WITH MARCHAND DE VIN SAUCE

makes 10 portions

10 beef strip steaks, well trimmed (5 to 6 oz/140 to 170 g each)

salt, as needed

cracked black peppercorns, as needed

vegetable oil, as needed

2 oz/60 g butter

20 fl oz/600 mL MARCHAND DE VIN SAUCE (recipe follows)

1 Season the steaks with salt and pepper and dip in oil. Allow any excess to drain away before placing on rods.

2 Place the steaks presentation side down on the grill or broiler rods. Grill or broil undisturbed for about 2 minutes. (Optional: Give each steak a quarter turn [90°] during broiling to achieve grill marks.)

3 Turn the steaks over and complete cooking to the desired doneness, about 2 to 4 minutes more (135°F/57°C for rare, 145°F/63°C for medium rare, 160°F/70°C for medium, or 170°F/75°C for well done).

4 Return the sauce to a simmer and finish with the butter. Serve the steaks at once with the sauce.

SAUCE MARCHAND DE VIN

makes 1 quart/1 liter

1 oz/30 g minced shallots

2 sprigs of thyme

1 bay leaf

½ tsp cracked black peppercorns

16 fl oz/480 mL dry red wine

1 qt/1 L JUS DE VEAU LIÉ (page 260) or DEMIGLACE (page 287)

4 oz/115 g unsalted butter, diced

1 Combine the shallots, thyme, bay leaf, peppercorns, and red wine and reduce the mixture until syrupy.

2 Add the demiglace and reduce until the sauce coats the back of a spoon. Strain the sauce.

3 Finish the sauce with the butter.

BROILED FLANK STEAK WITH BORDELAISE SAUCE

makes 10 portions

2 flank steaks (1½ to 2 lb/680 to 900 g each)

MARINADE

4 fl oz/120 mL vegetable oil

salt, as needed

pepper, as needed

2 tsp/10 mL paprika

BORDELAISE SAUCE (recipe follows)

1 Trim the flank steaks and remove all skin, membrane, and fat, if necessary.

2 Mix together all the ingredients for the marinade.

3 Pour the marinade over the steaks and marinate under refrigeration for 2 to 3 hours.

4 Broil in a preheated broiler for 3 to 5 minutes on each side. (Flank steak is most tender when cooked to 135°F/57°C for rare or 145°F/63°C for medium rare.)

5 Cut the flank steak into portions by slicing thinly on a diagonal, across the grain. Top with bordelaise sauce.

NOTE

Flank steak may be paired with a variety of sauces such as Mushroom Sauce (page 416), Corn and Pepper Sauce (page 417), Salsa Fresca (page 821), or Barbecue Sauce (page 290).

BORDELAISE SAUCE

makes 10 portions

1 oz/30 g minced shallots

2 thyme sprigs

1 bay leaf

½ tsp/3 mL cracked black peppercorns

16 fl oz/480 mL red wine

1 qt/1 L DEMIGLACE (page 287) or JUS DE VEAU LIÉ (page 260)

1 tbsp/15 mL lemon juice, or to taste

salt, as needed

pepper, as needed

4 oz/115 g diced or sliced butter

4 oz/115 g diced poached marrow (see page 371)

1 Combine the shallots, thyme, bay leaf, peppercorns, and red wine. Reduce by half over medium high heat to 8 fl oz/240 mL.

2 Add the demiglace or jus de veau and continue to simmer until the sauce has developed a good flavor and consistency.

3 Season the sauce with lemon juice, salt, and pepper. Finish by swirling in butter and folding in marrow.

BEEF TENDERLOIN WITH GARLIC GLAZE

makes 10 portions

3³⁄₄ lb/1.75 kg beef tenderloin

salt, as needed

pepper, as needed

GARLIC GLAZE

4 fl oz/120 mL glace de viande (see page 250)

6 oz/170 g puréed roasted garlic

SAUCE MARCHAND DE VIN (page 418)

1 Cut the tenderloin into 10 equal medallions, 5 to 6 oz/140 to 170 g each. Season with salt and pepper.

2 Combine all the ingredients for the garlic glaze. Season with salt and pepper.

3 Grill the medallions briefly on both sides to mark the exterior. Remove from the grill and butterfly each medallion.

4 Spread 1 oz/30 g of the garlic glaze on each medallion. Finish the medallions in a 400°F/205°C oven to the desired doneness, about 4 to 6 minutes more (135°F/57°C for rare, 145°F/63°C for medium rare, 160°F/70°C for medium, 170°F/75°C for well done). Brown the glaze lightly under a broiler if desired.

5 Serve the tenderloin with the sauce.

TENDERLOIN OF BEEF WITH BLUE CHEESE HERB CRUST

makes 10 portions

3³⁄₄ lb/1.75 kg beef tenderloin

salt, as needed

pepper, as needed

oil or clarified butter, as needed to sear

BLUE CHEESE HERB CRUST (recipe follows)

20 fl oz/600 mL DEMIGLACE (page 287) or JUS DE VEAU LIÉ (page 260)

1 Cut the tenderloin into 10 equal portions, 5 to 6 oz/140 to 170 g each. Season with salt and pepper.

2 At service, sear the medallions in the oil or butter over high heat on both sides, about 1 minute per side.

3 Pack ½ oz/15 g of the crumb mixture on top of each medallion. Bake in a 350° to 375°F/175° to 190°C oven to the desired doneness, about 4 to 6 minutes more (135°F/57°C for rare, 145°F/63°C for medium rare, 160°F/70°C for medium, or 170°F/75°C for well done). Brown the medallions under a salamander, if necessary.

4 Heat the jus de veau and pool it around each medallion.

BLUE CHEESE HERB CRUST

makes 10 portions

4 oz/115 g white bread crumbs

2¹⁄₄ oz/65 g blue cheese

½ oz/15 g chopped parsley

½ oz/15 g chopped chives

½ oz/15 g minced garlic

¼ tsp/1 mL ground white pepper

Process all ingredients to a fine crumb. Reserve and use as needed to coat broiled or roasted meats or poultry entrées.

BEEF TENDERLOIN WITH SCALLION BUTTER

makes 10 portions

3³/₄ lb/1.75 kg beef tenderloin

salt, as needed

pepper, as needed

vegetable oil, as needed

10 oz/300 g SCALLION BUTTER (recipe follows)

1 Cut the tenderloin into 10 equal medallions, 5 to 6 oz/ 140 to 170 g each.

2 Season the medallions with salt and pepper and dip in oil. Allow any excess to drain away before placing on rods.

3 Place the medallions presentation side down on the grill or broiler rods. Grill or broil undisturbed for about 2 minutes. (Optional: Give each medallion a quarter turn [90°] during broiling to achieve grill marks.)

4 Turn the medallions over and complete cooking to the desired doneness, about 2 to 4 minutes more (135°F/57°C for rare, 145°F/63°C for medium rare, 160°F/70°C for medium, 170°F/75°C for well done).

5 Top each medallion with a slice of the scallion butter; heat under a broiler or salamander until the butter begins to melt. Serve at once.

SCALLION BUTTER

makes 10 ounces/300 grams, or ten 1-ounce/30-gram portions

8 oz/225 g unsalted butter, room temperature

3 oz/85 g minced scallions (white and green portions)

2 tbsp/30 mL chopped parsley

¼ tsp/1 mL minced garlic

2 tsp/10 mL lemon juice

1 tsp/5 mL soy sauce

salt, as needed

pepper, as needed

1 Work the butter by hand or with a paddle attachment until it is soft. Add the remaining ingredients and blend well. Adjust the seasoning with salt and pepper.

2 The compound butter is ready to use now, or it may be rolled into a log or piped into shapes and chilled for later service.

Rosemary and Ginger Butter Prepare the butter as directed above and add 1 tbsp/15 mL minced rosemary, and 1 tbsp/15 mL minced ginger.

Cilantro and Lime Butter Prepare the butter as directed at left; substitute an equal amount of minced cilantro for the parsley and replace lemon juice with lime juice. Omit soy sauce. If desired, add 1 tsp/5 mL blanched minced lime zest.

Tarragon Butter Prepare the butter as directed above, substituting an equal amount of minced tarragon for the scallions. Omit the parsley and soy sauce.

STANDING RIB ROAST AU JUS

A TYPICAL OVEN-READY RIB ROAST, BONE-IN (ALSO REFERRED TO BY ITS NAMP NUMBER AS A 109), WEIGHS 20 LB/9 KG. DONENESS SHOULD BE DETERMINED BY USING AN INSTANT-READ THERMOMETER. ROASTING AT 350°F/175°C WILL TAKE 3¹/₂ TO 4 HOURS FOR RARE.

makes 25 to 30 portions

14 lb/6.3 kg beef rib roast, bone-in

salt, as needed

pepper, as needed

1¹/₂ lb/680 kg mirepoix

2 qt/2 L BROWN VEAL STOCK (page 252)

2¹/₂ oz/70 g arrowroot, diluted in cold stock or water (optional)

1 Season the beef with salt and pepper and roast to an internal temperature of 130°F/55°C.

2 Add the mirepoix about 30 minutes before the roast is done and let it brown.

3 Remove the roast and let it rest for 30 minutes.

4 Clarify the fat and reduce the pan drippings. Drain off the fat.

5 Deglaze the roasting pan with the stock. Simmer briefly, thicken with arrowroot slurry if desired, adjust seasoning, and strain.

ROAST DUCKLING WITH SAUCE BIGARADE

makes 10 portions

5 ducklings (about 3 lb/1.3 kg each)

salt, as needed

pepper, as needed

15 parsley stems

5 thyme sprigs

5 bay leaves

8 fl oz/240 mL BROWN DUCK STOCK (page 252) or BROWN VEAL STOCK (page 252)

SAUCE BIGARADE (recipe follows)

1 tbsp/15 mL orange zest julienne, blanched

30 pieces orange suprêmes

1 Rinse and trim the duckling, removing fat from body cavity (reserve for other use if desired). Place the duckling, breast side up, on a rack. Season it with salt and pepper. Place 5 parsley stems, 1 thyme sprig, and 1 bay leaf into the cavity of each bird.

2 Roast the duckling at 425°F/218°C until the juices run barely pink and the thigh meat registers 180°F/82°C. Remove the duckling from the pan and rest for at least 10 minutes before carving

3 To finish the sauce for service, degrease and deglaze the roasting pan with stock or water and strain the drippings into the bigarade sauce. Return the sauce to a simmer and adjust the seasoning if necessary. Finish the sauce with the zest and supremes.

4 Carve the duck for service by cutting away the breast from the rib and cutting the leg away from the body. Place the duck on a sizzler platter, overlapping the leg and breast portions, skin side facing up. Brush the ducklings with a small amount of the sauce and reheat until it is crisp in a 450°F/232°C oven.

5 Serve the ducklings on heated plates with the sauce.

SAUCE BIGARADE

makes 10 portions

3/4 oz/20 g sugar

1 tbsp/15 mL water

1 tbsp/30 mL white wine

1 fl oz/30 mL cider vinegar

2 fl oz/60 mL orange juice concentrate

2 oz/60 g red currant jelly

1 qt/1 L JUS DE CANARD or VEAU LIÉ (page 261) or DEMIGLACE (page 287)

salt, as needed

pepper, as needed

1 Cook the sugar and water in a saucepan over medium heat until the sugar is melted and a deep golden brown.

2 Add the wine, vinegar, orange juice concentrate, and currant jelly. Mix them well and simmer until reduced by half.

3 Add the demiglace (optional: add the strained drippings from the roasting pan if available) and simmer the sauce until a good flavor and consistency develops. Season with salt and pepper. Strain into a clean pan and keep hot for service.

PORK ROAST WITH JUS LIÉ

makes 10 portions

4¹/₂ lb/2 kg bone-in pork loin roast

¹/₂ oz/15 g minced garlic

1 tsp/5 mL minced rosemary leaves

salt, as needed

pepper, as needed

JUS LIÉ

4 oz/113.4 g small-dice onions

2 oz/small-dice carrots

2 oz/small-dice celery

4 fl oz/120 ml dry white wine

1 fl oz/30 ml tomato paste

1 qt/1 L BROWN PORK STOCK (page 252) or BROWN VEAL
   STOCK (page 252)

2 thyme sprigs

1 bay leaf

2 tbsp/30 mL arrowroot slurry, or as needed

1 Trim the pork loin and tie. Rub the roast with garlic, rosemary, salt, and pepper. Place the pork loin on a rack in a roasting pan.

2 Roast at 375°F/190°C for 1 hour, basting from time to time. Scatter the onions, carrots, and celery around the pork and continue to roast another 30 to 45 minutes or until a thermometer inserted in the center of the meat registers 160°F/70°C.

3 Remove the pork from the roasting pan and allow it to rest for 20 minutes before carving.

4 To prepare the jus lié, place the roasting pan on the stove-top and cook until the mirepoix is browned and the fat is clear. Pour off all the fat. Deglaze with the wine. Add the tomato paste and cook, stirring frequently, until it has a sweet aroma and brick red color, about 30 to 45 seconds.

5 Add the stock, stirring to release the fond completely. Add the thyme and bay leaf, and simmer the jus for about 20 to 30 minutes, or until it reaches the proper consistency and flavor. Add enough arrowroot or cornstarch slurry to thicken the sauce enough to coat the back of a spoon. Degrease and adjust seasoning.

6 Strain the jus lié through a fine mesh sieve and keep hot for service. Carve the pork loin into portions and serve with the jus lié.

BEEF WELLINGTON

makes 10 portions

1 beef tenderloin, 4 to 5 lb/1.75 to 2.25 kg

8 oz/225 g goose liver or foie gras pâté

2 oz/60 g truffle peelings, finely chopped

1 sheet PUFF PASTRY (page 942)

EGG WASH (page 874), as needed

20 fl oz/600 m MADEIRA SAUCE (recipe follows)

1 Sear the tenderloin and let cool. Spread with goose liver or foie gras pâté. Sprinkle with chopped truffles.

2 Roll dough out to ³/₁₆ in/5 mm thick. Wrap it around the tenderloin. Fold ends under. Place seam on bottom. Brush with egg wash.

3 Place on an oiled baking sheet. Bake at 350°F/175°C for about 40 minutes. Dough should be cooked thoroughly and golden brown.

4 Cut in ³/₄-in/2-cm slices. Serve the sauce on the side, in a gravy boat.

NOTE

A lighter style Beef Wellington may be prepared using phyllo dough.

MADEIRA SAUCE

makes 10 portions

20 fl oz/600 mL DEMIGLACE (page 287) or JUS DE VEAU LIÉ
   (page 260)

6 fl oz/180 mL Madeira

salt, as needed

pepper, as needed

2 oz/60 g diced butter

1 Bring the demiglace or jus de veau to a simmer, and reduce by one-fourth over medium heat.

2 Add the Madeira and simmer 2 to 3 minutes more, or until the sauce has a good flavor and consistency. Adjust seasoning with salt and pepper.

3 Swirl in butter over low heat just before serving.

SATEH OF CHICKEN

makes thirty 2 ounce/60 gram appetizer portions

4 lb/1.8 kg boneless chicken breast

MARINADE

4 fl oz/120 mL peanut oil

1 stalk lemongrass, minced

1 tbsp/15 mL minced garlic

1½ tsp/8 mL crushed chile peppers

1 tbsp/15 mL CURRY POWDER (page 353)

1 tbsp/15 mL honey

1 fl oz/30 mL nam pla or nuoc mam (Thai or Vietnamese fish sauce)

SPICY PEANUT SAUCE (recipe follows)

CUCUMBER RELISH (recipe follows)

1 Trim the chicken and cut into long thin strips.

2 Combine all of the marinade ingredients, add the meat, and let marinate under refrigeration for at least 2 hours and up to 12 hours.

3 Soak bamboo skewers in water for at least 10 minutes before you are ready to grill the satehs. Thread the chicken on the skewers, one strip per skewer. Skewered chicken can be returned to the marinade to hold until cooking time.

4 Place the skewered chicken on the grill or broiler rods. Grill or broil undisturbed for about 1 minute, turn and grill 1 minute more for medium rare, or as needed for the desired doneness. Serve the satehs with the sauce and relish.

see photograph on page 431

SPICY PEANUT SAUCE

makes 10 portions

1 fl oz/30 mL peanut oil

3 oz/85 g minced onion

½ oz/15 g minced garlic

1 oz/30 g minced lemongrass

1 kaffir lime leaf

½ tsp/3 mL crushed red pepper flakes

½ tsp/3 mL CURRY POWDER (page 353)

10 fl oz/300 mL coconut milk

2 oz/60 g peanut butter

1 oz/30 g tamarind paste

1 tbsp/15 mL nuoc mam (fish sauce)

1 tbsp/15 mL dark brown sugar

2 to 3 fl oz/60 to 90 mL CHICKEN STOCK (page 248), or as needed

2 tsp/10 mL lime juice

salt, as needed

pepper, as needed

1 Heat the oil. Add the onion, garlic, lemongrass, lime leaf, pepper flakes, and curry powder. Sauté until the mixture is well blended and aromatic, about 2 to 3 minutes.

2 Add the coconut milk, peanut butter, tamarind paste, fish sauce, brown sugar, and chicken stock. Simmer for 15 to 20 minutes, or until a good flavor develops. Adjust the consistency with chicken stock if necessary. Adjust the seasoning with lime juice, salt, and pepper to taste. Discard the lime leaf.

3 The sauce is ready to serve now or it may be cooled and stored for later service.

CUCUMBER RELISH

makes 10 portions

10 oz/280 g thin-slice cucumbers

5 oz/140 g thin-slice red onions

4 fl oz/120 mL rice wine vinegar

red pepper flakes, as needed

sugar, as needed

salt, as needed

pepper, as needed

1 Combine the cucumbers, onions, and vinegar. Toss to combine.

2 Adjust the seasoning to taste with red pepper flakes, sugar, salt, and pepper. Let the flavor develop for at least 1 hour under refrigeration. Serve chilled or at room temperature.

BEEF TERIYAKI (YAKINIKU)

makes thirty 2 ounce/60 gram appetizer portions

4 lb/1.8 kg beef tenderloin, loin, or top round, trimmed

1 pint/480 mL TERIYAKI MARINADE (page 356)

TERIYAKI SAUCE (recipe follows)

1 Cut the beef into 30 equal portions, 2 oz/60 g each. Combine with the marinade, turning to coat evenly, and marinate for at least 2 hours.

2 Place the beef on the grill or broiler rods. Grill or broil undisturbed for about 2 minutes.

3 Turn the beef over and complete cooking to the desired doneness, about 2 to 4 minutes more (135°F/57°C for rare, 145°F/63°C for medium rare, 160°F/70°C for medium, 170°F/75°C for well done).

4 Serve the beef at once with the teriyaki sauce.

TERIYAKI SAUCE

makes 3 pints/1.5 liters

1 qt/1 L CHICKEN STOCK (page 248)

1 pt/480 mL tamari sauce

7 oz/200 g sugar

4 fl oz/120 mL mirin (sweet rice wine)

4 oz/120 mL minced green onions

1 tbsp/15 mL minced ginger

1 tbsp/15 mL minced garlic

4 oz/120 mL sake

1 fl oz/30 mL rice vinegar

cornstarch slurry to thicken

1 Simmer the stock, tamari, sugar, mirin, onions, ginger, and garlic until well flavored, about 15 minutes.

2 Add the sake and vinegar to the sauce, thicken with the cornstarch slurry. The sauce should coat the back of a spoon. Keep warm.

SKEWERED BEEF AND SCALLIONS

makes 10 portions

3³/₄ lb/1.75 kg beef top butt or flank steak, trimmed

MARINADE

4 fl oz/120 mL soy sauce

1¹/₂ oz/45 g sugar

2 fl oz/60 mL sesame oil

¹/₂ oz/20 g minced garlic

¹/₂ oz/15 g minced ginger

1 tsp/5 mL ground black pepper

18 oz/510 g green onions (about 6 bunches), cut into 3¹/₂-in/ 9-cm pieces

1 Cut the meat into long thin strips, 4 x 1 x ⅛ in/ 10 x 2.5 x .5 cm.

2 Combine the ingredients for the marinade, add the beef, and marinate under refrigeration for 3 hours or overnight.

3 Soak bamboo skewers for 10 minutes. Thread the beef on the skewers, alternating with green onions.

4 Broil until medium rare.

RAZNJICI (PORK AND VEAL SKEWERS)

makes 10 portions

2 lb/900 g veal top round

2 lb/900 g pork loin

MARINADE

1³/₄ oz/50 g thinly sliced garlic

4 oz/115 g sliced onions

4 fl oz/120 mL vegetable oil

4 fl oz/120 mL lemon juice

2 tbsp/30 mL chopped parsley

salt, as needed

pepper, as needed

12 oz/340 g thinly sliced onions

DILL SAUCE (recipe follows)

1 Soak bamboo skewers for 10 minutes.

2 Cut the veal and pork into 1½-in/4-cm cubes, pat dry, and season with salt and pepper. Thread the meat on the soaked bamboo skewers.

3 Combine all the ingredients for the marinade and pour over the meat. Let marinate for 3 hours or up to overnight under refrigeration.

4 Allow excess marinade to drain from meat before grilling; blot if necessary. Place the meat on the grill or broiler rods. Grill or broil undisturbed for about 3 to 4 minutes. Turn the skewers over and complete cooking, about 3 to 4 minutes more. Brush the meat with additional marinade as it broils or grills.

5 Serve with the sliced onions and dill sauce.

NOTES

Cubed boneless lamb leg is sometimes used in place of the pork.

Serve with a cold sour-cream sauce (add chopped dill, minced shallots, lemon juice, salt, and pepper to sour cream and blend well; this is best if allowed to mellow overnight.)

Broiled Lamb Kebabs with Pimiento Butter Replace the veal and pork with an equal amount of boneless leg of lamb. Replace Dill Sauce with Pimiento Butter (page 404).

DILL SAUCE

makes 10 portions

3 oz/85 g butter

2 oz/60 g flour

1½ qt/1.4 L WHITE VEAL STOCK (page 249), hot

salt, as needed

pepper, as needed

8 fl oz/240 mL sour cream

3 tbsp/45 mL chopped dill

1 To prepare the dill sauce, cook the butter and flour to make a blond roux.

2 Add the stock, bring to a boil, then reduce to a simmer for 45 minutes, or as long as needed to make a smooth, flavorful velouté. Skim and adjust seasoning with salt and pepper as necessary throughout simmering time.

3 Strain the velouté and return to low heat. Temper the sour cream and add to the sauce. Add the dill. Return to just below a simmer (180°F/82°C), adjust the seasoning, and keep warm for service (165°F/73°C).

VEAL SHOULDER POÊLÉ

makes 10 portions

4 lb/1.8 kg boneless veal shoulder

salt, as needed

pepper, as needed

1/4 tsp/1 mL finely chopped rosemary

1/2 tsp/3 mL finely chopped basil

1/2 tsp/3 mL finely chopped thyme

1/2 tsp/3 mL finely chopped marjoram

2 tsp/10 mL minced garlic

2 oz/60 g clarified butter, or as needed

2 oz/60 g diced slab bacon or smoked ham

4 oz/115 g fine-dice onion

2 oz/60 g fine-dice carrot

2 oz/60 g fine-dice celery

1 oz/30 g tomato paste (optional)

8 fl oz/240 mL white wine

2 bay leaves

8 fl oz/240 mL BROWN VEAL STOCK (page 252)

cornstarch slurry, as needed

1 Butterfly the veal and season with salt and pepper. Mix the herbs and garlic together and spread this mixture evenly over the inside of the veal. Roll and tie the veal roast.

2 Prepare the matignon: Heat the butter over medium heat. Add the bacon or ham and cook for 1 or 2 minutes. Add the onions, carrots, and celery; cook until a light golden brown, about 10 to 12 minutes. Add tomato paste, if desired, and cook briefly.

3 Place the veal on top of the mirepoix and baste with some additional clarified butter.

4 Cover the pot and poêlé in 300°F/150°C oven, basting every 20 minutes for 60 to 70 minutes. Remove lid for the last 30 minutes to allow veal to brown.

5 Check for doneness: the meat should be tender when pierced with a fork. When done, remove the veal and keep warm.

6 Add the wine, bay leaves and stock to the pan and simmer for 20 minutes. Degrease if necessary.

7 Thicken with cornstarch and reduce more if necessary. Adjust the seasoning.

8 Carve the veal into portions and serve with the sauce.

LAMB CHOPS WITH CHILI BUTTER

makes 10 portions

30 lamb chops

salt, as needed

pepper, as needed

vegetable oil, as needed

10 oz/285 g CHILI BUTTER (recipe follows)

1 Season the lamb chops with salt and pepper and dip in oil. Allow any excess to drain away before placing on rods.

2 Place the lamb presentation side down first on the grill or broiler rods. Grill or broil undisturbed for about 2 minutes. (Optional: Give each chop a quarter turn [90°] during broiling to achieve grill marks.)

3 Turn the lamb chops over and complete cooking to the desired doneness, about 2 to 4 minutes more (135°F/57°C for rare, 145°F/63°C for medium rare, 160°F/70°C for medium, 170°F/75°C for well done).

4 Top each chop with a slice of the chili butter; heat under a broiler or salamander until the butter begins to melt. Serve at once.

CHILI BUTTER

makes 1 pound/450 grams, or sixteen 1-ounce/30-grams portions

1 lb/450 g unsalted butter, room temperature

1 tbsp/15 mL chili powder

1/2 tsp/3 mL ground cumin

1 1/2 tsp/8 mL paprika

1 tbsp/15 mL CHILI POWDER (page 353)

1 tbsp/15 mL chopped fresh oregano

1 1/2 tsp/8 mL Worcestershire sauce

1/4 tsp/1 mL Tabasco

1/4 tsp/1 mL garlic powder

1/4 tsp/1 mL onion powder

salt, as needed

pepper, as needed

1 Work the butter by hand or with a paddle attachment until it is soft. Add the remaining ingredients and blend well. Adjust the seasoning with salt and pepper.

2 The compound butter is ready to use now, or it may be rolled into a log or piped into shapes and chilled for later service.

LAMB CHOPS WITH ARTICHOKES

makes 10 portions

20 lamb chops, rib or loin (3 oz/85 g each)

MARINADE

4 fl oz/120 mL olive oil

2 fl oz/60 mL lemon juice

2 fl oz/60 mL soy sauce

1 tbsp chopped thyme

salt, as needed

pepper, as needed

ARTICHOKE AND ZUCCHINI SAUTÉ (recipe follows)

1 Trim the chops. Combine all the ingredients for the marinade and brush liberally onto the chops. Marinate under refrigeration for 1 to 2 hours. Allow any excess to drain away before placing on rods.

2 Place the lamb presentation side down on the grill or broiler rods. Grill or broil undisturbed for about 2 minutes. (Optional: Give each chop a quarter turn [90°] during broiling to achieve grill marks.)

3 Turn the lamb chops over and complete cooking to the desired doneness, about 2 to 4 minutes more (135°F/57°C for rare, 145°F/63°C for medium rare, 160°F/70°C for medium, 170°F/75°C for well done).

4 Serve the chops on a bed of the artichoke mixture. Garnish with the artichoke leaves.

see photograph on page 431

ARTICHOKE AND ZUCCHINI SAUTÉ

makes 10 portions

3 tbsp minced shallots

2 tsp minced garlic

2 fl oz/60 mL olive oil

12 oz/340 g zucchini, cut into 1/2-inch julienne

5 oz/140 g tomato concassé

10 cooked artichoke bottoms, sliced, leaves reserved

1 tbsp chopped peperoncini

salt, as needed

pepper, as needed

1 Sauté the shallots and garlic in the oil. Add the zucchini and sauté for 3 to 4 minutes, or until any moisture released by zucchini has cooked away.

2 Add the tomato concassé and artichokes. Continue to sauté until all ingredients are very hot, 3 to 4 minutes more. Season the mixture with the peperoncini and with salt and pepper to taste.

GRILLED LAMB CHOPS WITH CARAMELIZED GARLIC SAUCE

makes 10 portions

20 double rib lamb chops (3 oz/85 g each)

salt, as needed

pepper, as needed

olive oil, garlic flavored, as needed

CARAMELIZED GARLIC SAUCE (recipe follows)

1 Season the chops with salt and pepper and brush the chops with oil.

2 Place the lamb presentation side down first on the grill or broiler rods. Grill or broil undisturbed for about 2 minutes. (Optional: Give each chop a quarter turn [90°] during broiling to achieve grill marks.)

3 Turn the lamb chops over and complete cooking to the desired doneness, about 2 to 4 minutes more (135°F/57°C for rare, 145°F/63°C for medium rare, 160°F/70°C for medium, 170°F/75°C for well done).

4 Serve the chops at once with the caramelized garlic sauce.

CARAMELIZED GARLIC SAUCE

makes 10 portions

4 oz/115 g whole garlic cloves, peeled

2 oz/60 g clarified butter or oil

8 fl oz/240 mL white wine

1 pint/480 mL JUS D'AGNEAU LIÉ (page 261) or DEMIGLACE (page 287)

1 oz/30 g basil chiffonade

8 oz/225 g tomato concassé

salt, as needed

pepper, as needed

2 oz/60 g whole unsalted butter, diced

1 Blanch the garlic cloves in salted water, shock, and peel them. Cook them in 3 successive changes of water until tender.

2 Sauté the blanched garlic cloves in the butter until they are lightly browned. Deglaze the pan with the white wine and reduce to à sec.

3 Add the jus lié and any juices from the sizzler platter and reduce the mixture lightly.

4 Add the basil and tomato. Adjust seasoning. At service, swirl in the butter to finish the sauce.

GRILLED OR BROILED PORK CHOPS WITH SHERRY VINEGAR SAUCE

makes 10 portions

10 pork chops, 2 in/5.5 cm thick (10 oz/285 g each)

salt, as needed

pepper, as needed

oil, as needed

SHERRY VINEGAR SAUCE (recipe follows)

1 Trim the pork chops if necessary. Season with salt and pepper and brush lightly with oil.

2 Place the pork presentation side down on the grill or broiler rods. Grill or broil undisturbed for about 3 to 4 minutes. (Optional: Give each chop a quarter turn [90°] during broiling to achieve grill marks.)

3 Turn the pork chops over and complete cooking to medium or well done, about 3 to 4 minutes more (160°F/70°C for medium, 170°F/75°C for well done).

SHERRY VINEGAR SAUCE

makes 10 portions

2 fl oz/60 mL sherry wine vinegar

1½ oz/40 g dark brown sugar

24 fl oz/720 mL JUS DE VEAU LIÉ (page 260) or DEMIGLACE (page 287)

salt, as needed

pepper, as needed

1 Prepare a gastrique as follows: Cook the vinegar and sugar in a saucepan until the mixture comes to a boil and the sugar is completely dissolved.

2 Add the jus lié or demiglace to the gastrique away from the heat. Stir to combine, then return to a simmer over medium heat until reduced to a good flavor and consistency. Adjust the seasoning with salt and pepper and strain.

3 The sauce is ready to serve now or it may be cooled and stored for later service.

BAKED STUFFED PORK CHOPS

makes 10 portions

10 center-cut pork chops, 1½ in/4 cm thick

salt, to taste

pepper, to taste

STUFFING

2 oz/60 g vegetable oil or rendered bacon fat

4 oz/115 g minced onion

3 oz/85 g minced celery

2 tsp/10 mL minced garlic

24 oz/680 g dried bread cubes

1 tbsp/15 mL chopped parsley

1 tsp/5 mL rubbed sage, to taste

6 fl oz/180 mL CHICKEN STOCK (page 248), as needed

24 fl oz/720 mL JUS DE VEAU LIÉ (page 260) or DEMIGLACE (page 287)

1 Cut a pocket into each chop. Season with salt and pepper. Refrigerate until stuffing is properly prepared and cooled.

2 Heat the oil or bacon fat in a pan. Add the onion and cook until it is golden brown. Add the celery and garlic, and cook until the celery is limp. Remove them from the pan, spread out on a baking sheet, and allow this mixture to cool completely.

3 Combine the onion mixture with bread cubes, parsley, and sage. Add enough of the stock to make a stuffing that is moist but not wet. Chill the stuffing until it is 40°F/4°C.

4 Add the stuffing to the pork chops. Secure the chops by tying or closing with skewers.

5 Sear the pork chops in a sauté pan until golden on both sides. Remove to a baking sheet and finish cooking in a 350°F/175°C oven to an internal temperature of 160°F/70°C.

6 Pour off any excess oil or bacon fat from the pan. Add the jus lié or demiglace and bring to a simmer. Degrease the sauce if necessary. Adjust the seasoning to taste with salt and pepper if necessary.

7 Serve the chops with the sauce.

NOTES

Serve Sauce Robert (page 474) or Sauce Charcutière (page 475) with these chops, if desired.

The chops you cut should be at least ¾ in / 2 cm thick. For more information about cutting chops, refer to Chapter Sixteen, page 363.

ROAST LEG OF LAMB BOULANGÈRE

makes 10 portions

1 bone-in leg of lamb (14 to 16 lb/6.35 to 7.25 kg)

salt, as needed

pepper, as needed

1 oz/30 g garlic, slivered

4 lb/1.8 kg baking potatoes, sliced ⅛ in/5 mm thick

1 lb/450 g thinly sliced onions

24 fl oz/720 mL BROWN LAMB STOCK (page 252) or BROWN VEAL STOCK (page 252), hot, or as needed

1 qt/1 L JUS D'AGNEAU LIÉ (page 261), JUS DE VEAU LIÉ (page 260), or DEMIGLACE (page 287), hot

1 Season the lamb with salt and pepper and stud it with the slivered garlic.

2 Place the lamb on a rack in a roasting pan. Roast at 400°F/205°C for 1 hour, basting from time to time. Remove the lamb from the roasting pan and pour off the grease.

3 Layer the sliced potatoes and onions in the roasting pan. Season the layers with salt and pepper. Add enough stock to moisten well.

4 Place the lamb on the potatoes. Continue to roast to the desired doneness, another 30 to 45 minutes or until a thermometer inserted in the center of the meat registers 135°F/57°C for rare, 145°F/63°C for medium rare, 160°F/70°C for medium, or 170°F/75°C for well done. The potatoes should be tender.

5 Let the leg rest before carving it into portions. Serve with a portion of the potatoes and hot jus lié or demiglace.

Grilled Chicken Breast with Fennel Sauté

**Salmon Fillet with Smoked Salmon
and Horseradish Crust**

Sateh of Chicken

Lamb Chops with Artichokes

ROAST RACK OF LAMB PERSILLÉ

makes 10 portions

2 rack of lamb, frenched (2 lb/900 g each)

salt, as needed

pepper, as needed

1 tsp/5 mL chopped rosemary

1 tsp/5 mL chopped thyme

vegetable oil, as needed

PERSILLADE (recipe follows)

8 oz/225 g mirepoix

8 fl oz/240 mL BROWN LAMB STOCK (page 252) or BROWN VEAL STOCK (page 252)

arrowroot or cornstarch slurry, as needed (optional)

1 Season the lamb with salt and pepper and rub with rosemary, thyme, and oil.

2 Place the lamb on a rack in a roasting pan.

3 Roast at 400°F/205°C for 15 minutes, basting from time to time. Scatter the mirepoix around the lamb, reduce the heat to 325°F/175°C, and continue to roast to the desired doneness, another 15 to 20 minutes or until a thermometer inserted in the center of the meat registers 135°F/57°C for rare, 145°F/63°C for medium rare, 160°F/70°C for medium, or 170°F/75°C for well done.

4 To make the jus: Place the roasting pan on the stovetop and cook until the mirepoix is browned and the fat is clear. Pour off all the fat. Add the stock, stirring to release the fond completely. Simmer the jus for 20 to 30 minutes, or until it reaches the proper consistency and flavor. (Optional: Add enough arrowroot or cornstarch slurry to thicken the sauce enough to coat the back of a spoon.) Degrease and adjust seasoning. Strain through a fine mesh sieve.

5 Transfer the lamb to a sheet pan and spread the persillade on top of the lamb rack. Return the lamb to a 400°F/205°C oven until the crumbs lightly brown.

6 Cut the lamb into chops and serve with the jus.

PERSILLADE

makes 10 portions

5 oz/140 g fresh white bread crumbs

½ oz/15 g garlic, mashed to a paste

1 tbsp/15 mL chopped parsley

2 oz/60 g butter, melted

salt, as needed

Mix all ingredients together to make an evenly moistened mixture.

ROAST LEG OF LAMB WITH MINT SAUCE

makes 10 portions

1 boneless leg of lamb (about 6 lb/2.7 kg)

SALT HERBS (recipe follows)

½ oz/15 g minced garlic

vegetable oil, as needed

4 oz/115 g grams mirepoix, medium dice

MINT SAUCE

24 fl oz/720 mL JUS DE AGNEAU LIÉ (page 261) or DEMIGLACE (page 287)

2 oz/60 g mint stems or sprigs

salt, as needed

pepper, as needed

1 oz/30 g mint chiffonade

1 Rub the lamb on all sides with the salt herbs and garlic and marinate under refrigeration overnight.

2 Roll and tie the roast. Rub with oil and place on a rack in a roasting pan.

3 Roast at 350°F/175°C for 45 minutes, basting from time to time. Scatter the mirepoix around the lamb and continue to roast another 30 to 40 minutes or until a thermometer inserted in the center of the meat registers 135°F/57°C for rare, 145°F/63°C for medium rare, 160°F/70°C for medium, or 170°F/75°C for well done. Remove the lamb from the roasting pan and allow it to rest.

4 To make the mint sauce: Place the roasting pan on the stovetop and cook until the mirepoix is browned and the fat is clear. Pour off all the fat. Add the jus lié or demiglace, stirring to release the fond completely. Add the mint stems and simmer for 20 to 30 minutes, or until the sauce reaches the proper consistency and flavor. Degrease and adjust seasoning with salt and pepper. Strain through a fine mesh sieve. Finish with mint chiffonade.

5 Carve the lamb into portions and serve with mint sauce.

SALT HERBS

makes 2 tablespoons/30 milliliters

1 tbsp/15 mL salt

2 tsp/10 mL rosemary leaves

2 tsp/10 mL thyme leaves

3 bay leaves

¹/₂ tsp/3 mL pepper

1 Grind together the salt with the rosemary, thyme, bay leaves, and pepper in a grinder or with mortar and pestle until a fine powder forms.

2 Let the salt herbs rest 12 hours before using.

INDIAN GRILLED LAMB WITH MANGO CHUTNEY

makes 10 portions

6 lb/2.75 kg leg of lamb, boned and butterflied

MARINADE

1 tsp/5 mL ground green cardamom

1 tsp/5 mL ground cumin

¹/₂ tsp/3 mL ground nutmeg

4 oz/115 g minced onion

³/₄ oz /20 g minced garlic

³/₄ oz/20 g minced ginger

1 tsp/5 mL black pepper

4 fl oz/120 mL plain yogurt

MANGO CHUTNEY (recipe follows)

1 Trim the lamb and separate into individual muscles. Remove all interior fat and gristle. Cut the meat into long thin strips.

2 Prepare the marinade. Toast the cardamom and cumin lightly in a pan. Add the nutmeg, onions, garlic, ginger, and black pepper and sauté. Let cool. Add to the yogurt.

3 Pour the marinade over the lamb and turn to coat evenly. Marinate for 8 hours or overnight under refrigeration.

4 Thread the lamb onto skewers and allow excess marinade to drain away. Place the lamb on the grill or broiler rods. Grill or broil undisturbed for about 2 minutes. Turn the skewers over and complete cooking to the desired doneness, about 2 to 4 minutes more (135°F/57°C for rare, 145°F/63°C for medium rare, 160°F/70°C for medium, or 170°F/75°C for well done).

5 Serve the lamb at once with the chutney.

FRESH MANGO CHUTNEY

makes 10 portions

1 lb/450 g small-dice mangoes

1 fl oz/30 mL lime juice

2 tsp/10 ml chopped cilantro

1 tsp/5 mL minced ginger

¹/₂ tsp/3 mL minced jalapeños (optional)

salt, as needed

pepper, as needed

Combine all ingredients and let the chutney rest under refrigeration for up to 2 hours, to allow the flavors to marry. Adjust seasoning before serving if necessary with additional lime juice, salt, or pepper.

PAKISTANI-STYLE LAMB PATTIES

makes 10 portions

2 oz/60 g minced onions

1 fl oz/30 mL vegetable oil

2 tsp/10 mL minced garlic

2 oz/60 g soft white bread crumbs

3 lb/1.3 kg lean ground lamb

3 oz/85 g pine nuts, toasted

2 eggs, beaten

1 oz/30 g tahini

3 tbsp/45 mL chopped parsley

salt, as needed

pepper, as needed

1 tsp/5 mL ground coriander

2 tbsp/30 mL ground cumin

1 tsp/5 mL ground fennel seeds

2 tbsp/30 mL grated ginger

1 Sauté the onions in hot oil until they are translucent.

2 Add the garlic and sauté it briefly. Remove from the heat.

3 Soak the bread crumbs in water. Squeeze out any excess moisture.

4 Combine the bread crumbs and onions and garlic.

5 Add the lamb, pine nuts, beaten eggs, tahini, parsley, salt, pepper, spices, and ginger. Mix together gently but thoroughly.

6 Shape the mixture into patties and chill.

7 Place the patties on the grill or broiler rods. Grill or broil undisturbed for about 3 to 4 minutes. (Optional: Give each patty a quarter turn [90°] during broiling to achieve grill marks.) Turn the patties over and complete cooking to the desired doneness, about 2 to 4 minutes more (135°F/57°C for rare, 145°F/63°C for medium rare, 160°F/70°C for medium, or 170°F/75°C for well done).

BROILED CHICKEN BREAST

makes 10 portions

10 boneless chicken breast portions, skin on (7 oz/200 g each)

salt, as needed

pepper, as needed

vegetable oil, as needed

5 oz/140 g SUN-DRIED TOMATO AND OREGANO BUTTER (page 404), cut into 10 slices

1 Season the chicken with salt and pepper and dip in oil. Allow any excess to drain away before placing on rods.

2 Place the chicken presentation side down on the grill or broiler rods. Grill or broil undisturbed for about 3 to 4 minutes. (Optional: Give each breast a quarter turn [90°] during broiling to achieve grill marks.)

3 Turn the chicken over and complete cooking until done, about 4 to 5 minutes more (170°F/75°C for breast meat).

4 Top each portion with a slice of the sun-dried tomato and oregano butter; heat under a broiler or salamander until the butter begins to melt. Serve at once.

BARBECUED CHICKEN BREAST WITH BLACK BEAN SAUCE

makes 10 portions

10 chicken breast portions (7 oz/200 g each)

MARINADE

8 fl oz/240 mL apple cider

1 fl oz/30 mL cider vinegar

1/2 oz/15 g minced shallots

1 tsp/5 mL minced garlic

1 tsp/5 mL cracked black peppercorns

1 pint/480 mL BARBECUE SAUCE (page 290), or as needed

BLACK BEAN SAUCE (recipe follows), heated

1 Trim the chicken portions, removing skin and bones if desired.

2 Combine all the ingredients for the marinade. Add the chicken and turn to coat it evenly. Marinate the chicken under refrigeration for 1 to 2 hours.

3 Place the chicken presentation side down on the grill or broiler rods. Grill or broil undisturbed for about 2 minutes. (Optional: Give each portion a quarter turn [90°] during broiling to achieve grill marks.) Brush with barbecue sauce and turn the chicken over. Continue to turn the chicken, brushing with a light coat of barbecue sauce each time, until the chicken is done, about 6 to 8 minutes (170°F/75°C for breast meat).

4 Serve the chicken on heated plates with black bean sauce.

BLACK BEAN SAUCE

makes 10 portions

7 oz/200 g black beans, soaked overnight

40 fl oz/1.2 L CHICKEN STOCK (page 248)

1/2 oz/15 g diced bacon

3 oz/85 g diced onions

1/4 oz/7 g minced garlic

1/4 tsp/1 mL chopped oregano leaves

1/2 tsp/3 mL ground toasted cumin seeds

1/2 tsp/3 mL jalapeño, chopped

1 dried chile, or to taste

salt, as needed

pepper, as needed

1/2 oz/15 g chopped sun-dried tomatoes

1 fl oz/30 mL lemon juice, or as needed

1 tsp/5 mL sherry wine vinegar, or as needed

1 Simmer the beans in stock until tender.

2 Render the bacon over medium heat until it releases its fat. Add the onion, garlic, oregano, cumin, jalapeño and the dried chile. Continue to sauté over moderate heat, stirring occasionally, until the onions are limp and translucent, about 6 to 8 minutes. Add the remaining sauce ingredients to the beans.

3 Season the sauce with salt and pepper and cook for 10 to 15 minutes more. Remove the chile.

4 Purée a third of the beans. Add the purée back to the sauce along with the sun-dried tomatoes. Season with lemon juice and sherry vinegar.

BROILED CHICKEN TEX-MEX

makes 10 portions

10 chicken breast portions (7 oz/200 g each)

MARINADE

4 fl oz/120 mL vegetable oil

2 fl oz/60 mL cider vinegar

2 fl oz/60 mL lime juice

1 tbsp/25 mL chopped cilantro

1 tsp/5 mL minced garlic

1 tbsp/25 mL minced jalapeños

1 tsp/5 mL CHILI POWDER (page353)

1 tsp/5 mL ground cumin

1/2 tsp/3 mL salt, to taste

1/4 tsp pepper, to taste

10 oz/285 g CHILI BUTTER (page 426)

1 Trim the chicken and remove bone and skins if desired.

2 Combine the marinade ingredients and pour over the chicken. Turn to coat evenly. Marinate under refrigeration for 4 hours or overnight.

3 Remove the chicken from the marinade before grilling and allow any excess to drain away before placing on rods.

4 Place the chicken presentation side down first on the grill or broiler rods. Grill or broil undisturbed for about 3 minutes. (Optional: Give each breast portion a quarter turn (90°) during broiling to achieve grill marks.)

5 Turn the chicken over and complete cooking until done, about 3 to 4 minutes more (170°F/75°C for breast meat).

6 Top each portion with a slice of the chili butter, heat under a broiler or salamander until the butter begins to melt. Serve at once.

GRILLED CHICKEN BREAST WITH FENNEL SAUTÉ

makes 10 portions

MARINADE

olive oil, as needed

1/4 oz/7 g crushed garlic

1/4 tsp/1 mL cracked fennel seeds

1/2 tsp/3 mL salt

1/4 tsp/1 mL pepper

10 chicken breast portions (7 oz/200 g each)

FENNEL SAUTÉ (recipe follows)

1 Combine all the ingredients for the marinade, add the chicken, and marinate briefly.

2 Remove the chicken from the marinade and allow any excess to drain away. Place the chicken presentation side down on the grill or broiler rods. Grill or broil undisturbed for about 3 minutes. (Optional: Give each breast portion a quarter turn [90°] during broiling to achieve grill marks.)

3 Turn the chicken over and complete cooking until done, about 3 to 4 minutes more (170°F/75°C for breast meat).

4 Serve the chicken on a bed of fennel sauté. Garnish it with fennel leaves, if desired.

FENNEL SAUTÉ

makes 10 portions

24 oz/720 g fennel julienne

1 oz/30 g minced shallots

2 oz/60 g butter or as needed

1 fl oz/30 mL Pernod, or to taste

salt, as needed

pepper, as needed

1 Cook the fennel in boiling salted water until it is tender, about 4 to 5 minutes. Drain well.

2 Sweat the shallots in the butter. Add the fennel and sauté it until heated through, about 3 minutes.

3 Add the Pernod and season the fennel to taste with salt and pepper.

see photograph on page 430

GRILLED PAILLARDS OF CHICKEN WITH TARRAGON BUTTER

makes 10 portions

3³/₄ lb/1.7 kg boneless skinless chicken breast

MARINADE

2 oz/60 mL oil

1 tsp/5 mL salt

¹/₂ tsp/3 mL pepper

2 fl oz/60 mL lemon juice

2 tsp/10 mL chopped tarragon leaves

5 oz/150 g TARRAGON BUTTER (page 420)

1 Cut the chicken into 10 portions (5 to 6 oz/140 to 170 g each). Trim and pound the chicken into paillards.

2 Combine all the ingredients for the marinade, add the chicken, and marinate briefly.

3 Remove the chicken from the marinade and allow any excess to drain away. Place the chicken presentation side down on the grill or broiler rods. Grill or broil undisturbed for about 3 minutes. (Optional: Give each breast portion a quarter turn [90°] during broiling to achieve grill marks.)

4 Turn the chicken over and complete cooking until done, about 3 to 4 minutes more (170°F/75°C for breast meat).

5 Top each paillard with a rosette or slice of the tarragon butter and serve immediately.

Grilled Chicken Sandwich (See page 800.) Serve the chicken on a sliced baguette or club roll with pancetta, arugula, and aïoli (page 784). Garnish the sandwich as desired.

Grilled Chicken with Basil and Fresh Mozzarella Substitute chopped fresh basil for the tarragon in the marinade. Grill the chicken as indicated in the recipe. Top each grilled paillard with a fresh basil leaf and a slice of fresh mozzarella. Place the chicken under the broiler briefly before serving.

Grilled Chicken Fajitas Add ground cumin and chili powder to the marinade. Serve the chicken breasts with steamed flour tortillas, salsa, chopped onions, tomato, and lettuce, and other condiments as desired.

POÊLÉ OF CAPON WITH TOMATOES AND ARTICHOKES

makes 10 portions

1 capon (12 lb/5.5 kg)

1 tsp/5 mL salt

¹/₂ tsp/3 mL pepper

2 oz/30 g fresh herb stems or sprigs, as available or desired

8 oz/225 g matignon

2 oz/60 g clarified butter, or as needed

1 qt/1 L chicken stock for jus lié style sauces (see page 249) or JUS DE VEAU LIÉ (page 260), or DEMIGLACE (page 287)

arrowroot or cornstarch slurry, as needed

8 oz/225 g tomato concassé

8 oz 225 g artichoke bottoms, poached and sliced

2 tbsp/30 mL chopped parsley

2 tbsp/30 mL chopped chives

2 tbsp/30 mL chopped chervil

2 tbsp/30 mL chopped tarragon

1 Season the bird with salt and pepper and stuff the cavity with a bundle of fresh herbs. Truss the bird.

2 Prepare the matignon: Heat the butter over medium heat. Add the bacon or ham and cook for 1 or 2 minutes. Add the onions, carrots, and celery; cook until a light golden brown, about 10 to 12 minutes.

3 Place the capon on top of the matignon and baste with some additional clarified butter.

4 Cover the pot and poêlé in 300°F/150°C oven for about 2 hours, basting with pan drippings or additional butter, until a thermometer inserted in the thickest part of the thigh reads 180°F/82°C. (Remove lid during the last 30 minutes to allow capon to brown.) Remove the capon and let rest while finishing the pan sauce.

5 Place the poêléing pan on direct heat and bring the liquid to a boil. Reduce slightly. Pour off or skim away excess fat.

6 Add the stock, jus de veau, or demiglace and bring to a boil. (Optional: Add the arrowroot or cornstarch slurry to thicken the sauce enough to coat a spoon if using stock.) Degrease the sauce thoroughly.

7 Add the tomato concassé, artichoke bottoms, and chopped herbs. Adjust the seasoning.

8 Carve the capon and serve it with the sauce.

BREAST OF CHICKEN WITH CORN BREAD OYSTER STUFFING

makes 10 portions

10 chicken breast suprêmes (7 oz/200 g each)
CORN BREAD OYSTER STUFFING (recipe follows)
1 oz/30 g tomato paste
¼ oz/7 g roasted garlic
4 fl oz/120 mL red wine
1 pint/480 mL BROWN CHICKEN STOCK (page 252) or
    BROWN VEAL STOCK (page 252)
3 fl oz/90 mL heavy cream
salt, as needed
pepper, as needed
arrowroot or cornstarch slurry, as needed (optional)

1 Cut a pocket in each chicken breast, from the wing end. Season the chicken with salt and pepper. Place a portion of the oyster stuffing into each chicken breast, stuffing loosely into the pocket.

2 Place the stuffed chicken breasts on a rack in a roasting pan. Bake at 350°F/175°C, basting from time to time, for 25 to 30 minutes or until a thermometer inserted in the center of the meat registers 170°F/75°C. Remove the chicken breasts from the roasting pan and allow them to rest.

3 Place the roasting pan on the stovetop and cook until the fat is clear and meat drippings have reduced. Pour off the fat. Add the tomato paste and roasted garlic and cook out 2 minutes more. Whisk in the red wine, stirring well to release the reduced drippings. Add the stock and simmer the sauce for about 10 minutes, or until it reaches the proper consistency and flavor. Degrease, add heavy cream, and adjust seasoning with salt and pepper. (Optional: Add the slurry to thicken the sauce enough to coat the back of a spoon.) Strain through a fine mesh sieve.

4 Slice the breasts into medallions and place them on warm plates. Serve immediately with the sauce.

CORN BREAD AND OYSTER STUFFING

makes 10 portions

1 oz/30 g butter
2 oz/60 g minced green onions
3 oz/85 g minced red pepper
3 oz/85 g minced green pepper
1 oz/30 g minced celery
20 shucked oysters, juices reserved
6 oz/170 g CORN BREAD (page 921)
pepper, as needed

1 Heat the butter in a pan and add the green onions, red and green pepper, and celery and sweat them. Remove from the heat and let cool.

2 Heat the liquor from the oysters. Add the oysters and poach them gently for about 1 minute, just until the edges begin to curl. Remove the oysters from the liquor and let cool. Reserve the oyster liquor. Dice the oyster meat and reserve.

3 Crumble the corn bread and moisten it with the oyster liquor. Let cool to room temperature. Fold in diced oysters and vegetables and season the mixture with pepper.

CHICKEN LEGS WITH DUXELLES STUFFING

makes 10 portions

10 whole chicken legs (7 oz/200 g each)
salt, as needed
pepper, as needed
DUXELLES STUFFING (recipe follows)
2 oz/60 g melted butter, or as needed
1½ pints/720 mL SUPRÊME SAUCE (page 288), heated

1 Bone out the chicken legs. Lay the meat flat on parchment paper and fold the paper over the meat. Pound it flat with a mallet and season with salt and pepper.

2 Portion 3 oz/85 g of the duxelles stuffing onto each chicken leg. Fold the meat over the stuffing.

3 Brush the chicken legs with melted butter. Place on a rack in a roasting pan. Bake at 375°F/190°C, basting from time to time for 35 to 40 minutes or until a thermometer inserted in the center of the meat registers 180°F/82°C.

4 To serve, pool 2 oz /60 mL of sauce on a heated plate and place a chicken leg on top of the sauce.

DUXELLES STUFFING

makes 2 lb/900 g

6 oz/170 g minced shallots

2 oz/60 g clarified butter

2 lb/900 g white mushrooms, cut into small dice

1 tsp/5 mL salt

1/2 tsp/3 mL pepper

8 fl oz/240 mL reduced heavy cream

8 oz/225 g fresh bread crumbs

1 Sweat the shallots in the clarified butter for 5 to 6 minutes. Add the mushrooms and sauté them until dry to create a duxelles. Season the duxelles with the salt and pepper.

2 Add the heavy cream and simmer until thickened. Add the bread crumbs and combine well. Chill well before using to stuff meat, fish, or poultry.

BREAST OF CORNISH GAME HEN WITH A MUSHROOM STUFFING

makes 10 portions

10 Cornish game hens (20 oz/570 g each)

salt, as needed

pepper, as needed

MUSHROOM FORCEMEAT (recipe follows)

clarified butter, as needed

MADEIRA SAUCE (page 422)

1 Remove the breasts from the hens. Make them into suprêmes and reserve the leg and thigh meat to prepare the mushroom forcemeat stuffing. Refrigerate until needed.

2 Loosen the skin from the breast meat. Season with salt and pepper. Pipe about 2 oz/60 g of the mushroom forcemeat between the skin and breast meat. Smooth out the surface to spread the forcemeat evenly.

3 Place the suprêmes in a baking dish. Brush lightly with the clarified butter. Bake in a preheated 350°F/175°C oven for 25 minutes or to an internal temperature of 180°F/82°C. Baste with additional butter or any pan juices during baking time.

4 To serve, reheat the Madeira sauce and finish with whole butter, if desired. Coat each portion with the sauce and serve at once. (Optional: Slice the breast on a slight diagonal into 4 slices and fan the slices out on a warm plate.)

MUSHROOM FORCEMEAT FOR STUFFING

makes 10 portions

12 oz/340 g leg or thigh meat from Cornish game hen (see Notes)

salt, as needed

pepper, as needed

2 1/2 oz/70 g minced bacon

1 oz/30 g clarified butter or vegetable oil

10 oz/285 g minced white mushrooms

10 oz/285 g minced morels

2 tsp/10 mL minced shallots

2 tsp/10 mL minced garlic

5 thyme sprigs

2 1/2 bay leaves

1/4 oz/7 g sage leaves

4 fl oz/120 mL Madeira

1 whole egg

8 fl oz/240 mL heavy cream

1 Trim the meat and cut into small dice. Season with salt and pepper and refrigerate until needed.

2 Render the bacon in a sauteuse over medium heat. Add the butter and heat. Add the white mushrooms and the morels and sweat until barely tender. Add the shallots and garlic and sauté. Add the thyme, bay leaves, sage, and Madeira. Reduce until thickened. Remove and discard the bay leaves, thyme, and sage. Season with salt and pepper. Chill the mixture to below 40°F/4°C.

3 Process the diced meat with the egg to a paste, scraping down the bowl. Add the cream and pulse the machine on and off until the cream is just incorporated. Remove to a bowl. Fold in the cooled mushroom mixture. Hold chilled until ready to use.

NOTE

This forcemeat can be prepared using any lean diced poultry meat to replace the leg and thigh meat from the Cornish game hen.

PAN-SMOKED CHICKEN WITH APPLE AND GREEN PEPPERCORN SAUCE

makes 10 portions

10 chicken breast portions (6 oz/170 g each)

salt, as needed

pepper, as needed

MARINADE

8 fl oz/240 mL fresh apple cider

2 fl oz/60 mL apple cider vinegar

$1/2$ oz/15 g minced shallots

$1/4$ oz/7 g minced garlic

APPLE AND GREEN PEPPERCORN SAUCE (recipe follows)

1 Rinse chicken, pat dry, season with salt and pepper, and place in shallow hotel pan.

2 Combine the ingredients for the marinade and pour over the chicken, turning to coat evenly. Marinate under refrigeration for 3 hours or up to overnight.

3 Place the chicken on a rack and set it in a pan over lightly dampened hardwood chips. Cover tightly and heat in a 450°F/230°C oven until the smell of smoke is apparent. Smoke for 3 minutes from that point. Transfer the chicken to a baking pan and finish baking (without smoke) in a 350°F/175°C oven until done, about 8 to 10 minutes more (170°F/75°C for breast meat).

4 Serve at once with the apple and green peppercorn sauce.

Smoke-Roasted Chicken Breast with Barbecue Sauce Prepare the chicken as directed above, using the Barbecue Marinade (page 354) to replace the marinade shown here. Brush the chicken with Barbecue Sauce (page 290) before smoke roasting and during final baking. Serve with additional Barbecue Sauce if desired.

APPLE AND GREEN PEPPERCORN SAUCE

makes 10 portions

1 pint/480 mL apple cider

$3/4$ oz/20 g minced shallots

$1/4$ oz/7 g minced garlic

3/4 oz/20 g green peppercorns

24 fl oz/720 mL JUS DE VOLAILLE LIÉ (page 261), JUS DE VEAU LIÉ (page 260), or DEMIGLACE (page 287)

6 oz/170 g apple julienne or small-dice apple (tart apples such as Granny Smith preferred)

1 Combine the cider, shallots, garlic, and peppercorns and simmer until reduced to about 2 fl oz/60 mL.

2 Add the jus, bring the sauce back to a simmer, and reduce slightly to a good flavor and consistency.

3 Add the apples to the sauce. Adjust flavor and seasoning with salt and pepper, adding apple cider to thin if necessary.

ROAST TURKEY WITH CHESTNUT STUFFING

makes 12 servings

15 lb/6.75 kg turkey

salt, to taste

pepper, to taste

2 onions, peeled and quartered

12 to 15 parsley stems

butter or oil, as needed

6 oz/115 g diced onion

3 oz/85 g diced carrot

3 oz/85 g diced celery

2 oz/60 g flour

1 qt/1 L CHICKEN STOCK (page 248)

CHESTNUT STUFFING (recipe follows)

1 Season the turkey with salt and pepper. Place the quartered onions and parsley stems in the cavity. Rub with butter or oil, and truss.

2 Place the turkey on a rack in a roasting pan. Roast at 350°F/175°C for 3 hours, basting from time to time. Scatter the onions, carrots, and celery around the turkey and continue to roast another 45 to 60 minutes or until a thermometer inserted in the center of the thigh meat registers 180°F/82°C.

3 Remove the turkey from the roasting pan and allow it to rest while preparing the pan gravy.

4 Place the roasting pan on the stovetop and cook until the mirepoix is browned and the fat is clear. Pour off all but 1 oz/30 g of the fat. Add the flour and cook out roux for 4 to 5 minutes. Whisk in the stock until completely incorporated and smooth.

5 Simmer the gravy for 20 to 30 minutes, or until it reaches the proper consistency and flavor. Degrease and adjust seasoning. Strain through a fine mesh sieve.

6 Carve the turkey into portions and serve with the pan gravy and chestnut stuffing.

NOTE

Other stuffings may be substituted for this dressing. See Corn Bread and Oyster Stuffing (page 438) or Sausage Bread Stuffing (recipe follows).

CHESTNUT STUFFING

makes 12 servings

4 oz/115 g minced onions

4 oz/115 g rendered turkey or bacon fat, or clarified butter

1½ lb/680 g cubed day-old bread

4 fl oz/120 mL CHICKEN STOCK (page 248), hot

1 egg, beaten

2 tablespoons chopped parsley

salt, as needed

pepper, as needed

1 teaspoon chopped sage

8 oz/225 g peeled roasted chestnuts, chopped

1 Sauté the onion in bacon fat until tender.

2 Combine the bread cubes, chicken stock, and egg and add to the onion.

3 Add the parsley, salt, pepper, sage, and chestnuts. Mix them all well.

4 Place the stuffing in a buttered hotel pan and cover it with parchment paper. Bake the stuffing at 350°F/175°C for 45 minutes.

SAUSAGE BREAD STUFFING

makes 12 servings

1¼ lb/580 g diced crustless CHALLAH BREAD (page 896)

12 oz/340 g sweet Italian sausage

4 oz/115 g small-dice onion

2 oz/60 g small-dice celery

2 oz/60 g water chestnuts, quartered

2 oz/60 g chopped toasted pecans

1 oz/30 g chopped parsley

1 tbsp/15 mL chopped sage

8 fl oz/240 mL CHICKEN STOCK (page 248) or turkey stock (see page 248)

1 egg

salt, as needed

pepper, as needed

1 Dry the cubed bread in a warm oven (around 225°F/107°C) until crisp but not brown.

2 Crumble the sausage into a pan and sauté over medium-high heat, stirring from time to time until cooked through, about 4 minutes. Transfer the cooked sausage to absorbent paper to drain.

3 Pour off all but 1 tbsp/15 mL of fat from pan. Sauté the onion and celery in the fat, stirring often, until translucent, about 5 to 6 minutes.

4 Combine the stock and egg and blend (do not whip).

5 Add the remaining ingredients and allow the bread to absorb the liquid (adjust the consistency of the mixture with additional stock, if necessary). Adjust the seasoning and transfer to a buttered pan. Bake in a 350°F/175°C oven in a water bath until set and brown on top, 30 to 40 minutes.

BROILED BLUEFISH À L'ANGLAISE WITH MAÎTRE D'HÔTEL BUTTER

makes 10 portions

3³/₄ lb/1.75 kg bluefish fillets

salt, as needed

ground white pepper, as needed

lemon juice, as needed

4 oz/115 g butter, melted

1 oz/30 g fresh bread crumbs

1 oz/30 g MAÎTRE D'HÔTEL BUTTER (page 404)

1 Trim the bluefish and make 10 equal portons, 6 oz/170 g each. Season fillets with salt, pepper, and lemon juice.

2 Brush them with the melted butter; dip in the bread crumbs and gently press down on surface.

3 Place the fillets on an oiled sizzler platter and broil them until barely cooked through (flesh should be opaque and firm), about 3 to 4 minutes.

4 Top each fillet with a slice of the maître d'hôtel butter and pass under a broiler briefly to begin melting the butter. Serve at once.

BROILED STUFFED LOBSTER

makes 10 portions

5 lobsters (1¹/₂ lb/680 g each)

STUFFING

2 oz/60 g butter

10 oz/285 g minced onions

5 oz/140 g minced celery

1¹/₂ oz/45 g minced red pepper

1¹/₂ oz/45 g minced green pepper

8 oz/225 g bread crumbs

salt, as nedded

pepper, as needed

lemon wedges, as needed

drawn butter, as needed

1 Split the lobsters. Remove and reserve the coral and tomalley, if available, to add to the stuffing. Place the lobster on a grill rack, shell side up. Grill it until the shell is red. Remove it from the rack and reserve.

2 Melt the butter in a sauté pan. Sweat the vegetables for 5 to 6 minutes, stirring frequently. Remove from the heat. Add the tomalley and coral (if desired) and bread crumbs. Season with salt and pepper, and spoon the mixture into the body cavity of each lobster. (Do not place it over the tail meat.)

3 Place the lobsters on a sheet pan and finish in a 400°F/205°C oven for 6 minutes.

4 Crack the claws but leave the meat inside. Serve the lobster with lemon wedges and drawn butter.

NOTES

Remove the claw meat and mix it with the stuffing before placing it in the cavity. Shrimp or minced fish can also be added. Season the stuffing with Worcestershire sauce and dry sherry.

BLUEFISH WITH CREOLE MUSTARD SAUCE

makes 10 portions

3³/₄ lb/1.75 kg bluefish steaks (6 oz/170 g each)

salt, as needed

pepper, as needed

vegetable oil, as needed

CREOLE MUSTARD SAUCE (recipe follows)

1 Season the fish with salt and pepper and dip in oil. Allow any excess to drain away before placing in a hand rack. Place the hand rack on the grill or broiler rods. Grill or broil undisturbed for about 2 minutes.

2 Turn the fish over and complete cooking, about 2 to 4 minutes more (flesh should be opaque and firm).

3 Serve at once with the Creole mustard sauce.

NOTES

Grill mackerel, king fish, mahi mahi, or grouper instead of the bluefish.

Serve the fish with Horseradish Sauce (page 510) instead of the Creole Mustard Sauce.

CREOLE MUSTARD SAUCE

makes 10 servings

¹/₂ oz/15 g minced shallots

4 fl oz/120 mL cider vinegar

2 tsp/10 mL cracked black peppercorns

2 bay leaves

16 fl oz/480 mL dry white wine

4 fl oz/120 mL reduced heavy cream

1¹/₂ lb/680 g butter, softened

1 oz/30 g Dijon mustard

1 oz/30 g Creole mustard

1 oz/30 g mild mustard

1 Combine the shallots, vinegar, peppercorns, bay leaves, and wine. Reduce the mixture to 6 fl oz/180 mL.

2 Add the heavy cream and reduce the mixture by half. Strain the sauce and return it to the heat.

3 Whisk in the butter gradually over low heat. Add the mustards and adjust the seasoning. Keep warm for service.

BROILED LEMON SOLE ON A BED OF LEEKS

BROILED FOODS PREPARED IN THE MANNER SHOWN HERE ARE KNOWN AS *À L'ANGLAISE*, MEANING THEY ARE COATED WITH MELTED BUTTER AND BREAD CRUMBS.

makes 10 portions

3³/₄ lb/1.7 kg lemon sole fillet, or other flounder

lemon juice, as needed

salt, as needed

pepper, as needed

clarified butter, as needed

fresh white bread crumbs, as needed

1¹/₂ lb/680 g paysanne-cut leeks

4 fl oz/120 mL heavy cream

1 Cut the fish into 10 equal portions of 6 oz/170 g. Season the fish with lemon juice, salt, and pepper. Brush lightly with the butter.

2 Work a little additional butter into the bread crumbs to moisten them slightly. Coat the fish with the bread crumbs and place on an oiled sizzler plate.

3 Place the sizzler platter directly on broiler rods. Broil undisturbed for about 4 minutes, or until the fish is done and the topping is browned.

4 Stew the leeks in the butter until they are tender. Season them with salt and pepper and finish them with the cream. Serve the fish on a bed of stewed leeks.

SCALLION-STUDDED SWORDFISH WITH RED PEPPER COULIS

makes 10 portions

4 scallions, cut into quarters

3³/₄ lb/1.75 kg swordfish fillet, skin on

salt, as needed

pepper, as needed

3 fl oz/90 mL lemon juice

2 fl oz/60 mL vegetable oil

20 fl oz/570 mL ROASTED RED PEPPER COULIS (recipe follows)

1 Weave the scallion quarters lengthwise through the swordfish. Cut into 10 equal steaks (6 oz/170 g each). Season with salt, pepper, and lemon juice and dip in oil. Allow any excess to drain away before placing on rods.

2 Place the swordfish presentation side down on the grill or broiler rods. Grill or broil undisturbed for about 2 minutes. (Optional: Give each steak a quarter turn [90°] during broiling to achieve grill marks.)

3 Turn the swordfish over and complete cooking (flesh should be opaque and firm).

4 Serve the steaks with the red pepper coulis.

RED PEPPER COULIS

makes 2 quarts/2 liters

2 fl oz/60 mL olive oil

1 oz/30 g minced shallots

3 lb/1.35 kg chopped red peppers (peel, seed, and derib before chopping)

salt, as needed

pepper, as needed

8 fl oz/240 mL dry white wine

16 fl oz/480 mL CHICKEN STOCK (page 248)

4 to 6 fl oz/120 to 180 mL heavy cream (optional)

1 Sweat the shallots in the olive oil, stirring frequently until they are tender, about 2 minutes. Add the peppers and continue to sweat over medium heat until the peppers are very tender, about 12 minutes. Add salt and pepper to taste as the peppers sweat.

2 Deglaze the pan with the wine and let the wine reduce until nearly cooked away. Add the stock; simmer until reduced by half.

3 Purée the sauce in a food processor or blender until very smooth. (Optional: Add the cream to the puréed sauce and simmer 3 to 4 minutes more.) Adjust the seasoning with salt and pepper to taste.

FILLET OF MAHI MAHI WITH PINEAPPLE SALSA

makes 10 portions

3³/₄ lb/1.75 kg mahi mahi fillet or steak (5 to 6 oz/140 to 170 g each)

lime juice, as needed

salt, as needed

pepper, as needed

vegetable oil, as needed

PINEAPPLE SALSA (recipe follows), warm

1 Cut the mahi mahi into slices or steaks, 5 to 6 oz/140 to 170 g each. Sprinkle with lime juice and season with salt and pepper. Dip the fish into oil and allow any excess to drain away before placing on rods.

2 Place the mahi mahi presentation side down on the grill or broiler rods. Grill or broil undisturbed for about 2 minutes. (Optional: Give each piece a quarter turn [90°] during broiling to achieve grill marks.)

3 Turn the mahi mahi over and complete cooking, about 2 to 4 minutes more (flesh should be opaque and firm). Serve at once with warm pineapple salsa.

PINEAPPLE SALSA

makes 10 portions

10 oz/285 g small-dice pineapple

2 oz/60 g small-dice red onion, small dice

1 tsp/5 mL minced jalapeños

1 fl oz/20 mL lime juice

¹/₂ tsp/5 mL lime zest

1 fl oz/30 mL peanut oil

2 tbsp/30 mL chopped fresh basil

salt, as needed

pepper, as needed

Combine all ingredients, and allow to sit one hour before service.

GRILLED RED PERCH WITH LIME-TEQUILA VINAIGRETTE

makes 10 portions

3³/₄ lb/1.7 kg red perch fillet, skin attached

lime juice, as needed

salt, as needed

pepper, as needed

LIME-TEQUILA VINAIGRETTE (recipe follows)

30 grapefruit sûpremes

30 avocado slices

1 Cut the perch into portions, 5 to 6 oz/140 to 170 g each. Score the skin side of the fish with a sharp knife to create a crosshatch design. Sprinkle with lime juice and season with salt and pepper.

2 Place the perch, skin side down, on a sizzler platter. Coat it with 1 oz/30 mL of the vinaigrette. Place the platter directly on the broiler rods and broil for about 2 minutes. Turn the fish and finish cooking it, skin side up, 2 to 3 minutes more.

3 Serve the perch with slices of grapefruit and avocado.

LIME-TEQUILA VINAIGRETTE

makes 10 fluid ounces /300 milliliters

2 oz/60 mL rice wine vinegar

1 oz/30 mL lime juice

1 oz/30 mL tequila

salt, as needed

pepper, as needed

6 oz/180 mL safflower oil

2 tbsp/5 g chopped cilantro

2 oz/55 g fine-dice tomato concassé

Combine the vinegar, lime juice, tequila, salt, and pepper. Gradually whisk in the oil. Finish by folding in the cilantro and tomato. Adjust the seasoning with salt and pepper. Recombine the vinaigrette before serving, if it has separated as it sits.

GRILLED SWORDFISH WITH PEPPER CREAM SAUCE

makes 10 portions

3³/₄ lb/1.75 kg swordfish steak

salt, as needed

pepper, as needed

lemon juice, as needed

vegetable oil, as needed

1 Cut the swordfish into 10 equal steaks, 5 to 6 oz/140 to 170 g each. Season the with salt and pepper. Brush it with the lemon juice and oil. Allow any excess to drain away before placing on rods.

2 Place the swordfish presentation side down on the grill or broiler rods. Grill or broil undisturbed for about 2 minutes. (Optional: Give each steak a quarter turn [90°] during broiling to achieve grill marks.) Turn the swordfish over and complete cooking, about 2 to 4 minutes more.

3 Serve the swordfish with the sauce.

Salmon with Pepper Cream Sauce Substitute a 5- to 6-oz/ 140- to 170-g portion of salmon fillet or salmon steak.

Tuna with Pepper Cream Sauce Substitute a 5- to 6-oz/ 140- to 170-g) portion of tuna.

PEPPER CREAM SAUCE

makes 10 portions

14 fl oz/420 mL dry white wine

14 fl oz/420 mL FISH FUMET (page 253)

3 tbsp/45 mL drained and mashed green peppercorns

3 tbsp/45 mL cracked black peppercorns

3 tbsp/45 mL cracked white peppercorns

1 thyme sprig

2 bay leaves

6 fl oz/180 mL heavy cream, reduced

salt, as needed

pepper, as needed

1 oz/30 g chopped chives

1 Combine the wine, fumet, peppercorns, thyme, and bay leaves. Simmer to reduce the mixture by half. Remove the thyme and bay leaves. Add the cream and reduce it to sauce consistency. Adjust the seasoning with salt and pepper.

2 Add the chives to the sauce immediately prior to service.

GRILLED TUNA ON A BED OF ROASTED PEPPERS WITH BALSAMIC VINEGAR SAUCE

makes 10 portions

3³/₄ lb/1.75 kg tuna steak

salt, as needed

pepper, as needed

vegetable oil, as needed

ROASTED PEPPERS AND BALSAMIC VINEGAR SAUCE (recipe follows)

1 Cut the tuna into 10 equal steaks, 5 to 6 oz/140 to 170 g each. Season them with salt and pepper. Brush with the and oil. Allow any excess to drain away before placing on rods.

2 Place the tuna presentation side down on the grill or broiler rods. Grill or broil undisturbed for about 2 minutes. (Optional: Give each steak a quarter turn [90°] during broiling to achieve grill marks.) Turn the tuna over and complete cooking, about 2 to 4 minutes more.

3 Serve the tuna with the balsamic vinegar and pepper sauce.

NOTE

Substitute swordfish or mahi mahi or other firm meaty fish for the tuna.

ROASTED PEPPERS AND BALSAMIC VINEGAR SAUCE

makes 10 portions

8 fl oz/240 mL balsamic vinegar

8 fl oz/240 mL FISH STOCK (page 253)

2 oz/60 g tomato concassé

1 oz/30 g chopped herbs (thyme, tarragon, and/or chives, for example)

arrowroot slurry, as needed

2 oz/60 g enoki mushrooms

3 oz/85 g roasted green pepper julienne

3 oz/85 g roasted red pepper julienne

3 oz/85 g roasted yellow pepper julienne

Combine the vinegar, stock, tomato concassé, and herbs. Bring the mixture to a simmer and thicken it lightly with arrowroot slurry. Add the enoki mushrooms to the sauce. Add the peppers, and simmer the sauce for 2 to 3 minutes more. Adjust the seasoning with salt and pepper.

GRILLED TUNA WITH PECAN LIME BUTTER

makes 10 portions

3½ lb/1.75 kg tuna steak

MARINADE

6 fl oz/180 mL peanut oil

4 fl oz/120 mL champagne vinegar

1 tsp grated nutmeg

2 tbsp/30 mL oyster sauce

2 tsp/10 mL minced garlic

2 scallions, minced

4 fl oz/120 mL white wine

2 tbsp/30 mL chopped celery leaves

salt, as needed

pepper, as needed

PECAN LIME BUTTER (recipe follows)

1 Cut the tuna into 10 equal steaks, 5 to 6 oz/140 to 170 g each. Combine all the ingredients for the marinade and pour over the steaks. Marinate for 1 to 2 hours under refrigeration. Before placing on grill or broiler, allow the excess marinade to drain away.

2 Place the tuna presentation side down on the grill or broiler rods. Grill or broil undisturbed for about 2 minutes. (Optional: Give each steak a quarter turn [90°] during broiling to achieve grill marks.) Turn the tuna over and complete cooking, about 2 to 4 minutes more.

3 Top each tuna steak with a slice of the pecan lime butter; heat under a broiler or salamander until the butter begins to melt. Serve at once.

PECAN LIME BUTTER

makes 10 portions

8 oz/225 g butter, softened

1½ oz/45 g pecans, toasted and crushed fine

1½ fl oz/45 mL lime juice, or as needed

1 tbsp/15 mL prepared oyster sauce

1 tsp/15 mL minced garlic

1 tbsp/15 mL chopped celery leaves

1 tbsp/15 mL dry white wine

salt, as needed

pepper, as needed

1 Work the butter by hand or with a paddle attachment until it is soft. Add the remaining ingredients and blend well. Adjust the seasoning with salt and pepper.

2 The compound butter is ready to use now, or it may be rolled into a log or piped into shapes and chilled for later service.

SMOKED NOISETTES OF SALMON WITH HORSERADISH BEURRE BLANC

makes 10 portions

3¾ lb/1.7 kg salmon fillet

salt, as needed

pepper, as needed

clarified butter, as needed (optional)

horseradish, as needed

lemon juice, as needed

20 fl oz/600 mL BEURRE BLANC (page 283)

1 oz/30 g chopped parsley

1 Cut the salmon into 20 noisettes, 2 to 3 oz/60 to 85 g each. (Two noisettes is a single portion.)

2 Season the salmon with salt and pepper, brush lightly with butter, and reserve.

3 Add horseradish, lemon juice, salt, and pepper to taste to the beurre blanc and keep warm.

4 Place the salmon on a rack and set it in a pan over lightly dampened hardwood chips. Cover tightly and heat in a 450°F/230°C oven until the smell of smoke is apparent. Smoke for 3 minutes from that point. Transfer the salmon to a baking pan and finish baking (without smoke) in a 350°F/175°C oven until done, about 8 to 10 minutes more.

5 Serve at once with the horseradish beurre blanc.

SALMON FILLET WITH SMOKED SALMON AND HORSERADISH CRUST

makes 10 portions

3³/₄ lb/1.75 kg salmon fillet

MARINADE

2 fl oz/60 mL lime juice

2 tsp/10 mL minced shallots

2 tsp/10 mL minced garlic

2 tsp/10 mL peppercorns

CRUMB MIXTURE

¹/₄ tsp/1 mL minced shallots

¹/₂ tsp/3 mL minced garlic

3 oz/85 g butter

5 oz/140 g fresh bread crumbs

5 oz/140 g smoked salmon

1 oz/30 g prepared horseradish

20 fl oz/300 mL BEURRE BLANC (page 283) or RED PEPPER COULIS (page 444)

1 Cut the salmon into 10 portions, 5 to 6 oz/140 to 170 g each. Rub the salmon fillet with the lime juice, shallots, garlic, and crushed peppercorns.

2 To prepare the crumb mixture, sauté the shallots and garlic in the butter until aromatic. Combine all of the ingredients for the crumb mixture in a food processor and process to a fine consistency.

3 Portion the crumb mixture onto the salmon fillets and place on a rack on a baking sheet.

4 Bake at 350°F/175°C for 6 to 7 minutes, or until the salmon is cooked through (flesh should be opaque and firm).

5 Serve at once with the beurre blanc or coulis on heated plates.

see photograph on page 430

ROAST MONKFISH WITH NIÇOISE OLIVES AND PERNOD SAUCE

makes 10 portions

3¹/₂ lb/1.575 kg monkfish fillet

MARINADE

2 limes, juiced

1 tbsp/15 mL green peppercorns, mashed

1 tbsp/15 mL tarragon, chopped

1 tbsp/15 mL minced shallots

vegetable oil, as needed

1 tbsp/15 mL tomato paste

1 tbsp/15 mL Pernod

1 pt/480 mL BEURRE BLANC (page 283)

1 oz/30 g pitted and sliced Niçoise olives

1 Trim any connective tissure from the monkfish. Combine all the ingredients for the marinade. Pour the marinade over the monkfish and marinate for 15 to 30 minutes. Remove from the marinade and drain before roasting.

2 Sear the monkfish in hot oil over high heat on all sides. Transfer to a 400°F/205°C oven and roast until done (an internal temperature of 140°F/60°C). Keep the monkfish warm while finishing the sauce.

3 To prepare the sauce, sauté the tomato paste in a pan over high heat, stirring constantly, about 1 minute. Deglaze the pan with the Pernod. Add the beurre blanc and olives and return to a bare simmer. Adjust the seasoning if necessary.

4 Slice the monkfish into 10 portions; fan it out on a hot plate and serve with the sauce.

The cooking techniques presented
in this chapter rely on a fat or oil
as the cooking medium. As the
amount of fat is altered from
a thin film up to enough to
completely submerge foods,
different effects are achieved.

SAUTÉING, PAN FRYING, AND DEEP FRYING

SAUTÉING

Sautéing is a technique that cooks food rapidly in a little fat over relatively high heat. The term sauté *comes from the French verb* sauter, *or "to jump," and refers to the way foods sizzle and jump in a hot pan.*

Certain menu items, listed as seared/pan-seared, charred/pan-charred, or pan-broiled, are also essentially sautés. Those terms on a menu have come to suggest that even less oil is used than for a traditional sauté. They may indicate that the food is cooked extremely rare. Sautéed dishes typically include a sauce made with the drippings, or fond, left in the pan.

Searing may be a first step for some roasted, braised, or stewed foods. In other words, they are cooked quickly in a small amount of oil over direct heat. The difference between searing and sautéing is not how the technique is performed, but that these foods are not cooked completely as a result of being seared. Searing is used in these cooking methods as an effective way to develop flavor and color in these longer, slower cooking methods.

Stir frying, associated with Asian cooking and successfully adapted by innovative Western chefs, shares many similarities with sautéing. Foods are customarily cut into small pieces, usually strips, dice, or shreds, and cooked rapidly in a little oil. They are added to the pan in sequence; those requiring the longest cooking times are added first, those that cook quickly only at the last moment. The sauce for a stir fry, like that of a sauté, is made or finished in the pan to capture all of the dish's flavor.

SELECT AND PREPARE THE INGREDIENTS AND EQUIPMENT

SELECT CUTS FROM THE RIB OR LOIN, as well as portions of the leg, for beef, veal, lamb, pork, or large game animals. These cuts are the most tender. Poultry and game bird breasts are often preferred for sautéing. Firm or moderately textured fish are easier to sauté than very delicate fish. Shellfish, in and out of the shell, are also successfully sautéed.

Choose the cooking fat according to the flavor you want to create as well as food cost and availability. Oils (including olive, corn, canola, soy, or grapeseed oils) and clarified butter are the most commonly used cooking fats. Rendered fats, such as lard, bacon, and duck or goose fat, are appropriate for ethnic-style dishes.

The base for a pan sauce in sautéing may vary to suit the flavor of the main item. Brown sauces, such as demiglace or jus lié, veloutés, reduced stocks (thickened with a slurry if necessary), vegetable coulis, or tomato sauce may be used. Consult specific recipes.

A sauté pan has short sides and is wider than it is tall to encourage rapid moisture evaporation. It is made of a metal that responds quickly to rapid heat changes. Woks are used to prepare stir frys. Pan-seared and pan-broiled items are often prepared in heavy-gauge pans that retain heat, such as cast-iron pans. Have tongs or spatulas available to turn foods and remove them from the pan, as well as holding pans to reserve foods while a sauce is prepared or finished, and all appropriate service items (heated plates, garnishes, and accompaniments).

FOR A SINGLE ENTRÉE-SIZE PORTION, YOU WILL NEED:

one 6- to 8-ounce/140- to 225-gram boneless portion of meat, poultry, or seafood (adjust the portion size to account for bones, skin, or shell)

a small amount of a cooking fat or oil

salt and pepper, plus other seasonings as required

one 2- to 3-ounce/60- to 90-milliliter portion of sauce

1. Season the food and dredge or dust with flour if necessary.

Season foods with salt and pepper, as well as spice blends or rubs if appropriate, just before cooking to build flavor into the dish. Seasoning before cooking is more effective than simply adding salt and pepper at the end.

Flour helps produce a good surface color for some light or white meats, poultry, and fish. Dusting is optional. If done, be sure to coat the item evenly and shake off any excess.

2. Preheat the pan and add the cooking fat.

Heating the pan before adding oil is referred to as conditioning the pan. Add enough fat to lightly film the pan, adjusting the amount to suit the food and the pan's size and surface. The more natural marbling or fat present in the food, the less fat needed. Well-seasoned or nonstick pans may not require any fat beyond that which is already present in the food. Bring the pan and the cooking fat to the correct temperature before adding the food. This way the cooking process begins as soon as the food hits the hot pan. To sauté red meats and/or very thin meat pieces, heat the cooking fat until the surface ripples and looks hazy. Less intense heat is required for white meats, fish, and shellfish.

3. Immediately add the food to the pan. Sauté on the first side until browned or golden.

Make sure that each portion comes in direct contact with the fat in the pan, with no overlapping or touching. Let the food sauté undisturbed for several seconds up to a minute or two to develop the proper flavor and color in the finished sauté. The food may stick to the pan at first, but it will release itself by the time it is ready to be turned.

ABOVE *Skinless poultry breasts, fish fillets, and small cuts (émincé or shreds) are commonly dredged or dusted with flour.*

ABOVE *Clarified butter added to a properly conditioned pan comes to a good cooking temperature rapidly to sauté food without smoking. It also adds its own taste to the finished dish.*

ABOVE *Place the food's better-looking side, the presentation side, down onto the heated pan first for the best-looking sautéed foods. This side will be face up when the dish is presented to the guest.*

4. Turn the food and continue sautéing to the proper doneness.
Sautéed foods are usually turned only once so that the fond can develop in the pan. More frequent turning can disturb this process, although there are exceptions. Sautéed shrimp or meat cut into émincé, for example, may be repeatedly tossed or turned.

Adjust the heat under the sauté pan if necessary to complete cooking on the stovetop. In some cases, sautéed food may be finished in the oven, either in the sauté pan or in a baking dish, sizzler platter, or sheet pan.

Proper doneness in sautéed foods depends upon the food itself, safe food handling, and customer preference. Be sure to allow for some carryover cooking so that foods are not overdone by the time you are ready to put them on a plate. For more information, review Guidelines for Determining Doneness, page 350.

5. Remove the food from the pan when it is done, and make a sauce with the fond.
Transfer sautéed items to a warm holding area while a sauce is prepared directly in the pan.

To make a sauce incorporating the fond found in the sauté pan, first remove any excess fat or oil. Add aromatic ingredients or garnish items that need to be cooked. Then deglaze the pan, releasing the reduced drippings. Wine, cognac, broth, or water can be used for this step. Reduce the liquid.

The sauce base (such as a separately prepared sauce, a jus lié, a reduced stock, or vegetable purées or coulis) should be added to the pan and brought to a simmer. Cream, if called for, should be added along with the sauce base so that it can reduce properly along with the base. Some sauces may need to be additionally thickened before they are served; if so, add a small amount of a pure starch slurry until the correct consistency is reached.

ABOVE *Turning sautéing foods too frequently can prevent them from developing a good flavor and color, since the meat's temperature will drop each time the meat is turned. Chefs often encourage less experienced cooks to "let the food cook."*

ABOVE *Sweating, smothering, or browning aromatic ingredients releases their flavor.*

TOP *Adding a liquid like stock or wine releases the browned drippings, or fond, and gives the sauce a deep and customized flavor.*

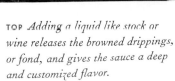

BOTTOM *Reducing the sauce concentrates the flavor and also thickens the sauce so that it coats the food well.*

6. Finish, garnish, and season the sauce and serve it with the sautéed food.

A pan sauce can be finished and garnished in several ways. It may be strained through a fine-mesh strainer for a very smooth texture before any finishing or garnishing ingredients are added. Simmer finishing and garnishing ingredients in the sauce long enough for them to be properly heated. Adjust the seasoning with salt, pepper, fresh herbs, juices, essences, purées, or similar items. If desired, a small amount of whole butter may be added just before serving to enrich the sauce.

After a final check to be sure the seasoning is correct, chefs often opt to return the main item (a chicken breast or veal scallop, for example) to the finished sauce briefly. This glazes and coats the item, as well as very gently reheating it. The sauce may be ladled in a pool on the plate and the food set on top. Or the sauce may be ladled over the food (nappé), or ladled around the food (cordon). Be sure to wipe away any drips with a clean cloth wrung out in hot water before the plate is sent to the dining room.

7. Evaluate the quality of the finished sautéed food.

The object of sautéing is to produce a flavorful exterior, resulting from proper browning, which serves to intensify the food's flavor. Weak flavor and color indicate that the food was sautéed at too low a temperature or that the pan was too crowded.

Good color depends on the food. When well sautéed, red meats and game will have a deep brown exterior. White meats (veal, pork, and poultry) will have a golden or amber exterior. Lean white fish will be pale gold when sautéed as skinless fillets, while firm fish steaks, like tuna, will take on a darker color. In any case, food should not be extremely pale or gray. Improper color is an indication that incorrect pan size or improper heat levels were used.

Only naturally tender foods should be sautéed, and after sautéing they should remain tender and moist. Excessive dryness is a sign that the food was overcooked, that it was cooked too far in advance and held too long, or that it was sautéed at a temperature higher than necessary.

TOP *Strain the sauce directly into a clean saucepan and return to a simmer.*

BOTTOM *Finishing ingredients, such as minced herbs, cream, or fortified wines, may all be added. A small amount of butter is often swirled into the sauce (monté au beurre) to add both flavor and body.*

10 chicken suprêmes (8 oz / 225 g each)

salt, as needed

pepper, as needed

flour, as needed (optional)

clarified butter, as needed

2 tbsp / 30 mL minced shallots

white wine, as needed to deglaze pan

FINES HERBES SAUCE (recipe follows on next page)

FINES HERBES (page 353)

SAUTÉED CHICKEN WITH FINES HERBES SAUCE

1 Trim the chicken suprêmes. Just before sautéing, blot dry and season with salt and pepper. Dredge in flour, if desired.

2 Sauté the chicken in the clarified butter on the first side until light golden, about 3 minutes. Turn the chicken and continue to sauté until done (170°F/75°C). Remove it and keep it warm.

3 Degrease the pan. Add the shallots and sauté until translucent.

4 Deglaze the pan with the white wine; reduce until nearly cooked away. Add the fines herbes sauce, simmer briefly, then strain into a clean pan. Add the fines herbes.

5 Serve the chicken with the sauce.

MAKES 10 PORTIONS

FINES HERBES SAUCE

clarified butter, as needed

½ oz / 15 g minced shallots

6 fl oz / 180 mL dry white wine

1 oz / 30 g parsley stems

1 oz / 30 g tarragon leaves and stems

1 oz / 30 g chervil stems

1 oz / 30 g chives

24 fl oz / 720 mL JUS DE VOLAILLE (page 261) or JUS DE VEAU LIÉ (page 260) or
  DEMIGLACE (page 287)

6 fl oz / 180 mL heavy cream

salt, as needed

pepper, as needed

1 Heat a small amount of butter in a saucepan. Add the shallots and sweat until translucent, about 2 to 3 minutes. Add the wine and herbs and simmer until nearly dry.

2 Add the jus lié or demiglace and bring to a simmer. Reduce slightly. Add the cream and
   continue to simmer to a good flavor and consistency, skimming as necessary. Adjust
   the seasoning with salt and pepper. Strain the sauce and hold warm, or chill and store
   for later service.

MAKES 10 PORTIONS (ABOUT 24 FLUID OUNCES/720 MILLILITERS)

PAN FRYING

Pan-fried foods have a richly textured crust and a moist flavorful interior, producing a dish of intriguing contrasts in texture and flavor. When a carefully selected sauce is paired with a dish, the effects can range from home-style to haute cuisine.

Pan-fried food is almost always coated — dusted with flour, coated with batter, or breaded. Food is fried in enough oil to come halfway or two thirds up its side; it is often cooked over less intense heat than in sautéing. The product is cooked more by the oil's heat than by direct contact with the pan. In pan frying, the hot oil seals the food's coated surface and thereby locks the natural juices inside. Because no juices are released and a larger amount of oil is involved, accompanying sauces are usually made separately.

Pan-fried food is usually portion-size or smaller. Select cuts that are naturally tender, as you would for a sauté; rib or loin cuts, the top round, or poultry breasts. Lean fish, such as sole or flounder, are well suited to this technique. Trim away any fat, silverskin, and gristle. Remove the skin and bones of poultry and fish fillets if necessary or desired. Cutlets are often pounded to give them an even thickness and to shorten cooking time. This means that the exterior will brown without overcooking in the same time that the meat cooks through. Be certain to season the food before adding a coating.

Ingredients for breading include flour, milk and/or beaten eggs, and bread crumbs or cornmeal. For instructions on Standard Breading, see page 349. Batters, such as beer batter, may also be prepared. Hold them at the correct temperature if made in advance.

The fat for pan frying must be able to reach high temperatures without breaking down or smoking. Vegetable oils, olive oil, and shortenings may all be used for pan frying. Lard, goose fat, and other rendered animal fats have a place in certain regional and ethnic dishes. The choice of fat makes a difference in the flavor of the finished dish.

The pan used must be large enough to hold foods in a single layer without touching one another. If the food is crowded, the temperature of the fat will drop quickly and a good crust will not form. Pans should be made of heavy gauge metal and should be able to transmit heat evenly. The sides should be higher than those appropriate for sautés to avoid splashing hot oil out of the pan as foods are added to the oil or turned during cooking. Have on hand a pan lined with absorbent toweling to blot away surface fat from fried foods. Tongs or slotted spatulas are typically used to turn foods. Select shallow, wide containers to hold coatings, breading, or batters.

FOR A SINGLE ENTRÉE-SIZE PORTION, YOU WILL NEED:

one 6- to 8-ounce/170- to 225-gram boneless portion of meat, poultry, or seafood (adjust the portion size to account for bones or skin)

enough cooking fat or oil to cover half to two thirds of the item being pan fried

standard breading, batter, or other coating

salt and pepper, plus other seasonings as required

one 2- to 3- ounce/60- to 90-milliliter portion of sauce

1. Dry and season the foods for pan frying, and coat as necessary.
Blot the food dry with absorbent toweling. Any moisture left on the surface could make the coating too moist. It will also break down the cooking fat more quickly, as well as causing it to splatter or foam over.

Seasonings are added before the coating. Foods are usually dipped in flour or a meal, then into a batter or into eggwash followed by a coating of bread crumbs. Coatings are applied just as the food is ready to go into the batter. Standard breading can be applied 3 or 4 hours in advance.

2. Heat the fat to the correct temperature.
The pan and the cooking fat must reach the correct temperature before the food is added. Otherwise, the crust's development will be slowed, and it may never achieve the desired crisp texture and golden brown color. As a rule of thumb, add enough fat to come one-half to two-thirds of the way up the food; the thinner the food, the less fat is required. When a faint haze or slight shimmer is noticeable, the fat is usually hot enough. To test the temperature, dip a corner of the food in the fat. If the fat is at about 350°F/175°C, it will bubble around the food, and the coating will start to brown within 45 seconds.

3. Add the food carefully to the hot fat and pan fry on the first side until a good crust and color are reached.
Exercise extreme caution at this point to prevent burns. Getting pan-fried foods evenly browned and crisped requires that the food be in direct contact with the hot fat. If foods are crowded, they may not develop good colors and textures. If there is not enough fat in the pan, the food may stick to the pan and tear, or the coating may come away.

When pan frying large quantities, skim or strain away any loose particles between batches. Add more fresh fat, or replace the fat to keep the level constant and to prevent smoking or foaming.

ABOVE *Season all components of the dish. This is especially important for food such as this cutlet, which will be breaded before cooking.*

ABOVE *In general, there should be enough cooking fat in the pan to allow the food to swim in the fat.*

ABOVE *Add the pieces to be pan fried to the oil carefully so that you don't splash yourself. Here the chef is laying cutlets in the pan gently to avoid creating a wave of hot oil.*

4. Turn the food once and continue to pan fry until the second side is golden and the food is properly cooked. Some foods, because they are thick or include bones or a stuffing, may need to be removed from the fat and placed in an oven to finish cooking. If they do need to go into the oven, be sure that they are not covered. A cover could cause steam to soften the crisp coating.

As with sautéed foods, it is difficult to give precise instructions for determining doneness in pan-fried foods, for the same reasons. In general, the thinner and more delicate the meat, the more quickly it will cook. Pan-fried items, even thin pieces, are subject to carryover cooking. It is thus best to slightly undercook. For more information, review Guidelines for Determining Doneness, page 350.

5. Drain or blot on clean absorbent paper or cloth. The food is ready to serve now, with a sauce if desired. Do not hold fried foods for more than a very brief period before serving. They tend to get soggy quickly.

Sauces for pan-fried foods are served under the food or separately to preserve the crust.

6. Evaluate the quality of the finished pan-fried food.

The object of pan frying is to produce a flavorful exterior with a crisp, brown crust, which acts as a barrier to retain juices and flavor. Because the food itself is not browned, the flavor will be different than if it had been sautéed. The color depends upon the food, the coating, and, to a certain extent, the thickness. Thin cuts of delicate meats (fish, shellfish, and poultry) should be golden to amber. Thicker pieces may take on a deeper color as a result of the longer cooking time. In no case should the food be extremely pale. A pale color indicates that incorrect heat levels or the wrong size pan were used.

Only naturally tender foods should be pan fried, and after cooking, the product should still be tender and moist. Excessive dryness means the food was allowed to overcook, was cooked too far in advance and held too long, or was cooked at a temperature higher than required.

ABOVE *Once a good crust and a pleasing color develop on the first side, carefully turn the food over, away from you to avoid splashing.*

ABOVE *The cutlets are briefly drained on a rack or paper toweling to blot away any excess surface fat. Season the food at this point if necessary, and serve it on a heated plate with sauce if desired.*

3¾ lb / 1.75 kg boneless veal top round

bread crumbs, as needed

salt, as needed

pepper, as needed

flour, as needed

egg wash, as needed

vegetable oil, for pan frying, as needed

PAN-FRIED VEAL CUTLETS

1 Trim the veal of any surface fat or silverskin. Cut the veal into 10 equal portions, 6 oz/170 g each. Pound the cutlets to an even thickness (about ¼ in/8 mm) between 2 pieces of plastic wrap, using a meat mallet.

2 Line a sheet pan with parchment and scatter a thin layer of crumbs over it if desired. Blot the cutlets dry and season with salt and pepper. Bread them by dipping them in flour and shaking off the excess, dipping into egg wash, transferring to the bread crumbs, and pressing the crumbs evenly over the surface. Transfer to the sheet pan. Continue breading as needed. If the bread crumbs start to clump together due to the egg wash, sieve the crumbs to remove clumps. (Breading may be done in advance; hold refrigerated but not covered for no more than 3 to 4 hours for best quality.)

3 Heat oil to a depth of about ⅛ in/30 mm over moderate heat until the oil is hot (350°F/175°C; a few bread crumbs will sizzle when dropped into the oil, but they should not immediately turn black or sink to the bottom of the pan).

4 Add the breaded cutlets to the hot oil. Pan fry on the first side for 2 to 3 minutes, or until golden brown and the cutlets release easily from the pan. Turn the cutlets once and finish cooking on the second side, 2 to 3 minutes.

5 Remove the cutlets from the oil and drain briefly on absorbent paper toweling. Serve with a sauce or other accompaniments.

MAKES 10 PORTIONS

DEEP FRYING

Deep-fried foods have many of the same characteristics as pan-fried foods, including a crisp, browned exterior and a moist, flavorful interior. Deep-fried foods, however, are cooked in enough fat or oil to completely submerge them.

In deep frying, significantly more fat is used than for either sautéing or pan frying. The food is almost always coated with a standard breading, a batter such as a tempura or beer batter, or a simple flour coating. The coating acts as a barrier between the fat and the food and also contributes flavor and texture contrast.

TO COOK RAPIDLY AND EVENLY, foods must be cut into a uniform size and shape and trimmed. Select cuts that are naturally tender; some typical choices include poultry, fish, and seafood. Remove the skin and bones of poultry and fish fillets if necessary or desired. Be certain to season the food before adding a coating. Deep frying is also suitable for croquettes and similar dishes made from a mixture of cooked, diced meats, fish, or poultry, bound with a heavy béchamel and breaded.

Breadings and coatings are common for deep-fried foods. Standard breading can be done up to three hours ahead and items held under refrigeration before frying, but ideally breading should be done as close to service as possible. For Standard Breading instructions, see page 349. A batter or plain flour coating is applied immediately before cooking.

Electric or gas deep fryers with baskets are typically used for deep frying, although it is also feasible to fry foods using a large pot. The sides should be high enough to prevent fat from foaming over or splashing, and wide enough to allow the chef to add and remove foods easily. Use a deep-fat frying thermometer to check the fat's temperature, regardless of whether you use an electric or gas fryer or a pot on a stovetop. Become familiar with the fryer's recovery time; that is, the time needed for the fat to regain the proper temperature after foods are added. The fat will lose temperature for a brief time. The more food added, the more the temperature will drop and the longer it will take to come back to the proper level.

Kitchens that must fry many kinds of food often have several different fryers to help prevent flavor transfer. Have a pan lined with absorbent toweling to blot fried foods before they are served. Tongs, spiders, and baskets are used to add foods to the fryer and remove them when properly cooked.

FOR AN ENTRÉE-SIZE PORTION, YOU WILL NEED:	*one 6- to 8-ounce/170- to 225-gram boneless portion of meat, poultry, or seafood*	*enough cooking fat or oil to completely submerge the foods being deep fried*	*salt and pepper, plus other seasonings as required*
		standard breading, batter, or other coating	*one 2- to 3-fluid ounce/60- to 90-milliliter portion of sauce*

HOW TO DEEP FRY

1. Heat the cooking fat to the proper temperature (generally 325° to 375°F/165° to 190°C).
The cooking fat must reach and maintain a nearly steady temperature throughout frying time to prepare crisp, flavorful, and non-greasy fried foods. Proper maintenance of oil will help extend its life. Old fats and oils have a darker color and more pronounced aroma than fresh oil. They may also smoke at a lower temperature and foam when foods are added. Be sure to strain or filter the oil properly after each meal period. Replenish the fryer's oil to the appropriate level if necessary.

2. Place the food directly into the fat and cook until done.

Two methods are used to deep fry foods. The choice depends on the food, the coating, and the intended result.

The swimming method is generally used for battered food. As soon as the food is coated with batter, it is carefully lowered into the

TOP *To coat prepared foods with batter, dust them with flour, then shake off the excess before dropping them into the batter.*

BOTTOM *Lift the food out of the batter with tongs and then lower it gently into the hot fat.*

hot oil using tongs. At first, the food will fall to the bottom of the fryer; as it cooks it swims back to the surface. It may be necessary to turn foods once they reach the surface for them to brown evenly.

The basket method is generally used for breaded items. Place the breaded food in a frying basket and then lower both the food and the basket into the hot fat. Once the food is cooked, use the basket to lift out the food. Foods that would tend to rise to the surface too rapidly are held down by setting a second basket on top of the food; this is known as the double-basket method.

Use all your senses as well as a thermometer to accurately judge internal doneness. For more information, review Guidelines for Determining Doneness, page 350.

Drain or blot foods on clean absorbent paper or cloth. The food is ready to serve now, with a sauce if desired.

ABOVE *Remove foods cooked by the swimming method with a skimmer or spider.*

3. Evaluate the quality of the finished deep-fried food.

Deep-fried foods should taste like the food, not like the fat used (or like other foods previously fried in the fat). Foods served very hot, directly from the frying kettle, have a better, less greasy taste. If the food tastes heavy, greasy, or strongly of another food, the fat was not hot enough, the fat was too old, or a strongly flavored food such as fish was fried in the same fat.

The texture of well-prepared deep-fried food is moist and tender on the interior, with a crisp, delicate crust. If the crust has become soggy, the food may have been held too long after cooking or, again, the oil was not at the correct temperature.

5 lb / 2.25 kg shrimp (21-25)

TEMPURA BATTER

1¹/₂ lb / 680 g all-purpose flour

1¹/₂ oz / 45 g baking powder

6 cups / 1.4 L cold water

4 fl oz / 120 mL sesame oil

vegetable oil for pan frying, as needed

salt, as needed

pepper, as needed

cornstarch for dusting, as needed

TEMPURA DIPPING SAUCE (recipe follows)

SHRIMP TEMPURA

1 Peel and devein the shrimp. Keep refrigerated or over ice until ready to coat with batter.

2 To make the batter, whisk together the flour and baking powder. Add the water and sesame oil all at once, and whisk until combined into a batter about the thickness of pancake batter and very smooth. Keep chilled until ready to prepare the tempura.

3 Heat the oil to 350°F/175°C in a deep fryer or tall pot. Blot the shrimp dry, season with salt and pepper, and dip in cornstarch and then in the batter. Deep fry in the oil until golden brown, about 4 to 5 minutes. Drain on absorbent paper.

4 Serve at once with dipping sauce.

MAKES 10 PORTIONS

TEMPURA DIPPING SAUCE

1 pt / 480 mL water

8 fl oz / 240 mL soy sauce

1 tbsp / 15 mL minced ginger

2 fl oz / 60 mL mirin (sweet rice wine)

³/₄ oz / 20 g katsuo dashi

Combine all of the ingredients. Let the flavors blend for at least 1 hour before serving.

TOMATO AND HERB SAUCE

makes 10 portions

clarified butter or oil for sautéing, as needed

1 oz/30 g minced shallots

12 oz/340 g small-dice tomato or tomato julienne

24 fl oz/720 mL JUS DE VEAU LIÉ (page 260) or DEMIGLACE (page 287)

1 tbsp/15 mL lemon juice, or as needed

salt, as needed

pepper, as needed

1 oz/30 g minced fresh herbs (thyme, chives, basil, oregano, or others)

4 oz/115 g diced or sliced butter

1 Heat the butter or oil and sauté the shallots until translucent, 2 to 3 minutes. Add the tomatoes and sauté until very hot and any juices they release have cooked away.

2 Add the jus lié or demiglace and continue to simmer until the sauce has developed a good flavor and consistency.

3 Season the sauce with lemon juice, salt, and pepper. Finish by swirling in herbs and butter. Keep warm for service or cool and store for later service.

NOISETTES OF PORK WITH WARM CABBAGE SALAD

makes 10 portions

3³⁄₄ lb/1.75 kg pork tenderloin

salt, as needed

pepper, as needed

clarified butter or oil for sautéing, as needed

6 fl oz/180 mL dry white wine, or as needed for deglazing

SHERRY VINEGAR SAUCE (page 428)

WARM CABBAGE SALAD (recipe follows)

1 Trim the tenderloins and cut into noisettes, 2 oz/60 g each. Shape in cheesecloth and keep chilled. When ready to sauté, blot to dry the surface and season with salt and pepper.

2 Heat a sauté pan, add the butter or oil, and sauté the pork about 2 minutes per side (160°F/70°C). Remove the noisettes from the pan and keep warm while completing the sauce.

3 Pour off the excess fat from the pan and add the white wine to deglaze the pan and cook down until nearly dry.

4 Add the sherry vinegar sauce and any juices released by the pork. Reduce to a good flavor and consistency. Adjust the seasoning with salt and pepper as needed.

5 Serve the cutlets on heated plates with the sauce and warm cabbage salad.

WARM CABBAGE SALAD

makes 10 portions

1³⁄₄ oz/50 g minced bacon

1 oz/30 g butter

3¹⁄₂ oz/100 g small-dice red onions

¹⁄₂ oz/15 g minced garlic

2 lb/900 g Savoy cabbage chiffonade

1³⁄₄ fl oz/50 mL sherry wine vinegar

1 oz/30 g sugar

1 tsp/5 mL caraway seeds

1 tbsp/15 mL chopped parsley

salt, as needed

pepper, as needed

1 Cook the bacon in a sauté pan over medium heat until the fat is rendered and the bacon is crisped. Remove the bacon with a slotted spoon, allowing the fat to drain back into the pan. Reserve the bacon.

2 Return the pan to the heat and add the butter. Add the onion and garlic, and sauté until they are translucent and tender, 2 to 3 minutes.

3 Add the cabbage to the pan, toss to coat evenly with the rendered fat, and sauté until limp, stirring frequently, about 6 to 8 minutes.

4 Add the vinegar, sugar, and caraway seeds, and bring to a simmer. Cook until cabbage is very hot and tender, 3 to 4 minutes more. Add the parsley. Adjust the seasoning with salt and pepper if necessary. Keep warm for service.

SAUTÉED MEDALLIONS OF PORK WITH WINTER FRUIT SAUCE

makes 10 portions

3³/₄ lb/1.75 kg boneless pork loin

salt, as needed

pepper, as needed

clarified butter or oil for sautéing, as needed

8 fl oz/240 mL dry white wine

WINTER FRUIT SAUCE (recipe follows)

1 Trim the pork loin and cut into medallions, 3 oz/85 g each. Shape in cheesecloth and keep chilled. When ready to sauté, blot to dry the surface and season with salt and pepper.

2 Heat a sauté pan, add the butter or oil, and sauté the pork about 2 minutes per side (160°F/70°C). Remove the medallions from the pan and keep warm while completing the sauce.

3 Pour off the excess fat from the pan, add the white wine to deglaze the pan, and cook down until nearly dry.

4 Add the winter fruit sauce and any juices released by the pork. Reduce to a good flavor and consistency. Adjust the seasoning with salt and pepper as needed.

5 Serve the medallions on heated plates with the sauce.

Pork Medallions with Apricots, Currants, and Pine Nuts Prepare as directed above, substituting the Apricot, Currant, and Pine Nut Sauce (see variation on Winter Fruit Sauce at right) for the Winter Fruit Sauce.

WINTER FRUIT SAUCE

makes 10 portions

10 fl oz/300 mL semi-dry white wine

3¹/₂ oz/100 g dried apricots (sulfur free)

1³/₄ oz/50 g dried cherries

2 fl oz/60 mL clarified butter or oil

1 oz/30 g minced shallots

5 oz/140 g small-diced Red Delicious apples

4 oz/113.4 g small-diced Bartlett pears

1³/₄ fl oz/52.5 mL brandy, apple-flavored

24 fl oz/720 mL BROWN PORK STOCK (page 252), JUS DE VEAU LIÉ (page 260), or DEMIGLACE (page 287)

2 tsp/10 mL lemon juice, or as needed

salt, as needed

pepper, as needed

1 Heat the wine in a small pan to just below a boil. Remove from the heat and add the dried fruit. Let the fruit soak in the wine (macerate) for 30 minutes. Drain the fruit and reserve the wine.

2 Heat the butter or oil in a saucepan and add the shallots. Sauté over medium heat until translucent, 1 to 2 minutes. Add the diced apples and pears and sauté until lightly browned.

3 Add the brandy to deglaze the pan and let it reduce until nearly cooked away. Add the reserved wine and reduce once more. Add the jus lié or demiglace and bring to a simmer. Simmer until reduced to a good flavor and consistency. Add the macerated dried fruit and adjust seasoning with lemon juice, salt, and pepper. Keep warm for service or cool and store for later service.

Apricot, Currant, and Pine Nut Sauce Prepare as directed above, substituting currants for the dried cherries and omitting the apples and pears. Finish the sauce by scattering toasted pine nuts over each portion while plating the food.

Chicken Provençal

Deep-Fried Squid

Noisettes of Pork with
Green Peppercorns and Pineapple

CHICKEN PROVENÇAL

makes 10 portions

10 boneless (or semi-boneless) chicken breast portions
(7 to 8 oz/200 to 225 g each)

salt, as needed

pepper, as needed

flour for dredging, as needed (optional)

clarified butter or olive or vegetable oil for sautéing, as needed

PROVENÇAL SAUCE

¼ oz/7 g minced garlic

3 anchovy fillets, mashed to a paste

12 oz/340 g tomato concassé

10 fl oz/300 mL dry white wine

24 fl oz/720 mL JUS DE VOLAILLE (page 261), JUS DE VEAU LIÉ
(page 260), or DEMIGLACE (page 287)

4 oz/115 g black olive slices or julienne

1 oz/30 g basil chiffonade

1 Trim the chicken breasts and french the wing bone for a
suprême; remove skin if desired. When ready to sauté,
blot to dry the surface and season with salt and pepper.
Dredge lightly in flour if desired, and shake off any
excess.

2 Heat a sauté pan, add the butter or oil, and sauté the
chicken 3 to 4 minutes per side or until done (170°F/
75°C). (Finish in a 350°F/175°C oven if necessary.)
Remove the chicken from the pan and keep warm while
completing the sauce.

3 Pour off the excess fat from the pan and add the garlic
and anchovies; sauté 30 to 40 seconds to release their
aroma. Add the tomatoes and continue to sauté until any
juices they release have cooked down. Add the wine to
deglaze the pan and simmer until nearly cooked away.

4 Add the jus lié or demiglace and any juices released by the
chicken. Reduce to a good flavor and consistency. Strain
into a clean pan and return to a simmer. Add the olives
and basil, return to a simmer, and adjust the seasoning
with salt and pepper as needed.

5 Return the chicken to the pan and turn to coat with the
sauce. Serve the chicken with the sauce on heated plates.

NOTES

You may elect to use different kinds of olives in this dish, introduce some
capers, or add other herbs, either in addition to or as a replacement for
the basil: Oregano, marjoram, chives, chervil, and thyme are all good
choices.

see photograph on page 478

PAN-SEARED BREAST OF CHICKEN GRAND-MÈRE WITH GREEN PEPPERCORN, PORT, AND MADEIRA SAUCE

makes 10 portions

10 boneless (or semi-boneless) chicken breast portions
(7 to 8 oz/200 to 225 g each)

salt, as needed

pepper, as needed

flour for dredging, as needed

clarified butter or vegetable oil for sautéing, as needed

GRAND-MÈRE GARNISH

5 oz/140 g clarified butter or oil

2 oz/60 g medium-dice slab bacon

1 lb/450 g parisienne-cut potatoes (use small melon baller)

30 peeled pearl onions, cooked until tender in salted water

4 oz/115 g quartered white mushrooms

GREEN PEPPERCORN, PORT, AND MADEIRA SAUCE
(recipe follows)

1 Trim the chicken breasts and french the wing bone for a
supreme; remove skin if desired. When ready to sauté,
blot to dry the surface and season with salt and pepper.
Dredge lightly in flour if desired, and shake off any
excess.

2 Heat a sauté pan, add the butter or oil, and sauté
the chicken 3 to 4 minutes per side or until done
(170°F/75°C). (Finish in a 350°F/175°C oven if
necessary.) Remove the chicken from the pan and keep
warm while completing the sauce.

3 Pour off the excess fat from the pan and add a little clarified butter or oil to the pan. Add the bacon and sauté until
golden brown and crisp. Remove the bacon with a slotted
spoon and reserve.

4 Add the potatoes to the same pan and sauté until golden
brown and crisped on the exterior, adding more butter if
necessary. Add the onions, mushrooms, and reserved
bacon and sauté until very hot. Adjust seasoning.

5 Serve the chicken breast with the grand-mère garnish and
the heated green peppercorn, Port, and Madeira sauce.

GREEN PEPPERCORN, PORT, AND MADEIRA SAUCE

makes 10 portions

1 oz/30 g minced shallots

2 thyme sprigs

1 bay leaf

½ tsp/3 mL cracked black peppercorns

6 fl oz/180 mL ruby Port

4 fl oz/120 mL Madeira

24 fl oz/720 mL JUS DE VOLAILLE (page 261), JUS DE VEAU LIÉ (page 260), or DEMIGLACE (page 287)

¾ oz/20 g drained green peppercorns

salt, as needed

4 oz/115 g diced or sliced butter

1 Combine the shallots, thyme, bay leaf, black peppercorns, Port, and Madeira. Reduce by half over medium high heat.

2 Add the jus lié or demiglace and continue to simmer until the sauce has developed a good flavor and consistency. Strain the sauce into a clean pan. Add the green peppercorns and return to a simmer.

3 Season the sauce with salt. Finish by batch or by portion by swirling in butter if desired.

BREAST OF CHICKEN CHARDONNAY

makes 10 portions

10 boneless (or semi-boneless) chicken breast portions (7 to 8 oz/200 to 225 g each)

salt, as needed

pepper, as needed

flour for dredging, as needed

clarified butter or oil, as needed

2 fl oz/60 mL dry white wine

CHARDONNAY AND LEEK SAUCE (recipe follows)

minced chives, as needed (optional)

1 Trim the chicken breasts and french the wing bone for a suprême; remove skin if desired. When ready to sauté, blot to dry the surface and season with salt and pepper. Dredge lightly in flour if desired, and shake off any excess.

2 Heat a sauté pan, add the butter or oil, and sauté the chicken 3 to 4 minutes per side or until done (170°F/75°C). (Finish in a 350°F/175°C oven if necessary.) Remove the chicken from the pan and keep warm while completing the sauce.

3 Pour off the excess fat from the pan and add the wine to deglaze the pan. Reduce until nearly cooked away. Add the chardonnay and leek sauce and any juices released by the chicken. Reduce to a good flavor and consistency. Add the chives, return to a simmer, and adjust the seasoning with salt and pepper as needed.

4 Serve the chicken with the sauce on heated plates.

CHARDONNAY AND LEEK SAUCE

makes 10 portions

clarified butter, as needed

½ oz/15 g minced shallots

1 lb/450 g sliced mushrooms

¾ lb/340 g sliced or paysanne-cut leeks

6 fl oz/180 mL Chardonnay

1 tbsp/15 mL mustard seeds

24 fl oz/720 mL JUS DE VOLAILLE (page 261), JUS DE VEAU LIÉ (page 260), or DEMIGLACE (page 287)

6 fl oz/180 mL heavy cream

salt, as needed

pepper, as needed

1 Heat a small amount of butter in a saucepan. Add the shallots, mushrooms, and leeks and sweat until translucent, about 2 to 3 minutes. Add the wine and mustard seeds and simmer until nearly dry.

2 Add the jus lié or demiglace and bring to a simmer. Reduce slightly. Add the cream and continue to simmer to a good flavor and consistency, skimming as necessary. Adjust the seasoning with salt and pepper. Keep the sauce hot for service, or chill and store for later service.

BREAST OF CHICKEN WITH DUXELLES STUFFING AND SUPRÊME SAUCE

makes 10 portions

10 boneless chicken breast portions (7 to 8 oz/200 to 225 g each)

salt, as needed

pepper, as needed

DUXELLES STUFFING (page 439)

flour for standard breading, as needed

egg wash for standard breading, as needed

bread crumbs for standard breading, as needed

clarified butter or oil for pan frying, as needed

20 fl oz/600 mL SUPRÊME SAUCE (page 289)

1 Trim the chicken breasts and remove skin if desired. Butterfly each breast portion and pound between sheets of parchment or plastic wrap to even thickness.

2 At the time of service or up to 3 hours in advance, blot to dry the chicken and season with salt and pepper. Fill each breast with a portion of the duxelles stuffing and roll the breast around the stuffing. Overlap the edges to form a seam.

3 Apply a standard breading: dredge the chicken in flour, dip in egg wash, and roll in bread crumbs. (Hold seam side down under refrigeration if breaded in advance.)

4 Heat about ½ in/16 mm of butter or oil to about 350°F/175°C over medium heat. Add the chicken to the hot oil seam side down first and pan fry for about 2 to 3 minutes, or until golden brown and crisp. Turn once, and finish pan frying on the second side, 3 minutes more or until an internal temperature of 170°F/75°C is reached. (Finish cooking in a 350°F/175°F oven once the crust is properly browned if preferred.)

5 Blot the chicken on absorbent paper briefly before serving on heated plates with the heated suprême sauce.

Chicken Suprêmes Maréchal Use semi-boneless chicken breast portions and french the wing bone to make a suprême; remove the skin but do not butterfly. Omit the stuffing and apply a standard breading. Pan fry as directed above. Serve with suprême sauce finished with cooked asparagus tips and truffle slices.

SOUTHERN FRIED CHICKEN WITH COUNTRY-STYLE GRAVY

makes 8 portions

4 fryer chickens

salt, as needed

pepper, as needed

1 qt/1 L buttermilk

4 oz/115 g mustard

1 tbsp/15 mL chopped tarragon leaves

2 oz/60 g flour for pan gravy, plus as needed for coating

vegetable oil for pan frying, as needed

24 fl oz/360 mL milk

1 Cut the chicken into eighths. Trim the chicken pieces and season well with salt and pepper.

2 Combine the buttermilk, mustard, and tarragon. Add the chicken pieces and turn until coated evenly. Let marinate under refrigeration for at least 4 hours or up to overnight.

3 Remove the chicken from the buttermilk and let it drain. Dredge the chicken in flour until well coated.

4 Heat about ½ in/16 cm of oil to about 350°F/175°C over medium heat. Add the chicken to the hot oil and pan fry on the first side for about 5 to 6 minutes, or until golden brown and crisp. Turn once, and finish pan frying on the second side, 7 to 8 minutes more or to an internal temperature of 170°F/75°C for breast portions, 180°F/82°C for thigh and leg portions. (Optional: Finish cooking in a 350°F/175°F oven if preferred.)

5 Blot the chicken pieces on absorbent paper and keep warm while preparing the pan gravy.

6 Pour off most of the oil from the pan, leaving about 2 fl oz/60 mL in the pan. Add 2 oz/60 g of flour for roux. Cook the roux, stirring frequently, until golden, about 5 to 6 minutes.

7 Add the milk to the roux, stirring well to remove all lumps. Simmer for 15 to 20 minutes, stirring and skimming as necessary. Adjust the seasoning with salt and pepper. Strain the gravy and keep hot for service.

8 Serve the chicken with the gravy.

TROUT AMANDINE

makes 10 portions

10 trout fillets (6 oz/170 g each)

salt, as needed

pepper, as needed

milk, as needed (optional)

flour, as needed

clarified butter or oil for sautéing, as needed

10 oz/285 g whole butter

5 oz/140 g slivered almonds

5 fl oz/150 mL juice lemon

2oz/60 g chopped parsley

1 Trim the trout as necessary. When ready to sauté, blot to dry, season with salt and pepper, dip into milk (optional), and dredge with flour, shaking off any excess.

2 Heat a sauté pan, add the clarified butter or oil, and sauté the trout about 2 minutes per side or until the flesh is opaque and firm (145°F/63°C). Remove the trout from the pan and keep warm while completing the sauce.

3 Pour off the excess fat from the pan and add whole butter (about 1 oz/30 g per portion), and cook until the butter begins to brown and has a nutty aroma.

4 Add the almonds and stir to coat them evenly with the butter. Add the lemon juice and swirl the pan to deglaze it. Add the parsley.

5 Serve the trout immediately on heated plates with the pan sauce.

SAUTÉED TROUT MEUNIÈRE

makes 10 portions

10 pan-dressed trout (10 oz/285 g each)

salt, as needed

pepper, as needed

flour, as needed

clarified butter or oil for sautéing, as needed

10 oz/300 g whole butter

2 fl oz/60 mL lemon juice

3 tbsp/45 mL chopped parsley

1 Rinse the trout, remove the head and tail if desired. Trim the trout as necessary. When ready to sauté, blot dry, season with salt and pepper, and dredge with flour, shaking off any excess.

2 Heat a sauté pan, add the butter or oil, and sauté the trout about 3 minutes per side or until the flesh is opaque and firm (145°F/63°C). Remove the trout from the pan and keep warm on heated plates while completing the sauce.

3 Pour off the excess fat from the pan and add whole butter (about 1 oz/30 g per portion); cook until the butter begins to brown and has a nutty aroma.

4 Add the lemon juice and swirl the pan to deglaze it. Add the parsley and immediately pour or spoon the pan sauce over the trout. Serve at once.

STIR-FRIED SCALLOPS

makes 10 portions

3³/₄ lb/1.75 kg bay scallops

salt, as needed

pepper, as needed

peanut or vegetable oil, as needed

2 oz/60 g minced ginger

1 oz/30 g minced garlic

10 oz/285 g oblique-cut zucchini

5 oz/140 g celery, sliced on the bias

10 oz/285 g red pepper julienne

10 oz/285 g yellow pepper julienne

10 oz/285 g green pepper julienne

10 oz/285 g snow peas

10 oz/285 g quartered mushrooms

3 oz/85 g sliced green onions

1 tsp/5 mL hot bean paste

1 tbsp/15 mL red bean paste

1 Pull the muscle tabs from the scallops. Just before stir frying, blot the scallops dry and season with salt and pepper.

2 Heat the oil in a wok, add the scallops to the oil and stir fry until the scallops lose their translucency, about 2 minutes.

3 Add the ginger, garlic, and zucchini to the wok and stir fry until very hot, about 2 minutes. Add the celery and stir fry 1 minute more. Add the peppers, snow peas, mushrooms, and green onions and continue to stir fry until the vegetables are all very hot, 1 minute more.

4 Push all the stir-fry ingredients up on the sides of the wok. Add the bean paste to the wok and stir fry until hot. Push the ingredients back into the bean paste and stir fry 1 minute more, tossing to coat evenly. Season with salt and pepper. Serve at once on heated plates.

PAN-FRIED GROUPER WITH MANGO BEURRE BLANC

makes 10 portions

3³/₄ lb/1.75 kg grouper fillets

salt, as needed

pepper, as needed

flour for standard breading, as needed

egg wash for standard breading, as needed

fresh bread crumbs for standard breading, as needed

vegetable oil for pan frying, as needed

MANGO BEURRE BLANC (recipe follows)

MANGO AVOCADO SALSA (recipe follows)

1. Trim the grouper and cut into 10 equal portions, 5 to 6 oz/ 140 to 170 g each. Season with salt and pepper.

2. At the time of service or up to 3 hours in advance, apply a standard breading to the grouper: Blot the grouper dry, dredge in flour, dip in egg wash, and roll in bread crumbs. (Hold under refrigeration if breaded in advance.)

3. Heat about ¼ in/8 mm of oil to about 350°F/175°C over medium heat. Add the grouper to the hot oil and pan fry on the first side for about 2 minutes, or until golden brown and crisp. Turn once, and finish pan frying on the second side, 1 to 2 minutes more or until an internal temperature of 145°F/63°C is reached. (Optional: Finish cooking in a 350°F/175°C oven if preferred.)

4. Blot the grouper on absorbent paper briefly before serving on heated plates with the beurre blanc and a portion of mango avocado salsa.

MANGO BEURRE BLANC

makes 10 portions

2 oz/60 g minced shallots

4 fl oz/120 mL dry white wine

1½ fl oz/45 mL lime juice

1½ oz/45 mL cider vinegar

4 oz/115 g small-dice mangos

4 fl oz/120 mL heavy cream (optional)

8 oz/225 g small-dice butter

salt, as needed

pepper, as needed

1. Combine the shallots, wine, lime juice, vinegar, and mangos and simmer until reduced by two-thirds. Add the cream, if desired, and simmer until the cream is lightly thickened. Purée this mixture and strain into a clean pan.

2. Add the butter a little at a time, swirling the pan or whisking constantly. When all butter is added, adjust seasoning with salt and pepper.

3. Hold the beurre blanc warm for service.

MANGO-AVOCADO SALSA

makes 10 portions

4 oz/115 g fine-dice mangos

3 oz/85 g fine-dice avocado

1½ fl oz/45 mL lime juice

1 oz/30 g fine-dice red bell peppers

1 oz/30 g fine-dice red onion

4 tsp/20 mL chopped cilantro

1 tsp/5 mL minced garlic

salt, as needed

pepper, as needed

1. Combine all items and let marinate for 1 hour.

2. Season and serve at room temperature.

PAN-FRIED HALIBUT WITH TOMATO CAPER SAUCE

makes 10 portions

3³/₄ lb/1.75 kg halibut fillets

salt, as needed

pepper, as needed

flour for standard breading, as needed

egg wash for standard breading, as needed

fresh bread crumbs for standard breading, as needed

vegetable oil for pan frying, as needed

TOMATO CAPER SAUCE (recipe follows)

1 Trim the halibut and cut into 10 equal portions, 5 to 6 oz/ 140 to 170 g each. Season with salt and pepper.

2 At the time of service or up to 3 hours in advance, apply a standard breading to the halibut: blot the halibut dry, dredge in flour, dip in egg wash, and roll in bread crumbs. (Hold under refrigeration if breaded in advance.)

3 Heat about ¼ in/8 mm of oil to about 350°F/175°C over medium heat. Add the halibut to the hot oil and pan fry on the first side for about 2 minutes, or until golden brown and crisp. Turn once, and finish pan frying on the second side, 1 to 2 minutes more or until an internal temperature of 145°F/63°C is reached. (Optional: Finish cooking in a 350°F/175°C oven if preferred.)

4 Blot the halibut on absorbent paper briefly before serving on heated plates with the tomato caper sauce.

NOTE

To give a different flavor and texture to the standard breading, replace from one-fourth to one-half of the bread crumbs with ground or finely chopped nuts (almonds, walnuts, or pecans, for example).

TOMATO CAPER SAUCE

makes 10 portions

olive oil, as needed

1 tsp/5 mL minced garlic

3 to 4 anchovy fillets (2 tsp/10 mL paste)

2 fl oz/60 mL dry white wine

1 tbsp/15 mL chopped capers

4 oz/115 g fine-dice tomato or tomato julienne

20 fl oz/600 mL TOMATO COULIS (page 289)

lemon juice, as needed

salt, as needed

pepper, as needed

2 tbsp/30 mL chopped parsley

1 Heat the olive oil in a pan. Add the garlic and anchovies and sauté, stirring frequently, until the garlic has a good aroma, about 2 minutes.

2 Add the white wine and deglaze the pan. Let the wine simmer until it has nearly cooked away.

3 Add the capers, tomato, and tomato coulis. Simmer until the sauce has a good flavor and consistency, about 15 minutes more.

4 Adjust the seasoning with lemon juice, salt, and pepper. Finish with parsley just before service. Keep the sauce hot for service, or cool and store for later service.

FLOUNDER STUFFED WITH CRABMEAT

makes 10 portions

3³/₄ lb/1.75 kg flounder fillets (6 oz/170 g each)

salt, as needed

pepper, as needed

CRABMEAT STUFFING (recipe follows)

flour, as needed

egg wash, as needed

fresh bread crumbs, as needed

butter or vegetable oil for pan frying, as needed

BEURRE BLANC (page 283)

1 Trim the flounder and cut into 10 equal portions, 5 to 6 oz/140 to 170 g each.

2 At the time of service or up to 3 hours in advance, blot to dry the surface and season with salt and pepper. Fill each fillet with a portion of the crabmeat stuffing and roll the fish around the stuffing. Overlap the edges to form a seam.

3 Apply a standard breading: dredge the flounder in flour, dip in egg wash, and roll in bread crumbs. (Hold seam side down under refrigeration if breaded in advance.)

4 Heat about ½ in/16 mm of butter or oil to about 350°F/175°C over medium heat. Add the flounder to the hot oil seam side down first and pan fry for about 2 minutes, or until golden brown and crisp. Turn once, and finish pan frying on the second side, 2 minutes more or until an internal temperature of 145°F/63°C is reached. (Finish cooking in a 350°F/175°C oven once the crust is properly browned, if preferred.)

5 Blot the flounder on absorbent paper briefly before serving on heated plates with the lemon beurre blanc.

CRABMEAT STUFFING

makes 10 portions

12 oz/340 g cooked crabmeat

1 oz/30 g minced shallots

3 oz/85 g minced green onions

1 oz/30 g butter

1 oz/30 g flour

6 fl oz/180 mL dry white wine

6 fl oz/180 mL heavy cream

2 tsp/10 mL chopped parsley

salt, as needed

pepper, as needed

1 Pick through the crabmeat carefully, removing any bits of shell or cartilage.

2 Sauté the shallots and green onions in the butter until tender and translucent, about 3 to 4 minutes. Add the flour and cook for 1 minute. Add the wine and cream and bring to a boil, simmering until the mixture is thick, stirring occasionally.

3 Fold in the crabmeat and parsley. Adjust the seasoning with salt and pepper. Chill to below 40°F/4°C.

FISHERMAN'S PLATTER

makes 10 portions

1¼ lb/570 g flounder

20 littleneck clams

20 oysters

20 shrimp (16/20 count)

10 oz/285 g sea scallops

lemon juice, as needed

salt, as needed

pepper, as needed

flour for standard breading, as needed

egg wash for standard breading, as needed

bread crumbs for standard breading, as needed

oil for pan frying, as needed

RÉMOULADE SAUCE (page 487)

1 Trim the flounder and cut into goujonettes, 1 oz/30 g each. Shuck the clams and oysters. Peel, devein, and butterfly the shrimp. Remove the muscle tabs from the scallops. Keep chilled until ready to bread.

2 At the time of service or up to 3 hours in advance, blot to dry the surface and season fish, oysters, clams, shrimp, and scallops with lemon juice, salt, and pepper. Apply a standard breading: dredge each piece in flour, dip in egg wash, and roll in bread crumbs. (Hold under refrigeration if breaded in advance.)

3 Heat about ½ in/16 mm of oil to about 350°F/175°C over medium heat. Add the fish and seafood to the hot oil and pan fry on the first side for about 2 minutes, or until golden brown and crisp. Turn once, and finish pan frying on the second side, 1 to 2 minutes more or until an internal temperature of 145°F/63°C is reached. (Finish cooking in a 350°F/175°C oven once the crust is properly browned, if preferred.)

4 Blot the fish and seafood on absorbent paper briefly before serving on heated plates with the remoulade sauce.

DEEP-FRIED BREADED SHRIMP

makes 10 portions

3½ lb/1.8 kg shrimp
salt, as needed
pepper, as needed
flour, as needed
egg wash, as needed
fresh white bread crumbs, as needed
20 fl oz/600 mL RÉMOULADE SAUCE (recipe follows)

1 Peel and devein the shrimp. Keep refrigerated or over ice until ready to coat with breading.

2 At the time of service or up to 3 hours in advance, apply a standard breading to the shrimp: Blot the shrimp dry, season with salt and pepper, dredge in flour, dip in egg wash, and roll in bread crumbs. (Hold under refrigeration if breaded in advance.)

3 Heat oil to 350°F/175°C in a deep fryer or tall pot. Place the shrimp in a fryer basket, lower into the oil, and deep-fry until golden brown, about 4 to 5 minutes. Drain on absorbent paper.

4 Serve at once with rémoulade sauce.

RÉMOULADE SAUCE

makes 15 portions

1½ pt/730 mL MAYONNAISE (page 767)
2 oz/60 g chopped capers
2 oz/ 60 g chopped cornichons
3 tbsp/45 mL chopped chives
3 tbsp/45 mL chopped chervil
3 tbsp/45 mL chopped tarragon
1 tbsp/15 mL Dijon mustard
1 tsp/5 mL anchovy paste
salt, as needed
Worcestershire sauce, as needed
Tabasco sauce, as needed

1 Combine all ingredients; mix together well.

2 Hold the sauce under refrigeration. Adjust the seasoning just before serving if necessary.

DEEP-FRIED SOLE ANGLAISE

makes 10 portions

3³/₄ lb/1.75 kg sole fillets

salt, as needed

pepper, as needed

lemon juice, as needed

flour for standard breading, as needed

egg wash for standard breading, as needed

bread crumbs for standard breading, as needed

20 parsley sprigs

RÉMOULADE SAUCE (page 487)

10 lemon wedges

1 Trim the sole and cut into 10 equal portions, 5 to 6 oz/140 to 170 g each. Keep refrigerated or over ice until ready to coat with breading.

2 At the time of service or up to 3 hours in advance, apply a standard breading to the sole: Blot the sole dry, season with salt and pepper, dredge the fish in flour, dip in egg wash, and roll in bread crumbs. (Hold under refrigeration if breaded in advance.)

3 Heat oil to 350°F/175°C in a deep fryer or tall pot. Place the sole in a fryer basket, lower into the oil, and deep-fry until golden brown, about 4 to 5 minutes. Drain on absorbent paper.

4 Deep-fry the parsley sprigs until crisp, about 45 seconds. Drain on absorbent paper.

5 Serve the sole at once with rémoulade sauce, lemon wedge, and fried parsley.

Deep-Fried Flounder Substitute an equal amount of flounder for the sole.

Deep-Fried Catfish Substitute an equal amount of catfish for the sole. Replace half of the bread crumbs with corn meal, if desired.

DEEP-FRIED SQUID

makes 10 portions

4 lb/1.8 kg squid

lemon juice, as needed

Worcestershire sauce, as needed

salt, as needed

pepper, as needed

flour for standard breading, as needed

eggwash for standard breading, as needed

Japanese-style bread crumbs for standard breading, as needed

20 fl oz/600 mL TOMATO SAUCE (page 272)

1 Clean squid and separate the tentacles from the body. Slice the body into rings, and divide into 10 equal portions, 5 to 6 oz/140 to 170 g each. Keep refrigerated or over ice until ready to coat with breading.

2 At the time of service or up to 3 hours in advance, apply a standard breading to the squid: Blot the tentacles and rings dry and season with lemon juice, Worcestershire, salt, and pepper. Dredge the squid in flour, dip in egg wash, and roll in bread crumbs. (Hold under refrigeration if breaded in advance.)

3 Heat oil to 350°F/175°C in a deep fryer or tall pot. Place the squid in a fryer basket, lower into the oil, and deep-fry until golden brown, about 3 to 4 minutes. Drain on absorbent paper.

4 Serve at once with tomato sauce.

see photograph on page 478

HOT AND SOUR FISH

3³/₄ lb/1.75 kg sole fillet

BATTER

1¹/₂ lb/680 g all-purpose flour

1¹/₂ oz/45 g baking powder

3 pints/720 mL cold water

4 fl oz/120 mL sesame oil

salt, as needed

pepper, as needed

flour for dredging, as needed

HOT AND SOUR SAUCE (recipe follows)

1 Trim the sole and cut into cubes or strips and divide into
   equal portions, 5 to 6 oz/140 to 170 g each. Keep refrigerated or over ice until ready to coat with batter.

2 To make the batter, whisk together the flour and baking
   powder. Add the water and sesame oil all at once, and
   whisk until combined into a batter about the thickness of
   pancake batter and very smooth. Keep chilled until ready
   to prepare the tempura.

3 Heat oil to 350°F/175°C in a deep fryer or tall pot. Blot
   the sole dry and season with salt and pepper. Dip in the
   flour, then into the batter. Carefully lower the pieces into
   the deep fryer with tongs and deep fry in the oil until
   golden brown, about 4 to 5 minutes. Drain on absorbent
   paper.

4 Serve at once with hot and sour sauce.

HOT AND SOUR SAUCE

oil, as needed

¹/₂ oz/15 g garlic, minced to a paste

4 oz/115 g fine-dice carrot

4 oz/115 g fine-dice celery

4 oz/115 g fine-dice tomato

4 oz/115 g fine-dice red pepper

1 oz/30 g tomato paste

2 fl oz/60 mL water

1¹/₂ fl oz/45 mL fish sauce

1 oz/30 g sugar

1 tbsp/15 mL Worcestershire sauce

2 fl oz/60 mL red wine vinegar

1 tbsp/ 15 mL red chili peppers

¹/₂ fl oz/15 mL soy sauce

3 tbsp/45 mL minced cilantro

salt, as needed

pepper, as needed

1 Heat the oil, add the garlic and vegetables, and stir fry
   until tender and translucent, about 3 minutes.

2 Add the tomato paste, water, fish sauce, and sugar and stir
   until evenly blended. Add the remaining ingredients and
   simmer for 15 to 20 minutes. Adjust the consistency with
   water if necessary. Adjust seasoning with salt and pepper.

SAUTÉING, PAN FRYING, AND DEEP FRYING   **489**

FLOUNDER À L'ORLY

3³/₄ lb/1.75 kg flounder fillets

vegetable oil, as needed

lemon juice, as needed

salt, as needed

pepper, as needed

flour, as needed

BEER BATTER (recipe follows)

20 fl oz/600 mL TOMATO SAUCE (page 272)

20 parsley sprigs

10 lemon wedges

1 Trim the flounder and cut into 10 equal portions, 5 to 6 oz/ 140 to 170 g each. Keep refrigerated or over ice until ready to coat with batter.

2 Heat the oil to 350°F/175°C in a deep fryer or tall pot.

3 At the time of service, blot the fish dry and season with lemon juice, salt, and pepper. Dip into the flour, shaking off any excess, then dip into the beer batter. Lower the fish into the hot oil with tongs and deep fry for 3 to 4 minutes, or until golden brown and cooked through.

4 Blot briefly on absorbent paper and serve at once with tomato sauce, parsley sprigs, and lemon wedge.

BEER BATTER

10 oz/285 g flour

¹/₂ tsp/2 mL baking powder

1 egg, separated

8 fl oz/240 mL beer

1 Whisk together the flour and baking powder. Add the egg yolk and beer all at once, and whisk until combined into a batter about the thickness of pancake batter and very smooth. Keep chilled until ready to prepare the fried food.

2 At the time of service, whip the reserved egg white to soft peaks. Fold the white into the batter and use at once.

Moist-heat techniques—steaming, cooking foods en papillote, shallow-poaching, deep-poaching, and simmering—rely on liquid and/or water vapor as the cooking medium. Monitoring cooking temperatures and times vigilantly and determining doneness accurately are key to a mastery of moist-heat methods.

STEAMING AND SUBMERSION COOKING

STEAMING

Cooked surrounded by water vapor in a closed cooking vessel, steamed foods have clean, clear flavors.

Steam circulating around the food provides an even, moist environment. Steaming is an efficient and highly effective way to prepare naturally tender fish and poultry. Properly steamed foods are plump, moist, and tender; they generally do not lose much of their original volume. They often have more intrinsic flavor than foods cooked by other methods because the cooking medium does not generally impart much of its own. Thus the flavor can be contrasted nicely with sauce. Colors also stay true.

FOR A SINGLE ENTRÉE PORTION, YOU WILL NEED:

a 6- to 8-ounce/170- to 225-gram portion of prepared meat, poultry or fish

enough steaming liquid to last throughout cooking time

salt and other seasonings for both the main item and the steaming liquid

additional finishing and garnishing ingredients

2 to 3 ounces/60 to 85 grams prepared sauce

SELECT AND PREPARE THE INGREDIENTS AND EQUIPMENT

NATURALLY TENDER FOODS of a size and shape that allow them to cook in a short amount of time are best for steaming. Cut food into the appropriate size, if necessary. Fish is generally made into fillets, though there are some classic presentations of whole fish. Poultry breast is often made into a suprême, a boneless skinless piece. Shellfish can be left in the shell, unless otherwise indicated; for example, scallops are customarily removed from the shell. Shrimp may also be peeled before steaming.

Many different liquids are used for steaming. Water is common, but a flavorful broth or stock, court bouillon, wine, or beer can also be used, especially if the steaming liquid is served along with the food. Adding such aromatic ingredients as herbs and spices, citrus zest, lemongrass, ginger, garlic, and mushrooms to the liquid also boosts its flavor as well as that of the food being steamed. Sometimes food is steamed on a bed of vegetables in a closed vessel, such as the tagine shown here; their natural moisture becomes part of the steam bath cooking

the food. Fillings, marinades, and wrappers can all be used in preparing steamed foods. Fish is sometimes wrapped in this way to keep it exceptionally moist.

Small amounts of food can be steamed using a small insert. Larger quantities, or foods that require different cooking times, are better prepared in a tiered steamer. Remember that it is important to allow enough room for steam to circulate completely around foods as they cook. This will encourage even, rapid cooking.

Pressure steamers, which reach higher temperatures than tiered steamers, and convection steamers are good choices for steaming large quantities. The chef can then prepare appropriately sized batches throughout a meal period or handle the more intense demands of a banquet or institutional feeding situation.

HOW TO STEAM

1. Bring the liquid and any additional aromatics to a full boil in a covered vessel.
Add enough liquid to the bottom of the steamer to last throughout cooking. Adding more liquid to the pot during cooking lowers the cooking temperature and lengthens the time needed to prepare steamed foods. If you must add liquid, preheat it.

2. Place the main item in the steamer in a single layer.
If cooking more than one layer of food at a time, use a tiered steamer. Foods may be placed on plates or in shallow dishes on the rack to collect any juices that might escape.

ABOVE *Just enough liquid is added to generate steam, not enough to poach the fish.*

ABOVE *Filleted fish sits on a bed of aromatic vegetables, including onions, tomatoes, and fennel, in a tagine.*

ABOVE *To ensure even cooking, foods should be placed in a single layer, not touching one another, so that the steam can circulate freely.*

3. Replace the lid and steam until done.

Adjust the heat to maintain even, moderate heat. Liquids do not need to be at a rolling boil in order to produce steam. In fact, rapid boiling may cause the liquid to cook away too fast.

Since steaming is done in a closed cooking vessel, it can be a little more difficult than in other methods to gauge how long foods need to cook. Recipes may tell how long to steam foods for the correct doneness. Still, it is important to check, starting at the earliest point at which the food might be done. Remember to tilt the lid away from you as you open it so that the steam will vent away from your face and hands.

4. Steamed foods should be cooked until they are just done and served immediately.

Steamed foods can easily become rubbery and dry, so be careful not to overcook. Any juices from the food should be nearly colorless. When done, the flesh of fish and shellfish loses its translucency, taking on a nearly opaque appearance. The shells of mollusks (mussels, clams, and oysters) open, and the flesh of the mollusks turns opaque and the edges curl. Crustaceans (shrimp, crab, and lobster) have a bright pink or red color when done. Poultry turns opaque, and the flesh offers little resistance when pressed with a fingertip.

Serve the food immediately on heated plates with an appropriate sauce, as desired, or as indicated by the recipe. Steamed food continues to cook after it comes out of the steamer. This underscores the importance of serving it immediately. Steamed foods take nicely to a sauce.

5. Evaluate the quality of the finished dish.

Evaluate the quality of steamed foods according to flavor, appearance, and texture. Because no initial browning of the food takes place, the flavor remains delicate. Any aromatics appropriate to the food's flavor should not be so intense as to overwhelm it. When properly done, the food's surface appears quite moist. Fish, especially salmon, should not have deposits of white albumin on the flesh, which indicates that it has been overcooked and/or cooked too quickly.

ABOVE *Once all the food is in the steamer, cover it with a tight lid. Avoid removing the lid unnecessarily. The drop in temperature will slow cooking time, affecting flavor and quality.*

ABOVE *Steamed foods are plump and moist when fully cooked. Foods suitable for steaming are naturally tender and remain tender unless overcooked.*

4 lb / 1.8 kg cod fillets, skin on

salt, as needed

pepper, as needed

FISH MARINADE (page 354), as needed

VEGETABLE BED

1 lb / 450 g sliced onions, sliced lengthwise

12 oz / 340 g sliced fennel, sliced crosswise

8 oz / 225 g celery julienne

2 lb / 450 g large-dice tomatoes (peel and seed before dicing)

2 oz/60 g preserved lemon (see Notes) or lemon zest, rinsed, cut into fine julienne

10 oz / 285 g artichoke hearts, halved

3 oz / 85 g caper berries, washed

1 qt / 1 L saffron-infused fish stock (see Notes)

2 fl oz / 60 mL extra-virgin olive oil

parsley, as needed

TAGINE OF COD

1 Cut the fish into 10 equal portions, 5 to 6 oz/140 to 170 g each. Score the fish fillets through the skin side in 2 or 3 places. Season them with salt and pepper.

2 Combine all the ingredients for the marinade. Spread the marinade over the fish fillets and marinate, refrigerated, for 1 to 2 hours.

3 Place the vegetable bed and stock in the bottom of a tagine. Season with salt and pepper. Bring the stock to a simmer. Place the fish on top of the vegetable bed and drizzle with the olive oil. Cover the tagine and steam in a 375°F/190°C oven until the fish is just done.

4 Serve the fish, along with the vegetables and broth, in a heated dish or bowl. Sprinkle the plate with chopped parsley and serve.

MAKES 10 PORTIONS

NOTES

To make preserved lemons, wash 3 lemons very well. Cut each one lengthwise in 6 wedges and remove all the seeds. Place the lemon wedges in a very clean jar. Add 2½ oz/70 g kosher salt and 5 fl oz/15 mL lemon juice and mix well. Add more lemon juice if necessary to just cover the lemons. Cover with a lid and refrigerate for at least a week before using, stirring the lemons every day or two to help dissolve the salt more. The lemons will stay preserved for up to a month or more in the refrigerator. Rinse the lemons under cold water and remove the seeds before using.

If you fillet your fish in-house, make a fish stock from the bones using the recipe for Fish Fumet or Stock on page 253. Add 1 tsp/5 mL saffron to a 1-gallon/3.75-L batch. If using purchased or prepared stock, add ¼ tsp/1 mL crushed saffron to a quart of stock and simmer until the stock is flavored and colored with the saffron, about 15 minutes.

COOKING EN PAPILLOTE

In this variation of steaming, which translates literally as "in paper," the main item and accompanying ingredients are wrapped in a parchment paper package and cooked in the steam produced by their own juices.

En papillote indicates a specific preparation, but there are similar dishes, known by regional names, throughout the world. The classic wrapper for a dish en papillote is parchment paper, but the effect is similar when aluminum foil; lettuce, plantain, grape, or banana leaves; corn husks; or similar wrappers are used to enclose foods as they cook. The wrapper traps the steam driven from the foods as they heat up — the dish is often presented to the guest still in its wrapper, and when the packet is opened, it releases a cloud of aromatic steam.

COOKING EN PAPILLOTE, like steaming, is suited to naturally tender foods, like chicken, fish, and shellfish. Trim and portion foods as required by recipe. They may be marinated or seared as an initial step, if appropriate. Marinades can add flavor and color; searing helps to assure that thicker cuts can cook more quickly as well as deepen both the flavor and color of the main item.

Some foods may be filled or stuffed.

Vegetables are usually included for moisture and steam as well as flavor, color, and texture. Cut the vegetables small, usually into thin slices, a fine julienne, or tiny dice, and sweat or blanch them, if necessary, to ensure that they will be fully cooked. Leave herbs in sprigs, cut them into a chiffonade, or mince them. Also, have available a

prepared sauce, reduced heavy cream, wine, or citrus juices as required by the recipe.

To cook en papillote, you will need parchment paper (or other wrappers as required by recipe), sizzler platters or baking sheets, and service items. Cut the wrapper large enough to allow the food and any additional ingredients to fit comfortably without overcrowding.

FOR A SINGLE ENTRÉE PORTION, YOU WILL NEED:	*a 4- to 6-ounce/115- to 170-gram portion of prepared meat, poultry, or fish*	*up to 1 ounce/30 grams of a cooking liquid (stock, sauce, wine) or enough naturally moist vegetables to produce steam*	*salt and other seasonings* *additional finishing and garnishing ingredients as desired (see recipes)*

HOW TO COOK EN PAPILLOTE

1. Assemble the packages.
Cut the parchment or other wrapper into heart shapes large enough to hold the food on one half of the heart, with a 1-inch margin of paper all the way around. Lightly oil or butter it on both sides to prevent it from burning. Place the food on one half of the paper or foil. Fold the other half over, then crimp the edges of the paper or foil or tie the packet securely to seal it.

ABOVE *Arrange a bed of vegetables, aromatics, or sauce on one half of the heart, square, or rectangle and top it with the main item.*

ABOVE *Crimping the edges of the package seals in the steam, so that it can properly cook the food.*

2. Place the package on a preheated sizzler platter or baking sheet and bake in a moderate oven. Serve immediately.
Bake the food until the package is puffed and the paper is browned. The oven temperature needs to be carefully monitored because delicate foods such as fish fillets can be overcooked quickly.

Foods prepared en papillote should be cooked until just done. This is difficult to gauge without experience, because you cannot open the package to apply the senses of sight and touch to determine doneness. If the food has been cut to the correct size or if it has been partially cooked in advance, it should be done when the package is very puffy and the paper is brown. Performing a few test runs of an en papillote dish will help establish a reliable cooking time for the dish, provided that the ingredients are consistently prepared beforehand.

As the package cools, it will begin to deflate, so serve en papillote dishes as soon as possible.

3. Evaluate the quality of the finished dish.
Meats, fish, and poultry prepared en papillote or by similar techniques should be cooked according to doneness standards for the kitchen or to guest preference (see the table on page 351). Sauces, cooking liquids, and other ingredients should also be have a full flavor and be properly cooked.

ABOVE *For a dramatic presentation, have the server cut open the package in front of the guest.*

1 lb / 450 g sea bass fillet

2 oz / 60 g butter

1¹/₂ pints / 720 mL VEGETABLE STOCK (page 254)

8 fl oz / 240 mL vermouth

2 lb / 900 g celeriac julienne

1 lb / 450 g thinly sliced red bliss potatoes

10¹/₂ oz / 300 g carrot julienne

10¹/₂ oz / 300 g cucumber julienne

1 lb / 450 g sea scallops, muscle tabs removed

1 recipe GREMOLATA (page 548)

1 tsp / 5 mL crushed black peppercorns

BASS AND SCALLOPS EN PAPILLOTE

1   Cut the bass into 10 equal portions, 1½ oz/45 g each. Refrigerate until needed.

2   Cut large heart shapes out of parchment paper. Lightly butter both sides of the paper.

3   Combine the stock and vermouth in a large saucepan and bring to a simmer. Individually blanch the celeriac, potatoes, and carrots in the stock mixture until tender. Drain the vegetables and toss together with the cucumber.

4   Arrange a bed of about 7 oz/210 g of the vegetables on one half of each paper heart. Top the vegetables with 1 portion of the bass and 1½ oz/45 g of the scallops. Top with about 1 tablespoon of the Gremolata and sprinkle with pepper.

5   Fold the top of the heart over the fish and vegetables. Crimp the edges of the paper to seal tightly. Refrigerate until needed.

6   For each serving, place 1 parchment package on a preheated sizzler pan or sheet pan and bake in a 425°F/220°C oven for 7 minutes. The package should be puffy and the paper brown. For a dramatic presentation, cut the package open in front of the diner.

MAKES 10 PORTIONS

NOTES
Add 2 tablespoons chopped sage and 4 teaspoons chopped rosemary to the Gremolata. Increase the anchovies to 5 fillets.

SHALLOW POACHING

Shallow poaching, like sautéing and grilling, is an à la minute technique. Foods are cooked in a combination of steam and simmering liquid.

Shallow-poached foods are partially submerged in liquid. It often contains an acid (wine or lemon juice). Aromatics, such as shallots and herbs, are added for more flavor. The pan is covered to capture some of the steam released by the liquid during cooking; the captured steam cooks the part of the food that is not directly in the liquid. A significant amount of flavor is transferred from the food to the cooking liquid. For maximum flavor, the cooking liquid *(cuisson)* is usually reduced and used as the base for a sauce. The acids give the sauce a bright, balanced flavor. Butter can be easily emulsified in the sauce, making beurre blanc is often the sauce of choice for shallow-poached foods.

FOR A SINGLE ENTRÉE PORTION, YOU WILL NEED:

a 4- to 6-ounce/115- to 170-gram portion of fish or chicken breast

1 to 2 ounces/30 to 60 grams butter

2 ounces/60 grams shallots

enough poaching liquid to last throughout cooking time (about 10 to 20 fluid ounces/300 to 600 milliliters)

salt and other seasonings for both the food and the poaching liquid

additional finishing ingredients, including prepared sauce, and garnishes

SELECT AND PREPARE THE INGREDIENTS AND EQUIPMENT

NATURALLY TENDER FOODS of a size and shape that allow for quick cooking are the ingredients that work best. Fish, shellfish, and chicken breasts are among the most common options for this cooking method.

Trim the main item as appropriate. Remove bones or skin from fish to make fillets, or suprêmes or boneless skinless breast portions from poultry. Fish fillets may be rolled or folded around a stuffing to form paupiettes (see Filling and Rolling Paupiettes), with the bone side of the fish showing on the exterior. Remove shellfish from the shell, if desired.

The liquid contributes flavor to the food as well as to the sauce prepared from the cooking liquid. Choose rich broths or stocks and add wine, vinegar, or citrus juice.

Cut aromatics fine or mince them. Other ingredients to be served along with the sauce as a garnish should be cut neatly into strips, dice, julienne, or chiffonade. These ingredients are often sweated or par-cooked first to develop the best possible flavor as well as to make certain that all parts of the finished dish are fully cooked at the same time.

The sauce may be a beurre blanc or sauce vin blanc (see page 503), or simply the reduced cooking liquids served as a broth.

Refer to specific recipes for additional suggestions or guidance.

Shallow poaching is done in a sauté pan or other shallow cooking vessel, such as a sautoir or rondeau. Select the pan or baking-dish carefully for shallow-poached dishes. If there is too much or too little space left around the food, food might over- or under-cook, or there may be too much or too little liquid for the sauce.

Buttered or oiled parchment is generally used to loosely cover the pan as the food cooks. It traps enough of the steam to cook the unexposed part of the food, but not so much that the cooking speed rises. A loose-fitting lid may also be used.

You may require a strainer for the sauce. You will also need utensils for handling the poached food, such as a slotted spatula, and heated plates for service.

FILLING AND ROLLING PAUPIETTES

Fish fillets are gently flattened between sheets of plastic wrap before being filled. (Trout is shown here.) This helps them cook evenly.

Spread cold filling evenly over the entire surface for paupiettes. Fillings are optional, but if used, they should be kept very cold until ready to cook.

Cut the food into portion size, remembering to include the filling to arrive at the total portion size. Here, the chef has cut the trout fillet in half after spreading the filling.

Fillings need to be fully encased. Here, the fish is rolled completely around the filling before transferring the paupiettes to a holding container for later service.

1. Butter the pan and add the aromatic ingredients.

Lightly butter a shallow pan and add aromatics to the pan to give the cooking liquid and finished sauce a good flavor. If they can cook completely in the time required, they can be added raw. Otherwise, cook them separately beforehand or sweat them lightly in the butter.

ABOVE *Although not always essential, butter is generally spread in an even layer in a cold pan or baking dish to add flavor and keep foods from sticking. Then, the aromatic ingredients are added in an even layer.*

2. Add the main item and the cooking liquid.

Season and set the main item on top of the aromatics, then pour the liquid around the item. It is not necessary in most cases to have the liquid already heated, though for large quantities, it may be helpful to do so. Be careful not to have it at a full boil.

ABOVE *The liquid's level should go no higher than halfway up the food; generally, less is required. If too much liquid is used, either a great deal of time will be needed to reduce it properly or only part of it will be usable in the sauce.*

3. Bring the liquid to a bare simmer over direct heat. Loosely cover the pan with parchment paper and finish cooking in a moderate oven.

The liquid is typically brought up to cooking speed over direct heat. On some occasions, however, it is preferable to perform the entire cooking operation in the oven. The quantity of food being prepared and available equipment will dictate what is most logical. Do not allow the liquid to boil at any time. A rapid boil will cook the food too quickly, affecting the quality of the dish.

Cook shallow-poached foods until just done (see the table on page 351). Fish and shellfish should appear opaque and feel slightly firm; the flesh of oysters, clams, and mussels should curl around the edges. Chicken suprêmes also appear opaque and should offer slight resistance when pressed with a fingertip when done.

ABOVE *It is best to finish poaching foods in the oven because oven heat is more even and gentle than direct heat. Finishing shallow poaching in the oven also frees burner space for other purposes.*

4. Remove the main item to a holding dish and prepare a sauce from the cooking liquid.

Cover the food loosely and keep it warm while making the sauce. Add the additional ingredients for the sauce to the cooking liquid, as directed in the recipe.

TO MAKE A BEURRE BLANC: reduce the cooking liquid until it is syrupy. (It may be strained into a separate pot at this point if desired.) With the reduced cooking liquid at a simmer, add pieces of cold butter a few at time. Keep the pan in motion as the butter is added, swirling it into the sauce as it melts.

TO MAKE A SAUCE VIN BLANC: reduce the cooking liquid and add the desired aromatics and an appropriately flavored velouté. Strain the sauce if necessary and finish with cream or a liaison and any additional garnishes.

For more information about preparing sauces for shallow-poached items, refer to specific recipes.

5. Evaluate the quality of the finished shallow-poached dish.

When well prepared, shallow-poached dishes reflect the flavor of both the food and the cooking liquid. Because acid and aromatic ingredients are included, the flavor is bright. The sauce adds a rich, complementary flavor. In general, foods appear moist, opaque, and relatively light in color. Fish should not have deposits of white albumin, which indicates that it has been overcooked or cooked too quickly.

Properly cooked shallow-poached foods are very tender and exceptionally moist. And because this technique is most often used with delicate foods, they have an almost fragile texture. If they are falling apart or dry, however, they have been overcooked.

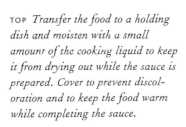

TOP *Transfer the food to a holding dish and moisten with a small amount of the cooking liquid to keep it from drying out while the sauce is prepared. Cover to prevent discoloration and to keep the food warm while completing the sauce.*

BOTTOM *Simmer the cooking liquid (cuisson) over direct heat to concentrate the flavor and thicken the liquid.*

TOP *A prepared fish velouté is being added to the reduced cuisson. Other options include reduced cream, vegetable purées, or butter.*

BOTTOM *To make a velvety smooth sauce, strain it through a fine-mesh sieve before service. Hold in a warm area or a steam table.*

ABOVE *Ladle the sauce over the food, garnish, and serve while still very hot.*

3¹/₂ lb / 1.6 kg skinless trout fillets

salt, as needed

pepper, as needed

1 lb / 450 g SALMON MOUSSELINE (page 847)

butter, as needed

2 tbsp / 30 mL minced shallots

4 fl oz / 120 mL dry white wine

8 fl oz / 240 mL FISH FUMET (page 253)

20 fl oz / 600 mL FISH VELOUTÉ (page 267)

8 fl oz / 240 mL heavy cream

POACHED TROUT PAUPIETTES WITH VIN BLANC SAUCE

1 Trim the trout fillets and portion at 6 oz/170 g each. Season the trout with the salt and pepper. Spread the mousseline in an even layer over the trout fillets and roll each piece up to make paupiettes.

2 Butter a pan and sprinkle it with the shallots. Place the paupiettes on the bed of shallots. Add the wine and fumet.

3 Bring the liquid to a simmer over direct heat.

4 Cover the paupiettes with buttered parchment paper and finish them in a 350°F/175°C oven.

5 Remove the paupiettes from the pan, loosely cover, and keep warm.

6 Reduce the cuisson; add the velouté and cream and simmer until flavorful and lightly thickened, about 5 minutes. Adjust the seasoning and strain the sauce if desired.

7 Serve the sauce with the paupiettes.

MAKES 10 PORTIONS

DEEP POACHING AND SIMMERING

Deep poaching and simmering are similar techniques. They both call for a food to be completely submerged in a liquid that is kept at a constant, moderate temperature.

The aim of deep poaching and simmering is the same — to produce foods that are moist and extremely tender. The distinguishing factors between the two methods are differences in cooking temperature and appropriate types of food. Deep poaching is done at a lower temperature and is better suited to naturally tender cuts of meat, poultry, or fish. Simmering occurs at slightly higher temperature so that the tougher cuts it is paired with can become tender and moist during cooking.

ITEMS TO BE DEEP POACHED should be naturally tender; those to be simmered need not be since the simmering process will tenderize them. Though portion-size cuts are often used — chicken quarters, for example — poached and simmered items also include whole dressed fish or whole birds, or large pieces of meat.

Wrap dressed fish in cheesecloth to protect it from breaking apart during cooking. Stuff the poultry, if desired, and truss it to help retain its shape. Stuff meats, if desired, and tie them to maintain their shape.

The liquid used in deep poaching and simmering should be well flavored. For meat and poultry, select a well-developed stock of the appropriate flavor. For fish and shellfish, use fish stock, fumet, wine, or a court bouillon.

Aromatic ingredients, such as herbs and spices, wine, vegetables, vegetable juice, or citrus zest, may be added to the cooking liquid to enhance the flavor of the finished dish. See specific recipes for instructions on preparing and adding these ingredients.

Deep-poached and simmered foods are often served with a sauce that is prepared separately. "Boiled" beef, for instance, is traditionally served with a horseradish sauce, and poached salmon is often served with a warm butter emulsion sauce, such as béarnaise or mousseline sauce. See specific recipes for sauce suggestions.

The pot used for deep poaching or simmering should hold the food, liquid, and aromatics comfortably, with enough room to allow the liquid to expand as it heats. There should also be enough space so that the surface can be skimmed if necessary throughout cooking. A tight-fitting lid may be helpful for bringing the liquid up to temperature, but it is not essential during deep poaching or simmering. Leaving a lid on throughout the cooking process may actually cause the liquid to become hotter than desired.

Other equipment that may be needed includes ladles or skimmers, holding containers to keep the foods warm, carving boards, and slicers. An instant-read thermometer is also helpful to monitor the temperature of the cooking liquid; it can be difficult to see the difference between a liquid at a perfect poaching temperature and one that is a degree or two away from a slow boil. The difference to the food can be quite important.

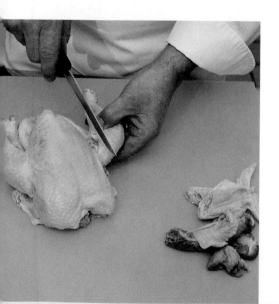

FOR A SINGLE ENTRÉE PORTION, YOU WILL NEED:

a 6-ounce/170-gram portion of fish, chicken, or meat

about 10 fluid ounces/300 milliliters of stock or other liquid

assorted vegetables

salt and other seasonings for both the food and the liquid

additional finishing ingredients, including prepared sauce, and garnishes

1. Combine the food with the liquid and bring to the correct cooking temperature.

Some foods are started off in cool liquid. Others are lowered into liquid that is already at poaching or simmering temperature. Poaching liquid should be at 160° to 185°F/70° to 82°C. The surface of the liquid may show some motion, sometimes called shivering, but no air bubbles should break the surface. Simmering liquid will have small bubbles gently breaking the surface and should be between 185° and 200°F/82° and 85°C.

2. Maintain the proper cooking speed throughout the poaching or simmering process until the item is done. Skim as necessary and adjust the seasoning throughout cooking time. If a cover is used, the cooking speed must be monitored regularly. Covering a pot creates pressure, which raises the temperature of the liquid. Setting the lid slightly ajar is a good precaution to be certain that the liquid does not inadvertently come to a boil.

ABOVE *Stock is added to wholesome trim and simmered to fortify the stock's flavor before adding the chicken pieces. Be sure to check the seasoning before adding the chicken.*

ABOVE *Be sure that the food is completely submerged in the liquid. If a part of the food is above the level of the cooking liquid, the cooking will be uneven and the finished product will not have the properly delicate color.*

TOP *Make sure the liquid does not boil. Check the temperature periodically with an instant-read thermometer and adjust the heat as necessary.*

BOTTOM *Skim the surface of the liquid throughout cooking time, if necessary. Skimming helps the dish develop attractive colors. It also keeps the broth from becoming too cloudy.*

3. Poach the food until properly done. Carefully remove it from the liquid.

Tests for doneness vary from one food type to another. Once cooked, a deep-poached or simmered food may be cut or sliced as necessary and served immediately with the appropriate sauce. It may also be held for a short period before serving.

To do so, transfer the food to a holding container, moisten it with some of the cooking liquid, and cover loosely to prevent it from drying out.

If a poached or simmered item is to be served cold, it may be desirable to slightly undercook it. Remove the pot from the heat and let the food cool in the poaching liquid, which will retain enough heat to complete the cooking process. Cool the liquid in an ice-water bath to prevent bacterial growth. Once it has reached room temperature, remove the food for any further preparation. The liquid may be used to poach or simmer other items.

4. Evaluate the quality of the finished dish.

When properly cooked, deep-poached or simmered poultry and meats are fork-tender, and any juices from poultry are nearly colorless. Poultry flesh takes on an evenly opaque appearance and offers little resistance when pressed with a fingertip. When whole birds are fully cooked, the legs move easily in the sockets.

When properly cooked, the flesh of fish and shellfish is slightly firm and has lost its translucency, taking on a nearly opaque appearance. Shellfish open and the edges of the flesh curl. Shrimp, crab, and lobster have a bright pink or red color.

Flavor, appearance, and texture are all important. In an ideal balance the aromatics, seasonings, and flavorings either bolster or complement the flavor of the food.

TOP *The chef is checking to see if the meat is fork-tender. Doneness may also be checked with an instant-read thermometer. Refer to the table on page 351.*

BOTTOM *After the finished chicken portions for service have been removed, strain the cooking liquid to remove the fortifying ingredients and aromatics.*

ABOVE *For this dish, several vegetables are added to the cooking liquid to form the garnish for the final dish. Long-cooking ingredients such as carrots, turnips, and potatoes have already been added. Leeks take less time to cook, so they are added last.*

ABOVE *Serve poached poultry or other items with the broth and garnishes and accompaniments. Or serve the broth separately as a soup course.*

2 broiler chickens (3 lb / 1.3 kg each)

3½ qt / 3.2 L CHICKEN STOCK (page 248), or as needed

1 bouquet garni

sachet d'épices, containing 3 chopped parsley stems, 1 bay leaf, ½ tsp/2 mL
   cracked black peppercorns, ½ tsp/2 mL fresh or dried thyme, and 1 garlic clove

8 oz / 225 g large-dice carrot

8 oz / 225 g large-dice parsnips

8 oz / 225 g large-dice celeriac

8 oz / 225 g large-dice yellow Finn potatoes

8 oz / 225 g large-dice leeks

1 tbsp / 15 mL salt

½ tsp / 3 mL pepper

1 oz / 30 g minced chives

POULE AU POT

1 Remove the backbones from the chickens and reserve. Cut the birds into quarters.

2 Bring the stock to a simmer. Place the chickens, backbones, necks, hearts, and gizzards, but not the liver, in a pot and add enough simmering stock to cover by 1 to 1½ inches. Return to a simmer over low heat. Add the bouquet garni and sachet. Simmer for about 45 minutes. Skim carefully throughout cooking time.

3 Transfer the chicken legs and breasts to a clean pot. Strain the broth over the chicken and return to a simmer over low heat for another 30 minutes. Discard the bouquet garni, necks, backbones, hearts, and gizzards.

4 Add the vegetables to the broth: carrots and parsnips first, celeriac after 5 minutes, potatoes after celeriac. Add the leeks last.

5 Continue to simmer, skimming as necessary, until the chicken is fork tender and all of the vegetables are tender.

6 Remove the chicken, and separate the drumsticks from the thighs. Cut the breast pieces in half on the bias. Finish the broth by seasoning with salt and pepper.

7 Arrange the chicken (a breast portion and either a drumstick or thigh) in a soup bowl with vegetables, ladle broth into the bowl, and finish with chives.

MAKES 8 PORTIONS

RECIPES

NEW ENGLAND BOILED DINNER

makes 25 portions

10 lb/4.5 kg corned beef brisket

2 lb/900 g beef tongue

1 gal/3.75 L WHITE BEEF STOCK (page 249)

sachet d'épices, containing 3 chopped parsley stems, 1 bay leaf, ½ tsp/2 mL cracked black peppercorns, ½ tsp/2 mL fresh or dried thyme, and 1 garlic clove

VEGETABLE GARNISH

50 red bliss potatoes, scrubbed

50 green cabbage wedges

50 pearl onions

50 pieces carrot tournés

50 pieces parsnip tournés

50 pieces rutabaga tournés

50 small beets, tournéed

12 oz/340 g green beans, cut into 2-in/5-cm lengths

HORSERADISH SAUCE

1½ qt/1.5 L BÉCHAMEL SAUCE (page 288)

12 fl oz/360 mL heavy cream

6 oz/170 g grated horseradish, as needed

1 Place the brisket and tongue in a pot with enough cold stock to cover them. Bring the stock to a slow simmer.

2 Add the sachet and continue to simmer gently, skimming as necessary, for about 3 hours, or until the meats are very tender. Remove the meats from the liquid and keep them warm and moist.

3 Cook the vegetables separately in the reserved cooking liquid.

4 To make the horseradish sauce, combine the sauce ingredients and heat the mixture.

5 Slice the meats and serve them with the vegetables and sauce.

GAISBURGER MARSCH (BOILED BEEF WITH SPÄTZLE AND POTATOES)

makes 10 portions

4 lb/1.8 kg beef shank meat, cut into ½-in/1-cm cubes

1½ gal/5.75 L WHITE BEEF STOCK (page 249)

2 lb 12 oz/1.3 kg medium-dice onion

2 bay leaves

1 clove

12 oz/340 g medium-dice leeks

1 lb/450 g medium-dice potatoes

3 oz/85 g butter

2 lb/900 g SPÄTZLE (page 717)

1 oz/30 g chopped parsley

salt, as needed

pepper, as needed

1 Blanch the beef shank meat, drain, and combine with the stock, 12 oz/340 g onion, the bay leaves, and clove, and simmer until 80 percent tender, about 45 minutes to 1 hour. Skim as necessary and adjust seasoning throughout cooking time.

2 Add the leeks and potatoes and cook until tender, about 20 more minutes.

3 Sauté the remaining 2 lb/900 g onions in the butter until brown, about 15 to 20 minutes. Add to the broth together with the spätzle and parsley, and season with salt and pepper.

4 Serve the beef and spätzle in a heated bowl or soup plate at once.

CORNED BEEF WITH CABBAGE AND WINTER VEGETABLES

makes 12 to 14 portions

10 lb/4.5 kg corned beef brisket, trimmed

3 qt/3 L WHITE BEEF STOCK (page 249) or water, cold

1 lb/450 g beets (skin on)

2 lb/900 g green cabbage wedges

1 lb/670 g potato tournés

1 lb/450 g carrot batonnets or tournés

1 lb/450 g turnip batonnets or tournés

1 lb/450 g pearl onions

salt, as needed

pepper, as needed

1 Split the brisket along the natural seam into two pieces.

2 Put the meat in a deep pot and add enough stock or water to cover the meat. Bring to a boil, skimming the surface as necessary. Reduce the heat to establish a slow simmer; continue simmering until meat is nearly fork tender, about 2½ hours.

3 While the corned beef is simmering, cook beets in simmering salted water until tender. Remove the beets and let them cool until they can be handled easily. Slip off or cut away the skin. Cut the beets into batonnet, tournés, or other shapes. Ladle some of the cooking liquid from the corned beef over the beets and reserve. (Beets must be reheated until very hot prior to serving.)

4 Add the cabbage, potato, carrot, turnip, and pearl onions to the corned beef and continue to simmer until the vegetables are fully cooked, tender, and flavorful and the corned beef is fork tender. Adjust seasoning with salt and pepper during cooking time.

5 Remove the corned beef from the cooking liquid and carve into slices. Serve on heated plates with the vegetables.

see photograph on page 519

POACHED TENDERLOIN WITH GREEN PEPPERCORN SABAYON

makes 10 portions

3¾ lb/1.75 kg trimmed beef tenderloin, tied

salt, as needed

pepper, as needed

2 qt/2 L WHITE BEEF STOCK (page 249), or as needed

1 bouquet garni

1 recipe GREEN PEPPERCORN SABAYON (recipe follows)

1 Season the beef well with salt and pepper.

2 Bring the stock to a simmer in a fish poacher or rondeau. Add the tenderloin and bouquet garni.

3 Poach the tenderloin until it reaches an internal temperature of 125° to 130°F/51°C for medium rare. Remove the tenderloin from the stock and keep it warm.

4 At the time of service, prepare the sabayon as directed and slice the tenderloin to make 4- to 5-oz/115- to 140-g portions.

5 Serve the sliced tenderloin with the sauce.

GREEN PEPPERCORN SABAYON

makes 10 portions

3 fl oz/90 mL reserved poaching liquid from tenderloin (recipe above)

5 egg yolks

2 fl oz/60 mL dry white wine

2 oz/60 g drained whole green peppercorns

salt, as needed

pepper, as needed

1 Combine 3 fl oz/90 mL cooking liquid from tenderloin with the egg yolks in a stainless-steel bowl. Add the wine and whip to combine.

2 Cook the yolks over simmering water, whipping constantly, until thick and foamy. Add the green peppercorns and adjust the seasoning with salt and pepper.

3 Serve the sauce immediately with sliced tenderloin.

POACHED BEEF TENDERLOIN WITH WINTER VEGETABLES

makes 10 portions

3¼ lb/1.75 kg trimmed beef tenderloin, tied

salt, as needed

pepper, as needed

2 qt/2 L BROWN VEAL STOCK (page 252), or as needed

1 bouquet garni

7 oz/200 g tournéed carrots, fully cooked

7 oz/200 g tournéed parsnips, fully cooked

7 oz/200 g tournéed potatoes , fully cooked

7 oz/200 g tournéed beets, fully cooked

1 recipe STUFFED CABBAGE BALLS (recipe follows)

chopped chives, for garnish

chopped parsley, for garnish

1 Season the beef well with salt and pepper.

2 Bring the stock to a simmer in a fish poacher or rondeau. Add the tenderloin and bouquet garni.

3 Poach the tenderloin until it reaches an internal temperature of 125° to 130°F/51°C for medium rare. Remove the tenderloin from the stock and keep it warm.

4 Strain (and clarify, if necessary—see Notes) the poaching broth. Add the cooked vegetables and cabbage balls to the broth and simmer gently until very hot. Adjust the seasoning.

5 Slice the tenderloin into portions. Serve in a heated bowl or soup plate surrounded by a portion of vegetables and cabbage balls. Ladle the hot broth into the bowl or plate. Sprinkle with chives and parsley, and fill the bowl with broth.

NOTES

If time allows, the tenderloin can be poached in advance and the broth clarified, as you would a consommé (pages 300–302). For every quart of poaching liquid, combine 12 oz/340 g lean ground beef (use trimmings from tenderloin if available), 10 oz/285 g ground or finely minced mirepoix, 1 egg white, 2 oz/60 g tomato purée, 1 tsp/5 mL salt, and ¼ tsp/ 1 mL cracked peppercorns. Mix these ingredients, chill them well, and combine with the poaching liquid. Simmer for 1 hour after the raft forms, then carefully remove and strain the consommé, disturbing the raft as little as possible.

see photograph on page 519

STUFFED CABBAGE BALLS

makes 10 portions

20 green cabbage leaves

¾ oz/20 g bacon

¾ oz/20 g garlic paste

1 tsp/5 mL caraway seeds

1 fl oz/30 mL apple cider vinegar

1 tsp/5 mL salt

11 oz/315 g green cabbage chiffonade

WHITE BEEF STOCK (page 249), as needed

salt, as needed

pepper, as needed

1 Bring a large pot of salted water to a boil. Add the cabbage leaves in batches; boil until tender and bright green, about 3 to 4 minutes. Refresh the cabbage leaves in cold water, let drain, and reserve.

2 Render the bacon in a sauté pan; add the garlic and sauté until aromatic, about 2 minutes. Add the caraway, vinegar, salt, and cabbage chiffonade. Sauté until the cabbage begins to wilt, about 2 to 3 minutes, stirring frequently.

3 Add the stock and simmer over low heat until the cabbage is very tender, 20 to 30 minutes. Add more stock as the cabbage cooks, if necessary. Adjust seasoning with salt and pepper.

4 To fill and close cabbage balls, lay one leaf on a work surface, place some of the filling on the leaf, and roll up, tucking in the edges to completely enclose the filling.

5 To reheat cabbage balls, steam, simmer in a small amount of stock, bake in a covered pan with a little added stock, or microwave.

BEEF AND PORK TAMALES

makes 10 portions

12 oz/340 g diced lean beef

12 oz/340 g diced lean pork

8 fl oz/240 mL prepared Enchilada Sauce

½ oz/15 g CHILI POWDER (page 353), or as needed

salt, as needed

4 oz/115 g dried corn husks

12 oz/340 g masa harina

14 fl oz/415 mL water or BROWN VEAL STOCK (page 252)

4 oz/115 g lard or vegetable shortening

¾ tsp/4 mL baking powder

1 recipe SALSA VERDE (recipe follows)

1 Combine the beef, pork and enchilada sauce in a heavy pot. Cook over medium heat until the meat is nearly done, about 15 minutes. The meat should be tender and mixture should be fairly dry. Season with chili powder and salt to taste. Reserve and cool.

2 Soak the corn husks in hot water to make them pliable.

3 Mix the masa harina with water or stock, lard, baking powder, and salt. Beat until smooth and fluffy.

4 Drain the corn husks. Lay 1 or 2 husks on the work surface. The husks should be about 5 inches wide.

5 Place 2 tbsp/30 mL of masa mixture on the smooth side of a corn husk and spread over the lower two thirds of the husk, leaving 1 inch of space on each side.

6 Place 1 tbsp/15 mL of meat mixture lengthwise down center of masa. Roll the husk tightly. Fold the excess husk under. Tie with a strip of corn husk if necessary.

7 Steam the tamales, seam side down, for 40 to 50 minutes. Serve with salsa verde.

NOTES

The filling and the dough can be prepared 1 day in advance. The tamales can be rolled and steamed up to 3 hours in advance. Once steamed, they hold well either directly in the steamer or in a perforated pan set over a hot-water bath. Because of the wrapper and the high fat content of the filling, the tamales will stay moist.

Cooked black or pinto beans (4 oz/115 g) can be added as a variation.

SALSA VERDE

makes 10 portions

2 oz/60 g olive oil

6 oz/140 g diced onions

4 oz/115 g diced roasted jalapeños

¼ oz/7 g minced garlic

4 lb/3.8 kg tomatillos, husks off, halved

4 fl oz/120 mL CHICKEN STOCK (page 248), or as needed

2 tbsp/30 mL chopped mint

2 tbsp/30 mL chopped cilantro

1½ tsp/8 mL ground coriander

1 tsp/5 mL ground cumin

1 Heat the olive oil in a sauté pan. Sauté onions, jalapeños, and garlic in the oil. Add tomatillos and chicken stock and cook until soft.

2 Purée the sauce and add mint, cilantro, coriander, and cumin. Cool the sauce. Serve with tamales on the side.

CHICKEN EUGENE

makes 10 servings

2 tbsp/30 mL minced shallots, sweated

10 chicken breast portions (6 oz/170 g each)

1 pint/480 mL CHICKEN STOCK (page 248)

5 fl oz/150 mL dry white wine

salt, as needed

pepper, as needed

1 recipe ROYAL GLAÇAGE (page 523)

10 slices French bread

10 oz/285 g butter, or as needed

10 oz/285 g fluted mushroom caps

10 thin slices ham

1. Place the shallots in a buttered sautoir. Place the suprêmes on top of the shallots. Add the stock, wine, salt, and pepper.

2. Bring the liquid to a simmer and poach the chicken until it is done (165°F/72°C). Remove the chicken, reserving the liquid (cuisson). Keep the chicken warm while finishing the royal glaçage.

3. Transfer the chicken to a sizzler platter or sheet pan.

4. Coat the suprêmes with the sauce. Place them under a broiler and broil until golden.

5. To prepare the crouton, sauté the French bread on both sides in butter until golden. Sauté the mushroom caps in the butter.

6. Place the sauced chicken on a crouton topped with a ham slice. Garnish it with mushroom caps.

POACHED CHICKEN BREAST WITH TARRAGON SAUCE

makes 10 portions

2 oz/60 g butter, or as needed

2 oz/60 g minced shallots

10 chicken breast portions (6 oz/170 g each)

4 fl oz/120 mL CHICKEN STOCK (page 248)

6 fl oz/180 mL dry white wine

20 fl oz/600 mL CHICKEN VELOUTÉ (page 266)

1 tbsp/15 mL chopped tarragon leaves

4 fl oz/120 mL heavy cream

salt, as needed

pepper, as needed

1. Butter a shallow pan and sprinkle with shallots. Add the suprêmes, stock, and wine.

2. Bring to a simmer and cover with parchment paper.

3. Poach in the oven at 350°F/175°C until done (165°F/72°C).

4. Remove the chicken to a holding container, cover with the paper, and keep warm.

5. Strain the poaching liquid and reduce to one quarter of the original volume. Add the velouté and tarragon and reduce until a good sauce consistency is reached. Add the heavy cream and season with salt and pepper.

6. Serve the sauce over the chicken breasts.

POACHED CHICKEN FLORENTINE

makes 10 portions

2 oz/60 g butter

2 oz/60 g minced shallots

10 boneless, skinless chicken breast portions (4 to 6 oz/115 to 140 g each)

10 fl oz/300 mL dry white wine

1 pint/480 mL CHICKEN STOCK (page 248)

1½ pints/720 mL MORNAY SAUCE (page 282)

1¾ lb/800 g cooked, squeezed, and chopped spinach

2 oz/60 g butter

3 oz/85 g grated Parmesan cheese

1 Butter a pan and sprinkle with shallots. Add chicken breasts, wine, and stock and bring to a simmer. Cover with parchment paper and poach in a 350°F/175°C oven until done, about 15 minutes (165°F/72°C).

2 Remove chicken breasts to a holding container and keep warm.

3 Strain the poaching liquid and reduce until syrupy. Add the Mornay sauce and reduce until a good sauce consistency is reached.

4 Sauté the spinach in the butter to reheat if necessary.

5 Place a portion of spinach (2½ oz/70 g) on a heated plate, top with a portion of chicken, and coat with a portion of sauce (2 fl oz/60 mL). Top with a sprinkling of Parmesan. Broil in a salamander or broiler lightly to brown cheese. Serve at once.

POACHED CORNISH GAME HEN WITH STAR ANISE

makes 10 portions

5 Rock Cornish game hens (1 lb 12 oz/780 g each)

salt, to taste

pepper to taste

10 bay leaves

10 thyme sprigs

¼ tsp/1 mL caraway seeds

30 parsley stems

2 qt/2 L CHICKEN STOCK (page 248) or CHICKEN CONSOMMÉ ROYALE (page 330), or as needed

20 star anise

10 oz/285 g carrot battonet, blanched

10 oz/285 g turnip battonet, blanched

10 oz/285 g parsnip battonet, blanched

10 oz/285 g yellow squash battonet, blanched

10 oz/285 g cucumber battonet, blanched

1¼ lb/570 g cooked rice

10 oz/285 g scallions, cut to 2½- to 3-in/60- to 75-mm lengths

2 oz/60 g chopped chives

1 Trim the game hens and rub with salt and pepper. Stuff the cavities with bay leaves, thyme, caraway seeds, and parsley stems, and truss.

2 Place the hens in a large pot and add enough stock or consommé to cover them. Add the star anise. Cover with parchment paper and simmer gently.

3 When nearly done, add the blanched vegetables to reheat them.

4 Add the rice just before service. Sprinkle the hens with the scallions and chives. Serve it in the casserole, if appropriate.

NEW ENGLAND SHORE DINNER

10 oz/285 g small-dice onions

3 oz/85 g butter

½ oz/15 g minced garlic cloves

1 tsp/5 mL dried thyme leaves

2 bay leaves

1 pt/480 mL CHICKEN STOCK (page 248), or as needed

3 ears corn on the cob, husked and quartered

3 lobsters (1 to 1½ lb/450 to 670 g each)

20 littleneck or cherrystone clams

20 mussels, scrubbed and debearded

10 red bliss potatoes, cooked

1¼ lb/570 g cod fillet, cut into ten 2-oz/60-g pieces

5 oz/140 g leeks, split and washed

20 pearl onions, cooked

5 oz/140 g sea scallops

8 oz/225 g zucchini battonet

1 Sweat the onions in the butter. Add the garlic and sauté it until the aroma is apparent.

2 Add the thyme, bay leaves, and stock; bring to a simmer.

3 Arrange the following ingredients in the following order in a flameproof casserole. Bottom layer: corn, lobster, clams, mussels, potatoes. Top layer: cod, leeks, onions, scallops, zucchini. Add the liquid.

4 Cover and steam all of the ingredients over direct heat or in a 350°F/175°C oven until the seafood is cooked through, 20 to 25 minutes.

5 Arrange the fish, seafood, and vegetables on a heated platter, or serve it directly from the casserole.

FILLET OF SNAPPER EN PAPILLOTE

3¾ lb/1.75 kg red snapper fillet, skinless

10 oz/285 g butter

salt, to taste

pepper, to taste

1 pt/480 mL FISH VELOUTÉ (page 267)

4 fl oz/120 mL dry white wine

2 tbsp/30 mL minced shallots

5 oz/140 g thin-sliced scallions

5 oz/140 g sliced or quartered mushrooms

1 Cut the fish into 10 equal portions, 6 oz/170 g each. Cut 10 pieces of parchment paper into heart shapes large enough to enclose the fillets. Butter both sides of the parchment paper.

2 Heat a sauté pan. Add the remaining butter. Season the fish pieces with salt and pepper and sear briefly on the flesh side only. Remove from the pan.

3 Place a portion of velouté (1 to 1½ fl oz/30 to 45 mL) on one side of the parchment heart. Place a portion of fish on top. Sprinkle with the wine, shallots, and scallions. Shingle the sliced mushrooms on top.

4 Fold the paper over and seal the sides tightly.

5 Place the bag on a hot, buttered sizzler platter.

6 Place in a 400° to 425°F/205° to 220°C oven for 5 to 8 minutes, or until fish is cooked through. Serve immediately in the paper.

PAUPIETTES OF TROUT WITH SAFFRON

makes 10 portions

20 skinless trout fillets (about 4 oz/115 g each)

salt, to taste

pepper, to taste

1 recipe TROUT MOUSSELINE (recipe follows)

butter for pan, as needed

1/2 oz/15 g minced shallots

2 fl oz/60 mL dry white wine, or as needed

4 fl oz/120 mL FISH FUMET (page 253), or as needed

1 pt/480 mL FISH VELOUTÉ (page 267)

7 oz/200 g tomato concassé

2 tbsp/30 mL chopped chives

10 oz/385 g spinach

1 Trim the trout and portion at 6 oz/170 g each. Pound lightly to an even thickness. Season the trout with the salt and pepper. Spread the mousseline in an even layer over the fish portions and roll up to form paupiettes.

2 Butter a pan and sprinkle it with the shallots. Place the paupiettes on the bed of shallots. Add the wine and fumet.

3 Bring the liquid to a simmer over direct heat. Cover the trout with buttered parchment paper and finish it in a 350°F/175°C oven.

4 Remove the trout from the pan, cover loosely, and keep it warm.

5 Reduce the cuisson; add the velouté and simmer until flavorful and lightly thickened, about 5 minutes. Adjust the seasoning and strain the sauce if desired. Finish the sauce with tomatoes and chives.

6 Serve the fish on a bed of spinach with the sauce.

TROUT MOUSSELINE

makes 10 ounces/280 grams

pinch saffron threads, pulverized

2 fl oz/60 mL heavy cream

7 oz/200 g trout fillet scraps, skinless boneless

1 egg white

1 tsp salt/5 mL, or as needed

white pepper, as needed

1 Heat the saffron in the cream and let steep for 30 minutes. Chill well.

2 Place the trout scraps and egg white in a food processor with a steel blade. Process to a fine paste, scraping down the sides of the bowl as needed. Add the saffron infusion, salt, and pepper, pulsing the processor on and off to blend.

3 Make a test quenelle and adjust the forcemeat as necessary.

4 Push the mousseline through a sieve, if desired. Hold under refrigeration until ready to use

Sole Mousseline Substitute sole for the trout. Omit the saffron.

POACHED SEA BASS WITH CLAMS, BACON, AND PEPPERS

makes 10 portions

butter, as needed

3³/₄ lb/1.75 kg sea bass fillet

50 littleneck clams, thoroughly scrubbed

4 fl oz/120 mL dry white wine

5 fl oz/150 mL CHICKEN STOCK (page 248)

5 fl oz/150 mL clam juice

8 oz/225 g green pepper julienne, blanched

10 oz/285 g bacon, minced, rendered crisp

salt, as needed

pepper, as needed

1 tbsp/15 mL chopped chives

1 Lightly butter a sautoir. Add the fish and clams. Add the wine, stock, and clam juice. Cover the fish with buttered parchment paper. Bring the liquid just barely to a simmer.

2 Transfer the sautoir to a 350°F/175°C oven and poach the fish and clams until the fish is slightly underdone and the clams are just barely open, about 10 to 12 minutes. Remove the fish and clams and keep them warm.

3 Strain the cuisson and reduce it. Whip in enough cold butter to lightly thicken the sauce.

4 Add the peppers and bacon. Adjust the seasoning with salt and pepper.

5 Ladle the sauce over the fish and clams. Garnish with the chives and serve.

Seafood Poached in a Saffron Broth with Fennel

Corned Beef with Cabbage and Winter Vegetables

Poached Tenderloin of Beef

POACHED STRIPED BASS WITH WATERCRESS SAUCE

makes 10 portions

3³/₄ lb/1.75 kg sea bass fillet

salt, as needed

pepper, as needed

2 lb/900 g watercress, trimmed and rinsed

butter, as needed

5 fl oz/150 mL dry white wine, as needed

5 fl oz/150 mL FISH FUMET (page 253), or as needed

6 fl oz/180 mL heavy cream

lemon juice, as needed

1 Trim the sea bass and cut into 10 portions, about 6 oz/ 170 g each. Season them with salt and pepper.

2 Blanch the watercress leaves in boiling salted water until bright green. Drain, shock, and purée the watercress. Reserve until ready to prepare the sauce.

3 Butter a sautoir. Place the fish in the pan. Add enough wine and fumet to barely cover the fish. Cover the pan with buttered parchment paper. Heat the liquid to a simmer. Finish poaching the fish in a 350°F/175°C oven. Remove the bass, moisten it with cuisson, and keep it warm.

4 Reduce the cuisson. Add the heavy cream, lemon juice, and salt and pepper as needed. Reduce the sauce to a good sauce consistency. Add the watercress purée and return the sauce to a simmer.

5 Ladle the sauce around the fish and serve.

BOSTON SCROD WITH CREAM, CAPERS, AND TOMATOES

makes 10 portions

3³/₄ lb/1.75 kg scrod fillet

salt, as needed

pepper, as needed

1 tbsp/15 mL minced shallots

5 fl oz/150 mL dry white wine

5 fl oz/150 mL FISH FUMET (page 253)

6 fl oz/180 mL heavy cream, reduced by half

4 oz/115 g tomato concassé

1 fl oz/30 mL capers, drained

4 oz/115 g mushrooms, sliced, sautéed

3 oz/85 g butter

lemon juice, as needed

1 Trim the scrod and cut into 10 portions, about 6 oz/170 g each. Pound lightly to an even thickness. Season them with salt and pepper.

2 Butter a pan and sprinkle it with the shallots. Place the scrod on the bed of shallots. Add the wine and fumet.

3 Bring the liquid to a simmer over direct heat. Cover the scrod with buttered parchment paper and finish it in a 350°F/175°C oven, about 10 to 12 minutes. Transfer the fish to a holding vessel, cover with the parchment, and keep the fish warm while finishing the pan sauce.

4 Return the pan used to prepare the fish to high heat. Add the heavy cream to the cuisson and reduce over medium to high heat. Add the tomato concassé, capers, and mushrooms and simmer long enough for the sauce to develop a good flavor and consistency, 3 to 4 minutes. Whisk or swirl in the 3 oz/85 g butter, and adjust the seasoning with lemon juice, salt, and pepper.

5 Serve the scrod on heated plates with the sauce.

POACHED SOLE WITH SAFFRON SAUCE

makes 10 portions

3³/₄ lb/1.75 kg sole fillets

salt, as needed

pepper, as needed

1 oz/30 g butter

¹/₂ oz/15 g minced shallots

8 fl oz/240 mL dry white wine

10 fl oz/300 mL FISH FUMET (page 253)

1 pt/480 mL FISH VELOUTÉ (page 267)

4 fl oz/120 mL heavy cream

pinch of saffron threads, crushed

salt, as needed

GARNISH

2 oz/60 g butter, or as needed

1 lb/450 g small-dice zucchini

1 tbsp/15 mL mixed herbs, as needed

10 pieces fleurons (see Note)

1 Trim the sole and portion at 6 oz/170 g each. Pound lightly to an even thickness. Season the sole with the salt and pepper.

2 Butter a pan and sprinkle it with the shallots. Place the sole on the bed of shallots. Add the wine and fumet.

3 Bring the liquid to a simmer over direct heat. Cover the sole with buttered parchment paper and finish it in a 350°F/175°C oven.

4 Remove the sole from the pan, loosely cover, and keep it warm.

5 Reduce the cuisson and add the velouté, heavy cream, and saffron. Simmer the sauce until flavorful and lightly thickened, about 5 minutes. Adjust the seasoning and strain the sauce if desired.

6 To prepare the garnish, heat the butter in a sauté pan over medium high heat. Add the zucchini, stir or toss to coat with butter, and season with salt and pepper. Continue to sauté until the zucchini is tender, 3 to 4 minutes. Add the herbs and keep hot.

7 Serve the fish with sauce, portion of vegetables and a fleuron.

NOTE

To prepare the fleurons, roll out puff pastry ¹/₈ in/.25 cm thick. Cut into shapes with a crescent cutter. Place crescents on a parchment-lined baking sheet, brush with egg wash, and bake in a 400°F/202°C oven until crisp and browned.

POACHED SOLE WITH CAPERS AND TOMATOES

makes 10 portions

3³/₄ lb/1.75 kg sole fillets

salt, as needed

pepper, as needed

cayenne pepper, as needed

1 oz/30 g butter, softened

1 oz/30 g chopped shallots

8 fl oz/240 mL dry white wine

12 fl oz/360 mL FISH STOCK (page 253) or FISH FUMET (page 253)

2 tbsp/30 mL small capers

12 oz/340 g tomato concassé

10 oz/285 g mushrooms, sliced ¹/₈ in/4 mm thick

1 tbsp/15 mL FINES HERBES (page 353)

1 pt/480 mL FISH VELOUTÉ (page 267)

4 fl oz/120 mL heavy cream

3 fl oz/90 mL brandy (optional)

2 oz/60 g butter

1 Trim the sole and portion at 6 oz/170 g each. Pound lightly to an even thickness. Season the sole with the salt, pepper, and cayenne pepper.

2 Butter a sautoir and add the shallots and fish. Add the wine, stock, capers, tomatoes, mushrooms, and fines herbes and cover with parchment paper. Bring to a simmer. Place in a 350°F/175°C oven until the flesh turns opaque, 6 to 8 minutes (140°F/60°C internal temperature.). Remove the fish. Garnish, arrange on a serving platter, cover, and keep warm.

3 Reduce the poaching liquid (cuisson) by half. Add the velouté and cream and reduce until of sauce consistency. Add the brandy, if using, season, and finish with butter.

4 Drain weepage from the fish and add it to the sauce. Coat the fish with sauce.

POACHED SALMON WITH ASPARAGUS AND BASIL SAUCE

makes 10 portions

3³/₄ lb/1.75 kg salmon fillet

1¹/₂ lb/0.680 kg asparagus, peeled and blanched

4 fl oz/120 mL dry white wine

4 fl oz/120 mL FISH FUMET (page 253)

1 tbsp/15 mL chopped shallots

BASIL SAUCE

1¹/₂ oz/45 g shallots

1 tsp/5 mL garlic

¹/₂ oz/15 g butter

3 fl oz/90 mL dry vermouth

1 bay leaf

1 pint/480 mL FISH VELOUTÉ (page 267)

1 tbsp/15 mL cut chives

2 tbsp/30 mL basil chiffonade

3 fl oz/90 mL heavy cream

1 tsp/5 mL salt

GARNISH

5 oz/140 g tomato julienne

basil chiffonade

1. Cut the salmon into 5-oz/140-g portions. Wrap each salmon portion around a 2-oz/60-g bundle of asparagus. Shallow poach in wine, fumet, and shallots. Remove the fish from the poaching liquid and reduce the liquid.

2. To make the basil sauce, sauté the shallots and garlic in the butter. Add the vermouth and bay leaf. Reduce until syrupy (do not brown).

3. Add the velouté, chives, and basil. Simmer for about 10 minutes. Strain and finish with heavy cream and salt.

4. Add the basil sauce to the poaching liquid and adjust to a sauce consistency. Finish with the tomato julienne and basil chiffonade.

5. Serve the fish with the sauce.

PAUPIETTES OF SOLE VERONIQUE

makes 10 portions

3³/₄ lb/1.75 kg sole fillets

salt, as needed

pepper, as needed

12 oz/340 g SOLE MOUSSELINE (page 517)

1 tbsp/15 mL minced shallots

8 parsley stems, chopped

4 fl oz/120 mL dry white wine

5 fl oz/150 mL FISH FUMET (page 523)

1 recipe ROYAL GLAÇAGE (recipe follows)

10 oz/285 g green seedless grapes, peeled and heated, 3 to 4 per portion

1. Trim the sole and portion at 6 oz/170 g each. Pound lightly to an even thickness. Season the sole with the salt and pepper.

2. Divide the mousseline evenly among the fillets and roll them into paupiettes.

3. Butter a sautoir and add the shallots and parsley stems. Arrange the paupiettes on top. Add the wine and fumet and cover the fish with buttered parchment paper. Bring the liquid to a simmer. Finish the fish in a 350°F/175°C oven. Remove the paupiettes and keep them warm while finishing the sauce.

4. Place the paupiettes on a sizzler platter. Coat with glaçage. Brown under a salamander or broiler. Serve the fish immediately, garnished with grapes.

ROYAL GLAÇAGE

makes 10 portions

poaching liquid, if available
7 fl oz/210 mL FISH VELOUTÉ (page 267)
7 fl oz/210 mL HOLLANDAISE SAUCE (page 279)
7 fl oz/210 mL heavy cream

1 Reduce the poaching liquid, if available, until nearly dry. Strain the reduced cuisson into a bowl.

2 Have the velouté and hollandaise at the same temperature (about 170°F/75°C). Add them to the reduced cuisson and fold together.

3 Whip the cream to medium peaks and fold into the velouté and hollandaise. Keep warm.

POACHED RED SNAPPER VERACRUZ

makes 10 portions

3 fl oz/90 mL lime juice
3³/₄ lb/1.7 kg red snapper fillets
salt, as needed
pepper, as needed
6 fl oz/180 mL dry white wine
12 fl oz/360 mL CHICKEN STOCK (page 248)
1 qt/1 L SWEET SPANISH SAUCE (recipe follows)
2 jalapeño chiles, cut into julienne (optional)
3¹/₂ oz/100 g black olives, sliced (optional)
2 tbsp/30 mL capers, washed

1 Sprinkle the lime juice over fish and season lightly with salt and pepper.

2 Shallow poach the fish in the wine and stock, reduce the cuisson, and add the Spanish sauce. Adjust the seasoning.

3 Place the fish on the sauce. Garnish with chile strips, olives, and capers, and serve.

SWEET SPANISH SAUCE

makes 1 quart/1liter

2 poblano chiles, roasted and peeled
2 cloves garlic, peeled
1 red onion, peeled and quartered
2 tbsp/30 mL safflower oil
1 lb/450 g tomato concassé
¹/₂ tsp/3 mL oregano
4 oz/115 g tomato purée
1 tsp/5 mL sugar
1 tsp/5 mL vinegar
¹/₂ tsp/3 mL salt
¹/₄ tsp/1 mL black pepper

1 Remove the stems and seeds from the chiles.

2 Purée the garlic, onions, and chiles in a food processor.

3 Heat the oil, add the purée, and sauté. Add all the other ingredients. Heat the sauce and cook for 20 to 25 minutes. Adjust the seasoning.

SEAFOOD POACHED IN A SAFFRON BROTH WITH FENNEL

makes 10 portions

1 qt/1 L FISH FUMET (page 253)

1 tsp/5 ml saffron threads, crushed

sachet d'épices, containing 3 chopped parsley stems, 1 bay leaf, ½ tsp/2 mL cracked black peppercorns, ½ tsp/2 mL fresh or dried thyme, and 1 garlic clove

4 fl oz/120 mL Pernod

4 fl oz/120 mL dry white wine

1 lb/450 g fennel julienne

1 lb/450 g tomato concassé

3⅛ lb/1.4 kg assorted seafood

1 Combine the fumet, saffron, sachet, Pernod, wine, fennel, and tomato concassé. Simmer until the fennel is barely tender and the broth is well flavored.

2 At the time of service, heat the broth to a bare simmer. Add the seafood and poach it until just cooked through. Serve the fish in heated soup bowls.

see photograph on page 518

POACHED SALMON WITH DILL BUTTER

makes 10 portions

3¾ lb/1.7 kg salmon fillet

1 qt/1 L FISH FUMET (page 253) (see Note)

1 lb/450 g paysanne-cut celeriac or celery

1 lb/450 g paysanne-cut carrots

1 lb/450 g paysanne-cut leeks, whites only

40 pieces tournéed potatoes, cooked until tender

5 oz/140 g dill compound butter (see page 802)

1 Trim the salmon and cut into 10 portions, 6 oz/140 g each.

2 Bring the fumet to a simmer over low heat with the paysanne cut vegetables. When it reaches 165°F/72°C, add the salmon. Poach salmon in fumet until the fish is cooked (internal temperature of 140°F/41°C) and place in a soup plate with some of the potatoes and vegetables.

3 Ladle 4 ounces of fumet over fish and vegetables. Top the salmon with a slice of dill butter and serve at once.

NOTE

For this dish, you may substitute salmon bones when preparing a fish fumet, if available.

CHAPTER TWENTY

Braises and stews are often thought of as peasant dishes because they frequently call for less tender (and less expensive) main ingredients than do other techniques. These dishes have a robust, hearty flavor and are often considered fall and winter meals; however, by replacing traditional ingredients with poultry, fish, or shellfish, braises and stews can be faster to prepare, lighter in flavor and color, and appropriate for contemporary menus.

BRAISING AND STEWING

BRAISES

A good braise is a dish of great complexity and flavor concentration that is simply not possible with other cooking techniques.

One of the benefits of braising is that tough cuts become tender as the moist heat gently penetrates the meat and causes the connective tissues to soften. Another bonus is that flavor is released into the cooking liquid to become the accompanying sauce; thus, virtually all the flavor and nutrients are retained. The sauce also has exceptional body because of the slow cooking needed to break down tough connective tissues.

Tender foods, even delicate fish and shellfish, can also be braised. To properly braise these kinds of foods, the chef must use less cooking liquid, and must cook the food at a lower temperature and for a shorter time.

FOODS TO BE BRAISED are traditionally the more mature and less tender cuts. They are more deeply flavored than the tender foods used for sautéing and steaming. Trim away all excess fat, silverskin, and gristle. Braised foods are often, although not always, left in a single large piece that can be sliced or carved into portions. Marinate or stuff red meat and poultry, if desired. In general it's a good idea to truss or tie meat in order to maintain the proper shape. Food may also be wrapped in lettuce leaves or other coverings to help maintain the shape and prevent the food from breaking apart during cooking.

The cooking liquids usually consist of rich stock or a combination of a stock and a sauce (such as espagnole, demiglace, or velouté) suited to the main item's flavor. Broths, essences, or vegetable juices may also be used. Wine is often used to deglaze the pan before adding the braising liquid.

Aromatic vegetables, herbs, and other ingredients are sometimes added to the cooking liquid for more flavor. If they will be strained out of the sauce or puréed to thicken it, peeling and uniform cuts are not so important. When aromatic ingredients are intended as a garnish in the finished dish, however, they should be peeled, cut to a uniform size and shape, and added to the dish in sequence, so that all components finish cooking at the same time.

Tomatoes may be included to give the finished dish additional flavor and color. Tomato concassé, tomato purée, or tomato paste can all be used.

Prepare a sachet d'épices or bouquet garni, including spices, herbs, and other aromatic ingredients, as desired or required by the recipe.

Use roux, roux-thickened sauces, reductions, beurre manié, or a pure starch slurry to thicken the braising liquid for a sauce. Another approach to thickening is to purée the mirepoix and return it to the sauce.

Choose a heavy-gauge braising pan or rondeau with a lid, of a size and shape that best fits the meat or poultry, for slow even cooking. Use a large tilting kettle to prepare a batch suitable for volume service or banquets. Use a kitchen fork to test doneness and to remove the food from the sauce. A carving knife and other equipment to finish the sauce, such as a strainer and/or immersion blender, are also needed.

A whole garlic head can be roasted with a little oil to give a deeper, sweeter flavor to the dish.

FOR BRAISING A SINGLE ENTRÉE-SIZE PORTION OF MEAT, POULTRY, OR FISH, YOU WILL NEED:			
	an 8- to 10-ounce/225- to 285-gram portion of meat, poultry, or fish	*1 ounce/30 grams prepared aromatics (mirepoix and/or other vegetables)*	*additional finishing or garnishing ingredients as appropriate*
	3 to 5 fluid ounces/90 to 150 milliliters cooking liquid (brown stock, brown sauce, and/or other flavorful liquids such as wine)	*salt and other seasonings (sachet d'épices or bouquet garni, for example)*	

1. Prepare the main item for braising and season it.

Braising concentrates the natural flavors of the main item, cooking liquid, and added ingredients, but it is still important to season the food before beginning to cook. Long simmering times reduce the volume of liquid and make relatively small amounts of seasoning more intense. Taste and adjust for seasoning throughout the entire cooking process.

Some recipes for braises call for the main item to be dredged with flour before searing. This is done to develop some body in the sauce. Some chefs prefer to add flour in a measured amount to better control the dish's quality.

2. Heat the pan and oil and sear the seasoned main item on all sides to a deep brown.

Searing develops a rich color and builds flavor. Cook the main item, turning it as often as necessary, just until each side is well colored. Transfer it to a pan and keep warm while cooking the aromatic vegetables.

Some foods are seared only until their exterior stiffens without browning for a paler dish, sometimes referred to as a white braise.

Remove the meat or poultry from the braising pan and transfer it to a hotel pan. Hold it in a warm place while cooking the mirepoix and other aromatic ingredients.

3. Add the aromatic vegetables to the pan and cook.

Onions and leeks are typically added to the pan first and allowed to cook to the appropriate color—tender and translucent for a light-colored braise or a deep golden for a brown braise. Allow enough time to cook these ingredients properly. Other vegetables, herbs, and spices are added to the pan in sequence. They too should be allowed to cook in fat.

Acidic ingredients such as tomatoes or wine are often added to a braise. Acid helps to soften the tough tissues of some braised foods and adds a desirable flavor and color to the finished dish.

ABOVE *Salt and freshly ground pepper are important to flavor development, but spice blends or marinades can also be used to give a special flavor to a braise.*

ABOVE *Developing a rich brown color on the meat or poultry gives the finished braise a deep flavor and an appealing color. Remove the main item and add the aromatic vegetables to the same pot.*

ABOVE *Cook the tomato paste until it turns a deep rust color and smells sweet.*

4. (Optional) Add flour to prepare a roux if desired.

Some chefs prefer to add the flour at this point, instead of dusting the main item with flour, for better control over the ultimate consistency of the sauce. Others prefer to omit flour and use a starch slurry or puréed aromatic vegetables to thicken the sauce after the braise is complete.

5. Add the appropriate amount of cooking liquid and bring it up to a rapid simmer over direct heat.

In general, the liquid should cover the main item by one third to one half for a braise. These very general guidelines should be adapted to suit the characteristics of the main item. The more tender the cut, the less liquid required, because the cooking time will be shorter and there will be less chance for the liquid to reduce properly.

Taste the cooking liquid to be sure it is flavorful, and adjust seasoning if necessary. Bring the liquid just up to a simmer, not a true boil, stirring well, especially if flour was added to the aromatic vegetables.

ABOVE *Add enough flour to properly thicken the sauce as the braise or stew cooks, or use other methods to thicken the sauce, such as reduction, starch slurries, or pureed vegetables.*

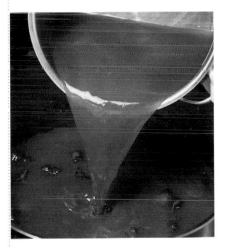

ABOVE *Add just enough liquid to keep the food moistened throughout the cooking time and to produce an adequate amount of sauce to serve with the finished dish.*

ABOVE *Adding the food back to the pot after the liquid is at a simmer keeps it from toughening.*

6. Add additional ingredients to the braise at the appropriate time so that all elements of the dish are evenly cooked.

Add the aromatics (such as roasted garlic, a sachet or bouquet, additional vegetables, or other ingredients) at the appropriate time. Add some early in the cooking process to infuse the dish with the flavor. Others may be added later on in the process to retain their flavor or texture.

7. Braise until the main item is fully cooked and tender.

Establish a slow simmer over direct heat, cover the pot, and finish cooking the braise in a moderate oven or over low direct heat. Stir, skim, and adjust the seasoning and the amount of liquid throughout cooking time.

Baste or turn the braising foods from time to time to keep all surfaces evenly moistened with the cooking liquid. As the liquid reduces on the food's surface, a deep glaze forms, further enhancing flavor. This also helps to ensure that the food is cooking evenly.

Remove the lid during the final part of the cooking time. This will cause the cooking liquid to reduce adequately so that the sauce will have a good consistency and flavor. Also, if the main item is turned frequently after the lid has been removed and is thus exposed to hot air, a glaze will form on the surface, providing a glossy sheen and good flavor.

Properly cooked braised foods are fork-tender. For foods that are portion size or smaller, check for doneness by cutting them with the side of a fork. Even though carryover cooking is not as big a factor for these dishes as it is for roasts, grills, and sautés, it is still easier to carve foods after they are allowed to rest for several minutes. Transfer the main item to a pan and keep it warm while finishing the sauce.

ABOVE *Adding roasted garlic at an early stage allows it to lend its flavor to the dish.*

ABOVE *To produce a very tender braise, keep the oven temperature moderate to low. Covering the pot allows the steam to condense on the lid and fall back onto the main item, moistening the food's exposed surfaces.*

ABOVE *Fork-tender braised foods slide easily from a kitchen fork inserted at the food's thickest part.*

8. Finish the sauce as necessary. Carve or slice the main item if necessary and serve with sauce and other accompaniments.

As the braised food rests, the sauce can be finished in a number of ways. Remove and discard the sachet d'épices or bouquet garni. Return the braising liquid to a simmer and degrease the sauce by skimming away any surface fat. Add any thickeners, such as arrowroot or cornstarch slurries, if necessary or desired. Or, strain out the vegetables and purée them; return the purée to the sauce as a thickener. Or, the sauce may be thickened by reducing it over medium heat to a good consistency. Once the correct consistency is reached, adjust the seasoning. (Note: The braise may be cooled and stored at this point for later service. Recombine the main item with the sauce to keep it moist and flavorful during storage.)

Many braises include vegetables, potatoes, or other components that are cooked along with the main item. These sauces are served unstrained. In other instances, the sauce is strained before it is served. Add any final finishing or garnishing ingredients just before serving the braise or stew.

9. Evaluate the quality of the finished braise.

Well-made braises have an intense flavor as a result of the long, gentle cooking, and a soft, almost melting texture. The main item's natural juices, along with the cooking liquid, become concentrated, providing both a deep flavor and a full-bodied sauce.

Braised foods have a deep color depending on the type of food. They should retain their natural shape, although a significant amount of volume is lost during cooking.

When done, braised foods are extremely tender, almost to the point at which they can be cut with a fork. They should not, however, be dry or fall into shreds. This would indicate that the food has been overcooked or cooked too rapidly at a high heat.

ABOVE *The mirepoix that is strained out may be puréed and returned to the sauce if it is still flavorful, or it may be discarded. Discard sachets or bouquets.*

ABOVE *Return the finished braised food to the finished sauce to hold it for service, or store it under refrigeration.*

10 lamb shanks (hind shank), well-trimmed (about 1 lb/450 g each)

salt, as needed

pepper, as needed

vegetable oil, as needed

8 oz / 225 g large-dice onions

4 oz / 115 g large-dice carrots

4 oz / 115 g large-dice celery

1 head garlic, halved and roasted

2 tbsp / 30 mL tomato paste

2 oz / 60 g flour for roux

1 pint / 480 mL dry red wine

2 qt / 2 L BROWN LAMB STOCK (page 252) or BROWN VEAL STOCK (page 252), hot

sachet d'épices, containing 3 to 4 sprigs parsley, $\frac{1}{2}$ tsp / 3 mL dried thyme, and $\frac{1}{2}$ tsp / 3 mL cracked black peppercorns

arrowroot slurry (optional), as needed

BRAISED LAMB SHANKS

1 Trim the lamb shanks of excess surface fat. Season them with salt and pepper.

2 Over medium to high heat, heat enough oil in a rondeau or brasier to liberally film the bottom until the oil starts to shimmer. Place the shanks carefully in the oil to sear to a deep brown on all sides. Remove the shanks to a pan and reserve.

3 Add the onions and carrots to the pan and cook, stirring from time to time, until golden brown. Add the celery and cook until barely translucent. Add the garlic and tomato paste and cook until the tomato paste turns a deeper color and gives off a sweet aroma, about 1 minute. If desired, stir in the flour to make a roux. Cook the roux for 4 to 5 minutes.

4 Add the wine to the pan, stirring to release any drippings. Reduce the wine by half. Whisk in the stock and bring to a simmer. Return the shanks to the pan along with any juices they may have released.

5 Bring to a gentle simmer over medium to low heat. Cover the pot and transfer it to a moderate oven (275°F/135°C). Braise the lamb shanks for 45 minutes. Add the sachet and degrease the liquid if necessary. Finish braising the lamb until fork-tender, 45 minutes more.

MAKES 10 PORTIONS

6   Transfer the lamb shanks to a hotel pan or other holding container and moisten with some of the cooking liquid. Keep warm while finishing the sauce.

7   To finish the sauce, continue to simmer the cooking liquid until it has a good flavor and consistency. Skim thoroughly to degrease the sauce. If necessary, it can be thickened lightly with arrowroot slurry. Adjust the seasoning with salt and pepper and strain. Keep hot for service.

8   Serve the lamb shanks with the sauce on heated plates.

NOTES

To prepare braised lamb shanks in advance and finish them by batches or à la minute, cool the shanks after they have been removed from the braising liquid. Once they are cool enough to handle, pull out the shank bone. Transfer the boneless shanks to a hotel pan. Cool, cover, and refrigerate. Finish the sauce. Cool and store the sauce separately in a bain-marie or other container.

To complete the shanks for service, ladle a small amount of a flavorful stock, remouillage, or broth on the shanks and reheat them in the oven. To complete the dish, reheat the amount of sauce needed in a sauté pan, add the reheated shanks, simmer briefly, and adjust the seasoning. Serve with side dishes or garnishes.

Foods that are braised on the bone have a wonderful flavor and texture but may be a challenge for the guest to eat. It is sometimes appropriate to remove the bones before service. Reheat the meat and hold it for service in a flavorful liquid.

STEWS

Stews share many similarities with braises, from the cuts of meat chosen to the texture of the finished dish. They differ from braises in that the foods are cut into bite-sized pieces and are cooked in more liquid.

Stews are often thought of as one-dish meals, producing a tender and highly flavored dish including not only meat, poultry, or seafood, but also a variety of vegetables in a redolent sauce. The sauce itself takes on a deeper flavor and body during stewing. It is also possible to finish a stew with cream, herbs, or a liaison of eggs and cream.

FOR A SINGLE ENTRÉE-SIZE PORTION OF MEAT, POULTRY, OR FISH STEW, YOU WILL NEED:	*an 8- to 10-ounce/225- to 285-gram portion of meat, poultry, or fish* *3 to 5 fluid ounces/90 to 150 milliliters of cooking liquid (stock, sauce, and/or other flavorful liquids such as wine)*	*1 ounce/30 grams prepared aromatics (mirepoix and/or other vegetables)* *salt and other seasonings (sachet d'épices or bouquet garni, for example)*	*additional finishing or garnishing ingredients (see individual recipes)*

SELECT AND PREPARE THE INGREDIENTS AND EQUIPMENT

STEWS ARE BASED ON the same cuts of meat, poultry, or fish as a braise. Trim the food of exterior and interior fat, gristle, and sinew. Divide larger cuts along seam lines to make it easier to cut against the grain for a more tender finished stew. The size of the cut will vary according to the style of stew, but typically they are bite-sized cubes. Season foods for stewing before cooking, using salt, pepper, marinades, or dry rubs to give the finished dish a good flavor.

Select the cooking liquid according to the food being stewed or the recipe's recommendation. Flavorful stocks or combinations of stocks and sauces, vegetable or fruit juices, or water may be used.

Stews often include vegetables, both as an aromatic component and as an integral component of the dish. Rinse, peel, and cut vegetables into uniform shapes so that they will cook properly. Keep the vegetables separated so that they can be added to the stew in the proper sequence.

Choose a heavy-gauge braising pan or rondeau with a lid for slow, even cooking. Have a ladle or skimmer available to skim the stew as it cooks. To test for doneness, use a table fork to cut a piece, or bite into a piece, to gauge its tenderness.

1. Heat the pan and oil and cook the seasoned main item on all sides, or combine the main item with the cooking liquid.

Some stews call for the meat or poultry to be dusted with flour and then cooked in hot oil just until it starts to stiffen with no browning. Other stews call for the main item to be cooked to a deep brown. Once the meat, poultry, or fish is properly colored, remove it from the pan and keep warm while sweating, smothering, or browning the aromatic vegetables, if desired, as explained for braising (page 528).

White stews, such as blanquette, do not call for the main item to be sautéed before the cooking liquid is added. Instead, a seasoned cooking liquid is added directly to the uncooked meat. Otherwise, the stewing liquid is added to the pan with the cooked aromatics and the main item is returned to the stew.

Stewed foods are typically completely covered with a cooking liquid throughout cooking time. The amount of liquid required varies from one cut of meat or poultry to another, however. Delicate or tender foods such as fish or shellfish may require very little added moisture to stew successfully. Tougher cuts may need proportionately more liquid for a longer cooking time as well as to soften tough tissues. Consult specific recipes for guidance.

2. Bring the liquid to a simmer over low heat, cover the pot, and finish the stew in a moderate oven or over low direct heat. Stir, skim, and adjust the seasoning and amount of liquid throughout cooking time.

Add any additional aromatics and vegetable garnish in sequence throughout the cooking time for a rich complex flavor and perfect texture. In some dishes, some or all of the garnish is prepared separately to maintain color. Add parcooked, blanched, or quick-cooking ingredients as close to service time as reasonable. Stir the stew occasionally, adjust the seasoning, and skim as necessary throughout cooking time.

Be sure to taste the cooking liquid before deciding what aromatics, if any, are needed. If the stock is very flavorful already, a bouquet garni or sachet may not be necessary.

ABOVE *Bring the cooking liquid to a simmer separately before pouring it over the prepared meat. This way the cooking liquid can be seasoned and the overall cooking time shortened. It also improves the texture of the dish.*

ABOVE *Skimming improves the flavor, color, and texture of the finished dish by removing impurities and solid particles. Keep a small bowl nearby to hold the skimmed scum.*

3. Stew the ingredients until fully cooked and tender to the bite. Properly cooked stewed foods should be easy to cut with the side of a table fork. Every component of the stew should be fully cooked and tender, including all vegetables. (Texture contrast, when desired, may be provided by a final garnish or side dish.) Discard the sachet d'épices or bouquet garni. Stews may be prepared to this point, then cooled and stored for later service. In this case, it is easy to lift any fat from the service once the stew has cooled.

The stewing liquid can be finished into a sauce, if desired. First, remove the solid ingredients with a slotted spoon or skimmer. Moisten them with a little of the cooking liquid, cover, and keep warm.

Strain the sauce if necessary and thicken by reducing it over direct heat. Add any additional thickeners, such as a prepared roux or a starch slurry, to the simmering sauce and continue to cook, skimming as necessary, until the sauce has a good flavor and consistency. Return the solid ingredients to the sauce and return the stew to a simmer.

4. Add any garnishing ingredients to the stew.
Many stews include a number of additional components, such as vegetables, mushrooms, potatoes, or dumplings. When these ingredients are cooked along with the main ingredient, their own flavors are improved as well as the flavor of the entire stew. However, in some instances, the chef may prefer to prepare some or all of these items separately, in order to make service more efficient or to produce a specific effect.

ABOVE *Before removing the veal to finish the sauce, check a few pieces to be sure that the meat is fully cooked and tender.*

ABOVE *To add cold roux to a simmering liquid, work the roux to break it up into small pieces, like a streusel topping, and then scatter it into the simmering cooking liquid.*

ABOVE *Cooking the garnish separately gives more control over the color of the garnish as well as its doneness. Here, mushrooms have been stewed gently in stock for rich flavor and an attractive color.*

5. Make the final adjustments to the stew's flavor and consistency. Add heavy cream or a liaison (page 242) to the stew as a finishing and enriching step. Adjust consistency by additional simmering or add a thickener such as slurry. Season with salt, pepper, lemon juice, or other ingredients. These ingredients are added to the stew either in batches or by individual portions.

6. Evaluate the quality of the stew. A well-made stew has a rich flavor and a soft, almost melting texture. The natural juices of the ingredients, along with the cooking liquid, become concentrated, and provide both good flavor and a full-bodied sauce. The major components in a stew retain their natural shape, although a certain amount of volume may lost during cooking. When done, a stew is extremely tender, almost to the point where it can be cut with a fork but not where it falls into shreds. This would indicate that the food has been overcooked.

TOP *The tempered liaison is added to the blanquette.*

BOTTOM *Wrap a lemon in cheesecloth before squeezing to keep seeds and pulp out of the sauce.*

ABOVE *The finished blanquette has a velvety sauce, and each ingredient is fully cooked but still retains its shape.*

4 lb / 1.8 kg boneless veal breast, shoulder, neck, or shank

salt, as needed

ground white pepper, as needed

2 qt / 1.9 L WHITE VEAL STOCK (page 249), CHICKEN STOCK (page 248), or
WHITE BEEF STOCK (page 249), hot

bouquet garni, containing 4 to 5 parsley stems, 2 sprigs thyme, and 1 bay leaf,
wrapped in leek leaves

8 oz / 225 g blonde or white roux (see pages 238–239)

1¾ lb / 800 kg white mushrooms, stewed in butter and/or stock until tender but
still white

12 oz / 340 g pearl onions, fully cooked

2 egg yolks

8 fl oz / 240 mL heavy cream

lemon juice, as needed

VEAL BLANQUETTE

1   Trim the veal and cut into 2-in/5-cm cubes. Season them with salt and pepper.

2   Heat the stock to a simmer and season as needed. Place the veal in a second pot and
pour the heated stock over it. Return to a simmer, stirring from time to time and skimming as necessary to remove impurities. Simmer for 1 hour and add the bouquet garni.
Continue to simmer until the veal is tender to the bite, 30 to 45 minutes more. Transfer
the veal to a pan and keep warm.

3   Add the roux to the simmering liquid, whisking to combine well, and return to a full
boil. Reduce the heat and simmer, stirring from time to time and skimming as necessary, until the sauce is thickened and flavorful, about 20 to 30 minutes.

4   Return the veal and any juices it has released to the sauce, along with the mushrooms
and pearl onions. Simmer until all of the ingredients are hot. (The stew may be cooled
and stored for later service. Return cooled stew to a simmer before adding the liaison.)

5   Combine the egg yolks and cream to make a liaison. Temper the liaison with some of
the simmering liquid, and add the tempered liaison to the stew. Return the stew to a
slow simmer and cook until the stew is lightly thickened and has reached 165°F/73°C.
Adjust the seasoning with salt, pepper, and lemon juice.

6   Serve the blanquette in heated bowls or plates.

MAKES 10 PORTIONS

HERBED STUFFING

makes 10 portions

2 oz/60 g unsalted butter

8 oz/225 g fine-dice onions

3 oz/85 g fine-dice celery

8 oz/225 g fine-dice mushrooms

5 oz/140 g small-dice bread

6 oz/140 g ground beef

6 oz/140 g ground pork

6 oz/140 g ground veal

1 egg

1/2 oz/15 g minced parsley

1/2 tsp/3 mL minced rosemary leaves

1/2 tsp/3 mL chopped basil

1/2 tsp/3 mL minced savory

1/2 tsp/3 mL minced sage

salt, as needed

pepper, as needed

1 Heat the butter and add the onions. Sauté, stirring frequently, until the onions are golden brown, about 5 to 6 minutes. Add the celery and mushrooms. Continue to cook until tender and translucent. Transfer to a bowl and cool.

2 Add the bread cubes, ground meats, egg, herbs, salt, and pepper, and mix until combined. Hold under refrigeration until ready to use.

BRAISED SHORT RIBS

makes 10 portions

10 beef short ribs (1 lb/450 g each)

salt, as needed

pepper, as needed

vegetable oil, as needed

8 oz/225 g mirepoix

4 fl oz/120 mL dry red wine

2 fl oz/60 mL tomato paste

8 fl oz/240 mL BROWN VEAL STOCK (page 252)

1 1/4 pt/600 mL DEMIGLACE (page 287), JUS DE VEAU LIÉ (page 260), or SAUCE ESPAGNOLE (page 287)

2 bay leaves

pinch dried thyme

3 fl oz/90 mL Madeira or sherry

1 Trim the short ribs and season them with salt and pepper.

2 Heat the oil in a rondeau or brasier until it starts to shimmer. Place the ribs carefully in the oil to sear to a deep brown on all sides. Remove to a separate pan and reserve.

3 Add the mirepoix to the first pan and cook, stirring from time to time, until the onions are golden brown, about 7 to 8 minutes. Add the tomato purée and cook until the it turns a deeper color and gives off a sweet aroma, about 1 minute.

4 Add the wine to the pan, stirring to release any drippings. Reduce by half. Return the ribs to the pan along with any juices they may have released. Add enough stock and demiglace, jus lié, or espagnol to cover them by two-thirds.

5 Bring to a gentle simmer over medium to low heat. Cover the pot and transfer it to a moderate oven (350°F/175°C). Braise the ribs for 1½ hours, turning occasionally to keep them evenly moistened.

6 Transfer the ribs to a hotel pan or other holding container and moisten with some of the cooking liquid. Keep warm while finishing the sauce.

7 To finish the sauce, continue to simmer the cooking liquid until it has a good flavor and consistency. Skim thoroughly to degrease the sauce. Adjust the seasoning with salt and pepper and strain. Add the Madeira or sherry to the entire batch or add it to portions at the time of service.

8 Serve the short ribs with the sauce on heated plates.

RECIPES

BEEF ROULADEN IN BURGUNDY SAUCE

makes 10 portions

3 lb/1.3 kg boneless bottom round, trimmed

salt, as needed

pepper, as needed

ROULADEN FILLING (recipe follows)

20 gherkins

flour for dredging, as needed

2 fl oz/60 mL vegetable oil, or as needed

6 oz/170 g small-dice onions

1 tsp/5 mL minced garlic

4 oz/115 g tomato purée

4 fl oz/120 mL Burgundy or other dry red wine

1 qt/1 L DEMIGLACE (page 287), JUS DE VEAU LIÉ (page 260), or SAUCE ESPAGNOLE (page 287)

1 Trim the beef and cut 20 portions weighing 2 oz/60 g each. Pound each piece to 1/4 in/6 mm. Season them with salt and pepper. Center 1 oz/30 g of filling on each piece, top with a gherkin, roll the beef around the filling, and secure with toothpicks or string. Dredge the beef in the flour and shake off any excess.

2 Heat oil in a rondeau or brasier until it starts to shimmer. Place the beef rolls carefully in the oil to sear to a deep brown on all sides. Remove to a separate pan and reserve.

3 Add the onions to the first pan and cook, stirring from time to time, until golden brown, about 7 to 8 minutes. Add the garlic and cook until aromatic, 1 minute more. Add the tomato purée and cook until it turns a deeper color and gives off a sweet aroma, about 1 minute.

4 Add the burgundy to the pan, stirring to release any drippings. Reduce by half. Return the beef rolls to the pan along with any juices they may have released. Add enough demiglace, jus lié, or espagnol to cover the rolls by two-thirds.

5 Bring to a gentle simmer over medium to low heat. Cover and braise in a 350°F/175°C oven for 1 to 1½ hours or until fork tender, turning occasionally to keep the beef evenly moistened.

6 Transfer the rouladen to a hotel pan, moisten with some of the cooking liquid, and keep warm.

7 To finish the sauce, continue to simmer the cooking liquid to a good flavor and consistency. Skim thoroughly to degrease the sauce. Adjust the seasoning with salt and pepper and strain over the finished rouladen. Keep hot for service.

8 Serve the rouladen with the sauce on heated plates.

ROULADEN STUFFING

makes 10 portions

3 oz/85 g minced onions

vegetable oil, as needed

8 oz/225 g bacon, chopped

4 oz/115 g chopped lean ham

2 oz/60 g ground beef

2 eggs, beaten

6 oz/170 g dry bread crumbs

1 tbsp/15 mL chopped parsley

salt, as needed

pepper, as needed

1 Sauté the onions in the oil until tender and translucent, about 4 to 5 minutes. Transfer to a bowl and let the onions cool.

2 Add the bacon, ham, ground beef and eggs to the onions and mix until evenly combined.

3 Add enough bread crumbs to tighten the filling; the mixture should hold together but still be moist. Season with parsley, salt, and pepper. Keep chilled until ready to fill rouladen.

YANKEE POT ROAST

makes 10 portions

4 lb/1.8 kg beef (top blade, bottom round, eye of round)

salt, as needed

pepper, as needed

oil, as needed

8 oz/225 g small-dice onions

6 oz/170 g tomato purée

8 oz/240 mL red wine

1½ pt/720 mL BROWN VEAL STOCK (page 252)

1½ pt/720 mL SAUCE ESPAGNOLE (page 287) or DEMIGLACE (page 287)

sachet d'épices, containing 3 to 4 sprigs parsley, ½ tsp/3 mL dried thyme, and ½ tsp/3 mL cracked black peppercorns

6 oz/170 g large-dice carrots or carrot tournés

6 oz/170 g large-dice turnips or turnip tournés

6 oz/170 g large-dice potatoes or potato tournés

6 oz/170 g large-dice parsnips or parsnip tournés

1 Trim the beef. Season it with salt and pepper. Tie the beef.

2 Heat oil in a rondeau or brasier and sear the beef to a deep brown on all sides. Remove the beef to a separate pan and reserve.

3 Add the onions to the first pan and cook, stirring from time to time, until golden brown, 6 to 8 minutes. Add the tomato purée and cook until it turns a deeper color and gives off a sweet aroma, about 1 minute.

4 Add the red wine to the pan, stirring to release any drippings. Reduce the wine by half. Return the beef to the pan along with any juices it may have released. Add enough stock and espagnol or demiglace to come about halfway up the beef.

5 Bring to a gentle simmer over medium to low heat. Cover the pot and transfer it to a moderate oven (350° to 375°F/175° to 190°C). Braise the beef for 1½ hours, turning occasionally to keep the beef evenly moistened. Add the sachet and degrease the liquid if necessary. Add the carrots, turnips, potatoes, and parsnips and finish braising until the beef is fork-tender and the vegetables are fully cooked, 35 to 45 minutes more.

6 Transfer the beef to a hotel pan or other holding container and moisten with some of the cooking liquid. Keep warm while finishing the sauce.

7 To finish the sauce, continue to simmer the cooking liquid until it has a good flavor and consistency. Skim thoroughly to degrease the sauce. Adjust the seasoning with salt and pepper. Keep hot for service.

8 Remove the string from the beef, slice it into portions, and serve on heated plates with the sauce and vegetables.

see photograph on page 547

SHAKER STUFFED FLANK STEAK

makes 10 portions

2 flank steaks (1½ to 2 lb/720 to 900 g each)

salt, as needed

pepper, as needed

HERBED STUFFING (recipe follows)

vegetable oil, as needed

6 oz/170 g mirepoix

2 tsp/10 mL tomato purée

6 fl oz/180 mL dry red wine

30 fl oz/900 mL BROWN VEAL STOCK (page 252)

arrowroot slurry, as needed

½ tsp/3 mL chopped tarragon

½ tsp/3 mL chopped chervil

1 Trim the flank steaks, butterfly, and pound them to an even thickness. Season them with salt and pepper. Center half of the stuffing on each steak, roll the steak around the stuffing, and tie to secure.

2 Heat the oil in a rondeau or brasier until it starts to shimmer. Place the steaks carefully in the oil to sear to a deep brown on all sides. Remove to a separate pan and reserve.

3 Add the mirepoix to the first pan and cook, stirring from time to time, until the onions are golden brown, about 7 to 8 minutes. Add the tomato purée and cook until it turns a deeper color and gives off a sweet aroma, about 1 minute.

4 Add the red wine to the pan, stirring to release any drippings. Reduce by half. Return the steaks to the pan along with any juices they may have released. Add enough stock to cover them by two-thirds.

5 Bring to a gentle simmer over medium to low heat. Cover the pot and transfer it to a moderate oven (350°F/175°C). Braise the steaks for 1½ hours or until fork tender, turning occasionally to keep them evenly moistened.

6 Transfer the steaks to a hotel pan or other holding container and moisten with some of the cooking liquid. Keep warm while finishing the sauce.

7 To finish the sauce, continue to simmer the cooking liquid to a good flavor and consistency. Skim thoroughly to degrease the sauce. Thicken as needed with arrowroot slurry and adjust the seasoning with salt and pepper and strain. Add the herbs to the entire batch or add them to portions at the time of service.

8 Remove the strings and slice the flank steaks into portions. Serve with the sauce on heated plates.

SAUERBRATEN

makes 10 portions

4 lb/1.8 kg boneless beef bottom round

salt, as needed

pepper, as needed

SAUERBRATEN MARINADE (recipe follows)

3 fl oz/90 mL vegetable oil

1 lb/450 g mirepoix

4 fl oz/120 mL tomato paste

3 qt/2.85 L BROWN VEAL STOCK (page 252)

3 oz/85 g gingersnaps, pulverized

1 Trim the beef and season it with salt and pepper. Tie the roast. Pour the marinade over the beef and marinate under refrigeration for 3 to 5 days, turning it twice each day.

2 Remove the beef from the marinade, drain, and blot dry. Strain the marinade and reserve.

3 Heat the oil in a rondeau or brasier until it starts to shimmer. Place the beef carefully in the oil to sear to a deep brown on all sides. Remove to a separate pan and reserve.

4 Add the mirepoix to the first pan and cook, stirring from time to time, until the onions are golden brown, about 7 to 8 minutes. Add the tomato paste and cook until it turns a deeper color and gives off a sweet aroma, about 1 minute.

5 Add the strained marinade to the pan, stirring to release any drippings. Reduce by half. Return the beef to the pan along with any juices it may have released. Add enough stock to cover it by two-thirds.

6 Bring to a gentle simmer over medium to low heat. Cover the pot and transfer it to a moderate oven (350°F/175°C). Braise the beef for 1½ hours, turning occasionally to keep it evenly moistened.

7 Transfer the beef to a hotel pan or other holding container and moisten with some of the cooking liquid. Keep warm while finishing the sauce.

8 To finish the sauce, continue to simmer the cooking liquid until it has a good flavor. Skim thoroughly to degrease the sauce. Add the gingersnaps and simmer until the sauce is thickened. Adjust the seasoning with salt and pepper and strain.

9 Remove the string from the beef, slice into portions, and serve with the sauce on heated plates.

SAUERBRATEN MARINADE

makes 2½ pints/1.2 liters

8 fl oz/240 mL dry red wine

8 fl oz/240 mL red wine vinegar

1 pt/480 mL water

8 oz/225 g sliced onions

8 black peppercorns

10 juniper berries

2 bay leaves

2 cloves

1 Combine all the ingredients for the marinade and bring to a boil. Cool to room temperature before combining with beef.

BRAISED OXTAILS

makes 12 portions

10 lb/4.5 kg oxtails

salt, as needed

pepper, as needed

oil, as needed

1 lb/450 g mirepoix

2 fl oz/60 mL tomato purée

1 qt/1 L dry red wine

1 qt/1 L BROWN VEAL STOCK (page 252), as needed

sachet d'épices, containing 3 to 4 sprigs parsley, ½ tsp/3 mL dried thyme, ½ tsp/3 mL cracked black peppercorns, 1 bay leaf, and 1 garlic clove

6 oz/170 g carrots tourné or batonnet

6 oz/170 g celeriac tourné or batonnet

6 oz/170 g white turnips tourné or batonnet

6 oz/170 g rutabaga tourné or batonnet

DEEP-FRIED ONIONS (recipe follows)

1 Trim the fat from the oxtails and cut into 2-in/5-cm cross sections and season them with salt and pepper.

2 Heat the oil in a rondeau or brasier until it starts to shimmer. Place the oxtails carefully in the oil to sear to a deep brown on all sides. Remove to a pan and reserve.

3 Add the mirepoix to the pan and cook, stirring from time to time, until the onions are golden brown, about 7 to 8 minutes. Add the tomato purée and cook until it turns a deeper color and gives off a sweet aroma, about 1 minute.

4 Add the wine to the pan, stirring to release any drippings. Reduce by half. Return the oxtails to the pan along with any juices they may have released. Add enough stock to cover them by two-thirds.

5 Bring to a gentle simmer over medium to low heat and add the sachet. Cover the pot and transfer it to a moderate oven (350°F/175°C). Braise the oxtails for 1½ hours and add the vegetables. Continue to braise until the meat is fork tender and the vegetables are fully cooked, turning the oxtails occasionally to keep them evenly moistened.

6 Transfer the oxtails to a hotel pan or other holding container and moisten with some of the cooking liquid. Keep warm while finishing the sauce.

7 To finish the sauce, continue to simmer the cooking liquid until it has a good flavor and consistency. Skim thoroughly to degrease the sauce. Adjust the seasoning with salt and pepper and strain.

8 Serve the oxtail with the sauce and vegetables on heated plates. Top with the deep-fried onions.

DEEP-FRIED ONIONS

makes 10 portions

12 oz/340 g onion julienne or thin rings
flour for dredging, as needed
salt, as needed

1 Heat the oil in a deep-fryer or a deep pot to 375°F/190°C.

2 Dredge the onions in flour and shake off any excess. Deep fry until golden brown. Drain on absorbent paper, season with salt, and keep warm until ready to serve.

ESTOUFFADE OF BEEF

makes 10 portions

4 lb/1.8 kg boneless beef shank or chuck
salt, as needed
pepper, as needed
2 to 3 fl oz/60 to 90 mL vegetable oil
12 oz/340 g small-dice onions
2 fl oz/60 mL tomato paste
2½ oz/70 g flour
1½ qt/1.5 L BROWN VEAL STOCK (page 252)
sachet d'épices, containing 3 to 4 sprigs parsley, ½ tsp/3 mL dried thyme, ½ tsp/3 mL cracked black peppercorns, 1 bay leaf, and 1 garlic clove
6 oz/170 g carrots tourné or batonnet
6 oz/170 g celery tourné or batonnet
6 oz/170 g turnips tourné or batonnet
6 oz/170 g pearl onions
4 oz/115 g peas
1 oz/30 g chopped parsley or chives (optional)

1 Trim the beef and cut into 2-in/5-cm cubes. Season them with salt and pepper.

2 Heat oil in a rondeau or brasier until it starts to shimmer. Place the beef (working in batches if necessary) carefully in the oil to sear to a deep brown on all sides. Remove the beef to a separate pan and reserve.

3 Add the onions to the first pan and cook, stirring from time to time, until they are golden brown. Add the tomato paste and cook until it turns a deeper color and gives off a sweet aroma, about 1 minute. Stir in the flour to make a roux. Cook the roux for 4 to 5 minutes.

4 Add the stock to the pan, whisking to work out any lumps. Return the beef to the pan along with any juices that may have been released.

5 Bring to a gentle simmer over medium to low heat and add the sachet. Cover the pot and continue to stew over low heat or transfer to a 350°F/190°C oven. Stew the beef for 45 minutes, stirring occasionally and skimming as necessary. Add the carrots, celery, turnips, and pearl onions and stew until the beef is tender to the bite and the vegetables are fully cooked, another 30 to 45 minutes.

6 Skim the stew thoroughly to degrease it. Remove and discard the sachet. Add the peas and simmer another 2 to 3 minutes, or until all of the ingredients are very hot. Adjust the seasoning with salt and pepper. Stir in the parsley or chives (or use to garnish individual portions) and serve the stew in heated bowls.

CHILI

makes 15 portions

5 lb/2.25 kg beef chuck or round

salt, as needed

pepper, as needed

vegetable oil, as needed

1½ lb/680 g small-dice onions

½ oz/15 g minced garlic

16 fl oz/480 mL canned tomato purée

1 qt/1 L BEEF BROTH (page 297)

8 oz/240 g diced green chiles

1¾ oz/50 g minced jalapeños

3 oz/85 g mild chili powder, or as needed

2 tbsp/30 mL hot chili powder, or as needed

6 tbsp/90 mL ground cumin, or as needed

3 tbsp/45 mL dried oregano

1 Trim the beef and cut into small dice. Season with salt and pepper.

2 Heat the oil in a pan over medium to high heat. Add the beef (work in batches if necessary to prevent overcrowding) and sear on all sides until well browned. Remove and reserve.

3 Add the onions and garlic to the pan and cook over medium heat, stirring from time to time, until the onions become a deep brown, about 12 to 15 minutes. Add the tomato purée and broth and bring to a boil. Return the beef and any juices it released to the pan and bring to a slow simmer. Cover the pot and stew either over very low heat or in a 325°F/165°C oven for 1 hour. Check the stew periodically, stirring and degreasing as necessary throughout cooking time.

4 Add the chiles, jalapeños, chili powders, 4 tbsp/60 mL of the ground cumin, and the oregano. Stew for 45 minutes, stirring frequently. Add the remaining ground cumin to taste and simmer for another 15 to 20 minutes, or until the meat is fork-tender and very flavorful, and the liquid has reduced and slightly thickened. Serve, or cool and store for later service.

5 To finish the chili, return it to a simmer. Taste the chili and adjust the seasoning if necessary with salt, pepper, ground cumin, or chili powder. Serve the chili in heated bowls, mugs, or soup plates.

CASSOULET

makes 12 portions

1½ lb/680 g boneless pork butt or loin

1½ lb/680 g boneless lamb shoulder, or leg, cut into 2-inch/5-cm cubes

salt, as needed

pepper, as needed

2 lb/900 g dried navy beans

3 qt/2.85 L CHICKEN STOCK (page 248)

1 lb/450 g slab bacon

1 lb/450 g garlic sausage

1 whole onion, peeled and halved

bouquet garni, containing 4 to 5 parsley stems, 2 sprigs thyme, 1 bay leaf, 2 to 3 garlic cloves, 1 celery stalk, wrapped in leek leaves

olive oil, as needed

8 oz/225 g small-dice onions

4 oz/115 g small-dice celery

1 oz/30 g chopped garlic

4 oz/115 g small-dice celery

8 fl oz/240 mL dry white wine

1 lb/450 g tomato concassé

1½ qt/1.4 L BROWN STOCK (page 252), as needed

sachet d'épices, containing 2 bay leaves and 10 peppercorns

6 whole legs duck confit (see Note)

6 oz/170 g bread crumbs (mie de pain)

2 oz/60 g parsley

1 Trim the pork and lamb and cut into bite-size pieces. Season them with salt and pepper. Reserve.

2 Sort and rinse the beans. Place them in a pot and add enough chicken stock to cover them by about 2 in/5 cm. Bring the stock to a simmer and cook the beans over low heat, skimming as necessary, for 30 minutes. Add the bacon and continue to simmer another 30 minutes. Add the garlic sausage, halved onion, and bouquet garni and continue to simmer until the beans are very tender and creamy, another 30 to 40 minutes. Remove and discard the sachet and halved onion. Hold the beans in their cooking liquid. Remove and reserve the bacon and and sausage.

3 Heat oil in a rondeau or brasier until it starts to shimmer. Place the pork and lamb carefully in the oil to sear to a deep brown on all sides. Remove to a pan and reserve.

4 Add the diced onions, celery, and garlic to the pan and cook, stirring from time to time, until limp and translucent, about 4 to 5 minutes. Add the wine and stir to deglaze the pan. Add the tomato concassé and cook until the juices released by the tomatoes have cooked down.

5 Return the reserved lamb and pork to the pan along with any juices they may have released. Add enough brown

stock to barely cover the meat. Return the stew to a slow simmer. Add the sachet, cover the pot, and transfer it to a 350°F/175°C oven and stew until the meat is tender to the bite, about 1 to 1¼ hours. Stir the stew from time to time and add more stock if necessary to keep the meat moistened.

6 Pull the meat from the duck legs, remove the skin, and pull or shred into bite-size pieces. Remove the rind from the reserved slab bacon and cut the bacon into small dice. Peel the sausage and slice it thin.

7 Arrange the duck, meat stew, bacon, and sausage in a casserole or other baking dish. Add the beans and some of their cooking liquid. Add the stewing liquid from the meats. The cassoulet should be very moist but not soupy. Top with a layer of breadcrumbs and bake in a 350°F/ 175°C oven until the breadcrumbs are golden brown and bubbling around the edges. Sprinkle with parsley and serve.

NOTE

To prepare duck confit, season duck legs liberally with salt and let them cure under refrigeration for 24 hours. Rinse the salt from the legs. Render enough duck fat to completely submerge the legs. Poach the duck in the fat until it reaches an internal temperature of 170°F/75°C. Remove from the heat; cool and store in the fat. Scrape excess fat from the duck before using or reheating.

CHOUCROUTE

makes 20 portions

5 lb/2.25 kg smoked pork loin

2½ lb/1.125 kg garlic sausage (optional)

10 oz/285 g sliced onions

1 oz/30 g minced garlic

8 oz/225 g Granny Smith apples, peeled, and cut into small dice

6 oz/170 g rendered goose fat, lard, or vegetable shortening

2½ lb/1.125 kg HOMEMADE SAUERKRAUT (recipe follows), rinsed in cool water

1 pt/480 mL CHICKEN STOCK (page 248)

8 fl oz/240 mL dry white wine

sachet d'épices, containing 3 to 4 sprigs parsley, ½ tsp/3 mL dried thyme, ½ tsp/3 mL cracked black peppercorns, and 6 juniper berries

1 whole carrot, peeled

12 oz oz/340 g finely grated Idaho or russet potatoes

salt, as needed

pepper, as needed

1 Trim the pork loin and tie if necessary. Prick the sausages in 5 or 6 places to prevent them from bursting.

2 Sauté the onions, garlic, and apples in the hot fat without browning them. Add the sauerkraut to the onions, garlic, and apples.

3 Add the chicken stock, wine, sachet, and carrot and stir. Bring the liquid up to a simmer.

4 Place the pork loin on top of the sauerkraut and add more stock if necessary to cover the pork by about one half. Cover the pan, and braise in a 350°F/175°C oven for approximately about 45 minutes. Add the sausages to the pan, return the cover, and continue to cook until the pork loin and sausages reach an internal temperature of 150°F/65°C, 15 to 20 minutes.

5 Transfer the pork loin and sausages to a holding pan and keep warm. Remove and discard the carrot and sachet.

6 Add the grated potato to the sauerkraut and cook it until the sauerkraut begins to bind and the potatoes are fully cooked, about 10 minutes. Season the sauerkraut with the salt and pepper.

7 Slice the pork loin and sausages and serve them on a bed of sauerkraut.

HOMEMADE SAUERKRAUT

makes about 2 gallons/7.5 liters

20 lbs/9 kg shredded green cabbage

8 oz/225 g kosher salt

1 Rough cut the shredded cabbage to 2-in/5-cm lengths. Toss the cabbage together with the salt until the salt is evenly distributed.

2 Line a food-grade plastic bucket with cheesecloth. Place the salted cabbage in the bucket and fold the cheesecloth over the top of the cabbage. Press firmly to pack the cabbage down and create an even surface.

3 Weight the top of the cabbage and cover this assembly with plastic wrap. Label with the date. Let the sauerkraut ferment at room temperature for 10 days. Remove the weights, cover well and refrigerate.

4 Rinse the sauerkraut in cool running water to remove a little of the excess salt before using.

Osso Buco Milanese

Couscous with Lamb
and Chicken Stew

Yankee Pot Roast

VEGETABLES, POTATOES, GRAINS AND LEGUMES, AND PASTA AND DUMPLINGS

From trimming and peeling to slicing and dicing, many vegetables and herbs need some kind of advance preparation before they are ready to serve or to use as an ingredient in a cooked dish. Various knife cuts are used to shape vegetables and herbs. A thorough mastery of knife skills includes the ability to prepare vegetables and herbs properly for cutting, to use a variety of cutting tools, and to make cuts that are uniform and precise.

MISE EN PLACE FOR VEGETABLES AND FRESH HERBS

CUTTING VEGETABLES AND FRESH HERBS

Make all vegetable cuts uniform in shape and size, so that they cook evenly and have a neat, attractive appearance.

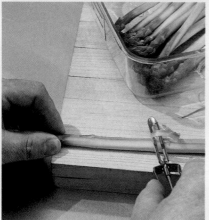

The best dishes begin with the best-quality produce. Review the information about purchasing and handling produce found in Chapter Eight. Handle fresh produce carefully to maintain its flavor, color, and nutritional value throughout all stages of preparation and cooking. One key to preserving quality in produce is to perform all cutting tasks as close as possible to cooking time.

Another important factor is the ability to select the right tool for the job, and to keep that tool in proper working condition. A steel should be on hand whenever you are cutting any food to periodically hone the knife's blade as you work. For a review of basic knife handling, see pages 80-86.

PEELING VEGETABLES

All fresh produce, even if it will be peeled before cutting, has to be washed well. Washing removes surface dirt and bacteria and other contaminants that might otherwise come in contact with cut surfaces by way of the knife or peeler. For the best shelf life, wash vegetables as close to preparation time as possible.

Not all vegetables require peeling before cooking, but when it is necessary, use a tool that will evenly and neatly remove the skin without taking off too much of the edible flesh.

Some vegetables and fruits have relatively thin skins or peels. Examples include carrots, parsnips, asparagus, apples, pears, and potatoes. Use a swivel-bladed peeler for these thin-skinned vegetables. These peelers can be used in both directions, so that skin or peel is removed on both the downward and upward strokes. A paring knife can be used in place of a peeler in some instances. Hold the blade's edge at a 20-degree angle to the vegetable's surface and shave the blade just under the surface to remove a thin layer.

Vegetables and fruits with thick or fibrous skins or heavy rinds are peeled with a knife. Paring knives are used for vegetables such as broccoli or turnips. Chef's knives are better for larger vegetables or those with very tough rinds such as celeriac or winter squash. Remove fibrous or tough skins from broccoli and similar vegetables by using a paring knife or swivel-bladed peeler to trim away the skin; often it can be pulled away after the initial cut.

Vegetables are trimmed to remove roots, cores, stems, or seeds. They may also be trimmed by slicing away one side of a round vegetable. This makes vegetable cutting tasks safer, since the vegetable will not roll or slip as it is cut. To produce very regular and precise cuts, such as julienne or dice, cut a slice from each side and both ends of the vegetable to make an even rectangle or square.

CHOPPING

Coarse chopping is generally used for mire-poix or similar flavoring ingredients that are to be strained out of the dish and discarded. It is also appropriate when cutting vegetables that will be puréed. Trim the root and stem ends and peel the vegetables if necessary. Slice or cut through the vegetables at nearly regular intervals until the cuts are relatively uniform. This need not be a perfectly neat cut, but all the pieces should be roughly the same size.

MINCING

Mincing is a very fine cut that is suitable for many vegetables and herbs. (Onions, garlic, and shallots may also be minced. For an illustration of this cutting technique, see pages 569–571).

Rinse and dry herbs well, and strip the leaves from the stems. Gather the leaves in a pile on a cutting board. Use your guiding hand to hold them in place. Position the knife so that it can slice through the pile. Coarsely chop.

Once the herbs are coarsely chopped, use the fingertips of your guiding hand to hold the tip of the chef's knife in contact with the cutting board. Keeping the tip of the blade against the cutting board, lower the knife firmly and rapidly, repeatedly cutting through the herbs. Continue cutting until the desired fineness is attained.

BELOW *Scallions and chives are minced differently. Rather than cutting repeatedly, slice them very fine.*

CHIFFONADE/SHREDDING

The chiffonade cut is used for leafy vegetables and herbs. The result is a fine shred, often used as a garnish or as a bed.

When cutting tight heads of greens such as Belgian endive or head cabbage, core the head and cut it in half, or quarters if it is large, to make cutting easier. For greens with large leaves, such as romaine, roll individual leaves into cylinders before cutting. Stack smaller leaves, such as basil, one on top of the other, then roll them into cylinders and cut. Use a chef's knife to make very fine, parallel cuts to produce fine shreds.

To shred or grate larger quantities, use a box grater or a food processor fitted with grating disks. An electric slicer can be used to shred cabbages and head lettuce.

ABOVE *For a very even shred, remove the core and any heavy ribs from cabbage before slicing.*

STANDARD VEGETABLE CUTS

THE STANDARD CUTS are illustrated here and on the following pages. The dimensions indicated are guidelines and may be modified as necessary. Determine the size of the cut by the requirements of the recipe or menu item, the nature of the vegetable being cut, the desired cooking time, and appearance.

FINE JULIENNE
$1/16$ x $1/16$ x 1 to 2 inches
(2 x 2 x 25 to 50 millimeters)

JULIENNE/ALLUMETTE*
$1/8$ x $1/8$ x 1 to 2 inches
(4 x 4 x 25 to 50 millimeters)

BATONNET
$1/4$ x $1/4$ x 2 to $2^1/2$ inches
(6 x 6 x 50 to 60 millimeters)

FINE BRUNOISE
$1/16$ x $1/16$ x $1/16$ inch
(2 x 2 x 2 millimeters)

BRUNOISE
$1/8$ x $1/8$ x $1/8$ inch
(4 x 4 x 4 millimeters)

SMALL DICE
$1/4$ x $1/4$ x $1/4$ inch
(6 x 6 x 6 millimeters)

MEDIUM DICE
$1/2$ x $1/2$ x $1/2$ inch
(12 x 12 x 12 millimeters)

LARGE DICE
$3/4$ x $3/4$ x $3/4$ inch
(20 x 20 x 20 millimeters)

*Allumette normally refers only to potatoes.

JULIENNE AND BATTONET

Julienne and batonnet are long, rectangular cuts. Related cuts are the standard pommes frites and pommes pont neuf cuts (both are names for French fries) and the allumette (or matchstick) cut. The difference between these cuts is the final size.

Trim and square off the vegetable by cutting a slice to make four straight sides.

Cut both ends to even the block off. These initial slices make it easier to produce even cuts. The trimmings can be used for stocks, soups, purées, or any preparation where the shape is not important.

Slice the vegetable lengthwise, using parallel cuts of the desired thickness. (See the table at left for dimensions.) Stack the slices, aligning the edges, and make parallel cuts of the same thickness through the stack.

DICING

Dicing produces cube shapes. Different preparations require different sizes of dice. The names given to the different size dice are fine brunoise/brunoise, and small, medium, and large dice. The table at left lists the dimensions.

Trim and cut the vegetable as for julienne or batonnet. Gather the julienne or batonnet pieces and cut through them crosswise at evenly spaced intervals.

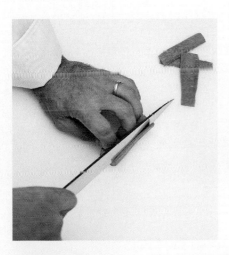

OTHER VEGETABLE CUTS

THE CUTS SHOWN HERE have been cut to precise standards for a more upscale presentation. They may be cut so that the natural shape of the vegetable is visible in each slice.

Tourné cuts (shown on page 567) may be the classic football shape shown here or modified to suit different vegetable types.

PAYSANNE
½ x ½ x ⅛ inch
(12 x 12 x 4 millimeters)

FERMIÈRE
Cut to desired thickness,
⅛ to ½ inch
(4 to 12 millimeters)

LOZENGE
Diamond shape,
½ x ½ x ⅛ inch
(12 x 12 x 4 millimeters)

RONDELLE
Cut to desired thickness,
⅛ to ½ inch
(4 to 12 millimeters)

TOURNÉ
Approximately 2 inches
(50 millimeters) long
with seven faces

MAKING PAYSANNE/ FERMIÈRE CUTS

Cuts produced in the paysanne (peasant) and fermière (farmer) style are generally used in dishes intended to have a rustic or home-style appeal. When used for traditional regional specialties, they may be cut in such a way that the shape of the vegetable's curved or uneven edges are still apparent in the finished cut. However, it is important to cut them all to the same thickness so that they will cook evenly.

In order to feature paysanne or fermière cuts as an ingredient in a classical dish or for a more upscale setting, square off the vegetable first and make large batonnet, ¾ in/20 mm thick. Cut the batonnet crosswise at ⅛-in/4-mm intervals.

For a more rustic presentation, cut the vegetable into halves, quarters, or eighths, depending on its size. The pieces should be roughly similar in dimension to a batonnet. Make even, thin crosswise cuts at roughly ⅛-in/4-mm intervals.

MAKING DIAMOND/ LOZENGE CUTS

The diamond, or lozenge, cut is similar to the paysanne. Instead of cutting batonnet, thinly slice the vegetable, then cut into strips of the appropriate width.

Trim and thinly slice the vegetable. Cut the slices into strips of the desired width. Make an initial bias cut to begin. This will leave some trim (reserve the trim for use in preparations that do not require a neat, decorative cut). Continue to make bias cuts, parallel to the first one.

MAKING ROUNDS/ RONDELLES

Rounds, or rondelles, are simple to cut. Just cut a cylindrical vegetable, such as a carrot or cucumber, crosswise. The basic round shape can be varied by cutting the vegetable on the bias to produce an elongated or oval disk or by slicing it in half for half-moons. If the vegetable is scored with a channel knife, flower shapes are produced. Trim and peel the vegetable if necessary. Make parallel slicing cuts through the vegetable at even intervals.

MAKING DIAGONAL/ BIAS CUTS

This cut is often used to prepare vegetables for stir fries and other Asian-style dishes because it exposes a greater surface area and shortens cooking time. To make a diagonal cut, place the peeled or trimmed vegetable on the work surface. Hold the blade so that it is cutting through the food on an angle. The wider the angle, the more elongated the cut surface will be. Continue making parallel cuts, adjusting the angle of the blade so that all the pieces are approximately the same size.

MAKING OBLIQUE OR ROLL CUTS

This cut is used primarily with long, cylindrical vegetables such as parsnips or carrots. Place the peeled vegetable on a cutting board. Make a diagonal cut to remove the stem end. Hold the knife in the same position and roll the vegetable a quarter-turn (approximately 90 degrees). Slice through it on the same diagonal, forming a piece with two angled edges.

Repeat until the entire vegetable has been cut.

DECORATIVE CUTS USING SPECIAL TECHNIQUES OR TOOLS

Decorative cuts can be an attractive visual component of a dish.

Basic tools like a paring knife or a swivel-bladed peeler (for curled or shaved Parmesan to top carpaccio or Caesar salad, for example) or Parisienne scoops or melon ballers (for balls of different sizes) can also be used to create special effects. More specialized tools including a mandoline, a Japanese "turner," an apple peeler, a ripple cutter, or a box grater can also be used for hand cutting. For large-volume operations, specialized cutting machines and tools are available. Be sure to read any instructions that come with special cutters, and use all the safety guards that come with them.

FLUTING

Fluting takes some practice to master, but it makes a very attractive garnish. It is customarily used on mushrooms.

Hold the mushroom between the thumb and forefinger of your guiding hand. Place the blade of a paring knife at an angle against the mushroom cap center. Rest the thumb of your cutting hand on the mushroom and use it to brace the knife. Rotate the knife toward the cap edge, to cut a shallow groove. At the same time the knife blade is cutting, turn the mushroom in the opposite direction with your guiding hand.

Turn the mushroom slightly and repeat the cutting steps. Continue until the entire cap is fluted. Pull away the trimmings. Trim away the stem.

FANNING

The fan cut uses one basic, easy-to-master cut to produce complicated-looking garnishes. It is used on both raw and cooked foods, such as pickles, strawberries, peach halves, avocados, zucchini, and other somewhat pliable vegetables and fruits.

Leaving the stem end intact, make a series of parallel lengthwise slices. Spread the cut fruit or vegetable into a fan shape.

WAFFLE/ GAUFRETTE

Use a mandoline to make waffle, or gaufrette, cuts. Potatoes, sweet potatoes, beets, and other large, relatively solid foods can be made into this cut. The blades of the mandoline are set so that the first pass of the vegetable doesn't actually cut away a slice but only makes grooves. The second pass, made at a 90-degree turn, makes a crosshatch pattern, as well as slicing away the first cut. Make the first pass, running the vegetable the entire length of the mandoline. Turn the vegetable 90 degrees and repeat the entire stroke. Repeat this procedure, turning the vegetable 90 degrees on each pass over the mandoline.

CUTTING TURNED/ TOURNÉ VEGETABLES

Turning vegetables (*tourner* in French) requires a series of cuts that simultaneously trim and shape the vegetable. The shape is similar to a small barrel or football. Peel the vegetable, if desired. and cut it into pieces of manageable size. Cut large round or oval vegetables, such as beets and potatoes, into quarters, sixths, or eighths (depending on the size), to form pieces slightly larger than 2 inches. Cut cylindrical vegetables, such as carrots, into 2-in/5-cm pieces.

Using a paring or tourné knife, carve the pieces into barrel or football shapes. The faces should be smooth, evenly spaced, and tapered so that both ends are narrower than the center.

PREPARATION TECHNIQUES FOR SPECIFIC VEGETABLES

A typical restaurant kitchen's vegetable and herb mise en place often includes vegetables that grow in layers, have seeds, grow in bulbs, or are otherwise unique.

ONIONS

Onions of all types taste best when they are cut as close as possible to the time when they will be used. The longer they sit, the more flavor and overall quality they lose. Once cut, onions develop a strong, sulfurous odor that can spoil a dish's aroma and appeal.

Use a paring knife to cut a thin slice away from the stem and root ends of the bulb. Catch the peel between the pad of your thumb and the flat side of your knife blade and pull away the peel. Trim away any brown spots from underlying layers if necessary before cutting the vegetable to the desired size or shape.

Leave the onion whole after peeling if you are preparing onion slices or rings. If you are cutting onion rings from a whole onion, be sure to hold the onion securely with your guiding hand. The rounded surface of the onion can slip on the cutting surface.

Cut the onion in half, making a cut that runs from the root end to the stem end in order to cut julienne or dice. As the accom-panying photograph shows, the root end, though trimmed, is still intact. This helps to hold the onion layers intact as it is sliced or diced. To cut julienne from a halved onion, make a V-shaped notch cut on either side of the root end.

An alternative peeling method is especially good for cutting and using the onion right away. Halve the onion lengthwise through the root before trimming and peel-ing. Trim the ends, leaving the root end intact if the onion will be diced, and pull away the skin from each half.

To dice or mince an onion half, lay it cut side down on a cutting board. Using a chef's knife, make a series of evenly spaced, parallel, lengthwise cuts with the tip of the knife, leaving the root end intact. Cuts spaced ¼ in/6 mm apart will make small dice; cuts spaced ½ in/12 mm or ¾ in/20 mm apart will produce medium or large dice.

Make two or three horizontal cuts par-allel to the work surface, from the stem end toward the root end, but do not cut all the way through. To complete the dice, make even, crosswise cuts working from stem end up to the root end, cutting through all lay-ers of the onion. Reserve any usable trim to use as mirepoix.

Some chefs prefer to cut onions by making a series of evenly spaced cuts that follow the natural curve of the onion. These cuts are sometimes referred to as radial cuts. Radial cuts result in even julienne or batonnet, which can then be cut crosswise into dice if desired.

GARLIC

Garlic has a distinctly different flavor, depending upon how it is cut. It can be purchased already peeled or chopped, but many chefs feel strongly that the loss in flavor and quality is not worth the convenience for all but volume cooking situations. Once cut, garlic (like onions) starts to take on a stronger flavor.

Mashed or minced garlic is called for in many preparations, so it is important to have enough prepared to last through a service period, but not so much that a significant amount has to be thrown out at the end of a shift. To prevent bacterial growth, store uncooked minced garlic covered in oil under refrigeration and use within 24 hours.

To separate the garlic cloves, wrap an entire head of garlic in a side towel and press down on the top. The cloves will break cleanly away from the root end. The towel keeps the papery skin from flying around the work area.

To loosen the skin from each clove, place it on the cutting board, place the flat side of the blade of a knife on top, and hit the blade, using a fist or the heel of your hand. Peel off the skin and remove the root end and any brown spots. At some times of the year and under certain storage conditions, the garlic may begin to sprout. Split the clove in half and remove the sprout for the best flavor.

Lay the skinned cloves on the cutting board and lay the flat of the knife blade over them. Using a motion similar to that for cracking the skin, hit the blade firmly with a fist or the heel of your hand. More force needs to be applied this time to crush the cloves.

Mince or chop the cloves fairly fine, using a rocking motion, as for herbs. To mash the garlic, hold the knife nearly flat against the cutting board and use the cutting edge to mash the garlic against the board. Repeat this step until the garlic is mashed to a paste. If desired, sprinkle the garlic with salt before mashing. The salt acts as an abrasive, speeding the mashing process and preventing the garlic from sticking to the knife blade. To mince large quantities of peeled garlic, use a food processor, if desired. Or crush and grind salt-sprinkled garlic to a paste with a mortar and pestle.

ROASTING GARLIC The flavor of garlic becomes rich, sweet, and smoky after roasting. Roasted garlic can be found as a component of vegetable or potato purées, marinades, glazes, and vinaigrettes, as well as a spread for grilled bread.

Place unpeeled heads of garlic in a small pan or sizzler platter. Some chefs like to place the garlic on a bed of salt. The salt holds the heat, roasting the garlic quickly and producing a drier texture. Instead of using a pan or sizzler platter, you may wrap whole heads of garlic in foil. The tip may be cut off each clove beforehand to make it easier to squeeze out the roasted garlic later. Or peel the cloves first, lightly oil them, and roast in a parchment-paper envelope.

Roast at a moderate temperature (350°F/175°C) until the garlic cloves are quite soft, usually 30 to 45 minutes. Any juices that run from the garlic will brown. The aroma should be sweet and pleasing, with no hints of harshness or sulfur. Separate the cloves and squeeze the roasted garlic from the skins or pass them through a food mill.

LEEKS

A leek grows in layers, trapping grit and sand between each layer, and one of the biggest concerns when working with leeks is removing every trace of dirt. Careful rinsing is essential.

To clean leeks, rinse off all the surface dirt, paying special attention to the roots, where dirt clings. Lay the leek on the cutting board, and using a chef's knife, trim away the heavy, dark green portion of the leaves. By cutting on an angle, you can avoid losing the tender light green portion of the leek. Reserve the dark green portion of the leek to make bouquet garni or for other uses.

Trim away most of the root end. Cut the leek lengthwise into halves, thirds, or quarters. Rinse the leek under running water to remove any remaining grit or sand.

Cut the leek into the desired shape. Leeks may be left in halves or quarters with the stem end still intact to make braised leeks. Or they may be cut into slices, chiffonade, julienne, dice, or paysanne-style cuts.

TOMATOES

Fresh and canned tomatoes are used in a number of dishes. Tomatoes can be cut into slices using a special tomato knife, which has a serrated blade, but a sharp chef's, utility, or paring knife also works well. Large quantities can be sliced on an electric slicer. Tomatoes have a skin that clings tight to the flesh and the interior contains pockets of seeds and juice. When the tomato is peeled, seeded, and chopped it is known as tomato concassé. The blanching technique for tomatoes is also used for peaches and nuts such as almonds and chestnuts. The techniques for seeding and chopping or dicing can be used for both fresh and canned tomatoes. Whole or sliced tomatoes can be roasted to intensify their flavor and change their texture.

PREPARING TOMATO CONCASSÉ

Tomato concassé is required in the preparation or finishing of many different sauces and dishes. Only enough should be made in advance to last through a single service period. Once peeled and chopped, tomatoes begin to lose some of their flavor and texture.

Cut an X into the bottom of the tomato. Some chefs also like to cut out the stem at this point to allow for better heat penetration. Others prefer to wait until the tomato has been blanched.

Bring a pot of water to a rolling boil. Drop the tomato into the water. After 10 to 15 seconds, depending on the tomato's age and ripeness, remove it with a slotted spoon, skimmer, or spider.

Immediately plunge the tomato into very cold or ice water. Pull away the skin. If the tomato was properly blanched, the skin will slip away easily and there will be very little flesh clinging to the skin.

Halve the tomato crosswise at its widest point. (Cut plum tomatoes lengthwise to seed them more easily.) Gently squeeze out the seeds.

Once the peel has been removed the flesh can be cut into dice or chopped into concassé of the desired size.

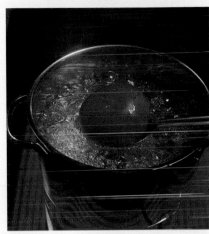

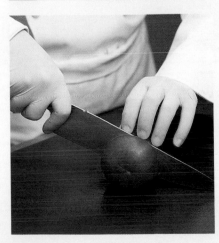

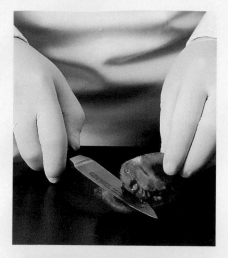

To prepare tomatoes so
that they can be cut into precise julienne,
dice, lozenge, or similar cuts, the tomato
flesh must be trimmed so that it has an
even thickness. Halve or quarter the peeled
tomato, cutting from stem to blossom end.

Using the tip of a knife, cut away any
seeds and membranes. This technique is
sometimes referred to as filleting. It is also
used for peppers and chiles. Cut the flesh
into julienne or other shapes, as desired.

FRESH PEPPERS AND CHILES

Peppers and chiles are used in dishes from
cuisines as diverse as those of Central and
South America, Thailand and other Asian
countries, Spain, and Hungary. As the interest in peppers and chiles has grown, many
special varieties have become available,
both fresh and dried. For more information
about working with dried chiles, see page
581. Whenever working with very hot chiles,
wear plastic gloves to protect your skin
from the irritating oils they contain.

CUTTING AND SEEDING FRESH
PEPPERS AND CHILES Cut through
the pepper from top to bottom. Continue to
cut it into quarters, especially if the pepper
is large.

Using the tip of a paring knife, cut
away the stem and the seeds. This cut
removes the least amount of usable pepper.
Chiles retain a good deal of their heat in
the seeds, ribs, and blossom ends. The degree
of heat can be controlled by adjusting how
much, if any, of these parts of the chile is
added to a dish.

You can make very fine, even julienne
or dice by filleting the pepper — that is,
removing the seeds and ribs — before cutting it. Cut away the top and bottom of the
pepper to create an even rectangle. Peel
away the skin, if desired, and then cut the
flesh into neat julienne or dice. Reserve any
edible scraps to use in coulis or to flavor
broths, stews, or court bouillons.

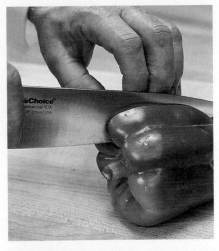

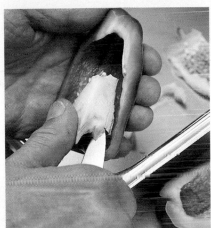

PEELING FRESH PEPPERS OR CHILES Peppers and chiles are often peeled before they are used in a dish, to improve the dish's flavor or texture, or both. The thin but relatively tough skin can be removed using swivel-bladed peelers or paring knives. This approach is often taken when the peppers are to be served raw, as in a salad or salsa, or in a dish that is intended to retain the pepper's sweet, fresh flavor. To peel raw peppers with a swivel-bladed peeler, first section the pepper with a knife, cutting along the folds to expose the skin. Then remove the core, seeds, and ribs and peel with a swivel-bladed peeler.

Peppers and chiles are often charred in a flame, broiled or grilled, or roasted in a very hot oven to produce a deep, rich flavor as well as to make the pepper easier to peel. To roast and peel small quantities of fresh peppers or chiles, hold the pepper over the flame of a gas burner with tongs or a kitchen fork, or place the pepper on a grill. Turn the pepper and roast it until the surface is evenly charred. Then place the pepper in a plastic or paper bag or covered bowl and let stand for at least 30 minutes to steam the skin loose. When the pepper is cool enough to handle, remove the charred skin, using a paring knife if necessary.

Larger quantities of peppers or chiles are often roasted in a hot oven or under a broiler, rather than charred individually in a flame. Halve the peppers or chiles and remove the stems, seeds, and ribs if desired. (The peppers or chiles may also be left whole.) Place cut side down on an oiled sheet pan. Place the pan in a very hot oven or under a broiler. Roast or broil until evenly charred. Remove from the oven or broiler and cover immediately, using an inverted sheet pan. Let stand for 30 minutes, to steam the peppers and make the skin easier to remove. Peel, using a paring knife if necessary.

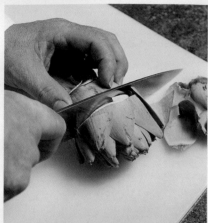

ARTICHOKES

Artichokes are members of the thistle family. Their leaves have sharp barbs, like thorns. The edible meat of the artichoke is found at the base of each leaf, which grows from a stem, as well as at the fleshy base of the vegetable, known as the bottom. Artichokes have a purple, feathery center — the "choke" — that is inedible in mature artichokes. The choke in baby artichokes may be tender enough to eat.

To prepare whole artichokes, first cut away the stem. The amount of stem removed is determined by how the artichoke is to be presented as well as by how tender or tough the stem is. Cutting the stem away even with the bottom of the artichoke makes a flat surface, so the artichoke will sit flat on the plate. If the artichoke is to be halved or quartered, some of the stem may be left intact. Peel the stem with a paring knife. Cut off the top of the artichoke. Snip the barbs from each leaf with kitchen scissors. Rub the cut surfaces with lemon juice to prevent browning, or hold the trimmed artichoke in acidulated water (a mixture of lemon juice and water). The artichoke can be simmered or steamed at this point, if desired, or the center of the artichoke, the choke, may be removed prior to cooking. To remove the choke, spread the leaves of the cooked or raw

artichoke open. The choke can now be scooped out using a spoon.

To prepare artichoke bottoms, pull away the leaves from around the stem and trim the stem as desired. Make a cut through the artichoke at its widest point, just above the artichoke bottom. Use a paring knife to trim the leaves away from the artichoke bottom. Finally, scoop out the choke with a spoon. Hold trimmed artichoke bottoms in acidulate water to prevent browning.

PEA PODS

Snow peas and sugar snap peas, depending upon the variety, often have a rather tough string that runs along one seam. This string should be removed before the peas are cooked. Snap off the stem end and pull. The string will come away easily.

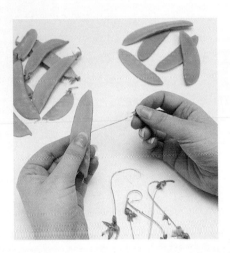

AVOCADO

Avocados have a rough, thick skin and a large pit. The flesh is soft enough to purée easily when they are properly ripened. Avocados, like potatoes, bananas, and artichokes, turn brown when they are exposed to air. To prevent browning, cut avocados as close to the time of service as possible. Citrus juices are often added to avocado, both to brighten the flavor of this rich but relatively bland food as well as to prevent the flesh from turning brown.

To remove the skin and pit from an avocado, hold it securely but gently with the fingertips of your guiding hand. Insert a knife blade into the bottom of the avocado. Turn the avocado against the knife blade to make a cut completely around it. The cut should pierce the skin and cut through the flesh up to the pit.

Again using your fingertips to avoid bruising the avocado, twist the two halves apart. Since it can be difficult to pick out the pit with your fingertips without mangling the flesh, scoop it out with a spoon, removing as little flesh as possible, or carefuly chop the heel of the knife into the pit, then twist and pull it free from the flesh. To remove the pit from the knife safely, use the edge of the cutting board or the lip of a container to pry the pit free.

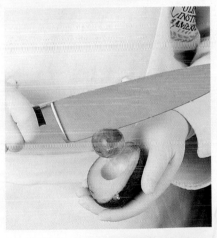

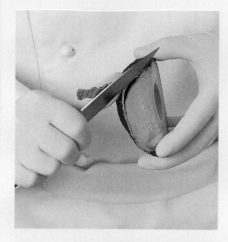

PEELING AND SLICING

AVOCADO To peel the avocado, catch the skin between the ball of your thumb and the flat side of a knife blade and pull it free from the flesh If the flesh is under-ripe, this may not be possible; in that case, use the knife to cut the skin away.

To slice the avocado, cut it lengthwise into wedges or slices. To dice the avocado, cut crosswise through the wedges. To dice an avocado while it is still in the skin, use the tip of a knife to score the flesh into dice of the desired size. Use the edge of a kitchen spoon to slice through the flesh. As the flesh is sliced away and lifted from the avocado, it is cut into dice. Make each layer as thick or as thin as desired.

ASPARAGUS

Young asparagus may need no further preparation than a simple trim to remove the very ends of the stalk, and a quick rinse. More mature asparagus may need to have the stalk trimmed a little more and partially peeled to remove the outer skin, which can be tough and stringy.

As asparagus matures, the stalk becomes tough. To remove the woody portion, bend the stalk gently until it snaps. Using a special asparagus peeler or a swivel-bladed peeler, peel the remaining stalk part-way up; this enhances palatability and also makes it easier to cook the asparagus evenly.

Asparagus may be tied into loose portion-size bundles to make it easier to remove them from boiling water when they are blanched or boiled. Don't tie them too tightly, or make the bundles more than a few inches in diameter. Otherwise the asparagus in the middle will not cook properly.

WORKING WITH DRIED VEGETABLES AND FRUITS

Dried vegetables and fruits have always been important in many cuisines. Drying makes foods suitable for long-term storage and concentrates their flavors.

Even today, some vegetables and fruits are too perishable to transport great distances or have a very short season. The rest of the year they can be had only in a preserved form. The flavor of dried chiles, mushrooms, tomatoes, and fruits such as apples, cherries, and raisins are special, even though those same ingredients may be purchased fresh throughout the year.

To get the most from these ingredients, recipes may often call for them to be rehydrated or "plumped" by letting them soak in a liquid. To rehydrate dried vegetables and fruits, check first for insect infestation and to remove any obvious debris or seriously blemished or moldy specimens. Place the vegetable or fruit in a bowl or other container and add enough boiling or very hot liquid (water, wine, fruit juices, or broth) to cover. Let the vegetable or fruit steep in the hot water for several minutes, until soft and plumped.

Pour off the liquid, reserving it, if desired, for use in another preparation. If necessary, strain it through a coffee filter or cheesecloth to remove any debris.

Other dried fruits and vegetables may be toasted or charred in a flame or on a griddle or heated pan to soften them. Some may be toasted and then rehydrated.

Toast dried chiles in the same manner as dried spices, nuts, and seeds, by tossing them in a dry skillet over moderate heat (see page 346). Or pass them repeatedly through a flame until toasted and softened. Scrape the pulp and seeds from the skin, or use the whole chile, according to the recipe. Break or cut open the chile and shake out the seeds. After toasting, rehydrate the chile in a hot liquid.

GENERAL GUIDELINES FOR VEGETABLE AND HERB MISE EN PLACE

One of the ways to distinguish a novice from a seasoned chef is the way each one approaches the task of cutting vegetables and herbs. The goal is consistency and speed. Without practice, it is impossible to achieve either.

To better approach vegetable mise en place, start by figuring out the proper timing of the work. Make a list and prioritize the tasks so that foods that can be prepared well in advance are done first, while those that lose good flavor or color when cut too early are done as close to service or cooking time as possible. Making such a list involves knowledge of the menu, of estimates for the meal periods (if known) for which the vegetables are being cut, and of standard kitchen practices for holding cut vegetables.

Think out the work carefully before beginning. Assemble all the tools needed, including containers to hold unprepped vegetables, prepped vegetables, usable trim, and trim that is not useful. Assemble the peelers, knives, and steel. Hone the knives (including the paring knife) at the start and during the work.

Wash vegetables and herbs before any initial trim work is done to avoid getting the work surface unnecessarily dirty. Spin dry leafy greens and herbs before they are cut.

Arrange the work in a logical flow, so that things are positioned within easy reach. This makes the work easier, faster, less wasteful, and more comfortable.

Keep all tools and the work surface clean and free from debris. Remove trim as it accumulates, before it has a chance to fall on the floor. Wipe down knife blades and cutting boards between phases of work. Sanitize all cutting and work surfaces when you switch from one food item to another. Wash your hands, too, and remember to use gloves if the vegetables will not be cooked before serving them to a guest.

In addition to the techniques and preparations already discussed, vegetable cookery often requires knowledge of other techniques —many of which can be found elsewhere in this book (see the box below).

Preparing leafy greens
(see pages 769–771)

Toasting spices, nuts, and seeds
(see page 346)

Zesting citrus fruit and cutting supremes
(see page 775)

Preparing fruits (see pages 774–778)

Marinades (see page 347)

Standard breading procedure
(see page 349)

CHAPTER TWENTY-TWO

Vegetables are far more important in contemporary menu planning than simply as a side dish. They can be the focal part of a meatless entrée. They can be selected and prepared to enhance another dish. Or they can be served as an appetizer or hors-d'oeuvre.

Buying vegetables that are at the peak of quality, observing proper storage and handling standards, and giving meticulous attention to the cooking process are vital to producing a vegetable dish that has strong appeal.

COOKING VEGETABLES

BOILING

Properly boiled vegetables have inviting flavors and vivid colors.

Boiling is a fundamental vegetable cooking technique that can result in a wide range of textures, colors, and flavors, depending upon how the technique is applied. Vegetables may be blanched, parcooked (or parboiled), or fully cooked. Boiled vegetables can be served chilled, added to another dish such as a stew to finish cooking, glazed or finished in butter or oil, or used to make a purée.

SELECT AND PREPARE THE INGREDIENTS AND EQUIPMENT

ALMOST ALL VEGETABLES can be boiled, as long as the appropriate modifications are made to the boiling process: green vegetables, including green beans, broccoli, and asparagus; leafy vegetables such as spinach and collard greens; red vegetables such as red cabbage or beets; yellow or orange vegetables like corn, carrots, pumpkins, and rutabagas; white vegetables such as cauliflower, turnips, or parsnips; dense or starchy vegetables such as winter squash; and delicate vegetables such as green peas or haricots verts.

Prepare vegetables for boiling by properly rinsing or scrubbing them to remove all traces of dirt. Vegetables may be trimmed and cut before cooking, or they may be cooked whole, according to the vegetable's nature as well as the intended presentation of the vegetable. If the vegetable has a tendency to turn brown once it is cut and exposed to the air (as artichokes do), try to cut the vegetable immediately before cooking, or hold the vegetable submerged in plain or acidulated water. Extended storage in water, once vegetables are peeled or cut, can rob them of flavor, texture, and nutritional value.

Vegetables boiled whole should be of a similar size, shape, and diameter to assure even cooking. If the vegetables are to be cut prior to boiling, the cuts should be uniform in size and shape to promote even cooking for a good flavor, appearance, and nutritional value.

Water is the most commonly used liquid for boiling, though other liquids may be used, depending on the desired flavor of the finished dish. Adding salt and other seasonings to the liquid enhances the flavor of a vegetable. Additional flavor and interest can be provided with finishing and garnishing ingredients.

Select the pot with a view to the amount of food being prepared. It should hold the vegetable, liquid, and aromatics comfortably, with enough room for the liquid to expand as it heats. Leave enough space for the surface to be skimmed if necessary. A tight-fitting lid is helpful for bringing the liquid up to temperature, but it is not essential. Leaving a lid on throughout the cooking process may shorten cooking time, but be sure to check the vegetables periodically to avoid overcooking them.

Other equipment that may be needed includes colanders or strainers for draining; equipment for cooling vegetables cooked in advance; holding containers to keep the vegetables warm; and spoons, ladles, or skimmers for cooking, tasting, and serving.

FOR 10 PORTIONS OF BOILED GREEN VEGETABLES, YOU WILL NEED:

2½ pounds / 1.15 kilograms prepped vegetables (weighed after trimming, peeling, and cutting)

plenty of salted boiling water

FOR 10 PORTIONS OF BOILED ROOT VEGETABLES, YOU WILL NEED:

2½ pounds / 1.15 kilograms prepped vegetables (weighed after trimming, peeling, and cutting)

enough salted cold water to generously cover the vegetables in the pot

FOR 10 PORTIONS OF BOILED RED OR WHITE VEGETABLES, YOU WILL NEED:

2½ pounds / 1.15 kilograms prepped vegetables (weighed after trimming, peeling, and cutting)

enough cold or boiling salted water to hold the vegetables without crowding

dash of vinegar, lemon juice, or other acid

HOW TO BOIL VEGETABLES

1. Season the cooking liquid and bring it to the proper cooking temperature before adding the prepared vegetables.

The amount of liquid required varies, depending on the type and amount of vegetable and the length of cooking time. In general, there should be enough water to hold the vegetables comfortably, without excessive crowding. Add salt and any other seasonings or aromatic ingredients to the liquid.

Bring the water to a rolling boil, except for dense or starchy root vegetables such as turnips and celeriac. These vegetables are started in cold water that is then brought to a boil so that they cook evenly.

For the best color in red cabbage, beets, and white vegetables like turnips or celeriac, return the cover to the pot. This helps retain acids that help to set color in these vegetables. Cover the pot while boiling orange and yellow vegetables (carrots and squash, for example), if desired. If preparing a green vegetable that will cook rapidly, such as peas or spinach, return the lid to the pot to help shorten cooking time. Denser green vegetables, such as broccoli, should be boiled uncovered for at least the first 2 to 3 minutes, to produce a good green color in the cooked vegetable.

ABOVE *Add the vegetables in small batches to keep the liquid's temperature from dropping dramatically.*

STEAMING

Steamed vegetables are cooked in a vapor bath to produce dishes that have pure, undiluted flavors.

Steaming shares many similarities with boiling as a cooking technique for vegetables. Any vegetable that can be boiled can also be steamed. It would be hard for most people to tell steamed and boiled carrots apart if they were presented side by side. But there are some differences. Since steaming cooks through direct contact with steam rather than liquid, steamed vegetables may be less soggy than some boiled vegetables. They are often viewed as having better nutritional value as well.

PREPARE VEGETABLES for steaming as you would for boiling. All vegetables should be properly rinsed or scrubbed, peeled, trimmed, and cut to shape as close to the time of service as is reasonable.

Although the most commonly used steaming liquid is water, flavorful stocks, broths, or other aromatic liquids are sometimes used to replace some or all of the water. The amount of liquid required depends on how long the vegetable will take to cook: the shorter the cooking time, the less liquid needed.

Salt, pepper, and other seasonings may be combined with the vegetables as they steam or as they are finished for service. Aromatic vegetables, spices, herbs, or citrus zest can be added to the steaming liquid to produce specific flavors. Steamed vegetables may be reheated or finished with flavorful oils, butter, heavy cream, or a sauce.

The quantity of vegetables being steamed determines the correct equipment. Small amounts can be steamed using an insert. Larger quantities, or vegetables that require different cooking times, are better

prepared in tiered steamers, pressure steamers, or convection steamers. It is important to allow enough room for steam to circulate completely around foods as they cook, to encourage even, rapid cooking.

In addition to steamers, it is important to have on hand the tools needed for handling the vegetables and for transferring them from the steamer to plates for service, or to holding containers. Also needed are containers to hold sauces, and spoons, ladles, and other serving utensils.

FOR 10 PORTIONS OF STEAMED VEGETABLES, YOU WILL NEED:	2½ pounds / 1.15 kilograms prepped vegetables (weight after trimming, peeling, and cutting)	enough cooking liquid to produce steam throughout the cooking time	seasonings to add to the vegetables and/or the cooking liquid

A convection or pressure steamer is suited to the more intense demands of a banquet or institutional feeding situation.

1. Bring the liquid to a full boil in the bottom of a covered steamer. Add the vegetables to the steamer in a single layer.

Before putting the steamer over direct heat, add any desired aromatics or seasonings to the steaming liquid so that they can release their flavor into the steam more effectively. As the liquid comes to a boil, it produces the steam to cook the vegetables. Cover the steamer to bring the liquid to a boil faster and trap the steam inside the vessel.

The vegetables should be arranged in a single layer on a steamer insert or tier to allow the steam to come into contact with all sides of the vegetable. Seasonings should be added to the vegetables before they go into the steamer for the best flavor development. Adding seasonings to the liquid at the beginning helps release their flavors.

2. Replace the cover, and steam the vegetable to the desired doneness. Doneness is determined by how the particular vegetable will be handled once it is steamed (see Determining Doneness in Vegetables on page 586). Steamed vegetables may be handled in the same ways as boiled vegetables.

3. Evaluate the quality of the finished steamed vegetable.

Properly steamed vegetables should have a good flavor and vibrant colors. Be sure to taste the vegetable to assess not only the flavor but also the texture. The textures may vary from very crisp (blanched vegetables) to tender enough to purée. Seasonings should enhance the flavor of the dish. Unless they are meant to be served chilled, vegetables should be very hot when served to the guest.

ABOVE *Once the vegetable is arranged over the boiling liquid, cover tightly to create an effective steam bath.*

ABOVE *Test the vegetable for doneness using all your senses (taste, sight, smell, touch).*

ABOVE *Steamed broccoli may be reheated by sautéing it with toasted garlic slivers.*

3½ lb / 1.6 kg broccoli (about 4 bunches)

salt, as needed

pepper, as needed

water, as needed

STEAMED BROCCOLI

1 Trim the broccoli, peel the stems, and cut into spears. Arrange the broccoli on a steamer rack or insert, and season with salt and pepper.

2 Bring the water to a full boil in the bottom of a tightly covered steamer. Add the broccoli, replace the cover, and steam the broccoli until tender, 5 to 7 minutes.

3 Remove broccoli from the steamer, adjust the seasoning, and serve immediately or cool and store for later service.

MAKES 10 PORTIONS

Broccoli and Toasted Garlic Sauté thinly sliced garlic in butter or oil until it is browned. Add the steamed broccoli and toss or roll the broccoli in the butter or oil until very hot. Adjust the seasoning with salt and pepper, as necessary. Serve at once.

PAN STEAMING

Pan steaming is a good à la minute technique for small batches or individual orders.

Pan-steamed vegetables are prepared in a covered pot with a relatively small amount of liquid. Usually the liquid barely covers the vegetables, and most of the cooking is done by the steam captured in the pan. Speed is a major advantage of this technique. Green vegetables that sometimes discolor when cooked in a covered pan, green beans for example, are done quickly enough to retain a bright color. Another advantage is that the reduced cooking liquids can be used to make a pan sauce or reduced to a glaze on vegetable.

SELECT AND PREPARE THE INGREDIENTS AND EQUIPMENT

VEGETABLES OF VIRTUALLY all sorts can be prepared by pan steaming. Inspect the vegetables for quality and freshness. It is a good idea to taste the vegetable before beginning to cook it, if possible. This can help determine which seasonings or cooking liquids to use, as well as how much. Very fresh locally grown vegetables may require very little additional seasoning, and they tend to cook more rapidly than mature vegetables, or those which have been stored under refrigeration for some time.

Rinse, trim, peel, and cut the vegetable as close to cooking time as possible for the best flavor and nutrition. All cuts should be precise and uniform for the best flavor and texture in the finished dish. Hold cut vegetables covered and under refrigeration when necessary.

Water is often used to prepare pan-steamed vegetables, but stocks or broths can be used for added flavor, if desired. Check the seasoning of any cooking liquid, adding salt or other flavorings, including

options such as wine, fruit juice, herbs, spices, or aromatic vegetables like leeks or shallots.

Sweeteners including white sugar, brown sugar, maple syrup, honey, or molasses can be added to glaze a vegetable if desired. If the cooking liquid will be used to prepare a pan sauce, have on hand additional seasonings or garnishes, thickeners, cream, or liaison, as indicated by recipe.

FOR 10 PORTIONS OF PAN-STEAMED VEGETABLES, YOU WILL NEED:

2½ pounds/1.15 kilograms prepped vegetables (weighs after trimming, peeling, and cutting)

enough seasoned cooking liquid to last throughout cooking time

additional ingredients or preparations as specified

HOW TO PAN STEAM VEGETABLES

1. Bring the cooking liquid to a simmer and season or flavor it as desired. Pan steaming is effective because vegetables are cooked very quickly before they lose significant flavor, color, texture, or nutritive value. To shorten the total amount of time the vegetables spend in the pan as they cook, some chefs like to have the liquid already at a simmer. In addition, this step permits the chef to steep the liquid with seasonings and aromatics. This infuses the cooking liquid and the steam for a more flavorful finished dish.

2. If desired, sweat or smother the vegetables and any aromatics in a cooking fat or in the cooking liquid. To add flavor to the finished dish, some recipes may call for shallots, ginger, or other aromatics to be gently cooked in fat or a liquid. Cook them until they have the desired color: tender and translucent for a subtle flavor or browned for a more robust flavor. At this time, add other ingredients as called for by the recipe, such as sweeteners to produce a glazed vegetable dish, herbs, or citrus juices. Consult specific recipes for guidance.

3. Pour or ladle enough cooking liquid into the pan to properly cook the vegetables. Very dense vegetables or large cuts will require more liquid than tender vegetables or small cuts. There may be a small amount of liquid left after cooking is complete; the pan should not cook dry, however. Check to see that the level of the cooking liquid is adequate throughout cooking time.

Covering the pan with a tight-fitting lid captures the steam released by the cooking liquid. The steam condenses on the lid and falls back onto the vegetables. This means that any flavors lost to the cooking liquid are retained.

4. Cover the pan and cook until the vegetable is done.
Covering the pan with a tight-fitting lid captures the steam released by the cooking liquid. The steam condenses on the lid, and falls back onto the vegetables. This means that any flavors lost to the cooking liquid are retained.

Pan-steamed vegetables can be cooked to a range of doneness, according to their intended use. They may be very lightly blanched, parcooked, or fully cooked (see Determining Doneness in Vegetables, page 586, for more information.) To check for proper doneness, bite or cut into a piece to evaluate its flavor and texture.

5. If desired, remove the cover and let the cooking liquid continue to reduce to make a glaze or a pan sauce. Glazed vegetables are left in the pan while the cooking liquid reduces to form a glaze. Before making a pan sauce, remove the vegetables from the pan if they are delicate or if they might overcook before the sauce is finished. Let the cooking liquid reduce until flavorful, and if necessary, add a starch slurry or beurre manié.

6. Evaluate the quality of the pan-steamed vegetable.
Look at the dish, smell it, and taste it. The vegetable cuts should look attractive, uniform, and neatly cut. The dish should smell appealing and reflect the seasonings and finishing or garnishing ingredients selected. The vegetables should be properly cooked and tender, flavorful, very hot, and well seasoned.

TOP *Sugar is added to the carrots to form a glaze as the cooking liquid cooks away.*

BOTTOM *For dense vegetables like these carrots, add enough liquid to nearly cover.*

ABOVE *Covering the pan captures the steam to help cook the vegetables quickly.*

ABOVE *The sugar added early in the cooking process has turned into syrup and reduced, along with the stock, to form a shiny glaze on the carrots.*

3 oz / 85 g butter

2¹/₂ lb / 1.15 kg oblique-cut carrots

sugar, as needed

salt, as needed

ground white pepper, as needed

12 fl oz / 360 mL CHICKEN STOCK (page 248) or VEGETABLE STOCK (page 254), hot

GLAZED CARROTS

1   Melt the butter in a sauté pan and add the carrots.

2   Cover the pan and lightly sweat the carrots, about 2 to 3 minutes.

3   Add the sugar, salt, pepper, and stock. Bring the stock to a simmer.

4   Cover the pan tightly and cook over low heat until the carrots are almost done, about 5 minutes for oblique cut.

5   Remove the cover and continue to simmer until the cooking liquid reduces to a glaze, 2 to 3 minutes more.

MAKES 10 PORTIONS

GRILLING AND BROILING

The intense heat of grills and broils gives vegetables a rich, bold flavor. The main restriction governing which vegetables can or cannot be broiled is their size.

Expanding the repertoire from a relatively short list, including summer squashes, peppers, and sliced onions, chefs have experimented and succeeded at grilling and broiling such tender vegetables as a tender-leaf head of raddichio to such dense and sturdy vegetables as winter squashes.

| FOR 10 PORTIONS OF GRILLED OR BROILED VEGETABLES, YOU WILL NEED: | 2½ pounds prepped vegetables (weight after trimming, peeling, and cutting) | oil, marinade, or glaze (optional) \ salt, pepper, and other seasonings | sauce and finishing or garnishing ingredients |

SELECT AND PREPARE THE INGREDIENTS AND EQUIPMENT

SELECT PERFECTLY FRESH VEGETABLES for the grill with no softening, discoloration, or wilting. Once selected, vegetables should be properly rinsed or scrubbed. Remove the peel or skin, core, and seeds if appropriate. Vegetables should be cut into uniform slices or other shapes before grilling or broiling.

High-moisture or tender vegetables can be grilled or broiled from the raw state; dense or starchy vegetables may require preliminary cooking to assure thorough cooking. Among the vegetables that can be grilled from the raw state are eggplant, zucchini, peppers, and mushrooms. Those vegetables that are typically par-cooked include fennel, sweet potatoes, carrots, and beets. Prepare the vegetables according to the type and desired result. Rinse, trim, peel, and cut into even pieces. Thread the vegetables on skewers, if desired.

Soft vegetables and precooked hard vegetables may be marinated briefly (15 to 30 minutes) before grilling or broiling. Longer marination could result in the vegetables' absorbing too much moisture.

If a marinade has been used, it may be served as a sauce with the cooked vegetables. Other possible sauces include salsa, soy sauce, a jus-based sauce, butter sauce, or cream sauce.

Maintain grills and broilers carefully. Scour the rods well with a wire grill brush between grilling different foods as well as after each service period to remove any buildup of charred food particles. Rub the rods lightly with a cloth dipped in vegetable oil to lubricate them before preheating the grill and throughout the service period.

1. Place the prepared vegetable directly on the grill or broiler rods. Vegetables can be seasoned with a marinade prior to grilling or broiling.

Allow excess marinade to drain from vegetables before grilling or broiling to prevent flare-ups. Vegetables can be seasoned during cooking by brushing on a light coat of glaze or marinade. Or, they may be seasoned after cooking; salt and pepper will not adhere well to all raw vegetables, but will to a vegetable that is hot from the grill or broiler. If there is a danger that the vegetables might stick easily to the rods or fall through, set them on a sizzler platter or in a hand-grill

2. Grill or broil the vegetables, turning as necessary, until properly cooked.

Turn grilled vegetables over after the first side has been marked or browned using a spatula or tongs. To create crosshatch marks, give the vegetables a 90-degree turn after the grill rods have made an imprint, then allow the rods to imprint again before flipping the vegetables to the second side. Complete the cooking time on the second side to produce a well-browned exterior.

Vegetables may be grilled only enough to mark and flavor them before they are used in another dish. They may be served hot, cool, or at room temperature. Thick cuts or high-starch vegetables can retain heat, even after they are removed from the grill or broiler. Allow enough margin for carry-over cooking to avoid overcooking.

3. Evaluate the quality of the finished grilled or broiled vegetable.

Grilled vegetables have a distinctive charred flavor. They usually have deeply browned exteriors, sometimes with marks from the rods. The interior is generally very tender, with an intense flavor. Grilled and broiled vegetables should be lightly browned on both sides, with well-browned crosshatch marks.

ABOVE *There will be some smoke, but there should not be any flare-ups as you grill.*

ABOVE *Marking the grilled vegetables with crosshatch marks.*

2½ lb / 1.15 kg shiitake mushrooms

10 green onions, left whole

SOY-SESAME GLAZE (recipe follows)

2 tbsp / 30 mL toasted sesame seeds

GRILLED SHIITAKE MUSHROOMS WITH SOY-SESAME GLAZE

1   Wipe the mushroom caps with a soft cloth to clean. If desired, slice large caps in half.

2   Add the mushrooms and green onions to the glaze and marinate at least 15 minutes or up to 1 hour.

3   Remove the mushrooms and green onions from the glaze, letting the excess drain away.

4   Grill the mushrooms and green onions on a preheated grill or broiler until they are marked on all sides and cooked through, about 2 minutes on each side.

5   Scatter with sesame seeds and serve at once.

MAKES 10 PORTIONS

NOTE
Once grilled, the mushrooms can be returned to the marinade, allowed to cool to room temperature, and added to salads or other dishes as a garnish.

SOY-SESAME GLAZE

4 fl oz / 120 mL soy sauce or tamari

2 fl oz / 60 mL water

2 fl oz / 60 mL peanut or corn oil

2 oz / 60 g tahini paste

1 tbsp / 15 mL sesame oil

1 tbsp / 15 mL minced garlic

2 tsp / 10 mL minced ginger

½ tsp / 3 mL crushed red pepper (optional)

Combine all ingredients. Keep refrigerated until ready to use.

ROASTING AND BAKING

Roasted or baked vegetables can be cooked whole or they may be cut to produce a browned exterior.

Vegetables are roasted for many different reasons. Thick-skinned vegetables such as winter squashes or eggplant can be roasted to make a richly flavored purée. Mirepoix and other aromatic vegetables are roasted to add an extra dimension of flavor and color to stocks, sauces, and other dishes. Tomatoes or peppers can be roasted to intensify their flavor and give them a drier texture.

Other baked vegetable dishes are prepared by combining vegetables with a cooking liquid (sauce, custard, or stock or broth). There are several famous potato dishes made in this manner (known as en casserole; see pages 648–652). The same techniques used to make those potato dishes may be applied to prepare vegetable casseroles, gratins, or flans.

FOR 10 PORTIONS OF ROASTED OR BAKED VEGETABLES, YOU WILL NEED:	*2½ pounds / 1.15 kilograms prepped vegetables (weight after trimming, peeling, and cutting)*	*oil, marinade, or glaze (optional)* *salt, pepper, and other seasonings*	*sauce and finishing or garnishing ingredients*

SELECT AND PREPARE THE INGREDIENTS AND EQUIPMENT

THICK-SKINNED WHOLE vegetables, such as potatoes and other root vegetables, winter squash, and eggplant, are well suited to roasting or baking. The skins protect the interior from drying or scorching. Roasting is also excellent for halved, cut, sliced, or diced vegetables, as well as vegetables that might otherwise be difficult to peel, such as peppers.

Rinse, peel, trim, and cut the vegetable, as necessary. To assure even cooking, cut vegetables into pieces of uniform size and shape. Toss the vegetables with oil to prevent excessive drying and scorching.

Marinades can enhance flavor and give extra protection to vegetables as they cook in the dry heat. Add seasonings or aromatics such as salt, pepper, spice blends, or garlic. Have available finishing ingredients (chopped fresh herbs, plain or flavored oils, whole or compound butter, reduced heavy cream, or a sauce), as desired or according to the particular recipe.

Have available roasting pans or sheet pans that can hold the vegetables correctly, with enough room for air to circulate freely, but not so much that juices from the food are likely to scorch. Some vegetables can also be set on roasting racks. For baked dishes, have available hotel pans or similar baking pans or dishes.

1. Prepare vegetables for roasting, as appropriate, by type or intended use and arrange in a baking or roasting pan.

Peel, halve, core, seed, and/or slice vegetables as necessary. Cut or sliced vegetables may be seasoned with salt, pepper, spices, juices, or marinades. Add some liquid to the pan to steam dense vegetables and to prevent them from becoming overly brown or scorching as they roast. Set vegetables on racks over the liquid, or directly in the liquid, as preferred.

2. Place the prepared vegetable in a hot or moderate oven and roast to the desired doneness. Serve immediately, hold for later use, or use as an ingredient in another dish.

The longer the roasting time — a factor determined by the type of vegetable, size and thickness, diameter of the cut, and its density — the lower the temperature of the oven. Vegetables may be roasted on sheet pans or in roasting pans or, in some cases, directly on the oven rack to allow the hot air to circulate readily. Generally, roasted vegetables are properly done when they can be

easily pierced with the tip of a knife or a kitchen fork. Vegetables should be rotated as they roast to promote even cooking because most ovens have hot spots. The placement of other items in the oven could also cause uneven cooking. Stir or turn the vegetables to keep those on the edge of the sheet pan from scorching.

Roasted vegetables are best served immediately on heated plates with finishing ingredients as desired. If the vegetables must be held, keep them uncovered in a warm spot for the shortest possible time.

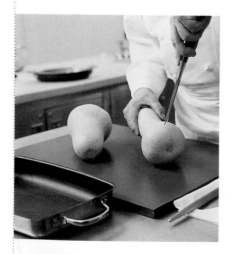

ABOVE *Vegetables roasted whole in the skin should be pierced to allow steam to vent. Otherwise, they could explode.*

ABOVE *For a method known as steam roasting or oven steaming, add a small amount of water and cover the pan with foil, if desired, to cook evenly and rapidly.*

ABOVE *If the pan was covered, remove the cover or foil during the final stage of cooking to develop a rich, roasted flavor and color.*

3. Evaluate the quality of the finished roasted or baked vegetable.

The aim of roasting and baking is to create intense flavor and a special texture. Browning produces the expected roasted flavor. The absence of added liquid means that the vegetable has a more intense flavor than otherwise.

The flesh of thick-skinned vegetables such as winter squash or eggplant should be soft enough to mash or purée easily.

ABOVE *Roasted vegetables are frequently puréed for use as ingredients in other items, such as soups or sauces.*

PURÉEING

Vegetables are often boiled, steamed, or baked until they are soft enough to make into a purée. Some are naturally soft or moist enough even when uncooked to make into a purée. The purée itself can be served as is or it may be used as a base for such dishes as vegetable timbales, custards, croquettes, or soufflés. It may also be used as an ingredient in other dishes or to flavor or color a sauce or soup.

If necessary or desired, cook the vegetables until the flesh is soft enough to mash easily. Cooked vegetables should be puréed while still very hot. Use a clean side towel to protect your hands as you work.

Cut away heavy or inedible peels, rinds, stems, or roots. Scoop or squeeze out seeds. Remove as little edible flesh as possible. Break or cut the vegetable in pieces sized properly for the puréeing equipment you are using.

Vegetables can range in texture from coarse to very smooth. Select the equipment to make the purée according to the way it will be used. A food mill, ricer, or sieve will remove fibers, skin, and seeds. These tools produce purées with a rather rough texture. Food processors can make quite smooth purées from cooked or raw vegetables that have already been trimmed, peeled, and seeded. If the vegetable is fibrous, the processor won't necessarily remove the strings, so the purée will need to be pushed

through a sieve. Blenders, immersion or countertop, and vertical chopping machines, can cut vegetables so fine that they produce a very smooth purée, though they too do not remove fibers and strings from some vegetables.

A vegetable purée can be finished by adjusting its seasoning, adding cream or butter, or blending it into other preparations. Or it may be cooled and stored for later use. Cool hot purées over an ice bath before wrapping and storing. Reheat cooled purées over gentle heat or in a bain-marie. Adjust seasonings and consistency before use or service.

4 lb / 1.8 kg butternut squash, scrubbed and left whole

4 oz / 115 g butter, at room temperature

4 fl oz / 120 mL heavy cream, hot

salt, as needed

pepper, as needed

BUTTERNUT SQUASH PURÉE

1 Pierce the squash and place it in a roasting pan. Add enough water to create steam during the initial roasting time. Cover with a lid or foil, if desired.

2 Roast at 375°F/190°C until the squash is extremely tender, about 1 hour. To check for doneness, pierce with a kitchen fork or paring knife. There should be no resistance. Remove the cover or foil during the final 15 minutes of cooking to brown the squash.

3 Remove from the oven. As soon as the squash can be safely handled (it should still be very hot), cut it in half and remove the seeds.

4 Scoop the flesh from the skin and purée it, using a food mill, blender, or food processor. If necessary, simmer the purée to reduce it.

5 Add the butter and cream and season to taste with salt and pepper. The purée is ready to use at once, or it may be properly cooled and held for later service.

MAKES 10 PORTIONS

SAUTÉING

Sautéing and its related technique stir frying may be used as the primary cooking techniques for vegetables as well as à la minute finishing techniques.

Boiled, steamed, or pan-steamed vegetables may be tossed or rolled in butter over high heat as a finishing step, or they may be cooked in a small amount of a flavorful liquid, sauce, or cream. Sautéed vegetables have a distinct flavor, primarily dependent upon the vegetable, but also influenced by the cooking fat that is chosen, as well as any additional finishing or garnishing ingredients.

Glazing is another finishing technique based upon the sautéing method. A small amount of butter and honey, sugar, or maple syrup is added to the vegetable as it reheats. The sugars liquefy and may be allowed to caramelize, coating the vegetable evenly to give it some sheen and a sweet flavor. Another way to glaze vegetables is to cook the vegetable in a lightly sweetened liquid, which when reduced, coats it with a glaze (see page 605).

SELECT AND PREPARE THE INGREDIENTS AND EQUIPMENT

RINSE, TRIM, AND PEEL the raw vegetable and cut it. Arugula, spinach, and other leafy greens, mushrooms, summer squashes, and onions may be sautéed or stir fried from the raw state. Drain greens and other vegetables that can hold excess moisture. This important step assures the best flavor, texture, and color in the finished dish.

Some vegetables will not cook completely when sautéed unless they are cooked by a separate method first. In this case, the vegetables are finished by the sautéing method. If necessary, partially or wholly cook the vegetable by boiling, steaming, or roasting.

Select a cooking fat to complement the flavor of the vegetable. Oils such as olive, peanut, canola, corn, or safflower can be used,

as well as whole or clarified butter, or rendered animal fat (lard, goose fat, bacon).

Optional seasonings and aromatics (salt, pepper, and lemon juice) can be used to adjust or heighten the flavor. Finely mince or chop fresh herbs and add them at the last moment. Small amounts of honey, sugar, maple syrup, or fruit juice, ingredients with a high sugar concentration, may be added to vegetables, generally near the end of the cooking time, to act as a glaze, giving additional flavor, sheen, and a golden color.

Take the quantity of food being sautéed into account when selecting the pan. It needs to be large enough to avoid overcrowding. If too much is put in the pan, the temperature will drop too quickly. On the other hand, the pan must not be too large either.

Certain materials are better at conducting heat with quick reaction to changes in temperature; others offer a more constant heat and do not react as quickly. There are benefits to both types of pan, and you will learn quickly which pan works best in which situation and with which food.

FOR 10 PORTIONS OF SAUTÉED VEGETABLES, YOU WILL NEED:	2½ pounds/1.15 kilograms prepped vegetables (weight after trimming, peeling, cutting, and blanching or parcooking; however, leafy green vegetables lose about	half their weight through moisture lost during sautéing, so begin with 4 lb/1.8 kg to prepare 10 portions) small amount of oil or other cooking fat	salt, pepper, and other seasonings sauce and finishing or garnishing ingredients

FOR 10 PORTIONS OF STIR-FRIED VEGETABLES, YOU WILL NEED:	2½ pounds/1.15 kilograms prepped vegetables (weight after trimming, peeling, and cutting)	small amount of oil or other cooking fat salt, pepper, and other seasonings	sauce or ingredients to make sauce (optional)

HOW TO SAUTÉ OR STIR FRY VEGETABLES

1. Heat the oil or fat and add any aromatic ingredients, as desired. Use only enough oil or fat to keep the pan lubricated and prevent the vegetable from burning. The cooking medium should be hot but not hazy or smoking. Vegetables require less intense heat than meat, poultry, and fish.

Some vegetable sautés and stir fries begin by cooking aromatic ingredients in the oil to add flavor to the finished dish.

2. Add the prepared vegetables to the pan.
If more than one type of vegetable is being cooked, as in a stir fry or vegetable medley, the vegetables should be added in sequence, beginning with those that require the longest cooking time and ending with those that require the least.

Do not over crowd the pan. To be of the best quality, sautéed vegetables should come into direct contact with the pan. For most vegetables, add only enough to make a relatively thin layer in the pan. Leafy greens can be loosely mounded in the pan, as they lose volume quickly while sautéing.

3. Add seasonings and continue to sauté or stir fry until the vegetables are fully cooked and flavorful. Turn or toss vegetables as needed. Some vegetables must be kept in nearly constant motion as they sauté; others develop a better flavor and color when turned only once or twice.

Use offset spatulas, tongs, or stir-frying tools to turn and lift vegetables as they sauté or stir fry.

4. Evaluate the quality of the finished sautéed or stir-fried vegetable. Each component of a sautéed vegetable dish should be cooked until done, very hot, and well seasoned. Be sure to check the temperature and seasoning of sautéed or stir-fried vegetables that are held for service in a steam table or other holding device.

FINISHING AND GLAZING VEGETABLES BY SAUTÉING

When vegetables are fully or partially cooked by steaming, boiling, or roasting, they can be sautéed just long enough to reheat them or to complete cooking them—a technique known as finishing.

Whole butter is a common choice for finishing vegetables, but other flavorful cooking fats such as extra-virgin olive oil or rendered bacon are also used to give a specific flavor to the dish. Vegetables may also be cooked in a small amount of heavy cream or a sauce, usually just enough to cling to the vegetables, in place of a cooking fat.

Heat the cooking fat, cream, or sauce over moderate heat. Add a small amount of sugar, honey, or other syrup to produce a sweet glaze, if desired. Garnishes may be added now or after the vegetables are heated through.

Add the prepared vegetables to the pan without crowding and stir, toss, or turn them until they are very hot and evenly coated. Taste them for proper doneness and seasoning, and serve at once.

TOP *Stir or toss sautéed vegetables as needed to prevent burning; keep stir-fried vegetables in constant motion. Sauté or stir fry until the vegetables are very hot and tender to the bite.*

BOTTOM *As vegetables sauté, they wilt or soften and the color intensifies. The arugula is a deeper, darker green than at the start of sautéing.*

ABOVE *Sautéed and stir-fried vegetable dishes should have an intense and appealing flavor.*

4 lb / 1.8 kg trimmed arugula

2 fl oz / 60 mL vegetable or olive oil

½ oz / 15 g minced shallots

¼ oz / 8 g minced garlic

salt, as needed

pepper, as needed

SAUTÉED ARUGULA

1 Rinse and drain the arugula, removing any tough or split stems.

2 Heat the oil in a sauté pan, add the shallots, and sauté until they begin to turn translucent, 1 to 2 minutes. Add the garlic and sauté until it begins to release its aroma.

3 Add the arugula, filling the pan (the arugula will wilt down as it sautés). Toss or turn the arugula as it sautés.

4 Sauté the arugula until it is completely wilted and tender and very hot. Season with salt and pepper and serve at once.

MAKES 10 PORTIONS

PAN FRYING

Pan-fried vegetables have a satisfying, crisp exterior that provides a pleasing contrast to the moist, flavorful interior.

Pan frying is similar to sautéing, the main difference being that, in pan frying, the amount of oil used as a cooking medium is greater than for sautéing. Also, any sauce served with pan-fried vegetables is made separately. The vegetables may be breaded or coated with flour or a batter.

RINSE, PEEL, TRIM, AND CUT the vegetable. Wholly or partially cook the vegetable, if necessary. Bread it with a standard breading, or coat it with flour or batter.

Clarified butter, most vegetable oils, shortening, and rendered animal fat (goose fat, lard, or foie gras fat) can all be used for pan frying. The cooking fat should come about halfway up the vegetables once they are placed in the pan.

Aromatics and seasonings may be added to the vegetable before or after cooking or they may be included in the breading or batter, if appropriate. In addition, a recipe may call for finishing ingredients, such as a compound butter, sauce, relish, or salsa.

The pan must be large enough to avoid overcrowding. If the pan is crowded, the oil's temperature will drop quickly and a good seal will not form. If this happens, the vegetable may absorb the oil and the breading can become soggy or even fall away in places.

Tongs, a skimmer, or a spider are also needed to remove the vegetable from the oil. Have a pan or platter lined with paper toweling to blot excess oil from the vegetable before service.

FOR 10 PORTIONS OF PAN-FRIED VEGETABLES, YOU WILL NEED:	2½ pounds/1.15 kilograms prepped vegetables (weight after trimming, peeling, and cutting), blanched, parcooked, or fully cooked, as necessary	coating ingredients, such as flour, egg wash, standard breading, or batter (optional)	salt, pepper, and other seasonings
		oil or other cooking fat	sauce and finishing or garnishing ingredients

HOW TO PAN FRY VEGETABLES

1. Heat the cooking fat in a heavy-gauge skillet, rondeau, or brazier. Add the vegetable carefully.
Pan frying requires high heat. When the cooking fat appears hazy or shimmering, it is hot enough. Monitor the heat of the fat to keep it even throughout cooking time.

For rapid cooking and for the best color, avoid crowding the vegetables in the pan. Add the vegetables gradually; too many vegetables added at once will lower the cooking temperature. Overcrowding also causes the coating to pull away from the vegetable.

2. Cook the vegetable over moderate to high heat until the first side becomes lightly browned and crisp. Turn the vegetable and complete the cooking on the second side.
Remove the vegetables from the fat and blot them briefly on absorbent paper toweling to absorb excess fat. Season the vegetables with salt and pepper away from the cooking fat, to help it last through successive batches. Skim away any bits of coating before adding the next batch.

3. Evaluate the quality of the finished pan-fried vegetable.
Properly done pan-fried vegetables have a golden or brown, crisp exterior, with the interior tender to the bite and very hot. The coating, if any, is crisp and light. Sauces or other accompaniments add complementary or contrasting flavor and texture.

ABOVE *Since zucchini cooks quickly, the fat can be at a higher temperature than for something denser or more fibrous. The shorter the necessary cooking time, the higher the heat may be.*

2½ lb / 1.15 kg trimmed zucchini

8 fl oz / 240 mL vegetable or olive oil, or as needed

salt, as needed

pepper, as needed

BEER BATTER (page 490)

20 fl oz / 600 mL TOMATO SAUCE (page 272), hot

PAN-FRIED ZUCCHINI

1 Slice the zucchini on the bias into ⅜-in/10-mm slices. Blot dry.

2 Heat ¼ in/6 mm of oil in a pan over medium heat.

3 Season the zucchini slices with salt and pepper and dip them into the batter to coat both sides evenly. Allow any excess batter to drain back into the bowl. Carefully lay the zucchini in the hot fat. Pan fry on the first side until browned. Turn carefully and complete cooking on the second side.

4 Remove the zucchini from the oil, blot on absorbent toweling, and season if necessary. Serve at once with tomato sauce.

MAKES 10 PORTIONS

DEEP FRYING

Perfectly fried vegetables are light and savory, and offer the chef a range of textures and flavors to showcase in appetizers, side dishes, garnishes, accompaniments, or entrees.

When vegetables are deep fried, the results can range from crisp, fragile chips to hearty croquettes with their crisp coating surrounding a moist, flavorful vegetable mixture. Tempura-style vegetables pair fresh vegetables with a light batter. Other batters, such as a beer batter, can also be used to coat vegetables before frying, as can coatings of bread crumbs or similar ingredients. (For deep-fried potatoes, see pages 657–659).

SELECT AND PREPARE THE INGREDIENTS AND EQUIPMENT

CHOOSE FRESH AND FLAVORFUL VEGETABLES and prepare them for frying according to the recipe's requirements or the intended style of service. All vegetables must be thoroughly rinsed, and in some cases scrubbed. Trim away tough or inedible skins, peels, cores, seeds, or roots. Cut or slice as required. When necessary, the vegetables may be parcooked before frying.

Dice, mince, or purée vegetables used in a croquette mixture, and use an appropriate binder to hold them together into a batter. Options include heavy béchamel or velouté, heavy cream, fresh cheeses, eggs, or bread crumbs.

Some fried vegetable preparations call for a standard breading (page 349) or batter. The batter should be applied just before the vegetable is fried.

Oils and other cooking fats used for frying must be able to reach a high temperature without smoking or breaking down. Vegetable oils, including corn oil, canola oil, or safflower oil have neutral flavors and high smoking points. Special oils may be used for a specific flavor. Olive oil or rendered duck or goose fat may be appropriate. Bring the frying oil or fat to the appropriate temperature before starting to fry.

Use either a frying kettle or deep fryer. Electric or gas deep fryers maintain an even temperature throughout cooking time and are efficient for menus that produce quantities of fried vegetables and other fried dishes. Baskets are used to lower some fried items into the oil and to remove them once cooked. For other fried foods, tongs are used to add the vegetables to the frying fat and a spider or skimmer is used to remove them.

Prepare a pan lined with absorbent paper to blot fried foods immediately after they complete cooking.

FOR 10 PORTIONS OF DEEP-FRIED VEGETABLES, YOU WILL NEED:

2½ pounds/1.15 kilograms prepped vegetables (weight after trimming, peeling, and cutting), blanched, parcooked, or fully cooked, as necessary

coating ingredients, such as flour, egg wash, standard breading, or batter (optional)

enough oil or other cooking fat to completely submerge the vegetable

salt, pepper, and other seasonings

sauce and finishing or garnishing ingredients

1. Heat the oil in a deep fryer or kettle. Add the vegetables to the hot oil using a basket, tongs, or a spider. The best temperature for deep frying most vegetables is about 350°F/175°C. Lower breaded vegetables into the oil using a basket. Be sure to leave room between larger pieces to prevent them from sticking to each other, and do not overcrowd the basket. Batter-coated vegetables should be dipped into the batter (in some cases, they should be dusted with flour before they are coated in batter) using tongs or a spider, then immediately lowered into the hot oil.

Adding the vegetables to the hot oil will lower the temperature of the oil for a time (this is known as recovery time), so adjust the size of the batches added to the oil to minimize the drop and shorten recovery time.

ABOVE *Use tongs to dip the vegetables into the batter for the swimming method of frying.*

2. Fry the vegetables until fully cooked. Remove and drain. Season if necessary.

Frying times vary according to the type of vegetable being fried. The vegetable (or vegetable mixture in the case of croquettes and fritters) should be fully cooked, tender, and hot. The coating, if any, should have a golden to brown color. Vegetables coated in breading and prepared by the basket method typically stay submerged until they are fully cooked, when they rise to the oil's surface. Use the basket to lift them from the oil. Hold the basket over the fryer briefly to allow the oil to drain back into the kettle.

Batter-coated vegetables fried using the swimming method may be turned as they fry to cook and brown them evenly. Use tongs, a spider, or similar tools to turn the vegetables, as well as to lift them from the oil when they are fully cooked.

Transfer fried vegetables to a paper-lined pan to blot them. Season them with salt, pepper, or spice blends now. Seasoning should never be done directly over the fryer, since these seasonings could hasten the breakdown of the frying oil. Fried vegetables are at their peak of quality now, and should be served right away. If necessary, they may be held for up to 15 minutes in a warm place (such as under a heat lamp).

3. Evaluate the quality of the finished deep-fried vegetable.

In general, the thinner the cut used for the vegetable, the crisper the finished dish will be. The exterior of the vegetable should be golden or brown in color, the flavor fresh and appealing. The coating, if any was used, should be an even thickness and not excessive in relation to the vegetable portion. The vegetable, as well as any coatings, should be properly seasoned and extremely hot.

ABOVE *Let excess oil drain from the vegetable back into the fryer before transferring it to a paper-lined pan to blot.*

oil for frying, as needed

2¹/₂ lb / 1.15 kg assorted prepped vegetables, cut as desired

tempura batter (see page 465), as needed, chilled

20 fl oz / 600 mL TEMPURA DIPPING SAUCE (page 465)

VEGETABLE TEMPURA

1 Heat the oil to 375°F/190°C.

2 Blot the vegetables dry, season, and coat evenly with the batter. Lower the batter-coated vegetables into the hot oil.

3 Deep fry the vegetables until the batter is golden brown and puffy. Turn them if necessary to brown and cook evenly. Remove them from the fryer with tongs or a spider and blot briefly on absorbent toweling. Season if necessary and serve at once.

4 Serve the vegetables with the dipping sauce.

MAKES 10 PORTIONS

STEWING AND BRAISING

Vegetable stews and braises include such delicate dishes as petit pois á la française and, on the other end of the spectrum, such sturdy and robust dishes as ratatouille and braised cabbage.

Stewed or braised vegetables literally cook in their own juices. The vegetables in a stew are customarily cut into small pieces, while those in a braise are in large pieces or are left whole. Occasionally, beurre manié or a starch slurry is added to the juices to give the dish more substance and to improve its appearance. The thickened sauce lightly coats the vegetable, providing an attractive sheen.

VEGETABLE STEWS AND BRAISES may be composed of one main ingredient, or a combination of vegetables. Braised fennel, for example, contains a single main ingredient; ratatouille is a stew that melds several different vegetables. Braises and stews generally include some aromatic ingredients, such as shallots or mirepoix, in addition to the main ingredient.

Prepare the vegetables according to the type and the desired result. Rinse, peel, trim, and cut the vegetables, as necessary. Blanch them to remove bitter flavors or to aid in removing peels.

The fat or oil chosen should have a good flavor, one that is appropriate to the dish. Vegetables that do not release a significant amount of liquid as they cook may need additional liquid, stock, wine, fumets, juices, or water, for example.

Prepare and use seasonings and aromatics, such as salt and pepper, shallots, garlic, minced herbs, spices, mirepoix, or matignon. Some dishes include a pork product (salt pork, bacon, or ham) or an acid (vinegar, citrus zest or juice, or wine) to develop a complex flavor in braised and stewed vegetable dishes.

Some recipes call for an added thickener such as a slurry of arrowroot, cornstarch, or potato starch, or beurre manié.

Various finishing ingredients, such as reduced heavy cream, a cream sauce, butter, or a liaison, may be added to give a vegetable stew a rich flavor, some sheen, and a smooth texture. A vegetable stew or braise may be garnished with bread crumbs and cheese to create a gratin, if desired.

The main piece of equipment needed for braising is a brasier or rondeau (or other deep, wide cooking vessel) with a lid. A skimmer or slotted spoon is used to remove properly braised or stewed vegetables from the pot before finishing the sauce. A strainer or immersion blender is used to finish the sauce.

FOR 10 PORTIONS OF STEWED OR BRAISED VEGETABLES, YOU WILL NEED:	3 to 3½ pounds / 1.5 to 1.8 kilograms prepped vegetables (weight after trimming, peeling, and cutting)	aromatic vegetables, seasonings, herbs, and spices flavorful cooking liquid	small amount of cooking fat finishing and garnishing ingredients

1. Cook the aromatic vegetables in a cooking fat, beginning with members of the onion family.

The aromatic vegetables in a light-colored stew or braise are cooked just until they start to become tender and release some of their natural juices. For other dishes, the aromatics are cooked to the desired stage of browness, ranging from a light golden color to a deep brown. Use enough oil to properly cook the aromatics without scorching them, and stir as needed to develop their flavor and color.

2. Add the remaining ingredients in order, stirring as necessary and adjusting the seasoning and consistency of the dish as it braises or stews.

Cook vegetable stews over gentle heat with the lid on to encourage them to release their flavor and to capture it in the cooking liquid. Braises may be cooked over direct heat or in the oven. If the cooking liquid cooks away too quickly, add more and lower the heat slightly. If the liquid does not reduce properly during cooking, remove the lid to encourage natural reduction.

ABOVE *Cooking members of the onion family first in a stew or braise develops a smooth, sweet taste in the dish. It also infuses the oil with onion flavor. The oil carries the flavor to all the ingredients in the dish.*

ABOVE *Peppers should be added early to cook until soft as well as to contribute their flavor throughout stewing.*

ABOVE *Eggplant absorbs flavors from other ingredients as it cooks. Allow enough time for it to become completely tender.*

3. Stew or braise the vegetable until it is flavorful, fully cooked, and fork tender. Serve immediately or hold for later use.

The stew or braise is ready to serve now, but it may be finished by preparing a sauce from the cooking liquid. To do so, remove the vegetable from the cooking liquid and thicken the liquid in one of the following ways:

- Reduce the liquid to a saucelike flavor and consistency and adjust the seasoning with salt and pepper.
- Purée some of the aromatic vegetables and return the purée to the cooking liquid.
- Add a starch slurry.
- Add a bit of beurre manié to the cooking liquid.

Serve as is on hot plates, or finish the vegetables with a gratin topping and brown under a salamander or broiler. Stewed and braised vegetables can be held for a longer time than other vegetables without losing significant quality. Hold them, loosely covered, in a steam table. They also may be cooled and held under refrigeration, then reheated as needed.

4. Evaluate the quality of the finished stewed or braised vegetable. Vegetable stews and braises have deep, concentrated flavors. They may be quite complex and include a wide variety of ingredients, like ratatouille, or they may be relatively simple, made from a single vegetable with some seasonings, like braised fennel. Stews and braises should be fork tender or, in some cases, meltingly soft.

ABOVE *Adjust the consistency of the stew as it simmers with additional stock, if the stew begins to appear dry.*

ABOVE *Ratatouille is a stew, so it should be moist but not soupy. All of the ingredients should be cooked and the colors of the dish should be attractive and vibrant.*

3 fl oz / 90 mL olive oil, or as needed

12 oz / 340 g diced red or white onions

¾ oz / 20 g minced garlic

1 oz / 30 g tomato paste

4 oz / 115 g medium-dice green pepper

1 lb / 450 g medium-dice eggplant

12 oz / 340 g medium-dice zucchini

6 oz / 170 g quartered or sliced mushrooms

8 oz / 225 g tomato concassé

4 fl oz / 120 mL CHICKEN STOCK (page 248), or VEGETABLE STOCK (page 254), or
   as needed

salt, as needed

pepper, as needed

chopped fresh herbs, as needed

RATATOUILLE

1 Heat the oil in a pan over medium heat. Add the onions and sauté until translucent, about 4 to 5 minutes. Add the garlic and sauté until it releases its aroma, about 1 minute.

2 Add the tomato paste and cook over medium heat until it turns a deeper color and gives off a sweet aroma, about 1 minute.

3 Add the rest of the vegetables in sequence: peppers, eggplant, zucchini, mushrooms, and finally tomatoes. Cook each vegetable until it starts to soften before adding the next.

4 Add a small amount of stock as necessary to stew the vegetables. They should be moist but not soupy.

5 Stew the vegetables until all are very tender and flavorful. Adjust the seasoning with salt and pepper and add the fresh herbs. The stew is ready to serve now, or it may be rapidly cooled and stored for later service.

MAKES 10 PORTIONS

GENERAL GUIDELINES FOR VEGETABLES

Each vegetable cookery technique produces specific and characteristic results and affects the flavor, texture, and nutritive value of the vegetable in different ways. The chef can take advantage of the full range of possibilities within a method to produce vegetable dishes specifically tailored to the operation's needs. Kitchens that rely on regional and seasonal produce can adapt a technique both to suit an ingredient's specific needs and to achieve an effect. For example, though acorn squash is often roasted or puréed, it can be gently stewed in cream or grilled and served with a salsa. Cucumbers, most commonly considered a vegetable to be eaten raw, may be steamed, sautéed, or even braised. The flavor, texture, and color differences produced in one vegetable when prepared by different techniques can be quite extraordinary.

Carefully handled vegetables maintain their flavor, color, texture, and nutritional value longer. Rinse leafy or delicate vegetables carefully to avoid bruising them, and dry them thoroughly. Scrub hardier vegetables before peeling. Be sure that all traces of dirt or grit have been removed.

In all cases, from a simple dish of steamed or boiled vegetables served seasoned but otherwise unadorned to a complex vegetable gratin, the best overall quality is assured by properly cooking vegetables to the appropriate doneness and serving them as soon as possible. The style of service and overall volume in a kitchen determines how much advance cooking and holding is desirable just as much as the nature of the vegetable and the cooking method does. Sautéed, stir-fried, pan-fried, and deep-fried dishes may be prepared just at the moment of service. Braises, stews, and purées are suited to batch cooking, since they are easier to hold and lose little, if any, of their flavor and texture when prepared in advance and reheated.

Vegetables should be seasoned with care, throughout cooking time. Check the seasoning of any vegetable dish carefully before it is served.

There are distinct differences in how tender a vegetable should be when it is properly cooked. Some vegetables, broccoli and green beans for example, are not considered properly cooked until they are quite tender. Others, such as snow peas and sugar snap peas, should always retain some bite (fully cooked but still firm). Preferences regarding the correct doneness of certain vegetables may vary from one part of the world to another and from one vegetable to another. In addition, there are different standards for different cooking techniques. For example, stir frying generally results in a very crisp texture, while baking or braising produces very tender vegetables.

There are several options for reheating vegetables:

In simmering stock or water. Place the vegetables in a sieve or perforated basket and lower it into a pot of simmering stock or water just long enough to heat the vegetables through. Drain and immediately finish the vegetables with butter, sauce, seasonings, and so on.

Another approach is to reheat the vegetables in a small amount of stock (with additional aromatics if desired). The stock will reduce to a glaze as the vegetables heat.

In the microwave. Generally best for small amounts. Evenly space the vegetables on a flat, round, or oval plate or other microwave-safe container. Some additional liquid may be needed to keep the vegetables moist. Cover with plastic and cut vents to allow the steam to escape, or with parchment paper. Reheat on the highest power setting for the shortest possible time, dress immediately, and serve.

By sautéing. Heat a small amount of olive oil, butter, cream, sauce, or glaze in a sauté pan and add the vegetables. Toss over medium-high heat until warmed through. Add seasonings if necessary and serve.

RECIPES

PAN-STEAMED CARROTS

makes 10 portions

water for pan steaming, as needed

salt, as needed

pepper, as needed

2 1/2 lb/1.15 kg sliced carrots

3 oz/85 g butter

1 tsp/5 mL chopped parsley, or as needed

1 Add about 1 in/25 mm water to a large pan, bring to a boil, and add seasonings. Add the carrots to the water, adding more water if necessary to barely cover the carrots. Bring the water to a boil. Cover the pan tightly, and reduce the heat slightly. Pan steam the carrots until they are fully cooked and tender to the bite, about 5 to 6 minutes for carrots sliced 1/4 in/6 mm thick.

2 When done, drain excess water from the pan. Return the carrots to the heat, add the butter and parsley, and season with salt and pepper. Stir or toss until the carrots are evenly coated and very hot. Serve at once.

Pecan Carrots Prepare the carrots as directed above. In step 2, add 3/4 oz/20 g minced shallots, 1 1/2 oz/45 g honey, and 3 oz/85 g chopped toasted pecans with the butter. Substitute minced chives for the parsley.

ASPARAGUS WITH ROASTED PEPPERS AND SHALLOT CHIPS

makes 10 portions

2 1/2 lb/1.15 kg trimmed asparagus

2 fl oz/60 mL olive oil

3 oz/85 g sliced shallots

4 oz/115 g roasted red pepper batonnet

salt, as needed

pepper, as needed

2 tsp/10 mL chopped oregano leaves, or as needed

1 Slice the asparagus on the bias into 2-in/5-cm pieces. Steam for 3 to 4 minutes or boil in salted water for 3 to 4 minutes, or until tender to the bite. Drain immediately, and if necessary, cool rapidly and hold for later service under refrigeration.

2 Heat the oil in a sauté pan over medium heat. Add the shallots and sauté until crisp and browned. Remove with a slotted spoon and blot on absorbent toweling.

3 Add the asparagus, peppers, salt, and pepper to the olive oil and sauté, tossing frequently, until heated. Add the oregano and heat another minute. Taste and adjust seasoning.

4 Serve with shallot chips scattered over the asparagus and red pepper mixture.

GREEN BEANS WITH WALNUTS

makes 10 portions

2¹/₂ lb/1.15 kg trimmed green beans

vegetable oil, as needed

¹/₄ oz/8 g minced shallots

1 tsp/5 mL minced garlic

4 fl oz/120 mL CHICKEN STOCK (page 248) or VEGETABLE STOCK (page 254), hot

salt, as needed

pepper, as needed

1 fl oz/30 mL walnut oil

2 tbsp/30 mL chopped toasted walnuts

2 tsp/10 mL minced chives

1 Cut the green beans on the bias, if desired.

2 Heat a little oil in a pan. Add the shallots and garlic and sauté until translucent, about 2 to 3 minutes. Add the green beans in an even layer and add the hot stock and salt and pepper. Return to a simmer.

3 Cover the pan and steam the beans until tender, about 4 to 5 minutes. Drain any excess cooking liquid. Toss the green beans with the walnut oil, walnuts, and chives. Serve at once.

MACÉDOINE OF VEGETABLES

makes 10 portions

2 oz/60 g large-dice mushrooms

¹/₂ oz/15 g minced shallots

butter, as needed

2 oz/60 g large-dice onions

4 oz/115 g large-dice celery

6 oz/170 g large-dice zucchini

6 oz/170 g large-dice yellow squash

6 oz/170 g large-dice carrots, steamed or boiled until tender

6 oz/170 g large-dice white turnips, steamed or boiled until tender

6 oz/170 g large-dice rutabagas, steamed or boiled until tender

2 oz/60 g small-dice red peppers

chopped chives, as needed

chopped tarragon, as needed

chopped basil, as needed

salt, as needed

pepper, as needed

1 Sauté the mushrooms and shallots in butter, stirring from time to time, until the moisture is reduced, about 2 to 3 minutes.

2 Add the onions and celery and sauté until the onions are translucent, about 5 minutes.

3 Add the zucchini and yellow squash and sauté until tender, about 2 to 3 minutes.

4 Add the remaining vegetables. Sauté them until heated through, 2 minutes more.

5 Add the herbs and toss to mix. Adjust the seasoning with salt and pepper. Serve at once or keep hot for service.

JARDINIÈRE VEGETABLES

makes 10 portions

9 oz/250 g carrot batonnet

9 oz/250 g celery batonnet

9 oz/250 g white turnip batonnet

9 oz/250 g shelled green peas

4 oz/115 g butter

salt, as needed

pepper, as needed

sugar, as needed

chopped parsley, as needed

1 Parcook the vegetables separately in boiling salted water until just barely tender. Drain them and, if necessary, submerge in ice-cold water to stop further cooking. Drain again until dry. Hold under refrigeration if the vegetables are to be finished later.

2 Heat the butter in a sauté pan. Add the vegetables (by individual portions or batches) and salt, pepper, and sugar. Toss or stir until the vegetables are evenly coated with the butter and very hot.

3 Add parsley and serve at once.

JULIENNED VEGETABLES

makes 10 portions

4 oz/115 g carrot julienne, blanched

4 oz/115 g celery julienne, blanched

4 oz/115 g leek julienne, blanched

2 oz/60 g butter

salt, as needed

pepper, as needed

1 Blanch the vegetables separately in boiling salted water, drain, shock, and drain again.

2 Reheat the vegetables by sautéing in butter.

3 Season to taste with salt and pepper and serve.

STEAMED SPAGHETTI SQUASH WITH SUMMER VEGETABLE COMPOTE

makes 10 portions

4 lb/1.8 kg spaghetti squash, whole

SUMMER VEGETABLE COMPOTE

2 oz/60 g small-dice onions

¹⁄₂ oz/15 g minced garlic

1 oz/30 g small-dice green peppers

vegetable oil, as needed

2 oz/60 g small-dice zucchini

2 oz/60 g small-dice mushrooms

2 fl oz/60 g mL tomato purée

2 oz/60 g tomato concassé

2 fl oz/60 mL dry white wine

2 fl oz/60 mL VEGETABLE STOCK (page 254)

chopped basil, as needed

chopped oregano, as needed

chopped parsley, as needed

salt, as needed

pepper, as needed

butter, as needed

1 Halve the squash and remove the seeds. Place the squash cut side down in a roasting pan. Add enough water to cover by one third. Cover with a lid or foil.

2 Roast at 375°F/190°C until the squash is extremely tender, about 1 hour. To check for doneness, pierce with a kitchen fork or paring knife. There should be no resistance.

3 While cooking the spaghetti squash, prepare the compote. Sauté the onions, garlic, and green peppers in the oil until the onions are translucent. Add the zucchini and mushrooms and sauté 2 to 3 minutes. Add the tomato purée, tomato concassé, wine, stock, basil, and oregano and simmer 5 minutes. Add the parsley, season with salt and pepper to taste, and hold for service.

4 When the spaghetti squash is cool enough to handle, scoop out the flesh, using a fork to separate it into strands. Reheat the squash by sautéing in butter over moderate heat, and season with salt and pepper. Serve with the vegetable compote.

CREAMED CORN

makes 10 portions

6 oz/170 g fine-dice leeks
1 pint/480 mL heavy cream
salt, as needed
pepper, as needed
ground nutmeg, as needed
1½ lb/675 g corn kernels, fresh or frozen
1 tbsp/15 mL chopped chervil, or as needed

1 Combine the leeks and the heavy cream in a saucepan, season with salt, pepper, and nutmeg, and simmer over medium heat until the cream has reduced by half.

2 Steam the corn kernels over boiling water until fully cooked, about 4 to 5 minutes. Add them to the leek mixture and simmer until a good flavor and consistency is reached, 2 to 3 minutes more.

3 Adjust the seasoning with salt and pepper. Add the chopped chervil. Serve now or hold hot for service.

BROCCOLI IN GARLIC SAUCE

makes 10 portions

2½ lb/1.15 kg broccoli florets or spears
4 fl oz/120 mL sherry
4 fl oz/120 mL rice vinegar
4 fl oz/120 mL soy sauce
2 tbsp/30 mL hot bean paste
2 tsp/10 mL sugar
8 fl oz/240 mL CHICKEN STOCK (page 248) or VEGETABLE STOCK (page 254)
2 fl oz/60 mL oil
½ oz/15 g minced ginger
2 oz/60 g minced garlic
½ oz/15 g chopped green onions
4 oz/115 g fine-dice or -julienne red pepper
cornstarch slurry, as needed

1 Blanch the broccoli in boiling salted water or steam for 2 minutes, or until broccoli is a vivid green but still firm. Drain boiled broccoli. If broccoli is being blanched in advance, refresh it in ice-cold water and drain again. Hold covered under refrigeration until ready to stir fry.

2 Combine the sherry, rice vinegar, soy sauce, hot bean paste, sugar, and stock. Reserve.

3 Heat the oil in a wok, add the ginger, garlic, and green onions, and stir fry until aromatic, about 1 minute. Add the red pepper and stir fry 1 minute more. Add the broccoli and stir fry until all of the ingredients are tender and very hot. Add the sherry mixture, bring to a boil, and add the cornstarch slurry gradually, just until the sauce is thickened enough to coat the vegetables. Adjust the seasoning if necessary. Serve at once on heated plates.

Corn Fritters

Braised Fennel in Butter

Grilled Vegetables

Oven-Roasted Tomatoes

GARDEN TREASURES

makes 10 portions

1 lb/450 g broccoli florets

2 lb/900 g medium-dice carrots

3 oz/85 g medium-dice celery

3 oz/85 g peanut or corn oil

4 tsp/20 mL minced ginger

4 tsp/20 mL minced garlic

2 oz/60 g mL green onions, sliced on the bias

1 lb/450 g medium-dice zucchini

1 lb/450 g medium-dice yellow squash

salt, as needed

ground white pepper, as needed

1 fl oz/30 mL sesame oil

1 Blanch the broccoli, carrots, and celery separately in boiling salted water; drain, shock, and drain again. Do not overcook.

2 Heat the oil in a wok, add the ginger, garlic, and green onions, and stir fry until aromatic, about 1 minute.

3 Add the broccoli, carrots, and celery and stir fry 2 to 3 minutes. Add the zucchini and yellow squash and stir fry, tossing, until tender.

4 Add salt, pepper, and sesame oil and mix together. Serve while very hot.

GLAZED ZUCCHINI

makes 10 portions

2 oz/60g ground salt pork

1 oz/30 g butter or oil, or as needed

2½ lb/1.15 kg zucchini tournés (or slices, batonnet, oblique)

salt, as needed

pepper, as needed

1 Heat the salt pork in a sauté pan over medium heat until the fat is rendered from the salt pork. Add the butter or oil.

2 Add the zucchini and salt and pepper. Sauté, stirring or tossing from time to time, until the zucchini is fully cooked, about 10 minutes.

3 Adjust the seasoning with salt and pepper to taste. Serve at once or keep hot for service.

GINGERED SNOW PEAS AND YELLOW SQUASH

makes 10 portions

6 fl oz/180 mL CHICKEN STOCK (page 248) or VEGETABLE STOCK (page 254), or as needed

2 tbsp/30 mL minced ginger

½ oz/15 g chopped shallots

2 tsp/10 mL minced garlic

salt, as needed

ground white pepper, as needed

1½ lb/680 g snow peas

12 oz/340 g medium-dice yellow squash

2 tbsp/30 mL chopped fresh chives

1 Combine the stock with the ginger, shallots, and garlic and simmer for 2 minutes. Add salt and pepper.

2 Add the snow peas and squash and return the stock to a simmer. Add more stock if necessary; the stock should come to a depth of about ½ in/12 mm in the pan. Cover the pan tightly and pan steam until the vegetables are tender, 2 to 3 minutes.

3 Adjust the seasoning with salt and pepper. Serve hot, scattered with fresh chives.

SHIITAKE MUSHROOMS WITH PEPPERS

makes 10 portions

2 fl oz/60 mL vegetable oil

½ tsp/2 mL hot bean paste

1 tbsp/15 mL red bean paste

3 oz/85 g celery julienne

1 lb/450 g stemmed shiitake mushrooms, caps sliced

½ oz/15 g minced ginger

½ oz/15 g minced garlic

2 oz/60 g scallion julienne

3 oz/85 g red pepper julienne

3 oz/85 g green pepper julienne

12 oz/340 g snow pea julienne

salt, as needed

pepper, as needed

1 Heat the oil in a wok. Stir fry the hot bean paste and red bean paste in the oil for 30 seconds.

2 Add the celery and mushrooms and stir fry for 3 to 4 minutes, or until the vegetables are very hot and barely tender.

3 Add the remaining ingredients and stir fry 2 to 3 minutes more. Adjust the seasoning with salt and pepper. Serve immediately.

SPINACH PANCAKES

makes 10 portions

2 lb/900 g leaf spinach

12 fl oz/360 mL milk

1 oz/30 g butter, melted

4 eggs

5 oz/140 g all-purpose flour

sugar, as needed

salt, as needed

pepper, as needed

ground nutmeg, as needed (optional)

vegetable oil for sautéing, as needed

1 Remove the stems from the spinach leaves. Rinse in several changes of water to remove all traces of sand or dirt. Blanch the spinach in boiling salted water or by steaming for 1 minute. Drain and rinse with cold water to stop cooking. Drain and squeeze the spinach to dry it. Chop coarsely, and reserve.

2 Combine the milk, butter, and eggs until evenly blended. Stir together the flour and sugar. Make a well in the center of the flour, pour in the milk mixture, and stir just until a smooth batter forms.

3 Combine the spinach with the batter and season with salt, pepper, and nutmeg to taste.

4 Heat a small amount of oil in a pan (or lightly oil a preheated griddle). Ladle 2 fl oz/60 mL batter into the hot pan for each pancake. Sauté for about 2 minutes on the first side, or until golden brown. Turn the pancake and complete cooking on the second side. Serve immediately or transfer to a holding pan and keep hot during service.

SUMMER SQUASH NOODLES

makes 10 portions

1 lb/450 g yellow squash julienne

12 oz/340 g zucchini julienne

12 oz/340 g leek julienne

salt, as needed

pepper, as needed

clarified butter or oil for sautéing, as needed

½ oz/15 g minced shallots

2 tbsp/60 mL minced herbs, such as tarragon, basil, cilantro, oregano

1 Toss the yellow squash, zucchini, and leeks together to mix evenly. Season with salt and pepper.

2 Heat butter or oil in a sauté pan over medium heat. Add the shallots and cook until aromatic, about 1 minute. Add the vegetables and sauté them, tossing or stirring to coat them with the butter or oil. Increase the heat to high and continue to sauté until the vegetables are tender and very hot, 3 to 4 minutes more.

3 Adjust the seasoning with salt and pepper and add the chopped herbs. Serve at once on heated plates or transfer to a holding pan and keep hot for service.

NOTE

Make the julienne cut extremely long for this dish, so that the vegetables look like noodles.

CORN FRITTERS

makes 12 portions (3 fritters per portion)

2¹/₂ lb/1.15 kg corn kernels (10 to 12 whole ears)
4 oz/115 g flour
2 oz/60 g sugar
1 tsp/5 mL salt, plus as needed
¹/₄ tsp/1 mL pepper
2 eggs, beaten
2 oz/60 g grated Cheddar (optional)
oil for pan frying, as needed

1 If using corn on the cob, cut the kernels from the ears of corn. Scrape the cobs well to release all the milk.

2 Blend the flour, sugar, salt, and pepper in a mixing bowl and make a well in the center. Blend the corn (along with the corn milk, if available), eggs, and cheese separately and add them to the flour mixture all at once. Stir just until a relatively smooth batter forms.

3 Heat about ¹/₂ in/12 mm of oil in a pan to 365°F/182°C and ladle 1 fl oz/30 mL of batter for each fritter into the hot oil.

4 Fry on the first side until golden brown, about 2 to 3 minutes. Turn once and finish frying on the second side, 2 minutes more. Blot on paper toweling, season with additional salt if necessary, and serve while very hot.

NOTES

Add diced red or green pepper to the batter if desired.

Add 1 to 2 tsp/ 5 to 10 mL chili powder to the dry ingredients if desired.

see photograph on page 624

GRILLED VEGETABLES PROVENÇAL-STYLE

makes 10 portions

1¹/₄ lb/570 g zucchini
1¹/₄ lb/570 g eggplant
2 oz/60 g garlic cloves
8 fl oz/240 mL olive oil, or as needed
2 tbsp/60 mL minced rosemary
6 oz/170 g onion slices
salt, as needed
pepper, as needed
6 oz/170 g green peppers
7 oz/170 g red peppers
4 oz/115 g tomato concassé
balsamic vinegar, as needed
1 oz/30 g basil chiffonade

1 Trim the zucchini and eggplant. Cut them into ¾-inch/2-cm thick slices (either on an elongated bias or lengthwise).

2 Put the garlic in a large, shallow pan and add enough oil to barely cover. Add the rosemary and simmer, partially covered, over very low heat, until the garlic is cooked but not falling apart, 15 to 20 minutes. Remove from the heat and cool to room temperature. Reserve.

3 Preheat a grill or broiler. Brush the zucchini, eggplant, and onion slices with the garlic-and-rosemary oil and season with salt and pepper. Place them on the grill and cook on the first side until browned. Turn once and complete cooking on the second side until the vegetables are fully cooked, about 3 minutes. Remove from the grill, cut into medium dice, and reserve.

4 Grill or broil the peppers until evenly charred on all sides. Remove from the grill and let the peppers cool. Remove the skin, core, seeds, and ribs. Cut the peppers into medium dice, and reserve.

5 Put garlic and 2 fl oz/60 mL of the remaining oil in a large, deep saucepan and heat over medium heat. Add the grilled vegetables and tomato concassé and stir gently to finish cooking the vegetables and blend the flavors. Adjust the seasoning with salt, pepper, and balsamic vinegar to taste. Fold in the basil or use it to garnish individual portions. Serve at once, or keep hot for service.

GRILLED VEGETABLES

makes 10 portions

2¹/₂ lb/1.15 kg assorted vegetables, according to season

MARINADE

8 fl oz/240 mL vegetable oil

2 fl oz/60 mL soy sauce

1 fl oz/30 mL lemon juice

¹/₄ oz/8 g minced garlic

¹/₂ tsp/3 mL whole fennel seeds

salt, as needed

pepper, as needed

1 Slice the vegetables into pieces thick enough to withstand the heat of the grill. If necessary, parcook or blanch the vegetables prior to grilling them.

2 Combine all the ingredients for the marinade. Coat the vegetables evenly with the marinade.

3 Remove the vegetables from the marinade, letting any excess drain completely. Place the vegetables on a hot grill and grill them on both sides (the time depends on the type of vegetable and the thickness of the cut). Turn each piece 90 degrees to create crosshatch marks, if desired. Turn the vegetables once and complete the cooking on the second side.

4 Serve the vegetables at once, or hold hot for later service.

see photograph on page 625

PARSNIP AND PEAR PURÉE

makes 10 portions

2 lb/900 g sliced parsnips

12 oz/340 g medium-dice Bartlett pears

4 fl oz/120 mL heavy cream, hot

salt, as needed

ground white pepper, as needed

1 Cook the parsnips and pears separately in boiling salted water until they are tender enough to mash with a fork. Drain and then dry in a warm oven or over low heat until the excess moisture has cooked away. Combine the pears and parsnips and purée them through a fine sieve or food mill.

2 Add the hot cream gradually to the puréed parsnips and pears and stir to form a smooth, light purée. Season the purée with salt and pepper to taste. Serve at once on heated plates (may be piped or spooned) or hold hot for service.

BAKED ACORN SQUASH WITH CRANBERRY-ORANGE COMPOTE

makes 12 portions

3¹/₄ lb/1.5 kg acorn squash (3 squash)

4 oz/115 g brown sugar, honey, or maple syrup

6 oz/170 g butter

salt, as needed

pepper, as needed

CRANBERRY-ORANGE COMPOTE (recipe follows)

1 Quarter the squash and remove the seeds. Place them cut side up on a baking sheet. Sprinkle the squash with sugar and dot with butter. Season with salt and pepper.

2 Cover the squash quarters with foil and bake in a 350°F/175°C oven for 1 to 1¹/₄ hours or until tender, basting periodically.

3 Serve the squash (still in the skin) on heated plates topped with the compote.

CRANBERRY-ORANGE COMPOTE

makes 1 pint/480 milliliters; 10 servings

1 lb/450 g cranberries

6 fl oz/180 mL orange juice concentrate

water, as needed

sugar, as needed

2 oz/60 g blanched orange zest

Combine the cranberries, orange juice, and enough water to barely cover the berries in a pan. Add sugar to taste. Simmer the berries over medium heat until they are softened and thickened. Add the orange zest. Serve hot.

OVEN-ROASTED TOMATOES

makes 10 portions

4½ lb/2 kg tomatoes

3 fl oz/90 mL extra-virgin olive oil

½ oz/15 g minced garlic

½ oz/15 g minced shallots

2 tsp/10 mL chopped basil

2 tsp/10 mL chopped oregano

1 tsp/5 mL chopped thyme

½ tsp/3 mL kosher salt

1 tsp/5 mL cracked pepper

1 Rinse the tomatoes and let dry. Remove the cores and cut to the desired shape (may be halved, quartered, cut into wedges, or sliced). Arrange in a single layer in a shallow pan.

2 Combine the oil, garlic, shallots, basil, oregano, thyme, salt, and pepper. Drizzle this mixture over the tomatoes and turn carefully to coat the tomatoes.

3 Arrange the tomatoes on racks set in sheet pans. Roast in a 275°F/135°C oven for 1 to 1½ hours, or until the tomatoes are dried and lightly browned.

4 The tomatoes are ready to serve or use as an ingredient in another dish, or they may be cooled on the rack and stored, covered, under refrigeration.

see photograph on page 625

BRAISED SAUERKRAUT

makes 10 portions

4 oz/115 g rendered pork or goose fat, or vegetable oil

8 oz/225 g small-dice onions

7 oz/200 g grated Golden Delicious apples

6 oz/170 g grated chef's potatoes

2½ lb/1.15 kg HOMEMADE SAUERKRAUT (page 545)

1 tsp/5 mL caraway seeds

12 juniper berries

1 qt/1 L BROWN PORK STOCK (page 252) or BROWN VEAL STOCK (page 252)

1 Heat pork fat in a large rondeau, add the onions and apples, and sweat until tender and translucent, about 8 to 10 minutes.

2 Add the potatoes and sweat a few minutes longer. Add the sauerkraut, caraway seeds, juniper berries, and stock, and bring to a boil. Cover and braise in a 325°F/165°C oven until the stock has nearly cooked away and the sauerkraut has a good flavor, about 1 to 1½ hours. If the sauerkraut is too liquid, place it on top of the stove and reduce the liquid as necessary. The sauerkraut is ready to serve now, or it may be properly cooled and stored for later service.

FRENCH-STYLE PEAS

makes 10 portions

2 oz/60 g pearl onions

4 oz/115 g butter

1¼ lb/560 g shelled green peas

12 oz/340 g Boston lettuce chiffonade

4 fl oz/120 mL CHICKEN STOCK (page 248)

salt, as needed

pepper, as needed

3 tbsp/45 mL flour

1 Bring a large pot of water to a rolling boil. Add the pearl onions and blanch for 1 minute. Remove the onions, rinse in cool water until they can be handled, and remove the skin.

2 Heat 2 oz/60 g the butter in a pan over low heat and add the pearl onions. Cook covered until they are tender and translucent, about 8 to 10 minutes.

3 Add the peas, lettuce, and stock to the onions. Season with salt and pepper to taste. Bring the stock to a gentle simmer and return the cover to the pan. Stew the peas until they are fully cooked and tender, about 3 to 4 minutes.

4 Blend the remaining butter with the flour and add gradually to the peas in small pieces until the cooking liquid is lightly thickened. Adjust the seasoning if necessary and serve on heated plates.

BRAISED FENNEL IN BUTTER

makes 10 portions

4¹/₂ lb/2 kg fennel

6 oz/170 g butter

12 fl oz/360 mL CHICKEN STOCK (page 248), or
VEGETABLE STOCK (page 254)

2 fl oz/60 mL lemon juice

salt, as needed

pepper, as needed

4 oz/115 g grated Parmesan

1 Cut the stems from the fennel and trim the root end. Cut from stem to root end to make halves or quarters, depending upon the size of the bulb. Bring a pot of salted water to a boil, add the fennel, and boil until partially cooked, about 6 minutes. Drain the fennel and reserve.

2 Heat half of the butter in a rondeau. Add the fennel and turn to coat evenly with the butter. Add the stock and season with lemon juice, salt, and pepper. Bring the stock to simmer, cover the pan, and braise the fennel in a 325°F/165°F oven until the fennel is very tender, but still holds its shape, about 45 minutes. The liquid should be nearly cooked away; if necessary, simmer over medium heat until it has reduced.

3 Remove the cover from the pan and scatter the Parmesan in an even layer over the fennel. Dot with the remainder of the butter.

4 Place the uncovered fennel in a 450°F/230°C oven or under a broiler until the butter and cheese form a golden crust. The fennel is ready to serve now.

see photograph on page 625

BRAISED ROMAINE

makes 10 portions

4¹/₂ lb/2 kg romaine lettuce heads

2¹/₂ oz/70 g butter

5 oz/140 g small-dice onions

5 oz/140 g thinly sliced carrots

10 fl oz/300 mL BROWN VEAL STOCK (page 252), CHICKEN STOCK (page 248), or VEGETABLE STOCK (page 254)

salt, as needed

pepper, as needed

6 oz/170 g slab bacon, sliced ¹/₈ in/4 mm thick

1 Remove or trim the outer lettuce leaves to remove any blemishes or wilted leaves. Trim the core. Bring a large pot of salted water to a boil. Blanch the lettuce in the water for 1 minute, until the color turns bright and the leaves are softened. Drain the lettuce, rinse in cold water to stop the cooking, and drain again. To make individual portions, cut the romaine into 10 equal portions lengthwise. Cut away the core. Roll up each portion into a cylinder, squeezing out excess water as you roll. To make larger portions that can be sliced for service, remove the larger outer leaves and arrange them to form a large rectangle on a sheet of plastic wrap or parchment. Remove the cores from the lettuce leaves and arrange the leaves evenly over the outer leaves. Roll up as for a jelly roll, squeezing to remove the water.

2 Heat the butter in a rondeau over moderate heat. Add the onions and carrots and sweat over low heat until they are tender and starting to release their juices into the butter, about 8 to 10 minutes. Add the romaine to the pan in an even layer. Add the stock and bring it to a simmer. Add salt and pepper. Top the romaine with slices of slab bacon.

3 Cover the pan and braise the lettuce in a 350°F/175°C oven for 25 to 30 minutes, or until the lettuce is very tender and the bacon is crisp. Remove the cover during the final 10 minutes of cooking time if necessary to properly reduce the cooking liquid and brown the bacon.

4 Remove the romaine from the braising liquid and keep warm. Degrease the liquid and adjust the seasoning with salt and pepper.

5 Serve the romaine with the sauce on heated plates.

BELGIAN ENDIVE À LA MEUNIÈRE

makes 10 portions

2¹/₂ lb/1.15 kg Belgian endive (10 heads)

salt, as needed

sugar, as needed

2 fl oz/60 mL lemon juice

milk, as needed

flour for dredging, as needed

clarified butter or oil for sautéing, as needed

3 oz/85 g whole butter

2 tbsp/30 mL chopped parsley

1 Remove any bruised or damaged outer endive leaves and trim the core of each endive. Bring a large pot of water to a boil and season with salt, sugar, and 1 tbsp/15 mL of the lemon juice. Add the endive and boil until partially cooked, about 3 minutes. Drain the endive well.

2 Pare and trim the endive cores with a sharp knife (there should be enough core left to hold the leaves together) and flatten each head slightly by pressing down on it with the palm of your hand.

3 To finish the endives, season them with salt and pepper, dip in milk and dredge in flour, shaking off the excess.

4 Sauté the endive in hot clarified butter or oil until crisp and brown on both sides, about 3 to 4 minutes total cooking time. Remove them from the pan and keep warm.

5 Pour off any excess butter or oil from the pan. Add the whole butter and cook over medium heat until the butter begins to brown and take on a nutty aroma. Add the remaining lemon juice and the parsley and swirl it until the mixture thickens slightly. Pour the pan sauce over the endive and serve immediately.

LEEK TIMBALE

makes 10 portions

1 oz/30 g butter

2¹/₂ lb/1.15 kg sliced leeks, white parts only

10 fl oz/300 mL CHICKEN STOCK (page 248) or VEGETABLE STOCK (page 254)

salt, as needed

pepper, as needed

4 oz/115 g grated Gruyère

12 eggs

5 egg whites

1¹/₂ pt/720 mL milk

few grains of ground nutmeg, as needed

softened butter for preparing molds, as needed

bread crumbs for preparing molds, as needed

1 Heat the butter in a sauté pan over low heat. Add the leeks and a small amount of the stock, enough to cover the leeks by one-third. Bring the stock to a simmer, add salt and pepper to taste, cover the pan, and stew the leeks until tender, about 12 to 15 minutes.

2 Purée the leeks in a food processor until smooth. Transfer the purée to a bowl and stir in the Gruyère, eggs, egg whites, and milk. Adjust the seasoning with salt, pepper, and nutmeg.

3 Coat 10 timbale molds with softened butter, dust with bread crumbs, and fill with the leek purée.

4 Place the molds in a hot water bath and bake in a 325°F/165°C oven until the timbales are set and a knife blade inserted near the center comes out clean, about 45 minutes.

5 Unmold onto heated plates for service.

The potato is one of the most versatile foods. It is found in nearly every menu category as the main component of appetizers, soups, entrées, and side dishes; it is also an important ingredient in such preparations as soufflés, pancakes, and breads.

COOKING POTATOES

POTATO VARIETIES

Potato varieties differ in starch and moisture content, skin and flesh color, and shape. Sweet potatoes and yams, although not botanically related to the potato, share several characteristics with it and can be treated in the same manner. Each technique produces a markedly different texture, flavor, and appearance. Knowing the natural characteristics of each kind of potato and the ways in which a particular technique can either enhance or detract from these characteristics is important to any chef.

The following categories, defined by moisture and starch content, help to clarify why specific types of potato are best when prepared with certain cooking techniques. As potatoes in all categories age, their starch content increases and their moisture content decreases.

LOW MOISTURE/HIGH STARCH

Potatoes in this category include Idaho or russet potatoes (also known as baking potatoes or bakers) and some fingerling varieties. The higher the starch content, the more granular and dry a potato is after it is cooked. The flesh is easy to flake or mash. These potatoes, desirable for baking and puréeing, are also good for frying because the low moisture content makes them less likely to splatter or absorb grease. Their low moisture and natural tendency to absorb moisture also make them a good choice for scalloped or other casserole-style potato dishes.

MODERATE MOISTURE AND STARCH

Potatoes in this category include so-called all-purpose potatoes, boiling potatoes, chef's potatoes, Maine potatoes, and US 1 potatoes. It also includes red-skinned potatoes, waxy yellow potatoes (e.g., Yellow Finn and Yukon Gold), and certain fingerling varieties. Potatoes with moderate amounts of moisture and starch tend to hold their shape even after they are cooked until tender. This makes them a good choice for boiling, steaming, sautéing, oven roasting, and braising or stewing. They are frequently used in potato salads and soups. Many chefs like to use waxy yellow potatoes for baking, puréeing, and casserole-style dishes because of their outstanding flavor.

HIGH MOISTURE/LOW STARCH

Potatoes in this category include new potatoes (any potato that is harvested when less than 1½ inches in diameter) and some fingerling varieties. The skin of a new potato is tender and does not need to be removed prior to cooking or eating. Their naturally sweet, fresh flavor is best showcased by simple techniques such as boiling, steaming, or oven roasting.

TIP!

IF YOU ARE UNSURE of the moisture/starch content of your potatoes, a simple test can be done to gauge the starch content. Prepare a brine of 11 parts water to 1 part salt. Place the potatoes in the brine. Those that float contain less starch.

BOILING POTATOES

Boiled potatoes are among the simplest of preparations, with a subtle, earthy flavor.

In the absence of a great number of aromatic or supporting flavors, attention must be focused on good technique and the careful selection and handling of the potato itself. Each potato variety has a unique texture and taste once boiled. Some potatoes hold their shape even when boiled until very tender and have a soft, smooth consistency. Others have a mealier consistency and a tendency to break apart when fully cooked. Both boiled and steamed potatoes can be cooked to a range of doneness: partially cooked for sautéed dishes, fully cooked for purées, or cooked and cooled for salads.

FOR 10 PORTIONS OF BOILED POTATOES, YOU WILL NEED:	*4 pounds/1.8 kilograms moderate- or high-moisture potatoes, weighed before peeling and cutting, or 3¼ pounds/ 1.5 kilograms prepped potatoes*	*enough cold liquid to completely submerge the potatoes*	*salt and other seasonings* *finishing and garnishing ingredients*

SELECT AND PREPARE THE INGREDIENTS AND EQUIPMENT

MODERATE- OR HIGH-MOISTURE potatoes are a good choice for dishes where the potatoes are presented whole since they hold their shape when boiled. Low-moisture potatoes are preferred for purées.

Scrub the potatoes or peel them and remove the eyes and sprouts. Potatoes may be peeled before boiling; tender-skinned fingerlings or new potatoes are usually prepared unpeeled, called *en chemise* in French. If the potatoes are to be cooked whole, try to make sure the shapes are similar in size. If necessary, cut the potatoes into regular, even shapes.

Green spots in a potato must be peeled away completely. The green color indicates the presence of a toxin called *solanine*, which is harmful when eaten in large quantities. This same toxin is present in the potato sprouts and eyes; they should be completely removed as well.

Raw potatoes will discolor after they are peeled, first turning light pink and eventually, dark gray or black. To prevent this discoloration, submerge peeled or cut raw potatoes in cold water until time to cook. When possible, use the soaking water to cook the potatoes so any nutrients leached into it are retained.

To ensure that potatoes cook evenly, start them in a cold liquid, usually water, though some recipes specify stock or milk for a special flavor, texture, or appearance. Salt is usually added to the cooking liquid. If using salt, add enough to enhance the potato's flavor. If parcooking, add slightly more salt than if fully cooking the potatoes.

Other optional ingredients include herbs and spices, which may be added for special effects. For example, saffron or turmeric gives boiled potatoes a golden color and a special flavor. Herbs are often added to the potatoes as they are reheated in butter—parslied new potatoes are a classic example.

Butter, cream, sour cream, and sauces are used to dress the potatoes after they are boiled and immediately before they are served. When potatoes are held briefly before service, these finishing ingredients may be used as the medium for reheating them.

The equipment needs for boiling potatoes are simple: a cooking pot large enough to hold the water and potatoes, a slotted spoon or colander for draining the potatoes, and holding containers. Sheet pans may be used to hold the potatoes in a single layer for quick cooling or drying.

STEAMING POTATOES

STEAMING CAN BE USED as an alternative to boiling. To properly steam potatoes, prepare them as for boiling, taking care to make even cuts or to select like-sized whole potatoes to cook in the same batch. The potatoes should be arranged in even layers on the racks or inserts to let the steam circulate completely and encourage thorough, rapid cooking.

Convection or pressure steamers are good for steaming large quantities of potatoes. They allow for the preparation of batches as needed throughout a meal period, and they are well suited to the intense demands of a banquet or institutional feeding situation.

When using a stovetop steamer, remember that the larger the potatoes, the longer the cooking time and the more liquid that will be required. Bring the cooking liquid in the bottom of the steamer to a rolling boil before adding the potato-filled inserts or tiers. The potatoes should be arranged so that the steam can circulate around the potatoes. Do not stack the potatoes or overcrowd the tiers or inserts.

Various herbs, spices, or aromatic vegetables may be added to the cooking liquid or directly to the potatoes to allow the steam to carry the flavor to the potatoes.

1. Place the potatoes in a pot of an appropriate size and cover completely with cold water. Add salt and/or other seasonings as necessary to the cooking liquid.

Starting the cooking process with cold liquid allows the heat to penetrate slowly and evenly, giving the potatoes a uniform texture without overcooking the exterior flesh.

2. Bring to a boil and cook at a simmer or low boil until the potatoes are done.

To test for doneness, taste a piece or pierce with the tines of a fork. If there is no resistance, the potatoes are properly cooked. If the potatoes are to be only partially cooked, there should be increasing resistance as the fork is inserted deeper into the potato. Do not use a knife to test for doneness because a knife simply slices through the potato, regardless of how done it is.

Drain the potatoes as soon as they are done and dry them to improve their flavor and texture. Potatoes can be dried by returning them to the pot and placing the pot, uncovered, over very low heat. Or spread them out in a single layer on a sheet pan and place the pan in a warm oven. Potatoes are sufficiently dried when steam no longer rises from them.

3. Evaluate the quality of the finished boiled potatoes.

A properly boiled potato has a delicate aroma and flavor and a soft texture. Boiled potatoes to be served as is should hold their shape but still be extremely tender. Seasonings added to the cooking water, as well as any additional finishing or garnishing ingredients, should be appropriate to the finished dish.

If the potatoes were cooked in the skin, remove the skin as soon as the potatoes are cool enough to handle. Use a paring knife to remove eyes or black spots.

To hold potatoes for a short time (less than an hour), cover them loosely with a damp, clean cloth and keep warm. Reheat the potatoes by tossing them in hot butter, submerging them in hot stock, or tossing them in hot cream or sauce. Potatoes can be cooled and held for use in a other preparations, such as salads, hash browns, stews, or soups.

ABOVE *The action on the surface of the liquid as the potatoes cook should show lazy bubbles breaking occasionally.*

ABOVE *Potatoes boiled to make into a purée may start to fall apart on their own.*

4 lb / 1.8 kg potatoes

salt, as needed

2 oz / 60 g butter

1 oz / 30 g chopped parsley

pepper, as needed

BOILED PARSLIED POTATOES

1 Scrub the potatoes and peel if desired. Cut the potatoes into equal-size pieces if necessary. (Hold peeled potatoes in cold water to prevent discoloration until it is time to
   cook them.)

2 Place the potatoes in a pot with enough cold water to cover them by about 2 in/5 cm.
   Add salt to taste. Gradually bring the water to a simmer over medium heat. Cover and
   simmer until the potatoes are easily pierced with a fork.

3 Drain the potatoes. Return them to the pot and let them dry briefly over very low heat
   until no more steam rises from the potatoes, or spread them out on a sheet pan and dry
   them in a low oven. If necessary, peel the potatoes as soon as they are cool enough to
   handle.

4 Heat the butter in a sauteuse over medium heat. Add the potatoes, rolling and tossing
   to coat them evenly with butter, and heat them through.

5 Add the parsley and salt and pepper to taste. Toss the potatoes to coat. Serve immediately.

MAKES 10 PORTIONS

PURÉEING
POTATOES

Puréed potatoes are an important basic preparation.

Puréed potatoes can be blended with milk and butter to make whipped potatoes, with egg yolks to make pommes duchesse potatoes or potato croquettes, or with pâte à choux to fry as pommes lorette.

Potatoes to be puréed are first cooked by boiling, steaming, or baking in the skin. After being puréed, the potatoes may be flavored with oil, butter, cream, garlic, or other vegetable purées.

LOW- TO MODERATE-MOISTURE potatoes, such as russets and waxy yellow potatoes, make the best purées. Have ready boiled or steamed potatoes that have been drained and dried and that are still very hot. Hot baked potatoes may also be used. In addition to salt and pepper, which are standard seasonings for puréed potatoes, many other ingredients may be added to the potatoes for special flavors.

All additional ingredients should be either heated to the same temperature as the purée or at room temperature. Choices include milk or cream, soft (not melted) butter, chicken or meat broth, garlic, shallots, scallions, horseradish, mustard, cheese, or purées of other vegetables, such as parsnip or celeriac. Egg yolks or pâte à choux are needed for duchesse and lorette potatoes.

A food mill or potato ricer gives the best texture for puréed potatoes. Use a hand-held potato masher for a coarser texture. Puréed potatoes may be blended with other ingredients by hand using a wooden spoon or with an electric mixer for whipped potatoes. A pastry bag with star and/or plain tips will be needed if the purée is to be decoratively piped onto plates or shaped in various ways.

| FOR 10 PORTIONS OF POTATO PURÉE, YOU WILL NEED: | *4 pounds/1.8 kilograms low-moisture potatoes, weighed before peeling and cutting, or 3 ¼ pounds/1.5 kilograms prepped potatoes* | *4 fluid ounces/120 milliliters milk or cream* | *salt, pepper, or other seasonings* |

1. Cook the potatoes until very tender by boiling, steaming, or baking. Warm the milk or cream.

Potatoes may be peeled and cubed before cooking to shorten cooking and drying time when boiling (see pages 635–636) or steaming (see page 636).

To bake potatoes for use in purées, leave them whole and in the skin. Season, pierce, and bake until very tender. When they are done, immediately halve them and scoop out the flesh. Use a clean side towel to protect your hands as you work.

2. Push hot drained and dried potatoes through a warmed food mill or ricer. For best results, the potatoes must be hot and the equipment heated. Do not use a blender or food processor. The texture of the potato will be broken down irreparably, resulting in a soupy, sticky product that will not hold its shape. Large quantities of potatoes may be run through a grinder directly into the bowl of a mixer.

3. Add seasonings and any additional ingredients, as desired or according to the recipe.

Be sure that other ingredients are at the correct temperature when added. Milk or cream should be at or near a simmer. Butter should be at room temperature. Season the potato purée carefully with salt and pepper. Stir or fold in such flavorings as puréed roasted garlic. Stir with a spoon by hand or use the paddle attachment of an electric mixer. Do not overwork; this will release too much starch from the potatoes, giving the purée a heavy, sticky consistency.

TOP *As you purée the potatoes, check to be sure that the bowl holding the purée is not overfull, as the chef is doing here.*

BOTTOM *The entire batch of potatoes has been puréed and can now be combined with finishing ingredients.*

ABOVE *Using a wooden spoon, rubber spatula, or a mixer with a paddle attachment, work the purée quickly just until it is smooth and all ingredients are blended.*

4. Pipe or spoon the potatoes into the desired shape.

Potato purée can be mounded or piped onto serving plates. Puréed potatoes may be held for service over a hot-water bath or in a steam table, covered directly on the surface with plastic wrap. Do not hold purées for too long, or the quality will begin to degrade.

5. Evaluate the quality of the finished puréed potatoes.

A good potato purée is smooth, light in texture, and able to hold its shape when dropped from a spoon. It should be a consistently creamy purée, with no evidence that fat has separated from the purée.

Purées to be used in dishes that are subsequently baked, sautéed, or deep-fried may be held under refrigeration for up to several hours. Once the final cooking is completed, they should be served immediately.

ABOVE *Here the potato purée has been blended to make duchesse potatoes. Pipe them into even portions on parchment-lined sheets.*

TOP *Duchesse potatoes may be brushed with egg wash before baking to give them a rich golden color.*

BOTTOM *Make smaller fresh batches throughout the period rather than one large batch at the start of service for the best flavor, texture, and color.*

4 lb / 1.8 kg potatoes

4 oz / 115 g butter, at room temperature

4 egg yolks, beaten

few grains of ground nutmeg

salt, as needed

pepper, as needed

egg wash, as needed

DUCHESSE POTATOES

1 Scrub the potatoes, peel, and cut into large pieces. Cook the potatoes by boiling or steaming until tender enough to mash easily. Drain and dry them over low heat or on a sheet pan in a 300°F/150°C oven until no more steam rises from them. (Alternatively, potatoes may be baked in their skins until very tender. Halve the potatoes and scoop out the flesh while it is still very hot.) While the potatoes are still hot, purée them through a food mill or potato ricer into a heated bowl.

2 Add the butter, egg yolks, nutmeg, and salt and pepper to taste to the potatoes and mix them in well.

3 Transfer the mixture to a piping bag and pipe the mixture into the desired shapes on a baking sheet lined with parchment paper. Brush lightly with egg wash. Bake at 375°F/190°C until the potatoes are golden brown and heated through, about 10 to 12 minutes. Serve as soon as possible.

MAKES 10 PORTIONS

BAKING AND ROASTING POTATOES

The classic baked potato is served in its crisp skin and garnished with butter, salt, pepper, and, perhaps, sour cream with chives.

When potatoes are cooked in an oven without any added liquid or steam, they develop an intense flavor and a dry, light texture. High-starch potatoes, like Idahos or russets, become mealy; the higher the moisture content of the potato, the creamier and moister the baked potato will be. Baked potatoes are often served as is, with their skins, but there are other uses and presentations for them. The flesh can be scooped from the shell and puréed. This purée can be served on its own, or returned to the hollowed-out skin in the preparation known as stuffed potatoes or twice-baked potatoes. When oven roasting, the potatoes are cooked in oil, butter, or rendered juices from a roasted item and cooked until browned on the outside and completely tender on the inside.

FOR 10 PORTIONS OF BAKED POTATOES, YOU WILL NEED:	10 baking potatoes (about 6 ounces/170 grams each) or 4 pounds/1.8 kilograms low-moisture or yellow waxy potatoes, scrubbed	salt or oil to lightly rub the skin of the potato (optional)	finishing and garnishing ingredients

FOR 10 PORTIONS OF OVEN-ROASTED POTATOES, YOU WILL NEED:	4 pounds/1.8 kilograms moderate- to high-moisture potatoes, weighed before peeling and cutting, or 3 ¼ pounds/ 1.5 kilograms prepped potatoes	enough cooking fat to lightly coat the potatoes salt and other seasonings	finishing and garnishing ingredients

LOW-MOISTURE POTATOES are generally best for baked potatoes, although yellow waxy potatoes also yield good results. Low- or high-moisture potatoes may be used for oven-roasting.

Scrub the potato well. For a relatively thick-skinned potato, a brush works well. For new potatoes, use a cloth. Blot the potatoes dry before placing them in a pan to prevent an excess of steam when the potatoes start to bake. Pierce the skin of the potato in a few places to allow the steam that builds up during baking to escape. Never wrap the potato in foil before baking; the result is similar to steaming. The skin will not become crisp, and there is a noticeable flavor difference. For the same reasons, baked potatoes cannot be prepared successfully in a microwave oven. Some chefs believe that baking potatoes on a bed of salt or rubbing the skin lightly with oil encourages the development of a crisp skin and delicate, fluffy interior.

For oven-roasted potatoes, scrub or peel the potatoes and cut them into the desired shape. Toss in fat (fat and drippings from roasted meats, oil, clarified butter, lard, goose fat, and so on) and season as desired with salt and pepper, fresh or dried herbs, or spices.

Equipment needs for baking potatoes are minimal. The only truly essential piece of equipment is the oven. Potatoes can be placed directly on the oven racks; they can also be arranged on sheet pans, which makes it easier to move them in and out of the oven, particularly when dealing with large quantities. Puréeing equipment such as a potato ricer or a food mill is also needed if stuffing the potatoes. Have available holding and serving pieces as necessary.

For oven-roasted potatoes, sheet pans or shallow roasting pans that can hold the potatoes in a single layer are needed. Also needed are utensils for stirring the potatoes as they roast and holding and serving pieces.

HOW TO BAKE OR ROAST POTATOES

1. Prepare the potatoes for roasting. To bake potatoes whole in the skin, scrub them, blot dry, and rub with oil or salt if desired. Pierce them with a fork to let steam escape as the potatoes bake; this prevents them from bursting. Whole potatoes may be placed on the oven racks or on sheet pans. If placed on sheet pans, turn the potatoes once during baking because the sides in contact with the pan may become slightly soggy.

Scrub and blot dry or peel potatoes for oven roasting and cut into a uniform shape if desired. Arrange the potatoes in a single layer on a sheet pan or in a roasting pan, not too tightly packed, or they will not brown properly.

2. Season the potatoes, pierce, and bake or roast the potatoes until tender.

It takes about 1 hour for a 6-oz/ 170-g potato to bake. To test for doneness, pierce the potato with a fork. If there is no resistance when it enters the flesh, the potato is done. The skin of a baked potato should be crisp, the flesh tender and fluffy with a fresh flavor.

Stir oven-roasted potatoes as often as necessary during the roasting time to ensure even browning. To test for doneness, taste a piece or pierce with a fork. Oven-roasted potatoes should be nicely browned and crisp on the outside, tender and moist on the inside.

Serve baked and oven-roasted potatoes immediately. If this is not possible, they can be held, uncovered, for less than an hour in a warm place. However, the steam trapped in the interior can cause the crisp skin to become soggy over time. Stuffed potatoes may be prepared in advance and held, covered, under refrigeration. Reheat and brown just prior to service.

3. Evaluate the quality of the finished baked or roasted potatoes.

A properly baked potato has very crisp skin and is tender enough to mash easily when fully cooked. Serve baked or roasted potatoes as soon as they are done. This assures the best possible flavor, good texture, and optimal service temperature.

ABOVE *Seasoning potatoes with salt just before they go into the oven gives the finished potato a better flavor and texture.*

ABOVE *Pierce the potatoes to release steam.*

TOP *A properly baked potato has a crisp skin that you can hear crackle. It should never feel or appear leathery or rubbery.*

BOTTOM *The flesh of a properly baked or roasted potato is very tender with a good flavor.*

10 baking potatoes (about 6 oz / 170 g each)

10 oz / 285 g sour cream

2 tbsp / 30 mL minced chives

salt, as needed

ground white pepper, as needed

10 oz / 285 g thinly sliced Spanish onion

2 oz / 60 g flour

2 oz / 60 g cornstarch

oil, for frying

BAKED POTATOES WITH FRIED ONIONS

1 Scrub the potatoes and blot dry. Pierce the potatoes with a kitchen fork or knife. Bake in a 425°F/220°C oven until very tender and cooked through, about 1 hour.

2 Blend the sour cream and chives, season with salt and peper, and reserve for service.

3 Separate the onion slices into rings.

4 Combine the flour and cornstarch, and add salt and pepper to taste. Add the onion rings and toss to coat well.

5 Heat the oil to 375°F/190°C and deep fry the onions until very crisp. Drain on paper toweling.

6 To serve, pinch or cut open the potato, place a dollop of chive sour cream on the flesh, and top with onions.

MAKES 10 PORTIONS

BAKING POTATOES EN CASSEROLE

*Potatoes en casserole are baked in combination
with cream or a custard. Scalloped potatoes,
au gratin potatoes, and dauphinoise potatoes
are all good examples.*

For potato dishes prepared en casserole,
peeled and sliced potatoes (either raw
or parcooked to speed baking time) are
combined with flavored heavy cream, a
sauce, or uncooked custard, and then slowly
baked until the potatoes are extremely
tender but set well enough to hold a
shape when cut for service.

LOW-MOISTURE POTATOES, because of their tendency to absorb liquid, produce casseroled potatoes that are very tender. Waxy yellow potatoes are also often prepared en casserole; these casseroled potatoes have a slightly more noticeable texture and a golden color.

Scrub and peel the potatoes and remove the eyes. Slice the potatoes thin, or cut into an even dice or tourné. Thoroughly dry raw potatoes that have been held in water before combining them with the other ingredients. Excess water can adversely affect the flavor and final texture of the dish. Blot dry parcooked potatoes.

Have the liquid component of the dish (cream, custard, or stock, for example) hot before combining it with the potatoes. This allows the dish to reach cooking temperature more quickly, thus shortening the cooking time.

Salt and pepper are basic for any in en casserole dish. Other spices are often required. Many of these dishes call for one or more grated cheeses, such as Gruyère and/or Parmesan.

Additional ingredients may be used to introduce color, flavor, and texture. Common options include herbs, mushrooms, mustard, and bread crumbs.

En casserole dishes are prepared in hotel pans or similar baking pans and dishes. Liberally grease the baking pan or dish with butter or oil to prevent sticking. Additional helpful but not necessarily essential equipment includes a mandoline for cutting evenly thin slices of potato and a large offset spatula for serving individual portions of the dish.

FOR 10 PORTIONS OF POTATOES EN CASSEROLE, YOU WILL NEED:

3¼ pounds / 1.5 kilograms low-moisture or waxy yellow potatoes, weighed before peeling and cutting, or 2¾ pounds / 1.25 kilograms prepped potatoes

24 to 30 fluid ounces / 720 to 900 milliliters liquid (milk, stock, or sauce)

2 to 3 eggs or egg yolks (optional)

4 to 5 ounces / 115 to 140 grams grated cheese or other topping (optional)

salt and other seasonings

finishing and garnishing ingredients

1. Slice low-moisture or waxy yellow potatoes. Par-cook in the liquid called for in the recipe, if desired. Scrub and peel the potatoes and slice them very thin, using a mandoline if available. Simmer the slices until cooked half way. Add adequate seasonings to flavor both the potatoes and the liquid.

2. Layer the potatoes in the greased pan or pans with the cooking liquid. Arrange raw or par-cooked potatoes in single layers, separating the slices so they will cook evenly.

Using a slotted spoon, transfer the potatoes in layers to the pan.

Add aromatic ingredients and seasonings, such as sliced garlic or salt and pepper, to each layer for the best distribution of flavor.

Pour the hot cooking liquid evenly over the potatoes. Have cream, sauces, and drippings very hot, custards heated but not at a boil. Shake the pan gently to distribute the liquid evenly between the layers.

TOP *A mandoline produces very thin, very even slices of potato quickly and efficiently.*

BOTTOM *Simmering the potatoes before layering them in the baking pan, shortens the cooking time.*

ABOVE *Spread the potatoes and milk evenly in a buttered baking pan. Note that the potatoes' starch has thickened the milk during simmering.*

ABOVE *For this dish, the chef has chosen to add a layer of grated cheese between the layers of potatoes.*

3. Add topping ingredients at the appropriate time to create a crust. Many en casserole dishes are referred to as gratins. The surface of the gratin gradually browns and forms a crust. Some recipes call for specific toppings, such as grated cheese or bread crumbs, to give the crust additional flavor and texture. This step can be performed now, or it can wait until after baking, as necessary.

4. Bake in a moderate (300° to 325°F/150° to 165°C) oven until the potatoes are just tender and the top is golden brown.

Bake at a moderate temperature to avoid curdling, especially with custards. A very creamy texture can be best achieved by baking en casserole dishes in a hot-water bath.

If the top begins to brown too quickly, reduce the oven temperature and sprinkle the dish lightly with milk or stock to moisten and cool it down. If the potatoes are done before the top browns, place the dish under a salamander or broiler briefly to brown.

These dishes can be held throughout a typical service period. Cover the dish loosely with foil and hold it in a warm place. If necessary, reheat the potatoes in an oven or brown them lightly under a salamander or broiler just before serving.

5. Evaluate the quality of the finished potatoes en casserole.

In a good potatoes en casserole, the potatoes are moist and tender; they hold their shape when cut into portions and placed on the plate. The sauce is thick and very smooth, not runny, grainy, or curdled.

ABOVE *Sprinkle toppings over the casserole as the final assembly step.*

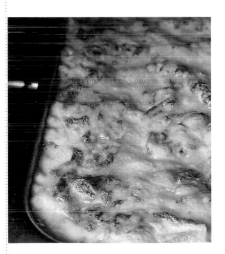

ABOVE *The cheese has melted, browned, and crisped to create an extra flavor dimension.*

ABOVE *These dishes are particularly suitable for banquet service because they are easy to divide into portions and serve.*

3¹⁄₄ lb / 1.5 kg low-moisture or waxy yellow potatoes

24 fl oz / 720 mL milk

salt, as needed

pepper, as needed

butter, as needed

5 oz / 140 g grated Cheddar

POTATOES AU GRATIN

1   Scrub the potatoes, peel, and remove any eyes or green spots. Slice very thin on a man-doline. If done in advance, hold sliced potatoes in cold water to cover under refrigeration. Drain and blot dry before proceeding.

2   Combine the potatoes, milk, salt, and pepper. Simmer the potatoes over low heat until par-cooked, about 10 minutes.

3   Butter a hotel pan.

4   Layer the potatoes and milk in the pan, seasoning each layer. Top with the grated cheese.

5   Cover the pan with foil and bake the potatoes (in a hot-water bath, if desired) at 350°F/175°C until tender, 45 minutes to 1 hour. Uncover and let the cheese brown lightly.

6   Remove the potatoes from the oven and let them rest 10 to 15 minutes before slicing into portions and serving.

MAKES 10 PORTIONS

SAUTÉING POTATOES

Home fries, Anna potatoes, potato pancakes, hash browns, rösti, and Lyonnaise potatoes are prepared by sautéing.

Sautéed potatoes combine a browned and crisp exterior with a tender moist interior. The cooking fat plays a significant role in the flavor of the finished dish, and choices range from the taste of Anna-style or rösti potatoes cooked in liberal amounts of butter to the more rustic flavor of hash browns or home fries sautéed in lard or goose fat. The key to successful sautéed potato dishes is in preparing the potatoes so that they become fully cooked just as the exterior has finished developing a good color and texture.

MODERATE-MOISTURE/
MODERATE-STARCH POTATOES
give the best texture and appearance. Scrub and peel the potatoes, and remove the eyes. Cut the potatoes into even slices, dice, julienne, tourné, or balls. If the potatoes are peeled and cut in advance, hold them submerged in cold water until it is time to cook them. Drain and blot them dry on absorbent toweling immediately before sautéing to avoid splattering. To shorten the cooking time, partially or fully cook the potatoes in advance by steaming or boiling. Drain and dry them as described on page 637.

Different kinds of cooking fat may be used, singly or in combination, for the best flavor in the finished dish. They include vegetable oil, olive oil, clarified butter, or rendered duck, goose, or bacon fat.

Season the potatoes with salt and pepper during cooking. A wide range of herbs and spices, vegetables, and meats can be combined with potatoes to produce a dish with a special appearance, flavor, or color. Among them are onions, shallots, and green onions; diced green and red peppers; or diced bacon or ham. Finishing ingredients, such as heated cream, melted butter, heated

sour cream, or grated cheese, may be added to the potatoes during the actual cooking process or after they have been cooked until tender.

Choose a sauté pan large enough to hold the potatoes without crowding. Cast-iron pans are especially good for potatoes because they can create a crust of exceptional crispness. Spatulas, serving pieces, and absorbent toweling for draining excess fat may also be necessary.

FOR 10 PORTIONS OF SAUTÉED POTATOES, YOU WILL NEED:	4 pounds/1.8 kilograms moderate-moisture potatoes, weighed before peeling and cutting, or 3 ¼ pounds/1.5 kilograms prepped potatoes	cooking fat (oil, clarified butter, or rendered duck, goose, or bacon fat)	salt and other seasonings finishing and garnishing ingredients

1. Prepare the potatoes for sautéing. Scrub and peel raw potatoes and cut, slice, or grate them into the desired shape. If the potatoes are held before cooking, drain and blot them dry before sautéing. Some dishes may call for the potatoes to be simmered until partially cooked either before or after they are sliced or cut.

2. Heat the fat in an appropriately sized pan. Add the potatoes to the hot fat and sauté until tender.

Be sure to use enough cooking fat to coat the pan generously, to prevent the potatoes from sticking and falling apart as they cook.

The fat must be hot, so that the crust begins to develop immediately. This crust assures the proper color, flavor, and texture and also helps prevent the potatoes from absorbing too much fat.

Stir the potatoes or shake the pan occasionally as the potatoes cook, to brown evenly. In general, add garnishes or finishing ingredients when the potatoes have almost finished cooking.

For the best flavor and texture, serve sautéed potatoes immediately after they are cooked. If necessary, however, they may be held for 5 to 10 minutes, uncovered, in a warm place.

3. Evaluate the quality of the finished sautéed potatoes.

Properly sautéed potatoes have a rich flavor from the browning of the potatoes as well as from the cooking fat itself. Use seasonings to bring out the flavor of the potatoes and garnishing and finishing ingredients that further enhance the flavor by adding their own flavors, textures, and colors to the finished presentation.

TOP *For Lyonnaise potatoes, cut thick slices and cook them in plenty of boiling salted water.*

BOTTOM *The potatoes have been partially cooked, as you can see by the slight color change around the exterior. The interior, which is still not cooked, is more opaque.*

ABOVE *Add other ingredients, such as onions, to the potatoes and turn them carefully, to preserve the potatoes' shape during cooking.*

ABOVE *Allow the potatoes to form a golden skin on all sides, though they will not have as uniform a color as deep-fried potatoes. Finish the potatoes by seasoning them well.*

4 lb / 1.8 kg chef's potatoes

vegetable oil, as needed

1 lb / 450 g sliced onions

salt, as needed

pepper, as needed

chopped parsley, as needed

LYONNAISE POTATOES

1 Scrub and peel the potatoes. Cut into slices or medium dice. Cook the potatoes in boiling salted water until partially cooked. Drain the potatoes and dry them over low heat or on a sheet pan in a 300°F/150°C oven.

2 Heat the oil in a pan. Add the onions and cook, stirring frequently, until lightly browned. Add the potatoes and season with salt and pepper.

3 Continue to sauté, stirring occasionally, until the potatoes are browned well on all sides and are tender to the bite. Garnish with parsley and serve.

MAKES 10 PORTIONS

DEEP FRYING POTATOES

French fries and steak fries as well as waffle-cut, matchstick, and soufflé potatoes are all deep-fried potatoes.

Deep-fried potatoes seem simple to make but must be done carefully if excellent quality is to be achieved. Most deep-fried potatoes prepared from the raw state are first blanched in oil heated to 300° to 325°F/150° to 162°C until tender and almost translucent. They are then drained thoroughly and held until just before service. At that time they are finished in oil heated to 350° to 375°F/167° to 190°C. Blanching assures that the finished potato has the proper color, texture, and flavor and that it cooks thoroughly without becoming greasy or scorched. It is especially important to blanch soufflé potatoes so that they puff adequately. Potatoes cut very thin (e.g., matchstick potatoes) can usually be cooked in a single step, without blanching. Deep-fried potatoes, such as lorette, croquette, and dauphine potatoes, are made from a puréed appareil.

LOW-MOISTURE POTATOES are best for deep frying. Scrub and peel the potatoes, and remove the eyes. Cut the potatoes into even slices, julienne, batonnet, or other cuts. If the potatoes are peeled and cut in advance of cooking, hold them submerged in cold water. Rinse the potatoes in several changes of cold water if indicated, and drain and dry them thoroughly to prevent splattering when they are added to the oil. Rinsing the potatoes in several changes of cold water removes the surface starch and helps prevent the potatoes from sticking together. Potatoes that are to be deep fried for such preparations as straw or matchstick potatoes, in particular, should be rinsed so they don't clump together as they cook. Potatoes used for deep-fried potato nests and cakes need the cohesiveness provided by the surface starch and should not be rinsed.

Choose a neutral oil with a high smoking point for frying the potatoes.

Deep-fried potatoes are customarily seasoned with salt after frying and prior to service. Condiments — catsup and malt vinegar are the most common — may be served with them.

Use either a frying kettle or a deep fryer. Electric or gas deep fryers are excellent for doing a great deal of deep frying because they maintain even temperatures. They are also put together in such a way that it is relatively easy to clean them and care for the oil properly.

Lacking a freestanding fryer, use a deep kettle or pot, such as a stockpot, instead. Use a thermometer to monitor and control the temperature. Once the correct frying temperature is reached, adjust the heat so that the temperature remains relatively constant.

Other equipment, such as baskets, tongs, spiders, and containers lined with absorbent toweling, are also needed.

| TO PREPARE 10 PORTIONS OF DEEP-FRIED POTATOES, YOU WILL NEED: | *2½ to 3 pounds / 1.15 to 1.3 kilograms potatoes, peeled and cut to shape* | *enough cooking oil to completely submerge the potatoes*

salt and other seasonings | *finishing or garnishing ingredients for service* |

HOW TO DEEP FRY POTATOES

1. Scrub, peel, cut, and rinse the potatoes for deep frying. Blanch them in hot oil.

Peel and cut the potatoes and hold them in cold water. Immediately before cooking, rinse several times in cold water, if indicated, and drain thoroughly. Blot dry. Heat the oil to 300° to 325°F/150° to 162°C. Blanch the potatoes until they are nearly cooked through but still relatively uncolored. Blanched potatoes may be held, covered, under refrigeration for up to several hours before finishing the cooking process. They may be frozen for 1 month.

ABOVE *Before lowering the potatoes into the hot fat, blot them dry on paper toweling. Be sure not to overload the basket.*

ABOVE *After blanching, drain the potatoes on absorbent toweling and hold them, covered and under refrigeration, until just before service.*

2. Deep fry the potatoes at 350° to 375°F/176° to 190°C until done.
Just before service, reheat the oil and deep fry the potatoes until evenly golden brown on all surfaces. Lift them from the cooking oil with a basket or spider and transfer to a pan lined with paper toweling to blot away excess oil. Season with salt and serve immediately. Deep-fried potatoes cannot be held successfully for more than a few minutes.

Add seasonings to the very hot fried potatoes as desired. Be sure to do this away from the oil used for frying to prolong the life of the oil.

3. Evaluate the quality of the finished deep-fried potatoes.
Bite into one of the pieces. Very thin potatoes, such as gaufrette (waffle-cut) potatoes, should be extremely crisp, almost to the point where they shatter when bitten. Thick-cut potatoes should have a crisp exterior and a tender, fluffy interior.

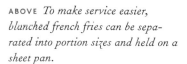

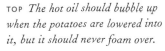

ABOVE *To make service easier, blanched french fries can be separated into portion sizes and held on a sheet pan.*

TOP *The hot oil should bubble up when the potatoes are lowered into it, but it should never foam over.*

BOTTOM *Lift the potatoes from the hot oil using the basket, and allow any excess oil to simply drain back into the fryer.*

ABOVE *A blotting setup should be part of the deep-frying mise en place. Replace the paper as necessary when it becomes soaked with oil.*

4 lb / 1.8 kg baking potatoes

vegetable oil

salt, as needed

FRENCH-FRIED POTATOES

1 Peel the potatoes, cut into the desired shape, and hold them in cold water until ready to cook. Rinse, drain, and dry thoroughly.

2 Heat the oil to 325°F/165°C. Add the potatoes, in batches, and blanch until just tender but not browned (time varies according to the size of cuts).

3 Drain well and transfer to pans lined with absorbent paper, scaling into portions if desired.

4 Just before service, reheat the oil to 375°F/190°C and finish the potatoes, frying until they are golden brown and cooked through. Drain well, season with salt to taste (away from the fryer), and serve immediately.

MAKES 10 PORTIONS

RECIPES

WHIPPED POTATOES

makes 10 portions

4 lb/1.8 kg baking potatoes

2¹⁄₂ oz/70 g butter, at room temperature

4 to 6 fl oz/120 to 180 mL milk or buttermilk, hot

salt, as needed

pepper, as needed

1 Scrub, peel, and cut the potatoes into large pieces. Cook them by boiling or steaming until tender enough to mash easily. Drain and dry them over low heat or on a sheet pan in a 300°F/50°C oven until no more steam rises from them. While the potatoes are still hot, purée them through a food mill or potato ricer into a heated bowl.

2 Add the butter and mix into the potatoes by hand or with the paddle or whip attachment of an electric mixer until just incorporated. Add the milk or buttermilk, salt, and pepper and whip by hand or mixer until smooth and light.

3 Serve the potatoes on heated plates by spooning them onto the plate, or transfer the mixture to a piping bag and pipe into the desired shapes.

NOTE

Alternatively, potatoes may be baked in their skins until very tender. Halve the potatoes and scoop out the flesh while it is still very hot.

EUROPEAN-STYLE POTATO SALAD

makes 10 portions

4 lb/1.8 kg waxy potatoes

salt, as needed

5 oz/140 g fine-dice onions

3 fl oz/90 mL red wine vinegar

8 fl oz/240 mL WHITE BEEF STOCK (page 249)

1¹⁄₂ fl oz/45 mL prepared mustard, or as needed

pepper, as needed

sugar, as needed

3 fl oz/90 mL vegetable oil

chopped parsley or chives, as needed

1 Scrub the potatoes and peel if desired. Place the potatoes in a pot with enough cold water to cover them by about 2 in/5 cm. Add salt to taste. Gradually bring the water to a simmer over medium heat. Cover and simmer until the potatoes are easily pierced with a fork.

2 Drain the potatoes. Return them to the pot and let them dry briefly over very low heat until no more steam rises from them, or spread them out on a sheet pan and dry them in a low oven. Peel and slice the potatoes as soon as they are cool enough to handle.

3 Combine the onions, vinegar, and stock. Bring the mixture to a boil. Add the mustard, with salt, pepper, and sugar to taste. Add the oil. Immediately pour the hot dressing over the hot potato slices.

4 Sprinkle the potato salad with the parsley or chives. Let stand for at least 1 hour before serving at room temperature, or properly cool and store for later service.

see photograph on page 664

BAKED STUFFED POTATOES

makes 10 portions

10 baking potatoes (about 6 oz/170 g each)

oil, as needed

salt, as needed

6 fl oz/180 mL milk, or as needed, hot

4 oz/115 g butter, softened

1 egg yolk

pepper, as needed

1 Scrub the potatoes and blot dry. Rub lightly with oil or salt, if desired. Pierce the potatoes with a kitchen fork or paring knife. Bake in a 425°F/220°C oven until very tender and cooked through, about 1 hour.

2 Slice away the tops of the potatoes and scoop out the flesh while it is still very hot. (Reserve the potato skins.) While the potatoes are still hot, purée them through a food mill or potato ricer into a heated bowl.

3 Mix in the milk by hand or with the whip attachment of an electric mixer until just incorporated. Add 2 oz/60 g of the butter, the egg yolks, and salt and pepper to taste and mix them in well by hand or with the mixer.

4 Transfer the mixture to a piping bag and pipe the mixture back into the potato skins. Dot the remaining butter on top of each potato. Bake at 425°F/220°C until the tops are lightly browned and the potatoes are very hot, about 10 minutes.

ROASTED POTATOES WITH GARLIC AND ROSEMARY

makes 10 portions

4 lb/1.8 kg red bliss potatoes

1 oz/30 mL olive oil

1 tbsp/15 mL minced garlic

1 tbsp/15 mL minced rosemary leaves

salt, as needed

pepper, as needed

1 Scrub and blot dry the potatoes. Peel if desired. Cut into halves or quarters if desired. If potatoes are peeled or cut in advance, hold them in cold water to prevent browning. Drain and blot them dry before cooking.

2 Combine the oil, garlic, rosemary, salt, and pepper in a large bowl. Add the potatoes and roll or toss until they are evenly coated. Transfer to an oiled sheet pan.

3 Bake in a 425°F/220°C oven until browned and tender enough to be easily pierced with a fork, about 40 to 45 minutes. Serve as soon after baking as possible on heated plates.

GLAZED SWEET POTATOES

makes 10 portions

4 lb/1.8 kg sweet potatoes

8 oz/225 g small-dice fresh pineapple

2 fl oz/60 mL lemon juice

8 oz/225 g sugar

1 tsp/5 mL ground cinnamon

2 oz/60 g butter

salt, as needed

pepper, as needed

1 Scrub and blot dry the potatoes. Arrange in a single layer on a sheet pan. Bake in a 375°F/190°C oven until very tender and cooked through, about 30 to 40 minutes.

2 Combine the pineapple, lemon juice, sugar, cinnamon, butter, salt, and pepper in a saucepan and bring to a simmer while the sweet potatoes are baking. Continue to cook until lightly thickened; keep warm.

3 As soon as the potatoes are cool enough to handle, peel them and cut into slices or large chunks. Arrange the sweet potatoes on a sheet pan. Pour the glaze over them and bake at 350°F/165°C until very hot, about 10 minutes. Serve on heated plates.

DAUPHINOISE POTATOES

makes 10 portions

3 1/2 lb/1.5 kg baking or waxy potatoes

24 fl oz/720 mL milk

salt, as needed

pepper, as needed

ground nutmeg, as needed (optional)

butter, as needed

1 garlic clove, crushed

2 eggs, beaten

5 oz/140 g grated Gruyère

1 Scrub the potatoes and peel them. Slice thin by hand or on a mandoline. If the potatoes are peeled or sliced in advance, hold them in water to prevent discoloration. Drain and dry them before cooking.

2 Simmer the potatoes, milk, salt, pepper, and nutmeg until the potatoes are nearly tender but not fully cooked, about 15 minutes.

3 Butter a hotel pan and rub it with the crushed garlic clove.

4 Lift the potatoes from the milk and arrange in layers in the pan. Blend the eggs into the milk and pour over the potatoes. Shake the pan slightly to settle the layers and distribute the milk evenly. Spread the cheese in an even layer over the potatoes.

5 Cover the potatoes and bake in a hot-water bath at 350°F/175°C until tender, 45 minutes to 1 hour. Uncover during the final 5 to 10 minutes of cooking to brown the cheese.

Savoyarde Potatoes Substitute an equal amount of stock, broth, or consommé for the milk.

SWEDISH-STYLE CANDIED POTATOES

makes 10 portions

4 lb/1.8 kg red bliss potatoes

salt, as needed

6 oz/170 g sugar

lemon juice, as needed

3 oz/85 g butter

pepper, as needed

1 Scrub and peel the potatoes. Cut the potatoes into equal-size pieces if necessary.

2 Place the potatoes in a pot with enough cold water to cover them by about 2 in/5 cm. Add salt to taste. Gradually bring the water to a simmer over medium heat. Cover and simmer until the potatoes are easily pierced with a fork.

3 Drain the potatoes. Return them to the pot and let them dry briefly over very low heat until no more steam rises from them, or spread them out on a sheet pan and dry them in a low oven.

4 Transfer the potatoes to a sauté pan, add the sugar and lemon juice, and cook over medium heat, occasionally tossing gently, until the potatoes are evenly coated and caramelized.

5 Add the butter, salt, and pepper to taste. Serve immediately.

NOTE

Hold peeled potatoes in cold water to prevent discoloration until it is time to cook them.

SWEET POTATOES BAKED IN CIDER WITH CURRANTS AND CINNAMON

makes 10 portions

4 lb/1.8 kg sweet potatoes

2 oz/60 g butter

1 oz/30 g minced shallots

8 fl oz/240 mL apple cider

2 oz/60 g currants

1 tsp/5 mL ground cinnamon

salt, as needed

pepper, as needed

1 Scrub the sweet potatoes and peel them. Slice thin by hand or on a mandoline.

2 Shingle the sweet potato slices in a well-buttered casserole or gratin dish. Sprinkle with the shallots. Add the cider. There should be enough to thoroughly moisten the potatoes. Add the currants, cinnamon, salt, and pepper.

3 Cover the sweet potatoes loosely with aluminum foil and bake at 325°F/165°C until the potatoes are very tender, about 35 to 40 minutes. Serve immediately.

HASH BROWN POTATOES

makes 10 portions

4 lb/1.8 kg chef's potatoes

vegetable oil, as needed

salt, as needed

pepper, as needed

chopped parsley, as needed

1 Scrub and peel the potatoes. Cook the potatoes in boiling salted water until partially cooked, about 20 minutes, depending upon the potatoes' size. Drain the potatoes and dry them over low heat or on a sheet pan in a 300°F/150°C oven. Peel the potatoes as soon as they are cool enough to handle and cut into slices or small or medium dice, or grate them.

2 Heat the oil in a pan. Add the potatoes and season with salt and pepper.

3 Sauté the potatoes until they are fully cooked and well browned on all sides, and are tender to the bite. Garnish with parsley and serve.

European-Style Potato Salad

Rösti Potatoes

Macaire Potatoes

Sweet Potato Chips

RISSOLÉE POTATOES

makes 10 portions

4 lb/1.8 kg chef's potatoes
clarified butter or vegetable oil, as needed
salt, as needed
pepper, as needed
chopped parsley, as needed

1 Scrub and peel the potatoes. Use a parisienne scoop to shape the potatoes into small balls. Simmer the potatoes in salted water until the potatoes are tender but not fully cooked, about 10 minutes.

2 Drain the potatoes. Return them to the pot and let them dry briefly over very low heat until no more steam rises from them, or spread them out on a sheet pan and dry them in a low oven.

3 Sauté the potatoes in hot butter or oil over high heat. Season with salt and pepper.

4 Sprinkle with parsley and serve.

NOTE

Hold peeled potatoes in cold water to prevent discoloration until it is time to cook them.

MACAIRE POTATOES

makes 10 portions

4 lb/1.8 kg baking potatoes
2 oz/60 g butter
salt, as needed
pepper, as needed
clarified butter or vegetable oil, as needed

1 Scrub and blot dry the potatoes. Season with salt. Pierce the skins in a few places with a paring knife or kitchen fork.

2 Bake in a 425°F/220°C oven until very tender and cooked through, about 1 hour.

3 Halve the potatoes, scoop out the flesh while it is still very hot, and transfer to a heated bowl. Mash the potatoes, butter, salt, and pepper together with a fork or wooden spoon until evenly blended. Shape into cakes.

4 Sauté the cakes in hot clarified butter or oil over medium heat until golden on both sides and very hot, about 2 to 3 minutes per side. Serve immediately.

see photograph on page 665

CHÂTEAU POTATOES

makes 10 portions

4 lb/1.8 kg chef's or waxy potatoes
clarified butter or oil for sautéing, as needed
chopped parsley, as needed
salt, as needed
pepper, as needed

1 Scrub the potatoes and peel if desired. Cut the potatoes into equal size tournés, about the size of an olive.

2 Sauté the potatoes in hot clarified butter or oil over moderate heat until tender with a golden exterior, about 8 to 10 minutes.

3 Sprinkle with parsley and season with salt and pepper to taste. Serve at once.

NOTE

Hold peeled potatoes in cold water to prevent discoloration until it is time to cook them.

POTATO PANCAKES

makes 10 portions

3 lb/1.35 kg chef's or waxy potatoes

1 lb/450 g onions

1 fl oz/30 mL lemon juice, or as needed

2 eggs, lightly beaten

1 oz/30 g all-purpose flour

1 oz/30 g matzo meal

salt, as needed

pepper, as needed

vegetable oil, as needed

1   Scrub and peel the potatoes. Remove the peel and core from the onions and quarter them. Grind or grate the potatoes and onions into a bowl (this should be done as close to cooking time as possible to prevent discoloration). Sprinkle with lemon juice and toss to coat evenly.

2   Wring the grated potatoes and onions in cheesecloth to remove excess moisture. Transfer to a bowl and stir in the eggs, flour, matzo meal, salt, and pepper.

3   Heat ¼ in/6 mm of oil in a griswold or cast-iron skillet over moderate heat.

4   Drop the potato batter into the hot oil by level serving spoons. Brown the pancakes on the first side, about 2 minutes. Turn them once and brown them on the second side, another 2 to 3 minutes. If necessary, the pancakes may be finished in a 375°F/190°C oven until browned and crisp. Blot the pancakes on absorbent toweling and serve as soon as possible.

ANNA POTATOES

makes 10 portions

4 lb/1.8 kg waxy potatoes

whole butter, as needed

clarified butter, as needed

salt, as needed

pepper, as needed

1   Scrub and peel the potatoes and trim them into uniform cylinders. Cut the cylinders into thin slices on a mandoline.

2   Liberally brush a sautoir with butter. Arrange the potato slices in concentric rings. Lightly brush each layer with clarified butter and season with salt and pepper.

3   Cover the potatoes and cook them over medium heat until the bottom layer is brown. Turn the potato cake and brown the other side. Place in a 400°F/205°C oven and cook until tender, about 30 to 35 minutes.

4   Drain off the excess butter and turn out the potato cake onto a platter. Slice and serve.

NOTE

Reserve the potato trim for use in purées or other applications.

POTATOES HASHED IN CREAM

makes 10 portions

4 lb/1.8 kg waxy potatoes

salt, as needed

24 fl oz/720 mL milk or half-and-half, hot

pepper, as needed

1 Scrub the potatoes. Place them in a pot with enough cold water to cover them by about 2 in/5 cm. Add salt to taste. Gradually bring the water to a simmer over medium heat. Cover and simmer until the potatoes are partially cooked (a fork inserted in the potato should meet resistance about ½ in/12 mm from the surface).

2 Drain the potatoes. Return them to the pot and let them dry briefly over very low heat until no more steam rises from them, or spread them out on a sheet pan and dry them in a low oven. Peel the potatoes as soon as they are cool enough to handle and cut them into small dice.

3 Simmer the potatoes and the heated milk or half-and-half over low heat until completely cooked and the cream is thickened, about 15 to 20 minutes more. Stir frequently to avoid scorching. Season to taste with salt and pepper and serve on heated plates.

RÖSTI POTATOES

makes 10 portions

4 lb/1.8 kg baking potatoes

salt, as needed

clarified butter, as needed

pepper, as needed

whole butter, as needed

1 Scrub the potatoes. Place them in a pot with enough cold water to cover them by about 2 in/5 cm. Add salt to taste. Gradually bring the water to a simmer over medium heat. Cover and simmer until the potatoes are partially cooked (a fork inserted in the potato should meet resistance about ½ in/12 mm from the surface).

2 Drain the potatoes. Return them to the pot and let them dry briefly over very low heat until no more steam rises from them, or spread them out on a sheet pan and dry them in a low oven. Peel the potatoes as soon as they are cool enough to handle and grate them on the coarse side of a grater.

3 Heat a sautoir over high heat. Ladle in some of the clarified butter. Layer the grated potato in the pan. Lightly drizzle each layer with a little additional butter and season with salt and pepper. Dot the outside edge with pieces of whole butter.

4 Cook the potatoes until they are golden brown and form a cake, about 4 to 5 minutes. Turn the entire cake, dot the edge with more whole butter, and cook the other side until the potatoes are fully cooked and tender and the crusts are golden brown and crisp. Turn the cake out of the pan, cut into portions, and serve on heated plates.

see photograph on page 664

BERNY POTATOES

makes 10 portions

4 lb/1.8 kg baking potatoes

2½ oz/70 g butter, softened

2 egg yolks, beaten

ground nutmeg, as needed

salt, as needed

pepper, as needed

2 oz/60 g chopped truffle

2 oz/60 g slivered almonds

2 oz/60 g bread crumbs

egg wash, as needed

vegetable oil, as needed

1 Scrub, peel, and cut the potatoes into large pieces. Cook them by boiling or steaming until tender enough to mash easily. Drain and dry them over low heat or on a sheet pan in a 300°F/150°C oven until no more steam rises from them. While the potatoes are still hot, purée them through a food mill or potato ricer into a heated bowl.

2 Add the butter and egg yolks, and nutmeg, salt, and pepper to taste to the potatoes and mix them in well by hand or with the whip attachment of an electric mixer. Fold in the truffles.

3 Combine the almonds and bread crumbs in a shallow container.

4 Shape 2-oz/60-g portions of the potato mixture into balls or other shapes, as desired. Dip the balls in the egg wash and then into the almond/bread crumb mixture. Arrange them in a frying basket.

5 Heat the oil to 375°F/190°C and lower the potatoes into the oil. Deep fry them until an even golden brown, 4 to 5 minutes. Blot them on absorbent paper and serve very hot on heated plates.

CROQUETTE POTATOES

makes 10 portions

4 lb/1.8 kg baking potatoes

2¹/₂ oz/70 g butter, softened

2 egg yolks, beaten

ground nutmeg, as needed

salt, as needed

pepper, as needed

flour, as needed

egg wash, as needed

bread crumbs, as needed

vegetable oil, for frying

1 Scrub, peel, and cut the potatoes into large pieces. Cook the potatoes by boiling or steaming until tender enough to mash easily. Drain and dry them over low heat or on a sheet pan in a 300°F/150°C oven until no more steam rises from them. While the potatoes are still hot, purée them through a food mill or potato ricer into a heated bowl.

2 Add the butter and egg yolks, and nutmeg, salt, and pepper to taste to the potatoes and mix them in well by hand or with the whip attachment of an electric mixer.

3 Transfer the mixture to a piping bag and pipe it into long ropes about 1 in/2 cm in diameter. Cut these ropes into 3-in/7-cm lengths. Coat with flour, egg wash, and bread crumbs.

4 Heat the oil to 375°F/190°C and deep fry the croquettes until golden brown and heated through, 3 to 4 minutes. Drain briefly on paper toweling and serve hot on heated plates.

LORETTE POTATOES

makes 10 portions

4 lb/1.8 kg baking potatoes

2¹/₂ oz/70 g butter, softened

2 egg yolks, beaten

ground nutmeg, as needed

salt, as needed

pepper, as needed

20 oz/570 g PÂTE À CHOUX (page 943), at room temperature

vegetable oil, as needed

1 Scrub, peel, and cut the potatoes into large pieces. Cook the potatoes by boiling or steaming until tender enough to mash easily. Drain and dry them over low heat or on a sheet pan in a 300°F/150°C oven until no more steam rises from them. While the potatoes are still hot, purée them through a food mill or potato ricer into a heated bowl.

2 Add the butter and egg yolks, and nutmeg, salt, and pepper to taste to the potatoes and mix them in well by hand or with the whip attachment of an electric mixer. Add the pâte à choux.

3 Transfer the mixture to a piping bag and pipe the mixture into crescent shapes on strips of parchment paper.

4 Heat the oil to 375°F/190°C and carefully lower the strips of paper into the fryer. When the lorettes have lifted off the paper, remove and discard the paper. Deep fry the lorettes until golden brown, turning if necessary to brown evenly. Remove from the oil, blot dry on absorbent paper, and serve very hot on heated plates.

POTATO NESTS

makes 10 portions

3¹/₂ lb/1.6 kg baking potatoes

vegetable oil, as needed

1 Scrub and peel the potatoes and hold them in cold water until ready to cook. Rinse, drain, and dry thoroughly just before cooking. Grate the potatoes into long, fine shreds on a mandoline.

2 Arrange the potatoes in the bottom of a potato-nest basket. Fit the top basket in place.

3 Heat the oil to 350°F/175°C and deep fry the potatoes until crisp, brown, and thoroughly cooked. Drain briefly and serve as soon as possible.

SWEET POTATO CHIPS

makes 10 portions

4 lb/1.8 kg sweet potatoes

vegetable oil, for frying

salt, as needed

pepper, as needed

lime juice, as needed (optional)

1   Scrub the sweet potatoes and peel them. Slice thin by hand or on a mandoline. Blot them dry before cooking.

2   Heat the oil to 325°F/165°C and fry the sweet potatoes by the basket method until they are tender, but not browned or crisp. Remove them from the oil, drain on absorbent toweling and hold until ready to finish for service.

3   At time of service, reheat the oil to 375°F/190°C and finish frying the potatoes until they are very crisp.

4   Drain well and blot on absorbent paper. Season with salt and pepper, and sprinkle with lime juice, if desired. Serve very hot on heated plates.

see photograph on page 665

SOUFFLÉED POTATOES

makes 10 portions

4 lb/1.18 kg baking potatoes

vegetable oil, as needed

salt, as needed

1   Scrub the potatoes and peel them, using a paring knife to produce a relatively uniform cylinder. Slice them very thin by hand or on a mandoline. If the potatoes are sliced in advance, hold them in water to prevent discoloration. Drain and dry them before cooking.

2   Heat the oil to 300°F/150°C. Add the potato slices in small batches. Shake the basket or pot carefully to prevent the potatoes from sticking. When the slices blister, remove and drain them in a single layer on absorbent toweling. Hold for service.

3   At time of service, reheat the oil to 375°F/190°C and add the blanched potato slices. Fry until puffed and golden. Drain well. Season with salt to taste and serve immediately.

One of the most dramatic changes on the culinary scene in recent years has been the rediscovery of grains and legumes. Everyday grains — wheat, corn, rice — are appearing in many new forms, and beans as well have become a familiar sight. In addition, exotic grains, such as millet and quinoa, and once-rarely seen beans, including flageolets and borlottis, are appearing more and more frequently.

COOKING GRAINS AND LEGUMES

SIMMERING WHOLE GRAINS AND LEGUMES

Grains and legumes are dried foods that must be properly rehydrated by cooking in stock or water before they can be eaten.

Although grains and legumes are often referred to as boiled, they are actually simmered or steamed. The high heat of a boiling liquid tends to toughen them. When the liquid is completely absorbed by a grain as it cooks, it is often referred to as steamed. Grains may also be cooked in a quantity of liquid greater than they can absorb. Once fully cooked, the excess liquid is drained.

SELECT AND PREPARE THE INGREDIENTS AND EQUIPMENT

SORT WHOLE GRAINS AND legumes carefully before cooking. Occasionally a few stones are mixed in, and they need to be removed. Spread out the grains or legumes in a single layer on a sheet pan and work from one end of the pan to the other systematically to spot and remove stones and moldy beans. Put the beans or legumes in a large pot or bowl and cover them with cold water. Any that float on the surface are too dry for culinary or nutritional purposes and should be removed and discarded. Drain the beans or legumes in a colander or sieve and then rinse well with cold running water to remove any dust.

Most legumes and some grains are soaked prior to cooking. Whole grains such as whole or scotch barley and wheat and

rye berries benefit from soaking, which softens the outer layer of bran. (Pearl barley, which has had the bran removed mechanically, does not need to be soaked.) Imported basmati and jasmine rice should be soaked to remove excess starch from the surface and prevent clumping. (Domestic basmati and jasmine rice do not need to be soaked.) Fine- or medium-grind bulgur wheat is steeped in boiling liquid for several minutes, until the grain softens enough to be chewed easily. Like bulgur, instant couscous is cooked by steeping in hot stock or water. (While couscous is a form of pasta rather than a grain, it is often thought of as one because of its texture and appearance.)

Whether or not to soak legumes is a subject of debate among chefs. Some

believe that most legumes, with a few notable exceptions (lentils, split peas, and black-eyed peas), are easier to prepare and produce a better-quality finished dish if they are soaked, because the skins soften slightly, allowing for more rapid and even cooking. Others find that soaking has no benefit beyond shortening the cooking time and that cooking legumes without soaking results in a creamier texture. If you choose to soak, there are two methods commonly used to soak legumes, the long soak and the short soak; except for time, there is no appreciable difference between them.

Place the sorted and rinsed legumes in a container and add enough cool water to cover them by a few inches. Let the legumes soak under refrigeration for 4 hours to overnight, depending on the legume.

Place the sorted and rinsed legumes in a pot and add enough water to cover by a few inches. Bring the water to a simmer. Remove the pot from direct heat and cover. Let the legumes steep for 1 hour.

Whether or not to use the soaking water as the cooking liquid is also a subject of debate. In addition to softening skins, soaking the legumes causes many of the oligosaccharides (indigestible complex sugars that can cause flatulence) in the legumes to be leached into the water. At the same time, small amounts of nutrients, flavor, and color are also leached into the water. When the soaking water is used as the cooking liquid, the nutrients, flavor, and color are retained, but so are the oligosaccharides.

Water, stock, and broth are common choices for the cooking liquid. Each type of grain or legume absorbs a different amount of liquid. (Refer to Common Ratios for Grains and Legumes, page 995, or to package or recipe instructions for details.) Grains often are cooked in an amount of liquid greater than they can actually absorb. This is especially desirable for grains that should remain separate, fluffy, and very dry after cooking. The amount of liquid required for legumes depends on the type and the age of the legume and its total cooking time. Legumes should be completely covered by liquid at all times. It is important to main-

tain this level throughout cooking. If the legumes are allowed to absorb all the liquid, they might break apart or scorch.

Legumes and grains have relatively subtle flavors that frequently require a boost. Ingredients that contribute to the dish's overall appeal usually need to be added. Salt needs to be added to the cooking liquid at the beginning (for grains) or near the end (for legumes) of cooking time to properly enhance natural flavors. Many spices and herbs are combined with grains and legumes either during or after cooking.

The equipment needs for simmering grains and legumes are quite simple: a pot large enough to allow for the expansion of the grain or legume, a colander or strainer if draining will be required, and holding and serving pieces.

FOR 10 PORTIONS OF WHOLE GRAINS OR LEGUMES, FOLLOW THIS FORMULA.	MAIN INGREDIENT OPTIONS INCLUDE:	COOKING LIQUID OPTIONS INCLUDE:	SEASONING OPTIONS INCLUDE:
	14 ounces/400 grams grain	*stock as needed to cover grain or legumes throughout cooking time*	*salt and pepper*
	12 ounces/340 grams legumes		*standard sachet d'épices or bouquet garni*
		water as needed to cover grain or legumes throughout cooking time	*mirepoix or other aromatic vegetables*

1. Combine the grain or legumes with the cooking liquid and bring to a full boil.

Legumes and most grains are usually combined with the liquid before bringing it to a boil, but some grains (quinoa, for instance) are added to the liquid only after it has come to a boil. Some seasonings are added at the beginning of the cooking period, others at the end. (Refer to specific recipes for details.)

2. Reduce the heat slightly to a simmer and cook the grain or legumes until done as desired.

Legumes and some grains need to be stirred occasionally as they cook to prevent scorching. Check the level of the cooking liquid and add more as necessary to keep the legumes or grain completely covered. To check for doneness, taste a grain or legume. Salt is typically added to legumes after they have become tender. Adding salt or acidic ingredients, such as citrus juices or vinegar, earlier can toughen the skin if added at the start of cooking time.

3. Drain the grain or legumes or let them cool in the cooking liquid. Finish and serve on heated plates or use in another preparation.

Legumes are often allowed to cool in their cooking liquid if they are to be used later. This keeps the skins tender. In many cases, the cooking liquid is an important ingredient in the finished dish.

If liquid is not entirely absorbed, drain the grain in a colander and suspend it over a pot. Cover the pot and let the grain steam dry for a few minutes over low heat. Use a fork to gently fluff the grain, but do not stir; stirring may cause starch granules to burst, creating a gluey texture.

Adjust the seasoning as necessary and appropriate with salt, pepper, and other ingredients. Hold the dish in a warm place, if necessary, until ready to serve.

4. Evaluate the quality of the finished boiled legume or whole grain. Grains are done when they are tender to the bite. They should be fluffy, with a sweet, nutty flavor. Legumes are done when they are completely tender and creamy on the inside but still retain their shape. They should be soft and easy to mash with a fork or spoon. Undercooking legumes is a common mistake.

TOP *Skim beans as they simmer to improve the flavor of the finished dish.*

BOTTOM *A bouquet garni is often added to the beans' cooking liquid as it comes to a boil.*

12 oz / 340 g white beans

vegetable oil, as needed

4 oz / 115 g chopped onion

1 fresh ham hock (optional)

3 qt / 3 L CHICKEN STOCK (page 248), or as needed

sachet d'épices, containing 3 chopped parsley stems, 1 bay leaf, ½ tsp/2 mL cracked
    black peppercorns, 1 sprig thyme or ½ tsp/2 mL dried thyme, and 1 garlic clove

salt, as needed

BOILED WHITE BEANS

1 Sort the beans and rinse well with cold water. Soak using the long or short method if
   desired. Drain soaked beans.

2 Heat the oil in a pot, add the onions, and sweat until tender and translucent, about 5 to
   6 minutes. Add the beans, ham hock (if using), stock to cover, and the sachet d'épices.
   Simmer the beans for 1 hour and add salt as needed. Continue to simmer until the
   beans are tender to the bite, about 20 to 30 minutes more.

3 The beans are ready to drain and finish at this point, or they may be cooled in their
   cooking liquid and stored for later use.

MAKES 10 PORTIONS

SIMMERING AND BOILING CEREALS AND MEALS

Culinary grains may undergo some type of processing (milling) before they reach the kitchen to produce meals and cereals.

When a whole grain is milled, it is broken down into successively smaller particles. Depending on the grain, the final result might be quite coarse (cracked wheat or groats) or quite fine (cornmeal or farina). Some grains are treated before milling.

Bulgur wheat, for example, is steamed and dried before it is crushed. Cereals include various forms of oats, buckwheat groats, and rye flakes, as well as cracked grains like bulgur. Meals include grits and polenta, farina, semolina, and cream of rice. Flours are even more finely ground (see page 203).

CEREALS AND MEALS VARY widely according to the way in which they are processed. Meals and cereals may be ground coarse or fine. The bran and germ may be left intact or removed. The type of grinding equipment affects both flavor and nutritional content. Coarser cereals produce a dense, porridge-like texture; finer grinds produce a smooth, even silky, texture similar to a pudding. All cereals and grains should have a fresh, appealing aroma. As they age, the natural oils can become rancid. Discard any cereals or meals that do not smell fresh.

Sort the meal to remove any debris before weighing it. Some cereals and grains should be rinsed before cooking. Others must be dry so that they can be added gradually to the cooking liquid.

Water, stock, or broth may be used as the cooking liquid, depending on the grain, the dish, and the menu. Cereals and grain meals are generally cooked in just as much liquid as they can absorb; each type of cereal or meal will absorb a different amount of liquid. (Refer to package or recipe directions for details.)

Salt is generally added to the cooking water, and sometimes spices or herbs are added as well. Taste and adjust the seasoning at the end of the cooking time. Grains tend to need considerable salt; otherwise they taste flat.

The pots for cooking the cereal or meal can be small or large, depending on the amount, but, in general, they should be heavy bottomed. A colander or strainer will be necessary if draining is required. Have holding and serving pieces on hand.

FOR 10 PORTIONS OF CEREALS OR MEALS, FOLLOW THIS FORMULA.	MAIN INGREDIENT OPTIONS INCLUDE:	COOKING LIQUID OPTIONS INCLUDE:	SEASONING AND FLAVORING OPTIONS INCLUDE:
	1 pound/450 grams cereal or cracked or flaked grain	*stock or broth*	*salt and pepper*
		water	*bouquet garni or sachet*
	1 pound/450 grams grain meal	*milk*	*aromatic vegetables, such as onions or garlic*
		a combination of liquids	*(or, for sweetened preparations, add sugar, honey, or other sweeteners)*

1. Depending on the grain, bring the liquid to a full boil and add the cereal or meal in a thin stream, stirring constantly or combine the cereal and liquid and bring to a boil. Salt and other seasonings may be added to the liquid as it comes to a boil, along with any other desired seasonings and aromatics.

2. Reduce the heat to establish a simmer and cook, stirring as necessary, until done.

Most cereals should be stirred occasionally as they cook to prevent scorching. Drag the spoon across the bottom of the pot and into the corners to release the cereal or meal as it cooks. The mixture will thicken noticeably while cooking. Some meals or cereals may become stiff enough to pull away from the sides of the pot and are relatively heavy in texture. Others remain fluid enough to pour easily.

3. Evaluate the quality of the finished cooked meal or cereal.

Polenta, porridges, and puddings made from grain meals will be thick, with a coarse to smooth consistency, depending on the cereal.

ABOVE *For better control, use a container to pour the measured meal or cereal into the liquid. Stirring helps prevent the grain from clumping together; this is especially important for meals, such as this polenta made from coarse cornmeal.*

ABOVE *Properly cooked grain meals should be liquid enough to pour when they are still warm and should have a relatively smooth, creamy texture.*

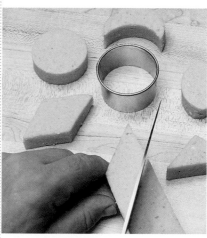

TOP *Polenta is often cooled to serve later. Line a sheet pan with plastic wrap, then spread the hot polenta into an even layer to help it cool more quickly.*

BOTTOM *Cooled cooked meals and cereals such as this polenta can be cut into a variety of shapes, then sautéed, grilled, baked, or pan fried before they are served.*

2½ qt / 2.5 L water

salt, as needed

1 lb / 450 g coarse yellow cornmeal

2 oz / 60 g butter

pepper, as needed

BASIC POLENTA

1 Bring the water to a boil and season with salt.

2 Add the cornmeal in a stream, stirring constantly until it has been all added. Simmer, stirring often, until done, about 45 minutes. When done, the polenta will pull away from the sides of the pot.

3 Remove the pot from the heat and blend in the butter. Adjust the seasoning with salt and pepper.

4 Serve at once as soft polenta. Or pour the polenta onto a greased or plastic wrap–lined half-sheet pan and refrigerate until cool enough to cut into shapes. Finish by sautéing, pan frying, grilling, or baking.

MAKES 10 PORTIONS

PILAF

Originally from the Middle East, pilaf (also called pilau*) is a grain dish in which the grain — usually rice—is first heated in a pan, either dry or in fat, and then combined with a hot liquid and cooked, covered, over direct heat or in the oven.*

Pilafs may be simple dishes, composed of only the grain and cooking liquid, or they may be quite substantial and include a wide range of additional ingredients, such as meats or shellfish, vegetables, nuts, or dried fruits. In pilaf the grains remain separate and take on a nutty flavor from the initial sautéing of the grain. The grain has a somewhat firmer texture than if it were prepared by boiling.

RICE IS THE GRAIN most frequently used to prepare a pilaf, though other grains, such as bulgur or barley, can also be used. Sort and, if necessary, rinse and air-dry the grain by spreading it out in a thin layer on a sheet pan.

A neutral-flavored vegetable oil is most often used to sweat the aromatics and sauté the grain, but a cooking fat that will contribute a flavor of its own, such as butter or rendered goose fat, may also be used.

Stock is generally the preferred cooking liquid. Bring the liquid to a boil in a separate pot before adding it to the grain to help shorten the cooking time. To impart a particular flavor and/or color, substitute vegetable or fruit juice or a vegetable coulis for up to half of the liquid. If the juice is acidic (tomato juice, for instance), the cooking time may need to be increased by as much as 15 to 20 minutes.

A member of the onion family, such as finely diced or minced onions, shallots, scallions, or leeks, is usually required for a pilaf. In addition to onions, bay leaf and thyme are commonly used for flavor. Other herbs and spices may also be added. Additional vegetables may be added to sweat along with the onion. Other ingredients, including seafood, meat, vegetables, and nuts, are often added. (Refer to recipes for details.)

A heavy-gauge pot of the appropriate size with a lid is required to allow steaming and to prevent scorching. Holding and serving pieces are also needed.

FOR 10 PORTIONS OF PILAF, FOLLOW THIS FORMULA.	MAIN INGREDIENT OPTIONS INCLUDE:	COOKING LIQUID OPTIONS INCLUDE:	SEASONING AND FLAVORING OPTIONS INCLUDE:
	14 ounces/400 grams rice, quinoa, or similar whole grains	*1¾ to 2 pints/840 to 960 milliliters stock, broth, or water for rice, quinoa, or similar whole grains*	*salt and pepper*
	12 ounces/340 grams orzo or similar small pasta shapes		*bay leaf, thyme, or other herbs*
	9 to 10 ounces/255 to 285 grams barley or lentils	*1 to 1¼ quarts/1 to 1.2 liters stock, broth, or water for orzo or similar small pasta shapes*	*onions or other aromatic vegetables*
		1¼ to 1½ quarts/1.2 to 1.4 liters stock, broth or water for barley or lentils	

1. Sweat the aromatic vegetables in fat or oil until softened. Add the grains and sauté, stirring frequently, until they are well coated with fat. Heating the grain in hot fat or oil begins to gelatinize the starches. This encourages the grains to remain separate after they are cooked. It also encourages the grain to pick up the flavor of the aromatics.

2. Heat the liquid, add it to the grain, and bring to a simmer. Cover the pot and complete the cooking in a moderate oven or over low heat on the stovetop.
Heating the liquid before adding it speeds up the cooking process. Stir the grain once or twice as it comes up to the simmer to prevent it from sticking to the pot bottom. Add any flavoring ingredients at this point.

When done, remove from the heat and let the pilaf rest, covered, for 5 minutes. The pilaf may cook either in the oven or on stovetop, with no significant difference in quality. Letting the pilaf rest allows it to absorb the remaining liquid and steam. Uncover and use a fork to fluff the grains and release the steam. Adjust the seasoning.

3. Evaluate the quality of the finished pilaf.
Test a few grains by biting into them. They should be tender but with a noticeable texture, not soft and mushy. In addition, the individual grains should separate easily. Pilafs that have been overcooked have a pasty flavor; the individual grains may be mushy or soggy and may clump together. Grains that have been undercooked or cooked in too little liquid are overly crunchy.

TOP *Be sure to allow the onions to cook until tender and translucent. Otherwise, their flavor might not be as sweet and aromatic as desired.*

BOTTOM *Heating the grain is sometimes referred to as parching.*

ABOVE *Bring the cooking liquid to a simmer over direct heat before adding it. Thyme sprigs, bay leaves, or other aromatics can be added for more flavor. Cover the pot and place it in the oven or leave it on the stovetop.*

ABOVE *When a pilaf is properly cooked, the grains will separate easily. There should be no liquid visible in the bottom of the pot.*

RICE PILAF

14 oz / 400 g long-grain white rice

1¹⁄₂ oz / 45 g clarified butter or vegetable oil

1 oz / 30 g minced onion

28 fl oz / 840 mL CHICKEN STOCK (page 248), hot

2 bay leaves

2 thyme sprigs

salt, as needed

pepper, as needed

1 Sort the rice and rinse in cool water if necessary or desired. Drain thoroughly.

2 Heat the butter or oil in a heavy-gauge pot over medium heat. Add the onion and sweat, stirring frequently, until translucent, about 5 to 6 minutes.

3 Add the rice and sauté, stirring frequently, until coated with butter or oil and heated through. Add the heated stock to the rice. Bring to a simmer, stirring the rice once or twice to prevent it from clumping together or sticking to the pot bottom.

4 Add the bay leaf, thyme, salt, and pepper. Cover the pot, and place it in a 350°F/175°C oven or leave it over low heat on the stovetop.

5 Cook until the grains are tender to the bite, about 15 to 20 minutes. Remove from the heat and let stand for 5 minutes. Uncover and using a fork, separate the grains and release the steam.

6 Adjust the seasoning with salt and pepper to taste and serve the pilaf on heated plates at once or keep hot for service.

MAKES 10 PORTIONS

Converted White Pilaf Substitute an equal amount of converted white rice for the long-grain white rice. Total cooking time is 28 minutes.

Long-Grain Brown Pilaf Substitute an equal amount of long-grain brown rice for the long-grain white rice. Increase the stock by 6 fl oz/180 mL. Total cooking time is 43 minutes.

Long-Grain White Rice (Carolina Rice) Pilaf Substitute an equal amount of converted white rice for the long-grain white rice. Total cooking time is 21 minutes.

White Texmati Pilaf Substitute an equal amount of white Texmati rice for the long-grain white rice. Reduce the amount of stock by 6 fl oz/180 mL. Total cooking time is 20 minutes.

Brown Texmati Pilaf Substitute an equal amount of brown Texmati rice for the long-grain white rice. Increase the amount of stock by 6 fl oz/180 mL. Total cooking time is 45 minutes.

Wild Rice Pilaf Substitute an equal amount of wild rice for the long-grain white rice. Increase the stock by 8 fl oz/240 mL. Total cooking time is 45 minutes.

Short-Grain Brown Rice Pilaf Substitute an equal amount of short-grain brown rice for the long-grain white rice. Increase the amount of stock by 8 fl oz/240 mL. Total cooking time is 45 minutes.

Wheat Berry Pilaf Substitute an equal amount of wheat berries for the long-grain white rice. Soak them overnight in cold water under refrigeration and drain before cooking. Increase the stock by 8 to 10 fl oz/240 to 300 mL. Total cooking time is 1 to 1½ hours.

Pearl Barley Pilaf Substitute an equal amount of pearl barley for the long-grain white rice. Total cooking time is 40 minutes.

Kasha Pilaf Substitute an equal amount of kasha for the long-grain white rice. Add 1 egg white to the kasha as it is sautéed in the butter or fat. Reduce the stock by 6 fl oz/180 mL. Total cooking time is 15 minutes.

Short-Grain White Rice (Valencia) Substitute an equal amount of short-grain white rice for the long-grain white rice. Increase the stock by 8 fl oz/240 mL. Total cooking time is 20 minutes.

RISOTTO

A classic risotto is a rich, creamy dish with a nearly porridge-like consistency, yet each individual grain of rice retains a distinct bite.

In the Italian dish risotto, the rice is parched as in the pilaf method, but the liquid is added and absorbed gradually while the grain is stirred almost constantly. The starch is slowly released during the cooking process, producing a creamy texture.

Grated cheese is often included, and vegetables, meats, or fish may be added to create a risotto that can be served as an appetizer or main course. Although risotto's preparation is relatively lengthy and requires constant attention, there are ways to streamline the process, making it suitable for restaurant service.

RISOTTO IS TRADITIONALLY MADE with special Italian varieties of medium-grain round rice. The best known of these is Arborio, but other varieties include Vialone Nano and Carnaroli. Other grains, including other long-grain or brown rices, barley, and wheat berries, or small pasta shapes, may also be prepared with this method, but the quality of the finished dish is not the same as a risotto made with an Italian medium-grain rice. The cooking time will be longer for brown rice and whole grains, and the amount of liquid required may be greater.

The cooking liquid most often suggested for risotto is a high-quality stock or broth. Measure the appropriate quantity of stock or broth and bring it to a simmer before starting to cook. Wine may replace a portion of the stock or broth in some formulas. The liquid should be brought to a simmer separately and seasoned if necessary. Simmering the stock first shortens the risotto's cooking time somewhat and provides an opportunity to add ingredients to infuse the broth with flavor and color. Opinions differ regarding whether the wine should be added early in cooking time or nearer the end. Some chefs prefer to combine the stock and wine and bring them to a simmer together to cook away the harsh flavor of raw wine and improve the dish's taste.

A member of the onion family, such as finely minced leeks, shallots, or onions, is usually included in a risotto. Other aromatic vegetables, including mushrooms, fennel, carrots, or celery, may be added to some dishes. They should be finely cut or sliced thin to release their flavors fully. Spices, such as saffron and fresh herbs, may also be added. Consult recipes for specific guidance.

Butter contributes a sweet, rich flavor to a risotto. Other fats and oils, especially olive oil, may also be used. Cheese, usually Parmesan or Romano, should be added as close to service time as possible to assure the best flavor. Meat, fish, poultry, or vegetables may be included. (Refer to specific recipes for more detail.)

A wide, heavy-gauge saucepan is best for making risotto. A spoon, preferably wooden, is needed for stirring, and if the risotto is to be cooled and finished later, a sheet pan or similar wide shallow pan is needed.

FOR 10 PORTIONS OF RISOTTO, FOLLOW THIS FORMULA.

MAIN INGREDIENT OPTIONS INCLUDE:

14 ounces/400 grams Arborio or other white or brown rices

12 ounces/340 grams orzo or similar small pasta shapes

12 ounces/340 grams fideo or similar thin noodles

COOKING LIQUID OPTIONS INCLUDE:

1¾ to 2 quarts/1.75 to 2 liters stock, broth, or water for white rices

1 to 1¼ quarts/1 to 1.2 liters stock, broth, or water for brown rices or pastas

(Optional: replace up to one-fourth of the cooking liquid with dry white wine)

SEASONING AND FLAVORING OPTIONS INCLUDE:

salt and pepper

bay leaf, thyme, or other herbs

onions or other aromatic vegetables

grated cheese

1. Sweat the aromatic ingredients in fat until translucent. Add the rice and parch it until well coated. Onions or other aromatic vegetables should be given sufficient time to sweat in the hot butter or oil to fully develop their flavor. In some risottos, a cooked onion purée is used instead of chopped onions. Spices, either left whole or ground, may be added at this point as well. (If using saffron, infuse it in the cooking liquid for best flavor and color.) Cooking the rice in the fat produces the correct finished texture in the risotto.

2. Add the simmering liquid in parts. Add about one-fourth to one-third of the cooking liquid to the parched rice and stir constantly over medium heat until the liquid is absorbed. Continue adding portions of the cooking liquid in this manner.

3. Stir constantly as the rice cooks. Stir until the entire amount of liquid has been incorporated, and the rice is fully cooked and the risotto is creamy and thick. The average cooking time for risotto prepared with Arborio rice is 20 minutes.

Although the best risotto is prepared from start to finish just prior to service, it is possible to partially cook the dish in advance.

ABOVE *Generally no more than one-third of the cooking liquid is added at any time.*

TOP *The dish is stirred constantly as the rice absorbs the liquid to develop the natural creaminess of the grains and to avoid scorching.*

BOTTOM *After the rice absorbs one-third of the liquid, the grains appear quite firm and distinct, and no real creaminess is in evidence yet.*

To do this, remove the risotto from the heat after the rice has absorbed two-thirds to three-fourths of the total amount of cooking liquid. Pour the risotto onto a sheet pan and spread it in an even layer. Cool it rapidly under refrigeration. To finish risotto held in this manner, return the risotto to a pot and heat it over medium heat. Add the final third or fourth of the cooking liquid and finish cooking until the risotto is creamy and the rice if fully cooked.

4. Add the finishing ingredients.
Some garnish ingredients may be added early in the cooking process so that they fully cook along with the risotto. Others may be cooked separately and added at the end. (Refer to specific recipes for details.) Add fresh herbs, if desired, adjust the seasoning to taste, and serve the risotto on heated plates.

5. Evaluate the quality of the finished risotto.
Italians describe a properly cooked risotto as *all'onda* (wavelike), meaning that the risotto has a creamy, almost porridge-like consistency but individual grains are slightly firm with a discernable texture. Risotto that has been cooked over high heat or too rapidly will not develop the proper consistency nor will it be adequately cooked.

ABOVE *After the rice absorbs the final portion of liquid, the grains appear more tender with a creamy, saucelike consistency.*

ABOVE *Stir butter and grated cheese or other finishing ingredients into the risotto vigorously over low heat until well blended and very hot. Cheese can become stringy if allowed to cook for too long at high temperatures.*

ABOVE *Risotto should be served as soon as possible after it is cooked for the best quality.*

2 oz / 60 g minced onions

2 oz / 60 g butter

14 oz / 420 g Arborio rice

1³/₄ qt / 1.6 L CHICKEN STOCK (page 248), hot

salt, to taste

pepper, to taste

RISOTTO

1 Sweat the onions in the butter until softened and translucent, about 6 to 8 minutes.

2 Add the rice and mix thoroughly with the butter. Cook, stirring, until a toasted aroma rises, about 1 minute.

3 Add one third of the stock to the rice, and cook, stirring constantly, until the rice has absorbed the stock. Repeat, adding the remaining stock in 2 more portions, allowing each to be absorbed before adding the next. Cook the risotto until the rice is tender but with a pleasing texture and most of the liquid is absorbed. The dish should be creamy. Season the risotto with salt and pepper to taste and serve at once.

Parmesan Risotto Prepare the risotto, replacing up to one quarter of the stock with a dry white wine. Add the wine to the stock as it heats to a simmer for the best flavor. Finish the risotto by adding 2 to 3 oz/60 to 85 g grated Parmesan and 1½ oz/45 g butter. Stir the risotto until evenly blended.

Wild Mushroom Risotto Soak 3 oz/85 g dried wild mushrooms in 8 fl oz/240 mL warm water for 30 minutes to 1 hour; drain the mushrooms and add along with the onions. Strain the soaking liquid through a paper filter to remove any sediment, measure it, and use it to replace an equal amount of the stock for the risotto.

Risi e Bisi Prepare the risotto and fold in 10 oz/170 g of steamed or boiled fresh green peas.

RECIPES

BASIC BOILED RICE

makes 10 portions

3 qt/2.75 L water, or as needed
salt, as needed
14 oz/400 g long-grain white rice

1 Bring the water to a rolling boil. Add salt to taste. There should be enough water to cover the rice.

2 Add the rice in a thin stream, stirring it with a fork to prevent the grains from clumping as they are added. When the water returns to a boil, reduce the heat to a simmer.

3 Simmer the rice until tender, about 15 minutes. Drain immediately in a colander and set the colander in the pot. Return to the heat to steam the rice dry for 5 minutes. Fluff with a fork and serve the rice on heated plates, or hold hot for service.

COCONUT RICE

makes 10 portions

1¹/₂ fl oz/45 mL butter or vegetable oil
14 oz/400 g long-grain white rice
1 pint/480 mL water
12 fl oz/360 mL unsweetened coconut milk
salt, as needed
pepper, as needed

1 Heat the butter or oil in a heavy-gauge pot over medium heat. Add the rice and sauté, stirring frequently, until coated with butter or oil and heated through.

2 Add the water and coconut milk to the rice. Bring to a simmer, stirring the rice once or twice to prevent it from clumping together or sticking to the pot bottom. Cover the pot, and place it in a 350°F/175°C oven or leave it over low heat on the stovetop.

3 Cook until the grains are tender to the bite, about 12 to 14 minutes. Remove from the heat and let stand for 5 minutes. Uncover and, using a fork, separate the grains and release the steam.

4 Adjust the seasoning with salt and pepper to taste and serve the pilaf on heated plates at once or keep hot for service.

BROWN RICE PILAF WITH PECANS AND SCALLIONS

makes 10 portions

14 oz/400 g brown rice
1¹/₂ oz/45 g butter or oil
2 oz/60 g minced onions
2¹/₂ pt/1.25 L CHICKEN STOCK (page 248), seasoned and hot
bouquet garni, containing 1 piece celery or leek, 2 to 3 thyme sprigs, 4 to 5 parsley stems, 1 garlic clove, 1 bay leaf
salt, as needed
pepper, as needed
2 oz/60 g chopped toasted pecans
2 oz/60 g sliced scallions

1 Sort the rice and rinse in cool water if necessary or desired. Drain thoroughly.

2 Heat the butter or oil in a heavy-gauge pot over medium heat. Add the onion and sweat, stirring frequently, until translucent, about 5 to 6 minutes.

3 Add the rice and sauté, stirring frequently, until coated with butter or oil and heated through. Add the heated stock to the rice. Bring to a simmer, stirring the rice once or twice to prevent it from clumping together or sticking to the pot bottom.

4 Add the bouquet garni, salt, and pepper. Cover the pot, and place it in a 350°F/175°C oven or leave it over low heat on the stovetop.

5 Cook until the grains are tender to the bite, about 45 minutes to 1 hour. Remove from the heat and let stand for 5 minutes. Uncover and using a fork, fold in the pecans and scallions while separating the grains and releasing the steam.

6 Adjust the seasoning with salt and pepper to taste and serve the pilaf on heated plates at once, or keep hot for service.

see photograph on page 694

RICE CROQUETTES

makes 10 portions

1 pt/480 mL CHICKEN STOCK (page 248) or VEGETABLE STOCK (page 254)

pinch of saffron threads, crushed

salt, as needed

pepper, as needed

½ oz/15 g butter or oil

1 oz/30 g chopped onions

6 oz/170 g short or medium grain white rice

HEAVY BÉCHAMEL (recipe follows)

3 oz/85 g grated Parmesan

3 egg yolks

dry bread crumbs for breading, as needed

cornmeal for breading, as needed

egg wash for breading, as needed

vegetable oil for frying, as needed

1 Simmer the stock and saffron over medium heat for 3 to 4 minutes. Season the stock with salt and pepper. Keep hot.

2 Heat the butter or oil in a heavy-gauge pot over medium heat. Add the rice and sauté, stirring frequently, until coated with butter or oil and heated through. Add the saffron-infused stock to the rice. Bring to a simmer, stirring the rice once or twice to prevent it from clumping together or sticking to the pot bottom. Cover the pot, and place it in a 350°F/175°C oven or leave it over low heat on the stovetop.

3 Cook until the grains are tender to the bite, about 12 to 14 minutes. Remove from the heat and let stand for 5 minutes. Uncover and, using a fork, separate the grains and release the steam. Adjust the seasoning with salt and pepper to taste.

4 Blend the rice with the béchamel, Parmesan, and egg yolks. Spread the mixture in an even layer on a buttered, parchment-lined sheet pan. Place a sheet of plastic wrap over the mixture and refrigerate for several hours or overnight to chill and firm the rice mixture.

5 Combine the bread crumbs and cornmeal (3 parts bread crumbs to 1 part cornmeal). Cut the rice into desired shapes and dip first into egg wash and then into the bread crumb mixture.

6 Heat the oil in a deep fryer to 350°F/175°C and deep fry the croquettes until golden, about 5 to 6 minutes. Drain briefly on absorbent paper toweling and serve at once on heated plates.

HEAVY BÉCHAMEL

makes 10 fluid ounces/300 milliliters

2 oz/60 g butter

2 oz/60 g flour

12 fl oz/360 mL milk

salt, as needed

pepper, as needed

1 Heat the butter over medium heat. Add the flour, and cook the mixture, stirring frequently, to make a blond roux, about 8 to 10 minutes.

2 Add the milk and stir with a whip to remove any lumps and bring up to a boil. Add salt and pepper and simmer the béchamel over low heat, stirring frequently and skimming as necessary, until the sauce is very thick and has no floury taste, about 30 minutes. Remove from the heat, adjust the seasoning if necessary, and strain through a fine wire-mesh sieve. Reserve or rapidly cool and store for later use.

POLENTA WITH PARMESAN CHEESE

makes 20 portions

1 oz/30 g minced shallots

2 tbsp/30 mL minced garlic

8 oz/225 g butter

3 qt/3 L CHICKEN STOCK (page 248)

salt, as needed

24 oz/680 g coarse yellow cornmeal

3 egg yolks

2 oz/60 g grated Parmesan

pepper, as needed

1 Sauté the shallots and garlic in 2 oz/60 g of the butter until translucent. Add the stock and bring to a boil. Season with salt.

2 Add the cornmeal in a stream, stirring constantly until it has all been added. Simmer, stirring often, until done, about 45 minutes. When done, the polenta will pull away from the sides of the pot.

3 Remove the pot from the heat and blend in the remaining butter, egg yolks, and cheese.

4 Serve at once as soft polenta. Or pour the polenta onto a greased half-sheet pan and refrigerate until cool enough to cut into shapes. Finish by sautéing, pan frying, grilling, or baking.

CILANTRO-LIME RICE

makes 10 portions

1 fl oz/30 mL vegetable oil

8 oz/225 g minced onions

1 tbsp/15 mL minced garlic

14 oz/400 g converted long-grain white rice

28 fl oz/840 mL CHICKEN STOCK (page 248), hot

1 fl oz/30 mL lime juice

2 tsp/10 mL grated lime zest

1/2 oz/15 g minced cilantro

salt, as needed

pepper, as needed

1 Heat the oil in a heavy-gauge pot over medium heat. Add the onion and sweat, stirring frequently, until translucent, about 5 to 6 minutes. Add the garlic and continue to sauté another minute.

2 Add the rice and sauté, stirring frequently, until coated with oil and heated through. Add the heated stock to the rice. Bring to a simmer, stirring the rice once or twice to prevent it from clumping together or sticking to the pot bottom. Cover the pot, and place it in a 350°F/175°C oven or leave it over low heat on the stovetop.

3 Cook until the grains are tender to the bite, about 12 to 14 minutes. Remove from the heat and let stand for 5 minutes. Uncover and, using a fork, separate the grains and release the steam. Stir in the lime juice, lime zest, and cilantro.

4 Adjust the seasoning with salt and pepper to taste and serve the pilaf on heated plates at once or keep hot for service.

NOTES

Adding lime juice or zest to the rice before it is fully cooked will interfere with proper cooking. The grain may never become fully tender.

HOPPIN' JOHN

makes 10 portions

8 oz/225 g dried black-eyed peas

salt, as needed

4 oz/115 g large-dice bacon

4 oz/115 g small-dice onions

4 oz/115 g small-dice peppers

1/4 oz/7 g minced garlic

1/2 tsp/3 mL crushed red pepper

8 oz/225 g long-grain rice

1 qt/1 L CHICKEN STOCK (page 248)

1 bay leaf

1 thyme sprig

pepper, as needed

1 Sort the black-eyed peas and rinse well with cold water. Simmer in enough water to cover for 30 to 35 minutes, or until they are barely tender to the bite. Add salt to taste about 10 minutes before the end of cooking time. Drain the black-eyed peas and reserve.

2 Render the bacon in a pot. Remove the crisped bacon with a slotted spoon and reserve. Add the onion and pepper and sweat, stirring frequently, until translucent, about 5 to 6 minutes. Add the garlic and crushed red pepper and continue to sauté another minute.

3 Add the rice and sauté, stirring frequently, until coated with oil and heated through. Add the heated stock and drained black-eyed peas to the rice. Bring to a simmer, stirring once or twice to prevent the rice from clumping together or sticking to the pot bottom. Add the bay leaf and thyme. Cover the pot, and place it in a 350°F/175°C oven or leave it over low heat on the stovetop.

4 Cook until the rice and black-eyed peas are tender to the bite, about 12 to 14 minutes. Remove from the heat and let stand for 5 minutes. Uncover and, using a fork, separate the grains and release the steam. Stir in reserved bacon.

5 Adjust the seasoning with salt and pepper to taste and serve the hoppin' John on heated plates at once or keep hot for service.

KASHA WITH SPICY MAPLE PECANS

makes 10 portions

2 egg whites, lightly beaten

12 oz/340 g kasha

1½ pt/720 mL CHICKEN STOCK (page 248) or VEGETABLE STOCK (page 254)

salt, as needed

1½ oz/45 g butter

3 oz/85 g toasted pecans, chopped

2 oz/60 g maple syrup

cayenne pepper, as needed

1 Combine the egg whites and kasha in a saucepan and cook over low heat, stirring constantly, for 2 minutes.

2 Add the stock, salt, and butter to the kasha and bring to a boil over high heat. Reduce the heat to low and simmer the kasha, covered, for about 15 minutes.

3 Remove the kasha from the heat and let it steam for about 5 minutes. Uncover and fluff the kasha by lifting it gently with 2 forks to remove any lumps.

4 While the kasha steams, place the pecans, maple syrup, and cayenne in a small skillet. Heat over low heat until the pecans are well coated and the maple syrup has reduced to a very thick consistency.

5 Scatter the spiced pecans over the kasha and serve.

COUSCOUS

makes 10 portions

1 lb/450 g couscous

salt, as needed

olive oil, as needed (optional)

1 Soak the couscous in enough warm water to cover for about 5 minutes.

2 Drain the couscous in a colander or the top of a couscousière and set it over a pot of simmering water or stew. Cover the pot and let the couscous steam for 3 to 4 minutes. Uncover the pot and stir the couscous with a fork to break up any lumps. Return the colander to the pot, cover, and continue to steam for 5 minutes more.

3 Fluff the couscous with a fork, and season it with salt to taste. Drizzle a small amount of olive oil over the couscous, if desired.

QUINOA PILAF WITH RED AND YELLOW PEPPERS

makes 10 portions

12 oz/340 g quinoa

1 fl oz/30 mL butter or vegetable oil

1 oz/30 g minced shallots

1 tbsp/15 mL finely minced garlic

1½ pt/720 mL CHICKEN STOCK (page 248)

1 bay leaf

1 thyme sprig

salt, as needed

3 oz/85 g diced roasted red pepper

3 oz/85 g diced roasted yellow pepper

pepper, as needed

1 Rinse the quinoa in cool water to remove the grain's bitter coating and let it drain.

2 Heat the butter or oil in a heavy-gauge pot over medium heat. Add the shallots and garlic and sweat over medium heat until translucent, about 2 minutes. Add the quinoa and sauté, stirring frequently, until coated with butter or oil and heated through. Add the stock to the quinoa. Bring to a simmer, stirring once or twice to prevent the quinoa from clumping together or sticking to the pot bottom. Add the bay leaf, thyme, and salt. Cover the pot, and place it in a 350°F/175°C oven or leave it over low heat on the stovetop.

3 Cook until the grains are tender to the bite, about 15 minutes. Remove from the heat and let stand for 5 minutes. Uncover and, using a fork, separate the grains and release the steam. Fold in the roasted peppers. Adjust the seasoning with salt and pepper to taste. Serve on heated plates or hold hot for service.

Brown Rice Pilaf with Pecans and Scallions

Saffron Risotto with Shrimp

Wild Rice Pilaf

Stewed Chickpeas with Tomato, Zucchini, and Cilantro

RISOTTO WITH ASPARAGUS TIPS

makes 10 portions

2¼ oz/65 g asparagus tips

2½ pints/1.25 L CHICKEN STOCK (page 248) or VEGETABLE STOCK (page 254), hot

salt, as needed

2 oz/60 g minced onions

2 oz/60 g clarified butter

14 oz/420 g Arborio rice

1½ oz/45 g minced parsley

4 oz/115 g whole butter, room temperature

4 oz/115 g grated Parmesan

pepper, as needed

1 Cook the asparagus tips in boiling salted water until tender and bright green, about 3 to 4 minutes. Drain and rinse in cold water to stop the cooking. Drain again and reserve.

2 Bring the stock to a simmer and season with salt.

3 Sweat the onions in the butter until softened and translucent, about 6 to 8 minutes.

4 Add the rice and mix thoroughly with the butter. Cook, stirring, until a toasted aroma rises, about 1 minute.

5 Add one third of the stock to the rice, and cook, stirring constantly, until the rice has absorbed the stock. Repeat with another third of the stock. Add the remaining stock and the asparagus tips and finish risotto until the rice is tender but with a pleasing texture and most of the liquid is absorbed.

6 Remove from the heat and stir in the parsley, whole butter, and Parmesan. Season the risotto with salt and pepper to taste and serve at once on heated plates.

RISOTTO WITH MUSSELS

makes 10 portions

5 lb/2.25 kg mussels

2½ pints/1.25 L FISH STOCK (page 253), hot

salt, as needed

pepper, as needed

2 oz/60 g minced onions

2 oz/60 g clarified butter

14 oz/420 g Arborio rice

1½ oz/45 g minced parsley

4 oz/115 g butter

1 Scrub and debeard the mussels. Steam them in a small amount of salted water in a covered pot until the shells open. Remove the mussel meat from the shells and reserve. Strain the cooking liquid.

2 Bring the stock and the cooking liquid from the mussels to a simmer and season with salt and pepper.

3 Sweat the onions in the butter until softened and translucent, about 6 to 8 minutes.

4 Add the rice and mix thoroughly with the butter. Cook, stirring, until a toasted aroma rises, about 1 minute.

5 Add one third of the stock to the rice, and cook, stirring constantly, until the rice has absorbed the stock. Repeat with another third of the stock. Add the remaining stock and the mussels and finish risotto until the rice is tender but with a pleasing texture and most of the liquid is absorbed.

6 Remove from the heat and stir in the parsley and whole butter. Season the risotto with salt and pepper to taste and serve at once on heated plates.

Risotto with Seafood Prepare the risotto as directed above, using 2¼ lb/1 kg combined cooked seafood, such as shrimp, mussels, crayfish, clams, or oysters.

SAFFRON RISOTTO WITH SHRIMP

makes 10 portions

2¹/₂ pt/1.25 L FISH STOCK (page 253) or CHICKEN STOCK (page 248)

pinch of saffron

salt, as needed

pepper, as needed

4 oz/115 g minced onions

3 oz/85 g clarified butter

¹/₄ oz/7 g minced garlic

14 oz/400 g Arborio rice

10 oz/285 g diced shrimp

2 bay leaves

2 tbsp/30 mL chopped parsley

2 oz/60 g whole butter, room temperature

1 Bring the stock and saffron to a simmer and season with salt and pepper.

2 Sweat the onions in the butter until softened and translucent, about 6 to 8 minutes. Add the garlic and continue to sauté until aromatic, 1 minute more.

3 Add the rice and mix thoroughly with the butter. Cook, stirring, until a toasted aroma rises, about 1 minute.

4 Add one third of the stock to the rice, and cook, stirring constantly, until the rice has absorbed the stock. Repeat with another third of the stock. Add the remaining stock and the shrimp and finish risotto until the rice is tender but with a pleasing texture and most of the liquid is absorbed and the shrimp has cooked through.

5 Remove from the heat and stir in the parsley and whole butter. Season the risotto with salt and pepper to taste and serve at once on heated plates.

see photograph on page 694

WILD RICE PILAF

makes 10 portions

¹/₂ oz/15 g butter or oil

4 oz/115 g diced onions

14 oz/400 g wild rice

2¹/₂ pt/1.25 L CHICKEN STOCK (page 248), hot

bay leaf

2 thyme sprigs

salt, as needed

pepper, as needed

1 Heat the butter or oil in a heavy-gauge pot over medium heat. Add the onions and sweat, stirring frequently, until translucent, about 5 to 6 minutes.

2 Add the rice and sauté, stirring frequently, until coated with butter or oil and heated through. Add the heated stock to the rice. Bring to a simmer, stirring the rice once or twice to prevent it from clumping together or sticking to the pot bottom.

3 Add the bay leaf, thyme, salt, and pepper. Cover the pot, and place it in a 350°F/175°C oven or leave it over low heat on the stovetop.

4 Cook until the grains are tender to the bite, about 30 to 45 minutes. Remove from the heat and let stand for 5 minutes. Uncover and, using a fork, separate the grains and release the steam.

5 Adjust the seasoning with salt and pepper to taste and serve the pilaf on heated plates at once or keep hot for service.

see photograph on page 695

MIDDLE EASTERN–STYLE CHICKPEAS

makes 10 portions

12 oz/340 g dry chickpeas

vegetable oil, as needed

6 oz/170 g chopped onion

3 qt/3 L CHICKEN STOCK (page 248), or as needed

½ oz/15 g minced garlic

SACHET FOR MIDDLE EASTERN–STYLE CHICKPEAS (recipe follows)

lemon juice, as needed

salt, as needed

pepper, as needed

1 Sort the chickpeas and rinse well with cold water. Soak using the long or short method if desired. Drain soaked chickpeas.

2 Heat the oil in a pot, add the onions and sweat until tender and translucent, about 5 to 6 minutes. Add the chickpeas and stock to cover. Bring the stock to a simmer.

3 While the chickpeas are simmering, heat the oil in a pan. Sauté the onions until they are tender and a light golden color, about 8 minutes. Add the garlic and continue to sauté another minute. After the chickpeas have simmered 3 to 3½ hours, add along with the sachet and salt to taste. Continue to simmer until the chickpeas are tender to the bite, about 1 hour more. Add lemon juice, salt, and pepper to taste.

4 The chickpeas are ready to drain and serve at this point, or they may be cooled in their cooking liquid and stored for later use.

SACHET FOR MIDDLE EASTERN–STYLE CHICKPEAS

makes 1 sachet

1½ tsp/7 mL cumin seed

1 tsp/5 mL coriander seed

½ tsp/2 mL ground ginger

½ tsp/2 mL cracked red pepper

5 cardamom pods

1 stick cinnamon

¼ tsp/1 mL mustard seed

½ tsp/1 mL cracked black peppercorns

Cut a square of cheesecloth large enough to hold the spices. Place the spices on the cheesecloth and tie into a bag with twine.

ROMAN-STYLE FAVA BEANS

makes 10 portions

12 oz/340 g dry fava beans

olive oil, as needed

4 oz/115 g diced pancetta

6 oz/170 g chopped onion

½ oz/15 g minced garlic

3 qt/3 L CHICKEN STOCK (page 248), or as needed

BOUQUET GARNI FOR ROMAN-STYLE FAVA BEANS (recipe follows)

Parmesan cheese rind (optional)

salt, as needed

red wine vinegar, as needed

1 Sort the fava beans and rinse well with cold water. Place them in a pot, cover with cold water, and bring to a boil. Remove from the heat and let them soak for 1 hour. While the beans are still warm, make a slit along the side of each bean and gently squeeze the bean from its skin. Discard the skin and cooking water.

2 Heat the oil in a pot, add the pancetta, and cook until the fat renders from the pancetta. Add onions and sweat until tender and translucent, about 5 to 6 minutes. Add the garlic and cook another minute.

3 Add the fava beans and stock to cover and bring the stock to a simmer. Add the bouquet garni, cheese rind (if using), and salt to taste. Continue to simmer until the fava beans are tender to the bite, about 35 to 45 minutes. Adjust the seasoning with vinegar, salt, and pepper.

4 The fava beans are ready to drain and serve at this point, or they may be cooled in their cooking liquid and stored for later use.

BOUQUET GARNI FOR ROMAN-STYLE FAVA BEANS

makes 1 bouquet

2 thyme sprigs

2 oregano sprigs

1 rosemary stem

½ tsp/2 mL cracked black peppercorns

2 leek leaves, 3 to 4 in/50 to 75 mm long

Sandwich the herbs and peppercorns between the leek leaves, and tie into a bundle with twine.

BLACK BEANS WITH PEPPERS AND CHORIZO

makes 10 portions

12 oz/340 g dry black beans

3 qt/2.8 L CHICKEN STOCK (page 248) or water, as needed

2 fl oz/60 mL vegetable oil

3 oz/85 g minced bacon

6 oz/170 g medium-dice onions

1/4 oz /7 g minced garlic

4 oz/115 g sliced chorizo

3 oz/85 g medium-dice red pepper

3 oz/85 g medium-dice green pepper

2 oz/60 g sliced scallions

chopped basil, as needed

chopped oregano, as needed

chopped cilantro, as needed

salt, as needed

pepper, as needed

sour cream (optional)

1   Sort black beans and rinse well with cold water. Cook the drained beans in enough stock or water to cover until tender to the bite, about 90 minutes. Set aside in their cooking liquid.

2   Heat the oil and add the bacon. Cook until the bacon is rendered. Add the onion and sauté until tender and lightly browned, about 8 minutes. Add the garlic and cook 1 minute more, stirring frequently.

3   Add the chorizo and red and green peppers and sauté, stirring frequently, until the peppers are tender, 6 to 8 minutes.

4   Drain the beans and add them with enough cooking liquid to keep them moist (the consistency should be that of a thick stew). Simmer the beans until all the flavors are developed and all the ingredients are heated through.

5   Add the scallions and herbs and adjust the seasoning with salt and pepper to taste. Serve the beans with sour cream, if desired.

BRAISED LENTILS WITH EGGPLANT AND MUSHROOMS

makes 10 portions

12 oz/340 g brown lentils

3 qt/2.8 L CHICKEN STOCK (page 248) or water, as needed

1 fl oz/30 mL olive oil

6 oz/170 g medium-dice onions

1/4 oz /7 g minced garlic

8 oz/225 g large-dice eggplant

4 oz/115 g trimmed mushrooms, sliced or quartered

1/2 tsp/3 mL ground cinnamon

1/2 tsp/3 mL ground turmeric

1/4 tsp/1 mL grated lemon zest

salt, as needed

pepper, as needed

GRATIN

4 oz/115 g fresh bread crumbs

2 oz/60 g melted butter

1   Sort the lentils and rinse well with cold water. Cook the lentils in enough water or stock to cover until tender, about 30 to 40 minutes. Drain, reserving the cooking liquid.

2   Heat the oil and add the onions. Sauté until tender and lightly browned, about 8 minutes. Add the garlic and cook 1 minute more, stirring frequently.

3   Add the eggplant, stirring to coat it evenly with oil. Add the mushrooms, cinnamon, turmeric, and lemon zest. Cook until the mushrooms begin to release their juices.

4   Add the lentils and enough cooking liquid to moisten them well. Cover the pan and place it in a 350°F/175°C oven. Braise for 15 minutes, or until the eggplant is completely tender. Adjust the seasoning with salt and pepper to taste.

5   Transfer the cooked lentils to individual gratin dishes or a baking pan. Combine the bread crumbs with the butter and place this gratin on top of the lentils. Return the pan to a hot oven and bake until a crust has developed and browned evenly. Serve directly in the gratin dishes, if used, or on heated plates, or hold hot for service.

STEWED CHICKPEAS WITH TOMATO, ZUCCHINI, AND CILANTRO

makes 10 portions

12 oz/340 g dry chickpeas

3 qt/2.8 L CHICKEN STOCK (page 248) or water, as needed

1 fl oz/30 mL olive oil

¼ oz/7 g minced garlic

6 oz/170 g small-dice zucchini

4 oz/115 g tomato concassé

1 oz/30 g chopped cilantro

salt, as needed

pepper, as needed

fresh lime juice, as needed

1 Sort the chickpeas and rinse well with cold water. Soak using the long or short method if desired. Drain soaked peas.

2 Cook the chickpeas in plenty of stock or water until they are tender, about 30 minutes. Reserve about 1 pint/480 mL of the cooking liquid. Drain in a colander, rubbing gently to remove the skins (discard the skins).

3 Heat the olive oil in a sauteuse. Add the garlic and cook until an aroma rises.

4 Add the zucchini and tomato concassé. Sauté the vegetables until the zucchini is tender and heated through, about 10 minutes.

5 Add the chickpeas to the sauteuse, along with enough cooking liquid to keep them moist. Stew until heated through. Add the cilantro and adjust the seasoning with cilantro, salt, pepper, and lime juice to taste.

see photograph on page 695

REFRIED BEANS

makes 10 portions

12 oz/340 g dry pinto beans

3 qt/3 L CHICKEN STOCK (page 248) or as needed

8 oz/225 g finely chopped onions

¼ oz/7 g minced garlic

6 oz/170 g bacon fat or lard

6 oz/170 g tomato concassé

salt, as needed

pepper, as needed

ground cumin, as needed

chili powder, as needed

5 oz/140 g grated Monterey jack

1 Cook the beans in the stock until they are very soft.

2 Sauté the onions and garlic in the bacon fat, add the tomato concassé, and cook for 2 minutes.

3 Add the cooked beans and continue to cook, mashing the beans with a spoon.

4 Season the beans to taste with salt, pepper, cumin, and chili powder. Top the beans with Monterey jack before serving and heat briefly under a salamander or broiler.

SOUTHWEST WHITE BEAN STEW

makes 10 portions

BOILED WHITE BEANS (page 675), drained

2 tsp/10 mL vegetable oil

6 oz/170 g chopped onions

4 oz/115 g small-dice peppers

2 oz/60 g diced jalapeños

1 oz/30 g minced garlic

2 fl oz/60 mL sherry wine vinegar

4 oz/115 g tomato concassé

2 tbsp/30 mL chopped cilantro

salt, as needed

pepper, as needed

1 Purée about 2 cups of the cooked beans, and combine with the remaining whole beans.

2 Heat the oil and add the onions, peppers, jalapeños, and garlic. Sauté until the onions are translucent.

3 Add the beans and sauté, stirring constantly, until the beans are heated through.

4 Add the vinegar and tomato concassé and continue to sauté until very hot.

5 Add the cilantro and adjust the seasoning with salt and pepper just before serving.

The immense popularity of pastas and dumplings is not at all surprising. Nutritious and highly versatile, these foods are an important element of most cuisines. They are based on ingredients that are inexpensive and easy to store: flours, meals, and eggs. They adapt well to a number of uses and can be found on contemporary menus as appetizers, entrées, salads, and even desserts.

COOKING PASTA AND DUMPLINGS

MAKING FRESH PASTA, NOODLES, AND DUMPLINGS

The formula for fresh pasta may be thought of as the "base" recipe to produce a stiff dough that can be endlessly varied to produce myriad shapes, flavors, and colors.

Dried and fresh noodles are both included in the general category of pasta. Pasta may be prepared fresh on the premises or purchased either fresh or dried. There are advantages to both fresh and dried pastas. Fresh pasta gives the chef freedom to create dishes with special flavors, colors, or shapes, or fillings, but it has a limited shelf life. Dried pasta can be stored almost indefinitely.

Changing the ratio of flour to liquid, or introducing other ingredients into a basic pasta formula, produces doughs and batters that are handled and cooked differently from the base recipe to produce dumplings. For example, the amount of liquid can be increased to create a soft batter for spätzle. This batter is cut off a spätzle board or dropped through a sieve or spätzle maker into simmering liquid. Adding a leavener to the basic pasta formula produces a soft batter that can be used for larger dumplings with a bread-like texture that are simmered in a stew or other liquid.

Although the term "dumpling" may mean something very specific to an individual or a particular ethnic group, it actually is a very broad category. Some dumplings are based on doughs and batters, others on ingredients ranging from bread to puréed potatoes. The popular Chinese dim sum, including steamed yeast doughs and fried egg rolls, is yet another category. Dumplings may be cooked in a variety of ways, according to type. They may be simmered in liquid, steamed, poached, baked, pan-fried, or deep-fried. A variety of ingredients can be used, depending on what sort of dumpling is being prepared. See the recipes included in this chapter for specific instructions.

FOR 10 PORTIONS OF FRESH PASTA, FOLLOW THIS FORMULA.	MAIN INGREDIENT:	TENDERIZING AND ENRICHING OPTIONS INCLUDE:	INGREDIENTS TO ADJUST SEASONING AND CONSISTENCY:
	1 pound / 450 grams all-purpose flour or mixtures of flours (equal to 1 pound)	*4 whole eggs* *1 fluid ounce / 30 milliliters oil (optional)*	*salt* *water* *other flavoring or garnishing ingredients as desired*

SELECT AND PREPARE THE INGREDIENTS AND EQUIPMENT

BECAUSE FLOUR PROVIDES the structure of pasta, it is important to choose one that has the necessary qualities for making the best possible dough. All-purpose flours can be used successfully for most fresh pasta. Whole-wheat flour, semolina, cornmeal, buckwheat flour, rye flour, ground legumes (chickpeas, for instance) and other special flours and meals can be used to replace a portion of the all-purpose flour, giving the pasta unique flavor, texture, and color. Experimentation is often the best way to determine how to use special flours. Refer to the recipes for guidance on flours, ratios, and substitutions.

Eggs are frequently included in fresh pasta to provide moisture, flavor, and structure. Different formulas may specify the use of either whole eggs, yolks, or whites. Because it is especially important to have the proper amount of moisture, many recipes call for water. Doughs that are too dry or too moist are difficult to roll out.

Neutral or flavored oil is often called for in pasta doughs because it helps keep the dough pliable and makes it easy to work with.

Salt is added to the dough to develop flavor. Additional ingredients, such as herbs, vegetable purées, or citrus zest, may be added to fresh pasta dough to change its color, flavor, or texture. If these added flavoring or coloring ingredients contain high moisture levels, it is necessary to adjust the basic formula, by either using additional flour or less water. Vegetable purées used for flavor or color are often dried by sautéing in order to concentrate their flavors.

Equipment needs for fresh pasta are very basic, though a few special pieces of equipment can make the job even simpler. At the very least, you will need your hands, a rolling pin, and a knife. Or use an electric mixer with a dough hook or a food processor to mix the dough, and a pasta rolling machine to roll it out. Cutting attachments that result in uniform cuts of pasta are available for the rolling machines.

1. Mix the ingredients to form a dough.

Pasta dough can be mixed by hand or by machine. For small batches, it may be just as efficient to mix the dough manually. Large batches, on the other hand, can be made much more easily with a food processor or electric mixer.

To mix the dough by hand, combine the flour and salt in a bowl and make a well in the center. Place the eggs, flavoring ingredients, and oil (if using) in the well. Working as rapidly as possible, gradually incorporate the flour into the liquid ingredients until a loose mass forms.

To mix in a food processor, place all the ingredients in the bowl of a food processor fitted with a steel blade. Process until blended.

The dough should look like a coarse meal that will cohere when pressed into a ball. Do not overprocess.

To mix in an electric mixer, place all the ingredients in the bowl of a mixer fitted with a dough hook. Mix at medium speed until the dough forms a smooth ball that pulls cleanly away from the bowl's sides.

As the dough is mixed, adjust the consistency with additional flour or water, to compensate for the variations in ingredients, humidity in the kitchen, or the addition of optional flavoring ingredients. For example, an herb purée, even if squeezed dry, will still add some additional moisture to the formula, so extra flour may be required. On very dry days, it may be necessary to add a few drops of water to reach the desired consistency.

2. Knead until the dough is properly developed. Let the dough rest before rolling and cutting.

Once mixed by hand, processor, or mixer, the dough should be turned out onto a floured work surface and kneaded until the texture becomes smooth and elastic. Gather and smooth the kneaded dough into a ball, cover, and let the dough relax at room temperature for at least 1 hour. If it is not sufficiently relaxed, it will be difficult to roll into thin sheets. This resting phase is particularly important if the dough is to be rolled by hand.

After resting, the fresh pasta dough is rolled into sheets.

ABOVE *Add water a few drops at a time to adjust consistency.*

ABOVE *Mixing dough by hand.*

ABOVE *Properly kneaded dough is uniform in texture.*

3. Roll the pasta dough into thin sheets and cut into the desired shapes. Hold properly if it is not to be cooked immediately.

Pasta and egg noodle doughs can be rolled and cut by hand or using a pasta machine. To roll by hand, flatten a piece of dough about the size of an orange on a flour-dusted work surface. Using a rolling pin, work from the center of the dough to the edges with a back-and-forth motion to roll and stretch the dough, turning it occasionally and dusting it with flour, to the desired thickness. Once rolled into sheets the pasta can be cut with a knife into thin strips for flat or ribbon-style pastas such as fettucine or linguine, or stamped with cutters into squares or circles to make filled pastas such as ravioli.

To roll by machine, see sidebar at right.

Fresh pasta and noodles can be held under refrigeration for up to 2 days. If the pasta is cut in long strands, sprinkle it with cornmeal, semolina, or rice flour to keep the strands from sticking together. Hold the pasta on trays lined with plastic, and cover it with plastic as well. Filled pastas should be held on lined sheet trays, arranged so that they are not touching.

If the pasta is to be stored for more than 2 days, roll it into loose nests and arrange on parchment-lined sheet trays. Set the trays in a warm, dry place for several days, until the pasta has hardened and dried. Once dried, pasta may be held, well wrapped, in a cool, dry place the same way as commercial dried pastas. Fresh pasta, especially filled pastas such as tortellini and ravioli, may also be frozen successfully.

4. Evaluate the quality of the finished fresh pasta dough.

In general, pasta dough should be smooth, fairly elastic, and just slightly moist to the touch. If the dough is either tacky (from excess moisture) or crumbly (too dry), it will be difficult to roll out properly. Experience is the best guide for determining when the proper consistency has been reached.

Depending on the finished product for which the fresh pasta is to be used, different characteristics are desirable. For example, filled pasta may require a dough that is slightly moister than that for flat pasta, such as fettuccine and linguine, so that the dough can adhere to itself when filled. Otherwise, some of the filling may escape from the pasta as it simmers.

ROLLING AND CUTTING FRESH PASTA BY MACHINE

Different machines have different methods of operation. These directions are for making pasta sheets with the common two-roller hand-operated machine. (Tube pastas, such as macaroni or ziti, are made by forcing the dough through a special die in an extrusion pasta maker.)

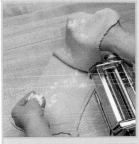

1. (TOP LEFT) *Cut off a piece of dough (the amount will vary, depending on the width of the machine) and flatten it; cover the rest. Set the rollers to the widest opening and begin to guide the dough through the machine, lightly flouring the dough as necessary to prevent sticking, to form a long, wide strip.*

2. (BOTTOM LEFT) *Fold the strip into thirds, like a letter, and run it through the rollers again. Repeat this step 1 or 2 times, folding the dough into thirds each time. If necessary, dust the dough with flour to keep it from sticking to the rollers and tearing.*

3. (TOP RIGHT) *Continue to roll the pasta through the machine, setting the rollers at a narrower setting each time, until the sheet of pasta is the desired thickness. The dough should feel smooth and not at all tacky. To prevent drying, keep it covered when not working with it.*

4. (BOTTOM RIGHT) *Cut the pasta as desired, using attachments for the machine or by hand.*

1 lb / 450 g all-purpose flour, or as needed

pinch of salt

4 eggs

1 fl oz / 30 mL water, or as needed

1 fl oz / 30 mL oil (optional)

FRESH EGG PASTA

1   Combine the flour and salt in a bowl and make a well in the center. Place the eggs, water, and oil, if using, in the well. Working as rapidly as possible, gradually pull the flour into the liquid ingredients and stir until a loose mass forms. As the dough is mixed, adjust the consistency with additional flour or water. (The dough may also be mixed in a food processor or electric mixer.)

2   Turn the dough out onto a floured work surface and knead until the texture becomes smooth and elastic. Gather and smooth the kneaded dough into a ball, cover, and let the dough relax at room temperature for at least 1 hour.

3   Roll the pasta dough into thin sheets and cut into the desired shapes by hand or using a pasta machine. The pasta is ready to cook now, or it may be held under refrigeration for up to 2 days.

MAKES 1½ POUNDS/680 GRAMS

Spinach Pasta Purée 6 oz/170 g spinach leaves, squeeze dry in cheesecloth, and add to the eggs; adjust the dough with additional flour as needed.

Saffron Pasta Steep 2 to 4 tsp/10 to 20 mL pulverized saffron threads in 1 fl oz/30 mL hot water and add to the eggs; adjust with additional flour as needed.

Citrus Pasta Add 4 tsp/20 mL finely grated lemon or orange zest to the eggs. Substitute 2 tbsp/30 mL citrus juice for the water; adjust with additional flour if needed.

Curried Pasta Add 2 to 4 tsp/10 to 20 mL Curry Powder (page 353) to the flour.

Herbed Pasta Add 2 to 3 oz/60 to 85 g chopped fresh herbs to the eggs; adjust with additional flour if needed.

Black Pepper Pasta Add 2 tsp/10 mL cracked black peppercorns to the flour.

Red Pepper Pasta Sauté 6 oz/170 g puréed roasted red pepper until reduced and dry. Cool and add to the eggs; adjust with additional flour if needed.

Tomato Pasta Sauté 3 oz/85 g tomato purée until reduced and dry. Cool and add to the eggs; adjust with additional flour if needed.

Pumpkin, Carrot, or Beet Pasta Sauté 6 oz/170 g puréed cooked pumpkin, carrots, or beets until reduced and dry. Cool and add to the eggs; adjust with additional flour if needed.

COOKING PASTA AND NOODLES

Pasta and noodles, both fresh and dried, are cooked in a large amount of salted water to ensure the best flavor and an even and appealing texture.

Some pastas and noodles cook very rapidly. Others take several minutes to cook properly. If you are working with an unfamiliar shape or style of pasta, be sure to consult any instructions on the packaging.

All pasta has the best flavor and texture if it is served as soon as possible after cooking. This is especially true of fresh pasta. However, there are appropriate techniques to hold cooked dried pastas to streamline cooking during service.

SELECT AND PREPARE THE INGREDIENTS AND EQUIPMENT

DRY AND FRESH PASTA AND NOODLES should be chosen according to the menu or recipe requirements. In general, 1¹/₂ lb/680 g is enough for 10 portions served as a side dish or a first course.

Water is the most common cooking liquid, although some preparations may call for stock. Salt, typically 1 oz/30 g for every gallon of water, is added to the water as it comes to a boil.

Choose a pot that is taller than it is wide for most pasta and noodles. Filled pasta may be prepared in pots that are wider than they are tall to make it easier to remove the pasta without breaking it apart. For large amounts of pasta, special pasta cookers, which resemble deep-fryers, are available. The pasta is placed in a wire basket with a handle and dropped into boiling or simmering water until cooked, then the basket is lifted out of the water, allowing the pasta to drain. Have available colanders, strainers, and skimmers to drain the pasta, as well as special cutting and shaping tools, such as a ravioli press or round cutters.

1. Bring a large amount of water to a rolling boil.

Allow about 1 gallon of water for every pound of pasta. Add about ¾ to 1 oz/20 to 30 g of salt to the cooking water. Taste the water before adding pasta. It should be noticeably salty, but not unpleasantly so.

2. Add the pasta and stir it to separate the strands or shapes.

Add flat or extruded pasta and noodles all at once to the boiling water. Long strands should be gently submerged into the water as they soften. Stir the pasta a few times to separate the strands or shapes to prevent them from sticking together. Lower filled pastas into the water and reduce the heat to a simmer throughout cooking time to keep the shapes from breaking apart.

3. Cook the pasta until it is properly cooked and tender. Drain in a colander immediately.

Some pastas and noodles cook very rapidly. Fresh pasta may cook in less than 3 minutes; dried pasta may take up to 8 minutes or longer, depending on the size and shape. If you are working with an unfamiliar shape or style of pasta, be sure to consult any instructions on the packaging. The most accurate test for doneness is to bite into a piece or strand, as well as to break apart a strand or piece and look at the interior. As pasta cooks, it becomes translucent throughout. An opaque core or center shows that the pasta is not completely cooked.

Drain the flat or extruded pasta or noodles through a colander, shaking gently to help the cooking water drain away. Tube shapes are prone to holding water; gently stirring them with gloved hands helps to drain away as much water as possible. (Note: Reserve some of the pasta water to adjust the sauce's consistency, if desired.) Filled pastas should be lifted from the cooking water gently with a spider or slotted spoon to avoid bursting them. They may be transferred to a colander to drain or blotted briefly to remove excess water.

Fresh pasta is best served immediately. It is ready to sauce or finish and serve now. Dried pasta may be properly cooled and stored for later service, as described in step 4.

ABOVE *Be sure to add salt to the pasta water for the best-tasting finished dish.*

ABOVE *Slide the dried pasta into the boiling water, letting it fall so the strands separate.*

4. (Optional) Rapidly cool and store the pasta, if appropriate or necessary and reheat portions or batches as necessary.

Because it takes longer to cook, dried pasta is sometimes cooked ahead of time and held for service. (Fresh pasta does not hold as well as dried pasta, and, since it cooks rapidly, it is usually feasible to cook it fresh to order during service.) If any pasta is prepared in advance and held, it should be slightly undercooked, so that it will not overcook during reheating.

To cool the pasta, rinse it thoroughly with cold water and drain it well. Toss the cooled pasta with a small amount of oil to keep the strands from clumping together during storage.

To reheat the pasta, bring some salted water to a boil. There should be enough water to generously cover the pasta, though not so much as is required for cooking the pasta. Lower the pasta into the water using a basket or by dropping it into the water, and let it simmer just long enough to heat through, depending upon the thickness of the pasta. Remove the pasta from the water and drain it well before finishing the pasta for service.

ABOVE *This pasta is not fully cooked. The strands do not have a uniform color and are not soft enough to drape easily.*

TOP *Now the pasta is fully cooked. The color is uniform and the strands fall easily from the spoon.*

BOTTOM *Toss well-drained pasta with just enough oil to lightly coat each strand. Hold under refrigeration.*

5. Evaluate the quality of the cooked pasta.

Properly cooked dried pasta is tender but with a discernible texture, a state known as *al dente* (Italian for "to the tooth"). Fresh pasta cooks rapidly, which makes it easy to overcook; it should be completely cooked and not raw or doughy. Pasta and noodles should remain separate if they were cooked correctly and stirred once or twice as they cook. Pasta that has been cooled and held should be properly cooked once reheated. Sauces and other finishing ingredients paired with pasta and noodles should be chosen to complement the shape or texture of the pasta (see General Guidelines on page 711).

6 qt / 5.75 L water

1½ oz / 45 g salt, or as needed

1½ lb / 450 g dry or fresh pasta

sauce or garnish (optional)

oil, for holding (optional)

BASIC BOILED PASTA

1 Bring the water and salt to a rolling boil in a large pot.

2 Add the pasta and stir well to separate the strands. Cook until tender but not soft. (Fresh pasta may cook in less than 3 minutes; dried pasta may take up to 8 minutes or longer, depending on the size and shape.)

3 Drain the pasta at once. Add any desired sauce or garnish at this point and serve. If the pasta is to be held, plunge it into an ice-water bath or rinse thoroughly with cold water to stop the cooking. Drain immediately and drizzle a small amount of vegetable oil over the pasta and toss it to prevent it from sticking together.

MAKES 10 PORTIONS

GENERAL GUIDELINES

PAIRING PASTA WITH SAUCES

Some pastas are dressed very simply, perhaps with only high-quality oil, salt, and pepper. More elaborate sauces are also used to prepare pasta dishes. Sauces are customarily selected to suit a particular type of pasta. Long, flat pastas, such as fettuccine or linguine, are generally served with smooth, light sauces, such as cream sauces, vegetable coulis, or butter-and-cheese combinations that coat the strands evenly. Tube pastas, such as elbow macaroni or ziti, and twisted pastas, such as fusilli, are normally paired with a more heavily textured sauce, such as a meat sauce or one with fresh vegetables, because these shapes are able to trap the sauce.

The flavor of the pasta is also an important consideration when choosing a sauce. The delicate flavor of fresh pasta is most successfully paired with a light oil-, cream-, or butter-based sauce. Heartier sauces and ragouts, such as those that include meats, are usually combined with dried pastas. Filled pastas require only a very light sauce, because the filling provides a certain amount of flavor and moisture of its own.

SERVING FRESH AND DRIED PASTA

Pasta dishes are suited to many different service styles. The speed and ease of preparing pasta makes it a good choice for à la carte restaurants; in fact, some restaurant kitchens include a separate pasta station on the hot-food line. When properly prepared, handled, and held, pasta can also be used for banquet and buffet service. Both the pasta and the accompanying sauces can be prepared in advance.

For à la carte service, cook or reheat the pasta as close to service time as possible. Since pasta loses heat rapidly, be sure to heat the bowls or plates on which it is to be served and serve it immediately.

For banquet service, use bowls or deep platters and mound the pasta to help conserve heat. Be sure to heat the serving pieces.

For buffet service, choose sturdy pastas that will hold up well. Fully preheat the steam table or heat lamps before placing the pasta on the buffet line. Cook, reheat, and/or finish the pasta as close to serving time as possible. Choose a hotel pan deep enough to contain the pasta comfortably, but not so large that the pasta is spread out in a thin layer, where it will lose heat and moisture rapidly. Even in a steam table, heat is lost rapidly. There is a limit to how long pasta dishes can be held successfully for buffet service. Holding them over heat for too long can cause the sauce to dry out and the pasta to begin to lose its texture.

RECIPES

PASTA ALLA CARBONARA

makes 10 portions

2¹/₂ lb/1.125 kg spaghetti

2 oz/60 g butter or oil

10 oz/285 g minced pancetta or bacon

8 egg yolks

12 fl oz/360 mL heavy cream

4 oz/115 g grated Parmesan, or as needed

salt, as needed

pepper, as needed

chopped parsley, as needed

1 Bring a large pot of salted water to a rolling boil. Add the spaghetti and stir a few times to separate the strands. Cook the pasta until it is tender to the bite but still retains some texture.

2 Drain the spaghetti in a colander. (Note: If the spaghetti is prepared in advance, rinse it with cold water, drain well, and rub a small amount of oil through the strands. Refrigerate until ready to serve. Reheat the pasta in boiling salted water and drain well while preparing the sauce.)

3 Heat the butter or oil in a sauteuse, add the pancetta or bacon, and sauté for 3 to 4 minutes or until the pancetta or bacon has rendered its fat. Add the drained cooked spaghetti and sauté until the spaghetti is very hot.

4 Blend the egg yolks with the cream and Parmesan. Add the egg mixture to the pasta. Cook the mixture gently, stirring constantly, until the sauce is heated through. Do not overheat, or it will curdle. Season to taste with salt and pepper.

5 Serve the spaghetti immediately on heated plates, sprinkled with chopped parsley and additional Parmesan, if desired.

see photograph on page 715

WILD MUSHROOMS AND ARTICHOKES OVER BLACK PEPPER PASTA

makes 10 portions

¹/₂ oz/15 g butter

¹/₂ oz/15 g minced shallots

6 oz/140 g sliced assorted mushrooms

2 fl oz/60 mL dry white wine

8 fl oz/240 mL heavy cream

2¹/₂ lb/1.125 kg BLACK PEPPER PASTA (page 706)

10 artichoke bottoms, cooked

8 oz/225 g tomato concassé

salt, as needed

chopped parsley, as needed

1 Melt the butter in a sauteuse and sauté the shallots until translucent, about 2 minutes. Add the mushrooms, and sauté until very hot, about 4 minutes. Add the wine and reduce until almost dry. Add the cream and reduce until slightly thickened.

2 Bring a large pot of salted water to a rolling boil. Add the pasta and stir a few times to separate the strands. Cook the pasta until it is tender to the bite but still retains some texture, about 3 to 4 minutes. Drain the pasta in a colander.

3 Add the artichoke bottoms and tomato concassé and heat until warmed through. Add the pasta and toss with the sauce until evenly coated and very hot. Adjust the seasoning with salt to taste.

4 Sprinkle with chopped parsley and serve at once on heated plates.

CHORIZO-FILLED RAVIOLI WITH TOMATO COULIS AND SALSA FRESCA

makes 10 portions

CHORIZO FILLING

5 oz/140 g cubed lean pork

2½ oz/70 g cooked rice

1 tsp/5 mL minced jalapeños, as needed

¼ oz/7 g minced garlic

10 oz/285 g chopped chorizo

salt, as needed

2 tsp/10 mL minced oregano

1 tsp/5 mL cider vinegar

½ tsp/3 mL chili powder

¼ tsp/1 mL cayenne

1½ lb/680 g FRESH EGG PASTA (page 706)

20 fl oz/600 mL TOMATO COULIS (see page 289), hot

20 fl oz/600 mL SALSA FRESCA (see page 821)

1 To make the filling, combine the pork and rice in a food processor and blend until smooth. Add the remaining filling ingredients and pulse the machine on and off until the ingredients are just combined. Remove the filling from the processor and refrigerate it.

2 Roll the pasta into thin sheets and cut the sheets into forty 3-in/75-mm circles. Keep the dough circles covered until they are ready to be filled.

3 Brush the pasta circles lightly with water. Place 1 tsp/ 5 mL filling on a pasta circle. Fold the circle in half and crimp the edges with the tines of a fork to seal.

4 Bring a large pot of salted water to a boil, reduce to a simmer, and add the ravioli. Simmer for about 5 minutes. Remove the ravioli with a spider or slotted spoon and drain or blot to remove excess water.

5 Pool 2 fl oz/60 mL coulis on a heated plate. Place 4 ravioli on the coulis, garnish with 1 tbsp/15 mL salsa, and serve.

see photograph on page 714

SHRIMP WITH CURRIED PASTA

makes 10 portions

30 oz/840 g shrimp

salt, as needed

pepper, as needed

vegetable oil, as needed

3 oz/85 g butter

1 oz/30 g minced shallots

4 fl oz/120 mL brandy

20 fl oz/570 mL FISH FUMET (page 253)

10 fl oz/300 mL heavy cream

2½ lb/1.125 kg CURRIED PASTA (page 706)

3 oz/85 g scallions, sliced on the bias

5 oz/140 g LOBSTER BUTTER (see page 802)

1 Season the shrimp to taste with salt and pepper. Heat the oil in a sauté pan and add the shrimp. Sauté until the shrimp are just cooked through, 4 to 5 minutes. Remove from the pan and reserve.

2 Add the butter to the oil until very hot. Add the shallots and sauté, stirring frequently until they are translucent, about 2 to 3 minutes. Deglaze with the brandy and reduce until the liquid cooks away. Add the fumet and cream. Let the mixture reduce until it lightly coats the back of a spoon. Keep warm until ready to combine with the pasta.

3 Bring the water and salt to a rolling boil in a large pot. Add the pasta and stir well to separate the strands. Cook until tender but not overly soft, 2 to 3 minutes. Drain the pasta at once.

4 Return the shrimp to the sauté pan and add the scallions. Stir or swirl in the lobster butter.

5 Add the drained pasta and toss or stir gently over medium heat until the pasta is coated and heated through. Adjust the seasoning with salt and pepper to taste, if necessary. Serve at once on heated plates.

see photograph on page 715

Lasagne di Carnevale Napolitana

Chorizo-Filled Ravioli with
Tomato Coulis and Salsa Fresca

Pasta Alla Carbonara

Shrimp with Curried Pasta

LASAGNE DI CARNEVALE NAPOLITANA

makes 10 portions

10 oz/285 g lasagne noodles

10 oz/285 g Italian sweet sausage

CHEESE FILLING

14 oz/400 g ricotta

4 oz/115 g grated Parmesan

salt, as needed

pepper, as needed

ground nutmeg, as needed (optional)

3 eggs

3/4 oz/20 g minced parsley

1 qt/1 L TOMATO SAUCE (page 272), with meat

10 oz/285 g mozzarella, sliced thin or shredded

4 oz/115 g grated Parmesan

1   Bring the water and salt to a rolling boil in a large pot.

2   Add the lasagne noodles and stir well to separate. Cook until tender but not overly soft, 8 minutes. Drain the lasagne at once and rinse with very cold water. Drain again and reserve.

3   Poach the sausage in water until cooked through, about 15 minutes. Remove the casing from the sausage and slice thin.

4   To make the cheese filling, combine all the filling ingredients and mix well.

5   To assemble the lasagne, spread a thin layer of tomato sauce in a large baking dish. Layer the ingredients beginning with a layer of noodles, arranged so that there is an overlap of about 3 in/75 mm at the sides of the pan. Spread with a layer of cheese filling about 1/4 in/5 mm thick, then a layer of sausage, a layer of sauce, a thin layer of the mozzarella, and a sprinkle of Parmesan. Continue layering the ingredients in this manner, reserving a portion of sauce and of Parmesan. Finish with a layer of noodles.

6   Fold the overhanging noodles over the top of the lasagne. Cover with the reserved sauce and top it with the reserved Parmesan.

7   Place the lasagne in a preheated 375°F/190°C oven and bake for 15 minutes. Reduce the heat to 325°F/165°C and bake for 45 minutes more. If the top browns too fast, cover it lightly with aluminum foil. The top should be a light golden brown when done.

8   Remove the lasagne from the oven and let it stand for 30 to 45 minutes before cutting into portions and serving on heated plates.

see photograph on page 714

GNOCCHI DI SEMOLINA GRATINATI

makes 20 portions

2 1/2 qt/2.5 L milk

1 tbsp/15 mL salt

1 lb/450 g semolina

8 oz/225 g butter

4 egg yolks, beaten

6 oz/170 g grated Parmesan, plus as needed for service

1   Bring the milk to a boil and season with salt. Add the semolina in a stream, stirring constantly until it all has been added. Simmer, stirring often, until done, about 20 minutes. Remove the pot from the heat and blend in 4 oz/ 115 g of the butter, egg yolks, and Parmesan.

2   Shape the gnocchi mixture into quenelles or spread it on a sheet pan to a thickness of 1/2 in/10 mm. Cool completely and cut as desired.

3   To serve the gnocchi, transfer them to liberally buttered baking dishes. Brush or drizzle with remaining melted butter and top with additional Parmesan. Bake in a hot oven or brown lightly under a broiler. Serve at once on heated plates.

GNOCCHI PIEDMONTESE

makes 10 portions

4 lb/1.75 g peeled russet potatoes

salt, as needed

1 oz/30 g butter

2 egg yolks

2 eggs

pepper, as needed

pinch of ground nutmeg (optional)

1 lb/450 g all-purpose flour, or as needed

2 oz/60 g butter

3 oz/85 g grated Parmesan

1 oz/30 g chopped parsley, or as needed

1 Scrub, peel, and cut the potatoes into equal-size pieces. Place the potatoes in a pot with enough cold water to cover them by about 2 in/5 cm. Add salt to taste. Gradually bring the water to a simmer over medium heat. Cover and simmer until the potatoes are easily pierced with a fork.

2 Drain the potatoes. Return them to the pot and let them dry briefly over very low heat until no more steam rises from the potatoes, or spread them out on a sheet pan and dry them in a low oven.

3 Push the potatoes through a rice or food mill while very hot. Add the butter, egg yolks, eggs, salt, pepper, and nutmeg (if using). Mix well. Incorporate enough of the flour to make a stiff dough.

4 Roll out the dough into cylinders about 1 in/25 mm in diameter. Cut the cylinders into pieces about 2 in/50 mm long. Roll over the tines of a fork, pressing and rolling the dough with your thumb.

5 Cook the gnocchi in simmering salted water for 2 to 3 minutes, or until they rise to the surface. Lift the gnocchi from the water with a slotted spoon or drain in a colander.

6 Heat the butter in a sauté pan, add the gnocchi, and toss until very hot and coated with butter. Add the Parmesan, parsley, salt, and pepper to taste. Serve at once on heated plates.

SPÄTZLE

makes 10 portions

2 eggs

3 fl oz/90 mL milk

salt, as needed

pepper, as needed

ground nutmeg, as needed (optional)

1 oz/30 g FINES HERBES (page 353)

6 oz/170 g flour

4 oz/115 g butter

1 Combine the eggs, milk, salt, pepper, nutmeg, if using, and fines herbes and mix well in a large bowl. Work in the flour by hand. Let the dough rest for 10 minutes.

2 Using a spätzle machine or other shaping technique, drop the dough into a large pot of boiling salted water. Simmer until done, about 5 to 6 minutes, and remove with a spider. The spätzle is ready to finish for service now, or they may be cooled in ice water, drained, and refrigerated for later service.

3 Sauté the spätzle in butter until very hot. Adjust the seasoning with salt and pepper and serve immediately on heated plates.

BREAD DUMPLINGS

makes 20 portions

2 lb/900 g white bread or rolls, with crust

4 oz/115 g butter

8 oz/225 g minced onions

8 oz/225 g flour

1 pt/480 mL milk, or as needed

10 eggs

1 oz/30 g minced parsley

salt, as needed

ground white pepper, as needed

ground nutmeg, as needed (optional)

1 Cut the bread or rolls into small dice. Dry them in a 250°F/120°C oven for 20 to 30 minutes.

2 Heat the butter in a sauté pan and add the onions, sautéing until lightly browned, about 8 to 10 minutes. Remove from the pan and cool.

3 Combine the dried rolls or bread, flour, and sautéed onions in a large bowl.

4 Combine the milk, eggs, parsley, salt, pepper, and nutmeg, if using, separately in another bowl.

5 Pour the liquid mixture into the dry mixture and blend together lightly. Let stand, covered, for 30 minutes. Add more milk if the bread is very dry.

6 Shape the mixture into 2-in/50-mm dumplings by hand.

7 Poach the dumplings in barely simmering salted water for 15 minutes. The dumplings are ready to serve now, or they may be left in the poaching liquid to hold hot for service. To serve, drain the dumplings with a slotted spoon or skimmer, and serve on heated plates.

BISCUIT DUMPLINGS

makes 30 pieces

1 lb/450 g all-purpose flour

4 tsp/20 mL baking powder

2 tsp/10 mL salt, or as needed

1 pt/480 mL milk

2 tbsp/30 mL chopped parsley (optional)

broth, soup, or stew for poaching dumplings, as needed

1 Sift together the flour, baking powder, and salt. Add the milk and parsley, if using, and mix in gently. Do not overmix. The consistency should be slightly softer than biscuit dough.

2 Drop 1-oz/30-g portions from a spoon about 1 in/50 mm apart into the broth, soup, or stew. Cover the pot and cook the dumplings for 20 to 25 minutes, or until they are cooked through.

HUSH PUPPIES

makes 10 portions

vegetable oil, lard, or bacon fat for frying, as needed

6 oz/170 g white cornmeal

1³/₄ oz/50 g flour

1 tsp/5 mL baking powder

pinch of salt

1 tsp/5 mL sugar

pinch of black pepper

pinch of cayenne

1 egg

4 fl oz/120 mL milk or buttermilk

1 tbsp/15 mL butter, melted

1 oz/30 g minced onion

¹/₄ oz/7 g minced garlic

1 Heat the oil, lard, or bacon fat in a deep-sided pan or skillet to 375°F/190°C.

2 Mix cornmeal, flour, baking powder, salt, sugar, black pepper, and cayenne together in a large bowl.

3 Beat the egg in a separate bowl. Stir in the milk or buttermilk, melted butter, onion, and garlic.

4 Stir the egg mixture into the cornmeal mixture to make a stiff batter.

5 Drop batter by heaping tablespoons into the hot oil until the skillet is full. Do not crowd.

6 When the hush puppies are golden brown, after about 5 to 6 minutes, remove from the oil with a slotted spoon and drain on paper towels. Serve at once on heated plates.

DIM SUM

DUMPLING SKINS

1 lb/450 g flour
8 fl oz/240 mL water, hot

FILLING

12 oz/340 g ground pork
8 oz/225 g shredded Chinese cabbage
2 oz/60 g chopped scallions
1 tsp/5 mL minced ginger
½ fl oz/15 mL soy sauce
½ fl oz/15 mL dark sesame oil
1 egg white
salt, as needed
white pepper, as needed

1 To prepare the dumpling skins, mix the flour and water to make a smooth batter. Let stand for 30 minutes. Divide the dough into ½-oz/15-g portions and roll each out into a thin circle.

2 To prepare the filling, combine all the filling ingredients and mix well. Check the consistency and seasoning of the filling by sautéing a small amount and tasting it.

3 Place 1 tbsp/15 mL of filling on a dumpling skin. Crimp and seal the edges tightly.

4 Steam the dumplings over boiling water until cooked through, about 8 minutes. Serve immediately.

Potstickers Use prepared wonton wrappers instead of preparing dough, if desired. Fill and seal dumplings as described above. Heat about ¼ in/5 mm oil in a skillet. Add the dumplings in a single layer, and pan-fry until the bottoms are very crisp and brown. Add enough stock, broth, or water, to come up ½ in/10 mm in the pan. Cover the pan and steam the potstickers for 6 to 8 minutes, or until the wrapper is translucent and tender. Serve at once.

COOKING PASTA AND DUMPLINGS   719

PART SIX

BREAKFAST AND GARDE MANGER

According to culinary lore, the chef's hat, with its many pleats, represents the many ways that a chef can prepare eggs. Eggs can be served at virtually any meal, as part of every course. They can be cooked in the shell, poached, fried, or scrambled, or prepared as omelets or soufflés; they add flavor and color to other dishes.

COOKING EGGS

COOKING EGGS IN THE SHELL

Although the term boiled *may appear in the name, eggs prepared in the shell should actually be cooked at a bare simmer for best results.*

Eggs are cooked in the shell to make hard- and soft-cooked eggs and coddled eggs. They may be served directly in the shell, for example, a soft-cooked egg for breakfast as shown above, or they may be shelled and used to make another preparation, such as deviled eggs, or as a garnish for salads or vegetable dishes.

SELECT AND PREPARE THE INGREDIENTS AND EQUIPMENT

CHECK EACH EGG CAREFULLY and discard any with cracked shells. Eggs should always be properly held under refrigeration until you are ready to cook them. To reduce cooking time for hard-cooked eggs, temper them in warm water for several minutes. Hard-cooked eggs are easiest to peel if the eggs are not extremely fresh; the fresher the egg, the more difficult the shell will be to remove neatly.

Select a pot deep enough for the eggs to be completely submerged in water. Have on hand a slotted spoon, skimmer, or spider to remove eggs from the water once they are cooked.

FOR 10 PORTIONS OF EGGS COOKED IN THE SHELL, YOU WILL NEED:	20 eggs (2 per portion)	plenty of simmering water to cook coddled, soft-, medium-, or hard-cooked eggs; plenty of cold	water to cover eggs if following the alternative hard-cooked method

HOW TO COOK EGGS IN THE SHELL

1. Place the eggs in a pot with enough water to completely submerge them.
It is common to have the water already at a simmer when preparing coddled and soft-cooked eggs. Hard-cooked eggs may be started in simmering or cold water. In either case, lower the eggs gently into the pot so they won't crack.

2. Bring (or return) the water to a simmer.
Do not allow the water to boil rapidly. Water that is at or close to a simmer will allow the eggs to cook evenly, without toughening the whites. In addition to toughening the whites, violent boiling could cause the eggshells to crack.

3. Start timing the cooking once the water reaches a simmer and cook to the desired doneness.
When shell eggs are added to a pot of simmering water, the water cools slightly. If hard-boiled eggs are started in cold water, the water must be heated up to a simmer before timing begins. Timing is started only when the water is at full cooking temperature. For example, a 3-minute egg cooks for 3 minutes from the time the water returns to a simmer after the egg has been added to the water. If the timing is started when the water is cold, the egg will not be properly cooked.

Hard-cooked eggs are easiest to peel while they are still warm. Place them under cold running water until they are cool enough to handle. Gently press down and roll the egg over a countertop to crack the shell before peeling. Peel the shell and membrane away with your fingers.

4. Evaluate the quality of the cooked egg.
The yolks of properly cooked soft-cooked eggs are warm but still runny, while those of medium-cooked eggs are partially coagulated. Medium- and soft-cooked eggs also have tender, coagulated whites. Properly hard-cooked eggs are completely and evenly coagulated with firm but tender, not tough, whites and no unsightly green ring surrounding the yolk.

The green ring is the result of a chemical reaction between the iron and sulfur naturally present in eggs forming green iron sulfide. Heat speeds up this reaction. The best way to prevent the green ring from forming is to watch the cooking time closely and not allow the eggs to boil longer than necessary. Quick cooling also helps keep the ring from forming.

HARD-COOKED EGGS

1 Place the eggs in a pot. Fill the pot with enough cold water to cover the eggs by 2 in / 50 mm.

2 Bring the water to a boil and immediately lower the temperature to a simmer. Begin timing the cooking at this point.

3 Cook small eggs for 12 minutes, medium eggs for 13 minutes, large eggs for 14 to 15 minutes, and extra large eggs for 15 minutes.

4 Cool the eggs quickly in cool water and peel as soon as possible.

MAKES 10 PORTIONS

Coddled Eggs Lower cold eggs into already simmering water and simmer for 30 seconds.

Soft-cooked Eggs Lower cold eggs into already simmering water and simmer for 3 to 4 minutes.

Medium-cooked Eggs Lower cold eggs into already simmering water and simmer for 5 to 7 minutes.

Alternative Method for Hard-cooked Eggs An alternative method calls for removing the pot holding the eggs from the heat when the water reaches a boil, covering them, and letting them stand in the hot water for 20 minutes.

see photograph on page 753

POACHING EGGS

The simplicity of the poached egg is its greatest asset, but as every chef knows, the simpler the dish, the more the chef's skill is on display.

Poached eggs are prepared by slipping shelled eggs into barely simmering water and gently cooking until the egg holds its shape. These tender and delicately set eggs form the basis of many dishes. Some familiar examples are Eggs Benedict or Florentine or poached eggs used as a topping for hash.

They may be served in baked potatoes or on croutons, with or without a sauce, or added as a garnish to broths or hearty soups.

Poached eggs can be prepared in advance and held safely throughout a typical service period to make the workload easier during service. Slightly underpoach the eggs, trim them, and hold them in cold water. At the time of service, reheat the eggs in simmering water.

PERFECTLY FRESH EGGS ARE BEST for poaching. The fresher the egg, the more centered the yolk, and the less likely the white is to spread and become ragged.

Eggs are most often poached in water, though other liquids, such as red wine, stock, or cream, can also be used. Add vinegar and salt to the water to encourage the egg protein to set faster. Otherwise, the egg whites can spread too much before they coagulate.

Other ingredients include seasonings, garnishes, and sauces as called for by the specific recipe.

Choose a pot that it is deep enough for the eggs to remain completely submerged. The size of the pan depends on the size of the batch. Have cups to hold the raw eggs, as well as a slotted spoon, skimmer, or spider for retrieving the eggs from the water, and absorbent toweling for blotting the eggs dry, a paring knife for trimming the eggs, and holding and serving pieces. An instant-read thermometer helps to accurately monitor the temperature of the water.

FOR 10 PORTIONS OF POACHED EGGS, YOU WILL NEED:	20 very fresh eggs (2 per portion), chilled until ready to poach	5 to 6 inches/13 to 15 centimeters simmering water	½ ounce/15 grams salt per gallon of water
		1 fluid ounce/30 milliliters vinegar per gallon of water	

HOW TO POACH EGGS

1. Bring water, vinegar, and salt to a simmer (180°F/82°C).
For the most attractive shape, like a teardrop, be sure that the water is deep enough. Fill a pan with water to a depth of 5 to 6 in/13 to 15 cm and season it with just enough vinegar and salt to prevent the egg whites from spreading. The vinegar and salt should be just barely perceptible, not enough that the poached egg tastes strongly of vinegar or salt. Two tablespoons of vinegar and 1 tablespoon of salt for each gallon of water are generally sufficient.

2. Add the shelled egg to the simmering water.
To reduce the chance of breaking an egg in the poaching liquid, break the eggs into cups. Use any eggs with broken yolks for other dishes. Discard any eggs that have blood spots on the yolks. Pour the egg from the cup into the poaching liquid.

Once added, the egg will drop to the bottom of the pot, then float to the top. The whites will set around the yolk, to create a teardrop shape. The more eggs added to the water, the more the temperature of the water will drop and the more time it will take to properly poach the egg. Working with smaller batches is actually more efficient.

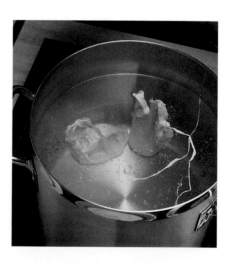

ABOVE *Slide the egg carefully into the water to keep the yolk intact.*

3. Remove the egg when done.
It generally takes about 3 to 4 minutes to properly poach an egg. Blot the egg on absorbent toweling to remove as much water as possible. If the whites appear ragged, trim them with a paring knife to give a neat appearance. The poached egg is ready to serve now.

To prepare eggs that will be chilled and held for later service, slightly undercook the eggs. Lift them from the poaching liquid, and submerge them in ice water until well chilled. Drain the eggs and hold them in a perforated pan until ready to reheat for service. To reheat the egg, lower it into simmering water for 30 to 60 seconds to finish cooking and properly reheat it.

Serve the egg while still very hot.

4. Evaluate the quality of the poached egg.
A properly poached egg is very tender with a regular, compact, oval shape. The white is set and opaque while the yolk is barely set (slightly thickened but still flowing).

ABOVE *Use a slotted spoon, skimmer, or spider to gently lift the egg from the water.*

ABOVE *To hold chilled poached eggs for later service, let them drain thoroughly in a perforated pan. Keep eggs safe under refrigeration.*

1 gal / 3.75 L water

1 tbsp / 15 mL salt

1 fl oz / 30 mL distilled white vinegar

20 eggs

POACHED EGGS

1 Combine the water, salt, and vinegar in a deep pan and bring it to a bare simmer.

2 Break each egg into a clean cup, and then slide the egg carefully into the poaching water. Cook for about 3 minutes, or until the whites are set and opaque.

3 Remove the eggs from the water with a slotted spoon, blot them on absorbent toweling, and trim the edges if desired. The eggs are ready to serve now, or they may be properly chilled and held for later service.

4 Serve the hot eggs at once on heated plates.

MAKES 10 PORTIONS

FRYING EGGS

Fried eggs call for perfectly fresh eggs, the correct heat level, an appropriate amount of cooking fat, and a deft hand.

Fried eggs American style may be served sunny side up (not turned) or over (turned once). Fried eggs may be basted with fat as they fry. Dishes like huevos rancheros, for example, feature fried eggs as part of a hearty dish of eggs, tortillas, and beans. The French prefer shirred eggs *(sur le plat)*, which are cooked in the oven with various garnishes.

| FOR 10 PORTIONS OF FRIED EGGS, YOU WILL NEED: | *20 very fresh eggs (2 per portion), refrigerated until ready to cook* | ONE OF THE FOLLOWING COOKING MEDIUM OPTIONS: *whole butter* *clarified butter* | *cooking oils* *rendered bacon fat* |

SELECT AND PREPARE THE INGREDIENTS AND EQUIPMENT

VERY FRESH EGGS are the only way to insure a rich flavor and good appearance in the finished dish. When very fresh eggs are broken onto a plate, the yolk sits high on the white near the white's center. The white is compact and thick and it holds the yolk in place. When the egg is fried, the white holds together in a neat shape and the yolk is more likely to stay intact. As eggs age, the white and yolk weaken and thin. To prepare eggs for frying, break them into clean cups. Any eggs with broken yolks can be reserved for another use. Hold the shelled eggs under refrigeration. (This may be done up to 1 hour in advance.)

Oils, whole or clarified butter, or rendered animal fat are used for frying, even if a nonstick surface is used. These cooking fats not only lubricate the pan, they can also add their own distinct flavor. Eggs are seasoned with salt and pepper as they cook for the best flavor.

Eggs are fried either in a sauté pan or on a griddle. In an operation where fried eggs are important on the menu, chefs often prefer to keep a set of pans reserved specifically for cooking eggs. Well seasoned black steel pans are suitable. Nonstick surfaces are also desirable. A spatula or palette knife is also needed for flipping and moving the eggs.

1. Heat the pan and the cooking fat over moderate heat.

Place a frying pan over medium heat. Add the cooking fat to the pan and continue to heat until the fat is hot. The ideal temperature range for frying an egg is 255° to 280°F/124° to 138°C, the same range at which butter sizzles without turning brown. If using a griddle, adjust its temperature and brush the surface with oil or other cooking fat. Temperature control is crucial. If the heat is too low, the egg will stick; if it is too high, the edges of the white may blister and brown before the rest of the egg is properly cooked.

2. Break the eggs into cups and slide into the hot fat.

Fried eggs should have intact yolks, unless the customer requests that they be broken. Breaking the egg first into a cup lets you reserve any uncooked eggs with broken yolks for other uses, and keeps bits of eggshell out of the pan. It also keeps your work area neat.

Slide or pour the egg out of the cup and into the pan.

3. Cook the egg until done as desired.

Eggs are done once the whites have coagulated; the yolks may be soft and runny or set. For eggs cooked over easy or over hard, flip the eggs or turn them with an offset spatula or palette knife. Some chefs baste the eggs with hot fat to set the top instead of turning them. Another alternative is to sprinkle a few drops of water on the egg, cover the pan, and let the water steam the eggs.

ABOVE *Eggs prepared sunny side up.*

4. Evaluate the quality of the finished fried eggs.

Properly fried eggs have shiny, tender, fully set whites and a fairly compact shape. They are not blistered or browned. The yolk should remain intact and should be centered in the egg. Yolks should be properly cooked, according to customer request or intended use.

20 eggs

whole or clarified butter, oil, or rendered bacon fat, as needed

salt, as needed

pepper, as needed

FRIED EGGS

1 Break the eggs into clean cups (1 egg per cup).

2 Heat the butter in a pan until very hot but not smoking. Slide the eggs into the pan and reduce the heat to medium-low or low.

3 When the egg whites have set, tilt the pan, allowing the fat to collect at the side of the pan, and baste the eggs with the fat as they cook. Season the eggs with salt and pepper and serve at once on heated plates.

MAKES 10 PORTIONS

Eggs Over Easy, Medium, or Hard Turn the eggs near the end of their cooking time with a spatula and cook them on the second side until done as desired (20 to 30 seconds for over easy, 1 minute for over medium, 2 minutes for over hard).

SCRAMBLING EGGS

Scrambled eggs are among the most popular egg dishes.

Scrambled eggs can be made in two ways: The eggs can be stirred constantly over low heat for a soft delicate curd and a creamy texture, or stirred less frequently as they cook for a larger curd and a firm texture. Whether prepared to order or to serve on a buffet line, scrambled eggs must be served hot, fresh, and moist.

FOR 10 PORTIONS OF SCRAMBLED EGGS, YOU WILL NEED:	*20 to 30 eggs (2 to 3 per portion)*	*up to ½ fluid ounce/15 milliliters water, milk, or cream (optional)* *salt and pepper as needed*	*½ to 1 fluid ounce/15 to 30 milliliters oil, clarified butter, or rendered fats*

SELECT AND PREPARE THE INGREDIENTS AND EQUIPMENT

CHOOSE EGGS THAT ARE FRESH with intact shells. The flavor of a fresh egg comes through in this dish, even though the shape of the egg is irrelevant for scrambled eggs.

Adding a small amount of water (about 2 tsp/10 mL per egg) or stock to the beaten eggs will make them puffier as the water turns to steam, although this addition is not strictly necessary. Milk or cream is also sometimes used to enrich the eggs as well.

Scrambled eggs can be seasoned with salt and pepper, and/or flavored or garnished with fresh herbs, cheese, sautéed vegetables, smoked fish, or truffles.

Eggs can be scrambled in a sauté pan or on a griddle. Nonstick surfaces make it easy to prepare scrambled eggs with a minimum amount of added fat. Black steel pans are appropriate, as long as they are properly maintained and seasoned. Pans used for eggs should be reserved for that use only, if possible. A table fork, wooden spoon, or spatula is needed for stirring the eggs as they cook. Have holding and serving pieces on hand.

1. Blend the eggs just until the yolks and whites are combined. Add liquid, if using, and seasonings.

Add water or other liquid ingredients if desired. Use a fork or a whip to break the eggs and blend them into a smooth, homogenous mixture. Add salt, pepper, and other seasonings at this time.

2. Preheat the pan and melt the butter. Cook the eggs over low heat.

Heat the pan and the cooking fat over medium heat. Pour the eggs into the pan; they should begin to coagulate almost immediately. Turn the heat down to low. Use the back of a table fork to stir the eggs as they cook. Keep both the pan and the fork in motion to produce small, softly set curds. The lower the heat and the more constant the agitation, the creamier the finished scrambled eggs are. In fact, they may be prepared by stirring them constantly over a water bath to prevent browning (a practice more common in European kitchens).

Add cream, if using, garnishes, cheeses, or flavoring ingredients once the eggs are completely set and fold these ingredients into the eggs over low heat, just until incorporated. Remove the eggs from the heat when slightly underdone; they will continue to cook slightly from the heat they retain.

3. Evaluate the quality of the finished scrambled eggs.

Properly prepared scrambled eggs have a soft, moist texture, creamy consistency, and delicate flavor. Moisture weeping from the eggs indicates that they were overcooked.

ABOVE *Do not whip in too much air.*

ABOVE *Scrambled eggs are constantly stirred from the pan's bottom and sides to achieve the proper creaminess.*

20 to 30 eggs

5 fl oz / 150 mL water or milk (optional)

salt, as needed

white pepper, as needed

butter (whole or clarified) for scrambling, as needed

SCRAMBLED EGGS

1 For each portion, break 2 to 3 eggs into a bowl. Add 1 tbsp/15 mL water or milk, if using. Season to taste with salt and pepper and whip until evenly blended.

2 Heat a pan over medium heat and add the butter. Heat over medium heat until hot, but not smoking.

3 Add the beaten eggs and cook over low heat, stirring frequently with the back of a fork or wooden spoon to release the eggs from the pan, until they are soft and creamy. Remove from the heat when fully cooked but still moist, and serve at once on heated plates.

MAKES 10 PORTIONS

MAKING OMELETS

As Auguste Escoffier put it, an omelet is "really a special type of scrambled egg enclosed in an envelope of coagulated egg and nothing else."

The rolled, or French-style, omelet as described by Auguste Escoffier is the style that may come to mind first. This type of omelet starts out like scrambled eggs, but when the eggs start to set, they are rolled over. A folded, or American-style, omelet is prepared in much the same manner, though it is often cooked on a griddle rather than in a pan and instead of being rolled, the American omelet is folded in half.

There are two other styles of omelets, both based upon a beaten mixture of eggs, cooked either over direct heat or in an oven. Flat omelets, known variously as farmer-style omelets, frittatas (Italian), or tortillas (Spanish), are a baked version. Instead of being stirred, as the American and French omelets are, this omelet is baked so that the finished dish is denser and easier to slice into portions (see page 748). Souffléed or puffy omelets are made from eggs first separated into yolks and whites. The beaten whites are folded into the beaten yolks and the dish is prepared by baking the omelet in a hot oven (see page 748).

WHOLE EGGS, SHELLED AND BLENDED just before they are scrambled, are the standard choice for most omelets, although some formulas indicate additional whites or yolks, or are made exclusively from whites. As with scrambled eggs, the ability of the egg to hold its shape is irrelevant, but fresh eggs are preferred for their flavor. Salt and pepper as well as herbs are used to season omelets. Clarified butter or oil is most common the cooking fat, though some ethnic style dishes may have a more authentic flavor if prepared with rendered fats, such as lard or goose fat.

Omelets may be filled or garnished with cheese, sautéed vegetables or potatoes, meats, and smoked fish, among other things. These fillings and garnishes are incorporated at the appropriate point to be certain they are fully cooked and hot when the eggs have finished cooking. Grated or crumbled cheeses will melt sufficiently from the heat of the eggs, and are often added just before an omelet is rolled or folded.

Rolled and souffléed omelets are made individually in omelet pans, which are basically small sauté pans. Omelet pans should either be well seasoned or have a nonstick surface. Treat pans carefully and avoid scratching a nonstick surface with metal. A fork, wooden spoon, or heat-resistant rubber spatula is also needed to stir the eggs as they cook.

FOR 1 INDIVIDUAL OMELET, YOU WILL NEED:	*2 to 3 eggs* *up to 2 teaspoons/10 milliliters water, stock, milk, or cream(optional)*	*salt, as needed* *pepper, as needed*	*½ to 1 fluid ounce/15 to 30 milliliters cooking fat, as needed*

HOW TO MAKE AN OMELET

1. Blend the eggs with any liquid, if using, salt, pepper, and seasonings. Like the eggs for scrambled eggs, these should be shelled and blended as close to cooking time as possible. Keep eggs refrigerated until needed. Be certain that the eggs are not cracked. Discard any eggs with broken shells.

For rolled, folded, or flat omelets, the yolks and whites should be evenly blended along with seasonings and any appropriate liquid.

For souffléed omelets, the eggs are separated into whites and yolks. The yolks are blended with seasonings and any liquid desired, then the whites are beaten to medium peak and folded into the yolk mixture.

2. Heat the pan and then add the oil or butter over high heat or in a hot oven. Add any appropriate garnishes at this time.

A portion-size omelet pan should be heated over high heat. Then, the butter or oil is added and allowed to heat as well. The fat should appear lightly hazy, but not smoking. Larger frittatas as well as souffléed omelets are started in a pan that is preheated over direct heat or in a hotel pan heated in the oven with the cooking fat before the eggs are added. Some garnish ingredients are added to the pan before the eggs; others are added when the curds are almost completely set. Consult recipes for more details about when to add specific ingredients.

3. Add the eggs and cook the omelet until the eggs are properly set. Add any additional fillings or garnishes, if desired.

For individually prepared rolled and folded omelets, keep the eggs in constant motion as the omelet cooks. Cook rolled and folded omelets over brisk heat to assure that the eggs begin to set almost immediately and don't stick to the pan. If using an omelet pan, use one hand to swirl the pan over the heat source and the other to stir the eggs from the bottom and sides of the pan with the back of a fork or a heat-resistant rubber spatula. Use a flexible spatula to turn and stir an omelet cooked on a griddle.

Individual flat omelets are usually started over high heat to set the first side. The egg mixture is poured into the pan and cooked without stirring. Flat omelets may be inverted and finished on the second side, still on the stovetop, or they can be finished by transferring them into a hot oven or under a broiler without first inverting the omelet. *Souffléed omelets* are typically baked in a hot oven throughout cooking time.

Garnishes for flat and souffléed omelets are added at the start of cooking time. For rolled or folded omelets, add fillings such as cheese when the curds are barely set.

ABOVE *Diced ham is sautéed first to develop its flavor more fully.*

ABOVE *Cook the eggs to the point at which soft curds begin to form before adding cheese to the omelet.*

ABOVE *The heat of the eggs warms and softens the cheese enough to make a satisfying filling.*

HOW TO ROLL A FRENCH-STYLE OMELET

4. Evaluate the quality of the finished omelet.

A rolled omelet should be oval in shape and golden-yellow in color with a creamy, moist interior. A folded omelet is a half-circle shape; the exterior is sometimes allowed to take on a very light golden color. A flat omelet should be dense but moist, able to be cut or sliced into portions yet still hold its shape. A souffléed omelet should be light and foamy with slight golden color on the upper surface; it starts to lose its volume rapidly after coming out of the oven, however.

Start by gently spreading or flattening the omelet in the pan to even it out for the best-looking rolled and folded omelets. Then roll the edge of the omelet nearest the handle toward the center and shake the pan to loosen the omelet. Roll the omelet out of the pan, completely encasing any filling (make sure the edges are caught neatly underneath the omelet), directly onto a heated plate. It may be necessary to shape the omelet with a clean towel.

30 eggs

salt, as needed

pepper, as needed

5 fl oz / 150 mL water, stock, milk, or cream (optional)

clarified butter or oil, as needed

filling, as needed (optional)

PLAIN ROLLED OMELET

1 For each portion, beat 3 eggs well and season with salt and pepper to taste. Add water, if desired.

2 Heat an omelet pan and melt the butter or oil over high heat, tilting the pan to coat the entire surface.

3 Pour the egg mixture into the pan and scramble it with the back of a fork or wooden spoon. Move the pan and utensil at the same time until the egg mixture has coagulated slightly. Add the filling at this point, if desired.

4 Let the egg mixture finish cooking without stirring.

5 Tilt the pan and slide a fork or spoon around the lip of the pan, under the omelet, to be sure it is not sticking. Slide the omelet to the front of the pan and use a fork or a wooden spoon to fold it inside to the center.

6 Turn the pan upside down, rolling the omelet onto the plate. The finished omelet should be oval shaped.

MAKES 10 PORTIONS

NOTES

An alternate method of filling an omelet is to slit open the top at this point and spoon a filling or sauce into the pocket. To give the omelet additional sheen, rub the surface lightly with butter.

SAVORY SOUFFLÉS

The preparation, assembly, and baking of a soufflé are not difficult tasks on their own. The tricky part is timing.

Soufflés, like omelets and quiches, are not strictly for breakfast; in fact, they are more typically part of the brunch, luncheon, or even the dinner menu, where small soufflés often appear as hot appetizers, a savory course, or as a dessert.

Although not inappropriate for breakfast, soufflés are seldom served then. The main reason is time. A common rule in the kitchen is that "the customer waits for the soufflé; the soufflé does not wait for the customer." Thus, tradition and common sense have relegated soufflés to more leisurely meals served later in the day. The kitchen staff and the front of the house must communicate well, to assure that the guest receives the soufflé while it is still puffy and hot.

FOR 1 INDIVIDUAL SOUFFLÉ, YOU WILL NEED THE FOLLOWING:	A BASE APPAREIL, SUCH AS:	A LIGHTENER:	SEASONINGS, FLAVORINGS, OR GARNISH OPTIONS SUCH AS:
	2 fluid ounces/60 milliliters heavy béchamel for savory soufflés	*2 fluid ounces/60 milliliters egg whites, beaten to soft peaks*	*salt and pepper*
	2 fluid ounces/60 milliliters pastry cream for sweet soufflés		*vegetables*
	2 fluid ounces/60 milliliters of a vegetable purée (consistency similar to béchamel)		*grated cheese*
			others as desired

THE BASIC COMPONENTS of any soufflé, sweet or savory, are the soufflé base and beaten egg whites. A heavy béchamel, often with the incorporation of additional egg yolks, is the base for many savory soufflés. Sweet soufflés are often based upon pastry cream. Other mixtures or preparations, such as vegetable purées can be used as the base, or they may be used to flavor a base. It is important that the base mixture provide enough structure to keep the soufflé from collapsing as soon as it is removed from the oven. The base may be flavored or garnished in many ways: with grated cheese, chopped spinach, or shellfish, for example.

Egg whites give both volume and structure to the soufflé. They should be carefully separated from the yolks and beaten to soft peaks just before they are folded into the base. The yolks may be incorporated into the soufflé base, or they may be reserved for other uses. Be sure to keep eggs well chilled at all times for wholesomeness and flavor.

A variety of sauces may be served with soufflés. Cheddar Sauce or Mornay Sauce (page 288), vegetable ragouts or coulis, or various tomato sauces (recipes on page 288) are appropriate for savory soufflés.

Soufflés are usually baked in ceramic or glass soufflé dishes or ramekins. For the best rise, the sides of the dish should be straight.

To prepare the molds, butter them lightly and thoroughly, dusting the sides and bottom with grated Parmesan or bread crumbs if desired. Use meticulously clean bowls and whips to beat the egg whites for the best volume in the finished soufflé.

The oven should be set to the appropriate temperature, generally 400° to 425°F/ 205° to 220°C for an individual portion. The temperature should be slightly lower for larger soufflés.

Other equipment needs include a whisk (or electric mixer) and bowls for whipping the egg whites, a spatula for combining the soufflé mixture, and a sheet pan for baking.

MAKE THE SAVORY SOUFFLÉ

1. Prepare the base and incorporate any additional ingredients and seasonings.

The base mixture for many savory soufflés is essentially a heavy béchamel (page 288). Additional egg yolks are often tempered into the hot base to provide extra richness, flavor, color, and structure. The base may be prepared in advance and held under refrigeration. For the best rise in the finished soufflé, have the base at room temperature, or else work it with a wooden spoon until it has softened. Flavoring ingredients such as puréed spinach are folded into the base until evenly blended.

ABOVE *The egg yolks are blended with some of the hot base to temper them.*

ABOVE *Flavoring ingredients, spinach here, are added to the base and folded in until evenly blended.*

2. Whip the egg whites to soft peaks. Fold the egg whites into the base. Soft peaks will produce the proper rise, texture, and structure in the finished soufflé. Add the beaten whites in two or three parts. The first addition will lighten the base so that subsequent additions will retain the maximum volume.

3. Fill the prepared molds as soon as the egg whites are folded into the base. Spoon or ladle the batter into the mold gently to avoid knocking air out of the batter. Be sure to wipe the rims and outside of the mold clean for a good, even rise. Bake the soufflés as soon as the eg whites are folded into the base.

4. Place the soufflés immediately in a hot (425°F/220°C) oven and bake until risen, cooked through, and browned. For even cooking and a good rise, place the molds on a sheet pan. The rack should be in the center of the oven. Do not disturb the soufflés as they bake. The drop in temperature when the oven door is opened could be enough to affect the soufflé. Remove individual soufflés from the oven when done, about 16 to 18 minutes. To check a soufflé for doneness, shake the dish very gently. The center should be firm and set. A toothpick carefully inserted into the side of the soufflé should come out clean.

5. Serve the soufflé immediately. Any accompanying sauce should be hot and ready in a dish. The server should be standing by, ready to serve the soufflés as soon as they come from the oven.

6. Evaluate the quality of the finished soufflé.
A properly prepared soufflé tastes of the primary flavoring ingredient and is puffy, well risen, and browned.

ABOVE *The egg whites are fully incorporated at this point.*

ABOVE *The soufflé dishes have been prepared in advance and arranged on a baking sheet as part of a complete mise en place.*

ABOVE *The soufflés should rise evenly and cleanly above the rim of the dish.*

butter, as needed

3 oz / 85 g grated Parmesan, plus as needed

SOUFFLÉ BASE (recipe follows on page 746)

10 oz / 285 g blanched chopped spinach

salt, as needed

pepper, as needed

10 egg whites

SPINACH SOUFFLÉ

1 Prepare the soufflé molds by brushing them liberally with softened butter. Lightly coat the interior of the mold with Parmesan.

2 For each portion, blend together 2 fl oz/60 mL soufflé base, 1 oz/30 g spinach, ⅓ oz/8 g Parmesan, salt, and pepper until the spinach is evenly distributed.

3 Beat 1 egg white for each soufflé to soft peaks. Fold about one-third of the beaten white into the base. Add the remaining white in one or two more additions.

4 Spoon the soufflé batter into the prepared molds to within ½ in/12 mm of the rim. Wipe the rim carefully to remove any batter. Tap the soufflés gently on the counter to settle the batter. Sprinkle the soufflé tops with the remaining Parmesan.

5 Place the soufflés on a sheet pan in a 425°F/220°C oven and bake undisturbed until puffy and a skewer inserted in the center comes out relatively clean, about 16 to 18 minutes. Serve immediately.

MAKES 10 PORTIONS

SOUFFLÉ BASE

makes 20 fluid ounces/600 milliliters

2 oz/60 g butter
2½ oz/75 g flour
24 fl oz/720 mL milk
salt, as needed
pepper, as needed
15 egg yolks

1 Heat the butter in a pan over medium heat and stir in the flour. Cook this roux over low to medium heat for 6 to 8 minutes, stirring frequently, to make a blond roux.

2 Add the milk, whisking well until the mixture is very smooth. Add salt and pepper to taste. Simmer over low heat, stirring constantly, for 15 to 20 minutes or until very thick and smooth.

3 Blend the yolks with some of the hot base to temper them. Return the tempered yolks to the base mixture and continue to simmer 3 to 4 minutes, stirring constantly. Do not allow the mixture to boil.

4 Adjust the seasoning with salt and pepper, and strain through a sieve if necessary. The base is ready to use now, or it may be properly cooled and stored for later use.

BREAKFAST AND GARDE MANGER

RECIPES

DEVILED EGGS

makes 10 portions

10 HARD-COOKED EGGS (page 724), cooled and peeled
6 fl oz/180 mL MAYONNAISE (page 767)
1 tbsp/15 mL prepared mustard
salt, as needed
pepper, as needed

1   Slice the eggs in half lengthwise. Separate the yolks from the whites. Set aside the whites until ready to fill.

2   Rub the yolks through a sieve into a bowl or food processor. Add the mayonnaise, mustard, salt, and pepper. Mix or process the ingredients into a smooth paste. The filling may be prepared in advance and held under refrigeration.

3   Transfer the yolk mixture to a pastry bag and pipe into the cavities of the egg whites.

NOTES

The eggs may be separated and the filling mixed in advance, but if they are not to be served immediately, the whites and the yolks should be held separately until as close as possible to service.

Substitute softened butter or compound butter, sour cream, puréed cottage cheese, softened cream cheese, yogurt, or crème fraîche for all or part of the mayonnaise.

Possible garnishes include chopped parsley, snipped chives, sliced scallion tops, dill sprigs, pimiento strips, chopped olives, caviar, shredded carrots, or dried oregano. Possible spice garnishes include ground toasted cumin seeds, cayenne, or crushed red pepper.

Deviled Eggs with Tomato Sauté 2 oz/60 g tomato concassé in a small amount of oil, just until any juices they release are cooked away, and add to the yolk mixture. Add a small amount of fresh or dried herbs (basil, oregano, sage, thyme) and/or ½ tsp/3 mL minced garlic or shallots to the tomatoes as they sauté, if desired.

Deviled Eggs with Greens Add 1 tsp/5 mL per yolk blanched and puréed spinach, watercress, sorrel, lettuce, or other greens to the yolk mixture.

Deviled Eggs with Vegetables Add small-dice cooked, raw, and/or marinated vegetables, such as celery, carrot, red onion, peppers, fennel, mushrooms, tomatoes, green beans, peas, corn, or eggplant, to the yolk mixture.

Deviled Eggs with Peppers Purée roasted red or green peppers, pimientos, and/or hot chilies and add to the yolk mixture. Add about ⅓ cup purée or to taste per 6 yolks.

Deviled Eggs with Cheese Add up to ¾ oz/25 g grated hard cheese or 2 oz/60 g soft cheese to the yolk mixture. Purée the filling well in a food processor.

Deviled Eggs with Fish or Shellfish Add about 4 oz /115 g finely diced fish or shellfish with any desired vegetables to the yolk mixture. Or make a paste of fish by puréeing it with butter, mayonnaise, or heavy cream. Use smoked fish (especially small pieces or trimmings), shrimp, crab, or lobster, or fresh or canned tuna or salmon.

PICKLED EGGS

makes 10 portions

10 HARD-COOKED EGGS (page 726), cooled and peeled
2 tsp/10 mL dry mustard
2 tsp/10 mL cornstarch
1½ pt/720 ml white wine vinegar
2 tsp/10 mL sugar
1 tsp/5 mL turmeric or CURRY POWDER (page 353)

1   Place the eggs in a stainless-steel mixing bowl and set aside.

2   In a small saucepan, dilute the mustard and cornstarch in 1 tbsp/15 mL cold water. Add the vinegar, sugar, and turmeric or curry powder. Bring the mixture to a boil over medium heat and simmer for 10 minutes.

3   Pour the mixture over the eggs. Cool the eggs and pickling solution to room temperature, then refrigerate overnight. The eggs are ready to serve at this point.

Red Pickled Eggs Replace 8 fl oz/240 mL of the vinegar with beet juice.

FARMER-STYLE OMELET

makes 10 portions

10 oz/285 g diced bacon or 5 fl oz/150 mL vegetable oil

10 oz/285 g minced onions

10 oz/285 g diced cooked potatoes

30 eggs

salt, as needed

pepper, as needed

1 To make an individual frittata, cook 1 oz/30 g bacon in a skillet until it is crisp or heat the oil in a skillet.

2 Add 1 oz/30 g of the onions and sauté over medium heat, stirring occasionally, until light golden brown, 10 to 12 minutes.

3 Add 1 oz/30 g of the potatoes and sauté until lightly browned, 5 minutes more.

4 Meanwhile, beat 3 eggs together with salt and pepper to taste. Pour them over the ingredients in the skillet and stir gently.

5 Reduce the heat to low, cover the skillet, and cook until the eggs are nearly set.

6 Remove the cover and place the skillet under a broiler to brown the eggs lightly. Serve at once on a heated plate.

SOUFFLÉED CHEDDAR OMELET

makes 10 portions

30 eggs

salt, as needed

pepper, as needed

5 oz/140 g grated sharp Cheddar

2 tbsp/30 mL minced chives

clarified butter or oil, as needed

1 To make an individual omelet, separate 3 eggs. Beat the yolks and season with salt and pepper to taste. Add the Cheddar and chives to the beaten yolks.

2 Beat the egg whites to medium peaks and fold them into the yolks.

3 Pour the eggs into a preheated well-oiled skillet. When the sides and bottom have set, finish the omelet in a hot oven until fully set and light golden on top. Serve immediately.

ENCHILADA OMELET

makes 10 portions

AVOCADO SAUCE

3 avocados

1 lime, juiced

1 tbsp/15 mL minced chives

4 tomatoes, peeled and seeded

2 tsp/10 mL chopped cilantro

$1/4$ tsp/1 mL Tabasco sauce

salt, as needed

pepper, as needed

30 eggs

oil or butter, as needed

FILLING

$3^1/2$ oz/100 g red pepper, julienne

$3^1/2$ oz/100 g yellow pepper, julienne

$3^1/2$ oz/100 g green pepper, julienne

$1^1/4$ lb/570 g grated jalapeño Jack cheese

1 To prepare the avocado sauce, purée all the ingredients until smooth. Set aside and keep cold.

2 Beat the eggs and strain if necessary. Set aside in a bain-marie held in an ice bath.

3 At the time of service, preheat omelet pans, adding oil or butter if necessary. Using a 6-fl oz/180-mL ladle, portion out eggs into pans. Cook until each omelet is set.

4 Add filling ingredients to individual omelets and roll the omelet.

5 Transfer to plates and ladle some of the sauce over each omelet.

EGGS BENEDICT

makes 10 portions

20 POACHED EGGS (page 730)
10 toasted English muffins, split and buttered
20 slices Canadian bacon, sliced and heated
1 pt/480 mL HOLLANDAISE SAUCE (page 279), warm

1 If eggs have been poached in advance, reheat in simmering water until warmed through. Blot on toweling and shape if necessary.

2 Toast English muffin halves until browned and top with sliced Canadian bacon. Top with eggs.

3 Ladle warm hollandaise over eggs.

Eggs Florentine Replace each slice of Canadian bacon with 2 oz/60 g spinach sautéed with shallots.

Poached Eggs American Style Brush toasted English muffins or bread with butter and top with sautéed slices of peeled tomato and poached egg. Coat with Cheddar cheese sauce and garnish with chopped bacon and parsley.

Poached Eggs with Chicken Liver Chasseur Brush toasted English muffins with butter and top with sautéed chicken livers, poached eggs, and Chasseur Sauce (page 287).

Poached Eggs Perdue Brush toasted English muffins with butter and top with chicken ragout, poached eggs, and asparagus tips.

Poached Egg with Smoked Salmon Replace the English muffins with toasted bagel halves, replace the Canadian bacon with smoked salmon slices, and top with the eggs. Serve with horseradish sauce.

BAKED EGGS WITH RATATOUILLE

makes 10 portions

clarified butter, as needed
1 lb/450 g RATATOUILLE (page 617), warm
10 eggs
salt, as needed
pepper, as needed
5 tsp/25 mL butter, cut into 10 pieces

1 Warm ten 6-fl oz/180-mL ceramic ramekins and brush them with clarified butter.

2 Divide the ratatouille evenly among the ramekins. Break an egg into each ramekin. Sprinkle with salt and pepper and top with a piece of butter.

3 Set the ramekins in a prepared bain-marie and cover with aluminum foil. Bake in a preheated 350° to 375°F/175° to 190°C oven until the egg whites are fully set, 4 to 5 minutes. Serve at once in the ramekins.

NOTES

Replace the ratatouille with chicken livers sautéed with sherry, mushroom ragout, or other savory fillings.

SHIRRED EGGS

makes 10 portions

butter, melted, as needed
20 eggs
salt, as needed
pepper, as needed
5 fl oz/150 mL heavy cream, hot
5 oz/140 g tomato concasse (optional)

1 For an individual portion, brush a gratin dish with melted butter.

2 Break 2 eggs into cups (reserve eggs for other uses if yolks break) and slide them into the dish. Cook over low to medium heat for 1 to 2 minutes or until the underside has set.

3 Season the eggs with salt and pepper to taste, add the cream and tomatoes, if desired, and bake in a 350°F/175°C oven until done, 4 to 5 minutes.

see photograph on page 753

SAVORY CHEESE SOUFFLÉ

makes 10 portions

butter, as needed

3 oz/85 g grated Parmesan, plus as needed for coating molds

20 fl oz/600 mL SOUFFLÉ BASE (page 746)

3 oz/85 g grated Gruyère or Emmentaler

salt, as needed

pepper, as needed

ground nutmeg as needed (optional)

10 egg whites

1 Prepare the soufflé molds by brushing them liberally with softened butter. Lightly coat the interior of the mold with Parmesan.

2 For each portion, blend together 2 fl oz/60 mL soufflé base, ⅓ oz/8 g Parmesan, ⅓ oz/8 g Gruyère, salt, pepper, and nutmeg, if using, until the cheeses are evenly distributed.

3 Beat the 1 egg white for each soufflé to soft peaks. Fold about one-third of white into the base. Add the remaining white in one or two more additions.

4 Spoon the soufflé batter into the prepared molds to within ½ in/12 mm of the rim. Wipe the rim carefully to remove any batter. Tap the soufflés gently on the counter to settle the batter. Sprinkle the soufflé tops with the remaining Parmesan.

5 Place the soufflés on a sheet pan in a 425°F/220°C oven and bake undisturbed until puffy and a skewer inserted in the center comes out relatively clean, about 16 to 18 minutes. Serve immediately.

CORN AND PEPPER PUDDING

makes 10 portions

5 oz/140 g fine-dice onions

butter or oil, as needed

2 oz/60 g red pepper julienne

2 oz/60 g yellow pepper julienne

2 oz/60 g green pepper julienne

minced jalapeños, as needed (optional)

1 pt/480 mL half-and-half or heavy cream

4 eggs

10 oz/285 g corn kernels, fresh or frozen and thawed

1 tsp/5 mL sugar

½ tsp/3 mL ground cumin

1½ tsp/8 mL chopped oregano

1 tsp/5 mL chopped basil

2 tsp/10 mL chopped cilantro

6 oz/170 g grated Monterey Jack

salt, as needed

pepper, as needed

1 Sauté the onions in butter or oil until translucent. Add the peppers and jalapeño to taste. Cover the pan and sweat the peppers until tender. Drain off any liquid.

2 Whisk together the half-and-half or cream and the eggs. Add the pepper mixture, corn, sugar, cumin, oregano, basil, cilantro, and Monterey Jack. Mix together well and season the mixture with salt and pepper to taste.

3 Butter a casserole or 10 ramekins and pour in the pudding mixture. Bake in a bain-marie in a preheated 350°F/175°C oven until a knife blade inserted in the center comes out clean (about 45 minutes for a single large pudding, 20 to 25 minutes for ramekins).

4 Let stand for 15 minutes. Cut a large pudding into wedges or squares and serve hot or at room temperature. Or serve the pudding in the ramekins or unmolded.

QUICHE LORRAINE

8 oz/225 g chopped slab bacon

butter or oil, as needed

12 fl oz/360 mL heavy cream or crème fraîche

3 eggs

salt, as needed

pepper, as needed

9-in/22.5-cm PIE CRUST (page 937), baked blind

1 Sauté the bacon in butter or oil until browned. Remove the bacon with a slotted spoon and drain.

2 Whisk together the heavy cream and eggs and season to taste with salt and pepper.

3 Scatter the bacon evenly over the crust. Add the custard mixture gradually, stirring it gently with the back of a fork to distribute the filling ingredients evenly.

4 Set the quiche pan on a sheet pan and bake in a preheated 350°F/175°C oven until a knife blade inserted in the center comes out clean, about 40 to 45 minutes. Serve hot or at room temperature.

NOTES

Quiche may also be baked without a pastry crust. Butter a shallow casserole or baking dish. Sprinkle it with grated Parmesan, if desired. Spread the filling ingredients over the casserole bottom. Pour the custard mixture on top. Bake the quiche in a bain-marie until a knife inserted near the center comes out clean.

Quiche may be baked in tartlet shells, timbale molds, or custard cups.

Replace the cream, completely or in part, with half-and-half or milk.

Spinach Quiche Substitute 1 lb/450 g spinach, blanched, squeezed dry, and coarsely chopped, for all or part of the bacon.

LEEK AND TOMATO QUICHE

2 oz/60 g green onions, white parts only, thinly sliced

8 oz/225 g leeks, white and light green parts, thinly sliced

butter or oil, as needed

10 oz/285 g tomato concassé

salt, as needed

cayenne, as needed

12 fl oz/360 mL heavy cream

3 eggs

3½ oz/100 g grated Monterey Jack, Gruyère, or Cheddar

2 tbsp/30 mL minced tarragon, basil, or other herbs

9-in/22.5-cm PIE CRUST (page 937), baked blind

1 Sauté the green onions and leeks in butter until translucent.

2 Add the tomato concassé and sauté until the liquid evaporates. Season with salt and cayenne to taste.

3 Whisk together the cream and eggs. Stir in the cheese and season it with the tarragon and more salt and cayenne to taste. Spoon the filling mixture into the crust. Add the custard mixture gradually, stirring it with a fork to distribute the filling ingredients evenly.

4 Set the quiche pan on a sheet pan and bake in a preheated 350°F/175°C oven until a knife blade inserted in the center comes out clean, about 40 to 45 minutes. Serve hot or at room temperature.

Asparagus and Sun-Dried Tomato Quiche

Hard-Cooked Eggs

Cheese Omelet

Shirred Eggs

SEAFOOD QUICHE

makes one 9-inch/22.5-centimeter quiche

3 eggs, beaten

12 fl oz/360 mL heavy cream

4 oz/115 g diced bacon

6 oz/170 g diced onions

4 oz/115 g grated Swiss cheese

8 oz/225 g cooked seafood (shrimp, lobster, or crab)

1 tbsp/15 mL chopped parsley

salt, as needed

pepper, as needed

one 9-in/22.5-cm PIE CRUST (page 937), baked blind

1   Combine eggs and cream and mix well.

2   Fry the bacon halfway, add the onions, and sauté until translucent. Drain, discarding the bacon fat, and let cool.

3   Mix the onions, cheese, seafood, parsley, and salt and pepper to taste with eggs and cream and pour into the crust.

4   Set the quiche pan on a sheet pan and bake in a preheated 350°F/175°C oven until firm and browned on top, about 40 to 45 minutes. Let rest 15 minutes. Serve hot or at room temperature.

ASPARAGUS AND SUN-DRIED TOMATO QUICHE

makes one 9-inch/22.5-centimeter quiche

2 oz/60 green onions, white parts only, thinly sliced

8 oz/225 g leeks, white and light green parts, thinly sliced

butter or oil, as needed

10 oz/285 g asparagus tips, blanched

salt, as needed

pepper, as needed

12 fl oz/360 mL milk

3 eggs

3¹/₂ oz/100 g farmer cheese

2 oz/60 g grated Parmesan

2 oz/60 g chopped sun-dried tomatoes

2 tbsp/30 mL FINES HERBES (page 353)

one 9-in/22.5-cm PIE CRUST (page 937), baked blind

1   Sauté the green onions and leeks in butter until translucent. Add the asparagus tips and toss until the tips are coated. Remove from the heat. Season to taste with salt and pepper.

2   Whisk together the milk and eggs. Stir in the farmer cheese, Parmesan, sun-dried tomatoes, and fines herbes. Season to taste with salt and pepper.

3   Spread the asparagus mixture evenly over the crust. Add the custard mixture gradually, stirring it with a fork to distribute the filling ingredients evenly.

4   Set the quiche pan on a sheet pan and bake in a preheated 350°F/175°C oven until a knife blade inserted in the center comes out clean, about 40 to 45 minutes. Serve hot or at room temperature.

see photograph on page 752

ARTICHOKE SOUFFLÉ

makes 10 portions

10 globe artichokes

lemon juice, as needed

salt, as needed

13 eggs, separated

10 oz/285 g grated Gruyère

24 fl oz/720 mL milk

2 tbsp/30 mL cornstarch

pepper, as needed

1   Trim the artichokes and cook in simmering water seasoned with lemon juice and salt until tender (see page 578). Scrape the flesh from the leaves, discard the choke, and reserve the bottoms.

2   Purée the artichoke meat, egg yolks, Gruyère, milk, and cornstarch in a food processor. Adjust the seasoning with salt and pepper to taste.

3   Beat the egg whites to soft peaks and fold into artichoke mixture in 3 additions. Pour the mixture into 10 greased soufflé ramekins.

4   Bake in a preheated 400°F/205°C oven until done, about 20 minutes. Serve at once.

WARM GOAT CHEESE MOUSSE

makes 10 portions

6 oz/170 g cream cheese, room temperature

9 oz/250 g goat cheese, room temperature

pepper, as needed

9 eggs

1½ pt/720 mL heavy cream

1 oz/30 g sliced chives

salt, as needed

40 seedless green grapes

1 Combine the cream cheese with 6 oz/170 g of the goat cheese, reserving the remainder for garnish, and pepper to taste in a food processor and process until the mixture is very smooth.

2 Add the eggs, 8 fl oz/240 mL of the cream, and half of the chives. Pulse the processor on and off until the ingredients are just blended. Divide the mixture among 10 buttered 2-oz/60-mL timbale molds and cover the molds with buttered parchment paper.

3 Place the ramekins in a bain-marie and bake in a preheated 325°F/165°C oven until a knife inserted near the center of a timbale comes away clean.

4 Reduce the remaining cream by half and season with salt and pepper to taste. Add the remaining chives and the grapes to the cream immediately before service.

5 Unmold the ramekins and coat the mousse with sauce. Garnish with the reserved goat cheese.

NOTE

Replace the goat cheese with other soft cheeses, such as Boursin, Brillat-Savarin, Camembert, or Brie.

FRENCH TOAST

makes 10 portions

30 slices CHALLAH (page 896)

1 qt/1 L milk

8 eggs

2 oz/60 g sugar

pinch ground cinnamon (optional)

pinch ground nutmeg (optional)

salt, as needed

vegetable oil, as needed

1 Slice the challah into ¼ to ½ in/6 to 12 mm thick slices. Let them dry on sheet pans overnight or in a 200°F/95°C oven for 1 hour.

2 Combine the milk, eggs, sugar, cinnamon, and nutmeg, if using, and salt to taste, and mix into a smooth batter. Refrigerate until needed.

3 Heat a skillet and grease with a small amount of vegetable oil or use a nonstick pan over moderate heat.

4 Dip the bread into the batter, coating the slices evenly. Fry the slices on one side until evenly browned, then turn and brown the other side.

5 Serve the French toast at once on heated plates.

NOTES

Serve with powdered sugar or cinnamon sugar, or butter and syrup or honey. Or garnish with toasted nuts (or add them to the syrup), fruit compound butter, seasoned syrup, warm fruit compote, or peanut butter.

POACHED EGGS MORNAY

20 toast rounds or ovals

melted butter, as needed

20 POACHED EGGS (page 730)

1 pt/480 mL MORNAY SAUCE (page 288)

3 oz/85 g grated Gruyère

1 Brush the toast with butter, and top with the poached eggs. Coat with the sauce and sprinkle with grated cheese.

2 Brown lightly under a broiler or salamander. Top with Mornay Sauce and grated Gruyère. Serve immediately.

Poached Eggs, Farmer Style Top the toast with a peeled tomato slices, boiled ham, creamed mushrooms, and poached eggs.

Poached Eggs with Mushrooms Fill tartlets with creamed mushrooms, top with poached eggs, and coat with Hollandaise Sauce (page 279).

Poached Eggs Massena Heat fresh artichoke bottoms and fill with Béarnaise Sauce (page 289). Top with poached eggs, coat with Tomato Sauce (page 272), and sprinkle with chopped parsley.

Poached Eggs on Hash Top corned beef or roast beef hash patties with poached eggs. Garnish with deep-fried parsley.

POACHED EGGS WITH EGGPLANT AND RICOTTA

24 oz/680 g eggplant, sliced into rounds (20 slices)

salt, as needed

flour, as needed

egg wash, as needed

bread crumbs, as needed

vegetable oil, for frying

5 oz/150 g ricotta

12 oz/340 g tomatoes, peeled and sliced (20 slices)

pepper, as needed

20 POACHED EGGS (page 730)

5 oz/150 g sliced Provolone (20 slices)

1 oz/30 g grated Parmesan

1 Salt the sliced eggplant liberally and let it drain in a colander for about 1 hour. Rinse and drain well. Blot dry and bread the eggplant, following the standard breading procedure (see page 349). Heat the oil to 375°F/190°C and deep fry the eggplant. Drain on paper toweling.

2 Top each eggplant slice with ricotta and a tomato slice. Season with salt and pepper to taste. Heat in a 350°F/175°C oven for 5 minutes.

3 Place poached eggs on top of the tomatoes. Top with a slice of Provolone and sprinkle with Parmesan. Brown under a broiler. Serve immediately.

CHEESE OMELET

30 eggs
salt, as needed
pepper, as needed
5 fl oz/ 150 mL water, stock, milk, or cream (optional)
clarified butter or oil, as needed
grated or diced cheese, such as Gruyère or Cheddar

1. For each portion, beat 3 eggs well and season with salt and pepper to taste. Add water, if desired.

2. Preheat an omelet pan and melt the clarified butter over high heat, tilting the pan to coat the entire surface.

3. Pour the egg mixture into the pan and scramble it with the back of a fork or wooden spoon. Move the pan and utensil at the same time until the egg mixture has coagulated slightly. Add ½ oz/15 g cheese per omelet.

4. Let the egg mixture finish cooking without stirring.

5. Tilt the pan and slide a fork or a spoon around the lip of the pan, under the omelet, to be sure it is not sticking. Slide the omelet to the front of the pan and use a fork or a wooden spoon to fold it inside to the center.

6. Turn the pan upside down, rolling the omelet onto the plate. The finished omelet should be oval-shaped.

Cheese and Vegetable Omelet Fill the omelet with goat cheese and sun-dried tomatoes, Gorgonzola and walnuts, cream cheese and olives, or Gruyère and sautéed leeks.

Meat and Cheese Omelet Fill each omelet with 1 oz/30 g diced meat (turkey, goose, or salami or other sausage) and 1 oz/30 g grated cheese. Add sun-dried tomatoes, herbs, or other flavorings, as desired.

Herb Omelet Omit the cheese. Sprinkle each omelet with 2 to 3 tsp/5 to 10 mL finely chopped fresh herbs before rolling.

Tomato Omelet Omit the cheese. Fill each omelet with 2 fl oz/60 mL relatively thick Tomato Coulis (page 289).

Omelet Florentine Omit the cheese. Fill each omelet with 1½ oz/45 g blanched spinach leaves sautéed with shallots and seasoned with salt and nutmeg.

Omelet Marcel Omit the cheese. For each omelet, sauté 3 oz/85 g sliced mushrooms and 1 oz/30 g sliced ham in butter. Roll the omelet, cut it lengthwise, and fill it with the mushroom mixture. Sprinkle the omelet with chopped chives.

Omelet Opera Omit the cheese. For each omelet, sauté 2 oz/60 g chicken livers in Madeira sauce (see page 422). Roll the omelet, cut it lengthwise, and fill it with the chicken livers. Garnish each omelet with 3 asparagus tips and spoon Hollandaise Sauce (page 279) on top.

Seafood Omelet Omit the cheese. Fill each omelet with 2 to 3 tsp/10 to 15 mL sour cream, crème fraîche, or yogurt with 2 oz/60 g cooked shrimp, smoked salmon, lobster, or other cooked and/or smoked fish, caviar, or seafood.

Shellfish Omelet Omit the cheese. Fill each omelet with 3 or 4 oysters, clams, or mussels, steamed briefly in butter with wine and shallots.

Western Omelet Omit the cheese. Fill each omelet with 1 oz/30 g *each* sautéed diced ham, red and green peppers, and onions. Add grated Monterey Jack or Cheddar if desired.

Spanish Omelet Omit the cheese. Fill each omelet with 2 oz/60 g tomato concassé or sauce and 1 oz/30 g *each* sautéed diced onions and green peppers.

Jelly Omelet Omit the cheese. Fill the omelet with 2 to 3 tbsp/30 to 45 mL jelly, chutney, or other preserved fruits.

see photograph on page 753

SCRAMBLED EGGS WITH CHEESE

makes 10 portions

20 to 30 eggs

5 fl oz/150 mL water or milk (optional)

salt, as needed

white pepper, as needed

grated Gruyère or Cheddar, as needed

5 oz/150 g butter or clarified butter

3 oz/90 mL cream (optional)

1 For each portion, break 2 to 3 eggs into a bowl. Add 1 tbsp/15 mL water or milk, if using. Season to taste with salt and pepper and whip well. Stir in ½ oz/15 g Gruyère.

2 Preheat the pan and add the butter or clarified butter over low heat.

3 Add the beaten eggs and stir with a fork or wooden spoon as they cook until they are soft and creamy. Add the cream, if using. Remove from the heat when slightly underdone and serve.

Scrambled Eggs Swedish Style Omit the cheese. For each portion, heat 1 tbsp/15 mL butter. Add 1 crushed juniper berry and 1 oz/30 g smoked salmon julienne. Add 2 to 3 beaten eggs and 1 tsp/5 mL chopped chives and scramble. Serve with toast.

Scrambled Eggs Hunter Style Omit the cheese. For each portion, sauté ¾ oz/20 g diced bacon. Add 2 to 3 beaten eggs and ½ tsp/3 mL chopped chives and scramble. Sauté ¼ tsp/1 mL minced shallots and 3 oz/85 g sliced mushrooms in butter. Season with salt and spoon on top of the eggs.

Scrambled Eggs with Bratwurst Omit the cheese. For each portion, season 2 peeled tomato slices with minced garlic, salt, and pepper and sauté them in butter on both sides. Scramble 2 to 3 eggs. Top the tomatoes with the scrambled eggs and 1 oz/30 g cooked sliced bratwurst.

Scrambled Eggs Gratiné Omit the cheese. For each portion, top 2 to 3 scrambled eggs with mornay sauce (see page 288), sprinkle with grated Gruyère, and brown lightly under the broiler.

Scrambled Eggs Greek Style Omit the cheese. For each portion, slice a Japanese eggplant lengthwise into ½-in/12-mm slices, season with salt, and sauté in oil. Sauté 1 oz/30 g tomato concassé with garlic, salt, and pepper to taste. Spoon 2 to 3 scrambled eggs on top of the eggplant slices and top the eggs with the tomato concassé.

HUEVOS RANCHEROS

makes 10 portions

10 fl oz/300 mL SALSA FRESCA (page 821), warm

10 corn tortillas, warm

20 FRIED EGGS (page 733)

5 oz/150 g grated Monterey Jack or Cheddar

sour cream, for serving

chopped cilantro, for serving

10 oz/285 g refried beans

1 Spoon some salsa over each corn tortilla. Top with 2 fried eggs and Monterey Jack. Garnish with sour cream and cilantro.

2 Serve immediately with refried beans.

CHAPTER TWENTY-SEVEN

Salads appear on the menu in so many different guises today that it is easy to imagine that salads were invented by this generation of chefs. In fact, fresh concoctions of seasoned herbs and lettuces have been relished in every part of the world, from the beginnings of recorded culinary history.

SALAD DRESSINGS AND SALADS

VINAIGRETTE

A vinaigrette is a cold sauce typically made from three parts oil and one part vinegar.

Vinaigrettes are thought of mainly as dressing for green salads, but they are used in many other ways as well: as a marinade for grilled or broiled foods; to dress salads made from pastas, grains, vegetables, and beans; as a dip; as a sauce served with hot or cold entrées and appetizers; or brushed on some sandwiches.

A vinaigrette is a temporary emulsion, made by blending the measured ingredients until they form a homogenous sauce. The sauce remains an emulsion for a only a short time, quickly separating back into oil and vinegar. To add flavor and help stabilize the sauce, an emulsifier is sometimes included.

FOR 2 QUARTS/2 LITERS OF VINAIGRETTE, YOU WILL NEED:

3 pints/1.42 liters oil

1 pint/480 milliliters vinegar

salt, pepper, and other seasonings

finishing and garnishing ingredients (optional)

SELECT AND PREPARE THE INGREDIENTS AND EQUIPMENT

A STANDARD VINAIGRETTE RATIO of three parts oil to one part acid works well as a starting point, but the vinaigrette needs to be tasted and evaluated whenever a change is made in the type of oil, acid, or specific flavoring ingredients.

Select the oil with an eye to both its flavor and cost. Oils used in salad dressings can be subtle or intensely flavored. Very strongly flavored oils are often blended with a quantity of less intense oils to produce a balanced flavor in the finished sauce. Oils may serve simply to carry the other flavors in the vinaigrette, or they may have readily identifiable flavors of their own.

The choice of vinegar ranges widely as well, from those made from wine, to fruit juice, to malted barley, to similar acidic liquids. Every vinegar has a different level of tartness or acidity. Both oils and vinegars can be flavored.

Additional vinaigrette ingredients include emulsifiers (egg yolks, mustard, roasted garlic, fruit or vegetable purées, or glace de viande) and such seasonings as salt, pepper, herbs, and spices.

Equipment needs for making vinaigrettes are minimal: measuring spoons or cups, a bowl, and a whisk or a blender, food processor, or standing mixer.

1. Combine the vinegar with the emulsifying and seasoning ingredients.
Adding the mustard, salt, pepper, herbs, or other ingredients to the vinegar is the easiest way to be sure that they are evenly dispersed throughout the sauce.

2. Add the oil.
The way the oil is added determines the consistency and appearance of the finished vinaigrette. Whisk in the oil or, to create a more stable vinaigrette, use a blender, immersion blender, standing mixer with a whip, or food processor. Vinaigrettes made by machine hold their emulsion longer than those that are simply whipped together.

3. Add any garnish and adjust the seasonings.
Crumbled cheese, fresh or dried fruits and vegetables, or other garnishes can be added, if desired.

As the vinaigrette sits, it will begin to separate. To be sure that the sauce is perfectly balanced on each salad, whip or stir the sauce before each use to recombine the oil and vinegar. Cover and store vinaigrettes under refrigeration when not using. For optimum flavor, make vinaigrettes in quantities that will last no longer than three days.

4. Evaluate the quality of the finished vinaigrette.
The challenge of making a good vinaigrette lies in achieving balance, a point at which the acidity of the vinegar or juice is tempered but not dominated by the richness of the oil. The flavor should be neither too sour nor too oily and the consistency of the sauce such that it clings nicely to the greens without looking or feeling greasy. The best way to check is to toss some of the salad with the vinaigrette, and then taste the sauce on the salad.

TOP *Blending the mustard, salt, and other seasonings into the vinegar helps to distribute them in the vinaigrette for an even flavor.*

BOTTOM *The vinegar is added all at once and stirred until the ingredients are blended.*

ABOVE *Adding the oil gradually while whisking constantly creates a thick, emulsified sauce.*

8 fl oz / 240 mL red wine vinegar

2 tsp / 10 mL mustard (optional)

$\frac{1}{2}$ oz / 15 g minced shallots

24 fl oz / 720 mL mild olive oil or canola oil

2 tsp / 10 mL salt

$\frac{1}{2}$ tsp / 5 mL black pepper

2 tsp / 10 mL sugar (optional)

3 tbsp / 45 mL minced fresh herbs, such as chives, parsley, tarragon (optional)

RED WINE VINAIGRETTE

1 Combine the vinegar, mustard, and shallots and let rest for 20 to 30 minutes. Whisk in the oil gradually.

2 Adjust the seasoning with salt and pepper, and add sugar, if using. Add the herbs, if desired.

MAKES 1 QUART/1 LITER

White Wine Vinaigrette Substitute white wine vinegar for the red wine vinegar.

FLAVORED OILS AND VINEGARS

Good-quality oils and vinegars can be infused with spices, aromatics, herbs, and fruits or vegetables to produce products with many applications.

They work well as condiments, or added in a drizzle or in droplets to add a bit of intense flavor and color to a plated dish. They are also excellent to use as dressings for vegetables, pastas, grains, or fruits. And of course, they can be used in vinaigrettes and other dressings for a special effect.

TO INFUSE OILS AND VINEGARS USE ONE OF THE FOLLOWING METHODS:

Heat the oil or vinegar very gently over low heat. The flavoring ingredients, such as citrus zest or garlic, may be added to the oil or vinegar as it warms. Let the oil or vinegar steep off the heat with the flavoring ingredients until cool, then pour into storage bottles or containers. Or, you may opt to heat the oil or vinegar without any added flavorings, then pour it over the flavoring ingredients and cool. Pour the infused oil or vinegar into storage bottles or containers.

Strain the vinegar or oil for a clearer final product, or leave the aromatics in for a more intense flavor. Add fresh aromatics after the oil or vinegar has steeped for several days to give an even more intense flavor, if desired.

Purée raw, blanched, or fully cooked vegetables, herbs, or fruits. Bring the purée to a simmer, reducing if necessary to concentrate flavors. Add the purée to the oil or vinegar and transfer to a storage container. Leave the oil or vinegar as is and use it like a purée or strain it to remove the fiber and pulp.

Combine room-temperature oils or vinegars with ground spices and transfer to a storage container. Let the mixture settle until the vinegar or oil is clear and the spices have settled in the bottom of the container. This is known as cold infusion.

Rest the flavored oil or vinegar under refrigeration for at least 3 hours and up to 36 hours. The time will vary according to the intensity of the flavoring ingredients and the intended use. Taste the oil or vinegar occasionally and, if necessary, strain or decant it into a clean bottle.

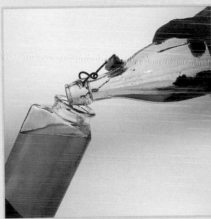
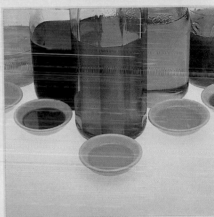

NOTE Fresh or raw ingredients such as garlic or shallots added to an oil or vinegar increase the risk of foodborne illness, especially if the infused oil or vinegar is not carefully stored. Although commercially prepared versions of flavored oil and vinegar are shelf stable, keep made-from-scratch versions stored under refrigeration. Use within a few days for the best flavor and color.

MAYONNAISE

Mayonnaise, because of its great versatility, is often included in the list of the basic, or grand, sauces prepared in the professional kitchen.

Mayonnaise is a cold sauce made by combining egg yolks with oil to form a stable emulsion. Unlike vinaigrette, this sauce does not break as it sits. Mayonnaise and sauces made with mayonnaise as a base can be used to dress salads or as a dip or spread. Among the famous mayonnaise-based sauces are Rémoulade, Sauce Verte (Green Mayonnaise), Aïoli (Garlic Mayonnaise), and Tartar Sauce.

FOR 1 QUART/1 LITER MAYONNAISE, YOU WILL NEED:	*3 fluid ounces/90 milliliters pasteurized egg yolks (3 large egg yolks)*	*1 to 2 fluid ounces/30 to 60 milliliters lemon juice, vinegar, or a combination 1½ pints/720 milliliters oil*	*1 fluid ounce/30 milliliters water*
	1½ pints/720 milliliters oil		*2 teaspoons/10 milliliters dry mustard (optional)*
			salt, pepper, and other seasonings

SELECT AND PREPARE THE INGREDIENTS AND EQUIPMENT

CLASSIC RECIPES FOR MAYONNAISE call for 6 to 8 ounces of oil to each egg yolk. Egg yolks provide both the liquid, which holds the oil droplets in suspension, and an emulsifier known as lecithin. To avoid any possible foodborne illnesses (such as those caused by *Salmonella* or *E. coli*), professional chefs should use pasteurized egg yolks.

Since mayonnaise is often intended as a base sauce that can be used for a variety of purposes, it is usually best to choose an oil that does not have a pronounced flavor of its own. There are exceptions to this general rule, however. For example, a mayonnaise made with extra-virgin olive oil or a nut oil would be appropriate to serve as a dip with a platter of grilled vegetables or crudités.

A small amount of mustard is often called for in mayonnaise. Though mustard is an emulsifier, its primary function in a mayonnaise is flavor. Various acids may also be used to prepare a mayonnaise, including lemon juice or wine or cider vinegars. The acid, along with water, is used to flavor the sauce as well as to provide additional moisture for the emulsification. When white vinegar is used, it also helps to keep the mayonnaise white. Additional flavoring ingredients, such as garlic or herbs, may also be needed as indicated.

Equipment needs for making mayonnaise are minimal: measuring spoons or cups, a bowl, and a whisk are appropriate for small quantities. For large batches, use a blender, food processor, or standing mixer. Mayonnaise sauces should be held in very clean storage containers.

1. Blend the yolks with a bit of water. Whisk the yolks and water together to loosen the eggs. Include lemon juice or vinegar and mustard at this point, if the recipe calls for those ingredients.

2. Add the oil a little at a time, whisking it in completely.
The oil must be whipped into the egg yolks so that it is broken up into very fine droplets. Adding the oil slowly allows a good emulsion to begin to form. If the oil is added too quickly, the droplets will be too large to emulsify properly, and the sauce will appear broken. Once about one fourth to one third of the oil has been properly blended into the egg mixture, start to increase the speed at which the oil is added.

When preparing mayonnaise in a mixer, add the oil in a thin stream as the machine runs. It is still true that the oil should be added more slowly at the beginning than at the end.

3. Adjust the thickness and flavor of the sauce by adding a bit more acid or water when incorporating the oil. The more oil that is added to the yolks, the thicker the sauce will become. Additional lemon juice, vinegar, or a little water are added when the mayonnaise becomes very thick. If this step is neglected, the sauce will become too thick to absorb any more oil.

ABOVE *Whisking the yolks with water prepares them to combine properly with the oil and form a good thick mayonnaise.*

ABOVE *Pour the oil into the whipped yolks while whisking constantly. Start pouring slowly and gradually increase the amount of oil.*

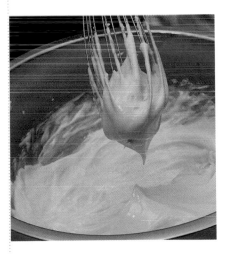

ABOVE *Continue adding oil until the amount specified in the recipe has been added. A finished mayonnaise should be thick enough to hold soft peaks.*

4. Add any additional flavoring or garnish ingredients at the point indicated in the recipe.

Aïoli, a garlic-flavored mayonnaise, calls for a good quantity of garlic to be included from the earliest stages of mixing. Other ingredients may be blended into the sauce once the oil is fully incorporated.

Keep mayonnaise refrigerated at all times once it is prepared. Transfer it to a storage container, cover it carefully, and label it with a date. Before using mayonnaise that has been stored, stir it gently and check the seasoning carefully. If the sauce needs to be thinned, add a bit of water.

5. Evaluate the quality of the finished mayonnaise.

A properly made mayonnaise has a mild and balanced flavor, without any predominance of acidic or oily flavors. It is thick, creamy, and completely homogenous in texture and appearance. The color is white or slightly off-white, not greenish or yellow.

Mayonnaise and similarly prepared dressings may break for a number of reasons: the oil was added too rapidly for the egg yolk to absorb it; the sauce was allowed to become too thick; the sauce became either too cold or too warm as it was being prepared.

A broken mayonnaise can be saved. Combine 1 fl oz/30 mL pasteurized egg with 1 tsp/5 mL water and beat until foamy. Gradually add the broken mayonnaise into the diluted yolk, whisking constantly until the mayonnaise regains a smooth, creamy appearance.

ABOVE *A basic mayonnaise can be flavored to produce rémoulade sauce (page 487) or Green Goddess Dressing (page 786).*

3 pasteurized egg yolks

1 fl oz / 30 mL water

1 fl oz / 30 mL white wine vinegar

2 tsp / 10 mL dry mustard

24 fl oz / 720 mL vegetable oil, olive oil, or mild peanut oil

salt, as needed

pepper, as needed

1 fl oz / 30 mL lemon juice, as needed

MAYONNAISE

1 Combine the yolks, water, vinegar, and mustard in a bowl. Mix well with a balloon whip until the mixture is slightly foamy.

2 Gradually add the oil in a thin stream, constantly beating with the whip, until the oil is incorporated and the mayonnaise is thick.

3 Adjust the flavor with salt, pepper, and lemon juice to taste.

4 Refrigerate the mayonnaise immediately.

MAKES 1 QUART/1 LITER

GREEN SALADS

Green salads provide a pleasant and refreshing counterpoint to the main attraction of the meal.

In its most basic form, a green salad (sometimes called a tossed salad, mixed salad, or garden salad) is made of one or more salad greens tossed with a dressing. Garnishes, such as other vegetables, croutons, and cheeses, are often included as well.

THE SALAD'S CHARACTER is determined by the greens that are selected. Greens are often grouped according to their flavors and/or textures, as follows:

mild and spicy greens

bitter greens or chicories

prepared mixes and blends of greens

herbs and flowers

Salad greens should be properly cleaned according to the method below. This is best done close to service time.

For more information on specific salad green varieties, see pages 165-67.

Commercially prepared salad blends are available today, but chefs can also create their own by combining lettuces from within one group or by selecting from among two or more groups.

A key piece of equipment in salad-making is the spinner. This tool, which comes in both hand-operated and large-scale electric versions, uses centrifugal force to spin the water away from the greens so that greens have a better flavor and dressing clings evenly to them.

FOR 10 PORTIONS OF SALAD, YOU WILL NEED:

30 ounces/850 grams salad greens

10 fluid ounces/300 milliliters vinaigrette or other salad dressing

garnishes, as desired

MAKE THE GREEN SALAD

1. Wash the greens thoroughly in plenty of cool water to remove all traces of dirt or sand.
Nothing is worse than a gritty salad or one that forces the diner to use a knife to cut the lettuce.

All greens, including prepackaged salad mixes and "triple-washed" bagged spinach, must be washed before serving. Change the water as often as necessary until absolutely no traces of dirt, grit, or sand are visible in the rinsing water.

Hydroponically raised greens, prepared mesclun mixes, and pre-rinsed spinach may need only a quick

plunge or rinse with cool water to refresh them.

Separate the lettuce or other heading greens into leaves. Loose heads and bunching greens will separate into individual leaves easily. Trim the coarse ribs or stem ends away if necessary.

To remove the core from heading lettuce, gently rap or push the core down onto a work surface. This will generally break the core away from the leaves. For tighter heads, it may be necessary to use a paring knife to cut out the core.

ABOVE *Fill a sink with cool water. Separate or loosen heading greens and dip them into the water. Plunging them gently in and out of the water will loosen the sand.*

2. Dry the greens completely.
Salad dressings cling best to well-dried greens. In addition, greens that are carefully dried before they are stored last longer. Use either a large-scale electric spinner for volume salad making or a hand basket for smaller batches. Clean and sanitize the spinner carefully after each use.

3. Store cleaned greens in tubs or other containers.
Once greens are cleaned and dried, keep them refrigerated until ready to dress and serve them. Use cleaned salad greens within a day or two.

Do not stack cleaned salad greens too deep; their own weight could bruise the leaves.

4. Cut or tear the lettuce into bite-size pieces.
Traditional salad-making manuals have always called for lettuces to be torn rather than cut to avoid discoloring, bruising, or crushing the leaf. The choice to either cut or tear lettuce is primarily a matter of personal style and preference. With today's high-carbon stainless-steel knives, discoloration is not a problem. As long as the blade is properly sharpened and a good cutting technique is used, the leaves will be sliced rather than crushed or bruised.

ABOVE *A spinner is the most effective tool to use for drying greens.*

ABOVE *Loosely wrap or cover the cleaned salad greens with dampened toweling to prevent them from wilting rapidly.*

5. Garnish and dress the salad.
The dressing's flavor should be appropriate to the salad ingredients, because the dressing serves to pull all the flavors together. Use delicate dressings with delicately flavored greens and more robust dressings with more strongly flavored greens. Consider the weight and coating capabilities of different dressings as well. Vinaigrettes coat lightly but evenly. Emulsified vinaigrette dressings and light mayonnaise dressings, which are thicker than vinaigrettes, tend to coat the ingredients more heavily.

Choose garnishes, if desired, according to the season and your desired presentation. Either toss these ingredients with the greens as they are being dressed or marinate them separately in a little vinaigrette and use them to top the salad.

To dress a salad, place the greens (about 3 oz/85 g or ³/₄ cup per serving) in a bowl and ladle a portion of salad dressing over them (2 to 3 tbsp/30 to 45 mL per serving). Tongs, spoons, or, if appropriate, gloved hands can all be used to toss the salad. Be sure each piece of lettuce is coated completely but lightly, with just enough dressing for the greens; if it pools on the plate, there is too much.

ABOVE *Use a lifting motion to toss the greens and dressing.*

MAKING CROUTONS

Croutons are often used as a garnish for salads as well as soups and stews. Croustades, crostini, rusks, and bruschetta are all types of crouton. Some are cut into slices, others into cubes or disks. Some are toasted, some deep-fried, some grilled, and some broiled. Large croutons made to act as the base for canapés, hors-d'oeuvre, and roasted or grilled meats reflect medieval European practices when plates were actually slabs of bread intended for consumption once they had been well dampened with juices and sauces from the meal.

TO PREPARE CROUTONS, *cut bread (crusts removed or not, as desired) into the desired size. Rub, spray, or toss the cubes or slices lightly with oil or clarified butter, if desired. Add salt and pepper.*

TO TOAST CROUTONS IN THE OVEN, *spread them in a single layer on a pan. Turn them from time to time to toast them evenly and check frequently to avoid scorching.*

TO DEEP FRY CROUTONS, *add the bread to hot clarified butter or oil. Fry until evenly browned and drain well on absorbent toweling. Add herbs or grated cheese while still hot.*

Good croutons are light in color, relatively greaseless, and well seasoned with a crisp, crunchy texture throughout.

30 oz / 850 g mixed greens, such as romaine, Bibb, Boston, red leaf, or green leaf

10 fl oz / 300 mL WHITE WINE VINAIGRETTE (page 762) or other dressing

MIXED GREEN SALAD

1 Rinse, trim, and dry the greens and tear or cut into bite-size pieces. Mix the greens and keep them well chilled until ready for service.

2 Place the lettuce (3 oz/85 g per portion) in a mixing bowl.

3 Add sufficient dressing to lightly coat the leaves. Toss the salad gently to coat it evenly.

4 Mound the lettuces on chilled salad plates and garnish them as desired.

MAKES 10 PORTIONS

FRUIT SALADS

Fruits have a variety of characteristics, making some fruit salads fairly sturdy, while others lose quality very rapidly.

Fruits that turn brown (apples, pears, and bananas) can be treated with fruit juice to keep them from oxidizing, as long as the flavor of the juice doesn't compete with the other ingredients in the salad.

Mixed fruit salads that include highly perishable fruits can be produced for volume operations by preparing the base from the least perishable fruits. More perishable items, such as raspberries, strawberries, or bananas, can then be combined with smaller batches or individual portions at the last moment, or they can be added as a garnish.

Fresh herbs such as mint, basil, or lemon thyme may be added to fruit salads as a garnish. Experiment to determine which herbs work best with the fruits selected for the salad.

To prepare fruit salads, you must learn how to peel, slice, or cut a variety of fruits, as shown on the following pages. Before working with any fruit, be sure it is properly rinsed. To avoid cross-contamination, clean and sanitize cutting boards and tools properly. Once fruits are cut, hold them under refrigeration until they are served.

APPLES

The cutting techniques demonstrated here on apples are also appropriate for other fruits and vegetables that have seeds in the interior, such as pears and vegetables like soft-skinned squashes.

Peel as thinly as possible, to avoid trim loss. To prevent discoloration of the cut surfaces of apples, as well as pears, peaches, and bananas, toss them in water that has been acidulated by adding a little fruit juice or vinegar. Choose a juice or vinegar with a flavor that complements the fruit's flavor. There shouldn't be so much acid that it overwhelms the fruit.

Slicing on a Mandoline

TOP *Use the tip of a paring knife to remove the stem and blossom ends.*

BOTTOM *Use a a paring knife or peeler to cut away the skin.*

TOP *Once the peel is removed, halve the apple from top to bottom and cut it into quarters.*

BOTTOM *To core the quarters, work from the stem end, angling your cut to the midpoint of the core, where it is deepest. Make a second cut working from the opposite direction.*

TOP *To cut very even slices, use a mandoline. Make slices from one side of the apple. Turn and repeat on the opposite side.*

BOTTOM *When the slices have been removed from both of the wider sides, slice the apple flesh from the narrow sides of the apple.*

Citrus fruits, including oranges, lemons, limes, and grapefruit, are used to add flavor, moisture, and color to dishes. They are also served as a functional garnish with some foods — for instance, a slice of lime with Cuban-style black bean soup or a wedge of lemon with broiled fish.

Before juicing citrus fruits, allow them to come to room temperature if possible. Roll the fruit under the palm of your hand on a cutting board or other work surface before juicing to break some of the membranes. This helps to release more juice. Remember to strain out the seeds and pith before using the juice, either by covering the fruit with cheesecloth before squeezing it or by straining it after juicing.

There are numerous special tools to juice citrus fruits including reamers, extractors, and hand-operated and electric juicers.

Citrus zest is the outer portion of the fruit's peel or rind. It is used to add color, texture, and flavor to dishes. The zest includes only the skin's brightly colored part, which contains much of the fruit's flavorful and aromatic volatile oils. It does not include the underlying white pith, which has a bitter taste. You can use the fine openings on a box grater to make grated zest, or a paring knife or zester.

Zest is often blanched before it is used in a dish, to remove any unpleasant bitter flavor. To blanch zest, cook it briefly in simmering water, then drain. Repeat as often as necessary; generally two to three blanchings are best. If a sweetened zest is desired, add sugar to the blanching water.

Cutting the flesh away from all the connective membranes of the fruit makes citrus suprêmes, also called sections or segments. Follow the natural curve of the fruit with your knife when removing the peel. Some flesh will adhere to the skin, but it should not be a very large amount. Squeeze the juice from the peel over the segments.

Making Citrus Sûpremes

TOP *A peeler removes very thin slices of zest.*

BOTTOM *Cut the zest into julienne or mince it with a chef's knife. Or use a zester to remove the zest as thin shreds in one step.*

TOP *Cut away both ends of the fruit, then use the midsection of the knife's cutting edge to cut the skin and pith completely away.*

BOTTOM *Slice next to the connective membrane on one side of each citrus segment. Twist the knife and use a scooping motion to cut out the citrus flesh.*

MANGO

A mango has a flat seed in the center of the flesh. The peel is left on to produce a special cut, known as the hedgehog cut, or the fruit may be peeled before cutting the flesh from the pit, if desired. If cut from the stem end to the pointed end of the mango, the flesh comes away from the pit more easily.

For the hedgehog cut, the mango is not peeled before the flesh is sliced from the pit. This technique can be used to prepare mangoes for salads or other uses, or it may be used for a decorative presentation on a fruit plate.

Hedgehog Cut

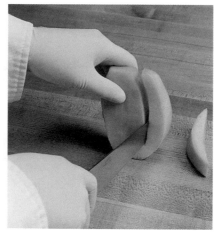

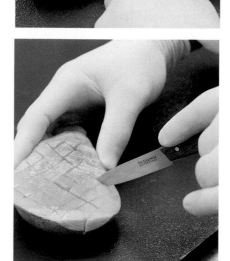

TOP *Peel the mango by making a series of cuts, removing as little edible fruit as possible.*

BOTTOM *Cut a slice from the other side of the pit, cutting as close to the pit as possible for the best yield.*

ABOVE *Cut the remaining flesh from the two narrow sides as shown, following the curve of the pit. Cube or slice the mango as desired.*

TOP *Cut the flesh on one of the wider sides away from the pit, following the natural curve of the fruit and cutting as close as possible to the pit.*

BOTTOM *Use the tip of a paring knife or a utility knife to score the flesh in a crosshatch pattern. The tip of the knife should not cut through the skin.*

PINEAPPLE

A pineapple has a thick, spiny skin. The flesh near the skin has "eyes" that should be completely removed before the flesh is used in a salad or other presentations.

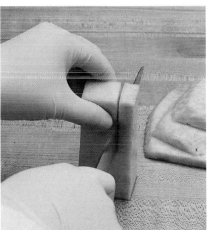

ABOVE *Turn the mango half inside out; it will look like a hedgehog. Slice the cubes away from the skin now, or present the fruit as is on a fruit plate.*

TOP *Slice away the pineapple top with a chef's knife, and cut a slice from the base of the pineapple.*

BOTTOM *Use a chef's knife to peel the pineapple. Make the cuts deep enough to remove the eyes but not so deep that a great deal of edible flesh is removed.*

TOP *For even slices or to make neat dice or cubes, slice the pineapple vertically at the desired thickness until you reach the core on the first side.*

BOTTOM *Turn the pineapple, and make slices from the opposite side as well as from both ends. Cut the slices into neat julienne or batonnet or dice as desired.*

MELONS

Melons are served in wedges, slices, cubes, or melon balls. The melons can be peeled before or after cutting. To make the melon more stable as you work, cut a slice from both ends of the melon. You may remove the entire rind before halving the melon and removing the seeds to streamline production of fruit plates and salads. Or you may prefer to leave the rind on. It is easier to prepare melon balls, for example, if the skin is left in place after halving the melon and removing the seeds.

Melon Balls

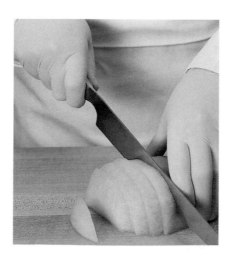

TOP *Use a utility or chef's knife to peel the skin away. The blade should follow the curve of the melon.*

BOTTOM *Cut the melon in half and scoop out the seeds.*

ABOVE *The melon can now be cut into even slices, which can then be cut crosswise to make neat cubes or dice.*

ABOVE *Alternatively, to make melon balls or for presentation as a melon half, cut through the equator of the melon. Scoop out the seeds with a spoon. The melon half may also be cut into wedges at this point.*

1 lb / 450 g cantaloupe balls

1 lb / 450 g honeydew balls

20 oz / 570 g prosciutto

1 fl oz / 30 g aged balsamic vinegar

cracked black pepper, as needed

SUMMER MELON SALAD WITH PROSCIUTTO

1 Cut the melon into balls as close as possible to service time. Keep chilled until service time.

2 Slice the prosciutto very thin and lay it out on a parchment-lined pan. Keep chilled until service time.

3 Arrange the melon and prosciutto on chilled plates and drizzle with balsamic vinegar. Scatter with cracked pepper. Serve at once.

MAKES 10 PORTIONS

WARM SALADS

Warm salad, known in French as *salade tiède*, is made by tossing the salad ingredients in a warm dressing, working over moderate to low heat. The salad should be just warmed through. Another approach is to use a chilled crisp salad as the bed for hot main items, such as grilled meat or fish.

VEGETABLE SALADS

Vegetables for these salads are prepared as required by the specific recipes. Some are simply rinsed and trimmed. Others need to be peeled, seeded, and cut to the appropriate shape. Some vegetables require an initial blanching to set colors and textures, while others must be fully cooked.

If the salad is to be served raw, the prepared vegetable or vegetables are simply combined with a vinaigrette or other dressing and allowed to rest long enough for the flavors to marry. When the vegetable or vegetables are partially or fully cooked, there are two methods for applying the dressing. In the first method, the vegetables are simply drained and combined with the dressing while they are still warm for faster flavor absorption. This works well for root vegetables such as carrots, beets, and parsnips, as well as leeks, onions, and potatoes. Some vegetables (especially green vegetables like broccoli or green beans) may discolor if they are combined with an acid in advance; in that case, refresh the vegetables before adding the dressing. Always be sure to thoroughly drain and blot dry the vegetables to avoid watering down the dressing.

POTATO SALADS

Potatoes must be cooked completely but not overcooked. High-moisture potatoes hold their shape after cooking better than low-moisture potatoes do.

The classic American potato salad is a creamy salad, dressed with mayonnaise. Other potato salads enjoyed around the world are often dressed with vinaigrette. In some traditional European-style recipes, the dressing may be based on bacon fat, olive oil, stock, or a combination of these ingredients. The dressing may actually be brought to a simmer before the potatoes are added for the best finished flavor.

PASTA AND GRAIN SALADS

Grains and pastas for salads should be fully cooked, but care should be taken to avoid overcooking. Grains and pasta will still be able to absorb some of the liquid in the dressing and can quickly become soggy.

If a pasta or grain salad is held for later service, be especially careful to check for seasoning before it is served. These salads have a tendency to go flat as they sit. Salt and pepper are important seasonings, of course, but others, such as vinegars, herbs, or citrus juices, can give a brighter flavor.

LEGUME SALADS

Dried beans should be cooked until they are tender to the bite. The center should be soft and creamy, and it is even possible that the skins may break open slightly. If a salad is made of several kinds of dried beans, it is important that beans with different cooking times be cooked separately to the correct doneness.

Unlike grains and pastas, which might become too soft as they sit in a dressing, beans will not soften any further. In fact, the acid in salad dressings will make the beans becomes tougher, even if they are fully cooked. Bean salads, therefore, should not be dressed and allowed to rest for extended periods. If the salad is used within four hours of preparation, however, there is little significant texture change.

COMPOSED SALADS

Composed salads are made by carefully arranging items on a plate, rather than tossing them together. They are usually main-course salads or appetizers, rather than an accompaniment. Although there are no specific rules governing the requirements for a composed salad, the following principles should be kept in mind:

- Consider how well each of the elements combines with the others. Contrasting flavors are intriguing. Conflicting flavors are a disaster.

- Repetition of a color or flavor can be successful if it contributes to the overall dish. But generally, too much of a good thing is simply too much.

- Each element of the dish should be so perfectly prepared that it could easily stand on its own. However, each part is enhanced by being in combination with the others.

- Components should be arranged in such a way that the textures and colors of the foods are most attractive to the eye.

RECIPES

BALSAMIC VINAIGRETTE

makes 1 quart/1 liter

4 fl oz/120 mL red wine vinegar

4 fl oz/120 mL balsamic vinegar

2 tsp/10 mL mustard (optional)

24 fl oz/720 mL mild olive oil

salt, as needed

pepper, as needed

3 tbsp/45 mL minced fresh herbs, such as chives, parsley, or tarragon (optional)

1 Combine the vinegars and the mustard, if using.

2 Whisk in the oil gradually.

3 Adjust the seasoning with salt and pepper to taste. Add the herbs, if desired.

VINAIGRETTE GOURMANDE

makes 12 fluid ounces/360 milliliters

1¹/₂ fl oz/45 mL sherry vinegar

1 fl oz/30 mL lemon juice

4 fl oz/20 mL olive oil

4 fl oz/120 mL vegetable oil

2 tbsp/30 mL minced chervil

2 tsp/10 mL minced tarragon

salt, as neeeded

pepper, as needed

1 Combine the vinegar and lemon juice.

2 Whisk in the oils gradually.

3 Add the chervil and tarragon and adjust the seasoning with salt and pepper to taste.

Walnut Oil and Red Wine Vinaigrette Substitute walnut oil for the vegetable oil and red wine vinegar for the sherry vinegar. Substitute parsley and chives for the chervil and tarragon.

MUSTARD-HERB VINAIGRETTE

makes 1 quart/1 liter

8 fl oz/240 mL white wine or cider vinegar

2 fl oz/60 mL Dijon mustard

2 tbsp/30 mL chopped parsley

¹/₂ tsp/2 mL onion powder

dash of garlic powder

2 tsp/10 mL sugar

2 tbsp/30 mL chopped herbs

salt, as needed

ground white pepper, as needed

24 fl oz/720 mL vegetable oil

water to adjust flavor, as needed

1 Combine the vinegar, mustard, parsley, onion powder, garlic powder, sugar, herbs, salt, and pepper.

2 Gradually incorporate the oil in a thin stream. Add a little water, as needed, to adjust the flavor.

3 Adjust the seasoning with salt and pepper to taste. Serve immediately or store under refrigeration.

PEANUT OIL AND MALT VINEGAR SALAD DRESSING

makes 1 quart/1 liter

20 fl oz/600 mL peanut oil

10 fl oz/300 mL malt vinegar

2 oz/60 g dark brown sugar, or as needed

2 tbsp/30 mL chopped tarragon

2 tbsp/30 mL chopped chives

2 tbsp/30 mL chopped parsley

2 tsp/10 mL minced garlic

salt, as needed

pepper, as needed

1 Combine the oil, vinegar, sugar, tarragon, chives, parsley, and garlic and mix well with a whisk. Let the dressing age for 24 hours before using.

2 Recombine the ingredients thoroughly and adjust the seasoning with salt and pepper to taste before service.

PESTO VINAIGRETTE

makes about 1 to 1½ quarts/1 to 1.5 liters

4 oz/115 g PESTO (recipe follows)
1 tsp/5 mL salt
pepper, as needed
8 fl oz/240 mL red wine vinegar
24 fl oz/720 mL olive or vegetable oil

1 Combine the pesto, salt, pepper, and vinegar.

2 Gradually incorporate the oil in a thin stream, mixing thoroughly. Adjust the seasoning with salt and pepper to taste.

3 Serve immediately or store under refrigeration for later service.

see photograph on page 789

PESTO

makes about 8 ounces/115 grams

2 oz/60 g basil leaves
3 tbsp/45 mL toasted pine nuts
¼ oz/7 g garlic paste
¼ oz/7 g salt, as needed
2 to 4 fl oz/60 to 120 mL olive oil
2 oz/60 g grated Parmesan cheese

1 Rinse the basil well, dry thoroughly, and chop coarsely. Transfer to a food processor or mortar and pestle. Grind the basil, pine nuts, garlic, and salt together, adding oil gradually, to form a thick paste of a saucelike consistency.

2 Adjust the seasoning with salt and add the Parmesan as close to service time as possible.

ROASTED GARLIC AND MUSTARD VINAIGRETTE

makes about 1 quart/1 liter

1 oz/30 g puréed roasted garlic
1 tsp/5 mL salt, or as needed
1 oz/30 g Dijon mustard
pepper, as needed
8 fl oz/240 mL red wine vinegar
24 fl oz/720 mL olive oil

1 Combine the garlic and salt and work into a paste. Combine the garlic mixture with the mustard, pepper, and vinegar.

2 Gradually incorporate the oil in a thin stream, mixing thoroughly. Adjust the seasoning with salt and pepper to taste.

3 Serve immediately or store under refrigeration for later service.

LEMON GARLIC VINAIGRETTE

makes about 1 quart/1 liter

6 fl oz/180 mL lemon juice
¼ oz/7 g garlic, mashed to a paste
1 tsp/5 mL minced rosemary
12 fl oz/360 mL olive oil
12 fl oz/360 mL salad oil
salt, as needed
pepper, as needed
sugar, as needed

1 Combine the lemon juice, garlic, and rosemary. Whisk in the oils gradually.

2 Adjust the seasoning with salt, pepper, and sugar to taste.

Lemon Parsley Vinaigrette Substitute ½ to ¾ oz/15 to 25 g minced parsley for the rosemary. Omit the garlic if desired.

LIME AND OLIVE OIL VINAIGRETTE

makes 1 quart/1 liter

2¹/₂ fl oz/75 mL lime juice

1¹/₂ fl oz/45 mL lemon juice

6 fl oz/180 mL Chardonnay

2 fl oz/60 mL white wine vinegar

1¹/₂ oz/45 g minced shallots

3 tbsp/45 mL cracked pink peppercorns

20 fl oz/600 mL extra-virgin olive oil

4 oz/115 g minced chives

salt, as needed

pepper, as needed

1 Combine the lime and lemon juices, Chardonnay, vinegar, shallots, and peppercorns. Whisk in the oil gradually.

2 Add the chives and adjust the seasoning with salt and pepper to taste.

CURRY VINAIGRETTE

makes 1 quart/1 liter

1¹/₂ pt/720 mL olive oil

3 tbsp/45 mL CURRY POWDER (page 353)

1 oz/30 g minced shallots

¹/₂ oz/15 g minced garlic

¹/₂ oz/15 g minced ginger

¹/₂ oz/15 g lemongrass, tender center portion only, minced

8 fl oz/240 mL cider vinegar

lemon juice, as needed

honey, as needed

salt, as needed

pepper, as needed

1 Heat 3 fl oz/90 mL of the oil over low heat. Add the curry powder, shallots, garlic, ginger and lemongrass. Continue to heat until the shallots are translucent. Remove from the heat and let cool.

2 Combine the cooled oil with the remaining oil and vinegar. Add lemon juice, honey, salt, and pepper to taste. Blend well.

see photograph on page 789

CATALINA FRENCH DRESSING

makes 1 quart/ 1 liter

3¹/₂ g/100 g pasteurized eggs

4 oz/115 g dark brown sugar

4 fl oz/120 mL cider vinegar

4 fl oz/120 mL paprika oil (see page 763)

2 tsp/10 mL Dijon mustard

¹/₄ tsp/1 mL garlic powder

¹/₄ tsp/1 mL onion powder

dash of ground allspice

12 fl oz/720 mL vegetable oil

salt, as needed

ground white pepper, as needed

1 Combine the eggs, sugar, vinegar, paprika oil, mustard, garlic powder, onion powder, and allspice and blend well.

2 Gradually incorporate the vegetable oil in a thin stream.

3 Adjust the seasoning with salt and pepper to taste.

AÏOLI

makes 1 quart/1 liter

2 egg yolks

¹/₄ oz/7 g garlic, mashed to a paste

1 fl oz/30 mL white wine vinegar

¹/₂ fl oz/15 mL water

1 tsp/5 mL dry mustard

1 pt/480 mL vegetable oil

10 fl oz/300 mL extra-virgin olive oil

salt, as needed

pepper, as needed

lemon juice, as needed

1 Combine the egg yolks, garlic, vinegar, water, and mustard in a bowl. Mix well with a balloon whip until the mixture is slightly foamy.

2 Gradually add the vegetable and olive oils in a thin stream, constantly beating with the whip, until they are incorporated and the mayonnaise is thick.

3 Adjust the flavor with salt, pepper, and lemon juice to taste.

4 Refrigerate immediately.

ANCHOVY CAPER MAYONNAISE

makes 1 quart/1 liter

1 qt/1 L MAYONNAISE (page 767)
3 fl oz/90 mL lemon juice, or as needed
1 tbsp/15 mL Dijon mustard
3/4 oz/25 g minced shallots
1 oz/30 g minced parsley
1 fl oz/30 mL minced nonpareil capers
1 oz/30 g minced anchovy fillets
salt, as needed
pepper, as needed

1 Combine the mayonnaise, lemon juice, mustard, shallots, parsley, capers, and anchovies and mix well.

2 Refrigerate until service. Stir to recombine. Adjust the seasoning with lemon juice, salt, and pepper to taste.

CREAMY BLACK PEPPERCORN DRESSING

makes 1 quart/1 liter

1 qt/.1 L MAYONNAISE (page 767)
3 to 4 oz/85 to 115 g Parmesan, or as needed
2 oz/60 g anchovy paste
1 oz/30 g garlic paste
1 tsp /5 mL salt, or as needed
2 tbsp/30 mL black peppercorns, coarsely ground

1 Combine all the ingredients and mix well.

2 Refrigerate until service time. Stir to recombine. Adjust the seasoning with salt and Parmesan to taste.

see photograph on page 789

BLUE CHEESE DRESSING

makes 1 quart/1 liter

4 oz/115 g crumbled blue cheese
1 pint/480 mL MAYONNAISE (page 767)
8 fl oz/240 mL sour cream
6 fl oz/180 mL buttermilk
3 fl oz/90 mL milk
1 tbsp/15 mL lemon juice, or as needed
1 oz/30 g puréed onions
1/4 oz/7 g garlic paste
Worcestershire sauce, as needed
salt, as needed
pepper, as needed

1 Combine the blue cheese, mayonnaise, sour cream, buttermilk, milk, lemon juice, onions, and garlic and mix to a smooth consistency.

2 Adjust the seasoning with lemon juice, Worcestershire sauce, salt, and pepper to taste.

3 Refrigerate until service.

CAESAR-STYLE DRESSING

makes 1 quart/1 liter

3 oz/85 g anchovy fillets
1/2 oz/15 g mild mustard
1/4 oz/7 g garlic paste
1 tbsp/15 mL Worcestershire sauce
6 fl oz/180 mL red wine vinegar
2 oz/60 g grated Parmesan
salt, as needed
1 tsp/5 mL ground black pepper, or as needed
18 fl oz/540 mL olive oil
2 tbsp/30 mL lemon juice, or as needed
1/2 tsp/2 mL Tabasco sauce, or as needed

1 Blend the anchovies, mustard, garlic paste, and Worcestershire to form a paste. Add the vinegar, Parmesan, salt, and pepper to taste and combine.

2 Gradually incorporate the oil in a thin stream.

3 Adjust the seasoning with pepper, lemon juice, and Tabasco sauce to taste. Serve immediately or refrigerate for later service.

CUCUMBER DRESSING

makes 1 quart/1 liter

12 oz/340 g thinly sliced cucumbers, peeled and seeded before slicing

2 fl oz/60 mL lemon juice

8 fl oz/240 mL sour cream

3 tbsp/45 mL minced dill

1 tbsp/15 mL sugar, or as needed

salt, as needed

ground white pepper, as needed

Tabasco sauce, as needed

1 Purée the cucumbers in a food processor.

2 Add the remaining ingredients and blend just until incorporated.

3 Adjust the seasoning with sugar, salt, and pepper. Serve immediately or refrigerate for later service.

GREEN GODDESS DRESSING

makes 1 quart/1 liter

2 oz/60 g spinach leaves

2 oz/60 g watercress leaves

1 tbsp/15 mL parsley leaves

1 tbsp/15 mL tarragon leaves

1 garlic clove, mashed to paste

4 oz/120 mL vegetable oil

12 fl oz/360 mL MAYONNAISE (page 767)

1 tbsp/15 mL mustard

salt, as needed

pepper, as needed

lemon juice, as needed

1 Purée the spinach, watercress, parsley, tarragon and garlic with the oil in a food processor. Combine with the mayonnaise and mustard.

2 Adjust the seasoning with salt, pepper, and lemon juice to taste.

3 Serve immediately or refrigerate for later service.

RANCH-STYLE DRESSING

makes 1 quart/1 liter

12 fl oz/360 mL sour cream

12 fl oz/360 mL MAYONNAISE (page 767)

8 fl oz/240 mL buttermilk

1 fl oz/30 mL lemon juice

2 fl oz/60 mL red wine vinegar

1/4 oz/7 g garlic paste

1 1/2 fl oz/45 mL Worcestershire sauce

1 tbsp/15 mL minced parsley

1 tbsp/15 mL minced chives

1 tbsp/15 mL minced shallots

1 tbsp/15 mL Dijon mustard

1 tsp/5 mL celery seed

1 Combine all the ingredients and mix well.

2 Serve immediately or refrigerate for later service.

TARTAR SAUCE

makes about 1 quart/1 liter

1 qt/1 L MAYONNAISE (page 767)

12 oz/360 g drained sweet pickle relish

2 oz/60 g minced capers

3 oz/85 g small-dice HARD-COOKED EGGS (page 726)

salt, as needed

ground white pepper, as needed

Worcestershire sauce, as needed

Tabasco sauce, as needed

1 Combine the mayonnaise, pickle relish, capers, and eggs and mix well. Adjust the seasoning with salt, pepper, Worcestershire, and Tabasco to taste.

2 Serve immediately or refrigerate for later service.

ROSEMARY GARLIC VINEGAR

makes 1 pint/480 milliliters

1 pt/480 mL white wine vinegar
3 to 4 peeled garlic cloves
6 to 8 rosemary sprigs
1 opal basil sprig (optional)
1 tbsp/15 mL whole black peppercorns

1 Heat the vinegar until slightly warm, about 120°F/49°C.

2 Thread the garlic on a skewer. Place it in a glass or plastic bottle with the rosemary, basil, if using, and peppercorns.

3 Pour the vinegar over the herbs and garlic.

4 Let cool. Close the bottle and hold under refrigeration.

5 Use as needed.

BASIL OIL

makes 1 pint/480 milliliters

3 oz/85 g basil leaves
1 oz/30 g flat-leaf parsley leaves
1 pt/480 mL olive oil

1 Blanch the basil and parsley leaves in salted water for 20 seconds. Shock and drain on paper towels.

2 Combine the blanched herbs with half of the oil in a blender and purée very fine. Add to the remaining oil. Strain through cheesecloth, if desired.

3 Transfer to a storage container or squirt bottle. Close the bottle and hold under refrigeration.

4 Use as needed.

NOTE
Substitute other herbs, such as chives, tarragon, chervil, or scallions, for the basil and parsley.

CINNAMON OIL

makes 1 pint/480 milliliters

19 fl oz/570 mL sunflower oil
12 sticks cinnamon, crushed
1 nutmeg, cracked

1 Heat the oil in a small saucepan with the cinnamon and nutmeg until about 150°F/65°C.

2 Remove from the heat and let cool.

3 Strain the oil into a bottle or other clean container.

4 Let cool. Close the bottle and hold under refrigeration.

5 Use as needed.

ORANGE OIL

makes 1 pint/480 milliliters

12 fl oz/360 mL olive oil
6 fl oz/170 mL extra-virgin olive oil
zest of 3 oranges, cut into strips

1 Combine the pure olive oil and the extra-virgin olive oil in a saucepan and heat to 140°F/60°C. Do not leave the oil. It warms very quickly.

2 Add the orange zest and infuse overnight in the refrigerator.

3 The next day, taste and strain out the zest if the flavor is good. Close the bottle and hold under refrigeration.

4 Use as needed.

Sherried Watercress and Apple Salad

Panzanella

Pesto Vinaigrette

Creamy Black Peppercorn Dressing

Curry Vinaigrette

Corn and Jícama Salad

CAESAR SALAD

makes 10 appetizer portions

20 oz 570 g romaine lettuce

10 oz 285 g garlic-flavored or plain croutons (see page 771)

DRESSING

¼ oz/7 g garlic paste

5 anchovy fillets

salt, as needed

pepper, as needed

2 oz/60 g pasteurized egg (whole egg or yolk)

2 fl oz/60 mL fresh lemon juice, or to taste

10 fl oz/300 mL extra-virgin olive oil

5 oz/170 g finely grated Parmesan cheese, or as needed

1 Separate the romaine into leaves. Clean and dry thoroughly. Tear or cut into pieces if necessary. Hold refrigerated until ready to serve.

2 Prepare croutons and hold until ready to serve.

3 To prepare each salad, mash about ⅛ tsp/50 cc garlic (½ clove), ½ anchovy fillet, salt, and pepper into a paste. Add 2 tsp/10 mL egg and 1 tsp/5 mL lemon juice, and blend. Add 1 fl oz/30 mL olive oil, whisking to form a thick dressing. Add 1 to 2 tbsp/30 to 60 mL grated Parmesan and 2½ oz/75 g of the prepared romaine. Toss until coated. Serve on chilled plates, topped with some croutons.

NOTES

If this salad is prepared tableside, be sure to clean and sanitize wooden bowls carefully after each use. The more traditional raw or coddled egg is replaced with a frozen pasteurized egg product, to help ensure the safety of the guest.

Grilled Chicken Caesar Salad Top a single portion of the Caesar Salad with a grilled chicken breast (a 4- to 5-ounce/115- to 140-gram) portion of chicken for a main course salad, a 2- to 3-ounce/60- to 85-gram portion for an appetizer portion).

WILTED SPINACH SALAD WITH WARM BACON VINAIGRETTE

makes 10 portions

WARM BACON VINAIGRETTE

8 oz/225 g diced bacon

1½ oz/45 g minced shallots

¼ oz/7 g garlic paste

4 oz/115 g brown sugar

3 oz/85 g cider vinegar

5 to 6 fl oz/150 to 180 mL vegetable oil

salt, as needed

cracked black peppercorns, as needed

1½ lb/680 g prepared spinach leaves

5 small-dice HARD-COOKED EGGS (page 726)

6 oz/170 g sliced mushrooms

3 oz/85 g thinly sliced red onion

4 oz/225 g croutons (see page 771), as needed

1 To make the vinaigrette, render the bacon. Remove from the pan and reserve. Add the shallots and garlic to the bacon fat and sweat. Blend in the brown sugar and melt it. Remove the pan from the heat. Whisk in the vinegar and oil. Season with salt and pepper to taste.

2 Arrange the spinach on a plate. Pour the hot dressing over the spinach. Top with the eggs, mushrooms, onion rings, croutons, and bacon.

3 Serve warm.

TROPICAL FRUIT SALAD

makes 10 portions

6 oz/170 g diced mango

6 oz/170 g diced pineapple

6 oz/170 g diced melon or melon balls

6 oz/170 g diced papaya

3 fl oz/90 mL orange juice

6 oz/170 g sliced bananas

2 oz/60 g shredded unsweetened coconut (optional)

1 Cut all the fruit as close as possible to service time. Toss the mango, pineapple, melon, and papaya together with the orange juice. Refrigerate until time of service.

2 Arrange the fruit salad on chilled plates and top with the bananas. Sprinkle with coconut, if desired, and serve at once.

NOTE

Substitute guava, passion fruit, star fruit, or other tropical fruits for those listed.

SHERRIED WATERCRESS AND APPLE SALAD

makes 10 portions

6 fl oz/180 mL vegetable oil

3 fl oz/90 mL sherry wine vinegar

1 tsp/5 mL brown sugar

salt, to taste

pepper, to taste

20 oz/340 g watercress, cleaned and stems trimmed

10 oz/285 g Golden Delicious apple julienne

3 oz/85 g diced celery

2 oz/60 g toasted walnut halves

1 Combine the oil, vinegar, sugar, salt, and pepper in a bowl and whisk until a lightly thickened vinaigrette forms.

2 Add the watercress, apples, and celery to the bowl and toss until evenly coated with the vinaigrette.

3 Scatter the toasted walnuts over the salad and serve at once.

SPINACH, AVOCADO, AND GRAPEFRUIT SALAD

makes 10 portions

1½ lb/680 g sliced avocados

1¾ lb/800 g grapefruit segments

2 lb/900 g spinach, cleaned and stems removed

BALSAMIC VINAIGRETTE (page 782), as needed

salt, as needed

pepper, as needed

1 Toss together the avocados and grapefruit segments. This will prevent the avocados from browning.

2 Toss the spinach with the vinaigrette, using only enough vinaigrette to coat the leaves very lightly. Adjust the seasoning with salt and pepper to taste.

3 Arrange the spinach on chilled plates. Top it with the avocados and grapefruit.

4 Drizzle additional dressing on the avocado mixture. Serve immediately.

TOMATO AND MOZZARELLA SALAD

makes 10 portions

3 lb/1.3 kg sliced tomatoes

20 oz/570 g sliced fresh mozzarella

10 fl oz/300 mL RED WINE VINAIGRETTE (page 762)

salt, as needed

¼ to ½ oz/8 to 15 g basil chiffonade

pepper, as needed

1 Place the tomatoes and mozzarella slices alternately on a plate and drizzle the vinaigrette over the top.

2 Adjust the seasoning with salt to taste. Garnish with the basil and pepper.

CARROT AND RAISIN SALAD

makes 10 portions

8 fl oz/240 mL water

2 tsp/10 mL sugar

1 tsp/5 mL salt, or as needed

1 tbsp/15 mL lemon juice

5 oz/140 g raisins

1½ lb/680 g grated carrots

3 fl oz/90 mL MAYONNAISE (page 767)

3 fl oz/90 mL WHITE WINE VINAIGRETTE (page 762)

1 Combine the water, sugar, salt, and lemon juice in a saucepan and bring to a boil. Pour over the raisins and steep until the raisins are plump. Drain and let cool.

2 Mix the raisins and carrots with the mayonnaise and vinaigrette.

3 Serve immediately or refrigerate for later service.

CELERIAC AND TART APPLE SALAD

makes 10 portions

DRESSING

3 fl oz/90 mL MAYONNAISE (page 767)

2 fl oz/60 mL crème fraîche

2 oz/60 g Dijon mustard

1 fl oz/30 mL lemon juice

salt, as needed

pepper, as needed

1½ lb/680 g celeriac

1 qt/1 L water, as needed

lemon juice, as needed

12 oz/340 g Granny Smith apples, peeled and diced

salt, as needed

pepper, as needed

1 To make the dressing, combine the mayonnaise, crème fraîche, mustard, and lemon juice and blend well. Adjust the seasoning with salt and pepper to taste.

2 Peel and cut the celeriac into julienne. (If the celeriac is cut in advance, hold it in water to which lemon juice has been added to keep the celeriac from turning brown.) When ready to blanch the celeriac, bring salted water to a simmer. Add 1 fl oz/30 mL lemon juice for each quart. Parcook celeriac about 2 minutes, drain, and refresh.

3 Toss the apples with the dressing. Add the celeriac and adjust the seasoning with salt, pepper, and lemon juice to taste.

4 Serve immediately or refrigerate for later service.

CUCUMBER YOGURT SALAD

makes 10 portions

1½ pt/720 mL plain yogurt

10 oz/285 g cucumber brunoise (peeled and seeded)

1 tbsp/15 mL minced green onions

1½ tsp/8 mL ground cumin, or as needed

salt, as needed

ground white pepper, as needed

1 Combine the yogurt, cucumbers, green onions, and cumin. Adjust the seasoning with salt, pepper, and more cumin if needed.

2 Serve immediately or refrigerate for later service.

CORN AND JÍCAMA SALAD

makes 10 portions

1½ lb/680 g corn kernels

1 lb/450 g jícama, peeled and cut into small dice

1 fl oz/30 mL lime juice

1 tsp/5 mL cilantro

pinch of cayenne

salt, as needed

white pepper, as needed

1 Combine the corn, jícama, lime juice, cilantro, and cayenne in a bowl and toss. Adjust the seasoning with salt and pepper to taste.

2 Serve immediately or refrigerate for later service.

see photograph on page 789

JÍCAMA SALAD

makes 10 portions

1½ lb/680 g jícama, peeled and cut into julienne

2 oz/60 g Granny Smith apples, peeled, cored, and cut into julienne

2 oz/60 g red pepper julienne

6 fl oz/180 mL yogurt

¾ tsp/4 g ground cumin

salt, as needed

pepper, as needed

1 Combine the jícama, apple, and red pepper in a medium bowl.

2 Mix together the yogurt and cumin in a small bowl. Adjust the seasoning with salt and pepper to taste. Pour over the jícama mixture and mix to combine.

3 Serve immediately or refrigerate for later service.

MEDITERRANEAN PEPPERS WITH LEMON THYME VINAIGRETTE

makes 10 portions

LEMON THYME VINAIGRETTE

6 fl oz/180 mL thyme-infused olive oil (see page 763)

2 fl oz/60 mL lemon juice

1 tbsp/15 mL minced thyme

1 tbsp/15 mL minced oregano

1 tbsp/15 mL minced parsley

1 tsp/5 mL minced shallots

salt, as needed

pepper, as needed

5 oz/140 g roasted red pepper julienne

5 oz/140 g roasted green pepper julienne

5 oz/140 g roasted yellow pepper julienne

7 oz/200 g tomato julienne

4 oz/115 g crumbled feta cheese

2 oz/60 g pitted Niçoise olives

1 oz/30 g drained capers

2 oz/60 g croutons (see page 771)

2 oz/60 g pine nuts, toasted

1 To make the vinaigrette, combine the olive oil, lemon juice, thyme, oregano, parsley, and shallots. Season with salt and pepper to taste.

2 Add the peppers, tomatoes, feta cheese, olives, and capers and combine evenly.

3 Let marinate 30 to 40 minutes at room temperature or up to 24 hours under refrigeration.

4 Serve topped with croutons and pine nuts.

WALDORF SALAD

makes 10 portions

1¼ lb/570 g large-dice apples

6 oz/170 g large-dice celery

3 oz/85 g MAYONNAISE (page 767)

salt, as needed

20 oz/570 g lettuce leaves

2 oz/60 g coarsely chopped walnuts

1 Combine the apples, celery, and mayonnaise. Season with salt to taste. Refrigerate.

2 Serve on a bed of lettuce. Top with walnuts.

COLESLAW

makes 10 portions

6 fl oz/180 mL sour cream

2 fl oz/60 mL MAYONNAISE (page 767)

2 fl oz/60 mL cider vinegar

1 tbsp/15 mL dry mustard

1½ oz/45 g sugar

2 tsp/10 g celery seed

salt, as needed

pepper, as needed

1½ lb/680 g shredded green cabbage

6 oz/170 g shredded carrots

1 Mix the sour cream, mayonnaise, vinegar, mustard, sugar, and celery seed together in a large bowl until smooth. Season with salt and pepper to taste.

2 Add the cabbage and carrots and toss until evenly coated.

3 Serve immediately or refrigerate for later service.

MIXED BEAN SALAD

makes 10 portions

10 oz/285 g cooked black beans, drained

10 oz/285 g cooked pinto or small red kidney beans, drained

10 oz/285 g cooked chickpeas, drained

5 oz/140 g cooked red lentils, drained

6 oz/170 g small-dice red onions

4 oz/115 g minced celery

2 tbsp/30 mL minced parsley

10 fl oz/285 mL VINAIGRETTE GOURMANDE (page 783)

salt, as needed

pepper, as needed

1 Combine the black beans, pinto beans, chickpeas, lentils, onions, celery, and parsley. Gently toss with the vinaigrette.

2 Marinate under refrigeration for 24 hours. Adjust the seasoning with salt and pepper to taste.

3 Serve immediately or refrigerate for later service.

WARM BLACK-EYED PEA SALAD

makes 10 portions

8 fl oz/240 mL olive oil

4 oz/115 g minced onions

¼ oz/7 g minced garlic

zest of 1 lemon

12 oz/340 g dried black-eyed peas, sorted and rinsed

1½ qt/1½ L CHICKEN STOCK (page 248)

2 rosemary sprigs

2 thyme sprigs

2 bay leaves

4 fl oz/120 mL lemon juice, as needed

¼ oz/8 g basil chiffonade

salt, as needed

pepper, as needed

1   Heat 1 fl oz/30 mL of the oil in a saucepan over high heat. Add the onions, half of the garlic, and the lemon zest and sauté until tender.

2   Add the peas, stock, rosemary, thyme, and bay leaves and bring to a boil. Reduce the heat and simmer until the peas are thoroughly tender, about 1 hour. Add water if necessary to keep the peas covered throughout the cooking time.

3   While the peas are cooking, combine the remaining oil and garlic, the lemon juice, and basil.

4   Drain the peas and remove and discard the rosemary, thyme, and bay leaves. Add the hot peas to the lemon basil vinaigrette and toss gently until evenly coated. Season with salt and pepper to taste.

5   Serve warm or at room temperature.

LENTIL SALAD

makes 10 portions

2 lb/900 g cooked brown or green lentils

6 oz/170 g minced green onions

6 oz/170 g chopped walnuts

6 fl oz/180 mL WHITE WINE VINAIGRETTE (page 762), or as needed

salt, as needed

pepper, as needed

1   Mix the lentils, green onions, and walnuts together. Add enough vinaigrette to coat. Season with salt and pepper to taste.

2   Serve immediately or refrigerate for later service.

CURRIED RICE SALAD

makes 10 portions

2 lb/900 g cooked long-grain rice

8 oz/225 g cooked green peas

4 oz/115 g diced onions

4 oz/115 g diced Granny Smith apples, peeled if desired

2 oz/60 g toasted pumpkin seeds

2 oz/60 g plumped golden raisins

6 fl oz/180 mL CURRY VINAIGRETTE (page 784), or as needed

salt, as needed

pepper, as needed

CURRY POWDER (page 353), as needed (optional)

1   Mix the rice, peas, onions, apples, pumpkin seeds, and raisins.

2   Toss lightly with the vinaigrette, adding just enough to moisten the rice. Adjust the seasoning with salt, pepper, and additional curry powder to taste, if desired.

3   Serve immediately or refrigerate for later service.

PANZANELLA

makes 10 portions

8 oz/225 g cubed stale or toasted Italian or French bread

1½ lb/680 kg large-dice tomatoes

2 tbsp/30 mL minced garlic

3 oz/85 g celery hearts, sliced thin on the bias

8 oz/225 g diced seeded cucumber

6 oz/170 g diced red pepper

6 oz/170 g diced yellow pepper

20 anchovy fillets, sliced (optional)

2 tbsp/30 mL drained capers

¼ oz/8 g coarsely chopped basil

10 fl oz/300 mL RED WINE VINAIGRETTE (page 762), or as needed

1   Combine the bread, tomatoes, garlic, celery, cucumber, peppers, anchovies, capers, and basil. Add the vinaigrette and toss to coat.

2   Serve immediately.

see photograph on page 788

MACARONI SALAD

makes 10 portions

2 lb/900 g cooked elbow macaroni, cooled

5 oz/140 g fine-dice celery

4 oz/115 g fine-dice onion

4 oz/115 g fine-dice green pepper

2 oz/60 g fine-dice red pepper

1 tsp/5 mL minced garlic

12 fl oz/360 mL MAYONNAISE (page 767) or MUSTARD-HERB
   VINAIGRETTE (page 782), or as needed

salt, as needed

pepper, as needed

1 Combine the macaroni, celery, onions, green pepper, red
   pepper, and garlic. Add just enough mayonnaise to coat.
   Adjust the seasoning with salt and pepper to taste.

2 Serve immediately or refrigerate for later service.

PASTA SALAD WITH PESTO VINAIGRETTE

makes 10 portions

2 lb/900 g cooked penne pasta, cooled

10 oz/285 g tomatoes, diced or cut into wedges

4 oz/115 g ham, diced or cut into julienne

2 oz/60 g olives, pitted and chopped

1 oz/30 g pine nuts, toasted

3 oz/85 g diced red onions or sweet onions

10 fl oz/285 mL PESTO VINAIGRETTE (page 782)

1 Combine all the ingredients.

2 Marinate several hours under refrigeration. Serve.

HAM SALAD

makes 20 portions

4 lb/1.9 kg diced or ground smoked ham

1 pt/480 mL MAYONNAISE (page 767)

2 to 3 oz/60 to 85 g sweet pickle relish

1 to 2 oz/30 to 60 g prepared mustard

pepper, as needed

1 Combine the ham, mayonnaise, relish, and mustard and
   mix well. Adjust the seasoning with pepper to taste.

2 Serve immediately or refrigerate for later service.

CHICKEN SALAD

makes 20 portions

4 lb/1.9 kg diced cooked chicken

1 pt/480 mL MAYONNAISE (page 767)

1½ lb/680 g minced celery

salt, as needed

pepper, as needed

poultry seasoning, as needed

1 Combine the chicken, mayonnaise, and celery and mix
   well. Adjust the seasoning with salt, pepper, and poultry
   seasoning to taste.

2 Serve immediately or refrigerate for later service.

EGG SALAD

makes 10 portions

2 lb/900 g small-dice HARD-COOKED EGGS (page 726)

4 oz/115 g MAYONNAISE (page 767)

6 oz/170 g minced celery

3 oz/85 g minced onions

salt, as needed

white pepper, as needed

½ tsp/3 mL garlic powder, as needed

1 tbsp/15 mL Dijon mustard, as needed

1 Combine the eggs, mayonnaise, celery, and onions and
   mix well. Season with salt, pepper, garlic powder, and
   mustard to taste.

2 Serve immediately or refrigerate for later service.

TUNA SALAD

makes 10 portions

1½ lb/680 g drained canned albacore tuna

10 fl oz/300 mL MAYONNAISE (page 767)

4 oz/115 g minced celery

4 oz/115 g minced onions

garlic powder, as needed

2 tsp/10 mL Worcestershire sauce, or as needed

salt, as needed

ground white pepper, as needed

½ tsp/3 mL dry mustard, as needed

1 Flake the tuna and place it in a large bowl. Add the mayonnaise, celery, and onions and mix well. Season with garlic powder, Worcestershire sauce, salt, pepper, and mustard to taste.

2 Serve immediately or refrigerate for later service.

SHRIMP SALAD

makes 20 portions

4 lb/1.9 kg cooked shrimp, peeled and deveined

1 pt/480 mL MAYONNAISE (page 767)

1 lb/450 g minced celery

6 oz/340 g fine-dice onion

salt, as needed

ground white pepper, as needed

1 Coarsely chop the shrimp (leave small shrimp whole).

2 Combine the shrimp, mayonnaise, celery, and onion and mix well. Adjust the seasoning with salt and pepper to taste.

3 Serve immediately or refrigerate for later service.

SEAFOOD RAVIGOTE

makes 10 portions

½ oz/15 g minced shallots

20 shrimp (16/20 count), peeled and deveined

10 frogs leg pairs, cut in half

10 oz/285 g bay scallops, outer muscle removed

10 fl oz/480 mL white wine

14 fl oz/415 mL FISH STOCK (page 253)

4 egg yolks

1 tbsp/15 mL prepared mustard

1 tbsp/15 mL lemon juice

8 fl oz/480 mL vegetable oil

1 tsp/5 mL FINES HERBES (page 353)

salt, as needed

pepper, as needed

20 cooked mussels

4 oz/115 g cucumber julienne

20 leaves Boston lettuce

20 tomato wedges

10 lemon wedges

1 Combine the shallots, shrimp, frogs legs, scallops, wine, and stock and bring to a simmer. Poach seafood until done.

2 Remove, cover, and refrigerate. Strain the poaching liquid.

3 Reduce the poaching liquid to 1½ fl oz/45 mL and transfer to a stainless-steel bowl. Add the egg yolks, mustard, and lemon juice and mix well.

4 Whisk in the oil, starting very slowly in the beginning and increasing the speed as the oil is absorbed and a thick vinaigrette forms. Add the herbs. Adjust the seasoning with salt and pepper to taste.

5 Remove the meat from the frogs legs and clean the mussels. Combine the seafood and sauce.

6 Mix the cucumber julienne with the vinaigrette.

7 Serve the seafood ravigote on the lettuce leaves, garnished with tomato, lemon, and cucumber.

POTATO SALAD

2¹/₂ lb/1.15 kg cooked red bliss potatoes, peeled and sliced

6 oz/170 g small-dice HARD-COOKED EGGS (page 726)

5 oz/140 g diced onions

5 oz/140 g diced celery

1 oz/30 g Dijon mustard, or as needed

1 pt/480 mL MAYONNAISE (page 767)

Worcestershire sauce, as needed

salt, as needed

pepper, as needed

1 Combine the potatoes, eggs, onions, and celery in a bowl. Mix the mustard with the mayonnaise and Worcestershire sauce to taste. Gently toss with the potato mixture. Adjust the seasoning with salt and pepper and more mustard to taste.

2 Serve immediately or refrigerate for later service.

CHEF SALAD

2 lb/900 g mixed greens

20 slices roast turkey, rolled tightly

20 slices salami, rolled tightly

20 slices ham, rolled tightly

5 HARD-COOKED EGGS (page 726), cut into wedges

10 oz/285 g Cheddar julienne

10 oz/285 g Gruyère julienne

10 tomato wedges

3 oz/85 g thin-sliced cucumber

3 oz/85 g thin-sliced carrot

10 fl oz/300 mL WHITE WINE VINAIGRETTE or RED WINE VINAIGRETTE (page 762)

2 tbsp/30 mL minced chives

1 Place the greens in a bowl or arrange them on a plate.

2 Arrange the meat, eggs, cheese, and vegetables on the lettuce.

3 Drizzle with the vinaigrette, top with the small-dice chives, and serve.

COBB SALAD

6 oz/170 g vegetable oil

2 oz/60 g cider vinegar

1 oz/30 g lemon juice

1 oz/30 g Dijon mustard

¹/₂ oz/15 g minced parsley

salt, as needed

pepper, as needed

2 lb/900 g shredded romaine lettuce

1 lb/450 g cubed roasted or smoked turkey breast

6 oz/170 g diced avocados

3 oz/85 g celery, sliced on the bias

2 oz/60 g green onions, sliced on the bias

10 oz/285 g crumbled blue cheese

10 strips bacon, fully cooked and diced

1 Blend the oil, vinegar, lemon juice, mustard, and parsley thoroughly in a large mixing bowl. Adjust the seasoning with salt and pepper to taste.

2 Add the lettuce and toss until combined. Divide the lettuce among bowls or platters.

3 Arrange the turkey, avocadoes, celery, and green onions on the bed of lettuce. Drizzle the dressing still remaining in the mixing bowl over the salad. Top with the blue cheese and bacon. Serve at once.

GREEK SALAD

2 lb/900 g prepared lettuce, such as romaine or green leaf

30 tomato wedges

6 oz/170 g cucumbers, sliced or diced

3 oz/85 g red onion, sliced into rings

5 oz/140 g crumbled feta cheese

3 oz/85 g pitted black olives

3 oz/85 g pitted green olives

12 fl oz/360 mL LEMON PARSLEY VINAIGRETTE (page 783)

1 Make beds of lettuce on plates or in bowls. Arrange the tomatoes, cucumber, onion rings, feta, and olives on the lettuce. Drizzle with the vinaigrette or toss in bowls.

2 Serve at once.

TACO SALAD

makes 10 portions

2¹/₂ lb/1.15 kg ground beef

TACO SAUCE (recipe follows)

2 lb/900 g iceberg lettuce chiffonade

10 corn or flour tortillas, fried and shaped into bowls

12 oz/340 g cooked pinto beans

12 oz/340 g cooked black beans

10 oz/285 g diced tomatoes

2 oz/60 g diced red onion

5 fl oz/150 mL sour cream

10 oz/285 g shredded Cheddar or Monterey Jack

20 pitted black olives

1 pt/480 mL SALSA FRESCA (page 821)

1 Brown the ground beef over medium heat, stirring and breaking up meat until it is fully cooked and no longer red or pink. Remove from the pan with a slotted spoon, drain well, and combine with the taco sauce. The mixture should hold together and be moist.

2 Lay a bed of lettuce in the bottom of each tortilla bowl. Layer with beans, beef and sauce mixture, tomatoes, onions, sour cream, cheese, olives, and salsa. Serve immediately.

TACO SAUCE

makes 24 fluid ounces/720 milliliters

4 fl oz/120 mL vegetable oil

2 oz/60 g small-dice onions

2 tsp/10 mL minced garlic

1 tbsp/15 mL dried oregano

1 oz/30 g ground cumin

1/2 oz/15 g CHILI POWDER (page 353)

12 fl oz/360 mL tomato purée

1 pt/480 mL CHICKEN STOCK (page 248)

salt, as needed

pepper, as needed

cornstarch slurry, as needed

1 Heat the oil in a pan. Add the onions and cook over medium heat, stirring frequently, until the onions are brown, about 10 to 12 minutes. Add the garlic and continue to sauté another 1 to 2 minutes.

2 Add the oregano, cumin, and chili powder and cook briefly. Add the tomato purée and continue to cook, stirring frequently, until the mixture is reduced, about 10 to 12 minutes.

3 Add the stock and simmer for 15 to 20 minutes, or until the sauce is well flavored. Adjust the seasoning with salt and pepper. Purée the sauce and strain if desired. Thicken with cornstarch slurry, if needed. The sauce is ready to use now, or it may be properly cooled and stored for later service.

Sandwiches find their place on nearly every menu, from elegant receptions and teas to substantial but casual meals. Built from four simple elements — bread, a spread, a filling, and a garnish — they exemplify the ways in which a global approach to cuisine can result in nearly endless variety.

SANDWICHES

ELEMENTS IN A SANDWICH

A sandwich can be open or closed, hot or cold. It can be small enough to serve as an hors-d'oeuvre or large enough to serve as an entreé.

Cold sandwiches include standard deli-style versions made from sliced meats or mayonnaise-dressed salads. Club sandwiches, also known as triple-decker sandwiches, are included in this category as well.

Hot sandwiches may feature a hot filling, such as hamburgers or pastrami. Others are grilled, like a Reuben sandwich or a melt. Sometimes a hot filling is mounded on bread and the sandwich is topped with a hot sauce.

BREADS

Bread for sandwiches runs a fairly wide gamut. Sliced white and wheat Pullman loaves are used to make many cold sandwiches. The tight crumb of a good Pullman makes it a particularly appropriate choice for delicate tea and finger sandwiches, since they can be sliced thin without crumbling. Tea and finger sandwiches must be made on fine-grained bread in order to be trimmed of their crusts and precisely cut into shapes and sizes that can be eaten in about two average bites. Whole-grain and peasant-style breads are not always as easy to slice thin.

Various breads, buns, rolls, and wrappers are used to make special sandwiches.

The characteristics of the bread and how it will fit with the sandwich should be considered. The bread should be firm enough and thick enough to hold the filling, but not so thick that the sandwich is too dry to enjoy.

Most breads can be sliced in advance of sandwich preparation as long as they are carefully covered to prevent drying. Toasting should be done immediately before assembling the sandwich. Some breads to choose from include:

Pullman loaves (white, wheat, or rye)

Peasant-style breads (pumpernickel, sourdough, pain de campagne, and boule)

Rolls (hard, soft, and Kaiser rolls)

Flatbreads (foccacia, pita, ciabatta, and lavash)

Wrappers (rice paper and egg-roll wrappers)

Flour and corn tortillas

SPREADS

Many sandwiches call for a spread applied directly to the bread. A fat-based spread (mayonnaise or butter, for instance) provides a barrier to keep the bread from getting soggy. Spreads also add moisture to a sandwich and help to hold it together as it is held and eaten. Some sandwich fillings include the spread in the filling mixture (for example, a mayonnaise-dressed tuna salad); there is no need then to add a spread when assembling the sandwich.

Spreads can be very simple and subtly flavored, or they may themselves bring a special flavor and texture to the sandwich. The following list of spreads includes some

classic choices as well as some that may not immediately spring to mind as sandwich spreads.

Mayonnaise (plain or flavored, such as aïoli and rouille) or creamy salad dressings

Plain or compound butters

Mustard or ketchup

Spreadable cheeses (ricotta, cream cheese, mascarpone, or crème fraîche)

Vegetable or herb spreads (hummus, tapenade, or pesto)

Tahini and nut butters

Jelly, jam, compotes, chutneys, and other fruit preserves

Avocado pulp or guacamole

Oils and vinaigrettes

MAKING FLAVORED BUTTERS

Flavored butters are used as a cold spread, particularly for canapés and finger sandwiches. They can also be used as a kind of sauce to finish grilled or broiled meats, boiled or steamed vegetables, pasta, or even other sauces.

Unsalted butter gives greater control over the seasoning of a compound butter. Taste the butter before using it to be sure that it is fresh and flavorful. The butter should be cool but soft enough to work easily with a wooden spoon or the paddle of an electric mixer. Incorporate the prepared flavorings into the softened butter evenly by hand or with a mixer or food processor. Scrape down the bowl of the processor or mixer and stir the butter a few times by hand before using it. Taste the butter to evaluate its quality. Use it immediately as a spread or roll and hold it for later. Bring the compound butter to room temperature before spreading or piping.

Compound butter has many different applications. To evaluate the butter, taste it as it will be presented to the guest. Sample a canapé or sandwich if it is to be used as a spread; toss some cooked vegetables with it if it is to be served as their sauce, and so forth. The flavor of creamy butter should be present, as should the flavors of the seasonings and finishing ingredients used.

Mound the butter evenly so that it runs across the width of the parchment paper. Fold the paper over the butter to completely cover it.

To produce an evenly round cylinder, use your thumbs to tighten the paper around the butter.

To keep the butter from developing a flat side during refrigeration, store it floating in an ice bath.

Once rolled, the butter is ready to slice into portions and can be held during service in ice water, ready to use as desired.

FILLINGS

Sandwich fillings are the focus of a sandwich. They may be cold or hot, substantial or minimal. It is as important to properly roast and slice turkey for club sandwiches as it is to be certain that the watercress for tea sandwiches is perfectly fresh and completely rinsed and dried.

The filling should determine how all the other elements of the sandwich are selected and prepared. Choices for fillings include the following:

Sliced roasted or simmered meats (beef, corned beef, pastrami, turkey, ham, pâtés, sausages)

Sliced cheeses

Grilled, roasted, or fresh vegetables

Grilled, pan-fried, or broiled burgers, sausages, fish, or poultry

Salads of meats, poultry, eggs, fish, or vegetables

GARNISHES

Colorful garnishes such as watercress and radish, as well as a decorative piping of the spread, complete this canapé for service.

Lettuce leaves, slices of tomato or onion, sprouts, marinated or brined peppers, and olives are just a few of the many ingredients that can be used to garnish sandwiches. These garnishes become part of the sandwich's overall structure, so choose them with some thought to the way they complement or contrast the main filling.

When sandwiches are plated, side garnishes may also be included. For example:

Green salad or side salad (potato salad, pasta salad, and coleslaw, for example)

Lettuce and sprouts

Sliced fresh vegetables

Pickle spears or olives

Dips, spreads, or relishes

Sliced fruits

PRESENTATION STYLES

A sandwich constructed with a top and a bottom slice of bread is known as a closed sandwich. A club sandwich has a third slice of bread. Still other sandwiches have only one slice of bread, which acts as a base; these are open-faced sandwiches.

Straight-edged sandwiches are created by cutting with a sandwich or bread knife into squares, rectangles, diamonds, or triangles. The yield is generally lower when preparing these shapes, making them slightly more expensive to produce.

Take the time to cut shapes in an exacting and uniform fashion so that they look their best when set in straight rows on platters or arranged on plates. Cut tea sandwiches as close to service as possible. If these sandwiches must be prepared ahead of time, hold them covered with damp cloths or in airtight containers for a few hours.

SANDWICH PRODUCTION GUIDELINES

Organize the work station carefully, whether preparing mise en place or assembling sandwiches for service. Everything needed should be within arm's reach. It helps to write a list of tasks with a priority or time sequence assigned to each.

Maximize the work flow by looking for ways to eliminate any unnecessary movements:

- Organize the work so that it moves in a direct line.
- Prepare spreads prior to service and have them at a spreadable consistency. Use a spatula to spread the entire surface of the bread.
- Slice breads and rolls prior to service for volume production. Whenever possible, toast, grill, or broil breads when ready to assemble the sandwich. If bread must be toasted in advance, hold the toast in a warm area, loosely covered.
- Prepare and portion fillings and garnishes in advance and hold them at the correct temperature. Clean and dry lettuce or other greens in advance.
- Grilled sandwiches such as a Reuben sandwich or croque monsieur can be fully assembled in advance of service, then grilled or heated to order.

RECIPES

CIA CLUB

makes 10 portions

30 slices bread

6 fl oz/180 mL MAYONNAISE (page 767), or as needed

10 red leaf lettuce leaves

20 oz/570 g thinly sliced turkey

20 oz/570 g thinly sliced ham

20 tomato slices

20 bacon strips, cooked and cut in half

1 Toast the slices of bread (for each sandwich, you will need 3 slices of bread). Spread mayonnaise on only 1 slice of toast for each sandwich.

2 Layer in this order: lettuce, turkey, ham, toast, more mayonnaise on both sides, more lettuce, tomato and bacon.

3 Top with toast with mayonnaise spread on the underside.

4 Secure the sandwich with sandwich picks, cut the sandwich into quarters, and serve.

see photograph on page 809

PHILLY HOAGIE

makes 10 portions

10 fl oz/285 mL olive oil

1 tbsp/15 mL chopped oregano

10 sub rolls (10 in/25 cm each)

1½ lb/680 g thinly sliced prosciutto

10 oz/285 g thinly sliced sweet cappicola

10 oz/285 g thinly sliced Genoa salami

20 oz/570 g thinly sliced provolone

5 oz/140 g shredded iceberg lettuce

30 tomato slices (sliced ⅛ in/4 mm thick)

30 onion slices (sliced 1/16 in/2 mm thick)

1 Mix together the olive oil and oregano to make a dressing.

2 For each sandwich, slice a roll open, leaving it hinged, and brush the inside of the roll with dressing.

3 Arrange some prosciutto, cappicola, salami, and provolone on the roll. Top with lettuce. Place 3 slices of tomato on top of the lettuce. Top with onions and additional dressing. Close the sandwich and serve.

ROASTED VEGETABLES IN PITA WITH ROASTED GARLIC TAHINI

makes 10 portions

FILLING

12 oz/340 g eggplant

olive oil, as needed

4 oz/115 g onions

salt, as needed

pepper, as needed

1 lb/450 g tomatoes

4 oz/115 g red peppers

4 oz/115 g green peppers

4 oz/115 g arugula, cleaned and trimmed

4 fl oz/120 mL olive oil, or as needed

2 fl oz/60 mL lemon juice, or as needed

1 tsp/5 mL roasted garlic paste

1 pt/480 mL tahini, or as needed

10 pita breads

1 Cut the eggplant in half lengthwise and rub the cut surface with oil. Peel the onion and cut into slices and rub with oil. Season the eggplant and onion with salt and pepper and roast on an oiled sheet pan at 375°F/190°C until they are tender and lightly browned, about 30 to 40 minutes. Scoop the flesh from the eggplant and cut into dice. Cut the onions into dice. Reserve.

2 Remove the core from the tomatoes and cut into slices ¼ to ½ in/6 to 12 mm thick. Rub lightly with olive oil, season with salt and pepper, and roast on a rack in a sheet pan in a 375°F/190°C oven until lightly browned, about 30 to 40 minutes.

3 Rub the peppers with oil and roast at 425°F/220°C or under a broiler until their skins are charred. Place in a covered bowl or bag and cool. Remove and discard the skin, seeds, and stems. Cut into small dice or julienne. Reserve.

4 Toss the eggplant, onions, tomatoes, red and green peppers, and arugula lightly with the olive oil, lemon juice, salt, and pepper as needed.

5 Blend the garlic with the tahini. Adjust the consistency with a little water or lemon juice and season with salt and pepper.

6 For each sandwich, cut a pita in half. Spoon some of the vegetables into each half. Drizzle some tahini over the open end. Serve 1 fl oz/30 mL of tahini sauce on the side. Serve immediately.

CHICKEN BURGER

2¹/₂ lb/1.15 kg ground chicken

6 oz/170 g bread crumbs

1 lb/450 g DUXELLES STUFFING (page 439), cooled

2 tbsp/30 mL chopped herbs, such as chives, oregano, basil, or parsley

1 tsp/5 mL salt

¹/₂ tsp/3 mL white pepper

10 oz/285 g thinly sliced provolone cheese

10 Kaiser rolls

4 fl oz/120 mL melted butter, or as needed

10 green or red leaf lettuce leaves

20 tomato slices

1 Gently mix the chicken, bread crumbs, duxelles, herbs, salt, and pepper. Form into patties.

2 Lightly butter a flat top or griddle. Brown the patties on both sides. Finish in a 350°F/175°C oven to an internal temperature of 160°F/70°C.

3 Prior to service, top each burger with provolone cheese and return to the oven to melt.

4 For each sandwich, slice a roll, leaving the bread hinged. Brush with melted butter, then grill.

5 Place a burger on the roll and serve open-faced with a leaf of lettuce and 2 slices of tomato.

see photograph on page 809

SLOPPY JOE

2 fl oz/50 mL vegetable oil, as needed

8 oz/225 g minced onion

4 oz/115 g minced celery

1 tsp/5 mL minced garlic

3 lb/1.3 kg ground beef

8 oz/225 g tomato concassé

1 pint/480 mL ketchup

1 pint/480 mL BEEF STOCK (page 249)

2 tbsp/30 mL Worcestershire sauce

2 tsp/10 mL dry mustard

salt, as needed

pepper, as needed

cayenne, as needed

10 Kaiser or hamburger rolls

1 Heat the oil in a saucepan. Add the onion and celery and sweat about 5 minutes. Add the garlic and continue to sweat 2 minutes.

2 Add the ground beef and cook until no longer pink. Drain off excess grease.

3 Stir in the tomato concassé, ketchup, stock, Worcestershire sauce, and mustard. Simmer 30 minutes, stirring occasionally. Check the consistency. Adjust the seasoning to taste with salt, pepper, and cayenne to taste.

4 For each sandwich, split open a roll and grill it. Serve the beef mixture on the grilled roll.

BARBECUED BEEF

4 lb/1.8 kg beef brisket
salt, as needed
pepper, as needed
20 fl oz/600 mL BARBECUE SAUCE (page 290)
10 hoagie or Kaiser rolls
4 fl oz/120 mL melted butter, or as needed

1 Season the brisket with salt and pepper, place on a rack in
   a roasting pan, and roast in a 325°F/165°C oven until
   fork tender, about 5 hours.

2 Cool. Trim off excess fat. Slice or shred the meat. Mix
   with the barbecue sauce and reheat to 160°F/70°C in a
   350°F/175°C oven or over medium heat on stovetop.

3 For each sandwich, slice a roll, leaving the bread hinged.
   Brush with melted butter, then grill.

4 Place barbecued beef on the grilled roll and serve open-
   faced.

TUNA MELT

makes 10 portions

2¹/₂ lb/1.15 kg TUNA SALAD (page 796)
20 slices bread
10 oz/285 g thinly sliced Swiss cheese
24 oz/115 g butter, as needed

1 For each sandwich, place 4 oz/115 g of tuna salad on a
   slice of bread. Top with cheese and another slice of bread.
   Lightly butter the outside of the sandwich.

2 Grill until golden brown on both sides. Cut into halves
   and serve at once on heated plates.

TURKEY SANDWICH WITH SWEET AND SOUR ONIONS

makes 10 portions

SWEET AND SOUR ONIONS

20 oz/570 g onion julienne
4 fl oz/120 mL clarified butter
4 fl oz/120 mL soy sauce
8 fl oz/240 mL duck sauce
4 fl oz/115 mL water
1/2 tsp/3 mL garlic powder, or as needed
ground ginger, or as needed

20 slices bread, lightly toasted
2¹/₂ lb/1.15 kg thinly sliced roast turkey
20 tomato slices
20 oz/570 g thinly sliced Swiss cheese

1 To prepare the onions, sauté them in clarified butter until
   transparent. Add the soy sauce, duck sauce, and water.
   Simmer until the onions are fully cooked and dry. Season
   with garlic powder and ginger to taste.

2 For each sandwich, spread some of the onion mixture on 2
   slices of toast. Cover with sliced turkey. Spread additional
   onion mixture over the turkey. Place tomatoes on top of
   the onion mixture, then cover tomatoes with Swiss cheese.

3 Bake in a 350°F/175°C oven until the sandwich is heated
   through and the cheese is melted. Serve open-faced.

Reuben Sandwich

Grilled Vegetable and Cheese Sandwich

CIA Club

Chicken Burger

WESTERN SANDWICH

makes 10 portions

10 eggs, beaten

8 fl oz/240 mL milk

10 oz/285 g fine-dice ham

4 oz/115 g minced onion

4 oz/115 g fine-dice green pepper

salt, as needed

pepper, as needed

3 oz/85 g butter, as needed

10 Kaiser rolls, warmed

1 Mix together the eggs, milk, ham, onion, green pepper, and salt and pepper to taste.

2 For each sandwich, melt some of the butter in an omelet pan over medium to high heat. Pour in 3 fl oz/90 mL of the egg mixture. Cook, stirring constantly, until the eggs are beginning to set. Turn over and cook until firm.

3 Serve on a warmed Kaiser roll.

CROQUE MONSIEUR

makes 10 portions

10 oz/285 g thinly sliced Gruyère

15 oz/425 g thinly sliced ham

20 slices white Pullman bread

2 tbsp/30 mL Dijon mustard

4 oz/115 g butter, as needed

1 For each sandwich, place 1 slice of Gruyère and 1 slice of ham on 1 slice of bread. Spread lightly with mustard. Place another slice of Gruyère on top and close with a second slice of bread. Butter the outside of the sandwich.

2 Lightly butter a flat top or pan. Grill the sandwich until golden brown. If necessary, place in the oven and continue cooking until cheese has melted. Serve immediately.

GRILLED VEGETABLE AND CHEESE SANDWICH

makes 10 portions

HERB MAYONNAISE

5 oz/140 g MAYONNAISE (page 767), or as needed

½ oz/15 g minced herbs (such as chives, dill, parsley, basil)

salt, as needed

pepper, as needed

20 slices whole-wheat bread

10 oz/285 g grilled eggplant slices (about the same size as the bread)

10 oz/285 g grilled eggplant slices

3 oz/85 g roasted green pepper julienne

3 oz/85 g red pepper julienne

20 tomato slices

10 oz/285 g thinly sliced Monterey Jack

4 oz/115 g room-temperature butter, or as needed

1 To prepare the herb mayonnaise, blend the mayonnaise and herbs. Add salt and pepper to taste. Reserve.

2 For each sandwich, spread 2 slices of bread with the mayonnaise mixture. Top one slice with eggplant, peppers, tomato, and cheese. Top with the second slice. Brush the outside of the sandwich with the butter.

3 Grill the sandwich on both sides until golden brown and crisp; the filling should be very hot. Slice in half and serve at once on a heated plate.

see photograph on page 808

REUBEN SANDWICH

makes 10 portions

RUSSIAN DRESSING

20 fl oz/600 mL MAYONNAISE (page 767)

6 fl oz/180 mL chili sauce

1½ oz/40 g horseradish

2 oz/60 g minced onions, blanched

1½ tsp/8 mL Worcestershire sauce

salt, as needed

pepper, as needed

20 oz/570 g thinly sliced Swiss cheese

2 lb/900 g thinly sliced corned beef

20 oz/570 g SAUERKRAUT (page 545)

20 slices rye bread

4 oz/115 g butter, at room temperature, or as needed

1 To prepare the dressing, mix together the mayonnaise, chili sauce, horseradish, onions, and Worcestershire sauce. Adjust the seasoning with salt and pepper to taste.

2 For each sandwich, layer the cheese, Russian dressing, a thin layer of corned beef, and the sauerkraut on 1 slice of bread. Top with more corned beef, more Russian dressing and a second slice of cheese. Top with a bread slice.

3 Butter both sides of the sandwich. Grill until golden brown on both sides. If necessary, finish in the oven to melt the cheese and heat through. Serve immediately.

see photograph on page 808

THREE CHEESE MELT

makes 10 portions

20 slices bread

20 oz/570 g thinly sliced Colby Cheddar

5 oz/140 g crumbled blue cheese

10 oz/285 g thinly sliced pepper Jack cheese

4 oz/115 g butter, or as needed

1 For each sandwich, top 1 slice of bread with 1 slice of Colby, ½ oz/15 g of crumbled blue cheese, 1 slice of pepper Jack cheese, and another slice of Colby. Top with a bread slice.

2 Brush the outside of the sandwich with butter and grill the sandwich until golden on both sides. If necessary, place in the oven and continue cooking until the cheese has melted. Cut into halves and serve at once on a heated plate.

WATERCRESS SANDWICH WITH HERB MAYONNAISE

makes 10 portions

HERB MAYONNAISE

5 fl oz/150 mL MAYONNAISE (page 767), or as needed

½ oz/15 g finely minced herbs (such as chives, parsley, or dill)

salt, as needed

pepper, as needed

20 thin slices white Pullman bread

3 oz/85 g watercress, cleaned and trimmed

1 To prepare the herb mayonnaise, blend the mayonnaise and herbs. Add salt and pepper to taste. Reserve.

2 For each sandwich, spread the bread with a little of the herb mayonnaise. Lay some watercress on 1 slice of the bread. Top with another slice. Cut into the desired shape and serve at once, or hold properly covered for no more than 2 hours.

CUCUMBER SANDWICH WITH HERBED CREAM CHEESE

makes 10 portions

6 oz/170 g cream cheese

2 tbsp/30 mL minced herbs

2 fl oz/60 mL heavy cream, or as needed

salt, as needed

pepper, as needed

20 thin slices bread

12 oz/340 g thinly sliced cucumbers

1 Blend the cream cheese and herbs with enough cream to get a smooth spreading consistency. Add salt and pepper to taste. Spread the cream cheese mix on the bread slices.

2 For each sandwich, place cucumber slices on 1 slice of the bread. Top with another slice of bread.

3 Cut into the desired shapes and serve at once, or hold properly covered for no more than 2 hours.

APPLE SANDWICH WITH CURRY MAYONNAISE

makes 10 portions

1 tbsp/15 mL CURRY POWDER (page 353)

5 fl oz/150 mL MAYONNAISE (page 767)

salt, as needed

pepper, as needed

20 thin slices white Pullman bread

1 lb/450 g thinly sliced Granny Smith apples (peeled before slicing)

1 Toast the curry powder. Cool. Blend into the mayonnaise and season with salt and pepper. Spread the curry mayonnaise on the bread slices.

2 For each sandwich, place apple slices on 1 slice of the bread. Top with another slice of bread.

3 Cut into the desired shapes and serve at once, or hold properly covered for no more than 2 hours.

GORGONZOLA AND PEAR SANDWICH

makes 10 portions

2 oz/85 g cream cheese

5 oz/140 g Gorgonzola

2 fl oz/60 mL heavy cream, or as needed

20 thin slices raisin pumpernickel bread

1 lb/450 g pears, peeled and sliced

1 Blend the cream cheese and Gorgonzola with enough cream to get a smooth spreading consistency. Spread the Gorgonzola mix on the bread slices.

2 For each sandwich, place pear slices on 1 slice of the bread. Top with another slice of bread.

3 Cut into the desired shape and serve at once, or hold properly covered for no more than 2 hours.

TOMATO SANDWICH WITH OREGANO SOUR CREAM

makes 10 portions

8 fl oz/240 mL sour cream

2 tbsp/30 mL minced oregano

salt, as needed

pepper, as needed

20 thin slices bread

1 lb/450 g tomatoes, sliced

1 Mix the sour cream and oregano. Adjust the seasoning with salt and pepper to taste. Spread the sour cream mix on the bread slices.

2 For each sandwich, place tomato slices on 1 slice of the bread. Top with another slice of bread.

3 Cut into the desired shape and serve at once, or hold properly covered for no more than 2 hours.

ELENA RUZ SANDWICH

makes 10 portions

20 slices brioche or challah

10 oz/285 g cream cheese

10 oz/285 g strawberry preserves

30 oz/850 g thinly sliced turkey

4 oz/115 g butter, or as needed

1 For each sandwich, spread 1 slice of brioche with cream cheese. Spread another slice with strawberry jam. Place turkey on the cheese and top with the other slice.

2 Butter both sides of the sandwich and grill until lightly golden.

3 Cut into the desired shape and serve at once, or hold properly covered for no more than 2 hours.

The distinction between an hors-d'oeuvre and an appetizer has more to do with how and when it is served than with the actual food being served. Hors-d'oeuvre are typically served as a prelude to a meal, while appetizers are usually the meal's first course.

HORS-D'OEUVRE AND APPETIZERS

HORS-D'OEUVRE

The term hors-d'oeuvre, from the French for "outside the meal," is universally recognized; we have not developed any exact equivalent in English capable of conveying as much information as this short French phrase.

Hors-d'oeuvre are meant to pique the taste buds and perk up the appetite. Foods served as hors-d'oeuvre should be:

- *Perfectly fresh.* Whether the chef begins with completely new items or uses the small pieces and trim from foods used elsewhere in the kitchen, this obvious guideline must be carefully observed.

- *Small enough to eat in one or two bites.* Some hors-d'oeuvre are often eaten with the fingers, while other hors-d'oeuvre may require a plate and a fork. With very few exceptions, hors-d'oeuvre do not require the use of a knife.

- *Attractive.* Because hors-d'oeuvre customarily precede the meal, they are considered a means of teasing the appetite. This is partially accomplished through visual appeal.

- *Designed to complement the meal that is to follow.* It is important to avoid serving too many foods of a similar taste or texture. For example, if the menu features a lobster bisque, lobster canapés may be inappropriate.

PRESENTING HORS-D'OEUVRE

The presentation of hors-d'oeuvre can extend from the elegance of butler-style service to the relative informality of a buffet, or it may be a combination of service styles. The type of hors-d'oeuvre as well as the requirements of a particular function determine how these foods are presented. These guidelines can assist the chef in hors-d'oeuvre presentation:

- Keep in mind the nature of the event as well as the menu that follows when selecting hors-d'oeuvre.

- Ice carvings and ice beds are often used to keep seafood and caviar very cold, as well as for their dramatic appeal. Be sure that the ice can drain properly and that heavy or large ice carvings are stable.

- Hors-d'oeuvre served on platters or passed on trays should be thoughtfully presented, so that the last hors-d'oeuvre on the plate is still attractively presented.

- Hors-d'oeuvre that are served with a sauce require serving utensils. In order to prevent the guest from having to juggle a plate, fork, and napkin while standing, these hors-d'oeuvre should ordinarily be limited to either buffet service or served as the prelude to a more elaborate meal.

- To ensure that hot hors-d'oeuvre stay hot, avoid combining hot and cold items on a single platter and have chafing dishes available for buffet service.

APPETIZERS

While hors-d'oeuvre are served separately from the main meal, appetizers are traditionally its first course.

The role of the appetizer on the contemporary menu is becoming increasingly important. Although the traditional pâté, smoked trout, or escargot with garlic butter may still be found, dishes based on pasta, grilled vegetables, and grains are receiving more exposure.

The usual admonition to "build" a menu from one course to the next calls for some logical connection between the appetizer and all the courses to follow. For every rule you read about what types of foods should or shouldn't constitute an appetizer, you will find at least one good exception. What most appetizers have in common is careful attention to portioning and sound technical execution and plating. Most appetizers are small portions of very flavorful foods, meant to take just enough edge off the appetite to permit thorough enjoyment of an entrée.

Classic hors-d'oeuvre can be served as appetizers by increasing the portion size slightly. Perennial favorites are perfectly fresh clams and oysters, for example, shucked as close to service time as possible and served with sauces designed to enhance their naturally briny flavor, or a classic shrimp cocktail, served with a cocktail sauce, salsa, or other pungent sauce.

Smoked fish, meat, or poultry; sausages, pâtés, terrines, and galantines; air-dried ham and beef sliced paper thin— all of these can be used to create appetizer plates, on their own with a few accompaniments or garnishes, or as a sampler plate.

Salads are also served as appetizers. Portion size may be changed or a different sauce or garnish substituted to vary the salad from season to season or to showcase a range of flavors and textures from other cuisines.

Warm and hot appetizers include small portions of pasta, such as tortellini or ravioli, served on their own or in a sauce or broth. Puff pastry shells can be cut into vols au vent or made into turnovers and filled with savory ragouts or foie gras. Broiled or grilled fish, shellfish, or poultry are often featured. Crêpes, blini, and other similar dishes are popular. Meatballs and other highly seasoned ground-meat appetizers are also frequent choices.

Vegetables are more important than ever as an appetizer. They are often presented very simply—for example, steamed artichokes with a dipping sauce, or chilled asparagus drizzled with a flavored oil, or a plate of grilled vegetables accompanied by an aïoli.

PREPARING AND PRESENTING APPETIZERS

In preparing and presenting appetizers, keep in mind the following guidelines:

- Keep the portion size appropriate. Generally, appetizers should be served in small portions.

- Season all appetizers with meticulous care. Appetizers are meant to stimulate the appetite, so seasoning is of the utmost importance. Don't overuse fresh herbs and other seasonings, however. It is all too easy to deaden the palate by overwhelming it with too much garlic or an extravagance of basil at the meal's start. Remember that other courses will follow this one.

- Keep garnishes to a minimum. Those garnishes that are used should serve to heighten the dish's appeal by adding flavor and texture, not just color.

- Serve all appetizers at the proper temperature. Remember to chill or warm plates.

- Slice, shape, and portion appetizers carefully, with just enough on the plate to make the appetizer interesting and appealing from start to finish but not so much that the guest is overwhelmed.

- Neatness always counts, but especially with appetizers. They can set the stage for the entire meal.

- When offering shared appetizers, consider how they will look when they come to the table. It may be more effective to split a shared plate in the kitchen, rather than leaving it to the guests to divide it themselves.

- Color, shape, and white space play a role in the overall composition of the plate. Choose the right size and shape serving pieces and provide the guest with everything necessary for the appetizer, including special utensils, dishes to hold empty shells or bones, and, if necessary, finger bowls.

COLD SAVORY MOUSSE

A cold savory mousse has many applications. Served unmolded, sliced as a loaf or terrine, or piped into a shell or as a topping, it can be featured as an hors-d'oeuvre, an appetizer, or a component in other dishes.

The French word *mousse* literally means "foam" or "froth." A mousse is prepared by gently folding whipped cream or egg whites into an intensely flavored base. The light, frothy mixture is chilled enough to set before it is served.

A cold mousse is not cooked after being assembled since heating the gelatin in the mousse would melt and deflate it. A hot mousse is a small portion of a mousseline forcemeat (see page 844) that has been molded in a fashion similar to a cold mousse before being cooked and served hot.

SELECT AND PREPARE THE INGREDIENTS AND EQUIPMENT

ALTHOUGH EACH BASE INGREDIENT MAY call for an adjustment in the amount of binder and aerator, the basic formula described below is a good checkpoint. It can and should be altered depending on the type of mousse being made and the intended use of the final product.

The mousse's main, or base, ingredient may be one or a combination of the following: finely ground or puréed cooked or smoked meats, fish, or poultry; cheese or a blend of cheeses (a spreadable cheese, such as goat cheese or cream cheese, is typically used); purées of vegetables (these may need to be reduced by sautéing to intensify flavor and drive off excess moisture).

All base ingredients should be properly seasoned before adding other ingredients,

and the seasoning rechecked once the mousse is prepared. Be sure to test at service temperature to make adjustments if necessary.

Some base ingredients are already stable enough to give finished mousse structure (e.g., cheeses). For base ingredients that are not as dense, formulas typically include a quantity of gelatin (see the sidebar on page 819). The amount of gelatin should be enough to keep the mousse in a shape. The more gelatin added, the firmer the finished mousse will be. Choose the quantity based upon presentation (a firmer mousse for slicing, a softer mousse for spooning or piping).

The lightener in a mousse can be a foam of whipped egg whites or heavy cream whipped to soft or medium peaks.

If the whites or cream is overbeaten, the mousse may start to "deflate" from its own weight as it sits.

Added seasonings, flavorings, and garnishes can run a wide gamut and should be chosen to suit the main ingredient's flavor.

Equipment needs for preparing a mousse include a food processor to work the main item into a purée or paste, and a whip or mixer with beaters to prepare egg whites and/or cream. Have a drum sieve on hand to strain the mousse if necessary. Prepare a cold ice bath to cool the mixture as well as the proper set-up for weighing and handling gelatin. Prepare various molds and serving dishes, or a pastry bag, to shape the finished mousse.

1. Prepare the main ingredients.
Purée the main ingredients in a food processor or grind them with a meat grinder. The base should have a consistency similar to pastry cream. It may be necessary to add a liquid or moist product such as velouté, béchamel, unwhipped cream, or mayonnaise to adjust the consistency. Cool the base over an ice bath, if the mixture is hotter than 90°F/32°C.

2. Add the gelatin, if necessary.
Usually, a binder is necessary to produce the correct body. Soften the gelatin in a cool liquid. This process is known as blooming. Warm the gelatin to about 90° to 110°F/32° to 43°C to dissolve the granules. Stir the melted gelatin into the base. Some main ingredients, such as cheese, may be sufficiently binding without gelatin.

3. Fold in the whipped cream and/or egg whites.
Beat the cream or egg whites to soft peaks for best results. Fold this aerator into the base carefully. Add about one-third of the whipped cream first to make it easier to fold in the remaining two-thirds. This technique keeps the maximum volume in the finished mousse.

ABOVE *For the best possible texture, sieve the puréed base. This removes any last bits of sinew or fiber for a very delicate end product.*

ABOVE *Blend the gelatin evenly throughout the entire base.*

TOP *Fold the whipped cream into the base until evenly blended and homogenous in color.*

BOTTOM *Salmon mousse has been piped into barquettes and garnished to make a completed hors-d'oeuvre.*

4. The mousse is ready to mold now. There are many different ways to use a mousse. It may be piped into barquette or tartlet molds, profiteroles, or endive spears, or used as the spread for a canapé. It may be spooned or piped into portion-size molds; some presentations call for the mousse to be unmolded before service while others call for the mousse to be presented directly in the mold. A mousse can also be layered into a terrine, unmolded, and sliced for presentation.

Refrigerate the mousse until needed, at least two hours if it is to be unmolded.

5. Evaluate the quality of the finished mousse.
A high-quality cold mousse should be fully flavored, delicately set, and very light in texture. The ingredients should be blended smoothly so that there are no streaks of cream or base. The color should be even and appealing.

WORKING WITH GELATIN

Gelatin is used to make aspic, to stabilize foams, and to thicken liquid-based mixtures that will be served cold. It is added to liquid in different concentrations to get different results. The concentration of gelatin, or gel strength, in a given liquid is best described in terms of ounces per gallon (or pint). Formulas for producing a variety of gel strengths can be found in the table below.

GEL STRENGTH FORMULAS

GEL STRENGTH	OUNCES PER GALLON	OUNCES PER PINT	POSSIBLE USES
Delicate Gel	2	0.25	When slicing is not required. Individual portions of meat, poultry, or fish bound by gelatin. Jellied consommés.
Coating Gel	4	0.5	Edible chaud-froid. Coating individual items.
Sliceable Gel	6–8	1	When product is to be sliced. Filling pâté en croûte, head cheese.
Firm Gel	10–12	1.25–1.5	Coating platters for a food show or competition. Cold mousse.

TOP LEFT *Weigh the gelatin carefully.*

BOTTOM LEFT *Rain or sprinkle the gelatin powder over a cool liquid. If the liquid is warm or hot, the gelatin will not soften properly. Scattering the gelatin over the surface of the liquid prevents the gelatin from forming clumps.*

TOP RIGHT *As the gelatin absorbs the liquid, each granule becomes enlarged. This is known as blooming.*

BOTTOM RIGHT *Warm the gelatin over a hot-water bath or in a microwave on low power to dissolve the granules. As the softened gelatin warms, the mixture will clear and become liquid enough to pour easily.*

24 oz / 680 g diced smoked salmon

8 fl oz / 240 mL FISH VELOUTÉ (page 267), cold

1 oz / 30 g powdered gelatin

8 fl oz/240 mL cold FISH STOCK (page 253) or water

salt, as needed

pepper, as needed

16 fl oz / 480 mL heavy cream, whipped to soft peaks

SMOKED SALMON MOUSSE

1 Combine the smoked salmon and velouté in a food processor and process to a smooth consistency. Push through a sieve and transfer to a bowl.

2 Combine the gelatin with the cold stock or water until the gelatin absorbs the liquid. Warm the gelatin over simmering water until the granules dissolve and the mixture reaches 90° to 110°F/32° to 43°C.

3 Blend the gelatin into the salmon mixture. Adjust the seasoning with salt and pepper to taste.

4 Fold in the whipped cream. Shape the mousse as desired. Refrigerate the mousse for at least 2 hours to firm it.

MAKES 10 PORTIONS

RECIPES

RED PEPPER MOUSSE IN ENDIVE

makes 30 pieces

3 oz/85 g minced onions

1/2 tsp/5 mL finely minced garlic

2 tbsp/30 mL vegetable oil

20 oz/670 g small-dice red peppers

8 fl oz/240 mL CHICKEN STOCK (page 248)

pinch crushed saffron threads

2 tbsp/30 mL tomato paste

salt, as needed

ground white pepper, as needed

1 tbsp/15 mL powdered gelatin

2 fl oz/60 mL white wine

6 fl oz/180 mL heavy cream, whipped to soft peaks

30 Belgian endive spears

30 red pepper slivers, for garnish

1 Sauté the onions and garlic in oil until golden. Add the red peppers, stock, saffron, tomato paste, and salt and pepper to taste. Simmer until all the ingredients are tender and liquid is reduced by half. Purée the mixture in a blender. Cool the base over an ice bath.

2 Soften the gelatin in the white wine for several minutes and then heat to 90° to 110°F/32° to 43°C to dissolve the granules. Stir into the base and blend to combine all ingredients well.

3 Cool the mixture over an ice bath until it mounds when dropped from a spoon. Fold the whipped cream into the mixture.

4 Pipe the mousse into the endive spears and garnish each with a sliver of red pepper.

BLUE CHEESE MOUSSE

makes 3 pounds/1.3 kilograms

1 1/4 lb/570 g blue cheese

3/4 lb/340 g cream cheese

1 tbsp/15 mL kosher salt

1/2 tsp/3 mL coarsely ground black pepper

12 fl oz/360 g heavy cream, whipped to soft peaks

1 Purée the blue cheese and cream cheese until very smooth. Season with salt and pepper.

2 Fold the whipped cream into the mousse until well blended, without lumps.

3 Use the mousse to prepare canapés or as a filling or dip.

Goat Cheese Mousse Substitute fresh goat cheese for the blue cheese.

SALSA FRESCA

SALSAS ARE MADE FROM UNCOOKED FRUITS OR VEGETABLES. THEY OFTEN INCLUDE AN ACID, SUCH AS CITRUS JUICE, VINEGAR, OR WINE, TO ADD A SHARP FLAVOR. SPICES, CHILES, AND HERBS ARE SOMETIMES ADDED TO GIVE THE SAUCE A POTENT FLAVOR AND A HIGHER-THAN-AVERAGE LEVEL OF HEAT.

makes 1 quart/1 liter

1 lb/450 g seeded and diced tomatoes

4 oz/115 g minced onions

4 oz/115 g diced green pepper

1/4 oz/7 g minced garlic

1/2 oz/15 g chopped cilantro

1 tsp/5 mL chopped fresh oregano

2 fl oz/60 mL lime juice

1/4 oz/7 g minced seeded jalapeño

1 fl oz/30 mL olive oil

salt, as needed

pepper, as needed

1 Combine all ingredients. Adjust the seasoning with salt and pepper to taste.

2 Use immediately or hold under refrigeration.

SALSA VERDE

makes 1 quart/1 liter

1/2 oz/15 g finely minced shallots

2 fl oz/60 mL red wine vinegar

salt, as needed

1 oz/30 g salt-packed anchovy fillets, rinsed, dried, and chopped

2 oz/60 g chopped flat leaf parsley

1/2 oz/15 g chopped chives

1/4 oz/7 g chopped chervil

4 tbsp/60 mL chopped thyme

2 tbsp/30 mL chopped capers

1 tbsp/15 mL finely chopped lemon zest

8 fl oz/240 mL pure olive oil

2 fl oz/60 mL extra-virgin olive oil

1 Cover the shallots with the vinegar in a small bowl and season with salt to taste. Let stand for about 20 minutes.

2 Combine the anchovies, chopped parsley, chives, chervil, thyme, capers, lemon zest, and olive oils. Add the shallots and vinegar. Taste and adjust seasoning with salt to taste.

3 Use immediately or hold under refrigeration.

PAPAYA BLACK BEAN SALSA

makes 1 quart/1 liter

7 oz/200 g cooked black beans

7 oz/200 g small-dice ripe papaya

2 oz/60 g small-dice red pepper

2 oz/60 g small-dice red onion

1/2 oz/15 g minced jalapeños, or as needed

1/4 oz/7 g chopped cilantro

2 tsp/10 mL dried Mexican oregano

2 tbsp/60 mL minced ginger

2 fl oz/60 mL olive oil

1 fl oz/30 mL lime juice

salt, as needed

pepper, as needed

1 Combine all the ingredients. Adjust the seasoning with salt and pepper to taste.

2 Use immediately or hold under refrigeration.

COCKTAIL SAUCE

makes 1 quart/1 liter

12 fl oz/360 mL prepared chili sauce

14 fl oz/420 mL prepared ketchup

1 fl oz/30 mL lemon juice

2 tbsp/30 mL sugar

2 tsp/10 mL Tabasco sauce

2 tsp/10 mL Worcestershire sauce

1/4 oz/7 g prepared horseradish

salt, as needed

pepper, as needed

1 Combine all the ingredients thoroughly.

2 Use immediately or hold under refrigeration. Stir the sauce and adjust the seasonings if necessary before serving.

CUMBERLAND SAUCE

makes 1 quart/1 liter

2 oranges

2 lemons

1/2 oz/15 g minced shallots

20 oz/570 g currant jelly

1 tbsp/15 mL dry mustard

12 fl oz/360 mL ruby Port

salt, as needed

pepper, as needed

pinch cayenne

pinch ground ginger

1 Remove the zest from the oranges and lemons and cut into julienne. Juice the oranges and lemons.

2 Blanch the shallots and orange and lemon zest in boiling water. Strain immediately.

3 Combine the orange and lemon juice, shallots, zest, and all the remaining ingredients and bring to a simmer. Simmer 5 to 10 minutes until syrupy. Let cool.

4 Use immediately or hold under refrigeration.

ASIAN DIPPING SAUCE

makes 1 quart/1 liter

1 pint/480 mL soy sauce

8 fl oz/240 mL rice vinegar

8 fl oz/240 mL water

1/2 oz/15 g minced garlic

2 oz/60 g minced scallions

2 tbsp/30 mL minced ginger

2 tsp/10 mL dry mustard

1 tsp/5 mL hot bean paste

2 fl oz/60 mL honey

salt, as needed

pepper, as needed

1 Combine all the ingredients thoroughly.

2 Use immediately or hold under refrigeration. Stir the dressing and adjust the seasonings if necessary before serving.

YOGURT CUCUMBER SAUCE

makes 1 quart/1 liter

1 pt/480 mL plain yogurt
1 lb/480 g small-dice cucumbers (peeled and seeded before dicing)
1 tbsp/15 mL minced garlic
2 tsp/10 mL ground cumin
1 tsp/5 mL ground turmeric
salt, as needed
ground white pepper, as needed

1 Place the yogurt in a cheesecloth-lined strainer. Set the strainer in a bowl and drain at least 8 hours under refrigeration.

2 Combine the yogurt and cucumber.

3 Add the garlic, cumin, turmeric, salt, and pepper. Adjust the seasoning with salt and pepper to taste.

4 The sauce can be served chunky or puréed until smooth. Use immediately or hold under refrigeration. Stir the dressing and adjust the seasonings if necessary before serving.

GUACAMOLE

makes 1 quart/1 liter

20 oz/570 g avocados, halved, pitted, and peeled
2 fl oz/60 mL lime juice
3 oz/85 g diced tomato (optional)
1/4 oz/7 g minced jalapeños
3 oz/85 g sliced green onions
4 tbsp/60 mL chopped cilantro
1 tsp/5 mL Tabasco sauce
salt, as needed
pepper, as needed

1 Push the avocados through a coarse sieve.

2 Combine the avocados, lime juice, tomato, jalapeños, green onions, cilantro and Tabasco and mix well. Taste for seasoning and adjust with lime juice, salt, and pepper.

3 Use immediately or cover tightly and refrigerate. It is best to make guacamole the same day as it is to be served.

HUMMUS

makes 1 quart/1 liter

1 1/2 lb/720 g cooked chickpeas, drained
4 oz/115 g tahini
6 fl oz/180 mL lemon juice, or as needed
2 fl oz/60 mL extra-virgin olive oil
1/2 oz/15 g minced garlic
salt, as needed
pepper, as needed

1 Purée the chickpeas with the tahini, lemon juice, olive oil, and garlic in a food processor in 2 batches until smooth. Add water to thin if needed. The hummus can be passed through a drum sieve, if desired, for a very smooth texture. Adjust seasoning with salt and pepper to taste.

2 Use immediately or cover tightly and refrigerate.

MUHAMMARA

This spicy hot pepper sauce made with peppers, walnuts, and pomegranate molasses comes from Aleppo in Syria. Pomegranate molasses is produced by cooking ripe pomegranates and sugar to a thick, jamlike consistency. Muhammara's flavor improves if it is made four or five days in advance and kept tightly closed in the refrigerator.

makes 1 quart/1 liter

3 oz/85 g coarsely ground walnuts
3 tbsp/45 mL fresh white bread crumbs
1 1/2 lb/720 g red peppers, peeled and seeded
1 fl oz/30 mL lemon juice, or as needed
4 tsp/20 mL pomegranate molasses
1/4 tsp/1 mL prepared red chili paste, or as needed
salt, as needed
pepper, as needed
1 tbsp/15 mL olive oil
1/4 tsp/1 mL ground cumin

1 Process the walnuts and bread crumbs in a food processor until finely ground. Add the peppers, lemon juice, and pomegranate molasses and purée until smooth and creamy. Add the chili paste and adjust the seasoning with lemon juice, chili paste, salt, and pepper to taste. Refrigerate, tightly covered, 4 or 5 days or at least overnight to allow flavors to mellow.

2 When ready to serve, decorate with a drizzle of olive oil and a light dusting of cumin.

TAPENADE

makes 10 portions

3 oz/85 g Niçoise olives, pitted

2 oz/60 g black olives, pitted

2 oz/60 g salt-packed anchovy fillets, rinsed and dried

1 oz/30 g capers, rinsed

$1/2$ oz/15 g minced garlic

lemon juice, as needed

extra-virgin olive oil, as needed

pepper, as needed

minced herbs, such as oregano or basil

1 Blend all the olives, the anchovies, capers, and garlic in a food processor, until chunky and easy to spread. Slowly incorporate lemon juice and olive oil to taste without overmixing. Tapenade needs to have texture and identifiable bits of olive.

2 Adjust the seasonings with pepper and more lemon juice, and olive oil to taste. Garnish with the herbs. Use immediately or cover tightly and refrigerate.

CHILI BUTTER

makes 1 pound /450 grams

1 tbsp/15 mL chili powder

1 tbsp/15 mL hot chili powder

$1/2$ tsp/2 mL sweet Hungarian paprika

$1/2$ tsp/2 mL ground cumin

1 tbsp/15 mL dried oregano

$1/2$ tsp/2 mL Worcestershire sauce

$1/4$ tsp/1 mL Tabasco sauce

$1/4$ tsp/1 mL garlic powder

$1/4$ tsp/1 mL onion powder

1 lb/450 g butter, softened

1 Heat the chili powders, paprika, and cumin in a dry pan to release their flavors.

2 Blend the heated spices with the remaining ingredients.

3 Pipe the chili butter into rosettes, using a pastry bag, or roll into a cylinder.

4 Refrigerate until needed.

PIMIENTO BUTTER

makes 1 pound/450 grams

12 oz/340 g butter, softened

$31/2$ oz/100 g minced pimientos

$1/4$ tsp/1 mL minced garlic

1 tbsp/15 mL lemon juice

salt, as needed

pepper, as needed

1 Blend the butter, pimientos, garlic, and lemon juice. Adjust the seasoning with salt and pepper to taste.

2 Pipe the pimiento butter into rosettes, using a pastry bag, or roll into a cylinder.

3 Refrigerate until needed.

GREEN ONION BUTTER

makes 1 pound/450 grams

1 lb/450 g butter, softened

3 oz/85 g minced green onions

$1/4$ tsp/1 mL minced garlic

1 tbsp/15 mL chopped parsley

1 tbsp /15 mL soy sauce

1 tbsp /15 mL lemon juice

salt, as needed

pepper, as needed

1 Blend the butter, green onions, garlic, parsley, soy sauce, and lemon juice. Adjust the seasoning with salt and pepper to taste.

2 Pipe the green onion butter into rosettes, using a pastry bag, or roll into a cylinder.

3 Refrigerate until needed.

CRANBERRY RELISH

makes 1 quart/1 liter

12 oz/340 g cranberries

3 fl oz/90 mL orange juice

3 fl oz/90 mL Triple Sec

3 oz/85 g sugar, or as needed

1 oz/30 g minced orange zest

10 oz/285 g orange suprêmes (see page 775)

salt, as needed

pepper, as needed

1 Combine the cranberries, orange juice, Triple Sec, sugar, and zest in a saucepan and stir to combine.

2 Cover and simmer 15 to 20 minutes, stirring occasionally.

3 When the berries burst and the liquid starts to thicken, remove from the heat and add the suprêmes. Taste for sweetness and adjust with sugar to taste. Use immediately or cool, cover tightly, and refrigerate.

SPICY MANGO CHUTNEY

makes 1 quart/1 liter

1 lb/450 g chopped mango

3 oz/85 g raisins

1/4 oz/7 g minced jalapeños

1/2 oz/15 g minced garlic

1 tbsp/15 mL minced ginger

5 oz/140 g dark brown sugar

1 fl oz/30 mL white wine vinegar

salt, as needed

pepper, as needed

1 tsp/5 mL turmeric

1 Combine the mangos, raisins, jalapeños, garlic, ginger, and brown sugar. Refrigerate 24 hours.

2 Add the vinegar, bring to a boil, and simmer 15 minutes.

3 Add the salt and pepper and simmer 10 minutes.

4 Add the turmeric and simmer 5 minutes.

5 Transfer to a clean storage container. Cover and refrigerate for up to 2 weeks.

CURRIED ONION RELISH

makes 1 quart/1 liter

1 lb/450 g small-dice onions

1/4 tsp/1 mL minced garlic

8 fl oz/240 mL white vinegar

6 oz/170 g sugar

salt, as needed

2 tbsp/30 mL pickling spice, tied into a sachet

1 tbsp/15 mL CURRY POWDER (page 353)

1 Combine all the ingredients and mix well.

2 Simmer, covered, in a small nonreactive saucepan, stirring often, for 30 minutes. Be careful not to scorch. Let cool.

3 Transfer to a clean storage container. Cover and refrigerate for up to 2 weeks.

MARINATED MACKEREL IN WHITE WINE

makes 10 portions

1 1/2 lb/680 g mackerel, drawn, head removed

MARINADE

1 pt/480 mL chablis

1 oz/30 g carrots, sliced thin

2 oz/60 g onions, sliced thin

salt, as needed

pepper, as needed

1 thyme sprig

4 bay leaves

3 to 4 parsley stems

1 Trim the fish and rinse it to remove all traces of blood. Drain well.

2 To make the marinade, combine all of the ingredients for the marinade. Bring to a boil and simmer, covered, for 45 minutes.

3 Place the mackerel in a poaching vessel. Pour the hot marinade over the fish and poach at 190°F/88°C for 8 to 10 minutes. Remove the pan from the heat. Cool the fish in the poaching liquid. Refrigerate.

4 Serve the fish chilled.

SEVICHE OF SCALLOPS

makes 10 portions

1¼ lb/570 g sea scallops, muscle tab removed, sliced thin

10 oz/285 g tomato concassé

6 fl oz/180 mL lemon or lime juice

3 oz/85 g red onions, cut into thin rings

2 oz/60 g bias-cut green onions

2 fl oz/60 mL olive oil

½ oz/15 g fine-dice jalapeño

1 tsp/5 mL mashed garlic

4 tbsp/30 mL chopped cilantro

salt, as needed

pepper, as needed

1 Combine all of the ingredients. Marinate the scallops for at least 4 hours or up to 12 hours.

2 Serve the seviche on chilled plates.

CARPACCIO OF SALMON

makes 10 portions

GREEN MAYONNAISE

2½ oz/70 g blanched spinach leaves

2 tsp/10 mL chopped parsley

2 tsp/10 mL chopped tarragon

2 tsp/10 mL chopped chives

2 tsp/10 mL chopped dill

1¼ pt/600 mL MAYONNAISE (page 767)

2 tbsp/30 mL lemon juice

salt, as needed

pepper, as needed

1½ lb/680 g salmon fillet

10 oz/285 g white mushrooms, sliced thin

4 fl oz/120 mL olive oil

1 To make the green mayonnaise, purée the spinach leaves, parsley, tarragon, chives, and dill in a blender. Mix the purée with the mayonnaise, lemon juice, and salt. Adjust the consistency with water if sauce is too thick and adjust the seasoning with salt and pepper to taste.

2 Slice the salmon into very thin pieces, arrange on a plate, and cover with plastic wrap.

3 Using a spoon, spread out the salmon to the edge of the plate in a thin, even layer. Remove the plastic wrap just before serving.

4 Garnish the salmon with mushrooms and sprinkle with pepper and oil.

5 Serve green mayonnaise on the side.

GRAVLAX

makes 20 portions

7 oz/200 g kosher salt

1 lb/450 g dark brown sugar

¾ oz/20 g cracked white peppercorns

3 oz/85 g chopped dill

2 fl oz/60 mL lemon juice

1 fl oz/30 mL olive oil

¾ fl oz/25 mL brandy

3 lb/1.3 kg salmon fillet

1 Combine the salt, brown sugar, peppercorns, and dill to make the dry cure.

2 Combine the lemon juice, olive oil, and brandy. Place the salmon on a piece of cheesecloth and brush this mixture on the salmon fillet.

3 Pack the cure evenly on the salmon fillet and wrap tightly.

4 Place the wrapped fillet in a pan, top with a second pan, and set a weight in the second pan. Refrigerate this assembly and let marinate for 3 days.

5 Unwrap the salmon and scrape off the cure.

6 Slice the salmon thinly on the bias to serve it.

SMOKED SALMON PLATTER SET-UP

makes 20 portions

1 smoked salmon fillet

3 hard-cooked eggs, whites and yolks separated and chopped fine

3 tbsp/45 mL capers, rinsed and drained

½ red onion, minced, rinsed

8 fl oz/240 mL mustard-dill sauce

French bread, toasted golden brown

cornichons

calamata olives

pepperoncini

1 Slice salmon very thin on a bias, starting from the tail.

2 Arrange the salmon on the plate and garnish with separate piles of the chopped egg white and yolks, capers and onions.

3 Drizzle the sauce over the smoked salmon and arrange the toasted bread, cornichons, olives, and pepperoncini around.

COLD POACHED SCALLOPS WITH TARRAGON VINAIGRETTE

makes 10 portions

1¼ lb/570 g bay scallops

1 pt/480 mL white wine

1 pt/480 mL FISH STOCK (page 253)

1½ oz/45 g minced shallots

TARRAGON VINAIGRETTE

4 fl oz/120 mL reduced cooking liquid from scallops

1 to 2 tsp/5 to 10 mL arrowroot, or as needed

4 fl oz/120 mL extra-virgin olive oil,

4 fl oz/120 mL tarragon vinegar

2 tsp/10 mL chopped tarragon

salt, as needed

pepper, as needed

GARNISH

10 oz/285 g blanched asparagus

5 oz/140 g tomato concassé

1 Shallow poach scallops in wine, stock, and shallots. Keep warm while finishing the vinaigrette.

2 Reduce the cooking liquid by half, and reserve amount required for vinaigrette.

3 To make the vinaigrette, bring the reserved cooking liquid to a simmer. Dilute the arrowroot in cold water and add as needed to very lightly thicken.

4 Add the oil, vinegar, tarragon, salt, and pepper. Keep warm.

5 Serve the scallops with the vinaigrette, asparagus, and tomatoes.

BROILED SHRIMP WITH GARLIC

makes 20 portions

8 oz/225 g dry bread crumbs

1 oz/15 g minced garlic

¼ oz/7 g chopped flat-leaf parsley

¼ oz/7 g chopped oregano

12 oz/340 g butter, melted

salt, as needed

pepper, as needed

3½ lb/1.6 kg shrimp (16 to 20 count), peeled and butterflied

1 Combine the bread crumbs, garlic, parsley, oregano, and 8 oz/225 g of the butter. Adjust the seasoning with salt and pepper to taste.

2 Arrange the shrimp on a gratin dish and brush them with the remaining butter.

3 Place 1 to 2 tsp/5 to 10 mL of the bread-crumb mixture on the shrimp and broil them under a broiler until they are very hot and cooked through. Serve.

CLAMS CASINO

makes 10 portions

4 oz/115 g diced bacon

4 oz/115 g minced onions

3 oz/85 g minced green peppers

3 oz/85 g minced red peppers

salt, as needed

pepper, as needed

Worcestershire sauce, as needed

1 lb/450 g butter

5 dozen littleneck or cherrystone clams

10 strips bacon, blanched and quartered

1 To make the casino butter, render the diced bacon until it is crisp. Add the onions and peppers and sauté until tender. Remove from the heat and let cool.

2 Adjust the seasoning with salt, pepper, and Worcestershire sauce to taste. Add the butter and blend until evenly mixed.

3 Scrub the clams and discard any that are open. Open the clams and loosen the meat from the shells. Top each clam with about 1 tsp/5 g of casino butter and a piece of blanched bacon. Broil the clams until the bacon is crisp and serve immediately.

Black Bean Cakes

Sushi

Gorgonzola Custards

Deviled Crab Cakes

Mussels Marinère

PAPER-WRAPPED CHICKEN

makes 80 pieces

STUFFING

3 lb/1.3 kg shredded chicken breast

4 oz/115 g minced green onions

1 tbsp/15 mL sugar

1 tbsp/15 mL sherry

2 fl oz/60 mL soy sauce

2 fl oz/60 mL sesame oil

1 tsp/5 mL salt

1 tsp/5 mL white pepper

1 egg

80 sheets rice paper (4 x 4-in/10 x 10-cm square)

vegetable oil, for frying

1 Combine all ingredients for the stuffing; mix together.

2 Soak a few pieces of rice paper at a time in room temperature water to soften. Place 1 tbsp/15 mL of filling on each piece of rice paper, roll in the traditional egg-roll shape, and seal. Or fold into a triangle.

3 Heat the oil to 350°F/175°C and deep fry the packets until golden brown. Drain on absorbent paper. Serve at once.

CORN CRÊPES WITH ASPARAGUS TIPS AND SMOKED SALMON

makes 10 portions

CORN CRÊPES

8 oz/225 g fresh or frozen corn kernels

4 oz/115 g flour

4 eggs

8 fl oz/240 mL milk

4 fl oz/120 mL water

salt, as needed

pepper, as needed

2 tsp/10 mL vegetable oil

vegetable oil, for frying

CORN SALAD

1 ½ lb/680 g fresh corn kernels

2 oz/60 g diced red peppers

2 oz/60 g diced green peppers

8 fl oz/240 mL WHITE WINE VINAIGRETTE (page 762)

2 tsp/10 mL chopped cilantro

2 tsp/10 mL chopped parsley

10 oz/285 g smoked salmon slices

20 oz/570 g cooked asparagus spears

1 pt/480 mL HOLLANDAISE SAUCE (page 279), finished with chives

1 To make the crêpes, mix all the ingredients together to form a batter, adjusting the consistency with more liquid or flour, as necessary.

2 Cook the crêpes in a heated and oiled crêpes pan. Turn and cook on second side, then remove to a plate. Stack the crêpes with parchment paper between each one to keep separate.

3 To make the corn salad, combine all the ingredients and let the flavors marry for 1 hour.

4 Cut a slit in each crêpe, roll into a cornucopia, and fill with salad.

5 Arrange the crêpes, salmon, and asparagus on a platter. Warm in the oven for 1 to 2 minutes.

6 Garnish the salmon with the hollandaise sauce. Serve at once.

Charcuterie, strictly speaking, refers to certain foods made from the pig, including sausage, smoked ham, bacon, head cheese, pâtés, and terrines. Garde manger, traditionally referred to as the kitchen's pantry or larder section, is where foods were kept cold during extended storage, as well as while being prepared as a cold presentation.

CHARCUTERIE AND GARDE MANGER

FORCEMEATS

Forcemeat, a basic component of such charcuterie and garde manger preparations as pâtés and terrines, is prepared by grinding lean meats together with fat and seasonings to form an emulsion.

There are four types of forcemeat. A mousseline-style forcemeat is prepared by combining delicate meats such as salmon or chicken with cream and eggs. A straight forcemeat calls for lean meats to be ground together with fatback. Country-style forcemeats have a coarser texture than other forcemeats and usually contain liver. Gratin forcemeats are similar to straight forcemeats with the following difference — a portion of the meat is seared, then cooled, before it is ground together with the other ingredients. Once puréed or ground together, forcemeats are mixed long enough to develop a uniform and sliceable texture. All four forcemeat styles have a number of applications in the professional kitchen: to prepare appetizers, to use as stuffings, or to produce garde manger specialty items, including pâtés, terrines, and galantines.

ALL NECESSARY INGREDIENTS and equipment used in preparing any force-meat must be scrupulously clean and well chilled at all times so that the lean meat and fats can combine properly. Refrigerate ingredients until they are ready to be used and hold them over a container of ice to keep the temperatures low during actual preparation. Equipment can be chilled in ice water.

Forcemeats are prepared with three basic components. The main, or dominant, meat provides the forcemeat's flavor and body. Fat is included to give a richness and smoothness; it may be either the fat that occurs naturally in a cut of meat, or it may be in the form of fatback or heavy cream. Seasonings are critical, especially salt. Salt not only enhances the forcemeat's flavor, it also plays a key role in developing the force-meat's texture and bind. Other seasonings may be added as desired.

Panadas for use in forcemeats: bread, milk, flour, rice, egg, and nonfat dried milk.

An additional component is sometimes required to help bind the forcemeat together, especially if the main item is delicate or when it is not finely ground. These binders may be eggs or egg whites, heavy cream, or a liaison of cream and eggs. Panadas are also used as binders. A panada is an ingredient or mixture used in forcemeats to help form a good emulsion. Bread panadas are made by soaking cubed bread in milk, in a ratio of one part bread to one part milk, until the bread has absorbed the milk. A flour panada is essentially a very heavy béchamel enriched with three to four egg yolks per 1 pint/480 mL of liquid. Pâte à Choux (page 945), rice, or nonfat dry milk powder all may be used as binders for forcemeats.

Garnishes are often folded into a forcemeat or arranged in the forcemeat as the pâté or terrine mold is filled. Options include such items as nuts, diced meats or vegetables, dried fruits, and truffles.

A variety of liners can be used when preparing terrines and pâtés. Thin sheets of fatback, ham, prosciutto, or vegetables are commonly used for terrines. Pâtés en croûte are baked in pastry-lined molds. The dough used for pâtés is by necessity a stronger dough than a normal pie dough, although the preparation technique is identical. (Pâté dough may also be used to prepare bar-quette molds). Flours other than bread flour, herbs, spices, or lemon zest may be added to change the flavor of the dough. For instructions for lining a pâté mold with dough, see page 856.

Aspic gelée is a well-seasoned, highly gelatinous, perfectly clarified stock. It is frequently strengthened by adding gelatin (either sheets or granular gelatin—see page 819). Aspic is applied to foods to prevent them from drying out and to preserve their moisture and freshness. When properly prepared, aspic sets firmly but still melts in the mouth. Aspic gelée made from white stock will be clear, with practically no color. When the base stock is brown, the aspic is amber or brown in color. Other colors may be achieved by adding an appropriate spice, herb, or vegetable purée.

Use a meat grinder to prepare most meats, although a food processor is adequate to grind delicate meats and fish. Be sure that the blade for either the grinder or the food processor is very sharp. Meats should be cut cleanly, never mangled or mashed, as they pass through the grinder.

Have an ice bath ready for mixing and holding the forcemeat. Forcemeats can be mixed by hand over ice with a spoon, in an electric mixer, or in a food processor. Some forcemeats are pushed through a drum sieve to remove any fibers or sinew. Once prepared, forcemeats can be shaped in a variety of molds, including earthenware molds known as terrines and hinged pâté molds, as well as a variety of specialty molds.

1. Follow sound sanitation procedures and maintain cold temperatures at all times.

Maintaining the correct temperature is important for more than the proper formation of an emulsion. These foods are often highly susceptible to contamination, due to handling, extended contact with equipment, and greater exposure to air. Pork, poultry, seafood, and dairy products begin to lose their quality and safety rapidly when they rise above 40°F/4°C. If the forcemeat seems to be approaching room temperature at any point in its preparation, it is too warm. Stop work and chill all ingredients and equipment. Resume work only after everything is below 40°F/4°C once more.

2. Grind foods properly.

Both the dominant meat and fatback (if used) must be properly ground before the forcemeat can be prepared. Some garnishes are also ground along with the meat and fat.

To prepare the meat for grinding, cut it into strips or cubes that will fit easily through the grinder's feed tube. Combine it with an adequate amount of salt and the desired seasonings and let the meat marinate under refrigeration for up to 4 hours. The salt will draw out proteins responsible for both flavor and texture development.

To prepare a grinder, choose the correct size die. For all but very delicate meats (fish and some types of organ meats, for example), begin with a die that has large or medium openings. Continue to grind through progressively smaller dies until the correct consistency is achieved. Remember to chill ingredients and equipment between successive grindings.

To use a grinder, guide the strips of meat and fatback into the feed tube. If they are the correct size, they will be drawn easily by the worm. If they stick to the feed tray or the sides of the feed tube, they can be aided through with a tamper, but do not force the foods through the feed tube with a tamper.

To use a food processor, cut the meat into small dice before seasoning it. Chill the blade and bowl of the food processor. Run the machine just long enough to grind the meat into a smooth paste. Pulsing the machine off and on and scraping down the sides of the bowl produces the most even texture.

3. Once the ingredients are properly ground, mix or process them combining the ground meat with a secondary binder, if desired.

A forcemeat is more than simply ground meat. In order to produce the desired texture, the ingredients

TOP *Add chilled egg whites to the ground salmon in a chilled food processor to begin developing the structure of the forcemeat.*
BOTTOM *Add cold cream gradually as the processor runs, for a smooth texture and flavor and to hold the salmon together after cooking.*

must be mixed long enough to develop a good bind. This may be done by hand over an ice bath, in a mixer, or in a food processor. Process the mixture to a smooth consistency. This encourages the forcemeat to hold together well when sliced.

4. Push the forcemeat through a drum sieve, if necessary.
Straight and gratin forcemeats are not typically put through a sieve. However, a mousseline forcemeat may be sieved to produce a very fine and delicate texture. Be sure that the forcemeat is very cold, and work rapidly to avoid warming the forcemeat.

5. Taste test the forcemeat for flavor and consistency.
Poach a bite-size portion of the forcemeat so that it can be evaluated (see the sidebar on quenelles on page 846). Be sure to taste test the forcemeat at serving temperature. If it is to be served cold, let the sample cool completely before tasting it. Make any necessary adjustments in the forcemeat. If it has a rubbery or tough consistency, add heavy cream; if it does not hold together properly, additional panada or egg whites may be necessary. Adjust the seasoning and flavoring ingredients as needed. Perform a new taste test after each adjustment until you are satisfied with the forcemeat.

TOP *Scrape down the sides of the processor bowl as you work to blend the ingredients thoroughly.*

BOTTOM *This forcemeat has a good texture and is ready to finish.*

ABOVE *Mousseline or other very delicate forcemeats may be pushed through a drum sieve* (tamis) *for the smoothest possible texture.*

Pork Tenderloin Roulade

Duck Terrine with Pistachios and Dried Cherries

Seafood Pâté en Croute

Pâté Grand-Mère

SEAFOOD PÂTÉ EN CROÛTE

makes one 2½-pound/2-kilogram mold, 18 to 20 slices

6 oz/170 g shrimp

6 oz/170 g crayfish tails

12 oz/340 g SALMON MOUSSELINE (page 847) (see Note)

2 tbsp/30 mL snipped chives

3 tbsp/45 mL chopped basil

1 oz/30 g small-dice truffle (optional)

1½ lb/680 g PÂTÉ DOUGH (recipe follows), flavored with saffron

dry nori sheets for liner, as needed

2 fl oz/60 mL egg beaten with 1 tbsp/15 mL milk

6 to 8 fl oz/180 to 240 mL ASPIC GELÉE (page 819)

1. Peel and devein the shrimp and crayfish tails. Cut into dice or julienne if desired, or leave whole. Chill to below 40°F/4°C.

2. Working over an ice bath, fold the shrimp, the crayfish, chives, and basil (and truffle, if using) into the mousseline by hand.

3. Roll out the dough into a rectangle, about ⅛ in/4 mm thick. Cut pieces to line the bottom and sides of a hinged pâté mold as shown at right; the dough should overhang all sides. Add a second liner of nori sheets if desired.

4. Pack the forcemeat into the lined mold. Fold the fatback (if used) back over the forcemeat. Fold the dough over, trim, and seal to completely encase the pâté.

5. Cut a cap piece and lay over the pâté, tucking the sides down into the mold. Cut and reinforce vent holes in the cap piece and brush the surface with egg wash. Roll a tube of aluminum foil (known as a chimney) to fit into the vent holes and keep them from closing during baking.

6. Bake at 450°F/230°C for 15 to 20 minutes, reduce the heat to 350°F/175°C, and finish baking to an internal temperature of 155°F/68°C, about 50 minutes.

7. Remove the pâté from the oven and let it cool to 90 to 100°F/36 to 38°C. Warm the aspic to 110°F/43°C and ladle it through a funnel into the pâté using the chimneys. Then remove and discard the chimneys.

8. Refrigerate the pâté for at least 24 hours before slicing and serving.

NOTE

When preparing the salmon mousseline as described on page 847, substitute 12 oz/340 g diced shrimp for an equal amount of salmon, if desired.

see photograph on page 853

TOP LEFT *Roll the dough out to an even thickness. Rolling it to the dimensions of a full sheet pan makes a square large enough to line and cover a standard pâté pan with the least dough wasted.*

BOTTOM LEFT *Cut the dough to line the interior, cutting away the excess from the corners as shown. Use the mold as a template.*

TOP RIGHT *Using a small ball of the leftover dough, gently but firmly press the dough together in the corners to form a tight seal.*

BOTTOM RIGHT *Tuck the edges of the top piece down into the mold. Once this step is complete, cut a vent to prevent the crust from splitting and add decorations made from dough, applying them with egg wash.*

PÂTÉ DOUGH

makes 2 pounds /900 grams

20 oz/570 g bread flour, sifted

1½ oz/45 g powdered milk

¼ oz/7 g baking powder

½ oz/15 g salt

3½ oz/100 g shortening

2½ oz/75 g butter

2 eggs

½ fl oz/15 mL vinegar

8 to 10 fl oz/240 to 300 mL milk

1 Place the flour, powdered milk, baking powder, salt, shortening, and butter in a food processor and pulse to a coarse meal. Add the eggs and vinegar and pulse for 5 seconds.

2 Transfer the dough to a mixer, add 4 to 5 oz/115 to 140 mL of the milk, and knead for 3 to 4 minutes on medium speed, until the dough forms a ball. Check consistency and add more milk if necessary.

3 Remove the dough from the mixer and knead by hand until smooth. Square off the dough and wrap in plastic. Let it rest for 30 minutes.

4 Roll out to the size of a sheet pan on a lightly floured surface.

5 Place the dough on a sheet pan lined with parchment paper, cover with another sheet of parchment paper, and wrap tightly with plastic wrap. The dough is ready to use to line a pâté mold, to cut into decorative shapes, or to make barquettes and tartlet molds.

NOTE

The flavor of the dough can be varied by adding ground spices or herbs, lemon zest, or grated cheese. Rye or whole wheat flour, or cornmeal, may be used to replace up to one third of the bread flour for a different flavor, texture, and appearance.

Saffron Pâté Dough Infuse a large pinch of saffron threads in 5 fl oz/150 mL of warm water. Reduce the milk in the formula to 3 to 5 fl oz/90 to 150 mL. Add the infused saffron water with the milk in Step 2.

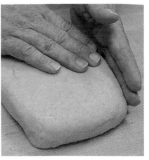

TOP LEFT *Cut the flour and fat together in a food processor, just until it looks like a coarse, damp meal.*

BOTTOM LEFT *The final kneading is done by hand on a lightly floured surface.*

ABOVE *Pat the dough into a square before allowing it to rest. This is known as blocking the dough.*

PÂTÉ SPICE

makes 14¾ ounces/425 grams

1½ oz/45 g white peppercorns

3 oz/85 g ground coriander

1¾ oz/50 g thyme

1¾ oz/50 g basil

3 oz/85 g cloves

1½ oz/45 g nutmeg

½ oz/15 g bay leaf

¾ oz/20 g mace

1 oz/30 g dried cèpes (porcini)

1 Combine all of the ingredients and grind them, using a mortar and pestle or spice grinder.

2 Transfer to an airtight container, cover, and store in a cool, dark place.

PART SEVEN

BAKING AND PASTRY

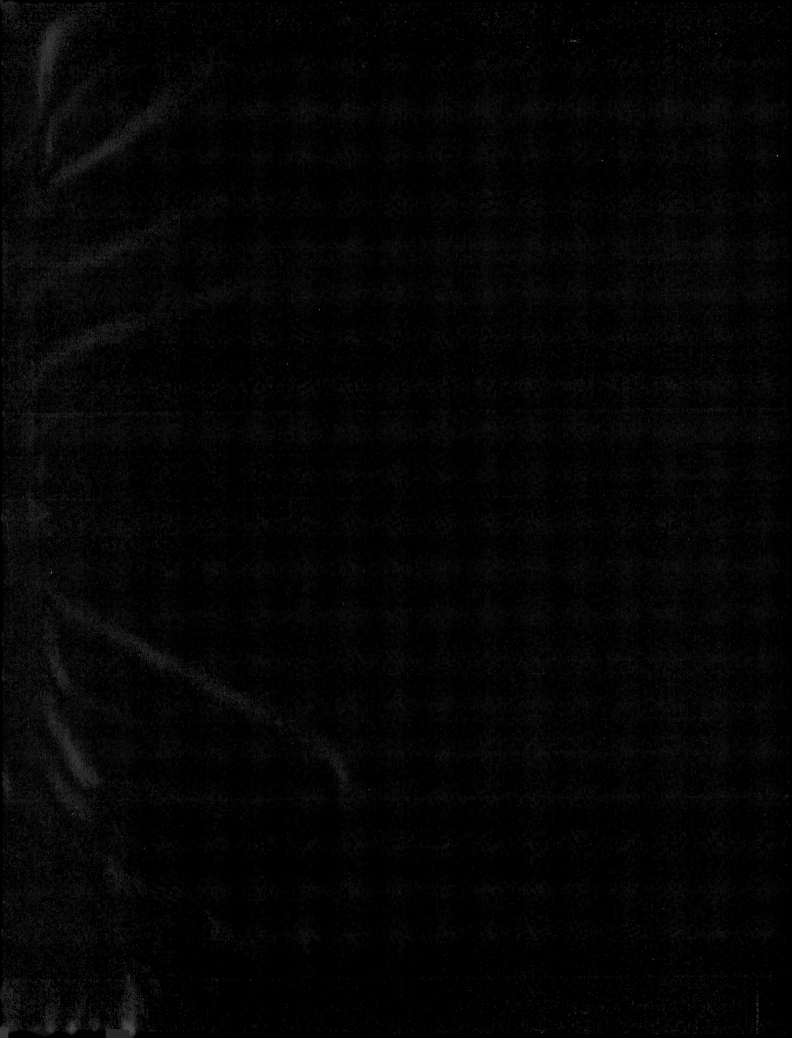

CHAPTER THIRTY-ONE

Baking depends on exact
measurements and precise
handling of ingredients and tools
to assure quality and consistency.

BAKING
MISE EN PLACE

THE FUNCTION OF INGREDIENTS IN BAKING

Each ingredient used in the bakeshop fulfills one or more basic functions: stabilizing, tenderizing, sweetening, leavening, flavoring, or thickening.

The basic ingredients used in baking typically fulfill more than one function in the finished product. Eggs, for example, can act as a stabilizer, tenderizer, leavener, or thickener. Butter is a tenderizer as well as a flavoring agent.

STABILIZERS

Stabilizers include ingredients containing protein. Protein provides structure, ensuring that the baked good does not collapse once it is removed from the oven. Flour, for example, functions as a strengthener because of its proteins. One of flour's proteins, gluten, is especially important in the production of yeast breads. Gluten develops into long, elastic strands during the mixing and kneading process. Because it is able to stretch without breaking, it traps the gases that result from the fermenting yeast in the dough to produce a light, even texture in the finished product.

The protein in eggs allows them to serve as a strengthener as well. Eggs are used in this way for meringues and cakes such as sponge cake, angel food, and chiffon that are made by the foaming method as well as in other ways where the combination mixing method is applied.

Starches, because of their absorbent qualities, are also important for overall stability. They are present in flours in differing percentages and are sometimes added in the form of cornstarch to further affect the texture of the finished product. The starch granules first swell in the presence of liquid. Then, as they are heated, they swell even more, trapping liquid or steam. As heat continues to set the starch into a stable structure, texture is also affected.

TENDERIZERS

Baking fats (butter, oil, hydrogenated shortening, lard) make baked goods tender and moist by surrounding long strands of gluten and breaking them up into shorter units. For this reason these high-fat ingredients are sometimes known as shorteners. Other ingredients that contain significant amounts of fat, such as cream or milk, sour cream, cream cheese, peanut butter, and egg yolks, function in the same way.

The way the fat is worked into the batter or dough affects the overall texture. Fats that are rubbed or rolled into doughs tend to separate the dough into large layers, creating a flaky texture. When the fat is thoroughly creamed together with sugar so that it can be mixed evenly throughout the batter, the texture is more cakelike.

SWEETENERS

Granulated sugar, superfine sugar, confectioners' sugar, and coarse sugar are all forms of sucrose, a sweetener. Sugar can do more than add flavor, however. It establishes the structure of some cakes or muffins. Cooked sugar improves the stability of a meringue. Granulated or powdered sugars as well as syrups (honey, corn syrup, molasses, maple syrup) attract moisture, helping to keep baked goods moist and prevent them from becoming stale.

LEAVENERS

Leaveners produce a desirable texture by introducing carbon dioxide into the batter or dough. This gas stretches the dough and creates small pockets. The three types of leaveners are chemical, organic, and physical.

Baking soda and baking powder are the primary chemical leaveners. In these leaveners, an alkaline ingredient (sodium bicarbonate or a combination of an alkali, an acid, and a starch) interacts with an acid (already present in baking powder or in an ingredient such as buttermilk, sour cream, yogurt, or chocolate). The alkalis and acids produce carbon dioxide when combined in the presence of liquid. When heated during baking, the carbon dioxide expands, giving the baked goods their characteristic texture, known as crumb. This process of expansion happens rapidly; hence, many items prepared with chemical leaveners are called quick breads.

Double-acting baking powder is so called because a first action occurs in the presence of moisture in the batter and a second action is initiated by the presence of heat. That is, the baking powder reacts once when it is mixed with the batter's liquids and again when the batter is placed in a hot oven.

Organic leaveners are based on yeast, a living organism that feeds on sugars, producing alcohol and carbon dioxide, the gas that lightens a dough to give it the proper texture. Unlike chemical leaveners, organic leaveners take a substantial amount of time to do their job. The yeast has to grow and reproduce sufficiently to fill the dough with air pockets. For this to take place, the temperature must be controlled carefully. Yeast will not function well below approximately 65° to 70°F/18° to 21°C, and above 140°F/60°C the yeast is destroyed.

Fresh or compressed yeast must be kept under refrigeration (ideally at 40°F/4°C) to maintain its viability; it may be held for only 7 to 10 days, or it may be frozen for longer storage. This type of yeast comes in cake form and is usually measured by weight rather than volume.

Active dry yeast and instant yeast are two types of granular yeast. They should be kept under refrigeration and must be kept dry until use. The yeast in an unopened package of active dry or instant yeast is in a completely dormant stage and may be stored in an unopened package for up to one year.

To substitute active dry yeast for compressed yeast, use 40 percent of the amount of compressed yeast called for in the recipe.

To substitute instant yeast, use 33 percent of the amount.

Sourdough starter also acts as a yeast-based leavener. In this case, the naturally occurring (or wild) yeast is allowed to incubate in a flour and water mixture. The mixture is left to ferment, or sour, over a period of days or weeks. With regular feedings of additional flour and water, the growing starter may be strengthened and maintained for regular use in the production of bread and other baked items. Some starters are kept alive for years.

Today, it is more common for some percentage of yeast to be added to a sourdough starter to produce a more uniform and reliable starter. The starter is allowed to ferment until it has soured. Part of this starter is used to prepare a dough. The remaining starter is generally replenished, either by adding flour and water or by returning a portion of the newly made dough to the starter.

The type of wild yeast present in the air differs from region to region. San Francisco, for example, is famous for its sourdough breads. The flavor of sourdoughs made in other locations may be noticeably different.

Steam, which is produced when liquids in a batter or dough are heated, is a physical leavener. Heat causes any air pockets in a batter or dough to expand. Steam is the leavening agent in sponge cakes and soufflés. It also plays a vital role in the production of puff pastry, croissants, and Danish pastry, where the steam is trapped between layers of dough, causing them to separate and rise. Other areas in which air

plays a vital role in leavening products is when air is incorporated into a batter through either whipping or creaming an ingredient or ingredients before they are incorporated into the final batter.

FLAVORINGS

Flavoring ingredients can range from extracts and essences to chocolate chips and chopped nuts. Dried fruits and fruit purées can also be considered flavorings. In general, flavoring ingredients do not have a great impact on the characteristics of the batter or dough as it is mixed, shaped, and baked.

THICKENERS

Sauces and puddings can be thickened by many ingredients, including eggs, gelatin, and starches such as flour, cornstarch, tapioca, or arrowroot. These thickeners may be used to lightly thicken a mixture, as for a sauce, or to produce something that is firmly set, like Bavarian cream.

The quantity and type of thickener, as well as how it is stirred or otherwise manipulated, will determine the properties of the finished product. For example, if a custard is cooked over direct heat and stirred constantly, the result will be a sauce that pours easily. The same custard cooked in a bain-marie with no stirring at all will set into a firm custard that can be sliced.

Typical thickeners are:

- **ARROWROOT AND CORNSTARCH.** These are generally preferred for thickening sauces, puddings, and fillings where a translucent effect is desired.

To dilute these thickeners before incorporating them with other ingredients, mix them with a small amount of a cool liquid. Tapioca starch is also commonly used to thicken pie fillings.

- FLOUR. Commonly used to thicken crème pâtisserie, for example. In order to prevent lumping, the flour (and sugar if used) may be stirred together and combined with a small amount of the liquid to form a slurry before being fully incorporated. Flour-thickened fillings are also often additionally thickened and enriched with eggs. The eggs must be tempered to prevent the filling from curdling.

- EGGS. Whole eggs or yolks are often used either alone or in conjunction with other thickeners. As the egg proteins begin to coagulate, the liquid becomes trapped in the network of set proteins, producing a smooth, rather thick texture, in which the sauce coats the back of a spoon when done.

- GELATIN. Used to produce light, delicate foams (Bavarian creams, mousses, stabilized whipped cream) that are firmly set. Such foams retain the shape of a mold even after unmolding and can be sliced. Available in both powder or sheets, gelatin must first be softened or bloomed in a cool liquid. Once the gelatin has absorbed the liquid, it is gently heated to melt the crystals, either by adding the softened gelatin to a hot mixture, such as a hot custard sauce, or by gently heating the gelatin over simmering water.

SCALING

The most accurate way to measure ingredients is to weigh them.

Even liquid ingredients are often, though not always, weighed. Various types of scales are used in the bakeshop, including balance-beam, spring-type, or electronic scales (for descriptions and illustrations, see pages 88–89 and 96–97). Other measuring tools, including volume measures and measuring spoons, are also required.

It is important to properly scale out each ingredient necessary to prepare the baked item. It is equally important to scale out the finished dough or batter to ensure that the proper amount is used for the pan size, mold, or individual portion. Not only does this contribute to the uniformity of products, it also decreases the possibility of uneven rising or browning caused by too much or too little dough in the pan.

The most accurate way to measure all ingredients, dry or liquid, is by weight on a scale.

SIFTING DRY INGREDIENTS

Dry ingredients used for most baked goods should be sifted before they are incorporated into the dough or batter.

Sifting aerates flour and confectioners' sugar, removing lumps and filtering out any impurities. Leavening ingredients and some flavoring ingredients (cocoa powder, for example) are more evenly distributed after sifting.

Sifting should take place after the ingredients have been properly scaled.

Dry ingredients are passed through a sieve onto a sheet of parchment paper. The paper can then be rolled into a cone, making it easier to add the dry ingredients to the batter or dough.

COOKING SUGAR

Applying heat to sugar changes its texture from a solid to a liquid and its color from white or clear to a deep gold or brown.

SIMPLE SYRUP

Simple syrups are an indispensable preparation in every pastry kitchen. They add flavor, moisture, and sweetness to sponge cakes before filling and finishing, act as a simple wash for puff pastry as it bakes to alter its flavor and texture, and serve as a poaching medium for fruits. Other flavoring ingredients, such as a sachet of cinnamon and clove, a pinch of saffron, or a split vanilla bean, may be added as the syrup comes to a boil. Various liquers may be added to the syrup for flavor, such as orange liquer, brandy, rum, or coffee-flavored liquer.

Use a candy thermometer for accuracy when cooking sugar.

COOKING SUGAR TO VARIOUS STAGES

When sugar is heated, it dissolves. As the sugar continues to cook to specific temperatures, the sugar syrup changes texture. At first, the syrup will cling together enough to form threads when a utensil is dipped into the syrup and pulled away. Eventually, the syrup will start to form into balls when it is removed from the heat. Each of the following stages has different applications in baking, pastry, and candy making:

234°F/112°C	thread
238°F/114°C	soft ball
248°F/120°C	firm ball
260°F/125°C	hard ball
275°F/135°C	soft crack
310°F/155°C	hard crack

A few basic rules apply when cooking sugar

- Use a heavy-gauge pot to prevent burning the sugar.

- Add an acid or an invert sugar, such as corn syrup, to prevent sugar crystals from forming.

- Brush down the side of the pot with a moist pastry brush; this will also help to prevent crystallization.

- Milk or other liquids to be added to the mixture need to be warmed before adding them to caramel.

- Add all liquids carefully, away from heat. The hot caramel will foam and splatter when a liquid is added.

TOP *Drop a small amount of the cooked sugar into ice water. Gather it into a ball. It should hold its shape.*

MIDDLE *When the sugar is cooked further, and a small amount is dropped into ice water, it hardens instantly. If it breaks apart without shattering, it is at the soft crack stage.*

BOTTOM *At the hard crack stage, sugar syrup dropped into ice water shatters when broken apart.*

WHIPPED CREAM OR CHANTILLY CREAM

Heavy cream can be whipped to soft, medium, or firm peaks for use in sweet and savory applications. It may be sweetened with powdered sugar and flavored with vanilla to produce chantilly cream.

Cream to be whipped must be well chilled, as should the bowl and whip. Working with cold cream and cold equipment helps to produce a more stable foam that is easier to fold into other products.

Begin by whipping the cream at a moderate and steady speed, working either by hand or with an electric mixer. Once the cream starts to thicken, increase the speed and continue to whip until the desired thickness and stiffness is reached. The various stages of whipped cream are as follows:

- **SOFT PEAK.** The cream is whipped just until it forms peaks that fall gently to one side when the beater is lifted. Soft peak cream is typically used as a sauce to pool under or spoon over desserts, or as the lightener for sweet and savory mousses with a smooth, creamy consistency.

- **MEDIUM PEAK.** As the cream passes through the soft peak stage, the cream becomes stiffer and holds peaks for a longer time and with less drooping when the beaters are lifted. Cream whipped to medium peaks is often used to cover cakes and tortes or to use as a garnish (either a dollop dropped from a spoon or a puff piped through a pastry bag). The peaks should not stand up perfectly straight, however, because the added agitation of spreading or piping the cream might overwhip and take on an undesirable, grainy appearance.

- **STIFF PEAKS.** When cream is beaten to stiff peaks, the foam loses some of its flexibility. This means that there is a good chance that the cream will start to break apart, eventually becoming very grainy and finally turning into butter. As cream reaches stiff peak stage, it will lose some of its gloss and velvety texture.

ABOVE *Soft peak whipped cream barely holds its shape. The peaks tip over when the beater is lifted.*

ABOVE *Medium peaks retain their shape when the beater is lifted from the bowl.*

ABOVE *When whipped up to or just past stiff peaks, the cream loses its sheen and starts to look grainy.*

WHIPPING EGG WHITES AND MAKING MERINGUES

Egg whites can be beaten into a foam to use as a leavener or lightener. Meringues are made by incorporating enough sugar to both stabilize and sweeten the foam.

There are several uses in the kitchen and the bakeshop for whipped egg whites. They are the leavener for soufflés and sponge cakes and they can be used to create the light texture in some mousses and bavarians.

Egg whites must be completely free of any trace of yolk. The separated whites whip to the greatest volume when they are at room temperature. Whites taken directly from refrigeration can be tempered by warming them over a bowl of hot water.

The bowl and whip must also be completely free of any grease or fat. Some chefs rinse the bowl and whip with white vinegar, followed by a rinse with very hot water, to remove all traces of grease. The bowl should be large enough to hold the beaten egg whites, which can triple in volume.

Begin whipping at a slow to moderate speed, just until the whites start to loosen and become foamy. Increase the speed and continue to whip until the whites hold soft or medium peaks (see Whipped Cream, at left). If egg whites are overbeaten, they become dull, grainy, and dry looking. Overbeaten egg whites collapse quickly as they are folded into a base or batter, adversely affecting the texture of the finished item.

SEPARATING WHOLE EGGS

Eggs separate most easily when they are taken directly from refrigeration. In addition to the cold eggs, you should have four well-cleaned containers on hand for separating eggs: one to catch the white as the egg is separated, plus three more to hold the clean whites, whites with some yolk, and yolks separately.

Crack the egg's shell and pull it apart into two halves. Pour the egg from one half into the other, allowing the white to fall into one of the containers. When all of the white has separated from the yolk, drop the yolk into a separate container. Examine the white in the bowl to be sure that it has no bits of yolk. If it is clean, drop it into a container that will hold only clean whites. If the white does have bits of yolk, transfer it to another container. These whites can be used in other dishes, where the whites need not be beaten to a foam.

Keep the eggs chilled as you work, and return them, labeled and dated, to refrigeration as soon as you have finished working with them.

Beat egg whites only if you are ready to use them immediately. For example, the whites for a soufflé are beaten and added to the base, then immediately baked for the best volume.

Adding sugar to beaten egg whites makes the foam more stable. These egg white foams are known as meringues. Meringues differ according to how the sugar is added to the whites.

To prepare any meringue, first separate the eggs carefully and be sure that the whites, the bowl, and the whip are all very clean. Different types of meringues are made in the following ways:

- **COMMON MERINGUE.** Beat the egg whites until frothy and then start to add the sugar, while whipping, in a gradual stream. Once all the sugar is added, whip the meringue to soft, medium, or stiff peak, as required by recipe. This type of meringue can be used to top a pie, to pipe and bake into shells or used to create borders and other decorations. Because the whites in a common meringue are not heated to a safe temperature, this style of meringue should be used for applications where it will be cooked, either by poaching or baking.

- **ITALIAN MERINGUE.** When a hot sugar syrup is whipped into egg whites, an Italian meringue is produced. This meringue requires more careful timing than a common meringue, but the end product has a finer grain and is much more stable. Prepare a sugar syrup and heat it to 250°F/121°C. As the syrup nears this temperature, beat the egg whites to soft peaks. Once the syrup is properly cooked, pour it gradually into the whites, while the mixer is running. Continue to beat the meringue until it holds soft, medium, or stiff peaks, as required. Italian meringue can be used to prepare baked shells, cookies, or left unbaked to use as a filling or as the base for Italian buttercream (page 963).

- **SWISS MERINGUE.** To prepare a Swiss meringue, combine the whites and sugar in a mixing bowl, and warm the mixture over simmering heat until it reaches 110° to 120°F/43° to 49°C, stirring frequently to be sure that the sugar is completely dissolved into the egg whites. Once the egg whites are warmed, transfer the bowl to a mixer and whip on moderate speed until the meringue has medium or stiff peaks, as required.

Preparing Meringue

TOP *Air begins to get trapped in egg whites and they look foamy.*

BOTTOM *Eggs whites whipped to soft peaks barely hold their shape.*

Topping with Meringue

Making Meringue Shells

TOP *Medium peak egg whites are glossy and soft, and hold the tracks from the whip.*

BOTTOM *Egg whites whipped to stiff peaks hold a well-defined shape.*

TOP *Spread and pipe the meringue onto a pie.*

BOTTOM *The high sugar content in a meringue makes it brown quickly in a hot oven or under a broiler.*

TOP *Meringues whipped to stiff peaks may be piped into shapes and warmed in a low oven until thoroughly dried.*

BOTTOM *Store finished meringues in air-tight containers.*

CHOOSING AND PREPARING PANS

Many different kinds of pans are used in baking. Picking the correct shape and size of the pan is essential to ensuring the right texture and appearance.

If a pan is too large, the cake or bread may not rise properly during baking and the edges may become overbaked. On the other hand, if a pan is too small, the item may not be properly baked through, and the appearance will also suffer.

Delicate batters, especially those for sponge cakes, jelly rolls, or cookies that are rich in eggs, sugar, and butter, are baked in pans that have been liberally greased (usually with hydrogenated shortening or a blend of shortening and flour), lined with parchment paper, and then greased again and dusted with flour.

As an exception to the general rule of greasing pans, angel food cake is baked in an ungreased tube pan. The batter must be able to adhere to the pan sides to produce a tall cake and give it stability until it is fully baked and cooled.

Lean doughs, such as pizza dough, hard rolls, and French and Italian breads, are baked in pans that are dusted with cornmeal. The cornmeal very slightly elevates the dough so that a good crust can form on all surfaces.

TOP *Shake a handful of flour into the greased pan and spread it around to coat all surfaces. Dump out the excess.*

BOTTOM *Line the bottom of cake or loaf pans with parchment paper to make it easier to unmold the baked item.*

SELECTING AND PREPARING OVENS

The success of baked goods depends in large part on baking them at the right temperature and in the right type of oven.

The type of oven used — conventional, hearth, convection, or steam-injected — has a direct impact on the color and texture of baked goods. In all cases, the oven should be fully preheated to the correct temperature.

A variety of ovens are described in Chapter 5, "Equipment Identification."

Do not overload the oven, or the air will not be able to circulate evenly. For even baking and browning, insert the racks in the center of a conventional oven. Baked goods that rise during baking, such as vol-au-vents made from puff pastry or éclairs made from pâté à choux, should be prepared in a conventional oven. Some cakes, muffins, and cookies may be baked in a convection oven. That way, larger batches may be baked in a single load. The forced movement of air allows each piece to bake evenly.

COOLING AND STORING BAKED GOODS

Cooling and storing baked goods properly is as important to the final quality of baked items as proper mixing and baking techniques.

Once an item is completely baked, it should be removed from the oven and, in most cases, allowed to cool briefly in the baking pan. The item then should be removed from the pan and allowed to cool completely on a rack. Placing the item on a rack allows air to circulate around all surfaces and prevents steam from condensing on the item.

Once cooled, baked goods can be either served immediately or stored in various ways, depending upon the product. Breads may be stored whole or sliced. They can be held for a short time on parchment-lined trays or in baskets. For longer storage, they should be wrapped well in plastic wrap. Most breads and cakes made from yeast dough can be frozen for longer storage. After thawing, they should be refreshed by reheating before service.

The major advantage of fresh baking is that preservatives are unnecessary, but some breads and cakes become stale rapidly, especially those made from lean doughs (hard rolls, Italian bread). Reheating these breads before service will refresh them. Microwave ovens, however, are not recommended for this purpose, because they can cause the bread to become tough and rubbery. (Richer doughs — Danish, muffins, and some cakes — may be successfully reheated in a microwave.)

Cakes are often prepared in advance and frozen. Ideally, they should not be filled and frosted until just before service, because most frostings and fillings do not stand up well after freezing and thawing. Baked goods thaw rapidly at room temperature. They should always be checked for a good, fresh flavor before they are served. Simple syrup is often brushed on the surface of a cake to refresh the flavor and add moisture.

USING PASTRY BAGS AND TIPS

Pastry bags and assorted tips are used to apply decorations, to add fillings to other foods, and as a portioning tool.

Pastry bags have many uses in the kitchen beyond decorating cakes. They are used to portion out batters such as pâté à choux or duchesse potatoes before baking, to fill pastry shells for éclairs or profiteroles, and to apply small amounts of garnish or finish ingredients on hors-d'oeuvre and canapés.

Expressing a frosting, batter, dough, or other soft mixture through a pastry bag is referred to as piping. It takes practice to develop the sure movements used to create decorative effects.

To fill a pastry bag, select the desired tip and position it securely in the pastry bag's opening or in a coupler. Fold down the bag's top to create a cuff, then transfer the buttercream to the bag with a spatula or spoon. Twist the bag to compress the mixture and to release any air pockets before beginning to pipe.

Use your dominant hand to hold the bag and squeeze out the contents of the bag. Use your other hand to guide and steady the tip. Release pressure on the bag as you lift it cleanly away to avoid making tails.

Clean reusable pastry bags and tips thoroughly immediately after use by washing them carefully in warm soapy water, then rinsing thoroughly. Be sure to turn the bag inside out to clean the interior before storage. In many kitchens and bakeshops, single-use pastry bags are used for reasons of sanitation.

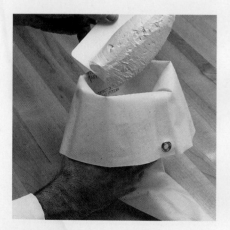

TOP LEFT *Support the bag with your free hand while filling it.*

BOTTOM LEFT *With one hand, press the buttercream down and out of the bag.*

TOP RIGHT *Wipe the bag dry with absorbent toweling before storing it.*

BOTTOM RIGHT *From the top: Rows 1 and 2 show a border design and individual rosettes made with a plain opening. Rows 3 and 4 show the same technique using a plain tip with a smaller opening. Rows 5 and 6 show the effect of two different-sized leaf tips. Rows 7 and 8 show rosettes made with a star tip and a shell border from the same tip. Other tips are also available.*

RECIPES

SOURDOUGH STARTER

6 pounds/2.75 kilograms

4 lb/1.8 kg hard wheat flour
2¼ lb/1 kg water, at 70°F/21°C

1 Combine 10 oz/285 g of the flour and 6 oz/170 g of water in a large bowl and blend, with clean hands or a utensil, until just combined.

2 Place dough in a food-grade plastic bucket or stainless steel bowl. Cover tightly with plastic wrap and allow to ferment at room temperature (68° to 76°F/20° to 24°C) until slightly bubbly with a faint sweet and fruity aroma, 2 to 3 days.

3 For the first refreshment, add 20 oz/510 g of flour and enough water to maintain the same consistency (about 10 to 12 oz/285 to 340 g). Cover tightly and allow to ferment at room temperature for 2 to 3 days more, or until bubbly with a stronger but still sweet and fruity aroma.

4 Refresh a second time with 30 oz/850 g of flour and enough water to maintain the same consistency (about 30 to 32 oz/850 to 900g). Cover tightly and allow to ferment at room temperature for 10 to 15 hours more, or until bubbly with a sweet and fruity aroma.

5 The starter is now ready to use.

NOTES

To keep the starter alive, add enough water and flour to replace the amount used. If the starter is not used frequently, refresh it every few days.

Keeping the starter under refrigeration will slow the yeast's fermentation and allow it to go for longer periods without refreshment.

The starter should never have a sour or pronounced vinegary aroma. If this type of aroma is detectable, begin to give regular refreshments every 2 to 3 days to restore the health of the starter.

Sourdough starters are highly acidic. Protect your hands by wearing plastic gloves or by preparing the dough in a mixer with a dough hook.

Rye Sourdough Starter Replace the hard wheat flour with rye flour.

SIMPLE SYRUP

makes 2 quarts/2 liters

2 qt/2 L water
1 lb/450 g sugar

1 Combine the water and sugar and bring to a boil.

2 Cool and reserve.

COMMON MERINGUE

makes 1½ pounds/680 grams

8 oz/225 g egg whites
1 lb/450 g sugar

1 Put the egg whites in the clean, grease-free bowl of a mixer and whisk on medium speed until very foamy, with air bubbles still visible and the whites still semi-translucent.

2 Start to gradually add the sugar, whisking constantly.

3 After all of the sugar has been incorporated, continue to beat on medium speed to the desired peak (soft, medium, or stiff), according to intended use.

SWISS MERINGUE

makes 1½ pounds/680 grams

8 oz/225 g egg whites
1 lb/450 g sugar

1 Put the egg whites and sugar in the clean, grease-free bowl of a mixer and stir together.

2 Place over a simmering hot water bath and stir frequently until the mixture reaches 110° to 120°F/43° to 49°C.

3 Beat on medium speed to the desired peak (soft, medium, or stiff), according to intended use.

ITALIAN MERINGUE

makes 1½ pounds/680 grams

1 lb/450 g sugar
4 fl oz/120 mL water
8 oz/225 g egg whites

1 Combine the sugar and water in a saucepan over moderate heat and bring the mixture to 240°F/116°C.

2 Put the egg whites in the bowl of a mixer and, starting to beat when the sugar reaches 230°F/110°C, beat the whites to the soft peak stage.

3 Add the sugar syrup to the egg whites in a thick steady stream while continuing to beat.

4 After all of the sugar syrup has been incorporated, continue to beat the mixture on medium speed to the desired peak (soft, medium, or firm), according to intended use.

EGG-AND-WATER WASH

EGG WASHES ARE AN IMPORTANT COMPONENT IN MANY BAKED GOODS; THEY HAVE A CONSIDERABLE EFFECT ON THE FINISHED APPEARANCE AND MAY ALSO AFFECT THE FLAVOR, MOUTH FEEL, AND TEXTURE.

AN EGG WASH MAY INCLUDE WHOLE EGGS, ONLY YOLKS, OR ONLY WHITES. THE WHITES MAY BE BLENDED WITH WATER, MILK, OR CREAM.

makes 1 pint/480 milliliters

8 oz/225 g eggs
4 fl oz/120 mL water

1 Combine the eggs and water in a bowl and whisk together until fully combined.

2 Use as indicated in the recipe. Washes should be applied in a light even coat. Be sure to brush away any pools of accumulated liquid.

Egg-and-Milk Wash Substitute milk for the water.

Egg-and-Heavy Cream Wash Substitute heavy cream for the water.

Egg Yolk-and-Heavy Cream Wash Substitute egg yolks for the eggs and heavy cream for the water.

CHAPTER THIRTY-TWO

Breads and rolls made from
yeast-raised doughs and batters
have a distinct aroma and flavor,
produced by the organic process
of the yeast's fermentation. The
effects vary from the simplicity
of a hearth-baked pizza to a
delicate egg-and-butter-enriched
brioche.

YEAST BREADS

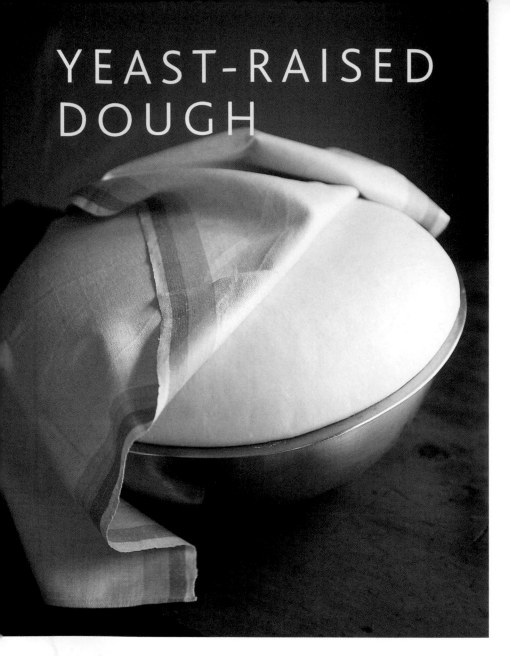

YEAST-RAISED DOUGH

An excellent yeast-raised bread requires not only the correct formula, but also good technique during mixing, kneading, proofing, shaping, and baking.

The earliest breads were flatbreads made by blending meals and water and baking in ovens or on griddles. Leavened bread did not become possible until the Egyptians, using the wheat that flourished in the fertile Nile River valley, discovered that certain doughs would ferment and rise and had a different texture when baked.

The Egyptians may not have been sure about what had caused the difference, but they were able to continue producing leavened cakes by preserving some of this fermented dough each day to combine with new batches. This is exactly the manner by which generations of people from all over the world practiced and continue to practice baking bread and how the American settlers kept their sourdough alive thousands of years later. Eventually, yeast itself was identified and methods for extracting and processing it were developed.

Yeast doughs may be divided into two categories: lean doughs and enriched doughs. Lean dough can be produced with only flour, yeast, salt, and water; in fact, it is the formula for a classic French baguette. Other ingredients such as spices, herbs, special flours, and/or dried nuts and fruits can be added to vary this dough, but they will not greatly change the basic texture.

Lean doughs contain only small amounts of sugar and fat, if any. Breads made from lean dough tend to have a chewier texture, more bite, and a crisp crust.

Hard rolls, French- and Italian-style breads, and whole wheat, rye, and pumpernickel breads are considered lean.

An enriched dough is produced by the addition of fat or tenderizing ingredients such as sugars or syrups, butter or oil, whole eggs or egg yolks, or milk or cream. Included in this category are soft roll dough, brioche, and challah. When fats are introduced, they change the dough's texture as well as the way in which dough behaves during mixing, kneading, shaping, and baking.

Enriched doughs have a cakelike texture after baking. They may be golden in color because of the use of eggs and butter, and the crust is usually very soft. The dough is usually softer and a little more difficult to work with during kneading and shaping than lean dough.

THE FOLLOWING FORMULA FOR A LEAN BREAD IS KNOWN AS A BAKER'S PERCENTAGE. THE BASIC INGREDIENTS ARE EXPRESSED AS PERCENTAGES, OR PARTS, BASED UPON THE WEIGHT OF THE FLOUR.

ADDITIONAL INGREDIENTS TO ENRICH OR FLAVOR THE DOUGH MAY BE ADDED, INCLUDING EGGS, BUTTER OR OIL, SUGAR, HERBS AND SPICES, CHEESES, NUTS, OR OLIVES. CONSULT SPECIFIC RECIPES FOR GUIDANCE.

100 parts wheat flour or a combination of wheat flour and other flours (bread, high gluten, or clear flour)

60 to 66 parts water or other liquid

2 parts yeast

2 parts salt

SELECT AND PREPARE THE INGREDIENTS AND EQUIPMENT

WHEAT FLOUR (all-purpose or bread flour, for instance) is the basis of most yeast-raised doughs. Wheat flours contain a high percentage of protein, which gives a good texture to lean doughs. A portion of the wheat

flour called for in a recipe may be replaced with other flours, such as rye, pumpernickel, or oat. Consult individual formulas and scale the flour carefully. It is generally not important to sift the flour for bread.

Yeast is an organic leavener, which must be alive in order to be effective. Bring the yeast to room temperature if necessary before preparing the dough.

Water, milk, or other liquids used in a bread formula should fall within a temperature range of 68° to 76°F/20° to 24°C for compressed (or fresh) yeast. The ideal water temperature for active dry yeast is 105° to 110°F/40° to 43°C.

The viability of yeast may be tested prior to use by proofing. To do so, combine the yeast with warm liquid and a small amount of flour or sugar. Let the mixture rest at room temperature until a thick surface foam forms. The foam indicates that the yeast is alive and can be used. If there is no foam, the yeast is dead and should be discarded.

Salt develops flavor in bread and also helps to control the action of the yeast. If salt is omitted, breads do not develop as good a color or texture.

The way a pan is prepared depends on the type of dough being used. For lean doughs, either line the pan with parchment paper or dust it with cornmeal or semolina flour (cornmeal is especially well suited to free-form loaves — baguettes or round loaves). For doughs with a higher percentage of milk, sugar, and fat, grease the pan or line it with parchment paper. For extremely rich doughs (brioche or challah, for example), grease, but do not line, the pan.

1. Combine the water and yeast in the bowl of an electric mixer.

Place the warm water or other liquid in the bowl of a mixer fitted with a dough hook. Add the yeast and mix thoroughly. If the sponge method is used or if the yeast should be proofed to test its power, combine the yeast with some liquid, some of the flour, and/or a small amount of sugar. Cover the bowl and let the yeast ferment in a warm place until frothy.

2. Add all the remaining ingredients to the yeast mixture.

Drop all of the flour into the bowl, followed by the salt and additional ingredients, such as eggs; butter or oil; sugars, syrups, or honey; spices or herbs. Because all of the ingredients are added at once, this mixing method is often referred to as the straight dough mixing method.

3. Mix until the dough starts to cohere into a ball. Knead the dough until it develops a smooth, elastic texture.

Blend by hand or in a mixer set at low speed. This mixes all of the ingredients into a homogenous, but very rough, dough. Once the dough has absorbed most of the flour, the mixer speed is increased to medium; this kneads the dough and develops the strands of gluten. This allows the dough to expand without breaking as the yeast ferments the dough and causes it to rise.

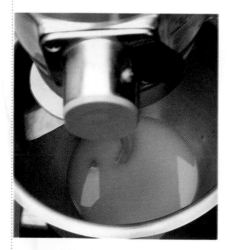

ABOVE *Combining the yeast and water rehydrates the yeast, an important step for both compressed and dry granulated yeasts.*

ABOVE *Add the remaining ingredients all at once for the straight mix method for yeast doughs.*

ABOVE *Mix the dough until it looks like a shaggy mass. It will begin to catch on the dough hook.*

Kneading can be done by hand on a well-floured surface by pushing the dough away from you with the heel of your hand and pulling it back into a ball with the fingertips. Dust the surface and the dough with flour as you work. The dough can also be kneaded directly in the mixer.

When the dough is properly kneaded, it changes appearance and becomes satiny and stretchy. Very lean doughs are quite firm to the touch and relatively dry. Richer doughs are soft and tacky.

4. Let the dough rise until nearly doubled or tripled, in what is known as the first fermentation.
Place the dough in a lightly oiled container and rub the surface with oil to keep it from drying out. Cover the dough with plastic wrap or clean cloths and let it rise in a warm area, away from drafts. Depending upon the type of dough and the conditions in the kitchen or bakeshop, the dough may double or triple in volume, often referred to as rising or proofing.

Test the dough to determine if it has risen sufficiently by pressing it with your finger. The indentation should remain; dough should not spring back into place. Doughs should be allowed to rise enough for the bread to have good texture. Dough that has not risen sufficiently (considered underfermented) will have a coarse texture and will be flat after it is baked. Dough that has risen too much due to overfermentation may have a sour taste, sometimes described as yeasty or as smelling or tasting like beer.

ABOVE *Properly kneaded dough releases from the hook and forms a ball that rolls around the bowl, sometimes known as clearing the side of the bowl.*

ABOVE *Oil the bowl and the dough to prevent a tough, dry skin from forming.*

ABOVE *The dough is more than doubled after the first proof, or rise.*

5. Fold the dough over, turn it out of the bowl onto a floured work surface, and scale into pieces. Push the dough down in a few places. This will gently expel the carbon dioxide, even out the overall temperature, and redistribute the yeast evenly. Then, fold the dough over on itself to further expel gases. Scale the dough into the appropriate size using a bench knife or chef's knife to cut the dough into equal-sized pieces. Weigh the pieces as you work to make certain all the rolls or loaves are consistent in size.

Once the dough is cut to size, round the dough into smooth balls by pulling the outer layer of each dough ball over the surface and pulling it taut on the bottom of the ball. Once the balls are formed, place them on a pan or floured surface;

cover and allow to rest briefly before they are shaped. This resting period allows the gluten strands to relax enough to make stretching the dough into the desired shape easier.

6. Shape the dough before baking and place in or on prepared pans or molds. Apply egg wash (optional) and proof the dough.

There are several ways to shape yeast doughs. They may be formed into loaves and placed in the pan or other mold in which they will be baked. Some breads, such as pizza and some round loaves, are formed and placed on cornmeal or parchment-lined sheet trays; these doughs are transferred into a deck or hearth oven with a peel. Once the dough is shaped, an egg wash (page 874) may be brushed over the surface.

Let the shaped dough rise, either in a warm, draft-free area, or in a proof box. This final rise is known as pan proofing.

The dough should be allowed to rise to about three quarters of the expected finished size during pan proofing. It will continue to rise slightly when it is in the oven. This additional rise is known as oven spring.

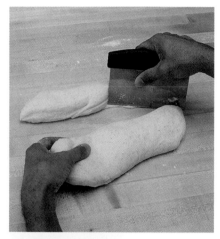

ABOVE *Fold the dough over on itself to release gases and redistribute the yeast.*

TOP *Use a bench knife or chef's knife to cut the dough into uniform pieces, according to the desired end result.*

BOTTOM *Use the edge of your hands to pull the outer layers into a smooth skin, stretching the dough and turning it clockwise as you work.*

ABOVE *Round loaves can be proofed in linen-lined molds or baskets.*

7. Score the bread and bake at the appropriate temperature until baked through.

Cutting a slash in the outer skin of a shaped loaf or roll permits the interior steam to escape. If it cannot, the pressure could cause the bread to burst open at the seam or some other spot. Use a sharp knife with a thin blade, a single-edged razor blade, or a special scoring tool known as a lamé.

To achieve a very crisp crust, use steam-generating ovens, if available. If not, brush or spray the loaves or rolls with water as they are put in the oven to simulate the effect.

Bake yeast doughs until they have a good aroma and a golden to brown color. Thumping the bread to see if it has a hollow sound is a common test for doneness. When this test is used in conjunction with other doneness indicators, such as the recipe's recommended baking time, smell, and appearance, it is effective.

8. Cool the bread on a rack before slicing and serving or before storing for later service.

Yeast-raised breads should not be cut until they have cooled thoroughly. To cut bread, use a serrated bread knife. Use gentle back and forth strokes to produce even slices without jagged surfaces.

9. Evaluate the quality of the bread.

Properly baked yeast-raised breads have a golden to deep-brown color and a fully developed crust. The use of special flours, such as rye or graham, influences the color. If, after baking, a bread or roll has a pale color, it is not completely baked or has been baked at too low a temperature. Doughs that have been brushed with egg wash or milk have a more tender and golden crust than others. Doughs that include butter and eggs are golden on the inside.

Breads made from yeast doughs should be fairly elastic but still easy to bite into. The higher the proportion of eggs and shorteners, such as butter or milk, the more tender the finished product.

The bread should not taste strongly of alcohol; if it does, it is an indication that the dough was not allowed sufficient time to proof before baking or that too much yeast was used. Doughs that do not include a sufficient amount of salt will have a bland flavor and strong alcohol odor.

ABOVE *Turn boules out of the shaping baskets onto a prepared pan and score the upper surface just before baking.*

ABOVE *Placing the loaves on racks allows air to circulate readily all around the loaf and prevents steam from condensing on the surfaces.*

3 lb / 1.3 kg water (68° to 76°F / 20° to 24°C)

⅓ oz / 10 g compressed yeast

5 lb / 2.25 kg bread flour

⅓ oz / 10 g salt

BASIC LEAN DOUGH

1 Combine the water and yeast in the bowl of an electric mixer and blend until the yeast is fully dissolved.

2 Add the flour and salt and mix, using the dough hook attachment, on low speed just to incorporate. Increase to medium speed and mix until the dough is smooth and elastic, 10 to 12 minutes.

3 Place the dough in a lightly oiled container, cover, and let rise until doubled in volume, about 75 minutes.

4 Fold the dough over on itself, pressing gently to expel the carbon dioxide in the bread. The dough is ready to scale and shape now.

MAKES 8 POUNDS/3.6 KILOGRAMS

Boules Prepare the lean dough as directed above. Scale the dough at 1 lb 8 oz/680 g per loaf. Round off the dough and place in a lined or floured mold or basket. Let the dough rise until it has increased to three quarters the desired finished size, about 20 to 30 minutes. Turn the proofed boules onto a parchment-lined sheet tray. Score the top of each loaf. Transfer to a 375°F/190°C oven and bake for 25 to 30 minutes, or until the crust is crisp and well browned and the loaf sounds hollow when the bottom is gently thumped. Cool on a rack before slicing and serving.

RECIPES

BAGUETTES

makes eight 1-pound/450-gram loaves

1 recipe BASIC LEAN DOUGH (page 882)
cornmeal, for dusting

1   Scale the prepared and properly proofed dough into
    1-lb/450-g pieces. Round off each piece and let rest about
    30 minutes before shaping.

2   To shape the baguette, flatten each ball of dough into a
    rectangle. Holding the narrow ends of the dough, lift and
    stretch the dough to elongate the rectangle, making its
    overall length about 8 in/20 cm. Roll the dough into a
    cylinder, pressing the seam closed with the edge of your
    palm. Transfer the dough, seam side down, to the pan or
    onto a parchment-lined sheet pan sprinkled with corn-
    meal. Let the loaves rise until increased by three fourths,
    about 1 hour.

3   Score each loaf in several places by making diagonal
    slashes just through the outer layer of dough.

4   Bake in a 425°F/220°C oven (with steam if available)
    until deep in color and hollow sounding when tapped on
    the bottom, about 30 minutes.

5   Remove loaves from the oven (and the pan, if used) and
    cool on a rack before serving.

    Hard Rolls Scale the dough into 1½-oz/45-g pieces. Round
    off and shape as directed for baguettes. Each hard roll
    should be about 4 in/10 cm long. Set on parchment-lined
    sheet pans. Let dough proof before baking (with steam,
    if possible). Just before baking, score rolls. Bake at
    450°F/230°C until golden brown and hollow sounding
    when tapped on the bottom, 12 to 13 minutes. Makes
    about 7 dozen rolls.

    Pizza Crust Scale the dough into 1-lb/450-g pieces. Round
    off dough and let rest for 20 minutes. Stretch into a circle
    about 10 in/25 cm in diameter and transfer to a pizza pan
    dusted with cornmeal. Add any desired toppings and bake
    at 450°F/230°C until the crust is golden brown on the
    edges and bottom and the toppings are very hot. Slice and
    serve at once. Makes enough dough for 8 pizza crusts.

see photograph on page 889

TOP LEFT *First, press the dough into a rectangle of an even thickness.*

BOTTOM LEFT *Next, lift the ends of the dough and allow its own weight to stretch it out.*

TOP RIGHT *Roll the stretched dough into a long cylinder, pressing the seams shut for the best finished loaf.*

BOTTOM RIGHT *Continue to roll and stretch the dough to the same length as the bread pan.*

SOURDOUGH BAGUETTES

makes eight 1-pound/450-gram loaves

3 lb/1.3 kg water (68° to 76°F / 20° to 24°C)

8 oz/225 g SOURDOUGH STARTER (page 873)

¼ oz/7 g compressed yeast

5 lb/2.25 kg bread flour

⅓ oz/10 g salt

1 Combine the water, starter, and yeast in the bowl of an electric mixer and blend until the yeast is fully dissolved.

2 Add the flour and salt and mix, using the dough hook attachment, on low speed just to incorporate. Increase to medium speed and mix until the dough is smooth and elastic, 10 to 12 minutes.

3 Place the dough in a lightly oiled container, cover, and let rise until doubled in volume, about 75 minutes.

4 Fold the dough over on itself, pressing gently to expel the carbon dioxide in the bread. Turn the dough out onto a floured work surface.

5 Scale the prepared and properly proofed dough into 1-lb/450-g pieces. Round off each piece, cover, and let rest about 15 to 20 minutes before shaping.

6 To shape the baguette, flatten each ball of dough into a rectangle. Holding the narrow ends of the dough, lift and stretch the dough to elongate the rectangle, making its overall length about 8 in/20 cm. Roll the dough into a cylinder, pressing the seam closed with the edge of your palm. Transfer the dough, seam side down, to the pan or onto a parchment-lined sheet pan sprinkled with cornmeal. Let the loaves rise until nearly doubled, about 1 hour. Just before baking, slash the dough in several places.

7 Bake in a 425°F/220°C oven (with steam if available) until deep in color and hollow sounding when tapped on the bottom, about 25 to 30 minutes.

8 Remove loaves from the pan and cool on rack.

FOCACCIA

makes twelve 10-ounce/285-gram loaves

1 recipe BASIC LEAN DOUGH (page 882)

olive oil, for brushing loaves, as needed

toppings, as needed (minced fresh herbs, sautéed onions, sliced tomatoes, etc.)

1 Scale the prepared and properly proofed dough into 10-oz/285-g pieces. Round off each piece and let rest about 30 minutes before shaping.

2 To shape the focaccia, flatten and stretch each ball of dough into a rectangle or a disk and place on a sheet pan sprinkled with cornmeal or brushed with oil. Let the loaves rise until doubled, about 30 to 40 minutes. Just before baking, dimple the focaccia with your fingertips. Brush generously with oil and scatter the desired topping over each focaccia.

3 Bake at 450°F/230°C until deep in color, about 30 minutes.

4 Remove loaves from the pan and cool on rack.

NOTE

Focaccia can be baked in a round or square pan as desired. Liberally brush the pan with olive oil before placing the focaccia into it to develop a richly flavored, crisp bottom crust.

TOP LEFT *Gently dimple the shaped focaccia dough with your fingertips.*

LEFT *Brush the focaccia with oil and sprinkle with herbs and seasonings, if desired.*

ABOVE *Cool on a rack.*

see photograph on page 888

CIABATTA

makes five 1-pound 8-ounce/680-gram loaves

3 lb 10 oz/1.6 kg water (68° to 76°F / 20° to 24°C)

1/3 oz/10 g compressed yeast

5 lb/2.25 kg bread flour

1/3 oz/10 g salt

olive oil for brushing loaf, as needed

kosher or sea salt, as needed

1 Combine the water and yeast in the bowl of an electric mixer and blend until the yeast is fully dissolved.

2 Add the flour and salt and mix, using the dough hook attachment, on low speed just to incorporate. Increase to medium speed and mix until the dough is smooth and elastic, 10 to 12 minutes.

3 Place the dough in a lightly oiled container, cover, and let rise until doubled in volume, about 75 minutes.

4 Turn the dough out of the bowl onto a well floured work surface. Scale the dough into 24-oz/680-g pieces and gently stretch each into a rectangle, about 10 in/25 cm long and 4 in/10 cm wide. Place on a lined baking sheet.

5 Bake in a 450°F/230°C oven (with steam if available) until deep in color, about 30 minutes.

6 Remove ciabatta from the pan, and if desired, immediately brush with olive oil and scatter salt over the surface. Cool on rack.

POTATO AND ROSEMARY BREAD

makes eight 2-pound/900-gram loaves

2 lb/900 g potatoes

1 3/4 lb/800 g water, at 68° to 76°F/20° to 24°C

1 1/4 oz/570 g compressed yeast

2 1/2 lb/1.15 kg all-purpose flour

2 1/2 lb/1.15 kg bread flour

8 oz/225 g whole-wheat flour

2 oz/60 g salt

5 1/2 lb/2.5 kg prefermented dough (see Notes)

1 oz/30 g minced rosemary

1 Peel the potatoes and cook in simmering salted water until tender. Put through a food mill or potato ricer and cool the potatoes to below 70°F/21°C.

2 Combine the water and yeast in the bowl of an electric mixer and blend until the yeast is fully dissolved.

3 Add the flours, potatoes, and salt and, using the dough hook attachment, mix on low speed just to incorporate. Add the prefermented dough and the rosemary, increase to medium speed, and mix until the dough is smooth and elastic, 10 to 12 minutes.

4 Place the dough in a lightly oiled container, cover, and let rise until it has doubled in volume, about 75 minutes.

5 Fold the dough over on itself and turn it out onto a floured work surface. Scale dough into eight 2-lb/900-g pieces and round off.

6 Set the round loaves on sheet pans lined with parchment or sprinkled with cornmeal and pan proof for 1 hour in a proof box or in a warm area. Just before baking, score the bread with several slashes.

7 Bake in a 430°F/221°C oven until deep in color and hollow sounding when tapped, about 70 minutes.

8 Remove loaves from pan and cool on racks.

NOTE

For the prefermented dough, prepare the Basic Lean Dough recipe (page 882). Once it has been pressed down, scale off 5 1/2 lb/2.5 kg. The dough is ready to use now as a prefermented dough in this recipe, or it may be tightly wrapped and held under refrigeration up to 24 hours in advance of mixing the Potato and Rosemary Bread.

MULTIGRAIN BREAD

makes twenty 1-pound 4-ounce/570-gram loaves

9 lb/4 kg milk, at 68° to 76°F/20° to 24°C

12 oz/340 g compressed yeast

8 oz/225 g cornmeal

10 lb/4.5 kg bread flour

1 lb/455 g bran

1 lb/455 g oatmeal

1 lb/455 g cracked wheat

8 oz/225 g whole wheat flour

2 oz/60 g molasses

1¼ lb/570 g sugar

12 oz/340 g butter

4 oz/115 g salt

1 Combine the milk and yeast in the bowl of an electric mixer and blend until the yeast is fully dissolved.

2 Add the remaining ingredients and, using the dough hook attachment, mix on low speed just to incorporate. Increase to medium speed and mix until the dough is smooth and elastic, 10 to 12 minutes.

3 Place the dough in a lightly oiled container, cover, and let rise until it has doubled in volume, about 75 minutes.

4 Turn the dough out onto a lightly floured work surface. Fold over the dough and scale it into twenty 1¼-lb/570-g pieces. Round the pieces, cover, and let rest for 10 minutes.

5 Re-shape the pieces into round loaves and place on sheet pans that have been lined with parchment and lightly dusted with cornmeal.

6 Proof the loaves in a proof box or, covered, in a warm area until double in size. Just before baking, slash the loaves.

7 Bake in a 380°F/195°C oven until deep in color and hollow sounding when tapped on the bottom, about 30 to 40 minutes.

8 Remove from the pans and cool on racks.

see photograph on page 889

PEASANT PECAN LOAF

makes eight 1-pound 4-ounce/570-gram loaves

3 lb/1.3 kg milk, at 68° to 76°F/20° to 24°C

4 oz/115 g compressed yeast

4½ lb/2 kg whole wheat flour

8 oz/225 g oatmeal

4¾ oz/130 g honey

4¾ oz/130 g butter

1 lb/450 g pecans

1¼ oz/35 g salt

1 lb/450 g raisins

1 Combine the milk and yeast in the bowl of an electric mixer and blend until the yeast is fully dissolved.

2 Add remaining ingredients except raisins and, using the dough hook attachment, mix on low speed just to incorporate. Increase to medium speed and mix for 8 minutes, add the raisins, and continue mixing until the dough is smooth and elastic, 2 to 4 minutes more.

3 Place the dough in a lightly oiled container, cover, and let rise until the dough has doubled in volume, about 75 minutes.

4 Scale into 1¼-lb/670-g pieces, round off, cover, and let rest for 15 to 20 minutes. Press each piece into a rectangle, stretching to the desired length (approximately the same length as the loaf pan). Roll each into a loaf, pressing the seam to seal the loaf. Place into lightly buttered loaf pans, seam side down. Let rise, covered, until nearly doubled in volume, about 45 minutes.

5 Bake at 375° to 390°F/175° to 200°C or until the loaves sound hollow when tapped on the bottom, about 35 minutes.

6 Let the bread cool in the loaf pans for several minutes, then remove from the pans and cool on racks.

RAISIN BREAD

makes seven 18-ounce/510-gram loaves

1 qt/1 L milk, at 68° to 76°F/20° to 24°C

4 oz/115 g compressed yeast

4 oz/115 g eggs

7¼ oz/205 g sugar

3¼ lb/1.5 kg bread flour

¼ oz/6 g ground cinnamon

½ oz/15 g salt

8 oz/225 g butter

2¾ lb/1.25 kg raisins

1 Combine the milk and yeast in the bowl of an electric mixer and blend until the yeast is fully dissolved. Add the remaining ingredients and mix using the dough hook attachment on low speed just to incorporate. Increase to medium speed and mix until the dough is smooth and elastic, 10 to 12 minutes.

2 Place the dough in a lightly oiled container, cover, and let rise until doubled in volume, about 75 minutes. Fold the dough over on itself, pressing gently to expel the carbon dioxide in the bread. Turn the dough out onto a floured work surface.

3 Scale the prepared and properly proofed dough into seven 18-oz/510-g pieces. Round off each piece, cover, and let rest about 15 to 20 minutes before shaping.

4 Press each piece into a rectangle, stretching to the desired length (approximately the same length as the loaf pan). Roll each into a loaf, pressing the seam to seal the loaf. Place into lightly buttered loaf pans, seam side down. Let rise, covered, until nearly doubled in volume, about 45 minutes.

5 Bake in a 380°F/195°C oven (with steam if available) until deep in color and hollow sounding when tapped on the bottom, about 35 minutes.

6 Remove loaves from the oven, cool in the pan for several minutes, then unmold the bread and finish on a rack before slicing and serving.

SUNFLOWER SEED BREAD

makes twelve 18-ounce/510-gram loaves

4 lb/1.8 kg milk, at 68° to 76°F/20° to 24°C

2 oz/60 g compressed yeast

4 oz/115 g honey

4 eggs

3 oz/85 g sugar

6½ lb/2.9 kg bread flour

12 oz/340 g bran flour

2 oz/60 g salt

6 oz/170 g butter

12 oz/340 g sunflower seeds, plus as needed for topping

EGG-AND-MILK WASH (page 874), as needed

1 Combine the milk and yeast in the bowl of an electric mixer and blend until the yeast is fully dissolved. Add the remaining ingredients, except the egg wash, and mix, using the dough hook attachment, on low speed just to incorporate. Increase to medium speed and mix until the dough is smooth and elastic, 10 to 12 minutes.

2 Place the dough in a lightly oiled container, cover, and let rise until doubled in volume, about 75 minutes. Fold the dough over on itself, pressing gently to expel the carbon dioxide in the bread. Turn the dough out onto a floured work surface.

3 Scale the prepared and properly proofed dough into twelve 18-oz/510-g pieces. Round off each piece, cover, and let rest about 15 to 20 minutes before shaping.

4 Press each piece into a rectangle, stretching to the desired length (approximately the same length as the loaf pan). Roll each into a loaf, pressing the seam to seal the loaf. Place into lightly buttered loaf pans, seam side down. Brush with egg wash and scatter surface of each loaf with additional sunflower seeds. Let rise, covered, until nearly doubled in volume, about 45 minutes. When they have risen, make several slashes on the surface of each loaf.

5 Bake in a 400°F/205°C oven until deep in color and hollow sounding when tapped on the bottom, about 35 minutes.

6 Remove loaves from the oven, cool in the pan for several minutes, then unmold the bread and finish on a rack before slicing and serving.

Sunflower Seed Rolls Scale the dough into pieces weighing 1½ oz/45 g. Round off and place on parchment-lined sheet pans. Brush with egg wash and scatter with additional sunflower seeds. Proof until nearly doubled in size. Bake until browned, about 25 minutes. Makes 11 dozen rolls.

Foccacia

Baguettes

Baguettes

Multigrain Bread

Challah

BUTTER KUCHEN

makes 3 half sheet pans

1 lb 8 oz/720 g bread flour

1 lb/450 g cake flour

2 oz/60 g compressed yeast

1 lb 3 oz/570 g milk, at 68° to 76°F/20° to 24°C

4½ oz /135 g eggs

5½ oz/165 g sugar

¼ oz/7.5 g salt

½ oz/15 g vanilla extract

finely chopped zest of 1 orange

12 oz/360 g butter, whipped until light and smooth

1 lb/450 g butter

½ tsp/2 mL ground cinnamon

pinch of ground nutmeg

sliced almonds, as needed

vanilla-flavored confectioners' sugar, for dusting

1 To make the sponge, combine the flours in the bowl of an electric mixer and make a well in the center. In a separate bowl, combine the yeast and warm milk and stir to dissolve the yeast. Pour into the center of the well. Stirring in the well only, incorporate enough flour to form a soft, sticky dough.

2 Cover the sponge with the unincorporated flour. Cover the bowl with plastic wrap and leave in a warm place until the sponge cracks through the surface of the flour.

3 Blend together the eggs, sugar, salt, vanilla, and orange zest. Add the egg mixture to the dough and, using the dough hook attachment, mix on medium speed.

4 Reduce the speed to low and add the whipped butter in small pieces, mixing until it is fully incorporated. Scrape down the side of the bowl as necessary.

5 Mix on medium speed until the dough is smooth and elastic, about 10 to 12 minutes. Place the dough in a lightly oiled container, cover, and let rise until doubled, about 1 hour.

6 Cream together the butter, cinnamon, and nutmeg for the topping and reserve.

7 Turn the dough out onto a lightly floured work surface. Fold the dough over and scale into three 1-lb 10-oz/735-g pieces, round off, and let rest briefly. Spread the dough out to completely cover the bottom of the half sheet pans.

8 Proof in a proof box or warm area until the dough has increased in size by two thirds, about 25 to 30 minutes. Press your fingers into the dough to make impressions, pipe the flavored butter into the impressions, and scatter sliced almonds over top. Proof in a warm area until double in size, about 15 minutes more.

9 Bake in a 400°F/205°C oven until golden brown, about 35 minutes.

10 Let cool completely in the pan. Slice and dust with vanilla-flavored powdered sugar.

SOFT DINNER ROLLS

makes 12 dozen 1-ounce/30-gram rolls

2½ lb/1.15 kg milk, at 68° to 76°F/20° to 24°C

6 oz /170 g compressed yeast

8 oz/225 g eggs

5½ lb/2.5 kg bread flour

2 oz/60 g salt

8 oz/225 g sugar

8 oz/225 g butter, at room temperature

EGG-AND-MILK WASH (page 874), as needed

1 Combine the milk and yeast in the bowl of an electric mixer and blend until the yeast is fully dissolved.

2 Add the remaining ingredients, except the egg wash, and, using the dough hook attachment, mix on low speed just to incorporate. Increase the speed to medium and mix until the dough is smooth and elastic, 10 to 12 minutes.

3 Place the dough in a lightly oiled container, cover, and let rise until the dough has doubled in volume, about 75 minutes.

4 Turn the dough out onto a lightly floured work surface. Fold the dough over, scale into 12 dozen 1-oz/30-g pieces, and round off. Cover and let rest for 10 minutes.

5 Shape the dough into rolls (see Notes) and place on sheet pans that have been lined with parchment. Brush lightly and evenly with egg wash. Cover and pan proof until nearly doubled, about 25 to 30 minutes. Brush with egg wash again just before baking, if desired.

6 Bake in a 375°F/190°C oven until deep golden brown, about 20 minutes.

7 Let cool on pan.

NOTES

The rolls may be shaped into knots, Parker House rolls, or cloverleaf rolls. To make knots, roll each ball of dough into a rope and then tie it into a knot or figure 8. For Parker House rolls, flatten a piece of dough, brush it with butter, and fold it in half. For cloverleaf rolls, arrange 3 small balls of dough in a triangular pattern. Place in muffin tins, if desired.

BRIOCHE

makes 9 dozen 1½-ounce/40-gram rolls

8 oz/225 g milk, at 68° to 76°F/20° to 24°C
3 oz/85 g compressed yeast
4 lb/1.75 kg bread flour
1½ oz/40 g salt
7 oz/200 g sugar
2½ lb/1.15 kg eggs
3 lb/1.3 kg butter, at room temperature
EGG-AND-MILK WASH (page 874), as needed

1 Combine the milk, yeast, and enough flour to form a soft, but not runny, dough. Place the remaining flour and dry ingredients on top of the sponge and allow to rest in a warm area until the yeast mixture rises enough to break through the dry ingredients.

2 Add 2 lb/900 g of the eggs and mix on low just until incorporated. Increase the speed to medium and mix for 7 minutes. Add the remaining eggs and continue to mix until all the eggs are incorporated and dough is smooth and elastic.

3 With the mixer on medium speed, slowly add the butter in small pieces and incorporate.

4 Place the dough in a lightly oiled container, cover and let rise until it has doubled in volume, about 75 minutes.

5 Fold over the dough, cover tightly, and refrigerate overnight.

6 Turn the dough out onto a lightly floured work surface. Scale the dough into 2-oz/60-g pieces for individual brioche. Round off, cover, and let rest 10 minutes. To shape the brioche, use the edge of your hand to pinch and roll off a teardrop-shaped piece of dough (about ½ oz/ 15 g). Round off the larger piece of dough and press a hole into the center. Insert the smaller piece, narrow end first, into the hole and place the brioche into lightly buttered brioche molds. Brush with egg wash and proof in a proof box or, covered, in a warm area until doubled in volume, about 25 to 30 minutes.

7 Bake in a 360°F/180°C oven for 35 minutes or until golden brown.

8 Cool in the molds for several minutes, then unmold and finish cooling on a rack.

NOTE

Brioche dough may be shaped into a pan loaf, braided as for challah, or rolled out and used to wrap meat, fish, cheese, or sausage.

CINNAMON RAISIN BUNS

makes 3 dozen buns

4 lb/1.8 kg SWEET DOUGH (recipe follows)
EGG-AND-MILK WASH (page 874), as needed
melted butter, as needed
raisins, as needed
cinnamon sugar, as needed
oil, as needed
apricot jam, as needed
fondant, as needed

1 Roll the dough into a rectangle; brush the long edge with egg wash and the remaining dough with melted butter.

2 Sprinkle the dough with raisins and cinnamon sugar, being careful not to cover the egg-washed area.

3 Roll the dough up like a jelly roll, sealing the egg-washed edge.

4 Cut into 3 dozen 2½ -oz/75-g slices and brush the tops with oil.

5 Place on a sheet pan, oiled side up, cover, and proof until double in size, about 20 minutes.

6 Bake in a 380° to 400°F/195° to 205°C oven until golden brown on all sides, about 25 to 30 minutes. Brush immediately with warm apricot jam. Drizzle with fondant. Let cool on the pan.

SWEET DOUGH

makes 11½ pounds/5.2 kilograms of dough

2 quarts/2 L milk, at 68° to 76°F/20° to 24°C
6 oz/170 g compressed yeast
1 lb/450 g eggs
1½ oz/45 g malt syrup
1 lb/450 g pastry flour
4½ lb/2 kg bread flour
¾ oz/20 g salt
8 oz/225 g sugar
½ oz/15 g ground cardamom
1 lb/450 g softened butter

Combine the milk and yeast in the bowl of an electric mixer and blend until the yeast is fully dissolved. Add the eggs and malt syrup and blend. Add the remaining ingredients and, using the dough hook attachment, mix on low speed just to incorporate. Increase the speed to medium and mix until the dough is smooth and elastic, 10 to 12 minutes. The dough may be shaped now or refrigerated for later use.

CROISSANTS

makes 9 dozen croissants

DOUGH

3¼ lb/1.5 kg milk, at 68° to 76°F/20° to 24°C

5 oz/140 g compressed yeast

5¼ lb/2.4 kg bread flour

4½ oz/125 g sugar

8 oz/225 g butter, softened

1½ oz/40 g salt

ROLL-IN

3 lb/1.3 kg butter

4 oz/115 g bread flour

EGG-AND-MILK WASH (page 874), as needed

1 To make the dough, combine the milk and yeast in the bowl of an electric mixer and blend until the yeast is fully dissolved.

2 Add the flour, sugar, butter, and salt and, using the dough hook attachment, mix on low speed just to incorporate. Increase the speed to medium and mix until the dough is smooth and elastic, 10 to 12 minutes.

3 Turn the dough out onto a floured work surface and pat it into a rectangle. Let the dough rest, covered, while preparing the roll-in.

4 To make the roll-in, combine the butter and flour in an electric mixer using the paddle attachment and pulsing on the lowest speed until the butter is broken into small pieces.

5 Increase the speed to medium-low and blend until the butter is smooth with no lumps but is still firm and cool to the touch.

6 Both the roll-in and the dough should be at 65°F/20°C. Roll out the butter between two pieces of lightly floured parchment paper until the roll-in is two thirds the size of the paper. Roll the dough out to the size of a sheet pan and place the roll-in on the dough so that two thirds of the dough is covered. Lock the butter into the dough by way of a 3-fold. The dough will have 5 layers: 3 of dough, 2 of butter. Seal the ends and sides.

7 Turn 90 degrees and roll out immediately to a rectangle twice the size of a sheet pan. Brush off extra flour. Give the dough another 3-fold, turn 90 degrees, and roll to fit the sheet pan. Cover and place in the refrigerator to rest for 20 to 30 minutes.

8 Repeat Step 6 two times. Mark the dough with 3 indentations to indicate the number of 3-folds that have been completed. Wrap in plastic and refrigerate overnight.

9 The next day, roll out the dough and cut to fit the width of a croissant cutter.

10 Roll up each croissant, starting at the wide end of the triangle. Place the croissants on a parchment-lined sheet pan, making sure the tip of the triangle is tucked on the underside of the rolled croissant. Curl the ends of the croissant around to the front, forming a C shape. Brush lightly and evenly with egg wash. Proof in a proof box or in a warm area until doubled in size, about 20 to 25 minutes.

11 Brush with egg wash again before baking, if desired, and bake in a 380°F/195°C oven until medium golden brown, about 28 minutes.

12 Let cool on the pans. Serve the same day.

NOTES

Dough has to be made 1 day in advance and allowed to rest overnight in the refrigerator.

The dough can be frozen for up to 3 weeks. Beyond that, the yeast loses its potency. Take frozen dough out of the freezer and place in the refrigerator to thaw 1 day before using.

COTTAGE DILL ROLLS

makes 6 dozen rolls

12 oz/340 g water, at 68° to 76°F/20° to 24°C

5 oz/140 g compressed yeast

5¼ lb/2.4 kg bread flour

3 lb/1.3 kg cottage cheese

4½ oz/125 g sugar

1½ oz/40 g minced onions

3 oz/85 g softened butter

1 oz/30 g salt

1 oz/30 g chopped dill

1 oz/30 g baking soda

6 oz/170 g eggs

pinch horseradish

melted butter, as needed

kosher salt, as needed

1 Combine the water and yeast in the bowl of an electric mixer and blend until the yeast is fully dissolved.

2 Add the remaining ingredients, except the melted butter and kosher salt, and, using the dough hook attachment, mix on low speed just to incorporate. Increase the speed to medium and mix until the dough is smooth and elastic, 10 to 12 minutes.

3 Place the dough in a lightly oiled container, cover, and let rise until the dough has doubled in volume, about 75 minutes.

4 Turn out onto a lightly floured work surface. Fold over the dough and scale into 6 dozen 1½-oz/45-g pieces. Round off the dough and let rest for 15 to 20 minutes. Reshape the rolls and place on parchment-lined sheet pans.

5 Proof in a proof box or in a warm area until doubled in size, about 25 to 30 minutes. Bake in a 380°F/195°C oven until light golden in color, about 20 minutes.

6 Brush the rolls with melted butter and sprinkle very lightly with kosher salt as soon as they are taken from the oven. Let cool on the pans.

DANISH DOUGH

makes 11¼ pounds/5 kilograms

2 lb/900 g milk, at 68° to 76°F/20° to 24°C

8 oz/225 g compressed yeast

10 oz/285 g sugar

1½ oz/40 g salt

8 oz/225 g butter

1 lb/450 g egg yolks

1½ lb/680 g pastry flour

3 lb/1.3 kg bread flour

¼ oz/8 g ground cardamom

3 lb/1.3 kg butter

EGG-AND-MILK WASH (page 874), as needed

1 Combine the milk and the yeast in the bowl of an electric mixer and blend until the yeast is fully dissolved.

2 Add the remaining ingredients, except the butter and egg wash, and, using the dough hook attachment, mix on low speed just to incorporate. Increase the speed to medium and mix until the dough is smooth and elastic, 10 to 12 minutes.

3 Place dough on a lightly floured sheet pan, cover, and refrigerate for 30 minutes.

4 Both the butter and the dough should be at 65°F/18°C as you work. If the dough becomes warm, stop work on the dough and chill before continuing to fold and roll it. Roll out the butter between two pieces of parchment paper that have been lightly dusted with bread flour until the butter is two thirds the size of the paper. Roll out the dough to the size of a sheet pan. The dough should be ½ inch/ 12 mm thick. Place the rolled butter on two thirds of the dough, fold in thirds to layer in the butter, and seal.

5 Turn the dough 90 degrees and roll out to give the first 3-fold. Refrigerate for 30 minutes to chill the dough if necessary, then return the dough to a lightly floured work surface, turning it so that the long edge of the dough is parallel to the edge of the work surface. Roll to about ½ in/12 mm thick and fold in thirds for the second 3-fold. Chill the dough if necessary, and repeat turning, rolling, and folding the dough once more, for a total of three 3-folds. The dough may be wrapped and chilled now for later use, or it may be rolled out and shaped into individual Danish.

GUGELHOPF

makes 9 lb/4 kg

SPONGE

1¹/₂ lb/680 g bread flour

1³/₄ oz/50 g compressed yeast

18 fl oz/540 mL milk, at 68° to 76°F/20° to 24°C

3 lb/1.3 kg bread flour

1 oz/30 g salt

¹/₂ oz/15 g malt syrup

10 oz/285 g sugar

10 oz/285 g eggs, room temperature

2 fl oz/60 mL milk

2 vanilla beans

¹/₂ oz/15 g lemon zest

³/₄ oz/20 g orange zest

10 oz/285 g butter, softened

3¹/₂ oz/100 g candied orange peel

1 lb/450 g raisins, plumped in rum

sliced almonds for lining pans, as needed

confectioners' sugar, as needed

1 To make the sponge, put 1¹/₂ lb/680 g bread flour in the bowl of an electric mixer and make a well in the center. In a separate bowl combine the yeast and warm milk and stir to dissolve the yeast. Pour into the center of the well. Stirring in the well only, incorporate enough flour to form a soft, sticky dough.

2 Cover the sponge with 3 lb/1.3 kg bread flour. Cover the bowl with plastic wrap and leave in a warm place until the sponge cracks through the surface of the flour.

3 Add the salt, malt syrup, sugar, eggs, milk, vanilla beans, lemon and orange zest, and butter to the sponge. Using the dough hook attachment, mix on low speed just to incorporate. Increase the speed to medium and mix until the dough is smooth and elastic, 10 to 12 minutes.

4 Place the dough in a lightly oiled bowl, cover, and let rest in a warm place until doubled, about 45 minutes. Blend the candied orange peel and raisins into the dough by kneading by hand until well incorporated. Scale into nine 1-lb/450-g pieces, round up, and let rest for 15 minutes.

5 Prepare the gugelhopf molds by brushing them liberally with butter and lining with sliced almonds. Pour out any almonds that do not cling to the sides of the pan.

6 Shape each piece into a ball and push a dowel or rolling pin into the center of the dough to create a hole. Place in gugelhopf pans. Proof in a proof box or in a warm area until the dough is almost up to the rim of the pan, about 35 minutes.

7 Brush the top of each cake with water and bake in a 400°F/205°C oven until golden brown, about 45 minutes. Cool slightly and unmold onto wire racks to finish cooling.

8 Dust with confectioners' sugar before slicing and serving.

STOLLEN

makes twenty-seven 1-pound/450-gram loaves

2¹/₂ lb/1.15 kg golden raisins

2¹/₂ lb/1.15 kg raisins

11 oz/315 g minced candied fruit

8 oz/225 g dark rum

2¹/₄ pt/1.1 L milk, at 85°F/30°C

7 oz/210 g compressed yeast

6 oz/170 g chopped almonds

4 lb/1.8 kg bread flour

2 lb/900 g cake flour

285 g/285 g sugar

2 lb/900 g unsalted butter, softened

¹/₄ oz/8 g ground cardamom

¹/₄ oz/8 g ground nutmeg

³/₄ oz/20 g salt

2 lb/900 g melted butter

2 lb/900 g VANILLA SUGAR (recipe follows)

1 Combine the raisins, candied fruit, and rum and let soak overnight at room temperature.

2 Combine the milk and yeast in the bowl of an electric mixer and blend until the yeast is fully dissolved.

3 Add the remaining ingredients, except for the melted butter and vanilla sugar, and, using the dough hook attachment, mix on low speed just to incorporate. Increase the speed to medium and mix until the dough is smooth and elastic, 10 to 12 minutes.

4 Place the dough in a lightly oiled container, cover, and let rise until it has doubled in volume, about 75 minutes.

5 Turn the dough out onto a lightly floured work surface. Fold over the dough and scale into 1¹/₂-lb/680-g pieces. Round off, and let rest for 10 to 15 minutes.

6 Press each piece into a rectangle, stretching to the desired length. Roll each into a loaf, pressing the seam to seal the loaf. Place onto parchment-lined sheet pans, seam side down, and brush with water. Proof in a proof box or in a warm area until the loaves increase by two thirds their original size.

7 Bake in a 380°F/195°C oven until golden brown, about 45 minutes. Immediately brush with melted butter and roll in vanilla sugar.

8 Cool the finished stollen on racks before slicing and serving or storing for later service.

VANILLA SUGAR

makes 2 pounds/900 grams

½ vanilla bean

2 lb/900 g sugar

1 Split the vanilla bean lengthwise and scrape out the seeds with the tip of a knife.

2 Blend the seeds into the sugar well. Cover the sugar and let the flavor develop for several hours before using.

BEAR CLAWS

makes 45 pastries

5 lb 10 oz/2.5 kg DANISH DOUGH (page 893)

EGG-AND-MILK WASH (page 874), as needed

filling of choice (see recipes at right)

1 To make up bear claw Danish, roll out the dough to ¼ in/63 cm thick. Cut the dough into 4 in × 8 in/10 cm × 20 cm rectangles.

2 Brush the long edges of each rectangle with egg wash. Place a 1½-oz/45-g strip of the filling down the center of the rectangle.

3 Fold the dough over the filling to form an 8-in × 2-in/20-cm × 5-cm rectangle and seal tightly along the egg-washed seam. Make 1-in/2.5-cm cuts at 2-in/5-cm intervals along the seam.

4 Place on parchment-lined pans, brush with egg wash, and proof in a proof box or in a warm area until doubled in size.

5 Brush with egg wash again and bake in a 385°F/196°C oven until golden brown, 15 to 20 minutes.

6 Let cool on the pans before serving or holding for later service.

CHEESE FILLING FOR DANISH

makes enough for 45 individual pastries; 4¼ pounds/1.9 kilograms

8 oz/225 g sugar

4 oz/115 g cornstarch

8 oz/225 g butter, softened

2½ lb/1.15 kg baker's cheese

½ oz/15 g salt

8 oz/225 g eggs

¼ oz/8 g vanilla extract

4 oz/115 g milk, or as needed

1 Whisk together the sugar and cornstarch in the bowl of an electric mixer. Add the butter and, using the paddle attachment, mix on low speed until just combined. Add the baker's cheese, salt, eggs, and vanilla extract and blend.

2 Add the milk gradually on low speed, adding a little more milk if necessary to produce a spreadable consistency.

3 The filling is ready to use now or it may be wrapped and stored under refrigeration for later use.

HAZELNUT FILLING FOR DANISH

makes enough for 45 pastries; 4¼ pounds/1.9 kilograms

12 oz/340 g almond paste

12 oz/340 g sugar

12 oz/340 g butter

2 lb/900 g ground lightly toasted hazelnuts

¼ oz/7 g ground cinnamon

1 Combine the almond paste and sugar in the bowl of an electric mixer and, using the paddle attachment, mix on medium speed, blending until smooth.

2 Add the butter and continue to blend on medium speed until fully incorporated. Blend in the hazelnuts and cinnamon, scraping down the bowl as necessary to blend evenly.

3 The filling is ready to use now or it may be wrapped and stored under refrigeration for later use.

NOTE

If it is necessary to make the filling more spreadable, add a mixture of 1 part water to 1 part egg white to obtain the desired consistency.

CHALLAH

makes twelve 12-ounce/340-gram loaves

2 lb/900 g water at 68° to 76°F/20° to 24°C

4 oz/115 g compressed yeast

8 oz/225 g vegetable oil

1 lb/450 g egg yolks

8 oz/225 g sugar

1½ oz/40 g salt

5¼ lb/2.4 kg bread flour

EGG-AND-CREAM WASH (page 874), as needed

1   Combine the water and yeast in the bowl of an electric mixer and blend until the yeast is fully dissolved.

2   Add the remaining ingredients except the egg wash and, using the dough hook, mix on low speed just to incorporate. Increase the speed to medium and mix until the dough is smooth and elastic, 10 to 12 minutes. Add more flour during mixing if necessary.

3   Place the dough in a lightly oiled container, cover, and let rise until the dough has doubled in volume, about 75 minutes.

4   Fold over and divide into two 4-lb 12-oz/2.15-kg pieces. Round off and let rest briefly. Divide each of the halves into thirty-six 2-oz/60-g pieces.

5   To braid a loaf, roll out 6 pieces into 8-in/20-cm-long strips that are thinner on the ends and thicker in the middle. Place all 6 strips on a lightly floured work surface with the tips at one end touching. Weave the strips together to form a braid until the bread is braided to the other end. Press the strips together to keep them from unraveling.

6   Place on a pan that has been lined with parchment and dusted with cornmeal. Proof in a proof box until about two-thirds the finished volume, about 30 minutes. If it is not possible to use a proof box, place in a warm area and let proof for 45 minutes to 1 hour. Brush all over with egg wash.

7   Bake in a 380°F/195°C oven until golden brown, 20 to 30 minutes.

8   Remove from the pan and cool on a rack before slicing and serving.

see photograph on page 889

Quick breads and cakes differ from yeast breads in that they are based on a batter, rather than a dough. Batters tend to be pourable (with the exception of batter for biscuits and similar quick breads). Batter for cakes and most quick breads often includes butter or oil, eggs, and milk or other liquids. The end result is a smooth mixture. When these batters are baked, a tender and delicate texture is formed to produce a wide range of products: muffins, biscuits, and scones are all examples of breakfast pastries made from batters. Simple cakes, such as pound cake and sponge cake, are also made from batters. The baker or pastry chef can enhance these simple items with a wide range of icings, glazes, fillings, and garnishes.

QUICK BREADS, CAKES, AND OTHER BATTERS

THE STRAIGHT-MIX METHOD

Quick breads, cakes, and muffins made by the straight-mix method are moist and cakelike in texture.

The straight-mix method calls for flour, oil or melted butter, eggs, milk or other liquids, salt, and, usually, a leavener. The exact proportion of ingredients varies widely from item to item. Changing the amount of liquid, eggs, or fat produces different textures and flavors. The cooking method also varies: Some items are cooked in a pan over direct heat; others are baked in the oven.

WHITE WHEAT FLOUR, either all-purpose or pastry, is generally used in this method. Pastry flour is often suggested to produce a more tender, cakelike product. Special flours such as cornmeal, graham flour, or oat flour also may be used to replace some or all of the white wheat flour in a recipe.

Milk, buttermilk, water, even the moisture from vegetables like zucchini can all add moisture to the recipe. The liquid should be carefully measured, either by weight or by volume; both methods of measure will be accurate.

The type of leavener, if used, depends upon the other ingredients as well as the final texture desired. Recipes typically call for the commonly used chemical leaveners, baking powder or baking soda. (Less often, physical leaveners, such as whipped egg whites, or an organic leavener, such as yeast or sourdough, are required.)

Fats, whether oil or butter, must be liquid when added to the batter. Butter should be melted and cooled to room temperature beforehand.

Salt and any other flavoring and garnishing ingredients should be carefully scaled and prepared as directed.

The type of pan and preparation for pans vary according to what is being prepared. For popovers, for example, popover pans or ramekins need to be buttered generously. Other baked goods may require a dusting of flour along with the butter. Use paper liners, if available, to line pans and muffin tins.

USE THE STRAIGHT-MIX METHOD

1. Sift the dry ingredients together.
Sifting the dry ingredients (flour, leavener, salt, and so forth) helps to distribute the leavener, salt, and dry flavoring ingredients, such as cocoa powder or ground spices, evenly in the batter. Sifting also removes any lumps, which would otherwise be difficult to blend into the batter smoothly. If the ingredients are properly sifted, the batter can be mixed quickly and evenly.

2. Combine all the liquid ingredients in a bowl.
Blend the liquid, eggs, and oil, along with any other liquid ingredients (such as vanilla extract). Blend until the ingredients are smooth but do not whip them into a foam.

3. Add the combined liquid ingredients to the combined dry ingredients.
Mix these batters as briefly as possible to ensure a light, delicate texture. The appearance and consistency of the batter will differ from one recipe to another. Batters for popovers and crêpes, for example, are usually thin enough to pour easily; others may be stiff enough to mound slightly, as in any kind of muffin.

Specific recipes may call for adding such ingredients as fresh or dried fruit or nuts. Fold them gently into the batter once it has been mixed and immediately before scaling the batter out for cooking or baking.

ABOVE *Add the combined wet ingredients all at once and blend in a mixer or by hand just until the dry ingredients are moistened. Scrape the bowl down once or twice to mix the batter evenly.*

4. Scale the batter into baking pans, popover pans, ramekins, a crêpe pan, or griddle.

Scale batters carefully and pour them into the pans, avoiding spillage or drips, which would burn on the sides of the pan. Some batters may be wrapped tightly and stored under refrigeration for later use.

5. Bake or cook the batter.

A skewer inserted near the center comes away clean, and the muffin, quick bread, or cake pulls away slightly from the pan's edges.

Griddle cakes, such as crepes and pancakes, should also take on a golden color. Their texture will vary, according to the type of batter you made and the leavener chosen, if any.

6. Evaluate the quality of the finished item.

The important characteristics are appearance, texture, and flavor. During baking, muffins and quick breads should rise to create a dome-shaped upper crust. The crust may develop a crack. The edges may become slightly darker than the center, but they should not shrink too far away from the pan's sides. The texture should be even throughout the product's interior, with a cakelike crumb. Well-made quick breads are moist but not wet. The flavor is well developed and appropriate to the ingredients used. The batter must be well mixed in order to ensure that there are no leavener or flour pockets.

Properly baked muffins, quick breads, and cakes are golden brown and spring back when pressed with a fingertip. Some muffins and quick breads normally develop a crack on their upper crust during baking. Griddled cakes, such as crêpes, should be browned, but still tender.

TOP *Crêpes are typically prepared in a small, flat, round pan. Brush with butter to prevent sticking, or use a nonstick surface.*

BOTTOM *A ladle is a good tool to properly portion the batter into the pan.*

TOP *Check the doneness of crêpes or pancakes by carefully lifting one edge and peeking underneath.*

BOTTOM *Use either a spatula or a flipping motion to turn crêpes and finish cooking on the second side.*

ABOVE *Crêpes may be made in advance. First let them cool on parchment-lined pans, then stack them with parchment paper in between each crêpe. Refrigerate or freeze for later use.*

8 oz / 225 g eggs

1 pt / 480 mL heavy cream

8 oz / 225 g milk

$\frac{1}{2}$ oz / 15 g oil

8 oz / 225 g all-purpose flour

2 oz / 60 g confectioners' sugar

salt, as needed

vanilla extract, as needed

rum, as needed (optional)

DESSERT CRÊPES

1   Combine the eggs, cream, milk, and oil and beat just until blended.

2   Sift together the flour, sugar, and salt and place in a mixing bowl.

3   Add the wet ingredients and mix until smooth, scraping down the bowl as necessary.

4   Add the vanilla and rum, if using, to taste. Stir just until the ingredients are blended into a relatively smooth batter. (The batter may be prepared in advance to this point and held under refrigeration up to 12 hours. Strain the batter if necessary before preparing crêpes.)

5   Add a small amount of batter to a preheated buttered crêpe pan, swirling the pan to coat the bottom with batter.

6   Cook over medium heat. When set, turn over and finish on the other side. The crêpes may be cooled, then stacked between parchment paper and wrapped for refrigerated or frozen storage. Thaw frozen crêpes before filling and folding.

7   Fill as desired, roll or fold, or use in other desserts (see Crêpes Suzette, page 919).

MAKES 20 TO 30 CRÊPES

RUBBED-DOUGH METHOD

Biscuits, scones, and soda breads have a distinctly flaky texture — the result of rubbing together, but not blending, the fat and flour.

Biscuits, scones, and soda breads can be prepared using a rubbed-dough method. The ingredients are not blended into a smooth batter. Instead, the fat (butter, shortening, or lard are common) is chilled and then rubbed into the flour to create the layers that produce a flaky baked item. As a biscuit or similarly prepared cake or bread bakes, steam trapped by the layers in the dough gives some additional rise to the product.

FLOUR, A SOLID FAT, and a very cold liquid are the basic components of most rubbed-dough products. All-purpose white wheat flour or a combination of wheat and other flours should be properly weighed and sifted. If a leavener is required, it should be weighed or measured and blended evenly throughout the flour either by sifting the leavener with the flour or by blending with a whip. Other dry ingredients (salt, spices, etc.) are typically scaled out and blended with the flour in the same manner.

The fat is kept very cold so that it will not easily blend with the dry ingredients. Cut the butter or lard into pieces, and chill it while assembling the rest of the ingredients. Shortening and lard may be included in these recipes, as well as butter. These solid baking fats should be broken or cut into pieces and kept cool.

Typically these recipes call for significantly less liquid, and the liquid, like the fat, should also be very cold to further inhibit the fat from blending evenly with the flour. Water, milk, and buttermilk are all common ingredients.

Pans need to be greased or lined with parchment paper. Sharp knives or biscuit cutters may be used to shape the dough before baking. Ovens should be properly preheated and the rack adjusted to the center position in conventional ovens. Cooling racks should be available.

USE THE RUBBED-DOUGH METHOD

1. Combine the dry ingredients in a bowl and blend.
Sift or blend the dry ingredients well before adding the fat. Good results are achieved when the dough is worked as little as possible, and blending the dry ingredients now cuts down on mixing time later.

2. Rub cold butter or other shortening into the dry ingredients.
Have the butter or shortening cold enough that it is still solid enough to be worked into the flour without blending the mixture into a smooth dough. Add the fat to the dry ingredients all at once, and rub them into the fat. This technique is quite similar to that used to prepare pie doughs. If the fat is worked into the flour too thoroughly, the end result will not be as flaky and delicate as desired.

ABOVE *Use your fingertips to rub the butter into the dry ingredients for the flakiest biscuits.*

3. Add the liquid ingredients and blend into a dough.
Once the fat is worked into the flour until the mixture resembles coarse meal, add the blended wet ingredients, mixing them together just until they begin to cohere or form a shaggy mass. Do not overwork once the liquid is added; vigorous or prolonged mixing will result in a tough product.

4. Transfer the dough onto a floured work surface and gather it into a ball. Pat the ball of dough by hand or roll it out to the desired thickness. Use light but even pressure while rolling out the dough. Keep the edges of the dough straight for a better yield from the finished dough. It is important that the dough be evenly thick, generally about ½ in/12 mm for biscuits.

Some biscuits require no kneading or rolling. These are simply dropped from a spoon onto a baking sheet.

TOP *Make a well in the center of the dry ingredients and pour in the liquid ingredients.*

BOTTOM *Working the ingredients into a shaggy mass with your hands makes it easier to gauge when the dough is properly mixed or to see if you need to adjust the amount of flour or liquid.*

ABOVE *Lightly dust with flour to keep your hands or the rolling pin from sticking.*

TOP *Use long smooth strokes, stopping at the edge of the dough to avoid compressing the layers of dough too much.*

BOTTOM *Draw a line of the same dimensions as a sheet pan on the floured surface around the dough to make it easy to roll out the dough to the correct size.*

5. (Optional) Fold and roll the dough to laminate it.

To laminate the dough, fold it into thirds, like a letter, or fourths, like a book. After the dough is folded, turn it 90 degrees so that the long side is parallel to the edge of the work surface. Roll the dough out to the desired thickness once more. Repeat the process of folding, turning, and rolling the dough twice for a total of 3 folds.

6. Scale and shape the dough, place on prepared pans, and bake or cook until done.

Cut the dough, using a biscuit cutter or a sharp knife, to the desired shape or size. Place the biscuits on prepared baking sheets. The closer together the biscuits are placed, the softer and less well developed the side crusts will be.

Once the dough has been shaped, it may be brushed with an egg wash before baking, if desired, in order to enhance the final appearance. Some doughs are cooked on a griddle, although most are baked in an oven.

When done, the tops of the product should be evenly browned and have no appearance of moisture on the sides. Remove the biscuits from the oven. These baked items are often served warm from the oven, although they may also be cooled and stored for later service. If necessary, reheat stored biscuits or scones to improve their flavor.

7. Evaluate the quality of the finished item.

Well-made biscuits and scones have a delicate texture, either flaky or cakelike, depending on how thoroughly the fat was blended into the flour. The crust is often more fully developed than in other quick breads.

ABOVE *An optional step known as laminating calls for the dough to be folded either in thirds, like a letter, or fourths, like a book.*

ABOVE *Scale and shape the dough. Place on prepared pans, leaving about 2 inches/5 centimeters between them for crisp sides, or leave them almost touching for softer sides.*

6 lb / 2.7 kg all-purpose flour

6 oz / 170 g baking powder

1¹/₂ oz / 40 g salt

8 oz / 225 g sugar

1¹/₂ lb / 680 g butter, cut into walnut-size pieces, cold

40 oz / 1.15 kg buttermilk, cold

24 oz / 680 g milk, cold

BUTTERMILK BISCUITS

1 Blend together the flour, baking powder, salt, and sugar.

2 Rub in the butter until the mixture looks like a coarse meal. There may be some pea-sized pieces of butter remaining.

3 Add the buttermilk and milk and mix to a shaggy mass.

4 Roll out the dough ½ in / 12 mm thick and fold it into thirds. Turn the dough 90 degrees.

5 Roll out the dough ½ in / 12 mm thick and fold the dough in fourths. Turn the dough 90 degrees. Roll out and repeat the four fold.

6 Roll out the dough ½ in / 12 mm thick and cut with a 2-in / 50-mm biscuit cutter. Place biscuits on a parchment-lined sheet pan.

7 Bake at 425°F / 220°C until golden brown, 20 to 22 minutes.

MAKES 6 DOZEN BISCUITS

THE CREAMING METHOD

Pound cakes, cheesecakes, muffins, quick breads, and some cookies are prepared using the creaming method. These have an exceptionally fine crumb and a texture that holds up well and slices evenly.

The creaming method gets its name from the initial mixing action, which calls for the baker to blend the fat and sugar until very smooth, light, and creamy. The remaining ingredients are added in sequence to produce a very smooth batter. Recipes for different products will include different proportions of ingredients to create a wide variety of baked goods.

THE BASIC COMPONENTS for baked items made by the creaming method are flour, butter, sugar, and eggs. Some recipes may also include a liquid, such as milk. Leaveners, if required, are generally chemical leaveners, such as baking soda or baking powder.

Measure the flour and other dry ingredients by weighing them for the most consistent results. Once measured, sift together the dry ingredients to blend them and to remove any lumps. Additional dry ingredients, other than flour and leaveners, may include cocoa powder or ground spices.

Butter is the most common baking fat for creaming method recipes, but shortening or even lard may be used, according to recipe. The fat should be pliable, but not liquid, so that it can aerate properly. Allow the butter or other fat to come to room temperature, or beat it with the paddle attachment of a mixer to soften it slightly. The fat should be softened, but not warm enough to melt.

The sugar used in creaming recipes is often granulated white sugar, although brown sugar or powdered sugar may be used in some recipes. It is the act of beating the granules of sugar into the fat that produces the final texture.

Eggs are often included in the recipe. Allow the eggs to come to room temperature to avoid breaking the creamed butter and sugar mixture.

Flavorings, such as vanilla extract or chocolate, should be at room temperature. Chocolate is typically melted and allowed to cool slightly before blended into the batter.

Generally, pans are greased and lightly floured or greased, lined with parchment that has been cut to size, and then greased again.

USE THE CREAMING METHOD

1. Sift the dry ingredients together. Sifting the dry ingredients onto a piece of parchment paper makes it easier to add them to the mixer.

2. Cream together the fat and sugar and blend them on medium speed until the mixture is smooth, light, and creamy.
Creaming can be done in a mixer, using the paddle attachment, or by hand. Scrape down the sides and bottom of the bowl occasionally as you work. Do not undermix.

ABOVE *When properly creamed, the butter and sugar will be light in both color and texture and very smooth.*

3. Gradually add the eggs to the creamed mixture.

Add the eggs gradually, beating them into the batter thoroughly and scraping down the bowl between additions. The eggs should be at room temperature when added to the creamed mixture. If not, they may cause the mixture to appear curdled, like a broken Hollandaise. If this should happen, continue to mix, without adding more eggs, until the mixture looks completely smooth again. Then resume adding the eggs.

4. Add the sifted dry ingredients, alternating with the liquid ingredients, if any, on low speed. Mix until the batter is very smooth.

If the recipe calls for no liquid ingredients, the sifted dry ingredients are added to the creamed butter/sugar/egg mixture all at once. If the recipe does call for the addition of liquid ingredients, such as milk, add the dry and liquid ingredients in an alternating sequence, beginning with the dry ingredients. Add one-third of the dry ingredients, followed by about one-third of the liquid ingredients, mixing until smooth and scraping down the bowl after each addition. Repeat this sequence until all of the dry and liquid ingredients have been incorporated. Increase the speed to medium and finish beating the batter. It should be extremely smooth and light, with no trace of lumps. Once the batter is fully blended, add any flavoring or garnishing ingredients.

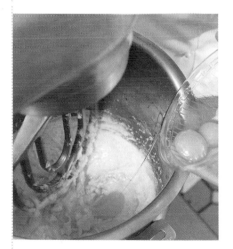

ABOVE *Add the eggs in parts, and continue to beat until all are incorporated, scraping down the bowl to mix evenly between additions.*

ABOVE *Pound cake does not include any added liquids, so the flour is added all at once and blended into the batter until smooth.*

TOP *To make a marble cake, first melt chocolate and cool slightly, then mix with a small quantity of the batter in a separate bowl.*

BOTTOM *Fold the chocolate batter gently into the plain batter just until streaked throughout. For a marble effect, do not blend in completely.*

5. Scale off the batter into prepared baking pans and bake at the appropriate temperature until done. Scaling assures uniformity of size and results. Grease the pans or grease and flour them, or line with parchment.

Bake creamed batters until the cake springs back when pressed lightly with a fingertip and the edges have begun to shrink from the sides of the pan. A wooden or metal skewer inserted into the center should come out clean, with no moist particles clinging to it.

Remove the cake from the oven, set it on a cooling rack, and cool it before removing it from the pan. It is ready to serve now, or it may be wrapped and stored under refrigeration or in the freezer.

6. Evaluate the quality of the finished item.

The crust of baked products made with the creaming method is usually slightly darker than the interior. The high proportion of eggs, butter, and sugar causes this browning action. If properly mixed, the cake will rise evenly, without a noticeable center hump or dip. Nor will it have tunnels or air pockets. Cakes that do not rise adequately have been either over-mixed or undermixed.

This type of cake has a moist, delicate, and regular crumb when cut. The flavor should always reflect that of the major components and flavoring ingredients.

ABOVE *For accurately scaled cakes, set the pan on the scale and set it to zero (tare) before adding the batter to the pan.*

ABOVE *Some chefs like to cut a slit in the cake just after a crust begins to form to prevent cracking.*

1 lb / 450 g all-purpose flour

1 tsp / 5 mL baking powder

1 tsp / 5 mL salt

1 lb / 450 g sugar

1 lb / 450 g butter

1 lb / 450 g eggs

1 tsp / 5 mL vanilla extract

6 oz / 180 g bittersweet chocolate, melted

MARBLEIZED POUND CAKE

1 Sift together the flour, baking powder, and salt on to a piece of parchment.

2 Cream together the sugar and butter until light.

3 Add the eggs slowly, fully incorporating them and scraping down the side of the bowl after each addition. Blend in the vanilla.

4 Add the sifted dry ingredients, mixing just to incorporate.

5 Divide the batter in half. Temper the melted chocolate into half of the batter.

6 Using a folding motion, gently blend the chocolate and vanilla batters, but incorporate only until they are nicely marbleized.

7 Thoroughly grease 2 loaf pans. Carefully divide the batter evenly between the pans.

8 Bake at 375°F/190°C. After about 15 minutes, or when a skin has formed on the baking cakes, make a slit down the center of the cakes with a sharp paring knife to create a uniform crack. Continue baking until a tester inserted in the center of each cake comes out clean.

9 Remove the cakes from the oven, set them on a cooling rack, and let them cool. Remove them from the pans. Serve or wrap them and store under refrigeration or in the freezer.

MAKES 2 LOAVES

THE FOAMING METHOD

Cakes made by the foaming method are extremely delicate, yet quite resilient; in some cases, cakes made by this method may be rolled, as in the classic holiday dessert, Bûche de Noël.

A foam of whole eggs, egg yolks, or egg whites provides the structure for genoise, angel food cake, and chiffon cakes, and for some small cakes such as madeleines and langues-de-chat. There are two versions of the foaming method. In one method, used for genoise, the eggs and sugar are heated before they are beaten into a foam. In the other, used for angel food and chiffon cakes, a basic meringue is prepared using cold egg whites and sugar. The foaming method is also used for preparing meringue, a mixture made of egg whites and sugar beaten until thickened.

EGGS, SUGAR, AND FLOUR are the principal components of a foam cake. Some recipes call for whole eggs, others for whites or yolks only, and still others call both both yolks and whites, added at different points in mixing. Eggs are easiest to separate when they are chilled, but should be warmed before mixing or beating. Review the material on separating eggs on page 867.

Sugar is incorporated by blending it with the eggs. Scale sugar carefully. Flour should be sifted, along with any other dry ingredients, such as an added leavener, ground spices, or finely ground nuts. Some formulas call for the addition of butter. In this case, melt the butter and allow it to cool to room temperature. This action will prevent hot butter from deflating the delicate batter. Vanilla extract or other liquid flavorings are generally added to the batter just before it is scaled into the prepared pans, so they should also be scaled and ready to avoid any delays during the mixing of the batter.

Pan preparation is especially important when the foaming method is used. The pans must be prepared ahead of time, so that the batter can be poured immediately into them and placed in the oven. Otherwise, the beaten egg product, which acts as the leavening, would begin to collapse after mixing. Pans may be greased and floured, or greased, lined with parchment paper, and greased again. Pans for angel food and chiffon cakes are not greased at all, since these cakes must adhere to the sides of the pan.

In order to properly mix foam cakes, you may also need a simmering water bath to heat the eggs and dissolve the sugar before they are beaten to a foam. Whips and rubber scrapers may be used to fold the flour into the egg foam.

1. Sift the dry ingredients together. It is important that the dry ingredients be scaled and sifted before the eggs are beaten. They must be combined with the eggs as soon as the eggs have reached their maximum volume, as they begin to lose volume after they are beaten.

2. Combine the eggs and sugar. For the warm foaming method, shown here, combine the eggs (whole, yolk, or whites) with sugar in a bowl and heat it to about 100°F/38°C and stir or whip to completely dissolve the sugar, increase the volume, and develop a finer grain.

For the cold foaming method, combine the eggs and sugar in a mixing bowl.

3. Beat the eggs and sugar to a foam. Once the eggs and sugar are combined, whip them on medium to high speed until a thick foam forms. (This step is done on the mixer, not over the hot-water bath.) A point will come when the foam does not appear to be increasing in volume. The mixture should form a ribbon as it falls from the whip. The eggs are properly beaten at that point.

4. Gently fold in the sifted dry ingredients. This is often done by hand, although some chefs add them on the machine using the lowest possible speed and turning the machine on and off, if necessary. Do not overwork the batter at this point, as the foam could start to deflate, resulting in a flat, dense cake.

ABOVE *Place the bowl over a hot-water bath and heat. Use a whip to blend the sugar and eggs constantly as they heat.*

TOP *The eggs and sugar at the start of mixing time are still a deep yellow and relatively thin.*

BOTTOM *When the eggs and sugar reach full volume, they are light in color and thick enough to show tracks as the beater passes through the foam.*

ABOVE *Use the parchment paper holding the sifted dry ingredients to transfer them to the bowl. Gently fold them into the batter.*

5. Add other ingredients, such as butter, flavoring, or finishing ingredients. If butter or another shortening is required, add it after the dry ingredients have been properly incorporated. These ingredients should be warm so that they are evenly distributed throughout the batter. Temper the ingredients by blending them with a little batter to retain maximum volume.

6. Scale off the batter into prepared baking pans and bake until done. The cake should rise evenly during baking. When it is properly baked, it will just begin to shrink away from the sides of the pan. The surface should spring back when lightly pressed.

Remove the cake from the oven and let it cool briefly in the pan. Remove it from the pan and let it cool completely on a rack. Angel food and chiffon cakes should be allowed to cool completely, upside down, in the pan before unmolding so that they retain their full volume.

7. Evaluate the quality of the finished product.

Cakes prepared by the foaming method are often more spongy than other cakes, although they do have a discernible crumb. Angel food and chiffon cakes are the spongiest of these types. The limited amount of shortening used gives these cakes a slightly dry texture, which is why they are often moistened with simple syrup. Even though there is a large proportion of eggs in foamed cakes, there should not be a marked egg flavor.

TOP *Combine flavoring with melted butter. This is then tempered with a small amount of batter. Otherwise the butter could cause the foam to collapse as it is added.*

BOTTOM *Fold the tempered butter into the batter carefully but thoroughly.*

ABOVE *Wear a glove when using your fingertips to check the doneness of a cake.*

3 ³/₄ lb / 1.7 kg eggs

1 lb 14 oz / 850 g sugar

1 lb 6 oz / 625 g all-purpose or cake flour

8 oz / 225 g cornstarch

10 oz / 285 g melted butter

¹/₂ fl oz / 15 mL vanilla extract

VANILLA SPONGE (GENOISE)

1 Combine the eggs and sugar in a mixing bowl and heat to 110°F/43°C over a double boiler.

2 Sift the flour and cornstarch together 2 times.

3 Whip the eggs until the foam is 3 times its original volume and is no longer increasing in volume.

4 Fold in the flour and cornstarch. Fold in the butter and vanilla extract.

5 Bake the cakes at 375°F/190°C for 30 minutes or until top is firm to the touch.

6 Remove the cakes from the oven and cool on a rack for several minutes. Remove the cakes from the pans and continue to cool to room temperature on racks. The cakes are ready to serve now, or to finish as desired. They may be wrapped and held under refrigeration for up to 3 days or frozen for up to 6 weeks.

MAKES EIGHT 8-INCH/20-CENTIMETER CAKES

NOTE

This cake is shown on page 912, filled and iced with a buttercream and garnished with toasted sliced almonds.

GENERAL GUIDELINES FOR ASSEMBLING CAKES

Cakes and tortes show the importance of mastering basic components. By combining cakes with a variety of properly made icings, fillings, glazes, and garnishes, the skill of the baker or pastry chef is highlighted on the dessert menu.

Before assembly, prepare all the basic components and have everything at the correct temperature. Cakes should be properly baked and cooled. Fillings should be prepared and held at the correct temperature. For example, a mousse or Bavarian cream should be used immediately after it has been prepared. Have buttercreams cool but pliable. They may be beaten briefly to improve their texture and spreadability. Prepare any syrups or glazes that are required. Other elements used to fill and finish cakes include fresh fruit garnishes, powdered sugar, cocoa powder, chocolate, or marzipan decorations.

Palette knives or spatulas are used to ice and fill a cake or torte. Use a pastry brush to apply syrups or certain glazes. Set a rack in a sheet pan to hold cakes as they are glazed. Some cakes are filled and then chilled in a mold such as a springform pan or a ring mold until they are ready to be decorated. These molds should be lined with plastic to make unmolding easier. Assemble pastry bags with assorted tips or parchment cones to create different borders, write messages, or apply other decorations. A turntable makes this work easier. Cardboard circles and other pieces required for display or service of the finished cake should be on hand.

Use a knife with a long blade to cut the cake into layers. Be sure to use the entire length of the blade to make the cut. The cut should be level and even, parallel to the work surface. Trim the edges of the cake, if necessary, and brush away any loose crumbs.

Moisten the layers with simple syrup, if desired, and place the first layer on a cake circle to make it easier to work with. Placing the cake circle on a turntable makes it even easier. Use a small dollop of icing or filling to keep the cake from sliding on the cardboard, or to keep the cardboard circle from slipping on the turntable.

To fill the cake layers, spread the filling evenly on the top of the first layer and top with a second layer. To work on a cardboard circle or turntable, spread an even thickness of filling on each layer. Stack a cake layer on top of the filled layer and line it up evenly. Press lightly to remove any air pockets and secure the layers. To work in a ring mold, arrange the first layer in the mold, add filling, and top with another layer. Repeat the sequence as required to prepare a layer cake or torte of more than 2 layers.

Cakes that are filled in a mold are refrigerated until the filling is firm enough to unmold. When you are ready to finish them, remove them carefully from the mold and transfer to a cardboard circle and then onto a turntable.

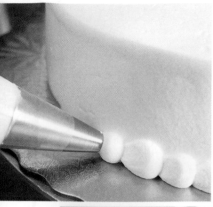

Spread a thin even layer of icing on the cake's top and then the sides. This layer of icing is sometimes referred to as the crumb coat. It is used to seal the outside of the cake and keep crumbs out of the top layer of icing. Apply a second layer of icing over the crumb coat. Use level, even strokes to smooth it out. To smooth the sides of the cake, hold the palette knife perpendicular to the cake turntable, and turn the cake, holding the knife still, until the sides are even and smooth. Once the sides are smoothly iced, apply a layer of whipped cream to the top of the cake, spreading it into a smooth even coating.

Various techniques for finishing the torte can be used alone or in combination. You may use fine cake crumbs of a contrasting color to create an edge for the cake. Gently press them along the cake's bottom. Scatter the crumbs evenly over the top of the cake, if desired.

Very lightly score the cake's top by pressing the edge of a long straight-edged knife into the icing to mark the slices. Place decorations, such as chocolate circles and whipped cream or buttercream rosettes, so that each slice will have a share of the decoration.

RECIPES

BUTTERMILK PANCAKES

makes 60 portions

7³/₄ lb/3.5 kg all-purpose flour
6 oz/170 g baking powder
1¹/₂ oz/40 g baking soda
1¹/₄ oz/47 g salt
1 lb 9 oz/700 g sugar
5 lb/2.25 kg eggs
6 qt/5.7 mL buttermilk
1¹/₂ lb/680 g melted batter
clarified butter or oil, as needed

1 Sift together the flour, baking powder, baking soda, salt, and sugar into a large bowl and make a well in the center.

2 Combine the eggs with the buttermilk and mix well. Pour all at once into the center of the dry ingredients. Slowly mix, using a whisk in a controlled circular motion.

3 Add the butter when about three fourths of the dry ingredients are moistened. Continue only until butter is worked in. Do not overmix. The batter is ready to use now, or it may be held under refrigeration for up to 12 hours.

4 To prepare pancakes, preheat a griddle to 350°F/175°C and grease with clarified butter or oil. Ladle 2 fl oz/60 mL batter for each pancake onto the griddle. Turn once, when bubbles break on the upper surface and the bottom is golden brown, about 2 minutes. Finish cooking on the second side, about 1 minute. Serve at once.

Basic Waffles Replace the whole eggs with separated eggs. Mix the egg yolks with buttermilk, and continue with Steps 2 and 3. Beat the egg whites to medium-stiff peaks. Fold the beaten egg whites into the finished batter. Preheat a waffle iron to 350°F/175°C and grease lightly with oil. Ladle the batter into the waffle iron, close it, and cook the waffles until golden brown and cooked through, about 3 to 4 minutes. (Amount of batter required will vary according to the size of the waffle iron.)

Banana Pancakes Omit 1 qt/1 L of the buttermilk. Add 3 lb/1.3 kg chopped bananas.

Chocolate Chip Pancakes Lightly dust 3 lb/1.3 kg small chocolate chips with flour. Fold the chocolate chips and 1 lb/450 g toasted pecans or walnuts into the finished batter.

Blueberry Pancakes Fold 3 lb/1.3 kg blueberries into the batter just before making the pancakes.

Oatmeal Pancakes or Waffles Replace 1 lb/450 g of flour with 1½ lb/680 g oatmeal, 2 tbsp/30 mL cinnamon, 2 tsp/10 mL nutmeg, and 1 tsp/5mL cloves.

Corn Pancakes Replace 2 lb/900 g of the flour with an equal amount of yellow cornmeal. Fold 3 lb/1.3 kg corn kernels into the batter. Add corn kernels and proceed as for pancakes above.

CRÊPES SUZETTE

makes 6 portions

1¹/₂ oz/45 g sugar
6 oz/180 g butter, cubed
1¹/₂ oz/45 g grated orange zest
3 fl oz/90 mL orange juice
18 DESSERT CRÊPES (page 901)
3 fl oz/90 mL Grand Marnier
3 fl oz/90 mL brandy or Cognac

1 Place a preheated suzette pan on a réchaud.

2 Sprinkle sugar evenly across the bottom of the suzette pan without allowing the spoon to touch the bottom; this may cause the sugar to crystallize.

3 As the sugar begins to caramelize, add the butter to the outside edges of the pan and gently shake the pan; this allows the butter to evenly temper and blend with the sugar.

4 Add the orange zest and shake the pan gently to thoroughly blend all the ingredients and become a light orange caramel color.

5 Pour the orange juice on the outside edges of the pan slowly, allowing it to temper and blend with the sugar.

6 Shake the pan gently, incorporating all the ingredients and allowing the sauce to thicken.

7 Sandwich the crêpe between a fork and a spoon and place the crêpe into the sauce. Flip the crêpe over to coat the other side.

8 Repeat with the remaining crêpes, moving quickly so the sauce does not become too thick.

9 Remove the pan from the réchaud and add the Grand Marnier. Do not flame it. Return the pan to the réchaud and shake gently.

10 Slide the pan back and forth over the front edge of the réchaud, allowing the pan to get hot.

11 Remove the pan, add the brandy, and tip the pan slightly to flame the brandy. Shake the pan until the flame dies.

12 Plate 3 crêpes per portion, shingling one over the other, and coat with sauce.

FRUIT FRITTERS

makes 10 portions

2 eggs
1 oz/30 g sugar
6 fl oz/180 mL white wine
6 fl oz/180 mL apple juice
pinch salt
$^1/_2$ tsp/2 mL grated lemon zest
$^1/_2$ tsp/2 mL grated orange zest
12 oz/340 g sifted all-purpose flour
4 lb/1.8 g fruit, prepared
oil, for frying
20 fl oz/600 mL FRUIT COULIS (page 987)
6 fl oz/180 mL whipped cream (optional)

1 Combine the eggs and sugar in the bowl of an electric mixer and beat lightly using the whisk attachment on medium speed.

2 Add the wine, apple juice, salt, and lemon and orange zest and combine.

3 Add the flour and blend until smooth.

4 Dip the fruit in the batter and deep fry at 350°F/175°C until golden brown. Drain on absorbent paper.

5 Serve with fruit sauce and whipped cream, if desired.

Strawberry Fritters Dip 4 lb/1.8 g hulled strawberries into heated and strained strawberry preserves, roll in chopped almonds or toasted coconut, then dip them in the batter. Fry as directed above.

BANANA NUT BREAD

makes four 2-pound/900-gram loaves

2 lb/900 g all-purpose flour
$^1/_2$ oz/15 g baking soda
$1^1/_2$ tsp/7 mL salt
12 oz/340 g butter, at room temperature
1 lb/450 g sugar
11 oz/315 g eggs, room temperature
8 oz/225 g milk, at room temperature
3 lb/1.3 kg mashed bananas
1 tbsp/15 mL vanilla extract
5 oz/140 g chopped toasted walnuts

1 Sift together the flour, baking soda, and salt.

2 Cream together the butter and sugar in an electric mixer, using the paddle attachment on medium speed, until light and smooth.

3 Add the eggs slowly on low speed, fully incorporating the eggs and scraping down the sides of the bowl after each addition.

4 Add the milk, alternating with the dry ingredients, in 3 additions, scraping down the sides of the bowl as necessary. Blend in the bananas, vanilla, and nuts.

5 Grease 4 loaf pans. Scale 1 lb 14 oz/850 g of batter into each loaf pan.

6 Bake in a 350°F/175°C oven until a skewer inserted in the center comes out clean, about 65 to 70 minutes.

BLUEBERRY MUFFINS

makes 5 dozen muffins

$1^3/_4$ lb/800 g all-purpose or cake flour
1 oz/30 g baking powder
1 lb/450 g butter
1 lb/450 g confectioners' sugar
$^1/_2$ oz/15 g salt
1 lb/450 g eggs
1 lb/450 g milk
1 lb 6 oz/625 g blueberries (fresh or frozen)

1 Sift together the flour and baking powder.

2 Cream together the butter, sugar, and salt in the bowl of an electric mixer. Using the paddle attachment, beat on medium speed until light and smooth.

3 Add the eggs slowly on low speed, fully incorporating and scraping down the sides of the bowl after each addition.

4 Add the milk, alternating with the dry ingredients, in 3 additions, scraping down the sides of the bowl as necessary. Gently fold in the blueberries, using a large rubber spatula.

5 Grease or line the muffin tins with paper liners. Scale 2 oz/60 g of batter per muffin.

6 Bake at 400°F/205°C until light brown on top, about 20 minutes.

7 Let cool slightly in the pan. Remove muffins from the pan and serve warm, or let cool completely, wrap tightly, and store at room temperature for 2 days or freeze for up to 1 month.

see photograph on page 925

BRAN MUFFINS

makes 4 dozen muffins

1½ lb/680 g all-purpose flour

1½ oz/40 g baking powder

8 oz/225 g bran

8 oz/225 g butter

1 lb/450 g sugar

½ oz/15 g salt

1 lb/450 g eggs

1 pt/480 mL milk

4 oz/115 g honey

4 oz/115 g molasses

1 Sift together the flour and baking powder. Add the bran to the sifted flour mixture and combine with a whip to distribute the bran evenly.

2 Cream together the shortening, sugar, and salt, in the bowl of an electric mixer. Using the paddle attachment, beat on medium speed until light and smooth. Add the eggs and beat on medium speed, scraping down the bowl as necessary, until smooth.

3 Add the milk and the dry ingredients in alternating turns, scraping down the sides of the bowl as necessary and mixing until just incorporated. Blend in the honey and molasses.

4 Grease the muffin tins or line with paper liners. Scale 2 oz/60 g of batter per muffin.

5 Bake at 400°F/205°C until light brown on top, about 20 minutes.

6 Let cool slightly in the pan. Remove muffins from the pan and serve warm, or let cool completely, wrap tightly, and store at room temperature for 2 days or freeze for up to 1 month.

CORN MUFFINS

makes 3 dozen muffins

1¼ lb/570 g sugar

¾ oz/20 g salt

1½ lb/680 g all-purpose flour

10 oz/285 g yellow cornmeal

1 oz/30 g baking powder

9 oz/255 g eggs, lightly beaten

20 fl oz/600 mL milk

12 oz/340 g corn oil

2 tbsp/30 mL orange juice concentrate, at room temperature

1 Preheat the oven to 350°F/175°C and place the empty muffin tins inside to heat.

2 Combine the sugar, salt, flour, cornmeal, and baking powder in the bowl of an electric mixer and stir to blend.

3 In a separate bowl thoroughly combine the remaining ingredients.

4 Add the wet ingredients to the dry ingredients. Using the paddle attachment, mix on low speed. Scrape down the sides of the bowl and blend until fully incorporated.

5 Remove the hot tins from the oven and spray with non-stick baking spray. Scale 3 oz/85 g per muffin and bake until golden brown, 10 to 15 minutes.

6 Let cool slightly in the pan. Remove from the pan and serve warm, or let cool completely, wrap tightly, and store at room temperature for 2 days or freeze for up to 1 month.

Corn Bread Heat a half sheet pan in the oven. When hot, remove from the oven and spray with nonstick baking spray. Fill the pan with 1¼ qt/1.2 L of batter and bake in a 350°F/175°C oven until golden brown, 45 minutes to 1 hour. Let cool in the pan for 1 hour. Serve or wrap tightly and store at room temperature for 2 days or freeze for up to 1 month.

DATE NUT BREAD

makes 5 loaves

2½ lb/1.15 kg all-purpose flour

½ tsp/2 mL ground cardamom

½ tsp/2 mL ground cinnamon

1 oz/30 g baking powder

⅓ oz/9 g baking soda

½ oz/15 g salt

9 oz/255 g butter

1¼ lb/570 g light brown sugar

9 oz/255 g eggs

36 fl oz/1.1 L water

1 lb/450 g chopped toasted pecans

2¼ lb/1 kg chopped dates

1 Sift together the flour, cardamom, cinnamon, baking powder, baking soda, and salt.

2 Cream together the butter and sugar in the bowl of an electric mixer. Using the paddle attachment, beat on medium speed until light and smooth.

3 Add the eggs slowly on low speed, fully incorporating and scraping down the sides of the bowl after each addition.

4 Add the water, alternating with the sifted dry ingredients, in 3 additions, scraping down the sides of the bowl as necessary. Blend in the chopped nuts and dates.

5 Grease 5 loaf pans. Scale 1 lb 14 oz/850 g of the batter into each pan. Bake in a 350°F/175°C oven until a skewer inserted in the center of each loaf comes out clean, 1 to 1½ hours.

6 Let cool in the pan and serve, or wrap tightly and store at room temperature for 2 days or freeze for up to 1 month.

see photograph on page 924

PUMPKIN BREAD

makes 4 loaves

2 lb/900 g all-purpose flour

2 tsp/10 mL baking powder

4 tsp/20 mL baking soda

1 tbsp/15 mL salt

2 tsp/10 mL ground cinnamon

14 oz/400 g oil

2¾ lb/1.25 kg sugar

2 lb/900 g pumpkin purée

1 lb/450 g eggs

13 oz/370 g water

7 oz/200 g chopped toasted pecans

1 Sift together the flour, baking powder, baking soda, salt, and cinnamon.

2 Combine the oil, sugar, pumpkin purée, eggs, and water in the bowl of an electric mixer. Using the paddle attachment, blend on low speed until fully incorporated.

3 Add the sifted dry ingredients to the oil mixture and blend until just incorporated, scraping the sides of the bowl as necessary. Blend in the nuts.

4 Grease 4 loaf pans. Scale 1 lb 14 oz/850 g of batter into each pan.

5 Bake in a 350°F/175°C oven until a skewer inserted near the center of each loaf comes out clean and the center of the loaves spring back when gently pressed, 1 to 1½ hours.

6 Cool the bread in the pan for a few minutes. Remove from the pans and cool on a rack before slicing and serving or wrapping for storage.

IRISH SODA BREAD

2¹⁄₂ lb/1.15 kg all-purpose flour

2¹⁄₂ oz/70 g baking powder

6 oz/170 g sugar

¹⁄₄ oz/7 g salt

5¹⁄₂ oz/155 g butter

6 oz/170 g currants

¹⁄₂ oz/15 g caraway seeds

26 fl oz/780 mL milk

1 Sift together the flour, baking powder, sugar, and salt.

2 Gently rub the butter into the dry ingredients using your fingertips.

3 Add the currants and caraway seeds and toss together with the mixture.

4 Add the milk and blend until it forms a shaggy mass.

5 Turn the dough out onto a lightly floured work surface and knead for 20 seconds.

6 Scale into 1 lb/450 g portions and round. Place on a parchment-lined sheet pan. Dust the tops of the loaves lightly with flour and, using a paring knife, press an × gently onto top surface of each loaf.

7 Bake in a 425°F/220°C oven until browned and baked through, 45 to 60 minutes. To test for doneness, insert a wooden skewer into the thickest part of the loaf. The skewer should not have any crumbs clinging to it.

8 Remove the loaves from the pan and let cool completely on a wire rack before slicing and serving.

DRIED CHERRY SCONES

1 lb 14 oz/850 g all-purpose or cake flour

1¹⁄₂ oz/40 g baking powder

1 oz/30 g sugar

¹⁄₂ oz/15 g salt

10 oz/285 g butter

6 oz/170 g dried cherries

6 fl oz/180 g buttermilk

6 fl oz/180 mL milk

2 eggs

1 Sift together the flour, baking powder, sugar, and salt.

2 Gently rub the butter into the dry ingredients using your fingertips.

3 Add the dried cherries and toss together with the mixture.

4 Mix together the buttermilk, milk, and eggs. Add the buttermilk mixture to the dough and fully combine.

5 Place the dough on a lightly floured work surface and roll out ¾ in/20 mm thick. Using a biscuit cutter, cut into 15 rounds. Place on a parchment-lined sheet pan.

6 Bake in a 400°F/205°C oven until golden brown.

7 Remove the scones from the pan and let cool on a wire rack before serving.

NOTES

Replace the dried cherries with other dried fruits, such as dried apricot, currants, or cranberries.

Add 1 tbsp/15 mL citrus zest (lemon, orange, or lime).

Blueberry Muffins

Chocolate XS Cake

Angel Food Cake

Cheesecake

Date Nut Bread

GERMAN CHOCOLATE CAKE

makes one 9-inch/23-centimeter cake

1½ oz/40 g cocoa

5 oz/140 g all-purpose or cake flour

1 tsp/5 mL baking soda

¼ tsp/1 mL salt

4 oz/115 g butter

7 oz/200 g granulated sugar

4 oz/115 g light brown sugar

1½ tsp/7 mL vanilla extract

2 eggs

8 fl oz/240 mL buttermilk

1 recipe GERMAN CHOCOLATE CAKE ICING (page 993)

2 oz/60 g chocolate shavings

1 Sift together the cocoa, cake flour, baking soda, and salt.

2 Cream together the butter, sugar, light brown sugar, and vanilla in the bowl of an electric mixer. Using the paddle attachment, beat on medium speed until light and smooth.

3 Add the eggs slowly on low speed, fully incorporating and scraping down the sides of the bowl after each addition.

4 Add the buttermilk, alternating with the sifted dry ingredients, in 3 additions, scraping down the sides of the bowl as necessary.

5 Grease two 9-in/23-cm pans and line the bottoms with parchment. Scale half of the batter into each pan.

6 Bake in a 350°F/175°C oven until a skewer inserted near the center of the cake comes out clean, 45 to 55 minutes.

7 Let cool slightly in the pan. Remove from the pans and let cool completely on a wire rack. The layers are ready to frost and fill, or wrap them in plastic wrap and store under refrigeration for 2 days or store in the freezer for up to 1 month.

8 Place one layer of cake on a cardboard circle and fill with 12 oz/340 g icing. Set the second layer on the filled layer. Ice the cake with the remaining icing. Mark the cake into 12 portions. Garnish with shaved chocolate.

DEVIL'S FUDGE CAKE

makes six 9-inch/23-centimeter cakes

2 lb/900 g all-purpose or cake flour

8 oz/225 g cocoa

3½ lb/1.6 kg sugar

1½ oz/40 g salt

1½ oz/40 g baking powder

½ oz/15 g baking soda

⅛ oz/4 g ground cinnamon

1 lb/450 g emulsified shortening

44 fl oz/1.3 L skim milk

1½ lb/680 g eggs

1 Combine the flour, cocoa, sugar, salt, baking powder, baking soda, cinnamon, shortening, and 20 fl oz/600 mL of the milk in the bowl of an electric mixer. Using the paddle attachment, beat on medium speed for 4 minutes.

2 Combine the eggs and the remaining milk.

3 Add the egg mixture to the flour mixture in 3 batches, mixing on medium speed for 2 minutes after each addition.

4 Grease six 9-in/23-cm cake pans and line the bottom of each pan with parchment. Scale 1¾ lb/800 g of batter into each pan.

5 Bake in a 350°F/175°C oven until the cake is firm to the touch and begins to pull away from the sides of the pan, about 25 minutes.

CHEESECAKE

makes two 10-inch/25-centimeter cakes

1 recipe GRAHAM CRACKER CRUST (recipe follows)
1½ lb/680 g sugar
4 oz/115 g cornstarch
5 lb/2.25 kg cream cheese
1 lb/450 g eggs
2 oz/60 g egg yolks
1oz/30 g vanilla extract
¼ oz/7 g grated lemon zest
10 fl oz/300 mL heavy cream

1 Coat the pans with a light film of softened butter and line with parchment. Divide the graham cracker crust evenly between the two pans and press into an even layer. Evenly divide the mixture between the prepared pans and firmly press to compact and evenly distribute. Bake in a 350°F/175°C oven for approximately 7 minutes, or until lightly golden brown. Remove the pans from the oven and allow to cool completely before filling.

2 Sift together the sugar and cornstarch.

3 Cream together the sugar mixture and the cream cheese in the bowl of an electric mixer. Using the paddle attachment, beat on medium speed until smooth.

4 Combine the eggs, egg yolks, vanilla, and lemon zest and add one fourth of the mixture at a time, fully incorporating and scraping down the sides of the bowl after each addition.

5 Add the heavy cream, scraping down the sides of the bowl as necessary

6 Divide the batter evenly between the pans. Bake in a water bath in a 300°F/150°C oven until the center is set, 60 to 90 minutes. Refrigerate the cakes overnight. Unmold and serve.

Marble Cheesecake Prepare the batter and fill the molds as directed above, reserving 10 fl oz/300 mL of the batter separately. Add 4 oz/115 g melted chocolate to the reserved batter. Pipe chocolate batter into the cakes and swirl in.

see photograph on page 924

GRAHAM CRACKER CRUST

makes enough to line two 10-inch/25-centimeter or three 8-inch/20-centimeter cake pans

1 lb/450 g graham crackers
6 oz/170 g sugar
9 oz/255 g butter, melted

1 Process the graham crackers and sugar in a food processor fitted with a metal chopping blade until the crackers are finely ground. Add the melted butter and pulse until just incorporated.

ANGEL FOOD CAKE

makes five 8-inch/20-centimeter cakes

2 lb/900 g sugar
13 oz/370 g cake flour
¼ oz/7 oz salt
2 lb/900 g egg whites
¼ oz/7 oz cream of tartar
1 tsp/5 mL vanilla extract

1 Sift together 1 lb/450 g of the sugar with the cake flour and salt.

2 Combine the egg whites and cream of tartar in the bowl of an electric mixer fitted with the whip attachment and beat until frothy with the mixer on medium speed.

3 With the mixer on high speed gradually add the remaining sugar to the beaten egg whites and beat to medium-stiff peaks.

4 Quickly and gently fold the sifted dry ingredients into the beaten egg whites. Fold in the vanilla.

5 Divide the batter evenly among five ungreased tube cake pans.

6 Bake in a 350°F/175°C oven for 35 to 40 minutes or until cake springs back when lightly touched.

7 Remove the cakes from the oven and allow to cool completely in their pans, upside down on a rack. Unmold the cakes from the pans when they are completely cooled. The cakes are ready to serve now, or wrap and hold under refrigeration for later use.

see photograph on page 924

CHOCOLATE SPONGE CAKE

makes five 10-inch/25-centimeter or eight 8-inch/20-centimeter cakes

1 lb/450 g all-purpose or cake flour

8 oz/225 g cornstarch

6 oz/170 g cocoa

1/2 tsp/2 mL baking soda

3 1/4 lb/1.47 kg eggs

1 lb 14 oz/850 g sugar

5 oz/140 g melted butter

1 Sift together the flour, cornstarch, cocoa, and baking soda 3 times.

2 Combine the eggs and sugar in the bowl of a mixer and, whisking constantly, heat over a hot-water bath to 110°F/43°C.

3 Put the bowl on the machine. Using the whisk attachment on high speed, beat to maximum volume.

4 Reduce the mixer speed to medium and beat for 5 minutes more.

5 Gently fold the sifted dry ingredients into the meringue.

6 Temper the melted butter into the batter and gently fold to incorporate.

7 Grease five 10-in/25-cm or eight 8-in/20-cm cake pans and line with parchment. Divide the batter evenly among the pans.

8 Bake in a 350°F/175°C oven until the cake springs back when lightly touched in the center and it begins to pull away from the sides of the pan, about 30 minutes. Cool the cakes in the pans on a cooling rack, then unmold and finish cooling. The cakes are ready to ice and fill now, or they may be wrapped and held under refrigeration for up to 2 days or frozen for up to 1 month. (Thaw frozen cakes under refrigeration overnight before filling and icing.)

SPONGE ROULADE

makes 1 sheet pan

8 oz/225 g egg yolks

5 oz/145 g sugar

8 oz/225 g egg whites

6 oz/170 g sifted all-purpose or cake flour

1 Combine the egg yolks with 2 oz/60 g of the sugar in the bowl of an electric mixer. Using the whisk attachment, beat on medium speed until thick and light in color.

2 In another bowl, beat the egg whites with the remaining sugar to medium peaks.

3 Gently blend a small portion of the egg whites into the egg yolks. Fold the remaining egg whites into the lightened yolk mixture.

4 Fold the sifted flour into the egg mixture.

5 Gently spread the batter evenly on a parchment-lined sheet pan.

6 Bake in a 425°F/220°C oven until the center of the cake springs back when gently pressed and golden in color, 10 to 15 minutes.

7 Immediately after baking, remove the cake from the pan and place in a cool sheet pan to prevent the cake from drying out.

8 Let cool completely before using, or wrap in plastic wrap and store at room temperature for 2 days or freeze for up to 1 month.

Chocolate Sponge Roulade Reduce the amount of cake flour to 4½ oz/125 g and sift together with 1½ oz/40 g cocoa.

CHOCOLATE XS CAKE

makes two 10-inch/25-centimeter or three 8-inch/20-centimeter cakes

14 oz/400 g butter

10 oz/285 g confectioners' sugar

6¹/₂ oz/185 g eggs

10¹/₂ oz/300 g egg yolks

16¹/₂ oz/465 g melted bittersweet chocolate

14 oz/400 g egg whites

4 oz/115 g sugar

5 oz/140 g bread flour, sifted

14 oz/400 g ground toasted almonds

1 lb/450 g apricot jam, warmed and strained

3 lb/1.3 kg BASIC GANACHE (page 992)

1 Cream together the butter and confectioners' sugar in the bowl of an electric mixer. Using the paddle attachment on medium speed, beat until light and smooth.

2 Add the eggs and egg yolks and beat slowly on low speed, fully incorporating and scraping down the sides of the bowl after each addition.

3 Add the warm melted chocolate all at once and quickly incorporate, scraping down the sides of the bowl as necessary.

4 Combine the egg whites and the sugar in another mixer bowl. Using the whip attachment, beat on high speed to medium peaks.

5 Fold the meringue into the creamed mixture.

6 Fold the sifted bread flour and the almonds into the batter.

7 Grease two 10-in/25-cm or three 8-in/20-cm cake pans and line them with parchment. Divide the batter evenly among the pans.

8 Bake in a 350°F/175°C oven until the center of the cakes spring back when lightly touched, 45 to 50 minutes. Remove from the oven and cool in the pans on racks. Unmold the cakes and finish cooling on racks. The cakes are ready to fill and glaze now, or they may be wrapped and stored under refrigeration for up to 2 days or frozen for up to 1 month. (Thaw frozen cakes under refrigeration overnight.)

9 Slice each cake evenly in 2 layers. Spread a thin layer of apricot jam on one layer, and top with a second layer of cake. Brush the sides of the cake with more apricot jam. Repeat for the second cake. Wrap and refrigerate the cake until the jam becomes firm.

10 Place half of the ganache in a stainless steel bowl. Using a wooden spoon, beat vigorously until it becomes thick. Coat the outside of the cake with a thin layer of the beaten ganache. Refrigerate the cake overnight or until the ganache is hard.

11 Warm the remaining ganache to 110°F/43°C. Set the filled cakes on a rack in a sheet pan. Pour the warmed ganache over the cakes. Let the glaze firm for 15 minutes, and mark for 16 slices. Pipe a decoration on each slice with the remaining ganache, if desired.

see photograph on page 925

BLACK FOREST CAKE

makes one 10-inch/25-centimeter cake

one 10-in/25-cm CHOCOLATE SPONGE CAKE (page 928)
8 fl oz/240 mL kirsch-flavored SIMPLE SYRUP (page 873)
1 lb 8 oz/680 g chocolate whipped cream
8 oz/225 g preserved cherries
1 lb/450 g kirsch-flavored whipped cream
2 oz/60 g chocolate shavings
confectioners' sugar, as needed

1 Slice the sponge cake into 3 even layers.

2 Soak the layers with syrup.

3 Coat the first layer of sponge with a thin coating of chocolate whipped cream and pipe 3 concentric rings of chocolate whipped cream. Reserve 16 cherries for garnish and place the remaining cherries in the chocolate whipped cream rings.

4 Top with a second layer of sponge. Coat with chocolate whipped cream.

5 Top with the last layer of sponge. Ice the cake with kirsch-flavored whipped cream and mark for 16 portions.

6 Pipe a dollop of kirsch-flavored whipped cream on each portion and top each with one of the reserved cherries.

7 Garnish the center of the torte with the chocolate shavings and dust with confectioners' sugar. Trim the bottom edge of the torte with chocolate shavings.

BAVARIAN CREAM TORTE

makes one 8-inch/20-centimeter torte

one 8-inch VANILLA SPONGE CAKE (page 916)
6 fl oz/180 mL SIMPLE SYRUP (page 873)
2 lb/900 g STRAWBERRY BAVARIAN CREAM (page 974)
8 oz/225 g sliced strawberries for filling
2 pt/900 g heavy cream, whipped
strawberries for garnish, whole or halved, as needed

1 Prepare cake rings by lining with plastic wrap.

2 Slice the cake horizontally into 3 layers.

3 Place a cake layer on the bottom of the cake ring and brush it with simple syrup.

4 Add 1 lb/450 g of Bavarian cream on top of the cake. Add strawberry filling. Top with a second layer of cake, brushing with simple syrup. Add another layer of Bavarian cream, and top with the third layer of cake. Brush with syrup. Cover the cake with plastic wrap and press the layers gently into the mold.

5 Chill the cake for at least 8 hours or place in the freezer for up to 1 month. (Thaw frozen cakes under refrigeration before finishing and serving.)

6 Remove the cakes from the rings and remove the plastic wrap. Ice with whipped cream, and mark each for 10 portions.

7 Pipe a dollop of whipped cream on each marked slice and garnish each dollop with a strawberry.

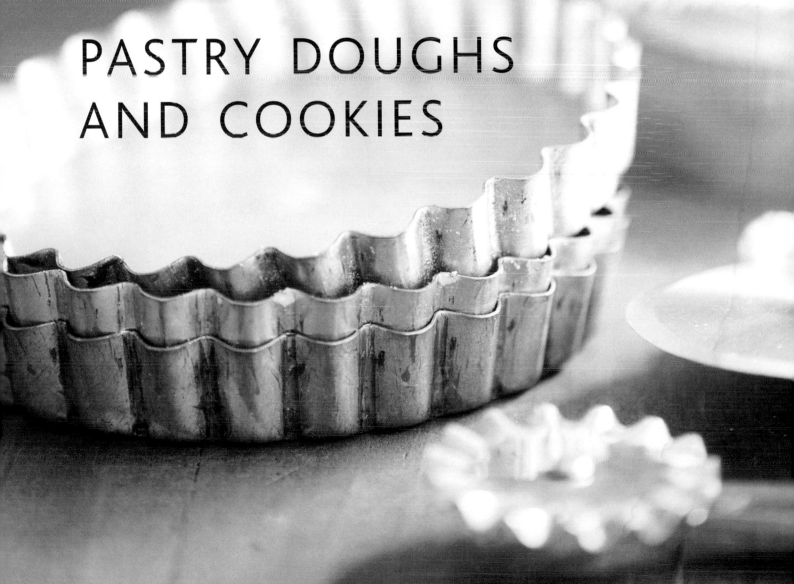

All chefs should be able to prepare and work with a variety of doughs to create both sweet and savory items ranging from pastries and pies to cookies. The same pie crust, for example, can be paired with sweetened fresh apples for an apple pie or with a cheese-flavored custard to make quiche. Individually sized pastries and cookies may be served outside a meal, as hors d'oeuvre or reception food, or to conclude the meal as a friandise or mignardise. Or they may be featured as a part of the regular menu offerings as an entrée, an appetizer, or a dessert.

PASTRY DOUGHS AND COOKIES

BASIC PIE DOUGH

Basic pie dough is often called "3-2-1 dough," because it is composed of three parts flour, two parts fat, and one part water (by weight). When properly made, the crust is flaky and crisp.

The characteristic flaky texture of baked pie dough is developed by rubbing together the fat and the flour, rather than blending them into a smooth dough. Flakes of fat should remain visible as the dough is mixed. The larger the fat flakes before the liquid is added, the larger the flakes will be in the baked dough. If the fat is worked more thoroughly into the flour, the result will be a pie crust with a very small flake; this type of dough is sometimes described as mealy.

ALL-PURPOSE OR PASTRY flour is used in pie doughs because of its low protein content, which results in a tender crust. Since these flours have a tendency to clump together, they must be sifted.

The fat may be shortening, butter, or lard. It should be cut or broken into large lumps, about the size of walnuts, before it is added to the flour and chilled. Cream cheese or sour cream is called for in some doughs to replace some of the butter or shortening.

The liquid for pie dough is customarily water, but milk or cream may also be used. Because of the fat in milk and cream, the amount of fat in the overall formula needs to be decreased if these ingredients are used. The liquid should be very cold to achieve the proper flaky texture. It is also a good idea to dissolve the salt in the liquid so that it is evenly distributed.

Some of the flour can be replaced with ground nuts. Eggs are added to some doughs for a golden color and a firmer texture. Adding sugar to a basic pie dough produces a dough known as pâte sucrée, which is sweet and darker in color than basic pie dough, with a crumbly texture.

Fruit fillings are used for many pies, tarts, and strudels. They are usually prepared with sliced and peeled fresh fruit. The fruit is typically combined with sugar and a starch (flour, arrowroot, cornstarch, or tapioca) to produce a flavorful filling with enough body to slice into neat portions. Cooked fruit fillings and custard, cream, or pudding fillings should be prepared in advance as directed in specific recipes. Hold all fillings at the correct temperature for the best flavor and consistency in the finished pie or tart.

Prepare any toppings, including crumb toppings and meringues, or glazes, such as melted chocolate or apricot jam. Egg wash is often applied to crusts and should be blended in advance and applied with a pastry brush.

Generally pies are baked in a relatively deep pan with sloping sides that can hold large amounts of filling. Tarts are usually prepared in thin, straight-sided pans, often with removable bottoms. Have on hand parchment paper and additional pie or tart pans or pie weights (metal pellets, dry beans, or dry rice) if the crust is to be baked blind. Filled pies should be baked on sheet pans to catch any drips. Cool pies on cooling racks.

1. Combine the flour and the fat.
Cut the fat into the dough either by hand, by using a mixer with the paddle attachment, or with a pastry knife. For flaky pie dough, leave the fat pieces rather large, about the size of nickels or dimes. For mealy pie dough, continue to blend the mixture until it resembles a coarse meal and has begun to take on a slightly yellow color.

2. Add the cold water to the dough and combine.
Add the liquid all at once to the flour-and-fat mixture. Toss the mixture with a lifting motion until the dough is evenly moistened. Turn the dough out onto a lightly floured work surface and press into a compact, flat disk. Wrap the dough in plastic and refrigerate until firm enough to roll out easily. Chilling allows the dough to relax, the fat to firm up, and the starches present in the flour to completely absorb the liquid.

3. Roll out the dough.
Turn out the dough onto a floured work surface. Lightly dust the surface of the dough with additional flour. Using even strokes, roll the dough into the desired thickness and shape. Turn it occasionally to produce an even shape and to keep it from sticking to the work surface. Work from the center toward the edges, rolling in different directions. Cut the dough, if necessary, to fit the pan. Brush away all flour from the surface. (The flour could cause the dough to bake unevenly or to scorch.) Transfer the dough to a pan and fit it gently into the corners. Use a ball of scrap dough to press out any air pockets.

TOP *Rub the fat into the dry ingredients.*

BOTTOM *Large pieces of fat make a flaky pie dough (top). Small pieces of fat make a mealy pie dough (bottom).*

ABOVE *Using a rolling pin, roll in one direction on a diagonal. Then switch hands and roll in the opposite direction.*

4. Line the pie or tart pan with the dough.

Carefully transfer the rolled dough into the pan. Position the dough so that it completely covers the entire pan. Settle the dough into the pan, pressing the dough gently against the pan. Trim the excess dough from the rim, leaving enough to seal a top crust in place, if necessary, or to prepare a fluted or raised edge for a single-crusted pie or tart.

TOP *Lift the dough with the rolling pin to place it in a pan.*

BOTTOM *Use a scrap of dough to gently press the dough into the corners of the pan.*

5. Finish and fill the pie crust as desired. Some pies and tarts are filled, then baked. Others call for the crust to be baked separately, either baked blind or full baked (see Blind Baking, page 936). To add a fruit filling to an unbaked pie shell, combine the filling ingredients and mound them in the shell. Custard-type fillings should be carefully poured into the shell to just below the rim of the pan.

Some pies, especially fresh fruit pies, have a top crust as well as a bottom crust. Roll out the top crust in the same manner as for the bottom crust. Cut slashes in the top crust to allow steam to escape, and carefully lay the top crust over the pie. Press the dough in place around the rim to seal the top and bottom crusts. Trim away excess overhang, and pinch or crimp the edges.

Pies and, less frequently, tarts may be finished with a lattice crust, made by cutting strips of dough and laying them on top of the filling to make a grid. Seal and crimp the edges

ABOVE *The fruit will settle and lose some volume as the pie bakes.*

as for a double-crusted pie. Crumb toppings should be applied in an even layer over the surface of the filling.

Another frequent pie topping is meringue, which is piped onto the pie in a decorative pattern or simply mounded and peaked. The meringue is then quickly browned in a very hot oven. If properly applied, it will not lift away from the filling or form visible moisture beads on the surface.

TOP *The top crust for a double-crusted pie should be vented. Decorative cuts are made to allow steam to escape during baking.*

BOTTOM *Brush the crust completely and evenly with egg wash and be sure that there are no puddles.*

6. Bake the pie or pie crust.

For a double-crusted pie, brush the top crust very lightly with egg wash and bake the pie on a sheet pan in a hot oven (425°F/205°C) until done. In general, pies and tarts are baked just until the crust begins to take on a golden color. The presence of such ingredients as egg yolks, milk, butter, or sugar contribute a richer golden to golden-brown color. The dough should appear dry. If the dough has been rolled out unevenly, the thicker portions may appear moist, indicating that the dough is not fully baked.

Fruit fillings should be tender with thickened juices. Custard fillings should be fully set, but not cooked to the point at which the surface cracks or shrinks away from the crust.

7. Evaluate the quality of the finished pie or crust.

The texture of the crust is determined in large part by the mixing method. If the fat has been worked into the dough completely, the finished crust will have a fine crumb. If the fat has been briefly rubbed into the flour, the dough will be flaky. If the dough has been underbaked, the texture may be gummy or even rubbery. If it has been overbaked, it may be tough.

The flavor of the dough depends for the most part on the type of fat used. Pie doughs made with vegetable shortening have a nearly neutral flavor. If lard has been used, the dough tastes slightly of that fat. Butter, or a combination of butter and shortening, may be used to introduce a butter flavor.

BLIND BAKING

The procedure for preparing a prebaked pie or tart shell is known as blind baking. The dough is rolled out, fitted into the pan, and pierced in several places with the tines of a fork (this step is known as docking) to prevent blisters from forming in the dough as it bakes.

The pastry is then covered with parchment paper and an empty pie pan is set on top of the paper (this is known as "double panning").

The pans are placed upside down in the oven. This procedure prevents the dough from shrinking back down the pan's edges and keeps it from blistering. The dough is baked in a moderate oven until it is set and appears dry, but not golden.

Another method for blind baking is to place a sheet of parchment paper over the dough after docking and then fill it with pie weights or dried beans before baking. Once the shell is baked, it may be coated with melted chocolate or warmed, strained jam to prevent the crust from becoming soggy. Various fillings may be used. In a classic example, pastry cream is spread on the prebaked shell and then covered with fresh fruit.

2 lb / 900 g shortening

3 lb / 1.3 kg pastry flour

1 oz / 30 g salt

1 lb / 450 g cold water

PIE CRUST (3-2-1 DOUGH)

1 Gently rub the shortening into the flour using your fingertips to form large flakes for an extremely flaky crust, or until it looks like a coarse meal for a finer crumb.

2 Dissolve the salt in the water.

3 Add the water to the flour-shortening mixture and mix just enough to form a dry, crumbly dough. It should be moist enough to hold together when pressed into a ball.

4 Turn the dough out onto a floured work surface and shape into a even rectangle. Wrap the dough with plastic and chill for 20 to 30 minutes. The dough is ready to roll out now, or it may be held under refrigeration for up to 3 days or frozen for up to 6 weeks. (Thaw frozen dough under refrigeration before rolling it out.)

5 Scale the dough out as necessary, using about 1 oz/30 g of dough per 1 in/25 mm of pie pan diameter.

6 To roll out the dough, work on a floured surface and roll the dough into the desired shape and thickness using smooth, even strokes. Transfer the dough to a prepared pie, tart, or tartlet pan. The shell is ready to fill or bake blind now.

MAKES 5 DOUBLE-CRUST 9-INCH/23-CENTIMETER PIES

LAMINATED DOUGHS

Although laminated doughs—Danish, croissant, and puff pastry—are the most technically advanced of the ones covered in this chapter, they are not difficult to master if the directions are followed carefully.

Proper mixing methods and rolling techniques and temperature control are essential to producing laminated doughs that are flaky and delicate after baking. Pastries based on these doughs, especially those made from puff pastry, are often referred to as individual pastries.

The techniques for preparing these three doughs are similar. Danish and croissant doughs include yeast; puff pastry (pâte feuilletée) and blitz puff pastry do not have an added leavener. In all four instances, the dough is layered with butter (in a roll-in) in such a manner that several layers are produced once the dough is properly folded and rolled.

SELECT AND PREPARE THE INGREDIENTS AND EQUIPMENT

LAMINATED DOUGHS ARE MADE from a basic dough — either a lean yeast dough (for croissant), yeast dough enriched with milk and eggs (for Danish), or an unyeasted dough (for puff pastry) — combined with a roll-in. Consult Chapter Thirty-Two for more information about preparing ingredients for yeast doughs. The dough should be properly fermented, if yeast is included, and allowed enough time to relax so that it can be rolled out.

The roll-in for laminated doughs is made from butter or a combination of butter or shortening. A small amount of flour may be added to the roll-in. The butter or shortening should be chilled but not extremely hard as the roll-in is mixed. Once it is blended, the roll-in must be chilled until it has firmed but is not brittle.

In addition to bowls and mixers, you will need a large, level work surface and a rolling pin. For the best rise, texture, and flavor in the finished baked item, you will need a pastry brush to remove excess flour from the dough as it is folded. The dough is transferred to sheet pans lined with parchment to chill it as it is worked. Once it is properly rolled into sheets, the dough is cut into shape using cutters or sharp knives.

1. Combine the ingredients for the dough and knead.

Mix the dough according to the specific recipe, knead, and, if yeast is included, let the dough rise. Roll and stretch the dough into a rectangle on a parchment-lined sheet pan. A 5½-lb/2.5-kg piece of dough will cover a full-size sheet pan and be about ¼ in/16 mm. Cover the dough with plastic and let rest while preparing the roll-in.

2. Mix the roll-in.

Mix the roll-in using a mixer fitted with the paddle attachment or a food processor or knead by hand. To use a mixer, mix the flour and butter at low speed. To use a food processor, blend the ingredients with on-off pulses. To knead by hand, sprinkle the flour over the butter and work it in lightly. In all cases the butter and flour should be well blended and the roll-in pliable and smooth. Roll into a rectangle about 15 in/38 cm long, 9 in/23 cm wide, and ½ in/15 mm thick between 2 pieces of parchment. Chill the roll-in long enough to firm it if necessary.

3. Combine the dough and the roll-in and lock the roll-in in place.

Have the roll-in and the dough at the same temperature. Turn the dough out onto a lightly floured work surface, with the long edge parallel to the edge of the work surface. Position the roll-in on the dough so that one third of the dough is uncovered, leaving a ½-in/12-mm border on the other three sides. Fold the uncovered dough portion in toward the center of the rectangle, as for a letter. Brush away any excess flour (flour left on the dough will interfere with proper layer formation). Fold the opposite end over, and use your fingertips to weld the seams together.

TOP *Brush away the flour from the dough as it is folded.*

BOTTOM *Use your fingertips to seal the seams along the narrow ends.*

TOP *The first stage of a four-fold.*

BOTTOM *The second stage of a four-fold.*

Once the roll-in is locked in place, you may proceed to laminate the dough as described in the following steps. If necessary, chill the dough long enough for the roll-in to firm up after locking in the roll-in and between laminations. It is essential to completely chill the dough if it starts to warm up. If the dough is worked long enough for the butter (or other fat) to become warm, it will be absorbed into the dough, instead of remaining in a separate layer. This will reduce the number of layers and could give the dough a rubbery or gummy texture.

4. Laminate the dough by turning, rolling, and folding it.
After locking in the roll-in, turn the dough 90 degrees, so that the long edge is again parallel to the edge of the work surface. Roll out the dough into a rectangle, lightly dusting the dough and the work surface, if necessary, to prevent the dough from sticking. Once the dough is rolled out, completely brush away all excess surface flour and fold the dough using a three- or a four-fold. For croissant and Danish, make 3 additional three-folds by folding the dough in the same way as described in Step 3 for encasing the roll-in. For puff pastry, fold the narrow ends of the dough in to meet at the center, and then fold the dough in half again; this technique is known as a four-fold, or a book-fold. The number of laminations varies according the type. Puff pastry generally calls for 4 four-folds.

After each fold is completed, check the dough to be certain that it is not becoming too warm. Both the dough and the lock-in should be cool to the touch and firm but not brittle. Allow the dough to firm briefly under refrigeration before turning and rolling out after each fold. Transfer the dough to a sheet pan and mark the dough with your fingertip to indicate the number of folds; cover and refrigerate it until cool and firm enough to roll out.

Be sure that the dough is given a 90-degree turn before it is rolled out once more. This turn is why successive folds are sometimes known as turns. Repeat this step, making the required number of three- or four-folds. Let the dough rest overnight before shaping it. Resting allows the gluten to relax. When the dough is formed for baking, it will hold its shape.

When working with these doughs, observe the following guidelines:

- Keep the dough chilled, taking out only the amount to be worked with at a given time. If the dough is too warm, the flakiness of the finished product will be reduced.
- Use a sharp knife when shaping or cutting the dough. Clean cuts ensure even rising. This is especially important for high, straight-sided pastry, such as vol-au-vent and bouchée.
- Do not run the rolling pin over the edge of the dough; this will destroy the layers at the edges and cause the dough to rise unevenly.
- Refrigerate puff pastry before baking. Chilling keeps the layers of dough and roll-in separate, assuring the best rise and flakiness.
- Save puff pastry scraps. They can be piled together and rolled out to use for pastries such as napoleons, where a substantial rise is not necessary.

5. Evaluate the quality of the finished product.

Properly laminated pastries have good volume and a deep-golden color, especially if they have been brushed with egg wash. Croissants and Danish do not usually rise as high as puff pastry, but they still have noticeable volume.

Puff pastry has a crisp and flaky texture. Danish pastry is usually more tender, and croissants are more resilient.

The predominant flavor should be a fresh, buttery taste. In some cases, shortening may be used; the flavor will be less buttery, but the rise is better.

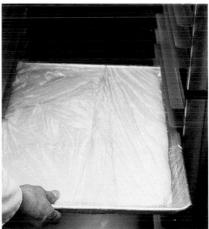

ᴛᴏᴘ *Mark the dough to show the number of completed folds.*

ʙᴏᴛᴛᴏᴍ *Return the wrapped dough to the refrigerator to cool whenever necessary.*

PHYLLO DOUGH

This dough, used to prepare strudel and baklava, is a very lean dough made only of flour and water and occasionally a small amount of oil. The dough is stretched and rolled until it is extremely thin. Butter, instead of being rolled into the dough, is melted and brushed onto the dough sheets before they are baked so that after baking, the result is similar to puff pastry.

Most kitchens purchase frozen phyllo dough. This dough needs sufficient time to thaw and come up to room temperature before it can be worked successfully. After phyllo is removed from its wrapping, cover it lightly with dampened towels and plastic. Otherwise, the phyllo can dry out quickly and become brittle enough to shatter.

For the best texture, spread bread crumbs, butter, or a combination of the two evenly over the dough to keep the layers separate as they bake. Use a spray bottle or brush to apply the butter or oil in an even coat.

Refrigerating phyllo pastries before baking helps the layers remain distinct and allows them to rise more as it bakes.

1 lb / 450 g cake flour

4 lb / 1.8 kg bread flour

2 oz / 60 g salt

5 lb / 2.25 g butter

2½ lb / 1.15 kg cold water

PUFF PASTRY

1 Sift together the cake and bread flours with the salt.

2 Gently rub 8 oz/115 g of the butter into 4 lb/1.8 kg of the sifted flour, using your fingertips.

3 Add the water and knead into a smooth dough.

4 Roll out the dough on a parchment-lined sheet pan to completely cover the pan. Cover the dough and refrigerate.

5 Combine the remaining butter with the remaining sifted flour in an electric mixer. Using the paddle attachment on low speed, blend until smooth.

6 Place the butter on a pan-size sheet of parchment and roll out to two thirds the size of the paper, and refrigerate. Do not allow it to become cold and brittle.

7 Remove the dough and the butter from the refrigerator when they are both at about the same temperature (65°F/18°C) and firmness.

8 Place the roll-in butter on the dough, leaving one third of the dough exposed. Fold the exposed piece of dough over the butter and fold the butter-covered dough over the top.

9 Turn the dough 90 degrees and roll it out to the size of a sheet pan.

10 Fold each of the ends of the dough to the center and then fold in half, to complete the first four-fold. Refrigerate for 15 minutes.

11 Remove the dough from the refrigerator and give it 2 more four-folds, first turning the dough 90 degrees. Let it rest for 20 minutes between each fold.

12 Roll the dough out to the desired thickness and cut into desired shapes. Or wrap tightly in plastic wrap and freeze until ready to use.

MAKES 5½ POUNDS/2.5 KILOGRAMS

PÂTE À CHOUX

Pâte à choux is a precooked batter, which expands into a hollow shell when baked. It can be filled, as for cream puffs, or not, as for gougère.

Pâte à choux is made by combining water, butter, flour, and eggs into a smooth batter, then shaping and baking it. The shapes expand during baking, to create a delicate shell. Pâte à choux is soft enough that a pastry bag can be used to pipe it into different shapes. Among the most common shapes are cream puffs, profiteroles, and éclairs.

SELECT AND PREPARE THE INGREDIENTS AND EQUIPMENT

BEFORE BEGINNING preparation, sift the flour and line the sheet pans with parchment. The pot selected for cooking the batter needs to be large enough to hold the liquid, fat and flour with enough room to be able to stir vigorously using a wooden spoon with no spillage. Assemble a mixer fitted with a mixing bowl and paddle attachment before the cooking process begins.

MAKE THE PÂTE À CHOUX

1. Bring the liquid and butter to a full boil. Add the flour and cook, stirring constantly.

Be sure to have the liquid at a rolling boil before adding the flour all at once. Cook until the mixture pulls away from the pan, forming a ball.

Transfer the mixture to a mixer bowl. Using the paddle attachment, mix the dough for a few minutes to cool it slightly. This will prevent the heat of the dough from cooking the eggs as they are worked into the mixture.

ABOVE *The mixture should be stirred even as the flour is being added to the pot to avoid the formation of lumps.*

ABOVE *The mixture is properly cooked.*

2. Add the eggs.

The eggs should be added gradually, in three or four additions, working the dough until it is smooth each time. Scrape down the sides and bottom of the bowl as necessary. Continue until all the eggs are incorporated.

3. Portion and bake the dough.

Pipe the dough onto prepared sheet pans according to the desired result. Bake until the dough is puffed and golden brown, with no beads of moisture on the sides. Begin by baking at a high temperature (375° to 400°F/190° to 204°C). Reduce the heat to 325°F/165°C once the dough begins to take on color. Continue to bake the pâte à choux until it is completely dry. Remove the pâte à choux from the oven. If the item is to be filled, slice it open and pull away any loose dough from the interior.

4. Evaluate the quality of the finished item.

When properly prepared and baked, pâte à choux has a definite golden color because of the high proportion of eggs. This color does not change drastically during baking. Properly baked pâte à choux appears perfectly dry, without moisture beads on the sides or top. It will swell to several times its original volume during baking.

Proper baking produces a dry, delicate texture. Remove the moist interior before adding filling for éclairs or puffs of any kind. Eggs are the predominant flavor of pâte à choux.

TOP *Add the eggs gradually.*

BOTTOM *Continue beating until the dough is shiny and able to form soft peaks.*

ABOVE *Pipe the dough onto a parchment-lined sheet pan.*

1 pint / 480 mL water, milk, or combination

8 oz / 225 g butter, cut into pieces

1 tsp / 5 mL salt

1 tsp / 5 mL sugar

12 oz / 340 g bread flour

4 to 6 eggs, as needed

PÂTE À CHOUX

1 Combine the water, butter, salt, and sugar in a saucepan and bring to a rolling boil.

2 Add the flour all at once, stirring constantly, until the mixture forms a ball and pulls away from the side of the pan.

3 Transfer the mixture to the bowl of an electric mixer and, using the paddle attachment on high speed, beat in the eggs one or two at a time, fully incorporating them and scraping down the sides of the bowl after each addition. Check the appearance and consistency after each addition. When the dough is a medium-stiff paste and has a shiny appearance, stop adding eggs.

4 Fill a pastry bag and pipe out dough as desired onto a parchment-lined sheet pan.

5 Bake in a 380°F/195°C oven until the structure has been formed and a little color has developed. Reduce the temperature to 325°F/165°C and bake until almost all the moisture has evaporated from the pâte à choux and it has a golden brown color.

MAKES 3¼ POUNDS/1.6 KILOGRAMS

Cookies are prepared in many different ways: piped, scooped, sliced, and molded, to name just a few. They are often served at receptions, as part of a dessert buffet, or with ice cream or sorbet. An assortment of cookies might be presented at the end of a meal, as an appealing extra.

Cookies contain a high percentage of sugar, so the oven temperature must be carefully regulated during baking. Convection ovens, which produce evenly baked items, are especially good for baking many kinds of cookies. Cookie doughs and batters can be prepared using different mixing methods. Some must be shaped and baked as soon as the batter or dough is prepared. Others need to be chilled before they are shaped. Prepare the dough or batter as directed in the recipe and assemble the tools needed to shape and bake the cookies.

Scooped and dropped cookies are shaped and baked as soon as the dough is mixed, so prepare baking sheets by lining them with parchment before mixing the dough. Use scoops or spoons to portion the dough uniformly, or they may be rolled into a log and sliced as for ice box cookies. Dropped cookies typically spread as they bake, so allow enough room for them to expand without touching each other. Arrange the cookies in even rows for even baking. Bake dropped cookies at 325° to 350°F/165° to 175°C until the bottoms are golden brown and the cookies are baked through but still moist. Cool on racks and store in tightly wrapped containers at room temperature, or freeze for longer storage.

TOP LEFT *Scoops are used to produce a consistent size for drop cookies.*

TOP RIGHT *Stiff doughs such as this one may be molded into a log by rolling on a floured work surface and scaled by slicing into portions.*

BOTTOM LEFT *Before baking, cookies are tight, compact mounds no matter which scaling method is used.*

BOTTOM RIGHT *Cookies will spread as they bake.*

Rolled and cut cookies are made from stiff doughs that are often allowed to chill briefly. While the dough chills, line sheet pans with parchment. Roll out the dough on a lightly floured work surface, using the same technique as described for rolling pie dough. Lightly dust the rolling pin as you work. For some cookies, the work surface and rolling pin can be dusted with powdered sugar. Very rich and delicate cookie batters can be rolled out between two sheets of parchment. When you have finished rolling, the dough should be even and generally no more than ⅛ to ⅙ in/2 to 4 mm thick. Be sure that the dough is not sticking to the work surface as you roll it out. Cutters of various shapes and sizes can be used, or the dough can be cut into shape with a knife. As you work, dip the cutter or knife blade into a small amount of flour or powdered sugar to keep it from sticking to the dough. Transfer the cookies to the baking sheet and bake in 350°F/175°C oven until the edges of the cookies just start to turn golden. Immediately transfer them to a cooling rack to prevent overcooking them. Store these cookies well wrapped or in airtight containers at room temperature. Shaped cookies are often glazed or iced. These coatings should be applied after the cookie is completely cooled. If the cookies are to be frozen for longer storage, freeze them plain and decorate or ice them after they have thawed.

Baked cookies must be wrapped tightly to maintain freshness.

Molded and sliced cookies, or *icebox cookies,* are made from a relatively stiff dough that is prepared and then shaped into a log. The log can then be pressed into ovals or squares. These logs are wrapped in parchment or plastic wrap and chilled until firm, at least 3 hours and up to 3 days. They may be frozen for longer storage; thaw frozen unbaked logs of dough under refrigeration. When you are ready to bake them, prepare sheet pans by greasing or lining them with parchment. Unwrap the log and slice it evenly to make cookies of the desired size. Arrange the cookies in neat rows, allowing enough space for the cookies to spread as they bake. Some recipes will spread a great deal, others will not. Once baked, the cookies should be cooled on racks and then properly stored in airtight containers or frozen for longer storage.

Biscotti or twice-baked cookies are a type of molded and sliced cookie. They are shaped into a half moon–shaped log directly on lined baking sheets and then baked. Once baked, the biscotti are sliced to make individual cookies. They are returned to the oven on parchment-lined sheet pans to lightly toast and dry.

TOP LEFT *Shaping the biscotti into a log before baking.*

LEFT *Using a serrated knife to slice the baked log.*

ABOVE *Finished biscotti, after toasting and drying during the second stage of baking.*

Piped cookies are shaped as soon as the dough is completed, so you should assemble all your equipment before starting to mix the batter. Pastry bags and tips should be assembled and the sheet pans should be greased or lined with parchment. When the dough is properly mixed, transfer it to the

The stencil used here is left in place as the tuiles bake and is removed once the cookies are done.

RIGHT *Drape the cookies on top of overturned glasses or similar molds to create cups.*

pastry bag with a rubber spatula and twist the top of the bag to express any air pockets. Squeeze the pastry bag to form a cookie and release the pressure on the bag once it is the desired size. Arrange the cookies in neat, even rows and leave some room for the cookies to spread as they bake.

Stenciled cookies are made from a very soft batter. The batter can be prepared and held while assembling the tools for shaping and baking. Stencils can be purchased or cut from sturdy cardboard. Line sheet pans with silicone baking mats, or use an inverted sheet pan that has been greased, floured, and then frozen. Freezing the pan helps the grease and flour to stick to the pan rather than coming off onto the cookie as it is stenciled. Lay the stencil on the prepared sheet pan and drop a spoonful of batter into the stencil. Spread it into an even layer with a small offset spatula or the back of a spoon. Remove the stencil and repeat until the sheet is filled. These cookies do not spread, but be sure to allow enough room so that the stencil will not disturb any already shaped cookies. Bake carefully, keeping a close eye on the cookies. Stenciled cookies should be removed from the baking pan immediately. They can be molded by draping them over glasses or rolling pins to create cups or the classic tuile shape.

RECIPES

SHORTBREAD FOR COOKIES OR CRUST

makes 14 pounds/6.35 kilograms

9 lb/2.7 kg all-purpose flour
$1/_2$ oz/15 g baking powder
$1/_2$ oz/15 g salt
4 lb/1.8 kg butter
$2^1/_2$ lb/1.15 kg sugar
$17^1/_2$ oz/500 g eggs
vanilla extract, to taste

1 Sift together the flour, baking powder, and salt and set aside.

2 Cream together the butter and sugar in an electric mixer, using the paddle attachment on medium speed, until light and smooth.

3 Combine the eggs and vanilla and add slowly to the butter-sugar mixture, fully incorporating and scraping down the sides of the bowl after each addition.

4 Add the sifted dry ingredients, mixing just to incorporate and scraping down the sides of the bowl as necessary.

5 Turn the dough out onto a lightly floured work surface and press into a flat disk. Wrap the dough tightly and refrigerate until firm enough to roll out. The dough may be held under refrigeration for up to 2 days or frozen for up to 3 weeks.

6 To prepare cookies, roll the dough to an even thickness, about $1/_8$ to $1/_4$ inch/3 to 6 mm thick and cut to the desired shape. Bake cookies at 350°F/175°C for 10 to 12 minutes, or until cooked through and the edges are a light golden. Cool on a rack before serving or storing in an airtight container.

7 To use dough for a crust, roll out as directed for pie dough on page 934.

APPLE PIE

makes one 10-inch/25-centimeter double-crusted pie

$1^1/_4$ lb/570 g PIE CRUST (page 937)
$2^1/_4$ oz/70 g granulated sugar
$1^1/_2$ oz/45 g brown sugar
$1/_2$ oz/15 g tapioca
$1/_2$ oz/15 g cornstarch
$1/_2$ tsp/3 mL ground cinnamon
$1/_4$ tsp/1 mL ground nutmeg
1 lb 8 oz/680 g sliced Granny Smith apples
1 lb 8 oz/680 g sliced Golden Delicious apples
$3/_4$ fl oz/20 mL lemon juice
$1/_2$ oz/15 g butter

PIE SHINE
1 oz/30 g corn syrup (light)
1 oz/30 g SIMPLE SYRUP (page 873)

1 Divide the dough into 2 pieces. Roll out the bottom crust and line a 10-in/25-cm pie pan. Trim away any excess if necessary.

2 Combine the granulated sugar, brown sugar, tapioca, cornstarch, cinnamon, and nutmeg. Add the sliced apples and toss until the slices are evenly coated. Sprinkle the lemon juice over the apples and toss briefly. Pile the apples in the pie plate, mounding them higher in the center than on the sides. Dot the apples with the butter.

3 Roll out the top crust and cut a vent in the crust. Transfer to the filled pie. Seal the top and bottom crusts by crimping them together.

4 Bake at 425°F/220°C for 15 minutes. Reduce the heat to 350°F/175°C and continue baking until the crust is browned and baked through, the juices in the filling have thickened, and the apples are tender, 30 to 40 minutes.

5 To prepare the pie shine, combine the corn and simple syrups and brush over the top of the pie. Bake in a 525°F/275°C oven until the top is browned, about 2 minutes more. Remove at once and let the pie cool before slicing and serving.

LEMON MERINGUE PIE FILLING

makes 7 pounds 13.5 ounces/3.5 kilograms

2 qt/2 L water

2 lb/900 g sugar

½ oz/15 g salt

10 fl oz/300 mL lemon juice

1 oz/30 g grated lemon zest

6 oz/170 g cornstarch

8 oz/225 g egg yolks

4 oz/115 g butter

1   Combine 1½ qt/1.4 L of the water and 1 lb/450 g of the sugar with the salt, lemon juice, and lemon zest in a saucepan and bring to a boil.

2   Combine the remaining sugar and the cornstarch and fully incorporate.

3   Combine the egg yolks with the remaining water and fully incorporate. Combine the sugar-cornstarch mixture with the egg yolk-water mixture and blend well.

4   When the lemon mixture comes to a boil, temper in the egg yolk mixture.

5   Return the mixture to a boil. Boil for 1 minute, stirring constantly.

6   Stir in the butter. Scale 1 lb 10 oz/735 g into a prebaked 10-in/25-cm pie shell. Refrigerate overnight before topping with meringue.

BLUEBERRY PIE FILLING

makes 9¼ pounds/4.2 kilograms

44 fl oz/1.3 L water

10 oz/255 g sugar

6 oz/170 g cornstarch

5 lb/2.25 kg fresh or frozen blueberries

1   Combine 1 qt/1 L of the water with 8 oz/225 g of the sugar in a saucepan and bring to a boil.

2   Combine the cornstarch with the remaining sugar and whisk to combine. Add the remaining water and blend.

3   Temper the cornstarch mixture into the hot sugar-water.

4   Return the mixture to a boil and boil for 1 minute.

5   Add the blueberries and mix to combine. Remove the filling from the heat and cool before filling pie shells. The filling may also be stored under refrigeration for later use.

PECAN PIE FILLING

makes 15 pounds 13 ounces/7 kilograms

2¼ lb/1 kg pecans

6 oz/170 g sugar

6 oz/170 g bread flour

9 lb/4 kg corn syrup

3 lb/1.3 kg eggs

1½ oz/40 g salt

1½ oz/40 g vanilla extract

10 oz/285 g melted butter

1   Scale out 4 oz/115 g of the pecans for each 9-in/23-cm pie and spread them in an even layer in the bottom of each unbaked pie crust.

2   Place the sugar and flour in a large stainless-steel bowl and whisk to combine. Add the corn syrup and blend.

3   Add the eggs, salt, and vanilla and stir until fully combined.

4   Blend in the melted butter.

5   Scale 1 lb 12 oz/800 g of mixture into each prepared pie shell.

6   Bake in a 400°F/205°C oven until the filling has set and the crust is a golden brown, about 40 minutes.

7   Let cool completely before serving.

CHERRY PIE FILLING

makes 13 pounds 5 ounces/6 kilograms, enough to fill four 10-inch/ 25-centimeter pies

40 fl oz/1.25 L water

1 qt/1 L cherry juice

1½ lb/680 g sugar

6 oz/170 g cornstarch

2 oz/60 g clear gel

10 lb/4.5 kg thawed and drained frozen cherries

1   Combine 1 qt/1 L of the water with the cherry juice and the sugar in a saucepan and bring to a boil.

2   Combine the cornstarch and clear gel and whisk to combine. Blend in the remaining water.

3   Temper the cornstarch mixture into the hot cherry juice mixture.

4   Return the mixture to a boil and boil for 1 minute.

5   Add cherries and mix to combine. Remove the filling from the heat and cool before filling pie shells. The filling may also be stored under refrigeration for later use.

INDIVIDUAL FRUIT TARTLETS

makes ten 4-inch/10-centimeter tartlets

1¼ lb/570 g PUFF PASTRY (page 942)

1½ lb/680 g sliced POACHED PEARS (recipe follows)

3½ oz/100 g cookie crumbs

2 tbsp/30 mL cinnamon sugar

3 oz/85 g melted and strained apricot jam

2 oz/60 g toasted sliced almonds

1. Roll the dough out ⅛ in/30 mm thick. Line 10 greased 4-in/10-cm tartlet molds and trim the edges.

2. Sprinkle the cookie crumbs on top of the dough.

3. Arrange the poached fruit in the tartlets and sprinkle with the cinnamon sugar.

4. Bake in a 350°F/175°C oven until the crust is golden brown, about 30 minutes.

5. Cool the tartlets slightly, brush with the apricot jam, and garnish with the sliced almonds.

POACHED PEARS

makes 10 portions

10 medium pears (about 5 oz/140 g each)

SIMPLE SYRUP (page 873), as needed

1. Peel the pears and remove the cores. Pears may be left whole with the stem intact, or halved, as preferred.

2. Place the pears in a sauce pot and add enough simple syrup to completely submerge them. Bring to a bare simmer over low heat (170°F/75°C) and simmer until the pears are very tender. Let cool in the poaching liquid, drain, and serve as desired.

Port-Poached Pears Replace half of the simple syrup with ruby port wine. If desired, add a sachet containing 1 whole clove, 2 to 3 slices of fresh ginger, and a small piece of cinnamon.

LINZERTORTE

makes four 10-inch/25-centimeter tortes

1 lb 14 oz/850 g all-purpose or cake flour

½ oz/15 g ground cinnamon

½ oz/15 g baking powder

4 oz/115 g fine cake crumbs

1½ lb/680 g butter

1 lb 2 oz/510 g sugar

4½ oz/125 g eggs

½ tsp/2 mL vanilla extract

12 oz/340 g ground toasted hazelnuts

2½ lb/1.15 g raspberry jam

20 oz/570 g fresh or frozen raspberries

12 oz/340 g melted and strained apricot jam

sliced, toasted almonds, as needed

1. Sift together the flour, cinnamon, baking powder, and cake crumbs and set aside.

2. Cream together the butter and sugar in an electric mixer using the paddle attachment on medium speed until light and smooth.

3. Combine the eggs and vanilla. Add the egg mixture slowly to the creamed mixture on low speed, fully incorporating it and scraping down the sides of the bowl after each addition.

4. Add the sifted dry ingredients and blend until just combined. Blend in the hazelnuts.

5. Wrap the dough in plastic wrap and refrigerate until firm enough to work with, about 30 minutes.

6. Roll out the dough to ¼ in/6 mm on a lightly floured work surface and cut into four 10-in/25-cm-diameter circles.

7. Line the bottoms of four 10-in/25-cm tart or cake pans with parchment and then the linzer dough circle.

8. Blend together the raspberry jam and the fresh or frozen raspberries. Evenly divide the mixture among the dough-lined pans. Spread the raspberry mixture in an even layer, starting from the center and working out to ½ in/12 mm from the edge of the pan.

9. Roll out the remaining dough to ⅛ in/4 mm on a lightly floured work surface and cut into strips ½ in/12 mm wide. Use the strips to form a lattice top on each of the tarts.

10. Bake at 350°F/175°C until light golden brown, 40 minutes.

11. Allow the tarts to cool completely in their pans. Remove the tarts from the pans, brush the top and sides with warm apricot jam, and press the sliced, toasted almonds to the side and upper edge.

see photograph on page 955

ALMOND ANISE BISCOTTI

makes 32 biscotti

10 oz/285 g all-purpose or bread flour

1 tsp/5 mL baking soda

3 eggs

6½ oz/180 g sugar

¼ tsp/1 mL salt

1 tsp/5 mL anise extract

7 oz/200 g whole almonds

2 tbsp/30 mL anise seeds

1 Place the flour and baking soda in a stainless-steel bowl and whisk to combine.

2 Whip the eggs, sugar, salt, and anise extract in an electric mixer using the whip attachment on high speed, until light and thick.

3 Blend in the flour mixture on low speed, mixing until just incorporated.

4 Add the almonds and anise seeds and blend until fully combined, scraping down the sides of the bowl as necessary.

5 Spread the dough in a strip 4 × 16 in/10 × 40 cm on a parchment-lined sheet pan.

6 Bake in a 300°F/150°C oven until light golden brown, about 1 hour.

7 Remove the pan from the oven and let cool for 5 to 10 minutes. Lower the oven temperature to 275°F/135°C.

8 Using a serrated knife cut the strip crosswise into ⅛-in/4-mm slices.

9 Place the sliced cookies back on the parchment-lined sheet pan and bake, turning over halfway through the baking time, until golden brown and crisp, 20 to 25 minutes.

10 Cool the cookies on a wire rack and store in an airtight container for up to two weeks.

Orange Biscotti Replace the anise extract with 1 tsp/5 mL vanilla extract and ¼ tsp/1 mL almond extract; replace the whole almonds with slivered almonds; and replace the anise seeds with 3 tbsp/45 mL grated orange zest and 3 oz/85 g finely chopped candied orange peel.

LEMON COOKIES

makes 5 dozen cookies

12½ oz/355 g butter

10½ oz/300 g confectioners' sugar

12 oz/340 g egg yolks

2 tbsp/30 mL grated lemon zest

1 lb ½ oz/470 g all-purpose or pastry flour, sifted

1 Place the butter and sugar in an electric mixer. Using the paddle attachment on medium speed, cream together until light and smooth.

2 Add the egg yolks slowly on low speed, fully incorporating and scraping down the sides of the bowl after each addition. Blend in the lemon zest.

3 Add the flour, mixing just to incorporate and scraping down the sides of the bowl as necessary.

4 Using a plain tip, pipe out cookies from a pastry bag onto parchment-lined sheet pans.

5 Bake in a 400°F/205°C oven until lightly browned, 8 to 10 minutes.

6 Let the cookies cool slightly on the pan. Remove from the pan and let cool completely on a wire rack.

7 Cookies may be stored in an airtight container for up to two weeks.

LADYFINGERS

makes 1½ pounds/680 grams

6 egg yolks

6½ oz/185 g sugar

6 egg whites

6 oz/170 g all-purpose or cake flour, sifted

1 Combine the egg yolks and 2 oz/60 g of the sugar in an electric mixer. Using the whip attachment on high speed, beat together until stiff and thick, 8 to 10 minutes.

2 In another mixer bowl, combine the egg whites and the remaining sugar. Using the whip attachment on high speed, beat to medium peaks.

3 Fold one third of the meringue mixture into the yolk mixture.

4 Fold the remaining meringue into the yolk mixture until incorporated.

5 Gradually fold in the flour.

6 Using a plain tip, pipe the batter onto parchment-lined sheet pans to the desired length.

7 Bake in a 400°F/205°C oven until golden brown, 15 minutes.

8 Allow the cookies to cool completely on the pans on wire racks.

9 Cookies may be stored in an airtight container for up to one week.

Chocolate Ladyfingers Substitute 2 oz/60 g of cocoa powder for 2 oz/60 g of the cake flour.

FLORENTINES

makes thirty-seven 1-ounce/30-gram cookies

7 oz/200 g butter
4 oz/115 g sugar
5 oz/140 g honey
5 oz/140 g milk
4 oz/115 g slivered almonds
4 oz/115 g sliced almonds
8 oz/225 g small diced candied fruit
19 whole glazed cherries, halved
tempered chocolate, as needed

1 Combine the butter, sugar, honey, and milk in a saucepan and cook to 245°F/119°C.

2 Add the almonds and candied fruit and fully combine.

3 Using a small round scoop, about 3 in/7.5 cm in diameter, portion into bun pans. Place a glazed cherry half in the center of each.

4 Bake in a 360°F/180°C oven until light golden brown, 12 to 15 minutes.

5 Let cool completely.

6 Spread some of the tempered chocolate on the bottom of each cookie and mark with a cake comb in a wave pattern.

7 Cookies may be stored in an airtight container for up to two weeks.

NOTES

If baked on a flat sheet pan, push the mixture back in shape with a 3-in/7.5-cm ring halfway through the baking.

Nutcrackers Use 8 oz/225 g toasted hazelnuts instead of almonds.

HERMIT COOKIES

makes 7½ dozen cookies

2½ lb/1.15 kg all-purpose or cake flour
¾ oz/20 g baking soda
¼ oz/8 g ground allspice
¼ oz/8 g ground cinnamon
⅜ oz/12 g salt
4 oz/115 g butter
8 oz/225 g shortening
1½ lb/680 g sugar
6 oz/170 g molasses
6 oz/170 g eggs
5 oz/140 g water
1 lb/450 g raisins

1 Sift together the flour, baking soda, allspice, cinnamon, and salt and set aside.

2 Place the butter, shortening, sugar, and molasses in an electric mixer. Using the paddle attachment on medium speed, cream together until light and smooth.

3 Add the eggs slowly on low speed, fully incorporating and scraping down the sides of the bowl after each addition.

4 Add the water, alternating with the dry ingredients, in 3 additions, scraping down the sides of the bowl as necessary. Blend in the raisins.

5 Scale into 12-oz/340-g portions and roll each into a log 1½ in/3.8 cm in diameter. Cut each roll into eight 1½-oz/40-g pieces and place them on parchment-lined sheet pans.

6 Bake in a 360°F/180°C oven until golden brown, 18 to 20 minutes.

7 After baking, transfer the cookies from the pans to wire racks and allow them to cool completely.

8 Cookies may be stored in an airtight container for up to two weeks.

Chocolate Chunk Cookies

Fudge Brownies

Almond Macaroons

Linzertorte

Toffee Chip Brazil Nut Cookies

Mudd Slide Cookies

HAZELNUT FLORENTINES

makes 29 1/2 ounces/840 grams

7 oz/200 g heavy cream

8 oz/225 g sugar

2 oz/60 g butter

12 oz/340 g ground toasted hazelnuts

1/2 oz/15 g all-purpose or cake flour

1 Combine the cream, sugar, and butter in a saucepan and bring to a boil.

2 Add 5 oz/140 g of the hazelnuts and the flour, and bring back to a boil.

3 Add the remaining hazelnuts, and remove from the heat.

4 Spread out on parchment paper in thin 10-in/25-cm circles.

5 Bake in a 350°F/175°C oven.

6 Allow the florentines to cool slightly before cutting into 16 equal wedges each.

7 Cookies may be stored in an airtight container for up to two weeks.

FUDGE BROWNIES

makes sixty 2-inch/5-centimeter square brownies

1 1/2 lb/680 g bittersweet chocolate

2 1/4 lb/1 kg butter

1 lb 14 oz/850 g eggs

4 1/2 lb/2 kg sugar

1 oz/30 g vanilla extract

1/2 oz/15 g salt

1 1/2 lb/680 g all-purpose flour, sifted

GANACHE (page 992) for glaze, warmed

1 Melt the chocolate and butter together carefully over a warm-water bath and stir to combine.

2 Combine the eggs, sugar, vanilla, and salt in an electric mixer. Using the whip attachment, beat on high speed until thick and light.

3 Temper the chocolate-butter mixture into the egg mixture.

4 Gently fold in the flour.

5 Pour the batter into a parchment-lined sheet pan and sprinkle the remaining nuts on top.

6 Bake in a 350°F/175°C oven until firm to the touch, 30 minutes.

7 Allow the brownies to cool completely in the pan on a wire rack. Pour warmed ganache over them for a glaze.

8 Slice the brownies into 2-in/5-cm square portions.

9 Brownies may be stored in an airtight container for up to 3 days.

see photograph on page 954

ALMOND MACAROONS

makes 19 cookies (2 ounces/60 grams each)

1 lb/450 g sugar

1 lb/450 g almond paste

7 oz/200 g egg whites

1 tsp/5 mL vanilla extract

1 drop almond extract

19 blanched almond halves

granulated sugar, as needed

1 Blend together the sugar and almond paste in an electric mixer, using the paddle attachment on medium speed, until fully combined.

2 Gradually add the egg whites to the mixture on medium speed, fully blending and scraping down the bowl after each addition, until the mixture forms a stiff batter. Blend in the vanilla extract and almond extract.

3 Pipe, using a plain tip, into 2-oz/60-g rounds onto a parchment-lined sheet pan and place a blanched almond half in the center of each cookie.

4 Sprinkle the tops of the piped cookies with granulated sugar and bake in a 350°F/175°C convection oven, rotating the tray halfway through baking. Bake until light golden brown. Remove the cookies from the tray and allow to cool completely on a wire rack. Cookies may be stored for up to 1 week.

see photograph on page 954

MUDD SLIDE COOKIES

makes 12 dozen cookies (2½ ounces/75 grams per cookie)

2 lb/900 g unsweetened chocolate

6 lb/2.75 kg bittersweet chocolate

1 lb/450 g butter

32 eggs

6 lb/2.75 kg sugar

1 oz/30 g coffee extract

1 oz/30 g vanilla extract

1 lb/450 g cake flour

1½ oz/40 g baking powder

½ oz/15 g salt

1 lb 5 oz/600 g walnuts

4 lb 8 oz/2 kg chocolate chips

1   Finely chop the unsweetened and bittersweet chocolates and melt together with the butter in a stainless-steel bowl set over a pan of barely simmering water. Remove from the heat and set aside.

2   Beat together the eggs, sugar, coffee extract, and vanilla extract in a mixer, using the wire whip attachment, on high speed for 5 minutes or until thick in texture and light in color. Add the chocolate mixture all at once to the egg mixture and blend together. Scrape down the bowl as necessary.

3   Sift together the flour, baking powder, and salt and blend into the mixture, scraping down the bowl as necessary. Add the walnuts and chocolate chips and mix just until blended.

4   Portion into 2-lb/900-g logs, wrap in parchment paper, and store in the freezer or under refrigeration until needed.

5   Cut logs into 2½-oz/75-g pieces and place on parchment-lined sheet pans.

6   Bake in a 350°F/175°C oven for 14 minutes, or until golden brown. Remove the cookies from the tray and allow to cool completely on a wire rack. Cookies may be stored for up to 1 week.

see photograph on page 955

TOFFEE CHIP BRAZIL NUT COOKIES

makes 12 dozen cookies (2½ ounces/75 grams each)

3 lb 8 oz/1.6 kg butter, softened

2 lb 4 oz/1 kg sugar

1 lb 10 oz/735 g light brown sugar

1¾ oz/50 g salt

1 lb/450 g eggs

1¼ oz/37 g vanilla extract

5 lb 4 oz/2.3 kg pastry flour

1 oz/30 g baking soda

2 lb/900 g toffee chips or chunks

1 lb 12 oz/800 g Brazil nuts, coarsely chopped

1   Cream together the butter, sugars, and salt in a mixer on medium speed, using the paddle attachment.

2   Gradually blend in the eggs, fully incorporating and scraping down the bowl after each addition. Blend in the vanilla.

3   Sift together the flour and baking soda.

4   Blend the sifted dry ingredients into the creamed mixture on medium speed just until combined.

5   Blend in the toffee chips and Brazil nuts.

6   Portion into 2 lb/900 g logs, wrap in parchment paper, and store in the freezer or under refrigeration until needed.

7   Cut logs into 2½-oz/75-g pieces and place on parchment-lined sheet pans.

8   Bake in a 350°F/175°C oven for 14 minutes, or until golden brown.

9   Remove the cookies from the tray and allow them to cool completely on a wire rack. Cookies may be stored in an airtight container for up to 1 week.

see photograph on page 955

CHOCOLATE CHUNK COOKIES

makes 4 dozen 2½-ounce/75-gram cookies

1 lb 12 oz/800 g all-purpose flour

½ oz/15 g baking soda

¼ oz/7 g salt

1 lb/450 g butter

1 lb 2 oz/510 g granulated sugar

12 oz /340 g light brown sugar

12 oz/340 g eggs

¾ fl oz/20 mL vanilla extract

2 lb/900 g chocolate chunks

6 oz/170 g chopped pecans

1 Sift together the flour, baking soda, and salt and set aside.

2 Place the butter, granulated sugar, and brown sugar in an electric mixer. Using the paddle attachment on medium speed, cream together until light and smooth.

3 Add the eggs slowly, fully incorporating and scraping down the sides of the bowl after each addition. Add the vanilla.

4 Add the dry ingredients and blend just to combine, scraping down the sides of the bowl as necessary. Blend in the chocolate chunks and nuts.

5 Scale into 2½-oz/75-g portions and drop onto parchment-lined sheet pans.

6 Bake in a 350°F/175°C oven until the edges of the cookies are lightly browned, 8 to 10 minutes.

7 Remove the pans from the oven and allow the cookies to cool slightly on the pans. Transfer the cookies from the pans to wire racks and allow them to cool completely.

8 Cookies may be stored in an airtight container for up to two weeks.

see photograph on page 954

OATMEAL RAISIN COOKIES

makes forty-six 1-ounce/30-gram cookies

13½ oz/365 g all-purpose flour

1 tsp/5 mL baking soda

½ tsp/2 mL baking powder

1 tsp/5 mL salt

⅛ tsp/.5 mL ground cloves

¼ tsp/1 mL ground cinnamon

¼ tsp/1 mL ground allspice

8 oz/225 g butter

12 oz/340 g light brown sugar

2 oz/60 g granulated sugar

3 eggs

8 oz/225 g rolled oats

4 oz/115 g raisins

1 Sift together the flour, baking soda, baking powder, salt, ground cloves, cinnamon, and allspice and set aside.

2 Cream together the butter, brown sugar, and granulated sugar in an electric mixer, using the paddle attachment on medium speed, until light and smooth.

3 Add the eggs slowly on low speed, fully incorporating and scraping down the sides of the bowl after each addition.

4 Blend in the sifted dry ingredients, mixing just to incorporate. Blend in the rolled oats and raisins.

5 Divide the dough in half. Roll each half into a log 23 in/ 60 cm long. Wrap the logs and refrigerate until firm. Slice each log into 1-in/25-mm pieces and place them on parchment-lined sheet pans. Or, after the batter is mixed, scoop the dough directly onto the pans, using a stainless-steel 1-oz/30-g scoop.

6 Bake in a 350°F/175°C oven until the cookies are golden brown, 15 to 18 minutes. Remove the cookies from the pans and cool on a wire rack. Store in an airtight container for up to 2 weeks.

The difference between a plain baked item and a fancy pastry often relies on the presence of an icing or filling, a sauce, or a glaze. The ability to prepare a number of basic sauces and creams makes it possible to give basic cakes a great deal of variety without a great deal of effort.

ICINGS, DESSERT SAUCES, AND CREAMS

BUTTERCREAM

Buttercreams are made by blending softened butter into an egg-and-sugar base. Italian buttercream, pictured here, is made by combining beaten egg whites with a hot sugar syrup, then whipping in butter.

Buttercreams make elegant cakes and tortes. The manner in which the eggs and sugar are combined, as well as whether whole eggs, egg yolks, or egg whites are used, produces a variety of icings. There are other icing options beyond buttercream, such as whipped or chantilly cream, cream cheese icing, and others. Consult specific recipes for further information and suggestions. Icings can be used to fill cakes and pastries in addition to coating them. Another type of icing, referred to as a glaze, can also be applied to cakes and pastries. Glazes are explained in greater detail on page 982.

MEASURE AND ASSEMBLE all the ingredients for the buttercream. Hold eggs under refrigeration to keep them safe. Separate eggs if necessary (see Separating Eggs, page 867).

Buttercreams typically call for granulated sugar. Sift the sugar if necessary to work out any lumps.

The butter should be cut or broken into small pieces and softened before it is added to the buttercream. Unsalted butter is typically preferred for its subtle, creamy taste.

Flavorings such as extracts, cordials, liqueurs, chocolate, or fruit purées should be prepared in advance and kept at the appropriate temperature.

An electric mixer with a whip attachment will be needed to mix the buttercream. Use an instant-read or candy thermometer to check the temperature of the egg mixture as it is heated. Have a plastic or rubber scraper at hand, as well as storage and service items as necessary.

MAKE THE BUTTERCREAM

1. Prepare the base for the buttercream. Different styles of buttercream have different bases. A common meringue is used to prepare Swiss buttercream (egg whites are whipped with sugar until firm peaks form). German buttercream is made from a room-temperature pastry cream base beaten until smooth and light. French buttercream's base is prepared by heating yolks and sugar to 145°F/63°C over simmering water and then whipping until a thick foam forms and the mixture cools to room temperature.

An Italian buttercream requires an Italian meringue as its base. To prepare the meringue, combine the sugar and water in a saucepan and bring to a boil. Continue to boil the sugar syrup until the temperature reaches 250°F/121°C without stirring. Use a wet pastry brush to wipe down the sides of the pan to dissolve any sugar crystals that splashed onto the sides.

If the crystals remain, they will act as seeds and cause the syrup to crystallize. Use a candy thermometer to check the temperature of the syrup. This stage is also known as the soft-ball stage. When the syrup reaches the correct temperature, it should be immediately added to the egg whites.

ABOVE *Use as little water as possible when washing down the sides.*

2. Combine the syrup and the egg whites.

As the sugar syrup cooks, whip the egg whites on medium speed. The ideal is to have the egg whites reach soft peaks at the same time that the syrup reaches 250°F/121°C. With the machine still running, gradually pour the hot sugar syrup in a thin stream into the whites. Continue to beat the mixture until a firm meringue is formed and the mixture has cooled to room temperature. If the meringue is too hot, it will melt the butter as it is added. Check the temperature by feeling the side of the bowl. It should be cool to the touch.

3. Gradually add softened butter to the base and beat the mixture until a smooth, light buttercream is formed.

Have the butter in small bits at room temperature so that it can be beaten into the meringue easily. As the butter is incorporated, the buttercream thickens. Once smooth and light, the buttercream is ready to apply to a prepared cake, or it may be stored under refrigeration for later use. Buttercream takes on other flavors and odors readily and must, therefore, be tightly wrapped before storing. Allow chilled buttercream to return to room temperature and beat it using the paddle attachment until very smooth and light before using it to fill or frost a cake.

4. Evaluate the quality of the buttercream.

Buttercreams should be perfectly smooth and soft enough to spread easily and have a good flavor. They should be sweet, but not overly sweet, and should taste primarily of sweet butter. There should be no detectable grains or pieces of sugar or any lumps of butter.

ABOVE *Add the syrup so that it pours down the side of the bowl rather than onto the whip, to prevent splattering.*

ABOVE *As the butter is whipped into the meringue, the buttercream thickens and becomes very smooth and glossy.*

ABOVE *Buttercream may be held covered under refrigeration for up to 7 days, or frozen for 2 to 3 months.*

1 lb 6 oz / 625 g sugar

7 oz / 200 g water

1 lb / 450 g egg whites

4 lb / 1.8 kg butter, diced, at room temperature

ITALIAN BUTTERCREAM

1 Combine 12 oz/340 g of the sugar with the water in a heavy saucepan. Cook over medium high heat to 250°F/121°C (soft ball stage) while occasionally brushing down the sides of the pan with a wet pastry brush to dissolve any sugar crystals forming on the side of the pan. Pour immediately into a clean measuring cup or pitcher with a pouring spout.

2 While the sugar is cooking, place the egg whites in a mixing bowl and beat using the whip attachment, until foamy. Gradually add the remaining sugar and continue to whip until medium stiff peaks form.

3 With the mixer running, add the hot syrup to the meringue in a slow steady stream.

4 Continue to whip until mixture has cooled to room temperature, 5 to 10 minutes.

5 Add the butter a few pieces at a time, until smooth and spreadable. The buttercream is ready to use now, or it may be held covered under refrigeration for up to 7 days, or frozen for 2 to 3 months.

MAKES 6½ POUNDS/3 KILOGRAMS (RECIPE CAN BE HALVED IF DESIRED)

NOTE

Thaw frozen buttercream in the refrigerator for several hours before using. Refrigerated or thawed buttercream should be beaten by hand or with the paddle attachment until smooth and spreadable.

VANILLA SAUCE

Vanilla sauce, sometimes known as custard sauce or sauce anglaise, is the basis for a number of sauces, fillings, creams, and frozen desserts.

Vanilla sauce is made by blending eggs, milk or cream, and sugar. When these ingredients are stirred together over low heat until the mixture begins to thicken, the result is a smooth, pourable sauce. Those same ingredients, combined and then baked in a hot-water bath, produce a custard.

If a thickener such as flour or cornstarch is added to the sauce, vanilla sauce becomes a pastry cream. Add some whipped cream and gelatin to stabilize the mixture, and you have a Bavarian cream. A frozen Bavarian cream is better known as a frozen soufflé or parfait. And, if you cool and then churn the sauce as it freezes, it becomes ice cream.

This delicate sauce requires careful handling to prevent curdling. Once it is cooked, it has to be cooled as quickly as possible to below 40°F/4°C and held under refrigeration to prevent food contamination or food-borne illness.

SELECT AND PREPARE THE INGREDIENTS AND EQUIPMENT

DIFFERENCES DO EXIST among vanilla sauce formulas. Some recipes may include whole milk, while others call for heavy cream, light cream, or a combination of cream and milk. Some recipes use only egg yolks; others use whole eggs or a blend of whole eggs and egg yolks. Some recipes call for a vanilla bean to flavor the sauce; others rely upon vanilla extract.

It is especially important to have all the necessary equipment assembled before beginning, including a heavy-bottomed pot or a bain-marie, a fine mesh sieve or conical sieve, and containers to hold the finished sauce during cooling and storing. To cool the sauce rapidly and safely, have an ice bath prepared.

MAKE THE VANILLA SAUCE

1. Combine the milk with half of the sugar (and the vanilla bean, if using) and bring to a simmer.

Heating the milk or cream with the sugar dissolves the sugar for a smoother, silkier finished texture. If a vanilla bean is used to flavor the sauce, add the seeds and the empty pod to the milk, or cream, and sugar as it heats. (If desired, vanilla extract may be used instead of vanilla beans. Add the extract just before the sauce is strained in Step 5.) Heat just to the boiling point. Keep an eye on the milk as it heats since it can easily boil over as it nears the boiling point.

2. Combine the egg yolks or eggs with the remaining sugar in a stainless-steel bowl.

Beating the eggs and sugar together helps prevent the eggs from scrambling when they are combined with the hot milk or cream. Blend the ingredients well, using a whip, for long enough to dissolve the sugar into the eggs.

ABOVE *Split the vanilla bean with the tip of a paring knife and scrape out the seeds.*

ABOVE *Add both the vanilla seeds and the pod to the cream and/or milk as it comes to a simmer.*

ABOVE *Blending some of the sugar into the yolks makes it less likely that the yolks will overcook when the hot milk or cream is blended into them.*

3. Combine the hot milk or cream mixture with the eggs.

To produce a smooth sauce, temper the egg yolks with a portion of the boiling milk mixture. Ladle the hot milk into the egg mixture a little at a time, stirring constantly, until about one-third of the milk or cream mixture has been blended into the eggs.

Return the tempered egg mixture to the pot. Continue to cook the sauce over low heat until it begins to thicken. Stir the sauce constantly to prevent it from overcooking. Do not let the sauce come to a boil, because the egg yolks will coagulate well below the boiling point. The idea is to create a soft gel that will coat the back of a wooden spoon. The temperature of the sauce should not go above 180°F/82°C.

5. Strain the sauce and cool the sauce.

Once the sauce coats the back of a wooden spoon, strain it immediately through a conical sieve into a container. Cool the sauce in an ice-water bath if it is to be held for later storage or served cold, stirring frequently as it cools, and refrigerate it immediately. Placing a piece of plastic wrap on the surface prevents a skin from forming.

6. Evaluate the quality of the finished sauce or custard.

A good vanilla sauce is thick and glossy and coats the back of a wooden spoon. It shows no signs of curdling. This sauce should have a smooth, luxurious mouth feel with a well-balanced flavor, neither too sweet nor too eggy.

ABOVE *Temper the egg mixture with the hot milk or cream.*

TOP *Add the yolks back to the pot and continue to cook, stirring constantly.*

BOTTOM *Strain the sauce into a container set in an ice-water bath to cool this delicate sauce quickly and safely.*

ABOVE *The sauce is thickened and glossy and evenly coats a spoon, all signs of good quality in a vanilla sauce.*

1 pt / 480 mL milk

1 pt / 480 mL heavy cream

1 vanilla bean, split and scraped

8 oz / 240 g sugar

9 oz / 270 g egg yolks

VANILLA SAUCE

1 Heat the milk, cream, vanilla bean pod and seeds, and half the sugar until the mixture reaches the boiling point.

2 Combine the egg yolks and the rest of the sugar and temper the mixture into the hot milk.

3 Stirring constantly, heat slowly to 180°F/82°C.

4 Remove cream immediately from the stove and strain through a conical sieve, directly into a container set in an ice bath.

MAKES 1 QUART/1 LITER

NOTES

Sauce can be made over a water bath for more control of the heat source.

1 tbsp/15 mL of vanilla extract may be substituted for the vanilla bean. Add it just before straining the sauce.

All milk or light cream can be used in place of heavy cream.

PASTRY CREAM

Pastry cream, or crème patisserie, *is a vanilla sauce thickened with a starch. As a basic preparation, it is part of the mise en place for many kitchen desserts.*

Denser than custards and creams, pastry cream is used to fill napoleons, éclairs, and Boston cream pie and to fill certain fruit tarts. It may also be used as a soufflé base.

Eggs, sugar, cornstarch, and milk and/or cream are cooked together into a very thick, smooth mixture. The method outlined here includes cornstarch as a thickener. Other formulas use flour instead of cornstarch.

SELECT AND PREPARE THE INGREDIENTS AND EQUIPMENT

MILK, SUGAR, EGGS, and a starch (usually cornstarch) are cooked together, then flavored and finished with vanilla and butter.

Whole milk produces a good flavor and texture in the finished pastry cream. Carefully measure the milk. Granulated sugar is used to sweeten the pastry. The starch may be cornstarch, arrowroot, or flour. When substituting one starch for another, consult the conversion information on page 241.

A combination of whole eggs and egg yolks is added to give richness, body, and color to the sauce. Observe all safe food handling procedures for eggs. Separate yolks from whites carefully, and reserve the clean whites for use in meringues or other applications.

Pastry cream is generally flavored with vanilla extract, although a vanilla bean and its seeds can be added to the milk as it heats. (See Vanilla Sauce, page 965, for more details on preparing and using a vanilla bean.)

Pastry cream is cooked in a nonreactive saucepan such as stainless steel to avoid discoloring the sauce. Be sure the pan has a heavy, level bottom. Use a whip to incorporate ingredients and a wooden spoon to stir the pastry cream as it cooks. The cream can be poured into a bain-marie or for more rapid cooling, a hotel pan. Prepare an ice bath to hold the bain-marie or hotel pan before beginning to cook the pastry cream.

1. Combine the milk with half of the sugar (and the vanilla bean, if using) and bring to the boiling point.

Bringing the milk and sugar just to a boil dissolves the sugar into the milk and infuses it with vanilla, if the bean and seeds are added at this point. Other flavorings may be added at this point to infuse the milk, if desired. Heating the milk also shortens the simmering time once the eggs and starch are added to the milk. This helps to prevent scorching, a concern with any starch-thickened cream.

2. Blend the remaining sugar and cornstarch and add the eggs. Temper the egg mixture with some of the hot milk.

Stir together the sugar with the starch to disperse it evenly and work out any lumps. Add the eggs and blend until smooth. Combining the eggs with sugar and starch increases the temperature at which the eggs thicken. This helps to prevent them from overcooking as the cream returns to a simmer.

Whisking constantly, pour some of hot milk mixture into the egg mixture to temper it. Return the tempered eggs to the pot and continue to cook, stirring constantly, until it reaches a full boil. The pastry cream will become very thick; when done, the wires of the whisk will leave traces.

ABOVE *The egg mixture is tempered with the hot milk mixture.*

ABOVE *Pastry cream is thicker than vanilla sauce and less prone to scrambling because it contains a starch.*

3. Add the butter and flavorings if not using a vanilla bean.
Remove the pastry cream from the heat. Remove the vanilla bean pod, if using. Transfer the cream to a clean container and cool it quickly over an ice bath.

Some chefs sprinkle sugar on the surface of the cream to prevent the formation of a skin; others dot it with additional butter or place a sheet of plastic wrap or parchment paper directly on the surface. If plastic wrap or parchment is used, be sure to pierce several ventilation holes to allow heat to escape.

Properly cooled pastry cream may be lightened by folding in whipped cream. This variation is called diplomat cream. It is also used as the basis for a German buttercream.

4. Evaluate the quality of the finished pastry cream.
Good-quality pastry cream should be smooth and dense, with a pleasing level of sweetness. The vanilla should enhance the flavors of the eggs, milk, and sugar. Pastry cream has a noticeable texture, but it should not feel gritty or pasty.

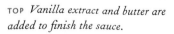

TOP *Vanilla extract and butter are added to finish the sauce.*

BOTTOM *Transfer the pastry cream to a hotel pan and spread into an even layer. Set this pan over a second pan that is filled with ice, to quickly cool the pastry cream.*

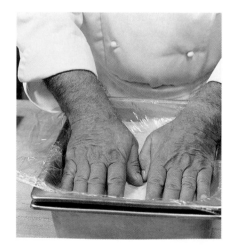

ABOVE *Once the pastry cream has cooled to 40°F/4°C, cover it with a piece of plastic or parchment before refrigerating. Be sure that the plastic is in direct contact with the cream's surface.*

2 lb / 960 g milk

8 oz / 240 g sugar

3 oz / 90 g cornstarch

6 to 8 eggs

1 tbsp / 15 mL vanilla extract

3 oz / 80 g butter

PASTRY CREAM

1 Combine the milk with half the sugar in a saucepan and bring to a boil.

2 Combine the remaining sugar with the cornstarch, add the eggs, and mix until smooth.

3 Temper the egg mixture into the hot milk and bring to a full boil, stirring constantly.

4 Remove from the heat and stir in the vanilla and butter. Transfer to a clean container, place a piece of plastic wrap directly on the pastry cream, and let cool.

5 The pastry cream is ready to use now, or it may be thoroughly cooled and stored for later use.

MAKES 1 QUART/1 LITER

BAVARIAN CREAM

Bavarian creams are incredibly versatile. They lend themselves to a wide range of flavors, and they may be used on their own or as a filling for pastries, tortes, pies, and cakes.

These delicate creams are made by stabilizing a vanilla sauce with gelatin and then lightening the mixture with whipped cream and beaten egg whites. Among possible flavorings are fruits (raspberries, bananas, and mangoes, to name a small sampling), chocolate, nuts, and many liqueurs, such as Grand Marnier or Kahlúa.

TO MAKE A BAVARIAN CREAM, YOU WILL NEED:	*gelatin*	*flavorings*	*heavy cream, whipped*
	water	*Vanilla Sauce (page 967)*	

SELECT AND PREPARE THE INGREDIENTS

HAVE EVERYTHING READY before you start. Measure all the ingredients and assemble the mise en place. The gelatin should be bloomed in the water or in a flavoring, and the heavy cream should be whipped to a very soft peak and reserved in the refrigerator.

1. Combine the vanilla sauce with bloomed gelatin and any flavoring ingredients.

Bloom the gelatin in water or in the flavoring that is going to be used for the Bavarian cream. Prepare the vanilla sauce. Warm the cold sauce to room temperature before adding gelatin.

2. Cool the base to 75°F/24°C over an ice bath.

Place the base over ice and let it cool, stirring constantly until it starts to gel. The mixture may mound very slightly when dropped back onto the surface of the Bavarian from a whisk or spoon.

3. Fold in the whipped cream gently but thoroughly. The Bavarian is ready to mold and chill (or freeze) for later service.

Once the cream is folded in, Bavarians can be molded and chilled or frozen as parfaits or frozen soufflés. They are often used as a filling for cakes and tortes.

Allow several hours for the gelatin in the Bavarian to set up.

4. Evaluate the quality of the finished Bavarian cream.

A well-made Bavarian cream is smooth and creamy with no lumps. It should be firm enough to hold its shape when sliced or spooned up.

TOP *Soften the gelatin (strawberry purée is used here) and melt it over simmering water.*

BOTTOM *Add the melted gelatin and strawberry mixture to the vanilla sauce and whisk until evenly blended.*

ABOVE *As soon as the Bavarian base is cooled to the gel point, remove it from the ice bath.*

ABOVE *Fold in the whipped cream.*

1 oz / 30 g gelatin

8 oz / 225 g water

1 qt / 1 L heavy cream

1 qt / 1 L Vanilla Sauce (page 967)

flavoring, to taste

BAVARIAN CREAM

1 Place the gelatin in a small stainless-steel bowl and add the water. Let stand for 15 minutes, or until the gelatin has fully bloomed.

2 Melt the bloomed gelatin slowly over a hot-water bath to 105° to 110°F/40° to 43°C.

3 Whip the cream to soft peaks and hold, covered, under refrigeration.

4 Combine the vanilla sauce and the flavoring. Taste and adjust the flavoring.

5 Combine the flavored vanilla sauce and the gelatin. Stir over an ice-water bath to 75°F/24°C. Fold in the whipped cream.

6 Pour immediately into prepared molds. Refrigerate or freeze until set.

MAKES FILLING FOR TWO 10-INCH CAKES

NOTES

To prepare the Bavarian Cake, as shown on page 987, refer to the recipe on page 930.

Strawberry Bavarian Replace the water with strawberry purée.

MOUSSE

A well-prepared mousse can become the signature dessert for a restaurant. It may be presented in different containers, such as tuile cups, hollowed fruits, or special glasses.

Mousses usually do not contain gelatin as a stabilizer. Opinions vary as to whether the base should be added to the whipped cream, as is done here, or the cream should be folded into the base. Both methods yield a light, delicate mousse.

FLAVOR A MOUSSE with ingredients such as chocolate, fruit purées or juices, vanilla, or flavored syrups. Whatever the flavoring ingredient may be, it should be at room temperature and liquid enough to fold together with whipped cream and/or egg whites without deflating those foams. To prepare chocolate, chop it into small pieces and melt it properly over simmering water or in the microwave. Let it cool to room temperature, when it should still be pourable.

Eggs, both yolks and whites, are called for in some mousse recipes. Consult the recipe and prepare the eggs as directed. Separate yolks and whites carefully, keeping whites free of all traces of yolk. Whites generally whip to a greater volume if they are at room temperature.

Cream should be kept very cold and whipped just to soft or medium peaks. Keep whipped cream very cold if it is prepared in advance.

Use a very clean bowl and whip to beat the egg whites. Have a simmering water bath ready to cook the eggs and sugar together. For the best volume in the whipped cream, chill the bowl and beaters before whipping the cream. Use a rubber spatula to fold the mousse together. Have molds arranged to fill with the finished mousse, if desired.

MAKE THE MOUSSE

1. Prepare the flavor ingredients for the mousse and cool.
Some mousse flavorings are made from pureed fruit, sweetened as necessary and strained to remove any fibers or seeds. Chocolate, one of the most popular mousse flavors, is prepared by chopping the chocolate. A quantity of butter is added to the chocolate and they are melted together over simmering water. Take care to avoid dropping any water into the chocolate as it melts. Adding butter to the chocolate now makes it easier to melt.

The flavor base should be soft enough to stir easily with a wooden spoon and very smooth. Blend the ingredients together using a wooden spoon. Let cool to room temperature before use.

2. Heat the egg yolks and sugar to 145°F/63°C for 15 seconds, whisking constantly.
Combine the egg yolks and sugar in a saucepan and place over a hot-water bath. Whip together until thick and light. The mixture will fall in ribbons from the whip when the base has reached the correct consistency. At this time, flavoring ingredients can be added.

ABOVE *Heat the egg yolks and sugar to 145°F/63°C.*

3. Beat the egg whites with the remaining sugar to stiff peaks and fold the egg whites into the egg yolk mixture.

Beat the egg whites in a completely clean and dry bowl. Beat the eggs at a moderate speed at first to begin to separate the protein strands. Add the sugar in small increments with the mixer on high speed until the peaks of the beaten whites remain stiff and do not droop when the beater is pulled from the bowl. The whites should still appear shiny, not dry.

Gently fold to keep the maximum amount of volume. Some chefs like to add the whites to the yolks in two or more additions, so that the first addition lightens the base. That way, less volume is lost from subsequent additions.

4. Fold the flavoring ingredients and whipped cream into the egg mixture.

Working carefully, gently incorporate the flavorings. Use a lifting and folding motion to avoid deflating the mousse. It is important that the flavoring be liquid enough to blend easily. Continue to fold in the flavoring just until there are no streaks in the mixture.

The finished mousse should be well blended but still retain as much volume as possible. At this point the mousse is ready for service or may be stored under refrigeration, covered, for a short period of time before service. The mousse may be scooped or piped into molds or containers for presentation.

5. Evaluate the quality of the finished mousse.

A well-made mousse should have an intense, identifiable flavor, with added smoothness and richness from the cream. The color should be even throughout each portion. Mousses have a light, foamy texture due to the addition of both beaten egg whites and whipped cream. When the whites and cream are beaten properly, the texture is very smooth and fine.

ABOVE *Fold the egg whites into the egg yolks.*

ABOVE *Chocolate and butter were melted over simmering water. The chocolate is still quite liquid so that it doesn't deflate the mousse.*

ABOVE *Pipe the finished mousse into a mold or serving container.*

10 oz / 300 g bittersweet chocolate

1½ oz / 45 g butter

5 egg yolks

1 oz / 30 g water

2 oz / 60 g sugar

5 egg whites

8 oz / 240 g heavy cream, whipped

rum, to taste

CHOCOLATE MOUSSE

1 Combine the chocolate and butter and melt over a hot-water bath.

2 Combine the egg yolks with half of the water and half of the sugar and whisk over a hot-water bath to 145°F/63°C for 15 seconds. Remove from the heat and whip until cool.

3 Combine the egg whites with the remaining sugar and whisk over a hot water bath to 145°F/63°C. Remove the whites from the heat and beat to full volume. Continue beating until cool.

4 Using a large rubber spatula, fold the egg whites into the egg yolks.

5 Fold the butter-chocolate mixture into the egg mixture.

6 Fold in the whipped cream and the flavoring.

MAKES 30 OUNCES/850 GRAMS (ABOUT 7 CUPS)

GANACHE

Ganache has many uses. It may be used as a sauce or to glaze a cake, or it may be whipped and used as a filling and/or icing. Ganache can also be made with a stiffer consistency, chilled, and rolled into truffles.

Light ganache is sometimes used as a chocolate sauce. There are a number of different recipes for this all-time favorite dessert sauce, and by varying the propor-

tions in the recipe so that there is more chocolate in relation to the amount of milk or cream, a harder ganache can be made. This hard ganache can be paddled and used for icing or filling. Adding an even greater amount of chocolate will produce the heavy ganache used to prepare chocolate truffles.

SHAVING OR CUTTING chocolate for ganache into very small pieces facilitates even melting. One of the most efficient ways to chop chocolate is to use a serrated knife; the serration causes the chocolate to break into small shards as it is cut. Use the best-quality chocolate available to be sure of a smooth, richly flavored sauce. Place the chopped chocolate into a heatproof bowl. Place the cream in a saucepan and bring to a boil.

MAKE THE GANACHE

1. Combine the cream and chocolate. Heat the cream and pour it over the chocolate. Allow the mixture to stand, undisturbed, for a few minutes.

ABOVE *Add the hot cream to the finely chopped chocolate.*

2. Stir the mixture until the chocolate is completely melted.
At this point, add any desired flavoring (e.g., flavored liqueurs, cognac, extracts, or essences). The sauce is ready to be used now, or it may be refrigerated for later use.

ABOVE *Gently stir the chocolate and hot cream together.*

3. Evaluate the quality of the finished ganache.
Ganache should be intensely flavored, with the chocolate flavor enriched and smoothed by the addition of cream. The texture should be completely smooth and dense. The more chocolate in the ganache, the denser the texture will be. Ganache is very glossy when warmed and used as a glaze. When cooled and whipped, it becomes more opaque and matte, lightening in color somewhat. Ingredients added to flavor or garnish the sauce should be appropriate to the sauce without masking or overwhelming the chocolate's flavor.

1 qt / 1 L heavy cream

4 lb / 1 kg 920 g finely chopped chocolate

LIGHT GANACHE

1 Bring the cream to a boil.

2 Remove cream from the heat, pour it over the chocolate, and stir constantly until the chocolate is completely melted.

3 Store, covered, in the refrigerator.

MAKES 6 POUNDS/2.75 KILOGRAMS

NOTE

Adjust the amount of chocolate to achieve desired consistency.

GENERAL GUIDELINES FOR ICINGS, GLAZES, AND SAUCES

ICINGS AND FILLINGS FOR CAKES AND PASTRIES

Buttercream and similar icings can be applied between cake layers or used to fill pastry shells. In addition to these filling options, the pastry chef can use a variety of jams, puddings, Bavarian or diplomat cream, mousses, or a light ganache that has been whipped until smooth and light. Whipped cream and chantilly cream can be used both to fill and to frost cakes and pastries. For more information, see General Guidelines for Assembling Cakes and Tortes on page 917.

DESSERT SAUCES

Vanilla sauce, chocolate sauce, fruit sauces, and caramel sauces are used to add flavor, moisture, and eye appeal to various desserts. In addition to their role as a dessert adornment, they are also used as a basic component of other items.

When plating desserts with a sauce, be certain that the sauce is at the desired temperature and that it has been tasted to check for any seasoning or flavoring adjustments. Sauces can be prepared in a variety of consistencies to complement a range of dessert items. Sauces can pooled on the plate, or drizzled or spooned over the main item. For some items, the sauce may be served separately and added at the table. A sauce can add a complementary or contrasting color, flavor, or texture to the plate. Smaller amounts of a second sauce may be used to add another level of interest, used more as a garnish than as a sauce.

TEMPERING FONDANT AND GLAZING

Fondant is used as the traditional glaze for many pastry items such as petit fours, éclairs, and doughnuts. For fondant to gain its glossy finish, it must be properly warmed until it is liquid enough to flow readily. This procedure is known as tempering. Most kitchens and bakeshops use purchased fondant. Plain fondant can be flavored or colored as desired, once it has been melted over simmering water. Keep the fondant warm as you work and be sure to have a complete glazing setup ready, as illustrated here. Small items are typically dipped into the fondant using a dipping fork or similar tool. Larger items are set on racks on sheet pans and the glaze is poured, ladled, spooned, or drizzled over the item.

BELOW LEFT *Place the fondant in a stainless-steel bowl. Heat over a hot-water bath to 105°F/40°C to melt the fondant.*

BOTTOM LEFT *Thin the fondant to the desired consistency by adding some warm water or other liquid.*

BELOW RIGHT *The fondant can be used to glaze pastries now by dipping them in the warm fondant.*

BOTTOM RIGHT *To make chocolate fondant, add melted chocolate to the warm fondant and blend in well.*

GLAZING CAKES, COOKIES, OR PASTRIES WITH GANACHE

Set a cake that is to be glazed with ganache on a cardboard round and seal-coat and chill it prior to glazing. Place the cake or cakes on a wire rack resting on a clean sheet pan. Have the ganache tepid so that it does not melt the crumb coating (if applied). It should not be so thin as to run off the cake. Pour or ladle the ganache over the cake. Using an offset spatula, quickly spread the ganache to completely enrobe the side of the cake. This step must be done quickly, before the ganache begins to set up, to avoid leaving marks of the spatula on the surface. Gently tap the wire rack on the sheet pan to facilitate the flow of any excess ganache off the cake.

MAKING TRUFFLES

Hard ganache (page 992) has a stiffer consistency and, when chilled, it can be shaped and rolled into truffles. Scoop the hard ganache onto a parchment-lined sheet pan and place in the refrigerator for 10 to 15 minutes, or until the ganache becomes firm again. Roll them into smooth balls. Refrigerate one more time to

TOP LEFT *Ladle the ganache over the center of the cake.*

BOTTOM LEFT *Prick any small air bubbles with a skewer or similar pointed tool.*

TOP RIGHT *Spread the ganache with an offset spatula quickly and lightly to encourage an even layer to form on the top and sides.*

BOTTOM RIGHT *Some of the remaining ganache may be piped through a parchment cone to decorate each portion.*

TOP FAR LEFT *Portion truffles using a small stainless-steel scoop and place balls of ganache on a parchment-lined sheet pan.*

BOTTOM FAR LEFT *Gently but quickly roll the truffles in the chocolate and place them back onto clean parchment.*

TOP MIDDLE *Smear a small amount of tempered chocolate into the palm of one gloved hand.*

BOTTOM MIDDLE *Roll the truffles in the tempered chocolate. Return to the parchment and allow the chocolate to harden completely. Coat each truffle a second time.*

TOP RIGHT *Truffles coated with tempered chocolate.*

be sure that the truffles are firm before rolling them in chopped nuts, cocoa powder, or confectioners' sugar. Truffles are also coated with tempered chocolate (page 984) to give them a glossy coating, as well as to give them a longer shelf life.

TEMPERING CHOCOLATE

Chocolate contains two distinct types of fat, which melt at different temperatures. In order to ensure that the chocolate will melt smoothly and harden evenly with a good shine, it must be tempered. This particular method of tempering is sometimes known as the seed method.

1. Chop the chocolate with a serrated knife and put it in a stainless steel bowl. Place the bowl over very low heat or barely simmering water, making sure that no moisture comes in contact with the chocolate. Stir the chocolate occasionally as it melts to keep it at an even temperature throughout.

2. Continue to heat the chocolate until it reaches a temperature between 105° and 110°F/40° and 43°C. Use an instant-read thermometer for the most accurate results.

3. Remove the chocolate from the heat. Add a large piece of unmelted chocolate (the seed) and stir it until the temperature drops to 87° to 92°F/30° to 33°C. If the chocolate drops below 85°F/29°C, it will be necessary to repeat the steps described here to gently reheat it to 92°F/33°C. If the chocolate scorches or becomes grainy, it can no longer be used. If any moisture comes in contact with the chocolate as it is being tempered, it will seize.

Tempered chocolate will evenly coat the back of a spoon and then harden into a shiny shell. Dried or fresh fruit or baked items can be dipped directly into the tempered chocolate with a dipping fork, or rolled in the tempered chocolate, or placed on a rack over a clean sheet pan and have the chocolate poured over it.

RECIPES

CRÈME CARAMEL

makes fourteen 4-ounce/115-gram portions

1 lb/450 g sugar
few drops of lemon juice
3 fl oz/90 mL water
1 qt/1 L milk
1 vanilla bean or 1 tbsp/5 mL vanilla extract
6 eggs, beaten
4 egg yolks

1 Prepare 14 ramekins by buttering the bottoms and sides.

2 Cook half of the sugar with the lemon juice in a heavy-bottomed saucepan over high heat, stirring constantly to a boil, making sure that all the sugar has dissolved. Allow to cook, covered, for 1 minute. Remove the cover, reduce the heat to medium flame, and cook to a rich golden brown. Add the water to the sugar off the heat.

3 Divide the caramel evenly among the ramekins.

4 To prepare the custard, bring the milk, vanilla bean, and half of the remaining sugar to the boiling point. Remove the mixture from the heat.

5 Combine the remaining sugar with the eggs and egg yolks.

6 Temper the egg mixture into the milk mixture. Add vanilla extract now if not using vanilla bean.

7 Divide the custard evenly among the ramekins and place in a water bath. Bake in a 325°F/165°C oven until the custard has set, about 1 hour. The custard will be firm but will jiggle when gently shaken.

8 Refrigerate overnight. (This allows the caramel to liquefy.) The custards are ready to serve at this point, or they may be stored, tightly wrapped, under refrigeration for up to 2 days.

9 Turn out onto a plate for service.

NOTE

Crème Caramel may also be prepared in a large casserole. The presentation is less dramatic but sometimes more practical for buffets or family-style seating.

CRÈME BRÛLÉE

makes twelve 5-ounce/140-gram portions

1½ qt/1.2 L heavy cream
½ vanilla bean
8 oz/225 g sugar
10 oz/285 g egg yolks, beaten
sugar, for crust

1 Combine the cream, vanilla bean, and half of the sugar in a heavy-bottomed stainless-steel saucepan and bring to a boil.

2 Whisk together the remaining sugar and the egg yolks in a stainless steel bowl.

3 Temper the egg mixture into the milk mixture and strain through a fine sieve.

4 Fill 12 ramekins seven eighths full and place them in a water bath.

5 Bake in a 325°F/165°C oven until just barely set, about 45 minutes. Let cool in the water bath. Remove, wipe the bottoms of the ramekins, and refrigerate overnight.

6 The custards are ready to be garnished and served at this point, or they may be stored, tightly wrapped, under refrigeration for up to 2 days.

7 To prepare for service, set the ramekins in a hotel pan filled with ice and cover the surface lightly with sugar.

8 Caramelize under the broiler and serve at once.

NOTES

Use a hand-held butane torch to caramelize the sugar if you prefer.

Crème Brûlée may be prepared in a large casserole. The presentation is less dramatic but sometimes more practical for buffets or family-style seating.

The cream can be infused with different flavors, such as coffee, ginger, or other spices. Fruit can be added to the bottom of the ramekins before baking.

BREAD AND BUTTER PUDDING

makes 15 portions

1½ lb/680 g stale bread

3 oz/85 g melted butter

4 oz/115 g raisins

1 qt/1 L milk

6 eggs, beaten

3 egg yolks, beaten

6 oz/170 g sugar

1   Prepare 15 custard cups by brushing them with softened butter.

2   Cut the bread into 1-inch cubes and drizzle with the melted butter.

3   Toast the bread cubes in a 350°F/175°C oven until lightly toasted, about 5 minutes.

4   Combine the toasted bread with the raisins and fill the buttered custard cups.

5   To prepare the custard, combine the milk, eggs, egg yolks, and sugar and mix well.

6   Pour the custard over the bread in the custard cups. Place in a water bath.

7   Bake in a 325°F/165°C oven until the custard is set, about 45 minutes. The custard will be firm but will still jiggle when gently shaken. Allow the puddings to cool completely.

8   The puddings are ready to serve at this point or they may be tightly wrapped in plastic wrap, refrigerated, and served chilled. Bread and butter pudding may be served in the ramekin or unmolded and plated.

9   The puddings may be stored, wrapped tightly, under refrigeration for up to 2 days.

VANILLA ICE CREAM

makes 4½ pounds/2 kilograms

1½ pt/720 mL milk

1½ pt/720 mL heavy cream

12 oz/340 g sugar

1 vanilla bean, split

12 egg yolks, beaten

1   Place the milk, cream, half of the sugar, and the vanilla bean in a saucepan. Bring the mixture to the boiling point.

2   Blend the egg yolks with the remaining sugar.

3   Temper the egg yolk mixture into the hot milk mixture. Heat to 180°F/82°C.

4   Strain through a fine-meshed strainer into a container in an ice bath. Allow the mixture to cool completely. Cover and refrigerate overnight.

5   Freeze in an ice cream freezer according to the manufacturer's instructions.

Chocolate Ice Cream To make chocolate ice cream, omit the vanilla bean and temper 4 oz/115 g of melted sweet chocolate and 4 oz/115 g of melted bitter chocolate into the warm, fully cooked base.

Pistachio Ice Cream To make pistachio ice cream, add 8 oz/115 g pistachio paste (a purchased product). Taste the base and add more paste if desired before churning and freezing.

see photograph on page 988

PETITS POTS DE CRÈME

6 oz/170 g sugar

12 fl oz/360 mL warm milk

12 fl oz/360 mL warm heavy cream

4½ oz/125 g eggs, beaten

1½ oz/40 g egg yolks, beaten

3 oz/85 g melted bittersweet chocolate

¼ fl oz/8 g vanilla extract

1 Place 4 oz/115 g of the sugar in a saucepan and cook, brushing down the sides of the pot with a wet pastry brush, to a dark amber color.

2 Add the milk and cream and bring the mixture to the boiling point, stirring until fully incorporated.

3 Combine the remaining sugar with the eggs and egg yolks.

4 Temper the egg mixture into the hot milk.

5 Add the chocolate and vanilla and strain through a fine-meshed sieve.

6 Fill 8 ramekins four fifths full and bake in a water bath in a 325°F/165°C oven until set, about 45 minutes. The custard will be firm but will jiggle when tapped.

7 Remove from the oven, let cool, wrap tightly, and refrigerate until fully chilled.

8 The custards are ready to serve at this point, or they may be stored, wrapped tightly, under refrigeration for up to 2 days.

NOTES
Serve with a dollop of unsweetened whipped cream and shaved chocolate or top with a chocolate-covered coffee bean.

BOURBON SAUCE

20 egg yolks

1¼ lb 4 oz/570 g sugar

10 fl oz/300 mL bourbon

22 oz/625 g heavy cream, whipped

1 Combine the egg yolks and sugar in a stainless-steel bowl over a simmering hot water bath. Whip until pale yellow and thick.

2 Remove the mixture from the water bath, add the bourbon, and chill thoroughly.

3 Fold the whipped cream into the cold sauce.

4 The sauce is ready to serve at this point, or may be stored, wrapped tightly, under refrigeration for up to 3 hours.

NOTES
Serve this sauce with cobblers, fritters, or other baked or fried desserts.

Orange Sauce Substitute an orange-flavored liqueur for the bourbon.

Coffee Sauce Substitute a coffee-flavored liqueur for the bourbon.

Mocha Sauce Substitute a coffee-flavored liqueur for half of the bourbon and a chocolate-flavored liqueur for the remaining half of the bourbon.

FRUIT COULIS

1 lb/450 g sugar, or as needed

1 lb/450 g fresh fruit (raspberries, strawberries, peaches, mango, etc.)

4 fl oz/120 mL lemon juice

cornstarch slurry, as needed (optional)

1 Slowly add the sugar to the fruit, tasting for sweetness and adjusting according to the sweetness of the fruit. Bring the mixture to a boil, purée, if desired, and strain.

2 Reduce the mixture over heat to the desired consistency and add the lemon juice.

3 Thicken with cornstarch (1 oz/30 g per qt/L), if desired.

4 The sauce is ready to serve at this point, or it may be stored, wrapped tightly, under refrigeration for up to 1 week.

Strawberry Bavarian Cake

Pistachio and Chocolate Ice Creams

Sabayon Sauce with Fresh Fruit

**Port-Poached Pear
with Caramel Sauce**

RASPBERRY SAUCE

makes 12³/₄ ounces/332 grams

2³/₄ oz/80 g sugar

3 fl.oz/90 mL burgundy wine

7 oz/200 g raspberry purée

1 Combine all the ingredients in a saucepan and simmer for 3 minutes. Strain.

2 Let cool before serving.

3 The sauce is ready to serve at this point, or may be stored, wrapped tightly, under refrigeration for up to 1 week.

SABAYON SAUCE

makes 1 quart/1 liter

9 oz/255 g egg yolks

9 oz/255 g sugar

6 fl.oz/180 mL white wine

12 oz/340 g heavy cream, whipped

1 Combine the egg yolks, sugar, and white wine in the bowl of an electric mixer.

2 Whip over a hot-water bath until it reaches 180°F/82°C. Remove from the heat and transfer to the mixer. Whip until cool.

3 Fold in the whipped cream.

4 Adjust consistency if necessary.

5 The sauce is ready to serve at this point.

NOTE

Serve sabayon sauce over a variety of fresh, seasonal fruits, such as berries.

see photograph on page 989

CINNAMON SAUCE

makes 2 ¹/₂ pints/1.2 liters

12 oz/340 g apple juice

6 oz/170 g sugar

12 oz/340 g water

4 oz/115 g orange juice

¹/₈ oz/4 g ground cinnamon

2 oz/60 g lemon juice

1¹/₄ oz/38 g clear gel

2 oz/60 g white rum

¹/₂ oz/15 g butter

1 Combine 8 oz/225 g of the apple juice with the sugar, water, orange juice, cinnamon, and lemon juice and bring to a boil.

2 Combine the remaining apple juice with the clear gel.

3 Temper the clear gel mixture into the hot sugar mixture.

4 Return the mixture to a boil and boil for 1 minute.

5 Remove from the heat and add the rum and butter. Cool and reserve.

6 The sauce is ready to serve at this point, or may be stored, wrapped tightly, under refrigeration for up to 1 week.

HAZELNUT SAUCE

makes 2 quarts/2 liters

2 qt/2 L VANILLA SAUCE (page 967), cooled

8 oz/225 g finely chopped toasted hazelnuts

2 oz/60 g finely chopped chocolate

2 fl oz/60 mL Frangelica

1 Combine all the ingredients and blend well.

2 Store, covered, under refrigeration until ready to use.

3 The sauce is ready to serve at this point, or may be stored, wrapped tightly, under refrigeration for up to 2 days.

CARAMEL SAUCE

makes 2 quarts/2 liters

1 qt/1 L heavy cream

13 oz/370 g corn syrup

1 lb 2 oz/510 g sugar

3 oz/85 g butter

1 Bring the cream to a boil and remove it from the heat.

2 Cook the corn syrup and sugar in a heavy-bottomed saucepan over medium heat to a golden caramel, stirring from time to time.

3 Stir in the butter, then carefully stir in the hot cream, working over low heat.

4 As soon as the cream is blended into the sauce, set the saucepan in an ice-water bath to stop the cooking process. The sauce is ready to serve now, or it may be cooled and held for later service. Reheat the sauce over low heat or in a bain-marie if necessary.

NOTE

This sauce is shown on page 989 as an accompaniment to Poached Pears (page 951).

see photograph on page 989

LEMON MOUSSE

makes 2½ pints/1.2 liters or twelve 3-ounce/85-gram portions

2 to 3 fl oz/60 to 90 mL oil, or as needed

2 to 3 oz/60 to 85 g confectioners' sugar

4 oz/115 g toasted finely chopped coconut

10 fl oz/300 mL milk

10 oz/285 g sugar

1 oz/30 g cornstarch

3½ oz/100 g pasteurized egg yolks

4½ fl oz/125 mL lemon juice

1 oz/30 g grated lemon zest

10 oz/285 g pasteurized egg whites

1 Prepare 12 molds by oiling them lightly and dusting with confectioners' sugar. Place the prepared molds on a parchment-lined sheet pan. Fill the bottoms of the molds with an even layer of coconut.

2 Place the milk in a heavy-bottomed stainless-steel saucepan over high heat. Combine half of the sugar with the cornstarch and blend well to break up any lumps in the cornstarch. Add the egg yolks and blend well.

3 Temper the yolk mixture into the milk mixture.

4 Bring the mixture to a boil. Add the lemon juice and zest.

5 Place the egg whites and the remaining sugar in the bowl of an electric mixer. Using the whip attachment, beat to soft peaks.

6 Fold the meringue into the egg yolk mixture and pipe into the prepared molds.

7 The mousse is ready to serve at this point. It may also be stored, wrapped tightly, under refrigeration for up to 2 days, or frozen for longer storage.

NOTES

The mousse may be piped directly into glasses or other serving pieces as desired, or it may be used as a filling for small pastries and tarts.

A small amount of bloomed and dissolved gelatin may be added to the mousse for greater stability.

LEMON CREAM (LEMON CURD)

makes 2½ pints/1.15 liters

7½ oz/215 g eggs

2 oz/60 g egg yolks

8 oz/225 g sugar

1 lb/450 g melted butter

4½ fl oz/135 mL lemon juice

2 tbsp/30 mL finely grated lemon zest

1 Combine the eggs, egg yolks, and sugar and cook, whisking constantly, over a a hot-water bath to 165°F/72°C and quite thick. Continue cooking for 3 minutes.

2 Remove the pot from the heat, whisk in the butter a few pieces at a time, and fold in the zest.

3 The curd is ready to serve at this point, or may be stored, wrapped tightly, under refrigeration for up to 2 days.

NOTE

The butter amount can be increased if a firmer consistency is desired

HARD GANACHE

makes 1½ pounds/680 grams

1 lb/450 g bittersweet chocolate

8 oz/225 g heavy cream

1 Finely chop the chocolate and place in a stainless-steel bowl.

2 Heat the cream to a boil and pour over the chocolate.

3 Gently stir the mixture until all the chocolate has melted and the mixture is completely smooth.

4 Cover with plastic wrap and refrigerate until cold and firm.

5 The ganache is ready to be formed into truffles (see page 983) at this point, or may be stored, wrapped tightly, under refrigeration for up to 1 week.

NOTES

Substitute white or milk chocolate for the bittersweet chocolate.

To make a richer ganache with a smoother, creamier mouth feel, add 2½ oz/70 g glucose and/or 2½ oz/70 g butter.

Flavor the ganache as desired with 1½ fl oz/45 mL of one or more of the following: dark rum; cherry-flavored cordials or liqueurs such as kirschwasser; orange-flavored liqueurs such as Grand Marnier; nut-flavored liqueurs such as Amaretto or Frangelico; or coffee-flavored liqueurs such as Kahlúa or Tia Maria.

GANACHE FOR GLAZING

makes 2 pounds 2½ ounces/978 grams

1½ lb/680 g bittersweet chocolate

1 lb/450 g heavy cream

2 oz/60 g corn syrup or glucose

1 Finely chop the chocolate and place in a stainless-steel bowl.

2 Heat the cream and corn syrup or glucose to a boil and pour over the chocolate.

3 Gently stir the mixture until all the chocolate has melted and the mixture is completely smooth.

FRENCH BUTTERCREAM

makes 1¾ pounds/800 grams

16 egg yolks

8 whole eggs

2¼ lb/1 kg 80 g sugar

8 oz/225 g water

3 lb/1.3 kg butter, diced, at room temperature

1 Combine the egg yolks, eggs, sugar, and water in the bowl of an electric mixer. Whisking constantly, warm over a hot-water bath to 145°F/63°C.

2 Put the bowl on the mixer and, using the whip attachment, beat on high speed to stiff peaks.

3 With the mixer on low speed, add the butter a few pieces at a time, until the cream is smooth and spreadable.

4 The buttercream is ready to use at this point. It may also be stored, wrapped tightly, under refrigeration for up to 7 days, or frozen for up to 3 months.

GERMAN BUTTERCREAM

makes 2¼ pounds/1 kilograms

1 lb/450 g butter
4 oz/115 g confectioners' sugar
1 lb/450 g PASTRY CREAM (page 971)

1 Cream together the butter and sugar in the bowl of an electric mixer, using the paddle attachment, on medium speed until light and smooth.

2 Gradually add the pastry cream and blend together, scraping down the sides of the bowl as necessary, until the cream is smooth and spreadable.

3 The buttercream is ready to use at this point. It may also be stored, wrapped tightly, under refrigeration for up to 7 days, or frozen for up to 3 months.

GERMAN CHOCOLATE CAKE ICING

makes 2 pounds/900 grams

7 oz/200 g sugar
2 oz/60 g water
8 oz/225 g unsweetened coconut milk, warm
2 eggs
1 tsp/5 mL vanilla extract
4 oz/115 g butter
4½ oz/125 g shredded unsweetened coconut, lightly toasted
4¾ oz/103 g finely chopped toasted pecans or walnuts

1 Cook the sugar and water in a heavy-bottomed saucepan over high heat, stirring constantly to a boil, making sure that all the sugar has dissolved. Allow to cook, covered, for 1 minute. Remove the cover, reduce the heat to medium flame, and cook to a rich golden brown. To stop the cooking process, shock the pot in an ice bath for 10 seconds. Add the coconut milk.

2 Whisk the eggs in a small bowl. Add the warm sugar mixture and whisk to blend. Return to the saucepan and gently heat to 180°F/82°C. Do not allow the mixture to boil. Remove from the heat and stir in the vanilla extract and butter. Stir in the coconut and nuts. Let cool until the frosting is spreadable.

3 The frosting is ready to use at this point, or may be stored, wrapped tightly, under refrigeration for up to 7 days.

DIPLOMAT CREAM

makes 2 quarts/2 liters or enough for twenty-four 2-inch/50-millimeter eclairs or twenty-four 2-inch/50-millimeter napoleons

¼ oz/8 g gelatin
2 oz/60 g brandy
1 lb/450 g PASTRY CREAM (page 971), cooled
1 lb/450 g heavy cream, soft whipped

1 Place the gelatin in a small stainless-steel bowl and add the brandy. Let stand until the gelatin has fully bloomed, about 15 minutes.

2 Melt the bloomed gelatin slowly over a hot-water bath to 105° to 110°F/40° to 43°C.

3 Quickly whisk the melted gelatin into the pastry cream.

4 Immediately fold in the whipped cream. Use immediately.

CREAM CHEESE ICING

makes 6 pounds/2.75 kilograms

3 lb/1.3 kg cream cheese
1½ lb/680 g butter
1¼ lb/680 g confectioners' sugar, sifted
vanilla extract, to taste

1 Blend the cream cheese and butter together in the bowl of an electric mixer, using the paddle attachment, on medium speed.

2 Add the sugar and blend on low speed just to incorporate. Increase to medium speed and cream until light and smooth. Add the vanilla.

3 If necessary, press through a sieve to remove any lumps.

4 The icing is ready to use at this point, or may be stored, wrapped tightly, under refrigeration for up to 7 days.

NOTE
Substitute lemon zest or Pernod for the vanilla extract.

APPENDIX

COOKING RATIOS AND TIMES FOR SELECTED GRAINS

TYPE	RATIO OF GRAIN TO LIQUID (CUPS)	APPROXIMATE YIELD (CUPS)*	COOKING TIME
Barley, pearled	1:2	4	35 to 45 minutes
Barley groats	1:2½	4	50 minutes to 1 hour
Buckwheat groats (kasha)	1:1½ to 2	2	12 to 20 minutes
Couscous[†]	———	1½ to 2	20 to 25 minutes
Hominy, whole[‡]	1:2½	3	2½ to 3 hours
Hominy grits	1:4	3	25 minutes
Millet	1:2	3	30 to 35 minutes
Oat groats	1:2	2	45 minutes to 1 hour
Polenta	1:3 to 3½	3	35 to 45 minutes
Rice, arborio (for risotto)	1:3	3	20 to 30 minutes
Rice, basmati	1:1½	3	25 minutes
Rice, converted	1:1¾	4	25 to 30 minutes
Rice, long-grain, brown	1:3	4	40 minutes
Rice, long-grain, white	1:1½ to 1¾	3	18 to 20 minutes
Rice, short-grain, brown	1:2½	4	35 to 40 minutes
Rice, short-grain, white	1:1 to 1½	3	20 to 30 minutes
Rice, wild	1:3	4	30 to 45 minutes
Rice, wild, pecan	1:1¾	4	20 minutes
Wheat berries	1:3	2	1 hour
Wheat, bulgur, soaked[§]	1:4	2	2 hours
Wheat, bulgur, pilaf[§]	1:2½	2	15 to 20 minutes
Wheat, cracked	1:2	3	20 minutes

*From 1 cup of uncooked grain.

[†] Grain should be soaked briefly in tepid water and then drained before it is steamed.

[‡] Grain should be soaked overnight in cold water and then drained before it is cooked.

[§] Grain may be cooked by covering it with boiling water and soaking it for 2 hours or cooking it by the pilaf method.

APPROXIMATE SOAKING AND COOKING TIMES
FOR SELECTED DRIED LEGUMES

TYPE	SOAKING TIME	COOKING TIME
Adzuki beans	4 hours	1 hour
Black beans	4 hours	1½ hours
Black-eyed peas*	———	1 hour
Chickpeas	4 hours	2 to 2½ hours
Fava beans	12 hours	3 hours
Great Northen beans	4 hours	1 hour
Kidney beans (red or white)	4 hours	1 hour
Lentils*	———	30 to 40 minutes
Lima beans	4 hours	1 to 1½ hours
Mung beans	4 hours	1 hour
Navy beans	4 hours	2 hours
Peas, split*	———	30 minutes
Peas, whole	4 hours	40 minutes
Pigeon peas*	———	30 minutes
Pink beans	4 hours	1 hour
Pinto beans	4 hours	1 to 1½ hours
Soybeans	12 hours	3 to 3½ hours

*Soaking is not necessary.

WEIGHT MEASURES CONVERSIONS

U.S.	METRIC*
¼ ounce	8 grams
½ ounce	15 grams
1 ounce	30 grams
4 ounces	115 grams
8 ounces (½ pound)	225 grams
16 ounces (1 pound)	450 grams
32 ounces (2 pounds)	900 grams
40 ounces (2¼ pounds)	1 kilogram

*Metric values have been rounded.

VOLUME MEASURES CONVERSIONS

U.S.	METRIC*
1 teaspoon	5 milliliters
1 tablespoon	15 milliliters
1 fluid ounce (2 tablespoons)	30 milliliters
2 fluid ounces (¼ cup)	60 milliliters
8 fluid ounces (1 cup)	240 milliliters
16 fluid ounces (1 pint)	480 milliliters
32 fluid ounces (1 quart)	950 milliliters (.95 liter)
128 fluid ounces (1 gallon)	3.75 liters

*Metric values have been rounded.

TEMPERATURE CONVERSIONS

DEGREES FAHRENHEIT (°F)	DEGREES CELSIUS (°C)*
32°	0°
40°	4°
140°	60°
150°	65°
160°	70°
170°	75°
212°	100°
275°	135°
300°	150°
325°	165°
350°	175°
375°	190°
400°	205°
425°	220°
450°	230°
475°	245°
500°	260°

*Celsius temperatures have been rounded.

WEIGHTS AND MEASURES EQUIVALENTS

Dash	less than $\frac{1}{8}$ teaspoon
3 teaspoons	1 tablespoon ($\frac{1}{2}$ fluid ounce)
2 tablespoons	$\frac{1}{8}$ cup (1 fluid ounce)
4 tablespoons	$\frac{1}{4}$ (2 fluid ounces)
5$\frac{1}{3}$ tablespoons	$\frac{1}{3}$ cup (2$\frac{2}{3}$ fluid ounces)
8 tablespoons	$\frac{1}{2}$ cup (4 fluid ounces)
10$\frac{2}{3}$ tablespoons	$\frac{2}{3}$ cup (5$\frac{1}{3}$ fluid ounces)
12 tablespoons	$\frac{3}{4}$ cup (6 fluid ounces)
14 tablespoons	$\frac{7}{8}$ cup (7 fluid ounces)
16 tablespoons	1 cup
1 gill	$\frac{1}{2}$ cup
1 cup	8 fluid ounces (240 milliliters)
2 cups	1 pint (480 milliliters)
2 pints	1 quart (approximately 1 liter)
4 quarts	1 gallon (3.75 liters)
8 quarts	1 peck (8.8 liters)
4 pecks	1 bushel (35 liters)
1 ounce	28.35 grams (rounded to 30)
16 ounces	1 pound (453.59 grams, rounded to 450)
1 kilogram	2.2 pounds

INFORMATION, HINTS, AND TIPS FOR CALCULATIONS

1 gallon = 4 quarts = 8 pints = 16 cups (8 fluid ounces) = 128 fluid ounces

1 fifth bottle = approximately 1$\frac{1}{2}$ pints or exactly 25.6 fluid ounces

1 measuring cup holds 8 fluid ounces (a coffee cup generally holds 6 fluid ounces)

1 egg white = 2 fluid ounces (average)

1 lemon = 1 to 1$\frac{1}{4}$ fluid ounces of juice

1 orange = 3 to 3$\frac{1}{4}$ fluid ounces of juice

To convert ounces and pounds to grams: multiply ounces by 28.35; multiply pounds by 453.59

To convert Fahrenheit to Celsius:

$$\frac{(°F - 32) \times 5}{9} = °C$$

To round to the next closest whole number, round up if final decimal is 5 or greater; round down if less than 5

GLOSSARY

A

abalone: A mollusk with a single shell and a large, edible adductor muscle.

aboyeur (Fr.): Expediter or announcer; a station in the brigade system. The aboyeur accepts orders from the dining room, relays them to the appropriate stations of the kitchen, and checks each plate before it leaves the kitchen.

acid: A substance having a sour or sharp flavor. Most foods are somewhat acidic. Foods generally referred to as acids include citrus juice, vinegar, and wine. A substance's degree of acidity is measured on the pH scale; acids have a pH of less than 7.

adulterated food: Food that has been contaminated to the point that it is considered unfit for human consumption.

aerobic bacteria: Bacteria that require the presence of oxygen to function.

aïoli (Fr.): Garlic mayonnaise. Also, in Italian, *allioli*; in Spanish, *aliolio*.

à la carte (Fr.): A menu in which the patron makes individual selections from various menu categories; each item is priced separately.

à l'anglaise: Foods that have been breaded and fried; foods that have been boiled.

albumen: The major protein in egg whites.

al dente (It.): Literally, "to the tooth"; refers to an item, such as pasta or vegetables, cooked until it is tender but still firm, not soft.

alkali: A substance that tests at higher than 7 on the pH scale. Alkalis are sometimes described as having a slightly soapy flavor. Olives and baking soda are some of the few alkaline foods.

allumette: Vegetables, potatoes, or other items cut into pieces the size and shape of matchsticks; ⅛ inch by ⅛ inch by 1 to 2 inches/3 mm by 3 mm by 25 to 50 mm is the standard.

amandine: Garnished with almonds.

amino acid: The basic molecular component of proteins; one of the essential dietary components.

amuse-gueule (Fr.): Chef's tasting; a small portion of something exotic, unusual, or otherwise special that is served when the guests in a restaurant are seated.

anaerobic bacteria: Bacteria that do not require oxygen to function.

angel food cake: A type of sponge cake made with egg whites that are beaten until stiff.

antioxidants: Substances that retard the breakdown of tissues in the presence of oxygen. May be added to food during processing or may occur naturally.

antipasto (It.): Literally, "before the pasta." Typically, a platter of cold hors-d'oeuvre that includes meats, olives, cheese, and vegetables.

apéritif (Fr.): A light alcoholic beverage consumed before the meal to stimulate the appetite.

appareil: A prepared mixture of ingredients used alone or as an ingredient in another preparation.

appetizer: Light foods served before a meal. These may be hot or cold, plated or served as finger food.

aquaculture: The farm-raising of fish or shellfish.

arborio: A high-starch, short-grain rice traditionally used in the preparation of risotto.

aromatics: Ingredients, such as herbs, spices, vegetables, citrus fruits, wines, and vinegars, used to enhance the flavor and fragrance of food.

aromatized wine: Fortified wine infused with any of a wide variety of aromatic plants or bitter herbs, roots, bark, or other plant parts (for example, vermouth).

arrowroot: A powdered starch made from a tropical root. Used primarily as a thickener. Remains clear when cooked.

as-purchased (AP) weight: The weight of an item before trimming or other preparation (as opposed to edible-portion [EP] weight).

aspic: A clear jelly made from stock (or occasionally from fruit or vegetable juices) thickened with gelatin. Used to coat foods or cubed and used as a garnish.

B

bacteria: Microscopic organisms. Some have beneficial properties; others can cause food-borne illnesses when contaminated foods are ingested.

baguette: A loaf of bread shaped into a long cylinder.

bain-marie: A water bath used to cook foods gently by surrounding the cooking vessel with simmering water. Also, a set of nesting pots with single, long handles used as a double boiler. Also, steam table inserts.

bake: To cook food by surrounding it with dry heat, as in an oven.

bake blind: To partially or completely bake an unfilled pastry crust.

baking powder: A chemical leavener made with an acidic ingredient and an alkaline one; most commonly these are sodium bicarbonate (baking soda) and cream of tartar. When exposed to liquid, it produces carbon dioxide gas, which leavens doughs and batters. Double-acting baking powder contains ingredients that produce two leavening reactions, one upon exposure to liquid, the second when heated.

baking soda: Sodium bicarbonate, a leavening agent that may be used in combination with an acidic ingredient such as sour milk or as a component of baking powder.

barbecue: To cook food by grilling it over a wood or charcoal fire. Usually some sort of marinade or sauce is brushed on the item during cooking.

bard: To cover a naturally lean meat with slabs or strips of fat, such as bacon or fatback, to baste it during roasting or braising. The fat is usually tied on with butcher's twine.

barquette: A boat-shaped tart or tartlet, which may have a sweet or savory filling.

baste: To moisten food during cooking with pan drippings, sauce, or other liquid. Basting prevents food from drying out.

batch cooking: A cooking technique in which appropriately sized batches of food are prepared several times throughout a service period so that a fresh supply of cooked items is always available.

baton/batonnet (Fr.): Items cut into pieces somewhat larger than allumette or julienne; ¼ inch by ¼ inch by 1 to 2 inches/6 mm by 6 mm by 25 to 50 mm is the standard. Translated to English as stick or small stick.

batter: A mixture of flour and liquid, sometimes with the inclusion of other ingredients. Batters vary in thickness but are generally semiliquid and thinner than doughs. Used in such preparations as cakes, quick breads, pancakes, and crêpes.

Bavarian cream, bavarois: A type of custard made from heavy cream and eggs; it is sweetened, flavored, and stabilized with gelatin.

béarnaise: A classic emulsion, similar to hollandaise, made with egg yolks. Also, a reduction of white wine, shallots, and tarragon. Also, butter finished with tarragon and chervil.

béchamel: A white sauce made of milk thickened with light roux and flavored with onion. One of the grand sauces.

bench-proof: In yeast dough production, to allow dough to rise after it is panned and just before it is baked.

beurre blanc (Fr.): Literally, "white butter." A classic emulsified sauce made with a reduction of white wine and shallots thickened with whole butter and possibly finished with fresh herbs or other seasonings.

beurre fondue (Fr.): Melted butter.

beurre manié (Fr.): Literally, "kneaded butter." A mixture of equal parts by weight of whole butter and flour, used to thicken gravies and sauces.

beurre noir (Fr.): Literally, "black butter." Butter that has been cooked to a very dark brown or nearly black. Also, a sauce made with browned butter, vinegar, chopped parsley, and capers. It is usually served with fish.

beurre noisette (Fr.): Literally, "hazelnut butter" or "brown butter." Whole butter that has been heated until browned.

binder: An ingredient or appareil used to thicken a sauce or hold together another mixture of ingredients.

bisque: A soup based on crustaceans or a vegetable purée. It is classically thickened with rice and usually finished with cream.

bivalve: A mollusk with two hinged shells. Examples are clams and oysters.

blanc: A preparation containing water, flour, onion, cloves, a bouquet garni, salt, and lemon juice. Used to cook vegetables such as mushrooms, celeriac, salsify, or cauliflower to keep them white.

blanch: To cook an item briefly in boiling water or hot fat before finishing or storing it.

blanquette: A white stew, usually of veal but sometimes of chicken or lamb. It is served after the sauce has been thickened with a liaison.

blend: A mixture of two or more flavors combined to achieve a particular flavor or quality. Also, to mix two or more ingredients together until combined.

blini: A silver-dollar-sized, yeast-raised buckwheat pancake.

bloom: To soften gelatin in warm liquid before use; a white coating that develops on chocolate.

boil: A cooking method in which items are immersed in liquid at or above the boiling point (212°F/100°C).

borscht (Rus.): A soup made from fresh beets and garnished with sour cream. May include an assortment of vegetables and/or meat, and may be served hot or cold.

botulism: A food-borne illness caused by toxins produced by the anaerobic bacterium *Clostridium botulinum*.

boucher (Fr.): Butcher.

bouillabaisse: A hearty fish and shellfish stew flavored with saffron. A traditional specialty of Marseilles, France.

bouillon (Fr.): Broth.

boulanger (Fr.): Baker, specifically of breads and other unsweetened doughs.

bouquet garni: A small bundle of herbs tied with string. It is used to flavor stocks, braises, and other preparations. Usually contains bay leaf, parsley, thyme, and possibly other aromatics.

braise: A cooking method in which the main item, usually meat, is seared in fat, then simmered in stock or another liquid in a covered vessel. The cooking liquid is then reduced and used as the basis of a sauce.

bran: The outer layer of a cereal grain and the part highest in fiber.

brandy: Spirit made by distilling wine or the fermented mash of fruit. May be aged in oak barrels.

brazier/braisier: A pan, designed specifically for braising, that usually has two handles and a tight-fitting lid. Often is round but may be square or rectangular.

bread: Food product made of flour, sugar, shortening, salt, and liquid leavened by the action of yeast.

brigade system: The kitchen organization system instituted by Georges-Auguste Escoffier. Each position has a station and well-defined responsibilities.

brine: A solution of salt, water, and seasonings, used to preserve foods.

brioche: A rich yeast dough traditionally baked in a fluted pan with a distinctive topknot of dough.

brisket: A cut of beef from the lower forequarter, best suited for long-cooking preparations such as braising. Corned beef is cured beef brisket.

broil: To cook by means of a radiant heat source placed above the food.

broiler: The piece of equipment used to broil foods.

broth: A flavorful, aromatic liquid made by simmering water or stock with meat, vegetables, and/or spices and herbs.

brown sauce: A sauce made from a brown stock and aromatics and thickened by roux, a pure starch slurry, and/or a reduction.

brown stock: An amber liquid produced by simmering browned bones and meat (usually veal or beef) with vegetables and aromatics (including caramelized mirepoix).

bruise: To partially crush a food item in order to release its flavor.

brunoise (Fr.): Small dice; ⅛-inch/3 mm square is the standard. For a brunoise cut, items are first cut in julienne, then cut crosswise. For a fine brunoise, 1/16-inch/1.5-mm square, cut items first in fine julienne.

butcher: A chef or purveyor who is responsible for butchering meats, poultry, and occasionally fish. In the brigade system, the butcher may also be responsible for breading meat and fish items and other mise-en-place operations involving meat.

butter: A semisolid fat made by churning cream.

buttercream: A mixture of butter, sugar, and eggs or custard. Used to garnish cakes and pastries.

butterfly: To cut an item (usually meat or seafood) and open out the edges like a book or the wings of a butterfly.

buttermilk: A dairy beverage with a slightly sour flavor similar to that of yogurt. Traditionally, the liquid by-product of butter churning, now usually made by culturing skim milk.

C

Cajun: A hearty cuisine based on French and southern influences; signature ingredients include spices, dark roux, pork fat, filé powder, green peppers, onions, and celery. Jambalaya is a traditional Cajun dish.

cake: A sweet product containing flour, sugar, salt, egg, milk, liquid, flavoring, shortening, and leavening agent.

calorie: A unit used to measure food energy. It is the amount of energy needed to raise the temperature of 1 gram of water by 1°C.

calzone (It.): A pizza that is stuffed with meats, vegetables, or cheese, folded over to resemble a large turnover, then baked or deep-fried.

Canadian bacon: Smoked pork loin.

canapé: An hors-d'oeuvre consisting of a small piece of bread or toast, often cut in a decorative shape, garnished with a savory spread or topping.

caramelization: The process of browning sugar in the presence of heat. The temperature range in which sugar caramelizes is approximately 320° to 360°F/160° to 182°C.

carbohydrate: One of the basic nutrients used by the body as a source of energy. Types include simple (sugars) and complex (starches and fibers).

carbon dioxide: A colorless, tasteless, edible gas obtained during fermentation or from the combination of soda and acid.

carry-over cooking: Heat retained in cooked foods that allows them to continue cooking even after removal from the cooking medium. Especially important to roasted foods.

casing: A synthetic or natural membrane (if natural, usually pig or sheep intestines) used to enclose sausage forcemeat.

casserole (Fr.): A lidded cooking vessel that is used in the oven; usually round with two handles. Also, food cooked in a casserole.

cassoulet: A stew of beans baked with pork or other meats, duck or goose confit, and seasonings.

caul fat: A fatty membrane from a pig or sheep intestine that resembles fine netting; used to bard roasts and pâtés and to encase sausage forcemeat.

cellulose: A complex carbohydrate; it is the main structural component of plant cells.

cephalopod: Marine creatures whose tentacles and arms are attached directly to their heads, such as squid and octopus.

chafing dish: A metal dish with a heating unit (flame or electric) used to keep foods warm and to cook foods at tableside or during buffet service.

champagne: A sparkling white wine produced in the Champagne region of France. The term is sometimes incorrectly applied to other sparkling wines.

charcuterie (Fr.): The preparation of pork and other meat items, such as hams, terrines, sausages, pâtés, and other forcemeats.

charcutière (Fr.): The person who prepares charcuterie items. À la charcutière, meaning in the style of the butcher's wife, refers to items (usually grilled meat) that are served with Sauce Robert and finished with a julienne of gherkins.

chateaubriand: A cut of meat from the thick end of the tenderloin.

chaud-froid (Fr.): Literally, "hot-cold." A sauce that is prepared hot but served cold as part of a buffet display, usually as a decorative coating for meats, poultry, or seafood. Classically made from béchamel, cream, or aspic.

cheesecloth: A light, fine mesh gauze used for straining liquids and making sachets.

chef de partie (Fr.): Station chef. In the brigade system, these are the line-cook positions, such as saucier, grillardin, etc.

chef de rang (Fr.): Front waiter. A demi-chef de rang is a back waiter or busboy.

chef de salle (Fr.): Headwaiter.

chef de service (Fr.): Director of service.

chef de vin (Fr.): Wine steward.

chef's potato: All-purpose potato.

chef's knife: An all-purpose knife used for chopping, slicing, and mincing; its blade is usually between 8 and 14 inches/20 and 36 cm long.

chemical leavener: An ingredient or combination of ingredients (such as baking soda or baking powder) whose chemical action is used to produce carbon dioxide gas to leaven baked goods.

cherrystone: A medium-sized, hard-shell clam indigenous to the East Coast of the United States; may be served raw or cooked.

chiffon: A cake made by the foaming method that contains a high percentage of eggs and sugar and relatively little if any fat.

chiffonade: Leafy vegetables or herbs cut into fine shreds; often used as a garnish.

chile: The fruit of certain types of capsicum peppers (not related to black pepper), used fresh or dry as a seasoning. Chiles come in many types (for example, jalapeño, serrano, poblano) and varying degrees of spiciness.

chili: A mixture such as chili powder, or a dish of the same name.

chili powder: Dried chiles that have been ground or crushed, often with other ground spices and herbs added.

chine: Backbone. A cut of meat that includes the backbone. Also, to separate the backbone and ribs to facilitate carving.

chinois: A conical sieve used for straining and puréeing foods.

cholesterol: A substance found exclusively in animal products such as meat, eggs, and cheese (dietary cholesterol) or in the blood (serum cholesterol).

chop: To cut into pieces of roughly the same size. Also, a small cut of meat including part of the rib.

choucroute (Fr.): Sauerkraut. *Choucroute garni* is sauerkraut garnished with various meats.

chowder: A thick soup that may be made from a variety of ingredients but usually contains potatoes.

ciguatera toxin: A toxin found in certain fish, otherwise harmless, that causes illness in humans when eaten. The poisoning is caused by the fish's diet and is not affected by cooking or freezing.

cioppino (It.): A fish stew usually made with white wine and tomatoes, believed to have originated in Genoa.

clarification: The process of removing solid impurities from a liquid (such as butter or stock). Also, a mixture of ground meat, egg whites, mirepoix, tomato purée, herbs, and spices used to clarify broth for consommé.

clarified butter: Butter from which the milk solids and water have been removed, leaving pure butterfat. Has a higher smoking point than whole butter but less butter flavor.

coagulation: The curdling or clumping of protein, usually due to the application of heat or acid.

coarse chop: A type of preparation in which food is cut into pieces of roughly the same size. Used for items such as mirepoix, where appearance is not important.

cocoa: The pods of the cacao tree, processed to remove the cocoa butter and ground into powder. Used as a flavoring.

cocotte (Fr.): Casserole. A cooking dish with a tight-fitting lid for braising or stewing. Also, a small ramekin used for cooking eggs. *En cocotte* is often interchangeable with *en casserole*.

coddled eggs: Eggs cooked in simmering water, in their shells or in ramekins or coddlers, until set.

colander: A perforated bowl, with or without a base or legs, used to strain or drain foods.

collagen: A fibrous protein found in the connective tissue of animals, used to make sausage casings as well as glue and gelatin. Breaks down into gelatin when cooked in a moist environment for an extended period of time.

combination method: A cooking method that involves the application of both dry and moist heat to the main item (for example, meats are seared in fat then simmered in a sauce for braising or stewing).

commis (Fr.): Apprentice. A cook who works under a chef de partie to learn the station and its responsibilities.

communard (Fr.): The kitchen position responsible for preparing staff meals.

complete protein: A food source that provides all of the essential amino acids in the correct ratio so that they can be used in the body for protein synthesis. Animal foods are considered complete proteins.

complex carbohydrate: A large molecule made up of long chains of sugar molecules. In food, these molecules are found in starches and fiber.

composed salad (Fr.): A salad in which the items are carefully arranged on a plate, rather than tossed together.

compote: A dish of fruit—fresh or dried—cooked in syrup flavored with spices or liqueur.

compound butter: Butter combined with herbs or other seasonings and usually used to sauce grilled or broiled items or vegetables.

concasser (Fr.): To pound or chop coarsely. Concassé usually refers to tomatoes that have been peeled, seeded, and chopped.

condiment: An aromatic mixture, such as pickles, chutney, and some sauces and relishes, that accompanies food. Usually kept on the table throughout service.

conduction: A method of heat transfer in which heat is transmitted through another substance. In cooking, when heat is transmitted to food through a pot or pan, oven racks, or grill rods.

confiserie (Fr.): Confectionery. A *confiseur* is a pâtissier specializing in, and responsible for, the production of candies and related items, such as petits fours.

confit: Meat (usually goose, duck, or pork) cooked and preserved in its own fat.

consommé: Broth that has been clarified using a mixture of ground meat, egg whites, and other ingredients that trap impurities.

convection: A method of heat transfer in which heat is transmitted through the circulation of air or water.

convection oven: An oven that employs convection currents by forcing hot air through fans so it circulates around food, cooking it quickly and evenly.

converted rice: Parboiled rice.

coquilles St. Jacques (Fr.): Scallops. Also, a dish of broiled scallops with any of several garnishes.

coral: Lobster roe, which is red or coral-colored when cooked.

cornichon (Fr.): A small, sour, pickled cucumber.

cornstarch: A fine, white powder milled from dried corn; used primarily as a thickener for sauce and occasionally as an ingredient in batters.

cottage cheese: The drained curd of soured cow's milk.

coulis: A thick purée, usually of vegetables but possibly of fruit. Traditionally refers to meat, fish, or shellfish purée; meat jus; or certain thick soups.

country-style: A term used to describe forcemeat that is coarse in texture, usually made from pork, pork fat, liver, and various garnishes.

court bouillon (Fr.): Literally, "short broth." An aromatic vegetable broth that usually includes an acidic ingredient, such as wine or vinegar; most commonly used for poaching fish.

couscous: Pellets of semolina usually cooked by steaming, traditionally in a couscoussière. Also, the stew with which this grain is traditionally served.

couscoussière: A set of nesting pots, similar to a steamer, used to cook couscous.

couverture: Fine semisweet chocolate used for coating and decorating. Its high cocoa butter content gives it a glossy appearance after tempering.

cream: The fatty component of milk; available with various fat contents. Also refers to a mixing method for batter cakes in which the sugar and fat are beaten together until they are light and fluffy before the other ingredients are added.

cream cheese: The drained, pressed curd of soured cream.

cream of tartar: A salt of tartaric acid used extensively in baking.

cream soup: Traditionally a soup based on a béchamel sauce. Loosely, any soup finished with cream, a cream variant such as sour cream, or a liaison; these soups are usually based on béchamel or velouté.

cream puff: A pastry made with pâte à choux, filled with crème pâtissière, and usually glazed. Also called *profiterole*.

crème Anglaise (Fr.): Custard.

crème brûlée (Fr.): Custard topped with sugar and caramelized under the broiler before service.

crème fraîche (Fr.): Heavy cream cultured to give it a thick consistency and a slightly tangy flavor. Used in hot preparations since it is less likely to curdle when heated than sour cream or yogurt.

crème pâtissière (Fr.): Literally, "pastry cream." Custard made with eggs, flour or other starches, milk, sugar, and flavorings, used to fill and garnish pastries or as the base for puddings, soufflés, and creams.

Creole: This sophisticated type of cooking is a combination of French, Spanish, and African cuisines; signature ingredients include butter, cream, tomatoes, filé powder, and green peppers, onions, and celery. Gumbo is a traditional Creole dish.

crêpe: A thin pancake made with egg batter; used in sweet and savory preparations.

croissant: A pastry consisting of a yeast dough with a butter roll-in, traditionally formed into a crescent shape.

cross contamination: The transference of disease-causing elements from one source to another through physical contact.

croustade: A small baked or fried edible container for meat, chicken, or other mixtures; usually made from pastry but may be made from potatoes or pasta.

croûte, en (Fr.): Encased in a bread or pastry crust.

crouton: A bread or pastry garnish, usually toasted or sautéed until crisp.

crumb: A term used to describe the texture of baked goods; for example, an item can be said to have a fine or coarse crumb.

crustacean: A class of hard-shelled arthropods, primarily aquatic, which includes edible species such as lobster, crab, shrimp, and crayfish.

cuisson (Fr.): Poaching liquid, including stock, fumet, court bouillon, or other liquid, which may be reduced and used as a base for the poached item's sauce.

curd: The semisolid portion of milk once it coagulates and separates.

cure: To preserve a food by salting, smoking, and/or drying.

curing salt: A mixture of 94 percent table salt (sodium chloride) and 6 percent sodium nitrite, used to preserve meats. Also known as *tinted curing mixture* or *TCM*.

curry: A mixture of spices used primarily in Indian cuisine. May include turmeric, coriander, cumin, cayenne or other chilies, cardamom, cinnamon, clove, fennel, fenugreek, ginger, and garlic. Also, a dish seasoned with curry.

custard (Fr.): A mixture of milk, beaten egg, and possibly other ingredients, such as sweet or savory flavorings, cooked with gentle heat, often in a bain-marie or double boiler.

D

daily values (DVS): Standard values developed by the Food and Drug Administration for use on food labels.

danger zone: The temperature range from 40° to 140°F/4° to 60°C, the most favorable condition for rapid growth of many pathogens.

Danish pastry: A pastry consisting of rich yeast dough with a butter roll-in, possibly filled with nuts, fruit, or other ingredients and iced. This pastry originated in Denmark.

daube: A meat stew braised in red wine, traditionally in a daubière, a specialized casserole with a tight-fitting lid and indentations to hold hot coals.

debeard: To remove the shaggy, inedible fibers from a mussel. These fibers anchor the mussel to its mooring.

deck oven: A variant of the conventional oven, in which the heat source is located underneath the deck or floor of the oven and the food is placed directly on the deck instead of on a rack.

deep fry: To cook food by immersion in hot fat; deep-fried foods are often coated with bread crumbs or batter before being cooked.

deep poach: To cook food gently in enough simmering liquid to completely submerge the food.

deglaze, déglacer: To use a liquid, such as wine, water, or stock, to dissolve food particles and/or caramelized drippings left in a pan after roasting or sautéing.

degrease, dégraisser: To skim the fat off the surface of a liquid, such as a stock or sauce.

demiglace (Fr.): Literally, "half-glaze." A mixture of equal proportions of brown stock and brown sauce that has been reduced by half. One of the grand sauces.

dépouillage (Fr.): To skim the surface of a cooking liquid, such as a stock or sauce. This action is simplified by placing the pot off center on the burner and skimming impurities as they collect at one side of the pot.

deviled: Meat, poultry, or other food seasoned with mustard, vinegar, and possibly other seasonings, coated with bread crumbs, and grilled.

dice: To cut ingredients into small cubes (¼ inch/6 mm for small, ½ inch/12 mm for medium, and ¾ inch/19 mm for large is the standard).

die: The plate in a meat grinder through which foods pass just before a blade cuts them. The size of the die's opening determines the fineness of the grind.

digestif (Fr.): A spirit usually consumed after dining as an aid to digestion. Examples include brandy and cognac.

direct heat: A method of heat transfer in which heat waves radiate from a source (for example, an open burner or grill) and travel directly to the item being heated with no conductor between heat source and food. Examples are grilling, broiling, and toasting. Also known as radiant heat.

dock: To cut the top of dough before baking to allow it to expand and/or to create a decorative effect.

doré (Fr.): Coated with egg yolk or cooked to a golden brown.

drawn: Describes a whole fish that has been scaled and gutted but still has its head, fins, and tail.

dredge: To coat food with a dry ingredient such as flour or bread crumbs.

dressed: Prepared for cooking. A dressed fish is gutted and scaled, and its head, tail, and fins are removed (same as pan-dressed). Dressed poultry is plucked, drawn, singed, trimmed, and trussed. Also, coated with dressing, as in a salad.

drum sieve: A sieve consisting of a screen stretched across a shallow cylinder of wood or aluminum. Also known as a tamis.

dry cure: A combination of salts and spices usually used before smoking to process meats and forcemeats.

dry sauté: To sauté without fat, usually using a nonstick pan.

dumpling: Any of a number of small soft dough or batter items, which are steamed, poached, or simmered (possibly on top of a stew); may be filled or plain.

durum: A species of hard wheat primarily milled into semolina for use in dried pasta.

dusting: Distributing a film of flour on pans or work surface.

Dutch oven: A kettle, usually of cast iron, used for stewing and braising on the stovetop or in the oven.

Dutch process: A method for treating cocoa powder with an alkali to reduce its acidity.

duxelles: An appareil of finely chopped mushrooms and shallots sautéed gently in butter.

E

éclair: A long, thin shell made of pâte à choux, filled with crème patissière and glazed with chocolate ganache.

edible-portion (EP) weight: The weight of an item after trimming and preparation (as opposed to the as-purchased [AP] weight).

egg wash: A mixture of beaten eggs (whole eggs, yolks, or whites) and a liquid, usually milk or water, used to coat baked goods to give them a sheen.

émincer (Fr.): To cut an item, usually meat, into very thin slices.

emulsion: A mixture of two or more liquids, one of which is a fat or oil and the other of which is water-based, so that tiny globules of one are suspended in the other. This may involve the use of stabilizers, such as egg or mustard. Emulsions may be temporary, permanent, or semipermanent.

endosperm: The inside portion of a grain, usually the largest portion, composed primarily of starch and protein.

entrecôte (Fr.): Literally, "between the ribs." A very tender steak cut from between the ninth and eleventh ribs of beef.

entremetier (Fr.): Vegetable chef/station. The position responsible for hot appetizers and often soups, vegetables, starches, and pastas; may also be responsible for egg dishes.

escalope (Fr.): Same as *scallop*; a small boneless piece of meat or fish of uniform thickness.

Espagnole sauce (Fr.): "Spanish sauce." Brown sauce made with brown stock, caramelized mirepoix, tomato purée, and seasonings.

essence: A concentrated flavoring extracted from an item, usually by infusion or distillation. Includes items such as vanilla and other extracts, concentrated stocks, and fumets.

estouffade (Fr.): Stew. Also, a type of brown stock based on pork knuckle and veal and beef bones that is often used in braises.

ethylene gas: A gas emitted by various fruits and vegetables; ethylene gas speeds ripening, maturing, and eventually rotting.

étouffé (Fr.): Literally, "smothered." Refers to food cooked by a method similar to braising, in which items are cooked with little or no added liquid in a pan with a tight-fitting lid. (Also *étuver, à l'étuvée*.)

evaporated milk: Unsweetened canned milk from which water has been removed before canning.

extrusion/extruding machine: A machine used to shape pasta. The dough is pushed out through perforated plates rather than being rolled.

F

fabrication: The butchering, cutting, and trimming of meat, poultry, fish, and game (large pieces or whole) into a variety of smaller cuts to prepare them to be cooked.

facultative bacteria: Bacteria that can survive both with and without oxygen.

farce (Fr.): Forcemeat or stuffing; *farci(e)* means "stuffed" in French.

farina (It.): Flour or fine meal of wheat.

fatback: Pork fat from the back of the pig, used primarily for barding.

fat: One of the basic nutrients used by the body to provide energy. Fats also carry flavor in food and give a feeling of fullness.

fermentation: The breakdown of carbohydrates into carbon dioxide gas and alcohol, usually through the action of yeast on sugar.

fiber, dietary fiber: The structural component of plants that is necessary to the human diet. Sometimes referred to as roughage.

filé: A thickener made from ground dried sassafras leaves; used primarily in gumbos.

fillet, filet: A boneless cut of meat, fish, or poultry.

fillet mignon: The expensive, boneless cut of beef from the small end of the tenderloin.

fines herbes: A mixture of herbs, usually parsley, chervil, tarragon, and chives.

first in, first out (FIFO): A fundamental storage principle based on stock rotation. Products are stored and used so that the oldest product is always used first.

fish poacher: A long, narrow pot with straight sides and possibly a perforated rack, used for poaching whole fish.

five-spice powder: A mixture of equal parts ground cinnamon, clove, fennel seed, star anise, and Szechwan peppercorns.

flatfish: A type of fish characterized by its flat body and having both eyes on one side of its head (for example, sole, plaice, and halibut).

flattop: A thick plate of cast iron or steel set over the heat source on a range; diffuses heat, making it more even than an open burner.

fleurons: Garnishes made from light puff pastry cut into oval, diamond, or crescent shapes and served with meat, fish, or soup.

Florentine, à la (Fr.): Dishes prepared in the style of Florence, Italy; denotes the use of spinach and sometimes cheese.

foaming method: Cake batters made by first preparing a foam of eggs, egg whites, or egg yolks with sugar. Little if any fat is included in the batter.

foie gras: The fattened liver of a duck or goose.

fold: To gently combine ingredients (especially foams) so as not to release trapped air bubbles. Also, to gently mix together two items, usually a light, airy mixture with a denser mixture. Also, the method of turning, rolling, and layering dough over on itself to produce a flaky texture.

fond (Fr.): Stock.

fondant: An icing made with sugar, water, and glucose; used primarily for pastry and confectionery.

food-borne illness: An illness in humans caused by the consumption of an adulterated food product. For an official determination that an outbreak of food-borne illness has occurred, two or more people must have become ill after eating the same food, and the outbreak must be confirmed by health officials.

food cost: Cost of all food purchased to prepare items for sale in a restaurant.

food mill: A type of strainer with a crank-operated, curved blade. It is used to purée soft foods.

food processor: A machine with interchangeable blades and disks and a removable bowl and lid separate from the motor housing. It can be used for a variety of tasks, including chopping, grinding, puréeing, emulsifying, kneading, slicing, shredding, and cutting into julienne.

forcemeat: A mixture of chopped or ground meat and other ingredients used for pâtés, sausages, and other preparations.

fork-tender: Degree of doneness in foods; fork-tender foods are easily pierced or cut by a fork, or should slide readily from a fork when lifted.

formula: A recipe, in which measurements for each ingredient may be given as percentages of the weight for the main ingredient.

fortified wine: Wine to which a spirit, usually brandy, has been added (for example, Marsala, Madeira, Port, or Sherry).

free-range: Refers to livestock that is raised unconfined.

frenching: The process of scraping meat from bones before cooking.

fricassée (Fr.): A stew of poultry or other white meat with a white sauce.

fritter: Sweet or savory food coated or mixed into batter and deep-fried. Also called *beignet*.

friturier (Fr.): Fry chef/station. The position responsible for all fried foods; it may be combined with the rôtisseur position.

fructose: A simple sugar found in fruits.

fumet (Fr.): A type of stock in which the main flavoring ingredient is allowed to cook in a covered pot with wine and aromatics. Fish fumet is the most common type.

G

galantine: Boned meat (usually poultry) that is stuffed, rolled, poached, and served cold, usually in aspic.

ganache: A filling made of heavy cream, chocolate, and/or other flavorings; may be used as a sauce, a glaze, or to make confections. Can range from soft to hard, depending on the amount of butter and cream.

garbure (Fr.): A thick vegetable soup usually containing beans, cabbage, and/or potatoes.

garde manger (Fr.): Pantry chef/station. The position responsible for cold-food preparation, including salads, cold appetizers, pâtés, etc.

garni (Fr.): Garnished.

garnish: An edible decoration or accompaniment to a dish.

gazpacho (Sp.): A cold soup made from vegetables, typically tomatoes, cucumbers, peppers, and onions.

gelatin: A protein-based substance found in animal bones and connective tissue. When dissolved in hot liquid and then cooled, it can be used as a thickener and stabilizer.

gelatinization: A phase in the process of thickening a liquid with starch in which the starch molecules swell to form a network that traps water molecules.

génoise (Fr.): A sponge cake made with whole eggs, used for petits fours, layer cakes, and other desserts.

germ: The embryo of a cereal grain, which is usually separated from the endosperm during milling because it contains oils that accelerate the spoilage of flours and meals.

gherkin: A small pickled cucumber.

giblets: Organs and other trim from poultry, including the liver, heart, gizzard, and neck.

glaçe (Fr.): Reduced stock; ice cream; icing.

glaçe(e) (Fr.): Glazed or iced.

glaze: To give an item a shiny surface by brushing it with sauce, aspic, icing, or another appareil. For meat, to coat with sauce and then brown in an oven or salamander.

glucose: A simple sugar; the preferred source of energy for the human body.

gluten: A protein that develops into long, elastic strands when hard wheat flour is moistened and agitated. Gluten gives yeast doughs their characteristic elasticity.

goujon (Fr.): Fish fillet cut in strips and usually breaded or batter-coated and then deep-fried. A goujonette is a smaller strip.

grand sauce: One of several basic sauces that are used in the preparation of many other small sauces. The grand sauces are demiglace, velouté, béchamel, hollandaise, and tomato. Also called mother sauce.

gratin (Fr.): Browned in an oven or under a salamander (au gratin, gratin de). Gratin can also refer to a forcemeat in which some portion of the dominant meat is sautéed and cooled before grinding.

gravlax: Raw salmon cured with salt, sugar, and fresh dill. A dish of Scandinavian origin.

griddle: A heavy metal surface, which may be either fitted with handles, built into a stove, or heated by its own gas or electric element. Cooking is done directly on the griddle.

grill: A cooking technique in which foods are cooked by a radiant heat source placed below the food. Also, the piece of equipment on which grilling is done. Grills may be fueled by gas, electricity, charcoal, or wood.

grill pan: A skillet with ridges that is used to simulate grilling on the stovetop.

grillardin (Fr.): Grill chef/station. The position responsible for all grilled foods; may be combined with the position of rôtisseur.

grissini (It.): Thin, crisp breadsticks.

griswold: A pot, similar to a rondeau, made of cast iron; may have a single short handle rather than the usual loop handles.

gumbo: A Creole soup/stew thickened with filé or okra.

H

haricot (Fr.): Literally, "bean." Haricots verts are green beans.

hash: Chopped, cooked meat, usually with potatoes and/or other vegetables, which is seasoned, bound with a sauce, and sautéed. Also, to chop.

Hazard Analysis Critical Control Point (HACCP): A monitoring system used to track foods from the time that they are received until they are served to consumers, to ensure that the foods are free from contamination. Standards and controls are established for time and temperature, as well as safe handling practices.

Heimlich maneuver: First aid for choking, involving the application of sudden, upward pressure on the upper abdomen to force a foreign object from the windpipe.

high-ratio cake: A cake in which the batter includes a high percentage of sugar in relation to other ingredients.

hollandaise: A classic emulsion sauce made with a vinegar reduction, egg yolks, and melted butter flavored with lemon juice. It is one of the grand sauces.

hollow-ground: A type of knife blade made by fusing two sheets of metal and beveling or fluting the edge.

hominy: Corn that has been milled or treated with a lye solution to remove the bran and germ.

homogenization: A process used to prevent the milkfat from separating out of milk products. The liquid is forced through an ultrafine mesh at high pressure, which breaks up fat globules, dispersing them evenly throughout the liquid.

hors-d'oeuvre (Fr.): Literally, "outside the work." An appetizer.

hotel pan: A rectangular metal pan in any of a number of standard sizes, with a lip that allows it to rest in a storage shelf or steam table.

hydrogenation: The process in which hydrogen atoms are added to an unsaturated fat molecule, making it partially or completely saturated, hence solid at room temperature.

hydroponics: A technique that involves growing vegetables in nutrient-enriched water rather than in soil.

hygiene: Conditions and practices followed to maintain health, including sanitation and personal cleanliness.

I

induction burner: A type of heating unit that relies on magnetic attraction between the cooktop and metals in the pot to generate the heat that cooks foods in the pan. Reaction time is significantly faster than with traditional burners.

infection: Contamination by a disease-causing agent, such as bacteria.

infusion: Steeping an aromatic or other item in liquid to extract its flavor. Also, the liquid resulting from this process.

instant-reading thermometer: A thermometer used to measure the internal temperature of foods. The stem is inserted in the food, producing an instant temperature read-out.

intoxication: Poisoning. A state of being tainted with toxins, particularly those produced by microorganisms that have infected food.

inventory: An itemized list of goods and equipment on hand, together with the estimated worth or cost.

invert sugar: Sugar that is mixed with water and acid and then heated. It is more soluble than normal sugar and doesn't crystallize easily.

J

jardinière: A mixture of vegetables.

julienne: Vegetables, potatoes, or other items cut into thin strips; ⅛ inch by ⅛ inch by 1 to 2 inches/3 mm by 3 mm by 25 to 50 mm is standard. Fine julienne is 1⁄16 inch by 1⁄16 inch by 1 to 2 inches/1.5 mm by 1.5 mm by 25 to 50 mm.

jus (Fr.): Juice. *Jus de viande* is meat gravy. Meat served au jus is served with its own juice or jus lié.

jus lié (Fr.): Meat juice thickened lightly with arrowroot or cornstarch.

K

kasha (Rus.): Buckwheat groats that have been hulled and crushed; usually prepared by boiling.

knead: The process of stretching dough repeatedly in order to give it a good consistency. Kneading also helps to ensure proper quality in the finished baked item.

kosher: Prepared in accordance with Jewish dietary laws.

kosher salt: Pure, refined salt used for pickling because it does not contain magnesium carbonate and thus does not cloud brine solutions. Also used to prepare kosher items. Also known as coarse salt or pickling salt.

L

lactose: The simple sugar found in milk.

laminate: To fold and roll a dough to create alternating layers of fat and dough.

lard: Rendered pork fat used for pastry and frying. Also, to insert small strips of fatback into naturally lean meats before roasting or braising. The process is done using a larding needle.

lardon (Fr.): A strip of fat used for larding; may be seasoned. Also *lardoon.*

leavener: Any ingredient or process that produces gas and causes the rising of baked goods.

lecithin: An emulsifier found in eggs and soybeans.

legume: The seeds of certain plants, including beans and peas, which are eaten for their earthy flavors and high nutritional value. Also, the French word for vegetable.

liaison: A mixture of egg yolks and cream used to thicken and enrich sauces. Also loosely applied to any appareil used as a thickener.

liqueur: A spirit flavored with fruit, spices, nuts, herbs, and/or seeds and usually sweetened.

littleneck: Small, hard-shell clams often eaten raw on the half shell; smaller than a cherrystone clam.

low-fat milk: Milk containing less than 2 percent fat.

lox: Salt-cured salmon.

lozenge cut: A knife cut in which foods are cut into small diamond shapes.

Lyonnaise (Fr.): Lyons style. Refers to a sauce made with onions and usually butter, white wine, vinegar, and demiglace. Lyonnaise potatoes are sautéed with onions and butter.

M

macaroon: Small cookies of nut paste (usually almond), sugar, and egg white.

Madeira: A Portuguese fortified wine that is treated with heat as it ages, giving it a distinctive flavor and brownish color.

Maillard reaction: A complex browning reaction that results in the particular flavor and color of foods that do not contain much sugar, including roasted meats. The reaction, which involves carbohydrates and amino acids, is named after the French scientist who first discovered it. There are low-temperature and high-temperature Maillard reactions; the high-temperature reaction starts at 310°F/155°C.

maître d'hôtel (Fr.): Dining room manager or food and beverage manager, informally called maître d'. This position oversees the dining-room or front-of-the-house staff. Also, a compound butter flavored with chopped parsley and lemon juice.

mandoline: A slicing device of stainless steel with carbon-steel blades. The blades may be adjusted to cut items into various shapes and thicknesses.

marbling: The intramuscular fat found in meat that makes the meat tender and juicy.

mark on a grill: To turn a food (without flipping it over) 90 degrees after it has been on the grill for several seconds to create the cross-hatching associated with grilled foods.

marinade: An appareil used before cooking to flavor and moisten foods; may be liquid or dry. Liquid marinades are usually based on an acidic ingredient, such as wine or vinegar; dry marinades are usually salt-based.

marzipan: A paste of ground almonds, sugar, and egg whites that is used to fill and decorate pastries.

matelote (Fr.): A fish stew traditionally made with eel.

matignon (Fr.): An edible mirepoix that is often used in poêléed dishes and is usually served with the finished dish. Typically, matignon includes two parts carrot, one part celery, one part leek, one part onion, one part mushroom (optional), and one part ham or bacon.

mayonnaise: A cold emulsion of oil, egg yolks, vinegar, mustard, and seasonings.

mechanical leavener: Air incorporated into a batter to act as a leavener. Usually, eggs or cream are whipped into a foam, then are folded into the batter.

medallion: A small, round scallop of meat.

meringue (Fr.): Egg whites beaten until they are stiff, then sweetened and possibly baked until stiff. Types include regular or common, Italian, and Swiss.

mesophilic: A term used to describe bacteria that thrive in temperatures between 60° and 100°F/16° and 43°C.

metabolism: The sum of chemical processes in living cells by which energy is provided and new material is assimilated.

meunière, à la: In the style of the miller's wife. Refers to a cooking technique for fish in which the item is dusted with flour, sautéed, and served with a sauce of beurre noisette, lemon juice, and parsley.

microwave oven: An oven in which electromagnetic waves (similar to radio waves) generated by a device called a magnetron penetrate food and cause the water molecules in it to oscillate. This rapid molecular motion generates heat, which cooks the food.

mie (Fr.): The soft part of bread (not the crust); mie de pain is fresh white-bread crumbs.

millet: A small, round, glutenless grain that is boiled or ground into flour.

milling: The process by which grain is ground into flour or meal.

mince: To chop into very small pieces.

mineral: An inorganic element that is an essential component of the diet. Provides no energy and is therefore referred to as a noncaloric nutrient.

minestrone: A vegetable soup that typically includes dried beans and pasta.

minute, à la (Fr.): Literally, "at the minute." A restaurant production approach in which dishes are not prepared until an order arrives in the kitchen.

mirepoix: A combination of chopped aromatic vegetables—usually two parts onion, one part carrot, and one part celery—used to flavor stocks, soups, braises, and stews.

mise en place (Fr.): Literally, "put in place." The preparation and assembly of ingredients, pans, utensils, and plates or serving pieces needed for a particular dish or service period.

mode, à la (Fr.): Literally, "in the style of" (often followed by de plus a descriptive phrase). Boeuf à la mode is braised beef; pie à la mode is served with ice cream.

molasses: The dark brown, sweet syrup that is a by-product of sugar cane refining.

mollusk: Any of a number of invertebrate animals with soft, unsegmented bodies usually enclosed in a hard shell; included are clams, oysters, and snails.

monosodium glutamate (MSG): A flavor enhancer without a distinct flavor of its own; used primarily in Chinese and processed foods. It may cause allergic reactions in some people.

monounsaturated fat: A fat with one available bonding site not filled with a hydrogen atom. Food sources include avocado, olives, and nuts.

monté au beurre (Fr.): Literally, "lifted with butter." Refers to a technique used to enrich sauces, thicken them slightly, and give them a glossy appearance by whisking in whole butter.

mousse (Fr.): A dish made with beaten egg whites and/or whipped cream folded into a flavored base appareil. May be sweet or savory.

mousseline (Fr.): A mousse. Also, a sauce made by folding whipped cream into hollandaise. Also, a very light forcemeat based on white meat or seafood lightened with cream and eggs.

N

napoleon: A pastry made of layered puff pastry rectangles filled with pastry cream and glazed with fondant.

nappé (Fr.): To coat with sauce; thickened.

nature (Fr.): Literally, "ungarnished" or "plain." Pommes natures are boiled potatoes.

navarin (Fr.): A stew, traditionally of lamb, with potatoes, onions, and possibly other vegetables.

new potato: A small, waxy potato that is usually prepared by boiling or steaming and is often eaten with its skin.

noisette (Fr.): Hazelnut. Also, a small portion of meat cut from the rib. Pommes noisette are tournéed potatoes browned in butter. Beurre noisette is browned butter.

nonbony fish: Fish whose skeletons are made of cartilage rather than hard bone (for example, shark, skate). Also called cartilaginous fish.

nouvelle cuisine (Fr.): Literally, "new cooking." A culinary movement emphasizing freshness and lightness of ingredients, classical preparations, and innovative combinations and presentation.

nutrient: A basic component of food used by the body for growth, repair, restoration, and energy. Includes carbohydrates, fats, proteins, water, vitamins, and minerals.

nutrition: The processes by which an organism takes in and uses food.

O

oblique cut, roll cut: A knife cut used primarily with long, cylindrical vegetables such as carrots. The item is cut on a diagonal, rolled 180 degrees, then cut on the same diagonal, producing a piece with two angled edges.

offal: Variety meats, including organs (brains, heart, kidneys, lungs, sweetbreads, tripe, tongue), head meat, tail, and feet.

offset spatula: A hand tool with a wide, bent blade set in a short handle, used to turn or lift foods from grills, broilers, or griddles.

oignon brûlé (Fr.): Literally, "burnt onion." A peeled, halved onion seared on a flattop or in a skillet and used to enhance the color of stock and consommé.

oignon piqué (Fr.): Literally, "pricked onion." A whole, peeled onion to which a bay leaf is attached, using a clove as a tack. It is used to flavor béchamel sauce and some soups.

omega-3 fatty acids: Polyunsaturated fatty acids that may reduce the risk of heart disease and tumor growth, stimulate the immune system, and lower blood pressure; they occur in fatty fish, dark green leafy vegetables, and certain nuts and oils.

omelet: Beaten egg that is cooked in butter in a specialized pan or skillet and then rolled or folded into an oval. Omelets may be filled with a variety of ingredients before or after rolling.

organic leavener: Yeast. A living organism operates by fermenting sugar to produce carbon dioxide gas, causing the batter to rise.

organ meat: Meat from an organ, rather than the muscle tissue of an animal.

oven spring: The rapid initial rise of yeast doughs when placed in a hot oven. Heat accelerates the growth of the yeast, which produces more carbon dioxide gas and also causes this gas to expand.

P

paella (Sp.): A dish of rice cooked with onion, tomato, garlic, vegetables, and various meats, including chicken, chorizo, shellfish, and possibly other types. A paella pan is a specialized pan for cooking paella; it is wide and shallow and usually has two loop handles.

paillard (Fr.): A scallop of meat pounded until thin; usually grilled.

palette knife: A flexible, round-tipped knife used to turn pancakes and grilled foods and to spread fillings and glazes; may have a serrated edge. Also called *metal spatula*.

panada: An appareil based on starch (such as flour or crumbs) moistened with a liquid, used as a binder.

pan-broiling: A cooking method similar to dry sautéing that simulates broiling by cooking an item in a hot pan with little or no fat.

pan-dressed: Portion-size whole fish, dressed.

pan frying: A cooking method in which items are cooked in deep fat in a skillet; this generally involves more fat than sautéing or stir frying but less than deep frying.

pan gravy: A sauce made by deglazing pan drippings from a roast and combining them with a roux or other starch and additional stock.

pan-steaming: A method of cooking foods in a very small amount of liquid in a covered pan over direct heat.

papillote, en (Fr.): Refers to a moist-heat cooking method similar to steaming, in which items are enclosed in parchment and cooked in the oven.

parchment: Heat-resistant paper used in cooking for such preparations as lining baking pans, cooking items en papillote, and covering items during shallow poaching.

parcook: To partially cook an item before storing or finishing by another method; may be the same as blanching.

Parisienne scoop: A small tool used for scooping balls out of vegetable or fruit. Also called a *melon baller*.

par stock: The amount of stock (food and other supplies) necessary to cover operating needs between deliveries.

pasta (It.): Literally, "dough" or "paste." Noodles made from a dough of flour (often semolina) and water or eggs that is kneaded, rolled, and cut or extruded, then cooked by boiling.

pasteurization: A process in which milk products are heated to kill microorganisms that could contaminate the milk.

pastry bag: A bag—usually made of plastic, canvas, or nylon—that can be fitted with plain or decorative tips and used to pipe out icings and puréed foods.

pâte (Fr.): Noodles or pasta. Also, dough or batter.

pâté (Fr.): A rich forcemeat of meat, game, poultry, seafood, and/or vegetables, baked in pastry or in a mold or dish.

pâte à choux: Cream puff paste, made by boiling a mixture of water, butter, and flour, then beating in whole eggs.

pâte brisée: Short pastry for pie crusts.

pâté de campagne: Country-style pâté, with a coarse texture.

pâté en croûte: Pâté baked in a pastry crust.

pâte feuilletée: Puff pastry.

pâte sucrée: Sweet short pastry.

pathogen: A disease-causing microorganism.

pâtissier (Fr.): Pastry chef. This station is responsible for baked items, pastries, and desserts. This is often a separate area of the kitchen.

paupiette: A fillet or scallop of fish or meat that is rolled up around a stuffing and poached or braised.

paysanne or fermier cut: A knife cut in which ingredients are cut into flat, square pieces; ½ inch by ½ inch by ⅛ inch/12 mm by 12 mm by 3 mm is the standard.

peel: A paddle used to transfer shaped doughs to a hearth or deck oven. Also, to remove the skin from a food item.

pesto (It.): A thick, puréed mixture of an herb, traditionally basil, and oil. Used as a sauce for pasta and other foods and as a garnish for soup. Pesto may also contain grated cheese, nuts or seeds, and other seasonings.

petit four: A bite-sized, iced and decorated cake.

pH scale: A scale with values from 0 to 14 representing degree of acidity. A measurement of 7 is neutral, 0 is most acidic and 14 is most alkaline. Chemically, pH measures the concentration of hydrogen ions.

phyllo dough: Pastry made with very thin sheets of a flour-and-water dough layered with butter and/or bread or cake crumbs; similar to strudel. Also called *filo*.

physical leavener: Name given to the action of steam when trapped in a dough.

phytochemicals: Naturally occurring compounds in plant foods that have antioxidant and disease-fighting properties.

pickling spice: A mixture of herbs and spices used to season pickles. Often includes dill weed and/or seed, coriander seed, cinnamon stick, peppercorns, bay leaves, and others.

pilaf: A technique for cooking grains in which the grain is sautéed briefly in butter, then simmered in stock or water with various seasonings. Also called *pilau, pilaw, pullao, pilav*.

pincé (Fr.): Refers to an item caramelized by sautéing; usually refers to a tomato product.

pluches: Whole herb leaves connected to a small bit of stem; often used as a garnish.

poach: To cook gently in simmering liquid that is 160° to 185°F/70° to 82°C.

poêlé: Used to refer to items cooked in their own juices (usually with the addition of a matignon, other aromatics, and melted butter) in a covered pot, usually in the oven. The technique is also called *butter roasting*.

poissonier (Fr.): Fish chef/station. The position responsible for fish items and their sauces; may be combined with the saucier position.

polenta (It.): Cornmeal mush.

polyunsaturated fat: A fat with more than one available bonding site not filled with a hydrogen atom. Food sources include corn, cottonseed, safflower, soy, and sunflower oils.

port: A fortified dessert wine. Vintage port is high-quality, unblended wine aged in the bottle for at least twelve years. Ruby port may be blended and is aged in wood for a short time. White port is made with white grapes.

pot-au-feu (Fr.): A classic French boiled dinner that typically includes poultry and beef, along with various root vegetables. The broth is often served as a first course, followed by the meats and vegetables.

prawn: A crustacean that closely resembles shrimp; often used as a general term for large shrimp.

presentation side: The side of a piece of meat, poultry, or fish that will be served facing up.

pressure steamer: A machine that cooks food using steam produced by heating water under pressure in a sealed compartment, allowing it to reach temperatures higher than boiling (212°F/100°C). The food is placed in a sealed chamber that cannot be opened until the pressure has been released and the steam properly vented from the chamber.

primal cuts: The portions produced by the initial cutting of an animal carcass. Cuts are determined standards that may vary by country and animal. Primal cuts are further broken down into smaller, more manageable cuts.

printanière: A garnish of spring vegetables.

prix fixe (Fr.): Literally, "fixed price." A type of menu in which a complete meal is offered for a preset price. The menu may offer several choices for each course.

proof: To allow yeast dough to rise. A proof box is a sealed cabinet that allows control over both temperature and humidity.

protein: One of the basic nutrients needed by the body to maintain life, supply energy, build and repair tissues, form enzymes and hormones, and perform other essential functions. Protein can be obtained from animal and vegetable sources.

Provençal(e), à la Provençale: Dishes prepared in the style of Provence, France, often with garlic, tomatoes, and olive oil. May also contain anchovies, eggplant, mushrooms, olives, and onions.

pulse: The edible seed of a leguminous plant, such as a bean, lentil, or pea. Often referred to simply as legume.

purée: To process food by mashing, straining, or chopping it very finely in order to make it a smooth paste. Also, a product produced using this technique.

Q

quahog: A hard-shell clam larger than 3 inches/7.5 mm in diameter, usually used for chowder or fritters. Also called *quahaug*.

quatre épices (Fr.): Literally, "four spices." A finely ground spice mixture containing black peppercorns, nutmeg, cinnamon, cloves, and sometimes ginger. Used to flavor soups, stews, and vegetables.

quenelle (Fr.): A light, poached dumpling based on a forcemeat (usually chicken, veal, seafood, or game) bound with eggs that is shaped in an oval by using two spoons.

quick bread: Bread made with chemical leaveners, which work more quickly than yeast. Also called batter bread.

R

raft: A mixture of ingredients used to clarify consommé. The term refers to the fact that the ingredients rise to the surface and form a floating mass.

ragoût (Fr.): Stew.

ramekin: A small, ovenproof dish, usually ceramic. Also *ramequin*.

reach-in refrigerator: A refrigeration unit, or set of units, with pass-through doors. They are often used in the pantry area for storage of salads, cold hors-d'oeuvre, and other frequently used items.

reduce: To decrease the volume of a liquid by simmering or boiling; used to provide a thicker consistency and/or concentrated flavors.

reduction: The product that results when a liquid is reduced.

refresh: To plunge an item into, or run it under, cold water after blanching to prevent further cooking. Also known as shock.

remouillage (Fr.): Literally, "rewetting." A stock made from bones that have already been used for stock. Weaker than a first-quality stock, it is often reduced to make glaze.

render: To melt fat and clarify the drippings for use in sautéing or pan frying.

rest: To allow food to rest after roasting and before carving; this allows the juices to seep back into the meat fibers.

rich dough: A yeast dough that contains fats such as butter or egg yolks. May also contain sweeteners.

rillette: Potted meat, or meat that is slowly cooked in seasoned fat, then shredded or pounded with some of the fat into a paste. The mixture is packed in ramekins and covered with a thin layer of fat.

ring-top: A flattop with removable plates that can be opened to varying degrees to expose the food to more or less heat.

risotto: Rice that is sautéed briefly in butter with onions and possibly other aromatics, then combined with stock, which is added in several additions and stirred constantly, producing a creamy texture with grains that are still al dente.

roast: To cook in an oven or on a spit over a fire.

roe: Fish or shellfish eggs.

roll-in: Butter or a butter-based mixture that is placed between layers of pastry dough, which is then rolled and folded repeatedly to form numerous layers. When the dough is baked, the layers remain discrete, producing a very flaky, rich pastry.

rondeau: A shallow, wide, straight-sided pot with two loop handles.

rondelle: A knife cut that produces round or oval flat pieces; used on cylindrical vegetables or items trimmed into cylinders before cutting.

rôtisseur (Fr.): Roast chef/station. The position is responsible for all roasted foods and related sauces.

roulade (Fr.): A slice of meat or fish rolled around a stuffing. Also, filled and rolled sponge cake.

round: A cut of beef from the hind quarter that includes the top and bottom round, eye, and top sirloin. It is lean and usually braised or roasted. Also, in baking, to shape pieces of yeast dough into balls. This process stretches and relaxes the gluten and ensures even rising and a smooth crust.

round fish: A classification of fish based on skeletal type, characterized by a rounded body and eyes on opposite sides of its head.

roux (Fr.): An appareil containing equal parts of flour and fat (usually butter) used to thicken liquids. Roux is cooked to varying degrees (white, blond, or brown), depending on its intended use.

royale (Fr.): A consommé garnish made of unsweetened custard cut into decorative shapes.

rub: A combination of spices and herbs applied to foods as a marinade or flavorful crust. Dry rubs are generally based upon spices; wet rubs (sometimes known as *mops*) may include moist ingredients such as fresh herbs, vegetables, and fruit juice or broth if necessary to make a pasty consistency.

S

sabayon (Fr.): Wine custard. Sweetened egg yolks flavored with Marsala or other wine or liqueur, beaten in a double boiler until frothy. In Italian, *zabaglione*.

sachet d'épices (Fr.): Literally, "bag of spices." Aromatic ingredients, encased in cheesecloth, that are used to flavor stocks and other liquids. A standard sachet contains parsley stems, cracked peppercorns, dried thyme, and a bay leaf.

salt cod: Cod that has been salted, possibly smoked, and dried to preserve it.

saltpeter: Potassium nitrate. A component of curing salt, used to preserve meat. It gives certain cured meats their characteristic pink color.

sanitation: The maintenance of a clean food-preparation environment by healthy food workers.

sanitize: To kill pathogenic organisms by chemicals and/or moist heat.

sashimi (Jap.): Sliced raw fish that is served with such condiments as a julienne of daikon radish, pickled ginger, wasabi, and soy sauce.

saturated fat: A fat whose available bonding sites are entirely filled with hydrogen atoms. These tend to be solid at room temperature and are primarily of animal origin, though coconut oil, palm oil, and cocoa butter are vegetable sources of saturated fat. Animal sources include butter, meat, cheese, and eggs.

sauce: A liquid accompaniment to food.

sauce vin blanc (Fr.): Literally. "white wine sauce." Made by combining a reduced poaching liquid (typically containing wine) with prepared hollandaise, velouté, or diced butter.

saucier (Fr.): Sauté chef/station. The chef de partie responsible for all sautéed items and their sauces.

sausage: A forcemeat mixture shaped into patties or links, typically highly seasoned.

sauté: To cook quickly in a small amount of fat in a pan on the range top.

sauteuse: A shallow skillet with sloping sides and a single, long handle. Used for sautéing. Referred to generically as sauté pan.

sautoir: A shallow skillet with straight sides and a single, long handle. Used for sautéing. Referred to generically as sauté pan.

savory: Not sweet. Also, the name of a course (savory) served after dessert and before port in traditional British meals. Also, a family of herbs (including summer and winter savory).

scald: To heat a liquid, usually milk or cream, to just below the boiling point. May also refer to blanching fruits and vegetables.

scale: To measure ingredients by weighing, or to divide dough or batter into portions by weight. Also, to remove the scales from fish.

scaler: Tool used to scrape fish scales from fish. Used by scraping against direction in which scales lie flat, working from tail to head.

scallop: A bivalve whose adductor muscle (the muscle that keeps its shells closed) and roe are eaten. Also, a thin slice of meat.

score: To cut the surface of an item at regular intervals to allow it to cook evenly.

scrapple: A boiled mixture of pork trimmings, buckwheat, and cornmeal.

sear: To brown the surface of food in fat over high heat before finishing by another method (for example, braising or roasting) in order to add flavor.

sea salt: Salt produced by evaporating seawater. Available refined or unrefined, crystallized or ground. Also known as *sel gris* (French for "gray salt").

seasoning: Adding an ingredient to give foods a particular flavor. Also, the process by which a protective coating is built up on the interior of a pan.

semolina: The coarsely milled hard wheat endosperm used for gnocchi, some pasta, and couscous.

shallow-poach: To cook gently in a shallow pan of simmering liquid. The liquid is often reduced and used as the basis of a sauce.

sheet pan: A flat baking pan, often with a rolled lip, used to cook foods in the oven.

shelf life: The amount of time in storage that a product can maintain its quality.

shellfish: Various types of marine life consumed as food, including univalves, bivalves, cephalopods, and crustaceans.

sherry: A fortified Spanish wine.

shirred egg: An egg cooked with butter (and often cream) in a ramekin.

sieve: A container made of a perforated material, such as wire mesh, used to drain, rice, or purée foods.

silverskin: The tough connective tissue that surrounds certain muscles.

simmer: To maintain the temperature of a liquid just below boiling. Also, to cook in simmering liquid. The temperature range for simmering is 185° to 200°F/82° to 85°C.

simple carbohydrate: Any of a number of small carbohydrate molecules (mono- and disaccharides), including fructose, lactose, maltose, and sucrose.

simple syrup: A mixture of water and sugar (with additional flavorings or aromatics as desired), heated until the sugar dissolves. Used to moisten cakes or to poach fruits.

single-stage technique: A cooking technique involving only one cooking method—for example, boiling or sautéing—as opposed to more than one method, as in braising.

skim: To remove impurities from the surface of a liquid, such as stock or soup, during cooking.

skim milk: Milk from which all but 0.5 percent of the milkfat has been removed.

slurry: A starch such as arrowroot, cornstarch, or potato starch dispersed in cold liquid to prevent it from forming lumps when added to hot liquid as a thickener.

small sauce: A sauce that is a derivative of any of the grand sauces.

smoker: An enclosed area in which foods are held on racks or hooks and allowed to remain in a smoke bath at the appropriate temperature.

smoke roasting: A method for roasting foods in which items are placed on a rack in a pan containing wood chips that smolder, emitting smoke, when the pan is placed on the range top or in the oven.

smoking: Any of several methods for preserving and flavoring foods by exposing them to smoke. Methods include cold-smoking (in which smoked items are not fully cooked), hot-smoking (in which the items are cooked), and smoke-roasting.

smoking point: The temperature at which a fat begins to break when heated.

smother: To cook in af covered pan with little liquid over low heat.

sodium: An alkaline metal element necessary in small quantities for human nutrition; one of the components of most salts used in cooking.

sommelier (Fr.): Wine steward or waiter.

sorbet (Fr.): Sherbet. A frozen dessert made with fruit juice or another flavoring, a sweetener (usually sugar), and beaten egg whites, which prevent the formation of large ice crystals.

soufflé (Fr.): Literally, "puffed." A preparation made with a sauce base (usually béchamel for savory soufflés, pastry cream for sweet ones), whipped egg whites, and flavorings. The egg whites cause the soufflé to puff during cooking.

sourdough: Yeast dough leavened with a fermented starter instead of, or in addition to, fresh yeast. Some starters are kept alive by "feeding" them with additional flour and water.

sous chef (Fr.): Literally, "underchef." The chef who is second in command in a kitchen; usually responsible for scheduling, filling in for the chef, and assisting the chefs de partie as necessary.

spa cooking: A cooking style that focuses on producing high-quality, well-presented dishes that are nutritionally sound and low in calories, fat, sodium, and cholesterol.

spätzle (Ger.): A soft noodle or small dumpling made by dropping bits of a prepared batter into simmering liquid.

spice: An aromatic vegetable substance, usually dried.

spider: A long-handled skimmer used to remove items from hot liquid or fat and to skim the surface of liquids.

spit-roast: To roast an item on a large skewer or spit over, or in front of, an open flame or other radiant heat source.

sponge: A thick yeast batter that is allowed to ferment and develop a light, spongy consistency and is then combined with other ingredients to form a yeast dough.

sponge cake: A sweet batter product that is leavened with beaten egg foam. Also called *génoise*.

springform pan: A round, straight-sided pan whose sides are formed by a hoop that can be unclamped and detached from its base.

stabilizer: An ingredient (usually a protein or plant product) that is added to an emulsion to prevent it from separating (for example, egg yolks, cream, or mustard). Also, an ingredient, such as gelatin, that is used in various desserts to prevent them from separating (for example, Bavarian creams).

standard breading procedure: The assembly-line procedure in which items are dredged in flour, dipped in beaten egg, then coated with crumbs before being pan-fried or deep-fried.

Staphylococcus aureus: A type of facultative bacteria that can cause food-borne illness. It is particularly dangerous because it produces toxins that cannot be destroyed by heat.

steak: A portion-size (or larger) cut of meat, poultry, or fish made by cutting across the grain of a muscle or a muscle group. May be boneless or bone-in.

steamer: A set of stacked pots with perforations in the bottom of each pot. They fit over a larger pot that is filled with boiling or simmering water. Also, a perforated insert made of metal or bamboo that can be used in a pot to steam foods.

steaming: A cooking method in which items are cooked in a vapor bath created by boiling water or other liquids.

steam-jacketed kettle: A kettle with double-layered walls, between which steam circulates, providing even heat for cooking stocks, soups, and sauces. These kettles may be insulated, spigoted, and/or tilting. The latter are also called *trunnion kettles*.

steel: A tool used to hone knife blades. It is usually made of steel but may be ceramic, glass, or diamond-impregnated metal.

steep: To allow an ingredient to sit in warm or hot liquid to extract flavor or impurities, or to soften the item.

stew: A cooking method nearly identical to braising but generally involving smaller pieces of meat and hence a shorter cooking time. Stewed items also may be blanched, rather than seared, to give the finished product a pale color. Also, a dish prepared by using the stewing method.

stir frying: A cooking method similar to sautéing in which items are cooked over very high heat, using little fat. Usually this is done in a wok, and the food is kept moving constantly.

stock: A flavorful liquid prepared by simmering meat, poultry, seafood, and/or vegetables in water with aromatics until their flavor is extracted. It is used as a base for soups, sauces, and other preparations.

stockpot: A large, straight-sided pot that is taller than it is wide. Used for making stocks and soups. Some have spigots. Also called *marmite*.

stone-ground: A term used to describe meal or flour milled between grindstones. This method of grinding retains more nutrients than other methods.

straight: A forcemeat combining pork and pork fat with another meat in equal parts that is made by grinding the mixture together.

straight mix method: The dough-mixing method in which all ingredients are combined at once by hand or machine.

strain: To pass a liquid through a sieve or screen to remove particles.

suprême (Fr.): The breast fillet and wing of chicken or other poultry. *Sauce suprême* is chicken velouté enriched with cream.

sweat: To cook an item, usually vegetables, in a covered pan in a small amount of fat until it softens and releases moisture.

sweetbreads: The thymus glands of young animals, usually calves, but also lambs or pigs. Usually sold in pairs.

swiss: To pound meat, usually beef, with flour and seasonings; this breaks up the muscle fibers, tenderizing the meat.

syrup: Sugar that is dissolved in liquid, usually water, possibly with the addition of flavorings such as spices or citrus zests.

T

table d'hôte (Fr.): A fixed-price menu with a single price for an entire meal based on entrée selection.

table salt: Refined, granulated salt. May be fortified with iodine and treated with magnesium carbonate to prevent clumping.

table wine: Still red, white, and rosé wines containing between 7 and 14 percent alcohol.

tart: A pie without a top crust. May be sweet or savory. A *tartlet* is a small, single-serving tart.

temper: To heat gently and gradually. May refer to the process of incorporating hot liquid into a liaison to gradually raise its temperature. May also refer to the proper method for melting chocolate.

tempura (Jap.): Seafood and/or vegetables that are coated with a light batter and deep-fried.

tenderloin: A boneless cut of meat, usually beef or pork, from the loin. Usually the most tender and expensive cut.

terrine: A loaf of forcemeat, similar to a pâté, but cooked in a covered mold in a bain-marie. Also, the mold used to cook such items, usually an oval shape made of ceramic.

thermophilic: Heat-loving. A term used to describe bacteria that thrive within the temperature range from 110° to 171°F/43° to 77°C.

thickener: An ingredient used to give additional body to liquids. Arrowroot, cornstarch, gelatin, roux, and beurre manié are examples of thickeners.

tilting kettle: A large, relatively shallow, tilting pot used for braising, stewing, and occasionally steaming.

timbale: A small pail-shaped mold used to shape rice, custards, mousselines, and other items. Also, a preparation made in such a mold.

tomalley: Lobster liver, which is olive green in color.

tomato sauce: A sauce prepared by simmering tomatoes in a liquid (water or broth) with aromatics. One of the grand sauces.

total utilization: The principle advocating the use of as much of a product as possible in order to reduce waste and increase profits.

tournant (Fr.): Roundsman or swing cook. A kitchen staff member who works as needed throughout the kitchen.

tourner: To cut items, usually vegetables, into barrel, olive, or football shapes. Tournéed foods should have five or seven sides or faces.

toxin: A naturally occurring poison, particularly those produced by the metabolic activity of living organisms, such as bacteria.

tranche (Fr.): A slice or cut of meat, fish, or poultry.

trash fish: Fish that have traditionally been considered unusable. Also called *junk fish* or *underutilized fish*.

Trichinella spiralis: A spiral-shaped parasitic worm that invades the intestines and muscle tissue. Transmitted primarily through infected pork that has not been cooked sufficiently.

tripe: The edible stomach lining of a cow or other ruminant. Honeycomb tripe comes from the second stomach and has a honeycomb-like texture.

truss: To tie up meat or poultry with string before cooking it in order to give it a compact shape for more even cooking and better appearance.

tuber: The fleshy root, stem, or rhizome of a plant, able to grow into a new plant. Some, such as potatoes, are eaten as vegetables.

tuile (Fr.): Literally, "tile." A thin, waferlike cookie (or food cut to resemble this cookie). Tuiles are frequently shaped while warm and still pliable by pressing them into molds or draping them over rolling pins or dowels.

tunneling: A fault in baked batter products caused by overmixing. The finished product is riddled with large holes or tunnels.

U

umami (Jap.): Describes a savory, meaty taste; often associated with monosodium glutamate (MSG).

univalve: A single-shelled mollusk, such as abalone and sea urchin.

unsaturated fat: A fat with at least one available bonding site not filled with a hydrogen atom. These may be monounsaturated or polyunsaturated. They tend to be liquid at room temperature and are primarily of vegetable origin.

V

vanilla sauce: Custard sauce made from milk or cream, sugar, and eggs, flavored with vanilla.

variety meat: Meat from a part of an animal other than the muscle; for example, organ meats.

vegetable soup: A broth- or water-based soup made primarily with vegetables; may include meats, legumes, and noodles and may be clear or thick.

vegetarian: An individual who has adopted a specific diet (or lifestyle) that reduces or eliminates animal products. Vegans eat no foods derived in any way from animals. Lacto-ovo-vegetarians include dairy products and eggs in their diet. Ovo-vegetarians include eggs in their diet.

velouté: A sauce of white stock (chicken, veal, seafood) thickened with white roux. One of the grand sauces. Also, a cream soup made with a velouté sauce base and flavorings (usually puréed) that is usually finished with a liaison.

venison: Meat from large game animals. Often used to refer specifically to deer meat.

vertical chopping machine (VCM): A machine, similar to a blender, that has rotating blades used to grind, whip, emulsify, or blend foods.

vinaigrette (Fr.): A cold sauce of oil and vinegar, usually with various flavorings. It is a temporary emulsion. The standard proportion is three parts oil to one part vinegar.

virus: A type of pathogenic microorganism that can be transmitted in food. Viruses cause such illnesses as measles, chicken pox, infectious hepatitis, and colds.

vitamins: Any of various nutritionally essential organic substances that do not provide energy but usually act as regulators in metabolic processes.

W

waffle: A crisp, pancakelike batter product that is cooked in a specialized griddle that gives the finished product a textured pattern, usually a grid. Also a special vegetable cut that produces a grid or basket-weave pattern. Also known as *gaufrette*.

walk-in refrigerator: A refrigeration unit large enough to walk into. It is occasionally large enough to maintain zones of varying temperature and humidity to store a variety of foods properly. Some have reach-in doors as well. Some are large enough to accommodate rolling carts as well as many shelves of goods.

wasabi (Jap.): Horseradish.

whey: The liquid left after curds have formed in milk.

whip: To beat an item, such as cream or egg whites, to incorporate air. Also, a special tool for whipping made of looped wire attached to a handle.

white chocolate: Cocoa butter flavored with sugar and milk solids. It does not contain any cocoa solids, so it does not have the characteristic brown color of regular chocolate.

white mirepoix: Mirepoix that does not include carrots and may include chipped mushrooms or mushroom trimmings. It is used for pale or white sauces and stocks.

white stock: A light-colored stock made with bones that have not been browned.

whole grain: An unmilled or unprocessed grain.

whole-wheat flour: Flour milled from the whole grain, including the bran and germ. *Graham flour* is a whole-wheat flour named after Sylvester Graham, a nineteenth-century American dietary reformer.

wok (Chin.): A round-bottomed pan, usually made of rolled steel, that is used for nearly all cooking methods in Chinese cuisine.

Y

yam: A large tuber that grows in tropical and subtropical climates; it has starchy, pale-yellow flesh. The name *yam* is also given to the (botanically unrelated) sweet potato.

yeast: Microscopic fungus whose metabolic processes are responsible for fermentation. It is used for leavening bread and in the making of cheese, beer, and wine.

yogurt: Milk cultured with bacteria to give it a slightly thick consistency and sour flavor.

Z

zest: The thin, brightly colored outer part of citrus rind. It contains volatile oils, making it ideal for use as a flavoring.

READINGS AND RESOURCES

FOOD HISTORY

American Food: The Gastronomic Story. Evan Jones. Overlook, 1992.

Cod: A Biography of the Fish That Changed the World. Mark Kurlansky. Walker, 1997.

Consuming Passions: The Anthropology of Eating. Peter Farb and George Armelagos. Pocket, 1983.

Culture and Cuisine: A Journey Through the History of Food. Jean-François Revel. Translated by Helen R. Lane. Da Capo, 1984.

The Deipnosophists (Banquet of the Learned). Athenaeus of Naucratis. Translated by C. D. Yonge. Henry G. Bohn, 1854.

Eating in America: A History. Waverley Root and Richard de Rochemont. Ecco, 1995.

Fabulous Feasts: Medieval Cookery and Ceremony. Madeleine Pelner Cosman. Braziller, 1978.

Food and Drink Through the Ages, 2,500 B.C. to 1937 A.D. Barbara Feret. Maggs Brothers, 1937.

Food in History. Reay Tannahill. Random House, 1995.

Gastronomy: The Anthropology of Food and Food Habits. Margaret L. Arnott, ed. Mouton, 1976.

Kitchens and Table: A Bedside History of Eating in the Western World. Colin Clair. Abelard-Schuman, 1965.

Much Depends on Dinner: The Extraordinary History and Mythology, Allure and Obsessions, Perils and Taboos, of an Ordinary Meal. Margaret Visser. Grove/Atlantic, 1999.

Our Sustainable Table. Robert Clark, ed. North Point, 1990.

The Pantropheon: or, A History of Food and Its Preparation in Ancient Times. Alexis Soyer. Paddington, 1977.

Platine on Right Pleasure and Good Health: A Critical Edition and Translation of De Honesta Voluptate et Valetudine. Mary Ella Milham, ed. MRTS, 1998.

The Rituals of Dinner: The Origins, Evolution, Eccentricities, and Meanings of Table Manners. Margaret Visser. Viking Penguin, 1992.

The Roman Cookery of Apicius: A Treasury of Gourmet Recipes and Herbal Cookery. Translated and adapted by John Edwards. Hartly & Marks, 1984.

The Travels of Marco Polo. Maria Bellonci. Translated by Teresa Waugh. Facts on File, 1984.

Why We Eat What We Eat: How Columbus Changed the Way the World Eats. Raymond Sokolov. Simon & Schuster, 1993.

A Woman's Place Is in the Kitchen: The Evolution of Women Chefs. Ann Cooper. John Wiley & Sons, 1998.

SANITATION AND SAFETY

Applied Foodservice Sanitation Textbook. 4th ed. Educational Foundation of the National Restaurant Association, 1993.

Basic Food Sanitation. The Culinary Institute of America, 1993.

HACCP: Reference Book. Educational Foundation of the National Restaurant Association, 1993.

CHEMISTRY OF COOKING

CookWise: The Secrets of Cooking Revealed. Shirley Corriher. Morrow/Avon, 1997.

The Curious Cook. Harold McGee. Hungry Minds, 1992.

The Experimental Study of Food. 2nd ed. Campbell Penfield Griswold. Houghton Mifflin, 1979.

Food Science. 3rd ed. Helen Charley. Macmillan, 1994.

On Food and Cooking: The Science and Lore of the Kitchen. Harold McGee. Simon and Schuster, 1997.

EQUIPMENT AND MISE EN PLACE

The Chef's Book of Formulas, Yields and Sizes. 2nd ed. Arno Schmidt. John Wiley & Sons, 1996.

Food Equipment Facts: A Handbook for the Foodservice Industry. 2nd ed. Carl Scriven and James Stevens. John Wiley & Sons, 1989.

The New Cook's Catalogue: The Definitive Guide to Cooking Equipment. Emily Aronson, Florence Fabricant, and Burt Wolf. Knopf, 2000.

The Professional Chef's Knife Kit. 2nd ed. The Culinary Institute of America. John Wiley & Sons, 1999.

The Williams-Sonoma Cookbook and Guide to Kitchenware. Chuck Williams. Random House, 1986.

GENERAL PRODUCT IDENTIFICATION

DICTIONARIES AND ENCYCLOPEDIAS

Asian Ingredients: A Guide to the Foodstuffs of China, Japan, Korea, Thailand, and Vietnam. Bruce Cost. Harper, 2000.

The Chef's Companion: A Concise Dictionary of Culinary Terms. 2nd ed. Elizabeth Riely. John Wiley & Sons, 1996.

A Concise Encyclopedia of Gastronomy. André Louis Simon. Overlook, 1983.

The Cook's Ingredients. Philip Dowell and Adrian Bailey. Reader's Digest Association, 1990.

The Encyclopedia of American Food and Drink. John F. Mariani. Lebhar-Friedman, 1999.

The Encyclopedia of Asian Food and Cooking. Jacki Passmore. Hearst, 1991.

Food. André Simon. Burke, 1949.

Food: An Informal Dictionary. Waverley Root. Simon and Schuster, 1980.

Food Lover's Companion. 4th ed. Sharon Herbst. Barron's, 2001.

Gastronomy. Jay Jacobs. Newsweek Books, 1975.

Gastronomy of France. Raymond Oliver. Translated by Claud Durrell. Wine & Food Society with World Publishing, 1967.

Gastronomy of Italy. Anna Del Conte. Prentice-Hall, 1988.

Herings Dictionary of Classical and Modern Cookery. Walter Bickel. French and European Publications, 1981.

Knight's Foodservice Dictionary. John B. Knight and Charles A. Salter, eds. John Wiley & Sons, 1987.

Larousse Gastronomique. Jenifer Harvey Lang, ed. Crown, 1988.

The Master Dictionary of Food and Wine. 2nd ed. Joyce Rubash. John Wiley & Sons, 1996.

The Oxford Companion to Food. Alan Davidson. Oxford University Press, 1999.

Patisserie: An Encyclopedia of Cakes, Pastries, Cookies, Biscuits, Chocolate, Confectionery and Desserts. Aaron Maree. HarperCollins, 1994.

Tastings: The Best from Ketchup to Caviar: 31 Pantry Basics and How They Rate with the Experts. Jenifer Harvey Lang. Crown, 1986.

The Von Welantz Guide to Ethnic Ingredients. Diana and Paul von Welanetz. Warner, 1987.

The World Encyclopedia of Food. Patrick L. Coyle. Facts on File, 1982.

MEATS, POULTRY, AND GAME

The Meat Buyers Guide. National Association of Meat Purveyors, 1992.

The Meat We Eat. 13th ed. John R. Romans. Interstate, 1994.

FISH AND SHELLFISH

The Complete Cookbook of American Fish and Shellfish. 2nd ed. John F. Nicolas. John Wiley & Sons, 1990.

The Encyclopedia of Fish Cookery. A. J. McClane. Henry Holt, 1977.

Fish and Shellfish. James Peterson. Morrow, 1996.

McClane's Fish Buyer's Guide. A. J. McClane. Henry Holt, 1990.

FRUITS AND VEGETABLES

The Blue Goose Buying Guide for Fresh Fruits, Vegetables, Herbs and Nuts. 9th ed. Castle and Cook, 1990.

The Foodservice Guide to Fresh Produce. Produce Marketing Association. Produce Marketing Association, 1987.

Rodale's Illustrated Encyclopedia of Herbs. Random House, 1997.

Uncommon Fruits and Vegetables: A Commonsense Guide. Elizabeth Schneider. Morrow/Avon, 1998.

CHEESES

Cheese: A Guide to the World of Cheese and Cheese-Making. Bruno Battistotti. Facts on File, 1984.

Cheese Buyer's Handbook. Daniel O'Keefe. McGraw-Hill, 1978.

The Cheese Companion: The Connoisseur's Guide. Judy Ridgway. Running Press, 1999.

Cheese Primer. Steven Jenkins. Workman Publishers, 1996.

Cheeses of the World. U.S. Department of Agriculture. Peter Smith, 1986.

The World of Cheese. Evan Jones. Knopf, 1978.

NONPERISHABLE GOODS

The Book of Coffee and Tea. 2nd ed. Joel Schapira, David Schapira, and Karl Schapira. St. Martin's, 1996.

The Complete Book of Spices: A Practical Guide to Spices and Aromatic Seeds. Jill Norman. Viking, 1995.

Spices, Salt and Aromatics in the English Kitchen. Elizabeth David. Penguin, 1972.

GENERAL AND CLASSICAL COOKERY

The Chef's Compendium of Professional Recipes. 3rd ed. John Fuller, Edward Renold, and David Faskett. Butterworth-Heinemann, 1992.

Classical Cooking the Modern Way. 3rd ed. Eugene Pauli. John Wiley & Sons, 1999.

Guide Culinaire: The Complete Guide to the Art of Modern Cooking. Auguste Escoffier. Translated by H. L. Cracknell and R. J. Kaufmann. John Wiley & Sons, 1979.

Cooking Essentials for the New Professional Chef. The Food and Beverage Instititute. Mary D. Donovan, ed. John Wiley & Sons, 1997.

Cooking for the Professional Chef. Kenneth C. Wolfe. Delmar, 1982.

Cuisine Actuelle. Victor Gielisse. Taylor Publications, 1992.

Culinary Artistry. Andrew Dornenberg and Karen Page. John Wiley & Sons, 1991.

Culinary Olympics Cookbook: U.S. Team Recipes from the International Culinary Olympics. Ferdinand E. Metz and the U.S. Team. Steve M. Weiss, ed. Cahners, 1983.

Dining in France. Christian Millau. Stewart, Tabori & Chang, 1986.

Escoffier: The Complete Guide to the Art of Modern Cookery. Auguste Escoffier. John Wiley and Sons, 1995.

Escoffier Cook Book. Auguste Escoffier. Crown, 1941.

The Essential Cook Book. Terence Conran, Caroline Conran, and Simon Hopkinson. Crown, 1980.

Essentials of Cooking. James Peterson. Artisan, 2000.

The Grand Masters of French Cuisine. Selected and adapted by Celine Vence and Robert Courtine. Putnam, 1978.

Foods of the World. Time-Life Books, 1971.

Great Chefs of France. Anthony Blake and Quentin Crewe. Harry N. Abrams, 1978.

Introductory Foods. 11th ed. Marion Bennion. Prentice-Hall, 1999.

Jacques Pepin's Art of Cooking. Jacques Pepin. 2 vols. Knopf, 1987.

James Beard's Theory and Practice of Good Cooking. Random House, 1990.

Jewish Cooking in America. Joan Nathan. Alfred A. Knopf, 1998.

La Technique. Jacques Pepin. Simon & Schuster, 1989.

Le Répertoire de la Cuisine. Louis Saulnier. Barron's, 1977.

Ma Gastronomie. Ferdinand Point. Translated by Frank Kulla and Patricia S. Kulla. Lyceum, 1974.

Paul Bocuse's French Cooking. Paul Bocuse. Translated by Colette Rossant. Pantheon, 1987.

The Physiology of Taste, or Meditations on Transcendental Gastronomy. Jean-Anthelme Brillat-Savarin. Counterpoint, 2000.

GARDE MANGER AND CHARCUTERIE

The Art of Making Sausages, Pâtés, and Other Charcuterie. Jane Grigson. Knopf, 1968.

Garde Manger: The Art and Craft of the Cold Kitchen. Culinary Institute of America. John Wiley & Sons, 2000.

Pâtés and Terrines. Frederich W. Elhart. Hearst, 1984.

SOUPS AND SAUCES

Sauces: Classical and Contemporary Sauce Making. James Peterson. John Wiley & Sons, 1998.

Soups for the Professional Chef. Terence Janericco. John Wiley & Sons, 1993.

The Saucier's Apprentice: A Modern Guide to Classic French Sauces for the Home. Raymond A. Sokolov. Knopf, 1980.

Splendid Soups. James Peterson. John Wiley & Sons, 2001.

FRUIT AND VEGETABLE COOKERY

Charlie Trotter's Vegetables. Charlie Trotter. Ten Speed Press, 1996.

Jane Grigson's Fruit Book. Jane Grigson. Atheneum, 1982.

Jane Grigson's Vegetable Book. Jane Grigson. Viking Penguin, 1981.

Roger Vergé's Vegetables in the French Style. Roger Vergé. Artisan, 1994.

Vegetarian Cooking for Everyone. Deborah Madison. Broadway, 1997.

Vegetables. James Peterson. Morrow, 1998.

NUTRITION AND NUTRITIONAL COOKERY

Choices for a Healthy Heart. Joseph C. Piscatella. Workman, 1988.

Food and Culture in America: A Nutrition Handbook. Pamela Goyan Kittler and Kathryn P. Sucher. Wadsworth, 1997.

Handbook of the Nutritional Value of Foods in Common Units. U.S. Department of Agriculture. Dover, 1986.

In Good Taste. Victor Gielisse. Simon & Schuster, 1998.

Jane Brody's Good Food Book: Living the High-Carbohydrate Way. Jane Brody. Norton, 1985.

The Mediterranean Diet Cookbook: A Delicious Alternative for Lifelong Health. Nancy Harmon Jenkins. Bantam, 1994.

The New Living Heart Diet. Michael E. DeBakey, Antonio M. Gotto Jr., Lynne W. Scott, and John P. Foreyt. Simon and Schuster, 1996.

Nutrition: Concepts and Controversies. 8th ed. Eleanor R. Whitney and Frances S. Sizer. Wadsworth, 1999.

The Professional Chef's Techniques of Healthy Cooking. 2nd ed. The Culinary Institute of America. Jennifer Armentrout, ed. John Wiley & Sons, 2000.

AMERICAN COOKERY

An American Bounty: Great Contemporary Cooking from the CIA. Culinary Institute of America. Mary Donovan, ed. Rizzoli, 1995.

Charlie Trotter's. Charlie Trotter. Ten Speed Press, 1994.

Chef Paul Prudhomme's Louisiana Kitchen. Paul Prudhomme. Morrow, 1984.

Chez Panisse Cooking. Paul Bertolli with Alice Waters. Peter Smith, 2000.

City Cuisine. Susan Feniger and Mary Sue Milliken. Morrow, 1989.

Epicurean Delight: The Life and Times of James Beard. Evan Jones. Knopf, 1990.

I Hear America Cooking. Betty Fussell. Viking Penguin, 1997.

Jasper White's Cooking from New England. Jasper White. Biscuit Books, 1998.

Jeremiah Tower's New American Classics. Jeremiah Tower. Harper & Row, 1986.

License to Grill. Chris Schlesinger and John Willoughby. Morrow, 1997.

The Mansion on Turtle Creek Cook Book. Dean Fearing. Grove-Atlantic, 1987.

The New York Times Cook Book. Craig Claiborne. Harper & Row, 1990.

Saveur Cooks Authentic American. Chronicle, 1998.

The Thrill of the Grill: Techniques, Recipes & Downhome Barbecue. Chris Schlesinger and John Willoughby. Morrow, 1997.

The Trellis Cookbook. Marcel Desaulniers. Simon and Schuster, 1992.

INTERNATIONAL COOKERY

LATIN AND CARIBBEAN

The Art of South American Cooking. Felipe Rojas-Lombardi. Harper, 1991.

The Book of Latin American Cooking. Elizabeth Lambert Ortiz. HarperCollins, 1994.

The Essential Cuisines of Mexico. Diana Kennedy. Crown, 2000.

Food and Life of Oaxaca. Zarela Martínez. Macmillan, 1997.

Food from My Heart: Cuisines of Mexico Remembered and Reimagined. Zarela Martínez. Hungry Minds, 1995.

Rick Bayless's Mexican Kitchen. Rick Bayless. Simon and
Schuster, 1996.

The Taste of Mexico. Patricia Quintana. Stewart, Tabori &
Chang, 1986.

EUROPEAN AND MEDITERRANEAN

The Art of Turkish Cooking. Neset Eren. Hippocrene Books,
1993.

The Belgian Cookbook. Nika Hazelton. Atheneum, 1977.

A Book of Mediterranean Food. Elizabeth David. Viking,
1988.

Classical and Contemporary Italian Cooking for Professionals.
Bruno Ellmer. John Wiley & Sons, 1990.

Classic Scandinavian Cooking. Nika Hazelton. Galahad, 1994.

The Classic Italian Cook Book. Marcella Hazan. Knopf, 1976.

The Cooking of the Eastern Mediterranean. Paula Wolfert.
HarperCollins, 1994.

*Cooking of the Southwest of France: A Collection of Traditional
and New Recipes from France's Magnificent Rustic Cuisine.*
Paula Wolfert. Harper, 1994.

Couscous and Other Good Food from Morocco. Paula Wolfert.
Harper, 1987.

Croatian Cuisine. Ruzica Kapetanovic and Alojzije
Kapetanovic. Associated, 1992.

The Czechoslovak Cookbook. Joza Brizova et al. Crown, 1965.

The Food and Cooking of Russia. Lesley Chamberlain. Viking
Penguin, 1989.

The Foods and Wines of Spain. Penelope Casas. Knopf, 1982.

French Provincial Cooking. Elizabeth David. Viking, 1999.

French Regional Cooking. Anne Willan. Morrow, 1981.

The German Cookbook. Mimi Sheraton. Random House, 1965.

George Lang's Cuisine of Hungary. George Lang. Wings, 1994.

Giuliano Bugialli's Classic Techniques of Italian Cooking.
Giuliano Bugialli. Simon & Schuster, 1982.

Greek Food. Rena Salamon. Harper, 1994.

Italian Food. Elizabeth David. Penguin, 1999.

The New Book of Middle Eastern Food. Claudia Roden. Knopf,
2000.

Pasta Classica: The Art of Italian Pasta Cooking. Julia Della
Croce. Chronicle, 1996.

*Paula Wolfert's World of Food: A Collection of Recipes from Her
Kitchen, Travels, and Friends.* Paula Wolfert. HarperCollins,
1994.

Pierre Franey's Cooking in France. Pierre Franey and Richard
Flaste. Knopf, 1994.

Please to the Table: The Russian Cookbook. Anya Von Bremzen.
Workman, 1990.

The Polish Cookbook. Z. Czerny. Vanous, 1982.

Roger Vergé's Cuisine of the South of France. Roger Vergé.
Translated by Roberta Smoler. Morrow, 1980.

Simple Cuisine. Jean-Georges Vongerichten. Hungry Minds,
1998.

The Taste of France: A Dictionary of French Food and Wine. Fay
Sharman. Houghton Mifflin, 1982.

A Taste of Morocco. Robert Carrier. Crown, 1987.

ASIAN

Classic Indian Cooking. Julie Sahin. Morrow/Avon, 1980.

Cracking the Coconut: Classic Thai Home Cooking. Su-Mei Yu.
Morrow/Avon, 2000.

The Foods of Vietnam. Nicole Routhier. Stewart, Tabori, &
Chang, 1999.

Japanese Cooking: A Simple Art. Shizuo Tsuji. Kodansha, 1980.

The Joy of Japanese Cooking. Kuwako Takahashi. C. E. Tuttle,
1992.

Madhur Jaffrey's Far Eastern Cookery. Madhur Jaffrey. Harper,
1989.

The Modern Art of Chinese Cooking. Barbara Tropp.
Morrow/Avon, 1982.

A Taste of Japan. Jenny Ridgewell. Raintree Steck-Vaughn,
1997.

Terrific Pacific Cookbook. Anya Von Bremzen and John
Welchman. Workman, 1995.

Traditional Korean Cooking. Chin-hwa Noh. Hollym
International, 1985.

BAKING AND PASTRY

The Baker's Manual. 4th ed. Joseph Amendola. John Wiley &
Sons, 1993.

The Bread Bible: Beth Hensperger's 300 Favorite Recipes. Beth
Hensperger. Chronicle, 1999.

Flatbreads and Flavors: A Culinary Atlas. Jeffrey Alford and
Naomi Duguid. Morrow/Avon, 1995.

Great Dessert Book. Christian Teubner and Sybil Schonfeldt.
Hearst, 1983.

*Nancy Silverton's Breads from the La Brea Bakery: Recipes for
the Connoisseur.* Nancy Silverton with Laurie Ochoa.
Random House, 1996.

The New International Confectioner. 5th ed. Wilfred J. France.
Virtue, 1987.

Nick Malgieri's Perfect Pastry. Nick Malgieri. Hungry Minds,
1998.

The Pie and Pastry Bible. Rose Levy Beranbaum. Simon and
Schuster, 1998.

Practical Baking. William J. Sultan. John Wiley & Sons, 1996.

The Professional Pastry Chef. 3rd ed. B. Friberg. John Wiley &
Sons, 1996.

Swiss Confectionery. 3rd ed. Richemont Bakers and
Confectioners Craft School, 1991.

Understanding Baking. 2nd ed. Joseph Amendola and Donald
E. Lundberg. John Wiley & Sons, 1992.

WINES AND SPIRITS

Exploring Wine: The Culinary Institute of America's Complete Guide to Wines of the World. 2nd ed. Steven Kolpan, Brian H. Smith, and Michael A. Weiss. John Wiley & Sons, 2001.

Great Wines Made Simple: Straight Talk from a Master Sommelier. Andrea Immer. Broadway, 2000.

Hugh Johnson's Modern Encyclopedia of Wine. 4th ed. Hugh Johnson. Simon & Schuster, 1998.

Larousse Encyclopedia of Wine. Christopher Foulkes, ed. Larousse, 1994.

Windows on the World Complete Wine Course: 2001 Edition. Kevin Zraly. Sterling, 2000.

BUSINESS AND MANAGEMENT

Becoming a Chef: With Recipes and Reflections from America's Leading Chefs. Andrew Dornenburg and Karen Page. John Wiley & Sons, 1995.

Cases in Hospitality Marketing and Management. 2nd ed. Robert C. Lewis. John Wiley and Sons, 1997.

Culinary Math. Linda Blocker, Julie Hill, and The Culinary Institute of America. John Wiley and Sons, 2002.

The Discipline of Market Leaders: Choose Your Customers, Narrow Your Focus, Dominate Your Market. Michael Treacy and Fred Wiersma. Addison-Wesley, 1995.

Food and Beverage Cost Control. Donald Bell. McCutchen, 1984.

Foodservice Organizations. 4th ed. Marion Spears. Prentice-Hall, 1999.

Lessons in Excellence from Charlie Trotter. Charlie Trotter. Ten Speed Press, 1999.

The Making of a Chef: Mastering the Heat at the CIA. Michael Ruhlman. Henry Holt, 1997.

Math Principles for Food Service Occupations. 3rd ed. Robert G. Haines. Delmar, 1995.

Math Workbook for Foodservice and Lodging. Hattie Crawford and Milton McDowell. John Wiley & Sons, 1988.

Principles of Food, Beverage & Labor Cost Controls. Paul Dittmer. John Wiley & Sons, 1999.

Principles of Marketing. 7th ed. Philip Kotler and Gary Armstong. Prentice-Hall, 1996.

Professional Table Service. Sylvia Meyer. Translated by Heinz Holtmann. John Wiley & Sons, 1993.

Recipes into Type: A Handbook for Cookbook Writers and Editors. Joan Whitman and Dolores Simon. HarperCollins, 1993.

Remarkable Service. The Culinary Institute of America. Ezra Eichelberger and Gary Allen, eds. John Wiley & Sons, 2001.

The Resource Guide for Food Writers. Gary Allen. Routledge, 1999.

The Successful Business Plan: Secrets and Strategies. 2nd ed. Rhonda Abrams. Rhonda, 1999.

What Every Supervisor Should Know. Lester Bittle and John Newstrom. McGraw-Hill, 1992.

PERIODICALS AND JOURNALS

American Brewer
Appellation
Art Culinaire
The Art of Eating
Beverage Digest
Beverage World
Bon Appétit
Brewer's Digest
Caterer and Hotelkeeper
Chef
Chocolate News
Chocolatier
Cooking for Profit
Cook's Illustrated
Cooking Light
Culinary Trends
Decanter
Food and Wine
Food Arts
Food for Thought
Food Management
Food Technology
Foodservice and Hospitality
Foodservice Director
Fresh Cup
Gastronomica
Gourmet
Herb Companion
Hospitality
Hospitality Design
Hotel and Motel Management
Hotels
IACP Food Forum
Lodging
Meat and Poultry
Modern Baking
Nation's Restaurant News
Nutrition Action Healthletter
Pizza Today
Prepared Foods
Restaurant Business
Restaurant Hospitality
Restaurant and Institutions
Saveur
Wine and Spirits
Wine Spectator
Wines and Vines

American Culinary Federation (ACF)
P.O. Box 3466
St. Augustine, FL 32085
(904) 824-4468
www.acfchefs.org

American Institute of Wine and Food (AIWF)
304 West Liberty, Suite 201
Louisville, KY 40202
(800) 274-2493
www.aiwf.org

Chefs Collaborative 2000
282 Moody Street, Suite 207
Waltham, MA 02453
(781) 736-0635
www.chefnet.com/cc2000

Chefs de Cuisine Association of America
155 East 55th Street, Suite 3028
New York, NY 10022
(212) 832-4939

International Council on Hotel/Restaurant and Institutional
   Education (CHRIE)
3205 Skipwith Road
Richmond, VA 23294
(804) 747-4971
www.chrie.org

International Association of Culinary Professionals (IACP)
304 West Liberty, Suite 201
Louisville, KY 40202
(502) 581-9786
www.chefnet.com/iacp

The James Beard Foundation
167 West 12th Street
New York, NY 10011
(212) 675-4984
www.jamesbeard.org

Les Dames d'Escoffier (LDEI), DC Chapter
P.O. Box 39237
Washington, DC 20016
(202) 973-2168
www.ldei.org

National Restaurant Association (NRA)
1200 17th Street, NW
Washington, DC 20036
(202) 331-5900
www.restaurant.org

Oldways Preservation and Exchange Trust
25 First Street
Cambridge, MA 01241
(617) 621-1230

Roundtable for Women in Foodservice
3022 West Eastwood
Chicago, IL 60625
(800) 898-2849

Share Our Strength (SOS)
1511 K Street, NW, Suite 94
Washington, DC 20005
(202) 393-2925

Women Chefs and Restaurateurs (WCR)
304 West Liberty, Suite 201
Louisville, KY 40202
(502) 581-0300
www.chefnet.com/wcr

RECIPE INDEX

Calcium, 39
Calories, 32
Canadian bacon, 119
Canapés, 802
Candy making, stages of, 865
Candy thermometer, 961
Canned foods, 229
Canning salt, 222
Canola oil, 212
Cantaloupes, 156
Captain (chef d'étage), 8
Caramel, adding ingredients to, 865
Caramelization, 51-52
Caraway seeds, 218
Carbohydrates, 32-33, 46
Carbon steel knife blades, 81
Carborundum stones, 84
Cardamom, 218
Career opportunities, 5-9
Caribbean cookery, resources for, 1019-1020
Carême, Marie-Antoine, 4, 5
Carnaroli rice, 686
Carob, 226
Carotenoids, 41
Carrots, 178
Carving, 412-414
Carving board, 407
Casaba melons, 156
Cashews, 216
Cassava flour, 241
Casserole-style potatoes, 634
Cast iron cookware, 91
Catering, 6
Catfish, 134
Cauliflower, 162
Cayenne pepper, 223
Celeriac, 178-179
Celery, 180
Celery seed, 218
Cephalopods, 140
Cereals, simmering and boiling, 676-679
Certification, 73-74
Challah, 877
Chanterelles, 167
Chantilly cream, 866, 960
Chapel, Alain, 5
Chapelure, 349
Charcuterie, 841-846
    resources for, 1019
Charcutière sauce, 284
Chard, 166
Charring, of peppers and chiles, 575
Chaud-froid, 819
Chayote squash, 163
Cheddar cheese, 196
Cheddar sauce, 743
Cheesecakes, creaming method for, 907-910
Cheesecloth, 90
Cheeses, 192-198
    for potatoes en casserole, 649
    in mousse, 817
    in omelets, 738
    in risotto, 685
    spreadable, 801
Chef attire, 72
Chef de cuisine, 7
Chef de vin, 8
Chef's knives, 83, 560
Chef's potatoes, 174
Chefs. See also Culinary professional; Professional chefs
    as businesspersons, 11-16
    executive, 7
Chemical contaminants, 56
Chemistry of cooking, resources for, 1017

Cherries, 159
Cherrystone clams, 141
Cherry tomatoes, 181
Chervil, 186
Chestnuts, 216
    preparing, 577
Chicken, 125-126
Chicken Chasseur, 285
Chiffonade cuts, 562
Chiffon cakes, 912, 915
    pans for, 913
Chile pepper flakes, 223
Chile peppers, 170, 171-172
Chiles
    preparing, 574-575
    toasted, 581
Chinois, 89
Chipotle peppers, 172
Chocolate, 225-226. See also Cocoa powder
    chopping, 980
    preparing for mousses, 976
    tempering, 984
Chocolate coating, 226
Chocolate fondant, 982
Chocolate sauce, light ganache as, 979
Chocolate truffles, 979
Cholesterol, 35-36
Choppers, 99
Chopping, of vegetables, 561
Chops
    cutting, 363
    veal, 115
Choron sauce, 274
Chuck, veal, 115
Chuck roast, beef, 109
Chutneys, 801
Cilantro, 186
Cinnamon, 218
Cippolini onions, 169
Citrus fruits, 151-153
    peeling and slicing, 775
Citrus zest, 775
Clams, 141
    cleaning and opening, 395-396
Clarified butter, 240, 452
Classical cookery, resources for, 1018-1019
Cleaning, 68. See also Food safety; Sanitation
    of copper pans, 91
    of pastry bags, 872
Cleaver, 83
Cloudberries, 150
Cloves, 218
Club sandwiches, 800, 803
Coarse white sugar, 224
Cocoa butter, 225, 226
Cocoa powder, storing, 226
Coconut oil, 212
Coconuts, 216
Cod, 134-135
Coddled eggs, 725, 726
Coffee, 228
Colanders, 89, 584, 677, 707
Cold-foods chef (garde-manger), 7
Cold sandwiches, 800
Cold savory mousse, 816-820
Cold soups, 329
Collard greens, 166
Colorado chiles, 171
Combi ovens, 102
Comice pears, 157
Commis, 7
Common meringue, 868
Common units of measure, conversion to, 25
Communard, 7
Communication skills, 15

Complete proteins, 37
Complex carbohydrates, 33
Composed salads, 780
Compotes, 801
Compound butters, 801, 802
Concassé, tomato, 573
Conch, 140
Concord grapes, 153
Condiments, 227
    for deep-fried potatoes, 658
Conduction, 49
Confectioner's sugar, 224
Conical sieve, 89, 964, 966
Consommé, 298-303
Consommé Brunoise, 298
Consommé Chasseur, 298
Consommé Célèstine, 298
Consommé Diplomate, 298
Consommé Grimaldi, 298
Consommé Julienne, 298
Consommé Mikado, 298
Consommé Printanier, 298
Consommé Royale, 298
Consultants, 8
Contamination. See also Food-borne illness
    of food, 56
    of forcemeats, 844
Continuing education, 10
Convection, 50
Convection ovens, 102, 946
Convection steamers, 101, 493, 589, 636
Converted rice, 204
Cooked foods, safe holding of, 64. See also Food safety
Cookery, resources for, 1018-1019
Cookie cutters, 946-947
Cookies
    creaming method for, 907-910
    glazing, 983
    guidelines for shaping and baking, 946-948
Cooking. See also Oven cooking; Stovetop cooking
    induction, 50
    microwave, 51
Cooking fats. See also Fats
    function of, 52-53
    for pan frying, 458
    for sautéing, 451
Cooking greens, 166-167
Cooking methods, 399-415
    beef, 112-114
    boiling vegetables, 584-587
    deep frying, 462-465
    deep poaching, 505-508
    en papillote, 496-499
    for pasta and noodles, 707-710
    grains and legumes, 671-689
    grilling and broiling, 400-404
    lamb and mutton, 123
    pan frying, 457-461
    pork, 121
    poultry, 128
    roasting, 405-411
    sautéing, 450-456
    shallow poaching, 500-504
    simmering, 505-508
    steaming, 492-495
    veal, 117
Cooking oils, 212
Cooking schools, 9
Cooking sprays, 213
Cookware, 90-95
Copper pans, care and cleaning of, 91
Copper pots, 90-91
Coral, 391
Cordials, 228-229
Coriander, 218

Corn, 205
    preparing, 577
Cornell food pyramid, 47
Cornish game hens, 126, 381
Cornmeal, 676, 703
Cornmeal dust, for baking pans, 870
Corn oil, 212
Cornstarch, 205, 228, 241, 863-864, 968
Corn syrup, 224, 865
Cost. See As-purchased cost (APC); Food/beverage costs
Cottonseed oil, 212
Country-style forcemeat, 842, 846
Court bouillons, 245
Couscous, 204, 672
Crab, 142
    cleaning, 394-395
Crabapples, 148
Cracked grains, 203
Cracked wheat, 204, 676
Cranberries, 150
Cranberry beans, 173
Cranberry tomatoes, 181
Crayfish, 142
    cleaning and picking, 394
Cream, 189-190. See also Buttercream
    chantilly, 866
    pastry, 968-971
    as a potato dressing, 636
    whipped, 866
Cream cheese icing, 960
Creamed corn, 577
Creaming method, 907-910
Cream puffs, 943
Creams, 959. See also Mousse
    Bavarian, 972-974
    buttercream, 960-963
Cream soups, 309-314
Crème fraîche, 192
Cremini mushrooms, 167
Crenshaw melons, 156
Crêpe pan, 93
Crêpes, 900
Croissant dough, 938-942
Crookneck squash, 163
Cross contamination, avoiding, 61-62
Crostini, 771
Croustades, 771
Croutons, making, 771
Crumb coat, 918
Crust
    of baked products, 910
    crisp, 881
    lattice, 935
Crustaceans, 140
Cryovac packing, 106
Cucumbers, 163
Cuisine, major figures in, 4
Cuisine classique, 5
Cuisson, 280
Culinary associations, 1022
Culinary historical figures, 4
Culinary Math, 30
Culinary profession, career opportunities in, 5-9
Culinary professional. See also Chefs; Professional chefs
    attributes of, 10-11
    process of becoming, 9-10
Cultured milk products, 189, 192
Cumin, 218
Cured pork, 120-121
Curing salt, 222
Curly endive, 165
Currants, 150
Currant tomatoes, 181
Custards, for pies, 933
Customer service, 16
Cut cookies, 946

Fish, 43, 46, 130-144. *See also* Fish
  fabrication; Shellfish
  breading for, 349
  for broths, 293
  commonly available, 133-139
  general guidelines for, 350-351
  grilling and broiling, 400-404
  in hearty broths, 307
  market forms of, 130
  mise en place for, 345-356
  roasting, 405-414
  seasonings for, 346-347
  stuffing for, 348
Fish bones, use in stocks, 245
Fish chef (poissonier), 7
Fish fabrication, 383-390
  cutting a fish, 384
  cutting fish into steaks, 385
  filleting, 386-390
  scaling and trimming fish, 383
Fish poacher, 93
Fish stocks, 246
Flageolets, 173
Flank steak, 111
Flatbreads, 801, 876
Flatfish, 133, 383
  cutting, 384
  filleting, 388
Flat omelets, 737, 738, 739
Flattop range, 101
Flavored butters, 802
Flavored syrups, 225
Flavorings. *See also* Seasonings
  for buttercream, 961
  in the creaming method, 908
  for mousses, 976, 977
  use in baking, 863
Flounder, 135
Flour, 203-205
  in the foaming method, 913
  for pie dough, 933
  rice, 241
  use in pasta, 703
  as a stabilizer, 862
  as a thickener, 864
  wheat, 877
Flour panadas, 843
Fluoride, 40
Fluting cuts, 566
Foam cakes, mixing, 913
Foaming method, 912-916
Foie gras, 127
Folded omelets, 738
Fondant, tempering, 982
Fonds de cuisine, 243
Food and beverage managers, 8
Food and Drug Administration
  (FDA), 35
  Model Food Code of, 64
Food/beverage costs, 13
Food-borne illness, 56-69
  chart of, 58-60
Food chopper, 99
Food contamination, 56
  avoiding, 61-62
Food cooling, safe, 64-65
Food Guide Pyramid, USDA, 42-45
Food handling. *See also* Sanitation
  careless, 61
  during fabrication, 358
Food history, resources for, 1017
Food mill, 89, 640
Food processors, 98, 601, 703
  use for forcemeats, 844
  for making pasta, 704
Food reception, safe, 63-64
Foods
  arranging, 64
  prepared, canned, and frozen, 229

Food safety, 56-69
Food science, basics of, 48-54
Food slicer, 99
Food storage, safe, 62-64. *See also*
  Storage
Food stylists, 9
Food writers, 9
Forcemeats, 842-845
  components of, 843
  molding, 846
  preparing, 844-846
  types of, 842
Forcemeat stuffings, 348
Fortified wines, 229, 260, 305
Four-fold, 940
Free-range poultry, 125
Freezing units, 63
French fries, 657
French knife, 83
French-style omelets, 737
  rolling, 740
Fresh cheeses, 193, 196
Fresh fruit pies, 935
Fresh fruits, yield calculations for,
  26
Fresh herbs, 183
  cutting, 560-565
  general guidelines for, 146-147
  mise en place for, 559-582
Fresh pasta
  process of making, 704-705
  serving, 711
Fresh peppers, preparing, 574-575
Fresh vegetables, yield calculations for,
  26
Fried eggs, 731-733
Frittatas, 737, 739
Front waiter (chef de rang), 8
Frozen desserts, 191
Frozen fish, 132
Frozen foods, 229
  safe thawing of, 65-67
Frozen phyllo dough, 941
Frozen soufflé, 964
Frozen yogurt, 191
Fructose, 33
Fruit cookery, resources for, 1019
Fruit drink mixes, 228
Fruit pies, 935
  fillings for, 933, 936
Fruit preserves, 801
Fruits, 43, 148-160. *See also* Citrus
  fruits; Dried fruits; Fresh fruits;
  Stone fruits; Tropical fruits
  in Bavarian creams, 972
  general guidelines for, 146-147
  general information chart for, 160
  in mousses, 976
  peeling, 560
  peeling and slicing, 773-778
  resources for, 1018
Fruit salads, 773-779
Fruit tarts, pastry cream for, 968
Fry chef (friturier), 7
Fryers, 101
Frying fats, 212
Frying kettle, 658
Full-service restaurants, 6
Fumets, 244, 245, 253
Fungi, 56-57

Gallia melons, 156
Game birds, 127
Game meats, 124
Ganache, 979-981
  glazing with, 983
Garde manger, 841-846
  resources for, 1019
Garden peas, 174

Garlic, 169
  preparation of, 570-571
Garlic-flavored mayonnaise, 766
Garlic powder, 219
Garnishes
  for appetizers, 816
  for bisques, 320
  for broths, 293
  for brown sauces, 260
  for cream soups, 310
  for forcemeats, 843, 846
  for omelets, 739
  for purée soups, 316
  for salads, 771
  for sandwiches, 803
  for soups, 328
  using pastry bags for, 872
  for vinaigrette, 761
Gaufrette cuts, 567
Geese, 126-127
Gelatin, 228
  in Bavarian creams, 973
  blooming, 818, 819, 973
  in mousse, 817, 818, 819
  as a thickener, 864
Gelatinization, 51-52
Gel strength formulas, 819
Genoise, 912
Ghee, 240
Ginger, 219
Glace, 250
Glace de viande, 250, 251, 276
Glazes, 960. *See also* Icings
  for cakes, cookies, and pastries, 983
  ganaches as, 980
  general guidelines for, 982-984
  vegetable, 593
Globe artichokes, 180
Glutinous rice, 204
Golden beets, 178
Golden delicious apples, 148
Gooseberries, 151
Goosefish, 136
Goujonette cuts, 390
Grading
  of eggs, 200
  of produce, 146
Graham flour, 204
Grain-based foods, 43
Grain-based stuffings, 348
Grains, 203-205
  cooking, 671-689
  cooking ratios and times for, 995
  in hearty broths, 307
  simmering, 672-675
  sorting, 672
Grain salads, 780
Grande cuisine, 5
Granny Smith apples, 149
Granulated sugar, 224, 961, 968
Grapefruit, 150, 152-153
Grapes, 153
Grapeseed oil, 212
Gratin dishes, 95
Gratin forcemeats, 842, 846
Grating cheeses, 196-197, 198
Gratins, 651
Gravad lox, 137
Gravy, preparing, 409-410
Green beans, 172
Green cabbage, 162
Greening apples, 149
Green onions, 169
Green peppercorns, 222, 223
Green peppers, preparing, 574-575
Greens
  cooking, 166-167
  drying, 770
  washing, 769

Green salad, 768-772
Green vegetables, in hearty broths, 307
Grenadins, 360
Griddle cakes, 900
Griddles, 93, 102-103, 731, 734
Grill chef (grillardin), 7
Grilling, 400-404
  of vegetables, 596-598
Grills, 102-103
  maintaining, 402, 596
Grinding
  of cereals and meals, 677
  of forcemeats, 844
  of meats, 375
Grinding equipment, 98-100
Grits, 205
Groats, 205, 676
Grouper, 136
Guacamole, 801
Guérard, Michel, 4

Habanero chiles, 171
Halibut, 136
Ham, 119
  carving, 414
Ham hocks, 120
Hand racks, 402
Hand tools, 87-88
Hand washing, 62, 68
Hanging meat, 108
Hard cheeses, 196, 198
Hard-cooked eggs, 725, 726
Hard ganache, 979, 983
Hard rolls, 877
Hard-shell clams, 141
Hard-shell crabs, 142
Haricots verts, 172
Hazard Analysis Critical Control
  Points (HACCP), 66-67
Hazelnuts, 216
Headwaiter (chef de salle), 8
Health, kitchen safety and, 69. *See also*
  Food-borne illness; Safety
Heart, 111
Hearty broths, 304-308
Heat transfer, 49-51
Hedgehog cut, 776
Heirloom potatoes, 175
Herb-flavored oils and vinegars, 763
Herbs, 183-186. *See also* Dried herbs;
  Fresh herbs
  adding to potatoes, 635-636
  in fruit salads, 773
  in hearty broths, 307
  mincing, 561
  in pasta dough, 704
  in pilaf, 681
  in risotto, 688
Herb spreads, 801
High-carbon stainless steel knife
  blades, 81
High-density lipoproteins (HDL), 36
High moisture/low starch potatoes,
  634, 640
Historical culinary figures, 4
Hollandaise sauce, 274, 275
Hollow-ground knife blades, 81
Home meal replacement, 6
Hominy, 205
Honey, 225, 862
Honeycomb tripe, 112
Honeydew melons, 156
Honing, of knives, 84-86
Hors-d'oeuvre, 813-814. *See also*
  Appetizers
  presenting, 814
Hot appetizers, 816
Hotel pans, 94
Hotels, career opportunities in, 5

PHOTOGRAPHY CREDITS

LORNA SMITH PHOTOGRAPHS:

6, 7, 8, 13, 20, 23, 26, 27, 28, 35, 38, 40, 49, 51, 52, 53, 61, 63, 64, 68, 70, 83, 89, 90, 93, 94, 98, 100, 108, 109, 133 (4 on right), 140 (3 on left), 148, 149, 150, 152, 153, 156, 157, 159, 161, 162, 163, 164, 165, 166, 168, 169, 170, 171, 172, 173, 174, 175, 178, 179, 180, 181, 183, 189, 199, 203, 204, 205, 206, 208, 213, 215, 216, 217, 218, 219, 220, 221, 223, 227, 228, 235, 237, 238, 240 (right), 241, 242, 244, 245, 247 (right), 249, 250, 253, 254, 256, 257, 258, 259, 263, 264, 265, 269, 270, 271, 275, 276, 277, 278, 281, 282, 288, 294, 295, 299, 300, 301 (2 on left), 302, 305, 306, 307, 308, 310, 311, 312, 313, 316, 317, 318, 321, 322, 323, 324, 326, 328, 329, 346, 347, 348, 349, 361, 362, 363, 364, 365, 366, 367, 375, 376, 377, 378, 379, 381, 382, 383 (left), 384, 385 (left), 386, 387, 389 (3 on right), 391, 392, 393, 395 (2 on right), 396, 401, 402, 403, 406, 408, 409, 410, 411, 412, 414, 443, 451, 452, 453, 454, 458, 459, 460, 463, 464, 487, 492, 493, 494, 498, 501, 502, 503, 506, 507, 508, 524, 527, 528, 529, 530, 533, 535, 536, 537, 560, 561, 562, 563, 564, 565, 566, 567, 568, 569, 570, 571 (6 on left), 572, 573, 574, 575 (3 on left and 1 on bottom right), 576, 577, 580 (right), 585, 586, 589, 591, 594, 596, 597, 600, 601, 603, 605, 608, 611, 615, 616, 618, 619, 622, 626, 629, 630, 631, 637, 640, 641, 642, 645, 646, 649, 650, 651, 655, 658, 659, 666, 667, 669, 672, 673, 674, 678, 687, 688, 693, 703, 708, 709, 717, 728, 729, 732, 735, 739, 740, 742, 743, 744, 760, 761, 763, 764, 765, 766, 769, 770, 771, 774, 775, 776, 777, 778, 801, 802, 803, 804 (2 on bottom), 819, 843, 846 (right), 851, 855, 864, 865, 866, 867, 868, 869, 870, 877, 899, 900, 903, 904, 905, 908, 909, 910, 913, 914, 915, 917, 918, 939, 940, 941, 943, 944, 946, 947, 948, 961, 962, 965, 966, 968, 969, 970, 972, 973, 976, 977, 980, 982, 983, 984

BEN FINK PHOTOGRAPHS:

Cover, end papers, 0-1, 3, 17, 31, 55, 76-77, 79, 96-97, 105, 129, 145, 154-155, 176-177, 184-185, 187, 194-195, 201, 210-211, 230-231, 233, 243, 255, 268, 274, 291, 292, 304, 309, 315, 320, 334-335, 337, 342-343, 345, 357, 399, 400, 405, 430-431, 449, 450, 457, 462, 478-479, 491, 496, 505, 518-519, 525, 526, 546-547, 556-557, 559, 583, 588, 592, 607, 613, 624-625, 633, 639, 648, 653, 657, 664-665, 671, 676, 680, 685, 694-695, 701, 702, 707, 714-715, 720-721, 723, 724, 727, 737, 752-753, 759, 768, 773, 788-789, 799, 800, 808-809, 813, 815, 828-829, 841, 842, 852-853, 858-859, 861, 875, 876, 888-889, 896, 897, 898, 902, 907, 912, 924-925, 931, 932, 954-955, 959, 960, 975, 979, 988-989

ELIZABETH CORBETT JOHNSON PHOTOGRAPHS:

60, 65, 69, 99 (bottom), 110, 111, 113, 115, 116, 117, 118, 119, 120, 122 (5 on right), 123, 124, 126, 127, 133 (left), 134, 135, 136, 137, 138, 139, 140 (right), 142 (bottom), 144, 165, 236, 240 (3 on left), 359, 360, 368, 369 (left), 383 (right), 571 (far right), 575 (top right), 578, 579, 580 (3 on left), 719, 818, 844, 845, 846 (left), 849, 856, 857, 880 (3 on right), 881, 883, 884

JOHN GRUBELL PHOTOGRAPHS:

10, 32, 37, 41, 99 (top), 131, 132, 141, 142 (top), 143, 239, 246, 247 (2 on left), 301 (3 on right), 369 (2 on right), 370, 371, 372, 373, 374, 380, 385, 388, 389 (2 on left), 390, 394, 395 (2 on left), 397, 398, 413, 682, 704, 705, 804 (top), 872, 878, 879, 880 (far left), 934, 935